101 951 639 9

Homeles

Eighth editio

ONE WEEK LOAN

D1493928

Andrew Arden QC is general editor of the *Encyclopaedia of Housing Law, Housing Law Reports* and *Journal of Housing Law*, as well as co-author of *Arden & Partington's Housing Law, Manual of Housing Law, Local Government Finance: Law and Practice* and *Local Government Constitutional and Administrative Law* (all published by Sweet & Maxwell). He has appeared in numerous leading cases in housing and homelessness law as well as in local government law. He is a full-time practitioner and head of Arden Chambers, London.

Emily Orme is a barrister at Arden Chambers in London. She practices in all areas of housing and local government law, and has a particular interest in homelessness and housing issues relating to children. Emily was part of the team that wrote the annotations to the Housing and Regeneration Act 2008 (*Current Law Annotated Statutes*) and she has written a number of articles, one of which, 'Child tenants – a minor problem', was cited in the Court of Appeal in *Alexander-David v Hammersmith & Fulham LBC* (2009).

Toby Vanhegan is a barrister at Arden Chambers in London specialising in housing law particularly homelessness, immigration and asylum, human rights and EU law. He has a particular knowledge and expertise in issues of eligibility, especially in the context of housing. He appeared in the European Court of Justice in the case of *Teixeira v Lambeth LBC and SSHD*. Toby has written articles for the *Journal of Housing Law* and *Legal Action* concerning freedom of movement of persons within the newly expanded EU. He speaks regularly at conferences and provides legal training courses.

The Legal Action Group is a national, independent charity which campaigns for equal access to justice for all members of society. Legal Action Group:
- provides support to the practice of lawyers and advisers
- inspires developments in that practice
- campaigns for improvements in the law and the administration of justice
- stimulates debate on how services should be delivered.

Homelessness and Allocations

A guide to the Housing Act 1996 Parts 6 and 7

EIGHTH EDITION

Andrew Arden QC, Emily Orme and
Toby Vanhegan

Legal Action Group
2010

arden
chambers

Eighth edition published in Great Britain 2010
by LAG Education and Service Trust Limited
242 Pentonville Road, London N1 9UN
www.lag.org.uk

First edition published 1982 as *The Homeless Persons Act* by Andrew Arden
Second edition published 1986 as *Homeless Persons – The Housing Act 1985 Part III* by Andrew Arden
Third edition published 1988 as *Homeless Persons – The Housing Act 1985 Part III* by Andrew Arden
Fourth edition published 1992 as *Homeless Persons* by Caroline Hunter and Siobhan McGrath
Fifth edition published 1997 as *Homelessness & Allocations – A Guide to the Housing Act 1996 Parts VI and VII* by Andrew Arden QC and Caroline Hunter
Sixth edition published 2002 as *Homelessness & Allocations – A Guide to the Housing Act 1996 Parts VI and VII* by Andrew Arden QC and Caroline Hunter
Revised sixth edition published 2003 as *Homelessness & Allocations – A Guide to the Housing Act 1996 Parts VI and VII* by Andrew Arden QC and Caroline Hunter
Seventh edition published in 2006 as *Homelessness & Allocations – A Guide to the Housing Act 1996 Parts VI and VII* by Andrew Arden QC, Caroline Hunter and Lindsay Johnson. © Andrew Arden and Caroline Hunter

© Andrew Arden QC 2010

British Library Cataloguing in Publication Data
a CIP catalogue record for this book is available from the British Library.

Crown copyright material is produces with the permission of the Controller of HMSO and the Queen's Printer for Scotland.

ISBN: 978 1 903307 74 8

Typeset by Regent Typesetting, London
Printed by Hobbs the Printer, Totton, Hants

Preface

In this, the eighth edition of this book, we have completely replaced the chapter on immigration (chapter 3), and expanded both chapter 11 (allocations) to cover allocations by registered providers of social housing and chapter 13 (other statutory provisions) to include housing for asylum-seekers. My new co-authors, Toby Vanhegan and Emily Orme, in addition to their work on other chapters, took first draft responsibility for, respectively, each of the first two of these, and jointly for the third. In addition, there are more than 80 new cases, including the important decisions of the House of Lords and Supreme Court in *Holmes-Moorhouse v Richmond-Upon-Thames RLBC* [2009] UKHL 7; [2009] HLR 34 (reasonably to be expected to reside with), *R (Ahmad) v Newham LBC* [2009] UKHL 14, [2009] HLR 31 (allocations), *Birmingham City Council v Ali; Moran v Manchester City Council* [2009] UKHL 36; [2009] 1 WLR 1506 (reasonable to continue to occupy accommodation), and available just in time (see 'Note on late developments' following this preface) – *Tomlinson v Birmingham CC* [2010] UKSC 8 (reviews and article 6), as well as of the Court of Appeal in *R (Weaver) v London and Quadrant Housing Trust* [2009] EWCA Civ 587 (registered providers and the Human Rights Act 1998).

There has also been supplementary guidance on homelessness and new guidance on allocations. As in the last edition, Welsh variations are footnoted to English guidance, for reasons of space: my apologies to practitioners in Wales; the decision is entirely numeric. Government websites are identified where available because changes are common and a constant eye needs to be kept out for them.

A book as old as this (the first edition was published in 1982) and especially one to which a number of co-authors have contributed over the years, does not merely run the risk of contradictions, obsolescent propositions, structural oddities and sometimes downright opaque wording (that doubtless made sense at the time) so much as it is guaranteed to suffer from many of these defects: on this occasion, the fresh eyes of my two new co-authors have generated much new thought about the book, for which I am most grateful, and have caused me to engage in closer review than for some years to try to eliminate such faults. I have no doubt some remain.

When this book was first published, domestic public law was considerably less well-known than it is today; of course, there was also much less law – both statutory and cases – on homelessness than there is today (and so little on allocations that it did not feature in its own right at all). At that time, many of the principles for which authority can today be found within homelessness and allocations case-law had to be drawn from outside those areas. For that reason, public law formed a discrete and early chapter of the book, containing relatively little law that was directly concerned with homelessness. The move to a later chapter (chapter 12) took place in the last edition, but the broad distinction between public law 'generally' and homelessness (and by then, of course, allocations) was largely maintained – which is to say that homelessness and allocations law was to be found in the other chapters, save for the purposes of illustration within chapter 12. In this edition, we have sought to integrate illustrations into the main body of the discussion of public law, recognising that homelessness and allocations law is part of it, and contributes to it, as well as being governed by it.

What I wrote in the preface to the last edition remains apt:

> That does not, however, mean that public law as an independent topic is no longer relevant. To the contrary, its own growth – partly in light of the Human Rights Act 1998 – continues apace and, so long as it does so, it has the capacity to roll over the specialist case law in any area to which it is applicable. In the ordinary case, the questions and answers may well today be found within the four walls of housing public law. When the envelope needs to be, or is, pushed out, recourse to a much wider range of public law decisions is available and may be the source of an unexpected assault. Familiarity with it remains an essential part of housing law – and homelessness – practice. In summary, it is probably less routinely necessary as an independent subject but more important when it raises its head as such.

The overall effect of the changes to chapter 12 is, I hope, less duplication, albeit at cost of more cross-reference. Likewise, we have sought to deal with topics such as available accommodation which it is reasonable to continue to occupy, and reasons, at single points in the book, also to avoid duplication (and perhaps contradiction).

That said, the philosophy of this book remains above all one of affording not only a full statement of the law but also a resource in which – hopefully – all relevant case-law continues to be available in one place. Having remarked in the preface to the last edition on the departure of some of the law on settled accommodation (for which it is necessary to refer back to the sixth edition), I added that

> ... the one thing this edition has not done is to have jettisoned its history entirely. ... A wholly new approach would almost certainly omit some (perhaps much) of the earlier case law and/or attention to some issues which are not currently in focus. Although that makes for a shorter and 'sharper' read, it has been my own experience that very little law does disappear for good and all, nor do issues do more than submerge for a period of time. A knowledge of how propositions of law originally emerged is always central to their understanding; if omitted or buried too deep, they may be unavailable to assist or one may be unprepared to resist them.

I illustrated this by reference to two older cases – *R v Beverley DC ex p McPhee* (1978) *Times* 26 October, and *R v Ealing LBC ex p Sidhu* (1982) 2 HLR 45, QBD – which had then recently been considered in the Court of Appeal; the latter formed a substantial part of the consideration of the House of Lords in *Ali and Moran* where, I am pleased to note, it received a much more sympathetic reception than it had at the Court of Appeal. By way of further illustration, we refer in this edition to the case of *R v Camden LBC ex p Gillan* (1988) 21 HLR 114, QBD, in the discussion of what has become the widespread practice of conducting inquiries by way of telephone interview (see para 9.62 below).

There has been another development on which I should also like to comment. For the first six editions, over a period of more than 20 years, I hope it will not be considered immodest if I say that this was the only book which addressed homeless (and allocations from 1996) in anything like the sort of full detail that a practitioner needs. From the last edition, it has been joined by another, also detailed work, *Housing Allocations and Homelessness* by Jan Luba QC and Liz Davies, the second edition of which was due to be published shortly before this. It is most welcome. Monopolies are always a bad thing, even one's own. In an area of law governing what may count amongst the most difficult conditions people can have to experience, where merits inevitably and rightly play a substantial part in the consideration of the courts, just as do the economic pressures on local authorities charged with resolving them (but not adequately funded to do so), the law is rarely, should not be, and hopefully never will be, 'fixed' or 'certain' beyond argument, at least in many (often critical) respects. Even with the best will in the world, even with the most conscious effort to do so, one author – even with co-authors – or one book cannot do full justice to all the different ways every case can be interpreted, let alone how it may be deployed. Once there are – at least – two books, or two teams, capacity to identify such 'room for manoeuvre' or 'tensions' increases exponentially. It may make for less simple solutions, but homelessness is inherently a complex problem, and deserves the maximum effort – as the volume of cases makes clear practitioners are more than willing to give it.

Of course, at a more human level, competition also cautions against complacency!

Andrew Arden QC
Arden Chambers
London
17 February 2010

Note on late developments

Tomlinson v Birmingham CC [2010] UKSC 8

The decision of the House of Lords in *Runa Begum v Tower Hamlets LBC* [2003] UKHL 5; [2003] 2 AC 430; [2003] HLR 32 is described in chapter 12 at paras 12.30 and 12.96–12.100. In short, it decided that, on the assumption (without deciding) that an appeal under section 204 was a determination of the homeless applicant's civil rights, within ECHR article 6, the requirements of that article were sufficiently met by an appeal to the county court confined to principles of domestic public law.

Runa Begum concerned suitability of accommodation offered. In *Tomlinson v Birmingham CC* [2010] UKSC 8, the issue was whether applicants had been warned, under Housing Act 1996 s193(5), of the consequences of refusal of an offer of accommodation, entitling the authority to consider that it had discharged its duty to them; the same issue arises under section193(7). The question arose because the applicants claimed not to have received relevant letters from the authority.

In *Tsfayo v UK* [2007] HLR 19, ECtHR, it was held that the question whether there was good reason for backdating a claim for housing benefit was a simple question of fact that should have been decided by an independent and impartial tribunal with full fact-finding jurisdiction, rather than one confined to judicial review principles, as distinct from an issue involving specialist knowledge or questions of housing policy (as in the determination of what comprises suitable accommodation). Following *Tsfayo*, it was therefore argued in *Tomlinson* that – distinguishing *Runa Begum* – whether or not letters had been received was likewise a simple question of fact which also entitled the applicants to a decision by an independent and impartial tribunal with full fact-finding jurisdiction.

The Supreme Court dismissed the claim. It held that:

(1) rights under Part 7 of the Housing Act 1996 are not civil rights engaging article 6, and

(2) *Runa Begum* applies even where the issue is a simple question of fact.

On the first issue, rights to accommodation were distinguished from the individual, economic right flowing from specific rules laid down in a statute which had been held to be civil rights in Strasbourg (as in *Tsfayo*). Lord Hope, giving the principal speech (with which Lady Hale and Lord Brown agreed)[1] said:

> The scheme which Part VII lays down can be seen, therefore, to have these characteristics. It provides a right to assistance if the relevant conditions are satisfied. But this is not a pecuniary right, nor is the benefit that is to be provided defined by the application of specific rules laid down by the statute. Even where the full homelessness duty arises under section 193, the content of the statutory duty lacks precise definition. There is no private law analogy. The duty is expressed in broad terms – to secure that 'accommodation is available' – which leave much to the discretionary administrative judgment of the authority. As Professor Ian Loveland, *Does Homelessness Decision-making Engage Article 6(1) of the European Convention on Human Rights?* [2003] EHRLR 176, 184 observes, no tightly defined rules are laid down. The legislative requirement is couched only in terms of broad principle (at [27]).

And:

> ... The present state of uncertainty as to whether the administration of social welfare benefits, such as those which are available to those who are homeless or threatened with homelessness, is unhealthy. It encourages litigation on issues that would not require to be addressed at all if their right to accommodation under section 193 did not give rise to a civil right within the meaning of article 6. The delay and expense that uncertainty on this issue gives rise to involves a waste of resources which would be much better deployed elsewhere in the public interest (at [32]).

Accordingly:

> ... I would be prepared now to hold that cases where the award of services or benefits in kind is not an individual right of which the applicant can consider himself the holder, but is dependent upon a series of evaluative judgments by the provider as to whether the statutory criteria are satisfied and how the need for it ought to be met, do not engage article 6(1). In my opinion they do not give rise to 'civil rights' within the autonomous meaning that is given to that expression for the purposes of that article. The appellants' right to accommodation

---

1   Lords Collins and Kerr gave their own concurring opinions.

under section 193 of the 1996 Act falls into that category. I would hold that article 6 was not engaged by the decisions that were taken in the appellants' cases by the reviewing officer (at [49]).

On the second issue, it was held that the principle in *Runa Begum* applies even where the question is a simple one of fact. Lord Hope said:

> I agree that the questions that had to be decided in these cases can be distinguished from the question that had to be decided in *Runa Begum*. . . . [T]he question in that case could not be said to be purely and simply one of fact as the question whether the accommodation was suitable was one for the expert assessment of the housing officer. But the subject matter of the decision appealed against here is exactly the same. The question whether or not the letters were received was just one among a number of questions that had to be addressed to determine whether the respondents' duty under section 193 had been discharged. They are dealt with together in section 193(5) in a way that shows that they are all interlinked. The scheme of the Act is that they are to be dealt with together both at the initial stage and, in the event of a review, by the reviewing officer. To separate out questions as to whether the formalities laid down by the subsection were complied with from those as to whether the accommodation was suitable would complicate a scheme which, in the interests of speed and economy, was designed to be simple to administer. Several of the further cases referred to in section 193(6) in which the authority ceases to be subject to the duty also raise issues that require the exercise of judgment. That is inherent in the entire structure of Part VII of the 1996 Act.

> The way the reviewing officers approached their task in these cases shows very clearly how the scheme works in practice. For ease of administration the review is entrusted to a single officer who is equipped to deal with issues as to the suitability of the accommodation that has been declined. An answer to the question whether or not the letters were received was incidental to a more searching and judgmental inquiry into the accommodation's suitability. It was, as Lord Bingham put it in *Runa Begum*, para 9(2), a staging post on the way to the much broader judgment that had to be made. These cases are quite different from *Tsfayo*, where no broad questions requiring professional knowledge or experience had to be addressed once the question whether there was good cause had been answered. In these circumstances I would hold that the ratio of the decision in *Runa Begum* should be applied and that the absence of a full fact-finding jurisdiction in the court to which an appeal lies under section 204 does not deprive it of what it needs to satisfy the requirements of article 6(1) (at [53–54]).

Contents

Table of cases

References in the right-hand column are to paragraph numbers.

Table of statutes

References in the right-hand column are to paragraph numbers.

Table of statutory instruments

References in the right-hand column are to paragraph numbers.

Table of European legislation

References in the right-hand column are to paragraph numbers.

Abbreviations

Legislation

AH(W) Regs 2003	Allocation of Housing (Wales) Regulations 2003
AIAA 1993	Asylum and Immigration Appeals Act 1993
A(IWA) Regs 2006	Accession (Immigration and Worker Authorisation) Regulations 2006
A(IWR) Regs 2006	Accession (Immigration and Worker Registration) Regulations 2006
BNA 1981	British Nationality Act 1981
CA 1989	Children Act 1989
CPR	Civil Procedure Rules 1998
EC Treaty	Treaty of Rome as amended by Treaty on European Union
ECHR	European Convention on Human Rights
EEA Regs 2006	Immigration (European Economic Area) Regulations 2006
Eligibility Regs 2006	Allocation of Housing and Homelessness (Eligibility) (England) Regulations 2006
HA	Housing Act
H&RA 2008	Housing and Regeneration Act 2008
H(HP)A 1977	Housing (Homeless Persons) Act 1977
HPA 1986	Housing and Planning Act 1986
HRA 1998	Human Rights Act 1998
H(W) Regs 2006	Homelessness (Wales) Regulations 2006
IA	Immgration Act
IAA 1999	Immigration and Asylum Act 1999
LGA 2000	Local Government Act 2000
NAA 1948	National Assistance Act 1948
NHSCCA 1990	National Health Service and Community Care Act 1990
NIAA 2002	Nationality, Immigration and Asylum Act 2002
PEA 1977	Protection from Eviction Act 1977
R(A)A 1976	Rent (Agriculture) Act 1976
Review Procedure Regs 1999	Allocation of Housing and Homelessness (Review Procedures) Regulations 1999

Other

COT	Certificate of Travel
ECJ	European Court of Justice
EEA	European Economic Area

ELR	exceptional leave to remain
EU	European Union
ILR	indefinite leave to remain
ISD	Immigration Status Document
NASS	National Asylum Support Service
UKBA	UK Borders Agency
UKRP	UK Residence Permit
WRS	worker registration scheme

CHAPTER 1

The policy of the provisions

continued

Introduction

1.1 This chapter outlines the history of the law on homelessness and allocations, from before the Housing (Homeless Persons) Act (H(HP)A) 1977 through the Housing Act (HA) 1996 Parts 6 and 7 – the present, principal Acts – to the Homelessness Act 2002.

1.2 Although Parts 6 and 7 are free-standing legislation – in the sense that they are neither consolidation nor amendment – and it may be unnecessary always to approach them by reference to their evolution, nonetheless both Parts are best understood historically. Their application needs to be informed not only by the case-law but also by the statutory provisions which preceded them, in respect of both that which was retained and that which was changed.

1.3 Thus, the Minister for Local Government, Housing and Urban Regeneration (Mr Curry) said of the changes to homelessness law made by the 1996 Act:

> We shall not go back to pre-1977 days. We shall keep the 1977 Act concepts of entitlement, homelessness, priority need, intentionality and local connection. Essentially, what we are changing is the way in which the duty is to be discharged.[1]

1.4 That discharge was closely interwoven with the allocation of local authority housing – Part 6 was the first big change in allocations law since 1935, when the concept of 'reasonable preference' for certain categories of housing need was introduced: in practice, however, allocations policy had been dominated by the homeless since H(HP)A 1977.

1.5 Since HA 1996, the Homelessness Act 2002 has again changed the shape of the law, introducing a new 'strategic' duty to formulate a response to homelessness and reshaping Part 6 to seek to include 'choice-based letting' within allocations law. Further changes have been made by regulations.

1.6 In this chapter, homelessness and allocations policy as embodied in law will be approached as follows:

a) National Assistance Act (NAA) 1948 Part 3;
b) H(HP)A 1977; Housing Act (HA) 1985 Part 3;
c) *Re Puhlhofer*;[2]
d) Housing and Planning Act (HPA) 1986;
e) Asylum and Immigration Appeals Act (AIAA) 1993;

---

1 *Hansard*, Standing Committee G, 12 March 1996, col 587.
2 *R v Hillingdon LBC ex p Puhlhofer* [1986] AC 484; 18 HLR 158, HL.

f)   *Ex p Awua;*[3]
g)   HA 1996 Parts 6 and 7;
h)   between Acts;
i)   Homelessness Act 2002;
j)   changes since the 2002 Act.

National Assistance Act 1948

1.7   The provisions of NAA 1948 s21(1) put local authorities under a duty to provide:

> . . . residential accommodation for persons who by reason of age, infirmity or any other circumstances are in need of care and attention which is not otherwise available to them, [and] temporary accommodation for persons who are in urgent need thereof, being need arising in circumstances which could not reasonably have been foreseen or in such other circumstances as the authority may in any particular case determine.

1.8   Homelessness law – starting with H(HP)A 1977 – replaces only the second limb of that duty, the duty to provide temporary accommodation in urgent need.[4]

1.9   The NAA 1948 duty extended to people ordinarily resident in the local authority's area.[5] The National Assistance Board (NAB) (later the Supplementary Benefits Commission (SBC)) had power to require an authority to provide accommodation where satisfied that such a person was in urgent need of it. The local authority was under a further duty to protect the property of a person to whom it provided assistance under these provisions.[6]

1.10 Local authority duties under NAA 1948 were exercised under the general guidance of the Minister, who was, for these purposes, the Minister of Health.[7]

1.11 This legal structure fell far short of imposing a full and permanent duty on local authorities to protect all homeless people. Rather, it provided for emergencies, especially unforeseeable emergencies.[8] The

3   *R v Brent LBC ex p Awua* [1996] 1 AC 55; 27 HLR 453, HL.
4   H(HP)A 1977 s20 and Schedule, repealing this part of NAA 1948 s21.
5   NAA 1948 s24.
6   NAA 1948 s24.
7   NAA 1948 s33, subsequently Local Authorities Social Services Act 1970 s7.
8   *Southwark LBC v Williams* [1971] 1 Ch 734, CA; see also Ministry of Health Circular 87/48 illustrating 'urgent and unforeseen need' as homelessness arising as a result of 'fire, flood or eviction'.

duration of accommodation, save where the NAB/SBC was involved, was a matter for the authority. It probably meant no more than for so long as the authority considered appropriate or necessary;[9] urgent need for temporary accommodation was not to be equated with a vital but continuing need for permanent accommodation.[10]

1.12　　The discretionary and temporary nature of this provision was the principal problem. Another problem was that of deciding on 'ordinary residence' in an area. Notoriously, and reminiscent of the Poor Laws which NAA 1948 repealed and replaced, authorities 'shuttled' homeless people between areas, claiming that they were ordinarily resident in another authority's area.

1.13　　Even more problematic was the division of responsibilities between different authorities within a single geographical area: homelessness provision was to be found in NAA 1948 and was regarded as a social services problem; the duty to provide housing in any area lay, however, with the authority having responsibility under the Housing Acts.[11] This problem was exacerbated by the re-organisation effected by the Local Government Act 1972 with effect from 1 April 1974. From that date, social services outside London, and in non-metropolitan areas, became the responsibility of county councils, while housing was the responsibility of the district council.[12] Even in London and the metropolitan areas, where social services and housing remained the responsibility of the same authority, different departments would usually handle the different responsibilities. In either event, this brought with it a different kind of shuttling, not in this case between different geographical areas, but between different authorities or different departments carrying out different functions in the same locality.

1.14　　This was an unsatisfactory division. Popular perception was changing – homelessness was no longer readily regarded as a symptom of personal or social inadequacy; it had come to be recognised as part of the continuing severe housing problem (whether this is described as a crude shortage of housing or as a shortage of adequate housing in the location where it is needed).[13]

9　*Bristol Corporation v Stockford* (1973), reported in Carnwath, *A guide to the Housing (Homeless Persons) Act 1977* (Knight's Annotated Acts, 1978).

10　*Roberts v Dorset CC* (1976) 75 LGR 462.

11　Formerly HA 1957 Part 5, now HA 1985 Part 2.

12　Formerly HA 1957 s1, as amended by Local Government Act 1972 s193 and Sch 22, now HA 1985 s1.

13　Significant contributions to this rise in awareness included those of J Sandford and K Loach, *Cathy come home* ('The Wednesday Play', 1966 television film);

1.15   The fact that children were commonly taken into care for no reason other than their parents' want of accommodation was itself a significant factor in the changing attitudes which produced the climate for H(HP)A 1977.

1.16   There are two other points to make concerning the pre-1977 Act position, both of them occurring in 1974. The first is largely technical. The Local Government Act 1972 contained an amendment to NAA 1948, additional to the redistribution of responsibilities in non-metropolitan areas. The amendment reduced to a mere power what had previously been a duty.[14] The secretary of state, however, was empowered to reimpose the duty by directive, and, following an outcry by voluntary and welfare workers, lawyers and others concerned with the homeless,[15] did so in February 1974.

1.17   Of more significance was the circular issued in February 1974, which came to be known as the 'Joint Circular',[16] directed both to social services departments and authorities, and to housing departments and authorities.

1.18   The Joint Circular had two main aims: first, it urged the transfer of such stock as was held by social services authorities and social services departments for the purpose of discharging their responsibilities towards the homeless, to housing authorities or departments; second, it identified what it described as 'priority groups' who were intended to enjoy a claim on local authority stock.

1.19   The definition of priority groups in the Joint Circular closely resembled the definition of priority need that was adopted in H(HP)A 1977 s2, subsequently in Housing Act 1985 s59 and, now, in HA 1996 s189:

> The Priority Groups comprise families with dependent children living with them or in care; and adult families or people living alone who either become homeless in an emergency such as fire or flooding or are vulnerable because of old age, disability, pregnancy or other special reasons. For these priority groups, the issue is not whether, but by what means, local authorities should provide accommodation

J Greve et al, *Homelessness in London* (Scottish Academic Press, 1971); Bryan Glastonbury, *Homeless near a thousand homes* (Allen & Unwin, 1971); F Berry, *Housing – the great British failure* (Charles Knight, 1974). Of less populist, but greater official, influence was the Cullingworth Report, *Council housing – purposes, procedures and priorities* (9th report of Housing Management Sub-committee of the Central Housing Advisory Committee, 1969).

14 Local Government Act 1972 s195 and Sch 23.

15 Partington, *Housing (Homeless Persons) Act 1977* (Sweet & Maxwell, 1978), introductory notes.

16 DoE Circular 18/74, DHSS Circular 4/74.

themselves or help those concerned to obtain accommodation in the private sector . . .

Where a family has children there is no acceptable alternative to accommodation in which the family can be together as a family. The social cost, personal hardship, the long-term damage to children, as well as the expense involved in receiving a child into care rules this out as an acceptable course, other than in the exceptional case when professional social work advice is that there are compelling reasons apart from homelessness for separating children from their family. The provision of shelter from which the husband is excluded is also not acceptable unless there are sound social reasons, as, for example, where a wife is seeking temporary refuge following matrimonial dispute and it is undesirable that she should be under pressure to return home.[17]

1.20 Notwithstanding this advice, many authorities failed to transfer responsibility from social services to housing, or to give the priority groups preference over their own, local priorities.[18] Accordingly, when a Liberal MP, Stephen Ross, was successful in the ballot for private members' bills, the government of the day supported him in introducing a Homeless Persons Bill and the opposition announced that it, too, would broadly support the measure. The bill was introduced and became law as the Housing (Homeless Persons) Act 1977.

Housing (Homeless Persons) Act 1977; Housing Act 1985 Part 3

1.21 These two Acts are taken together, as the Housing Act 1985 was an exercise of consolidation of housing law: as such, save so far as there were recommendations of the Law Commission (Cmnd 9515) to effect explicit changes (of which there were none relevant to the policy or the framework of the legislation), no substantive change in homelessness law was intended or achieved.

1.22 One clear aim of H(HP)A 1977 was to place responsibility for the homeless on district councils and the London borough councils.[19] Provision was made to transfer staff and stock from social services to housing: the Secretary of State for the Environment enjoyed power to compel the transfer of property and staff from one authority to

17 DoE Circular 18/74 paras 10–12.
18 *Hansard* HC Debs, 15 December 1975, Vol 902 cols 473–475.
19 H(HP)A 1977 s19.

another, not merely between London borough councils and district councils, but as between all 'relevant authorities', defined to include social service authorities.[20]

1.23 Another aim of H(HP)A 1977 was to provide a uniform and national definition of, or criterion for, the circumstances in which one authority could shift on to another responsibility for a homeless person, so as to end shuttling. These 'local connection' provisions included a positive link between employment and housing.[21]

1.24 The local connection provisions operated not so much to permit an authority to shift the burden of housing a homeless person on to another authority as to prevent it from doing so once the applicant was shown to have a local connection with the area of the authority to which s/he had applied. Thus, the authority for the area in which an applicant had only an employment connection had to house the applicant, even though s/he might have had no other connections with that area, for example, family or residence.

1.25 The most important provision of H(HP)A 1977, however, was the establishment of a national criterion which required local authorities to accommodate, or to secure accommodation for, those who:

a) were homeless;
b) were in priority need of accommodation; and
c) did not become homeless intentionally.

1.26 Leaving aside the resolution of responsibility embodied in the local connection provisions, the three key questions, therefore, became:

a) what was homelessness?
b) who was in priority need? and
c) when was homelessness intentional?

Homelessness

1.27 Defining homelessness is not easy, either as a matter of law or as a matter of policy.[22] The most literal approach is to deal with those without a roof over their heads. This is not only difficult to estimate, but is likely to exclude those with children as, commonly, some form of accommodation, however inadequate, is found for them.

---

20 H(HP)A 1977 s14; Housing (Consequential Provisions) Act 1985 s5 and Sch 4 para 8.
21 H(HP)A 1977 s18; HA 1985 s61.
22 This and the next paragraph are based largely on Partington, *Housing (Homeless Persons) Act 1977* (Sweet & Maxwell, 1978), introductory notes, subheading 'Definitions of homelessness and extent of homelessness'.

1.28   The most radical approach, advocated by Shelter, the National Campaign for the Homeless, was that a person was homeless if s/he lived 'in conditions so bad that a civilised family life is impossible': this was homelessness 'in the true sense of the word'.[23]

1.29   Another approach is to consider those families who have no home where they can reside together. This excludes both single people and childless couples, but it was at the core of the definition which was adopted.

1.30   Under H(HP)A 1977, Parliament started with legal rights of occupation: a person was homeless if there was no accommodation which s/he could occupy by virtue of an interest or estate, or contract, together with anyone else who usually resided with him/her either as a member of the family, or in circumstances in which it was reasonable for that person to reside with him/her.[24]

1.31   A person was also not to be regarded as homeless if s/he was in occupation in circumstances in which a court order was required for eviction, for example, tenants whose tenancies had been determined. A person was homeless, however, if s/he had been locked out of accommodation, had to leave the accommodation because of domestic violence, or, in the case of mobile homes and houseboats, if there was nowhere to park/moor accommodation and to live in it.[25]

Priority need

1.32   The definition of homelessness did not create any substantive housing rights on its own. It had to be read together with the definition of priority need.

1.33   Only homeless people with a priority need for accommodation received housing assistance under H(HP)A 1977 and Housing Act 1985:

- those with children who were residing, or who might reasonably be expected to reside, with either the applicant or with anyone with whom the applicant might be expected to reside;
- those who were residing, or who might reasonably be expected to reside, with someone who had become homeless as a result of an emergency;
- those who were residing, or who might reasonably be expected to reside, with someone who was vulnerable on account of age, handicap or other special reason; and

23 *The grief report* (Shelter, 1972).
24 H(HP)A 1977 s1; HA 1985 s58.
25 H(HP)A 1977 s1; HA 1985 s58.

- a person who was residing, or who might reasonably be expected to reside, with someone who was a pregnant woman.[26]

1.34   The important point to note was this: in determining whether or not there was a priority need, not only the applicant but anyone who might reasonably be expected to reside with him/her, regardless of whether they had hitherto lived together, had to be considered.

Intentional homelessness

1.35   Homeless people in priority need had acquired a prima facie right to accommodation. To have become homeless, however, did not necessarily mean that someone had been evicted: the person might have quit of his/her own accord.

1.36   This provoked a hostile local authority reaction to H(HP)A 1977 as a bill and, in turn, led to the inclusion of the 'intentional homelessness' provisions.

1.37   Infamously, the bill was to be described as a charter for 'scroungers and scrimshankers'.[27]

1.38   Mr G Cunningham acquired a notoriety that in earlier editions of this book was described as 'unenviable', but that has – it must be said – been given a degree of judicial sanction by the House of Lords decision in *R v Brent LBC ex p Awua*,[28] in which Lord Hoffmann, delivering the only substantive speech, suggested that local authorities could decide to provide only temporary accommodation to a pregnant woman and 'wait and see' whether or not the child is placed for adoption.

1.39   Foreshadowing this, Mr Cunningham had suggested that women would become pregnant to acquire a priority need and then terminate their pregnancies once housing had been secured.[29] 'Families who have hesitated in the past to make themselves homeless [as opposed to finding themselves homeless] need have no such reluctance now . . .'. 'It will mean chaos.' 'Fifty per cent of alleged claims of homelessness are "try-ons".'[30]

1.40   Parliament did not wholly give in to these fears. Under H(HP)A 1977, and then the Housing Act 1985, not everyone who voluntarily

26   H(HP)A 1977 s2; HA 1985 s59; cf, above, para 1.19.

27   Per Mr W R Rees-Davies, *Hansard* HC Debs, 18 February 1977, Vol 926 col 905.

28   [1996] 1 AC 55; 27 HLR 453, HL.

29   *Hansard* HC Debs, 8 July 1977, Vol 934 col 1689.

30   Quotes to be found in Widdowson, *Intentional homelessness* (Shelter, 1981), p6.

quit accommodation was considered to be homeless intentionally, from which it followed that some could quit and yet be entitled to assistance from a local authority. It is when this class – those who could quit of their own accord, and yet not be deemed homeless intentionally – is considered that there is to be found the last element that serves to define the remit of the 1977 and 1985 Acts.

1.41 For an authority to be permitted to find that someone had become homeless intentionally – and, thus, had forfeited his/her right to assistance – required four preconditions:

a) the applicant had to have ceased to occupy accommodation – so that those who had never had accommodation or last had it so long ago that it could not properly be taken into account, could not be homeless intentionally; *and*

b) the applicant had to have ceased to occupy accommodation in consequence of a deliberate act or omission – an act or omission in good faith, in ignorance of a material fact (for example, security of tenure or financial assistance towards housing costs), was not to be considered deliberate; *and*

c) the accommodation had to have been such that it was reasonable to continue to occupy it – although those who optimistically left bad physical conditions were faced with the qualification that, in determining whether or not it was reasonable to remain in occupation, a housing authority could take into account housing conditions in its area generally; *and*

d) the accommodation which had been quit had to have been 'available for the occupation' of the applicant.[31] Accommodation was only 'available for occupation' if it was available both for the homeless person and for anyone who might reasonably be expected to reside with him/her.[32] In determining who might reasonably be expected to live together, no account was to be taken of want of accommodation.[33]

1.42 It followed that people who had never been able to live together and who had to be deemed reasonably to be expected to do so – for example, the young couple who had to live apart for want of accommodation – and who acquired a priority need (for example, through pregnancy), could not be found to be intentionally homeless should one or other or both of them leave the separate accommodations in

---

31 H(HP)A 1977 s17; HA 1985 s60.

32 H(HP)A 1977 s16; HA 1985 s75.

33 *Re Islam* [1983] 1 AC 688; (1981) 1 HLR 107, HL.

which they had hitherto been living. Only those who had quit accommodation which was available both for themselves and for those with whom they might reasonably be expected to live could be deemed homeless intentionally.

Discharge

1.43   Homeless people, then, for whom it was the policy of H(HP)A 1977 to ensure that any authority with which there was a local connection provided substantive assistance, were those who had no accommodation (whether they gave it up of their own accord or not); who were in priority need of accommodation, which most commonly meant that they had children; and who did not quit accommodation which was available for themselves and for the whole of their family unit.

1.44   The right which such applicants acquired was not, however, the legal right to council housing itself. Rather, the authority's duty was to ensure that accommodation was made available for the applicant (and those who might reasonably be expected to reside with him/her). The authority might discharge this duty in any of the following ways:

a) by making available accommodation held by it under what is now Housing Act 1985 Part 2 (ie, the principal part of that Act under which council housing is held)[34] or under any other enactment (for example, housing acquired in the exercise of other functions, such as education, highways, etc); or

b) by securing that the applicant obtained accommodation from some other person; or

c) by giving such advice and assistance as would secure that accommodation was obtained from some other person.[35]

1.45   Of course, the principal burden was bound to be placed on the local authority's own stock. Since 1935,[36] local authorities had been under an obligation to 'secure that in the selection of their tenants a reasonable preference is given to persons who are occupying insanitary or overcrowded houses, have large families or are living under unsatisfactory housing conditions';[37] subject to this somewhat loose obligation, they were free to determine their own priorities. To this there

34   Formerly, HA 1957 Part 5.
35   H(HP)A 1977 s6(1); HA 1985 s69(1).
36   HA 1935 s51.
37   As consolidated in HA 1936 s85(2).

was now added a new group: those to whom authorities owed a duty under the homeless legislation.[38]

1.46   In principle, this did no more than require authorities to treat the homeless on the same footing as others, which in law was largely a matter of local choice. In practice, however, provision for the homeless was bound to make a significant impact – especially as no added money was made available to authorities under H(HP)A 1977.[39] Exacerbating the problem, public spending powers were severely restricted from 1980 onwards.[40] In addition, the introduction of security of tenure and the right to buy under the Housing Act 1980 Part 1,[41] meant that the stock of new housing available to local authorities was in decline. Inevitably, therefore, an increasing proportion of allocations went to homeless people.

Re Puhlhofer

1.47   With so much at stake for individuals, and authorities unable – and sometime unwilling – to fulfil the hope that the Act appeared to hold out, it was inevitable that the courts would be needed to broker the two main parties. Because of the structure of the rights and duties created by the legislation – and following a period during which it had been considered that challenges to authorities' decisions might be mounted by ordinary civil claim (in the county court or the High Court)[42] – it was held that this was a role that could only be fulfilled by way of judicial review in the High Court.[43]

1.48   What this led to was a very substantial number of cases in what has subsequently become the Administrative Court,[44] which hears judicial review applications at first instance.[45] Any analysis runs the

---

38 H(HP)A 1977 s6(2), amending HA 1957 s113(2), subsequently HA 1985 s22.

39 A point made by Lord Brightman in *R v Hillingdon LBC ex p Puhlhofer* [1986] AC 484; 18 HLR 158, HL.

40 Local Government, Planning and Land Act 1980; subsequently Local Government and Housing Act 1989. See now, the somewhat more liberal regime of Local Government Act 2003 Part 1.

41 See now HA 1985 Parts 4 and 5.

42 But see, now, chapter 12, for appeal to the county court on a point of law under HA 1996 s204.

43 Under RSC Order 53; *Cocks v Thanet DC* [1983] AC 286; 6 HLR 15, HL.

44 Formerly, the Crown Office List of the High Court.

45 By 1991, almost 20% of all cases in the Crown Office list were homelessness cases, second only to immigration: Bridges, Meszaros and Sunkin, *Judicial review in perspective* (Public Law Project, 1995).

risk of being subjective, but there was a popular perception that the High Court – and, on appeal, the Court of Appeal – so far from maintaining a consistent bias against the homeless, were not uncommonly helpful in their interpretation of the legislation, a perception which derives much support from many of the earlier decisions referred to in the body of this book.

1.49   One body of this judge-made law developed the obviously sensible notion that if a person was occupying accommodation so poor that it could be quit without a finding of intentionality, s/he ought to be treated as if already homeless. This in effect wrote into the definition of homelessness itself – with its reliance on rights of occupation[46] – a minimum standard below which any accommodation should be entirely disregarded, even if there was a right to occupy it.[47]

1.50   Another – related – body of judge-made law introduced the concept of 'settled accommodation'.[48] Only departure from settled accommodation could constitute intentionality, whether because of its condition, terms of occupation or temporary quality. Conversely, only acquisition of settled accommodation would, in normal circumstances, break a period of intentional homelessness and entitle an applicant to re-apply.

1.51   Sympathy – while on occasion expressed – was rarely to be seen in action, however, at the highest level, the House of Lords. Of the nine cases under the 1977/1985 legislation which reached the House of Lords,[49] the homeless were successful in only two of them.[50]

---

46   Above, para 1.30.

47   See *R v South Herefordshire DC ex p Miles* (1983) 17 HLR 82, QBD; *City of Gloucester v Miles* (1985) 17 HLR 292, CA; *R v Dinefwr BC ex p Marshall* (1984) 17 HLR 310, QBD; see also the judgment of Ackner LJ in *Re Puhlhofer* at the Court of Appeal (1985) 17 HLR 558.

48   The phrase was coined by Ackner LJ in *Din v Wandsworth LBC* at the Court of Appeal: [1983] 1 AC 657; 1 HLR 73, HL; see also *Dyson v Kerrier DC* [1980] 1 WLR 1205, CA. See below, chapter 6.

49   *Re Islam* [1983] 1 AC 688; (1981) 1 HLR 107, HL; *Din v Wandsworth LBC* [1983] 1 AC 657; 1 HLR 73; *Re Betts* [1983] 2 AC 613; 10 HLR 97; *Cocks v Thanet DC* [1983] AC 286; 6 HLR 15, HL; *Eastleigh BC v Walsh* [1985] 1 WLR 525; 17 HLR 392; *R v Hillingdon LBC ex p Puhlhofer* [1986] AC 484; 18 HLR 158, HL; *R v Oldham BC ex p G, R v Bexley LBC ex p Bentum, R v Tower Hamlets LBC ex p Begum* [1993] AC 509; 25 HLR 319; *R v Northavon DC ex p Smith* [1994] 2 AC 402; 26 HLR 659; *R v Brent LBC ex p Awua* [1996] 1 AC 55; 27 HLR 453, HL.

50   *Re Islam* [1983] 1 AC 688; (1981) 1 HLR 107, HL and *Eastleigh BC v Walsh* [1985] 1 WLR 525; 17 HLR 392. Of these, *Walsh* was part of a wider issue – the distinction between tenancy and licence – which was contemporaneously being reviewed (and recast) by the House of Lords: see *Street v Mountford* [1985] AC 809; 17 HLR 402.

1.52   One of those nine cases was *Re Puhlhofer*,[51] in which the equiparation of homelessness and want of intentionality[52] was firmly rejected.
No words such as 'appropriate' or 'reasonable' were to be imported
into the term 'accommodation' in H(HP)A 1977 s1/Housing Act
1985 s58 (definition of homelessness). The absence of any such qualification was described as something 'plainly and wisely' determined
by Parliament.

1.53   The House of Lords also took the opportunity forcefully to express
its concern about the 'prolific' use of judicial review in this area: the
courts should exercise great restraint when giving leave to proceed
by way of judicial review; the courts should be used to monitor the
actions of local authorities under the legislation only in exceptional
cases. The speech of Lord Brightman, in particular, expressed the
hope that there would be a lessening in the number of challenges
under the legislation.[53]

> My Lords, I am troubled at the prolific use of judicial review for the
> purpose of challenging the performance by local authorities of their
> functions under the Act of 1977. Parliament intended the local author-
> ity to be the judge of fact. The Act abounds with the formula when,
> or if the housing authority are satisfied as to this, or that, or have
> reason to believe this, or that. Although the action or inaction of a
> local authority is clearly susceptible to judicial review where they have
> misconstrued the Act, or abused their powers or otherwise acted per-
> versely, I think that great restraint should be exercised in giving leave
> to proceed by judicial review. The plight of the homeless is a desperate
> one, and the plight of the applicants in the present case commands
> the deepest sympathy. But it is not, in my opinion, appropriate that
> the remedy of judicial review, which is a discretionary remedy, should
> be made use of to monitor the actions of local authorities under the
> Act save in the exceptional case. The ground upon which the courts
> will review the exercise of an administrative discretion is abuse of
> power – eg bad faith, a mistake in construing the limits of the power,
> a procedural irregularity, or unreasonableness in the *Wednesbury*
> sense – unreasonableness verging on an absurdity: see the speech of
> Lord Scarman in *Reg v Secretary of State for the Environment, Ex parte
> Nottinghamshire CC*.[54] Where the existence or non-existence of a fact
> is left to the judgment and discretion of a public body and that fact
> involves a broad spectrum ranging from the obvious to the debatable
> to the just conceivable, it is the duty of the court to leave the decision

51 *R v Hillingdon LBC ex p Puhlhofer* [1986] AC 484; 18 HLR 158, HL.
52 Above, para 1.49.
53 At 518.
54 [1986] AC 240, 247–248 – see below, paras 12.13–12.16.

of that fact to the public body to whom Parliament has entrusted the decision-making power save in a case where it is obvious that the public body, consciously or unconsciously, are acting perversely.

. . . I express the hope that there will be a lessening in the number of challenges which are mounted against local authorities who are endeavouring, in extremely difficult circumstances, to perform their duties under the Homeless Persons Act with due regard for all their other housing problems.

1.54　Save for a relatively brief period, however, there was no appearance of any such reduction or indeed of a lower rate of success on the part of the homeless.

Housing and Planning Act 1986

1.55　In 1986, in direct response to *Puhlhofer*,[55] Parliament reacted to the judgment that it had been 'wise'[56] not to qualify the sort of accommodation the absence of which rendered a person homeless by amending the principal definition of homelessness to do just that, in effect to harmonise the criteria of homelessness and intentionality: the homeless were now those who, even if enjoying one of the qualifying rights of occupation, occupied accommodation so bad that it would not be reasonable to remain in occupation of it (having regard to the general housing circumstances of their area).[57]

1.56　This in substance preferred the High Court approach[58] to that of the House of Lords. In practical or applied terms, it meant that a person would now be homeless if s/he enjoyed no settled accommodation.[59]

1.57　The Housing and Planning Act 1986 also amended the Housing Act 1985 to ensure that accommodation provided under Part 3 met broadly the same minimum criteria, and likewise rejected critical observations by Lord Brightman in *Re Puhlhofer* in what had not otherwise proved to be an active area of controversy.[60] In substance

---

55　*R v Hillingdon LBC ex p Puhlhofer* [1986] AC 484; 18 HLR 158, HL.
56　Above, para 1.52.
57　HPA 1986 s14(2), amending HA 1985 s58. In Scotland, the equivalent amendment treated as already homeless those who were overcrowded under Scots law and in such circumstances that their health was endangered: Housing (Scotland) Act 1986 s21(2), amending H(HP)A 1977 s1(2).
58　Above, para 1.49.
59　Above, para 1.50.
60　In two cases, without drawing the same link that had been drawn between homelessness and non-intentionality, it had been held that accommodation

and in practice, therefore, it could now also be said that accommodation to be provided had to be settled.

1.58 It may be at this point that homelessness law reached its greatest coherence or cohesiveness – the lower courts had taken the parliamentary framework and, reinforced by the 1986 Act, fleshed it out to identify a level of accommodation to which all those in priority need were entitled, below which they could quit without being intentionally homeless or they continued to be homeless and entitled to the benefit of rehousing assistance under the Act, including priority in the allocation of local authority stock.

Asylum and Immigration Appeals Act 1993

1.59 For a period, homelessness and allocations law enjoyed a period of statutory stability.

1.60 Complaints of unfairness towards others awaiting public sector accommodation, or of an unduly liberal approach to intentionality, were met with revisions to the Code of Guidance issued by the Secretary of State for the Environment[61] but neither achieved – nor sought to achieve – any substantive differences in effect.

1.61 During the 1990s, however, there was growing antagonism towards asylum-seekers, many of whom remained in the United Kingdom for years before a final decision on a claim was reached. As persons lawfully in the country, they had at all times fallen within the protection of the legislation.[62] Under AIAA 1993, however, they were now placed on a different footing from other homeless people. Until the final determination of a claim for asylum, when authorities were bound to reach a new decision,[63] there would be no duty towards any asylum-seeker who had the benefit of some accommodation, however temporary. Likewise, accommodation to be provided did not have to be more than temporary.[64] In effect, therefore, asylum-seekers now enjoyed lesser rights, for the duration of their period as such.

to be provided had to be appropriate or suitable or habitable (having regard to the applicant and those to reside with him/her): *Parr v Wyre BC* (1982) 2 HLR 71, CA (disapproved in *Re Puhlhofer*), and *R v Ryedale DC ex p Smith* (1983) 16 HLR 66.

61 Under HA 1985 s71; see now HA 1996 s182.

62 *R v Hillingdon LBC ex p Streeting* [1980] 1 WLR 1425, CA; *R v Westminster CC ex p Castelli, Tristram-Garcia* (1996) 28 HLR 616, CA.

63 AIAA 1993 s4(4).

64 AIAA 1993 s4(4).

Ex p Awua

1.62   Leaving aside the policy of AIAA 1993, as a matter of law – or legal structure – that Act recognised what the courts, and the Housing and Planning Act 1986, had achieved in terms of quality of accommodation,[65] which is to say that it was that very achievement of which asylum-seekers were to be deprived.

1.63   This did not stop the House of Lords taking another crack at such minimum standards. The decision in *R v Brent LBC ex p Awua*[66] 'caught most people in the housing world somewhat by surprise. It said that a housing authority's duty could be discharged in as little as 28 days. The legal landscape . . . has, therefore, changed'. This was how the Minister for Local Government, Housing and Urban Regeneration, described the decision, noting that HA 1996 was neither introduced because of the *Awua* case nor was a response to it.[67]

1.64   In *Awua*, it was held that 'accommodation' in both Housing Act 1985 s58(1) (definition of homelessness) and s60(1) (definition of intentionality) meant no more than a place which could fairly be described as accommodation and which it would be reasonable, having regard to general housing conditions in the local housing authority's district, for the person in question to continue to occupy. Notwithstanding the 1986 Act amendments, there was no additional requirement that it should be permanent or settled.[68] The same was true of the accommodation which a local housing authority had to make available to an unintentionally homeless person under section 65(2); the accommodation had to be 'suitable', but there was no requirement of permanence.

1.65   Temporary accommodation was accordingly not per se unsuitable. If the tenure was so precarious that the person was likely to have to leave within 28 days without any alternative accommodation being available, then s/he remained threatened with homelessness[69] and the authority would not have discharged its duty. Otherwise, the period for which the accommodation was provided was a matter for the authority to decide.

1.66   This decision, at a stroke, swept away the concept of settled accommodation, save for the purpose of defining that class of accommodation which an intentionally homeless applicant would need to secure

---

65   Above, paras 1.48–1.50.
66   [1996] 1 AC 55; 27 HLR 453, HL.
67   *Hansard*, Standing Committee G, 19 March 1996, col 691.
68   Cf, above, paras 1.57–1.58.
69   HA 1985 s58(4); see now HA 1996 s175(4).

for him/herself before being entitled to re-apply.[70] It could no longer be used to identify accommodation which a person could quit without being found intentionally homeless or as the class of accommodation to which a qualifying applicant was entitled. The committee was not referred to – and did not refer to – AIAA 1993.[71]

Housing Act 1996 Parts 6 and 7

Policy

1.67 Not only was the Housing Act 1996 not a response to *Awua*, the Minister for Local Government, Housing and Urban Regeneration suggested that it went further than the government intended, by removing the safety net of immediate help that it was its new policy to provide,[72] in order to reduce the (increasing) proportion of (decreasing) local authority accommodation that was then being allocated to the homeless.

1.68   HA 1996 was foreshadowed by a Consultation Paper – *Access to Local Authority and Housing Association Tenancies* – in January 1994, which described:

> . . . two main methods of acquiring a local authority or housing association tenancy – by making a direct application to the landlord concerned (and usually going on the relevant waiting list until a suitable property becomes available), or by being accepted as statutorily 'homeless' by a local authority . . .[73]

1.69   Government research[74] published contemporaneously:

> . . . shows that people rehoused from the waiting list are in many important respects (such as income, employment status and previous tenure) similar to households through the homelessness route . . . But statutorily homeless households receive automatic priority over others . . . As a result, in some areas – particularly in parts of London – it is almost impossible for any applicant ever to be rehoused from the waiting list . . . Of those who did manage to get rehoused, people

70 Above, para 1.50.

71 See above, para 1.61.

72 *Hansard*, Standing Committee G, 21 March 1996, col 776. The Minister was aware of the implications of *Pepper v Hart* [1993] AC 625, HL, even if none too accurately, when he remarked, at ibid col 769: 'The Hon Gentleman should also know that what Ministers say during the passage of a Bill is taken into consideration in legal proceedings'.

73 January 1994 Consultation Paper, para 2.5.

74 *Routes into local authority housing*, DoE Housing Research Summary No 16, 1994.

using the waiting list route had to wait nearly twice as long . . . as people housed under the homelessness legislation . . .[75]

By giving the local authority a greater responsibility towards those who can demonstrate 'homelessness' than towards anyone else in housing need, the current legislation creates a perverse incentive for people to have themselves accepted by a local authority as homeless . . . In the great majority of cases, someone accepted as homeless is in fact occupying accommodation of some sort at the time he or she approached the authority. Indeed, the largest single category of households accepted as statutorily homeless are people living as licensees of parents, relatives or friends who are no longer willing or able to accommodate them . . . There is a growing belief that the homelessness provisions are frequently used as a quick route into a separate home . . .[76]

Against this background, the government is proposing measures to ensure fairer access to all parts of the rented housing sector. These include measures to prevent homelessness, to remove the distorting effect that the present provisions have on the allocation of housing, and to ensure that subsidised housing is equally available to all who genuinely need it, particularly couples seeking to establish a good home in which to start and raise a family.[77]

1.70   The proposals were threefold:

a)   to limit the extent of an authority's duties to the homeless;

b)   to limit local authority housing allocation to the homeless; and

c)   to encourage more advisory activity to help people find other accommodation.[78]

1.71   The idea was to provide an immediate safety net, while longer-term allocation to homeless people would be considered alongside others seeking council housing.[79] This would be achieved by new constraints on allocation, subject to 'broad principles' to be laid down by central government.[80]

1.72   The white paper on which the Act was based, *Our future homes*,[81] pursued the theme that homelessness was:

. . . usually a short term crisis . . . We are committed to maintaining an immediate safety net, but this should be separate from a fair system

---

75   January 1994 Consultation Paper, para 2.6.
76   January 1994 Consultation Paper, para 2.8.
77   January 1994 Consultation Paper, para 3.1.
78   January 1994 Consultation Paper, para 3.2.
79   January 1994 Consultation Paper, para 3.4.
80   January 1994 Consultation Paper, paras 20.2 and 22.1.
81   Cm 2901 (HMSO, June 1995).

of allocating long-term accommodation in a house or flat owned by a local authority or housing association . . .[82]

Local authorities will continue to have an immediate duty to secure accommodation for families and vulnerable individuals who have nowhere to go. Where such people are found to have no alternative available accommodation, the local housing authority will have to secure suitable accommodation for not less than twelve months.[83] The authority may continue to secure accommodation for longer than that, although after two years it must check that the household's housing circumstances have not changed . . . These arrangements are intended to tide people over the immediate crisis of homelessness, and to give them time to find longer-term accommodation . . .[84]

1.73 The white paper was followed in January 1996 by a linked consultation paper, *Allocation of housing accommodation by local authorities.* This introduced the ideas that were to become Part 6 of HA 1996, governing the waiting list. It identified changes proposed to Housing Act 1985 s22,[85] designed to 'create a single route into social housing',[86] in accordance with the policy[87] of putting '*all* those with long-term housing needs on the same footing, while providing a safety net for emergency and pressing needs' [emphasis in original]. It will be 'the only route into social housing allocated by local authorities; it will be dynamic, and will focus on basic underlying need rather than immediate emergency'.[88]

1.74 The consultation paper proposed to retain the long-established categories of those occupying insanitary or overcrowded housing, or living in unsatisfactory housing conditions,[89] to which it would add:

– those living in conditions of temporary or insecure tenure (including those at risk of losing accommodation, for example, tied accommodation);

82 *Our future homes* (see footnote 81,above), p36, claiming that over 40 per cent of local authority new tenancies – over 80 per cent in some London authorities – and over 25 per cent of allocations of housing association tenancies were going to those accepted under the homelessness legislation.

83 Later changed to two years: see HA 1996 s193(2). See also *Hansard*, Standing Committee G, 21 March 1996, col 776 – reflecting a concern that, even if renewable, one year would not provide sufficient security.

84 White paper, *Our future homes*, p37.

85 Above, paras 1.45 and 1.46.

86 *Hansard* (HC), Standing Committee G, 16th Sitting, 12 March 1996, Minister for Local Government, Housing and Urban Regeneration (Mr Curry), col 614.

87 White paper, *Our future homes*, chapter 6.

88 *Hansard* (HC), Standing Committee G, 15th Sitting, 12 March 1996, Minister for Local Government, Housing and Urban Regeneration (Mr Curry), col 588.

89 See above, para 1.45.

- families with dependent children or who are expecting a child ('recognising the importance of a stable home environment to children's development');
- households containing a person with an identified need for settled accommodation (for example, those who give or need to receive care or other personal circumstances); and
- those households with limited opportunities to secure settled accommodation (for example, low income), bearing in mind longer-term prospects.[90]

1.75   The principal policy change – to minimise the priority call of homeless people on local authority stock – may be addressed under its two heads: principal homelessness changes; and allocation changes. In addition, there were a number of other discrete changes.

Principal homelessness changes

1.76   The principal homelessness changes[91] were:

- persons subject to immigration control under the Asylum and Immigration Act 1996, unless of a class prescribed by the secretary of state, were no longer eligible under Part 7;[92] nor were others within any class prescribed by the secretary of state; nor were such persons to be taken into consideration when determining whether someone else was homeless, threatened with homelessness, or had a priority need for accommodation;[93]
- where the authority was satisfied that there was other suitable accommodation available in its area, the duty was limited to giving 'such advice and assistance as the authority consider is reasonably required to enable' the applicant to secure such accommodation;[94]
- in cases where such suitable accommodation was not available, the duty to secure that accommodation was made available to the applicant was limited to two years (although it could be continued in defined circumstances following a review, and – in default – a new application could otherwise be made);[95]

---

90   January 1996 Consultation Paper (see para 1.73, above), paras 26, 27, 28–31 and 33.
91   The exclusion of those subject to immigration control, introduced in 1993 (above, paras 1.59–1.61).
92   HA 1996 s185.
93   HA 1996 s185(4).
94   HA 1996 s197.
95   HA 1996 ss193 and 194.

– unless and until the authority could make an offer from its waiting list, the authority was prohibited from providing its own accommodation in discharge of functions under Part 7 for more than two years out of any three (whether continuously or in aggregate), unless it was hostel accommodation or accommodation privately leased by the authority from a private landlord.[96]

Allocations

1.77   Meanwhile, HA 1996 Part 6 provided that:

– local authorities were bound to comply with Part 6 when making any allocation decision, including the selection of their own tenants and making nominations to a registered social landlord;[97]
– allocation could also[98] only be to persons qualified on their housing register, which did not include a person subject to immigration control under the Asylum and Immigration Act 1996, unless of a class prescribed by the secretary of state, nor did it include others within any class prescribed by the secretary of state; qualification was otherwise within the discretion of the authority;[99]
– authorities had to adopt an allocation scheme for determining priority between applicants, including by whom decisions could be taken.

Subject to this, the scheme had to be framed to secure a reasonable preference not for the homeless to whom duties were owed per se but for:

a) those occupying insanitary or overcrowded housing, or otherwise living in insanitary conditions;
b) those living in temporary accommodation or on insecure terms;
c) families with dependent children;
d) households consisting of or including someone who was expecting a child;
e) households consisting of or including someone with a particular need for settled accommodation on medical or welfare grounds, with added preference under this heading to those who could not reasonably be expected to find their own settled accommodation in the near future; and

96 HA 1996 s207; this included housing associations or, as they were coming to be known by Part 1 of the same Act, registered social landlords.
97 HA 1996 s159.
98 See above, para 1.76.
99 HA 1996 s161.

f) households whose social or economic circumstances were such that they had difficulty in securing settled accommodation.[100]

Other changes

1.78   HA 1996 Part 6 included a number of ancillary provisions, including notification of entry on and removal from the register, review of entries and review of decisions.

1.79   Part 7 also effected a number of changes to homelessness law, of which the most significant were the introduction of a right to internal review and subsequent appeal to the county court.[101]

Between Acts

Restoration of priority to homeless people

1.80   HA 1996 Parts 6 and 7 had been in force for only a relatively short period of time when the general election of 1997 brought a new government into power.

1.81   One of its first acts was to restore priority to homeless people under HA 1996 Part 6. Using a power[102] to specify further descriptions of people to whom a preference should be given, the Allocation of Housing (Reasonable and Additional Preference) Regulations 1997[103] re-afforded[104] a reasonable preference to the unintentionally homeless towards whom a duty was owed under Part 7 or its predecessor provisions in the Housing Act 1985.

Asylum-seekers

1.82   The Immigration and Asylum Act 1999 set up an entirely separate national service (the National Asylum Support Service (NASS)) to deal with destitute asylum-seekers.[105] As a result, all asylum-seekers

---

100 HA 1996 s167(2).
101 HA 1996 ss202 and 204.
102 HA 1996 s167(3).
103 SI No 1902.
104 Cf above, para 1.45.
105 Now, for those who made their first asylum claim on or after 5 March 2007 dealt with under the New Asylum Model – see below, chapter 3; earlier applicants are known as 'legacy' cases and should have their asylum and support claims dealt with by the Casework Resolution Directorate (CRD).

whose claims were made on or after 3 April 2000 were taken out of HA 1996 Part 7.

The green paper

1.83　These changes were followed, in April 2000, by 'the first comprehensive review of housing policy for 23 years' – the green paper, *Quality and choice: a decent home for all* (DETR, 2000).

1.84　The green paper set out aims for reform in relation to both homelessness and allocations. The changes to the allocations provisions were given more prominence and made subject to an overall aim of encouraging 'social landlords to see themselves more as providers of a lettings service which is responsive to the needs and wishes of individuals rather than purely as housing "allocators"'.[106]

1.85　The aims were to ensure that lettings and transfer services:

a)　meet the long-term housing requirements of those who need social housing most, in a way which is sustainable both for individuals and the community;

b)　adopt a simple and customer-centred approach, empowering first-time applicants and existing tenants to make decisions in choosing housing which meets their requirements;

c)　make better use of the national housing stock, by widening the scope for lettings and transfers across local authority boundaries, and between local authorities and registered social landlords; and

d)　give local authorities more flexibility to build sustainable communities within the national context of extreme variations in local housing markets.[107]

1.86　The green paper's proposals for the reform of homelessness policy were intended to:

－　ensure that unintentionally homeless people in priority need are provided with temporary accommodation until they obtain settled accommodation (in either the public or private sector);

－　broaden the definition of priority need to ensure our most vulnerable citizens are protected by the homelessness safety net;

－　enable local authorities to use their own housing stock to provide temporary accommodation, without the current restriction that it may only be provided for two years in any three;

106　*Quality and choice: a decent home for all* (DETR, 2000), para 9.3.
107　*Quality and choice: a decent home for all*, para 9.4.

- give those housed in temporary accommodation a reasonable period in which they can exercise the same degree of customer choice of settled accommodation as is available to other people with urgent housing needs waiting on the housing register;
- allow local authorities greater flexibility to assist non-priority homeless households, particularly in areas of low demand; and
- encourage a more strategic approach to the prevention of homelessness and the rehousing of homeless households.[108]

1.87   Following consultation, the government published a response (*Quality and choice: a decent home for all – The way forward*, DETR, December 2000), explaining how it was 'taking the agenda forward'.[109] 'The principle of choice in lettings was broadly welcomed.'[110] Indeed, the move towards choice-based lettings was already being facilitated within the existing legal framework of HA 1996 Part 6, through a series of government-funded pilot schemes.[111] In relation to the homelessness proposals, 'there was almost unanimous support, from those who responded'.[112] Legislation was promised to implement both the allocation and the homelessness proposals.

1.88   This legislation originally formed part of the Homes Bill 2001, which also included provisions to improve the process of buying and selling homes through a requirement for a 'home-buyers pack'. The bill fell at committee stage in the House of Lords, as a result of the general election in May 2001. Following re-election, the government decided not to proceed immediately with the provisions relating to home-buying, but re-introduced those relating to homelessness and allocation, in the Homelessness Bill.

Priority need categories

1.89   Not all the elements of the green paper proposals required primary legislation, however. In particular, the green paper proposed extending the categories of priority need[113] to those leaving an institutional or care background, those fleeing domestic violence, and 16- and 17-year-olds. This could be achieved by statutory instrument, under HA 1996 s189(2).

---

108 *Quality and choice: a decent home for all*, para 9.42.
109 *The way forward*, p4.
110 *The way forward*, para 6.2.
111 *The way forward*, para 6.5.
112 *The way forward*, para 7.3.
113 *Quality and choice: a decent home for all*, paras 9.55 and 9.56.

1.90   An amendment was first made by the National Assembly for Wales on 1 March 2001.[114] In England, there was consultation on a draft statutory instrument during 2001, and it was not until 2002 that the changes were made, to coincide with the coming into force of the majority of the homelessness provisions in the Homelessness Act 2002.[115]

1.91   The Welsh and English provisions are not worded identically, illustrating an increasing divergence in housing policy following devolution.

Homelessness Act 2002

1.92   The Homelessness Act 2002 received Royal Assent on 26 February 2002.

Strategies

1.93   The green paper had emphasised the need for authorities to develop a more strategic approach to the prevention and redress of homelessness. This was embodied in Homelessness Act 2002 ss1–4, by a duty requiring each local housing authority to undertake a review of homelessness and to formulate an effective strategy to deal with it, in consultation with both social services (whether of the same authority or another) and other organisations.

Duties

1.94   One of the main changes of HA 1996 had been to limit the initial duty to house homeless people to a period of two years.[116] This limit was repealed by the Homelessness Act 2002, along with the limitation of use of an authority's stock to house the homeless.[117] Also repealed were the provisions of HA 1996 s197 which allowed the main duties to be avoided[118] if other suitable accommodation was available.[119]

---

114 Homeless Persons (Priority Need) (Wales) Order 2001 SI No 607.
115 See the Homelessness (Priority Need for Accommodation) (England) Order 2002 SI No 2051.
116 See para 1.76, above.
117 Homelessness Act 2002 s6.
118 See para 1.76, above.
119 Homelessness Act 2002 s9.

1.95   Nonetheless, the duty was not intended to last for an infinite time, and the circumstances which bring an authority's duty to an end under HA 1996 s193 were accordingly widened to allow more reliance on assured tenancies, and – in certain circumstances – even assured shorthold tenancies.[120]

Non-priority need applicants

1.96   Homelessness Act 2002 s5 also gave local authorities power to house the unintentionally homeless under HA 1996 Part 7, even where not in priority need.

Other changes

1.97   Further changes were made to the definitions of homelessness and intentionality, to ensure that any kind of violence – not only domestic violence – would mean that it is not reasonable to continue to occupy accommodation.[121] This helps, for example, those fleeing racial harassment or intimidation.

1.98   In addition, there was an extension in the jurisdiction of the county court to allow an applicant who is appealing against an authority's decision also to appeal to that court against a refusal by the authority to provide him/her with interim accommodation pending final outcome of the appeal process.[122]

1.99   The Homelessness Act 2002 made two other amendments to the review process: applicants are allowed both to accept an offer of accommodation and to challenge its suitability by way of review;[123] and the county court may itself extend the 21-day time limit for appealing.[124]

Allocations

1.100   The amendments to HA 1996 Part 6 almost all reflected the government's aim of bringing greater choice to the allocation process by local authorities.

---

120 Homelessness Act 2002 s7.
121 Homelessness Act 2002 s10.
122 Homelessness Act 2002 s11.
123 Homelessness Act 2002 s8(2).
124 Homelessness Act 2002 Sch 1 para 17.

1.101   One change was to bring transfer applications (whether within the stock of a single landlord or between the stocks of more than one landlord) into the ambit of HA 1996 Part 6.[125] This ensured both that existing tenants are dealt with on the same basis as new applicants and that their qualification for rehousing is not limited.[126]

1.102   The HA 1996 requirement to keep a housing register was abolished.[127]

> Removing the requirement to have a register is an important step in facilitating the development by local authorities of choice-based letting schemes that put the applicant at the centre of the decision-making process. We want to encourage authorities to move away from the rigid formulas of an often artificial points-based system, which typically becomes associated with allocation schemes based on the housing register.[128]

1.103   The government retained the ineligibility of persons from abroad for an allocation of housing.[129] In addition, the Homelessness Act 2002 and the green paper continued to reflect a widespread concern about anti-social behaviour, and the Act therefore contained provisions allowing those guilty of 'unacceptable behaviour serious enough to make him/her unsuitable to be a tenant' also to be excluded from social housing.[130]

1.104   The requirement that allocation schemes reflect housing need in some way was likewise not abandoned, and the Act retained the concept of the 'reasonable preference' to be given to certain groups, albeit subject to some changes.[131] Authorities' schemes are explicitly allowed to take into account financial resources, behaviour and local connection when determining preference and, even where those guilty of seriously unacceptable behaviour are not excluded from the allocation scheme altogether, they may be accorded no preference.

1.105   Changes were made to the ancillary provisions on notification and internal review, to allow an applicant to seek an internal review in relation to any decision about the facts of his/her case, including

---

125 Homelessness Act 2002 s13.
126 See *Quality and choice: a decent home for all* (DETR, 2000), para 9.8.
127 See para 1.77, above.
128 Standing Committee A, 12 July 2001, col 81, per Dr Alan Whitehead, Parliamentary Under-Secretary for Transport, Local Government and the Regions.
129 See para 1.77, above.
130 See para 1.77, above.
131 Including giving preference to all homeless people, whether in priority need or not, and whether or not they are intentionally homeless.

a decision that s/he is to be excluded or given no preference because of unacceptable behaviour.[132]

1.106   The Homelessness Act 2002 provisions still do not comprise a tightly-prescriptive framework and there remains considerable room for local variation:

> We believe the right way forward is for local authorities and registered social landlords to decide in the light of local circumstances, and drawing on the experiences of the pilot studies, the ways in which they should amend or develop their existing arrangements.[133]

Changes since the 2002 Act

1.107   Since the Homelessness Act 2002, the focus of government policy has been primarily on its implementation. One particular focus has been on the reduction in the use of bed and breakfast accommodation. In 2003, secondary legislation made it unlawful in England for local authorities to place families in bed and breakfast accommodation for more than six weeks.[134]

1.108   Other key changes have focused on issues of immigration and asylum. While it has already been noted that asylum-seekers were taken outside the existing statutory provisions in April 2000 by the establishment of NASS,[135] the question arose whether accommodation provided by NASS gave rise to a local connection under HA 1996 Part 7 if and when asylum-seekers achieved refugee status and were thus able to apply under Part 7. The House of Lords initially answered this question in the negative.[136] The government, concerned that refugees would overwhelmingly apply to areas of greatest housing stress in London and the south-east, reversed this decision by amendments to HA 1996 s199 contained in the Asylum and Immigration (Treatment of Claimants etc) Act 2004 s11.

1.109   Another immigration-related statutory change followed from the exclusion of ineligible persons when considering whether an applicant for Part 7 assistance was homeless, threatened with

---

132   Homelessness Act 2002 s14.

133   *The way forward* para 6.4.

134   Homelessness (Suitability of Accommodation) (England) Order 2003 SI No 3326. Similar (although not identical) limitations were introduced in Wales in 2006.

135   See para 1.82.

136   *Al-ameri v Kensington and Chelsea RLBC; Osmani v Harrow LBC* [2004] UKHL 4; [2004] HLR 20.

homelessness or in priority need.[137] This had been held to be incompatible with the family life provisions of article 8 of the European Convention on Human Rights.[138] In consequence, the Housing and Regeneration Act 2008 amended HA 1996 s185(4) so as to take such persons into account, except in those cases where, although eligible, the applicant[139] is subject to immigration control,[140] albeit that such an application would be known as a 'restricted case' to whom the authority owes a – somewhat lesser – duty by way of making a 'private accommodation offer',[141] and which is excluded from the reasonable preference afforded to the homeless under Part 6.[142]

1.110 The 2008 Act also made changes to the local connection provisions, so as to include employment in the armed forces and residence during such service as grounds for a local connection, where they had formerly been excluded.[143] No case-law[144] has, however, had the seminal effect of a *Puhlhofer*[145] or *Awua*,[146] with the possible exception of the Part 6 decision in *R (Ahmad) v Newham LBC*,[147] in which there are shades of Lord Brightman's speech in *Puhlhofer*[148] to be found in the speech of Lord Neuberger:[149]

> ... [A]s a general proposition, it is undesirable for the courts to get involved in questions of how priorities are accorded in housing allocation policies. Of course, there will be cases where the court has a duty to interfere, for instance if a policy does not comply with statutory requirements, or if it is plainly irrational. However, it seems unlikely that the legislature can have intended that Judges should embark on the exercise of telling authorities how to decide on priorities as

137 See above, para 1.76.
138 *R (Morris) v Westminster CC* [2005] EWCA Civ 1184; [2006] HLR 8.
139 Not being an EEA or Swiss national, who are fully eligible: see below, paras 3.11–3.12.
140 Ie, asylum-seekers, those with indefinite leave to remain: see below, paras 3.91–3.93.
141 Housing and Regeneration Act 2008 s314 and Sch 15 Part 1. The details of what this duty entails may be seen below, paras 5.7–5.8.
142 HA 1996 s167(2ZA), inserted by 2008 Act s314 and Sch 15 Part 1.
143 See below, para 7.16.
144 Other important decisions include *Birmingham CC v Ali, Moran v Manchester CC* [2009] UKHL 36 (see below, paras 4.13 and 4.70), and *Holmes-Moorhouse v Richmond upon Thames LBC* [2009] UKHL 7; [2009] HLR 34 (see below, para 5.26).
145 Above, paras 1.47–1.54.
146 Above, paras 1.62–1.66.
147 [2009] UKHL 14; [2009] HLR 31.
148 Above, para 1.53.
149 At [46–47].

between applicants in need of rehousing, save in relatively rare and extreme circumstances. Housing allocation policy is a difficult exercise which requires not only social and political sensitivity and judgment, but also local expertise and knowledge.

In relation to the provision of accommodation under the National Assistance Act 1948, my noble and learned friend, Baroness Hale of Richmond, then Hale LJ, said in *R (Wahid) v Tower Hamlets LBC*,[150] para 33, '[n]eed is a relative concept, which trained and experienced social workers are much better equipped to assess than are lawyers and courts, provided that they act rationally'. Precisely the same is true of relative housing needs under Part 6 of the 1996 Act, and trained and experienced local authority housing officers.

The provisions in outline

continued

Introduction

2.1   In this chapter, Housing Act (HA) 1996 Parts 6 and 7, as amended by the Homelessness Act 2002, will each be considered as a whole, in reverse order. The provisions are considered on their face; they are considered in detail in subsequent chapters.

2.2   HA 1996 Parts 6 and 7 extend to England and Wales. The provisions of the Housing (Homeless Persons) Act (H(HP)A) 1977 were consolidated in the Housing (Scotland) Act 1987 and, subject to amendment,[1] so remain. Provision is made to ensure that homelessness applications in England and Wales allow for connections with Scottish authorities.[2] In Northern Ireland, duties towards the homeless and those threatened with homelessness are imposed on the Northern Ireland Housing Executive by the Housing (Northern Ireland) Order 1988.[3]

2.3   In outline, HA 1996 Part 7 places an obligation on local housing authorities to secure that suitable accommodation is made available for a person:

– who is homeless;
– who is in priority need of accommodation;
– who did not become homeless intentionally,

but this is subject to the local connection provisions.[4] The obligation is the peak housing duty under HA 1996 Part 7. However, where discharge is by way of the allocation of a secure or introductory tenancy of an authority's own accommodation or nomination to such a tenancy of another authority or to an assured tenancy of a registered social landlord, it is subject to the provisions of HA 1996 Part 6.

---

1   Housing (Scotland) Act 1987 was amended by the Housing (Scotland) Act 2001. A major review of homelessness in Scotland (Scottish Executive Homelessness Task Force (2002) Final Report) led to further legislation in the Homelessness etc (Scotland) Act 2003. There has been increasing divergence between the law in Scotland and that in the rest of the UK. The 2003 Act provides for the eventual abolition of categories of priority need, so that a duty will be owed to all homeless persons. It also provides for continuing duties towards the intentionally homeless.

2   HA 1996 s201.

3   SI No 1990 (NI 23). This too has been subject to review by the Northern Ireland Housing Executive (NIHE) in 2001, and the order was amended to bring it more in line with HA 1996 Part 7 by the Housing (Northern Ireland) Order 2003 SI No 412 (NI 2). See also NIHE Homelessness Strategy 2002, available at: www.nihe.gov.uk/publications/reports/homeless02.pdf.

4   HA 1996 ss193(2) and 198(1).

2.4 Certain persons are ineligible for assistance on immigration grounds.[5] Special provision is made for those who, while eligible for assistance, are only homeless or in priority need by reference to others with whom they reside or might reasonably be expected to reside who are themselves ineligible.

2.5 There are also obligations in respect of those:

- who are not yet homeless;
- who do not have a priority need;
- who have a priority need but become homeless intentionally; and
- who are thought to be subject to the local connection provisions, pending determination of ultimate responsibility.

2.6 In addition, authorities have duties:

- to make enquiries;
- to notify the applicant of their decisions and the reasons for them; and
- to protect the property of the homeless.

There are ancillary provisions governing deception. There is provision for the funding of voluntary agencies. There is also provision for the internal review of decisions, and appeal to the county court on a point of law.

2.7 The approach adopted here is, first, to define the key concepts contained in HA 1996 Part 7, before matching them to the duties which Part 7 imposes, considering separately and under their own headings the ancillary provisions, review and appeal, and allocation under HA 1996 Part 6.

2.8 The definitions which must be considered are:

- 'authorities';
- 'immigration';
- 'homelessness';
- 'priority need';
- 'intentional homelessness'; and
- 'local connection'.

2.9 The duties which must be considered are:

- preliminary duties;
- principal duties; and
- local connection provisions.

5 HA 1996 s185. The detail is set out in regulations. For England see the Allocation of Housing and Homelessness (Eligibility) (England) Regulations 2006 SI No 1294 and, in Wales, see the Allocation of Housing (Wales) Regulations 2003 SI No 239 and the Homelessness (Wales) Regulations 2006 SI No 2646.

2.10   Further matters which must be considered are:
- protection of property;
- homelessness strategies;
- advice, information and voluntary organisations;
- Code of Guidance;
- review and appeal;
- criminal offences;
- co-operation between authorities; and
- allocation.

Authorities

2.11   HA 1996 Part 7 (s217) refers to three classes of authority:
- local housing authorities;
- relevant authorities; and
- social services authorities.

Local housing authority

2.12   'Local housing authority' means a district council except in London, where it means the London borough council or the Common Council of the City of London,[6] and in Wales, where it means the county or county borough council (Housing Act 1985 s1, as amended).[7] Unitary authorities under the Local Government Act 1992 or Local Government and Public Involvement in Health Act 2007 will have the functions conferred on them by order, which means that they, too, are housing authorities.[8]

Relevant authority

2.13   'Relevant authority' means, in England and Wales, a local housing authority and a social services authority.[9]

Social services authority

2.14   'Social services authority' means a non-metropolitan county council, a metropolitan district council, a London borough council or the

6   HA 1996 s230 and HA 1985 s1.
7   See also Local Government (Wales) Act 1994 s17.
8   Local Government (Changes for England) Regulations 1994 SI No 867.
9   HA 1996 s217.

Common Council of the City of London, and in Wales a county or county borough council.[10] Unitary authorities are, by order, also social services authorities.[11]

Immigration

2.15 Persons from abroad are ineligible for assistance if they are persons who are subject to immigration control under the Asylum and Immigration Act 1996, who have not been re-qualified by regulations.[12] No person who is excluded from entitlement to housing benefit by the Immigration and Asylum Act 1999 s115 may be re-included by such regulations.[13] In addition, the secretary of state may, by regulation, add categories of people who are to be treated as persons from abroad for these purposes.[14] Asylum-seekers, whose position was formerly governed separately by HA 1996 s186, are now governed by the regulations, as are other immigrants. Ineligible asylum-seekers may, however, be able to access accommodation from the UK Borders Agency[15] (formerly through the National Asylum Support Service);[16] and children in need – including those of ineligible persons from abroad – may be able to obtain assistance under local authority social service powers.[17] When deciding whether an eligible applicant is homeless or in priority need, provision is made governing whether persons who are themselves ineligible and subject to immigration control, and who either do not have leave to enter or remain in the UK or have leave subject to a condition of no recourse to public funds, may be

---

10 HA 1996 s217 and Local Authority Social Services Act 1970 s1, as amended.

11 Local Government (Changes for England) Regulations 1994 SI No 867.

12 HA 1996 s185(1) and (2).

13 HA 1996 s185(2A). Allocation of Housing and Homelessness (Eligibility) (England) Regulations (Eligibility Regs) 2006 SI No 1294, which came into force on 1 June 2006.

14 HA 1996 s185(3). See Eligibility Regs 2006, above.

15 The United Kingdom Borders Agency was set up in February 2008.

16 Below, paras 3.3 and 13.32–13.43. In July 2006. the Home Office announced that the National Asylum Support Service (NASS) no longer existed as a separate department. Asylum support is now administered by two separate routes. Those who made their first asylum claim on or after 5 March 2007 have their support processed by the New Asylum Model (NAM) 'case owner' who is processing their asylum claim. Applicants who claimed asylum before 5 March 2007, known as 'legacy' cases, should have their asylum and support claims dealt with by the Casework Resolution Directorate (CRD).

17 Below, paras 13.44–13.65.

taken into account.[18] Such persons are not taken into account if (but only if) the applicant is him/herself subject to immigration control (not including EEA and Swiss nationals for this purpose);[19] where reliance by an applicant is placed on such an ineligible member of his/her household, the case is known as a 'restricted case' and there are discrete provisions governing how a duty is to be discharged.[20]

Information

2.16   In order to reach a decision on the issue of eligibility, a local housing authority may seek such information as it requires from the secretary of state, who is bound to provide it (and, whether or not the original request for information was in writing, to provide it in writing if the authority, in writing, asks for it so to be provided).[21]

2.17   The secretary of state is under an additional duty to notify the authority in writing if it subsequently appears to him/her that any application, decision or other change of circumstance has affected the status of a person about whom s/he had previously provided information.[22]

Homelessness

2.18   A person is homeless for the purposes of HA 1996 Part 7 if s/he has no accommodation in the UK or elsewhere in the world, which is available for his/her occupation,[23] and which s/he is:

a)   entitled to occupy by virtue of an interest in it (for example, as tenant or owner or under an equitable interest); or

b)   entitled to occupy by virtue of a court order (for example, in the course of domestic proceedings); or

c)   entitled to occupy by virtue of an express or implied licence (for example, friendly or family arrangement, contractual licence); or

d)   actually occupying as a residence, 'by virtue of any enactment or rule of law giving him the right to remain in occupation or restricting the right of any other person to recover possession of it' (for example, between termination of tenancy and order for possession).[24]

18   HA 1996 s185(7).
19   HA 1996 s185(5).
20   HA 1996 s193(7AA); see below, para 3.75.
21   HA 1996 s187(1) and (2).
22   HA 1996 s187(3).
23   HA 1996 s175(1).
24   HA 1996 s175(1).

The provisions in outline 41

Available accommodation

2.19   Accommodation is only available for an applicant's occupation if it is available for him/her, together with any other person who normally resides with him/her as a member of his/her family, and any other person who might reasonably be expected to reside with him/her.[25]

Reasonable to continue to occupy

2.20   Accommodation is disregarded if it is not accommodation which it would be reasonable to continue to occupy,[26] for example, if it is in such bad condition that no one could be expected to stay in it. When deciding whether or not it would be reasonable for a person to remain in occupation, an authority to which application has been made can take into account the general housing circumstances prevailing in its area,[27] ie, to what extent others are having to live in bad conditions.

Violence

2.21   It is also not reasonable to continue to occupy accommodation if it is probable that to do so will lead to violence (domestic or otherwise) against the applicant, or against someone who normally resides with the applicant as a member of his/her family, or against anyone else who might reasonably be expected to reside with the applicant.[28]

2.22   'Violence' means violence from another person, or threats of violence from another person which are likely to be carried out.[29]

Domestic violence

2.23   Violence is domestic violence if it is from a person who is 'associated' with the victim.[30]

Associated people

2.24   People are associated if:
  a) they are or have been married to each other;
  b) they are or have been civil partners of each other;

25 HA 1996 s176.
26 HA 1996 s175(3).
27 HA 1996 s177(2).
28 HA 1996 s177(1).
29 HA 1996 s177(1A).
30 HA 1996 s177(1A).

c) they are cohabitants or former cohabitants (meaning a man and a woman who are living together without being married to one another or two people of the same sex who are living together without being civil partners);

d) they live or have lived in the same household;

e) they are relatives, meaning:

   i) parent, step-parent, child, step-child, grandparent or grand-child of a person or of that person's spouse, civil partner, former spouse; or former civil partner; or

   ii) sibling, aunt or uncle, niece or nephew of a person or that person's spouse, civil partner, former spouse or former civil partner, whether of full or half-blood, or by marriage or civil partnership;

f) they have or had formerly agreed to marry;

g) they have entered into a civil partnership agreement between them (whether or not that agreement has been terminated);

h) in relation to a child, each of the persons is a parent of the child, or has or has had parental responsibility (within the meaning of the Children Act (CA) 1989) for the child; and

i) in relation to a child who has been adopted (or subsequently freed from adoption), if one person is a natural parent or natural parent of a natural parent, and the other is the child, or is a person who has become a parent by adoption, or who has applied for an adoption order, or with whom the child was at any time placed for adoption.[31]

Unusable accommodation

2.25   In addition, a person is homeless if s/he has accommodation which s/he occupies or is entitled to occupy, and which is available for his/her occupation and reasonable to continue to occupy, but:

a) s/he cannot secure entry to it; or

b) the accommodation consists of a movable structure, vehicle or vessel, designed or adapted for living in, and there is no place where s/he is entitled or permitted both to place it and to reside in it, for example, houseboat, caravan.[32]

31   HA 1996 s178, as amended by Civil Partnership Act 2004 Sch 8.
32   HA 1996 s175(2).

Threatened with homelessness

2.26 A person is threatened with homelessness if it is likely that s/he will become homeless within 28 days.[33]

Priority need

2.27 A person has a priority need for accommodation if the authority is satisfied that:

a) the person has dependent children who are residing with, or who might reasonably be expected to reside with, him/her, for example, because the family is separated solely because of the need for accommodation; or

b) the person is homeless or threatened with homelessness as a result of any emergency such as flood, fire or any other disaster; or

c) the person, or any person who resides or who might reasonably be expected to reside with him/her, is vulnerable because of old age, mental illness, handicap or physical disability or other special reason; or

d) she is pregnant, or is a person who resides or might reasonably be expected to reside with a pregnant woman.[34]

Additional categories

2.28 The secretary of state[35] may specify further classes of person as having a priority need for accommodation, or amend or repeal any of the present classes.[36]

2.29 In England, the following additional classes have been specified:[37]

a) all 16- and 17-year-olds, provided they are not a relevant child, or a child to whom the local authority owes a duty to provide accommodation under the Children Act 1989 s20;[38]

---

33 HA 1996 s175(4).
34 HA 1996 s189(1).
35 In Wales, the power is exercisable by the National Assembly: National Assembly for Wales (Transfer of Functions) Order 1999 SI No 672.
36 HA 1996 s189(2).
37 Homelessness (Priority Need for Accommodation) (England) Order 2002 SI No 2051.
38 As defined by CA 1989 s23A. Relevant children remain the responsibility of social service authorities.

b) any person who is aged 18 to 20, other than a relevant student,[39] who at any time after reaching the age of 16 but while still under 18 was, but is no longer, looked after, accommodated or fostered;[40]
c) those who are vulnerable because they have previously been looked after, accommodated or fostered;
d) those who are vulnerable as a result of service in Her Majesty's regular armed forces;
e) those who are vulnerable as a result of having served a custodial sentence, having been committed for contempt of court or having been remanded in custody;
f) those who are vulnerable because they have had to cease to occupy accommodation because of violence or threats of violence which are likely to be carried out.

2.30   In Wales, this power has been exercised[41] to specify:
a) all those who are aged 18 or over, and under 21, if at any time while they were a child they were looked after, accommodated or fostered, or they are at particular risk of sexual or financial exploitation;
b) all 16- and 17-year-olds;
c) those without dependent children who have been subject to domestic violence, who are at risk of such violence or who would be if they returned home;
d) those who formerly served in the regular armed forces and have been homeless since leaving those forces;
e) former prisoners who have been homeless since leaving custody, provided they have a local connection[42] with the local housing authority.

Intentional homelessness

2.31   A person becomes intentionally homeless if s/he deliberately does or fails to do anything in consequence of which s/he ceases to occupy accommodation which is available for occupation, and which it would have been reasonable to continue to occupy.[43]

---

39   As defined by CA 1989 s24B(3).
40   The phrase 'looked after, accommodated or fostered' has the meaning given by CA 1989 s24(2).
41   Homeless Persons (Priority Need) (Wales) Order 2001 SI No 607.
42   See para 2.36, below.
43   HA 1996 s191(1).

2.32   A person becomes threatened with homelessness intentionally if s/he deliberately does or fails to do anything, the likely result of which is that s/he will be forced to leave accommodation which is available for occupation, and which it would have been reasonable to continue to occupy.[44]

2.33   These definitions incorporate a number of elements:

a) there must be a deliberate act or failure to act;

b) the act or omission must have a consequence;

c) the consequence must be that accommodation ceases or will cease to be occupied;

d) that accommodation must be or have been, 'accommodation available for [the] occupation' of the homeless person (see para 2.19, above); and

e) it must have been reasonable to continue in occupation of that accommodation (see para 2.20 onwards, above).

2.34   An act or omission in good faith, on the part of a person who was unaware of any relevant fact (for example, the availability of financial assistance towards rent, the right to remain in occupation after notice of seeking possession, notice to quit or expiry of tenancy), is not to be treated as deliberate for these purposes.[45]

Collusive arrangements

2.35   In addition, a person becomes homeless intentionally or threatened with homelessness intentionally if s/he enters into an arrangement under which s/he is required to cease to occupy accommodation, which it would have been reasonable for him/her to continue to occupy, the purpose of which arrangement is to enable him/her to qualify for assistance under HA 1996 Part 7, and there is no other, or independent, good reason for the actual or threatened homelessness.[46]

Local connection

2.36   A person has a local connection with an area if:

a) s/he is or was as a matter of choice normally resident in it; or

b) s/he is employed in the area; or

---

44 HA 1996 s196(1).
45 HA 1996 ss191(2) and 196(2).
46 HA 1996 ss191(3) and 196(3).

c) s/he has family associations with the area; or
d) there are other special circumstances which result in a local connection with the area.[47]

Residence of choice

2.37   Residence is not 'of choice' for these purposes if the person:[48]

a) became resident in it because s/he or any person who might reasonably be expected to reside with him/her was detained under the authority of any Act of Parliament (for example, prison or mental hospital); or
b) became resident in it in such other circumstances as the secretary of state may specify.[49]

Employment

2.38   A person is not employed in an area if[50] s/he falls within such other circumstances as the secretary of state may specify.[51]

Former asylum-seekers

2.39   A person has a local connection with an area if s/he was at any time provided with accommodation in that area under the Immigration and Asylum Act 1999 s95, unless either s/he was subsequently provided with accommodation in another local housing authority area under section 95 or else the accommodation was provided in an accommodation centre under the Nationality Immigration and Asylum Act 2002 s22.[52]

47 HA 1996 s199(1).
48 Residence arising from service in the armed forces was formerly also excluded, which remains the case for applications made before 1 December 2008: see below, para 7.16.
49 HA 1996 s199(3), (5).
50 Employment in the armed forces was formerly also excluded, which remains the case for applications made before December 1, 2008: see below, para 7.16.
51 HA 1996 s199(5). This power has not been exercised to date.
52 HA 1996 s199(6) and (7), added by Asylum and Immigration (Treatment of Claimants etc) Act 2004 s11. Note that the Nationality Immigration and Asylum Act 2002 s22 has not yet been brought into effect.

Preliminary duties

2.40   The preliminary duties described below arise where a person applies to a housing authority for accommodation, or for assistance in obtaining it, and the authority has reason to believe that s/he may be homeless or threatened with homelessness.[53]

2.41   There is no requirement for any particular form of application, or even that the application should be in writing.

2.42   The three main preliminary duties are:

a) to make enquiries;
b) to notify the applicant of the decision; and
c) in the case of an eligible homeless person in priority need, to accommodate pending the outcome of enquiries and the notification.

Enquiries

2.43   Where the authority has reason to believe that there is actual or threatened homelessness, then it must make enquiries:

a) such as are necessary to satisfy it whether the applicant is eligible for assistance (above, para 2.15); and
b) if so, whether any, and what, duties are owed to him/her under HA 1996 Part 7.[54]

2.44   The authority may also make further enquiries as to whether there is a local connection with the district of another authority.[55] Local connection enquiries about another area precede any enquiries made by an authority into the applicant's connection with its own area.

Notification of decision

2.45   If the authority is not satisfied as to eligibility, it need not proceed to make any further enquiries.

2.46   If it does make enquiries, then the authority must, on completion, notify the applicant of its decision and 'so far as any issue is decided against [the applicant's] interests' inform him/her of the reasons for it.[56]

53 HA 1996 s184(1).
54 HA 1996 s184(1).
55 HA 1996 s184(2).
56 HA 1996 s184(3).

2.47   If the decision is to notify another authority under the local connection provisions (below, para 2.77), the applicant must also be notified of this decision and its reasons.[57]

2.48   Notification must inform the applicant of the right to request a
review (within 21 days) (see para 2.114, below).[58]

2.49   Notification must be in writing.

2.50   If the applicant does not receive the notification, s/he will be
treated as having done so if the notice is made available at the authority's office for a reasonable period, for collection by or on behalf of
the applicant,[59] ie, the burden is on the applicant who does not receive the decision to go to the authority's office and ask for it.

Accommodation pending enquiries

2.51   Enquiries may take some time. If the authority has reason to believe
that the applicant may be homeless, and eligible for assistance, and
in priority need, then, pending its decision, the authority is obliged
to secure that accommodation is made available.[60]

2.52   This obligation is imposed on the authority to which the application has been made, whether or not the applicant may have a local
connection with another authority.[61]

2.53   The accommodation must be made available for the applicant and
for any other family member who normally resides with, or anyone
else who might reasonably be expected to reside with, him/her.[62]

2.54   The duty ceases on notification of a decision, even if the applicant
requests a review, although the authority still has power to house
pending the review.[63]

Principal duties

2.55   The extent of an authority's duty depends on its decision. Duties may
be considered as:

a) limited duties; and
b) full duties.

---

57   HA 1996 s184.
58   HA 1996 s184(5).
59   HA 1996 s184(6).
60   HA 1996 s188(1).
61   HA 1996 s188(2).
62   HA 1996 ss176 and 188(1).
63   HA 1996 s188(2) and (3).

Limited duties

Priority need but intentionally homeless

2.56 If the authority is satisfied that an applicant is homeless, and in priority need of accommodation, but it is also satisfied that s/he became homeless intentionally, then it has two duties:

a) to secure that temporary accommodation is made available for such period as it considers will give him/her a reasonable opportunity to secure his/her own accommodation;[64] and

b) to assess the applicant's housing needs and provide him/her (or secure that s/he is provided) with advice and assistance.[65]

The advice and assistance must include information about the likely availability in the authority's area of types of accommodation appropriate to the applicant's housing needs, including the location and sources of such types of accommodation.[66]

Accommodation

2.57 If the authority provides its own accommodation, it will not be secure unless and until the authority notifies the applicant otherwise,[67] which it may not do except in accordance with the allocation provisions (considered below at para 2.139 onwards).

2.58 If the authority secures accommodation through a landlord whose tenants are not secure, then this temporary accommodation will not be within any statutory protection at all for a year from when the authority first gave notification of its decision, or – if there is a review (or an appeal) – from its final determination, unless the tenant is notified by the landlord that it is to be regarded either as an assured shorthold or a fully assured tenancy.[68]

Priority need but threatened with homelessness intentionally

2.59 If the authority is satisfied that the applicant is threatened with homelessness intentionally, eligible for assistance and in priority need, then the advice and appropriate assistance duty (see above, para 2.56(b)) arises,[69] on the basis that once the homelessness itself

---

64   HA 1996 s190(2)(a).

65   HA 1996 s190(2)(b), (4).

66   HA 1996 s190(5), added by Homelessness Act 2002 Sch 1 para 10.

67   HA 1985 Sch 1 para 4, substituted by HA 1996 Sch 17 para 3.

68   HA 1996 s209(2).

69   HA 1996 s195(5)(b), (6), (7).

occurs, an application will entitle the applicant to a period of temporary accommodation (see para 10.54, below).

No priority need

2.60   If the authority is satisfied that the applicant is homeless – whether intentionally[70] or unintentionally[71] – or threatened with homelessness (intentionally or not),[72] and eligible for assistance, but it is also satisfied that s/he is not in priority need, it owes an identical advice and appropriate assistance duty (see above, para 2.56(b)) to the applicant.

2.61   In addition, if the authority is satisfied that the applicant is unintentionally homeless although not in priority need, then although there is no duty to secure that accommodation is made available for occupation by the applicant, there is power to do so.[73] Likewise, an applicant not in priority need who is unintentionally threatened with homelessness may benefit from reasonable steps taken by the authority to secure that accommodation does not cease to be available for his/her occupation.[74]

Priority need and unintentionally threatened with homelessness

2.62   If the authority decides that the applicant is threatened with homelessness, eligible for assistance and has a priority need, but did not become threatened with homelessness intentionally, its duty is to take reasonable steps to secure that accommodation does not cease to be available for his/her occupation,[75] ie, either to help him/her remain,[76] or else to have other accommodation waiting for him/her once homelessness occurs.

2.63   This duty cannot be used to prevent the authority itself obtaining vacant possession of any accommodation,[77] ie, the fact that the authority has this duty cannot be raised as a defence in any action by the authority against one of its own tenants.

70 HA 1996 s190(3).
71 HA 1996 s192.
72 HA 1996 s195(5)(a).
73 HA 1996 s190(3), as added by Homelessness Act 2002 s5.
74 HA 1996 s195(6).
75 HA 1996 s195(1) and (2).
76 HA 1996 s195(2).
77 HA 1996 s195(3).

2.64   If the authority provides its own accommodation when the home-lessness occurs, then HA 1996 s193 applies in the same way as it applies to those who apply when already homeless (see para 2.65 on-wards, below).[78]

Full duties

2.65   If the authority is satisfied that the applicant is homeless, eligible for assistance, in priority need, and not intentionally homeless, then its duty is (subject to the possibility of referral to another authority, see further below, para 2.77 onwards), to secure that accommoda-tion is made available for his/her occupation (and, therefore, for any other family member who normally resides with, or anyone else who might reasonably be expected to reside with, the applicant (see above, para 2.19).[79]

2.66   In addition, the authority must give the applicant a copy of the statement included in its allocation policy (see para 2.158, below) on offering choice to people allocated housing accommodation under HA 1996 Part 6.[80]

Securing accommodation

2.67   The duty to secure that accommodation is made available for the ap-plicant's occupation can be discharged by:

a)   making available suitable accommodation held by the authority under the Housing Act 1985 Part 2, or under any other powers; or

b)   securing that the applicant obtains suitable accommodation from some other person; or

c)   giving the applicant such advice and assistance as will secure that s/he obtains suitable accommodation from some other person.[81]

2.68   In deciding whether accommodation is suitable, the authority must have regard to the provisions of the Housing Acts 1985 and 2004 which govern hazardous housing, overcrowding and houses in multiple occupation;[82] the secretary of state has power to specify cir-cumstances in which accommodation is, or is not, to be regarded as

---

78   HA 1996 s195(4).
79   HA 1996 s193(2).
80   HA 1996 s193(3A).
81   HA 1996 s206(1).
82   HA 1996 s210(1).

suitable, and as to the matters which the authority must take into account or disregard when deciding suitability.[83]

Charges

2.69   Authorities have a general power to make reasonable charges for the provision of their own accommodation under the Housing Act 1985 Part 2.[84] HA 1996 Part 7 entitles them to make charges to a homeless person for accommodation which they provide, or for or towards accommodation which they arrange for some other person to provide, under HA 1996 Part 7.[85]

Out-of-area accommodation

2.70   So far as reasonably practicable, authorities are bound to secure accommodation within their own area.[86]

2.71   If the authority places an applicant in another area, it must give notice to the local housing authority with responsibility for that area, stating:

a) the name of the applicant;

b) the number and description of other members of his/her family normally residing with him/her, or of anyone else who might reasonably to be expected to reside with him/her;

c) the address;

d) the date on which the accommodation was made available to the applicant; and

e) what HA 1996 Part 7 function the authority was discharging when securing the accommodation for him/her.[87]

2.72   The notice must be given in writing within two weeks from when the accommodation was made available.[88]

---

83   HA 1996 s210(2). A number of statutory instruments have been made under this power see: Homelessness (Suitability of Accommodation) Order 1996 SI No 3204; Homelessness (Suitability of Accommodation) (England) Order 2003 SI No 3326; and Homelessness (Suitability of Accommodation) (Wales) Order 2006 SI No 650.

84   HA 1985 s24.

85   HA 1996 s206(2).

86   HA 1996 s208(1).

87   HA 1996 s208(2) and (3).

88   HA 1996 s208(4).

Security

2.73 Where an authority provides its own accommodation in discharge of the full duty, it is not secure (see para 2.57, above).

Discharge of duty

2.74 The duty is owed to an applicant until it is brought to an end by any of the circumstances set out in HA 1996 s193.[89]

2.75 Those circumstances are as follows:

a) if the applicant refuses an offer under HA 1996 Part 7, which the authority is satisfied is suitable for him/her (see para 2.69), and the authority has informed the applicant that it will regard itself as having discharged the duty;[90]

b) if the applicant ceases to be eligible for assistance (see para 2.15);[91]

c) if the applicant becomes homeless intentionally (see para 2.31) from HA 1996 Part 7 accommodation;[92]

d) if the applicant accepts an allocation under HA 1996 Part 6;[93]

e) if the applicant accepts an offer of an assured tenancy (other than an assured shorthold tenancy) from a private landlord, ie, one whose tenants are not secure;[94]

f) if the applicant voluntarily ceases to occupy HA 1996 Part 7 accommodation as an only or principal home;[95]

g) if the applicant, having been informed of the possible consequences of refusal, and of his/her right to request a review of the suitability of accommodation refused, refuses a written final offer of HA 1996 Part 6 allocation, and the authority is satisfied that the accommodation was suitable for him/her (see para 2.68), and that it was reasonable for him/her to accept it;[96]

h) if the applicant accepts a qualifying offer of an assured shorthold tenancy from a private landlord.[97] For this purpose, an applicant may reasonably be considered to accept an offer even though s/he is under a contractual or other obligation in respect of his/her

---

89 HA 1996 s193(3).
90 HA 1996 s193(5).
91 HA 1996 s193(6)(a).
92 HA 1996 s193(6)(b).
93 HA 1996 s193(6)(c).
94 HA 1996 s193(6)(cc).
95 HA 1996 s193(6)(d).
96 HA 1996 s193(7), (7A), (7F).
97 HA 1996 s193(7B).

existing accommodation, if (but only if) s/he can bring that other obligation to an end before s/he has to take up the offer.[98] For this purpose, an offer is qualifying if:

i) it is made with the approval of the authority, in pursuance of arrangements made by the authority with the landlord with a view to bringing the duty towards the applicant to an end;

ii) the offer is of a fixed-term tenancy; and

iii) it is accompanied by a statement in writing, which states the term of the tenancy being offered and explains in ordinary language that there is no obligation on the applicant to accept it but that if it is accepted the authority will cease to be under a duty to the applicant.[99]

Acceptance of a qualifying offer is only effective if the applicant signs a statement acknowledging that s/he has understood the authority's statement.[100] An authority may not make a qualifying offer unless satisfied that the accommodation is suitable for the applicant and that it is reasonable for him/her to accept the offer.[101] The applicant is free to reject a qualifying offer without affecting the duty owed to him/her under this section by the authority.[102]

Restricted cases

2.76   Where the duty arises by reference to a household member who is a restricted person (see para 2.15, above), the authority must, so far reasonably practicable, bring the full housing duty to an end by arranging for a private accommodation offer to be made.[103] This means an offer of an assured shorthold tenancy made by a private landlord to the applicant, which is made with the approval of the authority, in pursuance of arrangements made by the authority with the landlord with a view to bringing the authority's duty to an end; the tenancy must be a fixed tenancy for a period of at least 12 months.[104] The full housing duty ends if the applicant, having been informed of the possible consequences of refusal of the offer and the right to request a review of the suitability of the accommodation,[105] either accepts

---

98 HA 1996 s193(8).
99 HA 1996 s193(7D).
100 HA 1996 s193(7E).
101 HA 1996 s193(7F).
102 HA 1996 s193(7C).
103 HA 1996 s193(7AD).
104 HA 1996 s193(7AC).
105 HA 1996 s193(7AB).

or refuses a private accommodation offer.[106] Where it is not reasonably practical to bring the full housing duty to an end with a private accommodation offer, the local authority may discharge the duty in the same way as any other application.[107]

Local connection provisions

2.77 The local connection provisions allow one housing authority to shift the burden of making accommodation available on to another housing authority. The provisions apply when the authority is satisfied that the applicant is homeless (not merely threatened with homelessness), in priority need, and not homeless intentionally, and either:

a) the applicant was placed in accommodation in its area by another authority, in pursuance of HA 1996 Part 7 functions, within such period as may be prescribed[108] for this purpose[109] (see para 2.71, above, for the notification requirements imposed on that other authority at the time of the placement); or

b) the authority considers that all of the following conditions apply:

   i) neither the applicant nor anyone who might reasonably be expected to reside with him/her has a local connection (see para 2.36, above) with its area; and

   ii) the applicant or a person who might reasonably be expected to reside with him/her does have a local connection with the area of another housing authority; and

   iii) neither the applicant nor any person who might reasonably be expected to reside with him/her will run the risk of domestic violence in the area of the other authority.[110]

2.78 In addition, a local connection referral may not be made where the applicant or any person who might reasonably be expected to reside with him/her has suffered non-domestic violence in the area

---

106 HA 1996 s193(7AA).
107 HA 1996 s193(7AD).
108 By the secretary of state under HA 1996 s215. The relevant period is five years from the date of the placement together with the time between the date the application was initially made and the time the placement first became available: Allocation of Housing and Homelessness (Micsellaneous Provisions) (England) Regulations 2006 SI No 2527 and in Wales, Homelessness Regulations 2000 SI No 701 reg 6 (applied to Wales by the Homelessness (Wales) Regulations 2000 SI No 1079).
109 HA 1996 s198(4).
110 HA 1996 s198(1) and (2).

of the other authority and it is probable that the return to that area of the victim will lead to further violence of a similar kind against him/her.[111]

Violence and domestic violence

2.79   Violence and domestic violence are defined in the same terms as when determining whether or not it is reasonable to remain in occupation.[112] See above, paras 2.21–2.24.

Passing responsibility

2.80   The housing duty passes to the other authority if either set of conditions is satisfied.[113] The other authority's obligation is to house under HA 1996 s193.[114]

Retaining responsibility

2.81   The housing duty under HA 1996 s193 remains with the authority to which the application was made if neither set of conditions is satisfied.[115]

Interim accommodation and notification

2.82   Pending determination of final responsibility, the authority to which the application is made must provide temporary accommodation.[116]

2.83   Once the issue has been decided, it is for the authority to notify the applicant of the decision and of the reasons for it, as well as of his/her right to request a review (and the time within which it must be requested).[117] Notification is effected in the same way as under HA 1996 s184(6) – see para 2.50, above.[118]

---

111 HA 1996 s198(2A).
112 HA 1996 s198(3).
113 HA 1996 s200(4).
114 The same provisions apply under HA 1996 s200(5) as to continuation of accommodation pending review as apply if the case is referred to the other authority.
115 HA 1996 s200(3).
116 HA 1996 s200(1).
117 HA 1996 s200(2).
118 HA 1996 s200(6).

2.84   The temporary housing duty ceases when the notification is given, even if a review is requested, although the authority may continue to provide it pending review.[119]

Arbitration

2.85   These provisions are a breeding ground for differences of opinion between authorities. HA 1996 Part 7 provides elaborate machinery for the determination of disputes between them, by agreement or, if necessary, by reference to an independent arbitrator.[120]

2.86   An arbitration decision can itself be the subject of internal review, and thence appeal to the county court (see para 2.111 onwards, below).[121]

Protection of property

Duty

2.87   If an authority is or has been under a duty under HA 1996 s188 (see para 2.51, above), s190, s193, s195 (see para 2.56 onwards) or s200 (see para 2.80), it may also be under a duty to take reasonable steps to prevent the loss of an applicant's property, or prevent or mitigate damage to it.[122]

2.88   For these purposes, an applicant's personal property includes the personal property of any person reasonably expected to reside with him/her.[123]

2.89   The duty arises if the authority has reason to believe:

a) that there is a danger of loss of or damage to property because of the applicant's inability to protect or deal with it; and

b) that no other suitable arrangements have been or are being made.[124]

---

119 HA 1996 s200(5).
120 HA 1996 s198(5).
121 HA 1996 s198(5), s202(1)(d) and (e).
122 HA 1996 s211(2).
123 HA 1996 s211(5).
124 HA 1996 s211(1).

Power

2.90   If the authority has not been under one of the identified duties (see para 2.87, above), but has reason to believe that a relevant danger to property exists, for which there are no arrangements, it has power to protect property.[125]

Charges and terms

2.91   The authority can, however, decline to take action under these provisions other than on such conditions as it considers appropriate, including as to reasonable charges and the disposal of property.[126]

Power of entry

2.92   In connection with these provisions, the authority has power, at all reasonable times, to enter any premises which are or were the usual or last usual place of residence of the applicant, and to deal with his/her property in any way that is reasonably necessary, including by way of storage.[127]

Choice of storage

2.93   If the applicant asks the authority to move the property to a nominated location and the authority considers the request to be reasonable, the authority may discharge its responsibilities under these provisions by complying and, therefore, treating its responsibilities as being ended.[128]

Termination

2.94   Otherwise, the responsibilities end when the authority considers that there is no longer any danger of loss or damage by reason of the applicant's inability to protect or deal with his/her personal property, although, if the authority has provided storage, it may continue to do so.[129]

---

125 HA 1996 s211(3).
126 HA 1996 s211(4).
127 HA 1996 s212(1).
128 HA 1996 s212(2).
129 HA 1996 s212(3).

2.95   When the authority's responsibilities end, it must notify the applicant that they have done so and of the reasons why.[130] Notification may be given by delivery, or by leaving it or sending it to the applicant's last known address.[131]

Review

2.96   These provisions are not subject to internal review or appeal to the county court (see below, paras 2.111–2.128).

Homelessness strategies

2.97   The Homelessness Act 2002 imposed a new duty on local housing authorities to carry out a homelessness review (see para 2.100, below) in their areas and formulate and publish a homelessness strategy (see para 2.102, below) based on the results of that review.[132]

2.98   The first strategy must be published within 12 months of Homelessness Act 2002 s1 coming into force[133] and, thereafter, a new one must be published at least every five years.[134]

Authorities

2.99   Where it is a different authority, the social services authority (see para 2.14, above) for the area of the authority must afford such assistance in the review and in the formulation of the strategy as the housing authority may reasonably require.[135] The strategy must be taken into account by both the local housing authority and the social services authority in the exercise of their functions.[136]

130 HA 1996 s212(4).
131 HA 1996 s212(5).
132 Homelessness Act 2002 s1(1).
133 31 July 2003 (see the Homelessness Act 2002 (Commencement) (England) Order 2002 SI No 1799 article 2) and 30 September 2003 (see the Homelessness Act 2002 (Commencement) (Wales) Order 2002 SI No 1736 article 2).
134 Homelessness Act 2002 s1(3) and (4).
135 Homelessness Act 2002 s1(2).
136 Homelessness Act 2002 s1(5) and (6).

Review

2.100 For these purposes a homelessness review means a review of:

- the level, and likely future levels, of homelessness in the authority's area;
- the activities which are carried out in the area to:
  - prevent homelessness in the authority's area;
  - secure that accommodation is or will be available for people in the area who are or may become homeless; and
  - provide support for people in the area who are or may become homeless or who have been homeless and need support to prevent it happening again; and
- the resources available to the authority, the social services authority, other public authorities, voluntary organisations and other persons for such activities.[137]

2.101 On completion of the review, the authority must arrange for the results to be available for inspection at its principal office, at all reasonable hours, without charge, and provide (on payment of a reasonable charge, if required) a copy of the results.[138]

Strategy

2.102 A homelessness strategy means one formulated for:

- preventing homelessness in the authority's area;
- securing that sufficient accommodation is and will be available for people in the area who are or may become homeless; and
- securing that there is satisfactory provision of support for people in the area who are or who may become homeless or who have become homeless and need support to prevent them becoming homeless again.[139]

2.103 The strategy may include specific objectives to be pursued, and specific action planned to be taken in the course of the exercise of the authority's housing functions and also of the functions of the social services authority for the district.[140]

---

137 Homelessness Act 2002 s2(1) and (2).
138 Homelessness Act 2002 s2(3).
139 Homelessness Act 2002 s3(1).
140 Homelessness Act 2002 s3(2).

2.104   The strategy may also include specific action which the authority expects to be taken by any other public authority, voluntary organisation or other person, which or who can contribute to the objectives of the strategy, albeit only with the approval of the body or person in question.[141] The authority must consider how far the objectives of the strategy can be met by joint action between itself, the social services authority or any other body or persons.[142]

2.105   The strategy must be kept under review and may be modified.[143] Any modification must be published and, before adopting or modifying the strategy, the authority must consult such public or local authorities, voluntary organisations or other persons as it considers appropriate.[144]

2.106   A copy of the strategy must be available at the authority's principal office for inspection at all reasonable hours, free of charge, and provided to members of the public on request, on payment (if required) of a reasonable charge.[145]

Advice, information and voluntary organisations

2.107   HA 1996 Part 7 makes provision for giving grants, loans, premises or goods in kind to voluntary organisations concerned with the homeless.[146]

2.108   In addition, authorities have an obligation to ensure that advice and assistance about homelessness and its prevention are available to any person in their area, free of charge.[147] This duty would seem to be capable of being discharged by way of providing assistance (grant or loan, use of premises, furniture or other goods, or making staff available) through another person (not necessarily a voluntary organisation, although on the same terms and conditions as would apply to a voluntary organisation: HA 1996 s181(1)).[148]

---

141 Homelessness Act 2002 s3(3) and (4).
142 Homelessness Act 2002 s3(5).
143 Homelessness Act 2002 s3(6).
144 Homelessness Act 2002 s3(7) and (8).
145 Homelessness Act 2002 s3(8).
146 HA 1996 ss180 and 181.
147 HA 1996 s179(1).
148 HA 1996 s179(2) and (3).

Code of Guidance

2.109   In the exercise of their functions under HA 1996 Part 7, authorities are bound to have regard to such guidance as may from time to time be given by the secretary of state.[149] Under these provisions, the secretary of state has issued the Code of Guidance for England[150] and the Welsh Assembly Government has issued one applicable to Wales.

2.110   The meaning of the requirement to have regard to the Code is considered in chapter 12.

Review and appeal

Review

2.111   Applicants have a statutory right to request an internal review of any of the following decisions:

a) as to eligibility for assistance;[151]
b) as to the duty (if any) owed;[152]
c) to notify another authority under HA 1996 s198;[153]
d) as to whether the conditions for referral are met;[154]
e) as to what duty is owed following a local connection referral;[155] or
f) as to the suitability of accommodation offered in discharge of duty, including a HA 1996 Part 6 offer.[156]

2.112   The right of review does not, however, entitle the applicant to a review of an earlier review.[157]

Accommodation pending review

2.113   Pending the outcome of the review, the authority may – but is not under a duty to – provide accommodation for the applicant.[158]

---

149 HA 1996 s182.
150 See below, para 11.8 and appendix C.
151 See para 2.15.
152 See para 2.55 onwards.
153 See para 2.77.
154 See para 2.36.
155 See paras 2.80 and 2.81.
156 See para 2.75.
157 HA 1996 s202(2).
158 HA 1996 s188(3).

Request for review

2.114　A request for a review must be made within 21 days of notification[159] of decision, or such longer period as the authority may in writing allow.[160]

Review procedure

2.115　The secretary of state has power to regulate review procedure, including power to require that the review be conducted by a person of 'appropriate seniority . . . not involved in the original decision', and to prescribe the 'circumstances in which the applicant is entitled to an oral hearing, and whether and by whom [the applicant] may be represented at such a hearing'.[161]

Notification

2.116　The authority has to notify the applicant of the outcome of the review and, if it is adverse to his/her interests or confirms a local connection referral, of the reasons for it.[162] The authority must also notify the applicant of the right of appeal to the county court on a point of law.[163]

2.117　　If either of these requirements is not fulfilled, the notification is treated as not having been given.[164]

2.118　　Otherwise, notification is given in the same way as under HA 1996 s184 (see above, para 2.48).[165] The review may also need to be carried out, and notification given, within a period to be prescribed by the regulations.[166]

Appeal

2.119　An appeal lies to the county court if the applicant either:

a) is dissatisfied with the outcome of the review, or

b) has not been notified of the outcome within any time that may be prescribed.[167]

159 See paras 2.48, 2.75 and 2.83, above, for the duty to include this information in the notification.
160 HA 1996 s202(3).
161 HA 1996 s203(2).
162 HA 1996 s203(4).
163 HA 1996 s203(5).
164 HA 1996 s203(6).
165 HA 1996 s203(8).
166 HA 1996 s203(7).
167 HA 1996 s204(1).

2.120   Exercise of the right to a review is therefore an essential pre-condition of appeal.

2.121   Appeal lies only on a point of law, whether it arises from the original decision or from the decision on review (see chapter 12).[168]

Time for appeal

2.122   The appeal must be brought within 21 days of notification, or of when the applicant ought to have been notified of the outcome.[169] The court may give permission to appeal out of time where there is good reason for the applicant being unable to bring the appeal within the 21-day limit.[170]

Powers of court

2.123   The court may make such order as it thinks fit, confirming, quashing or varying the decision.[171]

Accommodation pending appeal

2.124   Pending an appeal (and any further appeal), the authority may, but is not obliged to, provide accommodation.[172]

2.125   If the authority refuses to do so, the applicant may appeal that decision to the county court[173] and the court may order that accommodation is made available pending the outcome of the appeal (or such earlier time as it may specify), and may confirm or quash the decision of the authority not to provide accommodation.[174]

2.126   In considering whether to confirm or quash the decision, the court must apply the principles applied by the High Court on an application for judicial review.[175]

2.127   If the court quashes the decision, it may order the authority to exercise the power to accommodate pending appeal in the applicant's case for such period as it specifies.[176]

---

168   HA 1996 s204(1).
169   HA 1996 s204(2).
170   HA 1996 s204(2A).
171   HA 1996 s204(3).
172   HA 1996 s204(4).
173   HA 1996 s204A.
174   HA 1996 s204A(4)(a), (b).
175   HA 1996 s204A(4).
176   HA 1996 s204A(5).

2.128   Such an order may, however, only be made if the court is satisfied that failure to exercise the accommodation power in accordance with its order would substantially prejudice the applicant's ability to pursue his/her substantive appeal.[177]

Criminal offences

2.129 It is a criminal offence knowingly or recklessly to make a statement which is false in a material particular, or knowingly to withhold information which an authority has reasonably required in connection with the exercise of its functions under HA 1996 Part 7, with intent to induce an authority to believe that the person making the statement, or any other person, is entitled to accommodation or assistance (or accommodation or assistance of a particular kind).[178]

2.130   The offence is punishable on summary conviction by a fine of up to level five on the standard scale,[179] ie, the standard scale for the time being under Criminal Justice Act 1982 s37.[180]

2.131   An applicant has a duty to notify an authority as soon as possible of any material change of facts material to his/her case, which occurs before s/he receives the notification of the authority's decision on his/her application.[181]

2.132   The authority is under a corresponding obligation to explain to an applicant, in ordinary language, the nature of this duty and the effect of the defence to a charge of non-compliance.[182] The defence is that no such explanation was given or that, although such an explanation was given, there is some other reasonable excuse for non-compliance.[183]

2.133   In the absence of such a defence, it is a criminal offence to fail to comply with the duty to notify the authority of material changes, punishable on summary conviction at level five on the standard scale (see para 2.130, above).

---

177 HA 1996 s204A(6)(a).
178 HA 1996 s214(1).
179 HA 1996 s214(4).
180 As a result of Criminal Justice Act 1991 s17 this is currently £5,000.
181 HA 1996 s214(2).
182 HA 1996 s214(2).
183 HA 1996 s214(3).

Co-operation between authorities

Co-operation

2.134 In the discharge of its functions under HA 1996 Part 7, a local housing authority may request assistance from another local housing authority, a new town corporation, a registered social landlord or housing action trust, or a Scottish local authority, development corporation, registered housing association or Scottish Homes.[184]

2.135 The authority may also ask a social services authority (in England, Wales or Scotland) to exercise any of its functions on its behalf.[185]

2.136 The other authority (or body) must co-operate with the housing authority by rendering such assistance as is reasonable in the circumstances.[186]

Referral

2.137 In addition, where a local authority has reason to believe that an applicant with whom children reside, or usually reside, may be ineligible for assistance (see para 2.15, above), may be homeless or may have become so intentionally (see para 2.31, above), or may be threatened with homelessness intentionally (see para 2.32, above), they must make arrangements for ensuring that the applicant is invited to consent to the referral of his/her case to the social services authority (or department in the case of a unitary authority) and, if consent is given, must make the social services authority/department aware of the facts of the case and the subsequent decision in relation to it.[187]

2.138 Following such a referral, the social services authority/department may request that the housing authority provide it with advice and assistance in the exercise of its functions under the Children Act 1989 Part 3 and the housing authority must provide it with such advice and assistance as is reasonable in all the circumstances.[188]

---

184 HA 1996 s213(1)(a) and (2).
185 HA 1996 s213(1)(b).
186 HA 1996 s213(1).
187 HA 1996 s213A(1), (2).
188 HA 1996 s213A (5), (6).

Allocation

2.139   When allocating housing, local housing authorities are obliged to comply with the provisions of HA 1996 Part 6.[189]

Meaning of allocation

2.140   For these purposes, 'allocation' means:

a) selecting a secure[190] or introductory tenant[191] for the authority's own accommodation. This includes notifying an existing tenant or licensee that his/her tenancy is to be secure,[192] for example, under the Housing Act 1985 Sch 1 para 2 (employment-related accommodation), para 5 (temporary accommodation for people taking up employment) or para 10 (student accommodation), as amended;

b) nominating a person to be a secure or introductory tenant of another. Nomination includes formal and informal arrangements;[193]

c) nominating (in the same sense as above) a person to be an assured tenant[194] of a registered social landlord.[195]

Excluded allocations

2.141   Allocations to existing secure or introductory tenants are excluded, unless the allocation involves a transfer of housing accommodation for that tenant, and the transfer is made on his/her application.[196]

2.142   There are various other cases which are not treated as an allocation:

a) succession and devolution on death, or assignment to a potential successor;

b) assignment by way of exchange;

c) vesting under a number of family or domestic law provisions; and

d) other cases as may be prescribed by regulations.[197]

189 HA 1996 s159(1).
190 HA 1985 Part 4.
191 HA 1996 Part 5, Chapter I.
192 HA 1996 s159(3).
193 HA 1996 s159(4).
194 HA 1988 Part 1.
195 HA 1996 Part 1; HA 1996 s159(2).
196 HA 1996 s159(5).
197 HA 1996 s160.

Eligibility

2.143   Any person may be allocated housing, provided that s/he is not ineligible under HA 1996 s160A.[198] An allocation may not be made to two or more persons jointly if one of them is ineligible.[199]

Persons from abroad

2.144   Persons subject to immigration control under the Asylum and Immigration Act 1996 are ineligible unless re-included by regulations.[200] The secretary of state may not include in regulations any person who is excluded from entitlement to housing benefit by Immigration and Asylum Act 1999 s115.[201] The secretary of state may prescribe other persons from abroad who are ineligible, either in relation to local housing authorities generally or any particular local housing authority.[202]

2.145   These provisions do not affect the eligibility of someone who is already a secure or introductory tenant or an assured tenant of housing accommodation allocated to him/her by a local housing authority.[203]

Unacceptable behaviour

2.146   A local authority may decide that an applicant is to be treated as ineligible if it is satisfied that:

  – the applicant or a member of his/her household has been guilty of unacceptable behaviour serious enough to make him/her unsuitable to be a tenant of the authority; and
  – by reason of the circumstances at the time his/her application is considered, s/he is unsuitable to be a tenant of the authority by reason of that behaviour.[204]

2.147   'Unacceptable behaviour' is that which would (if the applicant was a secure tenant of the authority) entitle the authority to a possession order under Housing Act 1985 s84 on any of grounds 1–7 of Schedule 2 to that Act, or behaviour by a member of the applicant's household, which would (if s/he were a person residing with a secure tenant of the authority) entitle the authority to such a possession order.[205]

---

198 HA 1996 s160A(1), (2).
199 HA 1996 s160A(1)(c).
200 HA 1996 s160A(3). See also above, para 2.15.
201 HA 1996 s160A(4).
202 HA 1996 s160A(5).
203 HA 1996 s160A(6).
204 HA 1996 s160A(7).
205 HA 1996 s160A(8).

Re-application

2.148 An applicant who is treated as ineligible because of unacceptable behaviour may (if s/he considers that s/he should no longer be so treated) make a fresh application.[206]

Notification

2.149 If the authority decides that the applicant is ineligible for an allocation, it must notify him/her of that decision and the ground(s) for it.[207]

2.150 Notification must be given in writing and, if not received by the applicant, shall be treated as having been given if it is made available at the authority's office for a reasonable period for collection by him/her or on his/her behalf.[208]

Applications

2.151 Authorities must ensure that there is free advice and information available in their area about the right to make an application for an allocation of housing.[209]

2.152 Authorities must also ensure that any necessary assistance in making an application is available free of charge to those who are likely to have difficulty in doing so without assistance.[210]

2.153 Authorities must also ensure that applicants are aware of their right to request information about the likely availability of accommodation (see para 2.165, below).[211]

2.154 Every application for an allocation of housing made in accordance with the procedural requirements of the authority's allocation scheme must be considered by the authority.[212] The fact that a person is an applicant for an allocation must not be divulged by the authority to any member of the public without the applicant's consent.[213]

206 HA 1996 s160A(11).
207 HA 1996 s160A(9).
208 HA 1996 s160A(10).
209 HA 1996 s166(1)(a).
210 HA 1996 s166(1)(b).
211 HA 1996 s166(2).
212 HA 1996 s166(3).
213 HA 1996 s166(4).

Priorities and procedures

2.155   The authority has to maintain an allocation 'scheme' governing both priorities and procedures (including all aspects of the allocation procedure, including by whom decisions may be made).[214]

Procedure

2.156   The scheme must be framed so as to give an applicant the right to request general information that will enable him/her to assess:

- how his/her application is likely to be treated under the scheme (including whether s/he is likely to be regarded as in one of the reasonable preference categories); and
- whether accommodation appropriate to his/her needs is likely to be made available to him/her and, if so, how long it is likely to be before such accommodation becomes available for allocation to him/her.[215]

Regulations

2.157   The secretary of state may require that the procedures are framed in accordance with such principles as s/he may prescribe.[216]

Choice policy

2.158   The scheme must include a statement of the authority's policy on offering people who are to be allocated housing:

a)   a choice of housing accommodation; or
b)   the opportunity to express preference about the housing accommodation to be allocated to them.[217]

Priority

2.159   The scheme must be framed so as to ensure that a reasonable preference is given to the following:

---

214   HA 1996 s167(1).
215   HA 1996 s167(4A)(a).
216   HA 1996 s167(5).
217   HA 1996 s167(1A).

a) people who are homeless (see para 2.18, above);
b) people who are owed a duty by an local housing authority under HA 1996 s190(2),[218] s193(2)[219] or s195(2)[220] (or under Housing Act 1985 s65(2) or s68(2)) or who are occupying accommodation secured by any such authority under HA 1996 s192(3);[221]
c) people occupying insanitary or overcrowded housing or otherwise living in unsatisfactory housing conditions;
d) people who need to move on medical or welfare grounds (including grounds relating to disability); and
e) people who need to move to a particular locality in the authority's area, where failure to meet that need would cause hardship to themselves or to others.[222]

2.160   The scheme may be framed so as to give additional preference to those within these categories who have an urgent housing need.[223]

2.161   The scheme may also include provision for determining priorities between those in the reasonable preference categories, taking into account:

- the financial resources available to a person to meet his/her housing costs;
- any behaviour of a person (or a member of his/her household) which affects his/her suitability to be a tenant;
- any local connection[224] which exists between a person and the authority's area.[225]

Unacceptable behaviour

2.162   The scheme does not have to provide for any preference to be given to an applicant where the authority is satisfied that:

- s/he, or a member of his/her household, have been guilty of unacceptable behaviour (as defined above, para 2.147) serious enough to make him/her unsuitable to be a tenant of the authority; and

---

218 See para 2.56, above.
219 See para 2.65, above.
220 See para 2.62, above.
221 See para 2.60, above.
222 HA 1996 s167(2), as amended by HA 2004 s223.
223 HA 1996 s167(2).
224 As defined in HA 1996 s199; see para 2.36, above.
225 HA 1996 s167(2A).

- in the circumstances at the time his/her case is considered, s/he deserves by reason of that behaviour not to be treated as a member of one of the groups to whom a reasonable preference is to be given.[226]

Regulations

2.163   The secretary of state has power to add to, amend or repeal any part of the list of those to whom a reasonable preference is to be accorded.[227] S/he also has power to specify factors which are not to be taken into account when allocating housing.[228]

Other allocations

2.164   Subject to the reasonable preference categories, the scheme may contain provisions about the allocation of particular accommodation to a person who makes a specific application for it and to people of a particular description, whether or not they are within the reasonable preference categories.[229]

Notification

2.165   The scheme must be framed so that an applicant is notified:

- in writing of any decision that s/he is a person being given no preference because of a decision as to behaviour under HA 1996 s167(2C) (see para 2.161, above); and
- of the right to request the authority to inform him/her about the facts of his/her case which are likely to be, or have been, taken into account in considering whether to allocate housing accommodation to him/her.[230]

Review

2.166   The scheme must include the right for applicants to request a review of a decision as to whether they are to be given no preference under HA 1996 s167(2C), about the facts of their case or that they are a person who is ineligible under section 160A (see para 2.143, above).[231]

226 HA 1996 s167(2C), (2D).
227 HA 1996 s167(3).
228 HA 1996 s167(4).
229 HA 1996 s167(2E).
230 HA 1996 s167(4A)(b), (c).
231 HA 1996 s167(4A)(d).

Change and consultation

2.167 Priorities and procedures are otherwise in the discretion of the authority.[232]

2.168 Before adopting or making any major policy change to a scheme, the authority must send a copy of it in draft to every registered social landlord with which they have nomination arrangements, and afford them a reasonable opportunity to comment.[233]

Code of Guidance

2.169 As under HA 1996 Part 7, there is provision for the secretary of state to issue guidance to which authorities must have regard.[234]

Co-operation

2.170 When an authority asks them to offer accommodation to people with priority under the authority's allocation scheme, registered social landlords are bound to co-operate to such extent as is reasonable in the circumstances.[235]

Information

2.171 An authority must publish a summary of its scheme and provide a copy of it, free of charge, to any member of the public who asks for it.[236] The full scheme must be made available for inspection at the authority's principal office and a copy must be made available to any member of the public who asks for it, on payment of a reasonable fee.[237]

2.172 When the authority makes a major policy alteration to its scheme, it has to take such steps as it considers reasonable to bring the effect of the alteration to the attention of those likely to be affected by it.[238]

---

232 HA 1996 s167(6).
233 HA 1996 s167(7).
234 HA 1996 s169.
235 HA 1996 s170.
236 HA 1996 s168(1).
237 HA 1996 s168(2).
238 HA 1996 s168(3).

Criminal offences

2.173   It is a criminal offence knowingly or recklessly to make a statement – in connection with the exercise by an authority of its functions under HA 1996 Part 6 – which is false in a material particular, or knowingly to withhold information which an authority has reasonably required in connection with the exercise of its functions under HA 1996 Part 6.[239]

2.174   The offence is punishable on summary conviction by a fine of up to level 5 on the standard scale,[240] ie, the standard scale for the time being under the Criminal Justice Act 1982 s37.[241]

---

239 HA 1996 s171(1).
240 HA 1996 s171(2).
241 Currently £5,000.

CHAPTER 3

Immigration

continued

3.138   Wales

Persons subject to immigration control • Persons not subject to immigration control

Introduction

3.1 In the last edition of this book, this chapter was called 'eligibility'. While that title would be correct were this book concerned only with homelessness, it is not correct when it comes to allocations, which define eligibility in terms of both immigration status and conduct, ie, applicants may also be disqualified from an allocation on grounds related to 'unacceptable behaviour';[1] that subject is dealt with below.[2]

3.2 Immigration status is a key topic in relation to both homelessness and allocations. In both cases, it is determinative of eligibility, excluding certain applicants from the protection of Housing Act (HA) 1996 Part 7 and the prospect of an allocation under Part 6.

3.3 That does not mean that no assistance will ever be available from a local authority to someone so disqualified; there remains the possibility of assistance under the National Assistance Act 1948, where an applicant is in need of care and attention (otherwise than as a result of destitution) – this is dealt with below.[3] In addition, some immigrants who are asylum-seekers disqualified from local authority assistance may be able to obtain housing help through the UK Borders Agency.[4] Furthermore, local authorities may have to give assistance to children in need, even though they or their parents are disqualified from housing assistance under Parts 6 and 7 of the 1996 Act.[5] There are also 'well-being powers' to assist under the Local Government Act 2000 Part 1, which may be exercisable in some circumstances.[6]

3.4 Even if an applicant is not ineligible for assistance under Part 7, there are, however, additional provisions which may exclude him/ her from temporary accommodation under some of the interim duties in Part 7; the same classes will also be excluded from assistance under the provisions mentioned in the last paragraph, ie, under

---

1 HA 1996 s160A (7)–(11).

2 Paras 11.28–11.41.

3 Paras 13.6–13.31.

4 Below, paras 3.101, 13.32–13.43. In July 2006 the Home Office announced that the National Asylum Support Service (NASS) no longer existed as a separate department. Asylum support is now administered by two separate routes. Those who made their first asylum claim on or after 5 March 2007 have their support processed by the New Asylum Model (NAM) case owner who is processing their asylum claim. Applicants who claimed asylum before 5 March 2007, known as legacy cases, should have their asylum and support claims dealt with by the Casework Resolution Directorate (CRD).

5 Below, paras 13.44–13.65.

6 Below, paras 13.66–13.71.

the National Assistance Act 1948, through the UK Borders Agency, under the Children Act 1989 or under the Local Government Act 2000. These classes are described in this chapter.[7]

3.5   Even if an applicant is not ineligible for assistance under Part 7, if qualification for assistance relies on family or household members who would themselves be ineligible, it may affect the duty placed on the authority: this is also dealt with below.[8] Likewise, it will affect priority in the allocation of housing under Part 6.[9]

3.6   Historically, the Housing (Homeless Persons) Act (H(HP)A) 1977) did not contain a test of eligibility. On the face of the Act, anyone could make an application. The Court of Appeal, however, expressed the view that the duty was owed only to a person making a homeless application who was lawfully in the country.[10] The consolidating Housing Act 1985 Part 3, which replaced H(HP)A 1977, likewise did not limit who could apply, but the Court of Appeal interpreted the provisions so that an authority owed no duty to an applicant for housing who was an illegal entrant.[11] It was also held that where – as a result of enquiries – the authority suspected that an applicant was an illegal entrant, it had a duty to inform the immigration authorities of its suspicion.[12]

3.7   The Asylum and Immigration Appeals Act 1993 was the first legislative provision explicitly to limit the rights of immigrants to housing assistance. The effect of its sections 4 and 5 was that authorities owed no duty to an asylum-seeker and his/her dependants if s/he had accommodation that was available for his/her occupation, however temporary, and which it would be reasonable for him/her to occupy. The Asylum and Immigration Act 1996 s9 additionally provided that an authority should not, so far as practicable, grant a tenancy or licence of housing accommodation to a person subject to immigration control, unless s/he is of a prescribed class.

3.8   These limitations were reproduced in HA 1996 Part 7, ss185 and 186, defining 'eligibility for assistance'. Subject to qualification and

---

7 Below, paras 3.120–3.122.

8 Below, paras 3.74–3.79.

9 Below, para 3.132.

10 *R v Hillingdon LBC ex p Streeting* [1980] 1 WLR 1425.

11 *London Borough of Tower Hamlets v Secretary of State for the Environment* [1993] QB 632; 25 HLR 524, CA.

12 See *London Borough of Tower Hamlets v Secretary of State for the Environment*, above.

exception, excluded persons from abroad under HA 1996 s185, and asylum-seekers under HA 1996 s186 were not eligible for assistance. A person ineligible for assistance could not receive 'the benefit of any function under . . . Part [7] relating to accommodation or assistance in obtaining accommodation',[13] although s/he could receive advice and assistance from any advisory service provided by the authority under its section 179 duty.[14]

3.9 Eligibility requirements were also introduced in Part 6 for allocations,[15] which, so far as concerns immigration, matched those for homelessness.

3.10 In this chapter, eligibility is accordingly considered for both homelessness and allocations. Before addressing each of these, in turn, below, it is first necessary to consider the detailed rules governing the relevant classes of the various immigration statuses which may be enjoyed by – or which may limit the rights of – applicants under either Part 6 or Part 7.

Immigration control

3.11 People in the UK are divided into two classes, persons who are subject to immigration control, and persons who are not subject to immigration control. The latter group includes all persons who have a right to reside in the UK.

Persons subject to immigration control

3.12 The term 'persons subject to immigration control' as used in both Parts 6[16] and 7[17] is based on immigration legislation[18] and means a person who, under the Immigration Act (IA) 1971, requires leave to enter or remain in the UK (whether or not such leave has been given). Generally speaking, this means anyone who requires a visa to come to the UK. It mainly applies to non-EEA (European Economic Area) nationals, but EEA nationals who are not exercising a right to

---

13 HA 1996 s183(2).

14 HA 1996 s183(3); see chapter 14.

15 See now HA 1996 s160A(1)–(6) as amended by the Homelessness Act 2002.

16 HA 1996 s160A(3).

17 HA 1996 s185(2).

18 Asylum and Immigration Act 1996 s13.

reside in the UK are also subject to immigration control[19] (although they are legally present).[20]

Persons not subject to immigration control

3.13　Persons not subject to immigration control form two groups. The first group consists of those who are exempt from the requirement to have leave to enter or remain in the UK.[21] This group is relatively unimportant for eligibility purposes and comprises three main classes:

a) Diplomats and certain staff of embassies and high commissions and their families who form part of their household;[22]

b) Members of UK armed forces, members of a Commonwealth or similar force undergoing training in the UK with the UK armed forces, and members of a visiting force coming to the UK at the invitation of the government;[23] and,

c) Members of the crew of a ship or aircraft, hired or under orders to depart as part of that ship's crew or to depart on the same or another aircraft within seven days of arrival in the UK.[24]

3.14　The second group is those who do not require leave to enter or remain in the UK, they include:

a) British citizens,

b) Commonwealth citizens with the right of abode in the UK,

c) EEA nationals who have a right to reside in the UK.

3.15　The Immigration Act 1971 expressly excludes (a) and (b) from the requirement to have leave to enter or remain in the UK,[25] but (c) was a later addition to the group to reflect the evolving nature of the European Union (EU).[26]

19　*Abdi v Barnet LBC and First Secretary of State; Ismail v Barnet LBC and First Secretary of State* [2006] EWCA Civ 383; [2006] HLR 23. See below, paras 3.36–3.71. See footnote 44 for members of the EEA.

20　*Abdirahman v Secretary of State for Work and Pensions* [2007] EWCA Civ 657; [2008] 1 WLR 254; [2007] 4 All ER 882, CA. A person who has temporary admission to the UK is also lawfully present: see *Szoma v Secretary of State for Work and Pensions* [2005] UKHL 64; [2006] 1 AC 564.

21　IA 1971 s8.

22　IA 1971 ss3 and 3A.

23　IA 1971 s8(4) and (6).

24　IA 1971 s8(1).

25　IA 1971 s1(1).

26　IA 1988 s7(1).

British citizenship

3.16 British citizenship is governed by the British Nationality Act (BNA) 1981. A person may become a British citizen in a variety of ways, which include the following. A person born in the UK after 1 January 1983 is a British citizen if at the time of the birth, his/her father or mother was a British citizen or settled in the UK.[27] In this context, 'settled' means that s/he has indefinite leave to remain or permanent residence in the UK. A person born in the UK after 1 January 1983 is entitled to be registered as a British citizen if, while s/he is a minor, his/her father or mother becomes a British citizen or becomes settled in the UK.[28] Otherwise, a person born in the UK after 1 January 1983 can apply for registration as a British citizen after s/he is ten years old, providing s/he has not been absent from the UK for more than 90 days a year.[29] Generally speaking, a person born outside the UK after 1 January 1983 will be a British citizen if at the time of the birth his/her father or mother was a British citizen.[30] A person may also apply for naturalisation[31] as a British citizen so long as s/he fulfils certain requirements set out in BNA 1981.[32]

The right of abode in the UK

3.17 Since the coming into force of BNA 1981,[33] the following now have the right of abode in the UK:

a) Persons who automatically became British citizens on the coming into force of BNA 1981.[34] These will include all the former citizens of the UK and Colonies who had a right of abode because they were 'patrials', ie, citizens of the UK and Colonies born, adopted, registered or naturalised in the UK, those with the necessary ancestral connections with the UK, and those who were ordinarily resident here for five years free of immigration restrictions;[35]

---

27 BNA 1981 s1(1).
28 BNA 1981 s1(3).
29 BNA 1981 s1(4).
30 BNA 1981 s2.
31 BNA 1981 s6.
32 BNA 1981 Sch 1.
33 On 1 January 1983.
34 BNA 1981 s11.
35 IA 1971 s2(1)(c) before amendment.

b) Commonwealth citizens[36] who immediately before commencement had the right of abode by virtue of having a parent who was
born in the UK under the now revoked IA 1971 s2(1)(d); and

(c) Female Commonwealth citizens who immediately before commencement had a right of abode under the now revoked IA 1971
s2(2) by virtue of their marriage to a patrial.[37]

The right to reside in the UK

3.18   The right to reside in the UK for EEA nationals derives from the EC
Treaty.[38] It is not an unconditional right.[39] The requirements to be
met are principally[40] set out in Directive 2004/38/EC[41] ('the Directive') which has been enacted into domestic law by the Immigration
(European Economic Area) Regulations (EEA Regs) 2006.[42] The EEA
Regs 2006 are not simply a repetition of the Directive. In situations
where the Directive gives a right to reside and the EEA Regs 2006 do
not, an applicant is entitled to rely on the Directive.[43] Conversely, if
the Directive does not give a right to reside but the EEA Regs 2006 do,
then an applicant can rely on those more favourable provisions.

3.19   There are two ways in which a person can have a right to reside
in the UK. These are either as an EEA[44] national who satisfies the rel-

36 Commonwealth citizens are all those who are citizens of the countries set out
in BNA 1981 Sch 3.

37 IA 1971 s2 before amendment. Patriality was conferred on certain citizens of
the UK and Colonies and certain other Commonwealth citizens.

38 The Treaty of Rome which established the Common Market in 1959, as
amended by the Maastricht Treaty or the Treaty on European Union, which
came into force on 1 November 1993.

39 EC Treaty article 18; *Minister voor Vreemdelingenzaken en Integratie v RNG Eind*,
Case C-291/05 at [28]; *Trojani v Centre public d'aide sociale de Bruxelles* (CPAS),
Case C-456/02, [2004] ECR I-7573 at paras [31] and [32]; *Zhu and Chen v
Secretary of State for the Home Department*, Case C-200/02, [2004] ECR I-9925 at
para [26]; *Ali v Secretary of State for the Home Department* [2006] EWCA Civ 484
at para [20].

40 Some rights of residence exist outside the scope of the Directive, see paras
3.55–3.60, below.

41 Of the European Parliament and of the Council of 29 April 2004, which came
into force on 30 April 2004.

42 SI No 1003, which came into force on 30 April 2006.

43 IA 1988 s7(1).

44 The EEA consists of the EU plus Norway, Iceland and Liechtenstein. The EU
consists of the EU15 Austria, Belgium, Denmark, Finland, France, Germany,
Greece, Ireland, Italy, Luxembourg, the Netherlands, Portugal, Spain, Sweden
and the UK, plus the countries which acceded on 1 May 2004, which are
Cyprus, the Czech Republic, Estonia, Hungary, Latvia, Lithuania, Malta,

evant conditions,[45] who is known as a 'qualified person'[46] in the EEA Regs 2006, or as a family member of an EEA national who either has a right to reside or has had a right to reside.

3.20 The right to reside exists independently of any residence documentation which is merely evidence of the right,[47] although a person who is in possession of such documentation may rely on article 12 of the EC Treaty in order to be granted social assistance.[48]

3.21 There are three types of right to reside:

a) initial right to reside,
b) extended right to reside,
c) permanent right to reside.

Initial right to reside

3.22 An EEA national must be admitted to the UK if s/he produces on arrival a valid national identity card or passport issued by an EEA State.[49] A person who is not an EEA national must produce on arrival a valid passport and an EEA family permit, a residence card or a permanent residence card.[50] An EEA family permit acts as a sort of entry clearance or visa for non-EEA nationals but its issue cannot be made subject to conditions that are more restrictive than those set out in the Directive.[51]

3.23 The initial right to reside lasts for no longer than three months and is on condition that the EEA national or his/her family member does not become an unreasonable burden on the social assistance system of the UK.[52] The phrase 'unreasonable burden' may be thought to imply that a temporary or short-term reliance on social assistance does not deprive a person of an initial right to reside. In England, a person who has an initial right to reside is ineligible under

---

Poland, Slovakia, Slovenia, plus the countries which acceded on 1 January 2007 (the A2), which are Bulgaria and Romania.

45 These are either set out in the directive or the EEA Regs 2006.

46 EEA Regs 2006 reg 6(1).

47 *Mario Lopes da Veiga v Staatssecretaris van Justitie*, Case 9/88; *Echternach and Moritz v Minister van Onderwijs en Wetenschappen*, Cases 389/87 and 390/87, at para [25].

48 *Trojani v Centre public d'aide sociale de Bruxelles* (CPAS), Case C-456/02; [2004] ECR I-7573 at para [43].

49 Directive 2004/38/EC article 5(1), EEA Regs 2006 reg 11(1).

50 EEA Regs 2006 reg 11(2), see also Directive 2004/38/EC article 5(2).

51 *Metock v Minister for Justice, Equality and Law Reform*, Case C-127/08.

52 Directive 2004/38/EC article 14(1), EEA Regs 2006 reg 13.

Parts 6[53] and 7.[54] In Wales, such a person is eligible under Parts 6[55] and 7,[56] so long as s/he is habitually resident in the UK although, in practice, the three-month period of the initial right of residence may well have expired by the time there has been a final determination of an application for assistance and the person's circumstances may be such that s/he has become an unreasonable burden on the social assistance system of the UK, thereby ceasing to have an initial right of residence in any event.

3.24   The term 'social assistance' is not defined in the Directive, or elsewhere in EU legislation, but has been considered by the European Court of Justice (ECJ), which has held that the grant of such assistance must essentially depend on need and not be linked to employment or contributions.[57] This is therefore likely to be considered to include social housing.[58]

Extended right to reside

3.25   There are five ways in which an EEA national may have an extended right to reside in the UK.[59] These are as a:

a) jobseeker,
b) worker,
c) self-employed person,
d) self-sufficient person, or
e) student.

A jobseeker

3.26   A jobseeker is a person who enters the UK in order to seek employment and can provide evidence that s/he is seeking employment and has a genuine chance of being engaged.[60] The European Court of Justice has held that after six months, a jobseeker must provide evidence that s/he is continuing to seek employment and has genuine chances

---

53 Allocation of Housing and Homelessness (Eligibility) (England) Regulations (Eligibility Regs) 2006 SI No 1294 reg 4(1)(b)(ii).
54 Eligibility Regs 2006 reg 6(1)(b)(ii).
55 Allocation of Housing (Wales) Regulations (AH(W) Regs) 2003 SI No 239 reg 5.
56 Homelessness (Wales) Regulations (H(W) Regs) 2006 SI No 2646 reg 4(1).
57 *Frilli v Belgium*, Case 1/72; [1972] ECR 457; [1973] CMLR 386.
58 By analogy, for the purposes of immigration law, the term 'public funds' is defined (Immigration Rules (HC 395) para 6) as including housing under HA 1996 Part 6 or Part 7 and HA 1985 Part 2.
59 EEA Regs 2006 reg 6(1).
60 EEA Regs 2006 reg 6(4).

of being engaged.[61] In English law, jobseekers are expressly excluded from eligibility under HA 1996 Parts 6[62] and 7.[63] In Wales, jobseekers are eligible under Parts 6[64] and 7,[65] so long as they are habitually resident in the UK.

A worker

3.27 There are three essential criteria which determine whether a person is a worker for the purposes of article 39 of the EC Treaty. First, the person must perform services of some economic value.[66] The activity must be real and genuine, to the exclusion of activity on such a small scale as to be regarded as purely marginal and ancillary.[67] Second, the performance of such services must be for and under the direction of another person. Any activity performed outside a relationship of subordination must be classified as an activity pursued in a self-employed capacity.[68]

3.28 Third, the person concerned must receive remuneration.[69] Neither the origin of the funds from which the remuneration is paid nor the limited amount of that remuneration can have any consequences with regard to whether or not the person is a worker.[70] The fact that the income from employment is lower than the minimum required for subsistence does not prevent the person in such employment from being regarded as a worker,[71] even if the person in question seeks to supplement that remuneration by other means of subsistence such as financial assistance drawn from the public funds[72] of the host Member State.[73]

---

61 *The Queen v Immigration Appeal Tribunal ex p Antonissen*, Case C-292/98; [1991] ECR I 745.

62 Eligibility Regs 2006 reg 4(1)(b)(i).

63 Eligibility Regs 2006 reg 6(1)(b)(i).

64 AH(W) Regs 2003 reg 5.

65 H(W) Regs 2006 reg 4(1).

66 *Lawrie-Blum v Land Baden Wurttemberg*, Case 66/85; [1986] ECR 2121.

67 *Vatsouras and Koupatantze v Arbeitgemeinschaft (ARGE) Nurnberg 900*, Cases C-22/08 and C-23/08; *Lawrie Blum*, above.

68 *Jany v Staatssecretaris van Justitie*, Case C-268/99 at [34].

69 *Vatsouras*, above, at para [25]; and *Lawrie-Blum*, above.

70 *Vatsouras*, above, at para [27].

71 *Levin v Staatssecretaris van Justitie*, Case 53/81.

72 For the purposes of UK immigration law, the term 'public funds' is defined in the Immigration Rules (HC 395) para 6 as including housing under HA 1996 Part 6 or Part 7 and HA 1985 Part 2.

73 *Kempf v Staatssecretaris van Justitie*, Case 139/85.

3.29   The fact that the employment is of short duration cannot, of itself, exclude the employee from being a worker.[74]

3.30   A person who is no longer working does not cease to be a worker if:[75]

a) s/he is temporarily unable to work as the result of an illness or accident;

b) s/he is in duly recorded involuntary unemployment after having been employed in the UK, provided that s/he has registered as a jobseeker with the relevant employment office; and

i) s/he was employed for one year or more before becoming unemployed,

ii) s/he has been unemployed for no more than six months, or,[76]

iii) s/he can provide evidence that s/he is seeking employment in the UK and has a genuine chance of being engaged;

c) s/he is involuntarily unemployed and has embarked on vocational training; or

d) s/he has voluntarily ceased working and embarked on vocational training that is related to his/her previous employment.

A self-employed person

3.31   A self-employed person means a person who establishes him/herself in another EEA State in order to pursue activity as a self-employed person in accordance with article 43 of the EC Treaty.[77] Essentially, this means a person who is working outside a relationship of subordination.[78]

3.32   The EEA Regs 2006 provide that a person who is no longer in self-employment shall not cease to be treated as a self-employed person if s/he is temporarily unable to pursue his/her activity as the result of an illness or accident.[79] This is much narrower than the provisions of the Directive[80] which allow a self-employed person to retain that status in the same way as a worker who is no longer working.

---

74 *Vatsouras*, above, at para [29]; *Ninni Orasche v Bundesminster für Wissenschaft, Verkehr und Kunst*, Case C-413/01; *Barry v Southwark LBC* [2008] EWCA Civ 1140; [2009] HLR 30.

75 EEA Regs 2006 reg 6(2).

76 There is dicta to the effect that these are alternatives, see *Barry*, above, per Lloyd LJ at [35]; see also Directive 2004/38/EC article 7(3).

77 EEA Regs 2006 reg 4(1)(b).

78 See *Jany*, above.

79 EEA Regs 2006 reg 6(3).

80 Directive 2004/38/EC article 7(3).

A self-sufficient person

3.33   A self-sufficient person is a person who has sufficient resources not to become a burden on the social assistance system of the UK during his/her period of residence, and has comprehensive sickness insurance cover in the UK.[81] The requirement not to become a burden on the social assistance system of the UK is not qualified, as in the case of a person who has an initial right to reside, which only requires that the person is not to be an 'unreasonable' burden.[82] A self-sufficient person is most unlikely to be eligible under Parts 6 and 7 because the need for social housing will mean that s/he has become a burden on the social assistance system of the UK and therefore cannot have a right to reside on the basis of self-sufficiency.[83]

A student

3.34   A student is a person who is enrolled at a private or public establishment which is included on the Department for Education and Skills' Register of Education and Training Providers or financed from public funds, for the principal purpose of following a course of study, including vocational training, who has comprehensive sickness insurance cover in the UK, and who assures the secretary of state, by means of a declaration, or by such equivalent means as the person may choose, that s/he has sufficient resources not to become a burden on the social assistance system of the UK during his/her period of residence.[84] This means that a person can have a right to reside as a student even if s/he subsequently becomes a burden on the social assistance system of the UK because the requirement is only that s/he assures the secretary of state that s/he will not become a burden during his/her residence, ie if his/her circumstances change. If a student can have a right of residence despite having a need for social housing, then s/he is likely to be eligible under both Parts 6[85] and 7,[86] so long s/he is habitually resident in the UK.

---

81   EEA Regs 2006 reg 4(1)(c).
82   Directive 2004/38/EC article 14(1); EEA Regs 2006 reg 13, see para 3.23, above.
83   By analogy, for the purposes of immigration law, 'public funds' is defined (Immigration Rules (HC 395) para 6) as including housing under HA 1996 Part 6 or Part 7 and HA 1985 Part 2.
84   Directive 2004/38/EC article 7(1)(c); EEA Regs 2006 reg 4(1)(d).
85   In England, Eligibility Regs 2006 reg 4(1); in Wales, AH(W) Regs 2003 reg 5(1).
86   In England, Eligibility Regs 2006 reg 6(1); in Wales, H(W) Regs 2006 4(1).

Permanent right to reside

3.35   An EEA national who has resided in the UK for a continuous period of five years has a permanent right to reside.[87] Family members who are not EEA nationals but who have resided with the EEA national for a continuous period of five years also obtain the right.[88]

3.36   Workers or self-employed persons who have stopped working (and their family members) also have a permanent right of residence.[89] The worker or self-employed person must have resided in the UK continuously for more than three years, must have worked for at least the last one of those years, and then stopped working at an age when s/he is entitled to a state pension or, in the case of an employed person, has ceased work to take early retirement.[90]

3.37   The definition also applies to a person who has stopped working as a result of a permanent incapacity to work and either s/he resided in the UK continuously for more than two years prior to the termination, or the incapacity is the result of an accident at work or an occupational disease that entitles him/her to a pension payable in full or in part by an institution in the UK.[91]

Residence documentation

3.38   An EEA national who has a right to reside in the UK is entitled to a registration certificate.[92] A non-EEA national who has a right to

87   Directive 2004/38/EC article 16(1); EEA Regs 2006 reg 15(1). In *Secretary of State for Work and Pensions v Maria Dias* [2009] EWCA Civ 807, the Court of Appeal referred to the European Court of Justice (ECJ) the question whether an EU citizen can count time spent in a host Member State, in possession of a residence permit but without a right to reside, towards the five years' continuous residence required under the Directive to be entitled to permanent residence; in *Secretary of State for Work and Pensions v Taous Lassal* [2009] EWCA Civ 157, the Court of Appeal referred to the ECJ the question whether an EEA national can count residence pursuant to EU secondary legislation that existed prior to the coming into force of the Directive, towards the five years' continuous residence required under the Directive to be entitled to permanent residence; after the Court of Appeal decision in *Shirley McCarthy v Secretary of State for the Home Department* [2008] EWCA Civ 641, the House of Lords has referred to the ECJ the question whether lawful residence in the UK as a British citizen can count as residence for the purpose of article 16(1) of the Directive.

88   Directive 2004/38/EC article 16(1); EEA Regs 2006 reg 15(1)(b).

89   Directive 2004/38/EC article 17; EEA Regs 2006 reg 15(1)(c) and (d).

90   Directive 2004/38/EC article 17; EEA Regs 2006 reg 5(2).

91   Directive 2004/38/EC article 17; EEA Regs 2006 reg 5(3).

92   Directive 2004/38/EC article 8; EEA Regs 2006 reg 16; the right to reside exists independently of any residence documentation which is merely evidence of the right, see *Mario Lopes da Veiga v Staatssecretaris van Justitie*, Case 9/88; *Echternach and Moritz v Minister van Onderwijs en Wetenschappen*, Cases

reside in the UK is entitled to a residence card.[93] A person with a permanent right of residence is entitled to a permanent residence document.[94]

Family members

3.39 The EEA Regs[95] define a family member as:

a) a spouse[96] or civil partner,

b) direct descendants including those of a spouse or civil partner who are:

   i) under 21, or

   ii) their dependants,

c) dependent[97] direct[98] relatives in his/her ascending line (ie, parents or grandparents) or those of his/her spouse or his/her civil partner, or

389/87 and 390/87, at para [25]; however a person who is in possession of such documentation may rely upon EC Treaty article 12 in order to be granted social assistance, see *Trojani v Centre public d'aide sociale de Bruxelles* (CPAS), Case C-456/02; [2004] ECR I-7573 at para [43]; there is currently a reference pending before the European Court of Justice to determine whether time spent in possession of a residence document, without a right to reside pursuant to EU law, can count towards permanent residence, see *Secretary of State for Work and Pensions v Maria Dias* [2009] EWCA Civ 807.

93 Directive 2004/38/EC article 10; EEA Regs 2006 reg 17.

94 Directive 2004/38/EC articles 19 and 20; EEA Regs 2006 reg 18; see also EEA Regs 2006 reg 2(1) which states that the document is only proof of the right of residence.

95 EEA Regs 2006 reg 7(1).

96 EEA Regs 2006 reg 7(1)(a). In *Diatta v Land Berlin* [1985] EUECJ R 267/83, the European Court of Justice held that a marital relationship continues until terminated by the competent authority and is not affected by the fact that the spouses live separately, even where they intend to divorce at a later date.

97 EEA Regs 2006 reg 7(1)(b)(ii); see *Jia v Migrationsverket*, Case C-1/05 at para [43], where the European Court of Justice held that 'dependant' means that the family member needs the material support of the EEA national or his/her spouse in order to meet his/her essential needs in the country of origin. The proof to establish such material support may be adduced by any appropriate means and is not confined to financial dependency; however see *Zhu and Chen v Secretary of State for the Home Department*, Case C-200/02; [2004] ECR I-9925, where the European Court of Justice held that the parent of a child had a right to reside in the UK even though the parent was not dependent upon the child but the child was dependent upon the parent.

98 *PG & VG* [2007] UKAIT 19, where it was held that 'direct' is not confined to the first generation but can include grandchildren, but does not include nieces, nephews, uncles and aunts. This approach was assumed to be correct in *Bigia & others v Entry Clearance Officer* [2009] EWCA Civ 79 at [4].

d) extended family members who have been issued with an EEA family permit, a registration certificate or a residence card and who satisfy the conditions in reg 8.[99]

3.40   An extended family member is treated as the family member of the relevant EEA national for so long as s/he holds a valid EEA family permit, a registration certificate or a residence card[100] and is one of the following:[101]

a) a relative of an EEA national or his/her spouse or civil partner, who is dependent on the EEA national or is a member of his/her household, and who
   i)   is residing in an EEA State in which the EEA national also resides, or
   ii) was so residing in an EEA State and is accompanying the EEA national to the UK or wishes to join him/her here, or
   iii) was so residing in an EEA State and has joined the EEA national in the UK and continues to be dependent or a member of his/her household;[102]

b) a relative of an EEA national or his/her spouse or civil partner, who strictly requires his/her personal care on serious health grounds;[103]

c) a relative of an EEA national who would meet the requirements for indefinite leave to enter or remain in the UK as a dependent relative of the EEA national if the EEA national were treated as a person present and settled in the UK;[104]

d) a partner of an EEA national who can prove that s/he is in a durable[105] relationship with the EEA national.[106]

3.41   A family member has a right to reside in the UK for so long as s/he remains the family member of an EEA national who has a right to reside in the UK.[107] The Directive provides that EEA nationals who are family members of an EEA national retain the right to reside on the

---

99 EEA Regs 2006.
100 EEA Regs 2006 reg 7(3).
101 EEA Regs 2006 reg 8.
102 EEA Regs 2006 reg 8(2).
103 EEA Regs 2006 reg 8(3).
104 EEA Regs 2006 reg 8(4).
105 The UKBA's Immigration Directorate Instructions suggest that a period of two years' cohabitation is required.
106 EEA Regs 2006 reg 8(5).
107 EEA Regs 2006 reg 14(2).

death or departure of the EEA national from the host Member State[108] or where there has been a divorce, annulment of marriage or termination of the registered partnership between the family member and the EEA national.[109] Under the Directive, family members who are not EEA nationals may also retain their right to reside.[110]

3.42   The EEA Regs 2006 provide that family members who are not EEA nationals may retain a right to reside in the following circumstances,[111] which are more restrictive than the Directive:

a) if the qualified person has died and the family member has resided in the UK for at least a year before the death and, if s/he were an EEA national, would be a worker, a self-employed person or a self-sufficient person or the family member of such a person;[112]

b) if the family member is the direct descendant of a qualified person who has died or left the UK, or is a direct descendant of that person's spouse or civil partner, and s/he was attending an educational course in the UK immediately before the qualified person died or left the UK, and continues to attend such a course;[113]

c) if the family member is the parent with actual custody of a child who satisfies (b) above;[114]

d) if the family member ceased to be such because s/he is divorced from the qualified person or their civil partnership has been terminated, s/he is not an EEA national but if s/he were, s/he would be a worker, a self-employed person or self-sufficient person or the family member of such a person, and either

   i) the marriage or civil partnership lasted for at least three years, and the couple resided for at least one year during its duration, or

   ii) the former spouse or civil partner has custody of a child of the qualified person, or

   iii) the former spouse or civil partner has the right of access to a child under the age of 18, and a court has ordered that such access must take place in the UK, or

   iv) the continued right of residence in the UK of the person is warranted by particularly difficult circumstances, for example, s/he

---

108 Directive 2004/38/EC article 12(1).
109 Directive 2004/38/EC article 13(1).
110 Directive 2004/38/EC article 12(2) and (3) and article 13(2).
111 EEA Regs 2006 reg 10.
112 EEA Regs 2006 reg 10(2).
113 EEA Regs 2006 reg 10(3).
114 EEA Regs 2006 reg 10(4).

or another family member having been a victim of domestic violence while the marriage or civil partnership was subsisting.[115]

A8 nationals

3.43   The Accession Treaty signed in Athens on 16 April 2003, provided
that ten countries[116] would accede to the European Union on 1 May
2004. The Treaty provides that existing Member States can, as a derogation from the usual position under EU law, regulate access to their
labour markets by nationals of the accession States, other than nationals of Cyprus and Malta. The States to which this derogation applies
are known as the 'A8' countries.

3.44   The derogation can be applied for a transitional period of five
years from 1 May 2004, with a provision for a further two years in the
case of disturbances to the labour market of the Member State. In
England and Wales, the derogation has now been extended until 30
April 2011.[117]

3.45   The Treaty was given domestic effect by the European Union (Accession) Act 2003[118] which gives the secretary of state the power to enact
regulations to permit the derogation. This resulted in the Accession (Immigration and Worker Registration) Regulations (A(IWR) Regs) 2004[119]
which have been unsuccessfully challenged as being unlawful.[120]

3.46   In certain respects, A8 nationals are worse off than nationals of
the original EEA States. A8 nationals who are subject to the worker
registration scheme (WRS) have no right to reside in the UK as work
seekers unless they are self-sufficient.[121] A8 nationals who are subject to the WRS only have a right to reside in the UK as a worker
if their employment is in accordance with the requirements of the
scheme.[122] A8 nationals who are subject to the WRS and who cease
to work in accordance with the requirements of the scheme cease to
have a right to reside in the UK as a worker.[123] If they cease to work

---

115 EEA Regs 2006 reg 10(5).
116 Cyprus, the Czech Republic, Estonia, Hungary, Latvia, Lithuania, Malta,
     Poland, Slovakia and Slovenia.
117 Accession (Immigration and Worker Registration) (Amendment) Regulations
     2009 SI No 892, which came into force on 29 April 2009.
118 It received Royal Assent on 13 November 2003.
119 SI No 1219.
120 *Zalewska v Department for Social Development (Northern Ireland)* [2008] UKHL
     67; [2008] 1 WLR 2602, HL(NI); *Putans v Tower Hamlets LBC* [2006] EWHC
     1634 (Ch); [2007] HLR 10.
121 A(IWR) Regs 2004 reg 4(2) and (3). See para 3.33, above.
122 A(IWR) Regs 2004 reg 5(2).
123 A(IWR) Regs 2004 reg 5(3) and (4).

within one month of the commencement of their employment with an authorised employer, they retain the right to reside as a worker until the end of that month. A8 nationals who are subject to the WRS are not entitled to the issue of registration certificates and cannot entitle non-EEA nationals to the issue of residence cards.[124]

The worker registration scheme

3.47 Most A8 nationals are only able to work as employed persons in the UK if they comply with the requirements of the WRS. The following exemptions apply:

a) Self-employed people are exempt from the WRS.[125]

b) A8 nationals are not subject to the WRS if on 30 April 2004 they had leave to enter or remain in the UK which was not subject to any condition restricting employment.[126]

c) The WRS does not apply to A8 nationals who have worked legally in the UK without interruption for a period of 12 months up to and including 30 April 2004.[127] This can include up to 30 days during which the A8 national was not working legally in the UK.

d) A8 nationals who work legally in the UK without interruption for a period of 12 months which ends after 30 April 2004 cease to be subject to the WRS.[128] This can also include up to 30 days during which the A8 national was not working legally in the UK.

e) A8 nationals are not subject to the WRS during any period in which they are members of a diplomatic mission or the family member of such a person.[129]

f) A8 nationals are exempt from the WRS if their employer is not based in the UK but they have been sent here to work on that employer's behalf.[130]

g) A8 nationals are exempt from the WRS if they are also UK nationals, Swiss nationals or nationals of another EEA State except Bulgaria and Romania.[131]

---

124 A(IWR) Regs 2004 reg 5(5).
125 A(IWR) Regs 2004 reg 1(2)(k) and 2(1). See paras 3.31–3.32, above.
126 A(IWR) Regs 2004 reg 2(2).
127 A(IWR) Regs 2004 reg 2(3) and (8).
128 A(IWR) Regs 2004 reg 2(4) and (8).
129 A(IWR) Regs 2004 reg 2(5A), inserted by the Accession (Worker Authorisation and Worker Registration) (Amendment) Regulations 2007 SI No 3012 reg 3(a) from 19 November 2007.
130 A(IWR) Regs 2004 reg 2(6)(a) and (9)(b).
131 A(IWR) Regs 2004 reg 2(5), as amended by the Accession (Immigration and Worker Authorisation) Regulations 2006 SI No 3317 reg 1(3), Sch 2 para 1(1), (2)(a), from 1 January 2007.

h) A8 nationals are also exempt from the WRS if they are the spouse, civil partner or child under 18 of a person who has leave to enter or remain in the UK that allows that person to work.[132]

i) A family member of a Swiss national or EEA national who has a right to reside in the UK is also exempt from the WRS. This does not include family members of nationals of the A8 or Bulgaria and Romania who are subject to the relevant scheme and who only have an initial right to reside under reg 13 of the EEA Regs 2006.[133]

3.48   A8 nationals who are not exempt must comply with the WRS. Their employment will give them a right to reside in the UK as a worker in any of the following circumstances:

a) they were working legally for an employer on 30 April 2004 and have not ceased working for that employer;[134]

b) they apply for a registration certificate authorising their work within one month of starting work for an employer and have not received a valid certificate, notice of refusal or ceased working for that employer;[135]

c) they have received a valid registration certificate authorising work for that employer and the certificate is still valid;[136] or,

d) they are within the first month of their employment.[137]

A2 nationals

3.49   The Treaty of Accession for Bulgaria and Romania was signed in Luxembourg on 25 April 2005. It provides for the accession of Bulgaria and Romania (the A2) to the European Union on 1 January 2007. During a transitional period of five years from 1 January 2007 to 31 December 2011, the existing Member States can regulate access to their labour markets by A2 workers and restrict their rights of residence.[138] There are also provisions for Member States to continue to maintain restrictions for a further two years in the case of disturbances to their labour markets.

132 A(IWR) Regs 2004 reg 2(5A), inserted by the Accession (Worker Authorisation and Worker Registration) (Amendment) Regulations 2009 SI No 2426 regs 1 and 3(a), from 2 October 2009.

133 A(IWR) Regs 2004 reg 2(6)(b), substituted by the Accession (Worker Authorisation and Worker Registration) (Amendment) Regulations 2009 SI No 2426 regs 1 and 3(b), from 2 October 2009.

134 A(IWR) Regs 2004 reg 7(2)(a).

135 A(IWR) Regs 2004 reg 7(2)(b).

136 A(IWR) Regs 2004 reg 7(2)(c).

137 A(IWR) Regs 2004 reg 7(3).

138 Annexes VI and VII of the Treaty of Accession.

3.50 The Treaty was given domestic effect by the European Union (Accessions) Act 2006. This gave the secretary of state the power to enact regulations to permit the derogation from the provisions of EU law relating to workers. The detail of the derogation is contained in the Accession (Immigration and Worker Authorisation) Regulations (A(IWA) Regs) 2006.[139]

3.51 A2 nationals are worse off than nationals of other EEA States. A2 nationals who are subject to worker authorisation have no right to reside in the UK as jobseekers[140] and will only have a right to reside as a worker when working in accordance with an accession worker authorisation document.[141] A2 nationals subject to worker authorisation will not retain a right to reside as a worker if they cease to work.[142] A2 nationals who are subject to worker authorisation are not entitled to the issue of registration certificates and cannot entitle non-EEA nationals to the issue of residence cards.[143] This does not apply to a highly skilled person who is seeking employment in the UK who is entitled to a registration certificate which states that s/he has unconditional access to the UK labour market. A highly skilled person is defined as someone who meets the requirements of the Highly Skilled Migrant Programme or holds a certain type of qualification.[144]

Worker authorisation

3.52 The way in which the derogation works is that certain A2 nationals are classified as 'subject to worker authorisation' and thereby restricted to authorised categories of employment.[145] The following exemptions apply:

a) Self-employed people are exempt.[146]

b) A2 nationals are not subject to worker authorisation if on 31 December 2006 they had leave to enter or remain in the UK which was not subject to any condition restricting employment.[147]

---

139 SI No 3317, which came into force on 1 January 2007.
140 A(IWA) Regs 2006 reg 6(2). See para 3.26, above.
141 A(IWA) Regs 2006 reg 6(1).
142 A(IWA) Regs 2006 reg 6(3).
143 A(IWA) Regs 2006 reg 7(1).
144 A(IWA) Regs 2006 regs 4 and 7(2).
145 A(IWA) Regs 2006 reg 1(2)(f); these are the categories of employment listed in the first column of the table in Sch 1.
146 A(IWA) Regs 2006 reg 1(2)(t), see paras 3.31–3.32, above.
147 A(IWA) Regs 2006 reg 2(2), as amended by the Accession (Immigration and Worker Authorisation) (Amendment) Regulations 2007 SI No 475 reg 2(1), (2)(a), from 16 March 2007.

c) Worker authorisation does not apply to A2 nationals who have worked legally in the UK without interruption throughout 2006.[148] This can include up to 30 days during which the A2 national was not working legally in the UK.

d) A2 nationals who work legally in the UK without interruption for a period of 12 months which ends after 31 December 2006, cease to be subject to worker authorisation.[149] This can also include up to 30 days during which the A2 national was not working legally in the UK.

e) A2 nationals are not subject to worker authorisation during any period in which they are members of a diplomatic mission or the family member of such a person.[150]

f) A2 nationals are also exempt if their employer is not based in the UK but they have been sent here to work on that employer's behalf.[151]

g) A2 nationals are not subject to worker authorisation if they are also nationals of the UK or an EEA State other than an A2 State. They are also exempt if they have a right of permanent residence.[152] This also applies if they are the spouse or civil partner of a national of the UK or of a person settled in the UK.[153]

h) A2 nationals are not subject to worker authorisation if they are the spouse, civil partner or child under 18 of a person who has leave to enter or remain in the UK which allows that person to work.[154]

i) A2 nationals are not subject to worker authorisation if they are family members of an EEA national who has a right to reside in the UK. This does not include family members of A2 nationals who are subject to worker authorisation. Neither does it include family members of a person who is exempt from worker authorisation because s/he is the family member of a self-employed person, a self-sufficient person or a student. A2 nationals are

---

148 A(IWA) Regs 2006 reg 2(3).
149 A(IWA) Regs 2006 reg 2(4) and 2(12)(c).
150 A(IWA) Regs 2006 reg 2(6A), inserted by the Accession (Worker Authorisation and Worker Registration) (Amendment) Regulations 2007 SI No 3012 reg 2(1), (2)(a), from 19 November 2007.
151 A(IWA) Regs 2006 reg 2(11) and (13)(a).
152 A(IWA) Regs 2006 reg 2(5) and (7).
153 A(IWA) Regs 2006 reg 2(6).
154 A(IWA) Regs 2006 reg 2(5A), inserted by the Accession (Worker Authorisation and Worker Registration) (Amendment) Regulations 2009 SI No 2426 regs 1 and 2(2)(a), from 2 October 2009.

nevertheless exempt if they are family members of a person who is self-employed, self-sufficient or a student.[155]

j) A2 nationals are not subject to worker authorisation if they are the spouse, civil partner or descendant of an A2 national who is working in accordance with the scheme, provided that the descendant is under 21 or dependent on the A2 worker.[156]

k) A2 nationals are not subject to worker authorisation if they are highly skilled persons and hold a registration certificate which states that they have unconditional access to the UK labour market.[157]

l) A2 nationals are not subject to worker authorisation if they are students, hold a registration certificate that permits employment for no more than 20 hours a week unless the work is vocational training or vacation work, and comply with that condition. This exemption is retained for four months after the end of the course of study.[158]

3.53 A2 nationals who are subject to worker authorisation must hold an accession worker authorisation document and work in accordance with the conditions set out in that document. Such a document can be:[159]

a) a passport or other travel document containing a visa which gives the holder the right to carry out a particular type of employment,

b) a seasonal agricultural card, or

c) an accession worker card.

3.54 An application for an accession worker card can be made in two circumstances. First, if the applicant can prove that the employment concerned is within an authorised category of employment.[160] Second, an application can be made by an authorised family member, in which

155 A(IWA) Regs 2006 reg 2(8), substituted by the Accession (Worker Authorisation and Worker Registration) (Amendment) Regulations 2007 SI No 3012 reg 2(1), (2)(b), from 19 November 2007, and amended by the Accession (Worker Authorisation and Worker Registration) (Amendment) Regulations 2009 SI No 2426 regs 1 and 2(2)(b), from 2 October 2009.

156 A(IWA) Regs 2006 reg 2(8A), inserted by the Accession (Worker Authorisation and Worker Registration) (Amendment) Regulations 2009 SI No 2426 regs 1 and 2(2)(c), from 2 October 2009.

157 A(IWA) Regs 2006 reg 2(9).

158 A(IWA) Regs 2006 reg 2(10), (10A) and (10B), substituted by the Accession (Immigration and Worker Authorisation) (Amendment) Regulations 2007 SI No 475 reg 2(1) and (2)(c), from 16 March 2007.

159 A(IWA) Regs 2006 reg 9(2).

160 A(IWA) Regs 2006 reg 10(1)(a).

case there is no restriction on the type of employment.[161] An authorised family member is a family member of an A2 national who is working in accordance with the scheme, unless the worker is only authorised to work by virtue of holding an accession worker card as an authorised family member, or the family member is the spouse or civil partner of the worker or his/her descendant who is under 21 or dependent.[162]

Other rights of residence

3.55   Rights of residence can exist outside the scope of the Directive. In *Chen*,[163] Mrs Chen and her husband were both Chinese nationals and worked for a company established in China but, for the purposes of work, Mr Chen travelled frequently to various Member States of the EU, in particular the UK.[164] Their daughter was born in Belfast and had Irish nationality.[165] She was dependent both emotionally and financially on her mother, Mrs Chen, who was her primary carer, and she received private medical and childcare services in the UK.[166] The European Court of Justice (ECJ) held that article 18 of the EC Treaty and Council Directive 90/364/EEC[167] confer on a minor who is him/herself an EEA national a right to reside for an indefinite period in a host Member State, where that minor is covered by appropriate sickness insurance and is in the care of a parent who is not an EEA national but who has sufficient resources for that minor not to become a burden on the public finances of the host Member State; in such circumstances, the parent who is the primary carer is also entitled to reside with the child in the host Member State.[168]

3.56   The ECJ has also based rights of residence on article 12 of Council Regulation 1612/68.[169] This provides that the child of a national of a Member State who is or has been employed in the territory of another Member State is to be admitted to that state's general educational,

---

161 A(IWA) Regs 2006 reg 10(1)(b).

162 A(IWA) Regs 2006 reg 3, substituted by the Accession (Worker Authorisation and Worker Registration) (Amendment) Regulations 2009 SI No 2426 regs 1 and 2(3), from 2 October 2009.

163 *Zhu and Chen v Secretary of State for the Home Department,* Case C-200/02; [2004] ECR I-9925.

164 *Zhu* at [7].

165 *Zhu* at [8].

166 *Zhu* at [12]–[14].

167 Of 28 June 1990.

168 *Zhu* at [41], [46] and [47].

169 Of 15 October 1968.

apprenticeship and vocational training courses on the same conditions as nationals of that state, if the child is residing in its territory.

3.57   In *Baumbast and R v Secretary of State for the Home Department*,[170] the ECJ held that children of an EU citizen who have installed themselves in a Member State during the exercise by their parent of rights of residence as a migrant worker are entitled to reside there in order to attend general educational courses. The ECJ also held that article 12 must be interpreted as entitling the parent who is the primary carer of those children, irrespective of nationality, to reside with them in order to facilitate the exercise of their right. It did not matter that the parents had divorced or that the parent who was an EU citizen had ceased to be a migrant worker in the host Member State.[171]

3.58   *Baumbast* was reconsidered by the ECJ in *Ibrahim*[172] and *Teixeira*,[173] two homelessness appeals referred by the Court of Appeal[174] to the ECJ, which heard them together. Ms Ibrahim was a Somali national, married to but separated from Mr Yusuf, a Danish citizen. They had four children, who were Danish. The two eldest were at school in the UK. Initially, Mr Yusuf worked but he then ceased to enjoy a right to reside as a worker and left to live in Eastern Europe. Although he returned to live in the UK, he never regained a right to reside. Ms Ibrahim did not work, was entirely reliant on means-tested benefits and had no medical insurance. She applied with her children for homelessness assistance under Part 7 but was refused on the basis that she had no right to reside under EU law.

3.59   Ms Teixeira was a Portuguese national. She came to the UK in 1989 with her husband, from whom she subsequently divorced. Her daughter was born in 1991. Ms Teixeira worked from 1989 to 1991, after which time she had intermittent periods of employment. She last worked in early 2005. Their daughter entered education in the UK at a time when Ms Teixeira was not a worker; in November 2006, she enrolled in a childcare course and, in March 2007, she went to live with her mother. In April 2007, Ms Teixeira applied under Part 7 but was refused on the basis that she had no right to reside.

---

170 Case C-413/99; [2002] ECR I-7091; [2002] 3 CMLR 23.

171 *Baumbast*, at [63] and [75].

172 Case C-310/08.

173 Case C-480/08.

174 *Harrow LBC and Secretary of State for the Home Department* [2008] EWCA Civ 386; [2009] HLR 2; and *Teixeira v Lambeth LBC and Secretary of State for the Home Department* [2008] EWCA Civ 1088; [2009] HLR 9.

3.60   The Advocate Generals in both references have delivered their Opinions.[175] They held that, where a child of an EU citizen is in education in a Member State in which that citizen is or has been employed as a migrant worker, the parent who is the child's primary carer enjoys a right of residence in the host Member State, derived from article 12. The right of residence of that parent is not subject to a requirement that the parent should have sufficient resources and comprehensive sickness insurance cover nor is it subject to a requirement that the parent should have been employed as a migrant worker in the host Member State when the child first entered education. It is sufficient for the child to have been installed in the host Member State during the exercise by a parent of rights of residence as a migrant worker in that State. The right of residence of the parent ends when the child reaches the age of majority, unless the circumstances of the individual case are such that it is appropriate for the child to continue to be looked after personally by that parent so as to ensure that the child is able to pursue and complete his/her education. The judgments of the ECJ in both references are awaited.

Habitual residence

3.61   The test of habitual residence applies to all persons from abroad who are not subject to immigration control and are returning to the UK. It therefore includes British citizens. The test focuses on the fact and nature of residence. Mere physical presence is insufficient, there needs to be an association between the individual and the place of residence. The most important factors governing habitual residence are the length, continuity and general nature of the actual residence.

3.62   A distinction should be made between applicants who have arrived in the UK for the first time, and those returning to resume a previous life here. The Code of Guidance[176] recommends that applicants who have been resident continuously for a two-year period[177] prior to their housing application will be habitually resident.[178] Enquiries will need to be conducted where an applicant has less than two years' continuous residence. Consideration should be given to why the applicant has come to the UK, whether s/he is joining friends or family, what

---

175   20 October 2009.

176   Homelessness Code of Guidance for Local Authorities, above, para 2.69 and appendix C below.

177   A period of about six months appears to be applied more regularly in practice.

178   Homelessness Code of Guidance for Local Authorities, para 9.16.

his/her plans are, his/her length of residence in the country s/he has left and where his/her centre of interest in located. Two conditions must be fulfilled.[179] There must be residence for an appreciable period of time such that it has become habitual and will or is likely to continue to be habitual.[180] Second, there must be a settled intention to reside.[181] Evidence of such intention might include bringing family or possessions to the UK.

3.63   An applicant who is returning to the UK after a period spent abroad, who it is established was previously habitually resident in the UK, and who now has a settled intention to return here, will be under no obligation to satisfy a further period of residence in the UK and will be immediately habitually resident.[182] There has to be a genuine resumption of the previous habitual residence. Relevant factors will focus on the length of absence from the UK and continuing links during that time.

Provision of information

3.64   If there are doubts about an applicant's immigration status, an authority can contact the UK Borders Agency (UKBA) to obtain relevant information. When a request is made, HA 1996 s187 places a duty on the secretary of state to provide a local authority with such information as it may require to enable it to determine whether a person is eligible for assistance under Part 7.

3.65   Annex 8 of the Code of Guidance[183] explains how to contact the Home Office Immigration and Nationality Directorate, now the UKBA.[184] Enquiries are dealt with by the Evidence and Enquiries Unit (EEU). The EEU's Local Authorities' Team will only assist once the authority has registered. This requires:

a) the name of the enquiring housing authority on headed paper,

b) the job title/status of the officer registering on behalf of the local housing authority,

c) the names of officers, and their job titles, who will be making the enquiries.

179 *Re J (a minor)* [1990] 2 AC 562 at 578F–G.
180 *Nessa v Chief Adjudication Officer* [1999] 4 All ER 677 at 682–683.
181 *Shah v Barnet LBC* [1983] 1 All ER 226.
182 *Swaddling v Adjudication Officer* [1999] All ER (EC) 217.
183 See appendix C.
184 UKBA was set up in February 2008.

3.66   Once registered, enquiries can be made by letter or fax, but replies will be returned by post. If the authority makes a written request, the secretary of state must confirm the information in writing.[185] The secretary of state is under a duty to update an authority in respect of any change in information that has been provided. Such a correction must be in writing, detail the change, the date on which the previous information became inaccurate and the reason why.[186]

3.67   If the response indicates that the applicant has an outstanding asylum claim, enquiries should be made to the Local Authority Communications Section of the UKBA.[187]

Homelessness – HA 1996 Part 7

3.68   Under Part 7, eligibility must be determined whenever an authority has reason to believe that an applicant may be homeless or threatened with homelessness.[188] The date for establishing whether an applicant is eligible is the date of the decision and not the date of application.[189] Where there is a review, it is the date of the review decision that is key.[190]

3.69   While an authority is entitled to reach its own decision as to an applicant's immigration status, any such decision is only for housing purposes and will be subject to a contrary decision by the immigration authorities.[191] An authority is entitled to take an immigration decision of the UKBA at face value and is not required to carry out its own further investigations to determine eligibility.[192]

3.70   Where a full housing duty has been accepted under HA 1996 s193(2),[193] an authority may revisit the issue of eligibility and will cease to be subject to the duty if an applicant ceases to be eligible.[194]

---

185   HA 1996 s187(2).
186   HA 1996 s187(3).
187   Enquiries used to be made to NASS LA Comms, but NASS no longer exists (see footnote 4, above).
188   HA 1996 s184(1)(a).
189   *R v Southwark LBC ex p Bediako* (1997) 30 HLR 22, QBD.
190   *Mohamed v Hammersmith and Fulham LBC* [2001] UKHL 57; [2002] 1 AC 547; [2002] HLR 7, HL.
191   *R v Westminster CC ex p Castelli and Tristan Garcia* (1996) 28 HLR 617, CA; *London Borough of Tower Hamlets v Secretary of State for the Environment* [1993] QB 632; 25 HLR 524, CA.
192   *R (Burns) v Southwark LBC* [2004] EWHC 1901 (Admin).
193   Below, paras 10.85–10.176.
194   HA 1996 s193(6)(a).

Other members of the household

3.71 Section 185(4) requires authorities also to consider the eligibility of household members. The section formerly required[195] authorities to disregard ineligible household members[196] when determining whether an eligible applicant was homeless or had a priority need. However, the provision was declared incompatible with article 14 when read with article 8 of the European Convention on Human Rights, to the extent that it required a dependent child or pregnant spouse of a British citizen, habitually resident in the UK but subject to immigration control, to be disregarded when determining whether the British citizen had a priority need for accommodation.[197]

3.72 Accordingly, the section was amended[198] so that it now[199] applies only to eligible applicants who are themselves subject to immigration control (except for EEA and Swiss nationals), for example, those granted refugee status, indefinite leave to remain or humanitarian protection.[200] When considering an application from such an applicant, authorities must continue to disregard any dependants or other household members who are ineligible for assistance for any reason, for the purpose of deciding whether the applicant is homeless or has a priority need[201] but, otherwise (ie, when the applicant is not him/herself a person subject to immigration control[202]), they are to be taken into account.

3.73 It follows that applicants who are not subject to immigration control, plus EEA and Swiss nationals, will now be able to rely on ineligible household members to qualify as homeless or in priority need,

---

195 In respect of all applications for accommodation or assistance in obtaining accommodation, within the meaning of HA 1996 s183, made before 2 March 2009.

196 For example, in *Ehiabor v Kensington & Chelsea RLBC* [2008] EWCA Civ 1074, the applicant could not rely on the dependent child to establish a priority need because the child, although born in the UK, was not a British citizen and therefore required leave to remain under the Immigration Act 1971 s1(2) and was subject to immigration control.

197 *R (Morris) v Westminster CC* [2005] EWCA Civ 1184; [2006] HLR 8.

198 By operation of the Housing and Regeneration Act 2008 s314 and Sch 15 Part 1.

199 In respect of all applications for accommodation or assistance in obtaining accommodation, within the meaning of HA 1996 s183, made on or after 2 March 2009.

200 Below, paras 3.82–3.97.

201 See the letter from the Department for Communities and Local Government to the Chief Housing Officers dated 16 February 2009 and the accompanying guidance note.

202 Above, para 3.12.

and confer an entitlement to be secured suitable accommodation under HA 1996 s193(2). Typically, ineligible household members who could confer priority need in this way are likely to be dependent children and pregnant women who have been granted leave with a condition of no recourse to public funds.[203]

3.74   This does not, however, give such applicants exactly the same rights as others. An application pursuant to which the authority would not be satisfied that the applicant had a priority need but for a 'restricted person' is called a 'restricted case'.[204] A restricted person is a person who is ineligible and subject to immigration control[205] who either does not have leave to enter or remain in the UK[206] or who has leave subject to a condition of no recourse to public funds.[207]

3.75   In a restricted case, the authority must, so far reasonably practicable, bring the full housing duty to an end by arranging for a private accommodation offer to be made.[208] This means an offer of an assured shorthold tenancy made by a private landlord to the applicant, which is made with the approval of the authority, in pursuance of arrangements made by the authority with the landlord with a view to bringing the authority's duty to an end; the tenancy must be a fixed tenancy for a period of at least 12 months.[209]

3.76   In a restricted case, the full housing duty ends if the applicant, having been informed of the possible consequences of refusal of the offer and the right to request a review of the suitability of the accommodation,[210] either accepts or refuses a private accommodation offer.[211]

3.77   Where it is not reasonably practical to bring the full housing duty to an end with a private accommodation offer, the local authority may discharge the duty in the same way as any other application; it would therefore be open to the authority to bring the duty to an end with a final offer of accommodation under HA 1996 Part 6.

---

203 For the purposes of UK immigration law, the term 'public funds' is defined in the Immigration Rules (HC 395) para 6 as including housing under HA 1996 Part 6 or Part 7 and HA 1985 Part 2.

204 HA 1996 s193(3B).

205 Above, para 3.12.

206 Above, para 3.12.

207 HA 1996 s184(7).

208 HA 1996 s193(7AD).

209 HA 1996 s193(7AC).

210 HA 1996 s193(7AB). What this means is considered further, in relation to non-restricted cases, below, paras 10.168–10.169.

211 HA 1996 s193(7AA).

3.78 Similar amendments have been made to section 195 in cases of threatened homelessness where the applicant is reliant on a household member who is ineligible and subject to immigration control[212] who either does not have leave to enter or remain in the UK or who has leave[213] subject to a condition of no recourse to public funds, which includes housing or assistance under HA 1985 Part 2 and HA 1996 Parts 6 and 7.[214]

3.79 If the authority decides that a duty is owed to the applicant under section 193(2) or section 195(2), but only because of a restricted person, it must inform the applicant that this was the basis for the decision,[215] identify the restricted person by name, and explain both why the person is a restricted person and that it is necessary to bring the duty to an end with a private accommodation offer.[216]

Homelessness assistance

3.80 The division into persons subject and not subject to immigration control set out above applies in both England and Wales. That, however, is not the end of the issue: the question remains who is actually eligible for assistance under HA 1996 Part 7 – and that differs between England[217] and Wales[218] in respect of both classes (subject, and not subject, to immigration control). Each must therefore be considered separately.

England

Persons subject to immigration control

3.81 For a person subject to immigration control to be eligible for actual assistance, s/he must fall within one of the prescribed classes.

---

212 Above, para 3.12.
213 Above, para 3.12.
214 Immigration Rules (HC 395) para 6.
215 HA 1996 s184(3A).
216 HA 1996 s184(3).
217 Eligibility Regs 2006, which came into force on 1 June 2006.
218 H(W) Regs 2006, see footnote 56, above, which came into force on 9 October 2006.

Class A

3.82   Class A[219] is a person who is recorded by the secretary of state as a refugee within the definition set out in article 1 of the Refugee Convention[220] and who has leave to enter or remain in the UK.

3.83   A refugee is any person who, owing to a well-founded fear of being persecuted for reasons of race, religion, nationality, membership of a particular social group or political opinion, is outside the country of his/her nationality and is unable or, owing to such fear, unwilling to avail him/herself of the protection of that country, or who, not having a nationality and being outside the country of his/her former habitual residence as a result of such events, is unable or, owing to such fear, unwilling to return to it.

3.84   A decision as to whether to recognise a person as a refugee must be taken in accordance with Council Directive 2004/83/EC[221] which lays down minimum standards for the qualification and status of third-country nationals or stateless persons as refugees or as persons who otherwise need international protection and the content of the protection granted. Such a decision is made by the UKBA.

3.85   Recognition as a refugee almost inevitably leads to a grant of leave to remain. Prior to 30 August 2005, refugees were granted indefinite leave to remain (ILR). From that date, the grant is normally five years' leave to remain. During the limited five-year period, refugee status can be reviewed and removed, for example, if there has been a change in circumstances in the refugee's country of origin or s/he has returned there. Normally there is no review at the end of the five-year period, but a review can be triggered if there is evidence of criminality or if an application for settlement is made after the initial period of leave has expired. At the end of the five-year period, the refugee qualifies for indefinite leave to remain in the UK.

3.86   From early 2002, application registration cards (ARCs) have been issued to asylum-seekers and their dependants during the asylum screening process. The ARC is a credit card sized form of identity. If an application for asylum is successful, the applicant will be given a letter from the UKBA which explains his/her position as a refugee and some of his/her rights in the UK. A refugee's national passport is not stamped, because s/he cannot use it without forfeiting his/

---

219 Eligibility Regs 2006 reg 5(1)(a).

220 The Convention relating to the Status of Refugees was adopted by a Conference of Plenipotentiaries of the United Nations on 28 July 1951 and entered into force on 21 April 1954.

221 Of 29 April 2004, which entered into force on 20 October 2004.

her refugee status. Instead, s/he will be issued with an Immigration Status Document (ISD). These were phased in during late 2003 and early 2004 and are an A4 sheet of paper, folded into four, confirming the immigration status of the holder. An ISD is also designed to hold a UK Residence Permit (UKRP). Since late 2003, the ink stamps that used to be endorsed in passports and travel documents have been progressively replaced by UKRPs which are issued to those granted more than six months' leave to enter or remain in the UK. The UKRP takes the form of a credit card sized sticker or vignette. It was introduced in accordance with EU Regulation 1030/2002 which requires EU countries that have opted in to this regulation to issue uniform format vignettes to all non-EEA nationals granted more than six months' leave to enter or remain. They are a security measure.

3.87 Refugees may apply for a refugee travel document, which looks like a passport. This is issued by the UKBA under the United Nations Convention relating to the Status of Refugees and the applicant's leave will be endorsed in the document on a UKRP vignette.

Class B

3.88 Class B[222] is a person who has exceptional leave to enter or remain in the UK granted outside the provisions of the Immigration Rules, whose leave to enter or remain is not subject to a condition requiring him/her to maintain and accommodate him/herself and any person who is dependent on him/her without recourse to public funds, which includes housing or assistance under HA 1985 Part 2, or HA 1996 Parts 6 and 7.[223]

3.89 Exceptional leave to enter or remain was abolished from 1 April 2003 and therefore only a dwindling group now has this status. Exceptional leave to remain (ELR) describes the leave granted to applicants who were not found to be refugees but who the Home Office, for humanitarian or compassionate reasons, determined it would not be right to require to return to their country of origin.

3.90 Persons with ELR should have a grant letter from the Home Office. They should also have their status stamped in their national passport. If they do not have a national passport, they will have been issued with an ISD containing a UKRP vignette. If such persons wish to travel but do not have a national passport, they may apply to the UKBA for a travel document known as a Certificate of Travel (COT).

---

222 Eligibility Regs 2006 reg 5(1)(b).
223 Immigration Rules (HC 395) para 6.

Class C

3.91 Class C[224] applies to a person who is habitually resident in the UK, the Channel Islands, the Isle of Man or the Republic of Ireland and whose leave to enter or remain in the UK is not subject to any limitation or condition, other than a person:

a) who has been given leave to enter or remain in the UK upon an undertaking given by his/her sponsor;

b) who has been resident in the UK, the Channel Islands, the Isle of Man or the Republic of Ireland for less than five years beginning on the date of entry or the date on which his/her sponsor gave the undertaking in respect of him/her, whichever date is the later; and

c) whose sponsor or, where there is more than one sponsor, at least one of whose sponsors, is still alive.

3.92 In summary, this class applies to any person with indefinite leave to remain in the UK unless that leave was granted on an undertaking by a sponsor less than five years ago and the sponsor is still alive.

3.93 Such a person should have a grant letter from the Home Office or UKBA. S/he should have a stamp or UKRP in his/her national passport which shows that s/he has ILR. S/he may also have an ISD or a COT with a UKRP vignette which shows his/her status.

Class D

3.94 Class D applies to a person who has humanitarian protection granted under the Immigration Rules.[225]

3.95 From 1 April 2003, the Home Office abolished ELR and replaced it with humanitarian protection (HP) and discretionary leave (DL). HP is granted to a person who, if removed, would face a serious risk to life or person arising from capital punishment, unlawful killing or torture or inhuman or degrading treatment or punishment in the country of return.[226] Although they do not qualify for refugee status, such persons would be at risk of treatment in violation of articles 2 or 3 of the European Convention on Human Rights. The requirements in relation to HP can now be found in the Immigration Rules.[227]

---

224 Eligibility Regs 2006 reg 5(1)(c).

225 Eligibility Regs 2006 reg 5(1)(d), substituted by the Allocation of Housing and Homelessness (Miscellaneous Provisions) (England) Regulations 2006 SI No 2527 reg 2(1) and (3), from 9 October 2006.

226 Immigration Rules para 339C.

227 Immigration Rules para 339C.

3.96   From 30 August 2005, if a person is granted HP, s/he is also granted leave to remain for five years, after which an application can be made for settlement when there is an automatic review of whether there is a continuing protection need.

3.97   Persons with HP should have a grant letter from the UKBA. Their ISD or national passport will contain a UKRP vignette granting leave for a period of five years. If they do not have a national passport, they may apply for a travel document or COT which, if issued, will contain the UKRP vignette.

Class E

3.98   Class E[228] applies to a person who is an asylum-seeker whose claim for asylum is recorded by the secretary of state as having been made before 3 April 2000 in the circumstances mentioned in one of the following paragraphs:

a) on arrival (other than on his/her re-entry) in the UK from a country outside the UK, the Channel Islands, the Isle of Man or the Republic of Ireland;

b) within three months from the day on which the secretary of state made a relevant declaration, and the applicant was in Great Britain on the day on which the declaration was made; or,

c) on or before 4 February 1996 by an applicant who was on 4 February 1996 entitled to benefit under regulation 7A of the Housing Benefit (General) Regulations 1987.[229]

3.99   For the purpose of Class E, asylum-seeker means a person who is at least 18 years old, who is in the UK, and who has made a claim for asylum. A claim for asylum means a claim that it would be contrary to the UK's obligations under the Refugee Convention for the applicant to be removed from, or required to leave, the UK. A person ceases to be an asylum-seeker when his/her claim for asylum is recorded by the secretary of state as having been decided, other than on appeal, or abandoned.

3.100   A relevant declaration means a declaration to the effect that the country of which the applicant is a national is subject to such a fundamental change of circumstances that the secretary of state would not normally order the return of a person to that country. The only claims for asylum currently affected are those made by nationals of Sierra Leone from 16 May to 16 August 1997, and those made by

228 Eligibility Regs 2006 reg 5(1)(e).
229 SI No 1971.

nationals of the Democratic Republic of Congo between 1 July and 1 October 1997.

3.101　The significance of 3 April 2000 is that a person who claimed asylum on arrival in the UK on or after that date was no longer supported by local authorities but by the National Asylum Support Service (NASS).[230]

3.102　Applicants who come within Class E are not automatically eligible for assistance. Section 186 of HA 1996 states that such a person or his/her dependant is not eligible if s/he has any accommodation in the UK, however temporary, available for his/her occupation, although it must be reasonable for the applicant to continue to occupy it.[231] For the purposes of this section, a person becomes an asylum-seeker at the time when his/her claim is recorded by the secretary of state as having been made and ceases to be an asylum-seeker when his/her claim is recorded as having been finally determined or abandoned. A dependant means a spouse or child under 18 and becomes such when the secretary of state records him/her as being a dependant of the asylum-seeker and ceases to be a dependant when the claimant ceases to be an asylum-seeker or, if earlier, when s/he is recorded by the secretary of state as ceasing to be a dependant. The section defines a claim for asylum as one made pursuant to the Refugee Convention.

Persons not subject to immigration control

3.103　Generally speaking, a person who is not subject to immigration control will only be eligible if s/he is habitually resident in the UK, but certain rights of residence are excluded and certain applicants are exempt from the habitual resident test.

3.104　A person who is not subject to immigration control is ineligible if:[232]

a) s/he is not habitually resident in the UK, the Channel Islands, the Isle of Man, or the Republic of Ireland;

b) his/her only right to reside in the UK is derived from his/her status as a jobseeker or the family member of a jobseeker, or is an initial right to reside; or

c) his/her only right to reside in the Channel Islands, the Isle of Man or the Republic of Ireland is a right equivalent to one of those mentioned in (b) above.

230　See footnote 4, above.

231　*Lismane v Hammersmith and Fulham LBC* (1998) 31 HLR 427, CA.

232　Eligibility Regs 2006 reg 6(1).

3.105 A person who is not subject to immigration control is exempt from the habitual residence test if s/he is:[233]

a) a worker;[234]

b) a self-employed person;[235]

c) an A8 or A2 worker who has a right to reside because s/he is complying with the relevant scheme;[236]

d) a person who is the family member of a person specified in (a) to (c) above;

e) a person with a right to reside permanently in the UK by virtue of regulation 15(1)(c), (d) or (e) of the EEA Regs [2006];[237]

f) a person who left the territory of Montserrat after 1 November 1995 because of the effect on that territory of a volcanic eruption;

g) a person who is in the UK as a result of his/her deportation, expulsion or other removal by compulsion of law from another country to the UK;

h) . . .;[238]

i) a person who arrived in Great Britain on or after 28 February 2009 but before 18 March 2011, who immediately before arriving in Great Britain had been resident in Zimbabwe, and who before leaving Zimbabwe had accepted an offer, made by Her Majesty's Government, to assist that person to settle in the UK.[239]

Wales

3.106 In Wales, as in England,[240] the issue of eligibility for actual assistance needs to be considered separately in relation to both those who are, and those who are not, subject to immigration control.[241]

---

233 Eligibility Regs 2006 reg 6(2).

234 Above, paras 3.27–3.30.

235 Above, paras 3.31–3.32.

236 Above, paras 3.43–3.54.

237 Above, paras 3.35–3.37.

238 Inserted by Allocation of Housing and Homelessness (Eligibility) (England) (Amendment) Regulations 2006 SI No 2007 reg 2(1) and (8), from 25 July 2006 at 4pm but ceasing to have effect on 31 January 2007.

239 Eligibility Regs 2006 reg 6(2)(i), inserted by Allocation of Housing and Homelessness (Eligibility) (England) (Amendment) Regulations 2009 SI No 358 reg 2(1) and (5), from 18 March 2009.

240 Above, paras 3.81–3.102.

241 H(W) Regs 2006, which came into force on 9 October 2006.

Persons subject to immigration control

3.107   A person who is subject to immigration control is eligible if s/he falls within one of the prescribed classes.[242]

Classes A to C

3.108   Classes A to C are almost identical to the equivalent Classes in the English regulations.[243]

Class D

3.109   Class D applies to a person who left the territory of Montserrat after 1 November 1995 because of the effect on that territory of a volcanic eruption.[244]

Class E

3.110   Class E[245] applies to a person who is habitually resident[246] in the Common Travel Area and who either is a national of a state which has ratified the European Convention on Social and Medical Assistance (ECSMA) made at Paris on 11 December 1953[247] or a state which has ratified the European Social Charter (CESC) made at Turin on 18 October 1961[248] who is lawfully present in the UK[249] or, before 3 April 2000, was owed a duty by a housing authority under HA 1985 Part 3 or HA 1996 Part 7, which is extant and is a national of a state which is a signatory to either of the two legislative instruments described above.

---

242 H(W) Regs 2006 reg 3.

243 Above, paras 3.82–3.93.

244 H(W) Regs 2006 reg 3(1)(d).

245 H(W) Regs 2006 reg 3(1)(e).

246 Above, paras 3.61–3.63.

247 The ECSMA signatories are Belgium, Denmark, Estonia, France, Germany, Greece, Iceland, Ireland, Italy, Luxembourg, Malta, the Netherlands, Norway, Portugal, Spain, Sweden, Turkey and the UK. Nationals of countries that have ratified ECSMA do not have an automatic right of residence in the UK, see *Yesiloz v Camden LBC and another* [2009] EWCA Civ 415.

248 The CESC includes Austria, Belgium, Croatia, Cyprus, the Czech Republic, Denmark, Finland, France, Germany, Greece, Hungary, Iceland, Ireland, Italy, Latvia, Liechtenstein (signed but not ratified), Luxembourg, Macedonia, Malta, the Netherlands, Norway, Poland, Portugal, Romania (signed but not ratified), Slovakia, Slovenia (signed but not ratified), Spain, Sweden, Switzerland (signed but not ratified), Turkey, Ukraine (signed but not ratified) and the UK.

249 It is possible to be lawfully present in the UK without a right to reside, see *Abdirahman v Secretary of State for Work and Pensions* [2007] EWCA Civ 657; [2008] 1 WLR 254.

Class F

3.111 Class F[250] applies to a person who is an asylum-seeker and who made a claim for asylum which is recorded by the secretary of state as having been made on his/her arrival (other than on his/her re-entry) in the UK from a country outside the Common Travel Area, and which has not been recorded by the secretary of state as having been either decided (other than on appeal) or abandoned.

Class G

3.112 Class G[251] applies to a person who is an asylum-seeker and who was in Great Britain when the secretary of state made a declaration to the effect that the country of which that person is a national is subject to such a fundamental change in circumstances that the secretary of state would not normally order the return of a person to that country, who made a claim for asylum which is recorded by the secretary of state as having been made within a period of three months from the day on which that declaration was made, and whose claim for asylum has not been recorded by the secretary of state as having been either decided (other than on appeal) or abandoned.

Class H

3.113 Class H[252] applies to a person who is an asylum-seeker and who made a relevant claim for asylum on or before 4 February 1996 and who was, on 4 February 1996, entitled to benefit under regulation 7A of the Housing Benefit (General) Regulations 1987.[253]

Class I

3.114 Class I[254] applies to a person who is on an income based jobseeker's allowance, an income related employment and support allowance,[255] or in receipt of income support and is eligible for that benefit other than because:

a) that person has limited leave to enter or remain in the UK which was given in accordance with the relevant Immigration Rules and

---

250 H(W) Regs 2006 reg 3(1)(f).
251 H(W) Regs 2006 reg 3(1)(g).
252 H(W) Regs 2006 reg 3(1)(h).
253 SI No 1971.
254 H(W) Regs 2006 reg 3(1)(i).
255 Inserted by Employment and Support Allowance (Consequential Provisions) (No 3) Regulations 2008 SI No 1879 reg 31(1) and (3), from 27 October 2008, see reg1(1).

that person is temporarily without funds because remittances to that person from abroad have been disrupted, or

b) that person has been deemed by regulation 3 of the Displaced Persons (Temporary Protection) Regulations 2005[256] to have been granted leave to enter or remain in the UK exceptionally for the purposes of the provision of means of subsistence.

Class J

3.115   Class J[257] applies to a person who has humanitarian protection granted under the Immigration Rules.[258]

Persons not subject to immigration control

3.116   As in England, persons not subject to immigration control will be eligible if they are habitually resident[259] in the UK, though some rights of residence are excluded, and some applicants are exempt from the habitual residence test.[260] A person not subject to immigration control will be ineligible if:

a) s/he is not habitually resident[261] in the UK, the Channel Islands, the Isle of Man or the Republic of Ireland; or

b) his/her right to reside in the UK, the Channel Islands, the Isle of Man or the Republic of Ireland is derived solely from Council Directive 90/364/EEC[262] or Council Directive 90/365/EEC.[263]

3.117   Council Directive 90/364/EEC confers a right to reside on EEA nationals and their family members who are covered by sickness insurance and have sufficient resources to avoid becoming a burden on the social assistance system of the host Member State during their period of residence.[264] Council Directive 90/365/EEC gives a right to reside to employees and self-employed persons who have ceased their occupational activity, along with their family members.[265]

---

256 SI No 1379.

257 H(W) Regs 2006 reg 3(1)(j).

258 Made pursuant to Immigration Act 1971 s3(2).

259 Above, paras 3.61–3.63.

260 H(W) Regs 2006 reg 4.

261 Above, paras 3.61–3.63.

262 Repealed on 30 April 2006 by Directive 2004/38/EC article 38(2).

263 Repealed on 30 April 2006 by Directive 2004/38/EC article 38(2).

264 Council Directive 90/364/EEC of 28 June 1990 article 1.

265 Council Directive 90/365/EEC of 28 June 1990 article 1.

3.118   Persons not subject to immigration control who are exempt from the habitual residence test are:[266]

a) a person who is a worker for the purposes of Council Regulation (EEC) No 1612/68[267] or (EEC) No 1251/70;[268]

b) an A8 national who is a worker in accordance with the worker registration scheme (WRS);[269]

c) a person with a right to reside pursuant to the EEA Regs which is derived from Council Directive 68/360/EEC,[270] 73/148/EEC[271] or 75/34/EEC;[272]

d) a person who left the territory of Montserrat after 1 November 1995 because of the effect on that territory of a volcanic eruption;

e) a person who arrived in Great Britain on or after 28 February 2009 but before 18 March 2011, who immediately before arriving in Great Britain had been resident in Zimbabwe and, before leaving Zimbabwe, who had accepted an offer, made by Her Majesty's Government, to assist that person to settle in the UK.[273]

3.119   A person will be treated as habitually resident in the UK, the Channel Islands, the Isle of Man or the Republic of Ireland only if s/he has a right to reside there.[274]

---

266 H(W) Regs 2006 reg 4(2).

267 Of 15 October 1968. Articles 10 and 11 were repealed on 30 April 2006 by Directive 2004/38/EC article 38(1).

268 Of 29 June 1970. This concerns the rights of workers to remain in the territory of a Member State after having been employed in that State.

269 Above, paras 3.47–3.48.

270 Of 15 October 1968. This abolished restrictions on movement and residence within the EU for workers of Member States and their families. It was repealed on 30 April 2006 by the Directive 2004/38/EC article 38(2).

271 Of 21 May 1973. This abolished restrictions on movement and residence within the EEC for nationals of Member States with regard to establishment and the provision of services. It was repealed on 30 April 2006 by Directive 2004/38/EC article 38(2).

272 Of 17 December 1974. This concerned the right of nationals of a Member State to remain in the territory of another Member State after having pursued therein an activity in a self-employed capacity. It was repealed on 30 April 2006 by Directive 2004/38/EC article 38(2).

273 H(W) Regs 2006 reg 4(2)(e), inserted by the Allocation of Housing and Homelessness (Eligibility) (Wales) Regulations 2009 SI No 393 reg 3, from 20 March 2009, see reg 1(1).

274 H(W) Regs 2006 reg 4(3). Above, paras 3.18–3.60.

Interim accommodation

3.120   Notwithstanding prima facie eligibility for homelessness assistance as set out above, the provisions of the Nationality, Immigration and Asylum Act (NIAA) 2002 Schedule 3 nonetheless disqualify certain classes of immigrant in both England and Wales from two classes of interim accommodation. These exclusions do not apply to British citizens or those who are under 18.[275] The classes of interm accommodation excluded are:

a) HA 1996 s188(3) accommodation pending review;[276]

b) HA 1996 s204(4) accommodation pending appeal to the county court.[277]

3.121   It may be noted that these classes are also disqualified from assistance under other statutory powers which may assist those who do not qualify under Part 7, considered below in chapter 13, ie, under

a) National Assistance Act 1948 ss21 and 29;[278]

b) Children Act 1989 ss17, 23C, 23CA,[279] 24A and 24B;[280]

c) Immigration and Asylum Act 1999;[281]

d) Local Government Act 2000 s2.[282]

3.122   The schedule excludes the following five classes of persons from eligibility:

a) The first class applies to a person who has been recognised as a refugee by an EEA State other than the UK. It also applies to a person who is the dependant of a person who is in the UK and who has such status.[283]

b) The second class applies to a person who has the nationality of an EEA State other than the UK, or who is the dependant of such a person.[284]

---

275 NIAA 2002 Sch 3 para 2(1)(a) and (b).

276 NIAA 2002 Sch 3 para 1(1)(j). See below, paras 10.33 to 10.44.

277 NIAA 2002 Sch 3 para 1(1)(j). See below, paras 12.196–12.200.

278 NIAA 2002 Sch 3 para 1(1)(a). See below, paras 13.6–13.31.

279 Inserted by Children and Young Persons Act 2008 s22(6). See below, paras 13.44–13.65.

280 NIAA 2002 Sch 3 para 1(1)(g). See below, paras 13.44–13.65.

281 NIAA 2002 Sch 3 para 1(1)(l). See below, paras 13.32–13.43.

282 NIAA 2002 Sch 3 para 1(1)(k). See below, paras 13.66–13.71.

283 NIAA 2002 Sch 3 para 2(4).

284 NIAA 2002 Sch 3 para 2(5).

c) The third class applies to a person who was, but is no longer, an asylum-seeker and who is not cooperating with removal directions. It also applies to the dependant of such a person.[285]

d) The fourth class applies to a person who is in the UK in breach of NIAA 2002 s11 and who is not an asylum-seeker.[286] In summary, this means anyone who is in the UK in breach of immigration laws, ie, who does not have a right to reside under EU law, does not have leave to enter or remain, does not have a right of abode, etc.

e) The fifth class applies to a person who, although his/her asylum claim has been rejected, continues to be treated as an asylum-seeker and accommodated by the UKBA because s/he has dependent children,[287] but the Home Secretary has certified that s/he has, without reasonable excuse, not taken reasonable steps to leave the UK voluntarily or place him/herself in a position in which s/he is able to leave the UK voluntarily. The person must have received the certificate and been given 14 days to act. It also applies to the dependants of such a person.[288]

Exceptions to ineligibility

3.123 A person who falls within one of these classes will not, however, be ineligible if the exercise of a power or the performance of a duty is necessary for the purpose of avoiding a breach of:

a) a person's rights under the European Convention on Human Rights (ECHR/'the Convention'),[289] or

b) a person's rights under the Community Treaties.[290]

3.124 The European Court of Human Rights has been sympathetic to arguments based on ECHR article 8.[291] It has held that the right to family life includes the right of a parent and child mutually to enjoy each other's company,[292] and has found a violation of that article where the

---

285 NIAA 2002 Sch 3 para 2(6).

286 NIAA 2002 Sch 3 para 2(7).

287 See below, paras 13.44–13.65.

288 NIAA 2002 Sch 3, para 2(7A), inserted by Asylum and Immigration Act 2004 s9 with effect from 1 December 2004, see Asylum and Immigration (Treatment of Claimants, etc) Act 2004 (Commencement No 2) Order 2004 SI No 2999.

289 See, generally, below, paras 12.95–12.106.

290 NIAA 2002 Sch 3 para 3.

291 See below, paras 12.101–12.103.

292 *Olsson v Sweden* (1988) 11 EHRR 259.

deportation of the applicant from the Netherlands would interrupt his intermittent contact with his daughter there.[293]

3.125   Conversely, the Court of Appeal has held that neither article 8 nor article 3[294] imposes a duty on the UK to provide support to foreign nationals who are in a position freely to return to their country of origin.[295] This principle was also applied in a case where the claimant had an undetermined human rights claim.[296] It has been held that the making of a purported fresh claim either for asylum or under article 3, by a claimant whose original claim had been rejected, did not always make it necessary for support to be provided in order to avoid a breach of the Convention. In considering the issue, the authority had to have regard to all the relevant circumstances, including where appropriate the matters which were alleged to constitute a fresh claim. It was necessary to proceed on a case by case basis considering the facts of each individual case with care.[297] Nevertheless, an authority does have the power to fund the costs of returning an applicant and his/her family to their country of origin.[298]

3.126   It would be unlawful to offer to fund the cost of return travel if this was not a viable option.[299] An authority must closely scrutinise any argument that a return to the country of origin would give rise to a breach of Convention rights.[300] It is important to take into account the potential effect of removal on each relevant family member and the impact on other family members. An authority should also take into account any relevant Home Office policy that concerns the issue of whether or not the claimant and his/her family will be able to remain in the UK.[301]

3.127   The exception governing EU Treaty rights has also been interpreted narrowly. It appears not to apply for the benefit of work seekers[302] but probably does assist workers.[303]

293 *Ciliz v Netherlands* [2000] 2 FLR 469.

294 See below, paras 12.95–12.105.

295 *R (K) v Lambeth LBC* [2003] EWCA Civ 1150; [2004] 1 WLR 272; [2004] HLR 15.

296 *Blackburn Smith v Lambeth LBC* [2007] EWHC 767 (Admin); (2007) 10 CCLR 252.

297 *R (AW) v Croydon LBC* [2005] EWHC 2950 (QB); (2005) 9 CCLR 252.

298 *R (Grant) v Lambeth LBC* [2005] 1 WLR 1781; [2005] HLR 27.

299 *R (J) v Enfield LBC* [2002] EWHC 432 (Admin).

300 *R (PB) v Haringey LBC and others* [2006] EWHC 2255 (Admin); [2007] HLR 13; (2007) 10 CCLR 99.

301 *R (Clue) v Birmingham CC* [2008] EWHC 3036 (Admin); (2009) 12 CCLR 79; see para 13.50, below.

302 *R (Mohamed) v Harrow LBC* [2005] EWHC 3194 (Admin); [2006] HLR 18.

303 *R (Conde) v Lambeth LBC* [2005] EWHC 62 (Admin).

Allocations – HA 1996 Part 6

3.128 The basic rule is that Part 6 is confined to allocations by authorities of secure or introductory tenancies, nominations by local authorities to registered social landlords for letting on assured tenancies, and transfers requested by tenants.[304] It does not cover, and the rules of eligibility do not apply to, the grant of or nomination to a tenancy or licence by a local authority which is not secure, or the nomination of a person to a tenancy or licence which is exempt from assured status.

3.129 Successions to and assignments of tenancies are also unaffected by eligibility because they do not involve the grant of rights of occupation by an authority.[305] Similarly unaffected are transfers of secure or introductory tenancies under the provisions of matrimonial and related domestic legislation,[306] and becoming a secure tenant following an introductory tenancy.[307]

3.130 Part 6 does not affect the eligibility of a person who is already a secure or introductory tenant, or an assured tenant of housing accommodation allocated to him/her by a local housing authority.[308] Under the legislation preceding the 1996 Act, when immigration was not explicitly addressed in the law governing either homelessness or allocations,[309] it was held that a tenancy granted to a person unlawfully in the UK was not void for that reason;[310] The same applies under Part 6: notwithstanding the prohibition in HA 1996 s167(8), it has been held that the grant of a tenancy, even though contrary to Part 6, is itself valid.[311]

3.131 The immigration status of members of the household of an applicant for an allocation under Part 6 is relevant, in particular when determining the size of the property to be allocated. It has long been said that Parliament cannot have intended to require housing authorities to house those who enter the country unlawfully.[312] Similarly, in

---

304 HA 1996 s159(2) and (5).
305 HA 1996 s160(2)(a)–(d).
306 HA 1996 s160(2)(e).
307 HA 1996 s160(3).
308 HA 1996 s159(5) as amended by HA 2002 s13.
309 Above, paras 3.6–3.8.
310 *Akinbolu v Hackney LBC* (1996) 29 HLR 259, CA.
311 See *Birmingham CC v Qasim* [2009] EWCA Civ 1080; [2010] HLR forthcoming.
312 *Tower Hamlets LBC v Secretary of State for the Environment* [1993] QB 632, per Sir Thomas Bingham at page 632; (1993) 25 HLR 524, CA; see also *R v Hillingdon LBC ex p Streeting* [1980] 1 WLR 1425.

Akinbolu,[313] it was held that it was proper to refuse to provide public sector housing to applicants who are illegal immigrants or overstayers. In *Ariemuguvbe*,[314] the appellant lived in a three-bedroom property with her husband, her five adult children (who had come to the UK from Nigeria but who had overstayed their visitor's visas) and three grandchildren. She contended that she was entitled to additional points under the authority's allocation scheme to take account of the five adult children.[315] The authority was held to be entitled to conclude that it was not appropriate to allocate a larger property to the appellant, because the five children were all independent adults, some having families of their own, who should have been able to make their own housing arrangements and also because they were subject to immigration control[316] in circumstances where providing accommodation for them would amount to them having recourse to public funds in breach of their conditions of entry to the UK.[317]

3.132   In a restricted case,[318] however, an applicant owed a full housing duty will not be entitled to a reasonable preference for an allocation of housing. In non-restricted cases, an applicant does enjoy such a preference.[319] Consequently, if an authority is considering making an offer of Part 6 accommodation to an applicant in a restricted case, it will need to take particular care to ensure that such an allocation would be in accordance with the priorities of its published allocation scheme.[320]

3.133   Authorities must consider eligibility at the point at which an applicant is considered for an allocation.[321] However, they should also consider eligibility at the time the applicant applies for an allocation because an applicant who is accepted into an allocation scheme has a

313 *Akinbolu v Hackney LBC* (1996) 29 HLR 259, CA, at 269.

314 *R (Ariemuguvbe) v Islington LBC* [2009] EWCA Civ 1308. The Court of Appeal overruled the decision in *R (Kimvono) v Tower Hamlets LBC* (2001) 33 HLR 78, QBD, in which neither *Tower Hamlets* nor *Akinbolu* had been cited and in which it had been held that the immigration status of the applicant's dependent child was irrelevant to the authority's duties under Part 6.

315 *Ariemuguvbe* at [2] and [3].

316 Above, para 3.12.

317 *Ariemuguvbe* at [19].

318 Above, paras 3.74–3.79.

319 HA 1996 s167(2ZA), and see below, para 11.56.

320 See para 17 of the guidance note that accompanied the Department for Communities and Local Government letter dated 16 February 2009, see above.

321 HA 1996 s160A.

reasonable expectation that s/he will be eligible to be allocated accommodation under it.[322]

3.134   Eligibility for an allocation of housing differs between England[323] and Wales.[324]

England

3.135   Eligibility for an allocation of housing depends on whether the applicant is a person subject to immigration control[325] or not subject to immigration control.[326]

Persons subject to immigration control

3.136   As with homelessness assistance, for a person subject to immigration control to be eligible, s/he must fall within one of the prescribed classes.[327] There are four such classes, A to D.[328] They are the same as Classes A to D in respect of homelessness assistance.[329]

Persons not subject to immigration control

3.137   With regard to persons who are not subject to immigration control, eligibility for an allocation of housing[330] is the same as eligibility under Part 7 of the HA 1996.[331]

Wales

3.138   As in England, eligibility for an allocation depends on whether the applicant is a person subject to immigration control[332] or not subject to immigration control.[333]

322 Code of Guidance on Allocation of Accommodation Choice Based Lettings para 3.10. This provision is unaffected by the statutory guidance on social housing allocation for local authorities in England, published in December 2009 (see its para 4).
323 Eligibility Regs 2006 regs 3 and 4.
324 AH(W) Regs 2003 regs 4 and 5.
325 Eligibility Regs 2006 reg 3.
326 Eligibility Regs 2006 reg 4.
327 Eligibility Regs 2006 reg 3(a) to (d).
328 Eligibility Regs 2006 reg 3(d), substituted by Allocation of Housing and Homelessness (Miscellaneous Provisions) (England) Regulations 2006 SI No 2527 reg 2(1) and (2), from 9 October 2006, see reg 1(1).
329 Above, paras 3.82–3.97.
330 Eligibility Regs 2006 reg 4.
331 Above, paras 3.103–3.105.
332 AH(W) Regs 2003 reg 4.
333 AH(W) Regs 2003 reg 5.

Persons subject to immigration control

3.139　A person who is subject to immigration control is eligible if s/he falls within one of the prescribed classes. There are five classes.

Classes A to C

3.140　Classes A to C are the same as those that apply to homelessness assistance.[334]

Class D

3.141　Class D[335] is the same as the Class E that applies under Part 7 of the HA 1996.[336]

Class D1

3.142　Class D1[337] applies to a person who has humanitarian protection granted under the Immigration Rules.[338]

Persons not subject to immigration control

3.143　In Wales, a person not subject to immigration control is eligible for an allocation[339] unless s/he falls within Class E, which applies to a person who is not habitually resident[340] in the Common Travel Area. The following persons are exempt from the habitual residence test and therefore cannot fall within Class E. Accordingly, they are eligible so long as they are not subject to immigration control.

a) a worker for the purposes of Council Regulation (EEC) No 1612/68[341] or No 1251/70,[342]

334　Above, para 3.108.

335　AH(W) Regs 2003 reg 4(d).

336　Above, para 3.110.

337　AH(W) Regs 2003 reg 4(e), inserted by Allocation of Housing (Wales) (Amendment) Regulations 2006 SI No 2645 reg 2(1) and (2)(b), from 9 October 2006, see regs 1(1) and 3.

338　Above, paras 3.94–3.97.

339　AH(W) Regs 2003 reg 5.

340　Above, paras 3.61–3.63.

341　Of 15 October 1968. This concerned the freedom of movement for workers within the EEC. Articles 10 and 11 have been repealed by Directive 2004/38/EC article 38(1), with effect from 30 April 2006.

342　Of 29 June 1970. This concerns the right of workers to remain in the territory of a Member State after having been employed in that State.

b) a person with a right to reside in the UK pursuant to the Immigration (European Economic Area) Order 2000[343] and derived from Council Directive 68/360/EEC[344] or 73/148/EEC,[345]

c) a person who left the territory of Montserrat after 1 November 1995 because of the effect on that territory of a volcanic eruption,

d) a person who arrived in Great Britain on or after 28 February 2009 but before 18 March 2011, immediately before arriving had been resident in Zimbabwe, and before leaving Zimbabwe had accepted an offer made by Her Majesty's Government to assist that person to settle in the UK.[346]

---

343 SI No 2326, which came into force on 2 October 2000 and was revoked, subject to certain savings, by Immigration (European Economic Area) Regulations 2006 SI No 1003, which came into force on 30 April 2006.

344 Of 15 October 1968. This abolished restrictions on movement and residence within the EEC for workers of Member States and their families. It was repealed by Directive 2004/38/EC article 38(2), with effect from 30 April 2006.

345 Of 21 May 1973. This abolished restrictions on movement and residence within the EEC for nationals of Member States with regard to establishment and the provision of services. It was repealed by Directive 2004/38/EC article 38(2), with effect from 30 April 2006.

346 AH(W) Regs 2003 reg 5(d), inserted by Allocation of Housing and Homelessness (Eligibility) (Wales) Regulations 2009 SI No 393 reg 2, from 20 March 2009, see reg 1(1).

Homelessness

continued

Introduction

4.1   This chapter considers the statutory definitions of 'homelessness' and of being 'threatened with homelessness'.

4.2   'Homelessness' is defined by the Housing Act (HA) 1996 s175 as:
a) accommodation, which is
b) available for the applicant's occupation, to which
c) there are rights of occupation (subsection (1)),
d) entry to or use of which is not restricted (subsection (2)), and which
e) it is reasonable for the applicant to continue to occupy (subsection (3)).[1]

4.3   The same terms also apply to:
f) what is meant by being threatened with homelessness (subsection (4)).

Accommodation

Location

4.4   Under HA 1985, only accommodation in England, Wales or Scotland was to be taken into account. This had not been stated explicitly in the original legislation – the Housing (Homeless Persons) Act 1977 – but had been accepted, albeit obiter, in *Streeting*[2] and was expressly enacted in HA 1985.

4.5   As departure from accommodation abroad could, however, qualify as intentional homelessness,[3] this did not commonly lead to any benefit. HA 1996 s175(1) now refers to accommodation in the UK or elsewhere.[4]

Nature

4.6   The term 'accommodation' has proved one of the most controversial under the homelessness legislation, not so much as between

---

1   See *Begum v Tower Hamlets LBC* (1999) 32 HLR 445, CA, for a discussion of the interaction of these different subsections.

2   *R v Hillingdon BC ex p Streeting* [1980] 1 WLR 1425, DC.

3   See *de Falco, Silvestri v Crawley BC* [1980] QB 460, CA, and other cases considered at paras 6.131–6.132, below.

4   See, eg, *Begum v Tower Hamlets LBC* (1999) 32 HLR 445, CA, where the accommodation in question was situated in Bangladesh.

applicant and authority, but between, on the one hand, the lower courts and the House of Lords, and, on the other, the House of Lords and Parliament.

Settled accommodation

4.7   Thus, between 1977 and 1986, there was a growing tendency on the part of the courts – High Court and Court of Appeal – to equiparate a want of accommodation with accommodation of such poor quality that it could be quit without a finding of intentionality. In this context a distinction was drawn for both purposes (and probably for the purpose of defining the duties owed by authorities) between 'settled' and 'unsettled' accommodation.

4.8   Both applications of this approach were firmly rejected by House of Lords, first in *Puhlhofer*,[5] and second in *Awua*.[6] In turn, this led to further legislation, first in the Housing and Planning Act 1986, and, to an extent, also under HA 1996 Part 7 itself.

4.9   In the more recent of these cases,[7] the House of Lords held that the only gloss on the word 'accommodation' which can properly be imported, other than pursuant to the statute itself (ie, availability and reasonableness to continue in occupation),[8] is that it must mean 'a place which can fairly be described as accommodation'.[9]

Non-qualifying accommodation

4.10   As an example of shelter which would have failed this test, Lord Brightman in *Puhlhofer* instanced Diogenes' tub.

4.11   In *Awua*, the modern equivalent was said to be the night shelter in *R v Waveney District Council ex p Bowers*,[10] in which the applicant could have had a bed if one was available but where he could not remain by day – and therefore had to walk the streets.[11]

4.12   In *Sidhu*,[12] it was held that a women's refuge was not accommodation, and so a woman who left her violent partner and found

---

5   *R v Hillingdon LBC ex p Puhlhofer* [1986] AC 484; 18 HLR 158, HL.

6   *R v Brent LBC ex p Awua* [1996] 1 AC 55; 27 HLR 453, HL.

7   *Awua*, above.

8   See paras 4.17–4.38 and 4.69–4.140, below.

9   *R v Brent LBC ex p Awua* [1996] 1 AC 55; 27 HLR 453, HL, per Lord Hoffmann at 461.

10   (1982) *Times* 25 May, QBD. Not cross-appealed on this point – see further [1983] QB 238; 4 HLR 118, CA.

11   *R v Brent LBC ex p Awua* [1996] 1 AC 55; 27 HLR 453, HL, at 459.

12   *R v Ealing LBC ex p Sidhu* (1982) 2 HLR 45, QBD.

temporary shelter in such a refuge was still homeless while residing there.[13]

4.13 In *Ali* and *Moran*,[14] the House of Lords concluded that *Sidhu* could probably not survive the decisions of the House in *Puhlhofer*[15] and *Awua*[16] as a matter of theory, although the effect of the decision was preserved by reference to sections 175(3) and 177, ie, that it would not normally be reasonable to continue to occupy accommodation in a women's refuge.[17] (The House of Lords also declined to comment on whether a prison cell or a hospital ward could amount to accommodation.)[18]

4.14 An applicant who occupies temporary accommodation provided to him/her pending enquiries, review or appeal under section 188 or section 204(4) is nevertheless homeless for the purpose of section 175(1), because to find otherwise would create the absurd result that a homeless person who is temporarily accommodated would not be entitled to benefit from Part 7.[19]

4.15 Where an authority granted a licence of accommodation in discharge of its functions under Part 7, the accommodation was not considered a 'dwelling' and therefore fell outside the ambit of the Protection from Eviction Act 1977,[20] although this conclusion was based on the policy of that Act rather than consideration of what is meant by homelessness.

4.16 Reference may also be made to *Miles*,[21] in which it was held that accommodation within the definition of homelessness means 'habitable'. This decision was followed by the majority in the Court of

13 *Sidhu* followed a county court decision, *Williams v Cynon Valley Council*, January 1980 *LAG Bulletin* 16, CC. In addition to *Bowers* (above, para 4.11 and footnote 10), other cases to consider the meaning of accommodation within the definition of homelessness before *Puhlhofer* and *Awua* were: *Parr v Wyre BC* (1982) 2 HLR 71, CA; *R v South Herefordshire DC ex p Miles* (1983) 17 HLR 82; *R v Preseli DC ex p Fisher* (1984) 17 HLR 147, QBD; and *R v Dinefwr BC ex p Marshall* (1984) 17 HLR 310, QBD.

14 *Birmingham City Council v Ali; Moran v Manchester City Council (Secretary of State for Communities and Local Government and another intervening)* [2009] UKHL 36; [2009] 1 WLR 1506 at [56].

15 *R v Hillingdon LBC ex p Puhlhofer* [1986] AC 484; 18 HLR 158, HL.

16 *R v Brent LBC ex p Awua* [1996] 1 AC 55; 27 HLR 453, HL.

17 Below, para 4.72.

18 *Stewart v Lambeth LBC* [2002] HLR 747; *R(B) v Southwark LBC* [2004] HLR 18.

19 *R (Alam) v London Borough of Tower Hamlets* [2009] EWHC 44 (Admin). Approved by the House of Lords in *Ali* at [54].

20 *Desnousse v Newham LBC, Paddington Churches Housing Association, Veni Properties Limited* [2006] EWCA Civ 547; [2006] HLR 38.

21 *City of Gloucester v Miles* (1985) 17 HLR 292, CA.

Appeal in *Puhlhofer*,[22] who were upheld by the House of Lords without reference to *Miles*; nor was the case mentioned in *Awua*.

Accommodation available for occupation

Accessibility

4.17   The requirement that accommodation is 'available for occupation' requires consideration of two elements:
  – 'practical accessibility'; and
  – 'legal accessibility'.[23]

4.18   The requirement also imports the need for accommodation to be available to other members of the applicant's household, as defined by HA 1996 s176.

Physical accessibility

4.19   To be practically accessible and accordingly available to an applicant, it must be possible for the applicant physically to access the accommodation, a question which includes whether an applicant can afford to return to accommodation overseas which is otherwise available.[24]

Legal accessibility

4.20   Legal accessibility will require consideration of issues such as whether an applicant is legally entitled to live in the country in which the accommodation is situated.

Immigration

4.21   HA 1996 s185(4) used[25] to require local housing authorities in England and Wales to disregard household members (including dependent children) who were ineligible[26] for housing assistance when

---

22   See (1985) 17 HLR 588.
23   See *Begum v Tower Hamlets LBC* (1999) 32 HLR 445, CA.
24   *Begum*, footnote 23, above. Although the authority had failed to consider this issue in the case, the Court of Appeal refused to quash the decision since the applicant had not raised the issue, and the authority was accordingly not required to investigate the matter (see para 9.100, below).
25   In respect of all applications for accommodation or assistance in obtaining accommodation within the meaning of HA 1996 s183, made before 2 March 2009.
26   Above, chapter 3.

considering whether any eligible housing applicant was homeless. This provision has now[27] been amended so that it applies only to an eligible applicant who is him/herself a person subject to immigration control,[28] for example, those granted refugee status,[29] indefinite leave to remain,[30] or humanitarian protection.[31] Accordingly, when considering an application from a person subject to immigration control (excluding for this purpose an EEA national[32] or Swiss national) who is eligible for assistance, a local authority must continue to disregard any dependants or other household members who are ineligible for assistance, when deciding whether the applicant is homeless.

4.22 The effect is that section 185(4) no longer applies to eligible[33] applicants who are not subject to immigration control,[34] for example, a British citizen,[35] a Commonwealth citizen with a right of abode in the UK,[36] or an EEA national or Swiss national with a right to reside in the UK.[37] This group of eligible applicants will be able to rely on ineligible household members, known as 'restricted persons'[38] to establish homelessness. A restricted person is someone who is not eligible for assistance under Part 7, who is subject to immigration control and who either does not have leave to enter or remain in the UK or who has leave subject to a condition of no recourse to public funds.

4.23 If the authority can be satisfied that the applicant is homeless only by taking into account the restricted person, the application is known as a 'restricted case'.[39] In those circumstances, the authority must, so far as reasonably practical, bring any section 193(2) duty to an end by arranging for an offer of an assured shorthold tenancy to be made to

---

27 By Housing and Regeneration Act 2008 s314 and Sch 15 Part I, in respect of all applications for accommodation or assistance in obtaining accommodation within the meaning of HA 1996 s183, made on or after 2 March 2009.
28 Above, para 3.12.
29 Above, paras 3.82–3.87.
30 Above, paras 3.91–3.93.
31 Above, paras 3.94–3.97.
32 Above, para 3.19.
33 Above, chapter 3.
34 Above, paras 3.13–3.60.
35 Above, para 3.16.
36 Above, para 3.17.
37 Above, paras 3.18–3.60.
38 HA 1996 s184(7).
39 HA 1996 s193(3B).

the applicant by a private landlord.[40] This is known as a private accommodation offer.[41]

Accommodation for whom?

4.24   By HA 1996 s176, accommodation is only 'available' if it is available for the applicant together with:

a)   any person who usually resides with him/her as a member of his/her family; or

b)   any other person who might reasonably be expected to do so (HA 1996 s176).

Code of Guidance

4.25   'Member of the family' is not defined. The Code of Guidance says that the expression will 'include those with close blood or marital relationships and cohabiting partners (including same sex partners)'.[42]

4.26   The Code continues that 'any other person' might cover a companion for an elderly or disabled person, or children being fostered by the applicant or a member of his/her family.[43]

4.27   The Code concludes:

> Persons who normally live with the applicant but who are unable to do so because there is no accommodation in which they can live together should be included in the assessment.[44]

Family

4.28   This approach echoes the decision of the House of Lords in *Islam*,[45] where the applicant lost his right to a shared room as a result of the arrival of his wife and four children from Bangladesh. A finding of intentionality was quashed by the House of Lords on the basis that what had been lost was not accommodation 'available for his occupation', meaning that of the applicant and his family.[46]

---

40   HA 1996 s193(7AD). See further below, paras 10.168–10.169.

41   HA 1996 s193(7AC). Above, para 3.75 and below, para 10.168.

42   Code of Guidance para 8.5. The Welsh Code (see para 13.3) does not contain any reference to same sex partners, but see *Fitzpatrick v Sterling Housing Association* [2001] 1 AC 27; (1999) 32 HLR 178, where a majority of the House of Lords accepted that same sex partners could be members of the family. Above, para 2.169 and appendix C below.

43   Code of Guidance para 8.5. See also Welsh Code para 13.3.

44   Code of Guidance para 8.6 See also Welsh Code para 13.4.

45   *R v Hillingdon LBC ex p Islam* [1983] 1 AC 688; 1 HLR 107, HL.

46   The argument in the Court of Appeal that Mr Islam had made the

4.29 Accordingly, a family which has never enjoyed accommodation in which there were rights of occupation for all of its members will at all times have been homeless. For example, a couple without a home of their own, each still living with his/her parents, will be able to claim a right to assistance under this Part as soon as a priority need is acquired. An authority wishing to resist the claim cannot resort to intentional homelessness based on a pregnancy itself, as this is precluded by *Islam*.[47]

4.30 Note, however, that an unborn child will not be a person with whom the applicant would be expected to reside. So the future housing needs of the unborn child need not be considered by the authority when determining homelessness,[48] save the extent to which it had otherwise rendered the mother's accommodation unavailable in her own right.

4.31 That does not make the pregnancy irrelevant. In *Rouf*,[49] it was held that an authority could not jump to the conclusion that accommodation would continue to be available to an applicant with an increasing family. See also *Ali*,[50] in which the court found the proposition that a single, small room was 'available' for a large family (applicant, wife and five children) 'quite extraordinary'.

4.32 In other cases, hopelessly inadequate accommodation had been held not to be accommodation it was reasonable to continue to occupy.[51]

4.33 A member of the family who usually resides with the applicant need not also be shown to do so reasonably.[52]

Others

4.34 The question of who is reasonably to be expected to reside with an applicant is a matter for the authority, challengeable on conventional

accommodation unavailable by bringing his family over was dismissed as 'circular . . . because that lack is the very circumstance which section 16 [of the Housing (Homeless Persons) Act 1977, subsequently HA 1985 s75, now s176] and the Act are designed to relieve'.

47 In *R v Eastleigh BC ex p Beattie (No 1)* (1983) 10 HLR 134, QBD, the court rejected out of hand a suggestion that pregnancy causing accommodation to cease to be reasonable to occupy could amount to intentionality.

48 See *R v Newham LBC ex p Dada* (1995) 27 HLR 502, CA.

49 *R v Tower Hamlets LBC ex p Rouf* (1989) 21 HLR 294, QBD.

50 *R v Westminster CC ex p Ali* (1983) 11 HLR 83, QBD.

51 See paras 4.103–4.113, below.

52 Compare *R v Hillingdon Homeless Persons Panel ex p Islam* (1981) *Times* 24 February QBD, not cross-appealed on the proposition, as it relates to priority need: see further para 6.9, below.

grounds of public law,[53] rather than a question of fact which a court can decide for itself: see *Ly.*[54]

4.35   In *Carr,*[55] it was held that the authority had erred in law in failing to consider whether the applicant's boyfriend – the father of her child – was a person with whom she might reasonably be expected to reside. The authority had wrongly reached its decision solely on the basis that they had not lived together at the applicant's last settled accommodation.

4.36   In *Okuneye,*[56] however, the fact that two people were intending or expecting to reside together did not mean that – when each departed from his and her separate accommodation – they were necessarily reasonably to be expected to reside together at that time. The authority was accordingly entitled to conclude that each had become homeless intentionally for ceasing to occupy available accommodation.

4.37   In *Ryder,*[57] the authority approached the question of whether a carer could reasonably be expected to reside with a disabled applicant by reference to whether the applicant was eligible for Disability Living Allowance. As the test for such an allowance was more stringent – and, it may be said, different – from what is now HA 1996 s176, the decision was quashed. Similarly, the authority in *Tonnicodi*[58] applied the wrong test – whether the applicant needed a live-in carer – rather than whether the carer was a person who might reasonably be expected to reside with the applicant.

4.38   In *Curtis,*[59] the applicant was occupying her former matrimonial home under a separation agreement which contained a cohabitation clause to the effect that if she cohabited or remarried the property would be sold. The applicant started to cohabit and her husband enforced the power of sale. The authority found the applicant to be homeless intentionally, a decision that was quashed because it had not considered availability in the statutory sense, ie, whether, if it was reasonable for her and her cohabitant to live together, the property was available to both of them (which it was not).

---

53   See chapter 12.

54   *R v Lambeth LBC ex p Ly* (1986) 19 HLR 51, QBD. Compare *R v Newham LBC ex p Khan and Hussain* (2000) 33 HLR 29, where a decision that a grandmother, her two daughters and their respective husbands and children did not usually reside together was quashed as *Wednesbury* unreasonable.

55   *R v Peterborough CC ex p Carr* (1990) 22 HLR 207, CA.

56   *R v Barking & Dagenham LBC ex p Okuneye* (1995) 28 HLR 174, QBD.

57   *R v Southwark LBC ex p Ryder* (1996) 28 HLR 56, QBD.

58   *R v Hackney LBC ex p Tonnicodi* (1997) 30 HLR 916, QBD.

59   *R v Wimborne DC ex p Curtis* (1985) 18 HLR 79, QBD.

Rights of occupation

4.39 If the applicant is not to be considered homeless, the applicant must be able to enjoy the benefit of one of three categories of occupational right (HA 1996 s175(1)):

a) occupation under interest or order;
b) occupation under express or implied licence; or
c) occupation by enactment or restriction.

4.40 Accommodation in a prison does not fall within any of these rights of occupation, as the prisoner has no enforceable right to occupy the cell.[60]

Occupation under interest or order

4.41 The right of occupation may be by virtue of an 'interest' in the accommodation: this would seem to mean a legal or equitable interest.

4.42 Those with a legal interest will include both owner-occupiers and tenants, whether under long leases or on short, periodic tenancies, and whether under an initially agreed contractual period or under the contract as statutorily extended by the Housing Acts 1985 and 1988 (secure tenants and assured tenants). If one of a pair of joint tenants unilaterally terminates the joint tenancy, regardless of the concurrence or knowledge of the other, the remaining joint tenant no longer has an interest in the property and therefore cannot be said to have a right of occupation as a tenant.[61]

4.43 Those with an equitable interest commonly include the spouse of an owner-occupier. Spouses, whether of owner-occupiers or of tenants, may also be given a right to occupy under an 'order of the court', ie, under matrimonial legislation.[62]

Occupation under express or implied licence

4.44 Lodgers will usually be licensees rather than tenants; flat-sharers may be only licensees rather than joint tenants; a child in the home of his/

---

60 *R (B) v Southwark LBC* [2003] EWHC; [2004] HLR 3 (see further para 4.132, below).
61 *Fletcher v Brent LBC* [2006] EWCA Civ 960; [2007] HLR 12; see further para 4.45, below.
62 Matrimonial Causes Act 1973 and the Family Law Act 1996.

her parents will be a licensee rather than a tenant or sub-tenant,[63] except in the most exceptional circumstances. An example might be where the house has been subdivided into two flats (whether self-contained or not), for one of which the parents are charging rent and there are no other criteria which lean against tenancy (such as sharing utilities).

4.45   Where the authority claims that an applicant has a licence to occupy accommodation, it must determine its precise nature. In *Fletcher*,[64] the applicant's wife terminated their joint tenancy by service of a notice to quit. The local authority nonetheless concluded that the applicant was not homeless; on appeal to the county court, the judge concluded that the applicant had some form of licence to occupy the property – the nature of which she decided that it was unnecessary for her to determine – and was therefore not homeless. The Court of Appeal, allowing a further appeal, remitted the case to the authority to determine whether a licence existed and, if so, on what terms.

Tied accommodation

4.46   Where the applicant's licence is as a service occupier and contingent on the contract of employment, there cannot be said to be a licence to occupy once the contract of employment has been terminated.

4.47   Even where the employer of a live-in house-keeper, having terminated the contract of employment, said that the applicant could return to occupy her room, the local authority was in error to conclude that she had a licence to occupy. The licence was dependent on a contract for employment which no longer existed.[65]

Occupation by enactment or restriction

4.48   The final category of 'right of occupation' is occupation as a residence by virtue of any enactment or rule of law giving the applicant the right to remain in occupation, or restricting the right of any other person to recover possession of it.

---

63   On the distinction between tenant and licensee, see the decisions in *Street v Mountford* [1985] AC 809; (1985) 17 HLR 402, HL and *AG Securities v Vaughan; Antoniades v Villiers* [1990] AC 417; (1988) 21 HLR 79, HL. See also Code of Guidance paras 8.9–8.13 on applicants asked to leave accommodation by family or friends.

64   *Fletcher v Brent LBC* [2006] EWCA Civ 960; [2007] HLR 12.

65   See *R v Kensington & Chelsea RLBC ex p Minton* (1988) 20 HLR 648, QBD and *Norris v Checksfield* (1991) 23 HLR 425, CA.

Actual occupation v right to occupy

4.49 This category predicates actual occupation, as distinct from a right to occupy, so that a person who walks out of accommodation occupied on this basis will be homeless, albeit possibly intentionally so (but see further below, 'Reasonable to continue to occupy' at para 4.69). In contrast, a person who walks out of a house in which s/he has an interest will, presuming it is available for his/her occupation (see para 4.62), not be homeless until such time as s/he divests him/herself of that interest, for example, by release or sale.

Protection from Eviction Act 1977

4.50 The definition closely follows the wording of Protection from Eviction Act (PEA) 1977 s1(1).

Rent Act protection

4.51 A tenant within the protection of the Rent Act 1977 will occupy by virtue of an interest until the determination of the tenancy; thereafter, s/he is a statutory tenant. A statutory tenancy is not an interest in land.[66] It is, however, a right of occupation by virtue of an enactment or rule of law, as well as one which gives the tenant the right to remain in occupation and which restricts the right of another to recover possession.

Secure/assured protection

4.52 The statutory tenant approach was abolished for secure and assured tenants under Housing Acts 1985 and 1988 in favour of a restriction on the landlord's right to determine the tenancy itself save by order of the court. Accordingly, the tenancy continues and, as such, occupation under that interest.

Tied accommodation

4.53 An agricultural worker in tied accommodation, enjoying the benefit of the Rent (Agriculture) Act (R(A)A) 1976, will usually occupy by virtue of a licence before its determination, and thereafter in the same way as a Rent Act statutory tenant. Those in tied accommodation who do not enjoy the benefit of R(A)A 1976 derive some temporary benefits under PEA 1977.[67]

---

66 *Keeves v Dean* [1924] 1 KB 685, CA.
67 See PEA 1977 s8(2) applying provisions of that Act to 'a person who, under the terms of his employment, had exclusive possession of any premises other than as a tenant . . .'.

Former long leaseholders

4.54   Long leaseholders usually continue to occupy beyond what would otherwise contractually be the termination of their interests by virtue of a statutorily extended tenancy, which is thus still an interest. They will subsequently become either statutory tenants under the Rent Act 1977 or assured tenants under the Housing Act 1988.[68]

Other tenants and licensees

4.55   PEA 1977 s3 itself prohibits the eviction – otherwise than by court proceedings – of former unprotected tenants and licensees,[69] those who had licences granted on or after 28 November 1980 which qualify as restricted contracts within the Rent Act 1977 s19, as well as certain service occupiers. All these people will occupy either by virtue of an interest or a licence until determination, and subsequently by virtue of an enactment restricting the right of another to recover possession.[70]

Spouses, civil partners and cohabitants

4.56   Even where the applicant is not the tenant, the Family Law Act 1996 Part 4[71] protects spouses, civil partners and some cohabitants (including those living together as civil partners) by giving them a right to remain in occupation, or restricting the right of another to recover possession.

Non-qualifying persons

4.57   Those who are left outside the definition altogether are:

a)   those who have been trespassers from the outset and remain so; and

---

68   Landlord and Tenant Act 1954 Part I, Local Government and Housing Act 1989 Sch 10.

69   Other than excluded tenants and licensees: see PEA 1977 s3(2B). Note that, by judicial extension, temporary accommodation provided under what is now HA 1996 s188 (pending enquiries) is incapable of qualifying under PEA 1977 s3: see *Mohamed v Manek* (1995) 27 HLR 439 CA; see also *Desnousse v Newham LBC* [2006] EWCA Civ 547, [2006] HLR 38, holding that *Manek* was binding in relation to HA 1996, and that it applied to HA 1996 s190 (for the intentionally homeless). It is, however, unclear whether this proposition applies (as it was said in *Manek* to apply) to both tenancies and licences so provided, or only to licences (a difference expressly raised and left open by the court in *Desnousse*).

70   PEA 1977 ss2 and 3, as amended by HA 1980 s69(1) and HA 1988 s30.

71   As amended by the Civil Partnership Act 2004.

b) those who have excluded tenancies and licences which have been brought to an end;[72] or who are otherwise excluded from PEA 1977.[73]

4.58   It follows that 'squatters' properly so-called, as distinct from those to whom a licence to occupy has been granted, are statutorily homeless even though no possession order may yet have been made against them, for, even though they may have the benefit of a roof over their heads, they have no accommodation within any of the classes specified.

4.59   An applicant who occupies temporary accommodation provided to him/her pending enquiries, review or appeal under section 188 or section 204(4) is nevertheless homeless for the purpose of section 175(1) because to find otherwise would create the absurd result that a homeless person who is temporarily accommodated would be unable to benefit from the protection of Part 7.[74]

Timing

4.60   The right not to be evicted otherwise than by court proceedings in PEA 1977 s3 confers protection until execution of a possession order by the court bailiff in accordance with the relevant court rules.[75]

4.61   In *Sacupima*,[76] it was held that the same applied under the Civil Procedure Rules and, therefore, under HA 1996 s175(1)(c).[77] Accordingly, an assured tenant[78] does not become homeless for the purposes of section 175(1)(c) until the warrant for possession against him/her is executed.[79]

---

72   *R v Blankley* [1979] Crim LR 166 and see PEA 1977 s3(2B).

73   Cf, above, footnote 69.

74   *R (Alam) v London Borough of Tower Hamlets* [2009] EWHC 44 (Admin). Approved by the House of Lords in *Birmingham City Council v Ali; Moran v Manchester City Council (Secretary of State for Communities and Local Government and another intervening)* [2009] UKHL 36; [2009] 1 WLR 1506 at [54], above, para.4.14.

75   *Hanniff v Robinson* [1993] QB 419, CA. The relevant county court rules are CCR Order 26 r17, retained in force under the CPR.

76   *R v Newham LBC ex p Sacupima* (2000) 33 HLR 1, CA. See also *R v Newham LBC ex p Khan* (2000) 33 HLR 29, QBD.

77   HA 1996 s230 defines 'enactment' as including subordinate legislation.

78   Entitled to remain in occupation under HA 1988 s5 until a court order is made. The same argument will apply to secure tenancies: see HA 1985 s82.

79   In these circumstances, however, the applicant will be threatened with homelessness: see para 4.143, below.

Restriction on entry or use

Entry prevented

4.62   A person is also homeless if s/he 'cannot secure entry to' his/her accommodation.[80]

4.63   This provision is primarily intended to benefit the illegally-evicted tenant or occupier, but covers anyone else who for some reason cannot immediately be restored to occupation of a home to which s/he has a legal entitlement, for example, because of occupation by squatters.[81]

4.64   This provision has not proved to be of as much practical use as was intended, because authorities have tended to consider that unless the applicant uses available legal remedies to re-enter, s/he will be considered intentionally homeless, albeit possibly provided with temporary assistance until an order from the court is obtained.

4.65   Authorities should, however, have no rigid policy to this effect,[82] for there may be circumstances in which, although legal redress exists, both the benefits to be gained from using it and the circumstances generally suggest that it would be inappropriate, for example, illegal eviction by a resident landlord who will shortly recover possession in any event, where tensions are such that it is impracticable for the tenant to remain in the property.

Moveable structures

4.66   A person is also homeless if his/her accommodation consists of a moveable structure, vehicle or vessel designed or adapted for human habitation, and there is no place where the applicant is entitled or permitted both to place it and to reside in it, for example, a mobile home, caravan or house-boat.[83]

4.67   In *Roberts*,[84] travelling showmen were considered to be neither homeless nor threatened with homelessness while moving between

---

80   HA 1996 s175(2)(a).

81   Code of Guidance para 8.16; Welsh Code para 13.9. It does not include the situation where an applicant cannot travel to accommodation (which is otherwise available): *Begum v Tower Hamlets LBC* (1999) 32 HLR 445, CA.

82   See, eg, *British Oxygen Co Ltd v Minister of Technology* [1971] AC 610, HL; *Re Betts* [1983] 2 AC 613; 10 HLR 97, HL; *Attorney-General ex rel Tilley v Wandsworth LBC* [1981] 1 WLR 854, CA; *R v Warwickshire CC ex p Williams* [1995] COD 182, QBD; *R v North Yorkshire CC ex p Hargreaves* (1997) 96 LGR 39, QBD.

83   HA 1996 s175(2)(b).

84   *R v Chiltern DC ex p Roberts et al* (1990) 23 HLR 387, QBD.

fairgrounds during the fairground season, residing at each ground in caravans on a temporary basis. 'Reside' does not require permanence: it means 'live' or 'occupy'.

4.68   In *Smith v Wokingham DC*,[85] a county court considered that a caravan parked on land belonging to a county council, without express permission but in which the applicant and his family had lived for two-and-a-half years, had been the subject of an acquiescence sufficient to constitute permission for the purpose of what is now HA 1996 s175(2)(b).

Reasonable to continue to occupy

4.69   A person is homeless if his/her accommodation is such that it is not reasonable to continue to occupy it.[86] There is a relationship between reasonableness to continue to occupy and suitability of accommodation.[87] Therefore, case-law on one of these issues may be relevant to the other.[88]

4.70   The test is satisfied only if it is reasonable for the applicant to occupy the accommodation indefinitely, or at least for as long as s/he otherwise would if the authority did not intervene to rehouse him/her: *Ali* and *Moran*.[89] Thus, an applicant will be homeless long before the situation becomes so bad that it is not reasonable for him/her to occupy the accommodation for another night.[90] What this recognises is that accommodation which it may be unreasonable for a person to occupy for a long period, may nonetheless be reasonable for him/her to occupy for a short period.[91]

85 April 1980 *LAG Bulletin* 92, CC. See also *Higgs v Brighton and Hove BC* [2003] EWCA Civ 895; [2004] HLR 2.
86 HA 1996 s175(3). This element of the definition was introduced into HA 1985 as s58(2A), by Housing and Planning Act 1986 s14(2), as a parliamentary response to the House of Lords decision in *R v Hillingdon LBC ex p Puhlhofer* [1986] AC 484, 18 HLR 158, HL.
87 See below, paras 10.118–10.149.
88 *Harouki v Kensington & Chelsea RLBC* [2007] EWCA Civ 1000; [2008] HLR 16. This is also implicit in *Birmingham City Council v Ali; Moran v Manchester City Council (Secretary of State for Communities and Local Government)* [2009] UKHL 36; [2009] 1 WLR 1506 where the House of Lords came close to eliding the two concepts.
89 *Birmingham City Council v Ali; Moran v Manchester City Council (Secretary of State for Communities and Local Government)* [2009] UKHL 36; [2009] 1 WLR 1506 at [37].
90 *Ali*, see footnote 89, above, at [40].
91 *Ali* at [42].

4.71   The test is linked to 'suitability':[92] accommodation which is not reasonable for an applicant to continue to occupy may nevertheless be suitable for the time being; there are degrees of suitability and what is suitable for occupation in the short term may not be suitable in the longer term.[93] The point in time at which accommodation which it is not reasonable for an applicant to continue to occupy becomes unsuitable is primarily for the authority to decide, and involves taking into account matters such as the severe constraints on budgets and personnel and the very limited number of satisfactory properties for large families.[94]

4.72   On the same basis, a woman who has left her home because of domestic or other violence[95] normally remains homeless even if she has found a temporary haven in a women's refugee[96] because it would usually not be reasonable for her to continue to occupy her place in the refuge indefinitely,[97] ie, for as long as she would have to occupy it if the authority did not intervene to rehouse her.[98]

4.73   The test of reasonableness to continue to occupy does not apply only to accommodation which is actually occupied: continuation refers to the entitlement rather than the occupation. Accordingly, a person is homeless if it is – or if it would not be – reasonable to occupy the accommodation, whether or not in prior occupation of it, or in occupation of it at the time of the application or decision. Any other approach would mean that if the circumstances were so bad that the applicant had left, s/he might in theory at least be found not to be homeless,[99] where s/he would be found homeless if the circumstances were such that, while unreasonable to continue to occupy the accommodation, they were not so bad that the applicant had actually left it. Such a result could not have been intended: *Maloba*.[100]

4.74   Whether it would have been reasonable for an applicant to continue to occupy accommodation for the purposes of HA 1996 s191(1)

---

92 Below, paras 10.118–10.149.

93 *Ali*, see footnote 89, above, at [47].

94 *Ali* and *Moran* at [50].

95 Below, paras 4.82–4.92.

96 *Ali* at [65].

97 *Ali* and *Moran* at [52].

98 *Ali* and *Moran* at [46].

99 In *Begum v Tower Hamlets LBC* (1999) 32 HLR 445, CA, at [41], while taking the contrary view of the statutory provisions, it was said that no reasonable authority could reach such a decision.

100 *Waltham Forest LBC v Maloba* [2007] EWCA Civ 1281; [2008] HLR 26, rejecting the majority obiter conclusion in *Begum*, in favour of the minority view.

is to be determined at a time before the deliberate acts or omissions which led to the loss of that accommodation. In answering this question, an authority must ignore those acts or omissions: *Denton*.[101]

4.75 The term 'reasonable to continue to occupy' is governed by HA 1996 s177, as to both:

a) violence (s177(1) and (1A)); and

b) the general housing circumstances of the area (s177(2)).

4.76 The secretary of state has power to specify other circumstances in which it is or is not to be regarded as reasonable to continue to occupy accommodation, and matters (other than the general housing circumstances of the area) which are to be taken into account when determining whether or not it is reasonable to continue in occupation (s177(3)).[102]

4.77 These additional considerations are not exhaustive of matters to be taken into account in determining whether or not it is reasonable to continue in occupation: *Duro-Rama*.[103] The question is not limited to consideration of the size, structural quality and amenities of accommodation.[104] It follows that, in addition to violence and the general housing circumstances of the area and any other considerations that may be specified by the secretary of state, there is a wide range of other matters which may affect the issue.

4.78 Subject to the provisions of section 177(2), which allows regard to be had to the general housing circumstances of the area, the question whether it is reasonable to continue to occupy has been described as subjective, and not susceptible to a generalised or objective standard: *McManus*.[105] This does not mean wholly subjective in the view of the applicant, but has been construed as meaning that the issue has to be determined on all the facts of the case: not, on the one hand, determined simply by reference to local conditions or the local authority's policy, nor, on the other, looked at from the perspective of the applicant alone, so that the role of other persons or factors is ignored.[106] (This approach is consistent with *Ahmed*,[107] which concerned HA

---

101 *Denton v Southwark LBC* [2007] EWCA Civ 623; [2008] HLR 11.

102 See para 4.122, below, as to the regulations which have been issued.

103 *R v Hammersmith & Fulham LBC ex p Duro-Rama* (1983) 9 HLR 71, QBD.

104 *Waltham Forest LBC v Maloba* [2007] EWCA Civ 1281; [2008] HLR 26.

105 *R v Brent LBC ex p McManus* (1993) 25 HLR 643, QBD.

106 *Denton v Southwark LBC* [2007] EWCA Civ 623; [2008] HLR 11, at [13], [30] and [31].

107 *Ahmed v Leicester City Council* [2007] EWCA Civ 843; [2008] HLR 6.

1996 s193(7F),[108] in which it was held that an applicant's genuine belief that it was not reasonable to accept an offer of accommodation was not conclusive of whether it was reasonable to do so; if the authority has evidence which entitles it to consider that the belief was not objectively reasonable, even if that evidence was not available to the applicant at the time of the refusal, the authority may nonetheless decide that it was reasonable for the applicant to accept the offer. It would seem that a similar approach may therefore be available in relation to section 177).

4.79   The question is not, however, whether it is reasonable to leave accommodation, but whether or not it is reasonable to continue to occupy it.[109] The distinction is significant: it will commonly be reasonable (in the sense of not being unreasonable) to leave somewhere; what has to be sustained is the proposition that it is positively not reasonable to stay.

4.80   There is no presumption that an applicant's current accommodation is unsuitable, such as to impose a burden on the authority to rebut it: *McCarthy*.[110]

4.81   Whether or not it is reasonable to continue to occupy accommodation relates not only to the applicant but also to any other person who might reasonably be expected to reside with him/her: *Bishop*.[111] This must be as true of a person residing with the applicant as a member of the family.

Violence

4.82   It is not reasonable to continue to occupy accommodation if, even though there may be a legal entitlement to do so, it is 'probable' that occupation of it will lead to domestic or other violence or to threats of such violence which are likely to be carried out:

a) against the applicant; or

b) against any person who usually resides with the applicant, or against any person who might reasonably be expected to reside with the applicant.[112]

---

108 Below, para 10.170.
109 See *R v Kensington & Chelsea RLBC ex p Bayani* (1990) 22 HLR 406, CA; see also *R v Gravesham BC ex p Winchester* (1986) 18 HLR 208, QBD.
110 *R v Sedgemoor DC ex p McCarthy* (1996) 28 HLR 608, QBD.
111 *R v Westminster CC ex p Bishop* (1993) 25 HLR 459, CA.
112 HA 1996 s177(1), (1A).

4.83   In *Danesh*[113] it was held that 'violence' means actual physical violence
        and does not include threats of violence or acts or gestures which lead
        a person to fear physical violence; the probability of violence is to be
        assessed objectively by the person carrying out the assessment.

Violence

4.84   It is not necessary to show an actual history of violence. The test may
        be satisfied by the lower standard, ie, threats by someone likely to
        carry them out. Many authorities fail to observe this important dis-
        tinction, and require a high standard of proof of actual violence in the
        past, as evidence of both probability and likelihood. As this section
        draws a careful distinction, so also must authorities.

4.85   The position is not the same as failure to use legal redress in
        connection with 'entry prevented'.[114] Authorities are not to concern
        themselves with what steps to prevent the violence applicants should
        (in the authority's view) take or could have taken: *Bond*.[115]

4.86   Therefore, when determining whether it is reasonable to con-
        tinue to occupy under HA 1996 s177, an authority may consider only
        whether it was probable that continued occupation of the property
        would lead to violence or the threat of violence.[116] Whether a victim
        of violence had failed to take measures to prevent the violence (such
        as contacting the police or taking out an injunction) is irrelevant,
        although, if the victim does in fact take preventative measures which
        will probably prove effective in preventing actual or threatened vio-
        lence, the level of risk of violence may factually be reduced below
        probability. Those are the questions which an authority must ask it-
        self; it may not assume that such measures will be taken or, if taken,
        that they will be effective.[117]

---

113 *Danesh v Kensington and Chelsea RLBC* [2006] EWCA Civ 1404; [2007] HLR 17.

114 Above, para 4.65.

115 *Bond v Leicester CC* [2001] EWCA Civ 1544; [2002] HLR 6, CA. See also Code of
     Guidance para 8.22 and Welsh Code para 13.24. Compare the earlier decisions
     of *R v Eastleigh BC ex p Evans* (1984) 17 HLR 515, QBD; *R v Purbeck DC ex
     p Cadney* (1985) 17 HLR 534; and *R v Wandsworth LBC ex p Nimako-Boateng*
     (1984) 11 HLR 95, QBD.

116 *Bond v Leicester CC* [2001] EWCA Civ 1544; [2002] HLR 6, CA.

117 *Bond*, footnote 116, above. The earlier decision in *R v Wandsworth LBC ex p
     Nimako-Boateng* (1984) 11 HLR 95, QBD, in which it had been held that an
     authority could conclude that it would be reasonable for a woman to continue
     to occupy accommodation – notwithstanding domestic violence – by reference
     to the remedies otherwise available to her for her protection, was decided
     under HA 1985 s58, now HA 1996 s175(3), at a time when the question of
     reasonableness was at large, rather than statutorily defined as it now is in

Threats

4.87   The only test that an authority may apply to establish whether threats are likely to be carried out is likewise what is probable: see *Bond*.[118] See also Code of Guidance, para 8.22:[119]

> . . . an assessment of the likelihood of a threat of violence being carried out should not be based solely on whether there has been actual violence in the past.

Residing with applicant

4.88   The violence need not be against the applicant but could be against any person who usually resides with him/her or against any person who might reasonably be expected to do so. See under 'Accommodation available for occupation' (paras 4.17–4.38), and note that the person to whom the violence is shown need not be residing with the applicant as a member of his/her family, so that, for example, a carer could qualify.

Domestic violence

4.89   Domestic violence is not confined to that between spouses or cohabitants. It may come from any person with whom the applicant or other person who is the subject of it is associated.[120] The Code of Guidance[121] suggests that 'domestic violence' should be understood to include threatening behaviour, violence or abuse (psychological, physical, sexual, financial or emotional) between associated persons.

4.90   'Person associated' is defined to include:

a) married or formerly married persons;
b) civil partners or former civil partners;
c) cohabitants and former cohabitants;[122]
d) persons who live or who have lived in the same household;[123]

---

s177. Accordingly, *Nimako-Boateng* was distinguished in *Bond*, as was the decision to like effect in *R v Purbeck DC ex p Cadney* (1985) 17 HLR 534.

118   *Bond v Leicester CC* [2001] EWCA Civ 1544; [2002] HLR 6, CA.
119   See Welsh Code para 13.19.
120   HA 1996 s177(1A), as amended by Civil Partnership Act 2004.
121   Para 8.21.
122   Defined in HA 1996 s178(3) to mean a man and a woman who, though not married to one another, are living together as husband and wife. Since amendment by the Civil Partnership Act 2004, it also includes two people of the same sex living together as if they are civil partners.
123   This is wide enough to cover flat-sharers or a carer sharing the same house.

e) relatives;[124]
f) those who have agreed to marry (or had done so);
g) those who have entered into a civil partnership agreement (or had done so); and
h) persons who are associated because each of them is a parent of a child, or has or has had, parental responsibility for that child.[125]

4.91 HA 1996 s178(2) and (2A) contains detailed provisions governing association arising out of adoptions.

Other violence

4.92 The Homelessness Act 2002 extended the application of HA 1996 s177 to 'other violence', ie, from someone not associated with the victim, covering, for example, those suffering from violent racial harassment or witnesses in trials who have been intimidated by violence or threats of violence. This is a significant extension. Formerly, violence from non-associated persons was only relevant to the question of reasonableness 'at large'.[126] An authority considering reasonableness at large could take into account whether an applicant could obtain protection from violence through the courts or by seeking a transfer.[127] Incorporation into HA 1996 s177, means that the proper approach to the availability of alternative remedies will be the same as set out in *Bond*.[128]

General housing circumstances of area

4.93 The comparison between accommodation occupied and the general circumstances prevailing in relation to housing accommodation in the district of the authority to which an application has been made[129]

---

124 Defined in HA 1996 s178(3) to include parents and step-parents, children and step-children, siblings and step-siblings, grandparents and grandchildren, uncles, aunts, nephews and nieces, whether of the person the subject of the violence or his/her spouse/civil partner or former spouse/civil partner or of persons living or formerly living together as husband and wife or as if they were civil partners, and whether by full-blood, half-blood or by marriage or civil partnership.

125 Within the meaning of the Children Act 1989, under which – in addition to parents – guardians appointed under s5 and those who have a residence order under s8 may have parental responsibility (see Children Act 1989 ss5 and 12): HA 1996 s178(3).

126 *R v Hillingdon LBC ex p H* (1988) 20 HLR 554, QBD.

127 See, eg, *R v Newham LBC ex p McIlroy* (1991) 23 HLR 570, QBD.

128 See para 4.86, above.

129 HA 1996 s177(2).

is one of the central concepts of homelessness law, albeit that most of it was developed in relation to intentionality.

4.94   Indeed, it initially bore not at all on the definition of homelessness, although it was in practice being applied by the courts at the point in the evolution of the law (see para 4.7, above, in relation to accommodation) at which an equiparation was being made between being homeless and the occupation of accommodation so poor that it could be left without a finding of intentionality.

4.95   *Awua*[130] notwithstanding, it is very difficult indeed to conceive that Parliament intended anything other than the importation of an identical criterion when it adopted the exact same phraseology for use in the definition (HA 1985 s58) of homelessness as had long existed in relation to intentionality (HA 1985 s60), ie, whether or not it was reasonable to continue to occupy, subject to the general housing conditions of the area.[131]

4.96   The comparison is between current accommodation, wherever situated, and conditions in the area of the authority to which application is made.[132]

4.97   HA 1996 s177(2) requires the authority to carry out a balancing act between the housing conditions in the authority's area and the accommodation quit, although whether or not it is reasonable to continue to occupy accommodation involves other questions, such as the pattern of life followed by the applicant: *Monaf*.[133] Such comparisons should only be made, however, where relevant to a case.[134]

4.98   The decision in *Tickner v Mole Valley DC*,[135] in which the applicants were evicted from a caravan site because they refused to pay increased rents which they thought excessive in view of the conditions on the site, turned on what is now section 177(2), albeit in the context of intentionality:

130 *R v Brent LBC ex p Awua* [1996] 1 AC 55; 27 HLR 453, HL.

131 Housing and Planning Act 1986 s14(2); see also para 4.75, above. See also *R v Wandsworth LBC ex p Wingrove*, and *R v Wandsworth LBC ex p Mansoor* [1996] 3 All ER 913; 29 HLR 801, CA. See also *Begum v Tower Hamlets LBC* (1999) 32 HLR 445, CA, at p319/H ('[T]he plain intention of Parliament was to enable a local authority to determine the question of homelessness . . . without having to go on to the corresponding question in the test of intentional homelessness . . .') and at p326/A–B.

132 *R v Tower Hamlets LBC ex p Monaf* (1988) 20 HLR 529, CA.

133 See footnote 132, above. See also *R v Newham LBC ex p Ajayi* (1994) 28 HLR 25, QBD, referring to matters 'of social history and national status', such as where children were born and how long a person has lived somewhere.

134 *R v Newham LBC ex p Tower Hamlets LBC* (1990) 23 HLR 62, CA.

135 August 1980 *LAG Bulletin* 187, CA.

That is what influenced this authority here. They had long waiting lists for housing. On those lists there were young couples waiting to be married: or young married couples sometimes staying with their in-laws: or people in poor accommodation. All those people were on the housing waiting lists – people who had been waiting for housing for years. The council thought it would be extremely unfair to all those on the waiting lists if these caravan dwellers – by coming in in this way – jumped the queue, when they were well able to pay the rent for the caravans and stay on. Those were perfectly legitimate considerations for the local authority to consider.[136]

4.99   In order to rely on this provision, the authority need not consider in great detail all the information on housing conditions in its area, but may have regard to 'the generally prevailing standard of accommodation in their area, with which people have to be satisfied'.[137]

Other reasons

4.100   There is an infinite number of reasons why people may not wish to remain in accommodation; accordingly, there is no simple test of reasonableness.[138]

Location

4.101   The question is not confined to matters relating to the accommodation in itself, but can extend to its location: *Homes*.[139]

Permanence

4.102   The fact that the accommodation is not permanent is not relevant to whether or not it is reasonable to continue the occupation: *Begum*.[140]

Physical conditions

4.103   Physical conditions may produce circumstances in which it is not reasonable to continue to occupy accommodation.

4.104   It is clear that, before an applicant can claim with confidence that it would not be reasonable to continue to occupy accommodation on

---

136   The same judge – Lord Denning MR – in *de Falco, Silvestri v Crawley BC* [1980] QB 460, CA, described the provision as a 'ray of hope', allowing the authority to say: 'You ought to have stayed where you were before. You ought not to have landed yourself on us when it would have been reasonable for you to stay where you were.'

137   Per Lord Denning MR in *Tickner*, above, para 4.98 and footnote 135.

138   See Code of Guidance para 8.18; Welsh Code para 13.13.

139   *R v Wycombe DC ex p Homes* (1988) 22 HLR 150, QBD.

140   *Begum v Tower Hamlets LBC* (1999) 32 HLR 445, CA.

the ground of its physical condition, the accommodation will have to be very poor indeed, although in some cases (for example, a wheelchair user) the physical characteristics of the accommodation may make it per se unsuitable for the particular applicant.[141]

4.105   In *Miles*,[142] a hut approximately 20 feet by 10 feet, with two rooms, infested by rats, and with no mains services (although services were available in a nearby caravan occupied by relatives), was held to constitute accommodation of which an authority could consider it reasonable for the applicant to continue in occupation, at a time when there were two adults and two children living in it, albeit that it was on the 'borderline' of what was reasonable and would cross the borderline into what no authority could consider reasonable on the birth of a third child.

4.106   In *Fisher*,[143] the applicant and her children had been living in temporary accommodation. For a period they lived in a caravan. Immediately before her application, they lived on a boat, without bath, shower, WC, electricity, hot water system or kitchen with a sink. There was one cabin, which was kitchen, living room and bedroom combined, and she occupied it with her children and two friends. This was held not to amount to accommodation of which it was reasonable to continue in occupation.

4.107   In *Winchester*,[144] the applicant and his family had left accommodation in Alderney. Among the reasons for leaving was that the accommodation was in an appalling state of disrepair, suffering from damp and a dangerous outside staircase and balcony. The family was found to be intentionally homeless. The decision of the local authority that it would have been reasonable to remain was not considered to be unreasonable or perverse.

4.108   In *Dee*,[145] a decision that it would have been reasonable for a young woman and her new baby to occupy a pre-fabricated beach bungalow which suffered severe damp problems was quashed because the authority had given too much weight to the fact that the property was not considered to be unfit for human habitation and too little to the medical advice which had been given to the applicant.[146]

141 Code of Guidance para 8.34; Welsh Code para 13.13.
142 *R v South Herefordshire DC ex p Miles* (1983) 17 HLR 82, QBD.
143 *R v Preseli DC ex p Fisher* (1984) 17 HLR 147, QBD.
144 *R v Gravesham BC ex p Winchester* (1986) 18 HLR 208, QBD.
145 *R v Medina BC ex p Dee* (1992) 24 HLR 562, QBD.
146 See also the discussion of *Shala v Birmingham CC* [2007] EWCA Civ 624; [2008] HLR 8 at para 5.36, below, the principle of which must apply in the same way to issues of suitability having regard to medical conditions.

4.109   In *Ben-El-Mabrouk*,[147] the want of adequate means of escape from fire did not necessarily mean that it was not reasonable for a couple with a small baby to stay in occupation of a fifth-floor flat in a house in multiple occupation (HMO), although a delay in rehousing the family under the provisions of the Land Compensation Act 1973 might itself (in the absence of an explanation from the authority) have been challengeable.

4.110   In *Puhlhofer*,[148] at the Court of Appeal, Ackner LJ's view as to whether or not the applicants had any accommodation (within the meaning of the legislation) at all[149] was based in part on the question whether or not it would have been reasonable to continue to occupy it. He considered that accommodation for the applicant, his wife and two children in one room in a guesthouse, with no cooking or laundry facilities, was still such that it could have been reasonable to continue to occupy it in the light of the authority's evidence that there were at least 44 families on the council's waiting list for two-bedroomed accommodation considered to be of higher priority.

Overcrowding

4.111   Overcrowding is a relevant consideration: *Beattie (No 1)*.[150] An authority cannot refuse to consider an application simply because the accommodation is not statutorily overcrowded: *Alouat*.[151] However, the authority is entitled to take into account the fact that the property is not statutorily overcrowded: *Beattie (No 2)*.[152] Even if it is, this does not prevent it being reasonable for an applicant to continue to occupy the accommodation.[153]

4.112   In *Ali*,[154] even if accommodation had been 'available', it was said:

> ... that anyone should regard it as reasonable that a family of that size should live in one room 10ft x 12ft in size, or thereabouts, is

147 *R v Kensington & Chelsea RLBC ex p Youssef Ben-El-Mabrouk* (1995) 27 HLR 564, CA.

148 (1985) 17 HLR 588, CA.

149 See above, para 4.8.

150 *R v Eastleigh BC ex p Beattie (No 1)* (1983) 10 HLR 134, QBD.

151 *R v Westminster CC ex p Alouat* (1989) 21 HLR 477, QBD. See also Code of Guidance para 8.28; Welsh Code para 13.13.

152 *R v Eastleigh BC ex p Beattie (No 2)* (1984) 17 HLR 168, QBD. See also, on overcrowding, *Krishnan v Hillingdon LBC* January 1981 *LAG Bulletin* 137, QBD; *R v Tower Hamlets LBC ex p Ojo* (1991) 23 HLR 488, QBD; and *R v Tower Hamlets LBC ex p Bibi* (1991) 23 HLR 500, QBD.

153 *Harouki v Kensington & Chelsea RLBC* [2007] EWCA Civ 1000; [2008] HLR 16.

154 *R v Westminster CC ex p Ali* (1983) 11 HLR 83, QBD.

something which I find astonishing. However, the matter has to be seen in the light of s17(4) [now HA 1996 s177(2)] which requires that reasonableness must take account of the general circumstances prevailing in relation to housing in the area. No evidence has been placed before me that accommodation in the area of the Westminster City Council is so desperately short that it is reasonable to accept overcrowding of this degree. In the absence of such evidence I am driven to the conclusion that this question could not properly have been determined against the applicant.

4.113 In *Osei*,[155] it was held that, even if the applicant's flat in Madrid had been overcrowded when he surrendered his tenancy, it was open to the authority to conclude that it was reasonable for him and his family to continue to occupy it until he had secured alternative accommodation for his family in London.

Legal conditions

4.114 The fact that accommodation had been obtained by deception meant that it would not have been reasonable to remain in occupation of it: *Gliddon*.[156]

4.115 In *Knight*,[157] and in *Li*,[158] once service occupancies had been ended and there could be no defence to an action for possession, the authorities were not able to consider that occupiers should reasonably have remained in occupation pending proceedings.

4.116 Although these decisions are difficult to reconcile with the definition of rights of occupation (including the right to remain in occupation under an enactment),[159] the Code of Guidance, issued under Housing Act 1985 s71, discouraged authorities from requiring possession orders where there would be no defence. In *Ugbo*,[160] the authority's failure to consider such guidance (and the implications of the fact that that applicant was only an assured shorthold tenant rather than a fully assured tenant) invalidated its decision on this issue.

4.117 The current Code[161] suggests that where the applicant is an assured shorthold tenant who has received proper notice (under HA 1988 s21)

---

155 *Osei v Southwark LBC* [2007] EWCA Civ 787; [2008] HLR 15.
156 *R v Exeter CC ex p Gliddon* (1984) 14 HLR 103, QBD.
157 *R v Portsmouth CC ex p Knight* (1983) 10 HLR 115, QBD.
158 *R v Surrey Heath BC ex p Li* (1984) 16 HLR 79, QBD.
159 See paras 4.48–4.59, above.
160 *R v Newham LBC ex p Ugbo* (1993) 26 HLR 263, QBD.
161 Code of Guidance para 8.32; Welsh Code para 13.15.

that the tenancy is to be terminated and the landlord intends to seek possession, and there is no defence to the possession proceedings, it is unlikely to be reasonable for the applicant to occupy the accommodation beyond the date given in the section 21 notice, unless s/he is taking steps to persuade the landlord to withdraw the notice.

4.118   *Ugbo* must be compared with *Jarvis*,[162] where the authority had considered the code but was held still to be entitled to reach the conclusion that it was reasonable to continue to occupy pending a court order following termination of an assured shorthold tenancy.

4.119   In *Minnett*,[163] the authority should have disregarded a departure one day before the date specified in a consent order for possession.

4.120   Given the decision in *Khan and Hussain*,[164] authorities should also consider cases where the applicant leaves between the possession order and physical eviction by the court bailiffs, even though s/he will not yet be homeless.[165]

Financial conditions and employment

4.121   Financial considerations raise the question of 'affordability': see *Hawthorne*,[166] in which the authority had to consider whether the applicant's failure to pay rent had been caused by the inadequacy of her financial resources.

4.122   The secretary of state has now required authorities to take affordability into account when determining whether or not it is reasonable to continue to occupy accommodation: Homelessness (Suitability of Accommodation) Order 1996.[167]

4.123   In reaching this decision, the authority must consider the financial resources available to a person, the costs of the accommodation, payments being made under a court order to a spouse or former spouse, any payments made to support children, whether under a court order or under the Child Support Act 1991, and the applicant's other reasonable living expenses.

4.124   The order contains a detailed list of financial resources which must be considered and accommodation costs, although authorities are not limited to considering only these resources or costs.

---

162 *R v Croydon LBC ex p Jarvis* (1993) 26 HLR 194, QBD; see too *R v Bradford CC ex p Parveen* (1996) 28 HLR 681, QBD.
163 *R v Mole Valley DC ex p Minnett* (1983) 12 HLR 49, QBD.
164 *R v Newham LBC ex p Khan and Hussain* (2000) 33 HLR 29.
165 *R v Newham LBC ex p Sacupima* (2000) 33 HLR 1, CA.
166 *R v Wandsworth LBC ex p Hawthorne* (1994) 27 HLR 59, CA.
167 SI No 3204 (see appendix B).

4.125   In determining the amount that an applicant requires for residual living costs, the Code of Guidance[168] suggests that authorities may wish to have regard to the amount of benefit to which the applicant would be entitled. The Code[169] makes it clear that affordability is always an issue which must be considered, and that the matters in the statutory instrument are but factors to be considered in that overall question.

4.126   This is consistent with case-law. In *Duro-Rama*,[170] issues of employment and the availability of benefits were held to be relevant considerations which the authority had ignored by confining itself to the matters set out in HA 1985 s60(4) (now HA 1996 s177(2)).

4.127   The first of these considerations reflects the comment of Lord Lowry in *Islam*,[171] that:

> There will, of course, and in the interests of mobility of labour ought to be, cases where the housing authority will . . . accept that it would not have been reasonable in the circumstances for the applicant to continue to occupy the accommodation which he has left.

4.128   To the same effect, in *Ashton*,[172] it was held that no reasonable authority would have allowed the provisions of what is now HA 1996 s177(2) to have governed a decision on intentionality where a middle-aged woman who had been unemployed for six years, and who had chronic active hepatitis, left settled accommodation to take up work in another area.

4.129   In *Griffiths*,[173] it was said that it cannot be assumed that income support is sufficient to meet housing costs.

4.130   Inadequacy of financial resources goes not merely to ability to pay the rent, but also to funding the necessities of life, including food: *Bibi*,[174] following *Tinn*.[175]

4.131   It is, however, for the authority not the court to assess whether or not accommodation is affordable: *Grossett*.[176]

---

168 Code of Guidance para 17.40; Welsh Code para 19.10.

169 Code of Guidance para 8.29; Welsh Code para 13.13.

170 *R v Hammersmith & Fulham LBC ex p Duro-Rama* (1983) 9 HLR 71, QBD.

171 *Re Islam* [1983] 1 AC 688; 1 HLR 107, HL.

172 *R v Winchester CC ex p Ashton* (1991) 24 HLR 520, CA.

173 *R v Shrewsbury BC ex p Griffiths* (1993) 25 HLR 613, QBD. See further *R v Hillingdon LBC ex p Tinn* (1988) 20 HLR 206, QBD; and *R v Camden LBC ex p Aranda* (1996) 28 HLR 672. Cf, *R v Westminster CC ex p Moklis Ali* (1996) 29 HLR 580, QBD.

174 *R v Islington LBC ex p Bibi* (1996) 29 HLR 498, QBD.

175 *R v Hillingdon LBC ex p Tinn* (1988) 20 HLR 206, QBD.

176 *R v Brent LBC ex p Grossett* (1994) 28 HLR 9, CA. See too *R v Brent LBC ex p Baruwa* (1997) 29 HLR 915, CA and *Bernard v Enfield LBC* [2001] EWCA Civ 1831, CA.

Type of accommodation

4.132   It has been held that accommodation in a prison cell is not accommodation which it is reasonable for the applicant to continue to occupy (where the applicant has the opportunity to obtain early release under a tagging scheme): B.[177]

4.133   The Code[178] suggests that some types of accommodation, for example, women's refuges, direct access hostels, and night shelters intended to provide very short-term temporary accommodation in a crisis, should not be regarded as reasonable for someone to continue to occupy in the medium and longer term. It may be that in some circumstances such accommodation should not be considered reasonable to occupy at all.[179]

Other considerations

4.134   In Bassett,[180] the court held that a woman who had followed her husband to Canada, notwithstanding the uncertainties of their prospects there, could not reasonably have remained in occupation of their secure council accommodation, when going to join him was her only chance of saving their marriage.

4.135   It would be wrong, however, to view this as anything more than an illustration of the proposition that it is the particular circumstances of applicant and household which are relevant.[181]

4.136   In Hearn,[182] the applicant's sense of isolation was held to be a factor relevant to deciding whether it was reasonable for her to continue to occupy premises.

4.137   In Healiss,[183] the authority failed to consider the applicant's reasons for concluding that it was not reasonable for her to continue in occupation of the accommodation of which she was a secure tenant, including repeated break-ins to empty flats in her block, two burglaries of her own flat, harassment involving strangers knocking at the door, stones thrown at windows, and shouting up to her windows at

---

177   R (B) v Southwark LBC [2003] EWHC 1678 (Admin); [2004] HLR 3. But cf, now, Ali and Moran, above, para 4.13, where the House of Lords expressly reserved the issue of whether prison could comprise accommodation at all.

178   Para 8.34; Welsh Code para 13.13.

179   See now Ali and Moran, para 4.13, above.

180   R v Basingstoke & Deane BC ex p Bassett (1983) 10 HLR 125, QBD.

181   Cf, above, R v Brent LBC ex p McManus (1993) 25 HLR 643, QBD; and R v Shrewsbury BC ex p Griffiths (1993) 25 HLR 613, QBD.

182   R v Swansea CC ex p Hearn (1990) 23 HLR 372, QBD.

183   R v Sefton MBC ex p Healiss (1994) 27 HLR 34, QBD.

all hours of the day and night; in addition, gangs of youths congregated on the stairway smoking what was assumed to be drugs, the first-floor landing was used as a latrine and smelled as such, and the applicant was too frightened to allow her child to play in the block and gardens.

4.138   In *Nimako-Boateng*,[184] however, the court upheld the decision of the authority that a woman could reasonably have remained in occupation of the matrimonial home in Ghana, even though her relationship with her husband had broken down. (The court noted that it had been given no information about Ghanaian domestic law, and assumed that the woman's rights would have been the same as under English law. There was no complaint of domestic violence.)[185] *Nimako-Boateng* was followed in *Evans*.[186]

4.139   In *Moncada*,[187] the applicant was divorced from his wife and had custody of his two sons. The court refused to interfere with a finding that, given the shortage of accommodation in London, it was reasonable for him to continue to live in the four-bedroomed matrimonial home, notwithstanding that his ex-wife and daughter also continued to live in it.

4.140   All violence and threats of violence, whatever their source, will now fall to be considered under HA 1996 s177[188] rather than – as previously – under section 175(2).[189]

Threatened with homelessness

4.141   A person is threatened with homelessness for the purposes of HA 1996 Part 7 if it is likely that s/he will become homeless within 28 days.[190]

4.142   This period of 28 days was originally referable to the 'normal' period granted by a court before a possession order would take effect.

---

184 *R v Wandsworth LBC ex p Nimako-Boateng* (1983) 11 HLR 95, QBD.
185 On the issue of domestic violence, as distinct from matrimonial breakdown, see now, however, *Bond*, above, para 4.85.
186 *R v Eastleigh BC ex p Evans* (1984) 17 HLR 515, QBD.
187 *R v Kensington & Chelsea RLBC ex p Moncada* (1996) 29 HLR 289, QBD.
188 See paras 4.82–4.92, above.
189 See, for example, *R v Hillingdon LBC ex p H* (1988) 20 HLR 559, QBD; *R v Northampton BC ex p Clarkson* (1992) 24 HLR 529, QBD; *R v Croydon LBC ex p Toth* (1987) 20 HLR 576, CA; and *R v Newham LBC ex p McIlory and McIlroy* (1991) 23 HLR 570, QBD.
190 HA 1996 s175(4).

Since 3 October 1980, however, courts have been obliged to make orders to take effect within 14 days, save where exceptional hardship would be caused: see HA 1980 s89, although this is applicable only where the court has no other discretion to suspend, for example, under the Rent Act 1977, HA 1985 or HA 1988.

4.143 Even once the date for possession has passed, the applicant will not be homeless until the warrant for possession is executed.[191] During this period, the applicant will, however, be threatened with homelessness.

4.144 There is no reason to draw any distinction of principle between the definitions of 'homelessness' and 'threatened with homelessness', other than the 28-day criterion: *Dyson*.[192] This seems to be based on a concession by counsel, but must surely be correct.

4.145 Once faced with an applicant who is threatened with homelessness, the authority must start making appropriate enquiries under HA 1996 s184.[193] The duty cannot be postponed until the applicant is actually homeless: *Khan and Hussain*.[194] If enquiries are made before the 28 days, they will be non-statutory: *Hunt*.[195]

---

191 See *R v Newham LBC ex p Sacupima* (2000) 33 HLR 1, CA.
192 *Dyson v Kerrier DC* [1980] 1 WLR 1206, at p1212, CA.
193 See chapter 9.
194 *R v Newham LBC ex p Khan and Hussain* (2000) 33 HLR 29, QBD.
195 *R v Rugby BC ex p Hunt* (1992) 26 HLR 1, QBD.

Priority need

continued

5.65   The English Regulations

16- and 17-year-olds • 18- to 20-year-old care leavers • Vulnerable care leavers • Vulnerable former members of the armed forces • Vulnerable former prisoners • Vulnerable due to fleeing violence

Introduction

5.1 There are no substantive rights or duties under Housing Act (HA) 1996 Part 7[1] unless the applicant has a 'priority need for accommodation'.

5.2 A homeless person or a person threatened with homelessness has a priority need for accommodation if the person is within one of the following categories:[2]

a) she is a pregnant woman, or a person with whom a pregnant woman resides or might reasonably be expected to reside;

b) s/he is a person with whom dependent children reside or might reasonably be expected to reside;

c) s/he is vulnerable as a result of old age, mental illness or handicap or physical disability or other special reason, or is someone with whom such a person resides or might reasonably be expected to reside;

d) s/he is homeless or threatened with homelessness as a result of an emergency such as flood, fire or other disaster.

5.3 These categories closely follow those described in DoE Circular 18/74 as the 'priority groups' who were to have the first claim on resources available:

> The Priority Groups comprise families with dependent children living with them, or in care; and adult families or people living alone who either become homeless in an emergency such as fire or flooding or are vulnerable because of old age, disability, pregnancy or other special reasons.[3]

5.4 The secretary of state may add to these categories,[4] which power has been exercised in relation to both England and Wales.[5]

5.5 A local authority cannot fetter its discretion by pre-determining that people within specified groups – for example, the single or childless homeless – should never be considered 'vulnerable' within category (c) in para 5.2, above).[6] Authorities are bound to provide advice and assistance even to those who are not in priority need.[7]

---

1 But see above, para 2.65, and below, paras 10.85–10.176. See now in particular the power to provide assistance for those in priority need but not intentionally homeless: para 10.44, below.

2 HA 1996 s189(1).

3 DoE Circular 18/74 para 10; see above, para 1.19.

4 HA 1996 s189(2).

5 See further paras 5.59–5.74, below.

6 See also para 12.44, below.

7 HA 1996 s192, see para 10.50, below.

Immigration

5.6   Section 185(4) used[8] to require local housing authorities in England and Wales to disregard household members (including dependent children) who were ineligible[9] for housing assistance, when considering whether any eligible housing applicant was in priority need. This provision has now[10] been amended so that it applies only to an eligible applicant who is him/herself a person subject to immigration control,[11] other than an EEA national[12] or Swiss national,[13] for example, those granted refugee status,[14] indefinite leave to remain,[15] or humanitarian protection. Accordingly, when considering an application from a person subject to immigration control who is eligible for assistance, other than those two excepted classes, a local authority must continue to disregard any dependants or other household members who are ineligible for assistance, when deciding whether the applicant is in priority need.

5.7   The effect is that section 185(4) no longer applies to eligible[16] applicants who are not subject to immigration control,[17] for example, a British citizen,[18] a Commonwealth citizen with a right of abode in the UK,[19] or an EEA national with a right to reside in the UK.[20] This group of eligible applicants will be able to rely on ineligible household members, known as 'restricted persons'[21] to establish priority need. A restricted person is someone who is not eligible for assistance under Part 7, who is subject to immigration control, and who

---

8   In respect of all applications for accommodation or assistance in obtaining accommodation within the meaning of HA 1996 s183, made before 2 March 2009.

9   Above, paras 3.68–3.79.

10 By Housing and Regeneration Act 2008 s314 and Sch 15 Part I, in respect of all applications for accommodation or assistance in obtaining accommodation within the meaning of HA 1996 s183, made on or after 2 March 2009.

11 Above, paras 3.11–3.12.

12 Above, para 3.12.

13 Above, para 3.12.

14 Above, paras 3.15–3.16.

15 Above, paras 3.91–3.93.

16 Above, paras 3.68–3.143.

17 Above, paras 3.13–3.15.

18 Above, para 3.16.

19 Above, para 3.17.

20 Above, paras 3.18–3.60.

21 HA 1996 s184(7).

either does not have leave to enter or remain in the UK or has leave subject to a condition of no recourse to public funds.

5.8   If the authority can only be satisfied that the applicant is in priority need by taking into account the restricted person, the application is known as a 'restricted case'.[22] In those circumstances, the authority must, so far as reasonably practical, bring any section 193(2) duty to an end by arranging for an offer of an assured shorthold tenancy to be made to the applicant by a private landlord.[23] This is known as a private accommodation offer.[24]

Pregnancy

5.9   Pregnancy at any stage qualifies as priority need. One of the objects of the Housing (Homeless Persons) Act 1977 was to eliminate the practice of some authorities, who refused to consider a woman's pregnancy as a factor until a given stage of pregnancy. Once the pregnancy is established, the priority need exists.

Dependent children

5.10   Dependent children do not qualify as being in priority need in their own right; nor will they qualify as vulnerable either because of their youth or because of any disability: *ex p G*.[25] Dependent children are expected to be provided for (with assistance where appropriate, ie, under Part 7) by those on whom they are dependent. The notion of a dependent child connotes a relationship akin to that of parent–child, so an applicant with a 17-year-old wife cannot claim to be in priority need under this category on the basis of her dependency on him.[26] Likewise, an 18-year-old applicant with a 17-year-old sibling was not in priority need under this category. However, where there is a greater age difference between siblings, giving rise to a truly dependent relationship much more akin to a parent–child relationship, priority need could still arise.[27]

22 HA 1996 s193(3B). See also above, para 3.74
23 HA 1996 s193(7AD). See further below, para 10.168.
24 HA 1996 s193(7AC). Above, para 3.75 and below, paras 10.168–10.169.
25 *R v Oldham BC ex p G, R v Bexley LBC ex p B, R v Tower Hamlets LBC ex p Begum* [1993] AC 509; (1993) 25 HLR 319, HL, and see para 9.17, below.
26 *Hackney LBC v Ekinci* [2001] EWCA Civ 776; [2002] HLR 2, CA.
27 *R (Lusamba) v Islington LBC* [2008] EWHC 1149 (Admin).

5.11   Children must be 'residing' with an applicant, not merely 'stay-ing', that is, some degree of permanence or regularity must exist.[28]

Alternative tests

5.12   The tests are alternative. In *Islam*,[29] not cross-appealed by the author-ity on this point,[30] the authority unsuccessfully contended that, if reliance were placed by an applicant on dependent children living with him/her, it was also necessary to show that such children might reasonably be expected to reside with him/her. If there are depend-ent children actually residing with the applicant at the date of the authority's decision (not the date of application),[31] it is not relevant to consider whether or not they are reasonably expected to do so.

5.13   Thus, in *Sidhu*,[32] the applicant and her children were living in a women's refuge.[33] The applicant had obtained an interim custody order from the county court but the authority still contended that it was entitled not to consider her to be in priority need until a full custody order was granted. The court rejected this argument. The full order was irrelevant (nor could the authority defer its decision in order to have time to assure itself that no change would take place in the future[34] – in that case, the remote prospect of the applicant los-ing custody at full hearing). The same may now be said of residence orders.[35]

5.14   An order of a court will, however, be relevant where an applicant's children are not currently residing with him/her, but are reasonably to be expected to do so, for example, where the applicant has won custody but cannot in practice take care of the children for want of accommodation.

---

28 See also *R v Lewisham LBC ex p Creppy* (1991) 24 HLR 121, CA and *R v Lambeth LBC ex p Bodunrin* (1992) 24 HLR 647, QBD.

29 *R v Hillingdon Homeless Persons Panel ex p Islam* (1981) *Times* 10 February, QBD.

30 *Re Islam* [1983] 1 AC 688; (1981) 1 HLR 107, HL.

31 See para 9.136.

32 *R v Ealing LBC ex p Sidhu* (1982) 2 HLR 45, QBD.

33 Above, paras 4.10–4.16.

34 A proposition approved in *Robinson v Hammersmith & Fulham LBC* [2006] EWCA Civ 1122; [2006] HLR 7. Below, para 9.133.

35 Under Children Act 1989 s8.

Dependence on applicant

5.15 There must be dependence on the applicant, so an applicant is not in priority need where children who reside with him/her are dependent on someone else.[36]

5.16 'Dependent' is not defined in HA 1996 Part 7. In *Amarfio*,[37] the Court of Appeal considered the Code of Guidance under HA 1985 Part 3 (reproduced in the current Code),[38] which referred to children under the age of 16 as dependent, together with those under the age of 19 either receiving full-time education or training or otherwise unable to support themselves. It was held that once a child has gone into full-time employment, s/he could not be dependent, and that a young person on a youth training scheme was in gainful employment by way of training and ought therefore to be regarded as being in full-time employment.

5.17 The court did recognise, however, that there may be circumstances where a 16- or 17-year-old, although not financially dependent on his/her parents, is sufficiently dependent on them in other respects to fall within the subsection.

5.18 In *Miah v Newham LBC*,[39] the authority had treated the Code of Guidance as limited to children up to their 18th birthday. The Court of Appeal held that the Code addresses children under 19 years old (who are in full-time education or training or otherwise unable to support themselves): the Code had been misinterpreted by the authority.

Separated parents

5.19 Where parents are separated, a child may divide his/her time between parents or others.[40] Three separate issues arise:

a) whether the child is dependent on the applicant;
b) whether the child resides with the applicant; and
c) if the child is not currently residing with the applicant, whether s/he may reasonably be expected to do so.

---

36 See *R v Westminster CC ex p Bishop* (1996) 29 HLR 546, QBD. See also *R v Camden LBC ex p Hersi* (2001) 33 HLR 52, QBD.

37 *R v Kensington & Chelsea RLBC ex p Amarfio* (1995) 27 HLR 543, CA.

38 Code of Guidance para 10.7; Welsh Code para 14.6. See appendix C.

39 [2001] EWCA Civ 487, CA.

40 See Code of Guidance paras 10.9–10.10; Welsh Code para 14.7.

Dependence on applicant

5.20   In *Vagliviello*,[41] the authority was held to have erred by applying the 'wholly and exclusively dependent' test. For the purposes of Housing Act 1985 s59, now HA 1996 s189, it is possible for a child to reside with and be dependent on more than one person, only one of whom may be applying for assistance.

5.21   In *Bishop*,[42] where parents had agreed that the children should split their time between each of them, the authority was entitled to conclude that the children were not dependent on one of them, the father. In reaching this decision, it took into account that the children were adequately housed with the mother, that she received income support and child benefit for them, and that the applicant, who was unemployed, did not have the financial means of supporting them.

Residing with applicant

5.22   In *Smith-Morse*,[43] the authority erred in applying a 'main' residence test, in addition to failing to consider the future as well as present arrangements for the child. On the other hand, in *McCarthy*,[44] the parents were divorced and, although there was a joint custody order, care and control had been given to the mother. Although it had been agreed that the children should spend three days per week with their father, this sort of 'staying access' did not equate to residence. It was considered that it would only be in very exceptional circumstances that a child might reside with both parents living apart, although this type of arrangement has become much more common since the Children Act 1989 came into force.[45]

5.23   The question is to be determined at the date the applicant becomes homeless. Where an application is made while the applicant is still only threatened with homelessness,[46] at which point s/he may still be residing with children, for example, before leaving the family home,

---

41   *R v Lambeth LBC ex p Vagliviello* (1990) 22 HLR 392, CA.

42   *R v Westminster CC ex p Bishop* (1996) 29 HLR 546, QBD.

43   *R v Kingswood BC ex p Smith-Morse* (1994) *Times* 8 December, QBD.

44   *R v Port Talbot BC ex p McCarthy* (1990) 23 HLR 208, CA.

45   See also *Holmes-Moorhouse v Richmond upon Thames LBC* [2009] UKHL 7; [2009] HLR 34. It was recognised that shared residence orders are much more common now. The policy reasons for a local authority not providing a family that previously lived under one roof with a second home are, however, considered to be overwhelming. See below, para 5.26.

46   Above, paras 4.141–4.145.

s/he will only be in priority need if the children will be residing with him/her once s/he is actually homeless, which may well not be the case if the authority provides no accommodation.[47]

Reasonably expected to reside

5.24 It was also held in *McCarthy*[48] that, while not bound to do so, the authority could conclude that children are usually reasonably to be expected to reside with the parent with care and control.

5.25 A joint residence order[49] does not mean that the children are reasonably to be expected to reside with both parents. In *Doyle*,[50] four children were to spend half the week with each parent under such a joint order. The father applied to the authority as homeless. The authority took the joint residence order into account but was still entitled to decide that the children could not reasonably be expected to reside with their father. In reaching this decision, the authority was entitled to take into account the shortage of housing stock in its area, and the under-occupation for part of each week that would result.

5.26 In *Holmes-Moorhouse v Richmond upon Thames LBC*,[51] the separated parents of four children agreed to a shared residence order pursuant to which the three youngest children would spend alternate weeks and half of each school holiday with the father. The father then applied to the local authority relying on the shared residence order to demonstrate priority need. The House of Lords held that whether children are reasonably expected to reside with an applicant is a matter for the local authority to decide and cannot be dictated by a residence order, although such an order is part of the material to which an authority should have regard when making its decision.[52] The question that the local authority should ask is whether it is reasonably to be expected, *in the context of a scheme for housing the homeless*, that children who already have a home with their mother should be able also to reside with their father, ie, asking that question in the context of a scheme for the allocation of a scarce resource.[53] Only

---

47 *Holmes-Moorhouse v Richmond upon Thames LBC* [2009] UKHL 7; [2009] HLR 34, at [20].

48 *R v Port Talbot BC ex p McCarthy* (1990) 23 HLR 208, CA.

49 Under Children Act 1989 s8.

50 *R v Oxford CC ex p Doyle* (1997) 30 HLR 506, QBD.

51 [2009] UKHL 7; [2009] HLR 34.

52 [2009] UKHL 7; [2009] HLR 34, at [17].

53 [2009] UKHL 7; [2009] HLR 34, at [9] and [14–16].

in exceptional circumstances[54] will it be reasonable to expect a child who has a home with one parent to be provided under HA 1996 Part 7 with another so that s/he can reside with both parents.

Children in social services care

5.27 The alternative limbs – 'are residing, or might reasonably be expected to reside' – avoid the difficulties which might otherwise arise where children are in temporary accommodation.

5.28 Where children are being looked after by the local social services authority, they may still be dependent on their parents and liaison with social services will be essential. 'Joint consideration with social services will ensure that the best interests of the applicant and the children are served.'[55]

Vulnerability

5.29 Whether someone is vulnerable, for one of the stated reasons,[56] is preferably approached as a composite question, rather than in two separate stages,[57] ie, rather than asking separately whether there is vulnerability at all and, discretely, whether it is attributable to any of those factors.[58]

---

54 [2009] UKHL 7; [2009] HLR 34, at [21], saying 'It seems to me that the likely needs of the children will have to be exceptional before a housing authority will decide that it is reasonable to expect an applicant to be provided with accommodation for them which will stand empty for at least half the time. I do not say that there may not be such a case; for example, if there is a child suffering from a disability which makes it imperative for care to be shared between separated parents. But such cases, in which that child (but not necessarily any sibling) might reasonably be expected to reside with both parents, will be unusual.'

55 Code of Guidance para 10.11; Welsh Code para 14.7.

56 Old age, mental illness or handicap or physical disability or other special reason.

57 *R v Kensington & Chelsea RLBC, Hammersmith & Fulham LBC, Westminster CC, and Islington LBC ex p Kihara and Others* (1996) 29 HLR 147, CA.

58 As the court had suggested in *R v Waveney DC ex p Bowers* [1983] QB 238; (1982) 4 HLR 118, CA. *Bowers* was not overruled by *Kihara*, but it was thought that the two-stage test was capable of causing confusion, where the composite approach would not. The composite approach was approved in *Osmani v Camden LBC* [2004] EWCA Civ 1706; [2005] HLR 22 and said to have been correctly applied in *Bellouti v Wandsworth LBC* [2005] EWCA Civ 602; [2005] HLR 46. See also *Crossley v Westminster CC* [2006] EWCA Civ 140; [2006] HLR 26.

5.30   For these purposes, vulnerability means 'less able to fend for himself than an ordinary homeless person so that injury or detriment to
him will result where a less vulnerable man will be able to cope without harmful effects': *Pereira*.[59] Detriment might include a significantly increased risk of suicide or of developing a serious ailment, but
it does not have to be measured in percentage terms.[60] The authority is not obliged to identify precisely the attributes of the ordinary
homeless person against whom the applicant is being compared.[61] It
makes no difference whether the authority expresses its conclusions
in terms of the applicant being at no greater risk of injury or detriment than the ordinary homeless person, or in terms of the applicant
being no less able to fend for him/herself than the ordinary homeless person: they are two ways of saying the same thing.[62]

5.31   The test in *Periera* was considered and approved in *Osmani*,[63] although the Court of Appeal stressed that the test is a judicial guide

59 *R v Camden LBC ex p Pereira* (1998) 31 HLR 317, CA at 330, applying *Bowers*
(footnote 58, above), overruling *R v Reigate and Banstead BC ex p Di Domenico*
(1987) 20 HLR 153, QBD and *Ortiz v Westminster CC* (1993) 27 HLR 364,
CA. These cases had added the gloss – amounting to a two-part test – that in
addition to being less able to fend when homeless, there had to be a lessened
ability to find and keep accommodation. In *R v Kensington & Chelsea RLBC,
Hammersmith & Fulham LBC, Westminster CC, and Islington LBC ex p Kihara
and Others* (1996) 29 HLR 147, CA, however, Simon Brown LJ doubted his
own proposition to this effect in *Ortiz* (although not the outcome on the facts),
which he had not intended to comprise a new statement of principle, and
Pereira disposed of it. The issue is whether the applicant is less able to fend
with the consequences of homelessness than a less vulnerable person, without
a risk of injury or detriment. The cases of *R v Bath CC ex p Sangermano* (1984)
17 HLR 94 (approved in *R v Wandsworth LBC ex p Banbury* (1986) 19 HLR
76) and *R v Lambeth LBC ex p Carroll* (1987) 20 HLR 142, which had referred
to vulnerability as being 'loosely in housing terms or the context of housing',
while not overruled, should not be taken to suggest anything other than
assessment of ability to cope without the risk of injury or detriment: *Pereira* at
330. See also *Osmani v Camden LBC* [2004] EWCA Civ 1706; [2005] HLR 22.

60 *Griffin v Westminster CC* [2004] EWCA Civ 108; [2004] HLR 32. In this context,
the previous edition of the Code of Guidance (2002, para 8.13) incorrectly
referred to whether the applicant 'would be likely to' suffer injury or detriment.
See now the amended current edition, para 10.13 and Welsh Code para 14.11.

61 *Tetteh v Kingston-upon-Thames RLBC* [2004] EWCA Civ 1775; [2005] HLR 21.
Cf *Hall v Wandsworth LBC; Carter v Wandsworth LBC* [2004] EWCA Civ 1740;
[2005] HLR 23, where the authority posed the wrong question.

62 *Bellouti v Wandsworth LBC* [2005] EWCA Civ 602; [2005] HLR 46.

63 *Osmani v Camden LBC* [2004] EWCA Civ 1706; [2005] HLR 22. The judgment
of Auld LJ in *Osmani* was described by Jonathon Parker LJ in *Bellouti v
Wandsworth LBC* [2005] EWCA Civ 602; [2005] HLR 46 at [57] as saying 'all
that (at least for present purposes) need be said or can be said on the matter' of
deciding whether an applicant is vulnerable.

not a statutory formulation. It is a necessarily imprecise exercise in comparison between the applicant and the 'ordinary homeless person'.

> Given that each authority is charged with local application of a national scheme of priorities but against its own burden of homeless persons and finite resources, such decisions are often likely to be highly judgmental. In the context of balancing the priorities of such persons a local housing authority is likely to be better placed in most instances for making such a judgment.[64]

5.32   The authority must, however, be careful to assess and apply it on the assumption that an applicant has become or will become street homeless, not on his/her ability to fend for him/herself while still housed.[65]

Old age

5.33   The Code suggests that authorities should consider whether old age is a factor which makes it hard for applicants to fend for themselves, and that all applications from people aged 60 or over should be considered carefully.[66]

Mental illness or handicap or physical disability

5.34   In considering vulnerability due to mental or physical illness or disability, the Code suggests that authorities should have regard to medical advice and – where appropriate – seek social services advice. It is for the local authority to decide whether to obtain its own advice in respect of medical reports relied on by a homeless applicant; there is no absolute requirement to refer an applicant's medical reports for evaluation by a medical adviser in every case; it depends on the facts in each case.[67] Local authorities are not, however, expected to make their own critical evaluation of an applicant's medical evidence and should have access to specialist advice where necessary.[68]

5.35   Where the authority does decide to refer the applicant's medical reports to an adviser for specialist advice, it must take care not to appear to be using the opinion of the medical adviser to provide or

---

64   Per Auld LJ at [38].
65   *Osmani*, footnote 63, above, per Auld LJ at [38].
66   Code of Guidance para 10.15; Welsh Code para 14.11.
67   *Simms v Islington LBC* [2008] EWCA Civ 1083; [2009] HLR 20.
68   *Shala v Birmingham CC* [2007] EWCA Civ 624; [2008] HLR 8.

support the authority's reasons for not finding a priority on medical grounds.

5.36   In *Shala v Birmingham CC*,[69] the applicant relied on a medical report from a psychiatrist. The local authority referred that report to its own medical adviser who, although a qualified medical practitioner, was not a qualified psychiatrist. Nor did the medical adviser examine the applicant in person. When evaluating the applicant's vulnerability on the grounds of mental illness, the authority nonetheless chose the opinion of the medical adviser over that of the applicant's psychiatrist. The Court of Appeal held that – although the local authority had done nothing wrong in obtaining medical advice – it had fallen into the trap of thinking that it was comparing like with like when looking at the medical opinions. The function of the medical adviser was to assist the authority in understanding the medical issues and to evaluate the applicant's expert evidence. In the absence of an examination of the patient, the medical adviser's evidence could not itself ordinarily constitute expert evidence. The review officer had failed to take the lack of examination by the medical adviser into account when considering the medical evidence.

5.37   The local authority should also consider the nature and extent of the illness or disability, the relationship between the illness or disability and the individual's housing difficulties, and the relationship between the illness or disability and other factors such as drug/alcohol misuse, offending behaviour, challenging behaviours, age and personality disorder.[70] In *Osmani*,[71] Auld LJ said that authorities should have regard to the particular debilitating effects of depressive disorders and the fragility of those suffering from them if suddenly deprived of the prop of their own home.

5.38   Particular reference is made in the Code[72] to those with mental health problems who have been discharged from psychiatric hospitals and local authority hostels. The need for effective liaison between housing, social services and health authorities is stressed.

---

69 [2007] EWCA Civ 624; [2008] HLR 8.

70 Code of Guidance para 10.16; Welsh Code para 14.13.

71 *Osmani v Camden LBC* [2004] EWCA Civ 1706; [2005] HLR 22 at [38] referring to the observations of Brooke LJ in *R v Newham LBC ex p Lumley* (2003) 33 HLR 111 at [63]. Cf *R (Yeter) v Enfield LBC* [2002] EWHC 2185 (Admin), where a decision that an applicant suffering from depression was not vulnerable – on the basis that an ordinary homeless person can be expected to suffer from depression so that the applicant was no more vulnerable than an ordinary homeless person – was upheld.

72 Code of Guidance para 10.17; Welsh Code para 14.14.

Authorities should also be sensitive to direct approaches from home-less discharged patients.

5.39　　Cases of vulnerability due solely to the problems of drink will not usually be attributable to one of the specified causes,[73] although an extreme case may amount to a mental or physical handicap or dis-ability. While in some cases vulnerability may be a medical question only, it may also be a question of housing and social welfare.[74] In all cases, the question must be determined by the local authority; it can-not merely 'rubber stamp' a decision of its medical officer of health or other medical experts.[75]

5.40　　In *Banbury*,[76] whether epilepsy amounted to vulnerability was said to be a question of fact and degree, which would be established if attacks occurred with intense regularity. In *Leek*,[77] a decision on the vulnerability of an epileptic – comprising refusal to reconsider an earlier decision – was quashed on the ground that the position of any particular sufferer may need to be re-assessed from time to time.

5.41　　A delusional condition which rendered the applicant unable to manage his own financial affairs made him vulnerable in *Dukic*.[78]

5.42　　In *Sangermano*,[79] the court distinguished between mental illness that is psychotic and mental handicap. The latter is not concerned with illness, but with subnormality or severe subnormality, although not all subnormality will necessarily amount to vulnerability.

5.43　　In the same case, it was held that where medical evidence of sub-normality is put before an authority, the authority ought either to accept it or make its own further enquiries. Furthermore, when de-termining priority need, the applicant's earlier rent arrears had been a wholly irrelevant consideration.

73　*R v Waveney DC ex p Bowers* [1983] QB 238; (1982) 4 HLR 118, CA. See also para 5.48, below, in relation to drug addiction.

74　*R v Lambeth LBC ex p Carroll* (1987) 20 HLR 142.

75　*R v Wandsworth LBC ex p Banbury* (1986) 19 HLR 76, QBD and *Osmani v Camden LBC* [2004] EWCA Civ 1706; [2005] HLR 22. Note, however, the comments of Auld LJ at [38] in *Osmani* stressing the need to look for and pay close regard to medical evidence submitted in support of applicants' claims of vulnerability on account of mental illness or handicap. Compare *Hall v Wandsworth LBC; Carter v Wandsworth LBC* [2004] EWCA Civ 1740; [2005] HLR 23, where the medical officer was entitled to advise that no further enquiries or specialist advice was required and *R v Newham LBC ex p Lumley* (2000) 33 HLR 11, QBD, where the medical officer failed to carry out adequate enquiries (see para 9.105, below).

76　*R v Wandsworth LBC ex p Banbury* (1986) 19 HLR 76, QBD.

77　*R v Sheffield CC ex p Leek* (1993) 26 HLR 669, CA.

78　*R v Greenwich LBC ex p Dukic* (1996) 29 HLR 87, QBD.

79　*R v Bath CC ex p Sangermano* (1984) 17 HLR 94.

5.44 The Code refers to those who are chronically sick, including those with HIV and AIDS.[80] It suggests that while some chronically sick people may have progressed to the point of physical or mental disability, they may also be vulnerable:

> because the manifestations or effects of their illness, or common attitudes to it, make it very difficult for them to find stable or suitable accommodation. This may be particularly true of people with AIDS, or even people who are infected with HIV without having any overt signs or symptoms if the nature of their infection is known.

Other special reason

5.45 In *Kihara*,[81] the court rejected an ejusdem generis[82] approach to 'other special reason', and the argument that, therefore, it was limited to the mental or physical characteristics of an applicant. The category is free-standing, unrestricted by any notion of physical or mental weakness other than that which is inherent in the word 'vulnerable'. It can comprise a combination of circumstances.[83]

5.46 The word 'special' imports the requirement that the housing difficulties faced by an applicant are of an unusual degree of gravity, enough to differentiate him/her from other homeless people. This does not include impecuniosity by itself, because an absence of means alone does not mark out one case from the generality of cases to a sufficient degree to render it 'special', ie, someone peculiarly in need of housing because of the risk of physical harm run from continuing homelessness.[84]

5.47 The expression 'other special reason,' however, does require examination of all the personal circumstances of an applicant, including physical or mental characteristics or disabilities, but not so limited. Accordingly, impecuniosity will be relevant as will be opportunities to raise money (for example, whether or not a person[85] is prohibited from employment), whether or not an applicant has family and friends and familiarity with the language, or – put another way – 'utter poverty and resourcelessness'.[86]

---

80 Code of Guidance para 10.32; Welsh Code para 14.18.

81 *R v Kensington & Chelsea RLBC, Hammersmith & Fulham LBC, Westminster CC, and Islington LBC ex p Kihara and Others* (1996) 29 HLR 147, CA.

82 Ie, of the same order.

83 *R v Waveney DC ex p Bowers* [1983] QB 238; (1982) 4 HLR 118, CA.

84 *R v Kensington & Chelsea RLBC, Hammersmith & Fulham LBC, Westminster CC, and Islington LBC ex p Kihara and Others* (1996) 29 HLR 147, CA.

85 By reason of immigration status.

86 *Kihara*, footnote 84, above, at 159.

5.48   In *Sangermano*,[87] the court considered that language difficulties on their own would not amount to a 'special reason' within what is now HA 1996 s189(1)(c). Drug addiction alone does not amount to a 'special reason', but a likelihood of relapse into such addiction may do so.[88]

Young people

5.49   The extension[89] to the categories of priority need covers many young people.[90] Not all will, however, qualify within the new categories, and the Code of Guidance[91] states that authorities should recognise that other young homeless people up to the age of 25 may be vulnerable and have priority need for a variety of reasons.

Multiple causes

5.50   In *Crossley*,[92] the applicant, as well as being a drug addict who was at risk of relapse and accordingly – it was contended – vulnerable for a 'special reason', had also been in care between the ages of 3 and 17 (which is an added category of vulnerability: see below, para 5.71). It was while in care that he had become a drug addict. The authority had failed to consider whether his vulnerability had arisen from the period in care. The court stated:[93]

> This appeal has not needed to address the question of how the decision-maker should deal with a case involving two of the prescribed causes of vulnerability – here, if the claimant is right, having been in care and some other special reason. We would nevertheless observe that where two such causes have produced a single set of effects, it would not seem consistent with Parliament's intention that the effects should be artificially distributed between the causes in arriving at a decision on the critical question of vulnerability.

---

87   *R v Bath CC ex p Sangermano* (1984) 17 HLR 94.
88   *Crossley v Westminster CC* [2006] EWCA Civ 140; [2006] HLR 26.
89   See para 5.4, above; see paras 5.59–5.74, below.
90   See paras 5.60–5.61 and 5.66–5.70, below.
91   Code of Guidance para 10.33; cf Welsh Code para 14.19, which does not specify a particular age. Other groups suggested include those fleeing harassment which does not amount to violence (para 10.34; Welsh Code para 14.22) and former asylum-seekers whose claim has been accepted or who have been given exceptional leave to remain (para 10.35).
92   *Crossley v Westminster CC* [2006] EWCA Civ 140; [2006] HLR 26.
93   At [31].

Emergency

5.51   This category of priority need is derived from earlier administrative guidance under the National Assistance Act 1948 s21(1)(b). HA 1996 Part 7 now requires that the event which causes the homelessness and the priority need must be both an emergency and a disaster.[94]

5.52   Fire and flood are not the only qualifying disasters. In *Noble v South Herefordshire DC*,[95] the words 'or any other disaster' (in the Housing (Homeless Persons) Act 1977 s2(1)(b)) were held to mean another disaster similar to flood or fire. The omission of the word 'any' in HA 1996 s189(1)(d) would not seem to affect this.

5.53   *Noble* was concerned with a demolition order under what is now HA 1985 Part 9. This was not considered to comprise a disaster similar to flood or fire, although on the facts of the case the occupiers had moved in after the demolition order had been made and it may be distinguishable in the case of a dangerous structure notice under the Building Act 1984 s77, or analogous powers, imposed without any real forewarning.[96] Where a demolition order under HA 1985 is imposed, however, its procedural provisions suggest that it would not qualify as an emergency, and an occupier will in any event usually be entitled to rehousing under the Land Compensation Act 1973 s39.[97]

5.54   The words 'other disaster' must be construed ejusdem generis.[98] Accordingly, a person who has been unlawfully evicted from his/her home is not in priority need within the subsection: it is not an

---

94 The need for the emergency to have caused the homelessness was illustrated in *Higgs v Brighton and Hove CC* [2003] EWCA Civ 895; [2004] HLR 2: although the loss of the applicant's caravan was an emergency (see para 5.55, below) it had not caused his homelessness; he was already homeless – prior to the loss – because the caravan was illegally sited (see para 4.69, above).

95 *Noble v South Herefordshire DC* (1983) 17 HLR 80, CA.

96 But compare the provisions of Greater London Council (General Powers) Act 1984 s39, below, para 5.56. If these were considered both to need, and to justify, deeming emergencies, it may be implied by the courts that other provisions of a like quality do not have the same effect.

97 See also *R v Kensington & Chelsea RLBC ex p Ben-El-Mabrouk* (1995) 27 HLR 564, CA (para 4.103, above), in which accommodation subject to action for want of means of escape from fire could reasonably continue to be occupied, pending rehousing under the Land Compensation Act 1973. The perceived need for GLC (General Powers) Act 1984 s39 (para 5.56, below) tends to support this result (where that Act does not apply).

98 *R v Bristol CC ex p Bradic* (1995) 27 HLR 584, CA (following *Noble v South Herefordshire DC* (1983) 17 HLR 80, CA. (As to ejusdem generis, see above, 5.45, footnote 82).

emergency similar to flood or fire: *Bradic*. The subsection is not confined to emergencies amounting to force majeure, however, but embraces all emergencies consisting of physical damage: *Bradic*.

5.55　　Where the applicant occupies a moving structure, such as a caravan, as his/her home, the disappearance of that structure is an emergency within the subsection because it involves the sudden and unexpected loss of his/her home in circumstances outside his/her control: *Higgs*.[99]

5.56　　The following people are statutorily deemed to have become homeless or threatened with homelessness as a result of emergency such as flood, fire or other disaster:[100]

a)　a person who resides in a building in outer London in respect of which an order has been made by a magistrates' court under the Greater London Council (General Powers) Act 1984 s37 that the occupants are to be removed because of its dangerous state;

b)　a person who resides in a building in inner or outer London whose occupants are in danger by reason of its proximity to a dangerous structure or building, within the Greater London Council (General Powers) Act 1984 s38(1), in respect of which an order has been made by the magistrates' court under section 38(2).

Alteration of categories

5.57　　The secretary of state and, in Wales, the National Assembly[101] can add further categories of priority need, or alter or remove existing categories,[102] although only after consultation with such associations representing authorities and such other persons as the secretary of state or Assembly considers appropriate.[103]

5.58　　In both Wales and England, the categories have been supplemented so as to reflect concerns about homelessness among young people, those leaving care, those leaving institutional settings, such as prison and the armed forces, and those fleeing violence. The regulations in each country are, however, worded differently.

99　*Higgs v Brighton and Hove CC* [2003] EWCA Civ 895; [2004] HLR 2.
100　GLC (General Powers) Act 1984 s39, as amended by HA 1996 Sch 17.
101　National Assembly for Wales (Transfer of Functions) Order 1999 SI No 672.
102　HA 1996 s189(2).
103　HA 1996 s189(3).

The Welsh Regulations[104]

5.59 The Homeless Persons (Priority Need) (Wales) Order 2001[105] came into effect on 1 March 2001. It specifies five additional categories of priority need.

18- to 20-year-olds[106]

5.60 All those who are aged 18 or over and under 21 are in priority need if at any time while they were a child they were looked after, accommodated or fostered[107] or are at particular risk of sexual or financial exploitation.[108]

16- and 17-year-olds

5.61 All 16- and 17-year-olds are to be considered in priority need.[109]

Persons fleeing domestic violence

5.62 Those without dependent children who have been subject to domestic violence,[110] are at risk of such violence, or who would be if they returned home, are in priority need.[111]

---

104 See Welsh Code paras 14.26–14.66.

105 SI No 607.

106 SI No 607 reg 3.

107 Defined as: 'being looked after by a local authority, ie, subject to a care order or voluntarily accommodated; accommodated by or on behalf of a voluntary organisation; accommodated in a private children's home; accommodated for a consecutive period of at least three months by a health authority, special health authority or local education authority or in any residential care home, nursing home, or mental nursing home, or in any accommodation provided by a National Health Service Trust; or, privately fostered': SI No 607 reg 3(2).

108 See, for example, *Kelly v Monklands DC* [1986] SLT 169 and *Wilson v Nithsdale DC* [1992] SLT 1131.

109 SI No 607 reg 4, and see the discussion at paras 5.60 and 5.62, below, for the discussion of *Robinson v Hammersmith & Fulham LBC* [2006] EWCA Civ 1122; [2006] HLR 7 to the effect that an authority cannot delay matters – whether by using mediation or otherwise – in such a way as to avert a duty because the applicant reaches 18.

110 Compare the English Regulations, referring to any type of violence (see para 5.74, below . Domestic violence is not defined, but see HA 1996 s177(1) (chapter 4, above).

111 SI No 607 reg 5.

Persons leaving the armed forces

5.63   A person is in priority need if s/he formerly served in the regular armed forces[112] and has been homeless since leaving those forces.[113]

Former prisoners

5.64   Former prisoners who have been homeless since leaving custody[114] are in priority need, provided they have a local connection[115] with the local housing authority.[116]

The English Regulations[117]

5.65   In England, the Homelessness (Priority Need for Accommodation) (England) Order 2002[118] came into force on 31 July 2002. It has six additional categories of priority need.[119]

16- and 17-year-olds

5.66   All 16- and 17-year-olds are in priority need provided they are not classified as a relevant child[120] (relevant children remain the responsibility of the social services authority) or are owed a duty by a local authority under the Children Act 1989 s20.[121] Whether a 16- or 17-year-old is a child in need for the purposes of the Children Act 1989, and accordingly owed a duty under section 20, is a mixed question of law and fact for the local authority to decide: *M*.[122] When considering whether to house a 16- or 17-year-old applicant under HA 1996

112 As defined by HA 1996 s199(4), see para 7.15, below.

113 SI No 607 reg 6.

114 A prisoner means 'any person for the time being detained in lawful custody as the result of a requirement imposed by a court that he or she be detained': ibid reg 7(2).

115 This is not defined for the purposes of the regulation, but presumably has the same meaning as HA 1996 s199, see further chapter 7.

116 SI No 607 reg 7(1).

117 See Code of Guidance paras 10.19–10.29 and 10.36–10.41.

118 SI No 2051.

119 SI No 2051 reg 3.

120 As defined by the Children Act 1989 s23A, ie, a child who has left care having been an eligible child. Eligible children are those in care who have been looked after for a prescribed period of time, ie, 13 weeks (see the Children (Leaving Care) (England) Regulations 2001 SI No 2874 reg 3).

121 *R (S) v Sutton LBC* [2007] EWCA Civ 790. See further para 13.44, below.

122 *R (M) v Hammersmith & Fulham LBC* [2008] UKHL 14; (2008) 4 All ER 271, HL, per Baroness Hale at [29].

s188 pending enquiries[123] a housing officer is not required to assess whether the applicant is a child in need. As a matter of good practice, if a housing officer, in the course of subsequent enquiries, identifies factors which make an applicant a candidate for designation as a child in need, it is the responsibility of that housing officer to refer the child to the social services department of the council, or to alert social services to his/her situation.[124] It is unlawful for a social services department to side-step their responsibilities under section 20 by assuming that a child in need can be suitably accommodated as a homeless person.[125]

5.67   If an authority's normal enquiry time would mean that an applicant will have turned 18 by the time of the decision, the authority cannot take the view that s/he will not be in priority need and refuse all assistance, nor simply provide accommodation until the birthday, even though, if enquiries in fact take the applicant to 18, s/he will not be in priority need at the time of the decision.[126] Nor may the authority postpone its decision to that date.[127] Nor can an authority take the benefit of an invalid decision which forces the applicant into a review, by which time the applicant has turned 18: the principle in *Mohamed v Hammersmith & Fulham LBC*,[128] that the reviewer takes into account all facts to the date of the review,[129] cannot apply in this way, for:

> If the original decision was unlawful . . . the review decision maker should have so held and made a decision that would have restored to the appellant the rights she would have had if the decision had been lawful.[130]

5.68   The Code of Guidance[131] suggests that for some young homeless applicants the most appropriate solution may be reconciliation with their

123 See chapter 10.

124 *R (M) v Hammersmith & Fulham LBC* [2008] UKHL 14; [2008] 4 All ER 271, HL, at [33], [36] and [42].

125 *R (S) v Sutton LBC* [2007] EWCA Civ 790. See also *R (M) v Hammersmith & Fulham LBC* [2008] UKHL 14; [2008] 4 All ER 271, HL, per Baroness Hale at [33] and [42]. Although there was no evidence of a deliberate policy, to seek 'to avoid its responsibilities under the 1989 Act by shifting them on to the housing department . . . would be unlawful.' The observation was made in connection with *any* duty under the 1989 Act, not s20 alone.

126 *Robinson v Hammersmith & Fulham LBC* [2006] EWCA Civ 1122; [2007] HLR 7.

127 *Robinson v Hammersmith & Fulham LBC*, above, even for a short period.

128 [2001] UKHL 57; [2002] HLR 7.

129 See para 9.176.

130 *Robinson v Hammersmith & Fulham LBC* [2006] EWCA Civ 1122 [2007] HLR 7, per Waller LJ at [32].

131 Para 12.8.

families so that they can return home. It recognises that in some cases, however, relationships may have broken down irretrievably, and in others that it may not be safe for a young person to return to the family home. Accordingly, any mediation or reconciliation will need careful brokering and social services should be involved.[132] Temporary accommodation may need to be provided while the process takes place.

5.69   If mediation would take an applicant beyond his/her 18th birthday, however, the authority is bound to reach its decision without awaiting the outcome, as – if unsuccessful – the effect would otherwise be to deprive the applicant of his/her right to a full duty.[133] Mediation and enquiries are separate processes:

> The two processes may of course proceed in parallel; and if mediation is successful while the section 184 inquiry process is still on foot, then of course there will be no need for the latter process to continue any further. On the other hand, a local housing authority has, in my judgment, no power to defer making inquiries pursuant to section 184 on the ground that there is a pending mediation.[134]

18- to 20-year-old care leavers

5.70   Any person who is aged 18 to 20 (other than a relevant student)[135] who at any time after reaching the age of 16, but while under 18, was, but is no longer, looked after, accommodated or fostered[136] is in priority need.

132 See also the obiter comments of Baroness Hale who approved the '. . . wisdom of this guidance . . .' in *R (M) v Hammersmith & Fulham LBC* [2008] UKHL 14; [2008] 4 All ER 271, HL at [27].

133 *Robinson v Hammersmith & Fulham LBC* [2006] EWCA Civ 1122; [2007] HLR 7.

134 *Robinson*, footnote 133, above, at [42], per Jonathan Parker LJ. See also per Jacob LJ at [45], who also relied on the s179 duty (below, para 14.18) to provide advice and information: 'A near-18-year-old who came to the authority could obviously not be properly be advised to mediate if the effect of mediation would be to delay the actual s184 decision past the 18th birthday.'

135 This is defined by the Children Act 1989, as a care leaver under 24 to whom the Children Act 1989 s24B(3) applies, who is in full-time further or higher education and whose term time accommodation is not available to him/her during a vacation. Relevant students remain the responsibility of social services authorities.

136 As defined by the Children Act 1989 s24, ie, looked after by a local authority (ie, has been subject to a care order or voluntarily accommodated); accommodated by or on behalf of a voluntary organisation; accommodated in a private children's home; accommodated for a consecutive period of at least three months by a health authority, special health authority, primary care trust or local education authority or in any care home or independent hospital or in any accommodation provided by the National Health Service Trust; or, privately fostered.

Vulnerable care leavers

5.71 Where a person has previously been looked after, accommodated or fostered,[137] s/he will be in priority need no matter what his/her age, if this has resulted in him/her being vulnerable.[138]

Vulnerable former members of the armed forces

5.72 Those who have been members of Her Majesty's regular armed forces[139] are in priority need, but only if they are vulnerable[140] as a result of that service.

Vulnerable former prisoners

5.73 A person who is vulnerable[141] as a result of having served a custodial sentence,[142] having been committed for contempt of court or having been remanded in custody[143] is also in priority need.

Vulnerable due to fleeing violence

5.74 If an applicant has had to cease to occupy accommodation because of violence[144] or threats of violence which are likely to be carried out, s/he will be in priority need if s/he is vulnerable[145] as a result.

---

137 See footnote 136, above.
138 As to whether someone is vulnerable, see paras 5.29–5.32, above. See also *Crossley v Westminster CC* [2006] EWCA Civ 140; [2006] HLR 26.
139 See HA 1996 s199(4), para 7.15, below.
140 As to whether someone is vulnerable, see paras 5.29–5.32, above.
141 See footnote 140, above.
142 Within the meaning of the Powers of Criminal Courts (Sentencing) Act 2000 s76.
143 Within the meaning of the Powers of Criminal Courts (Sentencing) Act 2000 s88(1)(b)–(d).
144 See the definition of violence in HA 1996 s177(1), paras 4.84–4.86, above.
145 As to whether someone is vulnerable, see paras 5.29–5.32, above.

Intentional homelessness

continued

Introduction

6.1 This chapter concerns the provision which has attracted most attention and controversy in homelessness law: intentional homelessness. Where a person is homeless intentionally, the only duty is to provide temporary accommodation for as long as the authority thinks is reasonable for the applicant to get his/her own accommodation.[1]

6.2 The principal definition of intentionality is the same under the Housing Act (HA) 1996 as it was under HA 1985. It was, however, extended by HA 1996 to include arrangements under which an applicant is required to cease to occupy accommodation which it would have been reasonable for him/her to continue to occupy, being an arrangement entered into so as to entitle him/her to assistance under HA 1996 Part 7, where there is no other good reason for the applicant to be homeless.[2]

Principal definition

6.3 A person is homeless intentionally if s/he has deliberately done or failed to do something in consequence of which s/he ceases to occupy accommodation which is available for his/her occupation and which it would have been reasonable for him/her to continue to occupy.[3]

6.4 A person is threatened with homelessness intentionally if s/he has deliberately done or failed to do something, the likely result of which is that s/he will be forced to leave accommodation which is available for his/her occupation and which it would have been reasonable for him/her to continue to occupy.[4] There is no reason for drawing any distinction of principle between the operation of the two definitions.[5]

6.5 Before an applicant can be considered homeless intentionally, the authority must satisfy itself that all the elements of this definition

---

1 See chapter 10.
2 HA 1996 s191(3). A further extension – to include persons to whom advice and assistance had been given under HA 1996 s197 (where the authority was satisfied that other suitable accommodation was available for the applicant's occupation in its area) but who failed to secure accommodation in circumstances where it was reasonable to be expected to do so (s191(4)) – was repealed by Homelessness Act 2002.
3 HA 1996 s191(1).
4 HA 1996 s196(1).
5 *Dyson v Kerrier DC* [1980] 1 WLR 1205, CA, at 1212. This seems to be based on a concession by counsel, but must surely be correct.

apply: thus, if the applicant left accommodation that was not available for his/her occupation, there can be no finding of intentionality.[6]

Elements of principal definition

6.6   The elements of the definition are:

a) the applicant must deliberately have done something or failed to do something;

b) the loss of accommodation must be in consequence of the act or omission;

c) there must be a cessation of occupation, as distinct from a failure to take up accommodation;

d) the accommodation must have been available for the occupation of the homeless person; and

e) it must have been reasonable for the homeless person to continue to occupy the accommodation.

6.7   Each of these elements, some of which are subject to further statutory definition or qualification, must be considered carefully and in the light of the case-law.

6.8   Before turning to these questions, however, there is one preliminary issue which requires discussion: that is, the question of whose conduct is to be taken into account, when an application is by or on behalf of more than one person.

Whose conduct?

6.9   A number of cases have considered how an authority should treat an application where one of the applicants, or a member of the applicant's household, has either already been adjudged homeless intentionally, or is susceptible to a finding of intentionality. The point tends to arouse strong passions for, as will be seen below,[7] the duty to a homeless person is also owed to anyone who might reasonably be expected to reside with him/her, which may well include the putatively intentionally homeless member of the household.[8]

6.10   The question was first considered in *Lewis*,[9] where a man quit his employment and lost his tied accommodation. He applied to

---

6   *Re Islam* [1983] 1 AC 688; (1981) 1 HLR 107, HL; see also, eg, *R v Eastleigh BC ex p Beattie (No 1)* (1983) 10 HLR 134, QBD.

7   See para 10.54, below.

8   See also the Code of Guidance para 11.9; Welsh Code para 15.11.

9   *R v North Devon DC ex p Lewis* [1981] 1 WLR 328, QBD.

the authority, which held that he had become homeless intention-ally.[10] Thereupon, the woman with whom he lived applied in her own name. The court rejected the authority's argument that it need only consider one application for the family unit as a whole: each applicant was entitled to individual consideration.[11]

6.11　　The court did, however, uphold the authority's argument that, in considering whether or not the women had become homeless intentionally, it could take into account conduct to which she had been a party, or in which she had acquiesced:

> In my view, the fact that the Act requires consideration of the family unit as a whole indicates that it would be perfectly proper in the ordinary case for the housing authority to look at the family as a whole and assume, in the absence of material which indicates to the contrary, where the conduct of one member of the family was such that he should be regarded as having become homeless intentionally, that was conduct to which the other members of the family were a party . . .
>
> If, however, at the end of the day because of material put before the housing authority by the wife, the housing authority are not satisfied that she was a party to the decision, they would have to regard her as not having become homeless intentionally. In argument the housing authority drew my attention to the difficulties which could arise in cases where the husband spent the rent on drink. If the wife acquiesced to his doing this then it seems to me it would be proper to regard her, as well as him, as having become homeless intentionally. If, on the other hand, she had done what she could to prevent the husband spending his money on drink instead of rent then she had not failed to do anything (the likely result of which would be that she would be forced to leave the accommodation) and it would not be right to regard her as having become homeless intentionally.

Burden

6.12　　This creates something of a shift in the normal burden that lies on an authority to make enquiries, because it imposes on an applicant seeking to avail him/herself of the principle of non-acquiescence something of a positive obligation to show why acquiescence should not be presumed.[12] See also *Caine*,[13] in which the Court of Appeal

---

10　See further below, paras 6.66–6.74.

11　See below, paras 9.38–9.39.

12　See chapter 9.

13　*R v Nottingham CC ex p Caine* (1995) 28 HLR 374, CA. See too *R v Hillingdon LBC ex p Thomas* (1987) 19 HLR 196, QBD.

held that the authority was entitled to look at the family as a whole, to infer that the applicant was aware that her partner had been withholding rent, and – even though there was no direct evidence that they had done so – to infer that the couple would have discussed the matter. The authority could not be criticised for proceeding on the basis that what it was considering was a normal family/couple in which such information would be shared.

Non-acquiescent applicants

6.13   *Lewis* was applied to the benefit of the applicant in *Sidhu*,[14] where the authority additionally sought to rely on an earlier finding of intentionality relating to rent arrears which had occurred while the applicant was still living with her husband, even though the couple had since separated.

6.14   *Lewis* was also applied to the applicant's benefit in *Beattie (No 2)*,[15] a case of non-payment of mortgage arrears,[16] even though the applicants were still living together as a couple, and in *Phillips*,[17] a case of rent arrears caused by the husband's drinking, likewise even though the applicants were still living together as a couple.

6.15   In *Trevena*,[18] a wife – the sole tenant of a flat – surrendered the tenancy in order to move in with another man in another town, leaving her husband in (unlawful) occupation. Possession proceedings had to be taken for his eviction. Subsequently, the couple were reconciled and he was able to rely on his lack of acquiescence in (indeed, opposition to) the surrender.

6.16   An attempt to raise a finding of intentionality against a wife for her husband's conduct, dating from before she even met him, was (unsurprisingly) rejected by the court in *Puhlhofer*.[19]

Findings of acquiescence

6.17   In *Thomas*,[20] however, Woolf J (who had decided *Lewis*), while restating the principle, upheld 'acquiescence' on the part of a male joint

---

14   *R v Ealing LBC ex p Sidhu* (1982) 2 HLR 45, QBD.

15   *R v Eastleigh BC ex p Beattie (No 2)* (1984) 17 HLR 168, QBD.

16   See further, paras 6.55–6.58, below.

17   *R v West Dorset DC ex p Phillips* (1984) 17 HLR 336, QBD.

18   *R v Penwith DC ex p Trevena* (1984) 17 HLR 526, QBD.

19   *R v Hillingdon LBC ex p Puhlhofer* (1985) 17 HLR 278, QBD, not appealed on this point; cf [1986] AC 484, CA and HL; (1985) 17 HLR 588, CA; (1986) 18 HLR 158, HL.

20   *R v Swansea CC ex p Thomas* (1983) 9 HLR 64, QBD.

tenant whose cohabitant had caused the loss of their council tenancy by nuisance and annoyance, even though he had been in prison both at the time of the conduct and at the time of the proceedings for possession.

6.18   The factors which influenced the court were:

a) that the man had been offered, but had declined, an opportunity to attend the hearing; and

b) that there was no evidence of attempts by him to persuade the woman to desist in the conduct, which had persisted up until the hearing.

6.19   In *Khatun*,[21] it was unsuccessfully argued on behalf of a Bangladeshi wife that she had not acquiesced in her husband's conduct in leaving accommodation which it would have been reasonable to continue to occupy, on the basis that – as a matter of culture and practice – she had no choice but to abide by her husband's decision. Dismissing the appeal, the court held that as the wife had been content to leave decisions to her spouse, and to co-operate in implementing those decisions, she could properly be regarded as having acquiesced.

Rent arrears

6.20   It may be the case, particularly in arrears cases, that the spouse has found out too late to be able to do anything about rent arrears. So, for example, arrears may be so substantial when s/he discovers them that simple awareness of the debt before homelessness cannot be said to amount to acquiescence: see *Spruce*.[22]

6.21   On the other hand, in *O'Connor (Barnet)*[23] the authority was entitled to conclude that there had been acquiescence, and in *Salmons*[24] the authority had addressed the critical question whether it was entitled to conclude that the applicant must have known about, or at least turned a blind eye to, the arrears, and was therefore entitled to reach the view that the applicant had either not been honest about his knowledge of the arrears, or that he had at the least been reckless about the true situation.

21 *R v Tower Hamlets LBC ex p Khatun* (1993) 27 HLR 344, CA.
22 *R v East Northamptonshire DC ex p Spruce* (1988) 20 HLR 508, QBD.
23 *R v Barnet LBC ex p O'Connor* (1990) 22 HLR 486, QBD.
24 *R v Ealing LBC ex p Salmons* (1990) 23 HLR 272, QBD.

Non-cohabitants

6.22   The acquiescence point is not confined to cohabitants. In *Smith v Bristol CC*,[25] a woman was held responsible for acts of nuisance caused by her son and lodgers, which resulted in her eviction. Similarly, the basis for the order for possession which resulted[26] in a finding of intentionality in *Devenport*[27] was conduct by the children of the family; conduct by children was included in the reasons for the finding of intentionality in *Ward*.[28]

6.23   In *Bannon*,[29] acquiescence was upheld in relation to nuisance by the family as a whole, where the applicant had either been a party to it or else had done nothing to prevent it. In *John*,[30] nuisance and annoyance by a lodger caused the eviction of the tenant even though it occurred only when she was out of the flat, and the lodger was both younger and considerably stronger than she, so that she was unable to control his behaviour. Her 'acquiescence' was the failure to evict him.[31]

6.24   An attempt to use the principle of non-acquiescence on behalf of child applicants failed on the basis that the children were not in priority need in their own right: *ex p G*.[32]

Deliberate act or omission

General principles

6.25   There is no requirement that a person deliberately became homeless, rather that s/he deliberately did (or failed to do) something as a result of which s/he became homeless. The word 'deliberate' only

---

25   See discussion at December 1981 *LAG Bulletin* 287.

26   But see below, para 6.25.

27   *Devenport v Salford CC* (1983) 8 HLR 54, CA.

28   *R v Southampton CC ex p Ward* (1984) 14 HLR 114, QBD.

29   *R v East Hertfordshire DC ex p Bannon* (1986) 18 HLR 515, QBD.

30   *R v Swansea CC ex p John* (1982) 9 HLR 56, QBD.

31   In *Darlington BC v Sterling* (1997) 29 HLR 309, CA, it was taken for granted that eviction on the grounds of nuisance and annoyance by – in that case – the tenant's son was capable of giving rise to a finding of intentionality (which should not, however, have prevented an order for possession being made against the tenant).

32   *R v Oldham MBC ex p G; R v Bexley LBC ex p B* (1993) 25 HLR 319, HL; see para 5.10, above. See also *R v Camden LBC ex p Hersi* (2001) 33 HLR 52, CA. On the applicability of the Children Act 1989 in such cases, see paras 13.44–13.65.

governs the act or omission: *Devenport*.[33] The link between the act and the homelessness must be judged objectively: *Robinson v Torbay BC*.[34]

Good faith

6.26 That said, 'an act or omission in good faith on the part of a person who was unaware of any relevant fact shall not be treated as deliberate' for the purposes of establishing intentional homelessness.[35] This provision introduces a subjective element into the analysis of intentionality.[36] Subsections 191(1) and (2) pose 'serial questions': whether an act is in good faith and in ignorance of relevant facts must be considered separately: *O'Connor (Kensington & Chelsea)*.[37] In that case, the authority had merged the two subsections and obscured the critical, good faith question.

6.27 If it is established that the applicant was unaware of a relevant fact, the question is not whether the ignorance was reasonable but whether it was in good faith.[38] Good faith includes circumstances where the applicant's ignorance of a relevant fact was due to his/her own unreasonable conduct[39] and where s/he could be said to have been foolish or imprudent.[40] The good faith requirement will not, however, be satisfied where an applicant has shut his/her eyes to the obvious, or has acted with wilful ignorance or on little more than a wing and a prayer.[41] The phrase 'good faith' carries the connotation of some kind of impropriety, or an element of misuse or abuse of the legislation.[42] Dishonesty will not constitute good faith.[43]

---

33 *Devenport v Salford CC* (1983) 8 HLR 54, CA. Cf the obiter comments of the Master of the Rolls in *R v Slough BC ex p Ealing LBC* [1981] QB 801, CA.

34 *Robinson v Torbay BC* [1982] 1 All ER 726, QBD.

35 HA 1996 ss191(2) and 196(2).

36 *R v Exeter CC ex p Tranckle* (1993) 26 HLR 244, CA. See the examples in the Code of Guidance para 11.27; Welsh Code para 15.9.

37 *O'Connor v Kensington & Chelsea RLBC* [2004] EWCA Civ 394; [2004] HLR 37.

38 *F v Birmingham CC* [2006] EWCA Civ 1427; [2007] HLR 18 at [17].

39 *F* at [17].

40 *Ugiagbe v Southwark LBC* [2009] EWCA Civ 31 at [26].

41 *F* at [17].

42 *Ugiagbe* at [27].

43 *Ugiagbe* at [27].

Ignorance of facts

6.28 An applicant's appreciation of the prospects of future housing can be treated as 'awareness of a relevant fact' for the purposes of section 191(2),[44] provided that it is sufficiently specific and provided that it is based on a degree of genuine investigation, not mere aspiration.[45] If the prospect of future housing rests on next to nothing but hope, it cannot be said that a decision falls into legal error by not invoking section 191(2) in the applicant's favour;[46] in such a case, the subsection is a non-starter and no specific reference to it is needed.[47]

6.29 In *Ugiagbe*,[48] the applicant was unaware of a relevant fact because she was ignorant of the fact that she could not be required to leave without a court order.[49]

6.30 However, it is ignorance of a relevant fact which must not have been deliberate, not ignorance of the legal consequences.[50] Where an applicant temporarily went to live with her mother while at college but was warned by her father that she would not be allowed to return, it was held that the authority had misdirected itself in disregarding her genuine belief that he did not mean it, ie, that she would be able to go back. The father's state of mind was a relevant fact and so his daughter's action – taken in genuine ignorance of her father's true intent – could not be classified as deliberate: *Wincentzen v Monklands DC*.[51]

6.31 Where a person was misled as to business prospects, which caused him to move abroad, it was unawareness of a relevant fact: *Lusi*.[52]

6.32 In *Sukhija*,[53] a distinction was drawn between a mistake of fact (which could be within the good faith defence) and a mere unfulfilled hope (which was held not to be). The decision that the applicant – who had come to England in the mistaken belief that she would be

---

44 *F v Birmingham CC* [2006] EWCA Civ 1427; [2007] HLR 18 at [17].

45 *R v Westminster CC ex p Obeid* (1996) 29 HLR 389 at 398; *Aw-Arden v Birmingham CC* [2005] EWCA Civ 1834 at [10] and [11].

46 *Aw-Arden* at [11].

47 *Aw-Arden* at [12].

48 *Ugiagbe v Southwark LBC* [2009] EWCA Civ 31 at [8].

49 For the facts, see further para 6.39, below.

50 *R v Eastleigh BC ex p Beattie (No 2)* (1984) 17 HLR 168, QBD; *R v Croydon LBC ex p Toth* (1988) 20 HLR 576, CA; cf *R v Mole Valley DC ex p Burton* (1988) 20 HLR 479, QBD, where the applicant's belief in assurances by her husband that they would be rehoused under a union agreement was held to be a belief of fact, not of law.

51 *Wincentzen v Monklands DC* (1988) SLT (Court of Session) 259; September 1988 *LAG Bulletin* 13.

52 *R v Hammersmith & Fulham RLBC ex p Lusi* (1991) 23 HLR 460, QBD.

53 *R v Ealing LBC ex p Sukhija* (1994) 26 HLR 726, QBD.

able to find employment and a home – was intentionally homeless was accordingly upheld. See also *Khatun*,[54] in which the applicant was described as having no more than an expectation of being able to live temporarily with her parents-in-law on her return to the UK, which was held not to be a fact to which the good faith defence could be applied.

6.33   In *Ashton*,[55] a middle-aged woman moved from her home in Tunbridge Wells to take up a temporary job in Winchester, where the authority provided her with a one-year tenancy subject to the exception in HA 1985 Sch 1 para 5.[56] After a year, the authority obtained possession of the premises. A finding that the applicant was intentionally homeless was quashed on the basis, inter alia, that, in leaving Tunbridge Wells, the applicant had acted in good faith because she was unaware that she would be unable to find either housing or employment after the initial year. Accordingly, her action in surrendering the tenancy at Tunbridge Wells should not have been treated as deliberate.

6.34   In *Conway*,[57] a woman erroneously but genuinely believed that she had a further period of a year in which to decide whether or not to extend her existing shorthold tenancy. This was ignorance of a material fact, ie, the time remaining in which to make her decision.

6.35   In *Obeid*,[58] the applicant had taken private-sector accommodation in the belief that her rent would be covered by housing benefit, in ignorance of (and without making enquiries about) the provisions of the (then) Housing Benefit Regulations 1987 which could limit her benefit to a proportion of her rent. This was held to be capable of constituting ignorance of a relevant fact.

6.36   In *Obeid*, Carnwath J, considering the decisions in *Lusi*[59] and *Sukhija*,[60] said at 398 that:

The effect of those judgments, as I understand them, is that an applicant's appreciation of the prospects of future housing or future

54 *R v Tower Hamlets LBC ex p Khatun* (1994) 27 HLR 465, CA.
55 *R v Winchester CC ex p Ashton* (1991) 24 HLR 48, QBD. The decision of Kennedy J was upheld by the Court of Appeal (see (1991) 24 HLR 520) on the additional basis that the respondents had given too much weight to the factors in what is now HA 1996 s177(1) when reaching their conclusion.
56 Temporary accommodation for people taking up employment.
57 *R v Christchurch BC ex p Conway* (1987) 19 HLR 238, QBD.
58 *R v Westminster CC ex p Obeid* (1996) 29 HLR 389, QBD.
59 *R v Hammersmith & Fulham RLBC ex p Lusi* (1991) 23 HLR 460, QBD; para 6.31, above.
60 *R v Ealing LBC ex p Sukhija* (1994) 26 HLR 726, QBD; para 6.32, above.

employment can be treated as 'awareness of a relevant fact' for the purposes of this subsection, provided it is sufficiently specific (that is related to specific employment or specific housing opportunities) and provided it is based on some genuine investigation and not mere 'aspiration'.

This statement was approved in *Aw-Aden*,[61] where the applicant's unfulfilled hope of finding employment in this country was insufficiently specific; rather, it was an aspiration.

6.37   Leaving settled accommodation to move into unsettled accommodation may form part of the circumstances amounting to intentional homelessness, under HA 1996 extended definition of intentionality: see further below.[62] Ignorance about the unsettled nature of intended accommodation would, however, amount to ignorance of a relevant fact and as such should mean that such a move would not be caught, because 'the purpose of the arrangement' implies an element of intention ('to enable [the applicant] to become entitled to assistance').

Carelessness v deliberate conduct

6.38   In deciding whether the ignorance is in good faith, an authority must distinguish between honest blundering or carelessness on the one hand, which can still amount to good faith conduct, and dishonesty, where there can be no question of good faith: *Lusi*;[63] *Ali and Bibi*.[64] The question is whether the action is taken in good faith, not whether it was reasonable.

6.39   In *Ugiagbe*,[65] the applicant was asked by her landlord to leave; she went to her local authority's 'One-Stop Shop' and was told to go to the Homeless Persons' Unit to get temporary accommodation; as she did not want to be treated as homeless, she returned to the property. Eventually, her landlord again asked her to leave, which she did, and she applied for homelessness assistance. Her conduct could be described as foolish or imprudent yet it was the opposite of bad faith because her subjective motivation in not going to the Homeless Persons' Unit was because she had been led to believe that she would be treated as homeless, which was the last thing she wanted.[66]

---

61 *Aw-Aden v Birmingham CC* [2005] EWCA Civ 1834.
62 See below, paras 6.146–6.151.
63 *R v Hammersmith & Fulham LBC ex p Lusi* (1991) 23 HLR 460, QBD.
64 *R v City of Westminster ex p Ali and Bibi* (1992) 25 HLR 109, QBD.
65 *Ugiagbe v Southwark LBC* [2009] EWCA Civ 31 at [3].
66 *Ugiagbe* at [25], [26] and [28].

6.40   In *F*,[67] the applicant surrendered a secure tenancy of a two-bedroom flat, ignoring advice from her social worker that she risked being found intentionally homeless, and took a tenancy of a three-bedroom house, from which she was evicted for arrears which accrued because she did not receive housing benefit. She was found, at best, to have proceeded on a wing and a prayer; her conduct was described as wilful ignorance or shutting her eyes to the obvious and she therefore could not satisfy the good faith test; section 191(2) did not arise for consideration.[68]

6.41   In *Rouf*,[69] a finding of intentionality against an applicant who returned to a flat that had been repossessed after an absence of three years, but who had nonetheless believed that it would still be available to him, was quashed. The authority had failed to consider whether the belief was genuine, wrongly approaching the question as one of reasonableness of conduct.

6.42   In *Onwudiwe*,[70] however, an unemployed applicant's conduct in taking on large mortgage commitments in order to fund a business for which there had been no market-testing took the case beyond the stage of honest incompetence and provided material on which it could be said that he was deliberately putting his house at risk.

6.43   In *Beattie (No 2)*,[71] persistent failure to pay mortgage arrears was upheld as deliberate, notwithstanding that the applicant had been advised by his solicitors that it would not be.

6.44   On the other hand, in *White*,[72] the applicant believed that the DHSS was, or ought to be, paying the whole of the interest element on the mortgage instalments by direct deduction from his benefit. In fact, his supplementary benefit entitlement was so low that it did not cover the full amount of the interest, so that arrears continued to mount. The court held that – for most of the period in question – the applicant was under a genuine misapprehension as to a relevant fact (whether or not the DHSS was paying the whole of the interest payments), and that he had acted in good faith in failing to make the payments himself. There was, accordingly, no deliberate omission and, in consequence, no intentional homelessness.

6.45   In *O'Connor (Kensington & Chelsea)*,[73] the applicant husband and wife believed that a friend, who was staying at their flat while they

---

67 *F v Birmingham CC* [2006] EWCA Civ 1427; [2007] HLR 18 at [9].

68 *F* at [19].

69 *R v Tower Hamlets LBC ex p Rouf* (1991) 23 HLR 460, QBD.

70 *R v Wandsworth LBC ex p Onwudiwe* (1993) 26 HLR 302, CA.

71 *R v Eastleigh BC ex p Beattie (No 2)* (1984) 17 HLR 168, QBD.

72 *White v Exeter CC*, December 1981 *LAG Bulletin* 287, QBD.

73 *O'Connor v Kensington & Chelsea RLBC* [2004] EWCA Civ 394; [2004] HLR 37.

were visiting Ireland for a funeral and while the husband recovered from depression, was paying the rent. He was not in fact doing so; a suspended possession order was obtained in their absence and subsequently enforced after their return. The Court of Appeal held that it is not necessary for the ignorance of the relevant fact to be reasonable before an omission qualifies to be treated as non-deliberate. A person's ignorance may well be due to unreasonable behaviour, yet what s/he does in consequence may still be in good faith. The dividing line is not at the point where an applicant's ignorance of a relevant fact is due to his/her own unreasonable conduct, but at the point where by shutting his/her eyes to the obvious s/he cannot be said to have acted in good faith.

Act causing loss of accommodation

6.46   The act of good faith referred to in HA 1996 s191(2) is the act or omission causing homelessness, which is the act that has to be considered under section 191(1).[74]

6.47   In *Stewart*,[75] the authority found that the deliberate act which caused the homelessness was the commission of a criminal act by the applicant, following which he was imprisoned and a warrant executed (without notice) on the basis of an earlier possession order for arrears. The authority accepted that, after his imprisonment, the applicant had made an arrangement with his sister to maintain the tenancy, but no rent was in fact paid under it. He sought to argue that the deliberate act or omission was the failure to pay the rent, which was an act in good faith because he had been unaware of a relevant fact, ie, his sister's failure to keep to the arrangement. The Court of Appeal held that, given a proper finding that the deliberate act which caused the homelessness was the offence, the subsequent acts in good faith were irrelevant and the authority was not obliged to investigate them.

6.48   Where the cause of homelessness was an applicant's inability to meet mortgage repayments as a result of a severe downturn in business, the homelessness was intentional because the mortgage itself had been obtained as a result of the applicant's fraudulent misrepresentation of her income: *Rughooputh*.[76]

---

74 Which is why it is important correctly to identify the date when the (putatively intentional) homelessness began, cf *O'Connor v Kensington & Chelsea RLBC* [2004] EWCA Civ 394; [2004] HLR 37. See also *Ugiagbe v Southwark LBC* [2009] EWCA Civ 31 at [6].

75 *Stewart v Lambeth LBC* [2002] EWCA Civ 753; [2002] HLR 40.

76 *R v Barnet LBC ex p Rughooputh* (1993) 25 HLR 607, CA.

6.49   In *Tranckle*,[77] however, the applicant entered into an imprudent financial arrangement in good faith, because she was unaware of the (un)reality of the prospects of success for the public house which she was purchasing, which had been concealed from her by the brewery.

6.50   In *Watchman*,[78] the applicant was a secure tenant who exercised the right to buy with the aid of a mortgage on which the repayments were significantly higher than the rent she had previously been paying and in respect of which there was a history of arrears. Her husband subsequently lost his job but, although he found another at a lower salary, mortgage arrears built up and the mortgagee repossessed the property. The review found that the applicant had become intentionally homeless by taking on the mortgage when it was inevitable that she would get into severe financial difficulties within a short time; her husband's employment problems had not caused the repossession but merely accelerated the inevitable eviction.[79] Upholding that decision, it was held that – when deciding whether an applicant is intentionally homeless where there are several potential causes of the homelessness – the authority has to make a careful judgement on the particular facts, to decide whether the homelessness is a likely consequence of a deliberate act on the part of the applicant, bearing in mind that it is the applicant's responsibility for the homelessness that is in question.[80] While the authority has to consider the time when the applicant in fact became homeless,[81] it is entitled to take account of events prior to that date.[82]

6.51   Ironically, it may even be the case that a person who takes the trouble to find out relevant facts, and reaches a decision on them, is more vulnerable to a finding of intentionality than a person who has omitted to make any such enquiries at all.[83]

Bad faith

6.52   Where bad faith is suspected, it has been suggested that it may not invariably be necessary to put the matter to the applicant (*Hobbs v Sutton*

---

77   *R v Exeter CC ex p Tranckle* (1993) 26 HLR 244, CA.

78   *Watchman v Ipswich BC* [2007] EWCA Civ 348; [2007] HLR 33 at [6].

79   *Watchman* at [9].

80   *Watchman* at [22].

81   *Din v Wandsworth LBC* [1983] 1 AC 657.

82   *Watchman* at [23].

83   *R v Westminster CC ex p Obeid* (1996) 29 HLR 389, QBD.

LBC),[84] but see *Moozary-Oraky*,[85] where good faith relative to awareness of housing benefit was considered to be a question of jurisdictional fact, without which no reasonable authority could reach a conclusion on intentionality, into which the authority was accordingly required to make explicit enquiry of the applicant (as to whether or not she had seen a letter informing her that her benefit had been stopped).

6.53   In *Joyce*,[86] the authority did not even ask the applicant why mortgage arrears had arisen. This failure was accordingly fatal to its decision on the basis that it had omitted to take something relevant into account, ie, the applicant's explanation or answer.

Illustrations

6.54   There is now a very large number of cases on intentionality, which can conveniently be approached under a series of headings, but it is essential to remember that these are all illustrative of the operation of the provisions rather than precedents on their facts.

Rent/mortgage arrears

6.55   The Code gives as an example of homelessness which should not be treated as deliberate:

> . . . where an applicant has lost his/her home or was obliged to sell it because of rent or mortgage arrears resulting from significant financial difficulties, and the applicant was genuinely unable to keep up the rent or mortgage payments even after claiming benefits, and no further financial help was available.[87]

6.56   This is to be contrasted with cases where an applicant:

> . . . chooses to sell his/her home in circumstances where he or she is under no risk of losing it, or has lost it because of wilful and persistent refusal to pay rent or mortgage repayments.[88]

6.57   The previous Code issued under Housing Act 1985 Part 3 was in similar terms. In *Hawthorne*,[89] it was considered not to misstate the

---

84 (1993) 26 HLR 132, CA.

85 *R v City of Westminster ex p Moozary-Oraky* (1993) 26 HLR 214, QBD.

86 *R v Wyre BC ex p Joyce* (1983) 11 HLR 73, QBD.

87 Code of Guidance para 11.18; Welsh Code para 15.6(ii).

88 Code of Guidance para 11.20(ii); Welsh Code para 15.7(i).

89 *R v Wandsworth LBC ex p Hawthorne* (1994) 27 HLR 59, CA. See also *Ekwuru v Westminster CC* [2003] EWCA Civ 1293; [2004] HLR 14, where arrears arose because of a housing benefit cap.

law. In *Bryant*,[90] it was said that the Code drew a distinction 'between those who can, or could reasonably be expected to, pay mortgage payments or rent but do not do so, and those who in reality cannot pay because of real financial difficulties'. It was a question of fact for the authority to decide into which category an applicant fell, open only to challenge on usual public law principles.[91]

6.58   Supplemental guidance[92] on intentional homelessness is specifically directed to applicants who are homeless following difficulties in meeting mortgage commitments, in the light of national economic circumstances. The guidance reminds authorities that they must not adopt general policies which seek to pre-define circumstances that do or do not amount to intentional homelessness or threatened homelessness,[93] and that nobody may be presumed to be homeless intentionally.[94] The decision-maker must look for the substantive cause of the homelessness; the effective cause will not always be the most immediate proximate cause.[95] An authority should not refuse to accommodate people whose homelessness has been brought about without fault on their part,[96] for example, if the home was not affordable because the applicant could not meet the cost of his/her mortgage commitments.[97]

Nuisance and annoyance

6.59   Nuisance and annoyance can clearly be considered 'deliberate' for this purpose.[98] In *ex p P*,[99] a finding of intentionality was upheld in

---

90 *R v Warrington BC ex p Bryant* (2001) JHL D5, QBD.

91 As to which, see chapter 12. See also *William v Wandsworth LBC; Bellamy v Hounslow LBC* [2006] EWCA Civ 535, on failure to make mortgage payments after taking out a further loan.

92 The Homelessness Code of Guidance for Local Authorities Supplementary Guidance on Intentional Homelessness was published in August 2009.

93 See Supplementary Guidance para 6, which refers to Code of Guidance para 11.5. See also below, para 12.44.

94 Supplementary Guidance para 8.

95 Supplementary Guidance para 8.

96 Supplementary Guidance para 7.

97 Supplementary Guidance para 11.

98 *Devenport v Salford CC* (1983) 8 HLR 54, CA; *R v Swansea CC ex p John* (1982) 9 HLR 56, QBD; and *R v East Hertfordshire DC ex p Bannon* (1986) 18 HLR 515, QBD. See also Code of Guidance para 11.20(v); Welsh Code para 15.5(iv).

99 *R v Hammersmith & Fulham LBC ex p P* (1989) 22 HLR 21, QBD.

relation to alleged criminal and anti-social behaviour[100] (confirmed by the authority's own enquiries) which had led to threats from the IRA that the applicants would be killed if they did not leave their accommodation.

6.60   In *Bell*,[101] a possession order was obtained against the applicant on the grounds of nuisance and annoyance. She was accepted by Wirral MBC as having a priority need because of the state of her mental health. Applying a test to be found in the Code of Guidance under Housing Act 1985 Part 3 – which referred to capacity to manage affairs[102] – the authority nonetheless found that she had become homeless intentionally. Her application for judicial review was dismissed. It was said to be one thing to be less able to fend for oneself (for the purpose of establishing vulnerability)[103] and another to be incapable of managing one's own affairs (for the purpose of intentionality); the two findings were accordingly not inconsistent.

6.61   In *Denton*,[104] the applicant's mother asked him to leave the family home because of his behaviour. The authority found that he had become homeless intentionally, a decision upheld by the Court of Appeal: when people live together, they must show appropriate respect for each other's needs and follow reasonable requests; there had been nothing inappropriate about the rules the mother had laid down.[105] It was relevant that the applicant's last accommodation had been a family home rather than rented accommodation because a child has no enforceable right to remain in his/her family home and therefore has to obey the house rules.[106] Accordingly, when deciding the issue of intentionality, the reasonableness of those rules should be considered.

100 In *Bristol CC v Mousah* (1997) 30 HLR 32, CA, allowing premises to be used in connection with the sale of drugs, even though the tenant was himself absent and was not charged, appears to have been presumed to be capable of giving rise to a finding of intentionality (which should not have prevented the making of an order for possession on the basis of 'reasonableness'; compare also the details of *Darlington BC v Sterling* (1997) 29 HLR 309, CA, summarised above at footnote 31).

101 *R v Wirral MBC ex p Bell* (1994) 27 HLR 234, QBD.

102 Now repeated in the current Code of Guidance para 11.17(ii); Welsh Code para 15.5(i).

103 See para 5.30, above.

104 *Denton v Southwark LBC* [2007] EWCA Civ 623; [2008] HLR 11 at [1].

105 *Denton* at [21].

106 *Denton* at [14].

Pregnancy

6.62 A person does not become homeless intentionally by becoming pregnant,[107] for example, because accommodation is lost (on account of size or for other reasons, such as terms of accommodation), or because it is the family home and the family reject the pregnant woman. (There is an alternative approach to the same point: in some cases, becoming pregnant will not so much have caused the loss of accommodation, as have rendered the accommodation unavailable for the applicant's occupation under HA 1996 s177. To render accommodation unavailable in the statutory sense is not to commit an act which can be treated as intentional homelessness.[108])

Failure to use other remedies

6.63 Two common examples of omission alleged to amount to intentional homelessness are:

a) failure by an evicted private tenant to take civil proceedings to secure re-entry; and

b) failure by a cohabitant or spouse to use domestic remedies.

Each of these examples merits closer consideration.

6.64 Under HA 1996 s175(2), 'a person is also homeless if he has accommodation but . . . he cannot secure entry to it'.[109] This defines as homeless a person who has been locked out of his/her home, and is generally taken to refer to the illegally-evicted occupier.[110] While it is open to an authority to treat an occupier who does not use his/her civil remedies as intentionally homeless, to adopt a policy that all such occupiers must do so would be illegal.[111]

6.65 Detailed provision is now made for cases of domestic and non-domestic violence,[112] and – since the decision in *Bond*[113] – it is clear that in such cases authorities cannot require an applicant to use civil remedies. A person who knows what can be done to prevent violence but deliberately fails to do it has not caused the probability of the domestic violence which makes the continued occupation of that

---

107 *R v Eastleigh BC ex p Beattie (No 1)* (1983) 10 HLR 134, QBD.

108 *Re Islam* [1983] 1 AC 688; (1981) 1 HLR 107, HL. See paras 4.17–4.38, above.

109 See paras 4.62–4.65, above.

110 Code of Guidance para 8.16; Welsh Code para 13.9.

111 See para 4.65, above.

112 See paras 4.82–4.92, above.

113 *Bond v Leicester CC* [2001] EWCA Civ 1544; (2002) HLR 6, CA.

accommodation unreasonable.[114] The probability of violence is to be assessed objectively, by the person carrying out the assessment.[115]

Loss of tied accommodation

6.66   Another common example is loss of tied accommodation.[116] It was not merely accepted in the High Court in *Lewis*[117] that the man's departure from his job, and consequent loss of accommodation, qualified as intentional, but an earlier (and otherwise unreported) challenge to that decision had been, albeit reluctantly, dismissed. Loss of tied accommodation also amounted to intentionality in *Goddard*,[118] and *Jennings*,[119] but the cases were fought on the meaning of 'in consequence' and are, as such, considered below.

6.67   Detailed consideration was given to this problem in *Williams*.[120] The manager of a public house was dismissed for stock and profit irregularities, which he denied. In the course of an appeals procedure, which he pursued with the assistance of his union representative, his employers offered him the choice of resigning or dismissal. He resigned and, while threatened with homelessness, applied to the local authority for accommodation.

6.68   The authority made enquiries of the former employers and concluded:

> My understanding of the circumstances of your resignation lead me to the conclusion that, had you not resigned, the end result would be the same, ie, that events leading up to your appeal against dismissal would be regarded as something 'the likely result of which is that you will be forced to leave accommodation which is available for your occupation and which it would have been reasonable for you to continue to occupy'.

The court interpreted this as:

> . . . saying it was intentional because he resigned. It also seems to go on to say that in any event 'even if you had not resigned you would

---

114 *Bond*, footnote 113, above, at para 33.

115 *Danesh v Kensington and Chelsea RLBC* [2006] EWCA Civ 1404; [2007] HLR 17.

116 See Code of Guidance para 11.20(vii); Welsh Code para. 15.7(vi). Note, however, the Code of Guidance at para 11.15, which states that the secretary of state considers that service personnel required to vacate service quarters as a result of taking up an option to give notice to leave the service should not be considered to have become homeless intentionally.

117 See para 6.10, above.

118 *Goddard v Torridge DC* January 1982 *LAG Bulletin* 9, QBD.

119 *Jennings v Northavon DC* January 1982 *LAG Bulletin* 9, QBD.

120 *R v Thurrock DC ex p Williams* (1981) 1 HLR 128, QBD.

have been dismissed because of your own faults.' In either event, it would have been an intentional homelessness.

6.69   During the course of the judgment, the court likened the position of the applicant to that of a person who had been constructively dismissed for the purposes of employment law:

> Had he gone to an industrial tribunal and complained that he had been unfairly dismissed, it would not have been open to the employers to say by way of answer . . . you resigned, because he would have been able to reply that he resigned only because he had been told that if he did not do so, he would be dismissed.

6.70   This is clearly one basis for distinguishing a resignation from dismissal. But what the authority was seeking to do was to say: either the applicant resigned (intentional homelessness) or he was dismissed (intentional homelessness), and it ignored the 'grey area' of dispute, which had led to the compromise.

6.71   The court analysed the case in stages. It asked:

- why the applicant was homeless (because there had been a possession order against him);
- why a possession order was made (because his contract of employment came to an end);
- why did it end (because he resigned);
- why did he resign (because if he did not do so, he would be dismissed);
- why would he have been dismissed, was it his fault (this was in dispute).

The authority was bound to reach a view as to fault, however hard it was for it to do so.

6.72   The court approved the authority's initial approach to 'job loss cases'. An act the consequences of which can be construed as a deliberate departure can qualify within the provisions; but someone who loses his/her job for incompetence, which will usually comprise a course of conduct spread over a period of time, cannot be said to be carrying out a deliberate act. This would seem to be because s/he would lack the necessary intention, or state of mind, in the absence of clear proof that a course of incompetent conduct had been adopted in order to provoke dismissal.

6.73   *Reeve*[121] was also a case on loss of tied accommodation, although it was as much on the meaning of 'in consequence' as 'deliberate'. A woman worked as a receptionist for a car hire firm and lived above

121   *R v Thanet DC ex p Reeve* (1981) 6 HLR 31, QBD.

the office. She was living with a man. She told her employers that he was not disqualified from driving. In fact he was, and when the employers found out they dismissed her. The authority found that she lost her accommodation because of the misconduct leading to loss of employment, which misconduct was the statement made to the employers.

6.74   This allegation was, at the time of dismissal and indeed at the time of the local authority's decision and of the hearing at the High Court, disputed. Nonetheless, the authority had investigated, and it had concluded that the dismissal was 'for that deliberate act of misconduct'. This was the crucial point of distinction from *Williams* (above):

> Some acts which a person does will lead indirectly to their becoming homeless ... Other acts will be sufficiently proximate to render the person within the category of those who become homeless intentionally ... It is my view that this case probably comes close to the borderline. For it to fall on the right side so far as the local authority are concerned it seems to me that the termination of the employment ... must be lawful. It must be some conduct on the part of the applicant which justifies the employer treating the contract as at an end ...

Sale of jointly owned home

6.75   In *Bellamy*,[122] the applicant was the joint owner of a property with her mother. She applied as homeless when the property was sold, having waived all rights to any of the proceeds of sale in favour of her mother. The authority found her intentionally homeless. On review, the authority rejected the applicant's assertion that she had intended her mother to be the sole owner of the property and concluded that the she had been aware that she had the right to object to the sale and had also been aware that – as a beneficial owner – she had a right to an interest in the property. They found that her failure to object to the sale constituted a deliberate act which caused her to become homeless.

6.76   The decision was quashed at first instance but restored by the Court of Appeal, which held that the authority had been entitled, on the basis of the evidence before it, to conclude that the appellant was a joint legal owner of the property with rights over it, including the right to object to the sale under the Trusts of Land and Appointment of Trustees Act 1996 ss14 and 15. The question for the judge had not been what the appellant and the mother intended when jointly

---

122 *William v Wandsworth LBC; Bellamy v Hounslow LBC* [2006] EWCA Civ 535; [2006] HLR 42.

purchasing the property but whether the authority had been obviously wrong in its understanding of that intention.

Overlap with 'reasonable to continue to occupy'

6.77 The question whether there has been a deliberate act or omission frequently overlaps with the question whether it was reasonable for the applicant to continue to occupy the accommodation.[123] Whether accommodation is accommodation which it would have been reasonable for an applicant to continue to occupy must of course be determined at a time before – and without regard to – the deliberate acts or omissions which led to the loss of that accommodation.[124]

6.78 In *Tinn*,[125] Kennedy J expressed the view that, as a matter of common sense, it cannot be reasonable for someone to continue to occupy accommodation the financial obligations in relation to which s/he can no longer discharge without so straining his/her resources as to deprive him/herself of the ordinary necessities of life.

6.79 Likewise, in *Hawthorne*,[126] the authority's omission to consider whether the applicant's failure to pay rent was caused by the inadequacy of her financial resources allowed her to succeed in her application to quash a finding of intentionality: it was a question the authority was bound to ask.

6.80 See also *Griffiths*,[127] in which the authority was held to have failed to have regard to the family's particular circumstances, and *Bibi*,[128] where the authority had failed to make a finding whether the applicant could reasonably have continued to occupy accommodation, in the light of her stated financial inability to feed her family.

6.81 On the other hand, in *Khan*,[129] the authority was entitled to reach the view that the applicants had not been forced to sell their previous home by reason of financial pressure and, in *Baruwa*,[130] it was said that deciding what were the necessities of life for any particular

---

123 See paras 4.121–4.131, above, and, in particular, now the Homelessness (Suitability of Accommodation) Order 1996 SI No 3204 (para 4.122) and paras 6.140–6.145, below.

124 *Denton v Southwark LBC* [2007] EWCA Civ 623; [2008] HLR 11 at [2] and [25].

125 *R v Hillingdon LBC ex p Tinn* (1988) 20 HLR 305, QBD.

126 *R v Wandsworth LBC ex p Hawthorne* (1994) 27 HLR 59, CA.

127 *R v Shrewsbury and Atcham BC ex p Griffiths* (1993) 25 HLR 613, QBD.

128 *R v Islington LBC ex p Bibi* (1996) 29 HLR 498, QBD.

129 *R v Westminster CC ex p Khan* (1991) 23 HLR 230, QBD. See also *R v Leeds CC ex p Adamiec* (1991) 24 HLR 138, QBD; and *R v Westminster CC ex p Moklis Ali* (1996) 29 HLR 580, QBD.

130 *R v Brent LBC ex p Baruwa* (1997) 29 HLR 915, CA.

family permitted a substantial 'margin of appreciation' for authorities. The authority was accordingly entitled to be satisfied that the applicant had sufficient income, given that – though no longer in work – she was spending £954 on a university course for herself and over £50 per week on nursery education for her child.

In consequence

6.82   The homelessness must be 'in consequence of' the deliberate act or omission. This is a question of 'cause and effect',[131] and the principal issue which has arisen is the attribution of present homelessness to past act or omission. That is to say, there is commonly an act which has or could have been the subject of a finding of intentionality and the argument then becomes whether or not it (that act or omission) is the cause of this homelessness. See also *Bashir Hassan*,[132] where the authority wrongly sought to rely on events which post-dated the onset of homelessness.

6.83   Where there are potentially multiple causes of an applicant's homelessness, the authority must make a careful judgment on the particular facts, looking to see whether homelessness is shown to have been a likely consequence of the applicant's deliberate act, bearing in mind that it is the applicant's own responsibility for his/her homelessness at which the statute is looking.[133] The precise question to be asked and answered relates to the time when the applicant in fact became homeless[134] but the authority is entitled to have regard to events prior to that date.[135]

Cause and effect

6.84   A causal link may continue to subsist following the act of intentionality even though the applicant ceases to be homeless in the interim, for example, because s/he finds some temporary accommodation from which s/he is subsequently evicted: *Awua*.[136]

---

131   *Dyson v Kerrier DC* [1980] 1 WLR 1205, CA; *Din v Wandsworth LBC* [1983] 1 AC 657; (1981) 1 HLR 73, HL.

132   *R v Islington LBC ex p Bashir Hassan* (1995) 27 HLR 485, although compare *R v Newham LBC ex p Campbell* (1993) 26 HLR 183.

133   *Watchman v Ipswich BC* [2007] EWCA Civ 348; [2007] HLR 33 at [22].

134   *Din v Wandsworth LBC* [1983] 1 AC 657.

135   *Watchman* at [23].

136   *R v Brent LBC ex p Awua* [1996] 1 AC 55; 27 HLR 453, HL. See also *Bratton v Croydon LBC* [2002] EWCA Civ 1494; [2002] All ER D 404.

6.85   The authority must look back to the original cause of the home-lessness and determine whether it was intentional.[137] This derives from the wording of the provisions and the distinction between tenses within what is now HA 1996 s191(1) ('is' homeless, but 'be-came' homeless intentionally; see also HA 1996 s189(2), 'has' a prior-ity need', and s191 'is homeless . . . and has a priority need, and did not become homeless intentionally').

6.86   In *Reeve*,[138] Woolf J said:

> It seems to me that the answer to the question of whether or not the council were entitled to take the view which they did of the applicant's conduct depends on the proper interpretation of s17(1) [now s191(1)]. It appears to me that the use of the words 'in consequence' in that subsection does raise problems of causation. Really, what is involved in deciding whether or not the applicant is right is a decision as to remoteness . . .

6.87   In *ex p P*,[139] Schiemann J observed that causation was a notorious minefield in jurisprudence and philosophy. The authority was en-titled to conclude that the misbehaviour of the applicants – resulting in threats from the IRA causing them to have to leave their home – was something 'in consequence of which' the applicants had ceased to occupy accommodation.

6.88   In *Hinds*,[140] the applicant undertook to leave the matrimonial home to avoid an ouster order; this led to termination of the secure tenancy. The authority's conclusion that his violence towards his wife had caused the loss of accommodation was upheld.

6.89   In *Aranda*,[141] the judge applied a 'but for' test. The applicant re-ceived a grant of £20,000 from the authority to give up a secure tenancy (so as to live in Columbia). The matters relied on by the authority, in-cluding the grant, were matters 'but for' which she might never have gone to Columbia at all, rather than matters but for which the appli-cant would have continued in occupation of the property in Colum-bia. Accordingly, they could not be considered deliberate acts which had caused the applicant's loss of (the Columbian) accommodation.

6.90   In *Robinson v Torbay BC*,[142] it was said that the loss of the home

---

137 *Din v Wandsworth LBC* [1983] 1 AC 657; (1981) 1 HLR 73, HL.
138 *R v Thanet DC ex p Reeve* (1981) 6 HLR 31, QBD.
139 *R v Hammersmith & Fulham LBC ex p P* (1989) 22 HLR 21, QBD.
140 *R v Islington LBC ex p Hinds* (1995) 28 HLR 302, CA.
141 *R v Camden LBC ex p Aranda* (1996) 28 HLR 672, QBD.
142 [1982] 1 All ER 726, QBD.

must be the 'reasonable result' of the deliberate act. This approach was adopted in *Reid*.[143]

6.91   Thus, in *R v Hounslow LBC ex p R*,[144] the applicant had terminated his tenancy when he was sentenced to seven years' imprisonment for indecent assault, as he could no longer pay his rent. In considering whether he was intentionally homeless, the test correctly applied was whether ceasing to occupy the accommodation would reasonably have been regarded at the time as a likely consequence of the deliberate conduct.

6.92   *Ex p R* was approved in *Stewart v Lambeth LBC*,[145] where the applicant lost his home after being convicted of drug dealing. In *Goodger v Ealing LBC*,[146] the Court of Appeal described the decision of a review panel that an applicant had become homeless intentionally by breaching a prohibition in his tenancy agreement against drug dealing from the property – which had led to a term of six years' imprisonment – as being the only decision possible in the circumstances, so much so that what might otherwise have been the procedural unfairness[147] of failing to disclose his housing file until a few days before the review hearing was irrelevant.

6.93   The decision in *City of Gloucester v Miles*[148] may also be considered to turn on cause and effect. The applicant had left her home for a period of time, but had not clearly or certainly quit it. During her absence, her estranged husband returned and caused damage which rendered the property entirely uninhabitable. As she was not a party to the vandalism, she had done nothing that could be classed as intentional, even though she might subsequently have lost the property either through failing to resume residence or because arrears had accrued and there was a threat of proceedings.

6.94   The authority must clearly act reasonably in regarding present homelessness as being caused by a departure from earlier accommodation. In *Krishnan*,[149] Birmingham City Council was putting pressure on owner-occupiers to reduce overcrowding in their premises.

---

143 *R v Westminster CC ex p Reid* (1994) 26 HLR 691, QBD.

144 (1997) 29 HLR 939, QBD.

145 *Stewart v Lambeth LBC* [2002] EWCA Civ 753, [2002] HLR 40.

146 [2002] EWCA Civ 751, [2003] HLR 6.

147 See para 12.57, below.

148 (1985) 17 HLR 292, CA, referred to in the Court of Appeal in *Puhlhofer* (1985) 17 HLR 558, CA, but not criticised either in that case at the House of Lords ([1986] AC 484; 18 HLR 158) or in *R v Brent LBC ex p Awua* [1996] 1 AC 55; 27 HLR 453, HL.

149 *Krishnan v Hillingdon LBC* January 1981 *LAG Bulletin* 137, QBD.

A family of relatives sharing the home were offered accommodation by another relative in Uxbridge, until such time as they could afford to buy their own house. At the same time, there was a possibility of promotion if the family could move to London. Subsequently, the Uxbridge relative decided to sell his house and move to Canada, at which point the family became homeless.

6.95 The authority considered that the family could reasonably have gone on occupying the Birmingham property – on which point its decision was not upheld – and took the view that the Uxbridge arrangement was only temporary.[150] On this, too, its decision was set aside by the court:

> I also hold that the Council's officers made insufficient enquiry as to the state of knowledge and expectations of the Plaintiff with regard to the availability of his accommodation at Uxbridge at the time when he moved here. Mrs Bates states in her note . . . that the Plaintiff did not deny that his accommodation at [Uxbridge] was temporary. That, however, was not the point. The word 'temporary' can aptly cover a considerable period. Thus, accommodation held on a tenancy for a year or more can rightly be described as temporary.
>
> As I have already indicated, the Plaintiff's expectation at the time when he moved . . . was that the accommodation there would be available for him for at least a year. It follows as it seems to me that if the Council's officers had been aware of that fact they might well have taken the view that the Plaintiff became homeless not because he moved to [Uxbridge] from . . . Birmingham, but because the Plaintiff's cousin changed his mind about the length of time for which he was willing to accommodate the Plaintiff and his family . . .

6.96 Similarly, in *Rose*,[151] although decided on the meaning of 'deliberate', the point may as easily be made that an earlier departure had not caused the homelessness: what had caused the homelessness was the loss of the intervening, temporary accommodation, which the applicant had not appreciated was – or was likely to be – temporary.

6.97 In *Gliddon*,[152] the applicants quit private-sector accommodation. Initially, they had been granted a tenancy. The landlord alleged that they had obtained it by deception and compelled them to enter into a licence agreement in substitution. It was the loss of accommodation under licence which was the immediate cause of the homelessness.

6.98 At first, the authority advised the applicants to await court proceedings for determination of their status; the court held that this was a

150 Ie, unsettled, cf, para 6.101, below.
151 *R v Wandsworth LBC ex p Rose* (1983) 11 HLR 105, QBD.
152 *R v Exeter CC ex p Gliddon* (1984) 14 HLR 103, QBD.

valid approach.[153] On the applicants' failure to follow this advice, however, the authority reached a new decision, based on the deception pursuant to which the accommodation had been obtained, and concluded that it had therefore been lost by the applicants' own fault.

6.99　　In the light of this finding of fact by the authority, however, the authority could no longer conclude that the applicants could reasonably have remained in occupation. Accordingly, the accommodation obtained by deception ought to have been ignored and the authority was obliged to look back instead to the loss of the applicants' previous accommodation.

Breaking the chain of causation

6.100　The question, then, becomes one of how the chain of causation between an act causing homelessness and current homelessness may be broken.

6.101　　Where the applicant has enjoyed a period of 'settled accommodation'[154] or 'other than temporary accommodation',[155] this will break the chain.[156] However, there is no reverse corollary: acquisition and loss of settled accommodation is not the only means of breaking the chain; the fact that what has been lost is unsettled does not mean that the applicant is still homeless intentionally.[157]

Settled accommodation

6.102　The concept of settled accommodation was developed by the judiciary – under the Housing (Homeless Persons) Act 1977 and under Housing Act 1985 Part 3 – and was used in a number of different contexts:

a) Housing Act 1985 s58(1) (definition of homelessness);

b) Housing Act 1985 s60(1) (intentionality: whether what was quit could give rise to a finding of intentionality/whether there had been a break in a period of intentionality);

c) Housing Act 1985 s65(2) (discharge of duty in relation to unintentionally homeless).

153　Below, paras 6.141–6.145.
154　*Din v Wandsworth LBC* [1983] 1 AC 657; (1981) 1 HLR 73, HL, per Lord Wilberforce, adopting Ackner LJ in the Court of Appeal.
155　*Din*, footnote 154, above, per Lord Lowry.
156　*R v Brent LBC ex p Awua* [1996] 1 AC 55; 27 HLR 453, HL. See also *Mohammed v Westminster CC* [2004] EWCA Civ 796; [2005] HLR 47.
157　Below, paras 6.118–6.130.

Following the decision in *Awua*,[158] however, the distinction between settled and unsettled accommodation is now only relevant to the question whether the chain of causation has been broken.[159]

6.103 In *Din*, where the concept of settled accommodation first emerged, it was said to be a question of 'fact and degree'.

6.104 A variety of circumstances may lead to accommodation being found to be unsettled. One relates to the physical conditions in the property, another, to the security of tenure which an applicant had, which is often linked to how long the applicant has occupied the accommodation.

Physical conditions

6.105 If these are very poor the accommodation will not be treated as settled.[160] In *Mohammed*,[161] one of the reasons accommodation occupied by the applicant was not settled was because it was severely overcrowded.

Security/temporal conditions

6.106 Most of the cases have turned on security.

6.107 *Ruffle*[162] concerned a family who had earlier applied to the authority and been found intentionally homeless. That decision was not contested. The applicants subsequently moved into the flat of a council tenant under an arrangement which was intended to be permanent but which broke down after a few months through no fault of their own. The family returned to the authority, which decided that they were still intentionally homeless because the intervening period had not 'been one in settled occupation which would give rise to a new cause of homelessness'.

---

158 *R v Brent LBC ex p Awua* [1996] 1 AC 55; 27 HLR 453, HL. See para 6.84, above.

159 See para 6.101, above. As it was the concept as already developed that was preserved by *Awua*, albeit only for this purpose, it is appropriate to consider pre-*Awua* cases alongside subsequent decisions.

160 See the early cases of *R v South Herefordshire DC ex p Miles* (1983) 17 HLR 82; *City of Gloucester v Miles* (1985) 17 HLR 292; *R v Dinefwr BC ex p Marshall* (1984) 17 HLR 310, which notwithstanding their disapproval in *R v Hillingdon LBC ex p Puhlhofer* [1986] AC 484, on the question of whether the accommodation was so physically poor the applicant was homeless, remain illustrative of when the physical condition of a property is so bad that it cannot be considered settled.

161 *Mohammed v Westminster CC* [2005] EWCA Civ 796; [2005] HLR 47. See para 6.116, below.

162 *R v Merton LBC ex p Ruffle* (1988) 21 HLR 361.

6.108   The applicants argued that the authority had asked the wrong question: it should have asked not whether the intervening accommodation was settled, but whether it was obviously temporary. There was a spectrum of accommodation of which 'settled' and 'obviously temporary' were only the extremes. The applicants contended that they needed only to have secured something more than the least secure type of accommodation in order to have ended homelessness and broken the chain, not the most secure.

6.109   The judge disagreed:[163]

> I think that one or the other term encompasses all states of accommodation. Thus, it is correct to contrast, as the various cases do, settled or permanent accommodation on the one hand with less than secure accommodation, variously described as precarious or temporary or transient on the other ... [For] the authority to ask themselves ... has the intervening period been one of settled accommodation occupation, involves asking the same question as whether the accommodation was only temporary. These questions are merely the opposite sides of the same coin.[164]

6.110   In *Evans*,[165] a couple left a secure tenancy for larger premises in the private sector, purportedly on a bed and breakfast basis. There was, however, a strong argument that they had full Rent Act protection. Following threats of – and actual – violence from their landlord, the couple left the new accommodation. The authority's decision that they were intentionally homeless was quashed because the authority had failed to consider whether the new accommodation, with security, had been settled.

6.111   Authorities are not bound to accept the applicant's view as to whether accommodation was settled. In *Cadney*,[166] a woman sought to rely on a period of three months during which she had moved out of the matrimonial home and into the home of another man. Their relationship was not successful and she left. She sought to rely on this as a period of intervening accommodation, because she had intended to stay with him permanently. The court considered this too

---

163 *Ruffle*, footnote 162, above, at 366.

164 Simon Brown J (given the later decision in *Awua*, somewhat presciently) contemplated an alternative analysis, which he considered contains possible tensions, of three possible types of accommodation: one so tenuous that it is discounted altogether; one which is sufficient to preclude homelessness; and a further type, 'settled' accommodation, which is required to break the chain of intentionality.

165 *R v Swansea CC ex p Evans* (1990) 22 HLR 467, CA.

166 *R v Purbeck DC ex p Cadney* (1985) 17 HLR 534, QBD.

subjective an approach. The authority had been entitled to take the view that it was a transient or precarious arrangement, ie, that an objective test could be applied.[167]

6.112 In *Ashton*,[168] the authority's decision that occupation of premises under a tenancy falling within the exception in Housing Act 1985 Sch 1 para 5[169] was not occupation of settled accommodation was upheld, entitling the authority to look back to the previous accommodation.

6.113 Length of time will be important in establishing whether accommodation is settled: see *Easom*,[170] in which it was open to the authority to conclude that accommodation was not settled – over several years – because the applicants had at all times been illegal immigrants to Australia who might have been deported at any moment.

6.114 In *Ajayi*,[171] Dyson J reiterated that whether accommodation was settled is a question of fact and degree. The applicant had lived with family friends (in the first instance for a period of 20 months, and in the second for some nine months) since leaving her family home in Nigeria. The authority concluded that in neither case had the accommodation been settled. The term 'settled accommodation' was an ordinary English expression, not a term of art. Although when the applicant moved in with her friends the duration of the accommodation had been uncertain, the authority was entitled – having regard to the circumstances – to conclude that it had been precarious.

6.115 The fact and degree test was restated in *Knight*,[172] where the question was whether occupation of a property under a six-month assured shorthold tenancy could amount to settled accommodation for the purpose of breaking the chain of causation. Although the Court of Appeal accepted that such occupation was capable of constituting settled accommodation, it did not as a matter of law always do so.[173] The question remained one of fact and degree to be determined by the authority. In the circumstances of the particular case, it was open to the authority to find that the accommodation was not settled, because the applicant had known from the outset that the tenancy was only for six months and would not be renewed.

---

167 See also *R v Merton LBC ex p Ruffle* (1988) 21 HLR 361.
168 *R v Winchester CC ex p Ashton* (1991) 24 HLR 48, QBD; (1991) 24 HLR 520, CA.
169 Temporary accommodation for persons taking up employment.
170 *R v Croydon LBC ex p Easom* (1992) 25 HLR 262, QBD.
171 *R v Hackney LBC ex p Ajayi* (1997) 30 HLR 473, QBD.
172 *Knight v Vale Royal BC* [2003] EWCA Civ 1258; [2004] HLR 9.
173 It was suggested, however, at [25] that, where accommodation is let on an assured shorthold tenancy, it is normally a significant pointer to it being settled.

Combination of factors

6.116   The applicant in *Mohammed*[174] also took an assured shorthold tenancy. She was evicted after 12 months because of a shortfall in housing benefit leading to arrears of rent. The authority on review considered that the accommodation was not settled for three reasons:

a) the applicant had obtained the accommodation with a view to making a second application to the authority as homeless;[175]

b) she could not afford the rent for the accommodation; and

c) the accommodation was overcrowded.

The Court of Appeal held that the reviewing officer was entitled to have regard to all these matters in reaching his decision.

6.117   An argument that a period of imprisonment could amount to settled accommodation was rejected in *Stewart*.[176]

Breaking the chain by other means

6.118   Whether acquisition of settled accommodation is the only means of breaking the causal link was expressly reserved in *Awua*.[177]

6.119   That question was considered by the Court of Appeal in *Fahia*.[178] The applicant had been found intentionally homeless by the authority and housed temporarily in a guest house. She remained in the guest house for over a year, her rent paid by housing benefit. A subsequent review of her housing benefit led to payments being cut and she was, in consequence, evicted from the guest house.

6.120   The authority decided that it had no new duty towards the applicant because the accommodation at the guest house did not constitute intervening settled accommodation such as to break the causal link with the applicant's original intentional homelessness.

6.121   The Court of Appeal rejected this approach and decided that events other than securing settled accommodation could break the chain; it remitted the case to the authority to decide whether the change in housing benefit had constituted such an event.

6.122   The court expressly approved the earlier decision in *Bassett*[179] as an example of a break in the chain of causation otherwise than by

174 *Mohammed v Westminster CC* [2005] EWCA Civ 796; [2005] HLR 47.

175 See now below, para 6.146.

176 *Stewart v Lambeth LBC* [2002] EWCA Civ 753; [2002] HLR 40.

177 *Stewart v Lambeth LBC* [2002] EWCA Civ 753; [2002] HLR 40.

178 *R v Harrow LBC ex p Fahia* (1997) 29 HLR 974, CA (not overruled by the House of Lords on this point, see [1998] 1 WLR 1396; (1998) 30 HLR 1124).

179 *R v Basingstoke & Deane BC ex p Bassett* (1983) 10 HLR 125, QBD.

settled accommodation. In that case, temporary accommodation had been lost not because of its temporary quality, but because the applicant had been staying with her sister-in-law and had to leave when she separated from her husband.

6.123   Although *Fahia* went to the House of Lords, the authority abandoned its appeal on this aspect.[180]

6.124   In subsequent cases, following *Fahia* at the Court of Appeal (and its approval of *Bassett*), it has been held that the subsequent event must be unconnected to the temporary nature of the accommodation.

6.125   Thus, in *Harvey*,[181] the applicant was evicted from his home for noise nuisance and moved in with a friend. After four months, the friend was taken into hospital and the applicant had to move out. The loss of the friend's accommodation did not break the chain of causation because it could not be said to be unconnected with the temporary or unsettled nature of the accommodation the applicant had been occupying.[182]

6.126   Likewise, in *Ajayi*,[183] the applicant left accommodation in Nigeria and moved to London where she stayed with various friends and acquaintances. She moved in with one friend in January 1996, at the same time as she discovered she was pregnant and, on the birth of the baby, was asked to leave. The chain of causation had not been broken. The real and effective cause of her homelessness was not the pregnancy but leaving her accommodation in Nigeria.

6.127   A term of imprisonment cannot amount to a supervening event which breaks the chain of causation.[184]

6.128   A slightly different question was posed in *Din*[185] – whether an act which at its inception was one causing intentional homelessness can cease to qualify as such merely through the passage of time, ie, whether it can become 'spent'?

6.129   In that case, a family were living in accommodation under extremely trying circumstances, and would ultimately have had to leave, but they were advised by the authority to remain in occupation until a

---

180 *R v Harrow LBC ex p Fahia* (1997) 29 HLR 974, CA, at p1130.

181 *R v Brighton BC ex p Harvey* (1997) 30 HLR 670, QBD.

182 For instance, because the hospitalisation was no different from being asked to leave, which could have happened at any time due to the temporary nature of the accommodation: *Harvey*, footnote 181, above, at 678.

183 *R v Hackney LBC ex p Ajayi* (1997) 30 HLR 473, QBD.

184 *Stewart v Lambeth LBC* [2002] EWCA Civ 753; [2002] HLR 40. See also above, para 6.117 – prison is not settled accommodation.

185 *Din v Wandsworth LBC* [1983] 1 AC 657; (1981) 1 HLR 73, HL.

court order was made.[186] It was common ground, at least on appeal, that if an application had been made immediately after the departure, the authority could have found the family to be homeless intentionally, because at that date it would have been reasonable to remain in occupation (see further below), whereas, on application at a later date, it was conceded by the authority that the family would by then have become homeless in any event, and not intentionally so.[187]

6.130 　During the interim period, the family had stayed with relatives and it was not argued that there had, on that account, been a break in the homelessness. Rather, it was argued that the original cause of homelessness had ceased to be effective because the family would have become homeless unintentionally by the time of application. This argument was upheld in the county court, but dismissed on appeal. The question was whether the present period of homelessness had, at its inception, been intentional. The fact that the applicants would have become homeless unintentionally by the date of application was simply irrelevant.[188]

Cessation of occupation

Accommodation abroad

6.131　The accommodation which has been lost can be accommodation abroad and the act causing its loss can be an act abroad.

6.132　In *de Falco*,[189] the reason given by the authority for finding intentional homelessness was that the family in question had come to the UK without arranging permanent accommodation. That reason was patently bad on its face. It was upheld by the Court of Appeal, however, by expanding it – against the factual background – to refer to a departure from accommodation in Italy. That this approach had been devised by the Court of Appeal was made clear in *Paris*,[190] where the authority used the same wording as in *de Falco* and was held to have erred because it had failed actually to consider the accommodation which had been quit and the circumstances of departure from it.

186　Below, paras 6.140–6.145.
187　There was no defence to the landlord's proposed proceedings for possession and the order would have already taken effect.
188　See also *R v Brent LBC ex p Yusuf* (1995) 29 HLR 48, QBD.
189　*De Falco, Silvestri v Crawley BC* [1980] QB 460, CA.
190　*R v Reigate and Banstead BC ex p Paris* (1984) 17 HLR 103, QBD.

Short-term accommodation

6.133 Where the authority is providing temporary housing pending a permanent allocation, its loss may lead to a finding of intentionality: *Hunt.*[191]

6.134 In *Conway*,[192] the applicant failed to renew a protected shorthold tenancy. It was held that this could amount to a deliberate omission (although on the facts, it had not been).[193]

Notional occupation

6.135 In *Islam*,[194] at the Court of Appeal, it was argued that the accommodation lost had not been available for the occupation of the applicant and his family (who had recently arrived from Bangladesh).[195] One of the grounds advanced for upholding the decision in the court below was therefore that the applicant – while living in a shared single room in Uxbridge – had at all material times nonetheless been in 'notional occupation' of the family home in Bangladesh, through his wife and children. Another suggestion was that the accommodation available for, and occupied by, the family was made up of the family home in Bangladesh and the room in Uxbridge.

6.136 The House of Lords rejected both of these approaches:

> The Master of the Rolls was . . . using the word occupation in an artificial sense, which . . . is quite inconsistent with its ordinary meaning and with the probably narrower sense in which it is used in the Act. When it speaks of occupying accommodation, the Act has in contemplation people who are residing in that accommodation . . .

6.137 Applicants may, however, be held to be occupying accommodation even though they are not physically residing in it. In *Khan*,[196] the applicants represented to immigration authorities that they would be living in a house, which the first applicant subsequently sold. The applicants never occupied the house although the first applicant's

---

191 *R v East Hertfordshire DC ex p Hunt* (1985) 18 HLR 51, QBD. The basis for the decision was politely criticised (described as 'heroic') in *Awua*, but the outcome remains correct. Furthermore, in such circumstances the authority will be considered to have discharged its duty to the applicant: see HA 1996 s193(6)(b) – below, para 10.152.

192 *R v Christchurch BC ex p Conway* (1987) 19 HLR 238, QBD.

193 See above, para 6.34.

194 *Re Islam* [1983] 1 AC 688; (1981) 1 HLR 107, HL.

195 See para 4.28, above.

196 *R v Westminster CC ex p Khan* (1991) 23 HLR 230, QBD.

family had done so. This was held to be sufficient occupation for the purposes of intentionality so that, on sale of the house, the applicants could be considered to have ceased to occupy it.

6.138   In *Lee-Lawrence*,[197] the applicant had to leave his home because it became uninhabitable following an arson attack. He accepted the offer of a tenancy elsewhere, on which he claimed housing benefit, but, when he subsequently applied as homeless, he asserted that he had never in fact occupied the new property. The Court of Appeal held that the fact that a person had a legal right to possession or held the keys was not, of itself, sufficient to establish occupation; nonetheless, those factors combined with the claim for housing benefit and other representations by the applicant that he had been resident in the premises, were sufficient to support a finding of occupancy.

Available for occupation

6.139   This has been considered in chapter 4.[198]

Reasonable to continue to occupy

6.140   It must have been reasonable to continue to occupy the accommodation which has been lost. This has also been considered in chapter 4,[199] to which reference should be made, but there are circumstances which are particular to findings of intentionality which merit mention. This is particularly true where advice has been given to the applicant by the authority prior to departure from the accommodation.[200]

6.141   In *Hughes*[201] it appeared that an alleged winter letting might not fall within the provisions of Rent Act 1977 Sch 15 case 13, so that there would be no mandatory ground for possession. The occupier was accordingly advised to await the outcome of proceedings but did not do so:

> The important point which this application raises . . . is the question as to what extent an authority exercising its powers under [the] Act is entitled to say to a person . . . 'You should remain in accommodation which you at present occupy and not leave that accommodation until there is a court order made against you requiring you to vacate . . .'

197 *Lee-Lawrence v Penwith DC* [2006] EWCA Civ 507.

198 Above, paras 4.17–4.38.

199 Above, paras 4.69–4.140.

200 See also *F v Birmingham CC* [2006] EWCA Civ 1427; [2007] HLR 18, above, para 6.40, and *Ugiagbe v Southwark LBC* [2009] EWCA Civ 31, above, para 6.39.

201 *R v Penwith DC ex p Hughes* August 1980 *LAG Bulletin* 187, QBD.

> [W]here there is a situation which is doubtful or difficult, it is rea-
> sonable for the authority to give advice to a person who is a prospec-
> tive candidate for assistance under the ... Act ... that they should not
> vacate the accommodation which they are at present occupying with-
> out the order of the court because otherwise they may be regarded as
> persons intentionally homeless.

6.142 In *Adamiec*,[202] the failure of an applicant to heed advice not to sell his
home resulted in a finding of intentionality which was upheld, as,
although he might ultimately have been forced to sell because of his
financial circumstances, that was a stage he had not yet reached.

6.143 Whether it is reasonable for an applicant to continue to occupy
the accommodation is to be judged at the time that the conduct in
consequence of which the accommodation was lost took place, not at
some later date when the applicant actually left the accommodation:
ex p P.[203]

6.144 Whether it is reasonable to continue to occupy may be affected by
whether alternative accommodation will be available if the applicants
remain in their present accommodation in the short term.[204] See
also *McIlory*,[205] in which Catholic applicants left accommodation in
Northern Ireland after being subjected to several years of harassment
by Protestant factions, culminating in a shooting incident. A finding
of intentionality was upheld on the ground that they had failed to
wait and see whether they would be rehoused by the Northern Ireland Housing Executive. This may be contrasted with *McManus*,[206]
where the applicant lived in a house in Belfast just off a road which
was the dividing line between the two main religious groups and
the scene of much sectarian violence. The applicant left her home
and went to London where she applied for homelessness assistance;
the authority found her to have become homeless intentionally. Her
challenge was successful: the authority should have examined the
effect of the situation in Belfast on the applicant and her daughter
and focused on the particular area of Belfast where they lived, which
the evidence suggested was particularly prone to the worst sectarian
violence in the city.[207]

---

202 *R v Leeds CC ex p Adamiec* (1991) 24 HLR 138, QBD. See too *R v Westminster
CC ex p Moklis Ali* (1996) 29 HLR 580, QBD.
203 *R v Hammersmith & Fulham LBC ex p P* (1989) 22 HLR 21, QBD. See also
Denton v Southwark LBC [2007] EWCA Civ 623; [2008] HLR 11.
204 *R v Hammersmith & Fulham LBC ex p P* (1989) 22 HLR 21, QBD.
205 *R v Newham LBC ex p McIlory* (1991) 23 HLR 570, QBD.
206 *R v Brent LBC ex p McManus* (1993) 25 HLR 643 at 645 and 646.
207 *McManus* at 648.

6.145   In *Wilson*,[208] the court, albeit with some hesitation, held that it had not been reasonable for a woman to remain in accommodation in Australia because (a) she had no legal permission to remain, and (b) she was pregnant and would shortly have reached the stage of pregnancy when she would not have been able to fly back to the UK.

Extended definition – collusive arrangements

6.146   Housing Act 1996 s191(3) contains the extended definition of intentionality, under which a person is to be treated as intentionally homeless if s/he enters into an arrangement pursuant to which s/he has to cease to occupy accommodation, which it would have been reasonable for him/her to continue to occupy,[209] and the purpose of the arrangement is to enable him/her to become entitled to assistance under HA 1996 Part 7, and there is no other good reason why the applicant is homeless.

6.147   This provision is aimed at arrangements designed to give an impression of being obliged to leave accommodation[210] which would have been reasonable to continue to occupy, so as to create an apparent right to assistance under Part 7.

6.148   If it would not have been accommodation which it was reasonable to continue to occupy in any event, the arrangement may be disregarded, although this would not prevent the authority looking back to the loss of any previous accommodation which may properly be considered to be the cause of the present homelessness.

6.149   The Code[211] suggests that collusion is not confined to those staying with friends or relatives, but can also arise between landlords and tenants:

> Housing authorities, while relying on experience, nonetheless need to be satisfied that collusion exists, and must not merely rely on hearsay or unfounded suspicions.[212]

6.150   Even if the subsection is prima facie applicable, there must also be no other 'good reason' for the homelessness. Examples of 'other good

---

208 *R v Hillingdon LBC ex p Wilson* (1983) 12 HLR 61, QBD.
209 See paras 4.69–4.140 and 6.140–6.145.
210 Note that it does not also have to have been 'available for . . . occupation'.
211 Code of Guidance para 11.28; Welsh Code para 15.10.
212 This is true for all decision-making (see chapter 9) but may be a particular problem in reaching decisions on collusion.

reasons' include overcrowding or an obvious breakdown in relationships between the applicant and the 'host' household or landlord.[213]

6.151 It seems that authorities do not frequently find collusive arrangements. A rare example is to be found in *Lomotey v Enfield LBC*,[214]
where the claimant surrendered her joint interest in a property to
her brother, who then evicted her.

---

213 Code of Guidance para 11.28; Welsh Code para. 15.10.
214 [2004] EWCA Civ 627; [2004] HLR 45.

CHAPTER 7

Local connection

Introduction

7.1　The local connection provisions of Housing Act (HA) 1996 Part 7 allow one authority to pass on to another the burden of securing that permanent accommodation is made available to an applicant. The provisions operate only in specified circumstances. It was one of the principal aims of the Housing (Homeless Persons) Act 1977 to end 'shuttling' homeless people between different local authorities, each alleging there was 'greater' connection with the other.[1] The provisions have been described[2] as 'curiously reminiscent of one of the features of the old Poor Law 1601, whereby paupers could be sent back to the parishes where they had a settlement'.

7.2　The local connection provisions represent a mixture of substance and procedure, and of binding law and voluntary agreement. In this chapter, reference will be made not only to Part 7 and the Code of Guidance (see appendix C), but also to the document known as the Local Authority Agreement[3] and a statutory instrument governing arbitration of disputes between authorities.[4]

7.3　It may be helpful to restate, in outline, how and when these provisions operate, before proceeding to consider them in detail. The local connection provisions exempt an authority to which application has been made (the 'notifying' authority) from the duty to secure that accommodation is made available under HA 1996 s193.[5] This duty passes to the 'notified' authority.[6]

7.4　The circumstances in which this may occur are set out in some detail:

　– there must be no local connection with the area of the notifying authority;
　– there must be a local connection with the area of the notified authority; and
　– there must be no risk of violence in the area of the notified authority.[7]

All three conditions must usually be fulfilled before the local connection provisions can be relied on. Part 7, however, introduced a new

---

1　See chapter 1.
2　*R v Slough BC ex p Ealing LBC* [1981] QB 801, CA, per Lord Denning MR.
3　See Code of Guidance annex 18, appendix C, below.
4　Homelessness (Decisions on Referrals) Order 1998 SI No 1578, see appendix B, below.
5　HA 1996 s200(1).
6　HA 1996 s200(4).
7　HA 1996 s198(2) and (2A).

condition for referral, where the applicant had previously applied to another authority – within a specified period – which authority had (in pursuance of its duties under Part 7) accommodated him/her in the area of the authority to which the applicant has now made a new application.[8] This condition is free-standing, ie, the authority to which the new application is made may make a referral back to the first authority regardless of whether any of the other conditions can be established.

7.5   In the event of a dispute between the two (or more) authorities, the first stage will be to try to resolve it by reference to the Local Authority Agreement.[9] In default of agreement, the matter must be referred to arbitration.[10] Pending the resolution of the dispute, principal responsibility for the homeless person or family rests with the authority to which application was initially made, ie, the notifying authority.[11]

7.6   The matters which must be considered are:

a) What is a local connection?
b) When are the local connection provisions applicable?
c) Procedure on prospective reference.
d) Resolution of disputes.
e) Post-resolution procedure.

What is a local connection?

7.7   The term 'local connection' is defined in HA 1996 s199.[12] A person may have a local connection with the district of an authority based on one of four grounds:

a) because s/he is, or in the past was, normally resident in it, and his/her residence is or was of his/her own choice;
b) because s/he is employed in it;
c) because of family associations; and
d) because of any special circumstances.[13]

---

8   HA 1996 s198(4).
9   HA 1996 s198(5).
10 HA 1996 s198(5).
11 HA 1996 s200(1).
12 It may be noted that the provisions do not apply in relation to the Isles of Scilly, where there is a requirement of residence of two years and six months during the previous three years: Homelessness (Isles of Scilly) Order 1997 SI No 797.
13 HA 1996 s199(1).

7.8   In addition, special provisions apply to applicants who have previously been housed by the UK Borders Agency (UKBA).[14]

7.9   It is important not to pay so much attention to the four grounds that insufficient regard is had to the words 'local connection' themselves: see *Re Betts*.[15]

7.10   In that case, the applicant was living with his family in the area of Blaby DC between 1978 and 1980. In August 1980, he got a job in Southampton, and moved into a houseboat in the area, where he was joined by his family. In October 1980, he was given a house by Eastleigh BC. Soon after, however, he lost his job through no fault of his own, fell into arrears with his rent, and was evicted. In February 1981, shortly before the order for possession expired, he applied under the Housing (Homeless Persons) Act 1977. Eastleigh BC referred the application to Blaby DC. The reason given for the decision was that the family had lived in Eastleigh BC's district for less than six months, and was not, accordingly, normally resident in its area. The applicant challenged this decision.

7.11   The Court of Appeal allowed the challenge.[16] The only reason given for the finding that the family was not normally resident in the area was that the family had lived in the area for less than six months, and this decision had been reached by rigid application of the Local Authority Agreement.[17] Normal residence was where a person intended to settle, not necessarily permanently or indefinitely, and a person may have more than one normal residence at different times. It requires consideration of many features of residence, not merely the application of a six-month, or any other arbitrary, period.

7.12   Allowing the authority's appeal, the House of Lords held that the fundamental question was whether or not the applicant had a local connection with the area. This meant more than 'normal residence'. Normal residence, and the other specified grounds of local connection, are subsidiary components of the formula to be applied. The formula is governed by the proposition that residence of any sort will be irrelevant unless and until it is such as to establish a local connection.[18]

---

14   The United Kingdom Borders Agency was set up in February 2008. Asylum support was previously administered by the National Asylum Support Service which was part of the Home Office. See paras 7.31–7.34, below; see further paras 13.32–13.43, below.

15   *Re Betts* [1983] 2 AC 613; (1983) 10 HLR 97, HL.

16   *Betts v Eastleigh BC* [1983] 1 WLR 774; (1983) 8 HLR 28, CA.

17   See below, paras 7.60–7.66.

18   This approach has been followed in *R v Islington LBC ex p Adigun* (1986) 20 HLR 600, QBD and *R v Westminster CC ex p Benniche* (1996) 29 HLR 230, CA.

7.13   The House of Lords did not dissent from the Court of Appeal's analysis of 'residence' (based on the decision in *R v Barnet LBC ex p Shah*,[19] under the Education Act 1962). Nor did it dissent from the proposition that a rigid application of the Local Authority Agreement would constitute a fetter on the authority's discretion.[20] The Agreement could, however, certainly be taken into account, and applied as a guideline, provided an authority does not shut out the particular facts of the individual case, ie, provided its *application* is given individual consideration.[21] In the present case, the House of Lords found that the authority had not misdirected itself in this respect.

Relevant time for determining local connection

7.14   When seeking to establish whether an applicant has a local connection with a particular area, the authority must look at the facts at the time of the decision. If there is a review of the decision,[22] it is the facts at the date of the review which must be considered.[23] An applicant may not have a local connection with an authority at the time of his/her application, but may acquire one subsequently, either prior to a decision or between decision and review, for example, by obtaining permanent employment or through normal residence in the area.[24]

Residence

7.15   Residence has to be 'of choice'.[25] There is no residence of choice if the applicant, or a person who might reasonably be expected to reside with him/her, is detained under the authority of any Act of Parliament.[26] Thus, prisoners (whether or not convicted) and those detained under the Mental Health Act 1983 will not acquire a local connection with the area in which the prison or hospital is situated.

---

19 [1983] 2 AC 309, HL.
20 See para 12.44, below.
21 See also *Ozbek v Ispwich BC* [2006] EWCA Civ 534; [2006] HLR 41, at [39] where Chadwick LJ stated that the need for a common basis of decision-making meant that there was an 'imperative for all authorities to apply the guidelines generally to all applications which come before them'.
22 See chapter 9.
23 *Mohamed v Hammersmith & Fulham RLBC* [2001] UKHL 57; [2002] HLR 7, HL.
24 See further para 9.180, below.
25 HA 1996 s199(1)(a).
26 HA 1996 s199(3).

The secretary of state has power to specify further circumstances in which residence is not to be considered 'of choice',[27] although this power has not been exercised.

7.16   Prior to 1 December 2008, residence resulting from service in the armed forces did not constitute residence 'of choice' for serving members of the armed forces.[28] This will still apply to applications made before 1 December 2008; for applications made on or after 1 December 2008, residence resulting from service in the armed forces is now to be treated as 'of choice' for the purposes of HA 1996 s199.[29]

7.17   In *Mohamed*,[30] the House of Lords considered whether occupation of interim accommodation provided[31] by a local authority during enquiries and pending review could amount to normal residence. Lord Slynn of Hadley, concluding that it did, said:

> . . . the prima facie meaning of normal residence is a place where at the relevant time the person in fact resides. That therefore is the question to be asked . . . So long as that place where he eats and sleeps is voluntarily accepted by him, the reason why he is there rather than somewhere else does not prevent that place from being his normal residence. He may not like it, he may prefer some other place, but that

27 HA 1996 s199(5).

28 The armed forces were defined as the Royal Navy, the regular armed forces as defined by Army Act 1955 s225, and the regular air forces as defined by Air Forces Act 1955 s223: HA 1996 s199(4). From 31 October 2009, the armed forces are defined as Royal Navy, the Royal Marines, the regular army or the Royal Air Force: Armed Forces Act 2006 s374. The repealed provision was addressed in *R v Vale of White Horse DC ex p Smith and Hay* (1984) 17 HLR 160, QBD, two cases heard together which considered the usual practice of the armed forces to allow a period of time after the termination of service before recovering possession of married quarters; it was held that the exclusion of residence as a result of service in the armed forces referred to the time residence commenced; a fresh residence after leaving the armed forces could be established, even in the same premises, but would not usually be established merely by holding over after the right to occupy married quarters had come to an end.

29 HA 1996 s199(2) repealed with effect from 1 December 2008. See also Circular 04/2009 *Housing Allocations – Members of the Armed Forces* from the Department for Communities and Local Government.

30 *Mohamed v Hammersmith & Fulham LBC* [2001] UKHL 57; [2002] HLR 7, HL. Cf *Al-ameri v Kensington & Chelsea RLBC; Osmani v Harrow LBC* [2004] UKHL 4; [2004] HLR 20 where accommodation provided by NASS to asylum-seekers was not residence of choice. The effect of this latter decision has now been statutorily overturned: see para 7.31, below.

31 Usually under HA 1996 s188(1) (see para. 10.5, below) but also potentially under s200(1) (see para 7.57, below) or s188(3) or s200(5) pending the review (see para 10.33, below).

place is for the relevant time the place where he normally resides . . . Where he is given interim accommodation by a local housing authority even more clearly is that the place where for the time being he is normally resident. The fact that it is provided subject to statutory duty does not . . . prevent it from being such.

7.18 The Local Authority Agreement suggests a working (or extended) definition of 'normal residence' as six months in an area during the previous 12 months, or not less than three years during the previous five-year period.[32] In *Re Betts*, this was described as 'eminently sensible and proper to have been included in the agreement'.

7.19 In *Smith and Hay*,[33] a period of a few months, some ten years before application, during which one of the spouses had been employed – and therefore resident – in an area, was considered to be too short necessarily to have established a local connection.

7.20 Compare, however, *Hughes*,[34] where the applicant had moved into the area to set up a permanent home with the man by whom she became pregnant. The relationship broke down owing to domestic violence after only two months and the applicant applied as homeless. A decision made some months later – during which the applicant had resided in a local women's aid refuge – that the applicant did not have a local connection with the area was quashed as one to which no reasonable authority could have come.

Employment

7.21 The Local Authority Agreement suggests that an authority should seek confirmation from the employer both of the employment and that it is not of a casual nature.[35] This implies that 'employment' is to be given a restrictive meaning, ie, one in the employ of another, but HA 1996 Part 7 does not suggest that self-employed people should be excluded or that employment need be full-time.

7.22 Given that employment is a subsidiary consideration, and merely one of the grounds for establishing a local connection,[36] it is clearly open to an authority to exclude casual work, but not, it is submitted, self-employment. In *Smith and Hay* (above), the same few months' employment, some ten years before the application, was described as

---

32 Local Authority Agreement para 4.1(i).
33 *R v Vale of White Horse DC ex p Smith and Hay* (1984) 17 HLR 160, QBD.
34 *R v Southwark LBC ex p Hughes* (1998) 30 HLR 1082, QBD.
35 Local Authority Agreement para 4.1(i).
36 See paras 7.9–7.13, above.

limited and of short duration and the authority did not err in finding that it did not give rise to a local connection.

7.23   A person used not to be regarded as employed in an area if s/he was serving in the regular armed forces,[37] or in such other circumstance as the secretary of state may by order specify.[38] (This power has not been exercised.) For applications made on or after 1 December 2008, a person serving as a member of the regular armed forces is regarded as employed so as to give rise to a local connection.[39]

Family associations

7.24   There is no statutory definition of the phrase 'family associations'. The Code of Guidance[40] suggests that, in addition to parents, adult children or siblings, it may include associations with family members such as step-parents, grandparents, grandchildren, aunts or uncles 'provided there are sufficiently close links in the form of frequent contact, commitment or dependency'. This goes further than the Local Authority Agreement which suggests that it arises where an applicant or a member of his/her household has parents, adult children, brothers or sisters currently residing in the area in question.[41] In *Avdic*,[42] a claim based on a first cousin once removed was insufficient.

7.25   The decision in *Avdic* is not, however, to be interpreted as limiting family associations to those mentioned in the Agreement: see *Ozbek*,[43] where it was said that the character of the family association was a least as relevant – if not more relevant – than the degree of

37   HA 1996 s199(2). This subsection was repealed with effect from 1 December 2008: Housing and Regeneration Act 2008 s315(a), s321(1) and Sch 16, and Housing and Regeneration Act 2008 (Commencement No 2 and Transitional, Saving and Transitory Provisions) Order 2008 SI No 3068.

38   HA 1996 s199(5).

39   Housing and Regeneration Act 2008 s315(a), s321(1) and Sch 16 and Housing and Regeneration Act 2008 (Commencement No 2 and Transitional, Saving and Transitory Provisions) Order 2008 SI No 3068 See also para 7.16, above.

40   Para 18.10.

41   Local Authority Agreement para 4.1(ii). It continues that 'only in exceptional circumstances would the residence of relatives other than those listed above be taken to establish a local connection'.

42   *R v Hammersmith & Fulham LBC ex p Avdic* (1996) 28 HLR 897, QBD; (1997) 30 HLR 1, CA.

43   *Ozbek v Ispwich BC* [2006] EWCA Civ 534; [2006] HLR 41. This is now reflected in the Code of Guidance, see previous para. See also the first instance decision of *Munting v Fulham LBC* [1998] JHL D91, where the authority had incorrectly concluded that a step-father could not be a close relative.

consanguinity.[44] In that case, the applicants sought to establish their local connection with the borough to which they had applied through brothers who had lived in the area for only 18 months, and cousins and other extended family members who had lived there for over five years. The relevant question for the authority in these circumstance was 'whether, in the particular circumstances of the individual case, the bond between the applicant and one or more members of the extended family was of such a nature that it would be appropriate to regard those members of the extended family as "near relatives" in the sense in which that concept is recognised in [the Local Authority Agreement]'.[45] The authority had correctly asked itself this question in reaching its conclusion that there was no local connection.

7.26   The Local Authority Agreement continues by saying that the relatives must have been resident for a period of at least five years and that the applicant must indicate a wish to be near them.[46] It also says that an applicant who objects to being referred to an area on account of family associations should not be so referred.[47]

7.27   Once a family association has been raised by the applicant, the authority should address the issue. A decision letter which failed to do so (after the issue had been raised) was held to be defective in *Khan*[48] (because it appeared from the letter that only residence had been addressed).

Other special circumstances

7.28   'Other special circumstances' is a phrase likewise left undefined in Part 7. The Code[49] suggests the example of the need to be near special medical or support services which are only available in a particular district. The Local Authority Agreement mentions[50] those who have been in prison or in hospital or those who wish to return to an area where they were brought up or had lived for a considerable length of

---

44 At [64].

45 At [49].

46 Local Authority Agreement para 4.1(ii).

47 Local Authority Agreement para 4.1(ii), but compare, *R v McCall and Others ex p Eastbourne BC*, unreported, but referred to at (1981) 8 HLR 48, QBD, in which it was observed that though the applicant's wishes are relevant, where other factors are equally balanced, they cannot override the words of the statute.

48 *R v Slough BC ex p Khan* (1995) 27 HLR 492, QBD.

49 Code of Guidance, para 18.10: Welsh Code, para. 20.7(iv).

50 Local Authority Agreement para 4.1(iii).

time in the past. It stresses that an authority must exercise its discretion when considering whether special circumstances apply.

7.29   In *Smith and Hay*,[51] one of the families attempted to place some reliance on membership of an evangelical church, around which their lives revolved. Following *Betts* (see para 7.9, above) – that the fundamental test is whether or not there is a local connection – the authority had not erred in concluding as a matter of fact that this association did not amount to a special circumstance giving rise to a local connection in their case. Nor does a mere desire not to return to an area with which the applicant has a local connection amount to a special circumstance giving rise to a local connection with a different area: *Adigun*.[52]

7.30   It has been said that family associations too weak to qualify under HA 1996 s199(1)(c) cannot amount to a special circumstance under this subsection: see *Khan* and *Avdic*.[53] This also seems too rigid. If a connection of importance exists, which could be based on what might also be described as a weak family association, it should not automatically rule out qualification as a special circumstance. Indeed, it would seem that if the exclusion of a range of family members from qualification as family association is correct, this category ought to be capable of catching it. That is not to say that a mere distant relation would automatically qualify as a connection under this head but, if the connection is of particular significance, nor should it automatically be disqualified.

Former asylum-seekers

7.31   In *Al-ameri*,[54] the House of Lords held that a former asylum-seeker who subsequently applied as homeless did not have a local connection with the area in which he had been provided with accommodation by NASS,[55] because residence in that accommodation was

---

51   *R v Vale of White Horse DC ex p Smith and Hay* (1984) 17 HLR 160, QBD. See also *R v Westminster CC ex p Benniche* (1996) 29 HLR 230, CA.

52   *R v Islington LBC ex p Adigun* (1986) 20 HLR 600, QBD.

53   *R v Slough BC ex p Khan* (1995) 27 HLR 492, QBD; *R v Hammersmith & Fulham LBC ex p Avdic* (1996) 28 HLR 897, QBD; (1997) 30 HLR 1, CA.

54   *Al-ameri v Kensington & Chelsea RLBC; Osmani v Harrow LBC* [2004] UKHL 4; [2004] HLR 20.

55   Above, paras 3.2–3.3 and 3.101. In July 2006, the Home Office announced that the National Asylum Support Service (NASS) no longer existed as a separate department. Asylum support is now administered by two separate routes. Those who made their first asylum claim on or after 5 March 2007 have their support processed by the New Asylum Model (NAM) 'case owner' who is

not 'of choice'.[56] Part 7 was amended by Asylum and Immigration (Treatment of Claimants etc) Act 2004 s11 to reverse the effect of this decision.[57]

7.32 By section 199(6) and (7), a person has a local connection with an authority's district if s/he was at any time provided with accommodation in that district under Immigration and Asylum Act 1999 s95[58] unless:

a) the applicant was subsequently provided with accommodation under section 95 in another authority's district; or

b) the accommodation was provided in an accommodation centre under Nationality, Immigration and Asylum Act 2002 s22.[59]

7.33 The amendments apply only to accommodation provided by the UK Borders Agency (UKBA) in England or Wales.[60] So, a former asylum-seeker who has been housed by UKBA in Scotland will not have a local connection in the district where the accommodation was provided.

7.34 In those circumstances – where a former asylum-seeker who has been housed by UKBA in Scotland[61] applies to an authority in England or Wales, and has no local connection with the authority to which s/he has applied nor any with an authority in Scotland – the principal housing duty under section 193[62] is disapplied.[63] Instead, the local authority has a discretion to secure accommodation for a reasonable period and may provide advice and assistance.[64]

---

processing their asylum claim. Applicants who claimed asylum before 5 March 2007, known as 'legacy' cases, should have their asylum and support claims dealt with by the Casework Resolution Directorate (CRD). See also below, paras 13.32–13.43.

56 See paras 7.15–7.20, above.

57 Given the statutory amendment, the absence of support from family and friends in the area in which an asylum-seeker has been housed by UKBA does not provide sufficient reason for an authority to decide against making a referral which it is otherwise entitled to make: *Ozbek v Ispwich BC* [2006] EWCA Civ 534; [2006] HLR 41.

58 See further paras 13.34–13.37, below, on the provision of accommodation by UKBA under this section.

59 This provision has not yet been brought into force.

60 See below, paras 13.34–13.37.

61 Other than in an accommodation centre under Nationality, Immigration and Asylum Act 2002 s22. This provision has not yet been brought into force.

62 See paras 10.85–10.176, below.

63 Asylum and Immigration (Treatment of Claimants etc) Act 2004 s11(2), (3)(a).

64 Asylum and Immigration (Treatment of Claimants etc) Act 2004 s11(3)(b). This discretion is framed in the same terms as the duty towards the intentionally homeless; see para 10.54, below.

When are the local connection provisions applicable?

7.35　The local connection provisions exempt an authority from duties under HA 1996 s193, ie, the responsibility for securing that housing is made available. They do not affect the provision of temporary accommodation for a person who is homeless and in priority need, but whom the authority to which application has been made has determined is homeless intentionally.[65]

7.36　It has been held that the local connection provisions are not applicable when the authority's duty arises because of threatened homelessness under HA 1996 s195(2). In *Williams v Exeter CC*,[66] a woman was occupying army property let to her husband, a serviceman, in the Exeter area. As such, she had no connection with Exeter on the basis of residence of choice, nor on any other ground. The Ministry of Defence secured an order for possession against her and, before it was executed, she applied to the authority.

7.37　The authority agreed that she was threatened with homelessness but referred her case to East Devon DC. As the applicant did not wish to leave the area, she challenged this decision, which is when it was held that the local connection provisions applied only when the duty arose under the Housing Act 1985 s65(2) (now HA 1996 s193), not under s195(2). It is unclear from the short report, however, whether the authority could have used the local connection provisions once actual homelessness occurred, or whether what was being held was that the structure of the provisions implies that if a decision is made while the applicant is still only threatened with homelessness, the local connection provisions will remain irrelevant once actual homelessness occurs. The former construction seems (much) more likely.

7.38　An authority will be entitled to rely on the local connection provisions when it is:

– satisfied that the applicant is homeless and in priority need;
– not satisfied that the applicant became homeless intentionally; and
– of the opinion that the conditions for referral apply.[67]

The conditions are that:

65　HA 1996 s198(1); *Delahaye v Oswestry BC* (1980) *Times* 28 July, QBD.
66　*Williams v Exeter CC* September 1981 *LAG Bulletin* 211.
67　HA 1996 s198(1).

a) neither the applicant nor any person who might reasonably be expected to reside with him/her has a local connection with their area; and

b) the applicant or a person who might reasonably be expected to reside with him/her does have a local connection with the area of another housing authority; and

c) neither the applicant nor any person who might reasonably be expected to reside with him/her will run the risk of domestic violence in that other authority's area.[68]

In addition, the conditions are not met if the applicant or any person who might reasonably be expected to reside with him/her has suffered non-domestic violence in the authority's area, and it is probable that the return to the area will lead to further violence of a similar kind against the victim.[69]

7.39   For the purposes of HA 1996 s198, 'violence' means actual physical violence and does not include threats of violence or acts or gestures which lead a person to fear physical violence.[70]

7.40   It is clear that all criteria must be satisfied. There must be:

a) no local connection with the one area; *and*

b) a local connection with the other area; *and*

c) no risk of domestic violence; *and*

d) no risk of non-domestic violence.

Thus, the procedure is unavailable if there is a local connection with the area to which application has been made, but the authority is of the opinion that the applicant has a greater or closer local connection elsewhere.[71] This was one of the mischiefs which the Housing (Homeless Persons) Act 1977 was intended to end.[72]

7.41   The decision to refer is discretionary and, as such, may be vulnerable to challenge if exercised unreasonably.[73] Given the discretionary nature of the exercise, authorities are under no obligation to

---

68 HA 1996 s198(2).

69 HA 1996 s198(2A).

70 *Danesh v Kensington & Chelsea RLBC* [2006] EWCA Civ 1404; [2006] HLR 17.

71 See *Re Betts* [1983] 2 AC 613; (1983) 10 HLR 97, HL; the House of Lords did not overrule the Court of Appeal on this point.

72 See chapter 1.

73 HA 1996 s184(2). *R v Newham LBC ex p Tower Hamlets LBC* (1990) 23 HLR 62, CA; *Ozbek v Ispwich BC* [2006] EWCA Civ 534; [2006] HLR 41. See also *R v East Devon DC ex p Robb* (1997) 30 HLR 922, QBD, where the authority failed to consider whether it had a discretion to refer the applicant.

investigate local connection, even where the applicant indicates that s/he wishes to live in another area.[74]

7.42   In *Tower Hamlets*,[75] a decision by Newham LBC to refer an applicant to Tower Hamlets LBC was quashed. The referral concerned a Bangladeshi man who had originally applied to Tower Hamlets LBC for housing but was found to be intentionally homeless. He subsequently applied to Newham LBC who found him not to be intentionally homeless. In reaching its decision, Newham LBC made a comparison between the housing conditions in Bangladesh and housing conditions in its own area. The Court of Appeal decided that a referring authority must satisfy itself that the applicant was homeless, in priority need and not intentionally homeless, but that if a finding of non-intentionality was flawed, to the extent that in appropriate judicial review proceedings it would have been quashed, the decision could not form a proper foundation for referral. Newham LBC's decision in the case was flawed, because it had failed to take account of the general circumstances prevailing in relation to housing in Tower Hamlets LBC.

7.43   The circumstances in which a person runs the risk of domestic violence or non-domestic violence are the same as those considered in relation to whether or not it would have been reasonable – on this ground – to continue to occupy accommodation, pursuant to HA 1996 s177.[76] The authority is under a positive duty to enquire whether the applicant is subject to such a risk.[77]

7.44   One point which may be made here relates to the interaction with intentional homelessness. It is not uncommon for women not merely to leave home on account of domestic violence, but to leave or try to leave the area. Some authorities who find that a person in these circumstances is not homeless intentionally, will nonetheless seek to refer her back. It is true that there is no necessary conflict between finding that a woman is homeless (perhaps on account of the domestic violence) and finding that she will not run the risk of domestic violence in the area from which she has fled. An authority can take the view that while domestic violence drove her out, the risk is no longer present. Nonetheless, it is a relatively sophisticated distinction, for which there ought to be a material basis, and it is clear that

---

74   *Hackney LBC v Sareen* [2003] EWCA Civ 351; [2003] HLR 54.

75   *R v Newham LBC ex p Tower Hamlets LBC* (1990) 23 HLR 62, CA. See also the Local Authority Agreement para 3.4, advising on this decision.

76   HA 1996 s198(3), see paras 4.82–4.92, above.

77   *Patterson v Greenwich LBC* (1993) 26 HLR 159, CA.

automatically to refer her back without considering this distinction will be a bad decision in law.

7.45   In this connection, it may be noted that in *Browne*,[78] which for these purposes and on this issue may be treated as if a local connection case,[79] the authority had not found intentional homelessness, but appeared to have addressed itself expressly to the point made in the last paragraph. In *Adigun*,[80] it was stressed that the task of determining whether or not there was a risk of domestic violence is one for the local authority. So long as there was material on which it could base its decision, the court would not intervene.

7.46   Although it is lawful for an authority to have a policy about how it may exercise its discretion, it cannot decide in advance that every applicant who qualifies for referral should be referred: *Carter*.[81]

7.47   If a person has no local connection with any housing authority in England, Wales or Scotland, s/he will be entitled to housing from the authority to which the application has been made.[82]

Additional application of provisions

7.48   By HA 1996 s198(4), the conditions for referral are deemed to be fulfilled – regardless therefore of local connection with the authority to which the application was made (on any of the foregoing grounds), and regardless of risk of domestic or other violence – if:

–   the applicant was placed by another authority in accommodation in the area of the authority to which the application has been made;

–   in discharge of its functions under Part 7;

–   within such period as may be prescribed.

7.49   The relevant period is five years from the date of the placement, together with the time between the date the application was initially made to the time the placement first became available.[83]

---

78 *R v Bristol CC ex p Browne* [1979] 1 WLR 1437, DC.

79 Below, paras 10.104 and 10.105.

80 *R v Islington LBC ex p Adigun* (1986) 20 HLR 600, QBD. See also *R v Newham LBC ex p Smith* (1996) 29 HLR 213, QBD.

81 *R v Harrow LBC ex p Carter* (1992) 26 HLR 32, QBD.

82 *R v Hillingdon LBC ex p Streeting* [1980] 1 WLR 1430, CA. Although note the limitations in relation to former asylum-seekers at para 7.30, above.

83 Allocation of Housing and Homelessness (Miscellaneous Provisions) (England) Regulations 2006 SI No 2527 and, in Wales, Homelessness Regulations 2000 SI No 701 reg 6 (applied to Wales by the Homelessness (Wales) Regulations 2000 SI No 1079).

7.50　The Welsh Code gives the following example:[84]

> ... where a housing authority accept a duty to secure that accommodation is available ... and place the household in accommodation which is outside their district, the placing housing authority retains 'responsibility' for that household in the event of a further application for assistance under Part 7 within a period of five years of the date when accommodation was first made available under the initial duty.

7.51　Note that in relation to eligible asylum-seekers[85] in England, the provisions are amended to permit a referral in any case where another authority has agreed to accept the referral and there is no risk of violence.[86]

Procedure on prospective reference

7.52　The obligation to house passes to the notified authority when the conditions for referral[87] are – or are deemed to be[88] – fulfilled.[89] The duty to make all preliminary enquiries into:

a) homelessness,
b) priority need, and
c) intentional homelessness

lies on the authority to which application is made.[90] This is so even if it becomes apparent that the local connection provisions may apply,[91] and even if the homeless person has already applied to the other authority and been rejected by it as homeless intentionally.[92]

7.53　Furthermore, even if the notified authority has already made a previous, different decision, it will be bound by the decision arising on the new application to the notifying authority. This leads to what

---

84　Welsh Code para 20.5. The English Code does not include any Guidance on this matter because of the repeal of the provisions by Allocation of Housing and Eligibility (England) Regulations 2006 SI No 1294, although they were subsequently re-introduced.

85　See paras 3.68–3.127, above.

86　Homelessness (Asylum-seekers) (Interim Period) (England) Order 1999 SI No 3126.

87　See para 7.41, above.

88　Under HA 1996 s198(4): see paras 7.48–7.51, above.

89　HA 1996 s200(2).

90　HA 1996 s194.

91　*Delahaye v Oswestry BC* (1980) *Times* 28 July, QBD.

92　*R v Slough BC ex p Ealing LBC* [1981] QB 801, CA, but see *R v Newham LBC ex p Tower Hamlets LBC* (1990) 23 HLR 62, CA.

has been described as a 'merry-go-round',[93] in which a person may apply to Authority A, be found homeless intentionally, move across to the area of Authority B, make a new application, be found homeless unintentionally and then be referred back for permanent housing to Authority A.[94]

7.54 A referral under HA 1996 s198 gives rise to a new section 193 duty, so that if an applicant applies to Authority A, is not found homeless intentionally but rejects its offer of accommodation, and then applies to Authority B which refers him/her back to Authority A, Authority A cannot rely on its earlier offer.[95]

7.55 An authority which finds an applicant homeless intentionally but wrongly refers the applicant to another authority, is not bound by its error; the erroneous reference may simply be ignored.[96] Because the local connection provisions are inapplicable if there is intentionality, it does not follow that the erroneous referral nullifies the intentionality decision.[97]

7.56 Until the completion of enquiries, the applicant will have been housed under HA 1996 s188.[98] This duty arises irrespective of local connection.[99]

7.57 If the authority concludes that the applicant is homeless, in priority need, and has not become homeless intentionally, but decides[100] to notify another authority of his/her application, it must notify the applicant of this and of its reasons.[101] Pending resolution of the issue, it is the duty of the notifying authority to continue to secure that accommodation is available for the applicant and his/her family.[102] So long as it remains under a duty towards the applicant, whether to accommodate pending enquiries or pending resolution of a local connection referral, the notifying authority also has duties in relation to the protection of the applicant's property.[103]

93 *R v Slough BC ex p Ealing LBC* [1981] QB 801, CA.
94 *R v Slough BC ex p Ealing LBC* [1981] QB 801, CA.
95 *R v Tower Hamlets LBC ex p Ali; R v Tower Hamlets LBC ex p Bibi* (1992) 25 HLR 158, CA (overruling *R v Hammersmith & Fulham LBC ex p O'Brian* (1985) 17 HLR 471, QBD on this point).
96 *Delahaye v Oswestry BC* (1980) *Times* 28 July, QBD.
97 This is consistent with the approach and decision in *Crawley BC v B* (2000) 32 HLR 636, CA, see paras 9.127–9.129, below.
98 Below, paras 10.5–10.13.
99 HA 1996 s188(2).
100 In its discretion, cf HA 1996 s184(2).
101 HA 1996 s184(4).
102 HA 1996 s200(1).
103 HA 1996 s211(2), see chapter 8.

Resolution of disputes

7.58   The question whether the conditions for referral of an application[104] are satisfied is to be determined by agreement between the notifying authority and the notified authority or, in default of agreement, in accordance with such arrangements as the secretary of state may direct, by order made by statutory instrument.[105] 'Arrangements' are those agreed by the authorities, or by associations of authorities, or in default of agreement such as appears to the secretary of state to be suitable, after consultation with the local authority associations and such other persons as s/he thinks appropriate.[106]

7.59   The current arrangements are to be found in the Homelessness (Decision on Referrals) Order 1998[107] and the agreement reached by the Association of London Government (ALG), the Convention of Scottish Local Authorities (CoSLA), the Local Government Association (LGA) and the Welsh Local Government Association (WLGA) in 2006 (the Local Authority Agreement).

Local Authority Agreement

7.60   The substantive provisions of the Local Authority Agreement in relation to the four grounds for local connections have been noted above. The Local Authority Agreement reminds authorities that, if there is any local connection with the area of the authority to which application is made, the local connection provisions will not be relevant, even though the household may have a greater local connection elsewhere. The degree of local connection is irrelevant except where an applicant

---

104 See above, para 7.41.

105 HA 1996 s198(5). This applies only to disputes about whether the applicant has a local connection. If an authority wishes to reject a referral, eg, because it believes the applicant should have been found intentionally homeless, it must do so by judicial review. In the absence of such a challenge, the authority cannot simply reject the referral: *R (Bantamagbari) v Westminster CC* [2003] EWHC 1350 (Admin); [2003] JHL D70.

106 HA 1996 s198(6).

107 SI No 1578. There is no order that directly deals with referrals to Scotland. See, however, the Homelessness (Decisions on Referrals) (Scotland) Order 1998 SI No 1603, made under Housing (Scotland) Act 1987 s33 and the Local Authority Agreement para 10.8, which provides for the appointment of a referee to be by CoSLA where the notified authority is in Scotland (in the case of referrals from England or Wales) and by the LGA where the referral is from Scotland to England or Wales.

has no local connection with the notifying authority but does have a local connection with more than one other local authority.[108]

7.61 The authority to which application has been made is urged to investigate all circumstances with the same thoroughness that it would use if it did not have it in mind to refer the application to another authority. These enquiries may be of another authority, one to which it may be making a referral, and such enquiries should be made as soon as possible.[109]

7.62 Where an applicant has a local connection with a number of authorities, the Local Authority Agreement says that the notifying authority should weigh up all relevant factors.[110] The Code of Guidance[111] suggests that the wishes of the applicant should be taken into account in deciding which authority to notify.

7.63 In *McCall*,[112] it was held that, although an arbitrator[113] will not – without the consent of the authorities – usually be entitled to apply the criteria set out in the Local Authority Agreement, if issues are evenly balanced it is proper for him/her to have regard to the wishes of the applicant. Indeed, where all other considerations give no indication one way or another, the court described it as 'perfectly reasonable and perfectly sensible, and within the spirit of the statutory provisions', to have regard to the wishes of the family.

7.64 Under the terms of the Local Authority Agreement, each authority should nominate one person to receive notifications of referral from other authorities.[114] Unless it has clear evidence to the contrary, the notified authority should accept all statements of the facts of the case as stated by the notifying authority.[115]

7.65 If the notified authority provides new information which causes the notifying authority to want to reconsider questions of homelessness, priority need or intentionality, the position will be the same as in other reconsideration cases.[116] The Local Authority Agreement

---

108 Local Authority Agreement para 4.11.
109 Local Authority Agreement para 5.1.
110 Local Authority Agreement para 4.11.
111 Code of Guidance para 18.14; Welsh Code para 20.10.
112 *R v McCall and Others ex p Eastbourne BC*, unreported, but referred to at (1981) 8 HLR 48, QBD, in which it was observed that though the applicant's wishes are relevant, where other factors are equally balanced, they cannot override the words of the statute.
113 Below, paras 7.67–7.73.
114 Local Authority Agreement para 6.2.
115 Local Authority Agreement para 6.3.
116 Below, paras 9.123–9.129.

stresses that the disputes procedures should be used only where there is a disagreement over the existence of a local connection, not for resolving disagreement on any other matter, and that – once enquiries have been completed – a challenge to the notifying authority's decision that the applicant is eligible, homeless, in priority need and not intentionally homeless can only be made by judicial review.[117]

7.66   If the Local Authority Agreement resolves the issue, then the notified authority should, if it has accepted responsibility, provide accommodation for the applicant and his/her family immediately. Once the notified authority has accepted responsibility, it is liable to repay the notifying authority for expenses incurred in the provision of temporary accommodation, although if the notifying authority has delayed unduly[118] the notified authority need only reimburse it for expenses incurred since notification of the referral was received.[119]

Arbitration

7.67   Where a notified authority disputes the referral, it should set down its reasons in full within ten days.[120] If there is still no agreement, the authorities must seek, within 21 days of receipt of the referral, to agree on an arbitrator who will make the decision.[121] The Local Government Association (LGA) maintains an independent panel of persons – generally known as referees – for this purpose.[122] In default of agreement as to the referee, the authorities must jointly request the chairman of the LGA or his/her nominee (the proper officer) to appoint a person from the panel.[123] If an arbitrator has not been appointed within six weeks of the date of notification, the notifying authority must request the proper officer to appoint a referee from the panel.[124]

7.68   The referee must invite written representations from both the notifying and the notified authority.[125] S/he may also invite further

---

117 Local Authority Agreement para 5.5. See also chapter 12.
118 Usually a period of more than 30 days from the date of initial application: Local Authority Agreement para 7.3.
119 Local Authority Agreement.
120 Local Authority Agreement para 10.2.
121 Homelessness (Decisions on Referrals) Order 1998 SI No 1578 Sch paras 1 and 2.
122 Homelessness (Decisions on Referrals) Order 1998 SI No 1578 Sch para 3.
123 Homelessness (Decisions on Referrals) Order 1998 SI No 1578 Sch para 4(1).
124 Homelessness (Decisions on Referrals) Order 1998 SI No 1578 Sch para 4(2).
125 Homelessness (Decisions on Referrals) Order 1998 SI No 1578 Sch para 5(2).

written representations from the authorities, written representations from any other person,[126] and oral representations from any person.[127]

7.69   The Local Authority Agreement suggests[128] that, where an oral hearing is necessary or more convenient (for example, where the applicant is illiterate, English is not his/her first language or further information is necessary to resolve the dispute), the notifying authority should be invited to present its case first, followed by the notified authority and any other persons whom the referee wishes to hear. It is for the referee to arrange the venue, although it is suggested that the offices of the notifying authority will often be the most convenient location.[129] Where a person has made oral representations, the referee may direct that reasonable travelling expenses are paid by either or both authorities.[130]

7.70   It is no part of the referee's duties to enquire into matters preceding a local connection reference: homelessness, eligibility, priority need or intentional homelessness.[131]

7.71   The referee must notify both authorities of his/her decision and the reasons for it.[132] The Local Authority Agreement[133] suggests a target of one month for the decision, from receipt of the authorities' written submissions. There is no obligation on the referee to notify the applicant of his/her decision: that is the notifying authority's duty.[134]

7.72   The previous regulations[135] specifically provided that the decision of the referee was final and binding on the authorities. No such provision is included in the current regulations, although the Local Authority Agreement does state[136] that it is binding on the participating

126 Most obviously the applicant, who the Local Authority Agreement suggests (para 13.4), should be supplied with copies of the authorities' submissions. Where representations are invited they may be made by someone, whether or not legally qualified, acting on behalf of the person: Homelessness (Decisions on Referrals) Order 1998 SI No 1578 Sch para 5(4).

127 Homelessness (Decisions on Referrals) Order 1998 SI No 1578 Sch para 5(3).

128 Local Authority Agreement para 14.1.

129 Local Authority Agreement para 14.2.

130 Homelessness (Decisions on Referrals) Order 1998 SI No 1578 Sch para 7(2).

131 *R v Slough BC ex p Ealing LBC* [1981] QB 801, CA.

132 Homelessness (Decisions on Referrals) Order 1998 SI No 1578 Sch para 6.

133 Local Authority Agreement para 13.5.

134 HA 1996 s200(2).

135 Housing (Homeless Persons) (Appropriate Arrangements) Order 1978 SI 1978 No 69.

136 Local Authority Agreement para 15.1.

authorities, subject to the applicant's right to review.[137] Once a referee has made the determination, s/he should not reopen the case, even though facts may be presented to him/her, unless it is to rectify an error arising from a mistake or omission.[138] The proviso that the decision is final and binding on the authority does not, however, prevent challenge on the grounds that the decision is ultra vires.[139]

7.73   The notifying and notified authorities each pay their own costs of the determination.[140] Unlike the 1978 order,[141] there is no explicit discretion for the referee to make a costs order against either party. The Local Authority Agreement suggests,[142] however, that the referee's fees and expenses, and any third party costs, would usually be recovered from the unsuccessful party to the dispute, although the referee may choose to apportion expenses between the authorities if s/he considers it warranted.

Post-resolution procedure

7.74   If the resolution of the dispute results in the burden of housing lying on the notified authority, it is still the duty of the notifying authority to provide notification of the result and the reasons for it, to the applicant.[143] The notification must also inform the applicant of his/her right to a review of whether the conditions[144] are met.[145] It is not entirely clear whether this review can encompass the 'decision' of the arbitrator. If it does, it would open the way to an applicant to appeal that decision to the county court on a point of law.[146]

7.75   If the burden of providing housing does not shift to the notified authority, it will remain with the notifying authority[147] and the principal housing duty under HA 1996 s193 will apply.[148] The mere fact

---

137 See para 9.153, below.

138 Local Authority Agreement para 19.1.

139 Below, chapter 12.

140 Homelessness (Decisions on Referrals) Order 1998 SI No 1578 Sch para 7(1).

141 Housing (Homeless Persons) (Appropriate Arrangements) Order 1978 SI No 69.

142 Local Authority Agreement para 18.3.

143 HA 1996 s200(2). See paras 9.142–9.148, below.

144 See para 7.41, above.

145 HA 1996 s202(1)(d).

146 HA 1996 s204. See chapter 12.

147 HA 1996 s200(3).

148 See chapter 10.

that an authority has unsuccessfully sought to shift the burden on to another authority is not, of course, any basis on which to alter the original decision that the applicant has not become homeless intentionally.[149] If the duty does pass to the notified authority, it will also be under a section 193 duty.[150]

149 *R v Beverley BC ex p McPhee* (1978) *Times* 26 October, QBD.
150 See paras 10.85–10.176.

CHAPTER 8

Protection of property

Introduction

8.1   Housing Act (HA) 1996 Part 7 makes provision for local housing authorities to take steps to protect the property of homeless people under HA 1996 s211, supplemented by section 212. These provisions – which appeared in both the Housing (Homeless Persons) Act 1977 and HA 1985 – are of considerable practical importance. Failure to take steps to protect the belongings of those who are homeless or threatened with homelessness can only have the effect of prolonging or worsening their economic position.

8.2   HA 1996 Part 7 contains:

a) a duty to protect property in some circumstances; and

b) a power to do so in others.

The discharge of this duty and the power[1] are not co-extensive with the discharge of housing duties under Part 7 and it is necessary, therefore, to consider these property provisions in their own detail. Authorities do not necessarily have to discharge duties themselves, but can contract them out: this is discussed at the start of Chapter 9.

To whom is a duty owed?

8.3   The duty is owed[2] to an applicant towards whom the authority has become subject to a housing duty under one of the following provisions of HA 1996:

– section 188 (accommodation pending enquiries);

– section 193 (full duty);

– section 190 (temporary accommodation for the intentionally homeless in priority need);

– section 195 (accommodation for those threatened with homelessness, in priority need and not so threatened intentionally); and

– section 200 (accommodation for those who are or have been the subject of a local connection issue).

In addition, the duty is owed under section 211(5) to someone who is reasonably to be expected to reside with the applicant, ie, for whom housing must also be provided.[3]

---

1   Both of which may be contracted out; see para 9.5, below.

2   HA 1996 s211(2).

3   See para 10.8, below.

When is the duty owed?

8.4   The duty is owed when the authority has reason to believe that:

a) by reason of his/her inability to protect or deal with it, there is a danger of loss of, or damage to, any personal property of the applicant, or other person to whom the duty is owed, and

b) no other suitable arrangements have been or are being made.[4]

'Danger' of loss or damage means a likelihood of harm not merely a possibility.[5]

8.5   The duty continues until the authority is of the opinion that there is no longer any reason to believe that there is a danger of loss of, or damage to, that property by reason of the applicant's inability to protect or deal with it, or that of someone else to whom the duty is owed.[6]

8.6   The duty is owed not only when the authority is subject to one of the prescribed housing duties, but also when it has been so subject.[7] For example, a person may be evicted from accommodation, and subsequently held to be homeless intentionally. The former landlord may have been willing to hold on to his/her property for a period of time. That period may be no longer than the period for which accommodation has been provided under HA 1996 s190(2)(a). If, after the expiry of section 190(2)(a) accommodation, the property duty has not expired, application may yet be made for assistance under section 211 and, if the relevant conditions are fulfilled, the authority will be obliged to provide that assistance.

8.7   Even when the property duty has expired, because the authority has formed the view that there is no further danger of loss of or damage to the property, or that the applicant is no longer unable to protect or deal with it, the authority has power to continue to protect that property.[8] Property may be kept in store, and the conditions on which it was taken into store will continue to have effect, with any necessary modifications.[9]

8.8   The Code of Guidance illustrates an inability to protect property with the example of a person who is ill or who cannot afford to have

4 HA 1996 s211(1).
5 *Deadman v Southwark LBC* (2001) 33 HLR 75, CA.
6 HA 1996 s212(3).
7 HA 1996 s211(2).
8 HA 1996 s212(3).
9 HA 1996 s212(3).

his/her property placed in store.[10] Similarly, a person could be deemed capable of taking back responsibility if s/he is no longer ill, or has obtained accommodation, or is able to afford the cost of storage.[11]

What is the duty?

8.9   The duty is to take reasonable steps to prevent loss or prevent or mitigate damage to the property.[12] In order to discharge the duty, the authority has power of entry on to private property.[13] At all reasonable times, staff may enter any premises which are 'the usual place of residence of the applicant or which were his last usual place of residence', and deal with his/her property in any way which is reasonably necessary, including by storing or arranging to store the property.[14]

8.10   The duty is owed in respect of 'personal property'. In *Roberts*,[15] there are dicta that it is likely that this would not extend to equipment used by an applicant in his/her business, at any rate where the business is conducted other than at the accommodation.

8.11   The authority generally has responsibility for arranging storage. It may, however, refuse to exercise the duty, except on appropriate conditions.[16] This means such conditions as it considers appropriate in a particular case, and can include conditions empowering it:

a) to charge for discharge of the duty; and
b) to dispose of the property in respect of which it discharged the duty, in such circumstances as may be specified.[17]

8.12   The Code suggests[18] that the authority might dispose of the property if it loses touch with the person concerned and is unable to trace him/her after a specified period. Whether or not a charge is made or a duty to store exists, the authority must, as bailee of the property, take reasonable care of it, and deliver it up when reasonably requested to do so. Failure to do this will render the authority liable to damages, even

---

10 Code of Guidance para 20.6; Welsh Code para 16.49.
11 Code of Guidance para 20.11; Welsh Code para 16.52.
12 HA 1996 s211(2).
13 Such provisions were also to be found in the National Assistance Act 1948 s48.
14 HA 1996 s212(1).
15 *R v Chiltern DC ex p Roberts et al* (1990) 23 HLR 387, QBD.
16 HA 1996 s211(4).
17 HA 1996 s211(4).
18 Code of Guidance para 20.10; Welsh Code para 16.51.

if the failure to deliver up is accidental, albeit a negligent accident.[19] The standard of care is high, and the burden of disproving negligence when damage has resulted from an accident lies on the authority, as bailee.[20]

8.13   The position set out in the above paragraphs may, however, be altered by Local Government (Miscellaneous Provisions) Act 1982 s41. That section applies wherever property comes into the possession of a local authority, after being found on premises owned or managed by it, or property has been deposited with the local authority and is not collected from it in accordance with the terms on which it was deposited.

8.14   Section 41 entitles the authority to give the owner or depositor of the property notice in writing that it requires him/her to collect the property by a date specified in the notice, and that if s/he does not do so the property will vest in the authority as from that date. If the person notified then fails to comply with the notice, the property does vest in the authority on that date.

8.15   The date to be specified is to be not less than one month from the date of the notice. When an authority finds property, as distinct from when property is deposited with it, and it appears to it that it is impossible to serve a notice, the property simply vests in it one month from the date when it so finds the property. In any other case, including deposit, when the authority is satisfied after reasonable enquiry that it is impossible to serve notice, the property simply vests in it six months after the property was deposited with it or six months from the date when the period from which the property was deposited with it expired, whichever is the later.

8.16   Perishable property, and property the continued storage of which would involve the authority in unreasonable expense or inconvenience, may, in any event, be sold or otherwise disposed of by the authority as it thinks fit. In such a case, the proceeds of sale vest in the authority on the same date as the property itself would have done were it not perishable or inconvenient or too expensive to store. If property is claimed by its owner prior to the date when it vests in the authority, s/he can collect it only on payment to the authority of its costs in storing the property, and in making enquiries or carrying out any of the other steps referred to in this section.

8.17   There is no express reference in the Local Government (Miscellaneous Provisions) Act 1982 to the provisions of the Housing (Home-

19   *Mitchell v Ealing LBC* [1979] QB 1.
20   *Port Swettenham Authority v TW Wu & Co* [1979] AC 580, PC.

less Persons) Act 1977, nor (by way of amendment) to HA 1985 nor HA 1996 Part 7. The courts may therefore consider that references to the Local Government (Miscellaneous Provisions) Act 1982 to 'property deposited' with the authority do not include property taken into safe-keeping under HA 1996 s211. If so, the Part 7 provisions only will apply. If not, the Local Government (Miscellaneous Provisions) Act 1982 makes it somewhat easier for authorities to limit the effect of their section 211 duties.

The power to protect property

8.18   The authority has power to take the identical steps to prevent loss of property, or to prevent or mitigate damage to it, as it is obliged to take under the duty described above, in any case where there is no duty to do so.[21] This power might benefit those not in priority need of accommodation, and also those who, though in priority need of accommodation, are only threatened with homelessness, and in respect of whom no decision on intentionality has yet been taken. Where the authority exercises this power, it has the same ancillary powers as in relation to the duty, ie, entry into premises, imposing conditions, etc.

Notification of cessation of responsibility

8.19   When the authority considers that it no longer has a duty or a power to protect property, it is obliged to notify the person towards whom it was subject to the duty, or in relation to whose property it has exercised the power:

a) that it has ceased to be subject to the duty, or to enjoy the power; and

b) why it is of the opinion that the duty or power has come to an end.[22]

The notification must be by personal delivery to the person to be notified or by leaving it or sending it by post to his/her last known address.[23]

---

21   HA 1996 s211(3).
22   HA 1996 s212(4).
23   HA 1996 s212(5).

CHAPTER 9

Homelessness decisions

continued

Introduction

9.1 The previous chapters have addressed the substantive law relating to homelessness. This and the following chapters are concerned with the procedure by which an applicant applies as homeless, the procedures to be followed by an authority on receipt of the application, the formal requirements concerning the decision-making process (including the right to request an internal review of an adverse decision), and the method by which the duty (if any) is discharged.

9.2 The next chapter is concerned with the discharge of any duty – this chapter is therefore concerned with the steps from application to decision and (if any) to review. This process involves a number of steps:

- application;
- enquiry into the application;
- initial decision;
- request for a review;
- further enquiries on review;
- 'minded to find' letter where necessary;
- review decision.

9.3 A number of points may be made at the outset. First, it is to be remembered that the body of homelessness law is organic and develops over time, whether court-led, by the introduction of new legislation and/or through the relationship between housing and other areas of public law.[1] The procedural aspects discussed in this chapter are therefore liable to change as issues are subjected to further scrutiny by the courts or are amended by Parliament to reflect cross-discipline policies.[2]

9.4 The second point of general significance is the question of who may discharge the various duties under Housing Act (HA) 1996 Part 7. It is common for decision-making in relation to homelessness to be delegated to an individual officer; the reviewing function – which must in any event be conducted by a person senior to the person carrying out the initial decision – is sometimes reserved to a panel rather than an individual, whether a panel of members, officers or both.

---

1 Cf the impact of immigration law and European law on the issue of eligibility (chapter 3) or the impact of human rights law on the extent of housing duties. See generally chapter 12.

2 Consider the impact of anti-social behaviour agenda on all aspects of housing law, including the issue of intentional homelessness (chapter 6) and allocations (chapter 11).

9.5   Under the Local Authorities (Contracting Out of Allocation of Housing and Homelessness Functions) Order 1996,[3] an authority may 'contract out' all or part[4] of its homelessness functions (including, for example, enquiries or reviews), save for functions relating to[5] the provision of advisory services,[6] assistance for voluntary organisations,[7] and the duty to co-operate with relevant housing authorities and bodies.[8] A contract may be for a period of up to ten years, but 'may be revoked at any time' by the authority.[9]

9.6   A third point should be made in relation to enquiries. Authorities are under obligations to conduct all relevant enquiries when an application is received: it would nonetheless be wrong to proceed on the basis that a failure to do so (or a defect in the enquiries process) is sufficient to vitiate the decision-making process.

9.7   The availability of a review of a decision provides an opportunity to remedy any perceived failure to conduct enquiries; indeed, it can be said positively to require the applicant to draw to the authority's attention all matters that s/he wishes to be considered or in relation to which s/he believes there to be a need for enquiries.[10]

9.8   Otherwise, although the substance of the duties on enquiries is discussed below in relation to the application itself,[11] the same principles as apply to enquiries are as relevant on review.

Applications

Who can apply?

9.9   Applications as homeless may in principle be made by any person who is lawfully in the country. 'Lawfully' in this context means 'not unlawfully', ie, someone who is not an offender under Immigration

---

3   SI No 3205. See further below, paras 12.47.
4   Deregulation and Contracting Out Act 1994 ss70(4) and 69(5).
5   Local Authorities (Contracting Out of Allocation of Housing and Homelessness Functions) Order 1996 SI No 3205 reg 3 and Sch 2.
6   See para 14.18, below.
7   See para 14.24, below.
8   See para 9.59, below.
9   Local Authorities (Contracting Out of Allocation of Housing and Homelessness Functions) Order 1996 reg 3 and Sch 2.
10   See *Bellouti v Wandsworth LBC* [2005] EWCA Civ 602; [2005] HLR 46.
11   Under HA 1996 s184(1).

Act 1971 s14 – see *Castelli and Tristran-Garcia, Tower Hamlets* and *Streeting*.[12]

9.10 Accordingly, 'applicant' under Part 7 means any person who applies to a local housing authority for accommodation, or for assistance in obtaining accommodation, whom the authority has reason to believe is or may be homeless, or threatened with homelessness.[13]

9.11 It follows that anyone – regardless as to whether s/he has a local connection with the authority (or any other authority in the UK)[14] – is entitled to make an application and refusal to permit him/her to do so is a breach of statutory duty.

9.12 There are, however, several exceptions to this general proposition.

Immigrants

9.13 A person unlawfully in the UK will not be permitted to make an application. An authority is entitled to reach its own decision as to whether or not an applicant for assistance is disqualified as such an illegal immigrant, albeit:

a) only for its own purposes; and

b) subject to a contrary decision by the Home Secretary.[15]

9.14 If, however, the immigration authorities later determine the issue of legality in the applicant's favour, or else decide not to take immigration action against him/her, s/he will cease to be an illegal immigrant for the purposes of Part 7, and will be entitled to apply. The issue of status then governs the question of eligibility.[16]

9.15 If a person has already been granted accommodation by the authority, questions of status do not serve to deprive him/her of his/her rights pursuant to the accommodation agreement: see *Akinbolu v Hackney LBC*.[17]

---

12 *R v Westminster CC ex p Castelli and Tristran-Garcia* (1996) 28 HLR 617, CA; *R v Secretary of State for the Environment ex p Tower Hamlets LBC* [1993] QB 632; 25 HLR 524, CA; *R v Hillingdon LBC ex p Streeting* [1980] 1 WLR 1425, CA. A person is lawfully here even where s/he has only been given temporary permission to enter, eg, as an asylum-seeker: *Szoma v Secretary of State for Department of Work and Pensions* [2005] UKHL 64; [2006] 1 All ER 1.

13 HA 1996 s183(1) and (2).

14 *R v Hillingdon LBC ex p Streeting* [1980] 1 WLR 1425, CA.

15 See *Castelli and Tristran-Garcia* and *ex p Tower Hamlets LBC*, above, footnote 12.

16 See chapter 3.

17 (1996) 29 HLR 259, CA.

9.16   In *Tower Hamlets*,[18] it was held – by concession – that, in addition to making enquiries of the immigration authorities and providing them with information, the authority was also under a positive duty to report suspected illegal immigrants to the immigration authorities.

Dependent children

9.17   A dependent child cannot apply in his/her own right: see *Garlick* and *Bentum*.[19] Children are expected to be provided for by those on whom they are dependent (where appropriate and qualifying, with assistance under Part 7).

9.18   The emphasis here is on 'dependent' children. The statutory scheme itself envisages the possibility of minors – 16- or 17-year-olds – applying as homeless.[20] It may be that subsequent enquiries reveal a connection with a family home, to which the minor can return, but the absence of such at the date of the application is sufficient to require an application to be received.

Capacity

9.19   A person must be capable of accepting or rejecting an offer of accommodation or assistance in order to qualify as an applicant: see *Begum*.[21] Thus, persons so disabled that they have neither the capacity themselves to apply nor to authorise an agent on their behalf do not qualify. There must be the capacity to understand and respond to the offer, and to undertake its responsibilities; whether or not a person so qualifies is a matter for the authority.

Transfers

9.20   In *Pattinson*,[22] it was suggested that an application for housing by an existing tenant of the authority is usually to be presumed to be an application for transfer, rather than for assistance under Part 7. That approach was, however, rejected in *ex p B*,[23] in which it was held

---

18   *R v Secretary of State for the Environment ex p Tower Hamlets LBC* [1993] QB 632; 25 HLR 524, CA.

19   *R v Oldham MBC ex p Garlick, R v Bexley LBC ex p Bentum, R v Tower Hamlets LBC ex p Begum* [1993] AC 509; 25 HLR 319, HL.

20   See Homelessness (Priority Need for Accommodation) (England) Order 2002 SI No 2051 articles 3 and 4, see above, paras 5.65–5.69.

21   *R v Tower Hamlets LBC ex p Begum* [1993] AC 509; 25 HLR 319, HL.

22   *R v Lambeth LBC ex p Pattinson* (1985) 28 HLR 214, QBD.

23   *R v Islington LBC ex p B* (1997) 30 HLR 706, QBD.

than an application for a transfer could overlap with what may on its facts require to be treated as an application as a homeless person. Although the point was not taken, the latter approach may be considered to have been put beyond doubt by the decision in *Ali*.[24]

9.21 The question in each case is whether the conditions are satisfied. Even if an existing tenant is accepted as homeless, however, an authority may continue to consider his/her transfer application and resolve the homelessness by that means.[25]

Repeat applications

9.22 This is an area which has attracted much litigation. Where an applicant who was refused assistance in the past, or in respect of whom a duty has been discharged because s/he abandoned accommodation offered by the authority following a previous application, applies again to the authority for assistance, there is a clear conflict between:

a) the absolute right of a person to make an application as homeless and the fact that the HA 1996 'does not place any express limitation on who can make an application or as to how many applications can be made';[26] and

b) the need to prevent repetitive applications on the same grounds which serve only to waste the authority's resources, which entitle the applicant to temporary accommodation[27] pending the authority's enquiries,[28] and which may have arisen as a result of the applicant's own actions – for example, because s/he refused accommodation previously offered to him/her by the authority.[29]

9.23 In some (if not all) cases, an authority will have to accept a repeat application. A number of separate questions arise:

a) Who may make a repeat application?

b) What needs to have occurred before an applicant can re-apply?

c) Where one member of a household has, or may be treated as having, become homeless intentionally, but another member

---

24 *Birmingham CC v Ali; Moran v Manchester CC (Secretary of State for Communities and Local Government and another intervening)* [2009] UKHL 36; [2009] HLR 41 at [56].

25 *Ali* and *Moran*, at para 4.71, above, and see also *R (Bilverstone) v Oxford CC* [2003] EWHC 2434 (Admin).

26 *R v North Devon DC ex p Lewis* [1981] 1 WLR 328, QBD, under HA 1985 Part 3.

27 See paras 10.5 onwards, below.

28 *Delahaye v Oswestry BC* (1980) *Times* 29 July, QBD.

29 *R v Westminster CC ex p Chambers* (1982) 6 HLR 15, QBD.

seeks 'separate treatment',[30] does s/he have to make a separate application, or does a duty to consider this issue arise whoever makes the application?

d) What is the position when there are applications to different authorities?

Who may make a repeat application?

9.24   A person who has become homeless intentionally[31] from accommodation provided under HA 1996 s193 or who loses its benefits for some other reason has a statutory right to re-apply.[32]

9.25   Other applicants, including those in respect of whom the authority has previously refused assistance and those who have previously refused assistance offered by the authority under Part 7, are not governed by statutory provisions and must therefore be considered in the light of the case-law.

What needs to have occurred before an applicant can re-apply?

9.26   In *Fahia*,[33] an applicant who had one year previously been found intentionally homeless made a new application for assistance. There had been no intervening settled accommodation.[34] The application was refused by the authority.

9.27   In the House of Lords, it was decided that, if an authority has reason to believe an applicant is homeless, the authority is bound to accept the application and make necessary enquiries. Lord Browne-Wilkinson said:

> [W]hen an applicant has been given temporary accommodation . . . and is then found to be intentionally homeless, he cannot then make a further application based on exactly the same facts as his earlier application . . . But those are very special cases when it is possible to say that there is no application before the local authority and therefore the mandatory duty under [HA 1996 s184] has not arisen. But in the present case there is no doubt that when Mrs Fahia made her further application for accommodation she was threatened with homelessness. Moreover in my judgment her application could not be treated as identical with the earlier 1994 application. She was relying on her eviction from the guesthouse which, for one year, she had been occupying as the direct licensee of the guesthouse proprietor, paying

30   See para 6.9 onwards, above.
31   See chapter 6.
32   HA 1996 s193(9). See further para 10.175, below.
33   *R v Harrow LBC ex p Fahia* [1998] 1 WLR 1396; 30 HLR 1124, HL.
34   Above, paras 6.102–6.117.

the rent for that accommodation . . . It is impossible to say that there has been no relevant change in circumstances at all.[35]

9.28 In the post-*Fahia* case of *J*,[36] the applicant was living with a friend who had asked her to leave. She was found not to be threatened with homelessness. More than a year later, when possession proceedings were issued against the friend, she re-applied. The authority refused to conduct any enquiries, contending that the application was on the same terms and that there had been no material change in circumstances. The decision was quashed. *Fahia* was authority for the proposition that an authority is not under a duty to make enquiries in relation to an application based on exactly the same facts as an earlier application but it did not entitle an authority to refuse to make enquiries where there had been a material change of circumstances. There had clearly been a material change in circumstances: possession proceedings against the friend were imminent.

9.29 In *Rikha Begum*,[37] the applicant, who had been living with her parents when she initially applied as homeless, refused an offer of accommodation made under HA 1996 s193 and the authority decided that it had discharged its duty towards her. She returned to live with her family. Nearly two years later, she re-applied. She claimed there had been a change in circumstances since her first application, because she had given birth to a second child[38] and other family members had come to live at her parents' home so that it was now overcrowded. The authority decided there had been no material change of circumstances and refused to accept an application. This was the wrong test: the authority ought to have asked whether the application was based on exactly the same facts as the previous application, not whether there had been a material change in circumstances.[39]

9.30 The decision in *Rikha Begum* potentially raises as many questions as it solves, for example, what constitutes a change of fact, when must

---

35 At WLR 1402/D–E; HLR 1130. *Delahaye v Oswestry BC* (1980) *Times* 29 July, QBD, which appeared to have decided to the contrary was distinguished on the basis of the requirement for there to be a change in the facts.

36 *R (J) v Waltham Forest LBC* [2002] EWHC 487 (Admin).

37 *Rikha Begum v Tower Hamlets LBC* [2005] EWCA Civ 340; [2005] HLR 34.

38 The child had been born between previous application and refusal of offer, and the decision by the authority that it had discharged its duty.

39 The decision in *Rikha Begum* settled the discussion as to whether the test was one of material change or any change, a discussion which had persisted since *Fahia* as several cases – not referred to in *Fahia* – had suggested that the material change test was to be preferred: see *R v Westminster CC ex p Chambers* (1982) 6 HLR 24, QBD; *R v Ealing LBC ex p McBain* [1985] 1 WLR 1351; 18 HLR 59, CA; *R v Southwark LBC ex p Campisi* (1998) 31 HLR 560, CA.

the change have occurred. Most importantly, the decision could have re-opened the flood-gates to repeat applications, which could not be summarily dismissed, regardless of how insignificant the factual change was.

9.31   To address those concerns, the Court of Appeal offered guidance to assist authorities in identifying when an application may be refused on the ground that it is not on exactly the same facts:

a) while it is for the applicant to identify in any subsequent application the facts which s/he contends render the application different from prior applications, it is for the authority to assess whether the circumstances of the two applications are exactly the same;

b) if a subsequent application for assistance purports to reveal new facts but those facts are, to the authority's knowledge (and without the need for further enquiry), not new, or else they are fanciful or trivial, the authority may reject the application as 'incompetent'; and,

c) if a subsequent application reveals new facts which, in the light of the information then available to the authority, are neither fanciful nor trivial, the authority must accept the application; it is not open to the authority to investigate the accuracy of the alleged new facts before deciding whether to treat the application as valid, even if it suspects (but does not know) that the new facts are inaccurate.

9.32   To determine whether a subsequent application is based on exactly the same facts as an earlier application, the comparison is not between the facts as they existed at the time of the original application and those existing at the time of the second application. Rather, it is between the circumstances as they were at the time of the authority's original decision (or review if there was one) on the earlier application and the circumstances revealed by the subsequent application.[40]

9.33   In *Gardiner v Haringey LBC*,[41] the applicant was a British national living in Columbia, where she had a house. Her daughter suffered from autism and needed care and support – including educational support – that was not available in Columbia. She came to the UK and applied to the authority as homeless. That authority refused the application because it was considered reasonable for the applicant to continue to occupy the house in Columbia and she was accordingly not homeless. Almost a year later, the applicant made another application to the authority and provided new information about her

40   *Rikha Begum* at [43].
41   *Gardiner v Haringey LBC* [2009] EWHC 2699 (Admin).

daughter's special needs and an updated medical report in support of the application. The new information included a statement that since the daughter had been in the UK she had demonstrated 'considerable and dramatic improvements'. The authority relied on *Rikha Begum*[42] in refusing to accept the application on the ground that there had been no change in the facts since the previous application. The claimant successfully applied for judicial review: the new material amounted to new facts which rendered it different from the earlier application.

9.34 There is a mild discrepancy within *Rikha Begum*: although reference is made to 'the date of the authority's decision'[43] as the appropriate date for comparison, there is also reference to 'the circumstances as they were known to be when the earlier application was disposed of' as the appropriate date for comparison;[44] and, when disposing of the appeal,[45] there is reference to the facts at the date of discharge of the original decision.

9.35 This discrepancy might seem to suggest that – where the original application was determined by way of discharge by the authority of its duty by means of an offer that was not accepted – the time for comparison is the date of discharge rather than of the authority's decision. That theory draws some support from *Griffin*,[46] in which a new application was properly held to have been based on the same facts: the change – relationship breakdown – had been known to the authority and taken into account at the time when the earlier offer of accommodation had been made, but had occurred subsequent to the decision on the original application.

9.36 Local connection may be considered in a class of its own. In *Ali and Bibi*,[47] it was held that, when the duty to house an applicant on a first application was discharged by reference to another authority under what is now HA 1996 s198, there was no discharge of duty (by the first authority) under what is now section 193. Accordingly, assuming there is no take-up of an accommodation offer from the other authority, the acquisition of a local connection entitles an applicant to re-apply.

---

42 [2005] EWCA Civ 340; [2005] HLR 34.
43 *Rikha Begum* at [43].
44 *Rikha Begum* at [44].
45 *Rikha Begum* at [54].
46 *R (Griffin) v Southwark LBC* [2004] EWHC 2463 (Admin).
47 *R v Tower Hamlets LBC ex p Ali; R v Tower Hamlets LBC ex p Bibi* (1992) 25 HLR 158, CA.

9.37   This is consistent with the early decision in *Wyness v Poole BC*,[48] in which the family declined to accept a reference to another authority, but 'made do' until one of its members had acquired employment and – thence – a local connection.

Applications by other family members

9.38   There is no bar to a family member of an unsuccessful applicant making a fresh application in his/her own name. Commonly this occurs where an applicant is found intentionally homeless and a member of his/her family claims not to have acquiesced in the act which gave rise to the intentionality.[49]

9.39   An application by another member of the family cannot, however, be used to circumvent a decision that the authority has discharged its duty towards the family.[50] It is considered irrelevant that the member of the family making the new application did not acquiesce in or agree to the refusal of accommodation which led to the decision that the duty had been discharged.

Applications to other authorities

9.40   In *R v Slough BC ex p Ealing LBC*,[51] two applicants had been found homeless intentionally in Slough. One applicant then moved and applied to Ealing, the other to Hillingdon; both authorities concluded that the applicants were not homeless intentionally. In each case, however, the local connection provisions entitled them to refer the applicants back to Slough.[52] It was held that Slough BC was bound by the unintentionally decisions of Ealing and Hillingdon.

9.41   There is therefore nothing to stop an applicant moving around until s/he finds an authority which concludes that s/he is not homeless intentionally, and – unless the second authority's decision can be vitiated as a matter of public law[53] – there is no way in which the authority fixed with final responsibility for the applicant can defeat the decision, even though it conflicts with its own original decision.

---

48   *Wyness v Poole DC* July 1979 *LAG Bulletin* 166, CC. The decision proceeded on 'change of circumstance'.

49   *R v North Devon DC ex p Lewis* [1981] 1 WLR 328. See also paras 6.13–6.16, above.

50   *R v Camden LBC ex p Hersi* (2001) 33 HLR 52, CA. See further para 10.150 onwards, below, on discharge of duty.

51   *R v Slough BC ex p Ealing LBC* [1981] QB 801, CA.

52   The case is a reminder that different authorities can reach different conclusions on the same question.

53   See paras 12.21–12.106, below.

9.42   The *ex p Ealing LBC* decision was applied in *ex p Camden LBC*,[54] which was on like facts. In its discretion, however, the court refused judicial review to quash the original authority's refusal to accept the referral, because the referring authority had failed to make adequate enquiries either of the applicant or of the other authority to resolve certain factual discrepancies between the applicant's statements to the two authorities. Authorities should therefore examine with care applications by people who have been declared homeless intentionally elsewhere. They should afford the first authority to which application was made (and who will bear the burden if a second application is successful) an opportunity to comment on any discrepancies between the applications.

9.43   The Court of Appeal went somewhat further in *ex p Tower Hamlets LBC*:[55] where an application is made to a second authority, that authority's enquiries should extend to examination of the reasons for the first authority's refusal to assist, and should take into account the general housing circumstances prevailing in the first authority's district, just as it may take into account the housing circumstances in its own.[56]

9.44   The principle derived from *ex p Ealing LBC* (see para 9.40, above) does not apply where the application to the second authority is made after the first authority had accepted a duty and made an offer: *O'Brian*.[57] Thus, if Slough BC had not found intentionality but had instead offered accommodation which the applicants had refused, leading Slough to decide that it had discharged its duty towards them, and the applicants had later applied to Ealing LBC and Hillingdon LBC which had referred them back under the local connection provisions, Slough BC could have relied on its prior offer as a discharge under what is now HA 1996 s193.[58]

---

54   *R v Tower Hamlets LBC ex p Camden LBC* (1988) 21 HLR 197, QBD.
55   *R v Newham LBC ex p Tower Hamlets LBC* (1990) 23 HLR 62, QBD.
56   See para 4.97, above.
57   *R v Hammersmith & Fulham LBC ex p O'Brian* (1985) 17 HLR 471, QBD.
58   Cf, para 9.36, above, for the converse position when the first authority has merely referred the applicant to another authority, and the applicant later reapplies on the basis of change of circumstance (acquisition of local connection), in which case there has been no prior discharge: *R v Tower Hamlets LBC ex p Ali; R v Tower Hamlets LBC ex p Bibi* (1992) 25 HLR 158, CA.

How to apply

9.45   Authorities have a duty to hear and adjudicate on applications made by people who are potentially homeless and they must therefore make provision to receive applications. In heavily populated areas, reasonable provision would be expected to comprise some form of 24-hour cover.[59] There is, however, no requirement that applications be in writing or in any particular form and an authority is therefore not at liberty to refuse an application on that basis.[60]

Provision of accommodation on application

9.46   Once an application has been received and accepted, the preliminary consideration for any local authority is whether it must provide accommodation pending the decision on the application, because the applicant appears to it to be eligible for assistance and in priority need.[61] The threshold test for provision of accommodation pending decision is very low:[62] it only requires authority to have 'reason to believe' that an applicant may be homeless, eligible for assistance and have a priority need for the duty to secure accommodation to be activated.[63]

9.47   A local housing authority can leave an applicant in current accommodation (where it remains available) in satisfaction of the duty under HA 1996 s188(1).[64] It is a question of fact, to be determined by the authority, as to how long accommodation will remain suitable.[65]

---

59   *R v Camden LBC ex p Gillan* (1988) 21 HLR 114, QBD.

60   *R v Chiltern DC ex p Roberts* (1990) 23 HLR 387, QBD. See also *R (Aweys) v Birmingham CC* [2007] EWHC 52 (Admin); [2007] HLR 27 (point not taken in Court of Appeal or House of Lords).

61   HA 1996 s188(1).

62   *R (M) v Hammersmith & Fulham LBC* [2006] EWCA Civ 917. The case was appealed to the House of Lords *R (M) v Hammersmith & Fulham LBC* [2008] UKHL 14; [2008] 4 All ER 271, HL see also para 5.66, above) but the point on the threshold for s188(1) was not in issue. A similar point on the threshold was made in the High Court in *R (Aweys) v Birmingham CC* [2007] EWHC 52 (Admin); [2007] HLR 27 but not pursued on appeal (see *Birmingham CC v Aweys and others* [2008] EWCA Civ 48; [2008] HLR 32 and later *Birmingham CC v Ali and others; Moran v Manchester CC* [2009] UKHL 36 [2009] HLR 41; see also para 9.47, below).

63   HA 1996 s188(1); see further below, paras 10.33–10.44.

64   *Birmingham CC v Ali and others; Moran v Manchester CC* [2009] UKHL 36; [2009] HLR 41; see below, para 10.23 and 10.96–10.97.

65   *Birmingham CC v Ali and others; Moran v Manchester CC* [2009] UKHL 36; [2009] HLR 41: see also HA 1996 ss188(1) and 206.

Enquiries

9.48 Once an application has been received, the next stage in the application process is for the authority to make enquiries into the application to determine what (if any) duty is owed. This section is concerned with the ambit and conduct of those enquiries.

The duty to make enquiries

9.49 The duty to make enquiries arises if the authority:

a) receives an application for accommodation or for assistance in obtaining accommodation; and

b) has 'reason to believe' that the applicant may be homeless or threatened with homelessness.[66]

(As noted, if the authority is additionally satisfied that there is reason to believe that the applicant may be eligible for assistance and in priority need, there is a duty to house pending a decision).[67]

9.50 These conditions arise relatively easily: the authority need only 'have reason to believe' that the applicant 'may' be homeless or threatened with homelessness.[68]

9.51 Failure to undertake the necessary enquiries does not, however, give rise to an action in damages: *Palmer.*[69]

9.52 Where there is no reason to believe that an applicant is yet threatened with homelessness, the duty to make enquiries has not been triggered and the authority cannot make a decision whether or not an applicant is threatened with homelessness intentionally: *Hunt.*[70]

9.53 In *Jarvis,*[71] notice that possession would be required of premises let on an assured shorthold tenancy was not of itself sufficient to trigger a duty under HA 1996 s184.

9.54 The enquiries must be sufficient to satisfy the authority whether the applicant is eligible for assistance and if so what (if any) duty is owed to him/her under Part 7.

---

66 HA 1996 s184(1).
67 Above, para 9.46; below, paras 10.5–10.13.
68 HA 1996 s184(1).
69 *R v Northavon DC ex p Palmer* (1995) 27 HLR 576, CA.
70 *R v Rugby BC ex p Hunt* (1992) 26 HLR 1, QBD.
71 *R v Croydon LBC ex p Jarvis* (1993) 26 HLR 194, QBD.

9.55   If the authority considers that there may be a local connection, it is still under a duty to make the preliminary[72] enquiries,[73] which are exclusively in the province of the authority to which application has been made: *ex p Ealing LBC*.[74] The authority may also make enquiries whether or not the applicant has a local connection with the area of another housing authority.[75] As referrals are discretionary, authorities are under no duty to investigate local connection, even where the applicant indicates that s/he wishes to live in another area,[76] although it is submitted that if the applicant gives the authority sufficient cause to think that a local connection referral is available, it should have reasons for refusing to do so.[77]

9.56   If local connection enquiries are to be made, the first must be whether the applicant has a local connection with the area of another authority rather than whether there is one with the authority to which the application has been made. If there is no such local connection, it will be irrelevant to consider whether or not there is one with the authority to which application has been made. People without a connection elsewhere remain the responsibility of that authority: *Streeting*.[78]

9.57   The authority can start local connection enquiries without awaiting the conclusion of its other enquiries, but the issue has to be determined by the date of the decision,[79] and it may become necessary to reconsider a decision to refer on local connection grounds if the other enquiries are prolonged,[80] as the connection itself may be based on factors arising during the enquiries.[81]

---

72 Above, para.9.54.

73 *Delahaye v Oswestry BC* (1980) *Times* 29 July, QBD.

74 *R v Slough BC ex p Ealing LBC* [1981] QB 801, CA; see para 9.41, above.

75 HA 1996 s184(2).

76 *Hackney LBC v Sareen* [2003] EWCA Civ 351; [2003] HLR 54.

77 In practice, of course, most authorities are keen to refer; that said, there can be reciprocal arrangements between authorities which militate against a referral and it remains to be considered whether this would be sufficient to justify a decision not to do so.

78 *R v Hillingdon LBC ex p Streeting* [1980] 1 WLR 1425, DC and CA. See further para 9.9 above.

79 *Mohamed v Hammersmith & Fulham LBC* [2001] UKHL 57; [2002] HLR 7, HL.

80 *R v Newham LBC ex p Smith* (1996) 29 HLR 213, QBD.

81 See *Mohamed*, above, footnote 79.

Who must make the enquiries?

9.58 The burden of making enquiries rests with the authority to whom the application was made. In the absence of contracting out,[82] the duty to enquire may not be delegated to another organisation but the authority may ask another housing authority or relevant body,[83] or a social services authority,[84] to assist in discharging the enquiry duty. This body is obliged to co-operate in the discharge of the function to which the request relates, to the extent that is reasonable in the circumstances.[85]

9.59 In *Gerrard*,[86] the authority had transferred all of its housing stock to a registered housing association, and had reached an agreement pursuant to which the association was to carry out the enquiries under what is now HA 1996 s184, on the basis of which enquiries the authority would make its decisions. Quashing the authority's decision that the applicant was not homeless, it was held that, although entitled under what is now HA 1996 s213 to enlist assistance from third parties (including a registered housing association) in making enquiries, the authority must nonetheless take an active and dominant role in the investigative process.

9.60 On the other hand, in *Woolgar*,[87] it was held that it is only the decision-making function which is exclusive to the authority, and so the investigative function involved in making enquiries could properly be delegated to an outside body (at least, one recognised by statute, such as a registered housing association, now registered provider or, in Wales, registered social landlord).[88]

---

82 See para 9.5, above.

83 New town corporation, registered provider (in Wales, registered social landlord) or housing action trust, or in Scotland a local authority, development corporation, or registered housing association: HA 1996 s213(2).

84 In the case of 16- and 17-year-olds, the Code of Guidance (para 6.19; Welsh Code para 14.30) recommends joint assessments with social services. See also *R (M) v Hammersmith & Fulham LBC* [2008] UKHL 14; [2008] 4 All ER 271, HL, para 5.66, above.

85 HA 1996 s213; see below, paras 12.114 and 14.12.

86 *R v West Dorset DC, West Dorset HA ex p Gerrard* (1994) 27 HLR 150, QBD. Both this and *Woolgar*, below, footnote 87, preceded the contracting out power – above, para 9.5.

87 *R v Hertsmere BC ex p Woolgar* (1995) 27 HLR 703, QBD.

88 HA 1996 s213(2)(a).

Conduct of enquiries

9.61 It is for the authority, not the courts, to determine how the necessary enquiries are made, including who should conduct interviews and what questions should be asked. Enquiries should nonetheless be carried out in a sympathetic way:[89] *Phillips*.[90]

9.62 Whether an interview is necessary is likewise primarily for the authority to decide. In *Tetteh*,[91] the applicant had set out his position in correspondence and there was nothing which required the authority to interview him; failure to do so could therefore not be seen to be a breach of the principles of natural justice.[92] A number of authorities – and/or contractors – now carry out interviews by telephone: while this may be proper where all that is needed is to establish or check facts, it is submitted that this will nonetheless not be sufficient where the matter under consideration calls for a face-to-face interview,[93] for example, vulnerability.[94] Thus, many people find it difficult to express themselves on the telephone, whether because of language difficulties or mental competence or through unease at being asked to talk about potentially sensitive issues without forewarning, as is often the case on receipt of a telephone call. Likewise, the interviewer is deprived of the ability to assess 'body language', a concept that may be difficult to describe but that is well-recognised and that is essential to the overall evaluative exercise in which the interviewer is

---

89 Previous versions of the Code referred to carrying out enquiries in a caring and sympathetic manner; the current version does not explicitly do so, but does refer to enquiries being carried out quickly and applicants having an opportunity to explain their circumstances fully: see para 6.15. The Welsh Code still refers to enquires being undertaken 'sympathetically': see para 12.5.

90 *R v West Dorset DC ex p Phillips* (1984) 17 HLR 336, QBD. See also comments in the decision in *R v Camden LBC ex p Gillan* (1988) 21 HLR 114, QBD. The change to the Code in England (see footnote 89, above) does not appear to derogate from these cases; the same conclusion would probably have been reached by the courts in any event, as a matter of construction of the Act and its purposes.

91 *Tetteh v Kingston upon Thames RLBC* [2004] EWCA Civ 1775; [2005] HLR 21.

92 Below, paras 12.56–60.

93 In *R v Camden LBC ex p Gillan* (1988) 21 HLR 114, QBD, the Divisional Court referred to the expectation of a 'face to face' opportunity to explain an applicant's situation, in contrast to a telephone-based system, and criticised the authority's 'cavalier treatment' of applicants who were required to explain their circumstances by telephone.

94 An authority must approach vulnerability with 'great care' – see *Crossley v Westminster CC* [2006] EWCA Civ 140; [2006] HLR 27, per Sedley LJ at [30].

engaged. It may be observed that the interviewee, too, is also deprived of the element of 'reading' the interviewer that is likewise central to comprehension (and to assessing reactions).[95] Furthermore, the interviewee may, without the knowledge of the interviewer, be distracted by other people or events;[96] indeed, the interviewee may be temporarily impaired, for example, through drink or drugs.[97]

9.63   Inconsistencies will frequently be found when someone's native language is not English: *Li*.[98] Previous editions of the Code recommended that authorities secure access to competent interpreters for the community languages of their area, but the current Code of Guidance makes no reference to this.[99]

9.64   Where there is doubt about the competence of an interpreter, the test is whether it has been shown that the interpreter is not – to the knowledge of the authority – competent to conduct the interview: *Jalika Begum*.[100]

9.65   In *Khatun*,[101] interviews with an applicant (without his/her own independent adviser or counsellor) were not inherently flawed on the basis that they had been conducted by an employee of the council who would be inclined to protect the employer's limited resources.[102]

95 An interviewee may – is likely to – wish to appear co-operative, and/or may be suggestible, at least to a point; in a telephone interview, s/he cannot gauge how his/her answers are impacting on the interviewer.

96 Particularly if the interview is with someone in an hostel, taking the call on a telephone in the common parts.

97 It is not impossible, including in cases such as those referred to in the previous footnotes, for there to be a mistake in identity, whether by misunderstanding or even deliberate conduct by a third party.

98 *R v Surrey Heath BC ex p Li* (1984) 16 HLR 79, QBD.

99 It does, however, suggest that information on homelessness procedures should be made available in the main languages spoken in the area, and that for languages less frequently spoken that there should be access to interpreters: para 6.10. Cf the Welsh Code para 12.6, which still recommends access to competent interpreters for the languages of communities in the authority's area.

100 *R v Tower Hamlets LBC ex p Begum* (1990) 24 HLR 188, QBD.

101 *R v Tower Hamlets LBC ex p Khatun* (1994) 27 HLR 465, CA.

102 Cf the 'fairness' discussions in *Runa Begum v Tower Hamlets LBC* [2003] UKHL 5; [2003] 2 AC 430; [2003] HLR 32; *Feld v Barnet LBC* [2005] EWCA Civ 1307; [2005] HLR 9 (see also see below, paras 9.167–9.169); *De-Winter Heald and others v Brent LBC* [2009] EWCA Civ 930; [2009] HLR 8. See below, para 12.62.

Ambit of enquiries

9.66   The burden of making enquiries is squarely on the authority.[103] Enquiries must cover all the relevant factors, for example, priority need,[104] or risk of domestic violence in another area.[105] Enquiries need not, however, amount to 'CID-type' enquiries.[106] The proper approach is summarised in *Winchester*:[107]

> The burden lies upon the local authority to make appropriate enquiries ... in a caring and sympathetic way ... These enquiries should be pursued rigorously and fairly albeit the authority are not under a duty to conduct detailed CID-type enquiries ... The applicant must be given an opportunity to explain matters which the local authority is minded to regard as weighing substantially against him ...

9.67   It follows that there are circumstances where a local housing authority may not need to make enquiries into some matters. For example, where possession has been ordered on the basis of arrears, the authority might not have to embark on enquiries before reaching a decision on intentionality unless there is material which suggests that it should do so.[108] Nor, when considering whether an applicant has been occupying settled accommodation, does an authority necessarily have to enquire into the legal character of that accommodation.[109] In *Gilby v Westminster CC*[110] the applicant occupied accommodation either as an unlawful subtenant or as a bare licensee. The question was whether the occupation constituted settled accommodation, for which purpose the relevant question was whether the applicant had the basis for a reasonable expectation of continued occupation. The difference between bare license and unlawful sub-tenancy was irrelevant to that question. In any event, the authority had determined that in either circumstance the accommodation was not settled.

103   *R v Woodspring DC ex p Walters* (1984) 16 HLR 73, QBD; *R v Reigate & Banstead DC ex p Paris* (1984) 17 HLR 103, QBD; *R v Barnet LBC ex p Babalola* (1995) 28 HLR 196, QBD; *R v Wandsworth LBC ex p Dodia* (1997) 30 HLR 562, QBD. See also Code of Guidance para 6.15; Welsh Code para 12.5.

104   *R v Ryedale DC ex p Smith* (1983) 16 HLR 66, QBD.

105   *Patterson v Greenwich LBC* (1993) 26 HLR 159, CA.

106   *Lally v Kensington and Chelsea RLBC* (1980) *Times* 27 March, QBD.

107   *R v Gravesham BC ex p Winchester* (1986) 18 HLR 208, QBD, at 214–215.

108   *Green v Croydon LBC* [2007] EWCA Civ 1367; [2008] HLR 28.

109   *Gilby v Westminster CC* [2007] EWCA Civ 604; [2008] HLR 7.

110   [2007] EWCA Civ 604; [2008] HLR 7.

9.68   Enquiries may extend to other departments within the authority, for example, the housing department (referable to an earlier tenancy): *Adair*.[111]

9.69   Where an application is made by an occupier of property owned by the authority, the duty to make enquiries does not, however, fetter any decision to recover possession. Thus, in *Grumbridge*,[112] a trespasser sought judicial review of the authority's decision to evict him before determining his application for housing. It was held that there was no requirement or statutory obligation on a housing authority to determine whether a person is either homeless or in priority need or, indeed, as to any of the other matters under (then) Part 3 of the Housing Act 1985 (now HA 1996 Part 7), before deciding whether to obtain possession of property.

9.70   Where the facts relating to an application are fairly placed before the applicant for him/her to agree, dispute or supplement, and the applicant agrees them, it is not unfair for the decision-maker or the reviewing officer to proceed on the basis that the agreed facts are accurate.[113]

Whose circumstances?

9.71   The section refers to 'a person making ... an application', and enquiries under HA 1996 s184[114] are whether 'he is' eligible for assistance, or whether 'he has a local connection' with another authority. The wording might therefore be said to suggest that it is only the applicant who is to be considered.

9.72   On the other hand, enquiries into the local connection of the applicant alone would not suffice, for the local connections of a person reasonably to be expected to reside with the applicant are relevant,[115]

---

111 *R v Camden LBC ex p Adair* (1996) 29 HLR 236, QBD.

112 *R v Barnet LBC ex p Grumbridge* (1992) 24 HLR 433, QBD.

113 *Rowley v Rugby BC* [2007] EWCA Civ 483; [2007] HLR 40. See para 9.199, below. See also *R (Lynch) v Lambeth LBC* [2007] HLR 15 at [32]: 'All the medical evidence was accepted, and the housing authority did not consider, either before the s184 or the review, that any further inquiries were necessary. No suggestion was made by the claimant or her advisers that further information should be sought, nor was any more offered. No response was made to the minded to find letter of the reviewing officer. In line with the decision of the *Cramp* case, . . . the Housing Authority were not unreasonable in failing to make further inquiries. It is difficult to envisage what other inquiries needed to be made, given the wealth of information with the original application.'

114 See para 9.48, above.

115 See para 7.32, above.

and priority need may likewise arise by reference to non-applicants.[116] The circumstances of a person reasonably to be expected to reside with the applicant may also affect the issue of intentionality, for example, if those circumstances meant that the accommodation which has been quit was not available, or not reasonable to be continued to be occupied.[117] The suitability of accommodation offered will also require regard to be had to those reasonably to be expected to reside with the applicant.[118]

9.73   It is submitted that it would introduce a surprising – and inconsistent – degree of legality or formality into Part 7 if anything turned on who actually approaches the authority or signs an application form.

9.74   It is suggested, therefore, that any person whose circumstances will, under Part 7, necessarily be taken into consideration in determining either eligibility for assistance or the level of that assistance, should be considered within the ambit of an application and its enquiries.[119]

Burden of proof

9.75   It is not for the applicant to 'prove' his/her homelessness. In *Walters*,[120] the applicant's solicitor gave the authority information which, if confirmed, would have led to a finding that the applicant was homeless; the authority said that she had not established that she was homeless. This wrongly treated the burden as being on the applicant to prove homelessness.

Relevant matters

9.76   It is a trite proposition that enquiries must cover all relevant matters.[121]

9.77   A relevant matter may evolve from the factual background provided by the applicant or of the authority's own motion. In *Paris*,[122]

---

116 See para 5.2, above.
117 See paras 6.77 and 6.140, above.
118 See para 10.141.
119 In turn, this could lead to a finding of unintentionally – where one member is or could be held to be have become homeless intentionally but another is or could not be; at that point, assuming there is at least a minimal degree of knowledge that the 'second' person is asking the authority for housing assistance, there is in substance an 'application', and that person is entitled to his/her separate consideration: see above, para 9.72.
120 *R v Woodspring DC ex p Walters* (1984) 16 HLR 73, QBD.
121 See below, paras 12.11 and 12.41–12.42.
122 *R v Reigate and Banstead BC ex p Paris* (1984) 17 HLR 103, QBD.

it was held that enquiries into matters relevant to a finding of intentionality have to be made whether or not the applicant provides information which suggests that there may be something to follow up, for example, whether or not the last accommodation occupied was available and whether it was reasonable to continue in occupation there.

9.78   An application of that principle can be found in *Silchenstedt*,[123] where the applicant was asked to leave accommodation consisting of two bedrooms on the ground of rent arrears but was offered alternative accommodation by the same landlord, which he refused on the ground that it was not suitable. The authority found the applicant intentionally homeless and that the alternative accommodation was available for him and reasonable for him to occupy.[124] The applicant successfully challenged the decision on the ground that the authority had not conducted sufficient enquiries into whether the current accommodation was suitable and reasonable for him to occupy.

9.79   By way of contrast, in *de Falco*,[125] the applicants gave their reason for leaving Italy as unemployment and did not put forward any material from which it might have been inferred that the accommodation that they had left was not accommodation which had been suitable for their occupation. The authority was held not to have erred in drawing the inference that what they had left had been suitable, even though it had made no express enquiry to this effect. *De Falco* was, however, an interlocutory application and was treated as such in *Paris*.[126] On this aspect, it is somewhat out of harmony with subsequent decisions.

9.80   In *Fisher*,[127] it was held that intentionality enquiries may have to go back over several years, to the last accommodation occupied by the applicant (if any) which was available and reasonable. See also *Iqbal*,[128] where insufficient enquiries were made as to the applicant's claim that he was a political refugee.

123 *R v Kensington and Chelsea RLBC ex p Silchenstedt* (1996) 29 HLR 728, QBD.

124 For reasons that are not apparent on the face of the report, the argument (described as 'legalistic, although it may be a perfectly proper, approach') that the applicant could not be homeless intentionally as a result of a failure to take up accommodation (above, para 6.6) 'has not been pressed in this application before me': *Silchenstedt*, at 731.

125 *De Falco, Silvestri v Crawley BC* [1980] QB 460, CA.

126 *R v Reigate and Banstead BC ex p Paris* (1984) 17 HLR 103, QBD.

127 *R v Preseli DC ex p Fisher* (1984) 17 HLR 147, QBD.

128 *R v Westminster CC ex p Iqbal* (1988) 22 HLR 215, QBD.

Adequacy of enquiries

9.81   The requirement to enquire into all relevant matters does not, however, mean that a failure to enquire into every matter raised will necessarily make the enquiry process flawed. What is relevant will be
different in every case. The duty to make enquiries means enquiries
appropriate to the facts known to the authority, or of which it ought
reasonably to have been aware.[129]

9.82   Enquiries can only be attacked as inadequate if they are enquiries that no reasonable authority could have failed to make; the court
should not intervene merely because further enquiries would have
been sensible or desirable, only if they were such that no reasonable authority could be satisfied had been sufficient – see *Costello*,[130]
Bayani,[131] *Kassam*.[132]

Examples – unsuccessful challenge

9.83   In *Adamiec*,[133] where the applicant alleged that he had been constrained to sell his home because of financial circumstances, the
court refused to quash the decision that he was intentionally homeless either on the basis that a reasonable authority would have further
tested the financial material before it or that a reasonable authority
would have made further enquiries.

9.84   Likewise in *Baruwa*,[134] where the applicant claimed she could not
afford her rent because of other necessary outgoings, the Court of
Appeal held that it was not necessary for the authority to investigate
every detail and every inconsistency in the income and expenditure
figures provided by the applicant before reaching its decision.[135]

9.85   In *Bariise*,[136] the applicant complained that insufficient enquiries
had been made into her allegations that those she had shared a house
with had stolen her food and had scolded her children, making them
cry. All the allegations were, however, known to the authority; there

---

129 *R v Sedgemoor DC ex p McCarthy* (1996) 28 HLR 608, QBD.

130 *R v Nottingham CC ex p Costello* (1989) 21 HLR 301, QBD.

131 *R v Kensington and Chelsea RLBC ex p Bayani* (1990) 22 HLR 406, CA.

132 *R v Kensington and Chelsea RLBC ex p Kassam* (1993) 26 HLR 455, QBD. See
also *R v Nottingham CC ex p Edwards* (1998) 31 HLR 33, QBD.

133 *R v Leeds CC ex p Adamiec* (1991) 24 HLR 138, QBD.

134 *R v Brent LBC ex p Baruwa* (1997) 29 HLR 915, CA.

135 Contrast *R v Tower Hamlets LBC ex p Ullah* (1992) 24 HLR 680, QBD, where
further enquiries were held to have been necessary, on very similar facts to
Baruwa.

136 *R v Brent LBC ex p Bariise* (1998) 31 HLR 50, CA.

were no further enquiries which the authority could usefully have made.

9.86   In *McDonagh*,[137] a failure to enquire into the applicant's British nationality could not be criticised, as the applicant had informed the authority that his family was a large Irish travelling family just arrived from Dublin, and only claimed to be British after the decision that he was intentionally homeless had been made.

9.87   In *Augustin*,[138] it could not be said – on the material before it – that the authority could not have been satisfied that the applicant was homeless intentionally. In the circumstances, it could not be said that it had not made necessary enquiries.

Examples – successful challenge

9.88   In *Beattie (No 2)*,[139] affidavit evidence in earlier proceedings was considered to be material which the authority ought to have taken into account, even though it had not expressly been referred to during the course of a further application.

9.89   In *Krishnan v Hillingdon LBC*,[140] the authority had made inadequate enquiries when it failed to chase up its letter to another authority, or to follow up the applicant's own description of pressure on him to leave his earlier accommodation because of overcrowding.

9.90   In *Phillips*,[141] the applicant burst out at her husband during their interview that she had always told him his drinking would get them into trouble. This was said not to be capable of being construed as acquiescence,[142] even by the most hard-hearted of officers; it was astonishing that the officer had not made further enquiries. If he had, for example, of social services, it would inevitably have led to the conclusion that the applicant could not be blamed.

9.91   In *Tickner v Mole Valley DC*,[143] Lord Denning MR criticised the enquiries made as to whether or not the applicants were actually homeless. The applicants, while living in mobile homes, had given permanent addresses to the site manager, on which the authority based its conclusion that they were not homeless:

> They made that finding because each couple gave their permanent address elsewhere. One gave a mother-in-law's address. Another

137 *R (McDonagh) v Hounslow LBC* [2004] EWHC 511 (Admin).
138 *R v Westminster CC ex p Augustin* (1993) 25 HLR 281, CA.
139 *R v Eastleigh BC ex p Beattie (No 2)* (1984) 17 HLR 168, QBD.
140 *Krishnan v Hillingdon LBC* June 1981 *LAG Bulletin* 137, QBD.
141 *R v West Dorset DC ex p Phillips* (1984) 17 HLR 336, QBD.
142 See para 6.14, above.
143 *Tickner v Mole Valley DC* August 1980 *LAG Bulletin* 187, CA.

gave a divorced husband's address. I think that was not sufficient. Enquiries should have been made at the addresses given as permanent addresses. If the mother-in-law was asked – or if the divorced husband was asked – the answer would have been: 'We are not going to have that person back.' So Mole Council should have found these couples were homeless.

9.92 As presaged above,[144] the right to review is likely to cure any deficiency or failure to conduct adequate enquiries. In *Cramp*,[145] Brooke LJ said:[146]

> Given the full-scale nature of the review, a court whose powers are limited to considering points of law should now be even more hesitant than the High Court was encouraged to be at the time of *ex p Bayani*[147] if the appellant's ground of appeal relates to a matter which the reviewing officer was never invited to consider, and which was not an obvious matter he should have considered.

9.93 Although *Cramp* has undoubtedly raised the bar which an applicant must cross in order to establish illegality on the grounds of the adequacy of enquiries, that is not to say that the issue can no longer be raised. Challenges are frequently pursued on the basis of failure to make enquiries and the obligation to do so remains extant and, if a failure to make an enquiry remains uncorrected on review, the right to challenge remains available.

9.94 The pre-*Cramp* case-law still provides useful guidance as to the matters which will influence the court's decision. It should, however, be read with the limitations of *Cramp* in mind.

Reliance on particular circumstances

9.95 If reliance is sought to be placed on some eventuality which is not to be taken for granted – for example, some idiosyncratic or uncommon circumstance which would alter the decision – but not even a suspicion of it has come to the authority's attention, it is much harder to complain of its failure to ask a relevant question.[148]

9.96 Advisers should therefore be careful to put all relevant matters before an authority. An authority will not be criticised for failing to

---

144 Para 9.7.

145 *Cramp v Hastings BC, Phillips v Camden LBC* [2005] EWCA Civ 1005; [2005] HLR 48.

146 *Cramp*, at [14].

147 *R v Kensington and Chelsea RLBC ex p Bayani* (1990) 22 HLR 406, CA.

148 See *Cramp*, above. See also *Bellouti v Wandsworth LBC* [2005] EWCA Civ 602; [2005] HLR 46.

make enquiries of someone they have no reason to believe will provide relevant information, for example, a doctor or a school where health or education were not apparently in issue, especially if an experienced adviser has not raised the point.

9.97 In *Holland*,[149] a couple applied as homeless. They had been living at a series of temporary addresses since leaving a caravan site, which the authority was satisfied had been quit in circumstances which amounted to intentional homelessness. At the Court of Appeal, the couple sought to rely on a suggestion that the man had enjoyed an intervening period of what would have been permanent accommodation in a boarding-house (because he and his wife had at that time separated), but which he had lost for reasons beyond his control, so that he could not be treated as being intentionally homeless. This argument was rejected: the authority had been given no reason to suspect that the accommodation might have been permanent or acceptable to the man, whose separation from his wife had never been mentioned.

9.98 In *Henderson*,[150] the applicants contended that they were unaware of material facts when they agreed to an order for possession being made against them; the authority could not, however, be faulted for failing to make appropriate enquiries when, on the facts available to it (including what it had been told by the applicants), it had no reason to be aware of this.

9.99 See also *Mahsood*,[151] in which it was held that the authority had no reason to be aware of the applicant's ignorance of housing benefit entitlement during a period of absence. See further *Cunha*,[152] where there had been little or no reference to the illness of the applicant's child as a reason for her return from Brazil and *Ajayi*,[153] where the authority had failed to enquire into 'important matters of social history and national status', such as for how long the applicant had been away from the UK and where her children were born, which failure led to an error in the way in which the application was considered.

9.100 In *Begum*,[154] although it was relevant to consider whether an applicant could afford to travel to accommodation in deciding whether it was available to her,[155] the challenge failed because the applicant

149 *R v Harrow LBC ex p Holland* (1982) 4 HLR 108, CA.
150 *R v Wandsworth LBC ex p Henderson* (1986) 18 HLR 522, QBD.
151 *R v Wycombe DC ex p Mahsood* (1988) 20 HLR 683, QBD.
152 *R v Kensington and Chelsea RLBC ex p Cunha* (1988) 21 HLR 16, QBD.
153 *R v Newham LBC ex p Ajayi* (1994) 28 HLR 25, QBD.
154 *Begum v Tower Hamlets LBC* (1999) 32 HLR 445, CA.
155 See para 4.19, above.

had not raised the issue, nor was it evident from any of the information before the authority that it was an issue. It was accordingly entitled to conclude without further enquiries that she could return to it.

Medical evidence

9.101   In cases where vulnerability is claimed for medical reasons, it will be both proper and a necessary part of an authority's enquiries to consider a medical opinion. The authority must, however, still decide the question of vulnerability for themselves: *Carroll*.[156]

9.102   A medical report obtained in pursuance of enquiries is not necessarily required to be disclosed to an applicant. In *R (Lynch) v Lambeth LBC*,[157] the authority made reference to extracts of its medical officer's report within the 'minded to find' letter sent in compliance with the Review Procedure Regulations 1999.[158] The applicant had the opportunity to make representations in response to the letter on any matter with which she disagreed, including the references to the medical officer's report. She did not do so. The failure by the authority to provide the applicant with a copy of the medical report was therefore 'not conclusive of any error of public law'.[159]

9.103   In *Sangermano*,[160] the authority ought either to have accepted medical evidence which was submitted by the applicant's advisers, or to have made its own further enquiries. Once medical evidence has been provided to an authority and properly considered, however, it is open to the authority to reject it.[161]

9.104   Medical evidence may also be rejected if it does not relate to a relevant time. In *Hijazi*,[162] a psychiatrist's opinion was rejected because it did not relate to the applicant's condition at the material time of his eviction.

9.105   In *Lumley*,[163] the authority was provided with a questionnaire completed by the applicant's GP which confirmed that the applicant suffered from severe depression for which he was on medication.

---

156   *R v Lambeth LBC ex p Carroll* (1987) 20 HLR 142, QBD; *Osmani v Camden LBC* [2004] EWCA Civ 1706; [2004] HLR 22.

157   [2006] EWHC 2737 (Admin); [2007] HLR 15.

158   Below, paras 9.161–9.192.

159   *R (Lynch) v Lambeth LBC* [2006] EWHC 2737 (Admin); [2007] HLR 15, at [33].

160   *R v Bath CC ex p Sangermano* (1984) 17 HLR 94, QBD.

161   *Noh v Hammersmith and Fulham LBC* [2001] JHL D54, CA.

162   *Hijazi v Kensington & Chelsea RLBC* [2003] EWCA Civ 692; [2003] HLR 73.

163   *R v Newham LBC ex p Lumley* (2001) 33 HLR 5, QBD.

The information was passed to the authority's medical officer, who was not qualified in psychiatric medicine, and who neither saw the applicant nor made any further enquiries. He concluded, without giving any reasons, that the applicant was not vulnerable on medical grounds. The enquiries made by the medical officer were held to be inadequate.

9.106   In *Kacar*,[164] however, the applicant claimed that it was not reasonable for him to continue to live away from London because of his wife's depression and phobia of being alone. His wife was not receiving any medical treatment, nor had she consulted her GP, nor had she spoken to her social worker. There were no further enquiries which a reasonable authority could have been expected to make; it had sufficient information to assess the seriousness of the wife's depression.

9.107   In *Shala v Birmingham CC*,[165] the applicants – a husband and wife – applied as homeless and asserted that the wife had mental health issues which meant that she had a priority need. Information was provided from a GP setting out the diagnosis and treatment of post-traumatic stress disorder and depression. The authority concluded that the wife was not in priority need. The couple asked for a review and obtained medical evidence from a psychiatrist stating that the wife was 'very depressed'. The local authority referred this to a medical adviser who provided an opinion that 'there was no particular assertion of severity' and no suggestion of admission to a psychiatric hospital or of other significant treatment being necessary. The medical adviser did not carry out any examination of the wife. Further information was subsequently provided as to the wife's vulnerability from the psychiatrist and the GP. None of that information was referred to the medical adviser . The authority upheld the original decision that there was no priority need.

9.108   On appeal, it was said that:

a) where an authority's medical expert lacks parity of qualification with the Appellant's expert, the authority 'must not fall into the trap of thinking that it is comparing like with like';[166] and,

b) if one medical expert advises on the implications of another expert's report without examining the patient, 'his advice cannot itself ordinarily constitute expert evidence of the applicant's condition'

---

164 *Kacar v Enfield LBC* (2001) 33 HLR 5, CA.
165 *Shala v Birmingham CC* [2007 EWCA Civ 624; [2008] HLR 8. See also para 5.36.
166 *Shala*, at [22].

and, if s/he does advise without examination 'the decision-maker needs to take the absence of an examination into account'.[167]

Blanket policies

9.109   A decision reached without proper enquiries will be invalid. A decision reached pursuant to a policy to treat all those evicted for arrears as homeless intentionally will be plainly void as a failure to exercise properly the duty to reach an individual decision: *Williams v Cynon Valley Council*.[168] Nor may an authority automatically or invariably treat as homeless intentionally all those who have been evicted from premises on grounds which reflect tenant default, for example, nuisance and annoyance; the authority must take the reasons for the eviction into account and look at the circumstances giving rise to the order.[169]

9.110   An authority must also bear in mind that some possession orders are within the discretion of the county court judge, who may have taken into account matters for which the applicant has no responsibility. In *Stubbs v Slough BC*,[170] a county court ordered the authority to reconsider its finding of intentionality because an element in the decision to order possession on the ground of nuisance had been the proximity of landlord and tenant, and their relationship, over which the tenant had no control.

Loss of employment

9.111   If the cause of an application is loss of employment, the authority must enquire why the job was lost: *Williams*.[171] Consider also *Cosmo*,[172] where there was a successful challenge on the ground that the authority had failed to make enquiries into whether the loss of accommodation was due to the failure of the applicant's business. In *Cunha*,[173] however, the claimant sought to require the authority to consider the difficulties in sustaining employment in Brazil before deciding that she had become intentionally homeless when she had left employment there to come to the UK; it was held that there was

---

167   *Shala*, at [22–23].
168   January 1980 *LAG Bulletin* 16, CC.
169   *Devenport v Salford CC* (1983) 8 HLR 54, CA; *R v Cardiff CC ex p John* (1982) 9 HLR 56, QBD.
170   January 1980 *LAG Bulletin* 16, CC.
171   *R v Thurrock DC ex p Williams* (1981) 1 HLR 128, QBD; see para 6.66, above.
172   *R v Camden LBC ex p Cosmo* (1997) 30 HLR 817, QBD.
173   *R v Kensington and Chelsea RLBC ex p Cunha* (1988) 21 HLR 16, QBD.

no requirement for the authority to enquire into local employment conditions in Brazil. Likewise in *Bayani*,[174] the failure of the local authority to make full enquiries into the applicant's employment situation in the Philippines was not fatal to its finding of intentionality.

Fairness

9.112   It is a trite proposition that fairness calls for all basic issues to be put to an applicant (that may be decided adversely to him/her). When conducting enquiries fairly, authorities are not bound to treat the issue as if in a court of law: *Ward*.[175] They act reasonably if they act on responsible material from responsible people who might reasonably be expected to provide a reliable account. An authority can rely on hearsay, in the sense that it is not obliged to confine itself to direct evidence, for example, where an authority relied on evidence from a social worker's supervisor, rather than the social worker herself.[176]

9.113   In *Goddard v Torridge DC*,[177] the authority discussed with the applicant's former employers the circumstances in which he had quit his job and, accordingly, had lost his tied accommodation, and went into these matters fully with the applicant on three separate occasions, which was sufficient for these purposes.

9.114   In the Divisional Court hearing in *Islam*,[178] an allegation of want of natural justice failed because – by the time of the decision – the authority had given the applicant the benefit of no fewer than six interviews. The judgment nonetheless takes for granted that a want of natural justice would be fatal to an authority's decision.

9.115   However, the authority is not obliged to put every detail to an applicant, although the applicant must have an opportunity to deal with at least the generality of material which will adversely affect him/her, which will usually mean matters of factual detail.[179]

9.116   A failure to ask why the applicant fell into mortgage arrears,[180] or a failure to enquire into the applicant's state of mind when she quit

---

174 *R v Kensington and Chelsea RLBC ex p Bayani* (1990) 22 HLR 406, CA.

175 *R v Southampton CC ex p Ward* (1984) 14 HLR 114, QBD.

176 *Ward*, footnote 175, above. See also *R v Nottingham CC ex p Costello* (1989) 21 HLR 301, QBD.

177 January 1982 *LAG Bulletin* 9, HC.

178 *R v Hillingdon Homeless Persons Panel ex p Islam* (1981) *Times* 10 February, QBD (not forming part of the subsequent appeals – see [1983] 1 AC 688, CA and HL; 1 HLR 107, HL).

179 On the requirements of fairness, see below, paras 12.56–12.60.

180 *R v Wyre BC ex p Joyce* (1983) 11 HLR 73, QBD.

her previous accommodation, ie, what she had believed about the accommodation that she was coming to (which turned out to be less than settled),[181] have both been held to have been errors on the part of an authority.

9.117   Where matters are put, they must be put to the applicant him/herself[182] and, if during interview, a record of the interview should be kept: *Brown*.[183]

9.118   All matters that are ultimately decided against the applicant should be put to the applicant,[184] whether the matter is related to an admission by the applicant of which s/he is aware[185] (regardless of whether it was provided on a 'confidential' basis)[186] or where the authority obtains information from a third party on which it intends to rely, such as a bank,[187] or information from the applicant's GP which is inconsistent with that which the applicant has him/herself provided.[188]

9.119   The duty is not, however, absolute. A finding of intentionality was upheld in *Reynolds*,[189] even though important but ultimately not decisive issues had not been put directly to the applicant, who had refused both a home visit and an interview and requested that all communication be made through her solicitors. Nor, in *Jaafer*,[190] was the authority required to put to the applicant its conclusion that her husband and child were illegal immigrants, as it had given her every opportunity to offer her version of events in an interview.

9.120   Where the facts are uncontested, there is no general obligation to inform each and every applicant in advance of any negative decision; this would place an unrealistically heavy burden on authorities: *Tetteh*.[191]

181 *R v Wandsworth LBC ex p Rose* (1983) 11 HLR 105, QBD.
182 *R v Tower Hamlets LBC ex p Saber* (1992) 24 HLR 611, QBD.
183 *R v Dacorum BC ex p Brown* (1989) 21 HLR 405, QBD.
184 *R v Tower Hamlets LBC ex p Rouf* (1989) 21 HLR 294, QBD.
185 *Robinson v Brent LBC* (1998) 31 HLR 1015, CA. See also *R v Wandsworth LBC ex p Dodia* (1997) 30 HLR 562, QBD and *R v Camden LBC ex p Mohammed* (1997) 30 HLR 315, CA on inconsistent statements given by applicants.
186 *R v Poole BC ex p Cooper* (1995) 27 HLR 605, QBD.
187 *R v Shrewsbury and Atcham BC ex p Griffiths* (1993) 25 HLR 613, QBD. See also *R v Brent LBC ex p McManus* (1993) 25 HLR 643, QBD and *R v Hackney LBC ex p Decordova* (1994) 27 HLR 108, QBD.
188 *R (Begum) v Tower Hamlets LBC* [2002] EWHC 633 (Admin); [2003] HLR 8.
189 *R v Sevenoaks DC ex p Reynolds* (1989) 22 HLR 250, CA.
190 *R v Westminster CC ex p Jaafer* (1997) 30 HLR 698, QBD.
191 *Tetteh v Kingston upon Thames RLBC* [2004] EWCA Civ 1775; [2005] HLR 21.

9.121   Nor is there an obligation to give the applicant the last word in every case. Whether or not it is unfair not to do so depends on the facts of the particular case. Thus in *Bellouti*,[192] medical evidence from the applicant's GP was submitted to the authority's medical adviser, who advised that it did not make the applicant vulnerable. Taking into account the evidence and the views of the medical adviser, a decision that the applicant was not vulnerable was upheld on review. The Court of Appeal held that the views of the medical adviser did not have to be put to the applicant, because they were not factual material obtained from a third party; all the authority had done was to refer material on which the applicant relied to its own medical adviser for comment. There was accordingly no unfairness in these comments not being shown to the applicant.

Doubt

9.122   If enquiries suggest that the applicant may have become homeless intentionally, but any doubt or uncertainty remains, the issue must be resolved in favour of the applicant.[193]

Further enquiries and reconsideration

9.123   Once a decision has been made, there is no statutory power to make further enquiries otherwise than by way of application for a review[194] or on a new application.[195] The local authority is entitled to take as its starting point the matters which the applicant has specifically raised on review.[196] If a decision taken has been adverse to an applicant, the authority can nonetheless re-open its enquiries of its own motion if it receives new information.[197] This will cure any defects in its earlier procedure, for example, failure to consider relevant matters. Where facts are agreed by an applicant, which facts form the basis of the

---

192 *Bellouti v Wandsworth LBC* [2005] EWCA Civ 602; [2005] HLR 46. See also *Hall v Wandsworth LBC; Carter v Wandsworth LBC* [2004] EWCA Civ 1740; [2005] HLR 23.

193 *R v North Devon DC ex p Lewis* [1981] 1 WLR 328, QBD; see also *R v Thurrock BC ex p Williams* (1982) 1 HLR 71, QBD and *R v Gravesham BC ex p Winchester* (1986) 18 HLR 208, QBD.

194 *Mohamed v Hammersmith & Fulham LBC* [2001] UKHL 57; [2002] HLR 7, HL.

195 *R v Lambeth LBC ex p Miah* (1994) 27 HLR 21, QBD.

196 *Williams v Birmingham CC* [2007] EWCA Civ 691; [2008] HLR 4.

197 Consider *R v Hambleton DC ex p Geoghan* [1985] JPL 394, QBD.

decision, the decision-maker is entitled to take the applicant's acceptance of the facts at face value.[198]

9.124   If the authority has power to reopen enquiries of its own motion,
then it is hard to see how any reasonable authority could refuse to
exercise it, ie, at the request of a disappointed applicant, provided
that the new information has some degree of credibility and could
(if accepted) affect the decision. If an authority refuses to do so, the
correct course is not to seek judicial review but to appeal the original
decision.[199]

9.125   In *Walsh*,[200] further enquiries led the authority to the conclusion
that an earlier account of being locked out of accommodation was
entirely false. While there was no right to make a new decision on the
same facts, the authority could do so if there was a material change,
including new facts or the ascertained falsity of former facts.

9.126   In *Dagou*,[201] however, it was suggested that only fraud and deception could entitle the authority to re-open enquiries once its decision
had been reached, although new information might still be relevant
to the accommodation which was to be provided.

9.127   In *Crawley BC v B*,[202] the authority decided initially that an applicant was not in priority need and had so notified her (without reaching a decision on intentionality). Subsequently, during an appeal, it
changed the priority need decision. It was still entitled to go on to
consider whether the applicant had become intentionally homeless.
This was, however, not so much a case of revising a decision as completing it. Some dicta in the case do, however, suggest that an authority may revisit a decision whenever, on public law grounds, it would
be reasonable to do so.[203]

9.128   *Crawley* was distinguished in *Sadiq*.[204] Once a duty had been
accepted under HA 1996 s193,[205] the section provides a complete
code of when an authority ceases to be subject to its requirements, so
that, for example, loss of priority need after acceptance of a section
193 duty does not entitle the authority to make a new decision that no
further duty is owed.

---

198 *Rowley v Rugby BC* [2007] EWCA Civ 483; [2007] HLR 40. See para 9.70, above.
199 *Demetri v Westminster CC* (2000) 32 HLR 470, CA and see para 9.160, below.
200 *R v Dacorum BC ex p Walsh* (1991) 24 HLR 401, QBD. Under HA 1985, there
      was no statutory review process.
201 *R v Southwark LBC ex p Dagou* (1995) 28 HLR 72, QBD.
202 (2000) 32 HLR 636, CA.
203 See per Buxton LJ at 645.
204 (2000) 33 HLR 47, QBD.
205 See para 10.85, below.

9.129   In *Porteous*,[206] however, the authority was permitted to change its decision even after a duty had been accepted under section 193. Rejecting the proposition in *Dagou*[207] that decisions could only be re-opened in cases of fraud or deception, they could also be revisited where the original decision was based on a fundamental mistake of fact.[208] Another way of putting the point is that a decision based on a material mistake of fact is likely to be considered void in public law:[209] as such, the decision on the application had in law not been reached, and there remained a duty to reach it.[210] Likewise in *Slaiman*,[211] the return of an applicant to her husband following domestic violence was held to go to the existence or non-existence of the original allegation of domestic violence, rather than comprising a change of circumstances arising after acceptance of a full duty.

Time-scales

9.130   Although there is no statutory requirement that enquiries be carried out within any specific time, the Code[212] says that authorities should deal with enquiries as quickly as possible. It suggests authorities should aim to achieve the following:

a) interview and carry out an initial assessment of the eligibility of applicants on the day of application;

b) wherever possible, complete enquiries and notify the applicant within 33 working days of accepting the duty to make enquiries.

9.131   The target does not entitle an authority to take the view that because enquiries take an average period of time, or are due to be completed with a target period, it owes no duty to a person whose priority need will be lost before that period expires, as where a young person with

---

206 *Porteous v West Dorset DC* [2004] EWCA Civ 244; [2004] HLR 30.

207 *R v Southwark LBC ex p Dagou* (1995) 28 HLR 72, QBD; above, para 9.126.

208 Both applicant and authority had operated under a fundamental mistake of fact relating to a tenancy which neither had realised the applicant still held.

209 Below, paras 12.35–12.37.

210 See *Islington LBC v Uckac* [2006] EWCA Civ 340; [2006] HLR 35 – albeit on concession.

211 *R (Slaiman) v Richmond upon Thames LBC* [2006] EWHC 329 (Admin); [2006] HLR 20.

212 Code of Guidance para 6.16. The Welsh Code para 12.22, suggests that authorities should set their own targets, and suggests illustratively: interview and assessment on the day of application, or first working day if made out of office hours; completion of enquiries as quickly as possible and within 33 working days; and issue of decision letter within three working days of completion of enquiries.

an automatic priority need because s/he is 16 or 17 years old[213] will turn 18 during that period.[214]

Decisions

Postponement

9.132 Although the obligation to reach a decision is not spelled out in the section, it is implicit: *Sidhu*.[215] An authority may not defer the obligation in the hope or expectation of a change in circumstances such as might reduce its duties, for example, by loss of priority need.[216]

9.133 Nor can an authority seek to use mediation (to reconcile a 17-year-old with his/her family) to prolong the decision-making process, so that the child turns 18 and loses his/her automatic priority need. Where mediation cannot take place without depriving the child of a right s/he would otherwise have had, the authority must take the view that its full duty has to be performed, although it may be able to use mediation in order to fulfil that duty.[217] Mediation and enquiries are entirely independent processes.[218]

9.134 If the issue is eligibility for accommodation,[219] there would in any

---

213 Above, para 5.61.

214 *Robinson v Hammersmith & Fulham LBC* [2006] EWCA Civ 1122; [2007] HLR 7, at [35].

215 *R v Ealing LBC ex p Sidhu* (1982) 2 HLR 45, QBD, approved in *Robinson v Hammersmith & Fulham LBC* [2006] EWCA Civ 1122; [2007] HLR 7, at [36].

216 *R v Ealing LBC ex p Sidhu* (1982) 2 HLR 45, QBD. A suggestion in the *Encyclopaedia of Housing Law and Practice*, Sweet & Maxwell, para 1-3590.7 that in an appropriate case, a de minimis deferral, perhaps a few days, may be permissible where there is a substantive basis (as distinct from speculation or a remote chance) for the authority to anticipate a material change was not disapproved, but 'in the case of a 17 year old child, it would not seem to me to be lawful for a local authority to postpone the taking of a decision even for a short period on the basis that by postponing that decision the child will have reached the age of 18 before the decision is taken': per Waller LJ in *Robinson v Hammersmith & Fulham LBC* at [38]. The effect would seem to be that – while the proposition *might* be correct in an appropriate case – it will not be if it will cause loss of the priority need (as where priority need will, absent other grounds, be lost on reaching 18, see para 5.60, above).

217 *Robinson v Hammersmith & Fulham LBC* [2006] EWCA Civ 1122; [2007] HLR 7, per Waller LJ at [41]. See further, below, para 10.104 on fulfilling the full duty through another person.

218 *Robinson v Hammersmith & Fulham LBC* [2006] EWCA Civ 1122; [2007] HLR 7, per Jonathan Parker LJ at [42] and [45].

219 See chapter 3.

event be no point in deferring because the authority's housing duty under HA 1996 Part 7 will cease if the applicant's eligibility ends.[220]

Material to be taken into account

9.135 Once the authority has completed its enquiries, it must make its decision. The decision must be taken on the basis of the information known to the authority at the time it is reached.

9.136 An applicant could not complain of a decision which failed to take into account a matter which only came to the knowledge of the authority after it had made its final decision: *Islam*.[221] If it comes to light after the initial decision, but before the review, it must be taken into account on the review.[222] If it comes to light after the review, the proper course would appear to be to put the further information before the authority for it to re-open its enquiries and to consider judicial review of a refusal to do so.[223] An authority must, however, take into account all that is relevant up to the date of its decision.

9.137 In *Crossley*,[224] the decision was so at odds with the evidence put before the authority that the authority must have failed to take it into account. As the court put it:[225]

> ... there were also stark facts, or appraisals of fact, pointing towards vulnerability for a statutorily recognised reason; and these the decision-maker had an obligation to acknowledge, take into account and evaluate along with everything else.

9.138 An authority must consider those matters which sensibly arise on the facts of a case. In *F*,[226] the applicant took a tenancy of a property that she could not afford and contended that she had made appropriate enquiries with the housing benefit department before doing so. The authority found that she had not acted in good faith when accepting the tenancy.[227] Although it had not explicitly been invited to consider whether the applicant had acted in good faith, it was a matter that was

---

220 HA 1996 s193(6)(a).
221 *R v Hillingdon Homeless Persons Panel ex p Islam* (1981) *Times* 24 February, QBD (not forming part of the subsequent appeals [1983] 1 AC 688; 1 HLR 107, HL).
222 See para 9.176, below.
223 See para 9.160, below.
224 *Crossley v Westminster CC* [2006] EWCA Civ 140; [2006] HLR 26.
225 At [28].
226 *F v Birmingham CC* [2006] EWCA Civ 1427; [2007] HLR 18.
227 Within the meaning of HA 1996 s191(2), above, paras 6.27–6.28.

sensibly capable of arising on the facts and therefore required consideration by the authority – which the authority had undertaken.

9.139 In *Elrify*,[228] the applicant applied as homeless by reason of overcrowding. Both in its original decision and on review, the authority had applied only one part of the statutory test for overcrowding under the Housing Act 1985 Part 10. The review decision was accordingly flawed because the authority had miscalculated the level of statutory overcrowding in the applicant's flat and had failed properly to apply the statutory test.

Own decision

9.140 The authority must reach its own decision. Even though other authorities from which an authority requests assistance must co-operate,[229] one authority cannot simply 'rubber-stamp' the decision of another: *Miles*.[230] There may, for example, be information about what has occurred between the two applications, such as a separation which means that intervening accommodation was 'settled' for the purposes of the separated parts of a family.[231]

9.141 This principle applies even to decisions of a court.[232] Thus, while an authority must take into consideration decisions by family courts relating to with whom children are to live, the authority is not bound by them but must reach its own decision in the context of its own duties in the (different) legislative context in which they arise: *Holmes-Moorhouse*.[233]

Notification

Reasons

9.142 Once the authority has reached its decision, it must notify the applicant.[234] While there will generally be no reason to distinguish between when the decision is made and notification of reasons, these

228 *Elrify v Westminster CC* [2007] EWCA Civ 332; [2007] HLR 36.
229 HA 1996 s213, and see below.
230 *R v South Herefordshire DC ex p Miles* (1983) 17 HLR 82, QBD. See also *Eren v Haringey LBC* [2007] EWCA Civ 409.
231 See para 6.100, above.
232 Otherwise than so far as they are decisions of a court directly relating to the decision, ie, appeal against it or on judicial review.
233 *Holmes-Moorhouse v Richmond upon Thames LBC* [2009] UKHL 7; [2009] HLR 34.
234 HA 1996 s184(3).

do not necessarily occur on the same date: ascertaining the date of the decision is essentially a question of fact.[235] If the authority decides an issue – relating either to eligibility or to level of duty – adversely to an applicant, it must also notify him/her of its reasons.[236]

Local connection

9.143 A decision to refer an application to another authority under the local connection provisions, and the reasons for doing so, must likewise be notified.[237]

Review

9.144 Notifications must inform applicants of the right to request a review of a decision and of the time within which the request must be made.[238]

Relationship of notification duty and substantive duty

9.145 Duties to notify and to give reasons for decisions arise independently of the substantive duties to which they refer: *R v Beverley BC ex p McPhee.*[239] It is not open to an authority to claim that it has no duty under, for example, HA 1996 s193[240] or s200,[241] on the basis that it has not yet given notice. To hold otherwise would in substance be to permit an authority to rely on its own wrong, ie, its failure to provide notice 'on completion' of enquiries.

Written notification

9.146 Notification, and reasons, must be given in writing; if not received by the applicant, notification will be treated as having been given only if made available at the authority's office for a reasonable time for collection by him/her or on his/her behalf.[242] This appears to be so

235 *Robinson v Hammersmith & Fulham LBC* [2006] EWCA Civ 1122; [2007] HLR 7, at [25], referring (at [24]) to *R v Beverley BC ex p McPhee* (1978) *Times* 27 October, QBD.
236 *Robinson v Hammersmith & Fulham LBC* [2006] EWCA Civ 1122; [2007] HLR 7. And see below, para 9.182.
237 HA 1996 s184(4).
238 HA 1996 s184(5); see further below.
239 (1978) *Times* 27 October, QBD.
240 See para 10.156, below.
241 See para 7.71, above.
242 HA 1996 s184(6).

even if a copy of the notice is sent by registered post to one of the authority's own hostels or other property.[243]

Restricted cases[244]

9.147 If the authority decides that a duty is owed under HA 1996 s193(2) or s195(2),[245] but only because of a restricted person, the notification is subject to additional requirements.[246] It must inform the applicant that the decision was reached on this basis, include the name of the restricted person, explain why the person is a restricted person, and explain the effect of section 193(7AD)[247] or, as the case may be, section 195(4A).[248]

Oral explanation

9.148 In cases where the applicant may have difficulty understanding the implications of the decision, authorities 'should consider arranging for a member of staff to provide and explain the notification in person'.[249]

Review

9.149 Neither the Housing (Homeless Persons) Act 1977 nor HA 1985 Part 3 made any provision for an applicant to seek an internal review of the authority's decision. The third edition of the Code of Guidance issued under HA 1985 Part 3 had, however, recommended[250] that authorities 'should have in place arrangements to review decisions on homelessness cases where an applicant wishes to appeal against the decision'. That recommendation is now a statutory requirement.[251] An applicant is statutorily entitled to request a review, provided that the decision complained of falls within those specified in HA 1996 s202(1). The right to request a review arises in relation to the following decisions.

---

243 The express requirement for writing was added to HA 1985 pursuant to Law Commission Recommendations (Cmnd 9515), No 5.
244 Above, paras 3.74–3.79.
245 Above, paras 3.79 and 7.36–7.37.
246 HA 1996 s184(3A).
247 Below, para 10.78.
248 Below, paras 10.68 and 10.78.
249 Code of Guidance para 6.23; Welsh Code para 12.28.
250 Para 9.6.
251 HA 1996 s202(4).

Eligibility[252]

9.150 A decision on eligibility may be reviewed.[253] This includes whether or not the applicant is a person subject to immigration control.[254]

Duties[255]

9.151 An applicant may also seek review of any decision on what, if any, duty is owed under HA 1996 ss190–193 and 195–196.[256]

9.152 This expressly encompasses whether or not the applicant is in priority need,[257] whether intentionally homeless,[258] whether a duty has ceased under HA 1996 s193(6) or (7),[259] and whether an applicant is threatened with homelessness or threatened with homelessness intentionally.[260] Whether an authority has complied with the requirement to notify the applicant of the consequences of refusal and the right to request a review under section 193(7) and (7A)[261] is also subject to review under this provision.[262]

Local connection[263]

9.153 Review may be sought of a number of local connection decisions.[264] The decision to notify another authority under HA 1996 s198(1) can

252 See generally chapter 3.
253 HA 1996 s202(1)(a).
254 See above, paras 3.81–3.102.
255 See generally chapter 10.
256 HA 1996 s202(1)(b).
257 HA 1996 ss190(3) and 192; and also by inference whether the applicant is homeless.
258 HA 1996 ss190(1) and 191.
259 HA 1996 s193 encompasses a decision that a duty, once owed, is no longer owed: *Warsame v Hounslow LBC* (1999) 32 HLR 335, CA. See further paras 10.156–10.159, below.
260 HA 1996 ss195 and 196.
261 See para 10.159, below.
262 *Tower Hamlets LBC v Rahanara Begum* [2005] EWCA Civ 116; [2006] HLR 9. The applicant had failed to seek internal review and the matter could not be raised as a defence to eviction proceedings being brought against her. Cf *R (Zaher) v Westminster CC* [2003] EWHC 101 (Admin), where the failure of the authority to inform the applicant of his right to review entitled him to challenge the decision on suitability by judicial review.
263 See generally chapter 7.
264 HA 1996 s202(1)(c), (d), (e). It may not be sought against a decision not to make a local connection referral: *Hackney LBC v Sareen* [2003] EWCA Civ 351; [2003] HLR 54.

be reviewed; the decision that the conditions for referral are met under section 198(5) can itself also be reviewed.

9.154   A decision that the conditions of referral are met may be reached either as a result of an agreement between the authorities, or as the result of an arbitration between them.[265] It may at first glance seem somewhat surprising to find provision for review of a decision that the conditions for referral are met, when it is statutorily provided that this is to be a matter for agreement or approved arbitration arrangements.[266] It needs, however, to be remembered that the applicant is him/herself party to neither agreement nor arbitration: this is accordingly his/her opportunity to dispute the outcome.

9.155   Third, decisions on how the duty is to be discharged may themselves be reviewed. This includes discharge both where the local connection referral conditions are met[267] and where they are not.[268]

Suitability and availability of offers

9.156   An applicant may seek a review of whether accommodation offered in discharge of duty under HA 1996 s190, s193[269] or s200 is 'suitable'.[270] An applicant may also seek a review of a decision of an authority as to the suitability of accommodation offered to him/her by way of a private accommodation offer,[271] ie, in a restricted case.[272]

9.157   It had formerly been held that, where an applicant accepted an offer of accommodation, s/he could not also seek a review as to its suitability: *Alghile*.[273] The result of this was that an applicant to whom an unsatisfactory offer of accommodation had been made had to face 'an unwholesome opportunity to gamble',[274] either to refuse

---

265 See paras 7.58–7.59, above.

266 See paras 7.58–7.59, above.

267 HA 1996 s200(4).

268 HA 1996 s200(3).

269 Including expressly HA 1996 s193(7) (see para 10.174, below) to clear up any residual doubt following the decision in *Warsame v Hounslow LBC* (1999) 32 HLR 335, CA, which had the effect of confining application of HA 1996 s202(1)(f) to the question of the suitability of an offer under section 193(6).

270 HA 1996 s202(1)(f); see paras 10.129–10.143, below.

271 HA 1996 s202(1)(g), inserted by Housing and Regeneration Act 2008 Sch 15 para 7.

272 Above, paras 3.74–3.79; para 9.147, above; paras 10.68–10.69, below.

273 *Alghile v Westminster CC* (2001) 33 HLR 57, CA, overruling *R v Kensington & Chelsea RLBC ex p Byfield* (1997) 31 HLR 913, QBD.

274 *Alghile v Westminster CC* [2001] EWCA Civ 363; (2001) 33 HLR 57 per Tuckey LJ at [28].

– which gave rise to the risk that, if unsuccessful on the review, the applicant would end up with nowhere to live – or to accept, which meant putting up with accommodation that s/he considered unsatisfactory.[275] There is, however, now a right to seek an internal review of the suitability of accommodation offered under HA 1996 s193(5) or (7).[276] The review is available whether or not the applicant has accepted the offer of accommodation.[277]

9.158   The date at which suitability of accommodation should be considered on a review will differ depending whether the accommodation is accepted or refused. If an offer of accommodation is accepted, then the authority should consider the facts at the date of review because the accommodation is still available.[278] Conversely, however, where an offer of accommodation has been refused, then the council has taken the decision that it has fulfilled its duty and the property will no longer be available; in those circumstances, the issue has to be tested by reference to the circumstances as they existed at the date of that decision.[279]

Further review

9.159   There is no right to request a review of a decision reached on an earlier review.[280]

9.160   Although HA 1996 s202(2) does not prevent an authority from further reconsidering a decision if asked and willing to do so, a refusal to exercise the discretion to reconsider has been held not to be judicially reviewable.[281] The correct forum for challenge remains by way of appeal to the county court of the original review decision.[282]

---

275 This contrasts with the outcome in *R v Wycombe DC ex p Hazeltine* (1993) 25 HLR 313, CA, see below, para 10.172.
276 HA 1996 s202(1A), added by Homelessness Act 2002 s8.
277 HA 1996 s202(1A), added by Homelessness Act 2002 s8.
278 *Omar v Westminster CC* [2008] EWCA Civ 421; [2008] HLR 36.
279 *Omar*, footnote 278, above, per Waller LJ at [25].
280 HA 1996 s202(2).
281 *R v Westminster CC ex p Ellioua* (1998) 31 HLR 440, CA. See also *R (C) v Lewisham LBC* [2003] EWCA Civ 927; [2004] HLR 4.
282 See *Demetri v Westminster CC* (2000) 32 HLR 470, CA as to the effects of reconsideration on time limits to appeal to the county court, discussed below, paras 12.167–12.169. See also above, para 9.124.

Review procedure

9.161   A request for a review should be made within 21 days of notification of a decision under HA 1996 s184.[283] The applicant must be told in the decision notification about the right to request a review;[284] if the notification does not do so, time cannot be considered to have started to run.

9.162   If the notification does inform the applicant of the right to review, then on the face of it, the applicant who fails to exercise it in time will lose it. The authority has power to extend time.[285] This discretion must be exercised in furtherance of its statutory purpose, which is to establish procedures and time limits necessary to enable the authority to manage its housing stock in an orderly way, and – where appropriate – to grant an indulgence to an applicant where the merits of his/her claim for review are deserving enough to override the failure to request a review in time. Accordingly, the authority is entitled but not bound to take into account the prospect of the review's success.[286]

9.163   The secretary of state has power to make regulations as to the procedure to be followed in connection with a review:[287] see the Allocation of Housing and Homelessness (Review Procedures) Regulations ('Review Procedure Regs') 1999.[288]

Identity of the reviewer

9.164   Regulations may require that the decision on review be made by a person of appropriate seniority who was not involved in the original decision.[289]

9.165   The Regulations[290] require that, when the original decision was made by an officer of the authority[291] and the review is also to be

---

283 HA 1996 s202(3).
284 HA 1996 s202(3). See para 9.144, above.
285 HA 1996 s202(3).
286 *R (C) v Lewisham LBC* [2003] EWCA Civ 927; [2004] HLR 4. See also *R (Slaiman) v Richmond upon Thames LBC* [2006] EWHC 329 (Admin); [2006] HLR 20.
287 HA 1996 s203(1).
288 Review Procedure Regs 1999 SI No 71.
289 HA 1996 s203(2)(a).
290 Review Procedure Regs 1999 reg 2.
291 The decision must be made by the authority by its executive (single member, committee, sub-committee or officer) to whom the function is delegated: see Local Government Act 2000 ss13–15 and Local Authorities (Functions and Responsibilities) Regulations 2000 SI No 2853.

carried out by an officer of the authority, the reviewing officer must be someone who was not involved in the original decision and who is senior to the original decision-maker:

> Seniority for these purposes means seniority in rank within the authority's organisational structure.[292]

9.166 The officer who is undertaking the review may, however, enlist the assistance of a more junior officer, even where that junior officer made the original decision.[293]

9.167 A view expressed by a more senior officer about the type of allocation for which an applicant qualified under the authority's Part 6 allocation scheme was not a decision for the purposes of regulation 2, nor could it be subject to a section 202 review, nor therefore did it disqualify a more junior officer from conducting the review: *Feld*.[294]

9.168 If elected members are involved in the review process,[295] the regulations set no particular requirements. The review function may be contracted out.[296]

9.169 In some circumstances, for example, following a county court appeal or where – following a finding that an original offer of accommodation was unsuitable – the applicant seeks to challenge a further offer, there may be more than one review on a single application. The fact that a review officer has conducted an earlier review does not prevent him/her from conducting a second review; there is no apparent bias in such circumstances and any actual unfairness can be cured on appeal to the county court: *Feld*.[297]

9.170 There is nothing in HA 1996 Part 7 that requires a decision whether or not to secure interim accommodation under HA 1996 s188(3) pending a review[298] to be made by an officer who is senior to the officer who made the original decision on the application.[299]

---

292 Code of Guidance para 19.8; Welsh Code para 21.7.

293 Review Procedure Regs 1999 reg 2; and see *Butler v Fareham BC* May 2001 *Legal Action* 24, CA.

294 *Feld v Barnet LBC; Pour v Westminster CC* [2004] EWCA Civ 1307; [2005] HLR 9.

295 These will now have to be members of the executive.

296 See para 9.5, above; and Code of Guidance para 19.8; Welsh Code para 21.7.

297 *Feld v Barnet LBC; Pour v Westminster CC* [2004] EWCA Civ 1307; [2005] HLR 9.

298 Below, para 9.196; below, paras 10.33–10.44.

299 *R (Abdi) v Lambeth LBC* [2007] EWHC 1565 (Admin); [2008] HLR 5.

Local connection reviews

9.171   While most reviews will be carried out by the authority to which the original homelessness application was made, an exception arises in the case of a review sought under HA 1996 s202(1)(d), that is, against a decision under HA 1996 s198(5) that the conditions for a local connection referral are met.[300] In these cases, the review must be carried out either:

a) jointly by the notifying and notified authorities where the decision was reached by agreement;[301] or

b) by a further referee, where the matter had been determined by a referee under the Homelessness (Decisions on Referrals) Order 1998.[302]

9.172   In the latter case, the further referee must be appointed within five working days.[303] If a referee is not appointed by agreement, then a person must be appointed in accordance with the Review Procedure Regs 1999.[304]

Impact of the Human Rights Act 1998

9.173   The review procedure is not the determination of a civil right for the purposes of article 6[305] of the European Convention on Human Rights.[306]

Procedure on review

9.174   Once the applicant has requested a review, the authority must notify the applicant that s/he – or someone acting on his/her behalf – may make representations in writing.[307]

9.175   The purpose of this requirement is to invite the applicant to state his/her grounds for requesting a review (if s/he has not already done

---

300 See paras 7.35–7.51, above.

301 Review Procedure Regs 1999 reg 1.

302 SI No 1578, see para 7.59, above.

303 Review Procedure Regs 1999 reg 7(1) and (2).

304 See Review Procedure Regs 1999 reg 7(2), (3) and (4).

305 'In the determination of his civil rights and obligations . . . everyone is entitled to a fair and public hearing within a reasonable time by an independent and impartial tribunal established by law . . .'.

306 See below, paras 12.96–12.100.

307 Review Procedure Regs 1999 reg 6(2)(a). Where the case concerns a local connection referral that has been referred to a referee (see para 9.171), it is the referee who must make the notification: reg 6(3)(a).

so) and to elicit any new information that the applicant may have in relation to it.[308] Where the applicant's legal representatives requested information from the authority prior to making representations, and the authority failed to provide the information or await the representations prior to making a review decision, the decision was unlawful.[309] If the applicant has not already been informed of the procedure to be followed,[310] then the notification must also set out what it is.[311]

9.176 The original regulations[312] required the reviewer to consider any representations made by the applicant and to carry out the review on the basis of the facts known to him/her at its date. The latter requirement is not explicit in the current Review Procedure Regs 1999.[313] This change notwithstanding, the reviewing officer 'is not simply considering whether the initial decision was right on the material before it at the date it was made. He may have regard to information relevant to the period before the decision but only obtained thereafter and to matters occurring after the initial decision': *Mohamed*.[314]

9.177 If there is a deficiency or irregularity in the original decision, or in the way it was made, but the reviewer is nonetheless minded to make a decision which is against the interests of the applicant, the reviewer must notify the applicant that s/he is so minded and of the reasons why, and that the applicant or someone on his/her behalf may make representations to the reviewer, orally or in writing or both, which representations the reviewer must consider.[315] This procedure is

---

308 Code of Guidance para 19.10; Welsh Code para 21.9.

309 *Aw-Aden v Birmingham CC* [2005] EWCA Civ 1834 at [21], although as the authority subsequently reconsidered the decision it was in fact upheld by the Court of Appeal.

310 Review Procedure Regs 1999 reg 6(2)(b) and (3)(b).

311 A requirement in the 1996 edition of the Code of Guidance that authorities should have an approved document setting out their procedure available to the public is not included in the present Code.

312 Allocation of Housing and Homelessness (Review Procedures and Amendment) Regulations 1996 SI No 3122 reg 8(1).

313 The former is included: Review Procedure Regs 1999 reg 8(1). Where the review is being conducted by a referee (see para 9.171) s/he must send any representations to both authorities involved and seek their comments: reg 7(5).

314 *Mohamed v Hammersmith & Fulham LBC* [2001] UKHL 57; [2002] HLR 7, HL at [26]. As to reviews of suitability, see above, paras 9.156–9.158.

315 Review Procedure Regs 1999 reg 8(1)(b) and (2). The Court of Appeal has assumed – without argument – that the wording of reg 8(2)(b) gives the applicant the right to choose how representations are made – orally, in writing, or orally and in writing: see *Lambeth LBC v Johnston* [2008] EWCA Civ 690; [2009] HLR 10 at [53]; and *Hall v Wandsworth LBC; Carter v Wandsworth LBC* [2004] EWCA Civ 1740; [2005] HLR 23 at [25]–[26].

capable of remedying any defect in the original decision letter and is suitable as a means for challenging the original decision of a local authority, rather than judicial review.[316]

9.178   The duty is two-fold: first, to consider whether there was a deficiency or irregularity in the original decision or in the manner in which it was made; second, if there was – and if the review officer is nonetheless minded to make a decision adverse to the applicant on one or more issues – to serve a 'minded to find' notice on the applicant explaining the reasons for the reviewer's provisional views.[317] The review officer is only under a duty to 'consider' the representations, not necessarily to give any notification or indication of that consideration.[318] Common sense dictates, however, that where consideration of deficiency and/or irregularity has taken place, but no reasons have been given for an adverse conclusion in relation to it, the review procedure could still be susceptible on public law grounds.[319] Accordingly, a local authority is effectively now required to state in every review decision letter why there is no deficiency or irregularity in the original decision, and consequently why no 'minded to find' letter was sent.

9.179   Neither 'deficiency' nor 'irregularity' is defined in the regulations.[320] 'Deficiency' is not confined to an error of law in the original decision; there is a deficiency if there is 'something lacking' in it which is of sufficient importance to the fairness of the procedure to justify the additional procedural safeguard: *Hall* and *Carter*.[321] Accordingly, a reviewing officer should apply regulation 8(2) whenever s/he considers that an important aspect of the case was either not addressed or was not addressed adequately by the original decision-maker. A lack of clarity as to whether the correct test of vulnerability[322] had been applied was one such deficiency.

9.180   If circumstances have changed between the original decision and decision on review,[323] reviewers will need to undertake further

---

316 *R (Lynch) v Lambeth LBC* [2007] HLR 15.

317 *Lambeth LBC v Johnston* [2008] EWCA Civ 690; [2009] HLR 10.

318 *Johnston*, footnote 317, above, per Rimer LJ at [51].

319 *Johnston*, per Rimer LJ at [54].

320 See Code of Guidance para 19.13; Welsh Code para 21.12, which suggests matters which might be included.

321 *Hall v Wandsworth LBC; Carter v Wandsworth LBC* [2004] EWCA Civ 1740; [2005] HLR 23. See now English Code of Guidance para 19.14, reflecting this decision. (The Welsh Code has not been amended since the decision.)

322 See paras 5.29–5.32, above.

323 As in *Mohamed v Hammersmith & Fulham LBC* [2001] UKHL 57; [2002] HLR 7, HL.

enquiries before reaching a decision and may need to serve a 'minded to find' letter.[324]

9.181   Applicants should be aware that it is not only new circumstances which count in his/her favour which are to be taken into account, but also any developments which adversely affect his/her entitlement.[325] A change of circumstances may yet lead to the loss of a qualifying element in the previous decision, for example, priority need.[326] In such a case, the requirement to allow further representations, including an oral hearing,[327] will apply.

9.182   An adverse change will not, however, cause the loss of an element in the first decision if that decision was itself unlawful. In *Robinson*,[328] the authority unlawfully decided that the applicant was not in priority need, notwithstanding that she was only 17 years old at the time.[329] By the time of the review, she was 18 and no longer in priority need. The authority unsuccessfully sought to uphold its original decision on that basis: the proper decision on the review was that an unlawful decision had been made such as to have denied the applicant her rights; she should therefore have been given the rights to which she was entitled had a lawful decision been made, and the reviewer should accordingly have found her to be in priority need.[330] The court applied the *dictum* of Chadwick LJ in *Crawley v B*[331] that

> . . . an applicant ought not to be deprived, by events which had occurred between the date of the original decision and the date of the appeal, of some benefit or advantage to which he would have been entitled if the original decision had been taken in accordance with the law.

324 *Banks v Kingston-Upon-Thames RLBC* [2008] EWCA Civ 1443; [2009] HLR 29. In the original decision, the applicant was found to be not homeless. Between the original decision and the review decision, the applicant was served with notice to quit by his landlord. The reviewer found that the applicant was homeless, and went on to consider the question of priority need without giving the applicant the opportunity to make representations on that issue, before deciding it against the applicant. The applicant successfully appealed to the Court of Appeal that the change in question under consideration invoked his right to receive a 'minded to find' letter in accordance with Review Procedure Regs 1999 reg 8(2).

325 See further below, para 9.189.

326 For example, a dependent child leaving home, death of a vulnerable co-resident.

327 Below, para 9.187.

328 *Robinson v Hammersmith & Fulham LBC* [2006] EWCA Civ 1122; [2007] HLR 7.

329 See para 5.67, above.

330 *Robinson v Hammersmith & Fulham LBC* [2006] EWCA Civ 1122; [2007] HLR 7, at [32].

331 (2000) 32 HLR 636, CA, at 651.

9.183   Points made earlier about enquiries before first decision are equally relevant here.[332] For example, if the reviewer fails to make sufficient enquiries into a matter or fails to make those enquiries that a reasonable authority would make, the decision is susceptible to challenge. The point of the review is to cure any defects in the original decision and therefore a failure to conduct sufficient enquiries can be resolved at this stage by the person conducting the review.

9.184   It is incumbent on the applicant to put forward the matters and evidence which s/he wishes to be taken into account: see *Cramp*.[333] This is particularly important where a 'minded to find' letter has been sent because a failure to challenge anything in it is likely to bar any argument on appeal that the authority had failed to carry out further enquiries in respect of the matters raised in the letter.[334]

9.185   Where an applicant deliberately withholds information so as to hinder the authority's enquiries, the authority is entitled to decide matters against the applicant on the basis that the threshold of satisfaction with the applicant's case cannot be reached.[335]

9.186   In *Bellouti*, 'it was for Mr Bellouti to put forward the material on which he relied in support of his assertion of priority need'.[336] Bearing in mind that a decision can only be based on the information available to the authority, there may therefore be difficulty complaining to the county court (on appeal) of a failure to make enquiries if a matter has not been raised before the review, at least sufficiently to put the reviewer on notice, or call for him/her to make such further enquiries as are necessary.

9.187   The review must be carried out fairly. Applicants should be given the opportunity to refute matters on which the authority wish to rely: *Robinson*.[337] In *Lomotey*,[338] there was no unfairness in failing to hold an oral hearing when requested, because the details of the case against the applicant had been discussed with her prior to the review. Likewise, comparison with other legislative review schemes suggests

---

332   Above, paras 9.48–9.132.

333   Para 9.92, above.

334   *R (Lynch) v Lambeth LBC* October 16, 2006; [2007] HLR 15.

335   *R (Abdi) v Lambeth LBC* [2007] EWHC 1565 (Admin); [2008] HLR 5. The applicant withheld information about her previous accommodation; the authority were entitled to decide that she was not homeless.

336   *Bellouti v Wandsworth LBC* [2005] EWCA Civ 602; [2005] HLR 46, at [59].

337   *Robinson v Brent LBC* (1998) 31 HLR 1015, CA. See further, para 9.118, on the fairness of conducting enquiries by authorities.

338   *Lomotey v Enfield LBC* [2004] EWCA Civ 627.

that the meaning of 'oral representations' does not amount to a right to an oral hearing.[339]

9.188　What comprises fairness in carrying out a review has to be determined having regard to the basis of the decision under review. In *Goodger*,[340] the authority's decision-making file was not disclosed to the applicant's advisers until a few days before the review. There was no procedural unfairness, however, as the applicant had known the case against him and the decision of intentional homelessness had been the only one possible in the circumstances.

9.189　As at the initial enquiry stage,[341] authorities may obtain expert medical opinion. If this raises new issues or contentious points on which the applicant has not been able to comment, s/he should normally be given a chance to do so in the interests of fairness. If, however, the advice is merely directed to assisting the authority to assess the weight to be given to evidence on matters which are already fully in play, there is no automatic obligation to disclose it to the applicant before the authority reaches its decision.[342]

Time

9.190　The Review Procedure Regs 1999[343] generally require authorities to notify applicants of their decision within eight weeks of the request for the review being made.[344]

9.191　The exceptions are: first, where an applicant is seeking to review an agreement between two authorities that the conditions for a local connection referral are met, in which case the decision must be notified within ten weeks;[345] second, where the review is being conducted by a referee,[346] the period is 12 weeks.[347]

339　See HA 1996 s143F and Demoted Tenancies (Review of Decisions) (England) Regulations 2004 SI No 1679; HA 1996 s129 and Introductory Tenants (Review) Regulations 1997 SI No 72.

340　*Goodger v Ealing LBC* [2002] EWCA Civ 751; [2003] HLR 6.

341　See para 9.101, above.

342　*Hall v Wandsworth LBC; Carter v Wandsworth LBC* [2004] EWCA Civ 1740; [2005] HLR 23. See also *Shala v Birmingham CC* [2007] EWCA Civ 624; [2008] HLR 8, in particular [19]–[23].

343　See para 9.163 and footnote 288, above.

344　Review Procedure Regs 1999 reg 9(1)(a).

345　Review Procedure Regs 1999 reg 9(1)(b).

346　See para 9.171, above.

347　Review Procedure Regs 1999 reg 9(1)(c). In such a case, the referee must notify the two authorities within 11 weeks (reg 9(3)), in order to give them time to notify the applicant.

9.192   The parties may, however, agree a longer period. The Code suggests that this may be appropriate where further enquiries are required about information which the applicant has provided or where an applicant has been invited to make oral representations which require additional time to arrange.[348]

Notification of review decision

9.193   The authority must notify the applicant of the outcome of the decision.[349]

9.194   Where the decision is against the interests of the applicant,[350] reasons for the decision must be included.[351]

9.195   The notification of the decision on the review must also inform the applicant of his/her right of appeal to the county court on a point of law.[352]

Housing pending review

9.196   This is considered in chapter 10.[353]

Reasons

9.197   Both the original decision and any decision reached on review must contain sufficient reasons.[354] In cases where there has been an internal review,[355] it is likely to be the reasons in the review decision which will be the focus of any challenge, although these may well rely on, reflect or be elaborated by, the first decision, which may therefore remain relevant. What is imported by the requirement to give reasons is considered below, in chapter 12.[356]

---

348 Code of Guidance para 19.16; Welsh Code para 21.15.
349 HA 1996 s203(4).
350 Identifying decisions to refer to another authority separately out of an abundance of caution, as the applicant may be presumed so to have considered it when s/he elected to seek a review under HA 1996 s203.
351 See para 9.197, below.
352 See chapter 12.
353 Paras 10.33–10.44.
354 HA 1996 ss184(3) and 203(4).
355 See para 9.194, above.
356 Paras 12.64–12.91.

CHAPTER 10

Part 7 discharge

continued

Introduction

10.1   The Housing Act (HA) 1996 Part 7 imposes duties on local authorities:

a) to make enquiries;
b) to make and notify decisions;
c) to protect property; and
d) to secure that accommodation is made available.

10.2   Duties relating to property have already been considered (see chapter 8) and so also have the duties to entertain applications, make enquiries and reach decisions (see chapter 9).

10.3   This chapter is accordingly concerned with the remaining duties. These will be considered under the following headings:

a) accommodation pending decision;
b) accommodation pending review;
c) duties to those not in priority need;
d) duties to the intentionally homeless;
e) duties on local connection referral;
f) duties to the unintentionally homeless; and
g) other statutory powers and duties.

Contracting out of functions

10.4   The power of an authority to contract out functions under Part 7 has been discussed at the start of chapter 9.

Accommodation pending decision

10.5   If the authority has reason to believe that the applicant may be eligible for assistance, homeless and in priority need, it has to secure that accommodation is made available for his/her occupation pending any decision that it may make as a result of its enquiries.[1] The test is exhaustive: the authority cannot qualify it by adding any further criteria, for example, that an applicant must be at risk of harm in his/her current accommodation if not provided with other accommodation pending the decision.[2]

---

1   HA 1996 s188(1).
2   *R (Kelly and Mehari) v Birmingham CC* [2009] EWHC 3240 (Admin).

10.6   The threshold in HA 1996 s188 is designedly low; the authority should provide the accommodation when it is needed and then make further enquiries[3] Even this threshold was not reached in *Burns*,[4] however, where the authority had no reason to believe that the applicant was eligible. The applicant, who had married an EU national, had been refused a residence permit by the Home Office, which refusal it was not unreasonable for the authority to take at face value. It was accordingly reasonable for the authority to have refused interim accommodation without making any further enquiries.

10.7   This duty exists irrespective of questions of local connection.[5]

10.8   The requirement to make accommodation available for the applicant's occupation is, by definition, a requirement to make it available for the applicant and for any person who might reasonably be expected to reside with him/her.[6]

10.9   An authority may discharge its duties pending enquiries not only by providing its own accommodation, but also by arranging for it to be provided by someone else, or by giving advice such as will secure that it is provided by someone else.[7] In discharging this duty, the authority is entitled to call for co-operation from other bodies, including a registered provider of social housing (in Wales, registered social landlord), or may arrange for social services or social work departments to discharge the duty on its behalf.[8]

10.10   The requirement calls for some action on the part of the authority. In *Sidhu*,[9] a women's refuge, not even in the same area, provided accommodation, but as the authority had not been involved in procuring it, it could not rely on it as a discharge of its duty.

10.11   The fact that the accommodation was in another area was not itself fundamental to the result, but it may not be without relevance. Many such refuges are funded by local authorities. In such circumstances, there are two reasons why accommodation provided voluntarily and other than at the arrangement of the authority may be less susceptible to challenge:

a) as a matter of practice, the refuge is not entirely independent of the authority; and

---

3   *R (M) v Hammersmith & Fulham LBC* [2008] UKHL 14; [2008] 1 WLR 535 at [36].

4   *R (Burns) v Southwark LBC* [2004] EWHC 1901 (Admin); [2004] JHL D105.

5   HA 1996 s188(2).

6   HA 1996 s176.

7   HA 1996 s206(1); see further below, para 10.98.

8   HA 1996 s213.

9   *R v Ealing LBC ex p Sidhu* (1982) 2 HLR 45, QBD.

b) the provision of funds for the refuge may be held to denote a sufficient degree of participation or assistance by the authority,[10] although probably only if the accommodation is provided at the express request of the authority, or it is agreed – or at the lowest 'understood' – that the organisation will accommodate those referred to it by the authority; anything more vague would probably not qualify.

10.12 The authority may require a person housed under this provision to pay such reasonable charges as it may determine, or to pay an amount towards the payment made by the authority to a third party for accommodation, for example, a contribution towards the cost of private sector accommodation.[11] The provision of assistance under HA 1996 Part 7 is not, however, contingent on ability to pay.[12]

10.13 In *Thrasyvoulou*,[13] an hotelier tried unsuccessfully to challenge a decision of the respondent authority designed to prevent the use of low-grade hotels – including his own – for the purpose of discharging its duty under the analogous provisions of the Housing Act 1985. The claim by the hotelier was held to have no foundation in public law. It was for the authority to decide which hotels it used in discharging its duty, an issue in which the applicant had no legal interest. Likewise, in *First Real Estates (UK) Ltd v Birmingham CC*,[14] the claimant had been successful in procuring the authority's agreement to licence a series of properties for use in connection with homelessness. Although a series of agreements could in principle be susceptible to judicial review, the power authorising the authority to enter into individual licence agreements was a contractual power governed by private law. The decision to terminate was therefore not susceptible to judicial review because it could not be right, in principle, to permit a claimant suing a public body for breach of contract to invoke public law. In any event, the claimant could not identify any statement which could have given rise to a legitimate expectation that the authority would not terminate any licence and could not show any detriment that he had suffered in reliance on any such representation.

---

10 It may depend on the circumstances, including the powers under which assistance was provided and the terms of assistance.
11 HA 1996 s206(2).
12 See further below, paras 10.97–10.98.
13 *R v Tower Hamlets LBC ex p Thrasyvoulou* (1990) 23 HLR 38, QBD.
14 [2009] EWHC 817 (Admin); [2009] JHL D93.

Security

10.14   In *Miah*,[15] *Buscombe*[16] and *Hayden*,[17] some doubt was cast on whether accommodation provided under the Housing (Homeless Persons) Act 1977 amounted to a tenancy or licence within the security provisions of what is now HA 1985 Part 4. In *Walsh*,[18] however, the authority's argument that any temporary accommodation so provided would necessarily be by way of licence was rejected by the House of Lords and the letting was held to amount to a tenancy.[19]

10.15   The importance of this issue is diminished[20] by the removal of security of tenure under the Housing Acts 1985[21] and 1988[22] for homeless applicants, although it may still bear on determination of right of occupation at common law, disrepair claims and whether or not court proceedings are required to evict an occupier.[23]

10.16   Where occupation is by way of licence, it has been held that accommodation provided under HA 1996 s188 – hostel-type accommodation or self-contained or otherwise – is not 'as a dwelling', so the protection of the Protection from Eviction Act (PEA) 1977 s3, requiring a court order before eviction, is not applicable.[24] Where the occupation is by way of tenancy, however, the applicability of PEA 1977 has been left open by the Court of Appeal.[25]

Quality

10.17   Under the Housing (Homeless Persons) Act 1977 and the Housing Act 1985, as unamended, there was no statutory requirement as to the quality of accommodation provided.[26]

---

15 *Family Housing Association v Miah* (1982) 5 HLR 94, CA.
16 *Restormel DC v Buscombe* (1982) 14 HLR 91, CA.
17 *Kensington and Chelsea RLBC v Hayden* (1984) 17 HLR 114, CA.
18 *Eastleigh DC v Walsh* [1985] 1 WLR 525; 17 HLR 392, HL.
19 See also *Street v Mountford* [1985] AC 809; 17 HLR 402, HL.
20 If not eliminated: see next paragraph.
21 HA 1985 Sch 1 para 4.
22 HA 1996 s209.
23 A homeless person who has been granted a daily licence to occupy a room with a lock in a local authority hostel is entitled to exclude trespassers: *Thomas v Director of Public Prosecutions*, QBD, 23 October 2009; (2009) *Times* 25 November.
24 *Mohamed v Manek and Royal Borough of Kensington and Chelsea* (1995) 27 HLR 439, CA; *Desnousse v Newham LBC* [2006] EWCA Civ 547; [2006] HLR 38.
25 See *Desnousse*.
26 *R v Hillingdon LBC ex p Puhlhofer* [1986] AC 484; (1986) 18 HLR 158, HL.

10.18 Under the Housing Act 1985, as amended by Housing and Planning Act 1986,[27] statutory requirements for suitability were introduced, but were not applicable to temporary accommodation pending enquiries. The suitability requirements[28] of HA 1996 are, however, applicable to every requirement to secure that accommodation is available, including the temporary duties.

10.19 When determining what constitutes 'suitable' accommodation, an authority must have regard to the slum clearance (Part 9), and overcrowding (Part 10) provisions of the Housing Act 1985 and Parts 1–4 of the Housing Act 2004 (housing conditions and control of houses in multiple occupation).[29] The secretary of state may by order add or exclude circumstances in which accommodation is or is not to be considered suitable, or considerations which may or may not be taken into account.[30] This power has been used to make affordability a matter which authorities must take into account when determining suitability: see Homelessness (Suitability of Accommodation) (England) Order 2003.[31] In addition, when determining the suitability of accommodation for asylum-seekers,[32] there is a requirement to have regard to the temporary nature of accommodation to be provided[33] and to exclude regard for any preference on the part of any member of the household being accommodated as to the locality of the accommodation.[34] In such cases, the authority is also required to have regard to the desirability in general of securing accommodation in areas in which there is a ready supply.[35]

10.20 Bed and breakfast accommodation is not in principle unsuitable,[36] nor is accommodation outside the authority's area but, in deciding the question of suitability, the authority must consider the individual needs of the applicant and his/her family, including needs as to work, education and health.[37] In England, the Homelessness

27 Section 14(3).
28 See HA 1996 ss206(1) and 210(1), and paras 10.118–10.149, below.
29 HA 1996 s210, as amended by Housing Act 2004 Sch 15; see para 10.119, below.
30 HA 1996, s210(2).
31 SI No 3326 (appendix B, below): see further, paras 10.127–10.128, below.
32 See generally above, chapter 3.
33 HA 1996 s210(1A)(a).
34 HA 1996 s210(1A)(b).
35 HA 1996 s206(1A).
36 See Code of Guidance para 7.6 suggesting its use in emergencies, but also stating that authorities should avoid using it wherever possible. See also Code of Guidance paras 17.24–17.38.
37 *R v Newham LBC ex p Sacupima* (2001) 33 HLR 1, QBD and 2, CA. See also *R v Newham LBC ex p Ojuri (No 3)* (1998) 31 HLR 452, QBD.

(Suitability of Accommodation) (England) Order 2003[38] limits the use of bed and breakfast accommodation: where it is afforded to families (including pregnant women) it is not to be regarded as suitable, save where there is no other accommodation available and then only for a period not exceeding six weeks (or periods not exceeding six weeks in total).[39] Limits on the use of bed and breakfast accommodation have also applied in Wales since 2007.[40]

10.21   A decision by Enfield LBC, in whose area the applicant had lived for the previous eight years since arriving as an asylum-seeker[41] and where her children were in school, to secure accommodation for an applicant in bed and breakfast accommodation in Birmingham, with which city the applicant had no connection, was held to be irrational and an infringement of the applicant's rights under European Convention on Human Rights article 8(1):[42] *Yumsak*.[43]

10.22   Accommodation which split a family between two hostels was held not to be suitable in *Surdonja*.[44] In *Flash*,[45] a one-bedroom flat provided to the applicant and her grandson was suitable: the grandson could sleep in the living room.

10.23   In *Ali* and *Moran*,[46] it was observed that 'what is regarded as suitable for discharging the interim duty may be rather different from what is regarded as suitable for discharging the more open-ended duty in section 193(2)'. This accords with two earlier decisions on the quality of temporary accommodation under the Housing (Homeless Persons) Act 1977, even though there was then no statutory suitability requirement,[47] although both related to temporary accommodation for the intentionally homeless.[48]

---

38 SI No 3326 (appendix B, below).
39 See further paras 10.127 and 10.128, below.
40 See Homelessness (Suitability of Accommodation) (Wales) Order 2006 SI No 650 and paras 10.129 and 10.132, below.
41 Acceptance of her refugee status, bringing an end to her assistance from the social services department of the council, prompted her homelessness application.
42 See paras 12.101–12.103, below.
43 *R (Yumsak) v Enfield LBC* [2002] EWHC 280 (Admin); [2002] JHL D38.
44 *R v Ealing LBC ex p Surdonja* (1998) 31 HLR 686, QBD.
45 *R (Flash) v Southwark LBC* [2004] EWHC 717 (Admin); [2004] JHL D60.
46 *Birmingham City Council v Ali; Moran v Manchester City Council (Secretary of State for Communities and Local Government and another intervening)* [2009] UKHL 36; [2009] 1 WLR 1506 at [18].
47 Above, para 10.17.
48 See para 10.54, below.

10.24   In *Gliddon*,[49] the authority was alleged to have been in breach of its temporary duty because the accommodation provided was in substantial disrepair, requiring works to prevent it becoming statutorily unfit for human habitation. It was held that the authority was entitled to have regard to the time for which accommodation was likely to be occupied when determining whether the accommodation was appropriate: while some quality of accommodation would fall below the line of acceptable discharge of even a temporary duty, accommodation needing works to pre-empt statutorily unfitness did not necessarily do so; accommodation so unfit that it is not even repairable, however, might well have been inadequate even for a temporary purpose.

10.25   In *Ward*,[50] accommodation on a caravan site described by a social worker as being in appalling condition was nonetheless an adequate discharge of the temporary duty, having regard to the family's wish to live on a site, rather than in a permanent structure.

Area

10.26   There are constraints on out-of-area placements, considered below in relation to the full duty,[51] which apply to discharge under this section.

Termination of accommodation

10.27   On occasion, in particular when enquiries have taken some time (for example, into accommodation abroad), a local authority will wish to terminate a right of occupation, either because it wants to move the applicant elsewhere or because of some default on the part of the applicant (for example, non-payment of charges, nuisance and annoyance, damage to property) or it will have to deal with the position which arises if another landlord providing accommodation on its behalf has taken or wants to take such, action.

10.28   It is clear that the authority may move the occupier, for example, for reasons of cost, provided the new accommodation is also suitable, and it is otherwise acting reasonably.

10.29   Where the accommodation is lost because of the applicant's default, it is not open to an authority to conclude that the applicant has

---

49 *R v Exeter CC ex p Gliddon* (1984) 14 HLR 103, QBD.
50 *R v Southampton CC ex p Ward* (1984) 14 HLR 114, QBD.
51 See para 10.112, below.

thereby become homeless intentionally, as this would not have been the accommodation the loss of which gives rise to the homelessness application requiring a decision: see *Din*.[52]

10.30   Intervening accommodation under this section does not create a new period of homelessness. This survives the decision in *Awua*,[53] where what had been lost, although interim in quality, was accommodation provided to the applicant (by another authority) in discharge of the full housing duty (ie, post-decision), withdrawn when that other authority offered – and the applicant refused – a more permanent offer.[54] Until a decision is reached, however, what is in issue is the loss of the accommodation that gave rise to the (as yet undetermined) application.

10.31   In such a case, the authority may nonetheless be able to conclude that it has discharged its duty under this section, and decline to provide further accommodation pursuant to it, by parity of reasoning with the decision under what is now HA 1996 s193 in *Chambers*,[55] albeit that it will still be bound to consider and discharge the appropriate duty following its decision under HA 1996 s184, relative to the accommodation lost which led to the homelessness which gave rise to the application.[56]

10.32   In reaching its decision on whether or not that loss amounted to intentionality, the loss of the intervening accommodation will therefore not be relevant,[57] save if and so far as the conduct involved can

---

52   *Din v Wandsworth LBC* [1983] 1 AC 657; 1 HLR 73, HL. Consider, too, that s193(6)(b) – below, para 10.152 – makes explicit provision for an authority to determine that its duty towards a homeless applicant – following a decision that the applicant is homeless, in priority need and not intentionally homeless – has been discharged in the event of becoming intentionally homeless from *that* accommodation; it would be anomalous to reach the same conclusion in relation to temporary accommodation *pending* a decision.

53   *R v Brent LBC ex p Awua* [1996] 1 AC 55; 27 HLR 453, HL.

54   See also *R v East Hertfordshire DC ex p Hunt* (1985) 18 HLR 51, QBD, the reasoning in which was criticised in *Awua* as 'heroic', but the result of which was not doubted. See now s193(6), (7): below, paras 10.152–10.167.

55   *R v Westminster CC ex p Chambers* (1982) 6 HLR 15, QBD; see para 10.154, below.

56   In *R v Kensington & Chelsea RLBC ex p Kujtim* (1999) 32 HLR 579; (1999) 2 CCLR 460, CA, the duty to provide accommodation under National Assistance Act 1948 s21 (see further chapter 13) was held not to be absolute. Where the applicant manifests a persistent and unequivocal refusal to observe the authority's reasonable requirements in relation to occupation of the accommodation, the authority is entitled to treat its duty as discharged and to refuse to provide further accommodation.

57   *R v Islington LBC ex p Hassan* (1995) 27 HLR 485, QBD.

properly be considered to have some evidential value in reaching a view on the earlier loss of accommodation, for example, analogous conduct.[58]

Accommodation pending review

10.33 Once the original decision has been notified to the applicant, the authority ceases to be under any duty to provide interim accommodation under HA 1996 s188,[59] even if a review is sought.[60] The duty is, however, replaced with a power to provide accommodation pending the review.[61]

10.34 Until amendment by Homelessness Act 2002, HA 1996 s188(3) only permitted an authority to 'continue to' house. This led to the argument that it could not be used where the applicant's temporary accommodation under section 188(1) had come to an end before a request to exercise the section 188(3) power was made. The repeal of the words 'continue to' is intended to close this gap. In particular, where an applicant has been found to be intentionally homeless, and accommodation has been provided under section 190(2)(a),[62] which comes to an end before the review is completed, the amended section 188(3) will permit authorities to provide accommodation pending outcome of the review.

10.35 Similar provisions apply where the applicant has been housed under HA 1996 s200 pending the outcome of a local connection referral: where the applicant seeks a review, the duty to house ceases and is replaced by a power.[63]

10.36 The authority is not obliged of its own motion to consider whether to exercise its power under HA 1996 s188(3) but may await a request from the applicant before deciding whether to do so.[64] As a refusal to house pending a review is not a decision that is itself susceptible to

---

58 See *R v Newham LBC ex p Campbell* (1993) 26 HLR 183, QBD.
59 See para 10.5, above.
60 HA 1996 s188(3).
61 HA 1996 s188(3). The observations on quality, area and termination made in relation to accommodation pending decision (above, paras 10.17–10.32) also apply to accommodation pending review.
62 See para 10.54, below.
63 HA 1996 s200(5).
64 *R (Ahmed) v Waltham Forest LBC* [2001] EWHC Admin 540, [2001] JHL D89.

the statutory review process, any challenge has to be by way of judicial review.[65]

10.37 As an applicant has an unfettered right to a review,[66] HA 1996 s188(3) does not envisage that the discretion to house pending review will be exercised as a matter of course. An authority may therefore decide to exercise the discretion only in exceptional circumstances: *Mohammed*.[67]

10.38 In exercising its discretion, the authority must balance the objective of maintaining fairness between other homeless persons – in circumstances where it has decided that no duty is owed to the applicant – and proper consideration of the possibility that the applicant may be right.[68]

10.39 In carrying out this balancing exercise, certain matters will always require consideration, although other matters may also be relevant:

- the merits of the case and the extent to which it can properly be said that the decision was one which was either contrary to the apparent merits or was one which involved a very fine balance of judgment;
- whether consideration is required of new material, information or argument which could have a real effect on the decision under review;
- the personal circumstances of the applicant and the consequences to him/her of a decision not to exercise the discretion.[69]

10.40 In *Lumley*,[70] Brooke LJ explained the merits of the case as meaning 'the merits of the applicant's case that the council's original decision was flawed'. In that case, the decision was quashed because the initial decision that the applicant was not in priority need was seriously flawed and the authority had failed to take these flaws into account when considering the exercise of its discretion to house pending review.

---

65 *R v Camden LBC ex p Mohammed* (1997) 30 HLR 315, QBD. See para 12.147, below.

66 Above, paras 9.149–9.158.

67 *R v Camden LBC ex p Mohammed* (1997) 30 HLR 315, QBD. See also *R v Hammersmith & Fulham LBC ex p Fleck* (1997) 30 HLR 679, QBD and *R v Newham LBC ex p Bautista* April 2001 *Legal Action* 22. See Code of Guidance para 15.19; Welsh Code para 21.24 on the need for flexibility.

68 *R v Camden LBC ex p Mohammed* (1997) 30 HLR 315, QBD.

69 *R v Camden LBC ex p Mohammed* (1997) 30 HLR 315, QBD.

70 *R v Newham LBC ex p Lumley* (2001) 33 HLR 11, CA.

10.41   In each case, the principles must be applied to the relevant facts and a properly reasoned decision provided.[71] In *Mohammed*,[72] the judge found that the council had considered the matters set out properly, but he nonetheless quashed its decision not to house the applicant pending review, because it had failed to give her an opportunity to explain inconsistencies in her statements and had therefore failed to take into account a relevant and material consideration in exercising its discretion.

10.42   In *Nacion*,[73] the Court of Appeal applied *Mohammed* to a decision under the discretion to house pending an appeal.[74] This issue is considered in chapter 12, below, as part of the machinery for enforcement of duties.[75]

10.43   In deciding when to terminate accommodation provided under HA 1996 s188(3) following an unsuccessful review, an authority must give the person reasonable notice so that s/he can have an opportunity to make alternative arrangements.[76]

10.44   It has been held that there is no requirement for a local housing authority to take into consideration possible duties owed to the children of an applicant under Children Act 1989, or the potential break-up of the family, when deciding whether to continue to provide accommodation under section 188(3).[77]

Duties without priority need

10.45   HA 1996 Part 7 distinguishes between those without priority need who are, and those who are not, intentionally homeless. It is a distinction which did not appear in Housing Act 1985 Part 3, as those without a priority need were in any event not entitled to substantive housing assistance, whether or not homeless intentionally.

---

71 See *R (Paul-Coker) v Southwark LBC* [2006] EWHC 497 (Admin); [2006] HLR 32.
72 (1997) 30 HLR 315, QBD.
73 *R v Brighton & Hove Council ex p Nacion* (1999) 31 HLR 1095, CA.
74 HA 1996 s204(4). But see now section 204A, allowing an appeal from such a refusal to be made to the county court itself – below, paras 12.196–12.202.
75 Para 12.202.
76 *R v Newham LBC ex p Ojuri (No 5)* (1998) 31 HLR 631, QBD.
77 *R (Hassan) v Croydon LBC* [2009] JHL D56, Admin Court.

Homelessness Act 2002

10.46   The distinction was designed for use in connection with the allocation provisions of Part 6 (see chapter 11). HA 1996 s167(3) gives the secretary of state power to make regulations specifying people to whom preference is to be given in allocating housing accommodation. By virtue of amendments under the Homelessness Act 2002, Part 6[78] now allows authorities to exclude from their allocation schemes those who are guilty of seriously unacceptable behaviour.[79]

10.47   The 2002 Act also built on this distinction by introducing a power to secure that accommodation is made available for those who are not in priority need and not intentionally homeless.[80]

10.48   There is, however, no right to seek an internal review of a refusal to exercise this discretion: a challenge would therefore have to be by way of judicial review.[81]

10.49   Where an applicant who is not in priority need is threatened with homelessness unintentionally, the authority may correspondingly take reasonable steps to secure that accommodation does not cease to be available to him/her.[82]

Advice and assistance

10.50   Having distinguished between those in priority need who are, and those who are not, intentionally homeless, the two relevant sections lead to the same Part 7 duty[83] in each case: ie to provide or secure that the applicant is provided with 'advice and assistance' in any attempts

---

78   See chapter 11, below.

79   See para 11.28, below. Accordingly, someone whose conduct qualifies as intentional homelessness, but not serious unacceptable behaviour, is eligible under Part 6.

80   HA 1996 s192(3), as amended. As this power to house falls within HA 1996 Part 7, authorities can accordingly now provide housing on a non-secure basis to this group (see para 10.111, below). Previously any allocation would have fallen within Part 6 and, as such, would have been or become secure (see chapter 11). Hence, authorities can now afford assistance to the homeless not in priority need, without needing to go as far as to provide full security. The observations on quality, area and termination made in relation to accommodation pending decision (above, paras 10.17–10.32) also apply to accommodation provided under this power.

81   See paras 12.113–12.114, below.

82   HA 1996 s195(6).

83   Ie as distinct from power.

the applicant may make to secure that accommodation becomes available for his/her occupation.[84]

10.51   Before advice and assistance are afforded, the applicant's housing needs must be assessed, and the advice and assistance must include information about the likely availability in the authority's district of types of accommodation appropriate to those needs.[85]

10.52   Even as strengthened by the Homelessness Act 2002, the right to advice and assistance is not of much substance or one therefore that is likely to be worth enforcing. In relation to the equivalent duty towards the intentionally homeless,[86] it has been held that, while an authority may provide financial assistance, there is no obligation so to do; a refusal to provide such assistance could only be challenged on conventional public law grounds: *Conville*.[87]

10.53   Nor does the right to advice and assistance give rise to a duty of care on the part of the authority to ensure that any accommodation towards which the applicant is directed is safe. Thus, in *Ephraim v Newham LBC*,[88] the plaintiff had been directed by the authority – by way of advice and assistance – to a guesthouse, a house in multiple occupation (HMO). She took up occupation in a bedsitting room in it. The HMO lacked proper fire precautions. Subsequently, there was a fire in the property and she suffered severe injuries. She sued, unsuccessfully alleging that Newham LBC was under a duty of care to satisfy itself that the premises to which it had referred her were reasonably safe, particularly in relation to fire. It was held that the imposition of such a duty would put the authority in the dilemma

---

84   HA 1996 s192(2) (unintentionally homeless) and s190(3) (intentionally homeless), as amended by the Homelessness Act 2002. See, on this, *Crawley v B* (2000) 32 HLR 636, CA, in which the authority – having made a decision that the applicant was not in priority need and therefore not gone on to consider intentionality – were still able to investigate and reach a conclusion on intentionality once the priority need had been successfully challenged; whether this could stand today in light of the power may be open to argument. Assistance could include paying a rent deposit: see Code of Guidance para 14.29; Welsh Code para 16.35.

85   HA 1996 s192(4) and (5) (unintentionally homeless) and s190(4) and (5) (intentionally homeless), added by the Homelessness Act 2002. See generally Code of Guidance para 14.4; Welsh Code paras 16.32–16.36. See also *R (Savage) v Hillingdon LBC* [2010] EWHC 88 (Admin).

86   See para 10.54, below.

87   *Conville v Richmond upon Thames LBC* [2005] EWHC 1430 (Admin); [2006] HLR 1, not appealed on this point, see [2006] EWCA Civ 718; [2006] HLR 45; see chapter 12.

88   *Ephraim v Newham LBC* (1992) 25 HLR 208, CA.

of having either to inspect a particular property, or else not advise people to seek available accommodation; it was more desirable that the authority should give advice which enables homeless people to obtain accommodation, even though some of the properties where they obtain accommodation might prove not to be properly equipped, than it was to restrict the range of advice and make it more difficult for homeless people to find housing.

Duties to the intentionally homeless

10.54 The same duty to provide advice and assistance arises when an applicant is homeless, in priority need, but has become homeless intentionally.[89] If in priority need, however, this class of applicant benefits from the additional duty imposed on the authority to secure that suitable[90] accommodation is made available for the applicant's occupation[91] – which means for the occupation of the applicant and of any person who might reasonably be expected to reside with him/her – 'for such period as they consider will give him a reasonable opportunity of himself securing accommodation for his occupation'.[92] As to 'suitable' accommodation, see above, paras 10.17–10.26.

10.55 An authority may discharge its duties under this provision not only by providing its own accommodation, but also by arranging for it to be provided by someone else, or by giving advice such as will secure that it is provided by someone else.[93]

10.56 The authority may require a person housed under this provision to pay such reasonable charges as it may determine, or to pay an amount towards the payment made by the authority to a third party for accommodation, for example, a contribution towards the cost of private sector accommodation.[94] The provision of assistance under Part 7 is not contingent on ability to pay.[95]

---

89 HA 1996 s190(2)(b), (4) and (5).
90 See HA 1996 ss205 and 206.
91 HA 1996 s176.
92 HA 1996 s190(2)(a).
93 HA 1996 s206(1); see further below, para 10.98.
94 HA 1996 s206(2).
95 *R v Secretary of State for Social Security ex p B & Joint Council for the Welfare of Immigrants* (1996) 29 HLR 129, CA. See further below, para 10.101.

Area

10.57 There are constraints on out-of-area placements, considered below in relation to the full duty,[96] which also apply to discharge under this section.

Security

10.58 Where accommodation is provided by the authority, it will not be secure.[97] If occupied under a licence, the accommodation will not be protected by the Protection from Eviction Act 1977 s3, and the applicant may be evicted without a court order, although this may not be so of accommodation provided under a tenancy.[98] Where the authority secures accommodation through the private sector, it will not be assured for a period of 12 months beginning on the date on which the applicant was notified of the decision,[99] unless the landlord notifies him/her to the contrary, either that it is to be a fully assured tenancy or an assured shorthold tenancy.[100] For these purposes, a private sector landlord is any landlord who is not within the Housing Act 1985 s80(1);[101] the term therefore includes registered providers of social housing.[102]

Time

10.59 This duty has given rise to a number of problems. The first question is from when does time run.

10.60 Whether or not an applicant seeks internal review does not affect this issue: time runs from the date of the decision regardless of whether an internal review is sought: *Conville*.[103]

---

96 See para 10.112, below.

97 HA 1985 Sch 1 para 4, as amended.

98 *Desnousse v Newham LBC* [2006] EWCA Civ 547; [2006] HLR 38; see above, para 10.16.

99 Or in the case of a review or appeal to the county court, of the date on which s/he is notified of the outcome of the review or of when the appeal is finally determined.

100 HA 1996 s209(2).

101 Ie, local authorities, new town corporations, housing action trusts, urban development corporations, or housing co-operatives within the meaning of HA 1985 s27B.

102 HA 1996 s217.

103 *Conville v Richmond upon Thames LBC* [2005] EWHC 1430 (Admin); [2006] HLR 1, not appealed on this point see [2006] EWCA Civ 718; [2006] HLR 45.

10.61   In *Dyson*,[104] the applicant was told on 21 May that she would be provided with one month's accommodation from 25 May (the date when her homelessness would actually occur). This decision appears to have been taken by an official but appears to have required ratification by a committee. The time was subsequently extended to 6 July, but it was not until 3 July that committee ratification was communicated to the applicant. Time was nonetheless held to run from the notification by the official, of which the letter of 3 July was mere confirmation.

10.62   In *de Falco*,[105] only four days had been allowed between notification of decision and the expiry of what is now HA 1996 s188 accommodation.

10.63   The Master of the Rolls thought that this period was probably adequate, having regard to several weeks in accommodation provided by the authority prior to its decision. He was, however, also influenced by the time during which the applicants had been accommodated between the issue of proceedings and the hearing before the Court of Appeal. As *de Falco* was the hearing of an interlocutory appeal for an interlocutory injunction to house until trial, he treated that matter as conclusive as a matter of the court's discretion.

10.64   The same point influenced Bridge LJ, although he was otherwise of the view that time prior to communication of the local authority's decision was irrelevant so that only time since that decision was communicated could count. As the purpose of the provisions is to give the applicant time to find somewhere else to live once it has been decided that the authority need not provide full assistance, this view seems preferable.[106]

10.65   The courts may be less generous towards an applicant who lives with another person who has previously been found homeless intentionally, and who has already enjoyed a period of HA 1996 s190(2)(a) accommodation, although such a person may indeed reapply and it seems to be an irresistible inference from *Lewis*[107] and the other cases on this point[108] that such a person will be entitled to a new period of

---

104   *Dyson v Kerrier DC* [1980] 1 WLR 120, CA.

105   *De Falco, Silvestri v Crawley BC* [1980] QB 460, CA.

106   Sir David Cairns thought that the decision was unreviewable, although this proposition does not find any support elsewhere and is wholly out of line with a more modern approach in public law.

107   *R v North Devon DC ex p Lewis* [1981] 1 WLR 328, QBD.

108   See paras 6.9–6.24, above. See also *R (Savage) v Hillingdon LBC* [2010] EWHC 88 (Admin), where it was held that it was for the authority to determine what period of time afforded a reasonable opportunity of securing accommodation.

section 190(2)(a) accommodation; it is strongly arguable that s/he can and should benefit from the reasoning of Bridge LJ in *de Falco*.

10.66   Some reconciliation of merits and principle may be found in the extent of acquiescence or participation in the act which results in the finding of intentionality and therefore the extent to which such finding should have been anticipated.

10.67   In *Smith v Bristol CC*,[109] a county court judge held that, even where a substantial period of warning had been given to the applicant, the authority was still obliged to give more time:

> I cannot accept that 'no time' can in any circumstances be a reasonable period . . . [A] reasonable time must be given to the applicant after she actually becomes homeless . . .

10.68   When an authority decides for how long it should secure that accommodation is available so as to give an applicant a reasonable opportunity of securing accommodation for him/herself, pursuant to its duty under HA 1996 s190(2)(a), it may not have regard to considerations peculiar to itself, ie the extent of its resources and other demands.[110] What is reasonable for these purposes is to be assessed by reference to the particular needs and circumstances of the applicant, including the possibilities open to him/her of obtaining accommodation; if the applicant is not making reasonable efforts to pursue such possibilities, however, that will be a strong indication that s/he should not be given more time; and, even if the applicant makes reasonable efforts, a moment will normally be reached when time will expire if those possibilities have not come to fruition.

Policies

10.69   A further problem is posed by 'policies'. In particular, the frequency with which all kinds of applicants receive identical offers of 28 days' accommodation suggests that many authorities operate a policy under this provision.[111]

10.70   If an inflexible policy can be proven, it can be set aside.[112] If, however, the 28-day rule is merely a guideline, reconsidered in each case, it is unlikely to be possible to set it aside.

109 December 1981 *LAG Bulletin* 287, CC.
110 *R (Conville) v Richmond upon Thames LBC* [2006] EWCA Civ 718; [2006] HLR 45.
111 In *Birmingham City Council v Ali; Moran v Manchester City Council (Secretary of State for Communities and Local Government and another intervening)* [2009] UKHL 36; [2009] 1 WLR 1506 at [17], Baroness Hale commented: 'We are told that up to six weeks is usually thought enough for this although there is no statutory limit.'
112 See paras 12.44–12.45, below.

10.71   The Code no longer suggests any particular time frame:[113]

> A few weeks may provide the applicant with a reasonable opportunity
> to secure accommodation for him or herself. However, some appli-
> cants might require longer, and others, particularly where the hous-
> ing authority provides pro-active and effective advice and assistance,
> might require less time.[114]

It continues that 'authorities will need to take account of local circumstances, including how readily other accommodation is available
in the district and have regard to the particular circumstances of the
applicant', including the resources available to him/her to provide
rent in advance or a rent deposit where this may be required by private landlords.[115]

10.72   The resources available to – or other demands on – an authority
are not relevant to the determination of what comprises a reasonable
'opportunity' for an applicant to secure his/her own accommodation.
While it is for the authority to decide what is a reasonable opportunity, subject to the usual principles of intervention,[116] the decision
remains one as to what is a reasonable opportunity from the perspective of the applicant, having regard to the applicant's circumstances
and such other matters as the availability of other accommodation.
However, the opportunity is no more than that; it can not be converted into a duty to provide long-term accommodation.[117]

10.73   This much is clear: an applicant's circumstances must be individually considered, and if it can be shown that the time allowed has
been reached without regard to them or was such a short period that
no authority could have considered that it gave the applicant a reasonable opportunity to find somewhere for him/herself, the courts
will order sufficient time.[118]

10.74   It would seem from *Monaf*[119] that – at least where the housing
authority is also a social services authority – the authority ought to
have regard to its duties under the Children Act 1989 s20(1)[120] when
determining this period. Prior to this stage, the housing authority

---

113 Previous editions referred to 28 days being adequate in most cases. The Welsh
      Code (para 16.39) still suggests that a 28-day period may provide a reasonable
      opportunity.
114 Code of Guidance para 14.28.
115 Code of Guidance para 14.28; Welsh Code para 16.29.
116 See chapter 12.
117 *Conville v Richmond upon Thames LBC* [2006] EWCA Civ 718; [2006] HLR 45.
118 *Lally v Kensington & Chelsea RLBC* (1980) *Times* 27 March, ChD.
119 *R v Tower Hamlets LBC ex p Monaf* (1988) 20 HLR 529, CA.
120 See para 13.51, below.

should in any event have sought the applicant's consent to refer the case to the social services authority,[121] so that the latter authority can consider exercise of its powers under the Children Act 1989.[122]

Threatened with homelessness

10.75 Where the authority is satisfied that an applicant is threatened with homelessness and eligible for assistance[123] the duties in section 195 apply.

10.76 If the authority is not satisfied that the applicant has a priority need,[124] or is satisfied that s/he has a priority need but is also satisfied that s/he became threatened with homelessness intentionally, it must provide him/her, or secure that s/he is provided with, advice and assistance in any attempts s/he may make to secure that accommodation does not cease to be available for his/her occupation.[125] The advice and assistance must include information about the likely availability in the authority's district of types of accommodation appropriate to the applicant's housing needs, including, in particular, the location and sources of such types of accommodation.[126] If the authority owes this duty because it is satisfied that the applicant has a priority need but became threatened with homelessness intentionally, of which decision the applicant seeks a review, the authority may secure that accommodation does not cease to be available for his/her occupation and, if s/he becomes homeless, secure that accommodation is available pending the decision on review.[127]

10.77 If the authority is not satisfied that the applicant has a priority need, nor satisfied that s/he became threatened with homelessness intentionally, the authority has power to take reasonable steps to secure that accommodation does not cease to be available for the applicant's occupation.[128]

---

121 See further section 213A, and para 13.61, below.
122 See further paras 13.44–13.65, below.
123 Above, chapter 3.
124 Even though the applicant is at this point only threatened with homelessness, priority need is to be determined as at the date when homelessness will occur: *Holmes-Moorhouse v Richmond upon Thames LBC* [2009] UKHL 7; [2009] HLR 34 – see above, paras 5.22–5.23.
125 HA 1996 s195(5).
126 HA 1996 s195(7).
127 HA 1996 s195(8).
128 HA 1996 s195(9).

10.78   If the authority is satisfied that the applicant has a priority need, and not satisfied that s/he became threatened with homelessness intentionally, it must take reasonable steps to secure that accommodation does not cease to be available for his/her occupation,[129] or, if the authority secures other accommodation, then HA 1996 193(3)–(9) apply as if the applicant was already homeless and the authority had a duty under section 193(2).[130] The position is adapted for restricted cases[131] of threatened homelessness: if other accommodation is secured, section 193(3)–(9) apply as if the applicant was only owed a duty under section 193(2) because s/he was a restricted case,[132] ie, the authority must, so far as is reasonably practicable, bring its duty to an end by making a private accommodation offer.[133]

10.79   Where the authority owes a duty under section 195, it must – except in a restricted case – give the applicant a copy of its allocation scheme.[134]

Duties where local connection referral

10.80   The allocation of housing responsibilities when the homeless person falls within the local connection provisions has been considered in chapter 7.

10.81   It is therefore only necessary to point out here that accommodation will not be secure.[135] The observations which have been made about temporary accommodation, including as to quality, area and termination,[136] apply here.

10.82   Where the authority to which the applicant is referred accepts the referral, the discussion relating to unintentionally homeless applicants will apply.[137]

10.83   If a local connection referral results in the transfer of the applicant to another authority, which had made an earlier offer under HA

---

129 HA 1996 s195(2).

130 HA 1996 s195(4).

131 HA 1996 s195(4A) and (4B) – ie, where the authority is only satisfied that the applicant is threatened with homelessness and eligible because of a restricted person: see above, paras 3.71–3.79.

132 Below, para 10.168.

133 HA 1996 s193(7AD). Above, para 10.168.

134 HA 1996 s195(3A).

135 HA 1985 Sch 1 para 4, as amended.

136 See above, paras 10.17–10.32.

137 See below, paras 10.85–10.176.

1996 s193, then – assuming that the earlier offer was sustainable as a discharge of duties[138] – the applicant will not be entitled to a further offer.[139]

10.84　On the other hand, if the authority to which the applicant is referred had earlier found that s/he was homeless intentionally, so that no earlier section 193 offer was made, it will usually be bound by the finding of unintentionality made by the second authority and will accordingly now be required to ensure that suitable accommodation is made available.[140]

Duties towards the unintentionally homeless

10.85　Duties towards those whom the authority is satisfied are eligible, homeless, in priority need and not intentionally homeless, are governed by HA 1996 s193.

10.86　Under that section, the duty towards the unintentionally homeless is to secure that accommodation is available for occupation by the applicant until the duty ceases in accordance with the section.[141]

10.87　'Available' means available in the statutory sense.[142]

10.88　A number of issues fall to be considered:

a) postponement of the duty;
b) means of discharge;
c) out-of-area placements;
d) suitability of accommodation;
e) cessation of duty.

10.89　Where the applicant is unintentionally threatened with homelessness, the duty is to take reasonable steps to secure that accommodation does not cease to be available to the applicant.[143]

Postponement of the duty

10.90　Discharge of the duty may not be postponed for any extraneous reason: see *Khalique*,[144] where the authority sought to postpone making an

---

138　See below, paras 10.98–10.149.
139　*R v Hammersmith & Fulham LBC ex p O'Brian* (1985) 17 HLR 471, QBD.
140　See para 10.99, below.
141　HA 1996 s193(2) and (3); s193(3) was amended by the Homelessness Act 2002 to remove the restriction on the duty to a period of two years.
142　HA 1996 s176; see paras 4.24–4.38, above.
143　HA 1996 s195(2); see also above, para 10.78.
144　*R v Tower Hamlets LBC ex p Khalique* (1994) 26 HLR 517, QBD.

offer of accommodation pending a reduction in arrears of rent owed by the applicant.[145] This does not mean that the applicant's arrears may not be taken into account when deciding whether or not to make a Part 6 allocation,[146] which is governed by its own provisions.[147]

10.91　　There are, however, apparently conflicting decisions as to whether the duty under HA 1996 s193 to secure suitable accommodation may be postponed, although these have tended to conflate the provision of suitable accommodation on a temporary basis with an allocation or other final offer of suitable accommodation.

10.92　　In *Anderson*,[148] the authority had failed to make any suitable offers to the applicant in 16 months since accepting that she was homeless because of overcrowding in her current accommodation. A number of offers of accommodation had been made, but it was accepted by the authority that these had been reasonably refused. One offer remained outstanding and subject to review.

10.93　　Moses J said:[149]

> The statutory scheme under the Housing Act shows that there is no time limit within which a housing authority is obliged under the statute to comply with a duty to secure available accommodation for those who fall within section 193 . . . The provisions within the Housing Act, which require housing authorities to put in place an allocations policy and to comply with that policy, are contained in Part 6 of the Housing Act. They demonstrate that there will be those to whom a duty is owed under section 193 of the Act who will not be housed immediately or within any particular time-limit. There may be those in respect of whom, the housing authority will be under an obligation, in accordance with their allocations policy, to give a greater priority.

10.94　　In *Sembi*,[150] the applicant, a woman of 52 who was confined to a wheelchair, was accepted as homeless and offered accommodation in a nursing home occupied mainly by the elderly and terminally ill. The authority accepted that the nursing home was not suitable in the long term but considered it suitable as temporary accommodation. The judge held that there had been no failure by the authority to discharge

---

145　See also *R v Newham LBC ex p Miah* (1995) 28 HLR 279, QBD.

146　Both *Khalique* and *Miah* preceded HA 1996: accordingly, discharge and offer of permanent accommodation were commonly synonymous. The proposition in the text applies the principle in *Khalique* to the provisions *post*-1996.

147　See below, para 11.41.

148　*R v Southwark LBC ex p Anderson* (1998) 32 HLR 96, QBD.

149　*R v Southwark LBC ex p Anderson* (1998) 32 HLR 96, QBD, at 98.

150　*R v Merton LBC ex p Sembi* (1999) 32 HLR 439, QBD.

its duty under HA 1996 s193. Jowitt J cited the passage from *Anderson* with approval.

10.95 However, in *Begum*,[151] Collins J held that duties under the HA 1996 – whether under section 193 or otherwise[152] – could not be deferred. Accordingly, the authority could not defer providing accommodation which was suitable for the applicant and his family, including for the applicant's mother who used a wheelchair. He accepted that where there were great difficulties in finding suitable accommodation, a court would not enforce the duty unreasonably, for example within a few days, but only provided that the authority was doing all that it could to comply with it.[153]

10.96 This conflict has in practice now been resolved by the House of Lords in *Ali* and *Moran*,[154] where a clearer distinction was drawn between the duty to secure that suitable accommodation is available for a homeless family under section 193(2) and allocation under Part 6. Thus, suitability for the purpose of section 193(2) does not imply permanence or security of tenure; there are degrees of suitability and what is suitable in the short term may not be suitable for a longer period; when the time comes that the applicant cannot continue to occupy his/her current accommodation for another night, the authority must act immediately.[155] Accordingly, Birmingham CC could decide that applicants were homeless even though they could remain in their current accommodation for a while.[156] When considering the question whether a local housing authority has left an applicant who occupies accommodation which it would not be reasonable for him/her to continue to occupy in that accommodation

---

151 *R v Newham LBC ex p Begum* (1999) 32 HLR 808, QBD. See also *R (Khan) v Newham LBC* [2001] EWHC Admin 589; October 2001 *Legal Action* 16, where Newham LBC conceded that it was in breach of the duty (through the provision of inadequate bed and breakfast-type accommodation), and a mandatory order requiring the authority to provide suitable accommodation within two months was made. Cf, *Begum v Tower Hamlets LBC* [2002] EWHC 633 (Admin), where, again, the authority acknowledged that the accommodation was unsuitable but the court refused to make a mandatory order in the absence of any evidence of the time within which suitable accommodation could be provided.

152 Ie, also under sections 188, 190 and 200.

153 The authority had not, however, done all that it could, because it had adopted a policy not to consider its own stock to discharge its duty under HA 1996 s193.

154 *Birmingham City Council v Ali; Moran v Manchester City Council (Secretary of State for Communities and Local Government and another intervening)* [2009] UKHL 36; [2009] 1 WLR 1506.

155 At [47].

156 At [48].

for too long a period, the question is primarily one for the authority; a court should normally be slow to accept that the authority has left an applicant in unsatisfactory accommodation for too long; in resolving this issue it is necessary to take account of the severe constraints on budgets and personnel, and the limited housing stock.[157]

10.97   The decision allows an authority to conclude that an applicant is already homeless, without necessarily providing fresh accommodation at once, on the basis that current accommodation is suitable in the short term: hence, there is no question of postponement of duty.

Means of discharge

10.98   By HA 1996 s206, a local authority may discharge its duty under section 193 in one of three ways:[158]

a) by securing that suitable accommodation provided by it is available for the applicant;

b) by securing that the applicant obtains suitable accommodation from some other person; or

c) by giving the applicant such advice and assistance as will secure that suitable accommodation is available from some other person.

10.99   The accommodation must be available in the statutory sense.[159] Suitability is discussed below (paras 10.118–10.149). As a matter of language, and construction, HA 1996 s206 is exhaustive of the means of providing accommodation, and so it cannot be used – even in conjunction with Local Government Act 1972 s111 – to guarantee the provision of accommodation by another.[160] In the case of eligible asylum-seekers[161] in England, authorities must, in discharging their duties, have regard to the desirability, in general, of securing accommodation in areas in which there is a ready supply of accommodation.[162]

10.100   The authority may require the applicant to pay reasonable charges in respect of its own accommodation or in relation to accommodation

---

157 At [50].

158 HA 1996 s206(1).

159 See paras 4.24–4.38, above.

160 *Crédit Suisse v Waltham Forest LBC* (1996) 29 HLR 115, CA.

161 See paras 3.98–3.102, above.

162 HA 1996 s206(1A), added by Homelessness (Asylum-seekers) (Interim Period) (England) Order 1999 SI No 3126. This is intended to encourage authorities in areas of high demand for social housing to seek accommodation outside the district: see 2002 edition of the Code of Guidance annex 12 para 7.

made available by someone else, for example, in the private sector.[163] If the authority provides its own accommodation, it can in any event make a reasonable charge under Housing Act 1985 s24.

10.101   The provision of assistance under HA 1996 Part 7 is not contingent on ability to pay.[164] There is, however, no reason why – even if the applicant is unable to make a payment – an authority should not reserve the right to payment, and a number of reasons why it should do so, and keep exercise of it under review, both during occupancy and for a period afterwards, for example, against a future change of fortunes on the part of an applicant.[165]

Resources

10.102   The issue of resources is not irrelevant to how an authority decides to discharge its duty. Thus, if an applicant has a particular and perhaps unusual need, the authority can – in deciding whether to meet it by purchasing a property on the open market – take into account the cost of doing so.[166] In *Calgin*,[167] the cost of providing accommodation was likewise held to be a factor the authority could take into account in deciding how to discharge its duty.

Advice and assistance

10.103   Advice and assistance such that the applicant secures accommodation from another under HA 1996 s206(1)(c) seems wide enough to cover advice and assistance leading to house purchase by an applicant who is financially able to undertake such a step.[168] It may also cover the provision of mediation designed to ensure that a 16- or 17-year-old applicant returns to live in his/her family home.[169]

---

163   HA 1996 s206(2).
164   *R v Secretary of State for Social Security ex p B and Joint Council for the Welfare of Immigrants* (1996) 29 HLR 129, CA.
165   It may be said that a record of the precise cost to the authority of the provision of free accommodation represents good accounting practice or, conversely, that to fail to record the cost of what is substantively a free service represents poor accounting practice.
166   *R v Lambeth LBC ex p Ekpo-Wedderburn* (1998) 31 HLR 498, QBD. See also *R v Lambeth LBC ex p A1* (1997) 30 HLR 933, CA, where the homeless applicant's challenge to a decision of the authority not to exercise its powers under HA 1985 ss9 and 17 to add to its stock failed.
167   *R (Calgin) v Enfield LBC* [2005] EWHC 1716 (Admin); [2006] HLR 4.
168   See Code of Guidance para 16.33, including through shared equity schemes: see Code of Guidance para 16.34. See Welsh Code para 18.38.
169   See *Robinson v Hammersmith & Fulham LBC* [2006] EWCA Civ 1122 at [39].

Discharge through another

10.104 Some other person, in the context of HA 1996 s206(1), may be a person or body – or an authority – abroad. In *Browne*,[170] a woman with no local connection with Bristol, and no local connection with the area of any other housing authority in England, Wales or Scotland, was offered assistance to return to her home town of Tralee, Eire, where the authorities were prepared to ensure that she was housed.

10.105 In order to sustain its decision, Bristol CC did not need to know the exact details of the accommodation to be made available to her.[171] The arrangement was, however, only appropriate once it was established by Bristol CC that, in its opinion, the woman ran no risk of domestic violence in Tralee. It would seem from the report that had there been a risk of domestic violence, the arrangement would not have been acceptable, for otherwise Bristol CC would have managed to circumvent the spirit of the local connection provisions,[172] even though, not being a referral to another authority in the UK, its letter did not apply.

10.106 In *Wyness v Poole BC*,[173] a county court rejected an attempt to house an applicant in the area of another authority, when the local connection provisions were inapplicable because of an employment connection, because living in the area of that other authority would have meant that the employment would have to be given up. The court held that no reasonable authority could so discharge the duty.[174]

10.107 In *Parr v Wyre BC*,[175] an authority sought to discharge its duty by securing an offer of accommodation in Birmingham, an area with which the applicants had no connection at all. There were no details available of the accommodation to be provided and the applicants had a limited time in which to accept. While it was common ground that discharge could be in another area (but consider now the provisions that govern out-of-area placements[176]), the Court of Appeal, distinguishing *Browne*, did not uphold the offer: the offer had to be of

---

170 *R v Bristol CC ex p Browne* [1979] 1 WLR 1437, DC.

171 The decision preceded the introduction of the requirement of suitability. Today, an authority would be bound to take steps to satisfy itself about suitability, even if only by appropriate enquiries – this accords with the approach taken in *Browne* to domestic violence: see text.

172 See para 7.45, above.

173 July 1979 *LAG Bulletin* 166, CC.

174 See also paras 10.112 and 10.117, below, on out-of-area placements.

175 (1982) 2 HLR 71, CA.

176 See paras 10.112–10.117, below.

'appropriate accommodation', in terms both of size of family and of area. In *Puhlhofer*,[177] however, the House of Lords rejected introduction of the qualification 'appropriate'.[178] Nonetheless, the result may well have been the same, so far as it related to relocation to another, altogether distant, area.[179]

10.108　　In *Cafun*,[180] the authority purported to discharge its duty by referring the applicant to another (neighbouring) authority with whom it had a reciprocal agreement. It failed to consider either whether accommodation in the neighbouring area would be suitable for the particular applicant, or the limits on out-of-area placements.[181] The decision was quashed.

10.109　　The provision of successful mediation which enables a 16- or 17-year-old applicant to return to live in the family home may be considered to secure 'accommodation from some other person'.[182]

10.110　　The authority may discharge the duty by securing an assured shorthold tenancy from a private sector landlord, although – having regard to the constraints on use of an assured shorthold as a final offer under section 193, in particular the requirement for consent from the applicant[183] – only in substance as a temporary or 'staged' measure. Accordingly, where an assured shorthold tenancy is being offered to an applicant otherwise than as a final offer, the authority should explain:

a) that the authority acknowledges that the accommodation would be temporary if the private landlord lawfully exercises his/her right to recover possession after the end of the fixed term; and

b) in that event and assuming that the applicant's circumstances have not materially changed, the authority would again become obliged to perform its duty under the section to secure that accommodation is available for occupation by the applicant: *Griffiths*.[184]

177　*R v Hillingdon LBC ex p Puhlhofer* [1986] AC 484; 18 HLR 158.

178　See paras 4.6–4.16, above.

179　*R (Yumsak) v Enfield LBC* [2002] EWHC 280 (Admin); [2002] JHL D38, in relation to discharge of the section 188 duty; see para 10.21, above. See also *R (Calgin) v Enfield LBC* [2005] EWHC 1716 (Admin); [2006] HLR 4, para 10.114, below.

180　*R (Cafun) v Bromley LBC* October 17, 2000, QBD (unreported).

181　See below, para 10.112.

182　See *Robinson v Hammersmith & Fulham LBC* [2006] EWCA Civ 1122 at [39].

183　See para 10.166.

184　*Griffiths v St Helens BC* [2006] EWCA Civ 160; [2006] HLR 29 at [42].

Discharge by authority

10.111 Although an authority may now use its own stock without limit of time to house an applicant under Part 7,[185] applicants do not become secure tenants, unless and until so notified.[186]

Out-of-area placements

10.112 'So far as reasonably practicable', the authority must secure accommodation in its own area.[187]

10.113 In *Sacupima*,[188] Latham LJ stated[189] that 'the clear and sensible purpose' of HA 1996 s208 is 'to ensure that so far as possible that authorities do not simply decant homeless persons into areas for which other authorities are responsible'. A failure to consider section 208 was a significant factor in rendering the decision in *Cafun*[190] unlawful.

10.114 In *Calgin*,[191] the authority, a London borough, had a policy of providing accommodation to some homeless households outside its district because of an acute shortage of affordable housing locally. The applicant was offered accommodation in Birmingham and challenged its suitability. On review, the authority decided that the accommodation was suitable and that its policy was not incompatible with section 208 because it was not reasonably practical to provide accommodation locally. The decision was upheld: it was for the authority to decide whether or not it was reasonably practical to obtain accommodation within its district, an assessment with which the court would only interfere on *Wednesbury* grounds.[192] The decision to use out-of-district accommodation for a small proportion of those seeking accommodation was not *Wednesbury* unreasonable.

---

185 Cf HA 1996 s207, which was repealed by the Homelessness Act 2002.

186 HA 1985 Sch 1 para 4, as amended. Notification that the tenancy is to be secure is an allocation under Part 6 (see para 11.13, below).

187 HA 1996 s208(1). Note that this requirement is disapplied in England in relation to eligible asylum-seekers, if there is written agreement with another authority that it may place asylum-seekers in its area: s208(1A) added by Homelessness (Asylum-seekers) (Interim Period) (England) Order 1999 SI No 3126.

188 *R v Newham LBC ex p Sacupima* (2001) 33 HLR 2, CA.

189 *R v Newham LBC ex p Sacupima* (2001) 33 HLR 2, CA, at [31].

190 See para 10.108, above.

191 *R (Calgin) v Enfield LBC* [2005] EWHC 1716 (Admin); [2006] HLR 4.

192 See chapter 12, below.

10.115 Under HA 1996 s208(2), if the authority accommodates someone in another area, it must – within 14 days of the accommodation being made available to the applicant[193] – give notice to the local housing authority for the area in which that accommodation is situated.

10.116 The notice must state:

- the name of the applicant;
- the number and description of the persons residing with the applicant;
- the address of the accommodation;
- the date on which it became available; and
- the function under which it was made available.[194]

10.117 The notification function is designed to allow the notified authority to refer the applicant back under the local connection provisions,[195] should a further application be made for assistance: as such, it is considered in chapter 7.[196]

Suitability of accommodation

10.118 The duty to provide suitable accommodation is a continuing one; authorities must consider any changes in circumstances which occur while they are discharging their duty: *Zaher*.[197]

Standard of accommodation

10.119 Suitability is statutorily governed by HA 1996 s210, which identifies considerations which must be taken into account – the law governing housing conditions, overcrowding and houses in multiple occupation (HMO).[198] The obligation is to 'have regard to' these provisions of the Housing Acts 1985 and 2004. The obligation was introduced by Housing and Planning Act 1986 s14, in direct response to the

---

193 HA 1996 s208(4).
194 HA 1996 s208(3). For example, under HA 1996 s193, s200 or s190.
195 See HA 1996 s198(4).
196 See para 7.48, above.
197 *R (Zaher) v Westminster CC* [2003] EWHC 101 (Admin).
198 In relation to eligible asylum-seekers in England, HA 1996 s210 is modified so that in considering whether accommodation is suitable the authority must have regard to the fact that the accommodation is to be temporary, pending the applicant's claim for asylum, and not have regard to any preference the applicant may have as to the locality of the accommodation: see Homelessness (Asylum-seekers) (Interim Period) (England) Order 1999 SI No 3126.

decision of the House of Lords in *Puhlhofer*,[199] in which both the Court of Appeal and the House of Lords had rejected the first instance decision that, inter alia, accommodation which was statutorily overcrowded was incapable of comprising accommodation for the purposes of what is now HA 1996 s175.

10.120   Even now, the wording is not strong enough to prevent an authority using overcrowded[200] or hazardous property[201] or an HMO which falls below standard, although it will vitiate a decision in which the authority had ignored these considerations – wilfully or because it was unaware of the relevant factual conditions; the wording is, however, sufficient to impose an obligation on the authority to justify its decision to use such substandard accommodation.[202]

10.121   In *Campbell*,[203] a cockroach-infested property was not suitable for the applicant, a decision which, on its facts, could still stand post-*Awua*. On the other hand, in *Jibril*,[204] an offer of a five-bedroom house with only one toilet – situated in the bathroom – to a family of 12 was held to be within the 'margin of appreciation' of that which an authority could consider suitable.

10.122   In *Khan*,[205] the authority conceded that a bed and breakfast property with communal kitchen and bathroom facilities – in which the applicant, his wife and their four children occupied two bedrooms on different floors – was unsuitable. Ordering the authority to find alternative accommodation, the judge stressed that bed and breakfast accommodation should only be used in the short term and that authorities should look for alternative ways to discharge their HA 1996 s193 duty. This has now been embodied in statutory constraints on use of bed and breakfast: see paras 10.127–10.128, below.

---

199   *Re Puhlhofer* [1986] AC 484; 18 HLR 158.

200   See *Harouki v Kensington & Chelsea RLBC* [2007] EWCA Civ 1000; [2008] HLR 16 in which it was considered that the wording of section 210 recognises that accommodation is not necessarily unsuitable because it is statutorily overcrowded.

201   The Code of Guidance para 17.15 recommends that, when determining the suitability of accommodation, authorities should, as a minimum, ensure that all accommodation if free of category 1 hazards under Housing Act 2004 Part 1.

202   Consider *Padfield v Minister of Agriculture, Fisheries & Food* [1968] AC 997, HL.

203   *R v Lambeth LBC ex p Campbell* (1994) 26 HLR 618, QBD.

204   *R v Camden LBC ex p Jibril* (1997) 29 HLR 785, QBD.

205   *R (Khan) v Newham LBC* [2001] EWHC Admin 589; [2001] JHL D90.

Asylum-seekers

10.123 In determining whether accommodation is suitable for an applicant who is an asylum-seeker, particular provisions apply.[206] When considering whether the accommodation is suitable for the applicant or any person who might reasonably be expected to reside with him/her, the authority must have regard to the fact that the accommodation is to be temporary pending the determination of the applicant's claim for asylum and must not have regard to any preference that the applicant, or any person who might reasonably be expected to reside with him/her, may have as to the locality in which the accommodation is to be secured.

Added considerations

10.124 The secretary of state has power to specify circumstances in which accommodation is (or is not) to be regarded as suitable and to specify other matters to be taken into account or disregarded.[207]

10.125 This power has been used to require authorities to take affordability into account when determining suitability: see Homelessness (Suitability of Accommodation) (England) Order 2003.[208] This order applies in both England and Wales.

10.126 This requires the authority to consider:

- the financial resources available to the person;
- the costs of the accommodation;
- payments being made under a court order to a spouse, former spouse;
- any payments made to support children, whether under a court order or under the Child Support Act 1991; and
- the applicant's other reasonable living expenses.[209]

206 HA 1996 s210(1A), inserted by the Homelessness (Asylum Seekers) (Interim Period) (England) Order 1999 SI No 3126 article 6.
207 HA 1996 s210(2).
208 SI No 3326 (appendix B, below).
209 See further paras 4.121 and 4.131, above. See also Code of Guidance paras 17.39–17.40; Welsh Code paras 19.9–19.10.

England

10.127 The power had also been used in England to restrict the use of bed and breakfast accommodation. The Homelessness (Suitability of Accommodation) (England) Order 2003[210] provides that bed and breakfast accommodation afforded to those with family commitments, including pregnant women, is not to be regarded as suitable, save where there is no other accommodation available, and then only for a period not exceeding six weeks (or periods not exceeding six weeks in total).[211]

10.128 Bed and breakfast accommodation is defined[212] as accommodation (whether or not breakfast is provided) which is not separate and self-contained and in which more than one household share one or more of the following:

a) a toilet;
b) personal washing facilities; or
c) cooking facilities.

Accommodation owned or managed by an authority, a registered provider of social housing or a voluntary organisation[213] is exempt from the prohibition.

Wales

10.129 The Homelessness (Suitability of Accommodation) (Wales) Order 2006 article 3[214] requires Welsh authorities to take into account the following additional matters when considering suitability of accommodation for a person in priority need:

a) the specific health needs of the person;
b) the proximity and accessibility of social services;
c) the proximity and accessibility of the support of the family or other support services; and
d) any disability of the person.

---

210 SI No 3326 (Suitability Order 2003, see appendix B). See Code of Guidance paras 17.24–17.35.
211 Where bed and breakfast accommodation is used for an applicant with family commitments, the Code of Guidance (para 17.29) advises that the applicant should be notified of the effect of the Suitability Order 2003, in particular the six-week limit. Where bed and breakfast accommodation is used, authorities should ensure that it is of a suitable standard: see Code of Guidance paras 17.36–17.38.
212 Suitability Order 2003 reg 2.
213 See para 14.24 as to the definition of voluntary organisation.
214 SI No 650 (Welsh Suitability Order).

10.130 In addition, since 2 April 2007, bed and breakfast accommodation[215] provided by a Welsh authority is not to be regarded as suitable for any homeless applicant unless it meets the 'basic standard'.[216]

10.131 Further, all bed and breakfast accommodation is to be regarded as unsuitable for pregnant women and minors save where occupation falls within the following circumstances:[217]

a) occupation of basic standard bed and breakfast for a period or a total of periods not exceeding two weeks;

b) occupation of higher standard[218] bed and breakfast for a period or a total of periods not exceeding six weeks;

c) occupation of basic standard small bed and breakfast[219] for a period or a total of periods not exceeding six weeks, where the local housing authority has, before the expiry of the two-week period referred to in (a) above, offered suitable alternative accommodation, but the person has chosen to remain in the bed and breakfast;

d) occupation of basic standard small bed and breakfast after exercising the choice referred to in (c), where the local housing authority has offered suitable alternative accommodation[220] before the end

215 For these purposes, bed and breakfast accommodation is defined in the same way as in England (see para 10.128, above), although there is a further exception for accommodation provided under the Care Standards Act 2003, and it is also a requirement that the accommodation is provided 'commercially' see Homelessness (Suitability of Accommodation) (Wales) Order 2006 SI No 650 article 2.

216 'Basic standard accommodation' means accommodation that:
   (a) complies with all statutory requirements (such as requirements relating to fire and gas safety, planning and licences for houses in multiple occupation, where applicable); and,
   (b) has a manager deemed by the local housing authority to be a fit and proper person with the ability to manage bed and breakfast accommodation: article 2.

217 Article 6(1). Note that periods in bed and breakfast accommodation prior to 2 April 2007 are not to be included in calculating the period of time spent in a bed and breakfast: article 6(4).

218 'Higher standard accommodation' means accommodation which meets the basic standard; and additionally the standards contained in the Schedule to the statutory instrument: article 2. The requirements of the Schedule set out minimum space and management standards and requirements as to the provision of facilities: see appendix B, below.

219 A bed and breakfast is small where the manager resides on the premises and it has fewer than seven bedrooms available for letting: article 2.

220 The offer must, in the case of households with dependent children or a pregnant woman, be of suitable self-contained accommodation. In the case of an applicant who is a minor, the offer must be of suitable accommodation with support: article 6(3).

of the six-week period referred to in (c) above, but the person has chosen to remain in the bed and breakfast;

e) occupation of higher standard small bed and breakfast, where the local housing authority has offered suitable alternative accommodation,[221] before the expiry of the six-week period referred to in (b), but the person has chosen to remain in the bed and breakfast.

10.132   Furthermore, since 7 April 2008, bed and breakfast accommodation is to be regarded as unsuitable for all persons who are in priority need, subject only to specified exceptions.[222] Shared accommodation[223] which does not meet the higher standard[224] will also be regarded as unsuitable, subject to the same exceptions.[225] The exceptions are as set out at (a)–(e) of para 10.131, above with the addition of the following:[226]

f) occupation of basic standard shared accommodation for a period, or a total of periods, not exceeding two weeks;

g) occupation, for a period or a total of periods not exceeding six weeks, of basic standard shared accommodation owned by a local housing authority or registered social landlord, where the local housing authority has offered suitable alternative accommodation before the expiry of the two week period referred to in (f), but the person has chosen to remain in the said accommodation.

---

221 The same requirements as under para (d) apply to the offer of suitable accommodation: article 6(3).

222 Article 7.

223 'Shared accommodation' means accommodation
   (a) which is not separate and self-contained premises; or
   (b) in which any of the following amenities is not available to the applicant or is shared by more than one household
      (i) a toilet;
      (ii) personal washing facilities;
      (iii) cooking facilities; or
   (c) which is not an establishment registered under the provisions of the Care Standards Act 2000.

224 See para 10.131, above, at (b).

225 Article 8. Local authorities and registered social landlords will not be subject to this requirement until 4 April 2011: article 10.

226 Article 9. Note that periods in shared accommodation prior to 7 April 2008 are not to be included in calculating the period of time spent in such accommodation: article 9(4).

Other considerations

10.133 In *Awua*,[227] it was said that suitability is primarily a matter of space and arrangement, but that other matters, such as whether the applicant can afford the rent, may also be material.[228] The statutory considerations (primary and subordinate) are accordingly not exhaustive. In *Maloba*,[229] on the related issue of whether accommodation was reasonable to continue to occupy, it was held that the question was not limited to consideration of the size, structural quality and amenities of accommodation. Thus, in *Kaur*,[230] before the statutory extension (see above, para 10.127), it had been held that accommodation secured for the applicant in the private sector was not suitable because the contractual rent exceeded the amount which would be met in housing benefit and the shortfall could not be afforded from the applicant's own resources.

Adaptations

10.134 The suitability of accommodation offered by an authority pursuant to HA 1996 s193(2) is not to be judged exclusively by reference to the condition of the accommodation at the time of the offer, so regard may be had to proposed adaptations or alterations provided that those proposals can fairly be regarded as certain, binding and enforceable; adaptations that are proposed after the date of the offer are, however, irrelevant to the question of suitability.[231]

Security

10.135 In *Wingrove* and *Mansoor*,[232] Evans LJ thought that the tenure, or time element, of suitability had to be proportionate to the circumstances of the case, including the needs of the applicant, for example the need for the applicant's children to remain in an area to attend the same school for a number of years. An assured shorthold tenancy

---

227 *R v Brent LBC ex p Awua* [1996] 1 AC 55; (1995) 27 HLR 453, HL.
228 This decision preceded the statutory instrument (see para 10.125, above) requiring authorities to take affordability into account.
229 *Waltham Forest LBC v Maloba* [2007] EWCA Civ 1281; [2008] HLR 26 at [59]–[61].
230 *R v Tower Hamlets LBC ex p Kaur* (1994) 26 HLR 597, QBD.
231 *Boreh v Ealing LBC* [2008] EWCA Civ 1176; [2009] HLR 22 at [31].
232 *R v Wandsworth LBC ex p Wingrove* and *R v Wandsworth LBC ex p Mansoor* [1997] QB 953, CA.

may be suitable: see *Wingrove* and *Mansoor*[233] and *Griffiths.*[234] Suitability for the purpose of HA 1996 s193(2) does not, however, imply permanence or security of tenure.[235]

Time

10.136   What is suitable may vary depending on the length of time that the applicant is likely to have to occupy the accommodation: it may be reasonable to expect an applicant to endure conditions for a few days which would be clearly unsuitable if they had to be tolerated for a number of weeks: see the discussion of *Ali* and *Moran* at para 10.96, above; see also *Begum*[236] and *Codona.*[237]

Personal circumstances

10.137   In *Omar,*[238] a political refugee was offered accommodation in a basement flat in an estate. The condition of the premises and the layout of the estate strongly reminded the applicant of the prisons in which she had been held and abused, to such an extent that she maintained that she would rather commit suicide than live there. The court held that the accommodation must be suitable for the person to whom the duty was owed, in determining which the authority should have regard to the relevant circumstances of the applicant as well as to the matters set out in HA 1996 s210.

10.138   *Omar* was considered in *Dolan,*[239] where the authority's decision to offer accommodation was flawed because it had separated out medical and social considerations and had not taken an overall view of the applicant's needs: 'the ultimate decision as to suitability must be the result of a composite assessment'.

---

233   *R v Wandsworth LBC ex p Wingrove* and *R v Wandsworth LBC ex p Mansoor* [1997] QB 953, CA, per Sir Thomas Bingham MR at 923G.

234   *Griffiths v St Helens BC* [2006] EWCA Civ 160; [2006] HLR 29.

235   *Birmingham City Council v Ali; Moran v Manchester City Council (Secretary of State for Communities and Local Government and another intervening)* [2009] UKHL 36; [2009] 1 WLR 1506 at [47].

236   *R v Newham LBC ex p Begum* (1999) 32 HLR 808, QBD.

237   *Codona v Mid-Bedfordshire DC* [2005] EWCA Civ 925; [2005] HLR 1. This will be particularly true in the case of bed and breakfast accommodation, see Code of Guidance paras 16.28 and 17.24–17.38, and the Suitability Order 2003, see paras 10.127 and 10.128, above, and from 2007 the Welsh Suitability Order 2006, see paras 10.129 and 10.132, above. See Welsh Code paras 18.41–18.44 but note that the Welsh Code does not currently reflect the Welsh Suitability Order.

238   *R v Brent LBC ex p Omar* (1991) 23 HLR 446, QBD.

239   *R v Lewisham LBC ex p Dolan* (1992) 25 HLR 68, QBD.

10.139   *Omar* was also considered in *Karaman*,[240] where the applicant's terror of her husband's domestic violence was such that the authority's decision to house her within two miles of where her husband was believed to be living was held to be *Wednesbury* unreasonable.

10.140   In *Slater*,[241] Ward LJ said of a young single mother who was fleeing domestic violence 'that the particular needs of the applicant, for example, to be protected from domestic violence and to be located near to support networks, are relevant when considering suitability'.

Family

10.141   An authority has a wide discretion to determine who is within an applicant's household.[242] In *Ariemuguvbe*,[243] the claimant was living in a three-bedroom property with her husband, five adult children who had come to the UK from Nigeria in 1998 and who had overstayed their visitor's visas, and three grandchildren. The claimant argued that the points allocated to her under the authority's allocation scheme should be increased to take account of the five adult children.[244] It was held that the authority was entitled to conclude that it was not appropriate to allocate a larger property to the claimant, because her five children were all independent adults, some having their own families, who should have been able to make their own housing arrangements; also, they were subject to immigration control[245] in circumstances where providing accommodation for them would amount to them having recourse to public funds in breach of their conditions of entry to the UK.[246]

Racial harassment

10.142   Issues of racial harassment and violence are also relevant. In *Abdul Subhan*,[247] Tower Hamlets LBC offered a Bangladeshi applicant accommodation in a block of flats in which there was active racial harassment. The authority had itself set up a Racial Incidents Panel, had been provided with details of incidents of racial harassment by

---

240 *R v Haringey LBC ex p Karaman* (1996) 29 HLR 366, QBD. Cf *R v Lambeth LBC ex p Woodburne* (1997) 29 HLR 836, QBD.
241 *Slater v Lewisham LBC* [2006] EWCA Civ 394; [2006] HLR 37 at [30].
242 *R (Ariemuguvbe) v London Borough of Islington* [2009] EWCA Civ 1308.
243 *Ariemuguvbe*.
244 *Ariemuguvbe*, at [2] and [3].
245 Above, para 3.12.
246 *Ariemuguvbe*, at [19].
247 *R v Tower Hamlets LBC ex p Abdul Subhan* (1992) 24 HLR 541, QBD; see also *R v Southwark LBC ex p Solomon* (1994) 26 HLR 693, QBD.

the local law centre, and had received reports from a research project set up by the Home Office Crime Prevention Unit. The decision to make the offer was quashed because the authority had failed to take into account the material on harassment which was before it.

Separation

10.143   While accommodation split into two rooms within a single hostel could be suitable, it was held in *Surdonja*[248] that two rooms split between two hostels a mile apart was not.

Location

10.144   Location will impact on suitability,[249] and an authority must consider how location will affect employment, education and healthcare for the applicant and his/her family.[250] In *Abdullah*,[251] the review officer had taken into account the appellant's submissions and the medical evidence provided and was entitled to conclude that the medical evidence meant no more than that it would be advantageous for the appellant to live near to her family and friends, rather than it being necessary for her to do so; it was also open to the reviewer to assume that social services would provide assistance where necessary, regardless of where the appellant lived.[252]

Gypsies

10.145   Where the applicant is a Gypsy, authorities must give special consideration to securing accommodation that will facilitate his/her traditional way of life: *Codona*.[253] Nonetheless, in *Codona*, the authority was unable to find any suitable accommodation other than bed and breakfast accommodation in the short term, and a decision that it was

---

248 *R v Ealing LBC ex p Surdonja* (1998) 31 HLR 686, QBD, a decision as to the suitability of accommodation provided under HA 1996 s188.

249 See also the discussion at paras 10.111–10.117, above, on discharging the duty by securing accommodation outside the authority's area.

250 *R v Newham LBC ex p Sacupima* (2001) 33 HLR 1, QBD and 2, CA; *R v Newham LBC ex p Ojuri (No 3)* (1998) 31 HLR 452, QBD; *R (Yumsak) v Enfield LBC* [2002] EWHC 280 (Admin); [2002] JHL D38. See also Code of Guidance para 16.38; Welsh Code para 18.40.

251 *Abdullah v Westminster CC* [2007] EWCA Civ 1566; [2007] JHL D89.

252 The decision in *Shala v Birmingham CC* [2007] EWCA Civ 624; [2008] HLR 8 was not considered: see above, para 5.36. While this may not have led to a different result, the same principles must surely apply to how the authority approaches the medical evidence.

253 *Codona v Mid-Bedfordshire DC* [2005] EWCA Civ 925; [2005] HLR 1. See also *R (Price) v Carmarthenshire CC* [2003] EWHC 42 (Admin).

suitable was not unlawful and did not violate the applicant's rights under European Convention on Human Rights articles 8 and 14.[254]

10.146　A person who has adopted a lifestyle similar to that of a Gypsy, but is not a Gypsy, is not entitled to the special protection afforded to Gypsies under human rights jurisprudence.[255]

Enquiries into suitability

10.147　Although there is no explicit statutory duty to enquire into questions of suitability, it is implicit: authorities cannot otherwise reach a decision that accommodation is suitable for the particular applicant. The principles developed in relation to HA 1996 s184 enquiries[256] therefore also apply to enquiries as to suitability: *Thomas*.[257]

Viewing property

10.148　Although recommended in the previous edition of the Code of Guidance,[258] there is no requirement that authorities provide applicants with an opportunity to view and comment on the suitability of any accommodation before moving into it or before a decision is made on its suitability: *Khatun*.[259] It is not oppressive, perverse or disproportionate to the fair and efficient administration of Part 7 for an authority to require an applicant who has not viewed a property to decide whether or not to accept it on pain of immediate cancellation of his/her current accommodation if s/he does not do so, as applicants can challenge suitability by internal review after moving in.[260]

Challenges to suitability

10.149　Challenge to the suitability of an offer is by review under HA 1996 s202[261] and appeal under section 204.[262] Save in exceptional

---

254　See also below, para 12.95.

255　*Steward v Kingston Upon Thames LBC* [2007] EWCA Civ 565; [2007] HLR 42.

256　See Chapter 9, above.

257　*R v Islington LBC ex p Thomas* (1997) 30 HLR 111, QBD. See also *R v South Holland DC ex p Baxter* (1998) 30 HLR 1069, QBD.

258　2002, Code of Guidance para 9.12 and see Welsh Code, para 16.19. The current edition (para 14.22) now only refers to a period of consideration when accommodation is offered under Part 6 in discharge of the section 193 duty (see para 10.154, below).

259　*Khatun v Newham LBC* [2004] EWCA Civ 55; [2004] HLR 29.

260　See para 10.174, below.

261　See para 10.174, below, and chapter 9.

262　See chapter 12.

circumstances, a decision on suitability of offer may not be challenged in a defence to eviction from temporary accommodation.[263]

Cessation of the duty

10.150 The duty under HA 1996 s193 will terminate in the following circumstances.

Eligibility

10.151 The duty will cease if the applicant ceases to be eligible for assistance,[264] for example, if his/her immigration status changes.[265]

Loss of accommodation

10.152 If the applicant becomes homeless intentionally from the accommodation made available, or otherwise voluntarily ceases to occupy it as his/her only or principal home,[266] the duty will cease.[267]

Offers

10.153 A number of instances terminate the duty through offers of accommodation outside of HA 1996 Part 7.

Section 193(5)

10.154 The duty ceases if the applicant is made an offer of suitable accommodation which s/he refuses, having been warned that the authority will regard itself as having discharged its duty if s/he does so and having been informed of the right to an internal review.[268] This provision operates to bring to an end the full housing duty regardless of whether the accommodation offered to the applicant is temporary

---

263 *Tower Hamlets LBC v Rahnara Begum* [2005] EWCA Civ 116; [2006] HLR 9.
264 See chapter 3.
265 HA 1996 s193(6)(a).
266 See *Crawley BC v Sawyer* (1998) 20 HLR 98, CA.
267 HA 1996 s193(6)(b) and (d).
268 HA 1996 s193(5). This condition even applies to an offer of an assured shorthold tenancy (see para 10.110, above) unless it is held out as an offer of a 'qualifying' offer under section 193(7B): see *Griffiths v St Helens BC* [2006] EWCA Civ 160; [2006] HLR 29; but this premises that the offer is only a stage in the rehousing exercise: see para 10.110, above. Section 193(5) embodies the effect of *R v Westminster CC ex p Chambers* (1982) 6 HLR 24, QBD; see para 10.31, above.

or permanent,[269] but see also para 10.110, above, and paras 10.164–10.167, below, where the offer is of an assured shorthold.

10.155 Where an authority has placed an applicant in temporary accommodation pursuant to its duty under HA 1996 s193(2), but that accommodation becomes unsuitable because of the applicant's change of circumstances, the authority's duty will cease under subsection (5) if the applicant refuses an offer of suitable alternative accommodation.[270] in *Muse*, the authority had not acted unfairly because it had followed the procedural safeguards set out in the subsection and had not led the applicant to believe that she was entitled to any additional procedural protection.[271]

10.156 The authority must notify the applicant that it considers the duty to have been discharged.[272] Since such notification comprises a decision as to what duty is owed to the applicant, ie that there is no duty because it has ceased,[273] it must comply with HA 1996 s184, which means that it must give reasons, inform the applicant of his/her right to a review and be in writing.[274]

Part 6 offer

10.157 The duty will cease if the applicant accepts an offer of accommodation under Part 6.[275]

10.158 The duty will also cease if the applicant, having been informed of the possible consequences of refusal and of his/her right to request a review of the suitability of the accommodation, refuses a final offer of accommodation under Part 6.[276] An offer is a final offer for this purpose if it is in writing and states that it is a final offer for the purposes of subsection (7) of HA 1996 s193.[277]

10.159 The exact wording of section 193(7) does not need to be used, provided that the notification contains every matter of substance which the subsection requires; the authority should, however, convey to the

---

269 *Griffiths v St Helens Council* [2006] EWCA Civ 160; [2006] HLR 29.

270 *Muse v Brent LBC* [2008] EWCA Civ 1447.

271 *Muse v Brent LBC* [2008] EWCA Civ 1447.

272 HA 1996 s193(5). Given the applicant's right to challenge the suitability of the offer, the reasons should encompass why the authority considers the accommodation to be suitable for the applicant. Surprisingly there is no express requirement that the notification has to be in writing.

273 HA 1996 s184(1).

274 See above, para 9.144.

275 HA 1996 s193(6)(c); see chapter 11.

276 HA 1996 s193(7).

277 HA 1996 s93(7A).

applicant that it is satisfied both that the accommodation is suitable for him/her and that it is reasonable for him/her to accept it.[278] In *Begum*,[279] the notification was inadequate because it merely stated that the accommodation offered was a reasonable and suitable offer of permanent accommodation.

10.160   A final offer of accommodation under Part 6 may not be made unless the authority is satisfied that the accommodation is suitable for the applicant and that is reasonable for him/her to accept it.[280] The questions of suitability and whether it is reasonable for the applicant to accept the offer must be considered separately.[281] In judging whether it is unreasonable to refuse an offer:

> . . . the decision-maker must have regard to all the personal characteristics of the applicant, her needs, her hopes and her fears and then taking account of those individual aspects, the subjective factors, ask whether it is reasonable, an objective test, for the applicant to accept. The test is whether a right-thinking local housing authority would conclude that it was reasonable that *this applicant* should have accepted the offer of *this* accommodation.[282]

10.161   An applicant's genuine belief that it was not reasonable to accept an offer of accommodation is not conclusive of whether it was reasonable to do so; if the authority has evidence which entitles it to consider that the belief was not objectively reasonable, even if that evidence was not available to the applicant at the time of the refusal, the authority may nonetheless decide that it was reasonable for the applicant to accept the offer: *Ahmed*.[283]

10.162   An offer under Part 6 which does not satisfy the requirements of subsection (7) may nonetheless serve to discharge the authority's duty if it satisfied the requirements of section 193(5) (above, paras 10.154–10.156).[284]

---

278 *Tower Hamlets LBC v Rahanara Begum* [2005] EWCA Civ 116; [2006] HLR 9 at [27], though that case concerned HA 1996 s193(7)(b) prior to its amendment by the Homelessness Act 2002.

279 *Rahanara Begum*, footnote 278, above.

280 HA 1996 s193(7F)(a).

281 *Slater v Lewisham LBC* [2006] EWCA Civ 934; [2006] HLR 37, where the authority had failed to apply its mind to the element of reasonableness.

282 Ward LJ in *Slater v Lewisham LBC* [2006] EWCA Civ 934; [2006] HLR 37 at [34] (italics in original).

283 *Ahmed v Leicester City Council* [2007] EWCA Civ 843; [2008] HLR 6.

284 *Omar v Birmingham City Council* [2007] EWCA Civ 610; [2007] HLR 43 at [29] and [36]; see also *Tower Hamlets LBC v Rahanara Begum* [2005] EWCA Civ 116; [2006] HLR 9 at [27], see para 10.159, above.

Assured tenancy

10.163 The duty will cease if the applicant accepts an offer of an assured (but not an assured shorthold) tenancy from a private landlord.[285]

Assured shorthold tenancy

10.164 The duty will cease if the applicant accepts a 'qualifying offer' of an assured shorthold.[286]

10.165 An offer qualifies if:

- it is made with the approval of the authority,[287] pursuant to arrangements made by the authority with the private landlord in order to bring the HA 1996 s193 duty to an end;
- the tenancy is a fixed-term tenancy;[288] and
- it is accompanied by a statement in writing, which states the term of the tenancy being offered and explains in ordinary language that there is no obligation to accept the offer, but that if it is accepted the duty under HA 1996 s193 will cease.[289]

10.166 An applicant is free to reject a qualifying offer without causing the duty under HA 1996 s193 to be discharged,[290] and acceptance is only effective if the applicant signs a statement acknowledging that s/he has read and understood the statement made with the offer.[291]

10.167 An offer of accommodation let on an assured shorthold tenancy which does not comply with the requirements of HA 1996 s193(7D) (above, para 10.165) cannot be a qualifying offer but, if refused, can nevertheless operate to bring the authority's duty under section 193(2) to an end under section 193(5), provided that the requirements of the latter subsection have been fulfilled, as qualified in the case of an assured shorthold (above, para 10.156).[292] If an applicant accepts an offer of an assured shorthold tenancy that is not a qualifying offer, and that accommodation subsequently ceases to be available, the authority will continue to owe him/her a duty under section

---

285 HA 1996 s193(6)(cc); as defined by HA 1996 s217(1).

286 HA 1996 s193(7B).

287 The offer may not be approved unless the authority is satisfied that the accommodation is suitable for the applicant and that it is reasonable for him/her to accept the offer: HA 1996 s193(7F)(b).

288 As defined by HA 1988 s45(1), ie, any tenancy other than a periodic tenancy.

289 HA 1996 s193(7D).

290 HA 1996 s193(7B).

291 HA 1996 s193(7E).

292 *Griffiths v St Helens Council* [2006] EWCA Civ 160; [2006] HLR 29.

193(2) (provided that the applicant's circumstances have not other-wise materially changed).[293]

Restricted cases

10.168   A restricted case[294] is one where the authority is only satisfied that the applicant is homeless, threatened with homelessness or in prior-ity need because of a restricted person.[295] If the authority only owes a full housing duty[296] to the applicant because of the restricted person, then, so far as reasonably practicable, it must bring the duty to an end by making a private accommodation offer.[297] Where it is not reasonably practicable to do so, the authority may discharge its duty under the other provisions of s193 but should continue to try to bring the duty to an end with a private accommodation offer.[298] A private accommodation offer is of an assured shorthold tenancy made by a private landlord to the applicant in relation to any accommodation which is, or may become, available for the applicant's occupation, which is made with the approval of the authority in pursuance of arrangements made by the authority with the landlord with a view to bringing the authority's duty to an end, and which tenancy is for a fixed term of at least 12 months.[299]

10.169   When making a private accommodation offer, the authority must inform the applicant of the possible consequences of refusal and of the right to request a review of the suitability of the accommoda-tion.[300] The duty ceases if the applicant either accepts or refuses the private accommodation offer.[301]

Reasonable refusals

10.170   An authority is not to make a final offer of accommodation under Part 6,[302] approve a private accommodation offer[303] or approve an

293 *Griffiths*, footnote 292, above.
294 HA 1996 s193(3B). Above, paras 3.71–3.79.
295 HA 1996 s184(7). Above, para 3.74.
296 Under HA 1996 s193(2).
297 HA 1996 s193(7AD).
298 Department of Communities and Local Government Guidance Note, 16 February 2009, para 14.
299 HA 1996 s193(7AC).
300 HA 1996 s193(7AB).
301 HA 1996 s193(7AA).
302 HA 1996 s193(7F)(a).
303 HA 1996 s193(7F)(ab), inserted by the Housing and Regeneration Act 2008

offer of an assured shorthold tenancy,[304] unless it is satisfied that the accommodation is suitable for the applicant and that it is reasonable for him/her to accept the offer.[305] An applicant may reasonably be expected to accept an offer, even though s/he is under contractual or other obligations in respect of his/her existing accommodation, provided s/he is able to bring those obligations to an end before s/he is required to take up the offer.[306]

Keeping offer open

10.171 In *Khatun*,[307] the Court of Appeal reviewed earlier cases in which it had been held that an offer (under HA 1985 Part 3) should remain open for consideration by the applicant for a reasonable time.[308] It was held that these did not support a proposition that the applicant's subjective views on suitability are a mandatory factor in the authority's decision-making process. Given the right to seek a review on suitability after moving in, authorities may insist that an applicant makes a decision whether or not to accept an offer at the time that it is made, without holding it open to afford him/her an opportunity to view it. The letter making the offer comprises the decision under HA 1996 s193(5) that the offer is suitable for the applicant, which pre-empts any opportunity for the applicant to make representations about it, whether based on viewing it or otherwise. The decision assumes that, at the time of making the offer, all the relevant information about suitability is known by the authority, or else that the review process (below, para 10.174) will cure any defects.

10.172 The position is different where the authority knows that admittedly relevant material, for example, medical evidence, is to be

---

s314 and Sch 15 Part 1 paras 1, 5(1) and (6), from 2 March 2009 except in relation to applications for an allocation of social housing or housing assistance or for accommodation made before that date, see the Housing and Regeneration Act 2008 (Commencement No 1 and Saving Provisions) Order 2009 SI No 415 article 2.

304 HA 1996 s193(7F)(b).

305 HA 1996 s193(7F).

306 HA 1996 s193(8).

307 *Khatun v Newham LBC* [2004] EWCA Civ 55; [2004] HLR 29.

308 *R v Wandsworth LBC ex p Lindsay* (1986) 18 HLR 502, QBD. The same had been held in *Parr v Wyre BC* (1982) 2 HLR 71, CA, which was disapproved in *R v Hillingdon LBC ex p Puhlhofer* [1986] AC 484; 18 HLR 158, HL, so far as it was based on the introduction of the word 'appropriate'. See also *R v Ealing LBC ex p Denny* (1995) 27 HLR 424, QBD.

produced. In *Hazeltine*,[309] the applicant challenged suitability on medical grounds; the authority agreed to keep the offer open, but only for a limited period, before the end of which it would not have received or evaluated the medical reports that it had requested from her. The authority's proposal was that, if she accepted the offer, she should abandon her challenge to it, but that, if she did not do so, the authority would determine the issue of suitability retrospectively, ie, if considered unsuitable she would get another offer, but if suitable she would not and the authority would take the position that it had discharged its duty to her. The court held that this procedure could not be regarded as fair.

10.173   Where an authority notifies an applicant that it has ceased to be subject to the duty under HA 1996 s193(2), because the applicant has refused an offer of suitable accommodation under section 193(5), the authority is not obliged to keep the accommodation available during the period when the applicant has the right to request a review or until the authority has reached its review decision.[310]

Review

10.174   There is now a right to seek an internal review of the suitability of accommodation offered under HA 1996 s193(5) or (7),[311] which may be exercised whether or not the applicant has accepted the offer of accommodation.[312] See generally chapter 12, below.

Re-application

10.175   A person towards whom the authority has been under a duty under this section, which is terminated, or ceases, may re-apply.[313]

10.176   This prevents an authority from simply relying on the previous discharge.[314] Rather, the authority must reconsider the case in full,

---

309   *R v Wycombe DC ex p Hazeltine* (1993) 25 HLR 313, CA. See *Khatun v Newham LBC* [2004] EWCA Civ 55; [2004] HLR 29 at [37] where *Hazeltine* was held to be consistent with the decision in that case.

310   *Osseily v Westminster City Council* [2007] EWCA Civ 1108; [2008] HLR 18 at [11].

311   HA 1996 s202(1A).

312   HA 1996 s202(1A); reversing the effect of *Alghile v Westminster CC* (2001) 33 HLR 57, CA, so as to afford the applicant the option of moving into the property while still contesting its suitability.

313   HA 1996 s193(9).

314   Cf paras 9.22–9.37, above. The case-law discussed there would suggest that, notwithstanding s193(9), an authority may refuse to accept a new application from an applicant who has refused a suitable offer of accommodation if the application is based on exactly the same facts.

so a new duty under this section will arise unless the authority can properly conclude that the applicant no longer fulfils the preconditions, for example, is no longer in priority need or is intentionally homeless.

Other statutory powers and duties

10.177 In addition to the duties that arise under HA 1996 Part 7, local authorities may have duties towards applicants under other legislation, particularly where the local housing authority is also the social services authority, for example, the National Assistance Act 1948 or the Children Act 1989. These are considered in chapter 13.

CHAPTER 11

Allocations

continued

Introduction

11.1   Local authorities hold the bulk of their housing stock under the Housing Act (HA) 1985 Part 2.

11.2   Until 1996, the only statutory constraints on the allocation of that stock were to be found in HA 1985 s22, which required that in the selection of tenants certain groups were to be given a reasonable preference, including homeless people, a formulation so loose that there was negligible case-law under it. Under HA 1985 Part 3, duties towards the homeless could be discharged by allocating housing held by the authority under HA 1985 Part 2 or any other power.[1]

11.3   The Housing Act 1996 was designed to reduce the proportion of permanent housing which went directly to homeless people, whether housing from an authority's own stock or by way of nomination to the stock of registered providers of social housing and, accordingly, repealed and replaced HA 1985 s22.[2] Homelessness was not per se a ground of preference, although the homeless could qualify along with others, on the grounds of, for example, unsatisfactory housing conditions, temporary or insecure housing, a particular need for settled accommodation, or social or economic circumstances which made it difficult for them to secure settled accommodation.[3]

11.4   The Housing Act 1996 also introduced a statutory requirement to maintain a housing register, which the authority could keep in such form as it thought fit and which it could, if it wished, maintain in common with other landlords, eg other social housing landlords.[4]

11.5   In 1997, a degree of direct priority for homeless people was restored in the allocation of permanent stock.[5] The Homelessness Act 2002 extensively amended Part 6,[6] primarily:

a) to remove the detailed requirements governing the housing register;

---

1   HA 1985 s69(1)(a).

2   See above, paras 1.68–1.75.

3   HA 1996 s167 as enacted.

4   See generally, HA 1996 ss162–166 as enacted; as to common registers, see HA 1996 s162(3).

5   Allocation of Housing (Reasonable and Additional Preference) Regulations 1997 SI No 1902.

6   The amendments came into force in Wales on 27 January 2003 (Homelessness Act 2002 (Commencement) (Wales) Order 2002 SI No 1736) and 31 January 2003 in England (Homelessness Act 2002 (Commencement No 3) (England) Order 2002 SI No 3114).

b) to remove the power of local authorities to impose blanket restrictions on groups of people;[7]

c) to introduce arrangements to exclude or give a lower priority to those guilty of 'serious unacceptable behaviour'; and

d) to advance the policy of more applicant choice in the allocation of housing.

11.6   This chapter addresses allocations under the following headings:

a) meaning of 'allocation';

b) qualifying persons;

c) applications for housing;

d) the allocation scheme;

e) internal reviews and challenges; and,

f) allocation of housing by registered providers of social housing.

11.7   Criminal offences which may be committed in relation to housing applications under HA 1996 Part 6 – as under Part 7 – are considered below in chapter 15.

11.8   The secretary of state has power – which has been exercised – to issue guidance to local authorities on the exercise of their functions under Part 6.[8]

11.9   The interaction of allocation schemes with other statutory duties, in particular the National Assistance Act 1948 s21 and the Children Act 1989 ss17 and 20, is considered below in chapter 13.

Meaning of 'allocation'

11.10   The provisions of HA 1996 Part 6 apply only to the allocation of housing accommodation, as defined by HA 1996 s159(2).

---

7 A practice facilitated by the wording of the former HA 1996 s161(4), which provided that authorities could decide what classes of persons were or were not 'qualifying persons' for the purposes of an allocation of housing.

8 *Code of Guidance for Local Housing Authorities in England – Allocation of Accommodation*, November 2002 ('old Code of Guidance'). Parts of that guidance have been replaced by *Fair and flexible: statutory guidance on social housing allocations for local authorities in England*, December 2009 ('new Code of Guidance') but otherwise remain in force – see below, appendix C. The new Code of Guidance replaces chapters 1, 2 and 6, paras 5.1–5.12, para 5.18 and paras 5.23–5.32 of chapter 5 and annexes 2, 4, 5, 6, 7, 8, 9 and 12 – see para 3 of the new Code. In Wales, see the *Code of Guidance for Local Authorities on Allocation of Accommodation and Homelessness*, April 2003, Welsh Assembly Government; no new guidance has been issued for Wales. It is available at: http://new.wales.gov.uk/topics/housingandcommunity/housing/ publications/ allocatehousingcode?lang=en.

Selecting a person to be a secure or introductory tenant

11.11 Any selection of a person to be a secure[9] or introductory tenant,[10] whether or not of property held under Housing Act 1985 Part 2, is an allocation, other than the grant of a tenancy which is exempt from security (and, therefore, also exempt from introductory status) by Housing Act 1985 Sch 1.[11] It has been held that selection is not synonymous with the grant of a tenancy:[12] the provisions accordingly govern how people are selected to become tenants, but the grant itself is a separate process under Housing Act 1985 Part 2; it follows that a grant that is not in accordance with the HA 1996 Part 6 allocations policy of the authority is not invalid[13] for that reason.[14]

11.12 For this purpose, 'tenancy' includes 'licence'.[15]

11.13 'Selection' includes notifying a tenant or licensee who is not currently secure that s/he is to become so.[16] The transition from introductory to secure tenant, effected by the passage of time,[17] is not, however, a further selection.

Nominations

11.14 Nomination of a person to be the secure or introductory tenant (or licensee) of another, for example, housing action trust, is an allocation.[18]

11.15 Likewise, the nomination of a person to be an assured tenant of a registered provider of social housing is an allocation: accordingly, this does not include a nomination to a tenancy that will not be assured

---

9 See HA 1985 Part 4.

10 Introductory tenancies were introduced by HA 1996 Part 5 Chapter 1.

11 HA 1996 s159(2)(a). Tenancies exempt from security are: long leases (over 21 years); introductory and demoted tenancies; accommodation for persons with temporary protection; accommodation provided in connection with employment; land acquired by the landlord for development; accommodation for the homeless, family intervention tenancies, temporary accommodation for persons taking up employment; leased premises from private landlords; temporary accommodation during works; agricultural holdings; licensed premises; student lettings; business lettings; and almshouses.

12 Ie, the disposal of stock by way of the grant of a tenancy, under HA 1985 s32.

13 Cf, below, para 11.55.

14 *Birmingham CC v Qasim* [2009] EWCA Civ 1080; [2010] HLR forthcoming.

15 HA 1996 s159(3); see HA 1985 s79(3).

16 HA 1996 s159(3). For example, under HA 1985 Sch 1 paras 4 (homeless persons), 5 (temporary accommodation for persons taking up employment) and 10 (student lettings), as amended by HA 1996 Schs 16 and 17.

17 See HA 1996 s125.

18 HA 1996 s159(2)(b).

under HA 1988 Sch 1,[19] but does include nomination to an assured shorthold.[20]

11.16   Nominations include those made in pursuance of an arrangement (whether or not legally enforceable) to require that accommodation is made available to a person or a number of persons nominated by the authority.[21]

11.17   These provisions reflect long-standing arrangements with housing associations and trusts to which funding has been provided under what is now HA 1996 s22, linked to a right on the part of an authority to nominate a proportion (or even all) of the tenants to a particular property, group of properties (for example, block of flats), or to an association's stock as a whole.

11.18   The wording of HA 1996 s159(4) is oxymoronic: if the entitlement is to 'require' that accommodation is made available to a person or number of persons, it is 'legally enforceable'. It may be that what was in mind is that a particular nomination is not legally enforceable, because such arrangements commonly work by way of proportions of voids, but the wording does not lend itself to this, because it is the arrangement that must 'require' – even if not 'legally enforceable'. To give the wording some meaning (within the apparent intention of the provision), therefore, it would seem that a voluntary nomination arrangement not made by deed and for which there is no consideration will still qualify.

Exemptions

11.19   HA 1996 s159(5)[22] exempts from these allocation provisions an allocation to anyone who is already a secure or introductory tenant (whether or not of the same landlord), unless the allocation involves a transfer of housing accommodation for that person which has been made on his/her application.[23] Those moved at the behest of

---

19 High rateable value tenancies; tenancies at a low rent; business tenancies; licensed premises; agricultural land and holdings; lettings to students; holiday lettings; accommodation for asylum-seekers; and accommodation for persons with temporary protection.

20 HA 1996 s159(2)(c).

21 HA 1996 s159(4).

22 As amended by the Homelessness Act 2002 s13.

23 Before amendment, transfers were also exempt. The re-inclusion within the provisions of transfer applications accords with the practice of many local authorities to deal with transfer applications on the same basis as those of new applicants (see, eg, *R v Islington LBC ex p Reilly and Mannix* (1998) 31 HLR 651, QBD).

the landlord – for example, for redevelopment – are exempt from the provisions.

11.20 Also exempt from Part 6 are the categories specified in HA 1996 s160:

a) succession to secure tenancy on death, or devolution of a fixed term in such circumstances that the tenancy remains secure;[24]
b) assignment by way of exchange of secure tenancy or to a person who could have succeeded to the tenancy;[25]
c) transfers of secure or introductory tenancies under the provisions of matrimonial and related domestic legislation;[26]
d) becoming a secure tenant following an introductory tenancy;[27]
e) succession to introductory tenancy;[28]
f) assignment of introductory tenancy to a person who could have succeeded to it.[29]

11.21 The secretary of state has power to prescribe other categories of allocation which will fall outside this Part, subject to restrictions or conditions, including by reference to a specific category or proportion of housing.[30]

11.22 This power has been exercised to exempt allocation of housing to:[31]

a) those entitled to rehousing under Land Compensation Act 1973 s39;[32] and
b) those whose homes are repurchased under Housing Act 1985 s554 or s555.[33]

---

24 See HA 1985 ss87–90.
25 HA 1985 s92.
26 For instance, Matrimonial Causes Act 1973 s24, Matrimonial and Family Proceedings Act 1984 s17, and Children Act 1989 Sch 1 para 1.
27 See HA 1996 s125.
28 HA 1996 s133.
29 HA 1996 s134.
30 HA 1996 s160(4) and (5).
31 Allocation of Housing (England) Regulations 2002 SI No 3264 reg 3 and Allocation of Housing (Wales) Regulations 2003 SI No 239 reg 3.
32 Following compulsory purchase or a number of specified actions leading to loss of the home, eg, a demolition order under HA 1985 or a prohibition order under HA 2004.
33 Repurchase of a designated defective dwelling.

Qualifying persons

11.23   The primary disqualification for an allocation is someone who is ineligible because of immigration status.[34] This has been considered in chapter 3.

11.24   If a person is disqualified, then the authority is not permitted to allocate a tenancy to him/her, even jointly with someone else who is qualified.[35]

11.25   This does not prevent an allocation to someone who is eligible, simply because a member of his/her household is not, but the ineligibility of members of the family may in some circumstances fall to be taken into account when determining an applicant's housing needs under an allocation scheme.[36]

11.26   Unless a person is ineligible, s/he may be allocated housing accommodation by an authority.[37]

Transfer applicants

11.27   Where an applicant is an existing secure or introductory tenant, or an assured tenant of housing accommodation allocated[38] to him/her by a local housing authority, s/he cannot be disqualified on the basis of his/her immigration status under HA 1996 s160A(3) or (5).[39]

Serious unacceptable behaviour

11.28   Additionally, local authorities may disqualify those who – or whose household members[40] – have been guilty of unacceptable behaviour serious enough to make them unsuitable to be tenants of the authority and who – in the circumstances at the time their application is considered – are unsuitable to be tenants of the authority because of the unacceptable behaviour.[41]

11.29   'Unacceptable behaviour' is defined as behaviour which would, if the person was either a secure tenant or a member of a secure tenant's household, entitle a landlord to a possession order under any

---

34   HA 1996 s160A(1).
35   HA 1996 s160A(1)(c).
36   See above, para 3.131.
37   HA 1996 s160A(2).
38   Above, para 11.15.
39   HA 1996 s160A(6).
40   'Household' is not defined, but is presumably wider than 'family'.
41   HA 1996 s160A(7).

of grounds 1 to 7 of Housing Act 1985 Sch 2.⁴² Accordingly, a former assured or protected tenant evicted on analogous grounds could be treated as disqualified. There need not have been an eviction on the particular ground, only behaviour which would entitle the landlord to a possession order.⁴³

11.30   Housing Act 1985 Sch 2 grounds 1 to 7 are the discretionary (fault) grounds for possession and, as such, the court has to be satisfied that it is reasonable to make a possession order before an order can be made.⁴⁴

11.31   The grounds are:

*Ground 1*⁴⁵ – Rent arrears or breach of tenancy.

*Ground 2*⁴⁶ – Behaviour which is likely to cause a nuisance or annoyance to those in the locality of the dwelling, or conviction for using the dwelling for immoral or illegal purposes or committing an indictable offence in or in the locality of the dwelling house.⁴⁷

*Ground 2A*⁴⁸ – Domestic violence causing a partner or other family member to leave the property.⁴⁹

*Ground 3*⁵⁰ – Deterioration of the dwelling-house due to waste, neglect or default.

---

42 HA 1996 s160A(8).
43 See old Code of Guidance para 4.21 – still in force, see para 11.7, above; Welsh Code para 3.16.
44 HA 1985 s84(2).
45 HA 1988 grounds 8, 10, 11 and 12; Rent Act 1977 case 1.
46 HA 1988 ground 14; Rent Act 1977 case 2.
47 A number of cases have relied on this ground and the Court of Appeal has either upheld possession orders or substituted possession where it has originally been refused: see *Kensington & Chelsea RLBC v Simmonds* (1996) 29 HLR 1; *Bristol CC v Mousah* (1997) 30 HLR 32; *Darlington LBC v Sterling* (1996) 29 HLR 310; *West Kent HA v Davies* (1998) 31 HLR 415; *Camden LBC v Gilsenan* (1998) 31 HLR 81; *Portsmouth BC v Bryant* (2000) 32 HLR 906; *Newcastle CC v Morrison* (2000) 32 HLR; *Lambeth LBC v Howard* (2001) 33 HLR 58; *New Charter HA v Ashcroft* [2004] EWCA Civ 310; [2004] HLR 36; *London and Quadrant Housing Trust v Root* [2005] EWCA Civ 43; [2005] HLR 28; *Manchester CC v Higgins* [2006] HLR 14; *Sandwell MBC v Hensley* [2008] HLR 22. These cases reflect a hardening of attitudes towards those guilty of anti-social behaviour and, in turn, make it easier for authorities to conclude that an applicant is disqualified on this ground, although authorities will need to be careful to consider each case and, in particular, the issue of reasonableness on its own merits not on the basis of policy. For the equivalent provision under HA 1988 Sch 2 ground 14, see eg, *Knowsley Housing Trust v Prescott* [2009] EWHC 924 (QB); [2009] L&TR 24.
48 HA 1988 ground 14A; there is no equivalent under the Rent Act 1977.
49 See *Camden LBC v Mallett* (2001) 33 HLR 20, CA.
50 HA 1988 ground 13; Rent Act 1977 case 3.

Ground 4[51] – Deterioration of furniture provided by the landlord due to ill-treatment;

Ground 5[52] – Tenancy induced by a false statement.[53]

Ground 6[54] – Premium received or paid in connection with a mutual exchange.

Ground 7[55] – Eviction from a dwelling within the curtilage of a building held for non-housing purposes due to conduct such that given the nature of the building it would not be right for occupation to continue.

11.32   The overriding test is whether the authority is satisfied that the applicant or member of his/her household has been guilty of behaviour 'serious enough to make [the applicant] unsuitable to be' its tenant, and that – in the circumstances at the time of his/her application – the applicant is (still) thus unsuitable. The fact that an order for possession has been made on a relevant ground will therefore not be sufficient.[56] Criminal convictions for drug-related offences can be sufficient.[57]

11.33   The criterion circumscribes the general power of exclusion, but is not the exclusion itself.[58] A fixed rule or practice to treat all those evicted on one of the relevant grounds as unsuitable will be unlawful;[59] indeed, given the separation in HA 1996 s160A(7) between past conduct and suitability at time of application, this proposition is likely to be strictly applied.

---

51   HA 1988 ground 15; Rent Act 1977 case 4.

52   HA 1988 ground 17; there is no equivalent under the Rent Act 1977.

53   Including those made as part of a homelessness application. Cf, *Rushcliffe BC v Watson* (1991) 24 HLR 124, CA; *Shrewsbury & Atcham BC v Evans* (1997) 30 HLR 123, CA; and *Lewisham LBC v Akinsola* (1999) 32 HLR 414, CA; *Waltham Forest LBC v Roberts* [2004] EWCA Civ 940; [2005] HLR 2.

54   There is no equivalent under the HA 1988 or Rent Act 1977, although in each case assignment may be prohibited or only allowed with consent, and hence an exchange in breach of the tenancy agreement.

55   There is no equivalent to this in either the HA 1988 or Rent Act 1977.

56   See old Code of Guidance para 4.22(ii) – still in force, see para 11.8, above; Welsh Code para 3.17(ii).

57   *R (Dixon) v Wandsworth LBC* [2007] EWHC 3075 (Admin).

58   Cf *Re Betts* [1983] 2 AC 613; 10 HLR 97, HL, above, para 7.9. See also the cases where authorities have successfully been challenged for concluding that an applicant had become homeless intentionally because a 'fault ground' for possession had led to an order against them, without addressing the conditions of what is now HA 1996 s191, and reaching a conclusion on the correct question for themselves (paras 9.109–9.110, above).

59   See para 12.44, below.

11.34 Housing Act 1985 Sch 2 grounds 1 to 7 are discretionary grounds for possession and as such the court has to be satisfied that it is reasonable to grant possession before an order can be made.[60] Authorities will therefore need to address this issue of reasonableness for themselves.[61] There is an oddity here, in that authorities may reach a public law decision (in particular, one that in itself is not so unreasonable as to be irrational or perverse)[62] on whether or not a county court would have found it reasonable to make the order.

11.35 Conduct leading to an outright, a suspended or a postponed order can suffice, because postponement and suspension are under Housing Act 1985 s85, which does not come into play unless an order under section 84 is available.

11.36 There is a difficult relationship here. In *Portsmouth CC v Bryant*,[63] it was said that: 'In deciding whether it is reasonable to make an order under section 84(2) the judge can properly take into account his/her power under section 85(2) to suspend that order.' The burden of this decision was that a court could decide to make an order because it had power to suspend or postpone knowing that it intended to do so, where if there were no such power it might not make an order at all.

11.37 It follows that there is a material difference between an outright order made under section 84 and one made in contemplation of the exercise of the section 85 power to suspend or postpone. On the face of it, any such order could suffice; on the other hand, if the conduct was such that a court would have been likely to suspend or postpone, it is tantamount to recognising that a court would have been operating from the premise that the conduct had not yet reached the point at which the occupier was – in terms of the overriding issue for the authority – unsuitable to be a tenant. In turn, it is submitted that this should impact on the overriding issue (whether or not the conduct was sufficient to make the applicant unsuitable to be a tenant). Accordingly, it must be the best practice for the authority to ask itself whether it was likely that an outright, suspended or postponed order would have been made: if one of the latter two, while it still has the right to treat the applicant as unsuitable, it should nonetheless be able to justify why.

60 HA 1985 s84(2).
61 The old Code of Guidance para 4.22(i) – still in force, see para 11.8, above – suggests that the authority will need to consider fully all the factors that a court would take into account in determining whether it was reasonable for an order to be granted. See Welsh Code para 3.17(i)(b).
62 Cf, below, paras 12.51–12.55.
63 (2000) 32 HLR 906, CA, per Simon Brown LJ at 916.

11.38 　　The old Code of Guidance suggests that the authority needs 'to be satisfied that, if a possession order were granted it would not be suspended by the court'.[64] It may be contended that this is an overstatement of the law; the essential issue is selection of tenants, to which conduct is, on the face of it, not irrelevant;[65] on the other hand, there is much practical merit in this reconciliation.

11.39 　　Relevant too would seem to be the distinction drawn in some of the anti-social behaviour cases between conduct by the tenant him/herself and conduct by a member of his/her household which s/he had failed to control, such that an outright order might be made in the first case but a suspended order in the second, depending on the degree of acquiescence.[66]

11.40 　　Thus, a transfer applicant against whom a suspended order has been made (which has not subsequently led to eviction) would prima facie still be suitable, even if the decision is that of the authority. Likewise, a person against whom a suspended order was made on the ground of, for example, nuisance and annoyance, but put into effect because of arrears,[67] would be in a different class from an applicant whose order was put into effect because of continued nuisance or annoyance.

11.41 　　Consider also the position of a former tenant who has abandoned a property owing several hundred pounds of arrears. On application for housing from the local authority, the authority may consider that the arrears are such that an order would have been made, so that the applicant can be considered to have committed unacceptable behaviour. The authority should, it is submitted, also consider whether it was an outright or a suspended order that would have been made if the tenant had decided not to abandon but had instead waited and defended a possession action based on the arrears.[68]

64　At para 4.22(ii): still in force – see para 11.8, above. See Welsh Code para 3.17(ii).

65　See also below, para 12.39.

66　See, eg, *Gallagher v Castle Vale HAT* [2001] EWCA Civ 944; 33 HLR 72; see also *Kensington & Chelsea RLBC v Simmonds* (1996) 29 HLR 507, CA, per Simon Brown LJ at 512; *Newcastle CC v Morrison* (2000) 32 HLR 891, CA; *Manchester CC v Higgins* [2005] EWCA Civ 1423; [2006] HLR 14 and *Knowsley Housing Trust v McMullen (by her litigation friend)* [2006] EWCA Civ 539; [2006] HLR43. Cf *London and Quadrant Housing Trust v Root* [2005] EWCA Civ 43; [2005] HLR 28.

67　See *Sheffield CC v Hopkins* [2001] EWCA Civ 1023; [2002] HLR 12.

68　See, eg, *Lambeth LBC v Henry* (2000) 32 HLR 874, CA.

Notification

11.42 Where an authority decides that an applicant is ineligible, it must notify[69] him/her of the decision and of the grounds for it in writing.[70] This duty is identical to that applicable to a decision on a homelessness application and the reasons for it: see chapters 9[71] and 12.[72]

Re-applications

11.43 Where an applicant is treated as ineligible due to serious unacceptable behaviour, s/he may make a fresh application if s/he considers that s/he should no longer be treated as ineligible,[73] for example, because rent arrears have been cleared or because someone who had been guilty of anti-social behaviour is no longer part of his/her household.[74]

11.44 Superficially, this might seem to suggest some analogy with the law on re-applications for assistance under HA 1996 Part 7.[75] This would, however, be wrong because, while the test – whether the application is made on exactly the same facts – in relation to a homelessness re-application is in principle a question for the authority to answer,[76] the obligation to reconsider qualification for an allocation arises when the applicant considers that s/he should no longer be treated as ineligible.

11.45 That said, it is unlikely that an authority must reconsider application after application, week in week out, each to be followed by a review,[77] without some basis for suggesting a relevant change. There are probably two broad approaches. Either the courts will oblige authorities to engage in consideration (and review), but they will be entitled to do no more than ask whether there has been a change 'in

---

69 If the notification is not received by the applicant, it is to be treated as having been received if it is made available at the authority's office for a reasonable period for collection: HA 1996 s160(10).

70 HA 1996 s160A(9) and (10).

71 Paras 9.132–9.148.

72 Paras 12.64–12.91.

73 HA 1996 s160A(11).

74 Cf, the distinction drawn above at para 11.39 – see *Gallagher v Castle Vale HAT* [2001] EWCA Civ 944; 33 HLR 72; *Kensington & Chelsea RLBC v Simmonds* (1996) 29 HLR 507, CA.

75 See paras 9.24–9.39, above.

76 See *Rikha Begum v Tower Hamlets LBC* [2005] EWCA Civ 340; [2005] HLR 34; paras 9.29–9.30, above.

77 See para 11.99, below.

the [applicant's] circumstances'[78] and what that change is, with the result that if the applicant fails to put forward anything which could justify reconsideration the same decision will follow,[79] or else the courts will impose a somewhat more rigorous test of whether 'a reasonable applicant' could consider that there had been any material change such as to lead him/her to consider that s/he should no longer be treated as ineligible, ie whether there is any basis for that conclusion. The latter seems the less likely.

11.46   In practice, the issue is only likely to get to court where there has been something that could lead the applicant to re-apply, both because a challenge will have to be by way of judicial review for which permission will be required, and in order to procure public funding to make a claim. Nonetheless, authorities need to determine a proper response to such applications. The safest course will be the former, ie, always to ask the applicant to identify the putative change and to ensure that it is considered (along with any other material changes, for example, to their own policies and/or stock availability).[80] The old Code of Guidance suggests that unless there has been a considerable lapse of time, it will be for the applicant to show that his/her circumstances or behaviour have changed,[81] ie, the first approach in para 11.45, above.

Existing applicants

11.47   The eligibility provisions of HA 1996 s160A came into force on 27 January 2003 in Wales and 31 January 2003 in England. All applicants who were on a local authority housing register immediately before that date, or who had made an application which had not yet been determined, were to be treated as persons who had applied for an allocation of housing,[82] which had the effect of applying the provisions of section 160A to them.

---

78 Cf, the wording of HA 1996 s160(7)(b).

79 Consider by way of analogy the homelessness cases where the applicant has failed to put forward a matter for the authority to enquire into – or something to put the authority on notice of an enquiry which needs to be made – above, paras 9.95–9.100.

80 See, in particular, HA 1996 s166(3); para 11.49, below.

81 Old Code of Guidance para 4.24: still in force – see para 11.8, above; Welsh Code para 3.19.

82 Homelessness Act 2002 s14(3).

Applications for housing

Housing register

11.48 Prior to amendment by Homelessness Act 2002 Act, HA 1996 Part 6 required all local authorities to establish and maintain a housing register. That requirement has now been repealed.

Consideration of applications

11.49 All applications must, if made in accordance with the procedures laid down in an authority's allocation scheme,[83] be considered by that authority.[84] It is a matter for the authority how it records that application and the information contained in it.

Advice and information

11.50 All authorities must make available, free of charge, advice and information about the right to make an application for an allocation of housing.[85] They must also provide the necessary assistance in making an application to those who are likely otherwise to have difficulty in doing so.[86]

11.51 All applicants must be informed of the right to request information about their applications,[87] and about any decisions made in relation to them,[88] and to seek an internal review.[89]

Disclosure of information

11.52 The fact that a person is an applicant for housing must not be disclosed – without the consent of the applicant – to any other member of the public.[90] The old Code of Guidance[91] states that this did

---

83 See para 11.53, below.

84 HA 1996 s166(3). Provided proper consideration has been given, a court will not interfere with the authority's findings or how it decides to treat the application : see, eg, *R (Heaney) v Lambeth LBC* [2006] EWHC 3332 (Admin).

85 HA 1996 s166(1)(a).

86 HA 1996 s166(1)(b).

87 Under HA 1996 s167(4A)(a), see paras 11.95 and 11.96, below.

88 Under HA 1996 s167(4A)(b), see para 11.98, below.

89 Under HA 1996 s167(4A)(c), see para 11.99, below.

90 HA 1996 s166(4).

91 See para 4.55: still in force – see para 11.8, above.

not preclude disclosure to housing officers, doctors, social workers or staff of registered social landlords (now, registered providers of social housing), 'although authorities will wish to preserve confidentiality and supply information only on a "need to know" basis'.[92] The new Code recommends that authorities should agree information-sharing protocols with registered providers of social housing in their district, covering issues such as rent arrears, anti-social behaviour and support needs.[93]

The allocation scheme

11.53   Each local housing authority must establish an allocation scheme for determining priorities between qualifying persons[94] and for the procedure to be followed[95] in allocating housing accommodation.[96]

Choice-based housing

11.54   The scheme must include a statement of the authority's policy on offering applicants a 'choice of housing accommodation' or 'the opportunity to express preferences' about the accommodation to be allocated to them.[97] The new Code of Guidance encourages allocation policies to provide for applicants to be given more of a say and a greater choice over the accommodation to which they are allocated as

92 Such information would arguably, in any event, be covered by the general principle that confidences should be preserved: see *Attorney-General v Guardian Newspapers (No 2)* [1990] 1 AC 109, HL; *R v Chief Constable of the North Wales Police ex p AB* [1999] QB 396, DC; *Woolgar v Chief Constable of Sussex Police* [2001] 1 WLR 25, CA; *Douglas v Hello! Ltd* [2001] QB 967, CA; and *Campbell v MGN Ltd* [2004] UKHL 22. It would also seem to engage ECHR article 8(1), ie, the right to respect for privacy. However, it is unlikely that disclosure to the relevant officers, professionals and other staff would be a breach of such confidence since it would not be 'unauthorised use of that information to the detriment of the party communicating it' (per Megarry J in *Coco v AN Clark (Engineers)* [1969] RPC 41, cited by Lord Griffiths in *Guardian (No 2)* at 268/C). While disclosure may prima facie be a breach of article 8(1), a proper disclosure would not be difficult to justify under article 8(2), see para 12.95, below.

93 Para 98. See also *Access to Housing: Information Sharing Protocol*, Housing Corporation, November 2007.

94 See paras 11.23–11.41, above.

95 'Procedure' includes all aspects of the allocation process including the persons or descriptions of persons by whom decisions are to be taken: HA 1996 s167(1).

96 HA 1996 s167(1).

97 HA 1996 s167(1A). See new Code of Guidance paras 24–25; Welsh Code paras 4.24–4.38.

this is the best way to ensure sustainable tenancies and to build settled, viable and inclusive communities.[98] This mirrors paragraph 5.3 of the old Code of Guidance, which is no longer in force.[99] The new Code refers to the forthcoming Equality Bill to put a clear emphasis on local authorities promoting and meeting equalities duties.[100]

Unlawful allocations

11.55 Allocation from the waiting list must be in accordance with the scheme.[101] An allocation which is not in accordance with the scheme will be ultra vires.[102] Notwithstanding what might be thought the obvious purpose of this provision to constrain lettings that are not in accordance with the scheme, it has been held that a non-compliant tenancy is nonetheless valid rather than void.[103]

Categories of reasonable preference

11.56 In establishing priorities, a reasonable preference must be given to:[104]

a) those who are homeless (within the meaning of Part 7);[105]

b) those who are owed a duty by any local housing authority under

---

98 New Code of Guidance para 24. Cf the Welsh Code, para 4.26, which does not advocate choice as strongly.

99 Above, para 11.8.

100 New Code of Guidance paras 21–22. See also cl 1 of the Equality Bill (currently at committee stage in the House of Lords) which provides that an authority to which it applies must have due regard to the desirability of exercising functions in a way that is designed to reduce the inequalities of outcome which result from socio-economic disadvantage. This will be a general, or 'target' duty (see cl 3) which will therefore only provide a basis for judicial review, not a cause of action at private law.

101 HA 1996 s167(8). See *Sarhadid v Camden LBC* [2004] EWCA Civ 1485; [2005] HLR 11; *R (Bibi) v Camden LBC* [2004] EWHC 2527 (Admin); [2005] HLR 18, where failures by the local authority to apply the scheme led to the quashing of its decisions. Cf *R (Osei) v Newham LBC* (2010) CO/12287/2008, 27 January 2010.

102 See *R v Macclesfield BC ex p Duddy* [2001] JHL D16, QBD (allocation to a former employee outside the provisions of the scheme).

103 *Birmingham CC v Qasim* [2009] EWCA Civ 1080; [2010] HLR forthcoming.

104 HA 1996 s167(2), as amended by Homelessness Act 2002 s16.

105 See chapter 4. The class is not qualified in any way (cf, s167(2)(b)), and therefore encompasses those who are homeless but not in priority need. There is no requirement that an applicant should have applied as homeless before an authority must consider whether or not s/he qualifies under this ground (again, cf subs (b)): *R (Alam) v Tower Hamlets LBC* [2009] EWHC 44 (Admin); [2009] JHL D47.

HA 1996 s190(2),[106] s193(2)[107] or s195(2)[108] (or under Housing Act 1985 s65(2) or s68(2))[109] or who are occupying accommodation secured under HA 1996 s192(3);[110]

c) those in insanitary or overcrowded housing or otherwise in unsatisfactory housing conditions;

d) those who need to move on medical or welfare grounds (including grounds relating to a disability);[111] and

e) those who need to move to a particular locality in the district of the authority, where failure to meet that need would cause hardship (to themselves or others).[112]

11.57   Reasonable preference must not be given to an applicant who only falls within any of the reasonable preference categories because of a restricted person.[113] A restricted person is someone who is ineligible,[114] subject to immigration control,[115] and who either does not have leave to enter or remain in the UK, or whose leave is subject to a condition to maintain and accommodate him/herself, and any

---

106 See para 10.54, above. This is the duty to those who are in priority need but intentionally homeless. Prior to this amendment, intentionally homeless people did not receive any statutory preference and many authorities either excluded them altogether or gave them little or no priority. Any exclusion or reduction of preference for this group must now be in accordance with HA 1996 s160A(7) (para 11.28, above) or s167(2A) or (2B) (see paras 11.62 and 11.63, below).

107 The duty to those who are eligible, in priority need and not intentionally homeless: see para 10.85, above.

108 The duty to those threatened with homelessness unintentionally: see para 10.89, above.

109 The equivalent duties under the HA 1985 to the unintentionally homeless.

110 Those unintentionally homeless who are not in priority need but who are offered housing under the discretionary power: see para 10.47, above.

111 The reference to disability was added by HA 2004 s223 because of concerns that local authorities were interpreting the need for a move on 'medical' grounds too narrowly. The old Code of Guidance (para 5.14: still in force – see para 11.8, above; Welsh Code para 4.12) envisages that those within this paragraph will not only include those with ongoing care and support needs, but also others such as care leavers or other vulnerable persons who need a secure base from which to build a stable life.

112 'This would include, for example, a person who needs to move to a different locality in order to give or receive care, to access specialised medical treatment, or to take up a particular employment or training opportunity': old Code of Guidance para 5.16: still in force – see para 11.8, above; Welsh Code para 4.14.

113 HA 1996 s167(2ZA), inserted by the Housing and Regeneration Act 2008 Sch 15 para 2.

114 Above, paras 3.71–3.79.

115 Above, para 3.12.

dependants, without recourse to public funds.[116] An authority should take care that their published allocation scheme reflects the particular position of restricted cases.[117]

11.58   The secretary of state has power to specify further categories or to amend or repeal any part of HA 1996 s167(2),[118] but this power has not been exercised in relation to the amended section 167(2).

11.59   Additional preference may be given to sub-groups within those groups, being persons with urgent housing needs.[119] This means giving those applicants 'additional weight' or 'an extra head start, but it does not require an allocation to be made to applicants entitled to it ahead of all others'.[120] The new Code of Guidance highlights the absence of any obligation to frame an allocation scheme so as to provide for additional preference, but reminds authorities to 'consider, in the light of local circumstances, whether there is a need to give effect to this provision'.[121]

11.60   There is no requirement for a local authority to frame an allocation scheme to provide for cumulative preference, ie affording greater priority to applicant who falls into more than one reasonable preference category.[122]

---

116 HA 1996 s184(7) and see above, para 3.74.

117 Department of Communities and Local Government Guidance Note, 16 February 2009, para 17.

118 HA 1996 s167(3).

119 HA 1996 s167(2). Examples given by the old Code of Guidance (para 5.18 – no longer in force, see para 11.8, above; Welsh Code para 4.20) include those owed a homelessness duty as a result of violence or threats of violence likely to be carried out and who as a result require urgent rehousing, and those who need to move because of urgent medical reasons. See also *R (Heaney) V Lambeth LBC* [2006] EWHC 3332 (Admin) where the applicant asserted that she had an urgent housing need arising out of the distress caused by continuing to live in a property in which one of her daughters had died and, as such, that she qualified within the authority's category for transfer on an urgent basis, a claim which the authority rejected. Recognising that the authority had set a high threshold for inclusion in the relevant category, and that it had considered all the evidence, the court held that the authority was entitled to reach the conclusion that the applicant did not meet the criteria.

120 *R (L and D) v Lambeth LBC* [2001] EWHC Admin 900; (2002) JHL D1 (upheld on appeal, *Lambeth LBC v A; Lambeth LBC v Lindsay* [2002] EWCA Civ 1084; [2002] HLR 57.

121 New Code of Guidance paras 18–19.

122 *R (Ahmad) v Newham LBC* [2009] UKHL 14; [2009] HLR 31. See also new Code of Guidance para 58. See further below, paras 11.73–11.83.

Considerations

11.61   For the purpose of defining how preference is to be awarded to those within these categories, an authority's allocation scheme may take into account:[123]

a) the financial resources open to an applicant to meet his/her housing costs;

b) any behaviour of an applicant (or a member of his/her household) which affects his/her suitability to be a tenant;[124]

c) any local connection[125] which exists between an applicant and the authority's area.[126]

11.62   The new Code of Guidance strongly recommends that when framing a scheme, a local authority should not only meet the requirements of the legislation, but should also take into account the particular needs and priorities of the local area.[127]

Anti-social behaviour

11.63   The allocation scheme need not, however, afford any preference at all for an applicant who – in the circumstances at the time his/her case is considered – does not deserve to be treated as a member of a group who are to be given preference, because s/he, or a member of his/her household, has been guilty of such serious unacceptable behaviour that s/he is unsuitable to be a tenant of the authority.[128] Such behaviour is defined in the same way as for ineligibility.[129] Authorities thus have a choice whether to exclude applicants altogether because of serious unacceptable behaviour,[130] or to permit them to join the allocation scheme but downgrade their preference.

11.64   Although HA 1996 s167(2C) refers to an applicant being 'guilty of unacceptable behaviour serious enough to make him unsuitable to be a tenant of the authority', the new Code of Guidance discusses

---

123   HA 1996 s167(2A).

124   See further below, paras 11.63–11.66.

125   As defined by HA 1996 s199; see paras 7.7–7.13.

126   Accordingly, a scheme is not unlawful because it includes reference to whether an applicant has a local connection when determining priority as between two applicants otherwise in the same band of priority: *R (Boolen) v Barking & Dagenham* [2009] EWHC 2196 (Admin); [2009] JHL D113.

127   See new Code of Guidance para 56.

128   HA 1996 s167(2B) and (2C).

129   See paras 11.28–11.41, above.

130   See para 11.28, above.

behaviour only in terms of 'good' and 'bad', defining 'bad' behaviour as including 'unacceptable behaviour which was not serious enough to justify a decision to treat the applicant as ineligible, or to give him/her no preference for an allocation, but which could be taken into account in assessing the level of priority which was deserved relative to other applicants'.[131]

11.65 An applicant must be notified in writing of a decision that s/he is a person to whom s167(2C) applies,[132] and of the grounds for it.[133] There is provision for review of such a decision: see below, paras 11.99–11.103.

11.66 The new Code also suggests that the provisions of HA 1996 s167(2C)–(2D) should be construed very widely, so that a local authority should be able to take account of good as well as bad behaviour, ie, so as to provide greater priority for those applicants who can demonstrate that they have been model tenants.[134]

Consultation

11.67 By HA 1996 s167(7), the authority must afford all registered providers of social housing with whom it has nomination arrangements the opportunity to comment on an allocation scheme before it is adopted or before it is altered in any way that reflects 'a major change of policy'. The expression 'major change of policy' is undefined.[135]

Reasonable preference

11.68 The requirement to give a 'reasonable preference' to certain groups was also to be found in Housing Act 1985 s22. In relation to that section, it was said that to give a reasonable preference means that the criteria must be an 'important factor in making a decision about the allocation of housing',[136] and that 'positive favour should be shown to

---

131 Para 67.
132 HA 1996 s167(4A)(b).
133 HA 1996 s167(4A)(c).
134 Para 67.
135 See new Code of Guidance para 95: registered providers of social housing should be 'involved at an early stage in developing allocation priorities and must be consulted on the allocation scheme'. See also Welsh Code para 5.12: 'major change of policy' would include any amendment that affects the relative priority of a large number of people being considered, and a significant alteration to procedures.
136 Per Tucker J in *R v Lambeth LBC ex p Ashley* (1996) 29 HLR 385, at 387.

applications which satisfy any of the relevant criteria'.[137] More recently, HA 1996 s167(2) has been said to provide those within it with a 'reasonable head start', although it still does not guarantee an allocation.[138] The test is whether they are given a reasonable preference relative to persons who are not so entitled; whether a preference is reasonable is a decision for the authority; a scheme may give reasonable preference to applicants who do not fall within section 167(2) provided that such non-statutory preferences do not dominate the scheme at the expense of the statutory preference categories.[139]

11.69   Reasonable preference does, however, imply a power to choose between different applicants on 'reasonable grounds . . . it is not unreasonable to prefer good tenants to bad tenants'.[140] There is therefore no reason why an authority's own principles of allocation should not include reference to arrears of rent[141] (but not, it is suggested, other categories of debt, such as arrears of local taxation).[142]

11.70   The secretary of state may specify factors which the local authority may not take into account when allocating housing accommodation.[143] This power has not been exercised.

11.71   Insofar as authorities can and do adopt their own policies, it is plainly the case that they cannot adopt policies so rigid as to fetter their consideration of the individual circumstances of particular applicants for housing.[144]

---

137 Per Judge LJ in *R v Wolverhampton MBC ex p Watters* (1997) 29 HLR 931, at 938.

138 See per Collins J in *R (A) v Lambeth LBC; R (Lindsay) v Lambeth LBC* [2002] EWCA Civ 1084; [2002] HLR 57 at [15].

139 *R (Lin) v Barnet LBC* [2007] EWCA Civ 132; [2007] HLR 30.

140 Per Carnwath J in *R v Newham LBC ex p Miah* (1995) 28 HLR 279, at 288.

141 *R v Newham LBC ex p Miah* (footnote 140, above); *R v Lambeth LBC ex p Njomo* (1996) 28 HLR 737; *R v Islington LBC ex p Aldabbagh* (1994) 27 HLR 271, QBD. See now HA 1996 s167(2A)(b), (2B) and (2C) specifically allowing behaviour to be taken into account; paras 11.62–11.63, above. They may also go to discretionary qualification under s160A(7); see para 11.28, above.

142 *R v Forest Heath DC ex p West and Lucas* (1991) 24 HLR 85, CA: all local taxpayers are to be treated the same way, regardless of their need for housing.

143 HA 1996 s167(4).

144 See *R v Canterbury CC ex p Gillespie* (1986) 19 HLR 7; *R v Bristol CC ex p Johns* (1992) 25 HLR 249, QBD; *R v Newham LBC ex p Campbell* (1993) 26 HLR 183, QBD; *R v Newham LBC ex p Watkins* (1993) 26 HLR 434, QBD; *R v Newham LBC ex p Dawson* (1994) 26 HLR 747, QBD; *R v Islington LBC ex p Aldabbagh* (1994) 27 HLR 271, QBD; *R v Lambeth LBC ex p Njomo* (1996) 28 HLR 737, QBD; *R v Southwark LBC ex p Melak* (1996) 29 HLR 223, QBD; *R v Gateshead MBC ex p Lauder* (1997) 29 HLR 360, QBD; and *R v Lambeth LBC ex p Ashley* (1996) 29 HLR 385, QBD. See also para 12.44, below.

11.72 The requirement to give a reasonable preference to the specified groups does not prevent an authority allocating a quota of all vacancies to one particular group (for example, homeless persons).[145]

R (Ahmad) v Newham LBC

11.73 A line of previous cases on reasonable preference within local authority allocation schemes was reversed by the House of Lords in *Ahmad*.[146] Those cases had held that a reasonable authority is bound to include within its scheme a mechanism for identifying, and giving added preference, to those with 'cumulative need,' ie, who qualified within more than one category of reasonable preference.[147]

11.74 In *Ahmad*, Newham LBC's allocations policy was challenged on two principal grounds: that it failed to determine priority between people in the reasonable preference groups in accordance with the gravity of their individual needs, ie, cumulative needs, and that the policy of allocating up to 5 per cent of properties advertised under the authority's choice-based lettings scheme to existing tenants (without a reasonable preference) who wished to transfer to another similar property failed to give reasonable preference to those within HA 1996 s167(2).

11.75 In both the High Court and the Court of Appeal, the scheme was held to be unlawful, principally because the mechanism for determining priority between those with a reasonable preference was by length of time since registration, not by relative need.[148] The scheme was also found to be unlawful because of the allocation of 5 per cent of properties to tenants seeking a transfer.

11.76 The House of Lords held that, in relation to the first ground of challenge (cumulative need), since HA 1996 s167(2) provides only that a local authority may afford additional preference to those within the priority groups who have an urgent need,[149] and section 167(2A) provides only that it may determine priorities between those within

---

145 *R v Islington LBC ex p Reilley and Mannix* (1998) 31 HLR 651, QBD; *R v Westminster LBC ex p Al-Khorsan* (2000) 33 HLR 6, QBD.

146 [2009] UKHL 14; [2009] HLR 31.

147 *R v Islington LBC ex p Reilly and Mannix* (1998) 31 HLR 651; *R v Westminster CC ex p. Al-Khorsan* (1999) 33 HLR 77; *R (A) v Lambeth LBC* [2002] EWCA Civ 1084; [2002] HLR 998. See also *R (Cali) (and others) v Waltham Forest LBC* [2006] EWHC 2950 (Admin); [2007] HLR 1. See, generally, the 7th edition of this book, at paras 11.70–11.83.

148 Per Richards LJ [2008] EWCA Civ 140 at [69].

149 See para 11.59, above.

priority groups by reference to other considerations,[150] an authority cannot be required to afford preference by reference to cumulative need.[151]

11.77   In relation to the second ground of challenge, the local authority was entitled to allocate properties to people who did not fall within a category of reasonable preference; HA 1996 s167(2) only requires that the categories set out in that subsection are given a 'reasonable preference' – it does not require that they should be given absolute priority over everyone else.[152] Moreover, allocating a proportion of the available housing stock to transfer applicants who were already tenants of the local authority neither increased nor decreased the available housing stock – the property left by the transferring tenant becomes available to others.[153]

11.78   The importance of the case is not merely the dismissal of the judicially created requirement of provision for cumulative need, but its statement about judicial intervention generally:

> . . . as a general proposition, it is undesirable for the courts to get involved in questions of how priorities are accorded in housing allocation policies. Of course, there will be cases where the court has a duty to interfere, for instance if a policy does not comply with statutory requirements, or if it is plainly irrational. However, it seems unlikely that the legislature can have intended that Judges should embark on the exercise of telling authorities how to decide on priorities as between applicants in need of rehousing, save in relatively rare and extreme circumstances. Housing allocation policy is a difficult exercise which requires not only social and political sensitivity and judgment, but also local expertise and knowledge.
>
> In relation to the provision of accommodation under the National Assistance Act 1948, my noble and learned friend, Baroness Hale of Richmond, then Hale LJ, said in *R (Wahid) v Tower Hamlets London Borough Council* [2002] EWCA Civ 287; [2003] HLR 13, para 33, '[n]eed is a relative concept, which trained and experienced social workers are much better equipped to assess than are lawyers and courts, provided that they act rationally'. Precisely the same is true of relative housing needs under Part 6 of the 1996 Act, and trained and experienced local authority housing officers.
>
> If section 167 carries with it the sort of requirements which can be said to be implied by the decisions of the Court of Appeal and the Deputy Judge in this case, then Judges would become involved in

---

150 See para 11.63, above.
151 See Baroness Hale at [14] and Lord Neuberger at [39–43].
152 See Baroness Hale at [18–19].
153 At [17–21].

considering details of housing allocation schemes in a way which would be both unrealistic and undesirable. Because of the multifarious factors involved, the large number of applicants, and the relatively small number of available properties at any one time, any scheme would be open to attack, and it would be a difficult and very time-consuming exercise for a Judge to decide whether the scheme before him was acceptable. If it was not, then the consequences would also often be unsatisfactory: either the authority would be in a state of some uncertainty as to how to reformulate the scheme, or the Judge would have to carry out the even more difficult and time-consuming (and indeed inappropriate) exercise of deciding how the scheme should be reformulated to render it acceptable. As Baroness Hale said, that point is well made by looking at the Deputy Judge's order in this case, which requires the Scheme to be reconsidered 'in accordance with the law set out in this judgment'.[154]

11.79   In contrast, in *Birmingham CC v Ali*,[155] the same committee of the House of Lords as in *Ahmad* – cognisant that in that case it has 'made it clear that the courts should be very slow indeed to interfere with a local housing authority's allocation policy, unless it breached the requirements of Part 6'[156] – nonetheless held that Birmingham CC's allocations policy was unlawful by reason of irrationality. Under that policy, where Birmingham accepted that a family was homeless because of overcrowding in or the condition of its current accommodation, so that a 'full' duty was owed,[157] the authority would discharge its duty under section 193(2) by leaving the family in the existing accommodation until suitable permanent accommodation could be found; they were, however, awarded a lower priority than where the authority placed a homeless family in temporary accommodation. There was little argument on this part of the case.[158] While the conclusion of the Court of Appeal that those who were homeless in their current accommodation could not lawfully be left in it under Part 7[159] was not supported by the House of Lords,[160] it was nonetheless held irrational on a 'relatively narrow aspect': the authority had not justified the difference in treatment – its 'bald statement' that 'those in greatest need are dealt with first' was insufficient; on the face of it, those in (their

154 Lord Neuberger, with whom the other members of the Committee agreed, at [46–48].
155 [2009] UKHL 36; [2009] HLR 41.
156 At [62].
157 Above, para 10.85–10.89.
158 See Baroness Hale at [57].
159 Above, paras 10.96 and 10.136.
160 At [61].

current) unsuitable accommodation were in greater need than those in other temporary accommodation which had not been subject to an unsuitability finding; if there was evidence to that effect, it had not been put forward.[161]

11.80   The new Code of Guidance may be said to welcome[162] – and reflects much of what was set out in – the *Ahmad* decision, although it recognises that, while there is no requirement for a local authority to prioritise as between applicants who have a reasonable preference, for practical purposes it is likely that an allocation scheme will need to have some sort of mechanism for determining levels of need between applicants for the purposes of administering the scheme.[163] The new Code recognises *Ahmad* as affording scope for authorities to develop schemes that are simpler, more transparent and easy to understand and operate,[164] including greater use of waiting time,[165] simple banding schemes[166] and the benefits of transfer schemes.[167]

Children

11.81   Where an authority – as it will invariably do – takes children into account for the purposes of determining priority and nature of accommodation under its Part 6 scheme, a residence order under Children Act 1989 s8 will be relevant in deciding whether or not a child is to be taken into account, but it is not determinative of the authority's allocation decision.[168]

Choice-based lettings

11.82   Subject to the 'reasonable preference' categories, the allocation scheme may contain provisions about the allocation of particular housing accommodation either to a person who makes a specific application for it or to persons of a particular description, whether or not within the reasonable preference groups.[169]

---

161 At [62–63].
162 See, eg, paras 57–59.
163 Para 63.
164 Para 62.
165 Para 65–66.
166 Para 71.
167 Para 79.
168 *R (Bibi) v Camden LBC* [2004] EWHC 2527 (Admin); [2005] HLR 18. See also *Holmes-Moorhouse v Richmond Upon Thames LBC* [2009] UKHL 14; [2009] HLR 34. See above, para 9.141.
169 HA 1996 s167(2E).

11.83   The first such provision – specific application – allows authorities to operate a system of advertising properties.[170] Allocation to persons 'of a particular description' governs local lettings schemes outside the general priorities of HA 1996 s167(2).[171] 'Where operating local lettings policies, housing authorities will need to ensure that, overall, reasonable preference for allocation is still given to applicants in the reasonable preference categories and that their local lettings policies do not discriminate, directly or indirectly, on racial or other equality grounds'.[172]

Procedure

11.84   Allocations are a matter for an authority's executive.[173]

11.85   The secretary of state may prescribe the principles of procedure to be followed when framing allocation schemes.[174]

11.86   In Wales, local housing authority officers must be included among the persons by whom allocation decisions can be taken, except where an express decision has been made not to delegate the decision, ie, to retain it as an executive decision.[175] In both England and Wales, elected members may not be involved in allocation decisions where the accommodation to be allocated, or the applicant's sole or main residence, is in the member's ward.[176]

Enquiries

11.87   Unlike under HA 1996 Part 7,[177] there is no express provision requiring an authority to make enquiries before determining an application.

---

170 Ie, where applicants can apply for particular properties which have been advertised as vacant by the housing authority: see new Code of Guidance para 84 (Welsh Code para 4.31) and para 11.54, above.

171 This might include, eg, giving priority to essential workers, to those without children in order to lower child densities on an estate: new Code of Guidance para 86; Welsh Code para 4.52.

172 New Code of Guidance para 86; Welsh Code para 4.52. See also *R (Ahmad) v Newham LBC* [2009] UKHL 14; [2009] HLR 31.

173 See above, para 9.165.

174 HA 1996 s167(5).

175 Local Housing Authorities (Prescribed Principles for Allocation Schemes) (Wales) Regulations 1997 SI No 45 reg 3 and Sch para 2.

176 1997 SI No 45 reg 3 and Sch para 1 and Allocation of Housing (Procedure) Regulations 1997 SI No 483 reg 3.

177 See paras 9.49–9.60, above.

Nevertheless, a body charged with a statutory function must make or cause to be made such enquiries as will allow it to be satisfied that it can properly discharge its role.[178]

11.88   In *Crowder,*[179] a decision that the applicant's daughter was no longer living with her – and that she should accordingly only be considered for single person's accommodation – was quashed because of the authority's failure to make adequate enquiries.

11.89   In *Maali,*[180] the authority's decision was quashed because of flaws in the medical assessment. The claimant, an asthmatic, occupied a third-floor maisonette under a secure tenancy granted by the authority. She occupied the property with her three children, the eldest of whom also suffered from asthma. She applied to the authority to be transferred to another property, contending that she and her eldest daughter were having difficulty climbing the stairs in the property and that therefore she fell within the emergency medical category (Group B) of the authority's allocation scheme.

11.90   In August 2003, the authority's housing medical adviser concluded that the claimant's and her child's medical conditions were not severe enough to justify the need for an emergency transfer because: (i) the fact that the claimant and her child had to climb stairs was positive because exercise helped alleviate the symptoms of asthma; and (ii) when the claimant's asthma worsened, she went to stay with friends in order to obtain help with childcare and would continue to do so even if transferred to another property. The authority accordingly assessed her as being within a mainstream category (Group D) of its allocation scheme.

11.91   The court concluded that the assessment was *Wednesbury* unreasonable. The medical adviser had wrongly attributed the claimant's stays with friends to a need for assistance with childcare rather than to the difficulties that she was experiencing in reaching the third floor. Nor was there any basis for the adviser's conclusion that, because exercise was beneficial to asthmatics, the climbing of stairs was positive.

---

178 See *R v Islington LBC ex p Thomas* (1997) 30 HLR 111, QBD, per Roger Henderson QC at 120 (in relation to whether accommodation provided under HA 1985 s65(2) was suitable). See also *Secretary of State for Education and Science v Tameside BC* [1977] AC 1014, per Lord Diplock at 1065.

179 *R v Oxford CC ex p Crowder* (1998) 31 HLR 485, QBD.

180 *R (Maali) v Lambeth LBC* [2003] EWHC 2231 (Admin).

Information

Scheme

11.92 Since the Housing Act 1980, authorities have been obliged to publish details of their allocation provisions: see HA 1985 s106. The details must be sufficient both to enable applicants to ascertain how the practices of a local authority will affect them and so that the legality of the practice may be determined.[181] Lack of publication does not, however, make a policy ultra vires.[182]

11.93 There is a similar and overlapping duty under HA 1996 Part 6, that an authority must publish a summary of its scheme and provide a copy of the summary free of charge to any member of the public who asks for one.[183] The authority must keep the full scheme available for inspection at its principal office, although a reasonable fee may be charged to any member of the public who asks for a copy.[184]

11.94 Where an authority makes an alteration to the scheme reflecting a major change in policy,[185] it must, within a reasonable period, take such steps as it considers reasonable to bring the effect of the alteration to the attention of those likely to be affected by it.[186]

Applications

11.95 The scheme must include a right for an applicant to request such general information as enables him/her to assess how his/her application is likely to be treated under the scheme. This must, in

181 *R (Faarah) v Southwark LBC* [2008] EWCA Civ 807; [2009] HLR 12 (how registration dates were determined). Cf *R (Yazar) v Southwark LBC* [2008] EWHC 515 (Admin): it was sufficient for a social services procedure for making housing nominations to be provided in a short and comprehensible form; nor did social services have to give reasons for refusing to make a nomination to housing unless asked to do so; and *R (Boolen) v Barking & Dagenham* [2009] EWHC 2196 (Admin) where the local authority was entitled to adopt its local connection policy so long as it was rational and like cases were treated alike: the policy did not have to be set out in the allocations scheme itself because it was not a central feature of the scheme. See also above, para 11.61.

182 *R v Newham LBC ex p Miah* (1995) 28 HLR 279.

183 HA 1996 s168(1). This is not confined to a member of the public in the authority's area.

184 HA 1996 s168(2).

185 Cf, para 11.64, above. The new Code of Guidance (paras 47–48) suggests that reasonable steps will depend on the nature of the allocation scheme. See Welsh Code para 5.12.

186 HA 1996 s168(3).

particular, include whether s/he is likely to be a member of a group to which a preference will be given.[187]

11.96   A person is also entitled to be given general information that will enable him/her to assess whether accommodation appropriate to his/her needs is likely to be made available to him/her and, if so, how long it is likely to be before housing accommodation actually becomes available.[188]

11.97   The old Code of Guidance suggests[189] that authorities which operate open advertising schemes, whereby applicants can apply for particular properties,[190] would usually be expected to provide them with details about properties which have been let: 'for example, what level of priority the successful applicants had, or the date on which they had applied to go on the housing authority's waiting list'.

11.98   The scheme must also afford an applicant the opportunity to request information about any decision about the facts of his/her case,[191] or, if s/he is a person to whom HA 1996 s167(2C) (unacceptable behaviour) applies,[192] information which is likely to be, or has been, taken into account in considering whether to allocate housing accommodation to him/her.[193]

Internal review and challenge

11.99   An applicant has the right to request an internal review of any decision taken under HA 1996 s167(4A)(b) (unacceptable conduct) or under section 160A(9) (eligibility, whether on the grounds of immigration status or conduct).[194] The authority must notify the applicant of the outcome of the review and the grounds for it.[195]

11.100   Prior to its repeal, HA 1996 s165 permitted regulations to be made governing the conduct of internal reviews under Part 6.[196] There is no

---

187 HA 1996 s167(4A)(a)(i).

188 HA 1996 s167(4A)(a)(ii). Additional to rights under the Data Protection Act 1998.

189 See para 5.57 – still in force, see para 11.8, above; Welsh Code para 4.32.

190 Above, paras 11.82–11.83.

191 For example, as to financial resources, previous behaviour or local connection under HA 1996 s167(2A): see para 11.62, above.

192 See para 11.63, above.

193 HA 1996 s167(4A)(b).

194 HA 1996 s167(4A)(d).

195 HA 1996 s167(4A)(d).

196 Allocation of Housing and Homelessness (Review Procedures) Regulations 1999 SI No 71.

such provision in connection with section 167(4A).[197] Authorities will nonetheless want to ensure that any review is fair to the applicant.[198] A decision on an application under Part 6 is not a determination of a civil right or obligation for the purposes of article 6 of the European Convention on Human Rights ('the Convention'/ECHR).[199]

11.101 There is no appeal to the county court against the review decision,[200] and any challenge has to be by way of judicial review.[201]

11.102 However, there is nothing to prevent authorities establishing a voluntary review or appeal process that goes beyond the statutory right to review.[202]

11.103 If the authority does add such a voluntary review process, it is likely to be considered necessary for anyone who is dissatisfied with the priority which s/he has been given to use this before seeking judicial review.[203]

Allocations by registered providers of social housing

11.104 Registered providers of social housing are obliged to co-operate with local housing authorities in offering accommodation to people with priority under the authority's allocation scheme, to such extent as is reasonable in the circumstances.[204] In practice, many local authorities now maintain no housing stock of their own, but have transferred it either to registered providers specially formed for the purpose, or to other providers, by way of large-scale voluntary stock transfers, in connection with which they will necessarily have reserved rights to ensure that they can discharge their homelessness duties, ie, by way of nomination. Even where the authority has retained some or all of its housing stock, it is likely also to have nomination arrangements

---

197 Nor does either the old or the new version of the Code of Guidance include any advice on their conduct. Cf the guidance in the Welsh Code at para 3.26.

198 Cf, para 12.56, below.

199 See paras 12.96–12.100, below.

200 Cf, paras 12.159–12.219, below.

201 See chapter 12.

202 See, eg, *R v Southwark LBC ex p Mason* (1999) 32 HLR 88, QBD (panel reviewing the suitability of offers).

203 See chapter 12, below. S/he could, of course, also complain to the Local Government Ombudsman – see para 12.220–12.226.

204 HA 1996 s 170. See also new Code of Guidance para 96.

with registered providers in its area.[205] Such registered providers are amongst the partners with which local authorities will normally evolve their homelessness strategies.[206]

11.105   Registered providers of social housing in England are regulated by Part 2 of the Housing and Regeneration Act (H&RA) 2008; those in Wales[207] are still regulated by HA 1996 Part 1.[208] Under the former, the Housing Corporation – which had regulated housing associations and trusts since the Housing Act 1974[209] – was abolished and replaced[210] by what is statutorily called the Office for Tenants and Social Landlords,[211] but known as the Tenant Services Authority (TSA).[212] Under the latter, regulation is, as it has been since 1 July 1 1999, performed by the National Assembly for Wales ('the Assembly').[213]

205 The new Code of Guidance recommends that local authorities ensure that they have nomination agreements in place and that those agreements are updated regularly to ensure that they reflect the changing housing market: para 97. See also *Effective Co-operation in Tackling Homelessness: Nomination Agreements and Exclusions* (November 2004, ODPM), identifying good practice in co-operation between housing authorities and registered providers of social housing in relation to nomination agreements and exclusions.

206 Below, paras 14.9–14.17. See also paras 93–95 of the new Code of Guidance, which recommends that local authorities involve registered providers of social housing from the early stages of strategic and operational development.

207 Still called registered social landlords under HA 1996 Part 1; the term registered provider is, however, used for both England and Wales.

208 Albeit amended in parts by H&RA 2008.

209 The original role of the Housing Corporation under HA 1964 was funding only, and only in relation to a small category of 'housing society' (cost rent and co-ownership).

210 H&RA 2008 s64. The Housing Corporation closed on 30 November 2008 and was replaced by the TSA from 1 December 2008, on which date the regulatory functions of the Housing Corporation transferred to the TSA: Transfer of Housing Corporation Functions (Modifications and Transitional Provisions) Order 2008 SI No 2839. Thereafter, the Housing Corporation was formally dissolved on 1 April 2009: see Housing Corporation (Dissolution) Order 2009 SI No 484.

211 H&RA 2008 s 81.

212 It is worth noting that, unlike the former Housing Corporation, the TSA does not have power to provide financial assistance to registered providers; that role is now undertaken by the Homes and Communities Agency (HCA).

213 National Assembly for Wales (Transfer of Functions) Order 1999 SI No 672. This is scheduled to be changed to the Welsh Ministers by H&RA 2008 s61 when brought into force. The original intention of the H&RA 2008 was to transfer the functions and powers from the 'relevant authority', ie the National Assembly for Wales, directly to the Welsh Ministers. In the absence of that transfer, the Welsh National Assembly remains the 'relevant authority' for the purposes of HA 1996 Part 1. The regulatory framework put in place by the Assembly in 2006 continues to apply to registered providers

11.106   It is not possible to describe either system of regulation here.[214] It suffices to say that registered providers are subject to regulatory regimes under one or other – 1996 or 2008 – Act. This means that, while not subject to direct statutory rules on allocation in the same way that local authorities are, their actions, including in relation to allocations, are nonetheless susceptible to review by their regulators and, in turn, susceptible to complaints to those regulators by those adversely affected by their actions and/or inaction.[215] Regulators have a range of sanctions available, including powers of inspection of performance by and/or enquiry into registered providers, extending ultimately to the de-registration or winding up of providers whose performance is inadequate.[216]

11.107   Complaints can also be made to an independent scheme approved by the secretary of state.[217] HA 1996 Sch 2 sets out the general provisions governing the membership, approval and registration of such a scheme. In England, the Housing Ombudsman Service (HOS) is the approved scheme of which every social landlord must be a member.[218] Failure to comply with the requirement to be a member of the scheme may result in an application to the High Court by the secretary of state for an order directing the provider to comply.[219] Where a complaint is made to the HOS, the ombudsman has the power to investigate and determine that complaint by reference to what is, in the opinion of the ombudsman, 'fair in all the circumstances of the case'.[220] If the complaint is upheld, the ombudsman has the power to

     in Wales until such time as it is replaced by the Assembly or any successor 'relevant authority'. It is anticipated that the amendments to the H&RA 2008 transferring the powers and functions of the Housing Corporation to the Welsh Ministers will be brought into force on 1 April 2010.

214 See, generally, Arden & Partington's *Housing Law* (Sweet & Maxwell), paras 1-203 onwards.

215 In some cases, contracts governing the transfer of stock from authorities to registered providers may themselves contain complaint provisions and – although not commonly – even provisions enabling direct enforcement, although this is unlikely to assist a would-be tenant complaining of failure to allocate and/or disappointed with the nature of an allocation so much as an existing tenant. In such circumstances, an existing tenant seeking a transfer may be able to avail him/herself of such provisions.

216 See H&RA 2008 Part 1 chapters 4, 6 and 7; HA 1996 Part 1 and Schedule 1.

217 HA 1996 Sch 2 para 3. In Wales, the function was transferred to the Public Services Ombudsman in 2006.

218 HA 1996 Sch 2 para 1(1). For further general information on how to make a complaint to the HOS, see the link at www.tenantservicesauthority.org/upload/pdf/Putting_things_right_20090106111709.pdf

219 HA 1996 Sch 2 para 1(2).

220 HA 1996 Sch 2 para 7.

order the relevant registered provider of social housing to pay compensation to the complainant or even to order that the member or the complainant is not to exercise or require the performance of contractual or other obligations or rights existing between them.[221] If the registered provider fails to comply with the ombudsman's determination, the ombudsman has the power to order the registered provider to publish that failure in such manner as s/he sees fit.[222] If the registered provider fails to comply with the order to publish, the ombudsman has the power to take such steps as s/he thinks appropriate to publish what the registered provider ought to have published and to recover from the registered provider the costs of doing so.[223]

11.108   Furthermore, it has been held that registered providers may qualify as public authorities within the Human Rights Act 1998, in respect of some aspects of their management of their social housing stock (including service of notice to quit or of seeking possession) and, in addition to the requirement to conform to the Convention rights, that they are also susceptible to the principles of domestic public law in respect of such activities, even if they would not otherwise be capable of challenge on that basis.[224] At the High Court in *Weaver*, those aspects explicitly included the allocation of social housing; while this was not overruled per se, it was not the basis on which the decision that such providers may be public authorities for the purposes of the 1998 Act was upheld: rather, it was held that service of notice to quit or to seek possession is a public function for the purposes of that Act, which means that registered providers are public authorities in respect of such service; while allocation was not directly in issue, however, it seems also to qualify; and, in *R (McIntyre) v Gentoo Group Ltd*,[225] it was held to include allocation. Whether or not other acts of management qualify may well depend on a detailed investigation into and assessment of the functions of allocating and managing housing of the particular registered provider.[226]

11.109   It follows from the foregoing that there may be much to be gained from familiarity with the regulatory requirements applicable

---

221 HA 1996 Sch 2 para 7(2).

222 HA 1996 Sch 2 para 7(3).

223 HA 1996 Sch 2 para 7(5).

224 *R (Weaver) v London & Quadrant Housing Trust* [2008] EWHC 1377 (Admin) and on appeal [2009] EWCA Civ 587. See above, para 12.8. The proposition as to susceptibility was conceded on appeal.

225 [2010] EWHC 5 (Admin), *Housing View*, 11 January 2010, in particular at [25].

226 *Weaver* at [68]–[72]. See also *Aston Cantlow and Wilmcote with Billisley Parochial Church Council v Wallbank* [2003] UKHL 37; [2004] 1 AC 546.

to allocations by registered providers under both English and Welsh regimes. What follows is only brief and introductory. This results from the timing of this edition, shortly after the transition of responsibility from the Housing Corporation to the TSA and at a time when there are imminent changes in standards and guidance. Its purpose, therefore, is to draw attention to what may be available on the basis of which to pursue an applicant's interests, rather than what is available, in the expectation that the adviser will follow up what has become available when the issue arises, and that it will be possible to offer more detailed information in a future edition of this book.

England

11.110　The statutory framework governing registered providers in England under H&RA 2008 is more detailed than that which applies under HA 1996 in Wales. The TSA enjoys a range of powers in relation to the provision of social housing, including that of setting standards, which may include requiring registered providers to comply with rules about, inter alia, allocation criteria,[227] in relation to which it may issue codes of practice amplifying the standard.[228] The secretary of state may issue a direction to the TSA to issue a standard, or about its content.[229] Critically, failure to meet a standard is a ground for the exercise of powers by the TSA,[230] including enforcement powers ranging from notices, fines and compensation, to orders to require the appointment of a manager over the whole of a registered provider's functions or such functions as are specified, or the transfer of such functions to another, and to the removal or suspension of officers or employees or their disqualification.[231]

11.111　Notwithstanding the transfer of regulatory powers to the TSA from the Housing Corporation on 1 December 2008,[232] the regulatory framework established by the Housing Corporation, including the Regulatory Code and Guidance,[233] continues to apply until such time as the TSA exercises its power to put a new regulatory framework in place. The TSA issued statutory consultation in November

227　H&RA 2008 s193(2)(a).
228　H&RA 2008 s195.
229　H&RA 2008 s197.
230　H&RA 2008 s198.
231　H&RA 2008 Part 1 chapter 7.
232　Above, para 11.105.
233　See *The Regulatory Code and Guidance*, August 2005 (Regulatory Code) available at www.housingcorp.gov.uk/upload/pdf/RegulatoryCode.pdf.

2009 on the standards that it is proposed that registered providers of social housing will have to meet from 1 April 2010, with a further two supplementary papers on the use of TSA powers and on consent to disposals of housing stock based on the same timeframe.

11.112   The TSA has indicated that it intends significantly to reduce and/ or remove requirements issued by the Housing Corporation by replacing the Regulatory Code and Guidance and removing thousands of individual regulatory consents and a number of Housing Corporation Circulars and Guidance Notes.[234] The closing date for responses is 5 February 2010: subsequent standards or guidance published pursuant to the consultation are therefore not available for inclusion in this book.

11.113   It is likely that the TSA will – as it has consulted – require registered providers to let their homes 'in a fair, transparent and efficient way' taking into account 'the housing needs and aspirations of tenants and potential tenants'.[235] Registered providers are also likely to be required to be able to demonstrate how their allocations processes make the best use of available housing and contribute to local authorities' strategic housing functions and sustainable communities, with a clear decision-making and appeals process.[236]

11.114   Until 1 April 2010, however, it is the Housing Corporation regulatory framework that remains applicable,[237] which framework includes not only regulatory codes and guidance, but also good practice notes[238] and circulars.[239]

11.115   In summary, that framework requires registered providers of social housing to work with local authorities to enable authorities to fulfil their duties to the homeless and people in priority housing

234 See *A new regulatory framework for social housing in England: A statutory consultation*, November 2009 (the New Framework), para 2.6: www. tenantservicesauthority.org/upload/pdf/statutory_consultation_web.pdf.

235 The New Framework, proposed new Tenancy Standard in Part 2, page 52.

236 The New Framework, proposed new Tenancy Standard in Part 2, page 52.

237 Together with paras 93–100 of the New Code of Guidance for local authorities: this contains encouragement, recommendations and guidance in relation to how closely local authorities and registered providers of social housing should work with each other in order to develop working partnerships so as to ensure the best use of social housing and the widest choice of accommodation for applicants.

238 See, eg, *Working with local authorities*, Practice Note 16, April 2008 available at www.housingcorp.gov.uk/upload/pdf/GPN_16_Working_with_local_authorities.pdf.

239 See, eg, *Tenancy Management: Eligibility and evictions*, Circular 02/07, April 2007 available at www.housingcorp.gov.uk/upload/pdf/Tenancy_management.pdf.

need,[240] and to show that their strategies and policies are responsive to their economic and social environment and link into regional and local housing strategies,[241] in particular that they:

a) adopt criteria for accepting and rejecting nominees and other applicants in consultation with the relevant local authority;[242]
b) exclude applicants from consideration only when their unacceptable behaviour is serious enough to make them unsuitable to be tenants[243] and only where they would not be unlawfully discriminated against;[244]
c) ensure that lettings policies are responsive to local authority housing duties, that they take account of the need to give reasonable priority to transfer applicants, including those from other providers, that they are responsive to national, regional and local mobility and exchange schemes, and that they are demonstrably fair and effectively controlled;[245]
d) ensure that new homes meet the long-term priority needs of the areas in which they are provided;[246]
e) co-operate and contribute to the strategic enabling role of local authorities;[247]
f) demonstrate contribution to neighbourhood renewal and regeneration, whether directly or through partnership, particularly in deprived areas; and[248]
g) demonstrate commitment to sustainable development and work towards incorporating economic, social and environmental objectives into their activities.[249]

Wales

11.116 The statutory framework governing registered providers in Wales under HA 1996 Part 1 has been the responsibility of the Assembly since 1 July 1999. The Assembly has responsibility for maintaining a register of providers, financial regulation, setting of performance

---

240 Regulatory Code para 3.6.
241 Regulatory Code para 3.7.
242 Regulatory Code para 3.6d.
243 Cf, above, paras 11.28–11.41.
244 Regulatory Code para 3.6e. See above, para 11.63.
245 Regulatory Code para 3.6f. See above, para 11.54.
246 Regulatory Code para 3.7a.
247 Regulatory Code para 3.7b.
248 Regulatory Code para 3.7c.
249 Regulatory Code para 3.7d.

standards and the power to issue guidance. Unlike the TSA, the Assembly has no enforcement powers to ensure that standards are maintained. The Assembly does, however, have responsibility for the provision of financial assistance.

11.117   In March 2006, the Assembly issued the *Regulatory Code for Housing Associations Registered in Wales* ('the Welsh Code'),[250] which continues to apply. There is no present indication that the Assembly intends to re-issue or update the Welsh Code.[251] The Welsh Code sets out the following 'key expectations' for registered providers in Wales so far as concerns allocations:

a) that providers should work in partnership with local authorities on allocation; and[252]

b) that providers should maintain a fair selection policy and seek a balance in allocation between the needs and preferences of both applicants and transferees, the need to maximise social inclusion, the need to build stable communities, and the need to make best use of publicly funded resources.[253]

---

250 Pursuant to HA 1996 s36.

251 A full copy of the code can be found at http://newydd.cymru.gov.uk/desh/publications/housing/regulatorycodehas/codee.pdf?lang=en&ts=1,

252 Welsh Code para 1.3.2.

253 Welsh Code para 1.3.3.

CHAPTER 12

Enforcement

Introduction

12.1   Housing Act (HA) 1996 Parts 6 and 7 both contain provision for *internal* review of decisions, which are considered elsewhere in this book.[1] This chapter is concerned with the *external* enforcement of an applicant's rights under both parts, ie, what an applicant, who remains dissatisfied with the decision of the authority after internal review, can do to challenge or change it by way of recourse to the courts.

12.2   A dissatisfied applicant for an allocation of housing under Part 6 may claim judicial review in the High Court to enforce his/her rights. Part 7, however, provides a statutory appeal to the county court[2] against a decision made on an internal review on a 'point of law',[3] and it is this procedure that will normally be used.[4]

12.3   The divergence is a practical one rather than substantive because an appeal on a point of law under these provisions confers on the county court a like jurisdiction to that available on a claim for judicial review, engaging the same legal basis for challenge.

12.4   This chapter is divided into two parts: the first contains the substantive law, applicable either on statutory appeal or on judicial review; the second deals with the procedural law, governing how to bring a claim in either court and when to do so. In an annex, a number of specimen documents have been produced, both to illustrate the principles under consideration here, and to assist when applying them.

Substantive law

Introduction

12.5   The general principles which underlie a challenge under Part 6 or Part 7 are those of administrative – or public – law, which have been largely, but far from exclusively,[5] developed in the course of

---

1   Discussed in chapter 11 (Part 6) and chapter 10 (Part 7), above.

2   HA 1996 s204.

3   It should be noted that the right to claim judicial review is subject to the usual requirements to obtain permission; an appeal under section 204 is, however, as of right. Consider *Manchester CC v Cochrane* [1999] 1 WLR 809, CA.

4   There are circumstances in which an applicant under Part 7 may seek judicial review of the authority's decision: these are considered below, para 12.113.

5   Consider the Court of Appeal decisions in *Crédit Suisse v Allerdale MBC; Same v Waltham Forest LBC* [1996] 4 All ER 129, CA, which were both appeals from decisions of the Commercial Court; *Boddington v British Transport Police* [1999] 2 AC 143, HL, was a criminal prosecution.

proceedings for judicial review, and which now comprise a significant area of law in its own right.[6] The overwhelming bulk of homelessness and allocations case-law is of this order, ie, an illustration of the operation of the principles of administrative law, in relation to the statutes governing homelessness and allocations.

12.6 This is so regardless of whether the challenge is brought by way of judicial review or as a statutory appeal. In judicial review, the courts are principally considering whether the decision reached can properly be said to be ultra vires, ie, outwith the powers of the body making the decision. Statutory appeals under HA 1996 s204 refer to a 'point of law', which, as mentioned above, applies the same principles as an application for judicial review.[7]

12.7 The underlying principles of administrative law are accordingly as relevant when determining appeals as on judicial review, and the jurisprudence that the courts develop in the contexts of appeals has itself added to the general body of administrative law, as well as contributed to the growth of housing law.

12.8 To the growth of administrative law there must now be added the obligations imposed on public bodies by the Human Rights Act (HRA) 1998 and the rights from the European Convention on Human Rights ('the Convention'/ECHR) that the Act imports into domestic law. This has three consequences: first, it adds to the categories of illegality – if an administrative law decision is unlawful under the provisions of HRA 1998, it is ultra vires in its own right; second, it reinforces and develops existing administrative law; third, public authorities within its purview, which include registered providers of social housing in respect of some aspects of their management of social housing stock (including service of notice to quit or of seeking possession), will, in addition to the requirement to conform to the Convention rights, also be susceptible to the principles of domestic public law, even if they would not otherwise be capable of challenge

6 See the two leading text-books in the area: Wade and Forsyth, *Administrative Law* (10th edn, OUP, 2009), and de Smith, Woolf and Jowell, *Judicial Review of Administrative Action* (6th edn, Sweet & Maxwell, 2009). See also Manning, *Judicial Review Proceedings* (LAG, 2nd edn, 2004).

7 *Nipa Begum v Tower Hamlets LBC* [2000] 1 WLR 306; (2000) 32 HLR 445, approved by the House of Lords in *Runa Begum v Tower Hamlets LBC* [2003] UKHL 5; [2003] 2 AC 430; [2003] HLR 32, see particularly Lord Bingham at [7]. *Runa Begum* was followed in *Tomlinson v Birmingham CC* [2010] UKSC 8: see 'Note on late developments' at the front of this book. See also, eg, *R v IRC ex p Preston* [1985] AC 835, HL.

on that basis.[8] At least so far as it has yet developed in housing law,[9] and even though it may be its less well-known point of reference, it is the second impact of HRA 1998 with which we are most concerned here – its own influence on the development of domestic administrative law.[10]

12.9   This developing (and expanding) body of 'administrative law' is that with which this part of this chapter is concerned. It addresses:

– the nature of a challenge;
– the general principles of administrative law;
– substantive grounds for challenge;
– procedural grounds for challenge.

12.10   This caveat should be entered at the start. Public law is not about absolutes: many aspects of it engage degrees of right and wrong, which will depend on the facts of the individual challenge: 'in law, context is everything'.[11]

12.11   Thus, a general duty to make enquiries will differ depending on the context: a duty to make enquiries under the homelessness provisions will import different practical obligations than will a duty to make enquiries into another, entirely different area, for example, a police enquiry into the commission of a crime (hence, the proposition that local authority enquiries do not have to amount to 'CID-type enquiries').[12] Likewise, and plainly, what is relevant to one area of activity will not be relevant to another.

12.12   Because administrative law derives from a variety of sources and is applied to (and therefore continues to be developed in relation to) a wide range of activities, many of which are very far from the specific issues raised by Parts 6 and 7, cases which have been developed in other areas do need to be treated with some caution: there may be much more room for manoeuvre over how they will function under Parts 6 and 7 than may at first appear. Decisions on the

---

8   *R (Weaver) v London & Quadrant Housing Trust* [2008] EWHC 1377 and on appeal [2009] EWCA Civ 587. The proposition as to susceptibility was conceded. The decision of the High Court that the public functions of registered providers extend to the management and allocation of social housing, while not overruled per se, was not the basis on which the decision that they are public authorities for the purposes of the 1998 Act was upheld: nonetheless, allocation would seem also to qualify as a public function (see in particular *Weaver* at [76]) and it is not difficult to argue that other acts of management will also do so.

9   Below, paras 12.95–12.106.

10 Below, paras 12.24–12.30.

11 *R (Daly) v Secretary of State for the Home Department* [2001] UKHL 26; [2001] 2 AC 532.

12 *Lally v Kensington & Chelsea RLBC* (1980) *Times* 26 March, QBD.

specific statutory provisions are one thing; decisions on principles of decision-making, another.

The nature of a challenge

12.13   At the heart of administrative law is the proposition that Parliament intends public bodies always to act properly, in the sense of reasonably and lawfully. The role of the courts is, however, supervisory rather than appellate: the court[13] must review the decision-making processes of the body in question, rather than determine for itself what decision the authority should make.[14] Provided that the authority does not err in how it reaches the decision,[15] the substance of the decision is for the authority, not for the court, and it is the authority's view or decision which must prevail.[16] There is rarely only one

13   Whether Administrative Court on judicial review or county court on appeal. The Court of Appeal has expressed its disapproval of county court judges who have overstepped their role (*Kruja v Enfield LBC* [2004] EWCA Civ 1769; [2005] HLR 13 – see para 12.151, below) and emphasised that decision-making on matters such as the vulnerability of applicants is for the local authority: *Osmani v Camden LBC* [2004] EWCA Civ 1706; [2005] HLR 22.

14   See, eg, *R v Northumberland Compensation Appeal Tribunal, ex p Shaw* [1952] 1 KB 338, CA, per Denning LJ at 346–7: 'The Court of King's Bench has an inherent jurisdiction to control all inferior tribunals, not in an appellate capacity but in a supervisory capacity. This control extends not only to seeing that the inferior tribunals keep within their jurisdiction, but also to seeing that they observe the law . . . The King's Bench does not substitute its own views for those of the tribunal, as a Court of Appeal would do. It leaves it to the tribunal to hear the case again, and in a proper case may command it to do so.' See also *R v Secretary of State for Trade and Industry ex p Lonrho plc* [1989] 1 WLR 525, per Lord Keith of Kinkel at 535: 'The question is not whether the Secretary of State came to . . . a conclusion which meets with the approval of the . . . Court but whether the discretion was properly exercised.' This is the same approach as the appellate court adopts when considering an appeal against a discretionary decision of a judge: eg, *Woodspring DC v Taylor* (1982) 4 HLR 95.

15   In any of the acknowledged senses – see para 12.17, below.

16   See, eg, *R v Secretary of State for the Home Department ex p Khawaja* [1984] AC 74, per Lord Scarman at 100, referring to the *Wednesbury* principle: 'The principle excluded the court from substituting its own view of the facts for that of the authority'; *R v Secretary of State for the Home Department ex p Brind* [1991] AC 696, per Lord Lowry at 767: 'The judges are not, generally speaking, equipped by training or experience or furnished with the necessary knowledge and advice, to decide the answer to an administrative problem where the scales are evenly balanced, but they have a much better chance of reaching the right answer where the question is put in a *Wednesbury* form'; see also *Wednesbury* itself, below, footnote 18 and para 12.21, where Lord Greene MR, at 234, refers to the court as 'a judicial authority which is concerned, and concerned only, to see whether the local authority have contravened the law by acting in excess of the powers which Parliament have confided in them'.

decision which an authority may reach: one individual's view of what is reasonable will often quite properly differ from that of another and Parliament has entrusted decision-making under Parts 6 and 7 to authorities, not to the courts.

12.14   In *Puhlhofer*,[17] Lord Brightman said, at 518:

I am troubled at the prolific use of judicial review for the purpose of challenging the performance by local authorities of their functions under the Act of 1977. Parliament intended the local authority to be the judge of fact. The Act abounds with the formula when, or if, the housing authority are satisfied as to this, or that, or have reason to believe this, or that. Although the action or inaction of a local authority is clearly susceptible to judicial review where they have misconstrued the Act, or abused their powers or otherwise acted perversely, I think that great restraint should be exercised in giving leave to proceed by judicial review. The plight of the homeless is a desperate one, and the plight of the applicants in the present case commands the deepest sympathy. But it is not, in my opinion, appropriate that the remedy of judicial review, which is a discretionary remedy, should be made use of to monitor the actions of local authorities under the Act save in the exceptional case. The ground upon which the courts will review the exercise of an administrative discretion is abuse of power, for example, bad faith, a mistake in construing the limits of the power, a procedural irregularity, or unreasonableness in the *Wednesbury*[18] sense – unreasonableness verging on an absurdity: see the speech of Lord Scarman in *R v Secretary of State for the Environment ex p Nottinghamshire CC.*[19] Where the existence or non-existence of a fact is left to the judgment and discretion of a public body and that fact involves a broad spectrum ranging from the obvious to the debatable to the just conceivable, it is the duty of the court to leave the decision of that fact to the public body to whom Parliament has entrusted the decision-making power save in a case where it is obvious that the public body, consciously or unconsciously, are acting perversely.

. . . I express the hope that there will be a lessening in the number of challenges which are mounted against local authorities who are endeavouring, in extremely difficult circumstances, to perform their duties under the Homeless Persons Act with due regard for all their other housing problems.[20]

---

17   *R v Hillingdon LBC ex p Puhlhofer* [1986] AC 484; (1986) 18 HLR 158.

18   *Associated Provincial Picture Houses Ltd v Wednesbury Corporation* [1948] 1 KB 223, CA.

19   *Nottinghamshire CC v Secretary of State for the Environment* [1986] 1 AC 240, HL.

20   The same principles apply on a statutory appeal – the county court must at all times bear in mind the public law exercise in which it is engaged: *Crawley LBC v B* (2000) 32 HLR 636, CA.

12.15 There are echoes of this in the Part 6 decision of the House of Lords in *R (Ahmad) v Newham LBC*.[21]

> 46. . . . [A] s a general proposition, it is undesirable for the courts to get involved in questions of how priorities are accorded in housing allocation policies. Of course, there will be cases where the court has a duty to interfere, for instance if a policy does not comply with statutory requirements, or if it is plainly irrational. However, it seems unlikely that the legislature can have intended that Judges should embark on the exercise of telling authorities how to decide on priorities as between applicants in need of rehousing, save in relatively rare and extreme circumstances. Housing allocation policy is a difficult exercise which requires not only social and political sensitivity and judgment, but also local expertise and knowledge.

> 47. In relation to the provision of accommodation under the National Assistance Act 1948, my noble and learned friend, Baroness Hale of Richmond, then Hale LJ, said in *R (Wahid) v Tower Hamlets LBC*[22] '[n]eed is a relative concept, which trained and experienced social workers are much better equipped to assess than are lawyers and courts, provided that they act rationally'. Precisely the same is true of relative housing needs under Part 6 of the 1996 Act, and trained and experienced local authority housing officers.

> 48. If section 167 carries with it the sort of requirements which can be said to be implied by the decisions of the Court of Appeal and the Deputy Judge in this case, then Judges would become involved in considering details of housing allocation schemes in a way which would be both unrealistic and undesirable. . . .

> . . .

> 55. This is not to say that there could never be circumstances in which a scheme, which complies with the statutory requirements, could be susceptible to judicial review on grounds of irrationality. Such a suggestion would be unmaintainable not least because it would represent an abdication of judicial responsibility. However, what is important is to emphasise that once a housing allocation scheme complies with the requirements of section 167 and any other statutory requirements, the courts should be very slow to interfere on the ground of alleged irrationality.

12.16 The discretion conferred by Parliament, which is embodied in this more limited,[23] supervisory approach, does not lead to the conclusion

---

21 [2009] UKHL 14; [2009] NPC 36.
22 [2002] EWCA Civ 287; [2003] HLR 13 at [33].
23 Than when an appeal approach allows a court to substitute its own view of the facts.

that an authority's decision under Part 6 or Part 7 is above reproach.[24] It is the purpose of public law to ensure that public authorities, entrusted with an apparently blanket power to reach 'subjective' decisions, nonetheless do so in accordance with the law. A discretionary decision may still be ultra vires and without effect in law: it may be unreasonable in the *Wednesbury* sense – ie, a decision which no reasonable authority, properly directing itself, could have reached; it may be a decision that is contrary to the law; it may be a decision which has been reached without affording the applicant his/her due procedural safeguards; or it may be a decision which is not based on all the relevant information.

Ultra vires

12.17   Local authorities may only act within their powers. If they do not do so, they are acting unlawfully, and their actions and decisions will be so treated[25] – this is the ultra vires doctrine and a decision so made will be unlawful because:

- on the face of the statute there was no authority to engage in the action at all; or
- the statute has been misconstrued; or
- the authority has misapplied the statute, for example, by failing to use the powers to implement the purpose of the statute; or
- a decision has been reached under the statute by reference to something which is irrelevant, or in ignorance of something which is relevant, to the way the power under the statute is intended to be operated.

12.18   If it can be shown that a public body such as a local authority has approached its decision unlawfully then, regardless of the reason, the decision will be void and the courts will not give effect to it.

12.19   The propositions in the last two paragraphs assume:

a) that there are no differences between the legal consequences of decisions which there was no power at all to take (ie, those which are said to be outside the four corners of a statute) and those which

---

24 See per Lord Wilberforce in *Secretary of State for Education and Science v Tameside MBC* [1977] AC 1014, HL, at 1047: 'The section is framed in a "subjective" form . . . This form of section is quite well-known and *at first sight* might seem to exclude judicial review . . .' (emphasis added).

25 Subject to issues of forum: cf *Wandsworth LBC v Winder* [1985] AC 461, HL; *Avon County Council v Buscott* [1988] QB 656, CA; and *LB Hackney v Lambourne* (1992) 25 HLR 172, CA; *Manchester CC v Cochrane* [1999] 1 WLR 809, CA.

there was power to take but which have been taken in some way improperly;[26] and

b) that once it is decided that a decision was ultra vires, it must be treated as if it had at all times been void for all purposes.

12.20 There have been several cases which have considered these two (overlapping) issues, and they are issues which will doubtless continue to be discussed.[27] For the purposes of this book, however, the propositions probably suffice in practice.[28]

The general principles of administrative law[29]

Wednesbury

12.21 The classic statement of the court's role and function when addressing public law issues is that of Lord Greene MR in *Wednesbury*:[30]

> What, then, is the power of the courts? They can only interfere with an act of executive authority if it be shown that the authority has contravened the law. It is for those who assert that the local authority has

---

26 See, in particular, *Crédit Suisse Plc v Allerdale MBC* [1997] QB 302, CA, per Neill LJ at 343: 'I know of no authority for the proposition that the *ultra vires* decisions of local authority can be classified into categories of invalidity . . .'

27 *Anisminic Ltd v Foreign Compensation Commission* [1969] 2 AC 147, HL, would nonetheless seem to be definitive: a decision wrongly reached, for whatever reason, was considered to be void and a nullity, because decision-makers have no jurisdiction to make unlawful decisions (see, in particular, per Lord Reid, at 171, using similar terms to describe unlawfulness as the classic definition by Lord Greene MR in *Wednesbury*, see para 12.21). In *Boddington v British Transport Police* [1999] 2 AC 143, HL, the majority of the Committee was not willing simply to assume invalidity for all purposes and at all times, because people would in the meantime have regulated their lives on the basis of a decision's validity.

28 It today appears to be accepted in homelessness law that a decision improperly taken may be retaken: see *Crawley LBC v B* (2000) 32 HLR 636, CA (see further below, para 12.207); *Porteous v West Dorset DC* [2004] EWCA Civ 244; HLR 30 at [7]–[9] (fundamental mistake of fact); and *Islington LBC v Uckac* [2006] EWCA Civ 340; [2006] HLR 35 (on mistake of fact, but by counsel's concession). Although the discussion in *Porteous* is in terms of revisiting and changing or rescinding an earlier decision, the basis of the argument in both cases was that the earlier decision was void and it is hard to see any other basis: unless void, the authority is what is known as functus officio, ie, it has no further function – it has had an application and it has reached its decision.

29 Some reliance in writing this section has been placed on Arden, Baker & Manning, *Local Government Constitutional and Administrative Law* (2nd edn, 2008, Sweet & Maxwell).

30 *Associated Provincial Picture Houses Ltd v Wednesbury Corporation* [1948] 1 KB 223, CA.

contravened the law to establish that proposition ... It is not to be assumed prima facie that responsible bodies like the local authority in this case will exceed their powers; but the court, whenever it is alleged that the local authority have contravened the law, must not substitute itself for that authority ... When an executive discretion is entrusted by Parliament to a body such as the local authority in this case, what appears to be an exercise of that discretion can only be challenged in the courts in a strictly limited class of case ... When discretion of this kind is granted the law recognises certain principles upon which that discretion must be exercised, but within the four corners of those principles the discretion ... is an absolute one and cannot be questioned in any court of law. What then are those principles? They are well understood. They are principles which the court looks to in considering any question of discretion of this kind. The exercise of such a discretion must be a real exercise of the discretion. If, in the statute conferring the discretion, there is to be found expressly or by implication matters which the authority exercising the discretion ought to have regard to, then in exercising the discretion it must have regard to those matters. Conversely, if the nature of the subject-matter and the general interpretation of the Act make it clear that certain matters would not be germane to the matter in question, the authority must disregard those irrelevant collateral matters. (at 228)

There have been in the cases expressions used relating to the sort of things that authorities must not do ... I am not sure myself whether the permissible grounds of attack cannot be defined under a single head ... Bad faith, dishonesty – those of course, stand by themselves – unreasonableness, attention given to extraneous circumstances, disregard of public policy and things like that have all been referred to, according to the facts of individual cases, as being matters which are relevant to the question. If they cannot all be confined under one head, they at any rate ... overlap to a very great extent. For instance, we have heard in this case a great deal about the meaning of the word 'unreasonable'.

It is true the discretion must be exercised reasonably. Now what does that mean? ... It has frequently been used and is frequently used as a general description of the things that must not be done ... A person entrusted with a discretion must ... direct himself properly in law. He must call his own attention to the matters which he is bound to consider. He must exclude from his consideration matters which are irrelevant to what he has to consider. If he does not obey those rules, he may truly be said, and often is said, to be acting 'unreasonably'. Similarly, there may be something so absurd that no sensible person could ever dream that it lay within the powers of the authority. Warrington LJ in *Short v Poole Corporation*[31] gave the example of the red-haired teacher, dismissed because she had red hair. That is

31 [1926] Ch 66.

unreasonable in one sense. In another sense it is taking into consideration extraneous matters. It is so unreasonable that it might almost be described as being done in bad faith; and, in fact, all these things run into one another . . . (at 229)

It is true to say that, if a decision on a competent matter is so unreasonable that no reasonable authority could ever have come to it, then the courts can interfere . . . But to prove a case of that kind would require something overwhelming . . . [The] proposition that the decision of the local authority can be upset if it is proved to be unreasonable, really meant that it must be proved to be unreasonable in the sense that the court considers it to be a decision that no reasonable body could have come to. It is not what the court considers unreasonable, a different thing altogether . . . The effect of the legislation is not to set up the court as an arbiter of the correctness of one view over another. It is the local authority that are set in that position and, provided they act, as they have acted, within the four corners of their jurisdiction, this court . . . cannot interfere . . . (at 230–231)

The court is entitled to investigate the action of the local authority with a view to seeing whether they have taken into account matters which they ought not to take into account, or, conversely, have refused to take into account or neglected to take into account matters which they ought to take into account. Once that question is answered in favour of the local authority, it may still be possible to say that, although the local authority have kept within the four corners of the matters which they ought to consider, they have nevertheless come to a conclusion so unreasonable that no reasonable authority could ever have come to it. In such a case, again, I think the court can interfere. The power of the court to interfere in each case is not as an appellate authority to override a decision of the local authority, but as a judicial authority which is concerned, and concerned only, to see whether the local authority have contravened the law by acting in excess of the powers which Parliament has confided in them. (at 233–234)

12.22 This statement, in particular the last passage, remains the cornerstone of domestic administrative law.

CCSU

12.23 The central principles of public law derived from Lord Greene's comments in *Wednesbury* were subsequently re-classified by Lord Diplock under the headings of 'illegality', 'irrationality' and 'procedural impropriety' in *CCSU*:[32]

---

32 *Council of Civil Service Unions v Minister for the Civil Service* [1985] 1 AC 374, HL (*CCSU*). The statement was described by Lord Scarman as 'a valuable and already "classical"' statement of the law, albeit 'certainly not exhaustive': *R v Secretary of State for the Environment ex p Nottinghamshire CC* [1986] AC 240, HL, at 249.

By 'illegality' as a ground of judicial review I mean that the decision-maker must understand correctly the law that regulates his decision-making power and must give effect to it. Whether he has or not is par excellence a justiciable question to be decided, in the event of dispute, by those persons, the judges, by whom the judicial power of the state is exercisable.

By 'irrationality' I mean what can by now be succinctly referred to as '*Wednesbury* unreasonableness' . . . It applies to a decision which is so outrageous in its defiance of logic or of accepted moral standards that no sensible person who had applied his mind to the question to be decided could have arrived at it. Whether a decision falls within this category is a question that judges by their training and experience should be well-equipped to answer, or else there would be something badly wrong with our judicial system . . . 'Irrationality' by now can stand upon its own feet as an accepted ground on which a decision may be attacked by judicial review.

I have described the third head as 'procedural impropriety' rather than failure to observe basic rules of natural justice or failure to act with procedural fairness towards the person who will be affected by the decision. This is because susceptibility to judicial review under this head covers also failure by an administrative tribunal to observe procedural rules that are expressly laid down in the legislative instrument by which its jurisdiction is conferred, even where such failure does not involve any denial of natural justice . . .

Human Rights Act 1998 and proportionality

12.24　As noted above,[33] HRA 1998 is relevant in two ways: first, in the sense that it imports specific articles of the ECHR ('the Convention'); second, because of its influence on the development of the principles of domestic administrative law. It is the second of these aspects which is relevant under this heading. The first is considered below[34].

12.25　In *CCSU*,[35] Lord Diplock had raised – but did not answer – the question whether or not the principle of 'proportionality'[36] might be imported into domestic law from Europe.[37]

33　Para 12.8.

34　Paras 12.70–80.

35　Above, para 12.23.

36　'Proportionality' is the doctrine that there has to be a reasonable relationship between the governmental (including local) action under review and its purpose in a given context.

37　At 410. What Lord Diplock had in mind was not the ECHR but EU law, in which proportionality also plays a substantial part. Some have considered that proportionality was in any event already inherent in *Wednesbury* unreasonableness: *R v Secretary of State Home Department ex p Leech* [1994] QB 198, CA; *R v Chief Constable of Sussex ex p International Trader's Ferry* [1999] 2 AC 418, HL.

12.26   From the early 1990s, doubt began to be cast on whether the *Wednesbury* test – affording a decision-maker a wide ambit of discretion – was suitable to deal with cases that involved what were recognisable as fundamental rights, and it began to be suggested that the *Wednesbury* test required adaptation so as to subject such cases to what has been called 'anxious scrutiny',[38] requiring a closer degree of factual scrutiny than the conventional *Wednesbury* approach.[39]

12.27   Comparing the differences, it has been observed that there are three potential approaches to the standard of review that may be applied when there is challenge on public law grounds:[40]

a) the conventional *Wednesbury* approach;

b) an approach based on fundamental rights which requires the court to 'insist that that fact be respected by the decision-maker, who is accordingly required to demonstrate either that his proposed action does not in truth interfere with the right, or, if it does, that there exist considerations which may reasonably be accepted as amounting to a substantial objective justification for the interference'; and

c) an approach based on claims which directly engage rights guaranteed by the ECHR, which requires the court to decide whether there has been a violation of a convention right.[41]

12.28 This trend towards different standards of review depending on the rights in issue appears to imply a weakening of the dominance of the *Wednesbury* test for determining public law challenges. In *Daly*,[42] Lord Steyn (although suggesting that in most cases the courts would

38 *R v Ministry of Defence ex p Smith* [1996] QB 517, CA; *Bugdaycay v Secretary of State for the Home Department* [1987] AC 514; sometimes referred to as 'Super-*Wednesbury*' – *Vilvarajah v UK* (1991) 14 EHRR 248, ECHR.

39 See *R v Ministry of Agriculture, Fisheries and Food ex p First City Trading Limited* [1997] 1 CMLR 250, QBD; see also *R v Secretary of State for Health ex p Eastside Cheese* [1999] 3 CMLR 123, CA.

40 *R (Mahmood) v Secretary of State for the Home Department* [2001] 1 WLR 840, CA.

41 Those categories were not 'hermitically sealed': 'There is, rather, what may be called a sliding scale of review; the graver the impact of the decision in question upon the individual affected by it, the more substantial the justification that will be required . . . [C]ases where, objectively, the individual is most gravely affected will be those where what we have come to call his fundamental rights are or are said to be put in jeopardy' (at [19]).

42 *R (Daly) v Secretary of State for the Home Department* [2001] UKHL 26; [2001] 2 AC 532. In *R (ProLife Alliance) v British Broadcasting Corporation* [2003] UKHL 23; [2004] 1 AC 185, Lord Walker extensively cited with approval the passages under consideration here: see [134]–[135]. See also per Lord Bingham in *A and others v Secretary of State for the Home Department; X and another v Secretary of State for the Home Department* [2004] UKHL 56; [2005] 2 AC 68, at [40].

reach the same conclusion regardless of the basis on which the decision was scrutinised) said that:

> ... the day will come when it will be more widely recognised that [*Wednesbury*] was an unfortunately retrogressive decision in English administrative law, insofar as it suggested that there are degrees of unreasonableness and that only a very extreme degree can bring an administrative decision within the legitimate scope of judicial invalidation. The depth of judicial review and the deference due to administrative discretion vary with the subject matter. It may well be, however, that the law can never be satisfied in any administrative field merely by a finding that the decision under review is not capricious or absurd.[43]

12.29   The reference to subject-matter is the key element for present purposes: see also Lord Steyn's comment in *Daly* that 'in law, context is everything'.[44] In *Runa Begum*,[45] it was held that it was appropriate for the decision-maker to make findings of fact without any scrutiny other than the usual grounds for judicial review, because homelessness decisions are administrative in nature and do not engage substantive Convention rights:[46] there was accordingly no need for any intensification of the traditional approach to review, or for anxious scrutiny[47] of, the decision.

12.30   What then is the current position? *Runa Begum* concludes that what may be called the highest standard of judicial scrutiny of the three identified[48] is not applicable to challenges under Part 7. It may even imply that nothing more than conventional *Wednesbury* is applicable. Nonetheless, it remains open to argument that housing is a fundamental right, within the 'middle' standard of review. Even if forced back to *Wednesbury*, that may not be the end of it: the *Wednesbury* approach is clearly under pressure or, as it has been put, the law is

---

43   Per Lord Cooke at [32]. The Court of Appeal has observed that 'the *Wednesbury* test is moving closer to proportionality' but also said that 'it is not for this court to perform the burial rights' – *R (Association of British Civilian Internees (Far East Region)) v Secretary of State for Defence* [2003] EWCA Civ 473; [2003] 3 WLR 80.

44   *Daly*, at [28].

45   *Runa Begum v Tower Hamlets LBC* [2003] UKHL 5; [2003] 2 AC 430; [2003] HLR 32. *Runa Begum* was followed in *Tomlinson v Birmingham CC* [2010] UKSC 8: see 'Note on late developments' at the front of this book.

46   See further below, paras 12.95–12.106.

47   See *R v Ministry of Agriculture, Fisheries and Food ex p First City Trading Limited* [1997] 1 CMLR 250, QBD; see also *R v Secretary of State for Health ex p Eastside Cheese* [1999] 3 CMLR 123, CA.

48   Above, para 12.27.

engaged in a 'long trek away from *Wednesbury* irrationality'.[49] Perhaps the simplest approach is to view the *Wednesbury* approach as an absolute minimum, whilst acknowledging that, sometimes, it will not be enough.

Grounds for challenge – practical classification

12.31 Having considered the general principles on which public law decisions may be challenged, we turn to consider the practical classification of grounds for challenge, utilising the *CCSU* classification,[50] supplemented by the specific (relevant) provisions of HRA 1998, to which attention has not yet been paid.[51]

12.32 As effectively recognised in *Wednesbury*,[52] when applied in a practical context, grounds tend to overlap one another: thus a failure to have regard to a relevant fact may also be an error of law; a failure to give reasons for a decision may not only be unlawful for failure to comply with the duty to do so but may also found a challenge based on the fairness of the procedure.[53]

12.33 Moreover, the distinction between a point of law (challengeable on administrative law principles) and a question of fact (which is not) is not a straightforward distinction and there will be cases where matters of pure fact arise:

> The cases do not support the proposition that *any* conclusion that a legal or statutory concept applies to a particular set of facts is a question of law, although in practice they permit considerable elasticity in their application.[54]

Illegality

Misdirection of law

12.34 A decision-maker must 'understand correctly the law that regulates his decision-making power and must give effect to it'[55], ie, s/he must

---

49 Per Lord Walker in *R (ProLife Alliance) v British Broadcasting Corporation* [2003] UKHL 23; [2004] 1 AC 185, at [131].

50 Above, para 12.23.

51 Cf, above, paras 12.24–12.30.

52 Above, para 12.21.

53 The overlapping nature of grounds is illustrated by the specimen documents annexed to this chapter.

54 *Adan v Newham LBC* [2001] EWCA Civ 1916; [2002] HLR 28, per Hale LJ at [66] (emphasis in original).

55 *CCSU* at 410F, per Lord Diplock.

understand and apply the law correctly. Thus in *Islam*,[56] the authority's misunderstanding of the test to be applied when determining whether a person was homeless intentionally under the Housing (Homeless Persons) Act 1977 was a misdirection of law sufficient to vitiate the decision.

Decisions must be based on the facts

12.35   While it is of the essence of *Puhlhofer*[57] that matters of fact are for the decision-maker, this does not mean that factual errors are irrelevant. In *Adan*,[58] Brooke LJ commented:[59]

> In very many cases, although it could be said that an administrative body had made a material mistake of fact the decision is vulnerable on other more conventional grounds: for procedural impropriety ... or because a factor had been taken into account which should not have been taken into account ... or because there was no evidence on which the decision could have been safely based ... What is quite clear is that a court of supervisory jurisdiction does not, without more, have the power to substitute its own view of the primary facts for the view reasonably adopted by the body to whom the fact-finding power has been entrusted.

12.36   If it can be shown that a decision proceeded on the basis of an incorrect understanding of the facts, that there was no evidence to support the finding of fact made, or that there was no account taken of the facts, there may be scope for a challenge on the basis that the decision was at odds with the factual matrix,[60] in particular where there are fundamental rights at stake.[61] It has also for some time been recognised that the court is entitled to decide what the facts are if they comprise 'precedent facts' or as they are sometimes called, 'jurisdictional facts',[62] ie, if the facts establish the right to exercise a power

56   *R v Hillingdon LBC ex p Islam* [1983] 1 AC 688, HL. See also *Anisminic Ltd v Foreign Compensation Commission* [1969] 2 AC 147, HL and *R (Q) v Secretary of State for the Home Department* [2003] EWCA Civ 364; [2004] QB 36.

57   Above, para 12.14.

58   *Adan v Newham LBC* [2001] EWCA Civ 1916; [2002] 1 WLR 2120.

59   At [41].

60   *Secretary of State for Education and Science v Tameside MBC* [1977] AC 1014, HL, at 1047.

61   In *R (Wilkinson) v Broadmoor Special Hospital Authority* [2001] EWCA Civ 1545; [2002] 1 WLR 419, it was suggested that, where fundamental rights were at issue, the court 'must now inevitably reach its own view' on the facts. See also *R (Murphy) v Secretary of State for the Home Department* [2005] EWHC 140 (Admin); [2005] 2 All ER 763.

62   Eg, *R v Secretary of State for the Environment ex p Powis* [1981] 1 WLR 584, per Dunn LJ at 595H.

or the obligation to perform a duty,[63] the court is entitled to reach a decision for itself as to what the facts are.[64] See also the discussion of the judgment of the Supreme Court in *Tomlinson v Birmingham CC*[65] in the 'Note on late developments' at the front of this book.

12.37   In *Tameside* at the Court of Appeal,[66] Scarman LJ suggested that an error of fact – not merely precedent fact – might be sufficient of itself to vitiate an authority's decision where that error could be said to be a 'misunderstanding or ignorance of an established and relevant fact': this approach has found significant subsequent support.[67] There are now several examples of administrative decisions quashed because they were reached on a material error[68] of fact,[69] although opinions differ as to whether they are examples of failing to take into account a relevant consideration,[70] a stand-alone

---

63   *R v Secretary of State for Home Department ex p Khawaja* [1984] AC 74. See also per Baroness Hale in *R (A) (FC) v Croydon LBC; R (M) (FC) v Lambeth LBC* [2009] UKSC 8, at [29–30].

64   See *Khawaja*, above, per Lord Wilberforce at 105; *R v Oldham BC ex p Garlick* [1993] AC 509, HL, per Lord Griffiths at 520E.

65   [2010] UKSC 8.

66   *Secretary of State for Education and Science v Tameside MBC* [1977] AC 1014 at 1030.

67   Lord Slynn, in *R v Criminal Injuries Compensation Board ex p A* [1999] 2 AC 330, accepted the existence of such a doctrine, a view he re-affirmed in *R (Alconbury Developments Ltd) v Secretary of State for the Environment, Transport and the Regions* [2001] UKHL 23; [2003] 2 AC 295 at [53], but in neither case was this reasoning adopted by the Committee and, in the first, Lord Slynn himself 'preferred' to decide the case on the alternative ground of breach of natural justice amounting to unfairness (at 345). In *E v Secretary of State for the Home Department* [2004] EWCA Civ 49; [2004] QB 1044, Carnwath LJ considers the history in some detail. How far the House of Lords can be said to have endorsed Scarman LJ's approach may be in some doubt: see *E* at [55].

68   Or 'fundamental mistake of fact': see *Porteous v West Dorset DC* [2004] EWCA Civ 244, per Mantell LJ at [9].

69   See also *Mason v Secretary of State for the Environment and Bromsgrove DC* (1983) JPL 332; *Jagendorf & Trott v Secretary of State for the Environment and Krasucki* (1986) JPL 771; *R v LB Hillingdon ex p Thomas* (1987) 19 HLR 196; *R v Legal Aid Committee No 10 (East Midlands) ex p McKenna* [1990] COD 358; (1989) *Times* 20 December; *Simplex GE (Holdings) Ltd v Secretary of State for the Environment* [1988] 3 PLR 25, CA; *R v London Residuary Body ex p ILEA* (1987) *Times* 3 July, CA. See also *R (Meredith) v Merthyr Tydfil CBC* [2002] EWHC 634 (Admin), unreported; *R (Kathro) v Rhondda Cynon Taff CBC* [2001] EWHC Admin 527; [2002] Env LR; *R (McLellan) v Bracknell Forest BC* [2001] EWCA Civ 1510; [2002] QB 1129.

70   *Secretary of State for Education and Science v MB Tameside* [1977] AC 1014, HL, per Lord Diplock at 1066F–1067A. See also *Crake v Supplementary Benefits Commission* [1982] 1 All ER 498 at 508, cited in *Aslam v South Bedfordshire DC* [2001] EWCA Civ 514; [2001] RVR 65, itself cited in *E & R v Secretary of State for the Home Department* [2004] EWCA Civ 49; [2004] QB 1044, at [38].

ground[71] or indeed as an aspect of fairness.[72] Nonetheless, it must be said that mistake of fact is still far from a generally accepted ground of judicial review.[73]

Taking into account irrelevant considerations

12.38　It is sufficient to void a decision on the basis that an irrelevant factor has been taken into account if the factor is significant, or potentially of influence, meaning that, if it had not been taken into account, the decision might have been different. The authority must take such steps as are reasonable to find out the relevant facts.[74] When housing is in issue, 'consideration of common humanity' is a relevant consideration in its own right.[75] While the resources available to an authority will be relevant to how it discharges its duty,[76]

71　*R (Alconbury Developments & Others) v Secretary of State for the Environment, Transport and the Regions* [2001] UKHL 23; [2003] 2 AC 295 at [53], [169]; *R v Criminal Injuries Compensation Board ex p A* [1999] 2 AC 330, at [344]; *Begum v Tower Hamlets LBC* [2003] UKHL 5; [2003] 2 AC 43, at [7]–[11].

72　*E v Secretary of State for the Home Department* [2004] EWCA Civ 49; [2004] QB 1044 and see further below, paras 12.56–12.60. 'What mattered was that, because of their failure, and through no fault of her own, the claimant had not had "a fair crack of the whip" (see *Fairmount Investments v Secretary of State* [1976] 1 WLR 1255, per Lord Russell at 1266/A). If it is said that this is taking "fairness" beyond its traditional role as an aspect of procedural irregularity it is no further than its use in cases such as *HTV Ltd v Price Commission* [1976] ICR 170, approved by the House of Lords in *R v IRC ex p Preston* [1985] AC 825, at 865–6). In our view, the time has now come to accept that a mistake of fact giving rise to unfairness is a separate head of challenge in an appeal on a point of law, at least in those statutory contexts where the parties share an interest in co-operating to achieve the correct result. Asylum law is undoubtedly such an area.' Per Carnwath LJ in *E* at [65]–[66].

73　See *Wandsworth v A* [2000] 1 WLR 1246, CA, at 1255/H–1256/C: 'While there may, possibly, be special considerations that apply in the more formalised area of planning inquiries . . . and while the duty of "anxious scrutiny" imposed in asylum cases by *R v Secretary of State for the Home Department ex p Bugdaycay* [[1987] AC 514, HL] renders those cases an uncertain guide for other areas of public law; none the less . . . there is still no general right to challenge the decision of a public body on an issue of fact alone. The law in this connection continues, in our respectful view, to be as stated for a unanimous House of Lords by Lord Brightman in *R v Hillingdon LBC ex p Puhlhofer . . .*'

74　Per Lord Diplock in *Secretary of State for Education and Science v Tameside MBC* [1977] AC 1014, HL, at p1065; see also *R v Lincolnshire CC and Wealden DC ex p Atkinson* [1995] 8 Admin LR 529, and *R v Hillingon LBC ex p McDonagh* (1998) 31 HLR 531.

75　*Ex p Atkinson, ex p McDonagh* (ibid); *R v Kerrier ex p Uzell* (1995) 71 P&CR 566; *R v Brighton & Hove Council ex p Marmont* (1998) 30 HLR 1046.

76　*R v Lambeth LBC ex p A & G* (1998) 30 HLR 933, CA. Consider, however, *Conville v Richmond upon Thames LBC* [2006] EWCA Civ 718; [2006] HLR 1, where it was held that financial considerations were not relevant when they are not relevant[77] to the question whether there is a duty at all.[78]

12.39   There is no general proposition which governs the question of what is a relevant consideration: the question is what the Act requires to be taken into account, not what the court thinks may be relevant.[79]

Disproportionate weight for relevant considerations

12.40   It is not just taking something irrelevant into account that may vitiate the decision but also giving disproportionate weight to a relevant consideration. In *Ashton*,[80] excessive reliance had been placed on the prevailing housing circumstances of the area when considering intentional homelessness;[81] the decision-maker had not appreciated

determining the period for which an authority must provide an applicant with accommodation under section 190(2)(a) to afford her/him 'reasonable opportunity to secure accommodation'. Nonetheless, homelessness and allocations must be considered in their context: 'But the social norm must be applied in the context of a scheme for allocating scarce resources. It is impossible to consider only what would be desirable in the interests of the family if resources were unlimited . . .'; 'There seems to me no reason in logic why the fact that Parliament has made the question of priority need turn upon whether a dependent child might reasonably be expected to reside with the applicant should require that question to be answered without regard to the purpose for which it is being asked, namely, to determine priority in the allocation of a scarce resource. To ignore that purpose would not be a rational social policy. It does not mean that a housing authority can say that it does not have the resources to comply with its obligations under the Act. Parliament has placed upon it the duty to house the homeless and has specified the priorities it should apply. But so far as the criteria for those priorities involve questions of judgment, it must surely take into account the overall purpose of the scheme.', per Lord Hoffmann in *Holmes-Moorhouse v Richmond upon Thames LBC* [2009] UKHL 7; [2009] HLR 34, at [12] and [16].

77   Save so far as it may be said that consideration of the general housing circumstances of an area as an element in a decision on homelessness, and on intentionality, might be said to import 'resources' by the back-door (see para 4.93, above).

78   Cf, *R v Birmingham CC ex p Tandy* [1999] 1 WLR 33, QBD, where it was said that to treat resources as relevant when deciding whether or not to approve a disabled facilities grant would be to downgrade a duty to a discretion. See, generally, *R v East Sussex CC ex p Tandy* [1998] AC 714, HL; see also *R v Bristol CC ex p Penfold* (1998) CCLR 315, QBD. Compare also *Conville v Richmond upon Thames LBC* [2006] EWCA Civ 718; [2006] HLR 1, and *Holmes-Moorhouse v Richmond upon Thames LBC* [2009] UKHL 7; [2009] HLR 34.

79   *Re Findlay* [1985] AC 318, HL, at 333; see also *R v Hillingdon LBC ex p McDonagh* (1999) 31 HLR 531.

80   *R v Winchester CC ex p Ashton* (1991) 24 HLR 520, CA.

81   Above, para 6.33.

that 'it is something that must be weighed carefully in the balance with the other factors upon which the decision . . . is reached'.

Failure to take into account relevant considerations

12.41   Just as taking into account the irrelevant may vitiate a decision, so may a failure to take into account the relevant, such as the effect of a medical condition on the need for a transfer from accommodation.[82] The authority must take reasonable steps to acquaint itself with what is relevant.[83] Some considerations derive from statute and therefore must be taken into account: consider the requirements under HA 1996 ss169(1) and 182(1) to have regard to Codes of Guidance issued by the secretary of state when determining applications under Parts 6 and 7, respectively.[84] If the decision-maker wrongly takes the view that a consideration is not relevant, and therefore has no regard to it, his/her decision cannot stand and s/he must be required to think again.[85]

12.42   A failure to take into account a relevant consideration will be sufficient to found a claim only if consideration of the relevant fact would have made a difference to the decision.[86]

Promoting the object of legislation[87]

12.43   Powers conferred for public purposes must be used in a way that Parliament can be presumed to have intended.[88] In *Khalique*,[89] the authority was entitled to provide temporary accommodation (in discharge of the Part 7 duty) provided the entitlement to permanent accommodation was not deferred so as 'to frustrate the purpose of the legislation and the rights which it gives to individuals, nor deferred or withheld for some improper or illicit reason'.[90]

---

82   *R v Islington LBC ex p Aldabbagh* (1995) 27 HLR 271.

83   Per Lord Diplock in *Secretary of State for Education and Science v Tameside MBC* [1977] AC 1014, HL, at 1065.

84   As to which, see *R v Wandsworth LBC ex p Hawthorne* [1994] 1 WLR 1442.

85   *Tesco Stores Ltd v Secretary of State for the Environment* [1995] 1 WLR 759, at 764G–H.

86   *R v Wandsworth LBC ex p Onwudiwe* [1994] COD 229; *R v Secretary of State for Health ex p Eastside Cheese Co* [1999] EuLR 968.

87   See, generally, *Padfield v Minister of Agriculture, Fisheries & Food* [1968] AC 997, HL; see also *Meade v Haringey LBC* [1979] 1 WLR 1, CA, and *R v Braintree DC ex p Halls* (2000) 32 HLR 770, CA.

88   *R v Tower Hamlets LBC ex p Chetnik Developments Ltd* [1988] AC 858, HL.

89   *R v Tower Hamlets LBC ex p Khalique* (1994) 26 HLR 517.

90   *Khalique* , at 522.

Fettering discretion

12.44   An authority must reach its own decision on each individual case; it may not fetter its discretion by approaching a decision with a pre-determined policy on how it will deal with cases that fall within a particular class.[91] That is not to say that – if good administration requires it – an authority cannot adopt a policy in order to guide the future exercise of its discretion. Where it does so, however, it must consider the application of that policy individually in every case where it is sought to make an exception.[92] This approach was adopted and applied by the House of Lords in *Re Betts*.[93]

12.45   A policy of requiring all applicants who were joint tenants of an authority to serve notice to quit (thereby terminating the tenancy) before they could be accepted as homeless owing to domestic violence under HA 1996 Part 7 was held to be unlawful in *Hammia*.[94]

Unlawful delegation or dictation

12.46   The authority cannot avoid its duties by adopting the decision of another body.[95] A distinction must be drawn, however, between adoption of the decision of another body and the proper use of others to assist in reaching a decision.[96] The authority may employ staff,[97] and have implied power to employ contractors or agents and to enter into contracts with them.[98] These resources can all be used when reaching a decision. What cannot be abdicated – save so far as statutorily permitted – is responsibility for the essential elements of a decision which are to determine what is to be done or what is to happen (in contrast to – even if overlapping with – *how* something is to be done), ie, the underlying decision rather than its day-to-day management.[99]

91   *British Oxygen Co Ltd v Minister of Technology* [1971] AC 610, HL. See also *R v Secretary of State for the Environment ex p Brent LBC* [1982] QB 593.

92   *British Oxygen Co Ltd v Minister of Technology* [1971] AC 610, HL, at [625E].

93   [1983] 2 AC 613; 10 HLR 97, HL; see chapter 8.

94   *R (Hammia) v Wandsworth LBC* [2005] EWHC 1127 (Admin); [2005] HLR 46.

95   *Lavender & Sons v Minister of Housing and Local Government* [1970] 1 WLR 1231.

96   In *R v West Dorset DC ex p Gerrard* (1994) 27 HLR 150, QBD, under HA 1985 Part 3, the authority could enlist the assistance of a third party but had to take the 'active and dominant' part in the investigative process. But cf the approach in *R v Hertsmere BC ex p Woolgar* (1995) 27 HLR 703, QBD, likewise under HA 1985 Part 3. The actual results are now overtaken by statutory provision: below, para 12.47.

97   Local Government Act 1972 s112.

98   *Crédit Suisse v Allerdale BC* [1997] QB 306, CA, at 346. There is now express power to contract, in Local Government (Contracts) Act 1997 s1.

99   *Crédit Suisse v Allerdale BC* [1995] 1 Lloyds LR 315, Comm Ct.

12.47   Statute may permit functions to be designated by order as capable of being exercised by others who are not members or employees of the authority.[100] Under this provision, the Local Authorities (Contracting Out of Allocation of Housing and Homelessness Functions) Order 1996[101] permits a wide range of functions under both Parts 6 and 7 to be contracted out, including enquiry and even decision-making on homelessness.[102]

The authority's decision must be reached properly

12.48 By statute,[103] it is the full authority which is entrusted with functions, including the function of reaching decisions, and only the authority can do so[104] – save so far as the authority is permitted to delegate it: the general power of delegation in local government (Local Government Act 1972 s101) permits delegation to a committee, sub-committee or officer. This power does not permit delegation to a single member, because there cannot be a committee or sub-committee of one.[105] It does, however, permit delegation to an officer, to be exercised in consultation with a member, so long as the member does not play the dominant role to the extent that the officer cannot be said to have reached the decision him/herself.[106]

12.49   Under the Local Government Act (LGA) 2000, however, local authorities now function in what may be described as two parts: an executive[107] and the full authority. Decisions not conferred on the authority by statute, statutory instrument or (where the matter is left to the authority to decide) under what is known as 'local choice',[108] *must* be taken by the executive.[109] Decisions on allocations and home-

100 Deregulation and Contracting Out Act 1994 s70. See chapter 10.
101 SI No 3205.
102 See chapter 9, above.
103 And subject to exceptions.
104 *Gardner v London Chatham and Dover Railway Co (No 1)* (1867) LR 2 Ch App 201; *Marshall v South Staffordshire Tramways Co* [1895] 2 Ch 36; *Parker v Camden LBC* [1986] 1 Ch 162, CA; *Crédit Suisse Plc v Waltham Forest LBC* [1997] QB 362, CA.
105 *R v Secretary of State for the Environment ex p Hillingdon LBC* [1986] 1 WLR 807, CA. There is statutory power to delegate to a single member in circumstances which do not apply here: see Local Government and Public Involvement in Health Act 2007 s236.
106 *R v Port Talbot BC ex p Jones* [1988] 2 All ER 208, QBD. See also *R v Tower Hamlets LBC ex p Khalique* (1994) 26 HLR 517.
107 Of one of a number of kinds: mayor and cabinet, leader and cabinet or (in Wales only) mayor and council executive – see LGA 2000 s11.
108 LGA 2000 s13(3)(b).
109 LGA 2000 s13(2) and (10).

lessness are – by this route – matters for the executive.[110] Decisions to
be taken by the executive may be dealt with in any way that the LGA
2000 permits, which includes delegation to an individual member of
the executive, or to a committee or sub-committee of the executive,
or to an officer (or, in some circumstances, an area committee not of
the executive but of the authority itself).[111]

12.50   A decision of an executive is treated as that of, and is binding on,
the authority;[112] it is not a delegation to the executive but a decision
taken on behalf of the authority:[113] the authority cannot 'overrule' it in
the way that, for example, it can 'overrule' one of its own committees
or officers (and could formerly overrule all committees and officers),
although it does have power to consider an executive decision and to
require the executive to reconsider it, whether or not – but probably
– by committee.[114] Nor, conversely, can the executive overrule a decision of the authority.[115]

12.51   A general category of 'appeals' is within the 'local choice' class.[116]
It does not seem that this includes reviews under Parts 6 and 7 because the fact that a review can take into account facts arising subsequent to the original decision[117] means that it is not exclusively
an 'appeal' and there remain issues of judgment that fall within the
'execution' of functions that should fall on the executive.

Irrationality

Wednesbury

12.52 As noted,[118] the authority may not reach a decision which no reasonable authority could have reached – such a decision, commonly

---

110 LGA 2000 s13 and Local Authorities (Functions and Responsibilities)
(England) Regulations 2000 SI No 2853.

111 LGA 2000 ss14–16 and 18.

112 LGA 2000 s13(9) and (10)(a).

113 LGA 2000 s13(9).

114 LGA 2000 s21. All authorities must maintain at least one 'overview and
scrutiny' committee to exercise such powers, on which the executive cannot
be represented; they may, however, maintain more than one, referable to
different functions.

115 This is implicit in the allocation of functions to the different parts of the
authority.

116 Local Authorities (Functions and Responsibilities) (England) Regulations 2000
SI No 2853 reg 3(1) and Sch 2 para 2.

117 *Mohamed v Hammersmith & Fulham LBC* [2001] UKHL 57; [2002] 1 AC 547. As
to decisions, see chapter 9.

118 Para 12.21.

referred to as a perverse decision, is conclusive evidence that the decision is irrational and therefore void. There is a high threshold to cross.

Bad faith/improper purposes or motives

12.53   A decision will be unlawful if it can be shown that the decision-maker acted in bad faith or was motivated by some aim or purpose that is not considered legitimate. This is part of the (obvious) principle that the decision-maker may not use the powers entrusted to him/her for purposes which fall outwith his authority.[119] Acting in bad faith stands alone as a ground and will automatically vitiate a decision.[120]

12.54   Although frequently alleged by dissatisfied applicants, both grounds are difficult to establish[121] and must be fully particularised and proven by the applicant.[122]

12.55   A power conferred on a local authority may not lawfully be exercised to promote the electoral advantage of a political party.[123] However, if several purposes are being pursued and the dominant purposes is legitimate, the decision will not be unlawful.[124]

Procedural impropriety

Fairness and article 6

12.56   A decision-maker must act fairly and in accordance with the principles of natural justice, which are supplemented and developed by article 6 of the ECHR.[125]

12.57   What constitutes fairness has been described as 'essentially an intuitive judgment'[126] and what it demands will depend on the context of the decision, the statute which confers the discretion on the decision-maker, and the legal and administrative system within which the decision is taken. Fairness will also commonly require that a person adversely affected by the decision should have an opportunity

---

119 *R v Tower Hamlets LBC ex p Chetnik Developments Ltd* [1988] AC 858, HL.

120 *Wednesbury*, see footnote 18, above; *Smith v East Elloe Rural DC* [1956] AC 736.

121 In *Cannock Chase DC v Kelly* [1978] 1 WLR 1, CA, it was suggested that the term should be used only in respect of a dishonest misuse of power.

122 *Cannock Chase DC v Kelly* [1978] 1 WLR 1.

123 *Magill v Porter* [2001] UKHL 67; [2002] 2 AC 357.

124 *Magill v Porter* [2001] UKHL 67; [2002] 2 AC 357.

125 As to which, see below, paras 12.96–12.100.

126 *R v Home Secretary ex p Doody* [1994] 1 AC 531, HL, at 560/D.

to make representations on his/her own behalf either before the decision is taken or with a view to procuring its modification; that requirement inevitably carries with it a need on the part of the applicant to be informed of the gist of the case which s/he has to answer.[127]

12.58 The influence of article 6 in this area generally has been considerable, but has not had a significant impact in relation to claims under Part 6 or 7, save for supplementing the pre-existing procedural safeguards.[128] Any defects which may exist in the statutory procedure for internal review are rectified by the right of an applicant to appeal to the county court or by judicial review.[129]

12.59 That is not to say that the existence of a statutory scheme will always be deemed sufficient. The courts may, if they consider the circumstances of the case justify it, impose more stringent requirements to ensure that a matter has been decided fairly.[130] Thus, while review of a homelessness decision has to be carried out by a senior officer not involved in the original decision,[131] mere compliance with this would per se not prevent a challenge to the review[132] if the reviewer – though senior and not involved – could, for other reasons,[133] be said to be biased against the applicant.

12.60 Leaving aside article 6, the principles of natural justice require both that no one should be a judge in his/her own cause (bias); and that an applicant has the right to be heard.[134]

127 *R v Home Secretary ex p Doody* [1994] 1 AC 531, HL, at 560/D.

128 Below, paras 12.96–12.100.

129 See also *R (Alconbury Developments Ltd) v Secretary of State for the Environment, Transport and the Regions* [2001] UKHL 23; [2003] 2 AC 295.

130 *Wiseman v Boreman* [1971] AC 297, HL; *R v Hull Prison Visitors ex p St Germain* [1979] 1 WLR 1401; *Lloyd v McMahon* [1987] AC 625; *R v Civil Service Appeal Board ex p Cunningham* [1991] 4 All ER 310; *R v Secretary of State for the Home Department ex p Doody et al* [1994] 1 AC 531, HL; *R v Higher Education Funding Council ex p Institute of Dental Surgery* [1994] 1 WLR 242; *R v Kensington & Chelsea RLBC ex p Grillo* (1995) 28 HLR 94, CA; and *R v Ministry of Defence ex p Murray* [1998] COD 134, QBD.

131 See HA 1996 s202 and Allocation of Housing and Homelessness Regulations 1999 SI No 71 reg 2 (see below, para 12.174).

132 Cf, *Feld v Barnet LBC* [2005] EWCA Civ 1307; [2005] HLR 9.

133 Eg, past contact/dealings suggesting something other than full disinterestedness, or even some private or personal reason.

134 *Ridge v Baldwin* [1964] AC 40, HL.

Bias

12.61 For a decision to be quashed on the ground of bias, it is not necessary to show that the decision-maker was in fact biased; it is sufficient for there to be an apparent bias. In *R v Gough*[135] it had been held that, in the absence of actual bias, the court should decide for itself whether, in all of the circumstances relevant to the issue of bias, there was a real danger that the decision-maker/decision-making body had been biased. In *Re Medicaments and Related Classes of Goods (No 2)*,[136] however, it was said that the court should ask whether a fair-minded and informed observer would conclude that there was a real possibility or danger of bias. The House of Lords has approved this 'modest adjustment of the test in *Gough*',[137] subject to the omission of the phrase 'real danger'; accordingly, the appropriate test for bias is now 'whether the fair-minded and informed observer, having considered the facts, would conclude that there was a real possibility that the tribunal was biased'.[138]

12.62 In *Feld*,[139] the authority had only one reviewing officer, who conducted both an initial review and a subsequent re-review following a successful complaint to the ombudsman (of which she was not the subject, and in the report on which she was not criticised). The applicant asserted that this gave rise to the appearance of bias. The Court of Appeal dismissed the claim. The fair-minded and informed observer would take into account that a decision under HA 1996 s202, is an administrative decision which Parliament has entrusted to senior local authority officers, who have received training; the observer would also consider the practical constraints (financial and administrative) imposed on local housing authorities. Taking those factors into account, there would not be said to have been any bias in the decision-making process, based either on the officer's conduct of the previous review or on the successful complaint to the ombudsman.[140]

---

135 [1993] AC 646, HL.

136 [2001] 1 WLR 700, CA.

137 See *Magill v Porter* [2001] UKHL 67; [2002] 2 AC 357, at [103].

138 *Magill*, at [103].

139 *Feld v Barnet LBC* [2005] EWCA Civ 1307; [2005] HLR 9.

140 'Adopting a balanced approach such an observer will accept that investigation by and even adverse comment from the Ombudsman is one of the slings and arrows of local government misfortune with which broad shouldered officials have to cope. [The officer] was not herself involved nor the subject of criticism. She could be expected to bear criticism of the department not only with fortitude but with indifference . . .': per Ward LJ at [49].

In *De-Winter Heald v Brent LBC*,[141] the Court of Appeal held that an objective and well informed observer would not think that there was a real danger of bias on the part of a contracted out reviewer, and therefore rejected the contention that the review decisions in the appeals were marred by apparent bias.

Right to be heard

12.63 This has two elements: first, to inform the party affected about what is being said; and second, to afford him/her the opportunity to answer it.[142] This does not equate to a requirement for an oral hearing – so as to require any internal review to be a full hearing[143] – but does require, where a decision is reached without an hearing, that the applicant is given an opportunity to put his/her case in response to adverse findings.[144]

Reasons

12.64 There is no general common law duty for public bodies to give reasons for their decisions. The internal review requirements in both Parts 6 and 7, however, contain express provision for reasons to be given for decisions.[145] A failure to provide reasons would give rise to a ground of challenge and would suffice to quash the decision.[146] However, it should be noted that the requirement to give reasons is a manifestation of the need for the applicant to be aware of the decision against him/her and to be able to challenge that decision if necessary,[147] so that it is the substance rather than the form that is of importance.

12.65 The latitude afforded does not, however, exempt the authority from the requirement to apply the facts to the legal background and

---

141 [2009] EWCA Civ 930; [2010] HLR 8.
142 *Board of Education v Rice* [1911] AC 179, HL; *Kanda v Government of the Federation of Malaya* [1962] AC 362, PC.
143 Consider *Runa Begum* and *Tomlinson v Birmingham CC*, above, paras 12.29–12.30.
144 This is not a limitless right and there is no absolute right to the last word: *Bellouti v Wandsworth LBC* [2005] EWCA Civ 602; [2005] HLR 46.
145 Sections 167(4A) and 203(4).
146 *R v Westminster CC ex p Ermakov* [1996] 2 All ER 302, CA. Reasons should be 'proper, adequate and intelligible': *Westminster CC v Great Portland Estates plc* [1985] 1 AC 661.
147 *R v Islington LBC ex p Hinds* (1995) 27 HLR 65.

reach a 'properly or adequately reasoned decision'.[148] In *Paul-Coker*, the applicant successfully claimed judicial review of the authority's decision to refuse her accommodation pending review, on the grounds that the authority had not applied the legal criteria to her circumstances and that there was a 'complete absence of any explanation or reasoning' in the authority's decision letter. This success, based on inadequacy of reasons, was 'an exceptional case'.[149]

12.66   The nature and extent of reasons must relate to the substantive issues raised by an applicant (or by an applicant's adviser): see *Re Poyser & Mills Arbitration*,[150] approved by the House of Lords in *Westminster CC v Great Portland Estates plc*,[151] and again in *Save Britain's Heritage v Secretary of State for the Environment*.[152] 'The reasons that are set out must be reasons which will not only be intelligible, but which deal with the substantive points that have been raised', per Megaw J in *Posyer*. 'The three criteria suggested in the dictum of Megaw J are that the reasons should be proper, intelligible and adequate', per Lord Bridge in *Save Britain's Heritage*. In *Edwin H Bradley & Sons Ltd v Secretary of State for the Environment*,[153] Glidewell J added to the dictum of Megaw J that reasons can be briefly stated (also approved in *Great Portland Estates*).

12.67   In *Baruwa*,[154] it was said to be:

> . . . trite law that where, as here, an authority is required to give reasons for its decision it is required to give reasons which are proper, adequate, and intelligible and enable the person affected to know why they have won or lost. That said, the law gives decision-makers a certain latitude in how they express themselves and will recognise that not all those taking decisions find it easy in the time available to express themselves with judicial exactitude.

12.68   The purpose of the obligation to give reasons is to enable the recipient to see whether they might be challengeable in law: see *Thornton*

---

148 *R (Paul-Coker) v Southwark LBC* [2006] EWHC 497 (Admin); [2006] HLR 32.
149 *R (Paul-Coker) v Southwark LBC* [2006] EWHC 497 (Admin); [2006] HLR 32, at [52].
150 [1964] 2 QB 467.
151 [1985] AC 661.
152 [1991] 1 WLR 153. See also *Givaudan v Minister of Housing and Local Government* [1967] 1 WLR 250; *Mountview Court Properties Ltd v Devlin* (1970) 21 P&CR 689.
153 (1982) 264 EG 926.
154 *R v Brent LBC ex p Baruwa* (1997) 29 HLR 915.

v Kirklees MBC.[155] In *Mohammed,*[156] Latham J considered the role of reasons in the light of the right to seek an internal review of the decision:

> ... the purpose to be served by the giving of such reasons ... is to enable the applicant to put before the local housing authority a proper case based upon a full understanding of the council's previous[157] decision to refuse accommodation.

12.69 The reasons should accordingly be sufficient to enable the applicant to form a view as to whether to challenge the decision on a point of law.[158] Merely stating the words of the Act 'parrot-fashion', with no substantive explanation for the decision, is insufficient.[159] Reasons should be in sufficient detail to show the principles on which the decision-maker has acted and that have led to his/her decision; they need not be elaborate nor need they deal with every argument presented in support of the case.[160] Not every factor which weighed with the decision-maker in the appraisal of the evidence has to be identified and explained, but the issues which were vital to the conclusion should be identified, and the manner in which they were resolved, explained.[161] The question is whether it is possible to understand the decision-maker's thought processes when s/he was making material findings.[162]

12.70 Authorities are entitled to give their reasons quite simply: 'their decision and their reasons are not to be analysed in minute detail. They are not to be gone through as it were with a fine-tooth comb. They are not to be criticised by saying: "They have not mentioned this

---

155 [1979] QB 626, CA, which appears to have been a judicial summary of counsel's submission, rather than a judicial observation in its own right. See further *R v Tynedale DC ex p Shield* (1987) 22 HLR 144, QBD.

156 *R v Camden LBC ex p Mohammed* (1997) 30 HLR 315, QBD at p323.

157 Ie, initial.

158 *Osmani v Camden LBC* [2004] EWCA Civ 1706; [2005] HLR 22 at [38.9]. See also *R v Croydon LBC* (1993) 26 HLR 286, at 291–292.

159 *R v Newham LBC ex p Lumley* (2000) 33 HLR 124: this was a concession by counsel, but is again obviously correct. See also para 9.104, above. The decision in *Kelly v Monklands DC* (1985) 12 July, Ct of Session (OH), that a mere recital of the words of the Act was sufficient, is unlikely to be followed unless the relevant factual issues for determination by the authority are both clear and confined to something which the wording of the Act serves to address.

160 *Eagil Trust Co. Ltd v Pigott Brown* [1985] 3 All ER 119.

161 *English v Emery Reimbold & Strick Ltd* [2002] EWCA Civ 605; [2002] 1 WLR 2409.

162 *R (Iran) and others v Secretary of State for the Home Department* [2005] EWCA Civ 982.

or that"': *Tickner v Mole Valley DC*.[163] In the context of a decision on review, it has been said that reasons contained in the decision letter are not to be treated as if they are statutes or judgments and that it is important to read a decision letter as a whole to get its full sense: *Osmani*.[164]

12.71   Nevertheless, if a decision-maker fails to address in his/her decision letter an issue 'so startling that one would not expect it to pass without individual comment', the court may be justified in inferring that it has not received any or any sufficient consideration: *Bariise*.[165]

12.72   In *Graham*,[166] Sir Thomas Bingham MR said:

> I readily accept that these difficult decisions are decisions for the housing authority and certainly a pedantic exegesis of letters of this kind would be inappropriate. There is, nonetheless, an obligation under the Act to give reasons and that must impose on the council a duty to give reasons which are intelligible and which convey to the applicant the reasons why the application has been rejected in such a way that if they disclose an error of reasoning the applicant may take such steps as may be indicated.

12.73   This passage was cited with approval in *Hinds*,[167] in which the duty was held to have been complied with because the reasons were intelligible and conveyed clearly to the applicant why his application had been rejected. In *Carpenter*,[168] the decision letter was considered 'manifestly defective' because it failed to address the reasons why the applicant had left his previous accommodation and, accordingly, defeated the purpose of the section, 'to enable someone who is entitled to a decision to see what the reasons are for that decision and to challenge those reasons if they are apparently inadequate'.

12.74   A court should not approve incomprehensible or misguided reasoning, but a judge should not adopt an unfair or unrealistic approach when considering or interpreting review decisions;[169] a decision can often survive despite the existence of an error in the reasoning

---

163 [1980] 2 April, CA transcript.

164 *Osmani v Camden LBC* [2004] EWCA Civ 1706; [2004] HLR 22. See also *William v Wandsworth LBC; Bellamy v Hounslow LBC* [2006] EWCA Civ 535; [2006] HLR 42.

165 *R v Brent LBC ex p Bariise* (1998) 31 HLR 50, CA, per Millett LJ at 58.

166 *R v Croydon LBC ex p Graham* (1993) 26 HLR 286, CA.

167 *R v Islington LBC ex p Hinds* (1996) 28 HLR 302, CA. See also *R v Camden LBC ex p Adair* (1996) 29 HLR 236, QBD and *R v Wandsworth LBC ex p Dodia* (1997) 30 HLR 562.

168 *R v Northampton BC ex p Carpenter* (1992) 25 HLR 349, QBD.

169 *Holmes-Moorhouse v Richmond upon Thames LBC* [2009] UKHL 7; [2009] HLR 34, at [47].

advanced to support it: for example, the error may be irrelevant to the outcome; it may be too trivial to affect the outcome; it may be obvious from the rest of the reasoning, read as a whole, that the decision would have been the same notwithstanding the error; there may be more than one reason for the conclusion, while the error only undermines one of the reasons; or, the decision may be the only one which could rationally have been reached: in all such cases, the error should not, save perhaps in wholly exceptional circumstances, justify the decision being quashed.[170]

12.75 Although they may be checked by people with legal experience or qualifications before they are sent out, review decisions are prepared by housing officers, who occupy a post of considerable responsibility and who have substantial experience in the housing field, but they are not lawyers; it is not therefore appropriate to subject their decisions to the same sort of analysis as may be applied to a contract drafted by solicitors, to an Act of Parliament, or to a court's judgment; rather, a benevolent approach should be adopted. Nor should the court take too technical view of the language used, or search for inconsistencies, or adopt a nit-picking approach when confronted with an appeal against a review decision.[171]

12.76 In *City of Gloucester v Miles*,[172] the Court of Appeal held that – to comply with the requirement to state reasons – a notification of intentional homelessness[173] ought to have stated:

a) that the authority was satisfied that the applicant for accommodation became homeless intentionally;

b) when s/he was considered to have become homeless;

c) why s/he was said to have become homeless at that time, ie, what is the deliberate act or omission in consequence of which it is concluded that at that time s/he ceased to occupy accommodation which was available for his/her occupation; and

d) that it would have been reasonable for him/her to continue to occupy that accommodation.

12.77 In *ex p H*,[174] it was held that, while the authority was entitled to express itself quite simply and could not be criticised for not having gone into great detail, it was nonetheless incumbent on it to say what

---

170 *Holmes-Moorhouse* at [51].

171 *Holmes-Moorhouse* at [50].

172 (1985) 17 HLR 292, CA.

173 See chapter 6.

174 *R v Hillingdon LBC ex p H* (1988) 20 HLR 559, QBD. See also *R v Southwark LBC ex p Davies* (1993) 26 HLR 677, QBD.

was the deliberate act or omission in consequence of which it had been concluded that the applicant had ceased to occupy accommodation available for his occupation and which it would have been reasonable for him to continue to occupy. In the context of the case, this had required more than a statement that he could have continued to occupy his council tenancy in Northern Ireland.

12.78   Likewise, in *Baruwa*,[175] the decision letter should have clarified why the applicant was regarded as having spent money on non-essential items and why the authority regarded this as having caused the applicant's homelessness. It is not necessary, however, that the decision letter set out arithmetical calculations or itemised qualifications of what an applicant could or could not afford.[176]

12.79   In *Monaf*,[177] the court quashed the decision of the authority on the basis that its letters did not disclose that it had carried out the proper balancing act called for, to determine whether or not it would have been reasonable for applicants to remain in accommodation in Bangladesh or to come back to the UK.

12.80   In *Adair*,[178] the court described a decision letter, which merely recited that the authority had taken into account all the evidence and that the applicant did not fall within any of the categories of priority need, as being completely devoid of reasoning and inadequate.[179] The decision letter should have set out why the applicant was considered not to be a vulnerable person in the light of the medical evidence which he had put forward.

12.81   In *Khan*,[180] a decision letter which addressed only one of a number of grounds on which local connection was being claimed was held to be defective. In *McCarthy*,[181] however, the decision letter was upheld, even though it had not dealt with the suitability of the applicant's current accommodation, because the applicant had not raised that issue with the authority.

12.82   In *O'Connor*,[182] the authority concluded that the applicants were intentionally homeless. Both initial and review decision letters, however, failed to identify the date at which the authority considered that

175 *R v Brent LBC ex p Baruwa* (1997) 29 HLR 915, CA. See also *Robinson v Brent LBC* (1998) 31 HLR 1015, CA.

176 *Bernard v Enfield LBC* [2001] EWCA Civ 1831, CA.

177 *R v Tower Hamlets LBC ex p Monaf* (1988) 20 HLR 529, CA.

178 *R v Camden LBC ex p Adair* (1996) 29 HLR 236, QBD.

179 See also *R v Brent LBC ex p Bariise* (1998) 31 HLR 50, CA, at 58.

180 *R v Slough BC ex p Khan* (1995) 27 HLR 492, QBD.

181 *R v Sedgemoor DC ex p McCarthy* (1996) 28 HLR 608, QBD.

182 *O'Connor v Kensington & Chelsea RLBC* [2004] EWCA Civ 394; [2004] HLR 37.

the homelessness had commenced and therefore had not considered whether the omission at that time had been in good faith. Although the letter was 'thoughtful and factually sound', the decision was quashed because it failed to address the questions raised by HA 1996 s191(2).

12.83   In *Augustin*,[183] it was held that a later letter from the authority could rectify the shortcomings of an earlier notification (which, however, was not itself considered defective, albeit 'sparse' – per Auld J in the court below – or 'cryptic' [and brief] – per Glidewell LJ in the Court of Appeal; the notification had given the applicant the information she needed).

12.84   The courts may be slow to intervene on the basis of want of adequate reasons unless the applicant, or his/her adviser, offers the authority an opportunity to remedy a defective decision letter, by way of a 'prompt request for details', to which the authority has failed to respond.[184] In judicial review cases, the pre-action protocol[185] requires a letter before action[186] and the same is expected before a county court appeal is launched.[187]

12.85   The issue of additional evidence to amplify reasons arises in the context of appeals where the person undertaking the review sometimes submits a witness statement containing further reasoning for his/her decision. Such evidence cannot be admitted as of right and great care must be taken when seeking to do so. Statements which are aimed at clarification and do not alter or contradict anything in the decision letter are, however, properly admitted.[188]

12.86   In *Graham*[189] and *Ermakov*,[190] the Court of Appeal held that – save in exceptional circumstances – the courts will not permit the reasons given in the notification to be supplemented.[191] In *John*,[192] however,

183 *R v Westminster CC ex p Augustin* (1993) 25 HLR 281, CA.
184 *R v Camden LBC ex p Mohammed* (1997) 30 HLR 315, at 323, cited with approval in *R v Newham LBC ex p Lumley* (2000) 33 HLR 124, at 136–137.
185 Below, para 12.177.
186 See para 12.118, below.
187 See para 12.171, below.
188 *Hijazi v Kensington & Chelsea RLBC* [2003] EWCA Civ 692; [2003] HLR 73. See also *Hall v Wandsworth LBC; Carter v Wandsworth LBC* [2004] EWCA Civ 1740; [2005] HLR 23.
189 *R v Croydon LBC ex p Graham* (1993) 26 HLR 286, CA.
190 *R v Westminster CC ex p Ermakov* (1995) 28 HLR 819, CA; see also *R v Southwark LBC ex p Dagou* (1995) 28 HLR 72, QBD.
191 These were pre-county court appeal, judicial review cases, but the same principles should apply.
192 *R v Cardiff CC ex p John* (1982) 9 HLR 56, QBD. Another judicial review, pre-appeal case.

non-disclosure of the proper reasons for the decision in the decision letter did not prevent the authority from relying on proper reasons and justifying its decision accordingly and, in *Hobbs*,[193] the Court of Appeal upheld the High Court decision to admit affidavit evidence amplifying and explaining earlier evidence as to reasons.

12.87   In *Baruwa*,[194] it was recognised that there are cases:

> ... where ... one could look at the affidavit[195] ... by way of amplification of the reasons for the decision. Looking at such an affidavit is often a sensible course and saves the bother and expense of going back to the decision-maker to make a new decision which will incorporate the material which appears in the affidavit.

12.88   Nonetheless, the courts have not invariably held authorities to the reasons given. The decision in *de Falco*[196] was, so far as relevant, that:

> ... the council is of the opinion that you became homeless intentionally because you came to this country without having ensured that you had permanent accommodation to come to.

12.89   This was clearly, and has since expressly been held to be, wrong.[197] The court upheld it by finding that the applicants were homeless intentionally because they had left accommodation (in Italy) before coming to this country.

12.90   In *Islam*,[198] at the Court of Appeal, the court was similarly willing to disregard the express words used by the authority, and consider whether there had been what in substance could be considered intentional homelessness. In *Chambers*,[199] the decision that applicants had become homeless intentionally was not sustainable, but relief was refused on the alternative approach that the authority had discharged its duties to the applicants by an earlier offer.

12.91   These earlier cases should be treated with some caution. *De Falco* could as easily be described as a decision (at an interlocutory hearing) on discretion. The result in *Islam* was, of course, overturned on appeal.[200] *Chambers* was explicitly a decision on relief (discretion).

---

193 *Hobbs v Sutton LBC* (1993) 26 HLR 132, CA. See also *R v Bradford CC ex p Parveen* (1996) 28 HLR 681, CA.

194 *R v Brent LBC ex p Baruwa* (1997) 29 HLR 915.

195 Or, witness statement or evidence on an appeal to the county court.

196 *De Falco, Silvestri v Crawley BC* [1980] QB 460, CA.

197 See para 6.132, above.

198 *R v Hillingdon LBC ex p Islam* [1983] 1 AC 688; 1 HLR 107, HL.

199 *R v Westminster CC ex p Chambers* (1982) 6 HLR 15, QBD.

200 *R v Hillingdon LBC ex p Islam* [1983] 1 AC 688; 1 HLR 107, HL, see para 6.136, above.

Legitimate expectation

12.92   The requirement of fairness means that an authority must respect any legitimate expectation which an applicant may enjoy.[201] Conventionally, legitimate expectation refers to a legitimate *procedural* expectation, ie, as to how a matter is to be handled, such as an assurance that no decision will be taken, at all or on an aspect of a matter, until there has been a further opportunity to comment or until the authority has managed to contact someone, or that it will only be taken by an officer of a particular level of seniority or by a panel (member or officer),[202] provided that to conform to the expectation would not interfere or conflict with the authority's statutory duty.[203]

12.93   At its most narrow, it may refer only to the procedure to be adopted before an existing right or privilege is removed,[204] although as the concept is a part of the overall duty of fairness, it may equally be used to infer the loss of an opportunity to acquire a benefit or advantage. This does not easily translate into a legitimate substantive expectation, ie, of a particular outcome of a decision-making process, as opposed to its procedure. For legitimate expectation to give rise to a substantive entitlement would require a clear and unambiguous representation, devoid of qualification, on which it was reasonable to rely.[205] However, there is no requirement that an applicant should detrimentally have changed his/her position in reliance on the promise.[206] The question is whether it would be an abuse of power to frustrate the legitimate expectation. It is for the court to determine whether there is a sufficient overriding interest to justify a departure from what has previously been promised.[207] In one case, the substantive right to take over a tenancy was upheld.[208]

12.94   No appeal to legitimate expectation can, however, widen an authority's duties under either Part 6 or Part 7.[209] Nonetheless, where

---

201 *R v North and East Devon Health Authority ex p Coughlan* [2001] QB 213.

202 *Schmidt v Secretary of State for Home Affairs* [1969] 2 Ch 149, CA; *R v Devon CC ex p Baker* [1995] 1 All ER 73, CA.

203 *R v Attorney General of Hong Kong ex p Ng Yuen Shiu* [1983] 2 AC 629, PC, at 638/f.

204 *Council of Civil Service Unions v Minister for the Civil Service* [1985] 1 AC 374, HL, per Lord Diplock at 413.

205 *R v IRC ex p MFK Underwriting* [1990] 1 WLR 1545, at 1569/G.

206 *R v Newham LBC ex p Bibi and Al-Nashed* [2001] EWCA Civ 607; (2001) 33 HLR 84.

207 *R v North and East Devon Health Authority ex p Coughlan* [2001] QB 213, CA.

208 *R v Lambeth LBC ex p Trabi* (1997) 30 HLR 975, QBD.

209 *R v Lambeth LBC ex p Ekpo-Wedderman* (1998) 31 HLR 498, QBD.

a promise of a 'permanent' home had been made to homeless applicants, a legitimate expectation had arisen which was sufficient to justify derogation from the authority's housing allocation scheme, and which required the authority to provide reasons if the expectation was not to be fulfilled.[210]

Human Rights Act 1998

12.95   The scheme of the Human Rights Act 1998 is to require all domestic legislation to be read and given effect (as far as is possible) in a manner that is compatible with the Convention rights contained in the Act[211] and to render it unlawful for a 'public authority',[212] including local authorities and registered providers of social housing in respect of some aspects of their management of their social housing stock, including service of notice to quit or of seeking possession,[213] to act in a way which is incompatible with one or more of the Convention rights.[214] A person who claims that a public authority has acted in such a way may bring proceedings against the authority or rely on the Convention right in any legal proceedings.[215] The Convention rights which are most obviously relevant to a claim brought against Part 6 or Part 7 decisions are:

Article 6 – Everyone, in the determination of his/her civil rights and obligations, is entitled to a fair and public hearing within a reasonable time by an independent and impartial tribunal established by law.

Article 8 – Rights to respect for private and family life and home, interference with which is permitted to the extent that it is in accordance with law and necessary in a democratic society in the interests of national security, public safety, economic well-being of the country, the prevention of disorder or crime, the protection of health or morals or the rights and freedoms of others.

---

210 *R v Newham LBC ex p Bibi and Al-Nashed* [2001] EWCA Civ 607; (2001) 33 HLR 84.

211 HRA 1998 s3(1). *Westminster CC v Morris; R (Badu) v Lambeth LBC and First Secretary of State* [2005] EWCA Civ 1184; [2006] HLR 8.

212 As defined in HRA 1998 s6(3).

213 *R (Weaver) v London & Quadrant Housing Trust* [2008] EWHC 1377 (Admin) and on appeal [2009] EWCA Civ 587, above, para 12.8: see also footnote 8 to that paragraph on other acts of management and allocation.

214 HRA 1998 s6(1).

215 HRA 1998 s7(1).

Article 14 – Prohibition on discrimination on grounds of sex, race, colour, language, religion, political or other opinion, national or social origin, association with a national minority, property, birth or other status.

Article 6

12.96   Internal reviews do not need to be compliant with article 6, as homelessness rights are not civil rights within it.[216]

12.97   Even if they were, it had been held in *Runa Begum*[217] that an internal review coupled with the right to an appeal to the county court under section 204 comprised compliance with article 6.

12.98   This may be contrasted with *Tsfayo*,[218] a challenge at the European Court of Human Rights to a decision of a housing benefit review board to refuse to find good reason for backdating a claim, in which it was held at Strasbourg – without doubting *Runa Begum* – that judicial review had not provided the claimant with access to a court of full jurisdiction for the purpose of article 6(1), because the question in issue for the board – which lacked independence[219] – was a simple one of fact, not involving professional knowledge or specialist experience; judicial review was considered an inappropriate jurisdiction for the resolution of factual issues.

12.99   On this issue, and although not necessary to the decision,[220] *Runa Begum* was followed in *Tomlinson v Birmingham CC*,[221] notwithstanding the decision in *Tsfayo*, where the only issue was whether the homeless person had received a letter warning her – in accordance with HA 1996 s193(5) – that if she did not accept the accommodation offered, the authority would consider that its duty had been discharged,[222] which it was contended was a matter of simple fact which *Tsfayo* required to be considered by a court of full jurisdiction. See 'Note on late developments' at the front of this book.

---

216   *Tomlinson v Birmingham CC* [2010] UKSC 8.

217   *Runa Begum v Tower Hamlets LBC* [2003] UKHL 5; [2003] 2 AC 430; [2003] HLR 32.

218   *Tsfayo v UK* [2007] HLR 19.

219   And perhaps impartiality: it was relevant to the decision that – had the claim been allowed – the authority (of some of whose members the board was comprised) would have received only 50% rather than 95% subsidy: at [19].

220   Because article 6 is in any event not engaged because homelessness rights are not civil rights: see above, para 12.96.

221   [2010] UKSC 8.

222   Above, paras 10.158–10.159.

12.100   Article 6 was also relied on in a challenge to the legality of contracting out review decisions.²²³ The Court of Appeal rejected the argument that a third party would be any less impartial than an employee of the authority; in any event, the authority accepted the contracted out review as its own decision and the availability of an appeal to the county court under HA 1996 s204 ensured compliance with article 6, following *Runa Begum.*²²⁴

Article 8

12.101   Article 8 does not comprise a right to housing to be provided by the state.²²⁵ Given this, it does not currently seem likely that a claim for breach of the right to respect for the home under article 8 will succeed²²⁶ where an authority has properly applied the provisions of Part 7 and reached the conclusion that there is no substantive duty to house an applicant, because the provisions of Part 7 are themselves compliant with ECHR (and, indeed, go further than any duties under article 8).

12.102   Thus, in *Hackney LBC v Ekinci,*²²⁷ the Court of Appeal rejected the applicant's argument that he was in priority need through his 17-year-old wife.²²⁸ Pill LJ said, at [16]:

> There is no breach of article 8(1) in Parliament enacting a scheme of priorities whereby applications for accommodation by homeless persons are to be determined by local housing authorities whose resources will inevitably be limited . . .

12.103   Claims may also be made under article 8 in relation to the right to respect for family life. Generally, social welfare measures provided

---

223 *De-Winter Heald and others v Brent LBC* [2009] EWCA Civ 930 at [4].

224 *Runa Begum v Tower Hamlets LBC* [2003] UKHL 5; [2003] 2 AC 430; [2003] HLR 32. Again, this is in any event overtaken by the decision in *Tomlinson v Birmingham CC* [2010] UKSC 8, that homelessness rights are not civil rights engaging article 6. See 'Note on late developments' at the front of this book.

225 *X v Federal Republic of Germany* (1965) 8 Yearbook of the ECHR 158; *Chapman v UK* (2001) 33 EHRR 18; (2001) 10 BHRC 48; *O'Rourke v UK* Application No 39022/97, ECJ. See also *Lambeth LBC v Kay; Leeds CC v Price* [2006] UKHL 10; [2006] 2 AC 465; [2006] HLR 22. Cf, *Mazari v Italy* (2000) 30 EHRR CD 218, suggesting that a right may arise in some limited, extreme circumstances, where there is a positive obligation towards the applicant under article 8.

226 See *R (Morris) v Newham LBC* [2002] EWHC 1262 (Admin), where a claim that the failure to comply with the authority's duty under HA 1996 s193 was a breach of ECHR article 8 and gave rise to a right to damages was rejected.

227 [2001] EWCA Civ 776; (2002) HLR 2, CA.

228 See, further, chapter 5.

by the state do not fall within the ambit of article 8, as they are not specifically designed to promote or protect family life.[229] Although this principle was applied to Part 7 generally in *Morris* and *Badu*,[230] the Court of Appeal considered that the particular section under consideration, section 185(4),[231] nonetheless fell within the ambit of article 8 'because it sets out to give effect to a legislative policy of preserving family life for the homeless'.

Article 14

12.104 Article 14 will be breached if it applies directly to another Convention right or if it can be said to fall within the ambit of another Convention right, even if no specific right under that article is said to have been breached.[232] Courts should approach article 14 in a structured way, considering: whether the facts fall within the ambit of one or more Convention rights;[233] whether there is a difference in treatment of the claimant and persons put forward for comparison; whether chosen comparators are in an analogous situation to the complainant; and, whether the difference in treatment has an objective and reasonable justification.[234]

229 See *R (Carson) v Secretary of State for Work and Pensions* [2003] EWCA Civ 797; [2003] 3 All ER 577 at [28], upheld [2005] UKHL 37; [2006] 1 AC 173. See also *R (Couronne & others) v (1) Crawley BC, (2) Secretary of State for Work and Pensions and (3) First Secretary of State; R (Bontemps & others) v Secretary of State for Work and Pensions* [2006] EWHC 1514 (Admin), in which the application of the 'habitual residence' test in deciding whether a homeless applicant is eligible (see chapter 3) was held to have nothing to do with promoting respect for private and/or family life; accordingly, the claimants' case was not within the ambit of article 8.

230 *Westminster CC v Morris; R (Badu) v Lambeth LBC and First Secretary of State* [2005] EWCA Civ 1184; [2006] HLR 8.

231 Section 185(4) provides that a person from abroad who is ineligible is to be disregarded in determining whether another person is homeless or in priority need (see para 3.71, above).

232 *M v Secretary of State for Work and Pensions* [2006] UKHL 11; [2006] 2 AC 91, at [11]–[14].

233 The right does not, however, have to be engaged – thus, even if no claim under article 8, there may be a claim under article 14 because the subject-matter is family, private life or home: *M v Secretary of State for Work and Pensions* [2006] UKHL 11; [2006] 2 AC 91, at [11]–[14].

234 *Wandsworth LBC v Michalak* [2002] EWCA Civ 271; [2003] 1 WLR 617 (see also *Ghaidan v Godin-Mendoza* [2004] UKHL 30; [2004] HLR 46). In *R (Carson) v Secretary of State for Work and Pensions* [2005] UKHL 37; [2006] 1 AC 173, Lord Nicholls said that the criteria derived from *Michalak* may not be appropriate in every case and that it may be appropriate simply to consider whether the alleged discrimination can withstand scrutiny.

12.105   In *Morris (No 2)*,[235] it was held that – in addition – the courts should ask whether any difference in treatment between the complainant and his/her comparator is based on one or more of the grounds set out in article 14.[236] Having found that HA 1996 s185(4)[237] fell within the ambit of article 8, the court went on to consider whether the section was in breach of articles 8 and 14. As the distinction in section 185(4) in effect discriminated on the ground of nationality, and could not be justified,[238] the section was declared incompatible with ECHR under HRA 1998 s4.[239]

12.106   In *R (RJM) v Secretary of State for Work and Pensions*,[240] the House of Lords accepted that being a homeless person was a 'personal characteristic', and accordingly that being a homeless person fell within the category of 'other status' within the meaning of article 14. In view of the reach of article 14,[241] the decision might yet, therefore, potentially have wider implications in future homelessness cases than has yet been realised.

Procedural law

Introduction

12.107 There are only two courts to which a dissatisfied applicant will be able to turn: the Administrative Court, by of proceedings for judicial review, and the county court, by way of a statutory appeal against a decision made under Part 7. In this section, we consider the procedure to be followed under each route of challenge.

---

235 *R (Morris) v Westminster CC & First Secretary of State* [2005] EWHC 2191 (Admin); [2005] HLR 7. The decision was upheld on appeal ([2005] EWCA Civ 1184; [2006] HLR 8).

236 See also *R (S) v Chief Constable of South Yorkshire Police* [2004] UKHL 39; [2004] 1 WLR 2196.

237 Above, para 370.

238 The government sought to justify the section on the basis that it was a necessary element of immigration control in order to prevent benefit tourism. This was rejected on the basis that the parent applicants in the cases (both of whom had children who were ineligible and were thus held not in priority need because of the application of section 185(4)) were both lawfully and habitually resident here.

239 Some changes were made as a result of the declaration – see para 3.71, above.

240 [2008] UKHL 63; [2009] 1 AC 311.

241 Above, para 12.104.

Which court?

12.108 Decisions made by local authorities under Parts 6 and 7 are administrative law decisions and therefore, without more, are prima facie justiciable by way of judicial review in the Administrative Court. Judicial review is, however, a remedy of 'last resort'[242] and the provision of a statutory appeal (or any form of alternative remedy) generally precludes recourse to it unless the case can in some way be distinguished from the category for which the appeal procedure is provided.[243] Thus, the existence of a scheme of internal review under both Parts 6 and 7 requires the applicant – save in exceptional cases – to pursue that review before going to court. More significantly for current purposes, the existence of a statutory appeal against a decision under Part 7 will generally preclude a dissatisfied Part 7 applicant from seeking to challenge that decision by proceedings for judicial review.

12.109 Examples of decisions outside Parts 6 and 7, where judicial review has proceeded notwithstanding the existence of an alternative – or internal – procedure, include cases where it is not the individual decision that is in issue but the underlying legality of a decision – for example, a policy – to which the individual case is a mere application,[244] and where the decision was made without jurisdiction or contained an error of law.[245]

12.110 In *R v East Yorkshire Borough of Beverley Housing Benefits Review Board ex p Hare*,[246] the court allowed judicial review proceedings to continue – and granted relief – even though the applicant had an alternative remedy by way of appeal (under the then provisions) to a housing benefit review board, because the point raised was in part a point of statutory interpretation of general importance on which it was therefore appropriate for the court to rule.

12.111 However, even these circumstances are unlikely to lead to the grant of permission to seek judicial review under Part 7 to a homeless person aggrieved by a decision on his/her application which

---

242 Ie, any proper alternative remedy should be exhausted before the Administrative Court will permit a case to be heard: *R v Hammersmith & Fulham LBC ex p Burkett* [2002] UKHL 23; [2002] 1 WLR 1593; *R (Bancoult) v Secretary of State for the Foreign and Commonwealth Office* [2001] QB 1067, CA.

243 *R v Secretary of State for the Home Department ex p Swati* [1986] 1 WLR 477, CA.

244 *R v Paddington Valuation Officer ex p Peachey Property Corporation Ltd* [1966] 1 QB 380, CA.

245 *R v Hillingdon LBC ex p Royco Homes Ltd* [1974] 1 QB 720, DC.

246 (1995) 27 HLR 637.

could otherwise be appealed to the county court,[247] because the appeal procedure itself – being on a 'point of law'[248] – embraces the same grounds as those on which judicial review would be available.[249]

12.112　The intention could not have been much clearer, to transfer the bulk of the work from the High Court to the county court.[250] Accordingly, permission to bring a challenge by way of judicial review was refused where the reason the applicant could not appeal to the county court was because s/he was out of time[251] to do so: while the court did not rule out *ever* granting permission where an applicant was out of time, the applicant would have to show 'really exceptional circumstances'.[252]

12.113　It would be wrong, however, to think that the High Court – through the Administrative Court – has nothing to do with homelessness. A number of Part 7 cases have come before it and the use of judicial review has been approved where:

- an authority refused to house pending an internal review;[253]
- an authority refused to consider a request for accommodation pending review;[254]
- the decision letter from the authority was so unsatisfactory, and the authority refused to rectify the deficiency in the letter, so that any internal review would be unfair to the applicant;[255]
- the challenge was to the legality of a policy of the authority: see *Byfield*,[256] in which the challenge was to a policy that applicants

---

247　The issue does not arise if the issue raised *cannot* be brought by way of appeal to the county court, as there is no 'alternative remedy'.

248　Section 204(1).

249　See below, para 12.150.

250　'Prior to 1997, many of these unhappy cases fell to be considered by nominated judges dealing with the Crown Office list. Such was the pressure that a particular deputy High Court judge sat almost continuously dealing with homelessness cases and other such cases frequently had to be referred to other deputy High Court judges. Therefore, Parliament incorporated into the Housing Act 1996 another route whereby complaints could be dealt with.' (per Tucker J in *R v Brent LBC ex p O'Connor* (1998) 31 HLR 923, QBD, at 924).

251　See para 12.121, below.

252　*R v Brent LBC ex p O'Connor* (1998) 31 HLR 923, QBD, at 925.

253　*R v Camden LBC ex p Mohammed* (1998) 30 HLR 315, QBD (see further para 12.147, below). Prior to the county court acquiring power to make an interim order to house (see para 12.197, below), this would also have been true of a refusal to house pending appeal to the county court.

254　*R (Casey) Restormel BC* [2007] EWHC 2554 (Admin); (2008) ACD 1.

255　*R v Camden LBC ex p Mohammed* (1998) 30 HLR 315, QBD.

256　(1997) 31 HLR 913, QBD. It is conceivable that such a challenge might be brought by an interested pressure group; see, eg, *R v Inland Revenue*

could not seek an internal review of the suitability of an offer of accommodation unless the offer was rejected; this was an unlawful fetter on their right to an internal review and was accordingly held properly to have been brought by way of judicial review;[257]

- the case raised an important matter of law: *Sadiq*;[258]
- an authority had not made a decision in response to a request for accommodation: *Lusamba*;[259]
- the decision was to refuse to make a local connection referral to another authority, which decision is not reviewable under s202: *Sareen*;[260]
- the authority refused to extend time to apply for an internal review under HA 1996 s202(3):[261] *Lewisham*;[262] *Slaiman*;[263]
- an appeal under HA 1996 s204 would not provide an effective remedy: in *Aguiar*,[264] the applicant received his costs on a compromised judicial review application, in part because the remedy being sought[265] would not have been available in appeal proceedings under HA 1996 s204;

Commissioners ex p National Federation of Self-employed and Small Businesses Ltd [1982] AC 617, HL; *R v Secretary of State for Social Services ex p Child Poverty Action Group* [1990] 2 QB 540, CA; *R v Her Majesty's Inspectorate of Pollution ex p Greenpeace Ltd* [1994] 4 All ER 329; *R v Secretary of State for Foreign and Commonwealth Affairs ex p World Development Movement Ltd* [1995] 1 WLR 386, QBD.

257 The substance of this decision was overruled in *Alghile v Westminster CC* [2001] EWCA Civ 363; 33 HLR 57; in turn, *Alghile* was overturned by the statutory amendment that permits an applicant to seek a review of accommodation while accepting it: HA 1996 s202(1A). These do not, however, affect the underlying point being made here, that a challenge to an unlawful policy may yet be brought by judicial review.

258 *R v Brent LBC ex p Sadiq* (2000) 33 HLR 47, QBD. Moses J, while acknowledging that the applicant should have sought a review and county court appeal, referred to the residual jurisdiction of the High Court and said that the case raised an important point (see para 9.128, above), which might well have had to be considered by the Court of Appeal in any event.

259 *R (Lusamba) v Islington LBC* [2008] EWHC 1149 (Admin). If, however, a decision is subsequently made by the authority, then there is no point in pursuing the substantive hearing.

260 *Hackney LBC v Sareen* [2003] EWCA Civ 351; [2003] HLR 54. See further para 9.153, above.

261 See chapter 10.

262 *R (C) v Lewisham LBC* [2003] EWCA Civ 927; [2004] HLR 4.

263 *R (Slaiman) v Richmond upon Thames LBC* [2006] EWHC 329 (Admin); [2006] HLR 20.

264 *R (Aguiar) v Newham LBC* [2002] EWHC 1325 (Admin).

265 An order that the authority carries out a section 202 review.

- the person seeking judicial review was a third party, not the applicant: in *Hammia*,[266] the authority applied a policy that victims of domestic violence, if a joint tenant of the authority, must first serve a notice to quit their existing home as a condition of acceptance as homeless; the applicant's husband, who lost his security of tenure because of the notice, successfully challenged this policy by proceedings for judicial review;
- following a local connection referral, the authority to which the applicant had been referred wished to challenge a substantive finding, for example, that the applicant is unintentionally homeless: *Bantamagbari*;[267]
- there were exceptional circumstances: *Van der Stolk*.[268]

12.114   In addition, there remain a number of circumstances, not yet considered by the courts, in which it is likely that judicial review will continue to be available, for example, where:

a)   in other circumstances two authorities are at odds (whether under the local connection provisions of HA 1996 ss200–201,[269] or the co-operation provisions of HA 1996 s213,[270] to which, again, the county court appeal procedure does not apply);

b)   what is in issue is discharge of the property duties, which are not subject to internal review or, therefore, to appeal (see HA 1996 ss211 and 212[271]);

c)   an applicant seeks an internal review on the facts alone, ie, without reference to a point of law, but the authority does not conduct the internal review (or notify the applicant of the outcome) within the prescribed time: there may need to be an application for judicial review to compel the authority to conduct the internal review

---

266   R *(Hammia) v Wandsworth LBC* [2005] EWHC 1127 (Admin); [2005] HLR 46.
267   R *(Bantamagbari) v Westminster CC* [2003] EWHC 1350 (Admin).
268   R *(Van der Stolk) v Camden LBC* [2002] EWHC 1261 (Admin), where the authority had failed properly to consider medical evidence provided after the time limit to appeal had passed and the applicant's mental health was deteriorating. See also R *(W) v Sheffield CC* [2005] EWHC 720 (Admin), where two local authorities were disputing responsibility for the applicant under the local connection provisions, and neither would house in the interim. '[T]he claimant having been caught between two stools and faced with an exceptional situation, I consider that it is appropriate, notwithstanding the existence of alternative remedies, to entertain judicial review proceedings': per Gibb J at [34].
269   See paras 7.35 onwards.
270   See chapter 13.
271   See chapter 8.

or to notify the applicant of the outcome, rather than appeal to the county court.[272]

12.115   Accordingly, judicial review is far from an obsolete process in cases under Parts 6 and 7. However, permission to pursue a judicial review for a 'pre-emptive' declaration in advance of any homelessness or threatened homelessness, that the applicant should not be considered intentionally homeless, while plainly not within the review or appeal provisions (for want of any decision), would seem likely to be refused.[273]

12.116   In the following paragraphs, therefore, the procedural steps to be followed when challenging a decision either in the Administrative Court – by way of judicial review against a decision under Part 6 or certain, limited, decisions under Part 7 – or the county court, by way of statutory appeal, are considered; see also the annex to this chapter for specimen documents.

Judicial review

Procedure

12.117   The procedure for claiming judicial review is contained in Civil Procedure Rules (CPR) Part 54.[274] Cases are now commonly – but not invariably – heard by a single High Court judge. All parties should comply with the pre-action protocol for judicial review. Compliance or non-compliance will be taken into account when giving directions for the case management of proceedings or when making an order for costs.[275] The protocol will not, however, be appropriate where there is an urgent need for an interim order, for example, to secure interim accommodation under HA 1996 s188(3).[276]

---

272 See further para 12.164, below.

273 See *R v Hillingdon LBC ex p Tinn* (1988) 20 HLR 305, QBD. Like every 'absolute' proposition, there may yet be exceptions, for example, where the court apprehends – with a degree of reason – *such* unlawful conduct by an authority that it feels impelled to intervene, even if the conditions for a prohibiting order are not fulfilled.

274 See also the accompanying Practice Direction and Senior Courts Act 1981 s31.

275 See Judicial Review Pre-action Protocol para 7 and CPR Costs Practice Direction.

276 Judicial Review Pre-action Protocol para 6. See further para 12.148 onwards on challenges to refusals to house pending internal review.

Letter before claim

12.118   The pre-action protocol requires that the claimant should send a letter to the defendant before making the claim, to identify the issues in dispute and to establish whether litigation can be avoided.[277] The letter should contain the date and details of the decision, act or omission being challenged and a clear summary of the facts on which the claim is based. It should also contain the details of any relevant information that the claimant is seeking to obtain and an explanation of why this is considered relevant.[278] The letter should set out a date for reply, which in most circumstances will be 14 days. A claim should not usually be made until the proposed reply date has passed.[279]

Letter of response

12.119   The authority should usually respond within 14 days.[280] If this is not possible, an interim reply should be sent and a reasonable extension proposed.[281] The reply must indicate clearly whether or not the claim is being conceded.[282] Failure to comply with the requirement to respond may lead to a costs order. In *R v Kensington & Chelsea RLBC ex p Ghebregiogis*,[283] a comprehensive letter before action had been sent to the authority by the applicant's solicitors explaining the applicant's position and dealing with the authority's adverse contentions, following which the applicant commenced judicial review proceedings. Just before the application for permission came on for hearing, the authority changed its mind. The applicant successfully sought his costs: the authority should properly have considered the case when it received the letter.

Permission

12.120   Permission must be sought to bring an application for judicial review.[284] Where a claim has become academic, it is only in ex-

---

277   Judicial Review Pre-action Protocol para 8. A suggested standard format is provided at annex A to the Protocol.
278   Judicial Review Pre-action Protocol para 10.
279   Judicial Review Pre-action Protocol para 12.
280   Judicial Review Pre-action Protocol para 13. A standard format letter is provided at annex B to the Protocol.
281   Judicial Review Pre-action Protocol para 14.
282   Judicial Review Pre-action Protocol paras 15 and 16.
283   (1994) 27 HLR 602, QBD.
284   The requirement for permission represents the most significant difference between the procedure to be followed on a claim for judicial review and an appeal under HA 1996 s204, which is as of right.

ceptional circumstances, and where there is good reason to do so in the public interest, that permission to claim judicial review will be granted; such exceptional circumstances include where a large number of similar cases either exist or are anticipated or where there is a discrete point of statutory construction which does not involve detailed consideration of the facts.[285]

Time

12.121 Application for permission must be made 'promptly and in any event within three months from the date when grounds for the application first arose' (CPR 54.5). The three-month period runs from the time when application for permission can first be made (CPR 54 Practice Direction 4.1).[286] The former explicit power (to be found in RSC Order 53 r4) to extend time for 'good reason' has not been retained, although the general jurisdiction of the court to extend time under CPR 3.1 is available. Any application to extend time must be set out in the claim form with grounds (CPR 54.5). The parties may not agree to extend time (CPR 54.5(2)), nor will the court be enthusiastic about granting permission when an application has grown stale.[287] Delay in obtaining legal aid may constitute an acceptable reason for granting permission belatedly.[288] Where the challenge is to the lawfulness of a policy and the relief sought is to restrain its further implementation, the need to ensure that a prima facie unlawful policy is discontinued is likely to comprise a good reason for extending time.[289]

12.122 When permission to pursue judicial review out of time is granted, it is not a final decision on the time question. The fact that the claim was out of time may still be raised at the full hearing of the application for judicial review itself.[290]

---

285 *R (McKenzie) v Waltham Forest LBC* [2009] EWHC 1097 (Admin).

286 When what is under challenge is a policy, time only begins to run when it affects the individual applicant: *R v Tower Hamlets LBC ex p Mohib Ali* (1993) 25 HLR 218, DC; *R v Newham LBC ex p Ajayi* (1994) 28 HLR 25.

287 See *R v Rochester CC ex p Trotman* (1983) *Times* 13 May.

288 *R v Stratford on Avon DC ex p Jackson* [1985] 1 WLR 1319, CA; see also *R v Dacorum BC ex p Brown* (1989) 21 HLR 405, QBD.

289 *R (Lin) v Barnet LBC* [2006] EWHC 1041 (Admin).

290 *R v Dairy Produce Quota Tribunal ex p Caswell* [1990] 2 AC 738, HL; caution should, however, be exercised when re-opening the issue of delay at the substantive hearing: *R (Lichfield Securities Ltd) v Lichfield DC* [2001] EWCA Civ 304; [2001] 3 PLR 33.

Form of application

12.123   An application must be made on form N461, in accordance with CPR Part 54. The claim form must include or be accompanied by a detailed statement of the grounds and a statement of the facts relied on.[291]

Supporting documents

12.124   In addition, any written evidence in support of the claim, a copy of the decision that the applicant[292] seeks to have quashed, any documents which will be relied on, copies of relevant statutory material and a list of essential documents for advance reading must also be supplied. Two copies of the relevant documents in a paginated and indexed bundle must be filed.[293] Where it is not possible to file all of the documents, the applicant must say which are to follow and explain why they are not currently available.

12.125   In the usual case, the applicant's full case will have to be made out in the initial application, without anticipating additional oral evidence or later elaboration. This makes the initial papers very important indeed. This means that the case must be made out from the outset.

Duty of care

12.126   There is a high duty of care on the part of all applicants to make full and frank disclosure in an application for permission, even if it is unhelpful to the case. Non-disclosure is not necessarily fatal if it causes no advantage to the applicant and no prejudice to the respondent but, even if it does not lead to the refusal of permission, it could still affect relief at the end of the day.[294] The obligation is to make full and candid disclosure of the material facts known to the applicant and to make proper enquiries before making the application; there is a breach of the disclosure duty if s/he has not disclosed any additional material facts which s/he would have known if s/he had made proper enquiries before making the application. [295] Proper

---

291   A form of N461, including the statement of grounds and statement of facts is annexed to this chapter.

292   Under the CPR, a person claiming judicial review is now (as in other cases) a claimant (see CPR Part 2.3(1): 'a claimant is a person who makes a claim' and CPR Part 54.1 referring to a 'claim for judicial review'); the term 'applicant' is, however, used in this book to denote applicant under either Part 6 or Part 7.

293   CPR Part 54.6 and PD para 5.7.

294   See *R v Wirral MBC ex p Bell* (1994) 27 HLR 234, QBD.

295   *R (Lawer) v Restormel BC* [2007] EWHC 2299 (Admin); [2008] HLR 20.

disclosure for this purpose means specifically identifying all relevant documents for the judge, taking him/her to the particular passages in the documents which are material and taking appropriate steps to ensure that the judge correctly appreciates the significance of what s/he is being asked to read; that burden of full and frank disclosure is more onerous where a telephone application is being made to a judge who has none of the papers before him/her, nor is it removed by giving informal notice to the other party.[296]

Service

12.127 The claim form (and accompanying documents) must be served on the defendant(s) within seven days of the date of issue,[297] together with an acknowledgment of service form, which must be filed by the respondent authority not more that 21 days after service of the claim form.[298]

Pre-permission response

12.128 In the acknowledgement of service, the defendant must set out a summary of the grounds for contesting the claim, any directions which will be sought and other applications which will be made at the permission stage. A respondent who does not return the acknowledgment of service form within 14 days of service will lose the right to take part in the permission hearing (although not the right to take part in the substantive application) without the court's express permission to do so.[299] A respondent authority may not apply to set aside permission where it has been served with the claim form,[300] but may do so where there has been a failure to serve by the applicant.[301]

Paper applications

12.129 Applications for permission to proceed will, unless the court directs otherwise, be decided by a judge without hearing oral submissions.

---

296 *R (Lawer) v Restormel BC* [2007] EWHC 2299 (Admin); [2008] HLR 20.
297 Where the relief sought in the claim form includes a declaration of incompatibility under Human Rights Act 1998 s4, the Crown must be given 21 days' notice and/or joined as an interested party or second defendant to the claim: CPR 19.4A(1), and see *R (Morris) v Westminster CC* [2003] EWHC 2266 (Admin); [2004] HLR 18.
298 CPR 54.8.
299 CPR 54.9.
300 CPR 54.13.
301 *R (Webb) v Bristol CC* [2001] EWHC Admin 696.

Interim applications

12.130　Any applications for interim relief should be made in accordance with CPR Parts 23 and 25 and may be considered with the application for permission. Even where an interim application – for example, to house pending the substantive hearing – is made at the same time as permission is sought, there does not have to be an oral hearing if the court does not consider it appropriate.[302] Failure to comply with any order of the court – or an undertaking given in lieu of an order – may amount to contempt of court.[303]

Attendance of respondent

12.131　The respondent authority does not need to attend any permission hearing, unless the court directs otherwise. Where it does so, the court will not generally make an order for costs against the applicant.[304]

Post-permission response

12.132　If permission is granted, the respondent must, within 35 days of service of the order granting permission, file and serve detailed grounds for contesting the claim and any written evidence on which reliance is to be placed.

Further stages

12.133　At least 21 days prior to the hearing, the applicant must file a full skeleton argument. The respondent must file a skeleton at least 14 days in advance. Where permission is, on the papers, refused or granted only subject to conditions or on certain grounds, the applicant may, within seven days, request that the decision be reconsidered at an oral hearing.[305] An appeal against a refusal of permission – generally or on specific grounds, or against conditions – lies to the Court of Appeal, but only with its permission.[306]

302　CPR 23.8.

303　See *R (Bempoa) v Southwark LBC* [2002] EWHC 153 (Admin), where, in proceedings under the National Assistance Act 1948 s21, the authority through its social services department undertook not to evict the applicant, pending an assessment of his needs. Notwithstanding this, the authority's housing department evicted him from his accommodation and refused to reinstate him. The undertaking bound all departments in the authority, which was held to be in contempt.

304　PD 54.8(6).

305　CPR 54.11 and 54.12.

306　CPR 52.15.

Disclosure

12.134 Application for disclosure of documents may be made (by either party) at the same time that permission is sought, or after it has been granted.[307] Unless the court makes an order for disclosure, it is not required.[308] On discovery, only material which is privileged – because it has been produced in the course of, or in anticipation of, the proceedings – may be withheld.

12.135 The applicant will accordingly be able to inspect the authority's minutes and memoranda dealing with his/her application. An examination of the authority's standing orders should be undertaken in every case, as these may reveal a want of authorised delegation or sub-delegation.[309] It may be said that few authorities can withstand such close legal scrutiny without revealing *some* flaws in their procedure, although these flaws may do no more than cause embarrassment (perhaps even only minor), without invalidating the whole process.

Further appeal

12.136 If permission is refused, the refusal may be appealed to the Court of Appeal; this must be pursued within seven days.[310] If successful, the Court of Appeal, rather than giving permission to appeal, may give permission to apply[311] and will usually order that the case should proceed in the High Court.[312] Appeals from a full judicial review application require permission from either the High Court, or – if refused – from the Court of Appeal.[313]

Costs

12.137 The general provisions concerning costs (ie, those contained in CPR 44.3) are applicable to judicial review proceedings. Accordingly, the usual order is for costs to follow the event so that the successful party will be able to recover costs.[314] However, the court has a broad

---

307 CPR 54.15.
308 PD 54.12(1).
309 Above, chapter 9.
310 CPR 52.15.
311 CPR 52.15(3).
312 CPR 52.15(4).
313 CPR 52.3(1). Permission may only be granted where there is a real prospect of success or some other compelling reason: CPR 52.3(6).
314 CPR 44.3(2)(a). See, eg, *Mendes & another v Southwark* LBC [2009] EWCA Civ 594; [2010] HLR 3, at [23] and [24].

discretion to take into account all factors, including the conduct of the parties, and so, where either party's conduct has prolonged litigation or has had the effect of increasing the costs burden on the other, the court may deprive the successful party of all or a proportion of the costs.[315] The courts will depart from the general rule on an issue-by-issue basis: where a party unsuccessfully raises an issue that takes up a significant part of the hearing, s/he may be denied costs in relation to that issue, even if successful in the claim overall.[316]

12.138   Publicly funded litigants should not be treated differently from those who are not; nonetheless, the consequences for solicitors who do such work is a factor which must be taken into account: it is one thing for solicitors who do a substantial amount of publicly funded work, and who have to fund the substantial overheads that sustaining a legal practice involves, to take the risk of being paid at lower rates if a publicly funded case turns out to be unsuccessful, but quite another for them to be unable to recover remuneration at inter partes rates in the event that the case is successful.[317]

12.139   If the court is satisfied that – but for the steps taken by an applicant's solicitor – a public authority would not have fulfilled its statutory duty, then the costs of taking those steps should, in principle, be recoverable from the public authority; the court should approach such a factual issue on a broad basis, after a comparatively short consideration of the facts and doing the best it can on the available material.[318]

12.140   Different considerations are likely to apply where a claim for judicial review is settled – most commonly, in the present context, where an authority agrees to withdraw its decision and reconsider it. It is not uncommon for the parties to agree the substance of the claim but remain in dispute over who is to bear the burden of costs. In

---

315 CPR 44.3(4), (5) and (6).

316 *AEI Rediffusion Music v Phonographic Performance Ltd* [1999] 1 WLR 1507, CA; *R (Bateman) v Legal Services Commission* [2001] EWHC 797 (Admin); [2002] ACD 29.

317 *R (E) v Governing Body of JFS and the Admissions Appeal Panel of JFS and others; R (E) v Governing Body of JFS and the Admissions Appeal Panel of JFS and others (United Synagogue)* [2009] UKSC 1 at [25]. The dicta of Scott Baker J in *R (Boxall) v Waltham Forest LBC* (2001) 4 CCLR 258, that the fact that the claimants were legally aided was immaterial when deciding what, if any, costs order to make between the parties in a case where they were successful, was approved.

318 *R v Hackney LBC ex p S*, unreported, 13 October 2000, para 6, cited in *R (Scott) v Hackney LBC* [2009] EWCA Civ 217.

Boxall,[319] guidance was given on the principles to be applied, additional to the point made above,[320] that it will ordinarily be irrelevant that the claimant is in receipt of public funding for his/her claim: the overriding objective is to do justice between the parties without incurring unnecessary court time and costs; how far the court will be prepared to look into the previously unresolved substantive issues will depend on the circumstances of the particular case, not least the amount of costs at stake and the conduct of the parties; in the absence of a good reason to make any other order, the fall-back position is to make no order as to costs; the court should take care not to discourage parties from settling judicial review proceedings. A reasonable and proportionate attempt must be made to analyse the situation and determine whether an order for costs is appropriate; a judge must not be tempted too readily to adopt the fall-back position of making no order.[321]

12.141   The court has power to order that costs be set off.[322] This may permit an order to set off costs against damages or costs to which a legally aided person has become or becomes entitled in the action; the set-off is no different from and no more extensive than the set-off available to or against parties who are not legally aided; the broad criterion is that the claims of both claimant and defendant claim are so closely connected that it would be inequitable to allow the claimant's claim without taking into account the defendant's claim;[323] the costs of and incidental to all proceedings in the High Court are in the discretion of the court.[324] While an assisted person is protected against the making of enforceable orders for payment of costs, that protection is not available to prevent an order for costs being set off.[325]

12.142   While there will rarely be claim and counterclaim in Part 6 and 7 cases,[326] the implication is that it may be possible to set off costs orders made in different judicial reviews, and perhaps even costs

---

319 *R (Boxall) v Waltham Forest LBC* (2001) 4 CCLR 258, QBD, approved in *Brawley v Marczynski & Business Lines Ltd* [2002] EWCA Civ 756; [2002] 4 All ER 1060.

320 Above, paras 12.137–12.139. .

321 *R (Scott) v Hackney LBC* [2009] EWCA Civ 217, at [51].

322 CPR 44.3(9).

323 *Lockley v National Blood Transfusion Service* [1992] 1 WLR 492, CA.

324 *R (Burkett) v Hammersmith & Fulham LBC* [2004] EWCA Civ 1342.

325 *Hill v Bailey* [2003] EWHC 2835 (Ch).

326 Whether formally so or in practice.

orders made in the county court against orders made in the High Court, if the proceedings are closely connected.

Burden of proof

12.143　As noted,[327] the burden of proof lies on a person seeking to show that a decision is void; the allegations must be both substantiated and particularised: *Wednesbury*[328] and *Cannock Chase DC v Kelly*.[329] Thus, it is never enough to say simply that the applicant is a homeless person and in priority need, because this would not be enough to raise the inference of a duty. The duty arises only when the authority is satisfied, or has reason to believe, or considers that the fact or state of affairs is as it is claimed to be. It must be alleged that it has refused or failed to reach a decision, or that such decision as has been reached must be treated by the courts as void, for want of compliance with such of the foregoing principles as are identified; the factual basis for this allegation must be set out.

Remedies and relief

Interim relief

12.144　Where a challenge is made by judicial review, the normal principle on an application for an interim injunction is that an order will be granted if it can be shown that the balance of convenience is in its favour.[330] In *de Falco, Silvestri v Crawley BC*,[331] however, Lord Denning MR said that it was necessary to show that – in a homeless person's action – there was a strong prima facie case of breach by the authority. The justification offered for this difference was that, almost invariably, the applicant would be unable to give a worthwhile undertaking in damages should s/he eventually lose, although the House of Lords had in *Cyanamid*[332] already included ability to give a meaningful undertaking in damages as a factor to be weighed up in determining the balance of convenience.

327　Above, para 12.123.

328　*Associated Provincial Picture Houses Ltd v Wednesbury Corporation* [1948] 1 KB 223, CA.

329　[1978] 1 WLR 1, CA.

330　*American Cyanamid v Ethicon* [1975] AC 396, HL; *Fellowes v Fisher* [1976] QB 122, CA.

331　*De Falco, Silvestri v Crawley BC* [1980] QB 460, CA.

332　*American Cyanamid v Ethicon* [1975] AC 396, HL.

12.145   The *de Falco* approach would also seem to conflict with Lord Denning MR's own approach in *Allen v Jambo Holdings Ltd*,[333] a case in which the owners of an aircraft sought discharge of a *Mareva* injunction on the ground that the plaintiff, who was legally-aided, could not give a valuable cross-undertaking in damages.

> It is said that whenever a *Mareva* injunction is granted the plaintiff has to give the cross-undertaking in damages. Suppose the widow should lose this case altogether. She is legally-aided. Her undertaking is worth nothing. I would not assent to that argument . . . A legally-aided plaintiff is by our statutes not to be in any worse position by reason of being legally-aided than any other plaintiff would be. I do not see why a poor plaintiff should be denied a *Mareva* injunction just because he is poor, whereas a rich plaintiff would get it . . .

12.146   In *R v Kensington and Chelsea RLBC ex p Hammell*,[334] it was contended by the authority that, following *Puhlhofer*,[335] it would be necessary to show something akin to 'exceptional circumstances' before an interim injunction could be granted. The court rejected this argument: interim relief is discretionary, although the discretion is one that must be exercised in accordance with principles of law; in a clear case of breach, there is therefore likely to be no issue of whether or not such relief should be granted. In *R v Cardiff CC ex p Barry*,[336] it was held that, as a strong prima facie case had to be made out for a court to grant leave to move for judicial review of an authority's decision, interim relief would be the usual concomitant of the grant of leave.

12.147   However, in relation to a challenge to a refusal to house pending review,[337] this approach was rejected in *R v Camden LBC ex p Mohammed*[338] (approved in *R v Brighton & Hove Council ex p Nacion*[339]) because a review is as of right, available to everyone who is the subject of an adverse decision, and so no prima facie case has to be made out.[340]

12.148   The principles on which the discretion to house pending review is to be exercised by the authority have been considered in chapter 10,

---

333   [1980] 1 WLR 1252, CA.
334   [1989] QB 518; (1988) 20 HLR 666, CA.
335   *R v Hillingdon LBC ex p Puhlhofer* [1986] AC 484; (1986) 18 HLR 158.
336   (1989) 22 HLR 261, CA.
337   Under the power in HA 1996 s188(3).
338   (1997) 30 HLR 315, QBD.
339   (1999) 31 HLR 1095, CA.
340   (1997) 30 HLR 315, at 320.

above;[341] their application to housing pending appeal[342] is considered below.[343] Whether the development of those principles will have an impact in other cases in which permission is sought to claim judicial review – on other grounds – is unclear, but there is no apparent reason why they should do so, or why *Hamell*[344] should not continue to apply.

12.149   Orders granted without notice should be for a defined and short period, though sometimes it may be appropriate to decline to make an immediate order and direct instead an oral hearing within one or two days. This would give the defendant the opportunity to mount an effective opposition to the application.[345]

Substantive hearing

12.150   The Administrative Court may:

– quash a decision (a quashing order);
– compel an authority to make a decision or a particular decision, or re-take a decision that has been quashed (a mandatory order);
– prohibit an authority from taking some action (a prohibiting order); or
– make a declaration (CPR 54.3(1)), for example, to declare a decision ultra vires, or void.

12.151   Although the Administrative Court, no more than the county court, cannot substitute its own decision for that of the authority, the findings of fact or law it makes may on occasion be such that there is only one decision that the authority can lawfully make, ie, with which it is left. In such cases, either directly or indirectly, the court will (in substance) order the authority to come to that decision.[346] Such circumstances would comprise circumstances in which the county court could use its powers to vary a decision instead of remitting the matter to the authority to reconsider.[347] It may also be that the Administrative Court would order the authority to come to a particular decision where it is necessary in order to restore a right of which the claimant has been unlawfully deprived.[348]

---

341 Above, para 10.39.
342 Under HA 1996 s204A.
343 Paras 12.197–12.200.
344 Above, para 12.146.
345 *R (Casey) v Restormel BC* [2007] EWHC 2554 (Admin); (2008) ACD 1.
346 See *Barty-King v Ministry of Defence* [1979] 2 All ER 80, ChD.
347 See paras 12.203–12.214.
348 Consider *Crawley LBC v B* (2000) 32 HLR 636, CA, at 651–652 – below, para

12.152 In an appropriate case, the Administrative Court may award damages as compensation for wrongful action or wrongful refusal to act.[349] This is not available where damages are the sole remedy claimed; the court must be satisfied that, if the claim had been made in a private law action, the claimant would have been awarded damages.

Refusal of relief

12.153 It is accepted in judicial review cases that a court may refuse relief, notwithstanding a finding of procedural error on the part of the authority, if the error would plainly have made no difference to the authority's decision.[350] This will not be so, however, if reconsideration merely *could* lead to a different decision, ie, it is not enough for the authority to assert that it could reach the same decision on reconsideration; the error must be such that it *would* have made no difference.[351]

Confidentiality

12.154 Both the High Court and the county court[352] have inherent jurisdiction to make an order granting anonymity to an applicant, and to support it with an order under the Contempt of Court Act 1981 s11 preventing publication of an applicant's name, address and photograph.[353] Such an order should be made, however, only where it can be shown that a failure to do so would render the attainment of justice doubtful or, in effect, impracticable.[354]

12.155 If no order is sought and obtained before proceeding, then:

a) no subsequent order could relate back, with the result that

b) it might become inappropriate to make an order in relation to the substantive proceedings themselves simply by reason of any publicity properly derived from preliminary proceedings.

12.207, and *Robinson v Hammersmith & Fulham LBC* [2006] EWCA Civ 1122; [2007] HLR 7, at [31], below, para 12.209.

349 CPR 54.3(2).

350 *R (Bibi) v Newham LBC* [2001] EWCA Civ 607; [2002] 1 WLR 237, at [40]: 'The court has two functions – assessing the legality of actions by administrators and, if it finds unlawfulness on the administrators' part, deciding what relief it should give.' See also *R v Secretary of State for the Environment ex p Walters; R v Brent LBC ex p O'Malley* (1997) 30 HLR 328, CA; *R v Islington LBC ex p B* (1997) 30 HLR 706, QBD.

351 See, by analogy in the context of statutory appeals under section 204.

352 *Norman v Mathews* (1916) 85 LJKB 857, *affirmed* (1916) 23 TLR 369, CA.

353 *R v Westminster CC ex p Castelli; R v Same ex p Tristran-Garcia* (1995) 27 HLR 125.

354 *In the matter of D* (1998) 1 CCLR 190, at 196K.

12.156   The proper course, therefore, is to apply to the court without notice under the Contempt of Court Act 1981 s11 at the same time as proceedings are to be issued, if appropriate asking for a hearing to be in camera. If there is power to make an order because the pre-conditions are satisfied, the court can grant it for a short time, for notice to be given to the press.[355] In some cases, it may be necessary for papers not to be lodged until the application can be dealt with immediately, so as to prevent disclosure by way of inspection of office documents.[356]

12.157   Additionally, the court has power under CPR 39.2(4) to order that the identity of any party or witness should not be disclosed if it considers non-disclosure necessary in order to protect the interests of that party or witness.

Minors

12.158   A court may also require reports not to identify parties for the purpose of protecting the interests of children indirectly involved in a case.[357]

Appeal to county court

Procedure

Point of law

12.159   An appeal to the county court lies on a point of law.[358]

12.160   'Point of law' includes 'not only matters of legal interpretation but also the full range of issues[359] which would otherwise be the subject of an application to the High Court for judicial review, such as procedural error and questions of vires, to which I add, also of irrationality and (in)adequacy of reasons'.[360]

12.161   The jurisdiction does not permit judges to reach their own decisions of fact; to do so is in excess of the statutory jurisdiction.[361]

---

355   *In the matter of D* (1998) 1 CCLR 190, at 196K.

356   *In the matter of D* (1998) 1 CCLR 190, at 196K.

357   See *Crawley BC v B* (2000) 32 HLR 636, CA, at 638. See CPR 39.2(2).

358   HA 1996 s204(1).

359   Cf, the first part of this chapter: Substantive law, paras 12.5–12.106.

360   *Nipa Begum v Tower Hamlets LBC* [2000] 1 WLR 306; (1999) 32 HLR 445, per Auld LJ at 452, approving the commentary to section 204 in *Encyclopaedia of Housing Law*. *Nipa Begum* was approved by the House of Lords in *Runa Begum v Tower Hamlets LBC* [2003] UKHL 5; [2003] 2 AC 430; [2003] HLR 32, see particularly Lord Bingham at [7].

361   *Kruja v Enfield LBC* [2004] EWCA Civ 1769; [2005] HLR 13. See also *Aw-Aden*

Where an authority considered that an applicant was not vulnerable[362] because of mental illness, it was not for the judge to conclude that he was mentally ill (and accordingly vulnerable): 'Some decision-makers might have arrived at a different conclusion. It is elementary that matters of that kind were not for the judge . . .'[363]

12.162 Yet although the absence of an appeal on issues of fact means that the internal review process does not provide an independent and impartial tribunal as required by ECHR article 6,[364] the right to a county court appeal on a point of law would nonetheless be sufficient safeguard to ensure compliance with article 6 even if article 6 were engaged.[365]

From what decision?

12.163 The point of law under challenge will usually be one made in relation to the internal review rather than the original decision, as any error on the original decision will either have been remedied or replaced on the review (with or without the same or an alternative error of law).

12.164 One exception to this is[366] if a time has been prescribed for notification of a decision on an internal review[367] and no such notification has been given (or, if notification has been given, if it does not comply with the minimum statutory requirements, ie, to give reasons and advise of the right to appeal and the time for appeal (see HA 1996 s203(4) and (5)) so that it is treated as not having been given: see HA 1996 s203(6)).

12.165 Another exception may be if the review simply ignores an original error which continues to have an effect, whether because it has been adopted or because – even if expressed differently – it influences how the court should construe the decision on review. In either event, however, the appeal must be on a point of law, whether it is in

---

v Birmingham CC [2005] EWCA Civ 1834, in which it was held that the judge had made inappropriate findings of fact.

362 And accordingly not in priority need – see chapter 5.

363 *Kruja v Enfield LBC* [2004] EWCA Civ 1769; [2005] HLR 13 at [23].

364 See further paras 12.96–12.100, above.

365 *Runa Begum v Tower Hamlets LBC* [2003] UKHL 5; [2003] 2 AC 430; [2003] HLR 32; *Tomlinson v Birmingham CC* [2010] UKSC 8. Article 6 is, however, not engaged: see paras 12.96–12.100, above and the 'Note on late developments' at the front of this book.

366 HA 1996 s204(1)(b).

367 HA 1996 s203(7).

relation to the internal review or – for want of review decision within time – in relation to the original decision.[368]

Review and reconsideration

12.166   There is no right to a review of a decision on an earlier review.[369] Not uncommonly, however, even where there has been a review, a local authority will be willing to reconsider its decision, for example, following receipt of a letter before action.[370] A complaint about the decision on such a reconsideration may still lie to the county court[371] if, but only if, the complaint can be described as still comprising an appeal from the original review decision[372] (which in turn will raise the issue of whether it is still in time).[373] In the alternative, it is possible that the decision to reconsider can in context be construed as a withdrawal of the original review decision.[374]

Time for appeal

12.167   The appeal must be brought within 21 days of the applicant being notified of the decision on the internal review, or when the applicant should have been so notified.[375] Where the court office is closed on the final day for lodging the appeal, the time is extended until the next day that the office is open.[376] Delivery of the notice of appeal is sufficient to constitute filing; there is no requirement that a court officer receive or authenticate the notice.[377]

Extension of time

12.168   The 21-day limit has been acknowledged as short, indeed 'draconian, as some might think'.[378] Prior to amendment by the Homelessness Act 2002 there was, however, no power for the court to extend time.[379]

---

368   HA 1996 s204(1).
369   HA 1996 s202(2).
370   Below, para 12.170.
371   *R v Westminster CC ex p Ellioua* (1998) 31 HLR 440, CA.
372   *Demetri v Westminster CC* [2000] 1 WLR 772, CA, at 780/A–B.
373   Below, para 12.167.
374   Below, para 12.170.
375   HA 1996 s204(2).
376   *Adan v Brent LBC* (1999) 32 HLR 848, CA.
377   *Van Aken v Camden LBC* [2002] EWCA Civ 1724; [2003] 1 WLR 684; [2003] HLR 33.
378   *R v Brent LBC ex p O'Connor* (1998) 31 HLR 923, QBD, per Tucker J at 925.
379   *Honig v Lewisham LBC* (1958) 122 JPJ 302; and *Gwynedd CC v Grunshaw* (1999) 32 HLR 610, CA. See also *O'Connor*, footnote 379, above.

By HA 1996 s204(2A), the county court now has power to extend time – before or after the 21-day period has expired – for 'good reason'. Delay in obtaining public funding to bring an appeal may well constitute an acceptable reason for extension of time.[380] Where the applicant was profoundly deaf and had been seeking legal assistance that she could understand and follow, there was a good reason for her appeal not to have been brought within the 21-day time limit.[381]

12.169 The merits of the appeal are irrelevant to deciding whether there is good reason to extend time; the merits come in at the next stage, having decided that there is a good reason, when the court has to decide whether it should exercise its discretion to extend time.[382]

Agreement to further review

12.170 Where an authority agrees to reconsider the review decision, it is possible that the agreement will in substance comprise an agreement on the part of the authority to revoke or withdraw its original decision. Alternatively, it may comprise an agreement to waive, extend or suspend the time limit for appeal from it, or to take no time point.[383] Such an agreement does, however, need to be clearly spelled out:[384] where an applicant seeking reconsideration is not represented, the authority should take it on itself to make clear the basis on which it is agreeing to reconsider and, in particular, should point out if time to appeal is not being extended.[385]

Letter before action

12.171 The provisions of CPR Part 52 do not require the applicant (or his legal advisers) to write a letter before action setting out his/her case on appeal. Prior to the introduction of the statutory appeal,[386] however – when challenges against adverse decisions were made by way

---

380 *R v Stratford on Avon DC ex p Jackson* [1985] 1 WLR 1319, CA; see also *R v Dacorum BC ex p Brown* (1989) 21 HLR 405, QBD.

381 *Barrett v Southwark LBC* [2008] EWHC 1568 (QB).

382 *Short v Birmingham CC* [2004] EWHC 2112 (QB); [2005] HLR 6.

383 *Demetri v Westminster CC* [2000] 1 WLR 772, CA, at 780/C–D and 781/E–G. An agreement to conduct a further review could constitute a good reason for the applicant being unable to bring the appeal in time, and would be likely to do so if public funding was not available until after its outcome.

384 *Demetri.*

385 *Demetri*, at 781/H–782/A.

386 And prior to the introduction of the requirement for a pre-action protocol letter in judicial review cases.

of judicial review – a letter before claim should have been written.[387] Given the introduction of a requirement for a pre-action letter in judicial review proceedings,[388] and the fact that the question of costs is a matter for the discretion of the court,[389] the same principles will apply (in the absence of special circumstances rendering such a letter impossible, or impracticable or pointless).

Costs

12.172   The general rule that costs should follow the event applies even where the matter is remitted to the authority for a fresh decision. It is not appropriate for the county court judge to refuse costs on the basis that it is considered inevitable that the authority will reach the same adverse decision (and that it will be upheld on review and appeal); it is inappropriate for the judge to reach any conclusion on that issue.[390]

12.173   The court has power to order that costs be set off.[391] The implication of this – discussed above – is that it may be possible to set off costs orders made in the county court against orders made in the High Court, if the proceedings are closely connected,[392] as well as costs against in other county court proceedings.

12.174   In *Maloba*,[393] the county court ordered the authority to pay two-thirds of the appellant's costs in relation to a section 204 appeal and refused the authority's application for a stay of enforcement pending the outcome of any future appeal against its fresh review decision, in which it hoped to be successful and therefore to secure a costs award in its favour, to be set off against those awarded against it in the present case.[394] The Court of Appeal accepted that the court's discretion was wide enough in principle to enable it to grant such a stay if it considers it just to do so, but refused to overturn the judge's decision.[395] It was cautious about introducing a general practice which would have the effect of depriving solicitors who acted for successful

---

387   *R v Horsham DC ex p Wenman* [1995] 1 WLR 680; *R v Secretary of State for the Home Department ex p Begum* [1995] COD 177.

388   Above, para 12.118.

389   See Senior Courts Act 1981 s51 and CPR 44.3.

390   *Rikha Begum v Tower Hamlets LBC* [2005] EWCA Civ 340; [2005] HLR 34.

391   CPR 44.3(9).

392   Above, paras 12.141–12.142.

393   *Waltham Forest LBC v Maloba* [2007] EWCA Civ 1281; [2008] HLR 26.

394   *Maloba* at [65].

395   *Maloba* at [71].

Legal Services Commission funded clients of being paid at normal commercial rates without being able to assess properly the potential wider consequences that this would have.[396]

12.175   It may be observed that it is hard to see that such an anticipatory order could ever be successful unless there was a history of unsuccessful challenges, in which the instant success was a rare or only occurrence. Even so, it would necessarily assume that the same solicitors would be acting, for those who had been successful should surely not properly be deprived of their success-based costs in the event that other solicitors pursued an unsuccessful case.

Wasted costs

12.176   In *Wilson*, a first-instance decision that non-legal officers of an authority could be ordered personally to pay costs, in substance for causing unnecessary legal expenditure by failing to respond to litigation, was overturned and held to have been wrongly made.[397] Lawyers, however, are susceptible to such orders ('wasted costs orders') under Senior Courts Act 1981 s51[398] and CPR 48.7.

12.177   It is appropriate to make a wasted costs order against a legal representative only if:

a) the legal representative acted improperly, unreasonably or negligently;[399]

b) the legal representative's conduct caused a party to incur unnecessary costs; and

c) it is just in all the circumstances to order him/her to compensate that party for the whole or part of the costs.[400]

12.178   The test is a moderately high one. Improper conduct is that which would attract a sanction from a professional body or which would fairly be stigmatised as being improper; unreasonable conduct is that which is vexatious or is designed to harass the other side rather than to advance a resolution of the case or which does not have a reasonable

---

396 *Maloba* at [73].

397 *R v Lambeth LBC ex p Wilson* (1997) 30 HLR 64, CA.

398 Inserted by Courts and Legal Services Act 1990 s4.

399 *KOO Golden East Mongolia v Bank of Nova Scotia* [2008] EWHC 1120 (QB), per Silber J; *Hallam Peel & Co v The London Borough of Southwark* [2008] EWCA Civ 1120.

400 The test derives from *Re A Barrister (wasted costs order) (No 1 of 1991)* [1992] 3 All ER 429, CA, and is now incorporated into the Practice Direction accompanying CPR Part 48 (at para 53.5).

explanation;[401] negligent conduct is not that which would found a common law action for damages,[402] but a question as to whether the legal representative conducted him/herself with the competence to be expected of a professional person.[403]

12.179   The rising tendency to seek an order for wasted costs was curtailed by the Court of Appeal in *Ridehalgh v Horsefield*,[404] where it was said that the courts should be anxious to avoid satellite litigation. Reinforcing the point, the House of Lords has held[405] that wasted costs orders should be confined to questions which are apt for summary disposal by the courts:[406]

> Save in the clearest case, applications against the lawyers acting for an opposing party are unlikely to be apt for summary determination, since any hearing to investigate the conduct of a complex action is itself likely to be expensive and time-consuming. The desirability of compensating litigating parties who have been put to unnecessary expense by the unjustified conduct of their opponents' lawyers is, without doubt, an important public interest, but it is, as the Court of Appeal pointed out in *Ridehalgh v Horsefield* . . . only one of the public interests which have to be considered.[407]

12.180   As a general rule, only matters such as failure to appear, conduct which leads to an otherwise avoidable step in the proceedings or the prolongation of a hearing by gross repetition or extreme slowness in the presentation of evidence or argument, wasting court time and abuse of process which results in excessive cost are apt for wasted costs.[408]

---

401 '[The] courts can be trusted to differentiate between errors of judgment and true negligence': *Arthur JS Hall & Co (a firm) v Simons* [2002] 1 AC 615, HL.

402 This is not negligence in any technical sense, see *Re Sternberg, Reed, Taylor and Gill* (1999) *Times* 26 July and *Dempsey v Johnstone* [2003] EWCA Civ 1134; [2003] All ER (D) 515.

403 See *Ridehalgh v Horsefield* [1994] Ch 2045, CA.

404 [1994] Ch 206, CA; see also *Re A Barrister (Wasted Costs Order)* [1993] QB 293, CA. See *Arthur JS Hall & Co v Simons* [2002] 1 AC 615 and *R v Camden LBC ex p Martin* [1997] 1 WLR 359, QBD, where it was held that there was no power to make a wasted costs order in favour of a person who elects to oppose an ex parte application for permission to seek judicial review.

405 *Medcalf v Mardell* [2002] UKHL 27, [2003] 1 AC 120.

406 See *Wall v Lefever* [1998] 1 FCR 605, CA, where wasted costs orders were said to provide a 'salutary and summary remedy' in clear cases. See also *R v Luton Family Proceedings Court Justices ex p R* [1998] 1 FCR 605.

407 *Medcalf v Mardell* [2002] UKHL 27; [2003] 1 AC 120, per Lord Bingham at [24].

408 *Medcalf*, approving *Harley v McDonald* [2001] 2 AC 678, PC.

12.181   Costs that arise as a consequence of difficulties with public funding are unlikely to lead to an order for wasted costs. Where a solicitor sought an adjournment on the day before the hearing because of difficulties with his client's funding, his failure was an error of judgment, not an act which attracted liability for wasted costs.[409]

12.182   Where a court refuses to make a wasted costs order, it will only be in very rare circumstances that an appeal court will intervene.[410]

Supporting documents

12.183   The appeal will need to be brought in accordance with CPR Part 52 and the associated Practice Direction. Three copies of the appellant's notice must be filed,[411] together with a copy of the skeleton argument,[412] the decision that is being appealed,[413] any witness statements, and bundles of any other relevant documents.[414] The grounds of appeal should be stated in the notice. Grounds not contained in the notice cannot be relied on at the hearing without the court's permission.[415]

12.184   Notwithstanding the discretion to amend the notice of appeal, the Court of Appeal has emphasised the importance of the grounds in setting the agenda for the appeal hearing and in enabling the respondent (and the court) to understand that agenda from the outset. Brooke LJ concluded that:

> It is thoroughly bad practice to state the barest possible grounds in the original notice of appeal . . ., and then to delay formulating and serving very substantial amended grounds of appeal for five months so that they surfaced for the first time less than a week before the appeal hearing.[416]

409 *Re a Solicitor (wasted costs order)* [1993] 2 FLR 959, CA.
410 *Persaud v Persaud* [2003] EWCA Civ 394; [2003] All ER (D) 80.
411 See form N161.
412 If this is impracticable, it may be filed within 14 days of filing the notice: CPR Part 52 PD 5.9.
413 Made under HA 1996 s203(4), see chapter 9.
414 Bundles must be prepared in accordance with CPR Part 52 PD 5.6, and should be limited to 'the documents which the appellant reasonably considers necessary to enable the appeal court to reach its decision on the hearing' (para 5.6A(1)(c)). See *Cramp v Hastings BC; Phillips v Camden LBC* [2005] EWCA Civ 1005; [2005] HLR 48: they should not generally include the whole of the housing file but only so much of it as is necessary for the court to reach its decision on the issues raised in the appeal.
415 CPR 52.11(5).
416 *Cramp v Hastings BC; Phillips v Camden LBC* [2005] EWCA Civ 1005; [2005] HLR 48, at [72].

Response

12.185 While a respondent's notice may be filed where a respondent seeks to uphold a decision for reasons different from, or additional to, those previously given,[417] this is unlikely to be appropriate in a homelessness appeal. If the review (or, on occasion, the original) decision is wrong, then the authority should consent to it being quashed, and proceed to make a fresh decision on the correct basis. The only obvious circumstance when the authority could ask the court to substitute one (wrong) decision with a fresh decision is if the fresh decision is the only decision open to the authority as a matter of law.[418] Where the respondent authority proposes to address arguments to the court, it must serve a respondent's skeleton argument no later than 21 days after it has been served with the appellant's skeleton argument.[419]

12.186 While an authority may well need to concede one or more elements of a challenge before the appeal comes to a hearing, the authority may not withdraw its decision so as to pre-empt the appeal if its continuance could lead to an enduring benefit to the applicant. Thus, in *Deugi*,[420] the applicant not only sought to quash the original decision but also sought a variation of it; its withdrawal would have deprived the applicant of the opportunity to seek the variation.

District judges

12.187 Once it was appreciated that the CPR permitted district judges to hear Part 52 appeals,[421] a new practice direction was introduced to prevent them doing so.[422]

Further appeal

12.188 Under the Access to Justice Act 1999 (Destination of Appeals) Order 2000,[423] the appropriate forum for appeal from a county court section 204 appeal is to the Court of Appeal. The basis for this requirement is that the section 204 appeal is itself an 'appeal' (from the decision of the authority), and so an appeal against the county court judge is a second appeal, to be determined by the Court of Appeal.

---

417 CPR 52.5.
418 Below, para 12.203–12.214.
419 CPR Part 52 PD 7.6 and 7.7.
420 *Tower Hamlets LBC v Deugi* [2006] EWCA Civ 159; [2006] HLR 28.
421 See the comments of Sir Richard Scott V-C in *Crawley BC v B* (2000) 32 HLR 636, CA.
422 CPR Part 2, PD 2B.9.
423 SI No 1071.

12.189   A consequence of the 'second appeal' status is that permission cannot be granted by the county court; it must be obtained from the Court of Appeal.[424] An application for permission to appeal must be made in accordance with CPR Part 52. Permission must be requested in an appellant's notice, which must be served within such period as directed by the lower court,[425] or – if no such direction is made – within 21 days of the decision being appealed.[426] Witness statements in support of an application for permission to appeal are only appropriate for relevant and admissible evidence (if any) going to the issue before the court and nothing else: submissions in support of the appeal are for advocates to make in skeleton arguments.[427]

12.190   Where a county court has ordered a further review and the authority seeks permission to appeal, the parties should agree that the obligation to undertake a fresh review be suspended pending outcome of the appeal. If agreement is not reached, an authority may apply to the Court of Appeal to stay the effect of the quashing order made by the county court. In the event that an authority does undertake a fresh review pending the appeal, however, it is verging on an abuse for the authority not to inform the Court of Appeal that it has done so.[428]

12.191   Permission to bring a second appeal will be granted only if the court is satisfied that:

a) the appeal raises an important point of principle or practice;[429] or
b) there is some other compelling reason for the appeal to be heard.[430]

12.192   Where an appeal raises an important point of principle which has not previously been determined, permission will normally be granted under CPR 52.13(2)(a).[431] When determining whether there is some other compelling reason to grant permission under CPR 52.13(b), the court should apply the following principles:

a) the prospects of success on appeal must be very high;
b) even where the prospects of success are very high, the court may

---

424 CPR 52.13(1).
425 Which may be longer or shorter than the period of 21 days required under the CPR: CPR 52.4(2)(a).
426 CPR 52.4.
427 *William v Wandsworth LBC; Bellamy v Hounslow LBC* [2006] EWCA Civ 535; [2006] HLR 42.
428 *William*, footnote 428, above.
429 CPR 52.13(2)(a).
430 CPR 52.13(2)(b).
431 *Uphill v BRB (Residuary) Ltd* [2005] EWCA Civ 60; [2005] 1 WLR 2070.

nonetheless conclude that justice does not require the appellant to have the opportunity of a second appeal; but, conversely,

c) if the prospects of success are not very high, there may nevertheless be a compelling reason for a second appeal if the court is satisfied that the first appeal was tainted by procedural irregularity such as to render it unfair.[432]

12.193　In the context of a homelessness appeal, permission was refused in *Azimi*,[433] where the decision of the county court was reached primarily on the facts. By contrast, in *Cramp*,[434] the Court of Appeal gave permission to appeal against a decision that an authority's enquiries had been inadequate because the appeal raised an important point of practice. Brooke LJ said:[435]

> In view of the amount of public money that is in issue in cases like this, it would in my judgment be quite wrong for this court to feel that the judgment in *Uphill*[436] represented a fetter on its power to put things right if it has occasion to believe that things are going wrong in an important way in the practical operation of the statutory scheme in Part 7 of the 1996 Act (up to and including the appeal on a point of law to the county court).

12.194　In *Elrify*,[437] it was pointed out that the second appeal is really only the first appeal from a judicial decision because the appeal to the county court is not in respect of a judicial decision but from the authority's review decision; this does not serve to disapply CPR 52.13 but does mean that the court can take a somewhat more relaxed approach to a second appeal in a homelessness case that has clear merits.[438]

12.195　On an appeal to the Court of Appeal, the primary question is normally not whether the county court judge deciding the first appeal was right, but whether the decision being appealed is right, or at least one that the decision-maker was entitled to reach.[439]

432　*Upill*, footnote 432, above.
433　*Azimi v Newham LBC* (2000) 33 HLR 51. See also *Ryde v Enfield LBC* [2005] EWCA Civ 1281 (no important point of principle or practice) and *Gentle v Wandsworth LBC* [2005] EWCA Civ 1377 (no obvious injustice).
434　*Cramp v Hastings BC; Phillips v Camden LBC* [2005] EWCA Civ 1005; [2005] HLR 48.
435　At [66].
436　Above, para 12.192.
437　*Elrify v Westminster CC* [2007] EWCA Civ 332; [2007] HLR 36.
438　*Elrify*, at [24].
439　*Danesh v Kensington and Chelsea RLBC* [2006] EWCA Civ 1404; [2007] HLR 17 at [30].

Remedies and relief

Interim relief

12.196   Authorities have power under HA 1996 s204(4) to house pending any appeal (and any subsequent appeal). Interim relief will not be needed on a county court appeal if the authority agrees to use this power.

12.197   Prior to amendment by the Homelessness Act 2002, if an authority refused to exercise this power, the county court could not grant an interim injunction because the applicant had no substantive rights to which an interim injunction could properly be said to be ancillary.[440] Under section 204A, however, an applicant with a right to appeal to the county court against a local authority's decision on review[441] may also appeal to the county court if the authority refuses to exercise its power to secure interim accommodation under section 204(4) or is only willing to do so for a limited period ending before the final determination of the main appeal.[442]

12.198   This right to appeal under section 204A may be exercised even before the applicant has appealed under section 204, provided the latter appeal is again the authority's decision on review: this excludes the possibility of a section 204A appeal where the applicant only has a right to appeal against the section 184 decision because the authority has not notified the review decision in time.[443] In those circumstances, judicial review is still the correct remedy.

12.199   However, as a matter of good practice, an applicant should include appeals under section 204 and section 204A in one appellant's notice[444] although, if this is not possible, the appeals may be included in separate appellant's notices.[445] An appeal under section 204A may[446] include an application for an order under section 204A(4)(a) requiring the authority to secure that accommodation is available for the applicant's occupation.[447] If the court makes such an order without notice, the appellant's notice must be served on the authority together with the order. Such an order will normally require the authority to secure that accommodation is available until a hearing

---

440   *Ali v Westminster CC* (1998) 31 HLR 349, CA.
441   HA 1996 s204A(1).
442   HA 1996 s204A(2).
443   HA 1006 s204(1)(b).
444   CPR Part 52 PD para 24.2(1).
445   CPR Part 52 PD para 24.2(2).
446   And usually will.
447   CPR Part 52 PD para 24.2(3).

date when the authority can make representations as to whether the order should be continued.[448]

12.200　The primary power given to the county court[449] is to order the authority to secure accommodation for the applicant pending determination of the appeal or such earlier time that the court may specify. The court is bound either to quash the authority's section 204(4) decision on accommodation pending appeal, or to confirm it.[450] If the county court decides to quash, it may order the authority to exercise the power for such period as may be specified in the order, up to but not beyond the determination of the main appeal.[451] The power may be exercised only if the court is satisfied that failure to exercise the section 204(4) power would substantially prejudice the applicant's ability to pursue the main appeal.

12.201　The Contempt of Court Act 1981 s2(2) uses a similar, although not identical, phrase of 'substantial risk that the course of justice will be seriously prejudiced'. In this context it has been held that:

> . . . 'substantial' as a qualification of 'risk' does not have the meaning 'weighty' but rather means 'not insubstantial' or 'not minimal'.[452]

12.202　In deciding whether to confirm or quash, the court must apply judicial review principles.[453] In effect, this means applying the approach to decisions to provide interim accommodation in *R v Camden LBC ex p Mohammed*,[454] and described above,[455] and so the court can order the provision of accommodation only if the authority has failed to direct itself in accordance with it: *Francis*.[456]

448　CPR Part 52 PD para 24.2(4).

449　HA 1996 s204A(4)(a).

450　HA 1996 s204A(4)(b).

451　HA 1996 s204A(5) and (6)(b).

452　Per Donaldson MR in *Attorney-General v New Group Newspapers Ltd* [1987] QB 1, CA.

453　HA 1996 s204A(4).

454　(1997) 30 HLR 315, QBD, as approved in *R v Brighton & Hove Council ex p Nacion* (1999) 31 HLR 1095, CA in relation to challenges under section 204 prior to the addition of section 204A (see para 12.147).

455　Above, para 10.39. When considering an application for interim accommodation pending an appeal against an authority's review decision, an authority must take into account the grounds of appeal: *Lewis v Havering LBC* [2006] EWCA Civ 1793; [2007] HLR 20.

456　*Francis v Kensington & Chelsea RLBC* [2003] EWCA Civ 443; [2003] HLR 50.

Powers on appeal

12.203 Under its appeal powers, the county court can confirm a decision, or quash it, and it can also vary the decision as it thinks fit.[457]

12.204 The power to vary gives the county court a somewhat wider range of powers than a court on judicial review.[458] This does not, however, empower the court to extend its scope beyond the 'point of law' (within the meaning given to that phrase that has already been considered).[459] It follows that the power can usually only be used to quash a decision, remitting the matter back to the authority for re-determination, unless – the point of law having been determined – there is only one decision which the authority could lawfully take.[460]

12.205 It may, however, be argued that – while the appeal is confined to a point of law – once the applicant has been successful on the appeal, the power to vary allows the court to substitute its own decision for that of the authority (even where matters of judgment or evaluation of facts are inherent). It is not a complete answer to this to say that, since the appeal itself has been on a point of law, there will not be the evidential material before the court on which to do so, because:

a) that will not be true in all cases (and would therefore merely limit the occasions when the power could be used); and

b) it is, in any event, a chicken-and-egg point, for if the court has the wider powers, then material can still be put before it even if only directed or relevant to the exercise of its powers.

12.206 Although this argument is consistent with Parliament having conferred wider powers on the county court than are available on judicial review,[461] it would nonetheless not seem to be available in most cases.[462] The 'decision' which the authority must take, and which the court has jurisdiction to vary, is a decision under HA 1996 s202(1), as

---

457 HA 1996 s204(3). Whether the court can refuse to grant relief when the appeal has been overtaken by events and is accordingly pointless is still open. Compare the obiter comments of Sedley LJ (the court can only refuse to grant relief where the appeal is an abuse of process) with those of Waller LJ (if the appeal is pointless the court ought to be able to make no order) in *O'Connor v Kensington & Chelsea RLBC* [2004] EWCA Civ 394; [2004] HLR 37.

458 As noted in *Begum v Tower Hamlets LBC* [2000] 1 WLR 306, at 313 F: see further para 12.160, above.

459 See paras 12.159–12.160, above.

460 Above, para 12.151.

461 Sedley LJ in *Begum* agreed with Auld LJ as to the ambit of the powers (see para 12.204, above): 'The jurisdiction of the county court is *at least* as wide as that of a court of judicial review' (at 327/B–C, emphasis added).

462 See further below, para 12.210.

to eligibility, suitability or local connection or – most relevantly here – 'as to what duty (if any) is owed' to the applicant, under the principal sections.

12.207   Thus, in *Crawley LBC v B*,[463] it was held that, once the existing decision had been quashed because of an error of law (admitted by the authority), the authority had to reconsider, which required it to make enquiries and reach a further decision. This will, of course, require the authority to establish (properly) whether or not it has reason to believe, or is of the opinion, or is satisfied as to a particular state of affairs. It is only once the relevant precondition (state of mind of the authority) exists, that the decision about duty can be taken:[464]

> The question, therefore, is whether the judge was entitled, or required, on the material before him, to do more than simply quash the decision . . . I would accept that, if that material had shown that the only decision as to its duty to provide accommodation or assistance that the Council, acting rationally, could reach was that the duty was that imposed by section 193(2) of the Act, the judge could properly have pre-empted further consideration by making an order to that effect . . .[465]

12.208 There is, however, an exception to this, where the power to vary may be used to substitute a decision in the applicant's favour, without remission back to the authority, in order to reinstate a benefit of which the applicant should not have been deprived:

> I would accept, also, that there could be circumstances in which a judge might properly take the view that an applicant ought not to be deprived, by events which had occurred between the date of the original decision and the date of the appeal, of some benefit or advantage to which he would have been entitled if the original decision had been taken in accordance with the law . . .[466]

---

463 *Crawley LBC v B* (2000) 32 HLR 636, CA.

464 'The decision that the authority has to make is . . . as to the category into which its duty falls under the 1996 Act. Although subject to the discipline of sections 202 and 204, that remains a decision based on the satisfaction of the authority as to the issues (which are issues of fact and judgment) of priority need and intentionality. As is well-established, a conclusion as to a public body's satisfaction can only be challenged on public law grounds . . . The application of the jurisprudence of public law to the process of decision-making in homelessness cases does not, therefore, necessarily lead to the conclusion that a decision, once taken, cannot be revisited.' (*Crawley LBC v B* (2000) 32 HLR 636, CA, per Buxton LJ at 645).

465 *Crawley LBC v B* (2000) 32 HLR 636, CA, per Chadwick LJ at 651.

466 *Crawley LBC v B* (2000) 32 HLR 636, CA, at 651–652.

12.209 This passage was adopted in *Robinson v Hammersmith & Fulham LBC*[467] in support of the proposition – in relation to a decision on a review – that:

> If the original decision was unlawful . . . the review decision maker should have so held and made a decision that would have restored to the appellant the rights she would have had if the decision had been lawful.

12.210 It would therefore seem that the power to vary does import an alternative to quashing a decision – and its remission to the authority – *either*:

a) where the variation relates to, reflects or rectifies the error of law itself, for example, where the decision can be identified in light of the authority's factual findings and/or evaluation, so that remission to the authority is unnecessary;[468] *or*

b) where it restores rights of which the applicant has been deprived.

12.211 Thus, in *Ekwuru*,[469] the authority could not, on the material before it, lawfully conclude that the applicant was intentionally homeless. The applicant had twice successfully appealed against the decision of the local authority, upheld on review, that he was intentionally homeless and on each occasion the decision had been quashed and remitted to the authority. Following the second appeal, the authority found him intentionally homeless and for a third time upheld this decision on review. On appeal, the county court judge again quashed the decision and remitted it. The applicant appealed against the failure of the judge to vary the decision. The Court of Appeal concluded that on the material before the authority at the date of the third review decision, it could not lawfully have concluded that the applicant was intentionally homeless. Accordingly, nothing could be gained by remitting the application for further investigation because there was no real prospect that the authority would discover further material which permitted it properly to conclude that the applicant was intentionally homeless. However, the circumstances of the case were described as 'exceptional'.[470]

---

467 [2006] EWCA Civ 1122, at [31].

468 Ie, where the only rational conclusion that the authority could reach is that proposed by the applicant: *Slater v Lewisham LBC* [2006] EWCA Civ 394.

469 *Ekwuru v Westminster CC* [2003] EWCA Civ 1293; [2004] HLR 14.

470 Per Schiemann LJ at [31].

12.212   In *Deugi*,[471] the authority's decision on eligibility and priority need was at issue on appeal, but the judge, having quashed the authority's decision, varied it to include a finding that the applicant was not intentionally homeless:

> The question for the judge was whether there was any real prospect that Tower Hamlets, acting rationally and with the benefit of further enquiry, might have been satisfied that Mrs Deugi was intentionally homeless.[472]

12.213   Only if there had been no such prospect could the judge could properly have varied the decision. On the facts of the case, however, there remained a possibility that further enquiries could yet have led to a finding of intentional homelessness, for which reason the decision could only be quashed.

12.214   In *Robinson*,[473] the initial decision ought to have been that the applicant was in priority need (because she was 17),[474] but she had turned 18 by the time of the review. On a strict application of *Mohamed*,[475] the review decision would therefore have concluded that the applicant was – regardless of the correctness of the first decision – not in priority need. The Court of Appeal in *Robinson* rejected this:

> I am not persuaded that the above passages[476] have any application to a situation such as the present. It was not in issue in *Mohamed* whether an unlawful decision by the original decision maker had denied rights to the person affected by the decision to which he would otherwise have been entitled.[477]

Damages

12.215   Damages can only be awarded in the county court in respect of a claim within its jurisdiction arising in contract or tort. An award of compensation is not one of the powers conferred on the county court in relation to a section 204 appeal.

---

471   *Tower Hamlets LBC v Deugi* [2006] EWCA Civ 159; [2006] HLR 28.
472   Per May LJ at [36]. This formulation was said (at [37]) 'to be seen as an amalgam of Chadwick LJ [in *Crawley v B*] and Schiemann LJ [in *Ekwuru*], [and] is intended to reflect the fact that this appeal process is in the nature of judicial review'.
473   [2006] EWCA Civ 1122.
474   Above, para 5.66.
475   *Mohamed v Hammersmith & Fulham LBC* [2001] UKHL 57; [2002] 1 AC 547 – above, paras 9.176–9.180.
476   From *Mohamed*.
477   At [31].

12.216 Notwithstanding some differences of opinion over the years,[478] no action will lie for breach of statutory duty for failure properly to perform duties under HA 1996 Part 7,[479] absent some separate cause of action, for example, negligence,[480] or indeed contract.[481]

Confidentiality

12.217 As noted above,[482] the court has inherent jurisdiction to make an order granting anonymity to an applicant. The same principles as discussed above in relation to judicial review proceedings are applicable here.[483]

Ancillary relief

12.218 Ancillary relief in the county court is available only where final relief is available.[484] It follows that if the authority has failed to carry out the review but the only basis for complaining about the original decision is on the facts, ie, if there is still no appeal to the county court on a point of law, then – notwithstanding the provisions of HA 1996 s204(1)[485] – the county court cannot make a mandatory order to require the authority to carry out the review.[486]

Refusal of relief

12.219 As in the Administrative Court on a claim for judicial review, a county court judge on a homelessness appeal may refuse relief on the basis that, notwithstanding a procedural error on the part of the authority, the error would have made no difference to the authority's decision. Where a court identifies procedural flaws in an authority's decision-making process, that decision may, however, only be upheld where the court is satisfied that a properly-directed authority

---

478 *Thornton v Kirklees MBC* [1979] QB 626, CA; *Cocks v Thanet DC* [1983] AC 286; 6 HLR 15, HL; *Mohram Ali v Tower Hamlets LBC* [1993] QB 407; (1992) 24 HLR 474, CA; *Tower Hamlets LBC v Abdi* (1992) 25 HLR 80, CA; *R v Lambeth LBC ex p Barnes* (1992) 25 HLR 140, QBD; *Hackney LBC v Lambourne* (1992) 25 HLR 172, CA; *R v Northavon DC ex p Palmer* (1995) 27 HLR 576, CA.

479 *O'Rourke v Camden LBC* [1998] AC 188, HL; *R (Morris) v Newham LBC* [2002] EWHC 1262 (Admin).

480 See further *Ephraim v Newham LBC* (1992) 25 HLR 207, CA.

481 For example, in respect of the conditions in accommodation occupied under contract (tenancy or licence), under which the authority is the landlord.

482 Above, para 12.154.

483 Above, paras 12.154–12.157.

484 County Courts Act 1984 s38.

485 Above, para 12.159.

486 Above, para 12.204.

would *inevitably* have reached the same decision. The test of inevitability is a strict test; regardless of how slight, if the possibility exists that a proper assessment of the circumstances might produce a different decision, the authority must conduct and consider such an assessment.[487]

Ombudsman

12.220   One further forum for challenge which may be mentioned[488] is the Local Government Ombudsman,[489] who may investigate claims of maladministration against local authorities, where the claimant can show that s/he has sustained injustice in consequence of the maladministration.[490]

12.221   Maladministration is not defined. In *Eastleigh BC*,[491] Lord Donaldson stated that:[492]

> . . . administration and maladministration in the context of the work of a local authority is concerned with the *manner* in which decisions by the authority are reached and the *manner* in which they are or are not implemented. Administration has nothing to do with the nature, quality or reasonableness of the decision itself.

12.222   The powers of the ombudsman in England were extended by the Local Government and Housing Act 1989[493] and by the Local Government and Public Involvement in Health Act 2007.[494] The latter extends jurisdiction in England from maladministration to include alleged or apparent maladministration in connection with the authority's administrative functions, alleged or apparent failure in a service which the authority has the function to provide, and alleged or apparent failure to provide such a service.[495]

---

487   *Ali v Newham LBC* [2002] HLR 20, CA.
488   For reasons of space, it is not practicable to describe the procedure here.
489   Local Government Act 1974, Part 3. In England this is called the Commission for Local Administration in England or the 'Ombudsman'.
490   Local Government Act 1974 s26.
491   *R v Local Commissioner for the South etc ex p Eastleigh BC* [1988] 1 QB 855, CA.
492   *Eastleigh BC* at 863E/F, as a summary of the decision in *R v Local Commissioner for Administration for the North etc ex p Bradford MBC* [1979] QB 287, CA. Emphasis in original.
493   Local Government Act 1972 Part 2, substituted by the Local Government and Housing Act 1989.
494   Part 9.
495   Local Government Act 1972 s26(1), substituted by Local Government and

12.223   The ombudsman can recommend that compensation be paid to a complainant. Where maladministration is found this will usually be ordered, and compensation has commonly been recommended in homelessness cases.

12.224   Complaint to the ombudsman may be particularly appropriate where there are delays in making decisions and inadequacies in decision letters. Even where the applicant is eventually adequately housed, it may be worth while proceeding with the complaint in order to obtain compensation.

12.225   Complaints must generally be made within 12 months of the maladministration complained of, although there is discretion to take complaints outside that period, if the ombudsman considers it reasonable so to do.[496]

12.226   In Wales, the Public Services Ombudsman for Wales has responsibility not only for local administration but also for the health service in Wales, social housing in Wales and for the functions of the former Welsh Administration Ombudsman. S/he therefore has power to investigate maladministration and service failure by the Welsh Assembly, Welsh health service, health service providers in Wales, local authorities in Wales and Welsh registered providers of social housing.[497] S/he has power to investigate[498] complaints by or on behalf of a person who claims to have suffered injustice or hardship[499] arising from maladministration by an authority in connection with a relevant action,[500] failure in a relevant service[501] provided by an authority and failure by an authority to provide a relevant service.[502] The Public Services Ombudsman for Wales also has power, subject to consultation, to issue guidance to local authorities about good administrative practice.[503]

Public Involvement in Health Act 2007 s173(2) with effect from 1 April 2008, by virtue of the Local Government and Public Involvement in Health Act 2007 (Commencement No 5 and Transitional, Saving and Transitory Provision) Order 2008 SI No 917 reg 2(1)(i).

496 Local Government Act 1974 s26(4).

497 Public Services Ombudsman (Wales) Act 2005 Sch 3.

498 Public Services Ombudsman (Wales) Act 2005 ss8 and 10.

499 Public Services Ombudsman (Wales) Act 2005 s4.

500 Public Services Ombudsman (Wales) Act 2005 s7(3).

501 Public Services Ombudsman (Wales) Act 2005 s7(4).

502 Public Services Ombudsman (Wales) Act 2005 s7.

503 Public Services Ombudsman (Wales) Act 2005 s31.

Specimen documents

12.227   The following are examples of the forms[504] and pleadings used in both judicial review proceedings, based on an allocation decision, and an appeal against a homelessness decision in the county court. The following specimens are included:

a) judicial review claim form;
b) judicial review statement of grounds and facts relied on;
c) judicial review acknowledgement of service;
d) judicial review summary grounds for contesting the claim;
e) county court appellant's notice;
f) county court grounds of appeal.

504 The forms in this section are all © Crown Copyright.

Judicial Review
Claim Form

For Court use only	
Administrative Court Reference No.	
Date filed	

In the High Court of Justice
Administrative Court

Seal

SECTION 1 Details of the claimant(s) and defendant(s)

Claimant(s) name and address(es)

name

JANE FIELDS

address

16A Maxwell Square
Warden
WAR16 1AB

Telephone no. 012557 932831   **Fax no.** n/a

E-mail address jane.fields@coldmale.co.uk

Claimant's or claimant's solicitors' address to which documents should be sent.

name

Leo & Nevil

address

2404 Nashville Road
Warden
WAR7 8QB

Telephone no. 012557 168932   **Fax no.** 012557 168933

E-mail address housing@leoandnevil.co.uk

Claimant's Counsel's details

name

John Clowns

address

Warden Drane Chambers
Warden Drane
Warden
WAR1 1AA

Telephone no. 012557 204204   **Fax no.** 012557 676767

E-mail address john.clowns@wardenchambers.com

1st Defendant

name

WARDEN DRANE DISTRICT COUNCIL

Defendant's or (where known) Defendant's solicitors' address to which documents should be sent.

name

Warden Drane DC – Legal Services

address

Civic Centre
Warden High Road
Warden
WAR1 9SX

Telephone no. 012557 132000   **Fax no.** 012557 132001

E-mail address legal@warden.gov.uk

2nd Defendant

name

Defendant's or (where known) Defendant's solicitors' address to which documents should be sent.

name

address

Telephone no.   **Fax no.**

E-mail address

SECTION 2 Details of other interested parties

Include name and address and, if appropriate, details of DX, telephone or fax numbers and e-mail

name

address

Telephone no.   Fax no.

E-mail address

name

address

Telephone no.   Fax no.

E-mail address

SECTION 3 Details of the decision to be judicially reviewed

Decision:

Failure by the respondent authority to operate a lawful allocations scheme and properly to afford the claimant appropriate preference within their allocation scheme.

Date of decision:

September 30, 2009 and continuing

Name and address of the court, tribunal, person or body who made the decision to be reviewed.

name

Housing Department Warden Drane DC

address

Civic Centre
Warden High Road
Warden
WAR1 9SX

SECTION 4 Permission to proceed with a claim for judicial review

I am seeking permission to proceed with my claim for Judicial Review.

Is this application being made under the terms of Section 18 Practice Direction 54 (Challenging removal)? ☐ Yes ☑ No

Are you making any other applications? If Yes, complete Section 7. ☐ Yes ☑ No

Is the claimant in receipt of a Community Legal Service Fund (CLSF) certificate? ☑ Yes ☐ No

Are you claiming exceptional urgency, or do you need this application determined within a certain time scale? If Yes, complete Form N463 and file this with your application. ☐ Yes ☑ No

Have you complied with the pre-action protocol? If No, give reasons for non-compliance in the box below. ☑ Yes ☐ No

Have you issued this claim in the region with which you have the closest connection? (Give any additional reasons for wanting it to be dealt with in this region in the box below). If No, give reasons in the box below. ☑ Yes ☐ No

Does the claim include any issues arising from the Human Rights Act 1998?
If Yes, state the articles which you contend have been breached in the box below.   ☐ Yes   ☑ No

SECTION 5 Detailed statement of grounds

☐ set out below   ☑ attached

SECTION 6 Details of remedy (including any interim remedy) being sought

1) A quashing order to quash the defendant's allocation scheme.

2) Further or alternatively, a declaration that the defendant's allocations scheme is unlawful in that it is incapable of affording the statutory preferences required by s. 167(2), Housing Act 1996.

3) Further or other relief.

4) Costs.

SECTION 7 Other applications

I wish to make an application for:-

SECTION 8 Statement of facts relied on

See attached statement of facts and grounds.

Statement of Truth

I believe (The claimant believes) that the facts stated in this claim form are true.

Full name_____

Name of claimant's solicitor's firm _____

Signed_____ Position or office held_____
　　　　Claimant ('s solicitor)　　　　　　　　　　　　　　(if signing on behalf of firm or company)

SECTION 9 Supporting documents

If you do not have a document that you intend to use to support your claim, identify it, give the date when you expect it to be available and give reasons why it is not currently available in the box below.

Please tick the papers you are filing with this claim form and any you will be filing later.

☑ Statement of grounds	☐ included	☑ attached
☑ Statement of the facts relied on	☐ included	☑ attached
☐ Application to extend the time limit for filing the claim form	☐ included	☐ attached
☐ Application for directions	☐ included	☐ attached

☑ Any written evidence in support of the claim or application to extend time

☐ Where the claim for judicial review relates to a decision of a court or tribunal, an approved copy of the reasons for reaching that decision

☑ Copies of any documents on which the claimant proposes to rely

☑ A copy of the legal aid or CSLF certificate *(if legally represented)*

☑ Copies of any relevant statutory material

☑ A list of essential documents for advance reading by the court *(with page references to the passages relied upon)*

If Section 18 Practice Direction 54 applies, please tick the relevant box(es) below to indicate which papers you are filing with this claim form:

☐ a copy of the removal directions and the decision to which the application relates	☐ included	☐ attached
☐ a copy of the documents served with the removal directions including any documents which contains the Immigration and Nationality Directorate's factual summary of the case	☐ included	☐ attached
☐ a detailed statement of the grounds	☐ included	☐ attached

Reasons why you have not supplied a document and date when you expect it to be available:-

Those documents not included herewith will follow within 14 days, once a full public funding certificate is in place.

Signed _____ Claimant ('s Solicitor)_____

IN THE HIGH COURT OF JUSTICE Claim No.
QUEEN'S BENCH DIVISION
ADMINISTRATIVE COURT

BETWEEN

THE QUEEN
(on the application of
JANE FIELDS) Claimant

–and–

WARDEN DRANE
DISTRICT COUNCIL Defendant

STATEMENT OF FACTS AND GROUNDS

STATEMENT OF FACTS

Introductory

1. The claimant is a 33 year old woman with 3 children – Sally (aged 15), Margaret (aged 14) and Peter (aged 11). Peter is quadriplegic and is confined to a wheel-chair. Sally suffers from severe attention-deficit and hyperactivity disorder. The claimant is unable to work as she is the sole carer of Peter.

2. On July 14, 2008, she applied to the defendant authority for accommodation under Pt 6, Housing Act 1996, and was duly registered on the authority's housing register.

Background

3. The claimant has resided in the authority's area since childhood. Until January 2008, she and her children lived in a house in the area.

4. In January 2008, the claimant left accommodation that she shared with her former partner, due to domestic violence. The claimant secured her current accommodation, which is a one-bedroom flat, occupied under a private-sector tenancy. The flat is located on the second-floor. There is no lift.

5. She applied to the authority as homeless under Pt 7, 1996 Act. The authority found that – although she was eligible for assistance and in priority need – the claimant was not homeless as she had accommodation that was available for her occupation and that is was reasonable for her to continue to occupy it. That decision was upheld on review and the claimant did not appeal.

6. The claimant applied to be registered on the authority's housing register. She provided medical evidence as to her children's medical needs and information on the overcrowded nature of her current accommodation, in particular that:

   (a) there are two teenage girls, a disabled boy and the claimant living in a one-bedroom flat, the girls share the only bedroom and the claimant and her son sleep in the living room;

   (b the bedroom is 8 foot x 8 foot – there is room for two single beds but no other furniture;

   (c) Sally's severe ADHD causes her to act impulsively and without regard to the consequences of her actions, this can have dangerous consequences in a confined space and places the other members of the household at risk; and,

   (d) the claimant has severe difficulties in taking Peter out of the flat as she has to carry him down two flights of stairs and return for his wheel-chair – although she is currently able to carry Peter, it is unlikely that she will be able to do so as he grows and develops.

7. In September 2008, the authority assessed the medical needs of Peter and Sally and visited the flat to assess its size and determine whether it was overcrowded. As a result of those assessments (and expert evidence obtained by the claimant), the authority found that both children had medical needs and that the family had a need for accommodation with an additional bedroom.

8. The current position is that the claimant is registered on the authority's housing register, awaiting an allocation of two-bedroom accommodation, in accordance with Pt 6, 1996 Act.

The authority's allocation scheme

9. The authority's allocation scheme operates, principally – but not exclusively – by means of 'choice-based lettings'. In broad terms, this means that applicants are given points to reflect their priority according to criteria set out under the scheme, and are informed of the types of property for which they are eligible. They may then bid for any properties of the appropriate type which are advertised as available to let. The bidding applicant with the highest number of points is then offered the property. It is estimated by the authority themselves that an applicant requires a minimum of 250 points before there is any realistic possibility that he will be able successfully to bid for accommodation.

10. In summary, the principal material provisions of the scheme are as follows.

11. Part 1 of the Scheme governs applications under Part 6 of the Housing Act 1996. The scheme provides that all applications are to be assessed using a points system.

12. Paragraphs 1.3 and 1.4 of the scheme make provision for various categories of applicant (those owed a duty as homeless under Pt 7, Housing Act 1996; young people leaving care; people moving to larger accommodation to foster or adopt a child; people with learning disabilities; applicants who

have successfully completed rehabilitation from drug or alcohol dependency) to be afforded 300 points, thereby essentially obtaining an overriding priority for accommodation.

Points for overcrowding

13. Where an applicant claims to reside in overcrowded accommodation, the application is referred to a panel which assesses the accommodation. The panel has power to award a maximum of 12 points. Those points are awarded on the basis of a space assessment; the scheme assumes that a room which is 60 square feet can accommodate two persons of any age and no account is taken of the sex of the occupants or their relationship to one another.

14. On the basis of the space assessment, the panel calculate the number of bedrooms required and may award an applicant three points for each extra bedroom required.

Medical and Welfare points

15. The scheme allows 10 points to be awarded on medical or welfare grounds. Paragraph. 2.4 provides:

> 'The panel may award a set 10 points on medical or welfare grounds. In calculating the amount of points (if any) to award, the panel shall have regard to any medical reports supplied but ultimately shall use their absolute discretion to award a household points on this basis.'

General points

16. All applicants are entitled to 'time points' awarded at the rate of 10 points for every year spent on the waiting list for accommodation.

17. Additionally, all applicants may receive 100 income points if they are 'unable (on financial grounds) to meet their own housing needs'.

18. Local connection points, at the rate of 50, are awarded to those applicants who live in the Borough and have done so by choice for two years.

19. The authority retains an absolute discretion to award up to 75 additional points, if it considers the circumstances justify doing so. Provision is also made for the award of other points, including for existing tenants of the authority who apply for a transfer to smaller accommodation.

The claimant's points

20. The claimant has been awarded the following points:

> 100 income points
> 50 residence points
> 10 time points
> 10 medical and welfare points
> 3 overcrowding points

21. The overcrowding panel calculated the claimant's entitlement to points on the basis that the household requires only one additional bedroom as the house comprises only four persons.

22. In assessing the need for medical and welfare points, the panel had regard to medical reports submitted in relation to both Peter and Sally. The panel accepted that both children had medical and welfare needs that were not being met in their current accommodation. On the basis of that conclusion they awarded the set 10 points.

23. The claimant has bid for a number of properties under the choice-based scheme, but 173 points has been insufficient for her bid to be successful.

Pre-claim correspondence

24. The claimant has been in correspondence with the authority since September 2008, seeking to negotiate the award of additional points. The claimant has sought to obtain three additional overcrowding points, on the basis that her household requires a three bedroom property. She has also sought to obtain additional medical and welfare points on the basis that two of her children have (accepted) medical and welfare needs, such that she should be entitled to a further 10 points on that basis.

25. The claimant has also asked the authority to exercise its residual discretion to award 50 further points on the grounds that her household's need for alternative accommodation is severe.

26. The authority has refused those requests. In letters dated December 12, 2008, February 14, 2009, and May 16, 2009, the authority has consistently stated that the claimant is not entitled to further points and has refused to exercise the residual discretion.

27. The only suggestions offered by the letters were that the claimant take up a council scheme to obtain a private sector tenancy or else move to another area where accommodation is in greater supply.

28. On June 20, 2009, the claimant's legal representatives sent the authority a pre-action protocol letter before action, which asserted (a) that the authority's allocation scheme was unlawful, alternatively (b) that the way in which the allocation scheme had been applied to the claimant was unlawful. The authority was invited to withdraw its scheme or to award the claimant sufficient points

STATEMENT OF GROUNDS

Allocations Law

29. The claimant and her children remain in the flat, awaiting an allocation of accommodation under Part 6. By 1996 Act, section 167(1) and (8), the authority may only lawfully allocate such accommodation in accordance with the provisions of its allocation scheme.

30. Those subsections provide that every local housing authority shall have an allocation scheme for determining priorities, and as to the procedure to be followed, in allocating housing accommodation (s167(1)) and that the authority may not allocate accommodation except in accordance with that scheme (s167(8)).

31. As a person who resides in overcrowded and unsatisfactory housing conditions and as a person who needs to move house on medical or welfare grounds, the claimant is entitled to a reasonable preference in the allocation of Part 6 accommodation. Section 167(2) and (2A) provide that such preference must be afforded to certain priority groups, in the following terms.

> '(2) As regards priorities, the scheme shall be framed so as to secure that reasonable preference is given to –
>
> . . .
>
> (c) people occupying unsanitary or overcrowded housing or otherwise living in unsatisfactory housing conditions;
> (d) people who need to move on medical or welfare grounds (including grounds relating to a disability); and
> . . .'.

The scheme may also be framed so as to give additional preference to particular descriptions of people within this subsection (being descriptions of people with urgent housing needs).'

32. Although the courts should be slow to interfere with the allocation policy of a local authority (*R (Ahmad) v Newham LBC* [2009] UKHL 14; [2009] HLR 31), where an allocation scheme is clearly irrational, even on a relatively narrow aspect, it should be struck down. The purpose of an allocation scheme should be justified properly and authorities should not rely on 'bald statements': *Birmingham CC v Ali; Moran v Manchester CC (Secretary of State for Communities and Local Government and another intervening)* [2009] UKHL 36; [2009] HLR 41.

GROUND ONE Error of law – no reasonable preference

33. The effect of the scheme is not to confer any reasonable preference at all on the claimant; unless and until the claimant has resided in the authority's area for two years, she has and will have no preference at all in practical terms.

34. The claimant has been awarded 10 points on medical grounds and a further 3 on the grounds of overcrowding. Those additional points give her no increased priority in practice; although the claimant and her family could remain in their current accommodation, when she is evicted or has to leave because she can no longer physically manage with her disabled son on the second floor, she will be entitled to apply as homeless and receive an additional 300 points.

35. The claimant and her family have no chance whatsoever of bidding successfully for a property unless or until they become homeless. Thus the claimant is in an even worse position than if she were to be evicted from her accommodation, as she would then receive 300 points as a homeless person.

36. In the context of the scheme, the award of a maximum 12 overcrowding points and 10 medical points is *de minimis* and has no effect on priority whatsoever, unless the applicant has a preference in another category.

37. The absence of any real preference can be seen by analysis of the points awarded to the claimant. Aside from the 10 medical points and the 3 over-crowding points, she has received 100 income points, 10 time points, 50 residence point (the maximum available).

38. Residency points are available to anyone who has resided in the author-ity's area for 2 years, regardless of whether or not that person is entitled to any statutory preference. Likewise, the income points are available to anyone, it seems, whose income is low. Waiting points are available to everyone.

39. Thus the only points which are related to the claimant's statutory right to a reasonable preference are the 13 points received for overcrowding and medical need. The claimant's 173 points have reached the maximum available to her, save for the possibility of 10 points a year for the next four years, giving her a maximum of 223. She will not be able to increase her points total at all, unless her circumstances change and she falls within another category of need.

40. The claimant's points total is at least 75 points short of any possibility of successfully bidding for a property under Part 6. The only option that the authority has been able to suggest is that, with three children, one of whom is disabled, she could move out of the area where she has lived since childhood.

41. To describe a scheme which operates in this way as securing a reasonable preference to persons who have a medical need or a need based on over-crowding (section 167(2)(c) and (d)), is a misuse of language.

GROUND TWO Error of law – frustrating the purpose of the 1996 Act

42. The provision of a maximum of 23 points to families with medical needs in overcrowded accommodation does not amount to the securing of a reasonable or any preference, and is contrary to – and frustrates – the scheme of Pt 6, 1996 Act.

43. It is plain from the scheme itself, from the correspondence referred to above, and indeed from the manner in which the scheme is operated, that the scheme is designed to keep families in overcrowded accommodation or with medical needs from being eligible for accommodation for as long as possible before permitting them sufficient points to have any prospect at all of bidding successfully for a tenancy under Part 6.

44. This is demonstrated by the following matters:
    (a) the availability of only 10 points on medical grounds;
    (b) the availability of only 12 points on the grounds of overcrowding, regardless of how overcrowded the property is;
    (c) the availability of 300 points where an alternative statutory preference category (homelessness) exists.

45. This is unlawful and conflicts with and frustrates the purposes of the 1996 Act, in particular the statutory intention concerning the statutory preference to be afforded to those with medical need or those in over-crowded accommodation.

GROUND THREE Irrationality – discretion

46. The scheme purports to confer 'additional preference' on persons who, in the absolute discretion of the defendant, have circumstances that give them 'urgent housing needs'. The only provision under the scheme for the award of additional points (other than waiting time) is the defendant's residual discretion to award up to 75 points. This is not a rational means by which to assess need, nor is it a rational means by which a person in the position of the claimant could ever achieve an additional preference, having regard to the maximum points available under the 'additional preference discretion'.

GROUND FOUR Policy applied unlawfully

47. In the alternative, if the policy is not unlawful, the application of the policy to the claimant's circumstances has been unlawful.

Failure to exercise the residual discretion

48. It is unlawful to fail to give any proper priority to the claimant's claim, not least because to do so requires her to remain in statutorily overcrowded accommodation that is fundamentally unsuitable to the medical needs of her household.

49. In the claimant's case, there were compelling factors which ought to have led to an exercise of discretion in her favour: namely the matters set out at paragraph 6, above.

Failure properly to assess the issue of overcrowding

50. The claimant has been awarded only 3 points on the grounds of overcrowding, on the basis that her household only requires one additional bedroom (*i.e.* two bedrooms in total). If that conclusion is correct, the claimant would be required to share a bedroom with her disabled son, while her two daughters – one of whom has a medical need – would also be required to share a room.

51. In concluding that two-bedroom accommodation would suffice for the claimant's household, the authority has acted irrationally and contrary to the medical evidence that was before it when making its decision on overcrowding.

GROUND FIVE Perversity

52. Further, or alternatively, the defendant's policy, and the treatment which the defendant has given to the claimant's application are both unreasonable in the *Wednesbury* sense.

John Clowns
Warden Drane Chambers, Warden Drane

Judicial Review **Acknowledgment of Service**	**In the High Court of Justice** **Administrative Court**	
	Claim No.	
Name and address of person to be served ┌name────── WARDEN DRANE DC ┌address────── Civic Centre Warden High Road Warden WAR1 96X	**Claimant(s)** *(including ref.)*	JANE FIELDS (LH/H/fields/01533)
	Defendant(s)	WARDEN DRANE DC (LE/HSG/FIELDS/86915)
	Interested **Parties**	

SECTION A
Tick the appropriate box

1. I intend to contest all of the claim ☒ ⎫
2. I intend to contest part of the claim ☐ ⎬ complete sections B, C, D and E
                                                     ⎭

3. I do not intend to contest the claim ☐ complete section E

4. The defendant (interested party) is a court or tribunal and **intends** to make a submission. ☐ complete sections B, C and E

5. The defendant (interested party) is a court or tribunal and **does not intend** to make a submission. ☐ complete sections B and E

Note: If the application seeks to judicially review the decision of a court or tribunal, the court or tribunal need only provide the Administrative Court with as much evidence as it can about the decision to help the Administrative Court perform its judicial function.

SECTION B
Insert the name and address of any person you consider should be added as an interested party.

┌name──────	┌name──────
┌address──────	┌address──────
┌Telephone no.────── ┌Fax no.──────	┌Telephone no.────── ┌Fax no.──────
┌E-mail address──────	┌E-mail address──────

SECTION C

Summary of grounds for contesting the claim. If you are contesting only part of the claim, set out which part before you give your grounds for contesting it. If you are a court or tribunal filing a submission, please indicate that this is the case.

Please see attached statement of grounds.

SECTION D

Give details of any directions you will be asking the court to make, or tick the box to indicate that a separate application notice is attached.

None.

If you are seeking a direction that this matter be heard at an Administrative Court venue other than that at which this claim was issued, you should complete, lodge and serve on all other parties Form N464 with this acknowledgment of service.

SECTION E

delete as appropriate	*(I believe)(The defendant believes) that the facts stated in this form are true. *I am duly authorised by the defendant to sign this statement.	(if signing on behalf of firm or company, court or tribunal)	Position or office held
(To be signed by you or by your solicitor or litigation friend)	Signed		Date

Give an address to which notices about this case can be sent to you

If you have instructed counsel, please give their name address and contact details below.

name	name
Legal Services	Claire Ronethun

address	address
Warden Drane DC Civic Centre Warden High Road Warden WAR1 96X	Smith Chambers 96 Smith Lane London ECR1 9SS

Telephone no	Fax no	Telephone no.	Fax no.
012557 132000	012557 132001	020 7999 8118	020 7999 8119

E-mail address	E-mail address
legal@warden.gov.uk	clairer@smithchambers.law.co.uk

Completed forms, together with a copy, should be lodged with the Administrative Court Office (court address, over the page), at which this claim was issued within 21 days of service of the claim upon you, and further copies should be served on the Claimant(s), any other Defendant(s) and any interested parties within 7 days of lodgement with the Court.

Administrative Court addresses

- Administrative Court in **London**

    Administrative Court Office, Room C315, Royal Courts of Justice, Strand, London, WC2A 2LL.

- Administrative Court in **Birmingham**

    Administrative Court Office, Birmingham Civil Justice Centre, Priory Courts, 33 Bull Street, Birmingham B4 6DS.

- Administrative Court in **Wales**

    Administrative Court Office, Cardiff Civil Justice Centre, 2 Park Street, Cardiff, CF10 1ET.

- Administrative Court in **Leeds**

    Administrative Court Office, Leeds Combined Court Centre, 1 Oxford Row, Leeds, LS1 3BG.

- Administrative Court in **Manchester**

    Administrative Court Office, Manchester Civil Justice Centre, 1 Bridge Street West, Manchester, M3 3FX.

IN THE HIGH COURT OF JUSTICE   Claim No.
QUEEN'S BENCH DIVISION
ADMINISTRATIVE COURT

BETWEEN

THE QUEEN
(on the application of
JANE FIELDS)   Claimant

–and–

WARDEN DRANE
DISTRICT COUNCIL   Defendant

SUMMARY GROUNDS FOR
CONTESTING THE CLAIM

Lawfulness of the allocations policy

1. The defendant's allocation policy is lawful and cannot successfully be challenged for the following reasons.

Error of law – reasonable preference

2. The scheme complies with the requirements of Pt 6, Housing Act 1996. A reasonable preference is afforded in accordance with section 167(2) and (2A) as all of the priority groups are afforded points that would not be available to persons who did not qualify under those categories.

3. It cannot be said that the preference awarded on overcrowding or medical grounds is not a reasonable preference. When affording a reasonable preference the requirement is that persons entitled to such a preference must be given a 'head start' over other applicants (*R (A) v Lambeth LBC* [2002] EWCA Civ 1084; [2002] HLR 57). The scheme achieves this by providing additional points for need arising on medical or overcrowding grounds.

4. In designing the allocations scheme the authority has determined – as it is entitled to do – that priority on those grounds should be given less (but still reasonable) preference when compared with other categories of need such as the homeless. The extent of the reasonable preference is a matter for the authority to determine and can be challenged only on *Wednesbury* grounds.

Error of law – frustration of the purpose of the 1996 Act

5. An additional preference is given to, *inter alia*, the homeless. That is permissible under the terms of the statute (s167) and accords with the

purpose of the interrelationship between Pts 6 and 7 of the Act. The authority cannot be criticised for deciding to award additional preference to the homeless over those in other priority groups.

6. It is absurd to suggest that the scheme is designed to keep families in overcrowded accommodation or with medical needs from being eligible for accommodation for as long as possible. Families falling within those groups are awarded additional points, thereby enhancing their possibility of successfully bidding for accommodation under the choice-based lettings scheme.

Irrationality – discretion

7. It is not irrational to have a residual discretion (*R v Islington LBC, ex p Reilly and Mannix* (1998) 31 HLR 651, QBD see also *R (Ahmad) v Newham LBC* [2009] UKHL 14; [2009] HLR 31), such a discretion is necessary to ensure that the scheme operates efficiently and can be adapted to unforeseen or individual circumstances.

Unlawful application of the policy

8. The authority's failure to exercise the residual discretion can only be challenged on *Wednesbury* grounds. It is for local authorities to determine the allocation of accommodation and they are afforded a wide margin of appreciation when doing so and when applying the scheme. It is not possible for the claimant to demonstrate that the decision not to exercise the residual discretion is so unreasonable as to be perverse.

9. Further, the issue of overcrowding has been considered in accordance with the scheme and the authority's policy for assessing overcrowding. There is no challenge to that policy and the claim under this head must fail. On the claimant's own case, the authority had regard to the medical evidence submitted and it is a matter for the authority – applying its policies – to determine the weight to be given to that medical evidence.

Challenge futile

10. In any event, the defendant is currently in the process of updating its scheme in accordance with its modernisation agenda and its commitment to continuous improvements in its services. It is envisaged that the new allocations scheme will be in place some time during 2010. The defendant cannot move any more quickly to replace its existing policy than this, whatever rulings the court may make on this application.

11. The claimant should wait for the adoption of the new policy and challenge that within 3 months of its adoption if she believes that she has grounds for so doing.

12. For those reasons, it is submitted that the claimant is not entitled to the relief claimed, or to any relief.

Claire Ronethun
Smith Chambers, London

Appellant's notice
(All appeals except small claims track appeals)

For Court use only	
Appeal Court Ref. No.	
Date filed	

Notes for guidance are available which will help you complete this form. Please read them carefully before you complete each section.

SEAL

Section 1   Details of the claim or case you are appealing against

Claim or Case no.   WXN1234

Name(s) of the   ☐ Claimant(s)   ☒ Applicant(s)   ☐ Petitioner(s)

JANE FIELDS

Name(s) of the   ☐ Defendant(s)   ☒ Respondent(s)

WARDEN DRANE DISTRICT COUNCIL

Details of the party appealing ('The Appellant')

Name

JANE FIELDS

Address (including postcode)

16A Maxwell Square	Tel No.	012557 932831
Warden	Fax	n/a
WAR16 6AB	E-mail	jane.fields@coldmale.co.uk

Details of the Respondent to the appeal

Name

WARDEN DRANE DISTRICT COUNCIL

Address (including postcode)

Housing Department Civic Centre Warden High Road Warden WAR1 96X	Tel No.	012557 132000
	Fax	012557 132001
	E-mail	housing@warden.gov.uk

Details of additional parties (if any) are attached   ☐Yes   ☒No

N161 Appellant's notice (July 2006)

Section 2 Details of the appeal

From which court is the appeal being brought?

☐ The County Court at

☐ High Court District Registry at

☐ The Royal Courts of Justice

☒ Other (please specify)

Decision of Warden Drane DC Housing Department

What is the name of the Judge whose decision you want to appeal?

n/a

What is the status of the Judge whose decision you want to appeal?

☐ District Judge or Deputy   ☐ Circuit Judge or Recorder

☐ Master or Deputy   ☐ High Court Judge or Deputy

What is the date of the decision you wish to appeal?

July 28, 2009

To which track, if any, was the claim or case allocated?

☐ Fast track

☐ Multi track

☒ Not allocated to a track

Nature of the decision you wish to appeal

☐ Case management decision   ☐ Grant or refusal of interim relief

☒ Final decision   ☐ A previous appeal decision

Section 3   Legal representation

Are you legally represented?   ☒Yes   ☐No
If 'Yes', please give details of your
solicitor below

Your solicitor's name

Leo & Nevil

Your solicitor's address (including postcode)

24204 Nashville Road Warden WAR7 8QB	Tel No.	012557 168932
	Fax	012557 168933
	E-mail	housing@leoandnevil.co.uk
	DX	896432 WARDEN 2
	Ref.	LN/h/fields/01532

Are you, the Appellant, in receipt of a Legal Aid Certificate
or a Community Legal Service Fund (CLSF) certificate?   ☒Yes   ☐No

Is the respondent legally represented?   ☒Yes   ☐No
If 'Yes', please give details of the
respondent's solicitor below

The respondent's solicitor's address (including postcode)

Legal Services Warden Drane DC Civic Centre Warden High Road Warden WAR1 96X	Tel No.	012557 132000
	Fax	012557 132001
	E-mail	legal@warden.gov.uk
	DX	162 WARDEN 1
	Ref.	LE/HSG/FIELDS/86914

Section 4   Permission to appeal

Do you need permission to appeal?   ☐Yes   ☒No

Has permission to appeal been granted ?

☐**Yes**   ☐**No**

Date of order granting permission	
Name of Judge granting permission	

I

the Appellant('s solicitor) seek permission to
appeal.

Section 5   Other information required for the appeal

Please set out the order (or part of the order) you wish to appeal

Decision of the respondent authority, dated July 28, 2009, that the appellant is homeless intentionally. A copy of the decision letter of that date is attached.

Does your appeal include any issues arising from the Human Rights Act 1998?   ☐Yes   ☒No

Are you asking for a stay of execution of any judgment against you?   ☐Yes   ☒No

If **'Yes'** you must complete **Part A of Section 8**

Have you lodged this notice with the court within 21 days of the date on which the Judge made the decision you wish to appeal?   ☒Yes   ☐No

If **'No'** you must complete **Part B of Section 8**

Are you making any other applications?   ☐Yes   ☒No

If **'Yes'** you must complete **Part C of Section 8**

Section 6   Grounds for appeal and arguments in support

Please state, in numbered paragraphs, **on a separate sheet** attached to this notice and entitled 'Grounds of Appeal' (also in the top right hand corner add your claim or case number and full name), why you are saying that the Judge who made the order you are appealing was wrong.

☒ The arguments (known as a 'Skeleton Argument') in support of the 'Grounds of Appeal will follow within 14 days of filing this Appellant's Notice

OR

☐ The arguments (known as a 'Skeleton Argument') in support of the 'Grounds of Appeal' are set out **on a separate sheet** and attached to this notice.

Section 7   What are you asking the Appeal Court to do?

I am asking the appeal court to:-
(please tick the appropriate box)

☐ set aside the order which I am appealing

☒ vary the order which I am appealing and substitute the following order. Set out in the following space the order you are asking for:-

> The court is asked to allow the appeal and vary the decision dated July 28, 2009, to record that the appellant is not intentionally homeless and that accordingly the respondent authority is under a full housing duty pursuant to s193, Housing Act 1996.
> Alternatively, the court is requested to quash the decision and remit it back to the authority for redetermination.

☐ order a new trial

Section 8   Other applications

Complete this section **only** if you are asking for orders **in addition** to the order asked for in Section 7.

Part A
I apply for a stay of execution because:

Part B

☐ I do not need an extension of time for filing my appeal notice because it has been filed within the extended time granted by the Judge whose decision I am appealing.

OR

☐ I apply for an extension of time for filing my appeal notice because (set out the reasons for the delay. You must also set out in Section 9 what steps you have taken since the decision you are appealing).

Part C
I apply for an order that:

because

Section 9   Evidence in support

In support of my application(s) in Section 8, I wish to rely upon the following evidence:

1.   Appellant's Witness Statement;

2.   Witness Statement of Becky Dodgson;

3.   Respondent's Housing Department files relating to the application including evidence submitted by the Appellant as to her reporting incidents of domestic violence to her doctor and to the police, and evidence as to the effect of her husband's violence on her daughter; and,

4.   Correspondence, including letters notifying decisions and in the conduct of a review, between the Respondent and the Appellant and/or her solicitors.

Statement of Truth

I believe (The appellant believes) that the facts stated in this section are true.

Full name	

Name of appellant's solicitor's firm	

signed		position or office held	
Appellant ('s solicitor)		(if signing on behalf of firm or company)	

Section 10   Supporting documents

To support your appeal you should file with this notice all relevant documents listed below. To show which documents you are filing, please tick the appropriate boxes.

If you do not have a document that you intend to use to support your appeal complete the box over the page.

☒ two additional copies of your appellant's notice for the appeal court;

☒ one copy of your appellant's notice for each of the respondents;

☐ one copy of your skeleton argument for each copy of the appellant's notice that is filed;

☐ a sealed *(stamped by the court)* copy of the order being appealed;

☒ a copy of any order giving or refusing permission to appeal, together with a copy of the Judge's reasons for allowing or refusing permission to appeal;

☒ any witness statements or affidavits in support of any application included in the appellant's notice;

☐ a copy of the order allocating the case to a track *(if any)*; and

☒ a copy of the legal aid or CLSF certificate *(if legally represented)*.

A bundle of documents for the appeal hearing containing copies of all the papers listed below:-

☐ a sealed copy *(stamped by the court)* of your appellant's notice;

☐ a sealed copy *(stamped by the court)* of the order being appealed;

☐ a copy of any order giving or refusing permission to appeal, together with a copy of the judge's reasons for allowing or refusing permission to appeal;

☐ any affidavit or witness statement filed in support of any application included in the appellant's notice;

☐ a copy of the skeleton argument;

☐ a transcript or note of judgment, and in cases where permission to appeal was given by the lower court or is not required those parts of any transcript of evidence which are directly relevant to any question at issue on the appeal;

☐ the claim form and statements of case (where relevant to the subject of the appeal);

☐ any application notice (or case management documentation) relevant to the subject of the appeal;

☐ in cases where the decision appealed was itself made on appeal (eg from district judge to circuit judge), the first order, the reasons given and the appellant's notice used to appeal from that order;

☐ in the case of judicial review or a statutory appeal, the original decision which was the subject of the application to the lower court;

☐ in cases where the appeal is from a Tribunal, a copy of the Tribunal's reasons for the decision, a copy of the decision reviewed by the Tribunal and the reasons for the original decision and any document filed with the Tribunal setting out the grounds of appeal from that decision;

☐ any other documents which are necessary to enable the appeal court to reach a decision; and

☐ such other documents as the court may direct.

Reasons why you have not supplied a document and date when you expect it to be available:-

Title of document and reason not supplied	Date when it will be supplied
Skeleton argument – due to limits on public funding, it has not been possible within the statutory timeframe to prepare a skeleton argument. Fully argued grounds have, however, been prepared.	Within 14 days
Witness statement – there has not been sufficient time, within the statutory timeframe, to obtain a witness statement from the appellant.	Within 14 days

Signed [   ] Appellant('s Solicitor)

IN THE WARDEN COUNTY COURT   Claim No. WXN1234
QUEEN'S BENCH DIVISION
ADMINISTRATIVE COURT

BETWEEN

JANE FIELDS   Appellant

–and–

WARDEN DRANE
DISTRICT COUNCIL   Respondent

GROUNDS OF APPEAL

This is an appeal under the Housing Act 1996 s204, against the decision of the authority's reviewing officer (under HA 1996 s202) to uphold the decision that the appellant had made herself homeless intentionally homeless from 1 Warden Lane, Warden, WD9 9ZX. A person is intentionally homeless if he deliberately does or fails to do anything in consequence of which he ceases to occupy settled accommodation which is available for his occupation and which it would have been reasonable for him to continue to occupy: HA 1996 s191(1).

GROUND ONE: The authority misdirected itself in law in finding that it would be reasonable for the appellant to continue to occupy the matrimonial home because she could exclude her husband

1.1 A person is homeless if he has no accommodation which he has a legal entitlement to occupy (s175(1)), but shall not be treated as having accommodation unless it is accommodation which it would be reasonable for him to continue to occupy: s175(3). Section 177(1) provides that a it is not reasonable for a person to continue to occupy accommodation if it is probable that such occupation will lead to domestic or other violence or threats of violence against him or a person who might reasonably be expected to reside with him.

1.2 The only question that an authority should ask when determining whether accommodation is suitable on the grounds of violence or threats of violence is whether it is probable that continued occupation of the accommodation will lead to violence or threats of violence against the applicant; it is irrelevant whether the applicant has or could have availed him/herself of any alternative remedies to address the domestic violence: *Bond v Leicester CC* [2001] EWCA Civ 1544; [2002] HLR 6 (see paras 6.18 onwards of the Homelessness Code of Guidance).

1.3 In its review decision letter the authority states that it would be reasonable for the Appellant to continue to occupy the matrimonial home because:

'*There are steps which Ms Fields may take to ask the court to oust her husband, John Jones, from their jointly owned property. It does not make sense to consider the first option in such cases to be rehousing by a local authority when a home-owner has suitable accommodation which they may use the process of law to secure and to protect them in residence there yet chooses not to do so.*'

1.4 In so finding, the authority misdirected itself in law by concluding that it was reasonable for the Appellant to continue to occupy the matrimonial home because the Appellant should have considered obtaining and/or obtained an injunction excluding her husband from the matrimonial home.

GROUND TWO: The authority gave inadequate reasons for finding that it was not probable that occupation of the marital home by the Appellant would lead to violence or threats of violence from her husband

2.1 Where on review under section 202 of the Housing Act 1996, a local authority confirms an earlier decision, it is required to give reasons for doing so: s.203(4), and see *R v Croydon LBC, ex p Graham* (1993) 26 HLR 286, CA, and *R v Brent LBC ex p Bariise* (1998) 31 HLR 50, CA.

2.2 In its decision letter, the authority disputes whether the Appellant would be at risk of violence from her husband were she to return to live at the matrimonial home:

That she says she is in fear – and for the sake of argument I am willing to accept that she is – does not mean that it is likely or probable that violence or threats of violence will be carried out. Just because Ms Field fears it does not make it so . . . Whilst I do not dispute Ms Field's version of past events, i.e. that violence occurred in the past, it does not mean that it is probable that domestic violence, other violence or threats of violence are likely to be carried out against her, or those who normally reside with her.

2.3 No reasons are given for not accepting the Appellant's belief that she would be subjected to violence or for disregarding the evidence submitted on her behalf and, accordingly, the authority has failed to provide any or any adequate reasoning for its decision.

GROUND THREE: the authority failed to make sufficient enquiries

3.1 The obligation on a reviewing officer is to have regard to all matters as they appear to him at the date of the review: *Sahardid v Camden LBC* [2004] EWCA Civ 1485; [2005] HLR 11. The officer is also under an obligation to make sufficient enquiries into all matters relevant to an application, including the risk of domestic violence (*Patterson v Greenwich LBC* (1993) 26 HLR 159, CA).

3.2 On September 9, 2008, representations were made on behalf of the appellant. Those representations detailed the appellant's history of violence from her husband and her concerns about the likely repetition of that violence since her husband was released from prison. The Appellant – and her then advisers – provided the authority with details of persons who could support her application and her account, including details of a next-door neighbour, Becky Dodgson, who was aware of the domestic violence suffered by the Appellant.

3.3 Once the issue of the husband's release from prison had been drawn to the authority's attention, it was obliged to make reasonable inquiries into the appellant's concern that there was a probability of threats of violence towards her. In failing to do so, the authority acted in breach of its duties under Part 7.

3.4 In circumstances where the authority was minded not to believe that the Appellant was at risk of domestic violence, it was incumbent on it to make enquiries of the neighbour in order to determine whether the Appellant's assertions could be corroborated. In failing to do so, the authority erred in law by failing to make sufficient enquiries into the Appellant's application.

GROUND FOUR: The authority failed to put adverse findings to the Appellant

4.1 In conducting its inquiries, the authority must put basic issues to the applicant that may be decided against him to enable him to comment on them (*R v Tower Hamlets LBC ex p Rouf* (1989) 21 HLR 294, QBD); the applicant must have an opportunity to deal with the generality of material which will adversely affect him: *R v Gravesham BC ex p Winchester* (1986) 18 HLR 208, QBD.

4.2 The authority found that it was not probable that the Appellant and her daughter were not at risk of violence or threats of violence if they returned to the property; in so finding they dismissed the evidence put forward by the Appellant as to her belief and the evidence put forward in support of the Appellant. That finding was a finding that was central to the authority's decision. The authority failed, however, to put that finding to the Appellant and in so doing breached the principles of natural justice and/ or acted unfairly towards the Appellant by failing to put adverse findings to her and allow her an opportunity to comment on them.

GROUND FIVE: Failure to have regard to relevant considerations

5.1 In the representations put to the authority on behalf of the appellant, the authority was informed that the appellant's husband had been released from prison and had been seen in the vicinity of 1 Warden Lane and had been associating with the appellant's neighbours.

5.2 The authority's decision letter is silent on this point or its effect. In failing to consider the effect which this would have on the appellant's application, the authority failed to have regard to a relevant consideration.

GROUND SIX: Error of fact

6.1 The authority made a number of findings when reaching its decision that the appellant did a deliberate act that rendered her intentionally homeless which are based on errors of fact.

6.2 In reaching its conclusions, the authority makes a number of key findings: '*You took no steps to oust your husband from the property*'; '*you did not report the alleged incidents to anyone'*, and *'Your daughter has not expressed any symptoms of being scared of your husband'*.

6.3 These findings are factually incorrect:

(a) the appellant did take steps to exclude her husband from the marital home, by contacting a solicitor and discussing her options regarding an exclusion order;

(b) the appellant did report incidents of domestic violence to the police and to her doctor; copies of the crime incident numbers and a letter from her doctor were supplied to the authority;

(c) the authority received evidence that the appellant's daughter was receiving counselling for stress consequent upon her experiences of violence from her husband.

6.4 Accordingly, the decision is based on errors of fact, which are so fundamental to the authority's conclusions that the decision that there was an intentional act cannot be said to be sustainable.

GROUND SEVEN: Reasonableness

7.1 When authorities make decisions, they must have regard to all relevant matters, ignore irrelevant matters and not come to a decision that no reasonable authority could make (*'Wednesbury* unreasonableness'): *Associated Provincial Picture House v Wednesbury Corporation* [1948] 1 KB 223, CA, *per* Lord Greene MR at 229, 234.

7.2 The decision that the accommodation at 1 Warden Lane Road was suitable as permanent accommodation was a decision which no reasonable authority, properly directing itself, could have reached, because, *inter alia*:

- the authority did not consider that accommodation which may be suitable on a temporary basis may not be suitable on a permanent basis;
- the authority did not have any or any adequate regard to the fact that the appellant's husband had been released from prison; and,
- the authority failed to have regard to the appellant's concerns for her own safety and that of her family.

7.3 Further or alternatively, the decision to dismiss the Appellant's belief that she would be subject to domestic violence were she to return was – on the basis of the facts and the evidence before the authority – a decision that no reasonable authority could have reached. Having regard to all the circumstances, the decision was so unreasonable as to be perverse.

John Clowns
Warden Drane Chambers, Warden Drane

CHAPTER 13

Other statutory provisions

Introduction

13.1   The National Assistance Act (NAA) 1948 was the direct precursor of homeless persons legislation.[1] That Act was also a precursor of the Children Act (CA) 1989.[2] Two factors have placed a greater emphasis on those Acts in recent years:

- the exclusion from housing assistance of categories of immigrant;[3] and
- the stricter controls on housing under the Housing Act (HA) 1996 Parts 6 and 7.[4]

13.2   This book is not a study of either the broader welfare provisions of NAA 1948 or the provisions for children under CA 1989. There is, however, an overlap: the facts of many of the recent cases under those two Acts often suggest circumstances that would, but for legislative change, formerly have been dealt with under homelessness legislation; many of those cases refer directly to that legislation. Also overlapping with homelessness is the asylum support scheme under the Immigration and Asylum Act (IAA) 1999.

13.3   In addition, because it has been held to be an available source of power with which to assist in appropriate circumstances, reference must also be made to the 'well-being' powers of the Local Government Act (LGA) 2000.

13.4   In this chapter, we therefore consider briefly the relevant provisions of the following Acts:

a) NAA 1948;
b) IAA 1999;
c) CA 1989; and
d) LGA 2000.

13.5   As with interim accommodation under Part 7 of HA 1996, however, it is important to note that some classes of immigrant are wholly excluded from assistance even under these provisions. These classes – and the exceptions from them, including the overarching exception for British citizens and persons under the age of 18,[5] and the human

---

1 See above, paras 1.7–1.20.
2 See NAA 1948 ss21 and 29, as enacted, amended to apply only to persons aged 18 and over by CA 1989 s108(5) and Sch 13 para 11; see the observations of Laws LJ in *R (A) v Lambeth LBC* [2001] EWCA Civ 1624; [2002] HLR 13; (2001) 4 CCLR 486 at [1].
3 See above, paras 1.59–1.61 and 1.82.
4 See above, paras 1.67–1.79.
5 Above, para 3.120.

rights/EC Treaty exceptions[6] – are the same as those who have been considered in chapter 3.[7]

National Assistance Act 1948

13.6   NAA 1948 s21(1), as amended provides that:

> ... a local authority may with the approval of the secretary of state, and to such extent as he may direct shall,[8] make arrangements for providing –
>
> (a) residential accommodation for persons aged eighteen or over who by reason of age, illness, disability or any other circumstances are in need of care and attention which is not otherwise available to them.

Assessment of need

13.7   Once an applicant has sought assistance from a local authority under NAA 1948 s21, and assuming s/he is not in the excluded class of immigrant,[9] the authority must assess his/her needs: National Health Service and Community Care Act (NHSCCA) 1990 s47. By section 47(1):

> ... where it appears to a local authority that any person for whom they may provide or arrange for the provision of community care services may be in need of such services, the authority –
>
> (a) shall carry out an assessment of his needs for those services; and
>
> (b) having regard to the results of the assessment, shall then decide whether his needs call for the provisions by them of any such services.

13.8   Community care services are defined in NHSCCA 1990 s46(3) and include services provided under NAA 1948 Part 3, therefore including section 21.[10]

---

6   Above, paras 3.123–3.126.

7   Above, paras 3.123–3.127.

8   The secretary of state has directed local authorities to make arrangements for persons who by reason of age, illness, disability or any other circumstance are in need of care and attention not otherwise available to them or who are in urgent need: see Circular LAC(93)10, Appendix 1.

9   Above, para 13.5 and paras 3.120–3.122.

10   Also included are services provided under the Health Services and Public Health Act 1968 s45, National Health Service Act 1977 s21 and Sch 8, and Mental Health Act 1983 s117.

13.9   A failure to carry out any – or an adequate – assessment may vitiate[11] the decision of an authority that it has discharged its duty under
section 21.[12] On the other hand, it is not a precondition of provision
of any temporary, interim accommodation under section 21 that an
assessment under NHSCCA 1990 s47 should have completed.[13]

13.10   An authority must carry out an assessment of an individual's
needs for community care services even where the individual has
made no request for such an assessment.[14] The first stage of the
assessment process obliges authorities to identify those needs which
could potentially be satisfied by the provision of a community care
service; these are known as 'presenting needs'.[15] The scope and depth
of an assessment will be determined in large measure by the complexity of the person's needs. The second stage is to decide which of
the individual's presenting needs call for the provision of community
care services.[16] There is no statutory requirement that assessments
be recorded in writing, although in practice all social services authorities[17] have pro forma assessment forms. The Court of Appeal[18] has
warned against subjecting such assessments to over zealous scrutiny
because they are of necessity prepared quickly by social workers who
would otherwise be performing their front line duties. Policy guidance states that there should be an initial review of the community
care needs of service users within three months of when help is first
provided or major changes are made to the services provided and,
thereafter, reviews should be at least scheduled annually.[19] A review
amounts to a reassessment and therefore the principles set out above
apply.[20]

11 See *R (P) v Newham LBC* [2001] JHL D20, QBD.
12 As to which see para 13.29–13.32, below.
13 *R (AA) v Lambeth LBC* [2001] EWHC Admin 741; (2002) 5 CCLR 36, QBD.
14 *R v Gloucester CC ex p RADAR* (1998) 1 CCLR 476.
15 Fair Access to Care Services (FACS) Policy Guidance 2002 para 13; the term
     is not used in the Unified and Fair System for Assessing and Managing Care
     (UFSAMC) 2002, which is the equivalent guidance in Wales.
16 NHSCCA 1990 s47(1)(b).
17 'Social services authority' is defined by Local Authority Social Services Act
     1970 s1 as the council of a non-metropolitan county, metropolitan district and
     London boroughs and the Common Council of the City of London: it therefore
     includes unitary authorities. In relation to Wales, 'social services authority'
     means the counties and county boroughs.
18 *R (Ireneschild) v Lambeth LBC* [2007] EWCA Civ 234; [2007] HLR 34.
19 FACS Policy Guidance 2002 para 60; UFSAMC 2002 para 2.54 onwards.
20 Above, para 13.9.

13.11   The Local Authority Social Services Act 1970 s7 provides that authorities shall, in the exercise of their social services functions – including the exercise of any discretion conferred by any relevant legislation – act under the general guidance of the secretary of state. In England, the most important guidance is the Fair Access to Care Services (FACS) Policy Guidance 2002. In Wales, the equivalent guidance is known as the Unified and Fair System for Assessing and Managing Care (UFSAMC) 2002. The guidance sets out eligibility criteria which help authorities to make consistent and sensible service provision decisions.

13.12   The duty to assess is triggered if the authority has knowledge that a person 'may' be in need of services.[21] This is a low threshold test.[22] The application of this test may lead to a reassessment of a person who is already in receipt of services. This is also known as a review.[23] The FACS Policy Guidance states that, when deciding whether a person appears to be in need of community care services, authorities should avoid screening individuals out of the assessment process before sufficient information is known.[24] Authorities cannot treat their eligibility criteria as exhaustively defining who may be owed a duty under NAA 1948 s21.[25] Subject to significant limitations, authorities are, however, entitled to take their available resources into account when framing their eligibility criteria: the availability of resources is not a legitimate reason for refusing to provide services where this would give rise to a breach of the service user's human rights;[26] there must be a full reassessment of needs before any decision can be taken to withdraw services;[27] resources cannot be determinative of what services are provided;[28] once an authority has indicated that a service should be provided, it is under a legal obligation to do so and cannot rely on budget difficulties as a basis for refusing.[29]

13.13   Accommodation under NAA 1948 s21 is only available to persons who (among other things) are in need of 'care and attention'.[30] The

---

21 NHSCCA 1990 s47(1).
22 *R v Bristol CC ex p Penfold* (1998) 1 CCLR 315.
23 Above, para 13.10.
24 FACS Policy Guidance 2002 para 30.
25 *R (N) v Lambeth LBC* [2006] EWHC 3427 (Admin); (2007) ACD 49.
26 *R (A and B, X and Y) v East Sussex CC* [2003] EWHC 167 (Admin); (2003) 6 CCLR 194 at [88].
27 *R v Gloucestershire CC ex p Barry* [1997] AC 584.
28 *R v Gloucestershire CC ex p Barry* [1997] AC 584.
29 *R v Gloucestershire CC ex p Barry* [1997] AC 584.
30 NAA 1948 s21(1)(a).

phrase is not statutorily defined. The courts have adopted a relatively generous approach.[31] In the context of psychiatric care, the Court of Appeal[32] concluded that the legal principles were clear: the question is whether the appellants' need for s21 care and attention by way of the provision of residential accommodation is made materially more acute by reason of their psychiatric disorder.

13.14   In *R(M)*,[33] there was a comprehensive review of the meaning of 'care and attention' in NAA 1948 s21. It was held that the natural and ordinary meaning of the words 'care and attention' in this context is 'looking after', which means doing something for the person being cared for which s/he cannot or should not be expected to do for himself; it might be household tasks, protection from risks, or personal care – such as feeding, washing or toileting; this is not an exhaustive list; the provision of medical care is, however, expressly excluded; nor does it include the provision of physical things such as accommodation, food or money, alone or together.[34]

13.15   Primary responsibility for the provision of services under NAA 1948 ss21 and 29 rests with the authority in which the relevant person is ordinarily resident.[35] The phrase ordinary residence was considered in *Shah*,[36] under the Education Act 1962: it was held that a person's long term future intentions or expectations are not relevant; the test is not what is a person's real home but whether a person can show a regular, habitual mode of life in a particular place, the continuity of which has persisted despite temporary absences; a person's attitude is only relevant in two respects – the residence must be voluntarily adopted and there must be a settled purpose in living in the particular residence.[37]

13.16   In urgent cases, the authority should consider exercising its power to make emergency provision for a person's needs pending the outcome of the assessment process.[38] An authority may temporarily provide a service without carrying out a prior assessment of needs if the condition of that person is such that s/he requires those services as

---

31   *R v Hammersmith LBC ex p M; R v Lambeth LBC ex p P and X; R v Westminster CC ex p A* (1997) 1 CCLR 85.

32   *R (Pajaziti and Pajaziti) v Lewisham LBC and Secretary of State for the Home Department (Interested Party)* [2007] EWCA Civ 1351.

33   *R (M) v Slough BC* [2008] UKHL 52; [2008] 1 WLR 1808.

34   *R (M) v Slough BC* [2008] UKHL 52; [2008] 1 WLR 1808 at [32].

35   NAA 1948 s24(1).

36   *R v Barnet LBC ex p Shah* [1983] 2 AC 309.

37   *R v Barnet LBC ex p Shah* [1983] 2 AC 309 at 349C.

38   NHSCCA 1990 s47(5); *R (AA) v Lambeth LBC* (2002) 5 CCLR 36.

a matter of urgency.[39] In such circumstances, the duty to assess still remains and an assessment should be done as soon as reasonably practicable.

Human rights exception

13.17 Where an asylum-seeker who is potentially eligible for assistance under NAA 1948 s21 is prima facie excluded by the Nationality, Immigration and Asylum Act (NIAA) 2002,[40] but seeks to rely on the human rights exception,[41] it has been said to be logical to ask the question whether support should be provided in order to avoid a violation of a Convention right before applying any eligibility criteria or assessing the applicant's need for care and attention.[42]

13.18 Thus, in *PB*,[43] the claimant was a homeless Jamaican woman and an illegal overstayer. She had contact with her oldest child who lived with his father in the UK but the other four children, all born in the UK, were the subject of care proceedings and not living with her at the time. The authority refused to assist her under NAA 1948 s21, on the basis that she could return to Jamaica. The High Court held that this decision was unlawful because the authority had not considered whether her right to respect for family life under article 8[44] would be breached if she were forced to leave the UK whilst care proceedings were pending.

13.19 In *Binomugisha*,[45] the authority withdrew CA 1989 [46] support from a 19-year-old failed asylum-seeker with mental health problems who had made a further application for leave to remain in the UK on the basis that it would be a breach of article 8 to remove him to Uganda. He claimed that the authority owed him a duty under the leaving care provisions of CA 1989 and under NAA 1948 s21. The Home Office had not yet made a decision on that application. The court held that where there is an outstanding article 8 claim, the question for the authority is whether that application was manifestly unfounded;

39 NHSCCA 1990 s47(5).
40 Sch 3, para 3.
41 Above, para 13.5; above, paras 3.123–3.126.
42 *R (N) v Lambeth LBC* [2006] EWHC 3427 (Admin); (2007) ACD 49.
43 *R (PB) v Haringey LBC and (1) Secretary of State for Health (2) Secretary of State for Communities and Local Government (Interested Parties)* [2006] EWHC 225 (Admin); [2007] HLR 13.
44 Above, para 12.101.
45 *R (Gordon Binomugisha) v Southwark LBC* [2006] EWHC 2254 (Admin).
46 Below, paras 13.44–13.65.

while responsibility for making decisions on such applications lay with the Home Office, pending that decision the authority would have to consider whether it was necessary to provide a service to prevent a breach of article 3 of the Convention.

13.20 Nonetheless, in *AW*,[47] it was held that a purported fresh claim either for asylum or under article 3, by an asylum-seeker whose original claim had been rejected, did not always make it necessary for support to be provided in order to avoid a breach of the Convention; in considering the issue, it was necessary for the public body concerned to have regard to all the relevant circumstances, including – where appropriate – the matters which were alleged to constitute a fresh claim; it was necessary to proceed on a case by case basis.[48] Accordingly, the human rights exception does not bite simply because a human rights claim has been made to the UK Borders Agency (UKBA): it only applies where the provision of community care service is necessary for the purpose of avoiding a breach of a person's human rights.[49]

Immigrants and asylum-seekers

13.21 Unless the person is re-qualified by the human rights exception,[50] NAA 1948 s21(1A), added by the IAA 1999 provides:

> A person to whom s115 of the Immigration and Asylum Act 1999 (exclusion from benefits) applies may not be provided with residential accommodation under subsection (1)(a) if his need for care and attention has arisen solely –
> (a) because he is destitute;[51] or
> (b) because of the physical effects or anticipated physical effects of his being destitute.[52]

47 *R (AW) v Croydon LBC* [2005] EWHC 2950 (QB).

48 *R (AW) v Croydon LBC* [2005] EWHC 2950 (QB). The decision on appeal did not affect this part of the judgment below – see *Croydon LBC & Hackney LBC v R (AW, A and Y)* [2007] EWCA Civ 266; (2007) 10 CCLR 189; (2007) BLGR 417.

49 NIAA 2002 Sch 3 para 3.

50 Above, paras 13.17–13.20.

51 The definition of destitution applied is that to be found in IAA 1999 s95: NAA 1948 s21(1B). In assessing whether a person is destitute, any assistance from the National Asylum Support Service under the IAA 1999 must be ignored by the authority.

52 Effectively reversing the decision in *R v Hammersmith & Fulham LBC ex p M* (1997) 30 HLR 10, in relation to those subject to immigration control.

13.22 The effect of this provision is to exclude those who are subject to immigration control (unless re-included by regulations[53]) from NAA 1948 s21, where their need for care and attention arises solely from destitution. Their needs are, instead, intended to be met under IAA 1999,[54] although assistance may be available under the CA 1989 in an appropriate case.[55] Local authorities have no power to provide any accommodation for non-asylum-seeking immigrants who are merely destitute, and who do not have children.

13.23 In the case of asylum-seekers whose need for care and attention does not arise because of destitution but, for example, because of disability, responsibility for meeting their care needs remains with the local authority under NAA 1948, s21.[56] This division of responsibilities has not been uncontentious. In *O v Wandsworth LBC*,[57] the secretary of state argued that an applicant subject to immigration control can only obtain assistance under NAA 1948 s21 if s/he would still need assistance without being destitute. The Court of Appeal rejected this in favour of the applicants' construction of the provision:

> They submit that if an applicant's need for care and attention is to any material extent made more acute by some circumstance other than the mere lack of accommodation and funds, then despite being subject to immigration control, he qualifies for assistance. Other relevant circumstances include, of course, age, illness and disability, all of which are expressly mentioned in section 21(1) itself. If, for example, an immigrant, as well as being destitute, is old, ill or disabled, he is likely to be yet more vulnerable and less well able to survive than if he were merely destitute.

Provision of housing accommodation

13.24 Once the local authority has assessed an applicant's needs as satisfying the criteria in NAA 1948 s21, it must provide accommodation on a continuing basis so long as the need of the applicant remains as originally assessed: *R v Kensington & Chelsea RLBC ex p Kujtim*.[58]

---

53 See further paras 3.10 and 3.11, above.
54 See para 3.3, above, and paras 13.32–13.43, below.
55 See paras 13.44–13.65, below.
56 *Westminster CC v National Asylum Support Service* [2002] UKHL 38; [2002] 1 WLR 2958. See also *R (Murua) v Croydon LBC* [2001] EWHC Admin 830; (2002) 5 CCLR 51, QBD; *R (Mani) v Lambeth LBC* [2003] EWCA Civ 836; [2004] HLR 5; (2003) 6 CCLR 376.
57 [2000] 1 WLR 2539; (2001) 33 HLR 39, CA. See also *R (M) v Slough BC* [2008] UKHL 52; [2008] 1 WLR 1808 where *O* was applied.
58 [1999] 4 All ER 161; 32 HLR 579, CA.

13.25   Residential accommodation may include 'ordinary' housing accommodation.[59] A duty to supply such accommodation will arise where a person needs care and attention, including housing accommodation, which is not otherwise available.

13.26   The need for care and attention remains, however, a pre-condition of the duty. In *Wahid*,[60] the applicant, who suffered from schizophrenia, lived in extremely overcrowded conditions with his wife and eight children. He was in receipt of medical treatment, which kept him mentally stable. The authority assessed that there was a risk of relapse that was exacerbated by his unsuitable accommodation. However, that risk did not amount to a present need for care and attention and his need for suitable accommodation was not urgent. The assessment had appropriately identified the applicant's need as liaison over his transfer application with the housing department, rather than the provision of accommodation.

13.27   The judgment recognises[61] the possible clash with HA 1996 s167:[62]

> . . . care must be taken to retain section 21 as a provision of last resort. Otherwise there is a danger that it will become a provision of principal resort, and will lead to the circumvention or sidelining of section 167 of the Housing Act and local housing authorities' policies for the allocation of housing to new and existing tenants. A need for better housing should not in general give rise to a duty under section 21. When construing and applying section 21, it is important to bear in mind the other provisions under which a housing authority is under a duty to provide accommodation.

Discharge of the duty

13.28   The duty under NAA 1948 s21 is not absolute. In *Kujtim*,[63] the applicant was placed in bed and breakfast accommodation by the author-

---

59   See *R v Bristol CC ex p Penfold* (1998) 1 CCLR 315, QBD; *R v Wigan MBC ex p Tammadge* (1998) 1 CCLR 581; *R (Batantu) v Islington LBC* (2001) 33 HLR 76; (2001) 4 CCLR 445, QBD; and *Khana v Southwark LBC* [2001] EWCA Civ 999; (2001) 4 CCLR 267. Cf, *R (Wahid) v Tower Hamlets LBC* [2001] EWHC Admin 641; (2001) 4 CCLR 455, QBD, where Stanley Burnton J doubted the correctness of the proposition but felt constrained by the existing case-law.

60   *R (Wahid) v Tower Hamlets LBC* [2001] EWHC Admin 641; (2001) 4 CCLR 455, QBD.

61   *R (Wahid) v Tower Hamlets LBC* [2001] EWHC Admin 641; (2001) 4 CCLR 455, QBD, at [32].

62   See para 11.611, above.

63   [1999] 4 All ER 161; 32 HLR 579; (1999) 2 CCLR 340, CA.

ity. He exhibited violent behaviour and made threats to staff. This was replicated in another hotel to which he was moved. The hotel refused to accommodate him any longer and the authority refused to provide him with further assistance. The Court of Appeal held that, where an applicant manifests a persistent and unequivocal refusal to observe the authority's reasonable requirements in relation to occupation of accommodation, the authority is entitled to treat its duty as discharged and to refuse to provide further accommodation. Before concluding that there is such a refusal, there should be careful consideration of an applicant's circumstances, and it is desirable that applicants should be given a final warning.

13.29   The duty may also be discharged by the unreasonable refusal of an offer of accommodation. In *Khana v Southwark LBC*,[64] the applicant was a severely disabled elderly Kurdish woman. She lived with her husband and daughter in the latter's one-bedroom flat. Following assessment, the authority offered her and her husband a placement in a residential home on the basis that it was the only form of residential accommodation that would meet her needs for care and attention. The offer was refused: the applicant said that they would only accept a two-bedroom, ground-floor flat, where the family could continue to live together. Given its conclusion as to needs, the authority was held to have discharged its duty and, in any event, the refusal was unreasonable and, as such, discharged the authority from any further duty, albeit only for so long as the refusal was maintained.

13.30   In *Patrick*,[65] the applicant had mental health difficulties; she was evicted on the grounds of neighbour nuisance. The respondent authority from whom she sought assistance decided that she was intentionally homeless and in due course evicted her from the temporary accommodation it had provided. Shortly afterwards, she started sleeping rough and lawyers wrote on her behalf, enclosing a doctor's letter confirming her significant psychiatric problems and requesting urgent accommodation. The authority refused, stating that it had offered the applicant accommodation in a charitable hostel for people with mental health problems, but that she had refused this offer.

13.31   This argument was rejected: an apparent refusal of accommodation by an applicant with psychiatric problems does not put an end to the authority's continuing duty to provide accommodation when the applicant may well have been labouring under a complete

---

64 [2001] EWCA Civ 999; (2001) 4 CCLR 267.
65 *R (Patrick) v Newham LBC* (2001) 4 CCLR 48.

misapprehension as to the nature of the accommodation.[66] If the authority wished to put an end to its duty under NAA 1948 s21, at the very least it ought to have ensured that the applicant was legally represented when the offer was made, to ensure that she understood not only the offer but also the legal consequences or potential legal consequences of refusing the offer.[67]

Immigration and Asylum Act 1999

13.32   The IAA 1999 Part 6 came into force on 3 April 2000. It excludes persons subject to immigration control[68] from social security benefits and most other welfare provisions.[69] At the same time, however, it also set up a scheme for asylum support. The National Asylum Support Service (NASS) was established within the Immigration and Nationality Directorate (IND) of the Home Office, to administer the scheme. In July 2006 the Home Office announced that NASS no longer existed as a separate department. Asylum support is now administered in two separate ways. Those who made their first asylum claim on or after 5 March 2007 have their support processed by the New Asylum Model (NAM) 'case owner' who is processing his/her asylum claim. Those who claimed before that date, are known as 'legacy cases' and have their asylum and support claims dealt with by the Casework Resolution Directorate (CRD). In April 2007, the Border and Immigration Agency (BIA) replaced the IND. BIA has now been replaced by the UK Border Agency (UKBA).

13.33   The EU has attempted to implement a common policy for the treatment of asylum-seekers across Europe by enacting Council Directive 2003/9/EC[70] which lays down minimum standards for their reception. The directive has been implemented into domestic law by amending the Immigration Rules[71] and enacting new regulations[72] which apply to a person whose claim for asylum is recorded on or after 5 February 2005.[73]

---

66   *R (Patrick) v Newham LBC* (2001) 4 CCLR 48, at [53D].
67   *R (Patrick) v Newham LBC* (2001) 4 CCLR 48, at [53H].
68   Above, para 3.12.
69   IAA 1999 s115.
70   The Directive came into force on 6 February 2003.
71   HC 395.
72   Asylum Seekers (Reception Conditions) Regulations 2005 SI No 7 and Asylum Support (Amendment) Regulations 2005 SI No 11.
73   Asylum Seekers (Reception Conditions) Regulations 2005 SI No 7 reg 1(2).

13.34   Under the IAA 1999 s95(1) the secretary of state may provide, or arrange for the provision of support for asylum-seekers or dependants of asylum-seekers who appear to him/her to be destitute or to be likely to become destitute within the prescribed period. That period is 14 days, or 56 days if they are already receiving asylum support.[74] The power to provide support is now a duty.[75] An asylum-seeker is a person who is not under 18 and has made a claim for asylum which has been recorded by the secretary of state but which has not been determined.[76] A claim for asylum means a claim that it would be contrary to the UK's obligations under the Refugee Convention, or under article 3 of the European Convention on Human Rights ('the Convention'/ECHR), for the claimant to be removed from, or required to leave, the UK.[77] Dependants include a spouse, a child of the claimant or the claimant's spouse, who is under 18 and dependent on the claimant,[78] and various other prescribed persons.[79]

13.35   Assistance under these provisions is in theory excluded in the case of some classes of immigrant, being those classes (subject to exceptions, including the overarching exception for British citizens and persons under the age of 18,[80] and the human rights/EC Treaty exceptions)[81] considered in chapter 3.[82] In practice, the UKBA does not usually apply these eligibility criteria when making asylum support decisions but applies the principles set out in these paragraphs.[83]

13.36   A person is destitute if s/he does not have adequate accommodation or any means of obtaining it, or s/he has adequate accommodation or the means of obtaining it, but cannot meet his/her other essential living needs.[84] This test involves a consideration of the claimant and his/her dependants.[85]

13.37   The secretary of state may not arrange or provide asylum support unless satisfied that the claim for asylum was made as soon as

---

74 Asylum Support Regulations (AS Regs) 2000 SI No 704 reg 7.
75 Asylum Seekers (Reception Conditions) Regulations 2005 SI No 7 reg 5.
76 IAA 1999 s94(1).
77 IAA 1999 s94(1).
78 IAA 1999 s94(1).
79 The list is set out in the AS Regs 2000 reg 2(4).
80 Above, para 3.120.
81 Above, para 3.123.
82 Above, paras 3.123–3.127.
83 Paras 13.34–13.43.
84 IAA 1999 s95(3).
85 IAA 1999 s95(4).

reasonably practicable after the person's arrival in the UK.[86] This does not apply if support is necessary to avoid a breach of the ECHR or if the household includes a dependent child who is under 18 years old.[87] The House of Lords has held that there would be a breach of article 3 of the ECHR when an individual faces an imminent prospect of serious suffering caused or materially aggravated by denial of shelter, food or the most basic necessities of life.[88] The UKBA has interpreted the judgment as meaning that it must provide support unless the asylum-seeker has accommodation.[89] The judgment, however, also requires the decision-maker to be satisfied that the asylum-seeker has some means of meeting their need for food and washing facilities.

13.38   The secretary of state may provide, or arrange for the provision of, temporary support to destitute asylum-seekers and their dependants until a decision is reached on eligibility for support under IAA 1999 s95.[90] This is usually in a hotel or hostel, arranged by one of the voluntary organisations funded by the Home Office, which are known as the Asylum Support Partnership (ASP), and provide reception assistance.

13.39   The secretary of state should arrange for the asylum-seeker to be offered support under IAA 1999 s95, as soon as it has been decided that s/he is eligible. This support can include providing accommodation that appears to be adequate for the needs of the supported person and his/her dependants, and providing for their essential living needs.[91] Before deciding what form of support to provide or continue to provide, the secretary of state must take certain matters into account and ignore others.[92] The asylum-seeker's resources must be taken into account when deciding the kind and level of support.[93]

13.40   An asylum-seeker stops being an asylum-seeker for support purposes 28 days after the secretary of state notifies him/her of a favourable asylum decision, or 21 days after notification of a refusal. If there is an appeal, the period ends 28 days after any final appeal is disposed of.[94] This does not apply if the asylum-seeker has a dependent child

86 Nationality, Immigration and Asylum Act 2002 s55(1).
87 Nationality, Immigration and Asylum Act 2002 s55(5).
88 *R (Limbuela) v Secretary of State for the Home Department (Shelter intervener)* [2005] UKHL 66; [2006] 1 AC 396.
89 Policy Bulletin 75, Version 7, 16 July 2007.
90 IAA 1999 s98.
91 IAA 1999 s96(1).
92 IAA 1999 s97(1), (2) and (4).
93 AS Regs 2000 reg 12.
94 IAA 1999 s94(3) and AS Regs 2000 reg 2(2).

under 18 in the household: in those circumstances, s/he continues to be treated as an asylum-seeker for support purposes so long as the child is under 18 and within the household.[95] An asylum-seeker will not benefit from this provision if s/he is a refused asylum-seeker with a dependent child under 18 but is refusing to leave the UK and the secretary of state has certified that this is the case.[96]

13.41 A person who is ineligible for asylum support under IAA 1999 s95 or s98 may nevertheless be entitled to what used to be known as 'hard cases' support.[97] Under IAA 1999 s4(1), the secretary of state has wide powers to provide, or arrange for the provision of, support to any person who has arrived in the UK and been granted temporary admission[98] or who has been detained, whether or not they are also a former asylum-seeker. Under IAA 1999 s4(2), the secretary of state may provide, or arrange for the provision of, facilities for the accommodation of a person if s/he was, but is no longer, an asylum-seeker, and his/her claim for asylum was rejected, if s/he can satisfy one of the five conditions set out in the applicable regulations.[99]

13.42 Those conditions are that:

a) s/he is taking all reasonable steps to leave the UK or place him/ herself in a position in which s/he is able to leave, which may include complying with attempts to obtain a travel document to facilitate his/her departure;

b) s/he is unable to leave the UK because s/he cannot travel for physical reasons or for some other medical reason;

c) s/he is unable to leave the UK because in the opinion of the secretary of state there is currently no viable route of return available;

d) s/he has made an application for judicial review of a decision in relation to his/her asylum claim,[100] and has been granted permission to proceed pursuant to CPR Part 54;

e) the provision of accommodation is necessary for the purpose of avoiding a breach of rights under the ECHR.[101]

95 IAA 1999 s94(5).

96 NIAA 2002 Sch 3 para 7A, substituted by the Asylum and Immigration (Treatment of Claimants, etc.) Act 2004, with effect from 1 December 2004.

97 IAA 1999 s4.

98 Immigration Act 1971 Sch 2 para 21.

99 Immigration and Asylum (Provision of Accommodation to Failed Asylum Seekers) Regulations (IA(PAFA) Regs) 2005 SI No. 930.

100 *R (NS) v First Tier Tribunal (Social Security Entitlement Chamber) and SSHD* [2009] EWHC (Admin), unreported, Stadlen J, on 6 November 2009.

101 IA(PAFA) Regs 2005 reg 3(2).

13.43   The power to provide support under IAA 1999 s4 is expressed as 'facilities for accommodation' so it may be provided in the form of accommodation with living expenses attached. Unlike support under IAA s95, it is not possible for an applicant to stay with a friend and only claim a subsistence allowance. The support is usually vouchers for living expenses with a room in a communal private rented house arranged by an accommodation provider. Sometimes the package is full board in hostel accommodation. The accommodation provider will issue weekly supermarket vouchers, which may be delivered to the applicant or s/he may need to collect them from an office. Unlike accommodation under IAA 1999 s95, there is no requirement for s4 accommodation to be adequate.

Children Act 1989

13.44   CA 1989 Part 3 confers general powers and imposes general duties on local authorities exercising social service functions in respect of children and families in their area.[102]

Children Act 1989 s17

13.45   Under CA 1989 s17(1), authorities are required to safeguard and promote the welfare of children within their area whom they assess as being in need and, insofar as is consistent with that duty, to promote the upbringing of such children by their families.[103] The section sets out only duties of a general character intended for the benefit of children in need in the area of the social services authority. Other duties – and specific duties in subsequent provisions of the Act – must be performed in each individual case by reference to the general duty which section 17(1) sets out, but section 17(1) does not itself impose an individual duty.[104]

13.46   This provision is excluded in the case of some classes of immigrant, being those classes (subject to exceptions, including the overarching exception for British citizens and persons under the age of

---

102 A local authority exercising a social services function in respect of children and families in their area is a 'children's services authority' as defined by the Children Act 2004, s65(1). This mirrors the definition of a 'social services authority' save for the addition of the Council of the Isles of Scilly. See para 13.10, above.

103 CA 1989 s17(1)(b).

104 *R (G) v Barnet LBC; R (W) v Lambeth LBC; R (A) v Lambeth LBC* [2003] UKHL 57; [2004] AC 208; [2004] HLR 10. See also paras 13.49 and 13.53.

18,[105] and the human rights/EC Treaty exceptions)[106] considered in chapter 3.[107] In view of the exception for persons under the age of 18, the exclusion has no effect on them, but it may prevent the use of section 17 for adult members of the family.

13.47   Although CA 1989 s17(1) is a general duty, when discharging it authorities have the specific powers and duties set out in Schedule 2 Part I, including assessment of the child's needs.[108] By section 17(6), such services may include assistance in kind or, in exceptional circumstances, cash, and may include the provision of accommodation, possibly together with family.[109] In *R (G) v Barnet LBC*,[110] the House of Lords held that it was unlawful for a local authority to adopt a general policy of only accommodating homeless children pursuant to their duty under CA 1989 s20[111] while refusing to exercise their power under section 17 to accommodate other members of the family. A child in need within section 17(10) is eligible for the provision of assistance, but has no absolute right to it.[112]

13.48   The provisions of CA 1989 s17(6), and in particular the inclusion of the power to provide accommodation,[113] should be read in light of the later published Local Authority Circular LAC (2003) 13, *Guidance on Accommodating Children in Need and Their Families* and the observations of Baroness Hale in *R (G) v Southwark LBC*,[114] highlighting that children in need of accommodation will almost always involve children needing to be accommodated with their families.

13.49   The assessment of need carried out under s17 should not be dealt with summarily and requires proper enquiry and consideration: *R (MM) v Lewisham LBC*.[115] In that case, the claimant, a 17-year-old girl,

---

105 Above, para.3.120.

106 Above, para 3.123.

107 Above, paras 3.123–3.127.

108 Section 17(2).

109 The Act was amended by the Adoption and Children Act 2002 s116(1) to include references to accommodation following the decision of the Court of Appeal in *R (A) v Lambeth LBC* [2001] EWCA Civ 1624; [2002] HLR 13, which suggested that there was no power to provide accommodation (although this was subsequently held to have been decided per incuriam: *R (W) v Lambeth LBC* [2002] EWCA Civ 613, (2002) 5 CCLR 203; [2002] HLR 41). See below, paras 13.68–13.69.

110 [2003] UKHL 57; [2004] AC 208; [2004] HLR 10. See also paras 13.45 and 13.53.

111 Below, paras 13.51–13.55.

112 *R (G) v Barnet LBC; R (W) v Lambeth LBC; R (A) v Lambeth LBC* [2003] UKHL 57; [2004] AC 208; [2004] HLR 10.

113 Adoption and Children Act 2002 s116(1).

114 [2009] UKHL 26; [2009] 1 WLR 1299 at [30].

115 *R (MM) v Lewisham LBC* [2009] EWHC 416 (Admin).

had been living in a women's refuge for four months when she was referred to the social services department of Lewisham LBC by a support worker at the refuge. The support worker informed the social services department that the reasons for the referral were that the claimant was fleeing domestic violence, vulnerable, lacking life-skills and was shortly to be placed in hostel accommodation. The social services department made no enquiries of its own and determined that the referral was 'vague'. Furthermore, it was decided that, as the claimant was in receipt of benefits and had accommodation provided for her, she was not a child in need under section 17 and was not therefore entitled to assistance from social services. The claimant applied for judicial review of that decision on the basis that the authority had failed to carry out a proper assessment. The High Court agreed that the decision could not stand. The consideration given to the referral was no more than 'cursory' and 'fell far below' the standard required by law.[116]

13.50   A local authority must consider the policy of the secretary of state when deciding whether to withdraw accommodation provided under section 17: *R (Clue) v Birmingham CC*.[117] In that case, the claimant and her eldest son were Jamaican citizens who had come to the UK as visitors and overstayed. The claimant was refused leave to remain. No action was taken to remove her and her son back to Jamaica. She subsequently had three more children in the UK. Accommodation for the entire family was being funded by the local authority under CA 1989 s17. After the birth of her youngest child, the claimant made a further application for leave to remain, by which time her eldest child had been continuously in the UK for seven years. The policy of the secretary of state for the Home Department was that it would normally be inappropriate forcibly to remove a family with a child who had been continuously in the country for seven years because such a child would, in most cases, have established ties which rendered it right and fair that the family should be allowed to remain. The authority nonetheless decided to withdraw funding for the accommodation and pay the cost of returning the family to Jamaica, even though no action had been taken by other authorities to remove the claimant and her family from the country. It was held that the authority was required by NIAA 2002 Sch 3 para 1 to determine whether this would breach the Convention rights of the claimant or any of her family

---

116 *R (MM) v Lewisham LBC* [2009] EWHC 416 (Admin), per Sir George Newman at [14].
117 *R (Clue) v Birmingham CC* [2008] EWHC 3036 (Admin); [2009] 1 FLR 838.

members. Although the policy was not binding, the authority was required to have regard to it, which it had failed to do.

Children Act 1989 s20

13.51   CA 1989 s20 provides:

> (1) Every local authority shall provide accommodation for any child in need within their area who appears to them to require accommodation as a result of:
>   (a) there being no person who has parental responsibility for him;
>   (b) his being lost or having been abandoned; or
>   (c) the person who has been caring for him being prevented (whether or not permanently, and for whatever reason) from providing him with suitable accommodation or care.
>   . . .
> (3) Every local authority shall provide accommodation for any child in need within their area who has reached the age of sixteen and whose welfare the authority consider is likely to be seriously prejudiced if they do not provide him with accommodation.

13.52   Section 20 imposes a duty on social services authorities to house children in the circumstances set out in CA 1989 s20(1) and to house young people in the circumstances set out in section 20(3). An authority may enter into arrangements with another local authority for assistance in the discharge of the duty under CA 1989 s20, but that does not permit it to pass the child 'from pillar to post' between authorities.[118] Whether a 16- or 17-year-old is a child in need for the purposes of the CA 1989, and accordingly owed a duty under section 20, is a question of fact for the court: *R (A) v Croydon LBC & (1) Secretary of State for the Home Department & (2) Children's Commissioner; R (M) v Lambeth LBC & (1) Secretary of State for the Home Department & (2) Children's Commissioner.*[119]

13.53   Where an authority provides a child with accommodation pursuant to its duty under section 20, it is not obliged by section 23(6)[120] to

---

118 *R (G) v Southwark LBC* [2009] UKHL 26; [2009] 1 WLR 1299, per Baroness Hale at [28].

119 [2009] UKSC 8. See, in particular, the opinions of Lady Hale at [14]–[33] and Lord Hope at [51]–[54].

120 Section 23(6) provides that an authority may provide accommodation with a child's family, relatives or any other suitable person and, so far as is reasonably practicable and consistent with the child's welfare, the authority must make the placement with a parent, person with parental responsibility, relative, friend, other person connected with him/her.

make arrangements to enable the child to live with a parent, relative, friend or other person connected with him/her.[121] Section 23(6) is concerned with placement of a child and assumes that the child's carer has accommodation which the child may share so as to live there.[122]

13.54   Section 20 imposes a strict duty to provide accommodation. Once a social services department has determined that it owes a duty to a child to provide accommodation under section 20, it cannot sidestep that duty by securing such accommodation pursuant to a different statutory provision such as CA 1989 s17 or HA 1996 part 7.[123]

13.55   However, for the duty to provide accommodation under CA 1989 s20 to be activated, notice must be given or a referral made to the social services authority; a social services authority cannot be criticised for not doing something that it had not been given notice it should be doing.[124]

Co-operation between social services and housing authorities

13.56   Just as housing authorities can seek the co-operation of social services authorities under Housing Act 1985 s213,[125] social services authorities can ask housing authorities to assist them, in which event the housing authority must comply with the request if it is compatible with its own statutory or other duties and obligations and does not unduly prejudice the discharge of any of its own functions.[126]

---

121 *R (G) v Barnet LBC; R (W) v Lambeth LBC; R (A) v Lambeth LBC* [2003] UKHL 57; [2004] AC 208; [2004] HLR 10. But see the obiter comments of Lord Nichols at [52] and [55]–[56] on the best interests of the child(ren) and the importance of maintaining the relationship between parent(s) and child(ren).

122 *R (G) v Barnet LBC; R (W) v Lambeth LBC; R (A) v Lambeth LBC* [2003] UKHL 57; [2004] AC 208; [2004] HLR 10. Accordingly it cannot be used to circumvent a finding of intentional homelessness. See also *R (McDonagh) v Hounslow LBC* [2004] EWHC 511 (Admin) and *R (Conde) v Lambeth LBC* [2005] EWHC 62 (Admin); [2005] HLR 29.

123 *R (S) v Sutton LBC* [2007] EWCA Civ 790 considered and applied in *R (G) v Southwark LBC* [2009] UKHL 26; [2009] 1 WLR 1299.

124 *R (M) v Hammersmith & Fulham LBC* [2008] UKHL 14; [2008] 1 WLR 535.

125 See para 9.58, above.

126 CA 1989 s27. See also Children Act 2004 s10 which places a duty on 'children's services authorities' (see above, footnote 101) to make arrangements to promote co-operation between the authority, relevant partners (including district authorities) and other persons or bodies engaged in activities in relation to children, to improve the well-being of children and young people in the authority's area.

13.57   This provision does not apply where one department of a local authority seeks help from another department of the same authority: *Byas*.[127]

13.58   In *Smith*,[128] the housing authority refused a request from the social services authority for assistance in housing a family with children whom the housing authority had previously found to be intentionally homeless. In the Court of Appeal, it was held that the housing authority could not simply refuse to help by reference to the finding of intentionality. The House of Lords allowed an appeal: although housing and social services authorities were expected to co-operate, if the housing authority could not assist – because no solution was forthcoming which did not unduly prejudice the discharge of its functions – then in the final analysis the children remained the responsibility of the social services authority.

13.59   A further specific referral and co-operation duty was imposed on local housing authorities by the Homelessness Act 2002.[129] The duty arises[130] where the local housing authority has reason to believe that a homeless applicant with children may be:

– ineligible for assistance;[131]
– homeless intentionally;[132] or
– threatened with homelessness intentionally.[133]

13.60   Given the low standard of satisfaction needed ('have reason to believe')[134], the housing authority may reach such a conclusion prior to a final decision on the homelessness application, and the procedures for referral put into place by CA 1989 s27 should commence prior to the applicant being notified of the decision under HA 1996 s184.[135]

13.61   In anticipation of this duty, the housing authority must have in place arrangements to invite the applicant to give his/her consent to a referral either to the social services authority for the area (where

---

127 *R v Tower Hamlets LBC ex p Byas* (1992) 25 HLR 105, CA.
128 *R v Northavon DC ex p Smith* [1994] 2 AC 402; 26 HLR 659, HL.
129 This followed the decision of the Court of Appeal in *R (A) v Lambeth LBC* [2001] EWCA Civ 1624; [2002] HLR 13; (2001) 4 CCLR 486, subsequently upheld in the House of Lords at [2003] UKHL 57; [2004] AC 208; [2004] HLR 10, see above, paras 13.45, 13.47 and 13.53.
130 HA 1996 s123A(1).
131 See chapter 3.
132 See chapter 6.
133 See para 6.4, above.
134 The same standard as triggers the homelessness enquiry duty; see para 9.50, above.
135 See para 9.142, above.

this is a separate authority) or to the social services department (in the case of a unitary authority).[136] Where consent to the referral is obtained, the social services authority/department must be made aware of the case and notified of any subsequent decision by the authority.[137]

13.62   The provisions in HA 1996 s213A(2) and (3) do not affect any other power to disclose information to social services, with or without the consent of the applicant, for example, where the housing authority receives information which might indicate that a child in the family is at risk of significant harm.[138]

13.63   Once the social services authority is made aware that an applicant is ineligible for assistance, homeless intentionally or threatened with homelessness intentionally, it may request the local housing authority to provide it with advice and assistance in the exercise of its functions under CA 1989 Part 3;[139] the housing authority must 'provide them with such advice and assistance as is reasonable in the circumstances'.[140]

13.64   In the case of a unitary authority, the authority must make arrangement for ensuring that the housing department provides the social services department with such advice and assistance as is reasonably requested.[141] The specific provision for unitary authorities means that while CA 1989 s27 will not apply to it,[142] this requirement to co-operate will do so.

13.65   These duties to provide advice and assistance are additional to those in CA 1989 s27.[143] The new duty of co-operation imposed by HA 1996 s213A does not reverse the position in *Smith*,[144] that where the housing authority/department is unable to provide any assistance, the ultimate responsibility for ensuring that the needs of the children are met remains with the social services authority/department.

---

136 HA 1996 s213(2)(a) and (3)(a).
137 HA 1996 s213A(2)(b) and (3)(b).
138 HA 1996 s213A(4). See also Code of Guidance para 13.7; Welsh Code para 17.4.
139 HA 1996 s213A(5).
140 HA 1996 s213A(5).
141 HA 1996 s213A(6).
142 See para 13.57, above.
143 See para 13.56, above.
144 See para 13.58, above. See also Code of Guidance para 13.9; Welsh Code para 17.7.

Local Government Act 2000

13.66   LGA 2000 s2 provides:

(1) Every local authority are to have power to do anything which they consider is likely to achieve any one or more of the following objects – ...
(b) the promotion or improvement of the social well being of their area.

13.67   The power may be exercised for the benefit of the whole or any part of the local authority's area,[145] or all or any persons resident or present in it.[146] This provision is, however, also excluded in the case of some classes of immigrant, being those classes (subject to exceptions, including the overarching exception for British citizens and persons under the age of 18,[147] and the human rights/EC Treaty exceptions)[148] considered in chapter 3.[149]

13.68   Well-being powers cannot be used where there is a prohibition, restriction or limitation on the authority's power to act 'contained in' any enactment, whenever passed or made.[150] The courts have, however, been reluctant to construe this broadly and have inclined against finding restrictions in the absence of an express exclusion.[151]

13.69   Following the Court of Appeal decision in *A*, in which it had been held that there was no power to provide accommodation under CA 1989 s17,[152] a further challenge to a refusal to assist was mounted in *R (J) v Enfield LBC*.[153] It was accepted that the authority had no power under CA 1989 to assist the applicant and her two-year-old daughter

145 LGA 2000 s2(2)(a).
146 LGA 2000 s2(2)(b).
147 Above, para 3.120.
148 Above, para 3.123.
149 Above, paras 3.123–3.127.
150 LGA 2000 s3(1).
151 *R (J) v Enfield LBC* [2002] EWHC Admin 432; [2002] HLR 38; *R (Theophilus) v Lewisham LBC* [2002] EWHC 1371 (Admin); [2002] 3 All ER 851; *R (W) v Lambeth LBC* [2002] EWCA Civ 613; (2002) 5 CCLR 203; [2002] HLR 41, per Brooke LJ at [75]; *R (Khan) v Oxfordshire County Council* [2004] EWCA Civ 309 [2004] HLR 41; *R (Grant) v Lambeth LBC* [2004] EWCA Civ 1711; [2005] HLR 27; *R (Richards) West Somerset Council* [2008] EWHC 3215 (Admin). The power under LGA 2000, s2 does not, however, authorise a local authority to promote its own economic well-being: *Brent LBC v Risk Management Partners LTD & (1) London Authorities Mutual Ltd & (2) Harrow LBC (interested Parties)* [2009] EWCA Civ 490.
152 *R (A) v Lambeth LBC* [2001] EWCA Civ 1624; [2002] HLR 13, see above, para 13.47 and footnote 109.
153 [2002] EWHC Admin 432; [2002] HLR 38; (2002) 5 CCLR 434.

by the provision of accommodation for them together; it was also
held that there was no power to provide assistance by way of payment
of financial assistance to obtain accommodation. Given that – on the
understanding of the law at that time[154] – no assistance could be provided which would keep the family together, it was common ground
between applicant and authority that the separation of the mother
and her child (by taking the child into local authority care) would
be a breach of ECHR article 8 (the right to respect for family life),[155]
unless there was another way in which assistance could be provided,
or the CA 1989 could be construed compatibly with the applicant's
right to respect for family life. At the instigation of the Secretary of
State for Health, however, the judge accepted instead that LGA 2000
s2 could be used in order to provide financial assistance.

13.70   While LGA 2000 s2 was plainly intended for a more strategic
use,[156] subsequent cases have affirmed its availability for this sort
of safety-net purpose. Thus, it has been held to afford power to an
authority to fund travel arrangements for a person unlawfully in the
UK, if exercising that power is necessary to avoid breaching the person's rights under the ECHR.[157]

13.71   J[158] went somewhat further than affirming availability: it also
held[159] that if it was the only way to avoid breach of the ECHR, an
authority was required to use LGA 2000 s2. However, this was overruled in *Morris*,[160] where it was likewise argued that – given the
prior declaration of incompatibility of HA 1996 s185(4) with ECHR
article 8[161] – the authority was obliged to provide assistance to the

---

154 In *R (W) v Lambeth LBC* [2002] EWCA Civ 613; (2002) 5 CCLR 203; [2002]
     HLR 41, the decision in *A* was held to have been per incuriam. Accordingly,
     the Court of Appeal in *W* did not find it necessary to consider use of the LGA
     2000 s2 power: see at [75]. Nor, when both *A* and *W* were considered by the
     House of Lords, were these powers dealt with at all.

155 See para 12.78, above. There is some doubt about this concession: see *R (W)
     v Lambeth LBC* [2002] EWCA Civ 613; (2002) 5 CCLR 203; [2002] HLR 41, at
     [85]–[86].

156 See the requirement in LGA 2000 s2(3) to have regard to the authority's
     community strategy (made under LGA 2000 s4) in determining whether and
     how to use the power.

157 *R (Grant) v Lambeth* LBC [2004] EWCA Civ 1711; [2005] HLR 57. See also *R
     (Theophilus) v Lewisham LBC* [2002] EWHC 1371 (Admin); [2002] 3 All ER 851,
     authorising a student loan to someone not otherwise entitled to assistance.

158 [2002] EWHC Admin 432; [2002] HLR 38; (2002) 5 CCLR 434.

159 At [58]. See also government guidance on section 2, *Power to Promote or Improve
     Economic, Social or Environmental Well-Being*, DETR (March 2001), para 25.

160 *R (Morris) v Westminster CC* [2005] EWCA Civ 1184; [2006] HLR 8.

161 See para 3.71, above.

applicants using alternative powers, including LGA 2000 s2. The Court of Appeal rejected this argument, and applied the decision of the House of Lords in *Hooper*,[162] that a power to make alternative provision could not become a duty simply because the principal power is subject to statutory restrictions which are incompatible with Convention rights.

---

162 [2005] UKHL 29; [2005] 1 WLR 1681. Compare the speeches of Lords Hoffmann, Hope and Brown.

CHAPTER 14

Strategy, aid and advice

Introduction

14.1   In this chapter, we consider what might be called the 'general' functions related to homelessness, imposed on local housing authorities for the benefit of their areas.

14.2   There are three such functions:

a) to maintain a homelessness strategy;
b) to provide advisory services; and
c) to provide assistance to the voluntary sector.

Homelessness strategies

14.3   By the Homelessness Act 2002 s1, all local housing authorities were required to carry out a homelessness review and formulate and publish a strategy based on that review.[1]

14.4   This exercise was to be carried out with the assistance of the local social services authority.[2] Both the housing and social services authorities have to take the strategy into account in exercising their functions.[3]

14.5   By the Homelessness Act 2002 s1(3) and (4), the first such strategy had to be drawn up within a year of the section coming into force,[4] and thereafter at least every five years.[5]

Reviews

14.6   A homelessness review is defined in the Homelessness Act 2002 s2 as a review of:

---

1 Homelessness Act 2002 s1(1). Para 20 of *Fair and Flexible: statutory guidance on social housing allocations for local authorities in England* (DCLG, December 2009) spells out the importance the government places on prevention of homelessness and the encouragement given to local authorities to use their allocations policies to assist with homeless strategies.

2 Homelessness Act 2002 s1(2). Within the meaning of the Local Authority Social Services Act 1970 (see para 2.14).

3 Homelessness Act 2002 s1(5) and (6).

4 That was by 31 July 2003 in England, and 30 September 2003 in Wales.

5 An English authority which has been categorised as an 'excellent authority' under an order made under the Local Government Act 2003, s99(4) (previously Comprehensive Performance Assessment, but now, since 1 April 2009, Comprehensive Area Assessment) is exempt from the requirement to publish further strategies: Local Authorities' Plans and Strategies (Disapplication) (England) Order 2005 SI No 157.

a) the current and likely future levels of homelessness in an authority's district;[6]
b) the activities carried out in the authority's area for:[7]
   i) preventing homelessness;
   ii) securing that accommodation is or will be available in the area
       for people who are or may become homeless; and
   iii) providing support[8] for such people or for those who have
       been homeless and need support to prevent it recurring; and
c) the resources available to the authority, the social services authority, other public authorities, voluntary organisations[9] and other
   persons for such activities.[10]

Guidance

14.7   Guidance on carrying out a review is available in *Homelessness strate-
        gies: a good practice handbook*.[11] The review should include an assess-
        ment of needs of all homeless people, including those who have
        become homeless intentionally and those who are not in priority
        need. The review of needs and audit of services should identify both
        where needs are not being met, and where there is unnecessary dupli-
        cation in the supply of services. The review of resources should cover
        staff, property and funding and include existing provision as well as
        plans for the future.

Publication

14.8   On completion of the review, an authority must arrange for the re-
        sults to be available for inspection by members of the public, at rea-
        sonable hours, without charge, and provide a copy on payment of a
        reasonable charge.[12]

Strategies

14.9   A homelessness strategy is defined in HA 2002 s3(1) as one formu-
        lated in order to:

---

6 See Code of Guidance paras 1.13–1.18.
7 See Code of Guidance paras 1.19–1.25.
8 Support means 'advice, information or assistance': Homelessness Act 2002 s4.
9 By Homelessness Act 2002 s4, this has the same definition as Housing Act
   1996 (HA 1996) s180(3): see para 14.24, below.
10 See Code of Guidance paras 1.25–1.29.
11 DTLR, February 2002. See, in particular, chapter 4. See also *Local authorities'
   homelessness strategies: evaluation and good practice* (ODPM, 2004).
12 Homelessness Act 2002 s2(3).

a) prevent homelessness in an authority's area;[13]
b) secure that accommodation is and will be available in that area for people who are or may become homeless; and
c) provide support[14] for such people or those who have been homeless and need support to prevent it recurring.

14.10   There is no requirement that specific objectives or plans, such as housing a proportion of homeless applicants outside an authority's district, should be included in the strategy. It is a matter of discretion for the authority whether or not to include such matters.[15]

Functions

14.11   The strategy may encompass specific objectives or action falling within both housing and social service functions.[16]

Partnership

14.12   The strategy may also include provision for action to be taken by other public authorities, voluntary organisations[17] or persons who might be capable of contributing to the achievement of any of the strategic objectives,[18] but only if given approval to include such provision by that contributing authority, organisation or person,[19] ie, an authority cannot rely on what others might do otherwise than with their consent.

14.13   In order to encourage partnership working, an authority is under a duty to positively consider the extent to which any of the objectives of the strategy can be achieved through action involving two or more of the local authority, social services authority, another public authority, any voluntary organisation or any person.[20]

---

13   On prevention, see further Code of Guidance chapter 2; Welsh Code chapter 10.
14   Support means 'advice information or assistance': Homelessness Act 2002 s4.
15   *R (Calgin) v Enfield LBC* [2005] EWHC 1716 (Admin); [2006] HLR 4.
16   Homelessness Act 2002 s3(2). See Code of Guidance annex 4 for a list of specific objectives and action that might be included. See also the guidance on developing action plans in *Local authorities' homelessness strategies: evaluation and good practice* (ODPM, 2004).
17   By Homelessness Act 2002 s4, this has the same definition as HA 1996 s180(3): see para 14.24, below.
18   See Code of Guidance annexes 3 and 6; Welsh Code annexes 17 and 18 for a list of other authorities, organisations and persons who may be able to contribute and specific action that might be expected to be taken by others.
19   Homelessness Act 2002 s3(3) and (4).
20   Homelessness Act 2002 s3(5).

Guidance

14.14 In addition to the needs assessment and audit of services emerging from the homelessness review, the strategy should include action on planning and implementing the strategy, including:[21]

a) the involvement of partner agencies – public, voluntary and private – in formulating and implementing the strategy;

b) consultation with other agencies in contact with homeless people, even if not involved in service provision;

c) consultation with service-users and other homeless people;

d) defining key aims and objectives of the strategy;

e) agreeing priorities for action;

f) a timetabled and costed programme;

g) identification of which agencies will do what and when;

h) mechanisms for joint and partnership work;

i) mechanisms of monitoring and evaluation of the strategy and individual elements of the programme, including targets and performance indicators; and

j) mechanisms for regular review and amendment of the strategy in the light of the monitoring and evaluation.

On strategies to prevent homelessness, further guidance is also available in *Homelessness prevention: a guide to good practice.*[22]

14.15 As the allocation of accommodation under Housing Act 1996 (HA 1996) Part 6 is one of the ways in which the main homelessness duty can be discharged, allocation policies and procedures should also be consistent with the local authority's homelessness strategy.[23]

Review of strategy

14.16 The strategy must be kept under review by the authority,[24] and may be modified.[25] Any modifications must be published.[26] Any public or local authorities, voluntary organisations or other persons as the

---

21 *Homelessness strategies: a good practice handbook* (DTLR, 2002), para 2.1.5.

22 DCLG, June 2006.

23 See para 54 of the new Code of Guidance on allocations. Note also that by para 55, the Code sets out the importance of allocation schemes being compatible with and flowing from an authority's sustainable community strategy (pursuant to Local Government Act 2000, s4).

24 See *Preventing Homelessness: A Strategy Health Check*, non-statutory guidance published in September 2006 by DCLG.

25 Homelessness Act 2002 s3(6).

26 Homelessness Act 2002 s3(7).

authority considers appropriate must be consulted prior to both adopting or modifying the strategy.[27]

Publication

14.17   The published strategy, and any modifications, must be available for inspection, at reasonable hours, without charge, by members of the public and available for purchase on payment of a reasonable charge.[28]

Provision of advisory services

14.18   HA 1996 s179[29] requires authorities to ensure that provision of advice and information about homelessness and the prevention of homelessness is available free of charge in their areas.

14.19   'Advice' and 'information' are not defined but the Code of Guidance[30] suggests that 'it will need to be wide ranging and comprehensive in its coverage and may require a full multi-disciplinary assessment ... Advice services should provide information on the range of housing options that are available in the district'. Such services may also include an advocacy service, which may include providing legal representation for people facing the loss of their home.[31] Where advice is provided by the authority, it is trite – but should be borne in mind – that accurate advice in the interests of the applicant must be given.[32]

14.20   The authority does not have to provide this service itself but may secure that it is provided on its behalf by or in partnership with some other organisation.[33]

---

27   Homelessness Act 2002 s3(8).

28   Homelessness Act 2002 s3(9).

29   See also HA 1996 s166, as amended by the Homelessness Act 2002, above, para 11.50.

30   Code of Guidance paras 2.10 and 2.11; Welsh Code paras 9.1 and 9.2.

31   Code of Guidance para 2.12.

32   *Robinson v Hammersmith & Fulham LBC* [2006] EWCA Civ 1122; [2007] HLR 7, per Jacob LJ at [45], considering – with reference to HA 1996 s179 – advice to mediate offered to a 17-year-old: 'A near 18 old who came to the authority could obviously not be properly be advised to mediate if the effect of mediation would be to delay the actual s184 decision past the 18th birthday' (thus causing the loss of automatic priority need – see para 5.67).

33   See further, Code of Guidance paras 2.17–2.19; Welsh Code paras 9.3–9.5.

14.21   To facilitate this, it may provide grants or loans to a person provid-ing the service on its behalf.[34] Assistance may also be given by way of the use of premises, furniture or other goods and even the services of staff.[35]

14.22   To ensure that they are providing an effective service to a high standard, housing authorities may wish to refer to the quality as-surance systems applied by the National Association of Citizens Advice Bureaux and the Shelter Network of housing advice centres, the national Disabled Housing Services Ltd (HoDis) accreditation scheme and the Community Legal Service Quality Mark. Housing authorities are also advised to monitor the provision of advisory ser-vices to ensure that they continue to meet the needs of all sections of the community and help deliver the aims of their homelessness strategy.[36]

14.23   The duty to provide advice and information to persons in the area is applicable even to those who are ineligible for assistance.[37]

Aid to voluntary organisations

14.24   Voluntary organisations have long played an important role in assist-ing homeless people. Bodies such as housing associations have pro-vided significant assistance to local authorities in the discharge of their obligations towards the homeless, especially those in 'special categories'. A voluntary organisation is, for the purposes of HA 1996 Part 7, a body whose activities are carried on otherwise than for profit, but not including a public or local authority.[38] This definition is wide enough to include housing associations and other non-profit-making social landlords.[39]

14.25   The powers permit the secretary of state, or local housing author-ities, to give money by way of grant or loan to such a voluntary organisation.[40]

---

34 HA 1996 s179(2).
35 HA 1996 s179(3); see paras 14.27–14.31, below, as to the terms of such assistance.
36 Code of Guidance para 2.20; Welsh Code para 9.13.
37 HA 1996 s183(3); see chapter 3.
38 HA 1996 s180(3).
39 *Goodman v Dolphin Square Trust Ltd* (1979) 38 P&CR 257, CA.
40 HA 1996 s180(1).

14.26   A local housing authority may also assist by letting a voluntary organisation use premises belonging to it, on such terms and conditions as may be agreed, and by making available furniture or other goods – by way of gift, loan or otherwise – or the services of staff employed by it.[41]

14.27   Assistance under HA 1996 s179 or s180 may be given on such terms and conditions as the secretary of state or authority may determine.[42]

14.28   No assistance of any kind is to be given, however, unless the voluntary organisation first gives an undertaking:

a) to use the money, furniture or other goods or premises made available to it for a purpose to be specified in the undertaking; and

b) that – if required to do so by the body providing the assistance – it will, within 21 days of notice served upon it, certify such information as may reasonably be required by the notice as to the manner in which assistance given to it is being used.[43]

14.29   In every case in which assistance is provided, the conditions must include a requirement that the voluntary organisation keeps proper books of account and has them audited in a specified manner, keeps records indicating how the assistance has been used, and submits accounts and records for inspection by the body providing the assistance.[44]

14.30   If it appears to the body providing the assistance that the voluntary organisation is not using the assistance for the purposes specified in the undertaking, it is obliged to take all reasonable steps to recover an amount of money equal to the amount of the assistance from the organisation.

14.31   No such amount is recoverable, however, unless there has first been served on the voluntary organisation a notice specifying the amount alleged to be recoverable and the basis on which it has been calculated.[45]

---

41 HA 1996 s180(2).
42 HA 1996 s181(2).
43 HA 1996 s181(3).
44 HA 1996 s181(4).
45 HA 1996 s181(5) and (6).

Criminal offences

Introduction

15.1   To prevent abuse of Housing Act (HA) 1996 Parts 6 and 7, some attempts to obtain accommodation are classified as criminal offences. There are three such offences:

a)   making a false statement;
b)   withholding information; and
c)   failing to notify changes.

15.2   Offences under these provisions are prosecuted in the magistrates' court, and carry a maximum fine of 'level 5 on the standard scale'.[1]

Making a false statement

15.3   This offence is committed by anyone – not only an applicant – who knowingly or recklessly makes a statement which is false in a material particular with intent to induce an authority, in connection with the exercise of its functions under HA 1996 Part 6 or Part 7, to believe that the person making the statement or any other person is homeless, threatened with homelessness, has a priority need, or did not become homeless or threatened with homelessness intentionally.[2]

15.4   The offence is sufficiently widely drafted to catch, for example, an adviser who makes representations on behalf of an applicant. Since the offence requires proof of intent to induce the authority to believe something which is not true, the prosecutor must, accordingly, include proof of such intent as part of the prosecution, so this would be a rare event. However, advisers should bear the possibility in mind when deciding in what terms to relay information to an authority.[3]

Withholding information

15.5   This offence is committed by anyone – again, not just an applicant – who knowingly withholds information which the authority has reasonably required him/her to give in connection with the exercise of

---

1   Currently £5,000: Criminal Justice Act 1982 s37(2), as amended by Criminal Justice Act 1991 s17(1).
2   HA 1996 ss171(1) and 214(1).
3   As a criminal offence, the standard of proof is beyond reasonable doubt but the element of intent may be proved by natural inference from acts.

its functions under HA 1996 Parts 6 and 7.[4] This is a widely drafted provision, allowing an authority to require information from, for example, a relative or a former landlord.

15.6   Under HA 1996 s214(1), however, an intent must be shown to induce the authority, in connection with the exercise of its Part 7 functions, to believe that the person withholding the information, or any other person, is entitled to accommodation or assistance. Accordingly, it is directed at the person withholding information that would be harmful to an applicant, rather than at someone who refuses to provide helpful information.

15.7   For this purpose, assistance means the benefit of any duty under HA 1996 Part 7, which relates to accommodation or to assistance in obtaining accommodation.[5] There is no equivalent limitation in HA 1996 s171(1).

Failure to notify changes

15.8   This offence arises only in relation to HA 1996 Part 7. It may be committed only by an applicant.

15.9   An applicant is under a positive duty to inform the authority as soon as possible of any change of facts material to his/her application, which occurs before the receipt of notification under HA 1996 s184 of its decision on his/her application.[6] This is even though the circumstances to be taken into account on an internal review include any that have changed between that decision and the decision on the review.[7] It follows that a failure to notify the authority of an adverse change – which the authority is entitled to take into account – would seem to be exempt from this obligation.[8]

15.10   The extent of obligation is less straightforward than the two offences previously considered. Of particular difficulty is the issue of what constitutes a 'material change of facts'. In accordance with

---

4   HA 1996 ss171(1) and 214(1).
5   See HA 1996 s183(2).
6   HA 1996 s214(2). The statutory language would not seem to be capable of being extended to the decision on the review, especially bearing in mind that as a criminal offence is involved, it is to be interpreted narrowly.
7   See para 9.176, above.
8   Although there is no reference to HA 1996 s214 in *Mohamed v Hammersmith & Fulham LBC* [2001] UKHL 57, [2002] HLR 7, it formed a substantive part of the argument and it would therefore seem that Lord Slynn's conclusion at [25] confirms this analysis: 'I find nothing in the statutory language which requires the review to be confined to the date of the initial application or determination.'

the usual principles of criminal law, the courts should interpret the provisions narrowly, ie in favour of the accused.

15.11   A related duty is imposed on authorities: to explain to an applicant, in ordinary language, the nature of his/her duty to notify them of material changes and that failure to do so is a criminal offence.[9] The Code of Guidance[10] suggests that this obligation is 'explained in ordinary language, and conveyed sensitively to avoid intimidating applicants'.

15.12   It is a defence for the applicant to show that s/he was not given such an explanation. It is also a defence to show that s/he had a reasonable excuse for non-compliance.[11]

9 HA 1996 s214(2).
10 At para 6.11; Welsh Code, para 12.71.
11 HA 1996 s214(3).

APPENDICES

continued

Statutes*

Housing Act 1985

LOCAL HOUSING AUTHORITIES

Local housing authorities

1   In this Act 'local housing authority' means a district council, a London borough council, the Common Council of the City of London a Welsh county council or county borough council or the Council of the Isles of Scilly.

The district of a local housing authority

2   (1) References in this Act to the district of a local housing authority are to the area of the council concerned, that is, to the district, London borough, the City of London the Welsh county or county borough, or the Isles of Scilly, as the case may be.

   (2) References in this Act to 'the local housing authority', in relation to land, are to the local housing authority in whose district the land is situated.
   . . .

OTHER AUTHORITIES AND BODIES

Other descriptions of authority

4   (1) In this Act –
   (a) 'housing authority' means a local housing authority, or a new town corporation;
   (b) 'new town corporation' means a development corporation or the new towns residuary body;
   (c) 'development corporation' means a development corporation established by an order made, or having effect as if made, under the New Towns Act 1981;
   (d) 'urban development corporation' means an urban development corporation established under Part 16 of the Local Government, Planning and Land Act 1980;
   (e) 'local authority' means a county, county borough, district or London borough council, the Common Council of the City of London or the Council of the Isles of Scilly, and in sections 43, 44 and 232 includes Broads Authority, and in sections 438, 441, 442, 443 and 458 includes the Broads Authority and a joint authority established by Part 4 of the Local Government Act 1985, an economic prosperity board, a combined authority, a joint waste authority and the London Fire and Emergency Planning Authority and in sections 45(2)(b), 50(2), 51(6), 80(1), 157(1), 171(2), . . . 573(1), paragraph 2(1) of Schedule 1, grounds 7 and 12 in Schedule 2, ground 5 in Schedule 3, paragraph 7(1) of Schedule 4, paragraph 5(1)(b) of Schedule 5 and Schedule 16 includes the . . . Broads Authority, a police authority established under section 3 of the Police Act 1996 . . . a joint authority established by Part 4 of the Local Government Act 1985, an economic prosperity board, a combined authority, a joint waste authority and the London Fire and Emergency Planning Authority;
   (f) 'housing action trust' means a housing action trust established under Part 3 of the Housing Act 1988.
   (g) 'new towns residuary body' means–

      (i) in relation to England, the Homes and Communities Agency so far as exercising functions in relation to anything transferred (or to be transferred) to it as mentioned in section 52(1)(a) to (d) of the Housing and Regeneration Act 2008; and

      (ii) in relation to Wales, the Welsh Ministers so far as exercising functions in relation to anything transferred (or to be transferred) to them as mentioned in section 36(1)(a) (i) to (iii) of the New Towns Act 1981.

(2) In this section –

    'combined authority' means a combined authority established under section 103 of the Local Democracy, Economic Development and Construction Act 2009;

    'economic prosperity board' means an economic prosperity board established under section 88 of that Act;

    'joint waste authority' means an authority established for an area in England by an order under section 207 of the Local Government and Public Involvement in Health Act 2007.[1]

---

1 Not yet in force. See Local Democracy, Economic Development and Construction Act 2009 s148(6).

Housing Act 1996

PART 6: ALLOCATION OF HOUSING ACCOMMODATION

INTRODUCTORY

Allocation of housing accommodation

159 (1) A local housing authority shall comply with the provisions of this Part in allocating housing accommodation.

(2) For the purposes of this Part a local housing authority allocate housing accommodation when they –

(a) select a person to be a secure or introductory tenant of housing accommodation held by them,

(b) nominate a person to be a secure or introductory tenant of housing accommodation held by another person, or

(c) nominate a person to be an assured tenant of housing accommodation held by a registered social landlord.

(3) The reference in subsection (2)(a) to selecting a person to be a secure tenant includes deciding to exercise any power to notify an existing tenant or licensee that his tenancy or licence is to be a secure tenancy.

(4) The references in subsection (2)(b) and (c) to nominating a person include nominating a person in pursuance of any arrangements (whether legally enforceable or not) to require that housing accommodation, or a specified amount of housing accommodation, is made available to a person or one of a number of persons nominated by the authority.

(5) The provisions of this Part do not apply to an allocation of housing to a person who is already a secure tenant unless the allocation involved a transfer of housing accommodation for that person and is made on his application.

. . .

(7) Subject to the provisions of this Part, a local housing authority may allocate housing accommodation in such manner as they consider appropriate.

Cases where provisions about allocation do not apply

160 (1) The provisions of this Part about the allocation of housing accommodation do not apply in the following cases.

(2) They do not apply where a secure tenancy –

(a) vests under section 89 of the Housing Act 1985 (succession to periodic secure tenancy on death of tenant),

(b) remains a secure tenancy by virtue of section 90 of that Act (devolution of term certain of secure tenancy on death of tenant),

(c) is assigned under section 92 of that Act (assignment of secure tenancy by way of exchange),

(d) is assigned to a person who would be qualified to succeed the secure tenant if the secure tenant died immediately before the assignment, or

(e) vests or is otherwise disposed of in pursuance of an order made under –

(i) section 24 of the Matrimonial Causes Act 1973 (property adjustment orders in connection with matrimonial proceedings),

(ii) section 17(1) of the Matrimonial and Family Proceedings Act 1984 (property adjustment orders after overseas divorce, etc),

(iii) paragraph 1 of Schedule 1 to the Children Act 1989 (orders for financial relief against parents), or

(iv) Part 2 of Schedule 5, or paragraph 9(2) or (3) of Schedule 7, to the Civil Partnership Act 2004 (property adjustments orders in connection with civil partnership proceedings or an overseas dissolution of civil partnership, etc).

(3) They do not apply where an introductory tenancy –

(a) becomes a secure tenancy on ceasing to be an introductory tenancy,

(b) vests under section 133(2) (succession to introductory tenancy on death of tenant),

(c) is assigned to a person who would be qualified to succeed the introductory tenant if the introductory tenant died immediately before the assignment, or

(d) vests or is otherwise disposed of in pursuance of an order made under –

(i) section 24 of the Matrimonial Causes Act 1973 (property adjustment orders in connection with matrimonial proceedings),

(ii) section 17(1) of the Matrimonial and Family Proceedings Act 1984 (property adjustment orders after overseas divorce, etc),

(iii) paragraph 1 of Schedule 1 to the Children Act 1989 (orders for financial relief against parents), or

(iv) Part 2 of Schedule 5, or paragraph 9(2) or (3) of Schedule 7, to the Civil Partnership Act 2004 (property adjustments orders in connection with civil partnership proceedings or an overseas dissolution of civil partnership, etc).

(4) They do not apply in such other cases as the Secretary of State may prescribe by regulations.

(5) The regulations may be framed so as to make the exclusion of the provisions of this Part about the allocation of housing accommodation subject to such restrictions or conditions as may be specified.

In particular, those provisions may be excluded –

(a) in relation to specified descriptions of persons, or

(b) in relation to housing accommodation of a specified description or a specified proportion of housing accommodation of any specified description.

ELIGIBILITY FOR ALLOCATION FOR HOUSING ACCOMMODATION

Allocation any to eligible persons

160A(1) A local housing authority shall not allocate housing accommodation –

(a) to a person from abroad who is ineligible for an allocation of housing accommodation by virtue of subsection (3) or (5);

(b) to a person who the authority have decided is to be treated as ineligible for such an allocation by virtue of subsection (7); or

(c) to two or more persons jointly if any of them is a person mentioned in paragraph (a) or (b).

(2) Except as provided by subsection (1), any person may be allocated housing accommodation by a local housing authority (whether on his application or otherwise).

(3) A person subject to immigration control within the meaning of the Asylum and immigration Act 1996 is (subject to subsection 6) ineligible for an

allocation of housing accommodation by a local housing authority unless he is of a class prescribed by regulations made by the Secretary of State.

(4) No person who is excluded from entitlement to housing benefit by section 115 of the Immigration and Asylum Act 1999 (exclusion of benefits) shall be included in any class prescribed under subsection (3).

(5) The Secretary of State may by regulations prescribe other classes of persons from abroad who are (subject to subsection (6) ineligible for an allocation of housing accommodation, either in relation to local housing authorities generally or any particular local housing authority.

(6) Nothing in subsections (3) or (5) affects the eligibility of a person who is already –
   (a) a secure or introductory tenant;
   (b) an assured tenant of housing accommodation allocated to him by a local housing authority.

(7) A local housing authority may decide that an applicant is to be treated as ineligible for an allocation of housing accommodation by them if they are satisfied that –
   (a) he, or a member of his household, has been guilty of unacceptable behaviour serious enough top make him unsuitable to be a tenant of the authority; and
   (b) in the circumstances at the time his application is considered, he is unsuitable to be a tenant of the authority by reason of that behaviour.

(8) The only behaviour which may be regarded by the authority as unacceptable for the purposes of subsection (7)(a) is –
   (a) behaviour of the person concerned which would (if he were a secure tenant of the authority) entitle the authority to a possession order under section 84 of the Housing Act 1985 on any ground mentioned in Part 1 of Schedule 2 of that Act (other than ground 8); or
   (b) behaviour of a member of his household which would (if he were a person residing with a secure tenant of the authority) entitle the authority to such a possession order.

(9) If a local housing authority decide that an applicant for housing accommodation –
   (a) is ineligible for an allocation by them by virtue of subsection (3) or (5); or
   (b) is to be treated as ineligible for such an allocation by virtue of subsection (7),
   they shall notify the applicant of their decision and the grounds for it.

(10) That notice shall be given in writing and, if not received by the applicant, shall be treated as having been given if it is made available at the authority's office for a reasonable period for collection by him or on his behalf.

(11) A person who is being treated by a local housing authority as ineligible by virtue of subsection (7) may (if he considers that he should no longer be treated as ineligible by the authority) make a fresh application to the authority for allocation of housing accommodation by them.

161   . . .
162   . . .
163   . . .
164   . . .
165   . . .

APPLICATIONS FOR HOUSING ACCOMMODATION

Applications for housing accommodation

166 (1) A local housing authority shall secure that –

(a) advice and information is available free of charge to persons in their district about the right to make an application for an allocation of housing accommodation; and

(b) any necessary assistance in making such an application is available free of charge to persons in their district who are likely to have difficulty in doing so without assistance.

(2) A local housing authority shall secure that an applicant for an allocation of housing accommodation is informed that he has the rights mentioned in section 167(4A).

(3) Every application made to a local housing authority for an allocation of housing accommodation shall (if made in accordance with the procedural requirements of the authority's allocation scheme) be considered by the authority.

(4) The fact that a person is an applicant for an allocation of housing accommodation shall not be divulged (without his consent) to any other member of the public.

(5) In this Part 'district' in relation to a local housing authority has the same meaning as the Housing Act 1985.

THE ALLOCATION SCHEME

Allocation in accordance with allocation scheme

167 (1) Every local housing authority shall have a scheme (their 'allocation scheme') for determining priorities, and as to the procedure to be followed, in allocating housing accommodation.

For this purpose 'procedure' includes all aspects of the allocation process, including the persons or descriptions of persons by whom decisions are to be taken.

(1A) The scheme shall include a statement of the authority's policy on offering people who are allocated housing accommodation –

(a) a choice of housing accommodation; or

(b) the opportunity to express preferences about the housing accommodation to be allocated to them.

(2) As regards priorities, the scheme shall, subject to subsection (2ZA), be framed so as to secure that reasonable preference is given to –

(a) people who are homeless (within the meaning of Part 7);

(b) people who are owed a duty by any local housing authority under section 190(2), 193(2) or 195(2) (under section 65(2) or 68(2) of the Housing Act 1985) or who are occupying accommodation secured by any such authority under section 192(3);

(c) people occupying insanitary or overcrowded housing or otherwise living in unsatisfactory housing conditions;

(d) people who need to move on medical or welfare grounds (including grounds relating to disability); and

(e) people who need to move to a particular locality in the district of the authority, where failure to meet that need would cause hardship (to themselves or to others).

The scheme may also be framed so as to give additional preference to particular descriptions of people within this subsection (being descriptions of people with urgent housing needs).

(2ZA) People are to be disregarded for the purposes of subsection (2) if they would not have fallen within paragraph (a) or (b) of that subsection without the local housing authority have had regard to a restricted person (within the meaning of Part 7).

(2A) The scheme may contain provision for determining priorities in allocating housing accommodation to people within subsection (2); and the factors which the scheme may allow to be taken into account include –

  (a) the financial resources available to a person to meet his housing costs;
  (b) any behaviour of a person (or of a member of his household) which affects his suitability to be a tenant;
  (c) any local connection (within the meaning of section 199) which exists between a person and the authority's district.

(2B) Nothing in subsection (2) requires the scheme to provide for any preference to be given to people the authority have decided are people to whom subsection (2C) applies.

(2C) This subsection applies to a person if the authority are satisfied that –

  (a) he, or a member of his household, has been guilty of unacceptable behaviour serious enough to make him unsuitable to be a tenant of the authority; and
  (b) in the circumstances at the time his case is considered, he deserves by reason of that behaviour not to be treated as a member of a group of people who are to be given preference by virtue of subsection (2).

(2D) Subsection (8) of section 160A applies for the purposes of subsection (2C)(a)above as it applies for the purposes of subsection (7)(a) of that section.

(2E) Subject to subsection (2), the scheme may contain provision about the allocation of particular housing accommodation –

  (a) to a person who makes a specific application for that accommodation;
  (b) to persons of a particular description (whether or not they are within subsection (2).

(3) The Secretary of State may by regulations –

  (a) specify further descriptions of people to whom preference is to be given as mentioned in subsection (2), or
  (b) amend or repeal any part of subsection (2).

(4) The Secretary of State may by regulations specify factors which a local housing authority shall not take into account in allocating housing accommodation.

(4A) The scheme shall be framed so as to secure that an applicant for an allocation of housing accommodation –

  (a) has the right to request such general information as will enable him to assess –

    (i) how his application is likely to be treated under the scheme (including in particular whether he is likely to be regarded as a member of a group of people who are to be given preference by virtue of subsection (2)); and
    (ii) whether housing accommodation appropriate to his needs is likely to be made available to him and, if so, how long it is likely to be before such accommodation becomes available for allocation to him;

(b) is notified in writing of any decision that he is a person to whom subsection (2C) applies and the grounds for it;

(c) has the right to request the authority to inform him of any decision about the facts of his case which is likely to be, or has been, taken into account in considering whether to allocate housing accommodation to him; and

(d) has the right to request a review of a decision mentioned in paragraph (b) or (c), or in section 160A(9), and to be informed of the decision on the review and the grounds for it.

(5) As regards the procedure to be followed, the scheme shall be framed in accordance with such principles as the Secretary of State may prescribe by regulations.

(6) Subject to the above provisions, and to any regulations made under them, the authority may decide on what principles the scheme is to be framed.

(7) Before adopting an allocation scheme, or making an alteration to their scheme reflecting a major change of policy, a local housing authority shall –

(a) send a copy of the draft scheme, or proposed alteration, to every registered social landlord with which they have nomination arrangements (see section 159(4)), and

(b) afford those persons a reasonable opportunity to comment on the proposals.

(8) A local housing authority shall not allocate housing accommodation except in accordance with their allocation scheme.

Information about allocation scheme

168 (1) A local housing authority shall publish a summary of their allocation scheme and provide a copy of the summary free of charge to any member of the public who asks for one.

(2) The authority shall make the scheme available for inspection at their principal office and shall provide a copy of the scheme, on payment of a reasonable fee, to any member of the public who asks for one.

(3) When the authority make an alteration to their scheme reflecting a major change of policy, they shall within a reasonable period of time take such steps as they consider reasonable to bring the effect of the alteration to the attention of those likely to be affected by it.

SUPPLEMENTARY

Guidance to authorities by the Secretary of State

169 (1) In the exercise of their functions under this Part, local housing authorities shall have regard to such guidance as may from time to time be given by the Secretary of State.

(2) The Secretary of State may give guidance generally or to specified descriptions of authorities.

Co-operation between registered social landlords and local housing authorities

170 Where a local housing authority so request, a registered social landlord shall co-operate to such extent as is reasonable in the circumstances in offering accommodation to people with priority under the authority's allocation scheme.

False statements and withholding information

171 (1) A person commits an offence if, in connection with the exercise by a local housing authority of their functions under this Part –

(a) he knowingly or recklessly makes a statement which is false in a material particular, or

(b) he knowingly withholds information which the authority have reasonably required him to give in connection with the exercise of those functions.

(2) A person guilty of an offence under this section is liable on summary conviction to a fine not exceeding level 5 on the standard scale.

Regulations

172 (1) Regulations under this Part shall be made by statutory instrument.

(2) No regulations shall be made under section 167(3) (regulations amending provisions about priorities in allocating housing accommodation) unless a draft of the regulations has been laid before and approved by a resolution of each House of Parliament.

(3) Any other regulations under this Part shall be subject to annulment in pursuance of a resolution of either House of Parliament.

(4) Regulations under this Part may contain such incidental, supplementary and transitional provisions as appear to the Secretary of State appropriate, and may make different provision for different cases including different provision for different areas.

Consequential amendments: Part 6

173 The enactments mentioned in Schedule 16 have effect with the amendments specified there which are consequential on the provisions of this Part.

Index of defined expressions: Part 6

174 The following Table shows provisions defining or otherwise explaining expressions used in this Part (other than provisions defining or explaining an expression used in the same section) –

allocation (of housing)	section 159(2)
allocation scheme	section 167
assured tenancy	section 230
district (of local housing authority)	section 165(5)
. . .	
introductory tenancy and introductory tenant	sections 230 and 124
local housing authority	section 230
. . .	
registered social landlord	sections 230 and 2
secure tenancy and secure tenant	section 230

PART 7: HOMELESSNESS

HOMELESSNESS AND THREATENED HOMELESSNESS

Homelessness and threatened homelessness

175 (1) A person is homeless if he has no accommodation available for his occupation, in the United Kingdom or elsewhere, which he –

(a) is entitled to occupy by virtue of an interest in it or by virtue of an order of a court,

(b) has an express or implied licence to occupy, or

(c) occupies as a residence by virtue of any enactment or rule of law giving him the right to remain in occupation or restricting the right of another person to recover possession.

(2) A person is also homeless if he has accommodation but –

(a) he cannot secure entry to it, or

(b) it consists of a moveable structure, vehicle or vessel designed or adapted for human habitation and there is no place where he is entitled or permitted both to place it and to reside in it.

(3) A person shall not be treated as having accommodation unless it is accommodation which it would be reasonable for him to continue to occupy.

(4) A person is threatened with homelessness if it is likely that he will become homeless within 28 days.

Meaning of accommodation available for occupation

176 Accommodation shall be regarded as available for a person's occupation only if it is available for occupation by him together with –

(a) any other person who normally resides with him as a member of his family, or

(b) any other person who might reasonably be expected to reside with him.

References in this Part to securing that accommodation is available for a person's occupation shall be construed accordingly.

Whether it is reasonable to continue to occupy accommodation

177 (1) It is not reasonable for a person to continue to occupy accommodation if it is probable that this will lead to domestic violence or other violence against him, or against –

(a) a person who normally resides with him as a member of his family, or

(b) any other person who might reasonably be expected to reside with him.

(1A) For this purpose 'violence' means –

(a) violence from another person; or

(b) threats of violence from another person which are likely to be carried out; and violence is 'domestic violence' if it is from a person associated with the victim.

(2) In determining whether it would be, or would have been, reasonable for a person to continue to occupy accommodation, regard may be had to the general circumstances prevailing in relation to housing in the district of the local housing authority to whom he has applied for accommodation or for assistance in obtaining accommodation.

(3) The Secretary of State may by order specify –

(a) other circumstances in which it is to be regarded as reasonable or not reasonable for a person to continue to occupy accommodation, and

(b) other matters to be taken into account or disregarded in determining whether it would be, or would have been, reasonable for a person to continue to occupy accommodation.

Meaning of associated person

178 (1) For the purposes of this Part, a person is associated with another person if –

    (a)   they are or have been married to each other;

    (aa)   they are or have been civil partners of each other;

    (b)   they are cohabitants or former cohabitants;

    (c)   they live or have lived in the same household;

    (d)   they are relatives;

    (e)   they have agreed to marry one another (whether or not that agreement has been terminated);

    (ea)   they have entered into a civil partnership agreement between them (whether or not that agreement has been terminated);

    (f)   in relation to a child, each of them is a parent of the child or has, or has had, parental responsibility for the child.

(2) If a child has been adopted or falls within subsection 2A, two persons are also associated with each other for the purposes of this Part if –

    (a) one is a natural parent of the child or a parent of such a natural parent, and

    (b) the other is the child or a person –

        (i)   who has become a parent of the child by virtue of an adoption order or who has applied for an adoption order, or

        (ii) with whom the child has at any time been placed for adoption.

(2A) A child falls within this subsection if –

    (a) an adoption agency, within the meaning of section 2 of the Adoption and Children Act 2002, is authorised to place him for adoption under section 19 of that Act (placing children with parental consent) or he has become the subject of an order under section 21 of that Act (placement orders), or

    (b) he is freed for adoption by virtue of an order made –

        (i)   in England and Wales, under section 18 of the Adoption Act 1976,

        (ii) in Scotland, under section 18 of the Adoption (Scotland) Act 1978, or

        (iii) in Northern Ireland, under Article 17(1) or 18(1) of the Adoption (Northern Ireland) Order 1987.

(3) In this section –

'adoption order' means an adoption order within the meaning of section 72(1) of the Adoption Act 1976 or section 46(1) of the Adoption and Children Act 2002;

'child' means a person under the age of 18 years;

'civil partnership agreement' has the meaning given by section 73 of the Civil Partnership Act 2004;

'cohabitants' means

    (a) a man and a woman who, although not married to each other, are living together as husband and wife, or

    (b) two people of the same sex who, although not civil partners of each other, are living together as if they were civil partners;

and 'former cohabitants' shall be construed accordingly;

'parental responsibility' has the same meaning as in the Children Act 1989; and

'relative', in relation to a person, means –

    (a) the father, mother, stepfather, stepmother, son, daughter, stepson, stepdaughter, grandmother, grandfather, grandson or granddaughter of that person or of that person's spouse, civil partner, former spouse or former civil partner, or

(b) the brother, sister, uncle, aunt, niece or nephew (whether of the full blood or of the half blood or whether by marriage or civil partnership) of that person or of that person's spouse, civil partner, or former spouse or former civil partner,

and includes, in relation to a person who is living or has lived with another person as husband and wife, a person who would fall within paragraph (a) or (b) if the parties were married to each other.

GENERAL FUNCTIONS IN RELATION TO HOMELESSNESS OR THREATENED HOMELESSNESS

Duty of local housing authority to provide advisory services

179 (1) Every local housing authority shall secure that advice and information about homelessness, and the prevention of homelessness, is available free of charge to any person in their district.

(2) The authority may give to any person by whom such advice and information is provided on behalf of the authority assistance by way of grant or loan.

(3) A local housing authority may also assist any such person –

(a) by permitting him to use premises belonging to the authority,

(b) by making available furniture or other goods, whether by way of gift, loan or otherwise, and

(c) by making available the services of staff employed by the authority.

Assistance for voluntary organisations

180 (1) The Secretary of State or a local housing authority may give assistance by way of grant or loan to voluntary organisations concerned with homelessness or matters relating to homelessness.

(2) A local housing authority may also assist any such organisation –

(a) by permitting them to use premises belonging to the authority,

(b) by making available furniture or other goods, whether by way of gift, loan or otherwise, and

(c) by making available the services of staff employed by the authority.

(3) A 'voluntary organisation' means a body (other than a public or local authority) whose activities are not carried on for profit.

Terms and conditions of assistance

181 (1) This section has effect as to the terms and conditions on which assistance is given under section 179 or 180.

(2) Assistance shall be on such terms, and subject to such conditions, as the person giving the assistance may determine.

(3) No assistance shall be given unless the person to whom it is given undertakes –

(a) to use the money, furniture or other goods or premises for a specified purpose, and

(b) to provide such information as may reasonably be required as to the manner in which the assistance is being used.

The person giving the assistance may require such information by notice in writing, which shall be complied with within 21 days beginning with the date on which the notice is served.

(4) The conditions subject to which assistance is given shall in all cases include conditions requiring the person to whom the assistance is given –

   (a) to keep proper books of account and have them audited in such manner as may be specified,

   (b) to keep records indicating how he has used the money, furniture or other goods or premises, and

   (c) to submit the books of account and records for inspection by the person giving the assistance.

(5) If it appears to the person giving the assistance that the person to whom it was given has failed to carry out his undertaking as to the purpose for which the assistance was to be used, he shall take all reasonable steps to recover from that person an amount equal to the amount of the assistance.

(6) He must first serve on the person to whom the assistance was given a notice specifying the amount which in his opinion is recoverable and the basis on which that amount has been calculated.

Guidance by the Secretary of State

182 (1) In the exercise of their functions relating to homelessness and the prevention of homelessness, a local housing authority or social services authority shall have regard to such guidance as may from time to time be given by the Secretary of State.

(2) The Secretary of State may give guidance either generally or to specified descriptions of authorities.

APPLICATION FOR ASSISTANCE IN CASE OF HOMELESSNESS OR THREATENED HOMELESSNESS

Application for assistance

183 (1) The following provisions of this Part apply where a person applies to a local housing authority for accommodation, or for assistance in obtaining accommodation, and the authority have reason to believe that he is or may be homeless or threatened with homelessness.

(2) In this Part –

   'applicant' means a person making such an application,

   'assistance under this Part' means the benefit of any function under the following provisions of this Part relating to accommodation or assistance in obtaining accommodation, and

   'eligible for assistance' means not excluded from such assistance by section 185 (persons from abroad not eligible for housing assistance) [or section 186 (asylum-seekers and their dependants)].[2]

(3) Nothing in this section or the following provisions of this Part affects a person's entitlement to advice and information under section 179 (duty to provide advisory services).

Inquiry into cases of homelessness or threatened homelessness

184(1)If the local housing authority have reason to believe that an applicant may be homeless or threatened with homelessness, they shall make such inquiries as

---

2   Words in square brackets repealed. Not yet in force: see Immigration and Asylum Act 1999 s170(4).

are necessary to satisfy themselves –
- (a) whether he is eligible for assistance, and
- (b) if so, whether any duty, and if so what duty, is owed to him under the following provisions of this Part.

(2) They may also make inquiries whether he has a local connection with the district of another local housing authority in England, Wales or Scotland.

(3) On completing their inquiries the authority shall notify the applicant of their decision and, so far as any issue is decided against his interests, inform him of the reasons for their decision.

(3A) If the authority decide that a duty is owed to he applicant under section 193(2) or 195(2) but would not have done so without having had regard to a restricted person, the notice under subsection (3) must also –
- (a) inform the applicant that their decision was reached on that basis,
- (b) include the name of the restricted person,
- (c) explain why the person is a restricted person, and
- (d) explain the effect of section 193(7AD) or (as the case may be) section 195(4A).

(4) If the authority have notified or intend to notify another local housing authority under section 198 (referral of cases), they shall at the same time notify the applicant of that decision and inform him of the reasons for it.

(5) A notice under subsection (3) or (4) shall also inform the applicant of his right to request a review of the decision and of the time within which such a request must be made (see section 202).

(6) Notice required to be given to a person under this section shall be given in writing and, if not received by him, shall be treated as having been given to him if it is made available at the authority's office for a reasonable period for collection by him or on his behalf.

(7) In this Part 'a restricted person' means a person –
- (a) who is not eligible for assistance under this Part,
- (b) who is subject to immigration control within the meaning of the Asylum and Immigration Act 1996, and
- (c) either –
  - (i) who does not have leave to enter or remain in the United Kingdom, or
  - (ii) whose leave to enter or remain in the United Kingdom is subject to a condition to maintain and accommodate himself, and any dependants, without recourse to public funds.

ELIGIBILITY FOR ASSISTANCE

Persons from abroad not eligible for housing assistance

185(1) A person is not eligible for assistance under this Part if he is a person from abroad who is ineligible for housing assistance.

(2) A person who is subject to immigration control within the meaning of the Asylum and Immigration Act 1996 is not eligible for housing assistance unless he is of a class prescribed by regulations made by the Secretary of State.

(2A) No person who is excluded from entitlement to housing benefit by section 115 of the Immigration and Asylum Act 1999 (exclusion from benefits) shall be included in any class prescribed under subsection (2).

(3) The Secretary of State may make provision by regulations as to other descriptions of persons who are to be treated for the purposes of this Part as persons from abroad who are ineligible for housing assistance.

(4) A person from abroad who is not eligible for housing assistance shall be disregarded in determining for the purposes of this Part whether a person falling within subsection (5) –
  (a) is homeless or threatened with homelessness, or
  (b) has a priority need for accommodation.

(5) A person falls within this subsection if the person –
  (a) falls within a class prescribed by regulations made under subsection (2); but
  (b) is not a national of an EEA State or Switzerland

Asylum-seekers and their dependants

186 (1) An asylum-seeker, or a dependant of an asylum-seeker who is not by virtue of section 185 a person from abroad who is ineligible for housing assistance, is not eligible for assistance under this Part if he has any accommodation in the United Kingdom, however temporary, available for his occupation.

(2) For the purposes of this section a person who makes a claim for asylum –
  (a) becomes an asylum-seeker at the time when his claim is recorded by the Secretary of State as having been made, and
  (b) ceases to be an asylum-seeker at the time when his claim is recorded by the Secretary of State as having been finally determined or abandoned.

(3) For the purposes of this section a person –
  (a) becomes a dependant of an asylum-seeker at the time when he is recorded by the Secretary of State as being a dependant of the asylum-seeker, and
  (b) ceases to be a dependant of an asylum-seeker at the time when the person whose dependant he is ceases to be an asylum-seeker or, if it is earlier, at the time when he is recorded by the Secretary of State as ceasing to be a dependant of the asylum-seeker.

(4) In relation to an asylum-seeker, 'dependant' means a person –
  (a) who is his spouse or a child of his under the age of eighteen, and
  (b) who has neither a right of abode in the United Kingdom nor indefinite leave under the Immigration Act 1971 to enter or remain in the United Kingdom.

(5) In this section a 'claim for asylum' means a claim made by a person that it would be contrary to the United Kingdom's obligations under the Convention relating to the Status of Refugees done at Geneva on 28th July 1951 and the Protocol to that Convention for him to be removed from, or required to leave, the United Kingdom.[3]

Provision of information by Secretary of State

187 (1) The Secretary of State shall, at the request of a local housing authority, provide the authority with such information as they may require –
  (a) as to whether a person is a person to whom section 115 of the Immigration and Asylum Act 1999 (exclusion from benefits) applies, and

---

3   Section 186 to be repealed by the Immigration and Asylum Act 1999. Not yet in force: see IAA 1999 s170(4).

(b) to enable them to determine whether such a person is eligible for assistance under this Part under section 185 (persons from abroad not eligible for housing assistance).

(2) Where that information is given otherwise than in writing, the Secretary of State shall confirm it in writing if a written request is made to him by the authority.

(3) If it appears to the Secretary of State that any application, decision or other change of circumstances has affected the status of a person about whom information was previously provided by him to a local housing authority under this section, he shall inform the authority in writing of that fact, the reason for it and the date on which the previous information became inaccurate.

INTERIM DUTY TO ACCOMMODATE

Interim duty to accommodate in case of apparent priority need

188 (1) If the local housing authority have reason to believe that an applicant may be homeless, eligible for assistance and have a priority need, they shall secure that accommodation is available for his occupation pending a decision as to the duty (if any) owed to him under the following provisions of this Part.

(2) The duty under this section arises irrespective of any possibility of the referral of the applicant's case to another local housing authority (see sections 198 to 200).

(3) The duty ceases when the authority's decision is notified to the applicant, even if the applicant requests a review of the decision (see section 202).

The authority may continue to secure that accommodation is available for the applicant's occupation pending a decision on a review.

Priority need for accommodation

189 (1) The following have a priority need for accommodation –

(a) a pregnant woman or a person with whom she resides or might reasonably be expected to reside;

(b) a person with whom dependent children reside or might reasonably be expected to reside;

(c) a person who is vulnerable as a result of old age, mental illness or handicap or physical disability or other special reason, or with whom such a person resides or might reasonably be expected to reside;

(d) a person who is homeless or threatened with homelessness as a result of an emergency such as flood, fire or other disaster.

(2) The Secretary of State may by order –

(a) specify further descriptions of persons as having a priority need for accommodation, and

(b) amend or repeal any part of subsection (1).

(3) Before making such an order the Secretary of State shall consult such associations representing relevant authorities, and such other persons, as he considers appropriate.

(4) No such order shall be made unless a draft of it has been approved by resolution of each House of Parliament.

DUTIES TO PERSONS FOUND TO BE HOMELESS OR THREATENED WITH HOMELESSNESS

Duties to persons becoming homeless intentionally

190 (1) This section applies where the local housing authority are satisfied that an applicant is homeless and is eligible for assistance but are also satisfied that he became homeless intentionally.

(2) If the authority are satisfied that the applicant has a priority need, they shall –

    (a) secure that accommodation is available for his occupation for such period as they consider will give him a reasonable opportunity of securing accommodation for his occupation, and

    (b) provide him with (or secure that he is provided with) advice and assistance in any attempts he may make to secure that accommodation becomes available for his occupation.

(3) If they are not satisfied that he has a priority need, they shall provide him with (or secure that he is provided with) advice and assistance in any attempts he may make to secure that accommodation becomes available for his occupation.

(4) The applicant's housing needs shall be assessed before advice and assistance is provided under subsection (2)(b) or (3).

(5) The advice and assistance provided under subsection (2)(b) or (3) must include information about the likely availability in the authority's district of types of accommodation appropriate to the applicant's housing needs (including, in particular, the location and sources of such types of accommodation).

Becoming homeless intentionally

191 (1) A person becomes homeless intentionally if he deliberately does or fails to do anything in consequence of which he ceases to occupy accommodation which is available for his occupation and which it would have been reasonable for him to continue to occupy.

(2) For the purposes of subsection (1) an act or omission in good faith on the part of a person who was unaware of any relevant fact shall not be treated as deliberate.

(3) A person shall be treated as becoming homeless intentionally if –

    (a) he enters into an arrangement under which he is required to cease to occupy accommodation which it would have been reasonable for him to continue to occupy, and

    (b) the purpose of the arrangement is to enable him to become entitled to assistance under this Part,

and there is no other good reason why he is homeless.

(4) . . .

Duty to persons not in priority need who are not homeless intentionally

192 (1) This section applies where the local housing authority –

    (a) are satisfied that an applicant is homeless and eligible for assistance, and

    (b) are not satisfied that he became homeless intentionally,

but are not satisfied that he has a priority need.

(2) The authority shall provide the applicant with (or secure that he is provided with) advice and assistance in any attempts he may make to secure that accommodation becomes available for his occupation.

(3) The authority may secure that accommodation is available for occupation by the applicant.

(4) The applicant's housing needs shall be addressed before advice and assistance is provided under subsection (2).

(5) The advice and assistance provided under subsection (2) must include information about the likely availability in the authority's district of types of accommodation appropriate to the applicant's housing needs (including, in particular, the location and sources of such types of accommodation).

Duty to persons with priority need who are not homeless intentionally

193 (1) This section applies where the local housing authority are satisfied that an applicant is homeless, eligible for assistance and has a priority need, and are not satisfied that he became homeless intentionally.

. . .

(2) Unless the authority refer the application to another local housing authority (see section 198), they shall secure that accommodation is available for occupation by the applicant.

(3) The authority are subject to the duty under this section until it ceases by virtue of this section.

(3A) The authority shall, on becoming subject to the duty under this section, in a case which is not a restricted case, give the applicant a copy of the statement included in their allocation scheme by virtue of section 167(1A) (policy on offering choice to people allocated housing accommodation under Part 6).

(3B) In this section 'a restricted case' means a case where the local housing authority would not be satisfied as mentioned in subsection (1) without having had regard to a restricted person.

. . .

(5) The local housing authority shall cease to be subject to the duty under this section if the applicant, having been informed by the authority of the possible consequence of refusal [and his right to request a review of the suitability of the accommodation], refuses an offer of accommodation which the authority are satisfied is suitable for him and the authority notify him that they regard themselves as having discharged their duty under this section.

(6) The local housing authority shall cease to be subject to the duty under this section if the applicant –

(a) ceases to be eligible for assistance,

(b) becomes homeless intentionally from the accommodation made available for his occupation,

(c) accepts an offer of accommodation under Part 6 (allocation of housing), or

(cc) accepts an offer of an assured tenancy (other than assured shorthold tenancy) from a private landlord,

(d) otherwise voluntarily ceases to occupy as his only or principal home the accommodation made available for his occupation.

(7) The local housing authority shall also cease to be subject to the duty under this section if the applicant, having been informed of the possible consequence of

refusal and of his right to request a review of the suitability of the accommodation, refuses a final offer for the purposes of subsection (7).

(7A) An offer of accommodation under Part 6 is a final offer for the purposes of subsection (7) if it is made in writing and states that it is a final offer for the purposes of subsection (7).

(7AA) In a restricted case the authority shall also cease to be subject to the duty under this section if the applicant, having been informed of the matters mentioned in subsection (7AB) –
   (a) accepts a private accommodation offer, or
   (b) refuses such an offer.

(7AB) The matters are –
   (a) the possible consequence of refusal of the offer, and
   (b) that the applicant has the right to request a review of the suitability of the accommodation.

(7AC) For the purposes of this section an offer is a private accommodation offer if –
   (a) it is an offer of an assured shorthold tenancy made by a private landlord to the applicant in relation to any accommodation which is, or may become, available for the applicant's occupation,
   (b) it is made, with the approval of the authority, in pursuance of arrangements made by the authority with the landlord with a view to bringing the authority's duty under this section to an end, and
   (c) the tenancy being offered is a fixed term tenancy (within the meaning of Part 1 of the Housing Act 1988) for a period of at least 12 months.

(7AD) In a restricted case the authority shall, so far as reasonably practicable, bring their duty under this section to an end as mentioned in subsection (7AA).

(7B) In a case which is not a restricted case, the authority shall also cease to be subject to the duty under this section if the applicant accepts a qualifying offer of an assured shorthold tenancy which is made by a private landlord in relation to any accommodation which is, or may become, available for the applicant's occupation.

(7C) In a case which is not a restricted case, the applicant is free to reject a qualifying offer without affecting the duty owed to him under this section by the authority.

(7D) For the purposes of subsection (7B) an offer of an assured shorthold tenancy is a qualifying offer if –
   (a) it is made, with the approval of the authority, in pursuance of arrangements made by the authority with the landlord with a view to bringing the authority's duty under this section to an end;
   (b) the tenancy being offered is a fixed term tenancy (within the meaning of Part 1 of the Housing Act 1988; and
   (c) it is accompanied by a statement in writing which states the term of the tenancy being offered and explains in ordinary language that –
      (i) there is no obligation to accept the offer, but
      (ii) if the offer is accepted the local authority will cease to be subject to the duty under this section in relation to the applicant.

(7E) An acceptance of a qualifying offer is only effective for the purposes of subsection (7B) if the applicant signs a statement acknowledging that he has understood the statement mentioned in subsection (7D).

(7F) The local housing authority shall not –

   (a)   make a final offer of accommodation under Part 6 for the purposes of subsection (7); or

   (ab) approve a private accommodation offer; or

   (b)   approve an offer of an assured shorthold tenancy for the purposes of subsection (7B),

unless they are satisfied that the accommodation is suitable for the applicant and that it is reasonable for him to accept the offer.

  (8) For the purposes of subsection (7F) an applicant may reasonably be expected to accept an offer . . . even though he is under contractual or other obligations in respect of his existing accommodation, provided he is able to bring those obligations to an end before he is required to take up the offer.

  (9) A person who ceases to be owed the duty under this section may make a fresh application to the authority for accommodation or assistance in obtaining accommodation.

194 . . .

Duties in case of threatened homelessness

195 (1) This section applies where the local housing authority are satisfied that an applicant is threatened with homelessness and is eligible for assistance.

  (2) If the authority –

   (a) are satisfied that he has a priority need, and

   (b) are not satisfied that he became threatened with homelessness intentionally,

they shall take reasonable steps to secure that accommodation does not cease to be available for his occupation.

   . . .

  (3) Subsection (2) does not affect any right of the authority, whether by virtue of a contract, enactment or rule of law, to secure vacant possession of any accommodation.

  (3A) The authority shall, on becoming subject to the duty under this section, in a case which is not a restricted threatened homelessness case, give the applicant a copy of the statement included in their allocation scheme by virtue of section 167(1A) (policy on offering choice to people allocated housing accommodation under Part 6).

  (4) Where, in a case which is not a restricted threatened homelessness case, in pursuance of the duty under subsection (2) the authority secure that accommodation other than that occupied by the applicant when he made his application is available for occupation by him, the provisions of section 193(3) to (9) (period for which duty owed) . . . apply, with any necessary modifications, in relation to the duty under this section as they apply in relation to the duty under section 193 in a case which is not a restricted case (within the meaning of that section).

  (4A) Where, in a restricted threatened homelessness case, in pursuance of the duty under subsection (2) the authority secure that accommodation other than that occupied by the applicant when he made his application is available for occupation by him, the provisions of section 193(3) to (9) (period for which duty owed) apply, with any necessary modifications, in relation to the duty under this section as they apply in relation to the duty under section 193 in a restricted case (within the meaning of that section).

(4B) In subsections (3A) to (4A) 'a restricted threatened homelessness case' means a case where the local housing authority would not be satisfied as mentioned in subsection (1) without having had regard to a restricted person.

(5) If the authority –
  (a) are not satisfied that the applicant has a priority need, or
  (b) are satisfied that he has a priority need but are also satisfied that he became threatened with homelessness intentionally,
  they shall provide him with (or secure that he is provided with) advice and assistance in any attempts he may make to secure that accommodation does not cease to be available for his occupation.

(6) The applicant's housing needs shall be assessed before advice and assistance is provided under subsection (5).

(7) The advice and assistance provided under subsection (5) must include information about the likely availability in the authority's district of types of accommodation appropriate to the applicant's housing needs (including, in particular, the location and sources of such types of accommodation).

(8) If the authority decide that they owe the applicant the duty under subsection (5) by virtue of paragraph (b) of that subsection, they may, pending a decision on a review of that decision –
  (a) secure that accommodation does not cease to be available for his occupation; and
  (b) if he becomes homeless, secure that accommodation is so available.

(9) If the authority –
  (a) are not satisfied that the applicant has a priority need; and
  (b) are not satisfied that he became threatened with homelessness intentionally,
  the authority may take reasonable steps to secure that accommodation does not cease to be available for the applicant's occupation.

Becoming threatened with homelessness intentionally

196 (1) A person becomes threatened with homelessness intentionally if he deliberately does or fails to do anything the likely result of which is that he will be forced to leave accommodation which is available for his occupation and which it would have been reasonable for him to continue to occupy.

(2) For the purposes of subsection (1) an act or omission in good faith on the part of a person who was unaware of any relevant fact shall not be treated as deliberate.

(3) A person shall be treated as becoming threatened with homelessness intentionally if –
  (a) he enters into an arrangement under which he is required to cease to occupy accommodation which it would have been reasonable for him to continue to occupy, and
  (b) the purpose of the arrangement is to enable him to become entitled to assistance under this Part,
  and there is no other good reason why he is threatened with homelessness.

(4) . . .

197　. . .

REFERRAL TO ANOTHER LOCAL HOUSING AUTHORITY
Referral of case to another local housing authority

198 (1) If the local housing authority would be subject to the duty under section 193 (accommodation for those with priority need who are not homeless intentionally) but consider that the conditions are met for referral of the case to another local housing authority, they may notify that other authority of their opinion.

. . .

(2) The conditions for referral of the case to another authority are met if –

  (a) neither the applicant nor any person who might reasonably be expected to reside with him has a local connection with the district of the authority to whom his application was made,

  (b) the applicant or a person who might reasonably be expected to reside with him has a local connection with the district of that other authority, and

  (c) neither the applicant nor any person who might reasonably be expected to reside with him will run the risk of domestic violence in that other district.

(2A) But the conditions for referral mentioned in subsection (2) are not met if –

  (a) the applicant or any person who might reasonably be expected to reside with him has suffered violence (other than domestic violence) in the district of the other authority; and

  (b) it is probable that the return to that district of the victim will lead to further violence of a similar kind against him.

(3) For this purposes of subsections (2) and (2A) 'violence' means –

  (a) violence from another person; or

  (b) threats of violence from another person which are likely to be carried out; and violence is 'domestic violence' if it is from a person who is associated with the victim.

(4) The conditions for referral of the case to another authority are also met if –

  (a) the applicant was on a previous application made to that other authority placed (in pursuance of their functions under this Part) in accommodation in the district of the authority to whom his application is now made, and

  (b) the previous application was within such period as may be prescribed of the present application.

(5) The question whether the conditions for referral of a case are satisfied shall be decided by agreement between the notifying authority and the notified authority or, in default of agreement, in accordance with such arrangements as the Secretary of State may direct by order.

(6) An order may direct that the arrangements shall be –

  (a) those agreed by any relevant authorities or associations of relevant authorities, or

  (b) in default of such agreement, such arrangements as appear to the Secretary of State to be suitable, after consultation with such associations representing relevant authorities, and such other persons, as he thinks appropriate.

(7) No such order shall be made unless a draft of the order has been approved by a resolution of each House of Parliament.

Local connection

199 (1) A person has a local connection with the district of a local housing authority if he has a connection with it –

(a) because he is, or in the past was, normally resident there, and that residence is or was of his own choice,

(b) because he is employed there,

(c) because of family associations, or

(d) because of special circumstances.

(2) . . .

(3) Residence in a district is not of a person's own choice if –

(a) . . .

(b) he, or a person who might reasonably be expected to reside with him, becomes resident there because he is detained under the authority of an Act of Parliament.

(4) . . .

(5) The Secretary of State may by order specify circumstances in which –

(a) a person is not to be treated as employed in a district, or

(b) residence in a district is not to be treated as of a person's own choice.

(6) A person has a local connection with the district of a local housing authority if he was (at any time) provided with accommodation in that district under section 95 of the Immigration and Asylum Act 1999 (support for asylum seekers).

(7) But subsection (6) does not apply –

(a) to the provision of accommodation for a person in a district of a local housing authority if he was subsequently provided with accommodation in the district of another local housing authority under section 95 of that Act, or

(b) to the provision of accommodation in an accommodation centre by virtue of section 22 of the Nationality, Immigration and Asylum Act 2002 (use of accommodation centres for section 95 support).

Duties to applicant whose case is considered for referral or referred

200 (1) Where a local housing authority notify an applicant that they intend to notify or have notified another local housing authority of their opinion that the conditions are met for the referral of his case to that other authority –

(a) they cease to be subject to any duty under section 188 (interim duty to accommodate in case of apparent priority need), and

(b) they are not subject to any duty under section 193 (the main housing duty),

but they shall secure that accommodation is available for occupation by the applicant until he is notified of the decision whether the conditions for referral of his case are met.

(2) When it has been decided whether the conditions for referral are met, the notifying authority shall notify the applicant of the decision and inform him of the reasons for it.

The notice shall also inform the applicant of his right to request a review of the decision and of the time within which such a request must be made.

(3) If it is decided that the conditions those for referral are not met, the notifying authority are subject to the duty under section 193 (the main housing duty).

(4) If it is decided that those conditions are met, the notified authority are subject to the duty under section 193 (the main housing duty).

(5) The duty under subsection (1), . . . ceases as provided in that subsection even if the applicant requests a review of the authority's decision (see section 202). The authority may secure that accommodation is available for the applicant's occupation pending the decision on a review.

(6) Notice required to be given to an applicant under this section shall be given in writing and, if not received by him, shall be treated as having been given to him if it is made available at the authority's office for a reasonable period for collection by him or on his behalf.

Application of referral provisions to cases arising in Scotland

201 Sections 198 and 200 (referral of application to another local housing authority and duties to applicant whose case is considered for referral or referred) apply –

(a) to applications referred by a local authority in Scotland in pursuance of sections 33 and 34 of the Housing (Scotland) Act 1987, and

(b) to persons whose applications are so transferred,

as they apply to cases arising under this Part (the reference in section 198 to this Part being construed as a reference to Part 2 of that Act).

RIGHT TO REQUEST REVIEW OF DECISION

Right to request review of decision

202 (1) An applicant has the right to request a review of –

(a) any decision of a local housing authority as to his eligibility for assistance,

(b) any decision of a local housing authority as to what duty (if any) is owed to him under sections 190 to 193 and 195 and 196 (duties to persons found to be homeless or threatened with homelessness),

(c) any decision of a local housing authority to notify another authority under section 198(1) (referral of cases),

(d) any decision under section 198(5) whether the conditions are met for the referral of his case,

(e) any decision under section 200(3) or (4) (decision as to duty owed to applicant whose case is considered for referral or referred),

(f) any decision of a local housing authority as to the suitability of accommodation offered to him in discharge of their duty under any of the provisions mentioned in paragraph (b) or (e) or as to the suitability of accommodation offered to him as mentioned in section 193(7), or

(g) any decision of a local housing authority as to the suitability of accommodation offered to him by way of a private accommodation offer (within the meaning of section 193).

(1A) An applicant who is offered accommodation as mentioned in section 193(5), (7) or (7AA) may under subsection (1)(f) or (as the case may be) (g) request a review of the suitability of the accommodation offered to him whether or not he has accepted the offer.

(2) There is no right to request a review of the decision reached on an earlier review.

(3) A request for review must be made before the end of the period of 21 days beginning with the day on which he is notified of the authority's decision or such longer period as the authority may in writing allow.

(4) On a request being duly made to them, the authority or authorities concerned shall review their decision.

Procedure on a review

203 (1) The Secretary of State may make provision by regulations as to the procedure to be followed in connection with a review under section 202.

Nothing in the following provisions affects the generality of this power.

(2) Provision may be made by regulations –

    (a) requiring the decision on review to be made by a person of appropriate seniority who was not involved in the original decision, and

    (b) as to the circumstances in which the applicant is entitled to an oral hearing, and whether and by whom he may be represented at such a hearing.

(3) The authority, or as the case may be either of the authorities, concerned shall notify the applicant of the decision on the review.

(4) If the decision is –

    (a) to confirm the original decision on any issue against the interests of the applicant, or

    (b) to confirm a previous decision –

        (i) to notify another authority under section 198 (referral of cases), or

        (ii) that the conditions are met for the referral of his case,

they shall also notify him of the reasons for the decision.

(5) In any case they shall inform the applicant of his right to appeal to a county court on a point of law, and of the period within which such an appeal must be made (see section 204).

(6) Notice of the decision shall not be treated as given unless and until subsection (5), and where applicable subsection (4), is complied with.

(7) Provision may be made by regulations as to the period within which the review must be carried out and notice given of the decision.

(8) Notice required to be given to a person under this section shall be given in writing and, if not received by him, shall be treated as having been given if it is made available at the authority's office for a reasonable period for collection by him or on his behalf.

Right of appeal to county court on point of law

204 (1) If an applicant who has requested a review under section 202 –

    (a) is dissatisfied with the decision on the review, or

    (b) is not notified of the decision on the review within the time prescribed under section 203,

he may appeal to the county court on any point of law arising from the decision or, as the case may be, the original decision.

(2) An appeal must be brought within 21 days of his being notified of the decision or, as the case may be, of the date on which he should have been notified of a decision on review.

(2A) The court may give permission for an appeal to be brought after the end of the period allowed by subsection (2), but only if it is satisfied –

(a) where permission is sought before the end of that period, that there is a good reason for the applicant to be unable to bring the appeal in time;

(b) where permission is sought after that time, that there was a good reason for the applicant's failure to bring the appeal in time and for any delay in applying for permission.

(3) On appeal the court may make such order confirming, quashing or varying the decision as it thinks fit.

(4) Where the authority were under a duty under section 188, 190 or 200 to secure that accommodation is available for the applicant's occupation, or had the power under section 195(8) to do so, they may secure that accommodation is so available –

(a) during the period for appealing under this section against the authority's decision, and

(b) if an appeal is brought, until the appeal (and any further appeal) is finally determined.

Section 204(4) appeals

204A(1) This section applies where an applicant has the right to appeal to the county court against a local authority's decision on review.

(2) If the applicant is dissatisfied with a decision by the authority –

(a) not to exercise their power under section 204(4) ('the section 204(4) power') in his case;

(b) to exercise that power for a limited period ending before the final determination by the county court of his appeal under section 204(1) ('the main appeal'); or

he may appeal to the county court against the decision.

(3) An appeal under this section may not be brought after the final determination by the county court of the main appeal.

(4) On an appeal under this section the court –

(a) may order the authority to secure that accommodation is available for the applicant's occupation until the determination of the appeal (or such earlier time as the court may specify); and

(b) shall confirm or quash the decision appealed against,

and in considering whether to confirm or quash the decision the court shall apply the principles applied by the High Court on application for judicial review.

(5) If the court quashes the decision it may order the authority to exercise the section 204(4) power in the applicant's case for such period as may be specified in the order.

(6) An order under subsection (5) –

(a) may only be made if the court is satisfied that failure to exercise the section 204(4) power in accordance with the order would substantially prejudice the applicant's ability to pursue the main appeal;

(b) may not specify any period ending after the final determination by the county court of the main appeal.

SUPPLEMENTARY PROVISIONS
Discharge of functions: introductory
205 (1) The following sections have effect in relation to the discharge by a local housing authority of their functions under this Part to secure that accommodation is available for the occupation of a person –

section 206 (general provisions),

. . .

section 208 (out-of-area placements),

section 209 (arrangements with private landlord).

(2) In sections 206 and 208 those functions are referred to as the authority's 'housing functions under this Part'.

Discharge of functions by local housing authorities
206 (1) A local housing authority may discharge their housing functions under this Part only in the following ways –

(a) by securing that suitable accommodation provided by them is available,

(b) by securing that he obtains suitable accommodation from some other person, or

(c) by giving him such advice and assistance as will secure that suitable accommodation is available from some other person.

(2) A local housing authority may require a person in relation to whom they are discharging such functions –

(a) to pay such reasonable charges as they may determine in respect of accommodation which they secure for his occupation (either by making it available themselves or otherwise), or

(b) to pay such reasonable amount as they may determine in respect of sums payable by them for accommodation made available by another person.

207 . . .

Discharge of functions: out-of-area placements
208 (1) So far as reasonably practicable a local housing authority shall in discharging their housing functions under this Part secure that accommodation is available for the occupation of the applicant in their district.

(2) If they secure that accommodation is available for the occupation of the applicant outside their district, they shall give notice to the local housing authority in whose district the accommodation is situated.

(3) The notice shall state –

(a) the name of the applicant,

(b) the number and description of other persons who normally reside with him as a member of his family or might reasonably be expected to reside with him,

(c) the address of the accommodation,

(d) the date on which the accommodation was made available to him, and

(e) which function under this Part the authority was discharging in securing that the accommodation is available for his occupation.

(4) The notice must be in writing, and must be given before the end of the period of 14 days beginning with the day on which the accommodation was made available to the applicant.

Discharge of interim duties: arrangement with private landlord

209 (1) This section applies where in pursuance of any of their housing functions under section 188, 190, 200 or 204(4) (interim duties) a local housing authority make arrangements with a private landlord to provide accommodation.

(2) A tenancy granted to the applicant in pursuance of the arrangements cannot be an assured tenancy before the end of the period of twelve months beginning with –

(a) the date on which the applicant was notified of the authority's decision under section 184(3) or 198(5); or

(b) if there is a review of that decision under section 202 or an appeal to the court under section 204, the date on which he is notified of the decision on review or the appeal is finally determined,

unless, before or during that period, the tenant is notified by the landlord (or in the case of joint landlords, at least one of them) that the tenancy is to regarded as an assured shorthold tenancy or an assured tenancy other than an assured shorthold tenancy.

Suitability of accommodation

210 (1) In determining for the purposes of this Part whether accommodation is suitable for a person, the local housing authority shall have regard to Parts 9 and 10 of the Housing Act 1985 (slum clearance and overcrowding) and Parts 1 to 4 of the Housing Act 2004.

(2) The Secretary of State may by order specify –

(a) circumstances in which accommodation is or is not to be regarded as suitable for a person, and

(b) matters to be taken into account or disregarded in determining whether accommodation is suitable for a person.

Protection of property of homeless persons and persons threatened with homelessness

211 (1) This section applies where a local housing authority have reason to believe that –

(a) there is danger of loss of, or damage to, any personal property of an applicant by reason of his inability to protect it or deal with it, and

(b) no other suitable arrangements have been or are being made.

(2) If the authority have become subject to a duty towards the applicant under –

section 188 (interim duty to accommodate),

section 190, 193 or 195 (duties to persons found to be homeless or threatened with homelessness), or

section 200 (duties to applicant whose case is considered for referral or referred),

then, whether or not they are still subject to such a duty, they shall take reasonable steps to prevent the loss of the property or prevent or mitigate damage to it.

(3) If they have not become subject to such a duty, they may take any steps they consider reasonable for that purpose.

(4) The authority may decline to take action under this section except upon such conditions as they consider appropriate in the particular case, which may include conditions as to –

(a) the making and recovery by the authority of reasonable charges for the action taken, or

(b) the disposal by the authority, in such circumstances as may be specified, of property in relation to which they have taken action.

(5) References in this section to personal property of the applicant include personal property of any person who might reasonably be expected to reside with him.

(6) Section 212 contains provisions supplementing this section.

Protection of property: supplementary provisions

212 (1) The authority may for the purposes of section 211 (protection of property of homeless persons or persons threatened with homelessness) –

(a) enter, at all reasonable times, any premises which are the usual place of residence of the applicant or which were his last usual place of residence, and

(b) deal with any personal property of his in any way which is reasonably necessary, in particular by storing it or arranging for its storage.

(2) Where the applicant asks the authority to move his property to a particular location nominated by him, the authority –

(a) may, if it appears to them that his request is reasonable, discharge their responsibilities under section 211 by doing as he asks, and

(b) having done so, have no further duty or power to take action under that section in relation to that property.

If such a request is made, the authority shall before complying with it inform the applicant of the consequence of their doing so.

(3) If no such request is made (or, if made, is not acted upon) the authority cease to have any duty or power to take action under section 211 when, in their opinion, there is no longer any reason to believe that there is a danger of loss of or damage to a person's personal property by reason of his inability to protect it or deal with it.

But property stored by virtue of their having taken such action may be kept in store and any conditions upon which it was taken into store continue to have effect, with any necessary modifications.

(4) Where the authority –

(a) cease to be subject to a duty to take action under section 211 in respect of an applicant's property, or

(b) cease to have power to take such action, having previously taken such action,

they shall notify the applicant of that fact and of the reason for it.

(5) The notification shall be given to the applicant –

(a) by delivering it to him, or

(b) by leaving it, or sending it to him, at his last known address.

(6) References in this section to personal property of the applicant include personal property of any person who might reasonably be expected to reside with him.

Co-operation between relevant housing authorities and bodies

213 (1) Where a local housing authority –

(a) request another relevant housing authority or body, in England, Wales or Scotland, to assist them in the discharge of their functions under this Part, or

    (b) request a social services authority, in England, Wales or Scotland, to exercise any of their functions in relation to a case which the local housing authority are dealing with under this Part,

the authority or body to whom the request is made shall co-operate in rendering such assistance in the discharge of the functions to which the request relates as is reasonable in the circumstances.

(2) In subsection (1)(a) 'relevant housing authority or body' means –

    (a) in relation to England and Wales, a local housing authority, a new town corporation, a registered social landlord or a housing action trust;

    (b) in relation to Scotland, a local authority, a development corporation, a registered housing association or Scottish Homes.

Expressions used in paragraph (a) have the same meaning as in the Housing Act 1985; and expressions used in paragraph (b) have the same meaning as in the Housing (Scotland) Act 1987.

(3) Subsection (1) above applies to a request by a local authority in Scotland under section 38 of the Housing (Scotland) Act 1987 as it applies to a request by a local housing authority in England and Wales (the references to this Part being construed, in relation to such a request, as references to Part 2 of that Act).

Co-operation in certain cases involving children

213A(1) This section applies where a local housing authority have reason to believe that an applicant with whom a person under the age of 18 normally resides, or might reasonably be expected to reside –

    (a) may be eligible for assistance;

    (b) may be homeless and may nave become so intentionally; or

    (c) may be threatened with homelessness intentionally.

(2) A local housing authority shall make arrangements for ensuring that, where this section applies –

    (a) the applicant is invited to consent to the referral of the essential facts of his case to the social services authority for the district of the housing authority (where that is a different authority); and

    (b) if the applicant has given that consent, the social services authority are made aware of those facts and of the subsequent decision of the housing authority in respect of his case.

(3) Where the local housing authority and the social services authority for a district are the same authority (a 'unitary authority'), that authority shall make arrangements for ensuring that, where this section applies –

    (a) the applicant is invited to consent to the referral to the social services department of the essential facts of his case; and

    (b) if the applicant has given that consent, the social services department is made aware of those facts and of the subsequent decision of the authority in respect of his case.

(4) Nothing in subsections (2) or (3) affects any power apart from this section to disclose information relating to the applicant's case to the social services authority or to the social services department (as the case may be) without the consent of the applicant.

(5) Where a social services authority –

    (a) are aware of a decision of a local housing authority that the applicant is ineligible for assistance, became homeless intentionally or became threatened with homelessness intentionally, and

(b) request the local housing authority to provide them with advice and assistance in the exercise of their social services functions under Part 3 of the Children Act 1989,

the local housing authority shall provide them with such advice and assistance as is reasonable in the circumstance.

(6) A unitary authority shall make arrangements for ensuring that, where they make a decision of s kind mentioned in subsection (5)(a), the housing department provide the social services department with such advice and assistance as the social services department may reasonably request.

(7) In this section, in relation to a unitary authority –
'the housing department' means those persons responsible for the exercise of their housing functions; and
'the social services department' means those persons responsible for the exercise of their social services functions under Part 3 of the Children Act 1989.

GENERAL PROVISIONS

False statements, withholding information and failure to disclose change of circumstances

214 (1) It is an offence for a person, with intent to induce a local housing authority to believe in connection with the exercise of their functions under this Part that he or another person is entitled to accommodation or assistance in accordance with the provisions of this Part, or is entitled to accommodation or assistance of a particular description –

(a) knowingly or recklessly to make a statement which is false in a material particular, or

(b) knowingly to withhold information which the authority have reasonably required him to give in connection with the exercise of those functions.

(2) If before an applicant receives notification of the local housing authority's decision on his application there is any change of facts material to his case, he shall notify the authority as soon as possible.
The authority shall explain to every applicant, in ordinary language, the duty imposed on him by this subsection and the effect of subsection (3).

(3) A person who fails to comply with subsection (2) commits an offence unless he shows that he was not given the explanation required by that subsection or that he had some other reasonable excuse for non-compliance.

(4) A person guilty of an offence under this section is liable on summary conviction to a fine not exceeding level 5 on the standard scale.

Regulations and orders

215 (1) In this Part 'prescribed' means prescribed by regulations of the Secretary of State.

(2) Regulations or an order under this Part may make different provision for different purposes, including different provision for different areas.

(3) Regulations or an order under this Part shall be made by statutory instrument.

(4) Unless required to be approved in draft, regulations or an order under this Part shall be subject to annulment in pursuance of a resolution of either House of Parliament.

Transitional and consequential matters

216 (1) The provisions of this Part have effect in place of the provisions of Part 3 of the Housing Act 1985 (housing the homeless) and shall be construed as one with that Act.

(2) Subject to any transitional provision contained in an order under section 232(4) (power to include transitional provision in commencement order), the provisions of this Part do not apply in relation to an applicant whose application for accommodation or assistance in obtaining accommodation was made before the commencement of this Part.

(3) The enactments mentioned in Schedule 17 have effect with the amendments specified there which are consequential on the provisions of this Part.

Minor definitions: Part 7

217 (1) In this Part, subject to subsection (2) –

'private landlord' means a landlord who is not within section 80(1) of the Housing Act 1985 (the landlord condition for secure tenancies);

'relevant authority' means a local housing authority or a social services authority; and

'social services authority' means a local authority for the purposes of the Local Authority Social Services Act 1970, as defined in section 1 of that Act.

(2) In this Part, in relation to Scotland –

(a) 'local housing authority' means a local authority within the meaning of the Housing (Scotland) Act 1988, and

(b) 'social services authority' means a local authority for the purposes of the Social Work (Scotland) Act 1968.

(3) References in this Part to the district of a local housing authority –

(a) have the same meaning in relation to an authority in England or Wales as in the Housing Act 1985, and

(b) in relation to an authority in Scotland, mean the area of the local authority concerned.

Index of defined expressions: Part 7

218 The following Table shows provisions defining or otherwise explaining expressions used in this Part (other than provisions defining or explaining an expression used in the same section) –

accommodation available for occupation	section 176
applicant	section 183(2)
assistance under this Part	section 183(2)
associated (in relation to a person)	section 178
assured tenancy and assured shorthold tenancy	section 230
district (of local housing authority)	section 217(3)
eligible for assistance	section 183(2)
homeless	section 175(1)

housing functions under this Part (in sections 206 and 208)	section 205(2)
intentionally homeless	section 191
intentionally threatened with homelessness	section 196
local connection	section 199
local housing authority –	
– in England and Wales	section 230
– in Scotland	section 217(2)(a)
. . .	. . .
Prescribed	section 215(1)
priority need	section 189
private landlord	section 217(1)
Reasonable to continue to occupy accommodation	section 177
registered social landlord	section 230
relevant authority	section 217(1)
restricted person	section 184(7)
social services authority	section 217(1) and (2)(b)
threatened with homelessness	section 175(4)

219–229   [*Not reproduced.*]

Minor definitions: general

230   In this Act –

'assured tenancy', 'assured shorthold tenancy' and 'assured agricultural occupancy' have the same meaning as in Part 1 of the Housing Act 1988;

'enactment' includes an enactment comprised in subordinate legislation (within the meaning of the Interpretation Act 1978);

'housing action trust' has the same meaning as in the Housing Act 1988;

'housing association' has the same meaning as in the Housing Associations Act 1985;

'introductory tenancy' and 'introductory tenant' have the same meaning as in Chapter 1 of Part 5 of this Act;

'local housing authority' has the same meaning as in the Housing Act 1985;

'registered social landlord' has the same meaning as in Part 1 of this Act;

'secure tenancy' and 'secure tenant' have the same meaning as in Part 4 of the Housing Act 1985.

. . .

Homelessness Act 2002

HOMELESSNESS REVIEWS AND STRATEGIES

Duty of local housing authority to formulate a homelessness strategy

1 (1) A local housing authority ('the authority') may from time to time –

    (a) carry out a homelessness review for their district; and

    (b) formulate and publish a homelessness strategy based on the results of that review.

  (2) The social services authority for the district of the authority (where that is a different local authority) shall give such assistance in connection with the exercise of the power under subsection (1) as the authority may reasonably require.

  (3) The authority shall exercise that power so as to ensure that the first homelessness strategy for their district is published within the period of twelve months beginning with the day on which this section comes into force.

  (4) The authority shall exercise that power so as to ensure that a new homelessness strategy for their district is published within the period of five years beginning with the day on which their last homelessness strategy was published.

  (5) A local housing authority shall take their homelessness strategy into account in the exercise of their functions.

  (6) A social services authority shall take the homelessness strategy for the district of a local housing authority into account in the exercise of their functions in relation to that district.

  (7) Nothing in subsection (5) or (6) affects any duty or requirement arising apart from this section.

Homelessness reviews

2 (1) For the purposes of this Act 'homelessness review' means a review by a local housing authority of –

    (a) the levels, and likely future levels, of homelessness in their district;

    (b) the activities which are carried out for any purpose mentioned in subsection (2) (or which contribute to their achievement); and

    (c) the resources available to the authority, the social services authority for their district, other public authorities, voluntary organisations and other persons for such activities.

  (2) Those purposes are –

    (a) preventing homelessness in the district of the authority;

    (b) securing that accommodation is or will be available for people in the district who are or may become homeless;

    (c) providing support for people in the district –

      (i) who are or may become homeless; or

      (ii) who have been homeless and need support to prevent them becoming homeless again.

  (3) A local housing authority shall, after completing a homelessness review –

    (a) arrange for the results of the review to be available at its principal office for inspection at all reasonable hours, without charge, by members of the public; and

    (b) provide (on payment if required by the authority of a reasonable charge) a copy of those results to any member of the public who asks for one.

Homelessness strategies

3 (1) For the purposes of this Act 'homelessness strategy' means a strategy formulated by a local housing authority for –

    (a) preventing homelessness in their district;

    (b) securing that sufficient accommodation is and will be available for people in their district who are or may become homeless;

    (c) securing the satisfactory provision of support for people in their district –

        (i) who are or may become homeless; or

        (ii) who have been homeless and need support to prevent them becoming homeless again.

(2) A homelessness strategy may include specific objectives to be pursued, and specific action planned to be taken, in the course of the exercise of –

    (a) the functions of the authority as a local housing authority; or

    (b) the functions of the social services authority for the district.

(3) A homelessness strategy may also include provision relating to specific action which the authority expects to be taken –

    (a) by any public authority with functions (not being functions mentioned in subsection (2)) which are capable of contributing to the achievement of any of the objectives mentioned in subsection (1); or

    (b) by any voluntary organisation or other person whose activities are capable of contributing to the achievement of any of those objectives.

(4) The inclusion in a homelessness strategy of any provision relating to action mentioned in subsection (3) requires the approval of the body or person concerned.

(5) In formulating a homelessness strategy the authority shall consider (among other things) the extent to which any of the objectives mentioned in subsection (1) can be achieved through action involving two or more of the bodies or other persons mentioned in subsections (2) and (3).

(6) The authority shall keep their homelessness strategy under review and may modify it from time to time.

(7) If the authority modify their homelessness strategy, they shall publish the modifications or the strategy as modified (as they consider most appropriate).

(8) Before adopting or modifying a homelessness strategy the authority shall consult such public or local authorities, voluntary organisations or other persons as they consider appropriate.

(9) The authority shall –

    (a) make a copy of everything published under section 1 or this section available at its principal office for inspection at all reasonable hours, without charge, by members of the public; and

    (b) provide (on payment if required by the authority of a reasonable charge) a copy of anything so published to any member of the public who asks for one.

Sections 1 to 3: interpretation

4 In sections 1 to 3 –

    'homeless' and 'homelessness' have the same meaning as in Part 7 of the Housing Act 1996 (in this Act referred to as 'the 1996 Act');

    'local housing authority' and 'district' have the same meaning as in the Housing Act 1985;

'social services authority' means a local authority for the purposes of the Local Authority Social Services Act 1970;

'support' means advice, information or assistance; and

'voluntary organisation' has the same meaning as in section 180(3) of the 1996 Act.

Statutory instruments*

*   All statutory instruments appear as amended up to date to January 2010. © Crown
    Copyright. Reproduced with the kind permission of HMSO and the Queen's Printer
    for Scotland.

The Homelessness (Suitability of Accommodation) Order 1996 SI No 3204

Citation and commencement

1   This Order may be cited as the Homelessness (Suitability of Accommodation) Order 1996 and shall come into force on 20th January 1997.

Matters to be taken into account

2   In determining whether it would be, or would have been, reasonable for a person to continue to occupy accommodation and in determining whether accommodation is suitable for a person there shall be taken into account whether or not the accommodation is affordable for that person and, in particular, the following matters –

(a) the financial resources available to that person, including, but not limited to –

  (i)   salary, fees and other remuneration;

  (ii) social security benefits;

  (iii) payments due under a court order for the making of periodical payments to a spouse or a former spouse, or to, or for the benefit of, a child;

  (iv) payments of child support maintenance due under the Child Support Act 1991;

  (v)   contributions to the costs in respect of the accommodation which are or were made or which might reasonably be expected to be, or have been, made by other members of his household;

  (vi) pensions

  (vii) financial assistance towards the costs in respect of the accommodation, including loans, provided by a local authority, voluntary organisation or other body;

  (viii) benefits derived from a policy of insurance;

  (ix) savings and other capital sums;

(b) the costs in respect of the accommodation, including, but not limited to, –

  (i)   payments of, or by way of, rent;

  (ii) payments in respect of a licence or permission to occupy the accommodation;

  (iii) mortgage costs;

  (iv) payments of, or by way of, service charges;

  (v)   mooring charges payable for a houseboat;

  (vi) where the accommodation is a caravan or a mobile home, payments in respect of the site on which it stands;

  (vii) the amount of council tax payable in respect of the accommodation;

  (viii) payments by way of deposit or security in respect of the accommodation;

  (ix) payments required by an accommodation agency;

(c) payments which that person is required to make under a court order for the making of periodical payments to a spouse or a former spouse, or to, or for the benefit of, a child and payments of child support maintenance required to be made under the Child Support Act 1991;

(d) that person's other reasonable living expenses.

The Local Authorities (Contracting Out of Allocation of Housing and Homelessness Functions) Order 1996 SI No 3205

Citation, commencement and interpretation

1 (1) This Order may be cited as the Local Authorities (Contracting Out of Allocation of Housing and Homelessness Functions) Order 1996.

(2) This article and article 3 of this Order shall come into force on 20th January 1997 and article 2 of this Order shall come into force on 1st April 1997.

(3) In this Order –
'the Act' means the Housing Act 1996;
'an authority' means a local housing authority as defined in the Housing Act 1985.

(4) Any expressions used in this Order which are also used in the Act have the same meaning as they have in the Act.

Contracting out of allocation of housing functions

2 Any function of an authority which is conferred by or under Part 6 of the Act allocation of housing accommodation), except one which is listed in Schedule 1 to this Order, may be exercised by, or by employees of, such person (if any) as may be authorised in that behalf by the authority whose function it is.

Contracting out of homelessness functions

3 Any function of an authority which is conferred by or under Part 7 of the Act (homelessness), except one which is listed in Schedule 2 to this Order, may be exercised by, or by employees of, such person (if any) as may be authorised in that behalf by the authority whose function it is.

SCHEDULE 1
Article 2

Allocation of housing functions of a local housing authority excluded from contracting out

Functions conferred by or under any of the following provisions of the Act:

(a) section 161(4) (classes of persons qualifying for allocations);

(b) section 162 (the housing register) so far as they relate to any decision about the form of the register;

(c) section 167 (allocation in accordance with allocation scheme) so far as they relate to adopting or altering an allocation scheme (including decisions on what principles the scheme is to be framed) and to the functions in subsection (7) of that section;

(d) section 168(2) (information about allocation scheme) so far as they relate to making the allocation scheme available for inspection at the authority's principal office.

SCHEDULE 2
Article 3

Homelessness functions of a local housing authority excluded from contracting out

Functions conferred by or under any of the following provisions of the Act:

(a) section 179(2) and (3) (duty of local housing authority to provide advisory services);

(b) section 180 (assistance for voluntary organisations);

(c) section 213 (co-operation between relevant housing authorities and bodies).

The Local Housing Authorities (Prescribed Principles for Allocation Schemes) (Wales) Regulations 1997 SI No 45

Citation, commencement and application

1 These Regulations may be cited as the Local Housing Authorities (Prescribed Principles for Allocation Schemes) (Wales) Regulations 1997 and shall come into force on 7th February 1997. They apply to Wales only.

Interpretation

2 In these Regulations –
'the Act' means the Housing Act 1996;
'allocation decision' means a decision to allocate housing accommodation;
'allocation scheme' means an allocation scheme within the meaning of section 167(1) of the Act;
'authority' means a Welsh local housing authority;
'delegation arrangements' means arrangements made under section 101(1) or (2) of the Local Government Act 1972 for the discharge of an authority's function of making allocation decisions;
'officer delegation arrangements' means delegation arrangements which arrange for the discharge (in whole or in part) of an authority's function of making allocation decisions, by an officer or a description of officers of the authority; and
'qualifying person', in relation to an authority, means a person who is qualified to be allocated housing accommodation by that authority.

Allocation scheme principles

3 As regards the procedure to be followed in allocating housing accommodation, the principles set out in the Schedule are prescribed as principles in accordance with which an authority's allocation scheme shall be framed.

SCHEDULE
Regulation 3

Allocation scheme principles

14 In relation to an allocation decision where either –
(a) the housing accommodation in question is situated in the electoral division for which a member is elected, or
(b) the qualifying person in question has his sole or main residence in the electoral division for which a member is elected,
that member shall not be included in the persons or descriptions of persons by whom the allocation decision is to be taken.

2 An officer or a description of officers of the authority shall be included in the persons or descriptions of persons by whom allocation decisions, or descriptions of allocation decisions, may be taken, except where the authority or a committee or sub-committee of the authority, as the case may be, has determined that no officer delegation arrangements shall be made.

The Allocation of Housing (Procedure) Regulations 1997 SI No 483

Citation and commencement

1   These Regulations may be cited as the Allocation of Housing (Procedure) Regulations 1997 and shall come into force on 1st April 1997.

Interpretation

2   In these Regulations –
'allocation decision' means a decision to allocate housing accommodation;
'authority' means a local housing authority in England;
'decision-making body' means an authority or a committee or sub-committee of an authority.

Allocation scheme procedure

3   (1) As regards the procedure to be followed, an authority's allocation scheme shall be framed in accordance with the principle prescribed in this regulation.

(2) A member of an authority who has been elected for the electoral division or ward in which –

(a) the housing accommodation in relation to which an allocation decision falls to be made is situated, or

(b) the person in relation to whom that decision falls to be made has his sole or main residence,

shall not, at the time the allocation decision is made, be included in the persons constituting the decision-making body.

The Homelessness (Isles of Scilly) Order 1997 SI No 797

Citation, commencement and interpretation
1 (1) This Order may be cited as the Homelessness (Isles of Scilly) Order 1997 and shall come into force on 3rd April 1997.

(2) In this Order –
'the Act' means the Housing Act 1996;
'the Council' means the Council of the Isles of Scilly.

Eligibility for assistance by the Council and local connection with the district of the Council
2 (1) Where –
   (a) a person applies to the Council for assistance under Part 7 of the Act (homelessness); or
   (b) a person applies to a local housing authority other than the Council for such assistance and, but for the provisions of paragraphs (2) and (3), the conditions specified in section 198(2) of the Act (referral of case to another authority) for referral of the case to the Council are satisfied,
   sections 183 to 218 of the Act shall be subject to the following provisions of this article.

(2) A person is not eligible for assistance by the Council if he has not been resident in the district of the Council for a period of two years and six months during the period of three years immediately prior to his application.

(3) Where a person is not excluded from assistance by the Council by paragraph (2) –
   (a) he has a local connection with the district of the Council; and
   (b) section 199 of the Act (local connection) shall not apply for the purpose of determining whether he has a local connection with the district of the Council.

The Homelessness (Decisions on Referrals) Order 1998 SI No 1578

Citation and commencement

1   This Order may be cited as the Homelessness (Decisions on Referrals) Order 1998 and shall come into force on the twenty eighth day after the day on which it is approved by resolution of each House of Parliament.

Arrangements for deciding whether conditions for referral are satisfied

2   The arrangements set out in the Schedule to this Order are those agreed by the Local Government Association, the Welsh Local Government Association, the Association of London Government and the Convention of Scottish Local Authorities, and shall be the arrangements for the purposes of section 198(5) and (6)(a) of the Housing Act 1996.

Revocation of order

3   (1) Subject to paragraph (2), the Housing (Homeless Persons) (Appropriate Arrangements) Order 1978 ('the 1978 Order') is hereby revoked.

(2) The 1978 Order shall remain in force for any case where a notified authority has received a notification under section 67(1) of the Housing Act 1985 or section 198(1) of the Housing Act 1996 (referral to another local housing authority) prior to the date on which this Order comes into force.

SCHEDULE
Article 2

The arrangements
Appointment of person by agreement between notifying authority and notified authority

1   Where the question whether the conditions for referral of a case are satisfied has not been decided by agreement between the notifying authority and the notified authority, the question shall be decided by a person appointed by those authorities.

Appointment of person other than by agreement between notifying authority and notified authority

2   If within a period of 21 days commencing on the day on which the notified authority receives a notification under section 198(1) of the Housing Act 1996 a person has not been appointed in accordance with paragraph 1, the question shall be decided by a person –
(a) from the panel constituted in accordance with paragraph 3, and
(b) appointed in accordance with paragraph 4.

3   (1) Subject to sub-paragraph (2), the Local Government Association shall establish and maintain a panel of persons from which a person may be appointed to decide the question whether the conditions for referral of a case are satisfied.

(2) The Local Government Association shall consult such other associations of relevant authorities as they think appropriate before –
(a) establishing the panel,

(b) inviting a person to join the panel after it has been established, and

(c) removing a person from the panel.

4 (1) The notifying authority and the notified authority shall jointly request the Chairman of the Local Government Association or his nominee ('the proper officer') to appoint a person from the panel.

(2) If within a period of six weeks commencing on the day on which the notified authority receives a notification under section 198(1) of the Housing Act 1996 a person has not been appointed, the notifying authority shall request the proper officer to appoint a person from the panel.

Procedural requirements

5 (1) Subject to the following provisions of this paragraph, the procedure for deciding whether the conditions for referral of a case are satisfied shall be determined by the appointed person.

(2) The appointed person shall invite written representations from the notifying authority and the notified authority.

(3) The appointed person may also invite –

(a) further written representations from the notifying authority and the notified authority,

(b) written representations from any other person, and

(c) oral representations from any person.

(4) If the appointed person invites representations from any person, those representations may be made by a person acting on his behalf, whether or not legally qualified.

Notification of decision

6   The appointed person shall notify his decision, and his reasons for it, in writing to the notifying authority and the notified authority.

Costs

7 (1) The notifying authority and the notified authority shall pay their own costs incurred in connection with the arrangements set out in this Schedule.

(2) Where a person has made oral representations, the appointed person may give directions as to the payment by the notifying authority or the notified authority or both authorities of any travelling expenses reasonably incurred by that person.

Meaning of 'appointed person'

8   In this Schedule 'appointed person' means a person appointed in accordance with paragraph 1 or 4.

The Allocation of Housing and Homelessness (Review Procedures) Regulations 1999 SI No 71

PART 1: GENERAL
Citation, commencement and interpretation

1 (1) These Regulations may be cited as the Allocation of Housing and Homelessness (Review Procedures) Regulations 1999 and shall come into force on 11th February 1999.

(2) In these Regulations –

'the authority' means the local housing authority which has made the decision whose review under section 164 or 202 has been requested;

'the Decisions on Referrals Order' means the Homelessness (Decisions on Referrals) Order 1998;

'the reviewer' means –

   (a) where the original decision falls within section 202(1)(a), (b), (c), (e) or (f), the authority;

   (b) where the original decision falls within section 202(1)(d) (a decision under section 198(5) whether the conditions are met for referral of a case) –

      (i) the notifying authority and the notified authority, where the review is carried out by those authorities;

      (ii) the person appointed to carry out the review in accordance with regulation 7, where the case falls within that regulation.

(3) In these Regulations, references to sections are references to sections of the Housing Act 1996.

Who is to make the decision on the review

2 Where the decision of the authority on a review of an original decision made by an officer of the authority is also to be made by an officer, that officer shall be someone who was not involved in the original decision and who is senior to the officer who made the original decision.

PART 2: THE HOUSING REGISTER
Notification of review procedure

3 Following a duly made request for a review under section 164, the authority shall –

   (a) notify the person concerned that he, or someone acting on his behalf, may make representations in writing to the authority in connection with the review; and

   (b) if they have not already done so, notify the person concerned of the procedure to be followed in connection with the review.

Procedure on a review

4 The authority shall, subject to compliance with the provisions of regulation 5, consider any representations made under regulation 3.

Notification of the decision on a review

5 The period within which the authority shall notify the person concerned of the decision on a review under section 164 is eight weeks from the day on which

the request for a review is made to the authority or such longer period as the authority and the person concerned may agree in writing.

PART 3: HOMELESSNESS
Request for a review and notification of review procedure

6 (1) A request for a review under section 202 shall be made –
   (a) to the authority, where the original decision falls within section 202(1)(a), (b), (c), (e) or (f);
   (b) to the notifying authority, where the original decision falls within section 202(1)(d) (a decision under section 198(5) whether the conditions are met for referral of a case).

(2) Except where a case falls within regulation 7, the authority to whom a request for a review under section 202 has been made shall –
   (a) notify the applicant that he, or someone acting on his behalf, may make representations in writing to the authority in connection with the review; and
   (b) if they have not already done so, notify the applicant of the procedure to be followed in connection with the review.

(3) Where a case falls within regulation 7, the person appointed in accordance with that regulation shall –
   (a) notify the applicant that he, or someone acting on his behalf, may make representations in writing to that person in connection with the review; and
   (b) notify the applicant of the procedure to be followed in connection with the review.

Initial procedure where the original decision was made under the Decisions on Referrals Order

7 (1) Where the original decision under section 198(5) (whether the conditions are met for the referral of the case) was made under the Decisions on Referrals Order, a review of that decision shall, subject to paragraph (2), be carried out by a person appointed by the notifying authority and the notified authority.

(2) If a person is not appointed in accordance with paragraph (1) within five working days from the day on which the request for a review is made, the review shall be carried out by a person –
   (a) from the panel constituted in accordance with paragraph 3 of the Schedule to the Decisions on Referrals Order ('the panel'), and
   (b) appointed in accordance with paragraph (3) below.

(3) The notifying authority shall within five working days from the end of the period specified in paragraph (2) request the chairman of the Local Government Association or his nominee ('the proper officer') to appoint a person from the panel and the proper officer shall do so within seven days of the request.

(4) The notifying authority and the notified authority shall within five working days of the appointment of the person appointed ('the appointed person') provide him with the reasons for the original decision and the information and evidence on which that decision was based.

(5) The appointed person shall –
   (a) send to the notifying authority and the notified authority any representations made under regulation 6; and
   (b) invite those authorities to respond to those representations.

(6) The appointed person shall not be the same person as the person who made the original decision.

(7) For the purposes of this regulation a working day is a day other than Saturday, Sunday, Christmas Day, Good Friday or a bank holiday.

Procedure on a review

8 (1) The reviewer shall, subject to compliance with the provisions of regulation 9, consider –
  (a) any representations made under regulation 6 and, in a case falling within regulation 7, any responses to them; and
  (b) any representations made under paragraph (2) below.

(2) If the reviewer considers that there is a deficiency or irregularity in the original decision, or in the manner in which it was made, but is minded nonetheless to make a decision which is against the interests of the applicant on one or more issues, the reviewer shall notify the applicant –
  (a) that the reviewer is so minded and the reasons why; and
  (b) that the applicant, or someone acting on his behalf, may make representations to the reviewer orally or in writing or both orally and in writing.

Notification of the decision on a review

9 (1) The period within which notice of the decision on a review under section 202 shall be given under section 203(3) to the applicant shall be –
  (a) eight weeks from the day on which the request for the review is made, where the original decision falls within section 202(1)(a), (b), (c), (e) or (f);
  (b) ten weeks from the day on which the request for the review is made, where the original decision falls within section 202(1)(d) and the review is carried out by the notifying authority and the notified authority;
  (c) twelve weeks from the day on which the request for the review is made in a case falling within regulation 7.

(2) The period specified in paragraph (1) may be such longer period as the applicant and the reviewer may agree in writing.

(3) In a case falling within paragraph (1)(c), the appointed person shall notify his decision on the review, and his reasons for it, in writing to the notifying authority and the notified authority within a period of eleven weeks from the day on which the request for the review is made, or within a period commencing on that day which is one week shorter than that agreed in accordance with paragraph (2).

PART 4: REVOCATION
Revocation and transitional provisions

10 (1) Subject to paragraph (2), the following provisions are hereby revoked –
  (a) regulations 2 to 8 of the Allocation of Housing and Homelessness (Review Procedures and Amendment) Regulations 1996;
  (b) the definition of 'the Review Regulations' in regulation 1(3) of the Allocation of Housing and Homelessness (Amendment) Regulations 1997 and regulation 6 of those Regulations.

(2) The provisions revoked by paragraph (1) shall continue in force in any case where a request for a review under section 164 or 202 is made prior to the date these Regulations come into force.

The Homelessness (Asylum-Seekers) (Interim Period) (England) Order 1999 SI No 3126

Citation, commencement and extent

1 (1) This Order may be cited as the Homelessness (Asylum-Seekers) (Interim Period) (England) Order 1999 and shall come into force on 6th December 1999.

   (2) This Order extends to England only.

Modification of Part 7 of the Housing Act 1996 for certain asylum-seekers

2   Part 7 of the Housing Act 1996 (homelessness) shall have effect in relation to asylum-seekers who are section 185(2) persons with the modifications specified in the following provisions of this Order.

Referrals to other local authorities

3   In section 198 (referral of case to another local housing authority) –

   (a) in subsection (3), after 'this purpose', there shall be inserted ', and for the purpose of subsection (4A)(c),'; and

   (b) after subsection (4), there shall be inserted –

      '(4A) The conditions for referral of the case to another authority are also met if –

         (a) the local housing authority to whom the application has been made and another housing authority have agreed that the case should be referred to that other authority;

         (b) that other authority has provided written confirmation of the agreement to the local housing authority; and

         (c) neither the applicant nor any person who might reasonably be expected to reside with him will run the risk of domestic violence in the district of that other authority.

      (4B) When reaching the agreement referred to in subsection (4A)(a), the local housing authority to whom the application was made and the other authority need not have regard to –

         (a) any preference that the applicant, or any person who might reasonably be expected to reside with him, may have as to the locality in which the accommodation is to be secured; or

         (b) whether the applicant, or any person who might reasonably be expected to reside with him, has a local connection with the district of any local housing authority.'.

Discharge of functions by local housing authorities

4   In section 206 (discharge of functions by local housing authorities), after subsection (1), there shall be inserted –

   '(1A) In discharging their housing functions under this Part, a local housing authority shall have regard to the desirability, in general, of securing accommodation in areas in which there is a ready supply of accommodation.'.

Out-of-area placements

5   In section 208 (discharge of functions: out-of-area placements), after subsection (1), there shall be inserted –

'(1A) Subsection (1) shall not apply where –

(a) the local housing authority and another housing authority have agreed that the local housing authority may secure that accommodation is available for the occupation of all or an agreed number of asylum-seekers who are section 185(2) persons in that other authority's district; and

(b) that other authority has provided written confirmation of the agreement to the local housing authority.'.

Suitability of accommodation

6   In section 210 (suitability of accommodation), after subsection (1), there shall be inserted –

'(1A) In determining for the purposes of this Part whether accommodation is suitable for an applicant, or any person who might reasonably be expected to reside with him, the local housing authority –

(a) shall also have regard to the fact that the accommodation is to be temporary pending the determination of the applicant's claim for asylum; and

(b) shall not have regard to any preference that the applicant, or any person who might reasonably be expected to reside with him, may have as to the locality in which the accommodation is to be secured.'.

The interim period

7   This Order shall cease to have effect on the date on which section 186 of the Housing Act 1996 (asylum-seekers and their dependants) is repealed by the Immigration and Asylum Act 1999 (as to which see section 117(5) of that Act).

The Homeless Persons (Priority Need) (Wales) Order 2001 SI No 607

Name, commencement and application
1 (1) The name of this Order is the Homeless Persons (Priority Need) (Wales) Order 2001 and it shall come into force on St. David's Day, March 1st 2001.

(2) This Order applies to Wales only.

Persons with priority need for accommodation
2 The descriptions of person specified in articles 3 to 7 have priority need for accommodation under section 189 of the Housing Act 1996.

A care leaver or person at particular risk of sexual or financial exploitation, 18 years or over but under the age of 21
3 (1) A person who –
 (a) is 18 years old or older but under the age of 21; and
 (b) at any time while still a child was, but is no longer, looked after, accommodated or fostered; or
 (c) is at particular risk of sexual or financial exploitation.

(2) In paragraph (1)(b) above 'looked after, accommodated or fostered' means:
 (a) looked after by a local authority;
 (b) accommodated by or on behalf of a voluntary organisation;
 (c) accommodated in a private children's home;
 (d) accommodated for a consecutive period of at least three months –
  (i) by any health authority, special health authority or local education authority, or
  (ii) in any residential care home, nursing home or mental nursing home or in any accommodation provided by a National Health Service Trust or NHS foundation trust; or
 (e) privately fostered.

A 16 or 17 year old
4 A person who is 16 or 17 years old.

A person fleeing domestic violence or threatened domestic violence
5 A person without dependant children who has been subject to domestic violence or is at risk of such violence, or if he or she returns home is at risk of domestic violence.

A person homeless after leaving the armed forces
6 (1) A person formerly serving in the regular armed forces of the Crown who has been homeless since leaving those forces.

(2) In paragraph (1) above the expression 'regular armed forces of the Crown' has the meaning given to it in section 199(4) of the Housing Act 1996.

A former prisoner homeless after being released from custody
7 (1) A former prisoner who has been homeless since leaving custody and who has a local connection with the area of the local housing authority.

(2) A 'prisoner' means any person for the time being detained in lawful custody as the result of a requirement imposed by a court that he or she be detained.

The Homelessness (Priority Need for Accommodation) (England) Order 2002 SI No 2051

Citation, commencement and interpretation

1 (1) This Order may be cited as the Homelessness (Priority Need for Accommodation) (England) Order 2002 and shall come into force on the day after the day on which it is made.

(2) This Order extends to England only.

(3) In this Order –

'looked after, accommodated or fostered' has the meaning given by section 24(2) of the Children Act 1989; and

'relevant student' means a person to whom section 24B(3) of that Act applies –

(a) who is in full-time further or higher education; and

(b) whose term-time accommodation is not available to him during a vacation.

Priority need for accommodation

2   The descriptions of person specified in the following articles have a priority need for accommodation for the purposes of Part 7 of the Housing Act 1996.

Children aged 16 or 17

3 (1) A person (other than a person to whom paragraph (2) below applies) aged sixteen or seventeen who is not a relevant child for the purposes of section 23A of the Children Act 1989.

(2) This paragraph applies to a person to whom a local authority owe a duty to provide accommodation under section 20 of that Act (provision of accommodation for children in need).

Young people under 21

4 (1) A person (other than a relevant student) who –

(a) is under twenty-one; and

(b) at any time after reaching the age of sixteen, but while still under eighteen, was, but is no longer, looked after, accommodated or fostered.

Vulnerability: institutional backgrounds

5 (1) A person (other than a relevant student) who has reached the age of twenty-one and who is vulnerable as a result of having been looked after, accommodated or fostered.

(2) A person who is vulnerable as a result of having been a member of Her Majesty's regular naval, military or air forces.

(3) A person who is vulnerable as a result of –

(a) having served a custodial sentence (within the meaning of section 76 of the Powers of Criminal Courts (Sentencing) Act 2000);

(b) having been committed for contempt of court or any other kindred offence;

(c) having been remanded in custody (within the meaning of paragraph (b), (c) or (d) of section 88(1) of that Act).

Vulnerability: fleeing violence or threats of violence

6 A person who is vulnerable as a result of ceasing to occupy accommodation by reason of violence from another person or threats of violence from another person which are likely to be carried out.

The Allocation of Housing (Wales) Regulations 2003 SI No 239

Citation, commencement and application

1 (1) These Regulations may be cited as the Allocation of Housing (Wales) Regulations 2003 and shall come into force on 29 January 2003.

(2) These Regulations apply to Wales only.

Interpretation

2 In these Regulations –

'the Act' (*'y Ddeddf'*) means the Housing Act 1996;

'the Common Travel Area' (*'Ardal Deithio Gyffredin'*) means the United Kingdom, the Channel Islands, the Isle of Man and the Republic of Ireland collectively; and

'the immigration rules' (*'y rheolau mewnfudo'*) mean the rules laid down as mentioned in section 3(2) of the Immigration Act 1971 (general provisions for regulation and control).

Cases where the provisions of Part 6 of the Act do not apply

3 The provisions of Part 6 of the Act about the allocation of housing accommodation do not apply in the following cases –

(a) where a local housing authority secures the provision of suitable alternative accommodation under section 39 of the Land Compensation Act 1973 (duty to rehouse residential occupiers);

(b) in relation to the grant of a secure tenancy under section 554 and 555 of the Housing Act 1985 (grant of tenancy to former owner-occupier or statutory tenant of defective dwelling-house).

Classes prescribed under section 160A(3) who are eligible persons

4 The following are classes of persons subject to immigration control prescribed for the purposes of section 160A(3) of the Act (persons prescribed as eligible for an allocation of housing accommodation by a local housing authority) –

(a) Class A – a person recorded by the Secretary of State as a refugee within the definition in Article 1 of the Convention relating to the Status of Refugees done at Geneva on 28th July 1951 as extended by Article 1(2) of the Protocol relating to the Status of Refugees done at New York on 31st January 1967;

(b) Class B – a person –

(i) who has been granted by the Secretary of State exceptional leave to enter or remain in the United Kingdom outside the provisions of the immigration rules; and

(ii) whose leave is not subject to a condition requiring them to maintain and accommodate themselves, and any person who is dependent on them, without recourse to public funds;

(c) Class C – a person who has current leave to enter or remain in the United Kingdom which is not subject to any limitation or condition and who is habitually resident in the Common Travel Area other than a person –

(i) who has been given leave to enter or remain in the United Kingdom upon an undertaking given by another person (that person's 'sponsor') in writing in pursuance of the immigration rules to be responsible for that person's maintenance and accommodation;

(ii) who has been resident in the United Kingdom for less than five years beginning on the date of entry or the date on which the above-mentioned undertaking was given in respect of that person, whichever date is the later; and

(iii) whose sponsor or, where is more than one sponsor, at least one of whose sponsors, is still alive;

(d) Class D – a person who is habitually resident in the Common Travel Area and who –

(i) is a national of a state which has ratified the European Convention on Social and Medical Assistance done at Paris on 11th December 1953 or a state which has ratified the European Social Charter done at Turin on 18th October 1961 and is lawfully present in the United Kingdom; or

(ii) before 3rd April 2000 was owed a duty by a housing authority under Part 3 of the Housing Act 1985 (housing the homeless) or Part 7 of the Act (homelessness) which is extant, and who is a national of a state which is a signatory to the European Convention on Social and Medical Assistance done at Paris on 11th December 1953 or a state which is a signatory to the European Social Charter done at Turin on 18th October 1961;

(e) Class D1 – a person who has humanitarian protection granted under the Immigration Rules.

Classes prescribed under section 160A(5) who are not eligible persons

5   The following is a class of persons, not being persons subject to immigration control, prescribed for the purposes of section 160A(5) of the Act (persons prescribed as ineligible for an allocation of housing accommodation) –

Class E – a person who is not habitually resident in the Common Travel Area other than –

(a) a worker for the purposes of Council Regulation (EEC) No 1612/68 or (EEC) No 1251/70;

(b) a person with a right to reside in the United Kingdom pursuant to the Immigration (European Economic Area) Order 2000 and derived from Council Directive No 68/360/EEC or No 73/148/EEC;

(c) a person who left the territory of Montserrat after 1st November 1995 because of the effect on that territory of a volcanic eruption.

(d) a person who –

(i) arrived in Great Britain on or after 28 February 2009 but before 18 March 2011;

(ii) immediately before arriving in Great Britain had been resident in Zimbabwe; and

(iii) before leaving Zimbabwe, had accepted an offer, made by Her Majesty's Government, to assist that person to settle in the United Kingdom.

Revocation

6   The Allocation of Housing (Wales) Regulations 2000 are revoked.

The Homelessness (Suitability of Accommodation) (Wales) Order 2006 SI No 650

Title, commencement and application

1 (1) The title of this Order is the Homelessness (Suitability of Accommodation) (Wales) Order 2006.

(2) Save as provided in paragraphs (3) and (4) of this Article, this Order comes into force on 3 April 2006.

(3) Articles 4, 5 and 6 of, and the Schedule to this Order come into force on 2 April 2007.

(4) Articles 7, 8, 9 and 10 of this Order come into force on 7 April 2008.

(5) This Order applies in relation to the duties of local housing authorities in Wales under Part 7 of the Housing Act 1996 (homelessness).

Interpretation

In this Order –

2   'the 1996 Act' ('*Deddf 1996*') means the Housing Act 1996; and any reference to a numbered section is a reference to a section of the Housing Act 1996;

'B&B accommodation' ('*llety Gwely a Brecwast*') means commercially provided accommodation (whether or not breakfast is included) –

(a) which is not separate and self-contained premises;

(b) in which any of the following amenities is not available to the applicant or is shared by more than one household –

(i) a toilet;

(ii) personal washing facilities;

(iii) cooking facilities;

(c) which is not accommodation which is owned or managed by a local housing authority, a registered social landlord or a voluntary organisation as defined in section 180(3) of the Housing Act 1996; or

(d) which is not an establishment registered under the provisions of the Care Standards Act 2000;

and 'B&B' ('*Gwely a Brecwast*') is to be construed accordingly;

'basic standard accommodation' ('*llety o safon sylfaenol*') means accommodation that –

(a) complies with all statutory requirements (such as requirements relating to fire and gas safety, planning and licences for houses in multiple occupation, where applicable); and

(b) has a manager deemed by the local housing authority to be a fit and proper person with the ability to manage B&B accommodation;

and 'basic standard' ('*safon sylfaenol*') is to be construed accordingly;

'higher standard accommodation' ('*llety o safon uwch*') means accommodation that meets –

(a) the basic standard; and

(b) the standards contained in the Schedule to this Order,

and 'higher standard' ('*safon uwch*') is to be construed accordingly;

'shared accommodation' ('*llety a rennir*') means accommodation –

(a) which is not separate and self-contained premises; or

(b) in which any of the following amenities is not available to the applicant or is shared by more than one household –
   (i) a toilet;
   (ii) personal washing facilities;
   (iii) cooking facilities; or
(c) which is not an establishment registered under the provisions of the Care Standards Act 2000;

'small B&B' ('*llety Gwely a Brecwast bach*') means –
   B&B accommodation –
   (i) where the manager resides on the premises; and
   (ii) which has fewer than 7 bedrooms available for letting.

PART 1: ADDITIONAL MATTERS TO BE TAKEN INTO ACCOUNT IN DETERMINING SUITABILITY

3   In determining for the purposes of Part 7 of the 1996 Act whether accommodation is suitable for a person in priority need there must be taken into account the following matters –
(a) the specific health needs of the person;
(b) the proximity and accessibility of social services;
(c) the proximity and accessibility of the support of the family or other support services; or
(d) any disability of the person.

PART 2: CIRCUMSTANCES APPLYING FROM 2 APRIL 2007 IN WHICH ACCOMMODATION IS NOT TO BE REGARDED AS SUITABLE

B&B accommodation used for housing a homeless person to meet the basic standard

4   For the purposes of Part 7 of the 1996 Act, B&B accommodation is not to be regarded as suitable unless it meets at least the basic standard.

B&B accommodation not to be regarded as suitable for a minor or a pregnant woman

5   For the purposes of Part 7 of the 1996 Act and subject to the exceptions contained in Article 6, B&B accommodation is not to be regarded as suitable for a person who is a minor or a pregnant woman.

Exceptions

6   (1) Article 5 does not apply where –
(a) the person occupies a basic standard B&B for a period, or a total of periods, which does not exceed 2 weeks;
(b) the person occupies a higher standard B&B for a period or a total of periods which does not exceed 6 weeks;
(c) the person occupies a basic standard small B&B for a period or a total of periods which does not exceed 6 weeks, and the local housing authority has, before the expiry of the two-week period referred to in sub-paragraph (a), offered suitable alternative accommodation, but the person has chosen to remain in the said B&B;

    (d) the person occupies a basic standard small B&B after exercising the choice referred to in sub-paragraph (c) above, and the local housing authority has offered suitable alternative accommodation before the end of the six-week period referred to in sub-paragraph (c) above, but the person has chosen to remain in the said B&B; or

    (e) the person occupies a higher standard small B&B, and the local housing authority has offered suitable alternative accommodation, before the expiry of the six-week period referred to in sub-paragraph (b) above, but the person has chosen to remain in the said B&B.

(2) If the suitable alternative accommodation offered for the purposes of paragraph (1) is shared, it must meet the higher standard.

(3) In the case of households with dependant children or a pregnant woman, the offer made under sub-paragraphs (d) or (e) must be of suitable self-contained accommodation. In the case of an applicant who is a minor, the offer must be of suitable accommodation with support.

(4) In calculating a period, or total period, of a person's occupation of B&B accommodation for the purposes of paragraph (1), there must be disregarded –

    (a) any period before 2 April 2007; and

    (b) where a local housing authority is subject to the duty under section 193 by virtue of section 200(4), any period before that authority became subject to that duty.

PART 3: EXTENSION FROM 7 APRIL 2008 TO ALL ACCOMMODATION PROVIDED IN DISCHARGE OF HOMELESSNESS FUNCTIONS

B&B accommodation not to be regarded as suitable for a homeless person in priority need

7   For the purposes of Part 7 of the 1996 Act and subject to the exceptions contained in article 9, B&B accommodation is not to be regarded as suitable for a person who is in priority need.

Shared accommodation to meet the higher standard

8   For the purposes of Part 7 of the 1996 Act and subject to the exceptions contained in articles 9 and 10, shared accommodation is not to be regarded as suitable for a person who is in priority need unless it meets the higher standard.

Exceptions

9 (1) Articles 7 and 8 do not apply where –

    (a) the person occupies basic standard B&B for a period, or a total of periods, which does not exceed 2 weeks;

    (b) the person occupies a higher standard B&B for a period or a total of periods which does not exceed 6 weeks;

    (c) the person occupies a basic standard small B&B for a period or a total of periods which does not exceed 6 weeks, and the local housing authority has, before the expiry of the two-week period referred to in sub-paragraph (a), offered suitable alternative accommodation, but the person has chosen to remain in the said B&B;

    (d) the person occupies a basic standard small B&B after exercising the choice referred to in sub-paragraph (c), and the local housing authority has offered suitable alternative accommodation before the end of the six-week period referred to in sub-paragraph (c) above, but the person has chosen to remain in the said B&B;

(e) the person occupies a higher standard small B&B, the local housing authority has offered suitable alternative accommodation, before the expiry of the six-week period referred to in sub-paragraph (b), but the person has chosen to remain in the said B&B: or

(f) the person occupies basic standard shared accommodation for a period, or a total of periods, which does not exceed 2 weeks;

(g) the person occupies, for a period or a total of periods which does not exceed 6 weeks, basic standard shared accommodation owned by a local housing authority or registered social landlord, and the local housing authority has offered suitable alternative accommodation before the expiry of the two-week period referred to in sub-paragraph (f), but the person has chosen to remain in the said accommodation.

(2) If the suitable alternative accommodation offered for the purposes of paragraph (1) is shared, it must meet the higher standard.

(3) In the case of households with dependant children or a pregnant woman, the offer made under sub-paragraphs (d) or (e) must be of suitable self-contained accommodation. In the case of an applicant who is a minor, the offer must be of suitable accommodation with support.

(4) In calculating a period, or total period, of a person's occupation of shared accommodation for the purposes of paragraph (1), there must be disregarded –

(a) any period before 7 April 2008; and

(b) where a local housing authority is subject to the duty under section 193 by virtue of section 200(4), any period before that authority became subject to that duty.

Delayed application to Social Housing

10   Article 7 is not to apply until 4 April 2011 to any property owned or managed by a local authority or registered social landlord and used for the purposes of Part 7 of the 1996 Act on 7 April 2008.

SCHEDULE
Higher standard

Minimum Space Standards

1   Space standards for sleeping accommodation

Room sizes where cooking facilities provided in a separate room or kitchen

Floor Area of Room	Maximum No of Persons
Not less than 6.5 square metres	1 person
Not less than 10.2 square metres	2 persons
Not less than 14.9 square metres	3 persons
Not less than 19.6 square metres	4 persons

Room sizes where cooking facilities provided within the room

Floor Area of Room	Maximum No of Persons
Not less than 10.2 square metres	1 person
Not less than 13.9 square metres	2 persons
Not less than 18.6 square metres	3 persons
Not less than 23.2 square metres	4 persons

For the purposes of the room size calculations above, a child less than 10 years old is treated as a half person.

(a) No room to be occupied by more than 4 persons, except where the occupants consent.

(b) No sharing of rooms for those of opposite genders, aged 10 or above unless they are living together as partners and both are over the age of consent, or where a parent or guardian elects to share with an older child.

(c) All rooms must have a floor to ceiling height of at least 2.1 metres over not less than 75% of the room area. Any part of the room where the ceiling height is less than 1.5 metres must be disregarded when calculating the floor area.

(d) Separate kitchens and bathrooms are unsuitable for sleeping accommodation.

Installation for heating

2   The premises must have adequate provision for heating. All habitable rooms and bath- or shower-rooms must have a heating system capable of maintaining the room at a minimum temperature of 18°C when the outside temperature is –1°C

Facilities for the storage, preparation and cooking of food within the unit

(1) In a unit of accommodation accommodating more than one person, the food preparation area provided within the unit must include the following facilities:

(a) four burners or hobs, conventional oven and grill, or two burners or hobs and a microwave with a built in oven and grill,

(b) a sink and integral drainer, with a constant supply of hot water and cold drinking water,

(c) a storage cupboard of a minimum capacity 0.2 cubic metres excluding storage beneath the sink,

(d) a refrigerator,

(e) a minimum of four 13-amp sockets (single or double) situated over the worktop,

(f) a worktop for food preparation of minimum dimensions 1 metre x 0.6 metre, and

(g) a minimum of 1 metre circulation space from facilities to other furniture in the room.

(2) In a unit of accommodation accommodating one person, the food preparation area provided within the unit of accommodation must include the following facilities:

As (a)–(g) above but (a) to have a minimum of two burners or hobs.

Storage, preparation and cooking of food in a shared facility

(1) Where food preparation areas are shared between more than one household there must be one set of kitchen facilities for:

(a) every 3 family households or fewer;

(b) every 5 single-person households or fewer. (For between 6 and 9 single-person households an additional oven or microwave is required.)

(c) every 10 persons or fewer where there is a mixture of family and single-person households within the same premises.

(2) Each set of shared facilities must provide the following facilities:

(a) as for unit accommodating more than one person except that cooking facilities must consist of 4 burners or hobs, conventional oven, grill and microwave,

(b) an electric kettle,

(c) a toaster.

The food preparation area used by the management may be included when calculating the ratio, provided it meets the criteria for storage, preparation and cooking of food in a shared facility.

Where residents have no access to kitchen facilities and the proprietor provides at least a breakfast and evening-meal for residents, the requirements for shared kitchen facilities will be deemed to have been met.

Additional facilities to be provided in each bedroom or within the total accommodation occupied exclusively by each household must include:

(a) a refrigerator; and

(b) lockable storage.

Alternatively, these may be provided elsewhere within the building.

Toilet and washing facilities

5 (1) Facilities for the exclusive use of the occupant or household must include:

(a) bath or shower,

(b) a wash hand basin with a constant supply of hot and cold water, and

(c) a water-closet either en-suite or in a separate room reserved for the exclusive use of individuals or households.

(2) Shared facilities must include:

(a) One water closet and wash hand basin with a constant supply of hot and cold water within the building for every five households or fewer. This must be located not more than one floor away from the intended users. For the first five households the water closet and wash hand basin may be in the shower or bathroom. All additional water closets and wash hand basins for occupancies of six households or more must be in a separate compartment.

(b) One bathroom or shower-room to be provided for every five persons. This must be located not more than one floor away from the intended users.

(c) In premises accommodating children under the age of 10, at least half of the bathing facilities must contain baths suitable for children.

The number of persons occupying a unit of accommodation with a water closet facility provided for their exclusive use is not to be included in the calculation for shared water closets.

Security

6   The entrance door to each unit of accommodation must be lockable and be capable of being unlocked from inside without the use of a key.

Common room(s)

7   Every premises must have a common room of at least 12 square metres unless all households have a living area separate from their sleeping area that is available for their exclusive use or the premises are for single person households only.

Management standard

8   (a) Each household must be issued with written 'house rules' which include details as to how sanctions will be applied. This document is to be approved by the local authority placing homeless households in the premises.

(b) Each household must be issued with written information relating to the premises including how to operate all installations, for example heating and hot water appliances and fire fighting equipment.

(c) Written information must be made available to residents relating to the local area including the location or contact details of local facilities, laundrettes, doctors' surgeries and schools.

(d) Residents must have access to their rooms at all times except when rooms are being cleaned or otherwise maintained. Provision must be made to accommodate residents at these times.

(e) Access is allowed for the appropriate officers of the local housing authority in whose area the premises are situated, and officers of any authority placing homeless households in the premises, to inspect the premises as and when they consider necessary, to ensure that the requirements are being complied with; and that the manager will allow such inspections to take place, if necessary without notice.

(f) Access is allowed for the officers of the local authority and authorised health and community workers for the area in which the premises are situated, to visit the occupiers of the premises and interview them in private in the room(s) they occupy.

(g) A manager with adequate day to day responsibility to ensure the good management of the property can be contacted at all times and that a notice giving the name, address and telephone number of the manager must be displayed in a readily visible position in the property.

(h) A clear emergency evacuation plan is in place setting out action upon hearing the fire alarm, escape routes and safe assembly points. The managers must ensure that each person newly arriving at the premises is told what to do in the event of a fire and about fire precautions provided.

(i) Each household must be issued with a complaints procedure which specifies how a complaint can be made. This information must also include where the complainant can obtain further advice and assistance.

The Allocation of Housing and Homelessness (Eligibility) (England) Regulations 2006 SI No 1294

Citation, commencement and application

1　(1) These Regulations may be cited as the Allocation of Housing and Homelessness (Eligibility) (England) Regulations 2006 and shall come into force on 1st June 2006.

(2) These Regulations apply to England only.

Interpretation

2　(1) In these Regulations –

'the 1996 Act' means the Housing Act 1996;

'the Accession Regulations 2004' means the Accession (Immigration and Worker Registration) Regulations 2004;

'the Accession Regulations 2006' means the Accession (Immigration and Worker Authorisation) Regulations 2006;

'the EEA Regulations' means the Immigration (European Economic Area) Regulations 2006;

'the Immigration Rules' means the rules laid down as mentioned in section 3(2) of the Immigration Act 1971 (general provisions for regulation and control);

'the Refugee Convention' means the Convention relating to the Status of Refugees done at Geneva on 28th July 1951, as extended by Article 1(2) of the Protocol relating to the Status of Refugees done at New York on 31st January 1967; and

'sponsor' means a person who has given an undertaking in writing for the purposes of the Immigration Rules to be responsible for the maintenance and accommodation of another person.

(2) For the purposes of these Regulations –

(a) 'jobseeker', 'self-employed person', and 'worker' have the same meaning as for the purposes of the definition of a 'qualified person' in regulation 6(1) of the EEA Regulations; and

(b) subject to paragraph (3), references to the family member of a jobseeker, self-employed person or worker shall be construed in accordance with regulation 7 of those Regulations.

(3) For the purposes of regulations 4(2)(d) and 6(2)(d) 'family member' does not include a person who is treated as a family member by virtue of regulation 7(3) of the EEA Regulations.

(4) For the purposes of regulations 4(2)(h) and 6(2)(h) 'the relevant period' means the period beginning at 4pm on 25 July 2006 and ending on 31st January 2007.

Persons subject to immigration control who are eligible for an allocation of housing accommodation

3　The following classes of persons subject to immigration control are persons who are eligible for an allocation of housing accommodation under Part 6 of the 1996 Act –

(a) Class A – a person who is recorded by the Secretary of State as a refugee within the definition in Article 1 of the Refugee Convention and who has leave to enter or remain in the United Kingdom;

(b) Class B – a person –
  (i) who has exceptional leave to enter or remain in the United Kingdom granted outside the provisions of the Immigration Rules; and
  (ii) who is not subject to a condition requiring him to maintain and accommodate himself, and any person who is dependent on him, without recourse to public funds;

(c) Class C – a person who is habitually resident in the United Kingdom, the Channel Islands, the Isle of Man or the Republic of Ireland and whose leave to enter or remain in the United Kingdom is not subject to any limitation or condition, other than a person –
  (i) who has been given leave to enter or remain in the United Kingdom upon an undertaking given by his sponsor;
  (ii) who has been resident in the United Kingdom, the Channel Islands, the Isle of Man or the Republic of Ireland for less than five years beginning on the date of entry or the date on which his sponsor gave the undertaking in respect of him, whichever date is the later; and
  (iii) whose sponsor or, where there is more than one sponsor, at least one of whose sponsors, is still alive; and

(d) Class D – a person who has humanitarian protection granted under the Immigration Rules.

Other persons from abroad who are ineligible for an allocation of housing accommodation

4 (1) A person who is not subject to immigration control is to be treated as a person from abroad who is ineligible for an allocation of housing accommodation under Part 6 of the 1996 Act if –

(a) subject to paragraph (2), he is not habitually resident in the United Kingdom, the Channel Islands, the Isle of Man, or the Republic of Ireland;

(b) his only right to reside in the United Kingdom –
  (i) is derived from his status as a jobseeker or the family member of a jobseeker; or
  (ii) is an initial right to reside for a period not exceeding three months under regulation 13 of the EEA Regulations; or

(c) his only right to reside in the Channel Islands, the Isle of Man or the Republic of Ireland is a right equivalent to one of those mentioned in sub-paragraph (b) which is derived from the Treaty establishing the European Community.

(2) The following are not to be treated as persons from abroad who are ineligible for an allocation of housing accommodation pursuant to paragraph (1)(a) –

(a) a worker;

(b) a self-employed person;

(c) a person who is treated as a worker for the purpose of the definition of 'qualified person' in regulation 6(1) of the EEA Regulations pursuant to either –

    (i) regulation 5 of the Accession Regulations 2004 (application of the 2006 Regulations in relation to accession State worker requiring registration) or

    (ii) regulation 6 of the Accession Regulations 2006 (right of residence of an accession State national subject to worker authorisation);

(d) a person who is the family member of a person specified in sub-paragraphs (a)–(c);

(e) a person with a right to reside permanently in the United Kingdom by virtue of regulation 15(c), (d) or (e) of the EEA Regulations;

(f) a person who left the territory of Montserrat after 1st November 1995 because of the effect on that territory of a volcanic eruption; . . .

(g) a person who is in the United Kingdom as a result of his deportation, expulsion or other removal by compulsion of law from another country to the United Kingdom; . . .

(h) during the relevant period, a person who left Lebanon on or after 12th July 2006 because of the armed conflict there; and

(i) a person who –

    (i) arrived in Great Britain on or after 28th February 2009 but before 18th March 2011;

    (ii) immediately before arriving in Great Britain had been resident in Zimbabwe; and

    (iii) before leaving Zimbabwe, had accepted an offer, made by Her Majesty's Government, to assist that person to settle in the United Kingdom.

Persons subject to immigration control who are eligible for housing assistance

5 (1) The following classes of persons subject to immigration control are persons who are eligible for housing assistance under Part 7 of the 1996 Act –

(a) Class A – a person who is recorded by the Secretary of State as a refugee within the definition in Article 1 of the Refugee Convention and who has leave to enter or remain in the United Kingdom;

(b) Class B – a person –

    (i) who has exceptional leave to enter or remain in the United Kingdom granted outside the provisions of the Immigration Rules; and

    (ii) whose leave to enter or remain is not subject to a condition requiring him to maintain and accommodate himself, and any person who is dependent on him, without recourse to public funds;

(c) Class C – a person who is habitually resident in the United Kingdom, the Channel Islands, the Isle of Man or the Republic of Ireland and whose leave to enter or remain in the United Kingdom is not subject to any limitation or condition, other than a person –

    (i) who has been given leave to enter or remain in the United Kingdom upon an undertaking given by his sponsor;

    (ii) who has been resident in the United Kingdom, the Channel Islands, the Isle of Man or the Republic of Ireland for less than five years beginning on the date of entry or the date on which his sponsor gave the undertaking in respect of him, whichever date is the later; and

    (iii) whose sponsor or, where there is more than one sponsor, at least one of whose sponsors, is still alive;

(d) Class D – a person who has humanitarian protection granted under the Immigration Rules; and

(e) Class E – a person who is an asylum-seeker whose claim for asylum is recorded by the Secretary of State as having been made before 3rd April 2000 and in the circumstances mentioned in one of the following paragraphs –

    (i) on arrival (other than on his re-entry) in the United Kingdom from a country outside the United Kingdom, the Channel Islands, the Isle of Man or the Republic of Ireland;

    (ii) within three months from the day on which the Secretary of State made a relevant declaration, and the applicant was in Great Britain on the day on which the declaration was made; or

    (iii) on or before 4th February 1996 by an applicant who was on 4th February 1996 entitled to benefit under regulation 7A of the Housing Benefit (General) Regulations 1987 (persons from abroad).

(2) For the purpose of paragraph (1)(e) –

    (a) 'asylum-seeker' means a person who is at least 18 years old, who is in the United Kingdom, and who has made a claim for asylum;

    (b) 'claim for asylum' means a claim that it would be contrary to the United Kingdom's obligations under the Refugee Convention for the claimant to be removed from, or required to leave, the United Kingdom;

    (c) 'relevant declaration' means a declaration to the effect that the country of which the applicant is a national is subject to such a fundamental change of circumstances that the Secretary of State would not normally order the return of a person to that country; and

    (d) subject to paragraph (3), a person ceases to be an asylum-seeker when his claim for asylum is recorded by the Secretary of State as having been decided (other than on appeal) or abandoned.

(3) For the purposes of paragraph (1)(e)(iii), a person does not cease to be an asylum-seeker as mentioned in paragraph (2)(d) while he is eligible for housing benefit by virtue of –

    (a) regulation 10(6) of the Housing Benefit Regulations 2006; or

    (b) regulation 10(6) of the Housing Benefit (Persons who have attained the qualifying age for state pension credit) Regulations 2006,

as modified in both cases by paragraph 6 of Schedule 3 to the Housing Benefit and Council Tax Benefit (Consequential Provisions) Regulations 2006.

Other persons from abroad who are ineligible for housing assistance

6 (1) A person who is not subject to immigration control is to be treated as a person from abroad who is ineligible for housing assistance under Part 7 of the 1996 Act if –

    (a) subject to paragraph (2), he is not habitually resident in the United Kingdom, the Channel Islands, the Isle of Man, or the Republic of Ireland;

    (b) his only right to reside in the United Kingdom –

        (i) is derived from his status as a jobseeker or the family member of a jobseeker; or

        (ii) is an initial right to reside for a period not exceeding three months under regulation 13 of the EEA Regulations; or

(c) his only right to reside in the Channel Islands, the Isle of Man or the Republic of Ireland is a right equivalent to one of those mentioned in sub-paragraph (b) which is derived from the Treaty establishing the European Community.

(2) The following are not to be treated as persons from abroad who are ineligible for housing assistance pursuant to paragraph (1)(a) –

(a) a worker;

(b) a self-employed person;

(c) a person who is treated as a worker for the purpose of the definition of 'qualified person' in regulation 6(1) of the EEA Regulations pursuant to either –

(i) regulation 5 of the Accession Regulations 2004 (application of the 2006 Regulations in relation to accession State worker requiring registration), or

(ii) regulation 6 of the Accession Regulations 2006 (right of residence of an accession State national subject to worker authorisation);

(d) a person who is the family member of a person specified in sub-paragraphs (a)–(c);

(e) a person with a right to reside permanently in the United Kingdom by virtue of regulation 15(c), (d) or (e) of the EEA Regulations;

(f) a person who left the territory of Montserrat after 1st November 1995 because of the effect on that territory of a volcanic eruption; . . .

(g) a person who is in the United Kingdom as a result of his deportation, expulsion or other removal by compulsion of law from another country to the United Kingdom; . . .

(h) during the relevant period, a person who left Lebanon on or after 12th July 2006 because of the armed conflict there; and

(i) a person who –

(i) arrived in Great Britain on or after 28th February 2009 but before 18th March 2011;

(ii) immediately before arriving in Great Britain had been resident in Zimbabwe; and

(iii) before leaving Zimbabwe, had accepted an offer, made by Her Majesty's Government, to assist that person to settle in the United Kingdom.

Revocation

7   Subject to regulation 8, the Regulations specified in column (1) of the Schedule are revoked to the extent mentioned in column (3) of the Schedule.

Transitional provisions

8   The revocations made by these Regulations shall not have effect in relation to an applicant whose application for –

(a) an allocation of housing accommodation under Part 6 of the 1996 Act; or

(b) housing assistance under Part 7 of the 1996 Act,

was made before 1st June 2006.

SCHEDULE
Regulation 7

Revocation schedule

(1) Regulations revoked	(2) References	(3) Extent of revocation
The Homelessness (England) Regulations 2000	SI 2000/701	The whole Regulations
The Allocation of Housing (England) Regulations 2002	SI 2002/3264	Regulations 4 and 5
The Allocation of Housing and Homelessness (Amendment) (England) Regulations 2004	SI 2004/1235	The whole Regulations
The Allocation of Housing and Homelessness (Amendment) (England) Regulations 2006	SI 2006/1093	The whole Regulations

The Homelessness (Wales) Regulations 2006 SI No 2646

Title, commencement and application

1 (1) The title of these Regulations is the Homelessness (Wales) Regulations 2006 and they come into force on 9 October 2006.

(2) These Regulations apply to Wales.

Interpretation

2 (1) In these Regulations –

'the 1971 Act' (*'Deddf 1971'*) means the Immigration Act 1971;

'the 1995 Act' (*'Deddf 1995'*) means the Jobseekers Act 1995;

'the 1996 Act' (*'Deddf 1996'*) means the Housing Act 1996;

'asylum-seeker' (*'ceisydd lloches'*) means a person who is not under 18 and who made a claim for asylum which is recorded by the Secretary of State as having been made before 3 April 2000 but which has not been determined;

'claim for asylum' (*'hawliad lloches'*) means a claim that it would be contrary to the United Kingdom's obligations under the Refugee Convention for the claimant to be removed from, or required to leave, the United Kingdom;

'the Common Travel Area' (*'Ardal Deithio Gyffredin'*) means the United Kingdom, the Channel Islands, the Isle of Man and the Republic of Ireland collectively;

'the immigration rules' (*'y rheolau mewnfudo'*) means the rules laid down as mentioned in section 3(2) of the 1971 Act (general provisions for regulation and control);

'limited leave' (*'caniatâd cyfyngedig'*) means leave under the 1971 Act to enter or remain in the United Kingdom which is limited as to duration; and

'the Refugee Convention' (*'y Confensiwn ynglyn â Ffoaduriaid'*) means the Convention relating to the Status of Refugees done at Geneva on 28 July 1951, as extended by Article 1(2) of the Protocol relating to the Status of Refugees done at New York on 31 January 1967.

(2) For the purposes of the definition of 'asylum-seeker', a claim for asylum is determined at the end of such period beginning –

(a) on the day on which the Secretary of State notifies the claimant of the decision on the claim; or

(b) if the claimant has appealed against the Secretary of State's decision, on the day on which the appeal is disposed of,

as may be prescribed under section 94(3) of the Immigration and Asylum Act 1999.

(3) For the purposes of regulations 3(1)(i) (Class I) –

(a) 'an income-based jobseeker's allowance' (*'lwfans ceisio gwaith ar sail incwm'*)means a jobseeker's allowance, payable under the 1995 Act, entitlement to which is based on the claimant satisfying conditions which include those set out in section 3 of the 1995 Act (the income-based conditions);

(b) 'income support' (*'cymhorthdal incwm'*) has the same meaning as in section 124 of the Social Security Contributions and Benefits Act 1992 (income support); . . .

(c) a person is on an income-based jobseeker's allowance on any day in respect of which an income-based jobseeker's allowance is payable to that person and on any day –

   (i) in respect of which that person satisfies the conditions for entitlement to an income-based jobseeker's allowance but where the allowance is not paid in accordance with section 19 of the 1995 Act (circumstances in which jobseeker's allowance is not payable); or

   (ii) which is a waiting day for the purposes of paragraph 4 of Schedule 1 to the 1995 Act (waiting days) and which falls immediately before a day in respect of which an income-based jobseeker's allowance is payable to that person or would be payable to that person but for section 19 of the 1995 Act; and

(d) 'an income-related employment and support allowance' means an employment and support allowance payable under Part 1 of the Welfare Reform Act 2007 entitlement to which is based on the claimant satisfying conditions which include those set out in Part 2 of Schedule 1 to that Act.

Classes of persons subject to immigration control who are eligible for housing assistance

3 (1) The following are classes of persons prescribed for the purposes of section 185(2) of the 1996 Act (persons subject to immigration control who are eligible for housing assistance) –

(a) Class A – a person recorded by the Secretary of State as a refugee within the definition in Article 1 of the Refugee Convention;

(b) Class B – a person –

   (i) who has been granted by the Secretary of State exceptional leave to enter or remain in the United Kingdom outside the provisions of the immigration rules; and

   (ii) whose leave is not subject to a condition requiring that person to maintain and accommodate themselves, and any person who is dependent on that person, without recourse to public funds;

(c) Class C – a person who has current leave to enter or remain in the United Kingdom which is not subject to any limitation or condition and who is habitually resident in the Common Travel Area other than a person –

   (i) who has been given leave to enter or remain in the United Kingdom upon an undertaking given by another person (that person's 'sponsor') in writing in pursuance of the immigration rules to be responsible for that person's maintenance and accommodation;

   (ii) who has been resident in the United Kingdom for less than five years beginning on the date of entry or the date on which the undertaking was given in respect of that person, whichever date is the later; and

   (iii) whose sponsor or, where there more than one sponsor, at least one of whose sponsors, is still alive;

(d) Class D –a person who left the territory of Montserrat after 1 November 1995 because of the effect on that territory of a volcanic eruption;

(e) Class E – a person who is habitually resident in the Common Travel Area and who –

   (i) is a national of a state which has ratified the European Convention on Social and Medical Assistance done at Paris on 11 December 1953 or a state which has ratified the European Social Charter done at Turin on 18 October 1961 and is lawfully present in the United Kingdom; or

   (ii) before 3 April 2000 was owed a duty by a housing authority under Part III of the Housing Act 1985 (housing and homeless) or Part 7 of the 1996 Act (homelessness) which is extant, and who is a national of a state which is a signatory to the European Convention on Social and Medical Assistance done at Paris on 11 December 1953 or a state which is a signatory to the European Social Charter done at Turin on 18 October 1961;

(f) Class F – a person who is an asylum-seeker and who made a claim for asylum –

   (i) which is recorded by the Secretary of State as having been made on his arrival (other than on his re-entry) in the United Kingdom from a country outside the Common Travel Area; and

   (ii) which has not been recorded by the Secretary of State as having been either decided (other than on appeal) or abandoned;

(g) Class G – a person who is an asylum-seeker and –

   (i) who was in Great Britain when the Secretary of State made a declaration to the effect that the country of which that person is a national is subject to such a fundamental change in circumstances that the Secretary of State would not normally order the return of a person to that country;

   (ii) who made a claim for asylum which is recorded by the Secretary of State as having been made within a period of three months from the day on which that declaration was made; and

   (iii) whose claim for asylum has not been recorded by the Secretary of State as having been either decided (other than on appeal) or abandoned;

(h) Class H – a person who is an asylum-seeker and –

   (i) who made a relevant claim for asylum on or before 4 February 1996; and

   (ii) who was, on 4 February 1996, entitled to benefit under regulation 7A of the Housing Benefit (General) Regulations 1987 (persons from abroad);

(i) Class I – a person who is on an income-based jobseeker's allowance, an income-related employment and support allowance or in receipt of income support and is eligible for that benefit other than because –

   (i) that person has limited leave to enter or remain in the United Kingdom which was given in accordance with the relevant immigration rules and that person is temporarily without funds because remittances to that person from abroad have been disrupted; or

   (ii) that person has been deemed by regulation 3 of the Displaced Persons (Temporary Protection) Regulations 2005 to have been granted leave to enter or remain in the United Kingdom exceptionally for the purposes of the provision of means of subsistence; and

(j) Class J – a person who has humanitarian protection granted under the Immigration Rules.

(2) In paragraph (1)(h)(i) (Class H), a relevant claim for asylum is a claim for asylum which –

   (a) has not been recorded by the Secretary of State as having been either decided (other than on appeal) or abandoned; or

(b) has been recorded as having been decided (other than on appeal) on or before 4 February 1996 and in respect of which an appeal is pending which –
  (i)   was pending on 5 February 1996; or
  (ii) was made within the time limits specified in the rules of procedure made under section 22 of the 1971 Act (procedure).
(3) In paragraph (1)(i)(i) (Class I), 'relevant immigration rules' (*'rheolau mewn-fudo perthnasol'*) means the immigration rules relating to –
  (a) there being or there needing to be no recourse
  (b) there being no charge on public funds.
(4) In paragraph (1)(i) (Class I), 'means of subsistence' (*'moddion byw'*) has the same meaning as in regulation 4 of the Displaced Persons (Temporary Protection) Regulations 2005.

Description of persons who are to be treated as persons from abroad ineligible for housing assistance

4 (1) The following are descriptions of persons, other than persons who are subject to immigration control, who are to be treated for the purposes of Part 7 of the 1996 Act (homelessness) as persons from abroad who are ineligible for housing assistance –
  (a) subject to paragraphs (2) and (3), a person who is not habitually resident in the United Kingdom, the Channel Islands, the Isle of Man or the Republic of Ireland;
  (b) a person whose right to reside in the United Kingdom, the Channel Islands, the Isle of Man or the Republic of Ireland is derived solely from Council Directive No 90/364/EEC or Council Directive No 90/365/EEC
(2) The following persons will not, however, be treated as persons from abroad who are ineligible pursuant to paragraph (1)(a) –
  (a) a person who is a worker for the purposes of Council Regulation (EEC) No 1612/68 or (EEC) No 1251/70;
  (b) a person who is an accession state worker requiring registration who is treated as a worker for the purpose of the definition of 'qualified person' in regulation 6 of the Immigration (European Economic Area) Regulations 2006 pursuant to regulation 5 of the Accession (Immigration and Worker Registration) Regulations 2004;
  (c) a person with a right to reside pursuant to the Immigration (European Economic Area) Regulations 2006, which is derived from Council Directive No 68/360/EEC, No 73/148/EEC or No 75/34/EEC;
  (d) a person who left the territory of Montserrat after 1 November 1995 because of the effect on that territory of a volcanic eruption;
  (e) a person who –
    (i)   arrived in Great Britain on or after 28 February 2009 but before 18 March 2011;
    (ii) immediately before arriving in Great Britain had been resident in Zimbabwe; and
    (iii) before leaving Zimbabwe, had accepted an offer, made by Her Majesty's Government, to assist that person to settle in the United Kingdom.

(3) A person will not be treated as habitually resident in the United Kingdom, the Channel Islands, the Isle of Man or the Republic of Ireland for the purposes of paragraph (1)(a) if he does not have a right to reside in the United Kingdom, the Channel Islands, the Isle of Man or the Republic of Ireland.

Transitional Provisions

5   The amendments made by these Regulations do not have effect in relation to an applicant whose application for housing assistance under Part 7 of the 1996 Act was made before 9 October 2006.

Revocation

6   The Homelessness (Wales) Regulations 2000 are hereby revoked.

Guidance*

Introduction to Codes

Owing to confines of space, the Welsh Code of Guidance for Local Authorities on Allocation of Accommodation and Homelessness issued in April 2003 has not been included. This Guidance is available at: http://wales.gov.uk/topics/housingandcommunity/housing/publications/allocatehousingcode/?skip=1&lang=en

In general terms, the Welsh Code is similar to the English Codes. The Welsh Code reflects the different approaches both to eligibility of persons from abroad (see chapter 3, above) and priority need (see chapter 5, above). Only the new English Code of Guidance on Allocations reflects the changed approach following *Ahmad* (see chapter 11, above). Attention is drawn to other significant differences in footnotes in the text of the English Codes.

The Welsh Code does not reflect changes on suitability of accommodation, introduced by the Welsh Assembly Government (see chapter 10, above).

Homelessness Code of Guidance for Local Authorities

CONTENTS

Chapters

Annexes

11. European groupings (EU, A8, EEA, Switzerland)

12. Rights to reside in the UK derived from EC law

13. Worker registration scheme

14. MOD Certificate: Certificate of cessation of entitlement for single personnel to occupy service living accommodation

15. MOD Certificate: Certificate of cessation of entitlement to occupy service families accommodation or substitute service families accommodation (SFA/SSFA)

16. Definition of overcrowding

17. Recommended minimum standards for bed and breakfast accommodation

18. Procedures for referrals of homeless applicants on the grounds of local connection with another local authority

CHAPTER 1
Homelessness reviews & strategies[1]

This chapter provides guidance on housing authorities' duties to carry out a homelessness review and to formulate and publish a strategy based on the results of that review.

DUTY TO FORMULATE A HOMELESSNESS STRATEGY

1.1   Section 1(1) of the Homelessness Act 2002 ('the 2002 Act') gives housing authorities the power to carry out a homelessness review for their district and formulate and publish a homelessness strategy based on the results of the review. This power can be exercised from time to time, however section 1(3) required housing authorities to publish their first homelessness strategy by 31 July 2003. Section 1(4) requires housing authorities to publish a new homelessness strategy, based on the results of a further homelessness review, within the period of five years beginning with the day on which their last homelessness strategy was published (there is an exemption from this requirement for local authorities categorised as an 'excellent authority', see paragraph 1.42). However, it is open to a housing authority to conduct homelessness reviews and strategies more frequently, if they wish.

1.2   For a homelessness strategy to be effective housing authorities need to ensure that it is consistent with other local plans and strategies and takes into account any wider relevant sub-regional or regional plans and strategies. There will be a lot of common ground between an authority's housing strategy (whether its own or a sub-regional one produced with neighbouring authorities) and its homelessness strategy. It is open to authorities to produce either separate housing and homelessness strategies or combine these in a single document where it is consistent to do so. It is also open to authorities, again where it would be consistent to do so, to consider producing a wider composite plan that includes not only the housing and homelessness strategies but also their Housing Revenue Account Business Plans and Home Energy Conservation Act report. The homelessness strategy should also link with other strategies and programmes that address the wide range of problems that can cause homelessness (see indicative list at Annex 2). It will be important to consider how these strategies and programmes can help achieve the objectives of the homelessness strategy and vice-versa.

1.3   Housing authorities are encouraged to take a broad view and consider the benefits of cross-boundary, sub-regional and regional co-operation. A county-wide approach will be particularly important in non-unitary authorities, where housing and homelessness services are provided by the district authority whilst other key services, such as social services and Supporting People, are delivered at the county level. Housing authorities should ensure that the homelessness strategy for their district forms part of a coherent approach to tackling homelessness with neighbouring authorities. Authorities may wish

---

1   This and the following four chapters provide more detail or reviews, strategies, prevention and joint working than is contained in chapters 8–10 of the Welsh Guidance. Welsh strategies should reflect the National Homelessness Strategy, Welsh Assembly Government, 2002, see Welsh Code, para 8.9.

to collaborate with neighbouring housing authorities to produce a joint homelessness strategy covering a sub-regional area. London boroughs are encouraged to work closely with the Greater London Authority when formulating their homelessness strategies.

1.4   When carrying out a review and formulating a strategy, housing authorities are encouraged to refer to *Homelessness Strategies: A good practice handbook, Local Authorities' Homelessness Strategies: Evaluation and Good Practice* and other relevant good practice documents published by the Office of the Deputy Prime Minister (see list of publications at Annex 1).

1.5   Housing authorities are reminded that when drawing up their strategies for preventing and tackling homelessness, they must consider the needs of all groups of people in their district who are homeless or likely to become homeless, including Gypsies and Travellers. Under section 225 of the *Housing Act 2004*, which supplements section 8 of the *Housing Act 1985*, when undertaking a review of housing needs in their district, local authorities are required to carry out an assessment of the accommodation needs of Gypsies and Travellers residing in or resorting to their district. Draft guidance on accommodation needs assessment for Gypsies and Travellers is available on the DCLG website, and will be finalised after further consultation in 2006.

Assistance from social services

1.6   In non-unitary districts, where the social services authority and the housing authority are different authorities, section 1(2) of the 2002 Act requires the social services authority to give the housing authority such assistance as may be reasonably required in carrying out a homelessness review and formulating and publishing a homelessness strategy. **Since a number of people who are homeless or at risk of homelessness will require social services support, it is unlikely that it would be possible for a housing authority to formulate an effective homelessness strategy without assistance from the social services authority. It will be necessary therefore in all cases for housing authorities to seek assistance from the social services authority.** In unitary authorities the authority will need to ensure that the social services department assists the housing department in carrying out a homelessness review and formulating and publishing a homelessness strategy.

1.7   The social services authority must comply with all requests for assistance from housing authorities within their district which are reasonable. Examples of the type of assistance that a housing authority may reasonably require from the social services authority when carrying out a review and formulating a strategy may include:

– information about current and likely future numbers of social services client groups who are likely to be homeless or at risk of homelessness e.g. young people in need, care leavers and those with community care needs;

– details of social services' current programme of activity, and the resources available to them, for meeting the accommodation needs of these groups;

– details of social services' current programme of activity, and the resources available to them, for providing support for vulnerable people who are homeless or likely to become homeless (and who may not currently be social services clients).

1.8   Effective co-operation will benefit both housing and social services authorities. See Chapter 5 for guidance on joint working with other agencies and
Chapter 13 for guidance on co-operation in cases involving children.

Taking the strategy into account

1.9   Sections 1(5) and (6) of the 2002 Act require housing and social services
authorities to take the homelessness strategy into account when exercising
their functions.

1.10 For a homelessness strategy to be effective it will need to be based on realistic
assumptions about how it will be delivered in practice. Whilst this will apply
in respect of all the agencies and organisations involved, the key players will
be the housing authority and the social services authority. Both authorities
will therefore need to ensure that, on the one hand, the assumptions in the
strategy about their future activities are realistic and, on the other, that in practice these activities are actually delivered through the operation of their statutory functions. When the strategy is formulated, the social services authority
(or social services department within a unitary authority) will need to work
closely with the housing authority (or department) to ensure that this can be
achieved. All contributors will need to take ownership of the strategy if it is to
be effective. Again, because of its crucial role in delivering the strategy, this
will be particularly important in the case of the social services authority (or
department).

HOMELESSNESS REVIEWS

1.11 Under section 2(1) of the 2002 Act a homelessness review means a review by
a housing authority of:

a) the levels, and likely future levels, of homelessness in their district;

b) the activities which are carried out for any the following purposes (or
which contribute to achieving any of them):

   i)   preventing homelessness in the housing authority's district;

   ii) securing that accommodation is or will be available for people in the
   district who are or may become homeless; and

   iii) providing support for people in the district:
   – who are or may become homeless; or
   – who have been homeless and need support to prevent them
   becoming homeless again;

c) the resources available to the housing authority, the social services authority for the district, other public authorities, voluntary organisations and
other persons for the activities outlined in (b) above.

1.12 The purpose of the review is to establish the extent of homelessness in the district, assess its likely extent in the future, and identify what is currently being
done, and by whom, and what level of resources are available, to prevent and
tackle homelessness.

a) Current levels, and likely future levels, of homelessness

1.13 Homelessness is defined by sections 175 to 178 of the 1996 Act (see Chapter
8 for guidance). The review must take account of **all** forms of homelessness
within the meaning of the 1996 Act, not just people who are unintentionally homeless and have a priority need for accommodation under Part 7. The

review should therefore consider a wide population of households who are homeless or at risk of homelessness, including those who might be more difficult to identify, including people sleeping rough, or those whose accommodation circumstances make them more likely than others to become homeless or to resort to sleeping rough.

1.14 The housing authority's own records of its activity under the homelessness legislation (Part 7 of the 1996 Act) will provide a baseline for assessing the number of people who are likely to become homeless and seek help directly from the housing authority. These records should give some indication as to why those accepted as statutorily homeless became homeless. Other useful sources of data on potential homelessness in the district may include:
   - records on rough sleeping;
   - estimates of people staying with friends/family on an insecure basis;
   - court records on possession orders;
   - records of evictions by the local authority and registered social landlords (RSLs);
   - local advice service records on homelessness cases;
   - hospital records of people homeless on discharge;
   - armed forces records of those homeless on discharge;
   - prison/probation service records of ex-prisoners homeless on discharge;
   - social services records of homeless families with children;
   - social services records of young people leaving care and children in need requiring accommodation;
   - records of Supporting People clients;
   - records available from hostels and refuges;
   - voluntary sector records, e.g. day centres, advice services;
   - records of asylum seekers being accommodated in the district by the National Asylum Support Service;
   - data from the national population census and housing authorities' own household surveys.

1.15 Some groups of people are likely to be more at risk of homelessness than others. These may include:
   - young people who have become estranged from their family; have been in care; have a history of abuse, running away or school exclusions; or whose parents have had mental health, alcohol or drug problems; (see chapter 12)
   - people from ethnic minority groups;
   - people with an institutionalised background, for example where they have spent time in prison or the armed forces;
   - former asylum seekers who have been given permission to stay in the UK and are no longer being accommodated by the National Asylum Support Service;
   - people who have experienced other problems that may increase the risk of homelessness including family/relationship breakdowns; domestic, racial or other violence; poor mental or physical health; drug and alcohol abuse; age-related problems and debt.

1.16 As part of the process of mapping and understanding the extent of current homelessness in the district, housing authorities may wish to develop a profile of those who have experienced homelessness. Elements within a profile may include:

- location of homelessness;
- reason(s) for homelessness;
- housing history including previous tenures and length of homelessness;
- ethnic background;
- other background (e.g. care provided by the local authority or other institution);
- age;
- gender and sexuality;
- disabilities;
- levels and types of debts;
- employment/benefits history;
- composition of household;
- vulnerability of applicant (or household members);
- support needs (housing-related or other);
- health/drug problems;
- immigration status;
- trends in any of these elements.

1.17 Housing authorities will also need to consider the range of factors which could affect future levels of homelessness in their district. Many of these will be similar to factors taken into account for the purpose of assessing housing needs in the district (e.g. as part of a broader housing strategy). Relevant factors in the district may include:
- the availability of affordable accommodation including housing provided by the housing authority and by RSLs;
- housing market analyses, including property prices and rent levels;
- the supply of accommodation in the private rented sector;
- the provision and effectiveness of housing advice;
- local voluntary and community sector services;
- the allocation policy of the housing authority;
- the lettings policies of RSLs;
- the effectiveness of nomination agreements between the housing authority and RSLs;
- the policy of the housing authority and RSLs on management of tenants' rent arrears and on seeking repossession;
- the efficiency of the housing authority's administration of housing benefit;
- the provision and effectiveness of housing-related support services;
- redevelopment and regeneration activity;
- unemployment;
- strength of the local economy;
- the local population (and demographic trends);
- the level of overcrowding;
- the rate of new household formation in the district;
- the level of inward migration (both national and international);
- the flow of itinerant population (i.e. Gypsies and Travellers) and availability of authorised sites;
- the number of people likely to be in housing need on leaving:
  - the armed forces,
  - residential care,

- local authority care,
- prison,
- hospital or
- accommodation provided by the National Asylum Support Service.

1.18 Individual cases of homelessness are often the result of a complex matrix of problems that may develop over time. In many cases homelessness may be triggered by individual circumstances (for example, relationship breakdown or unemployment) but it can also be the result of a failure in the housing market (for example, high rents in the private sector and a shortage of accommodation in the social sector) or a failure of the administrative system (for example, delays in the payment of housing benefit). In districts where the housing market and administrative systems are functioning well, the levels of homelessness are likely to be lower. All these factors will need to be taken into account when assessing the likely future levels of homelessness in the district.

b) Activities which are carried out

1.19 The public, private and voluntary sectors can all contribute, directly or indirectly, to the prevention of homelessness, the provision of accommodation and the provision of support for homeless people. When reviewing the activities which are being carried out for these purposes, the housing authority should consider the activities of **all** the various agencies and organisations, across all sectors, which are providing, or contributing to the provision of accommodation, support or relevant services in the district (Annex 3 provides an indicative list).

1.20 Having mapped all the current activities, the housing authority should consider whether these are appropriate and adequate to meet the aims of the strategy, and whether any changes or additional provision are needed.

Preventing homelessness

1.21 Gaining a good understanding of the causes of homelessness during the homelessness review process will help to inform the range of preventative measures that need to be put in place. Many statutory and non-statutory services can contribute to preventing homelessness. Housing authorities should adopt an open approach and recognise that there will be a broad range of organisations operating in fields other than housing, including, for example, health, education and employment, whose activities may help to prevent homelessness. Activities that contribute to preventing homelessness may include:

- advice services;
- mediation and reconciliation services;
- tenancy support schemes;
- proactive liaison with private sector landlords;
- rent deposit/guarantee schemes;
- management of social housing by the housing authority and by RSLs;
- debt counselling;
- Supporting People programme;
- social services support for vulnerable people;
- housing benefit administration;
- benefit liaison to young people delivered through Connexions;

- 'Sanctuary Schemes' to enable victims of domestic violence to stay in their homes;
- planning for the housing needs of people leaving institutions – e.g. local authority care, prison and the armed services.

Further guidance on preventing homelessness is provided in Chapter 2.

Securing accommodation

1.22   Housing authorities need to consider that a range of accommodation is likely to be required for people who are, or may become, homeless. Landlords, accommodation providers and housing developers across all sectors can contribute to the provision of accommodation in the district. Activities that contribute to securing that accommodation will be available for people who are homeless, or at risk of becoming homeless, may include:

- initiatives to increase the supply of new affordable accommodation in the district (e.g.: affordable housing secured through the planning system);
- provision of new housing for owner occupation;
- initiatives to increase the supply of specialist and/or supported accommodation;
- provision of accommodation from the housing authority's own stock;
- the proportion of lettings RSLs make available to the housing authority and to homeless people generally;
- programmes for the provision of hostel, foyer and refuge spaces;
- initiatives for maximising use of the private rented sector (e.g. rent deposit guarantee schemes and landlord/tenant mediation services);
- schemes for maximising access to affordable accommodation (e.g. rent guarantee schemes);
- local, regional and national mobility schemes (e.g. to assist tenants or homeless households to move to other areas, incentives to reduce under-occupation, and assistance to move into home ownership).

Further guidance on ensuring a sufficient supply of accommodation is provided in Chapter 3.

Providing support

1.23   As part of the review housing authorities should consider all the current activities which contribute to the provision of support for people in the district who are, or may become, homeless and people in the district who have been homeless and need support to prevent them becoming homeless again. The range of providers whose activities will be making a contribution to this area are likely to embrace the public, private and voluntary sectors.

1.24   As a starting point, the housing authority may wish to consider the level of services being provided under the Supporting People programme. Other activities which may be relevant are:

- social services support under the community care programme;
- social services support for children in need who require accommodation;
- social services support for young people at risk;
- housing advice services;
- tenancy support services;
- schemes which offer practical support for formerly homeless people (e.g. furniture schemes);
- day centres for homeless people;

- supported hostel provision;
- women's refuges;
- support for people to access health care services (e.g. registration with a GP practice);
- support for people with problems of alcohol or substance abuse;
- support for people with mental health problems;
- support for people with learning disabilities;
- support for people seeking employment, e.g. personal adviser through Connexions, Jobcentre Plus, voluntary sector organisations dealing with homelessness and worklessness;
- advocacy support.

Further guidance on securing support services is provided in Chapter 4.

c) Resources available for activities

1.25   As part of the homelessness review, the housing authority should consider the resources available for the activities set out in paragraph 1.11. The housing authority should consider not only its own resources (i.e. housing funding whether provided by central government or from authorities' own sources) but also those available for these purposes to the social services authority for their district, other public authorities, voluntary organisations and other persons. Annex 3 provides an indicative list of other authorities, organisations and persons whose activities may contribute to preventing and tackling homelessness.

Preventing homelessness

1.26   Housing authorities should invest their own resources in prevention services and measures since these are likely to produce direct net savings for the authority, for example through reduced processing of repeat homelessness applications, lower use of temporary accommodation and fewer social services interventions. Resources allocated to preventing homelessness will also help to reduce pressures on wider services, such as housing, health and employment, in the longer-term.

1.27   Resources available for the prevention of homelessness may include:
- staff or administrative budgets and resources available to the housing authority (e.g. related to the homeless persons unit, the housing advice service, the Supporting People programme, tenancy support etc.);
- the resources allocated within the housing authority for rent guarantee schemes and other preventative measures;
- the availability and quality of housing and homelessness advice in the district (e.g. number and location of advice centres);
- staff or administrative budgets and resources within other public bodies (e.g. social services authority, Primary Care Trust, local education authority) dedicated to activities that help prevent/tackle homelessness; and
- staff or administrative budgets and resources available to other agencies working to prevent homelessness in the district (e.g. housing advice services in the voluntary sector and agencies working with young people).

Securing accommodation

1.28   Resources available for securing that accommodation is, or will be, available may include:

- initiatives to increase the supply of new affordable accommodation in the district (e.g. bids for resources through the Regional Housing Strategy and Housing Corporation Approved Development Programme, cash incentive schemes, affordable housing secured through the planning system, other RSL developments, Private Finance Initiative or regeneration developments, self-funded developments, self build schemes, shared ownership schemes, Homebuy);
- initiatives to increase the supply of specialist and/or supported accommodation;
- staff or administrative budgets and resources to make better use of the existing social housing stock (e.g. working with RSLs, managing own housing stock, mobility schemes);
- staff or administrative budgets and resources for maximising use of the private rented sector (e.g. landlord fora and accreditation schemes, rent deposit/guarantee schemes);
- initiatives to enable people to remain in their homes (e.g. through housing renewal assistance and disabled facilities grants).

Providing support

1.29   Resources available for providing support may include:
- staff or administrative budgets and resources available through the Supporting People programme;
- other staff or administrative budgets and resources available to the housing authority, for example through general fund expenditure or the Housing Revenue Account;
- staff or administrative budgets and resources available to the social services authority (e.g. personnel working to meet the support needs of homeless people);
- staff or administrative budgets and resources available to other public authorities and voluntary and community sector agencies (e.g. Primary Care Trusts, Drug Action Teams, Sure Start, Connexions and others listed at Annex 3); and
- availability of supported accommodation units and floating support for homeless people.

Results of the review

1.30   Having completed a homelessness review, housing authorities must arrange for a copy of the results of the review to be made available at their principal office; these must be available to the public for inspection at all reasonable hours without charge. A copy of the results must also be made available to any member of the public, on request (for which a reasonable charge can be made).

HOMELESSNESS STRATEGIES

1.31   Having carried out a homelessness review the housing authority will be in a position to formulate its homelessness strategy based on the results of that review as required by s.1(1)(b) of the 2002 Act. In formulating its strategy a housing authority will need to consider the necessary levels of activity required to achieve the aims set out in the paragraph below and the sufficiency of the resources available to them as revealed by the review.

1.32 Under s.3(1) of the 2002 Act a homelessness strategy means a strategy for:

i) preventing homelessness in the district (see Chapter 2 for further guidance);

ii) securing that sufficient accommodation is and will be available for people in the district who are or may become homeless (see Chapter 3 for further guidance);

iii) securing the satisfactory provision of support for people in the district who are or may become homeless or who have been homeless and need support to prevent them becoming homeless again (see Chapter 4 for further guidance).

Specific objectives and actions for housing and social services authorities

1.33 A homelessness strategy may include specific objectives to be achieved and actions planned to be taken in the course of the exercise of the functions of the housing authority and the social services authority. This will apply equally in areas where the social services authority is not also the housing authority (for example, in district councils in county areas). Examples of specific objectives and actions for housing and social services authorities that might be included in a strategy are set out in Annex 4.

Specific action by others

1.34 A homelessness strategy can also include specific action which the housing authority expects to be taken by:

i) other public authorities;

ii) voluntary organisations; and

iii) other persons whose activities could contribute to achieving the strategy's objectives.

1.35 In all housing authority districts there will be a significant number of agencies whose activities address the wide range of needs and problems that can be linked to homelessness. These will be found across all sectors: public, private and voluntary. Housing authorities will need to seek the participation of all relevant agencies in the district in order to assist them in formulating and delivering an effective homelessness strategy that includes specific action that the housing authority expects to be taken by others.

1.36 In particular, housing authorities should enter into constructive partnerships with RSLs operating in their district. See Annex 5 for guidance on co-operation between housing authorities and RSLs.

1.37 An indicative list of the other public authorities, voluntary organisations and persons whose activities could contribute to achieving the strategy's objectives is at Annex 3. However, s.3(4) provides that a housing authority cannot include in a homelessness strategy any specific action expected to be taken by another body or organisation without their approval.

1.38 Examples of specific action that the housing authority might expect to be taken by others are provided at Annex 6.

Joint action

1.39 Section 3(5) of the 2002 Act requires housing authorities, when formulating a homelessness strategy, to consider (among other things) the extent to which any of the strategy's objectives could be achieved through joint action involving two or more of the persons or other bodies tackling homelessness in the district. This could include the housing authority, the social services authority, neighbouring housing authorities and any other public bodies working to alleviate homelessness within the district, for example, the National Offender Management Service. It might also include any other organisation or person whose activities could contribute to achieving the objectives of the homelessness strategy, for example, voluntary sector organisations working with homeless people, registered social landlords, and private landlords. The most effective strategies will be those which harness the potential of all the organisations and persons working to prevent and alleviate homelessness in the district, and which ensure that all the activities concerned are consistent and complementary. It will be important for all such organisations to take ownership of the strategy if they strive to help meet its objectives. See Chapter 5 for guidance on joint working with other agencies.

Action plans

1.40 As part of the homelessness strategy housing authorities should develop effective action plans, to help ensure that the objectives set out in the homelessness strategy are achieved. Action plans could include, for example, targets, milestones and arrangements for monitoring and evaluation. Good practice guidance on developing action plans is provided in the ODPM publication *'Local Authorities' Homelessness Strategies: Evaluation and Good Practice (2004)'*.

Need to consult on a strategy

1.41 Housing authorities must consult such public or local authorities, voluntary organisations or other persons as they consider appropriate before adopting or modifying a homelessness strategy. For a strategy to be effective it will need to involve every organisation and partnership whose activities contribute, or could contribute, in some way to achieving its objectives. As a minimum, therefore, it will be appropriate for all such organisations to be consulted on the strategy before it is adopted. It will be important to consult service users and homeless people themselves, or organisations representing their interests. Consultation with ethnic minority and faith-based groups will also be important in addressing the disproportionate representation of people from ethnic minority communities amongst homeless households. Annex 3 provides an indicative list of the types of authorities, organisations and people that the housing authority may wish to consult about a strategy.

Publishing a strategy

1.42 Under s.1(3) of the 2002 Act, housing authorities were required to publish their first homelessness strategy by 31 July 2003. Section 1(4) requires housing authorities to publish a new homelessness strategy, based on the results of a further homelessness review, within the period of five years beginning with the day on which their last homelessness strategy was published. However, those authorities which are categorised as an 'excellent authority' by the Secretary of State by virtue of the *Local Authorities' Plans and Strategies (Disapplication) (England) Order 2005* are exempt from this requirement. Housing authorities must make a copy of the strategy available to the public at their principal office, and this is to be available for inspection at all reasonable hours without charge. A copy must also be made available to any member of the public, on request (for which a reasonable charge can be made).

Keeping a strategy under review and modifying it

1.43 Housing authorities must keep their homelessness strategy under review and may modify it from time to time. Before modifying the strategy, they must consult on the same basis as required before adopting a strategy (see paragraph 1.41). If a strategy is modified, the housing authority must publish the modifications or the modified strategy and make copies available to the public on the same basis as required when adopting a strategy (see paragraph 1.42).

1.44 Circumstances that might prompt modification of a homelessness strategy include: transfer of the housing authority's housing stock to an RSL; the setting up of an Arms Length Management Organisation; a review of other, relevant local plans or strategies; new data sources on homelessness becoming available; a significant change in the levels or causes of homelessness; changes in either housing/homelessness/social security policy or legislation, or new factors that could contribute to a change in the levels or nature of homelessness in the district such as significant changes to the local economy (e.g. housing markets or levels of employment).

CHAPTER 2
Preventing homelessness

2.1 This chapter provides guidance on housing authorities' duties to have a strategy to prevent homelessness in their district and to ensure that advice and information about homelessness, and the prevention of homelessness, are available free of charge to anyone in their district. The chapter also provides some examples of the action housing authorities and their partners can take to tackle the more common causes of homelessness and to prevent homelessness recurring.

2.2 Preventing homelessness means providing people with the ways and means to meet their housing, and any housing-related support, needs in order to avoid experiencing homelessness. Effective prevention will enable a person to remain in their current home, where appropriate, to delay a need to move out of current accommodation so that a move into alternative accommodation can be planned in a timely way; to find alternative accommodation, or to sustain independent living.

2.3 The prevention of homelessness should be a key strategic aim which housing authorities and other partners pursue through the homelessness strategy. It is vital that individuals are encouraged to seek assistance at the earliest possible time when experiencing difficulties which may lead to homelessness. In many cases early, effective intervention can prevent homelessness occurring. Housing authorities are reminded that they must not avoid their obligations under Part 7 of the 1996 Act (including the duty to make inquiries under s.184, if they have reason to believe that an applicant may be homeless or threatened with homelessness), but it is open to them to suggest alternative solutions in cases of potential homelessness where these would be appropriate and acceptable to the applicant.

2.4   The Secretary of State considers that housing authorities should take steps to prevent homelessness wherever possible, offering a broad range of advice and assistance for those in housing need. It is also important that, where homelessness does occur and is being tackled, consideration is given to the factors which may cause repeat homelessness and action taken to prevent homelessness recurring.

2.5   Homelessness can have significant negative consequences for the people who experience it. At a personal level, homelessness can have a profound impact on health, education and employment prospects. At a social level, homelessness can impact on social cohesion and economic participation. Early intervention to prevent homelessness can therefore bring benefits for those concerned, including being engaged with essential services and increasing the likelihood that children will live in a more secure environment. Investment in prevention services can also produce direct cost savings for local authorities, for example through lower use of temporary accommodation and fewer social services interventions. Furthermore, measures to prevent homelessness will also help to reduce longer-term pressures on wider services, such as health and employment.

2.6   There are three stages where intervention can prevent homelessness:

early identification – by identifying categories of people who are at risk of homelessness and ensuring that accommodation and any necessary support are available to them in time to prevent homelessness. Early identification can target people who fall within known indicator groups (e.g. those leaving local authority care, prison, secure accommodation or the armed forces, or people at known or observed risk due to mental or physical health problems) even though they may not currently have a need for housing but for whom timely intervention can avoid homelessness when they leave their institutional environment and before they reach a crisis point;

pre-crisis intervention – this can take the form of: advice services and proactive intervention such as negotiation with landlords to enable people to retain their current tenancies. Such intervention is important even if it only delays the date when a person has to leave their home, as this may allow time to plan and manage a move to alternative accommodation;

preventing recurring homelessness – ensuring tenancy sustainment can be central to preventing repeat homelessness where there is an underlying need for support and the provision of accommodation by itself is insufficient to prevent homelessness.

STRATEGY TO PREVENT HOMELESSNESS

2.7   Under s.1 of the 2002 Act, local housing authorities must formulate and publish a homelessness strategy based on a review of homelessness for their district, and they must take the strategy into account when exercising their functions. (See Chapter 1 for guidance.) Under section 3(1)(a) of the 2002 Act a homelessness strategy must include, among other things, a strategy for preventing homelessness in the district. Gaining a thorough understanding of the causes of homelessness in a local area through the review process will help to inform the range of measures required to prevent homelessness. As part of the review, housing authorities must consider all the current activities in their area that contribute to the prevention of homelessness. They must also consider the resources available. Both activities and resources are likely to involve a wide range of providers working in the public, private and voluntary sectors.

2.8 In developing their homelessness strategies, housing authorities should consider the range of measures that need to be put in place to prevent homelessness. These will depend on local circumstances. Housing authorities are advised to adopt an open approach and recognise that there will be a broad range of organisations operating in fields other than housing, for example, in education, health and employment, whose activities may help to prevent homelessness. (See Chapter 1 for further guidance on carrying out a homelessness review and formulating a homelessness strategy).

ADVICE AND INFORMATION ABOUT HOMELESSNESS AND THE PREVENTION OF HOMELESSNESS

2.9 Under s.179(1) of the 1996 Act, housing authorities have a duty to secure that advice and information about homelessness, and the prevention of homelessness, are available free of charge to **any person** in their district. The provision of comprehensive advice will play an important part in delivering the housing authority's strategy for preventing homelessness in their district.

2.10 There is an enormous variety of reasons why people become homeless or find themselves threatened with homelessness. And, in many cases, there can be multiple reasons, and a complex chain of circumstances, that lead to homelessness. Some of these may relate to the housing market, for example, high rents and a shortage of affordable accommodation in the area, or to administrative systems, for example delays in the payment of benefits. Others may relate to personal circumstances, for example, relationship breakdown, a bereavement, long-term or acute ill health or loss of employment. The provision of advice and information to those at risk of homelessness will need to reflect this. It will need to be wide-ranging and comprehensive in its coverage and may require a full multi-disciplinary assessment.

2.11 Many people who face the potential loss of their current home will be seeking practical advice and assistance to help them remain in their accommodation or secure alternative accommodation. Some may be seeking to apply for assistance under the homelessness legislation without being aware of other options that could help them to secure accommodation. Advice services should provide information on the range of housing options that are available in the district. This might include options to enable people to stay in their existing accommodation, delay homelessness for long enough to allow a planned move, or access alternative accommodation in the private or social sectors. This 'housing options' approach is central to addressing housing need as a means of preventing homelessness.

2.12 Advice on the following issues may help to prevent homelessness:
 – tenants' rights and rights of occupation;
 – leaseholders' rights and service charges;
 – what to do about harassment and illegal eviction;
 – how to deal with possession proceedings;
 – rights to benefits (e.g. housing benefit) including assistance with making claims as required;
 – current rent levels;

- how to retrieve rent deposits;
- rent and mortgage arrears;
- how to manage debt;
- grants available for housing repair and/or adaptation;
- how to obtain accommodation in the private rented sector – e.g. details of landlords and letting agents within the district, including any accreditation schemes, and information on rent guarantee and deposit schemes;
- how to apply for an allocation of accommodation through the social housing waiting list or choice-based lettings scheme;
- how to apply to other social landlords for accommodation.

The advisory service might also include an advocacy service, which may include providing legal representation for people facing the loss of their home.

2.13   Housing authorities will need to ensure that the implications and likely outcomes of the available housing options are made clear to all applicants, including the distinction between having priority need for accommodation under Part 7 and having priority for an allocation of social housing under Part 6.

2.14   Advice services will need to be effectively linked to other relevant statutory and non-statutory service providers. As noted in paragraph 2.10 above, it is often a combination of factors that lead to homelessness, and housing authorities are advised to ensure that people who require advice of a wider or more specialist nature, for example, to address family and relationship breakdown, mental or physical health problems, drug and alcohol abuse, or worklessness are directed to other agencies who can provide the service they need. In situations where there is a history of child abuse or where there are child protection concerns, homelessness and housing organisations will need to work closely with the Local Safeguarding Children Board (LSCB).

2.15   The effectiveness of authorities' housing advice in preventing homelessness or the threat of homelessness is measured by Best Value Performance Indicator BVPI 213. Guidance on BVPI 213 is available at www.communities. gov.uk.

Accessibility

2.16   It is recommended that advisory services are well published and accessible to everyone in the district. Appropriate provision will need to be made to ensure accessibility for people with particular needs, including those with mobility difficulties, sight or hearing loss and learning difficulties, as well as those for whom English is not their first language.

Who provides the advice and information?

2.17   The legislation does not specify how housing authorities should ensure that advice and information on homelessness and the prevention of homelessness are made available. They could do this in a number of ways, for example:

i)   provide the service themselves;
ii)   ensure that it is provided by another organisation; or
iii) ensure that it is provided in partnership with another organisation.

2.18   The housing authority must ensure that the service is free of charge and available and accessible to everyone in their district. Securing the provision of an independent advisory service may help to avoid conflicts of interest. Private sector tenants may not naturally look to the housing authority for advice. Some young people may be reluctant to approach a statutory authority for advice, but they may feel more at ease in dealing with a more informal advisory service provided by the voluntary sector. People from different ethnic minority groups might also find advice more accessible if it is delivered through community or faith organisations. (See Chapter 21 for guidance on contracting out homelessness functions).

2.19 Under s.179(2), housing authorities may give grants or loans to other persons who are providing advice and information about homelessness and the prevention of homelessness on behalf of the housing authority. Under s.179(3), housing authorities may also assist such persons (e.g. voluntary organisations) by:

i) allowing them to use premises belonging to the housing authority,

ii) making available furniture or other goods, by way of gift, loan or some other arrangement, and

iii) making available the services of staff employed by the housing authority.

Standards of advice

2.20 Housing authorities should ensure that information provided is current, accurate and appropriate to the individual's circumstances. To ensure they are providing an effective service to a high standard, housing authorities may wish to refer to the quality assurance systems applied by the National Association of Citizens Advice Bureaux, the Shelter network of housing advice centres, the National Disabled Housing Services Ltd (HoDis) accreditation scheme and the Community Legal Service Quality Mark. Housing authorities are also advised to monitor the provision of advisory services to ensure they continue to meet the needs of all sections of the community and help deliver the aims of their homelessness strategy.

PREVENTING HOMELESSNESS IN SPECIFIC CIRCUMSTANCES

2.21 Some groups of people are likely to be more at risk of homelessness than others. These may include:

– young people who have become estranged from their family; have been in care and/or secure accommodation; have a history of abuse, running away or school exclusions; or whose parents have had mental health, alcohol or drug problems (see Chapter 12 for further guidance on 16 and 17 year olds);

– people from ethnic minority groups;

– people with an institutionalised background, for example where they have spent time in care, in prison or in the armed forces;

– former asylum seekers who have been given permission to stay in the UK and are no longer being accommodated by the National Asylum Support Service;

– people who have experienced other problems that may increase the risk of homelessness including family/relationship breakdowns; domestic, racial or other violence; poor mental or physical health; drug and alcohol misuse; age-related problems and debt.

2.22 In many cases homelessness can be prevented by identifying people who are in circumstances which put them at risk of homelessness, and by providing services which can enable them to remain in their current home. Homelessness can also be prevented by ensuring assistance is available at known risk points such as discharge from prison or hospital. Table 2.1 below gives examples of some of the measures that may help tackle some of the more common causes of homelessness. More detailed guidance is provided in Annex 7.

Table 2.1: Tackling common causes of homelessness

Cause	Action
Parents, relatives or friends not being able or willing to provide accommodation	Mediation services, usually contracted out by local authority to, for example, Relate, Youth Crime prevention and parenting programmes.
Relationship breakdown, including domestic violence	'Sanctuary' schemes, which allow domestic violence victims to remain in their homes where they choose to do so once security measures are in place.
Discharge from an institutional situation e.g. hospital, custody, residential treatment/care	Early planning for discharge between institutional staff and local housing providers, including assessing support needs. Proactive provision of advice by local housing authority on housing options (prior to discharge).
End of assured shorthold tenancy	Housing advice. Rent deposit or bond schemes to encourage landlords to let to potentially homeless people. Landlord-tenant mediation services, to resolve disputes about behaviour or repairs.
Mortgage and rent arrears	Debt counselling. Advocacy services in county court. Fast tracking housing benefit claims.
Person ill-equipped to sustain a tenancy	Advice and support under the Supporting People programme for vulnerable people at risk of homelessness, for example improving budgeting and 'life' skills.
Lack of information	Early and proactive intervention from local authority homelessness services to discuss options and offer assistance and advice.

2.23   Housing authorities should also work with housing providers to encourage them to seek to maintain and sustain tenancies by employing effective strategies for the prevention and management of rent arrears. Landlords should be encouraged to make early and personal contact with tenants in arrears and to assess whether there are any additional support needs and, where relevant, to establish that all benefits to which tenants are entitled are being claimed. Landlords should offer assistance and advice on welfare benefits and in making a claim, debt counselling and money advice either in-house or through a referral to an external agency and implement ways for recovering the money such as debt management plans or attachment to benefits or earnings orders. Possession action should only be taken as a last resort. See Annex 1 for ODPM guidance on *Improving the Effectiveness of Rent Arrears Management.*

PREVENTING HOMELESSNESS RECURRING

2.24 The underlying problems which led to homelessness in the first place have to be addressed in order to provide long-term solutions. Failure to address these root causes can lead to repeated episodes of homelessness. Recurring homelessness may be indicative of problems that are not being resolved by the provision of accommodation alone.

2.25 An effective approach to tackling recurring homelessness is likely to be based on:
  – effective monitoring that identifies housing applicants who are homeless or threatened with homelessness and who have previously been secured accommodation under the homelessness legislation (either by the same authority or another authority in a different area);
  – an analysis of the main causes of homelessness among housing applicants who have experienced homelessness more than once; and
  – the existence of support services (and, in particular, strong links with the local Supporting People strategy and services) for housing applicants who have experienced homelessness more than once, which tackle these causes and help the applicants to sustain tenancies or other forms of settled accommodation in the longer term.

2.26 Tenancy sustainment is central to preventing repeat homelessness and can include a range of interventions. It is closely linked with good housing management and the Supporting People programme. See Chapter 4 for further guidance on securing support services and the housing-related support services that can be funded through Supporting People.

2.27 Whilst tenancy sustainment is the eventual objective, there are some individuals who may not be able to sustain accommodation due to personal circumstances, for example mental health or substance misuse difficulties. Support will need to be provided to progress towards the time when they are able to maintain accommodation.

CHAPTER 3
Ensuring a sufficient supply of accommodation

3.1 This chapter provides guidance on options available to housing authorities to help increase the supply of new housing and maximise the use of the housing stock in their district.

3.2 Section 3(1)(b) of the *Homelessness Act 2002* provides that a homelessness strategy is a strategy for, amongst other things, securing that sufficient accommodation is and will be available for people who are or may become homeless. Chapter 16 provides guidance on the different ways in which housing authorities can ensure that suitable accommodation is available for applicants, for example by providing the accommodation themselves or by securing it from a private landlord or a registered social landlord.

3.3   Homelessness is significantly influenced by the availability of housing, and in particular affordable housing. A shortage of affordable housing can lead to increasing numbers of people being accommodated in temporary accommodation whilst waiting for settled housing to bring the main homelessness duty to an end. 'Settled housing' in this context will primarily be social housing and good quality private sector accommodation (see chapter 14 for further guidance on bringing the main homelessness (s. 193(2)) duty to an end.)

3.4   Although, in 2005, over 80% of people living in temporary accommodation were in self-contained homes they often lack certainty over how long they will live there. This can cause disruption to their lives, make it hard for them to put roots down in the community or to access important services. For example, they may face real difficulties in gaining access to a local GP or in enrolling their children in a local school. Many may already have faced disruption and become disconnected or moved away from existing services and support networks as a result of homelessness.

3.5   The Government's current target is to halve the number of households living in temporary accommodation by 2010. Increasing the supply of new affordable housing and making better use of existing social and private rented stock to provide settled homes will be critical for achieving this target, as will measures to prevent homelessness.

INCREASE SUPPLY OF NEW HOUSING

3.6   The *Sustainable Communities Plan* and *Sustainable Communities: Homes for All* set out how the Government is creating new communities and expanding existing communities in four areas in the wider South East. Taken together, these areas are expected to deliver an extra 200,000 homes above current planning totals.

3.7   At a regional level, local authorities have a key role to play to identify the priorities for housing in their region, to ensure these are reflected in regional housing strategies and to secure funding for their plans. Housing authorities will also need to ensure that housing strategies are aligned with regional economic and planning strategies.

3.8   There are a number of ways housing authorities can increase the supply of new housing. The main source of funding for the provision of affordable housing is the Housing Corporation's national Affordable Housing Programme (AHP), known formerly as the Approved Development Programme (ADP). From the 2006–2008 biannual bidding round, the AHP is open to both registered social landlords and non-registered bodies (e.g. developers). Bids continue to be assessed against a range of criteria including housing quality and value for money, and against regional and local priorities. Housing authorities will need to work closely with RSLs and others to make best use of this funding.

3.9   Another important means of providing affordable housing is through planning obligations, which are usually negotiated in the context of granting planning permission for new housing development. Planning obligations are generally secured by agreements made between a local authority and a developer under s.106 of the *Town and Country Planning Act 1990* and they are commonly referred to as 's.106 agreements'. Obligations may be appropriate where, for example, a planning objection to a proposed development cannot be overcome by the imposition of a condition. More detailed guidance on the use of s.106 agreements is contained in ODPM Circular 05/2005: Planning Obligations.

3.10 National guidance on planning and affordable housing is currently contained in Planning Policy Guidance Note 3 (PPG3): Housing, as supplemented by Circular 06/98. These documents provide advice to planning authorities about securing the provision of affordable housing either in kind or by financial contribution. They also remind local authorities when formulating local policy or determining planning applications to take account of the need to cater for a range of housing needs and to encourage the development of mixed and balanced communities in order to avoid areas of social exclusion.

3.11 PPG3 and Circular 06/98 are presently under review and a draft Planning Policy Statement 3 (PPS3): Housing was issued for consultation in December 2005. Following the publication of final PPS3, local planning authorities will be expected to ensure that policies in their Local Development Frameworks take into account the updated national planning policy framework for delivering the Government's housing objectives.

3.12 Planning authorities will need to ensure that their affordable housing policies are evidence-based, kept up to date over time, and applied consistently across developments to ensure that affordable housing is effectively and fairly delivered through this route.

MAXIMISING THE USE OF EXISTING HOUSING STOCK

3.13 A number of options are discussed below for how housing authorities might maximise the use of current housing stock.

The private rented sector

3.14 Some people living in the private rented sector can experience homelessness, but this sector can also provide solutions to homelessness. Homelessness statistics routinely show that the end of an assured shorthold tenancy (AST) is one of the top three reasons for loss of a settled home. Authorities are encouraged to work with landlords in their area to see how this can be addressed, for example, by offering mediation between landlord and tenant where relations have broken down, and negotiating to extend or renew ASTs where appropriate.

3.15 For many, renting in the private sector may offer a practical solution to their housing need (for example, it may offer more choice over location and type of property). Authorities are therefore encouraged to consider providing rent deposits, guarantees or rent in advance, to help households access this sector. They may also consider establishing Accreditation Schemes, whereby landlords voluntarily agree to a set of standards relating to the management or physical condition of privately rented accommodation to help increase the supply of private rented accommodation.

3.16 Many local authorities have used the private rented sector as a source of good quality, self-contained temporary accommodation. However, the private rented sector can also provide a source of settled accommodation, where qualifying offers of ASTs are accepted by households who are owed the main homelessness duty.

3.17 There is scope to make greater use of the private rented sector, either to help households avoid homelessness or to provide more settled homes for people living in temporary accommodation. Authorities are recommended to establish and maintain good relations with private sector landlords, for example through landlord fora. This can be effective in securing an improved supply of properties in the private rented sector for homeless, or potentially homeless, households.

3.18 It is also recommended that authorities review the extent to which qualifying offers of ASTs are being made to households in temporary accommodation in their area; whether there are any barriers to such offers being made or accepted and, if so, what additional steps would need to be taken to address those barriers.

Social housing

3.19 The Secretary of State considers that, generally, it is inappropriate for general needs social housing to be used as temporary accommodation for long periods, especially where such properties are able to be let as settled homes.

3.20 It is important that housing authorities work effectively with RSLs to help them prevent and tackle homelessness in the district. RSLs have a key role to play in sustaining tenancies, reducing evictions and abandonment, and preventing homelessness through their housing management functions. To ensure effective collaboration between themselves and partner RSLs operating in their district housing authorities are advised to consider establishing a nominations agreement. This would include the proportion of lettings that will be made available, any conditions that will apply, and how any disputes about suitability or eligibility will be resolved. Housing authorities are also advised to aim for any exclusion criteria (that may be applied to nominees by the RSL) to be kept to a minimum. Further guidance on co-operation between RSLs and housing authorities is at Annex 5.

3.21 There are a number of schemes and policies that social housing providers can implement to facilitate the effective management and use of the existing housing stock and to keep voids and re-let times to a minimum.

– **Mobility:** 'move UK' (formerly Housing Employment and Mobility Services) has been developed to offer social housing tenants and jobseekers more choice about where they live and work around the UK. Its services will open up new opportunities for people who wish to move. 'move UK' will have three main service components:

   (i) facilitated mobility services to social landlords and their tenants and applicants to help tenants and applicants to find new homes. This will continue and enhance the provision of the grant funded mobility previously provided by Housing Mobility and Exchange Services (HOMES) and LAWN (the Association of London Government scheme that helps tenants who want to, move out of London to areas of low demand);

   (ii) 'one stop shop' web-based information about available housing, neighbourhoods and job vacancies;

   (iii) web access to information on vacancies in social housing.

– **Cash Incentive Scheme** (CIS): although there is no obligation for a housing authority to provide a scheme, the main objectives of the Cash Incentive Scheme (CIS) are to release local authority accommodation required for letting to those in housing need, and to encourage sustainable home ownership. This is achieved by the payment of a grant to a local authority tenant to assist them in buying a property in the private sector.

- **The new HomeBuy scheme**: this scheme, which commenced on 1st April 2006, provides people with the opportunity to own a home based on equity sharing, whilst protecting the supply of social housing. Existing social tenants are one of the priority groups helped under the scheme, and any rented housing association/local authority home vacated by them will then be made available to others in priority housing need. The Social HomeBuy option, which allows housing association and local authority tenants to purchase a share in their rented home, will be voluntary. Landlords will be able to reinvest the proceeds in replacement social homes.

3.22 The Secretary of State also considers that where local authority or RSL stock is provided as temporary accommodation to discharge a main homelessness duty (owed under section 193(2)) the housing authority should give very careful consideration to the scope for allocating the accommodation as a secure or assured tenancy, as appropriate, especially where a household has been living in a particular property for anything other than a short-term emergency stay.

Choice-based lettings schemes

3.23 The expansion of choice-based lettings policy aims to achieve nationwide coverage by 2010. Local authorities are encouraged to work together, and with RSL partners, to develop sub-regional and regional choice-based lettings schemes which provide maximum choice and flexibility. Local authorities are encouraged to offer choice to homeless households, while ensuring that their schemes are designed so as not to provide a perverse incentive to applicants to make a homelessness application in order to increase their priority for housing. Housing authorities should also consider involving the private rented sector in their choice-based lettings schemes in order to maximise the housing options available.

Empty homes

3.24 Housing authorities are encouraged to adopt positive strategies for minimising empty homes, and other buildings that could provide residential accommodation, across all housing sectors and tenures within their district. A strategy for minimising empty homes might include schemes for tackling low demand social housing, bringing empty private sector properties back into use and bringing flats over shops into residential use.

3.25 Under the *Housing Act 2004* new provisions on Empty Dwelling Management Orders (EDMOs) are expected to be brought into force. EDMOs are a discretionary power for local authorities to use as part of their empty homes strategy. The new powers will allow local authorities to apply to a residential property tribunal for approval to make an interim EDMO lasting for up to 12 months. During this interim period, the authority may only place tenants in the house with the consent of the owner.

3.26 Local authorities also have the discretion to set the council tax discount on long term empty properties at any point between 50% and 0%, as well as at any point between 50% and 10% on second homes, taking into account local conditions.

Housing renewal

3.27   Housing renewal assistance can also assist in meeting the aims of the homelessness strategy. Under the *Regulatory Reform (Housing Assistance) (England and Wales) Order 2002*, local authorities have power to promote housing
renewal assistance to landlords, private homeowners and others to increase
the supply of a particular type of accommodation through converting under-
utilised accommodation to meet identified housing need within the district.
Empty homes, vacant accommodation above shops or commercial buildings
can be targeted for assistance. Housing renewal assistance can also enable
private homeowners to carry out essential repairs or improvements, and
remain in their home.

Disabled facilities grant

3.28   Uptake of the Disabled Facilities Grant – a mandatory entitlement administered by housing authorities for eligible disabled people in all housing tenures
– can enable homeowners to remain living an independent life at home, and
should be considered as part of an effective homelessness strategy. Authorities are required to give a decision within six months of receiving an application. The grant is subject to a maximum limit and is means tested to ensure
that funding goes to those most in need.

CHAPTER 4
Securing support services

4.1   **This chapter provides guidance on the importance of support services in preventing and tackling homelessness and outlines the types of housing-related
and other support services that might be required.**

4.2   A homelessness strategy is defined in section 3(1)(c) of the 2002 Act as (among
other things) a strategy for securing the satisfactory provision of support for
people in their district:
i)   who are or may become homeless; or
ii)   who have been homeless and need support to prevent them from becoming homeless again.

4.3   In formulating their homelessness strategies, housing authorities need to
recognise that for some households, homelessness cannot be tackled, or prevented, solely through the provision of accommodation. Some households will
require a range of support services, which may include housing-related support
to help them sustain their accommodation, as well as personal support relating
to factors such as relationship breakdown, domestic violence, mental health
problems, drug and alcohol addiction, poverty, debt and unemployment.

4.4   Support can help to prevent people who are at risk of homelessness from
becoming homeless at all. In other cases, where people have experienced
homelessness and been placed in temporary accommodation, the provision
of support may be essential to ensure that they are able to continue to enjoy a
reasonable quality of life and access the range of services they need to rebuild
their lives. The provision of support can also be important in helping formerly
homeless households to sustain settled housing and prevent homelessness
from recurring.

4.5 Solutions to homelessness should be based on a thorough assessment of the household's needs, including support needs. Housing authorities will need to establish effective links with the Supporting People team, the social services authority and other agencies (for example, Primary Care Trusts, the Criminal Justice Service, and voluntary and community organisations) to ensure that a joint assessment of an applicant's housing and support needs can be made where necessary. Such assessments should inform decisions on intervention to enable a household to remain in their home, placements in temporary accommodation and options for the provision of more settled accommodation that will bring the main homelessness duty to an end.

4.6 Where children and young people are involved, it is important that any solutions to homelessness address the issues they are facing and do not undermine any support they may already be receiving. In particular, housing authorities will need to establish effective links with children's services authorities and establish whether a Common Assessment Framework has been undertaken, and, if so, which agency will have relevant information about the child's or young person's needs.

STRATEGY TO SECURE PROVISION OF SUPPORT SERVICES

4.7 Section 1 of the 2002 Act requires housing authorities to carry out a homelessness review for their district. Gaining a thorough understanding of the causes of homelessness through the review process will help to inform the range of support provision required. As part of the review, housing authorities must consider all the current activities in their area which contribute to the provision of support for households who are, or may become, homeless, as well as people in the district who have been homeless and need support to prevent them becoming homeless again. They must also consider the resources available. Both activities and resources are likely to involve a range of providers working in the public, private and voluntary sectors. (See Chapter 1 for further guidance on carrying out a homelessness review and formulating a homelessness strategy).

4.8 In formulating their homelessness strategies housing authorities will need to consider the different types and level of support that households may require. Households who have experienced homelessness or who are at risk of homelessness may have diverse needs. Some households may only need information and advice in order to avoid experiencing homelessness, or becoming homeless again. Others, however, will need greater assistance including housing-related support and in some cases may require intensive support from a range of services.

INDIVIDUALS AT RISK OF HOMELESSNESS

4.9 Housing authorities should be aware that some individuals may be at particular risk of homelessness, for example young people leaving care, ex-offenders, former members of the armed forces, refugees, people with mental health problems or individuals leaving hospital, and may require a broader package of resettlement support. When developing their homelessness strategies, housing authorities should consider carefully how to work effectively to prevent homelessness amongst these groups and ensure that appropriate support is available. Early identification of people at risk will be crucial to preventing homelessness. Housing authorities should consider agreeing protocols for joint action with local agencies in order to assist with early identification and prevention measures.

4.10   Individuals at risk of homelessness may also include those who have never experienced homelessness in the past and for whom, with the appropriate support, homelessness can be avoided. These individuals may be at risk of homelessness due to specific problems such as managing debt or accessing benefits and require specialist advice which may be delivered through partner agencies such as Citizens Advice Bureaux or Jobcentre Plus. See Chapter 2 for guidance on preventing homelessness.

YOUNG PEOPLE

4.11   Many young people who have experienced homelessness may lack skills in managing their affairs and require help with managing a tenancy and operating a household budget. Those estranged from their family, particularly care leavers, may lack the advice and support normally available to young people from family, friends and other mentors. 16 and 17 year olds who are homeless and estranged from their family will be particularly vulnerable and in need of support. See Chapter 12 for further guidance on 16 and 17 years olds.

HOUSING-RELATED SUPPORT SERVICES

4.12   Housing-related support services have a key role in preventing homelessness occurring or recurring. The types of housing-related support that households who have experienced homelessness may need include:

  – *support in establishing a suitable home* – help, advice and support in finding and maintaining suitable accommodation for independent living in the community;
  – *support with daily living skills* – help, advice and training in the day-to-day skills needed for living independently, such as budgeting and cooking;
  – *support in accessing benefits, health and community care services* – information, advice and help in claiming benefits or accessing community care or health services;
  – *help in establishing and maintaining social support* – help in rebuilding or establishing social networks that can help counter isolation and help support independent living.

4.13   Services might be delivered through:

  – **floating support services** – using support workers who travel to clients' accommodation in order to provide support. These services can operate across all tenures and generally provide time-limited and low intensity support;
  – **short and medium stay housing with support** – including direct access schemes, night shelters, hostels, transitional housing and supported lodgings. Some of these services may specialise in supporting particular groups of individuals at risk of homelessness, such as vulnerable young people;
  – **long-stay supported housing services** – to provide ongoing support to those who are unable to live independently in the community.

4.14   Housing-related support can be funded through the Supporting People programme, and close co-operation between housing authorities and the

Supporting People team will be essential for ensuring effective support for households who have experienced homelessness, particularly through the local Commissioning Body and Core Strategy Group. Further information on housing-related support services is provided in separate guidance, *Supporting People – Guide to Accommodation and Support Options for Homeless Households* (ODPM, 2003).

OTHER SUPPORT SERVICES

4.15   Households who have experienced homelessness may need additional support services which are not directly housing-related and fall outside the scope of the Supporting People programme funding. Housing authorities will need to co-operate and work collaboratively with other departments within the authority and a wide range of statutory, voluntary and private sector agencies in order to ensure that the support which is required is provided. Joint working with commissioners/planners and providers of the following services will be particularly important:
   – health services;
   – drug/alcohol services including Drug Action Teams;
   – social services;
   – children's and young persons' services (e.g. Connexions, Sure Start children's centres, child care services);
   – voluntary and community sector service providers;
   – National Offender Management Service (incorporating the Prison Service and the Probation Service);
   – Youth Offending Teams;
   – Crime and Disorder Reduction Partnerships;
   – the Police;
   – education and training services;
   – the Employment Service (Jobcentre Plus);
   – grant making charities and trusts;
   – local strategic partnerships.

SUPPORT FOR HOUSEHOLDS IN TEMPORARY ACCOMMODATION

4.16   The provision of support to households placed in temporary accommodation is essential to ensure that they are able to continue to enjoy a reasonable quality of life and access the range of services they need. In formulating their homelessness strategies, housing authorities should consider what arrangements need to be in place to ensure that households placed in temporary accommodation, within their district or outside, are able to access relevant support services. In particular households will need to be able to access:
   – primary care services such as health visitors and GPs;
   – appropriate education services;
   – relevant social services; and
   – employment and training services.

4.17   Housing authorities will need to liaise and work collaboratively with the relevant service providers to ensure that appropriate arrangements are put in place and monitored. When households are placed in temporary accommodation, it is recommended that housing authorities offer to liaise with the relevant health, education and social services departments in the area in which the households are temporarily housed. Liaison will be particularly important in cases where households have to be accommodated in the district of another housing authority.

4.18 The Secretary of State recommends that housing authorities offer to liaise with the appropriate Primary Care Trust of all families with babies or young children who are placed in temporary accommodation, to ensure that they have the opportunity to receive health and developmental checks from health visitors and/or other primary health care professionals and can participate in vaccination programmes. It would be insufficient for an authority simply to provide such a family with details of health centres and GP practices in the area.

Notify

4.19 Authorities are encouraged to participate in any regional or sub-regional arrangements which facilitate the notification of other authorities and agencies about the location and support needs of households in temporary accommodation. When considering procedures for notifying the relevant agencies of placements in temporary accommodation, housing authorities may wish to have regard to NOTIFY – a web-based notification and information system administered by the Greater London Authority (GLA).

4.20 NOTIFY is designed to improve access to services for households placed in temporary accommodation. Its primary role is to notify relevant services of the placement or movement of households placed in temporary accommodation by London boroughs under the homelessness legislation. The system uses information provided by London borough housing departments to notify housing, education, social services and Primary Care Trusts about households placed in, moving between or leaving temporary accommodation. Information is contained in a database and updated weekly. Authorised users of the NOTIFY notifications website can view information held on NOTIFY at any time, by accessing that website. Relevant services receive a weekly email alert from NOTIFY, informing them of any unviewed notifications and reminding them to access the website. NOTIFY will also shortly provide access for each borough to its own operational management data. The system also has the capacity to analyse aggregated data both at borough and London level. For further information on NOTIFY see notifylondon.gov.uk or contact notify@london.gov.uk.

CHAPTER 5
Working with others

5.1 This chapter provides guidance to housing authorities on working in partnership with other agencies to deliver co-ordinated and effective services to tackle homelessness. It considers the range of organisations and people that contribute to preventing and tackling homelessness and provides examples of types of joint working. It also sets out the statutory provisions that require co-operation between various authorities.

5.2   Under s.3(5) of the 2002 Act, when formulating a homelessness strategy the housing authority must consider, among other things, the extent to which any of the strategy's objectives could be achieved through joint action involving two or more of the organisations tackling homelessness in the district. Whilst housing authorities are best placed to take the strategic lead in tackling homelessness, it is vital that as part of their homelessness strategies effective partnerships are developed with other organisations to deliver co-ordinated and more effective approaches to tackling homelessness locally that address not only housing need but all aspects of social need.

WHY JOINT WORKING?

5.3   At its best, joint working can result in higher quality and more efficient and cost-effective services. Joint working can:
   – expand the knowledge and expertise of partner agencies;
   – help to provide higher quality integrated services to clients with multiple needs;
   – help to ensure people who are homeless or at risk of homelessness do not fall through the net because no one agency can meet all their needs;
   – reduce wasteful referrals and duplicated work between agencies. For example, common procedures for assessing clients and exchanging information mean homeless people do not have to be repeatedly assessed by different agencies.

ORGANISATIONS/PEOPLE WORKING TO PREVENT AND TACKLE HOMELESSNESS

5.4   The most effective homelessness strategies will be those which harness the potential of all the organisations and persons working to prevent and tackle homelessness in the district, and which ensure that all the activities concerned are consistent and complementary. Joint working could involve the social services authority, the Primary Care Trust, other public bodies such as the National Offender Management Service, voluntary and community sector organisations, registered social landlords, private landlords, and any other relevant organisations. Housing authorities should also consider joint working with other agencies, for example, the Police and voluntary and community sector organisations, to tackle issues related to homelessness such as street drinking, begging, drug misuse and anti-social behaviour. Such collaborative working can help reduce the numbers of people sleeping rough and provide effective services targeted at those who are homeless or at risk of becoming homeless. Annex 3 provides an indicative list of other authorities, organisations and persons whose activities may contribute to preventing and tackling homelessness. Chapter 2 provides guidance on the range of activities that housing authorities might undertake in conjunction with other bodies in order to prevent homelessness.

5.5   Housing authorities should also consider developing cross-boundary partnerships to help tackle homelessness, for example with neighbouring local authorities and local strategic partnerships. Initiatives at regional, cross-regional and sub-regional level that address issues which cut across administrative boundaries may also be relevant – for example regional strategies for refugee integration or reducing re-offending.

TYPES OF JOINT WORKING

5.6   Joint working can take many forms. Examples of types of collaborative working that could help to achieve the objectives of a homelessness strategy might
include:

- establishment of a multi-agency forum for key practitioners and providers
  to share knowledge, information, ideas and complementary practices;
- clear links between the homelessness strategy and other key strategies
  such as Supporting People, and the NHS Local Delivery Plan;
- protocols for the referral of clients between services and sharing information between services – for example a joint protocol between hospital-
  based social workers and housing officers to address the housing needs of
  patients to be discharged from hospital;
- joint consideration of the needs of homeless people by housing and social
  services authorities under Part 7, the *Children Act 1989* and community
  care legislation;
- establishment of formal links with other services – for example with those
  provided by voluntary and community sector organisations;
- joint planning and commissioning of services;
- joint training;
- funding of joint posts, for example with the social services authority;
- senior housing representation on key corporate groups such as the Local
  Strategic Partnership (LSP) and the Crime and Disorder Reduction Partnership (CDRP);
- senior commitment from all stakeholders to joined-up working to ensure
  the homelessness strategy action plan is carried out;
- appropriate user involvement and consultation.

5.7   When offering housing advice and assistance, housing authorities should
consider devising screening procedures that identify at an early stage those
cases where there is a need for case-specific joint working. Authorities may
also wish to encourage their partner agencies to develop similar procedures.
Where there is a need for such an approach, authorities are encouraged to
adopt agreed protocols to ensure that appropriate action can be quickly initi-
ated. Early appraisal of all clients who may require multiple assessments, by
whichever authority is first approached, with agreed triggers and procedures
for further action, may help to prevent duplication of enquiries.

5.8   *Homelessness Strategies – A good practice handbook* (DTLR, March 2002) provides advice on successful joint working and the establishment of good links
between different agencies and programmes that can prevent and alleviate
homelessness. The handbook also signposts to other sources of guidance, for
example, on joint protocols, joint commissioning and joint assessments.

THE STATUTORY FRAMEWORK

5.9   The need for co-operation between statutory authorities is recognised in
legislation:

- s.213, s.213A and s.170 of the *Housing Act 1996;*
- s.1 of the *Homelessness Act 2002;*
- s.2 of the *Local Government Act 2000;*
- s.27 of the *Children Act 1989;*

- s.10, s.11 and s.13 of the *Children Act 2004;*
- s.47 of the *National Health Service* and *Community Care Act 1990;*
- s.27 and s.31 of the *Health Act 1999.*

These provisions are outlined in more detail below. However, the absence of a formal legal duty should not act as a barrier to joint working. Rather this should be predicated on meeting local needs and effectively implementing the homelessness strategy.

Housing Act 1996
Section 213

5.10 Where housing or inquiry duties arise under the 1996 Act a housing authority may seek co-operation from another relevant housing authority or body or a social services authority in England, Scotland or Wales. The authority or body to whom the request is made must co-operate to the extent that is reasonable in the circumstances. For this purpose, 'relevant housing authority or body' will include:

in England and Wales:
- another housing authority,
- a registered social landlord,
- a housing action trust, and

in Scotland:
- a local authority,
- a registered social landlord, and
- Scottish Homes.

5.11 The duty on the housing authority, body or social services authority receiving such a request to co-operate will depend on their other commitments and responsibilities. However, they cannot adopt a general policy of refusing such requests, and each case will need to be considered in the circumstances at the time.

5.12 Section 170 of the 1996 Act also provides that where a registered social landlord (RSL) has been requested by a housing authority to offer accommodation to people with priority under its allocation scheme, the RSL must co-operate to such extent as is reasonable in the circumstances. RSLs have a key role to play in preventing and tackling homelessness. See Annex 5 for guidance on co-operation between RSLs and housing authorities.

Section 213A

5.13 Section 213A applies where the housing authority has reason to believe than an applicant with whom a person under the age of 18 resides, or might normally be expected to reside, may be ineligible for assistance, or homeless, or threatened with homelessness, intentionally. Housing authorities are required to have arrangements in place to ensure that all such applicants are invited to agree to the housing authority notifying the social services authority of the essential facts of their case. This will give social services the opportunity to consider the circumstances of the child(ren) and family and plan any response that may be deemed by them to be appropriate. See Chapter 13 for further guidance on s.213A.

Local government acts

5.14   The promotion of well-being power contained in s.2 of the *Local Government Act 2000* gives local authorities substantial capacity for cross-boundary partnership working with other authorities and partners, such as the health and social services sectors. In particular, the power provides local authorities with increased scope to improve the social, economic and environmental well-being of their communities. Section 2(5) of the *Local Government Act 2000* makes it clear that local authorities may act in relation to and for the benefit of any person or area outside their own area if they consider that to do so is likely to promote or improve the social, economic or environmental well-being of their own area. This, therefore, provides scope for:

– co-operation between neighbouring local authorities and local strategic partnerships; and

– initiatives at regional, cross-regional and sub-regional level that address issues which cut across administrative boundaries.

It should be noted, however, that the s.2 power cannot be used by authorities to delegate, or contract out their functions. In order to do this, authorities will need to make use of specific powers such as those in s.101 of the *Local Government Act 1972* which provides for the joint exercise of functions between local authorities.

Children Act 1989

5.15   Under s.27 of the *Children Act 1989* ('the 1989 Act'), a local authority can ask a range of other statutory authorities, including a housing authority, to help them in delivering services for children and families, under their functions in Part 3 of the 1989 Act. Authorities must comply with such a request to the extent that it is compatible with their own statutory duties and other obligations, and does not unduly prejudice the discharge of any of their own functions. They cannot adopt a general policy of refusing such requests, and each case will need to be considered according to the circumstances at the time.

5.16   Children and young people should not be sent to and fro between different authorities (or between different departments within authorities). To provide an effective safety net for vulnerable young people who are homeless or at risk of homelessness, housing and social services will need to work together. Effective collaborative working will require clear corporate policies and departmental procedures agreed between the relevant departments. These should make provision for speedy resolution of any dispute as to which department should take responsibility for a particular case. Joint agreements should cover not only the assessment of clients, but should also reflect the strategic planning and delivery of provision to be set out in the local Children and Young People's Plan. Local Safeguarding Children Boards, which will co-ordinate and ensure the effectiveness of local work to safeguard and promote the welfare of children, may also be involved in drawing up policies and procedures to ensure effective inter-agency co-operation (see also paragraphs 5.17–5.20 below) and Chapter 13.

5.17   Under the 1989 Act, young people leaving care and 16/17 year old children assessed as in need are owed duties which may extend to the provision of accommodation. Where social services approach a housing authority for assistance in housing a young person, the housing authority must co-operate subject to the conditions referred to above in para 5.16. Whether a young person is accommodated under the auspices of the social services authority or the housing authority is a matter for individual authorities to determine in each case. Ideally the relationship of the two authorities should be symbiotic, with jointly agreed protocols in place in respect of the assessment of needs. In many cases the social services authority will have a continuing responsibility for the welfare of vulnerable young people and for assisting them in the transition to adulthood and independent living. Under the 1989 Act, these responsibilities can extend until the young person is aged 18 and in the case of care leavers until the age of 21 (or beyond that age if they are in an agreed programme of education and training). Thus, social services authorities can request assistance from housing authorities in meeting their obligations to provide accommodation for a young person and housing authorities can look to social services authorities to provide the support that young homeless applicants may require. In some cases, housing and social services authorities will both have responsibilities towards young people and will need to work together in order to ensure that an appropriate combination of housing and support is arranged to help the young person to live independently successfully.

Children Act 2004

5.18   The *Children Act 2004* ('the 2004 Act') provides the legislative support for the *Every Child Matters: Change for Children* programme which sets out a national framework for local change programmes to build services around the needs of children and young people. Improved outcomes for children will be driven by an analysis of local priorities and secured through more integrated front-line delivery such as multi-agency working, integrated processes such as the Common Assessment Framework, integrated strategy with joint planning and commissioning, and governance arrangements such as the creation of a Director of Children's Services and lead member for children's services.

5.19   To support the integration of systems to improve outcomes for children and young people by the creation of children's trusts, s.10 of the 2004 Act establishes a duty on county level and unitary authorities to make arrangements to promote co-operation between the authority, relevant partners (including district councils) and other persons or bodies engaged in activities in relation to children, to improve the well-being of children and young people in the authority's area. Relevant partners are required to co-operate with the authority. Section 11 of the 2004 Act requires a range of agencies – including county level and unitary authorities and district authorities where there are two tiers of local government – to make arrangements for ensuring that their functions are discharged having regard to the need to safeguard and promote the welfare of children. Section 13 of the 2004 Act requires county level and unitary authorities to set up a Local Safeguarding Children Board (LSCB) incorporating key organisations including district councils where relevant. As set out in s.14, the objective of the LSCB is to co-ordinate and ensure the effectiveness of what is done by each person or body represented on the board to safeguard and promote the welfare of children in that area.

5.20   The 2004 Act also makes provision for indexes containing basic information about children and young people to enable better sharing of information. In addition, each local authority is required to draw up a Children and Young

People's Plan (CYPP) by April 2006. The CYPP will be a single, strategic, over-arching plan for all services affecting children and young people. The CYPP and the process of joint planning should support local authorities and their partners as they work together. An integrated inspection framework is also being created with Joint Area Reviews assessing local areas' progress in improving outcomes.

The Department for Education and Skills has produced statutory guidance on the *Children Act 2004* which is available from **www.everychildmatters.gov.uk.**

National Health Service and Community Care Act 1990

5.21   Under the National Health Service (NHS) and Community Care Act 1990 ('the 1990 Act'), social services authorities are required to carry out an assessment of any person who may have a need for community care services. The purpose of the legislation is to ensure that the planning and assessment processes identify a person's full range of needs, including housing needs. Section 47 of the 1990 Act requires social service authorities to notify the housing authority if there appears to be a housing need when the assessment is carried out. The 'housing need', for example, may be for renovation or adaptation of the person's current accommodation or for alternative accommodation.

5.22   An assessment of vulnerability under the homelessness legislation will not necessarily mean that a client is eligible for social care services. Policy guidance on fair access to care services (FACS) was published on 2 June 2002 under guidance of local authority circular (LAC) (2002) 13. The guidance provides authorities with an eligibility framework for adult social care for them to use when setting and applying their eligibility criteria.

Health Act 1999

5.23   Section 27 of the *Health Act 1999* ('the 1999 Act') requires NHS bodies and local authorities to co-operate with one another in exercising their respective functions in order to secure and advance the health and welfare of the people of England and Wales.

5.24   Under s.31 of the 1999 Act, partnership arrangements can be designed to help break down the barriers between NHS and local authority services by removing existing constraints in the system and increasing flexibility in the provision and commissioning of services. The legislation introduces three flexibilities: pooled budgets, lead commissioning and integrated provision. Any health-related local authority function can be included in these partnerships, for example, housing, social services, education and leisure services.

National standards, local action: health and social care standards and planning framework 2005/06–2007/08

5.25   This document sets out the framework for all NHS organisations and social services authorities to use in planning over the financial years 2005/06–2007/08. It looks to Primary Care Trusts (PCTs) and local authorities to lead community partnership by even closer joint working to take forward the NHS Improvement Plan. Building on joint work on Local Strategic Partnerships (LSPs), they will need to work in partnership with other NHS organisations in preparing Local Delivery Plans (LDPs) for the period 2005/06 to 2007/08.

Mental health

5.26   The Mental Health National Service Framework (NSF 30/09/1999) addresses the mental health needs of working age adults up to 65. It sets out national standards; national service models; local action and national underpinning programmes for implementation; and a series of national milestones to assure progress, with performance indicators to support effective performance management. An organisational framework for providing integrated services and for commissioning services across the spectrum is also included.

5.27   The Government wants to ensure that people suffering from mental illness receive appropriate care and assistance, particularly those whose illness is severe and enduring. Research has shown that provision of suitable, settled housing is essential to the well-being of this vulnerable group. A key element in the spectrum of care and support is the development of a care plan under the Care Programme Approach (CPA). The initial assessment and ongoing reviews under the CPA must include an assessment of an individual's housing needs. It is essential that housing authorities liaise closely with social services authorities so that any provision of housing is appropriate to the needs of the individual, and meshes with the social and health care support that may be an essential part of the person's care programme.

5.28   This is equally important for young people up to the age of 18. Chapter 9 of the National Service Framework for Children, Young People and Maternity Services published in 2004 makes clear that use of the CPA is also a key marker of good practice for child and adolescent mental health services working with young people with high levels of mental health need.

CHAPTER 6
Applications, inquiries, decisions and notifications

6.1   This chapter provides guidance on dealing with applications for accommodation or assistance in obtaining accommodation; a housing authority's duty to carry out inquiries (where it has reason to believe an applicant may be homeless or threatened with homelessness); and, following inquiries, an authority's duty to notify an applicant of its decision.

APPLICATIONS FOR ASSISTANCE

6.2   Under s.184 of the 1996 Act, if a housing authority has reason to believe that a person applying to the authority for accommodation or assistance in obtaining accommodation may be homeless or threatened with homelessness, the authority must make such inquiries as are necessary to satisfy itself whether the applicant is eligible for assistance and if so, whether any duty, and if so what duty, is owed to that person under Part 7 of the 1996 Act. The definitions of 'homeless' and 'threatened with homelessness' are discussed in Chapter 8.

Preventing homelessness

6.3   Under s.179, housing authorities have a duty to ensure that advice and information about homelessness and the prevention of homelessness are available free of charge to anyone in their district (see Chapter 2 for further guidance on providing advice and information to prevent homelessness). In many cases early, effective intervention can prevent homelessness occurring. Many people who face the potential loss of their current home will be seeking practical advice and assistance to help them remain in their accommodation or secure alternative accommodation. Some may be seeking to apply for assistance under the homelessness legislation without being aware of other options that could help them to secure accommodation. Authorities should explain the various housing options that are available. These might include:

- advice and assistance (e.g. legal advice or mediation with a landlord) to enable them to remain in their current home;
- assistance (e.g. rent deposit or guarantee) to obtain accommodation in the private rented sector;
- an application for an allocation of long term social housing accommodation through a social housing waiting list or choice-based lettings scheme; or
- advice on how to apply to another social landlord for accommodation.

6.4   Housing authorities should ensure that the implications and likely outcomes of the available housing options are made clear to all applicants, including the distinction between having a priority need for accommodation under Part 7 and being in a 'reasonable preference' category for an allocation of housing under Part 6. Authorities must not avoid their obligations under Part 7 (especially the duty to make inquiries under s.184), but it is open to them to suggest alternative solutions in cases of potential homelessness where these would be appropriate and acceptable to the applicant.

Interim duty to accommodate

6.5   If a housing authority has reason to believe that an applicant may be eligible for assistance, homeless and have a priority need, the authority will have **an immediate duty under s.188 to ensure that suitable accommodation is available for the applicant** (and his or her household) pending the completion of the authority's inquiries and its decision as to what duty, if any, is owed to the applicant under Part 7 of the Act. Chapter 7 provides guidance on the interim duty to accommodate. Authorities are reminded that 'having reason to believe' is a lower test than 'being satisfied'.

Form of the application

6.6   Applications can be made by any adult to any department of the local authority and expressed in any particular form; they need not be expressed as explicitly seeking assistance under Part 7. Applications may also be made by a person acting on behalf of the applicant, for example, by a social worker or solicitor acting in a professional capacity, or by a relative or friend in circumstances where the applicant is unable to make an application themselves.

Applications to more than one housing authority

6.7   In some cases applicants may apply to more than one housing authority simultaneously and housing authorities will need to be alert to cases where an applicant is doing this. In such cases, where a housing authority has reason to believe that the applicant may be homeless or threatened with homelessness, it may wish to contact the other housing authorities involved, to agree which housing authority will take responsibility for conducting inquiries.

Where another housing authority has previously made decisions about an applicant's circumstances, a housing authority considering a fresh application may wish to have regard to those decisions. However, housing authorities should not rely solely on decisions made by another housing authority and will need to make their own inquiries in order to reach an independent decision on whether any duty, and if so which duty, is owed under Part 7. Any arrangements for the discharge of any of their functions by another housing authority must comply with s.101 of the *Local Government Act 1972*.

Service provision

6.8   A need for accommodation or assistance in obtaining accommodation can arise at anytime. Housing authorities will therefore need to provide access to advice and assistance at all times during normal office hours, and have arrangements in place for 24-hour emergency cover, e.g. by enabling telephone access to an appropriate duty officer. The police and other relevant services should be provided with details of how to access the service outside normal office hours.

6.9   In the interests of good administration, it is recommended that housing authorities should give proper consideration to the location of, and accessibility to, advice and information about homelessness and the prevention of homelessness, including the need to ensure privacy during interviews. Details of the service including the opening hours, address, telephone numbers and the 24-hour emergency contact should be well publicised within the housing authority's district.

6.10   Housing authorities should provide applicants with a clear and simple explanation of their procedures for handling applications and making decisions. It is recommended that this is provided in written form, for example as a leaflet, as well as orally. In order to ensure advice and assistance are accessible to everyone in the district, it is recommended that information is made available in the main languages spoken in the area, and that for languages less frequently spoken there is access to interpreters.[2] Applicants should be kept informed of the progress of their application and the timescales involved for making a decision on their case. They should also be given a realistic expectation of the assistance to which they may be entitled.

6.11   Under s.214, it is an offence for a person, knowingly or recklessly to make a false statement, or knowingly to withhold information, with intent to induce the authority to believe that he or she, or another person, is entitled to accommodation under Part 7. If, before the applicant receives notification of a decision, there is any change of facts material to his or her case, he or she must inform the housing authority of this as soon as possible. Housing authorities must ensure that all applicants are made aware of these obligations and that they are explained in ordinary language. Housing authorities are advised to ensure that the obligations are conveyed sensitively to avoid intimidating applicants.

---

2   The Welsh Code (para 12.6) recommends access to competent interpreters for the languages of communities in the authority's area: see para 9.63 above.

INQUIRIES

6.12 Under s.184, where a housing authority has reason to believe that an applicant may be homeless or threatened with homelessness, it must make inquiries to satisfy itself whether the applicant is eligible for assistance (see Chapter 9) and, if so, whether any duty and if so what duty is owed to him or her under Part 7. In order to determine this, the authority will need to establish whether the applicant is homeless or threatened with homelessness (see Chapter 8), whether he or she became homeless, or threatened with homelessness, intentionally (see Chapter 11) and whether he or she has a priority need for accommodation (see Chapter 10).

6.13 In addition to determining whether an applicant is owed any duty under Part 7, housing authorities are reminded that they have a **power** to provide further assistance to applicants who are eligible for assistance, homeless (or threatened with homelessness) unintentionally and do not have a priority need. Under s.192(3), housing authorities may secure that accommodation is available for applicants who are eligible, unintentionally homeless and do not have a priority need (see Chapter 15 for further guidance). Under s.195(9), housing authorities may take reasonable steps to secure that accommodation does not cease to be available for applicants who are eligible for assistance, unintentionally threatened with homelessness and do not have a priority need for accommodation (see paragraph 14.7 for guidance on steps to secure that accommodation does not cease to be available).

6.14 Under s.184(2), housing authorities may also make inquiries to decide whether the applicant has a local connection with another housing authority district in England, Wales or Scotland, but they are not required to do so. The possibility of a referral of an applicant to another housing authority can only arise where the applicant has been accepted as eligible for assistance, unintentionally homeless and having a priority need for accommodation (see Chapter 18 for guidance on local connection and referrals).

6.15 The obligation to make inquiries, and satisfy itself whether a duty is owed, rests with the housing authority and it is not for applicants to 'prove their case'. Applicants should always be given the opportunity to explain their circumstances fully, particularly on matters that could lead to a decision against their interests, for example, a decision that an applicant is intentionally homeless.[3]

6.16 Housing authorities should deal with inquiries as quickly as possible, whilst ensuring that they are thorough and, in any particular case, sufficient to enable the housing authority to satisfy itself what duty, if any, is owed or what other assistance can be offered. Housing authorities are obliged to begin inquiries as soon as they have reason to believe that an applicant may be homeless or threatened with homelessness and should aim to carry out an initial interview and preliminary assessment on the day an application is received. An early assessment will be vital to determine whether the housing authority has an immediate duty to secure accommodation under s.188 (see Chapter 7 for guidance on the interim duty to accommodate). Wherever possible, it is recommended that housing authorities aim to complete their inquiries and

---

3 The Welsh Code (para 12.5) still refers to inquiries being carried out 'sympathetically': see para 9.61 above.

notify the applicant of their decision within 33 working days of accepting a duty to make inquiries under s.184. In many cases it should be possible for authorities to complete the inquiries significantly earlier[4].

Violence

6.17   Under s.177, it is not reasonable for a person to continue to occupy accommodation if it is probable that this will lead to domestic or other violence against him or her, or against a person who normally resides with him or her as a member of his or her family, or any other person who might reasonably be expected to reside with him or her. Violence includes threats of violence from another person which are likely to be carried out. Inquiries into cases where violence is alleged will need careful handling. It is essential that inquiries do not provoke further violence. It is not advisable for the housing authority to approach the alleged perpetrator, since this could generate further violence, and may delay the assessment. Housing authorities may, however, wish to seek information from friends and relatives of the applicant, social services and the police, as appropriate. In some cases, corroborative evidence of actual or threatened violence may not be available, for example, because there were no adult witnesses and/or the applicant was too frightened or ashamed to report incidents to family, friends or the police. In many cases involving violence, the applicant may be in considerable distress and an officer trained in dealing with the particular circumstances should conduct the interview. Applicants should be given the option of being interviewed by an officer of the same sex if they so wish.

6.18   In cases where violence is a feature and the applicant may have a local connection elsewhere, the housing authority, in considering whether to notify another housing authority about a possible referral of the case, must be aware that s.198 provides that an applicant cannot be referred to another housing authority if he or she, or any person who might reasonably be expected to reside with him or her, would be at risk of violence in the district of the other housing authority (see Chapter 18 for guidance on referrals to another housing authority).

Support needs

6.19   16 and 17 year olds (including lone parents) who apply for housing assistance may also have care and support needs that need to be assessed. The Secretary of State recommends that housing authorities and social services authorities (and the relevant departments within unitary authorities) have arrangements in place for joint consideration of such young people's needs, whether the application is made initially to the housing department or social services department. See Chapter 12 for further guidance on 16 and 17 year olds.

Assistance from another authority or body

6.20   Under s. 213, a housing authority may request another relevant housing authority or body to assist them in the discharge of their functions under

---

4   The Welsh Code (para 12.22) recommends targets set by the local authority and suggest illustratively 33 days to decision and 3 days for notification: see para 9.130, above.

Part 7. In such cases the authority or body must co-operate in rendering such assistance in the discharge of the functions to which the request relates as is reasonable in the circumstances. For example, a housing authority may request another housing authority to co-operate in providing information about a previous application. See paragraph 5.10 for further guidance on s.213.

DECISIONS/NOTIFICATIONS

6.21 When a housing authority has completed its inquiries under s.184 it must notify the applicant in writing of its decision on the case. Where the decision is against the applicant's interests, e.g. a decision that he or she is ineligible for assistance, not homeless, not in priority need or homeless intentionally, the notification must explain clearly and fully the reasons for the decision. If the housing authority has decided that the conditions for referring the applicant's homelessness case to another housing authority have been met, they must notify the applicant of this and give their reasons for doing so.

6.22 All notifications must inform applicants of their right to request a review of the housing authority's decision and the time within which such a request must be made. At this stage, it is also recommended that housing authorities explain the review procedures. (See Chapter 19 for guidance on reviews of decisions and appeals to the county court).

6.23 It will be important to ensure that the applicant fully understands the decision and the nature of any housing duty that is owed. In cases where the applicant may have difficulty understanding the implications of the decision, it is recommended that housing authorities consider arranging for a member of staff to provide and explain the notification in person.

6.24 Under s.193(3A), where the housing authority accepts a duty to secure accommodation for an applicant under s.193(2), they must give the applicant a copy of the statement included in their allocation scheme of the housing authority's policy on offering people a choice of housing or the opportunity to express their preferences about the accommodation to be allocated to them. This statement is required to be included in the allocation scheme under s.167(1A).

6.25 Section 184(6) provides that where a notification is not received by an applicant, it can be treated as having been given to him or her, if it is made available at the housing authority's office for a reasonable period that would allow it to be collected by the applicant or by someone acting on his or her behalf.

WITHDRAWN APPLICATIONS

6.26 It is recommended that housing authorities have procedures in place for dealing with applications that are withdrawn or where someone fails to maintain contact with the housing authority after making an application. The Secretary of State considers that it would be reasonable to consider an application closed where there has been no contact with the applicant for three months or longer. Any further approach from the applicant after this time may need to be considered as a fresh application. Where an applicant renews contact within three months the housing authority will need to consider any change of circumstances that may affect the application.

FURTHER APPLICATIONS

6.27 There is no period of disqualification if someone wants to make a fresh application. Where a person whose application has been previously considered and determined under Part 7 makes a fresh application, the authority will need to decide whether there are any new facts in the fresh application which render it different from the earlier application. If no new facts are revealed, or any new facts are of a trivial nature, the authority would not be required to consider the new application. However, where the fresh application does reveal substantive new facts, the authority must treat the fresh application in the same way as it would any other application for accommodation or assistance in obtaining accommodation. Therefore, if the authority has reason to believe that the person is homeless, or threatened with homelessness, the authority should make inquiries under s.184 and decide whether any duty is owed under s.188(1).

CHAPTER 7
Interim duty to accommodate

7.1 This chapter provides guidance on housing authorities' interim duty to secure that accommodation is available for an applicant if they have reason to believe that the applicant may be homeless, eligible for assistance and has a priority need.

7.2 Section 188(1) imposes an interim duty on housing authorities to secure that accommodation is available for an applicant (and his or her household) pending their decision as to what duty, if any, is owed to the applicant under Part 7 of the Act if they have reason to believe that the applicant may:
a) be homeless,
b) be eligible for assistance, and
c) have a priority need.

7.3 The threshold for the duty is low as the local authority only has to have a reason to believe that the applicant **may** be homeless, eligible for assistance and have a priority need. (See paragraph 6.5 for guidance on the 'reason to believe' test.)

7.4 The s.188(1) duty applies even where the authority considers the applicant may not have a local connection with their district and may have one with the district of another housing authority (s.188(2)). Applicants cannot be referred to another housing authority unless the housing authority dealing with the application is satisfied that s.193 applies (i.e. the applicant is eligible for assistance, unintentionally homeless and has a priority need). (See Chapter 18 for guidance on referrals to other housing authorities.)

SUITABILITY OF ACCOMMODATION

7.5 The accommodation provided under s.188(1) must be suitable for the applicant and his or her household and the suitability requirements under s.206(1) and s.210(1) apply (see Chapter 17 for guidance on the suitability of accommodation). The applicant does not have the right to ask for a review of the housing authority's decision as to the suitability of accommodation secured under the interim duty, but housing authorities are reminded that such decisions could be subject to judicial review.

7.6   Housing authorities should avoid using Bed & Breakfast (B&B) accommodation wherever possible. Where B&B accommodation has been used in an emergency situation, applicants should be moved to more suitable accommodation as soon as possible. The *Homelessness (Suitability of Accommodation) (England) Order 2003* provides that B&B accommodation is not suitable accommodation for families with children and households that include a pregnant woman unless there is no alternative accommodation available and then only for a maximum of six weeks.

DISCHARGING THE INTERIM DUTY

7.7   Where the s.188(1) interim duty is being discharged, inquiries should be completed as quickly as possible to minimise uncertainty for the applicant and the period for which accommodation needs to be secured by the housing authority. (See Chapter 6 for guidance on inquiries).

7.8   Housing authorities can discharge their interim duty to secure accommodation by providing their own accommodation or by arranging that it is provided by some other person, or by providing advice and assistance so that it will be provided by some other person. (See Chapter 16 for more information on discharging the duty to secure accommodation).

ENDING THE INTERIM DUTY

7.9   The s.188(1) interim duty ends once the housing authority has notified the applicant of its decision as to what duty, if any, is owed to him or her under Part 7, even if the applicant requests a review of the decision.

7.10   Where, having completed their inquiries, the housing authority is satisfied that they are under no further duty to secure accommodation, they should give the applicant a reasonable period of notice to vacate the accommodation to enable him or her to make alternative accommodation arrangements for him/herself. The time allowed should be reasonable when judged against the circumstances of the applicant. Housing authorities should give the applicant time to consider whether to request a review of their decision and, if a review is requested, will need to consider whether to exercise their discretionary power under s.188(3) to secure that accommodation is available (see paragraph 7.13 below).

7.11   It has been established that, as a general rule, accommodation provided pending inquiries under s.184 does not create a tenancy or a licence under the *Protection from Eviction Act 1977*. The courts have applied this principle in cases where the accommodation provided was B&B accommodation in a hotel and where it was a self-contained flat. Consequently, where this general rule applies, housing authorities are required only to provide an applicant with reasonable notice to vacate accommodation provided under the interim duty, and do not need to apply for a possession order from the court. Authorities should note, however, that this general rule may be displaced by an agreement between the housing authority and the applicant, or if the occupation of the accommodation is allowed to continue on more than a transient basis.

7.12   In cases involving applicants who have children under 18 where the housing authority are satisfied that the applicant is ineligible for assistance, the housing authority must alert the social services authority, or social services department, as appropriate, to the case (see Chapter 13 for further guidance on co-operation with social services). Applicants should be invited to consent to social services being notified of the case, but in certain circumstances, for example where the housing authority are concerned about the welfare of the child, they should disclose information about the case even where consent has not been given.

ACCOMODATION PENDING A REVIEW

7.13   Where a review of a decision of a housing authority is requested under s.202, although there is no duty under s.188(1), under s.188(3) the housing authority has a discretionary power to provide accommodation pending the outcome of the review. Failure to consider exercising this discretionary power could be the subject of challenge by judicial review proceedings. Housing authorities are reminded that applicants have 21 days in which to request a review of a decision. (See Chapter 19 for guidance on review of decisions and Chapter 15 for guidance on powers to accommodate pending a review).

CHAPTER 8
Homeless or threatened with Homelessness

8.1   This chapter provides guidance on how to determine whether a person is 'homeless' or 'threatened with homelessness' for the purposes of Part 7.

8.2   Under s.184 of the 1996 Act, if a housing authority has reason to believe that a person applying to the housing authority for accommodation, or assistance in obtaining accommodation, may be homeless or threatened with homelessness, the housing authority must make inquiries to satisfy itself whether the applicant is eligible for assistance and if so, whether a duty is owed to that person under Part 7 of the 1996 Act (see Chapter 6 for guidance on applications for assistance).

THREATENED WITH HOMELESSNESS

8.3   Under s.175(4), a person is 'threatened with homelessness' if he or she is likely to become homeless within 28 days. In many cases, effective intervention can enable homelessness to be prevented or the loss of the current home to be delayed sufficiently to allow for a planned move. The Secretary of State considers that housing authorities should take steps to prevent homelessness wherever possible, offering a broad range of advice and assistance for those in housing need. Authorities should not wait until homelessness is a likelihood or is imminent before providing advice and assistance. (See Chapter 2 for guidance on preventing homelessness).

HOMELESS

8.4   There are a number of different factors that determine whether a person is homeless. Under s.175, a person is homeless if he or she has no accommodation in the UK or elsewhere which is available for his or her occupation and which that person has a legal right to occupy. A person is also homeless if he or she has accommodation but cannot secure entry to it, or the accommodation is a moveable structure, vehicle or vessel designed or adapted for human habitation (such as a caravan or house boat) and there is no place where it can be placed in order to provide accommodation. A person who has accommodation is to be treated as homeless where it would not be reasonable for him or her to continue to occupy that accommodation.

Available for occupation

8.5   Section 176 provides that accommodation shall be treated as available for a person's occupation only if it is available for occupation by him or her together with:

i)   any other person who normally resides with him or her as a member of the family, or

ii)   any other person who might reasonably be expected to reside with him or her.

The first group covers those members of the family who normally reside with the applicant. The phrase 'as a member of the family' although not defined, will include those with close blood or marital relationships and cohabiting partners (including same sex partners),[5] and, where such a person is an established member of the household, the accommodation must provide for him or her as well. The second group relates to any other person, and includes those who may not have been living as part of the household at the time of the application, but whom it would be reasonable to expect to live with the applicant as part of his or her household. Persons in the second group might include a companion for an elderly or disabled person, or children who are being fostered by the applicant or a member of his or her family. The second group will also include those members of the family who were not living as part of the household at the time of the application but who nonetheless might reasonably be expected to form part of it.

8.6   It is for the housing authority to assess whether any other person might reasonably be expected to live with the applicant and there will be a range of situations that the authority will need to consider. Persons who would normally live with the applicant but who are unable to do so because there is no accommodation in which they can all live together should be included in the assessment. When dealing with a family which has split up, housing authorities will need to take a decision as to which members of the family normally reside, or might be expected to reside, with the applicant. A court may have made a residence order indicating with whom the children are to live, but in many cases it will be a matter of agreement between the parents and a court will not have been involved.

Legal right to occupy accommodation

8.7   Under s.175(1), a person is homeless if he or she has no accommodation which he or she can legally occupy by virtue of:

i)   an interest in it (e.g. as an owner, lessee or tenant) or by virtue of a court order;

ii)   an express or implied licence to occupy it (e.g. as a lodger, as an employee with a service occupancy, or when living with a relative); or

---

5   The Welsh Code does not contain any reference to same sex partners.

iii) any enactment or rule of law giving him or her the right to remain in occupation or restricting the right of another person to recover possession (e.g. a person retaining possession as a statutory tenant under the Rent Acts where that person's contractual rights to occupy have expired or been terminated).

8.8 A person who has been occupying accommodation as a licencee whose licence has been terminated (and who does not have any other accommodation available for his or her occupation) is homeless because he or she no longer has a legal right to continue to occupy, despite the fact that that person may continue to occupy but as a trespasser. This may include, for example:

i) those required to leave hostels or hospitals; or

ii) former employees occupying premises under a service occupancy which is dependent upon contracts of employment which have ended.

People asked to leave accommodation by family or friends[6]

8.9 Some applicants may have been asked to leave their current accommodation by family or friends with whom they have been living. In such cases, the housing authority will need to consider carefully whether the applicant's licence to occupy the accommodation has in fact been revoked. Housing authorities may need to interview the parents or friends to establish whether they are genuinely revoking the licence to occupy and rendering the applicants homeless. Authorities are encouraged to be sensitive to situations where parents or carers may have been providing a home for a family member with support needs (for example a person with learning difficulties) for a number of years and who are genuinely finding it difficult to continue with that arrangement, but are reluctant to revoke their licence to occupy formally until alternative accommodation can be secured.

8.10 In some cases the applicant may be unable to stay in his or her accommodation and in others there may be scope for preventing or postponing homelessness, and providing the applicant with an opportunity to plan their future accommodation and pursue various housing options with assistance from the housing authority. However, housing authorities will need to be sensitive to the possibility that for some applicants it may not be safe for them to remain in, or return to, their home because of a risk of violence or abuse.

8.11 In areas of high demand for affordable housing, people living with family and friends may have genuine difficulties in finding alternative accommodation that can lead to friction and disputes within their current home, culminating in a threat of homelessness. In some cases external support, or the promise of assistance with alternative housing, may help to reduce tension and prevent homelessness. The use of family mediation services may assist here.

8.12 Housing authorities will also need to be alert to the possibility of collusion where family or friends agree to revoke a licence to occupy accommodation as part of an arrangement whose purpose is to enable the applicant to be entitled to assistance under Part 7. Some parents and children, for example, may seek to take advantage of the fact that 16 and 17 year old applicants have a priority need for accommodation (see also Chapter 11 on intentional homelessness).

6   There is no equivalent in the Welsh Code.

16 and 17 year olds[7]

8.13 The Secretary of State considers that, generally, it will be in the best interests of 16 and 17 year olds to live in the family home, unless it would be unsafe or unsuitable for them to do so because they would be at risk of violence or abuse. See Chapter 12 for further guidance on 16 and 17 year olds.

Tenant given notice

8.14 With certain exceptions, a person who has been occupying accommodation as a tenant and who has received a valid notice to quit, or notice that the landlord requires possession of the accommodation, would have the right to remain in occupation until a warrant for possession was executed (following the granting of an order for possession by the court). The exceptions are tenants with resident landlords and certain other tenants who do not benefit from the *Protection from Eviction Act 1977*. **However, authorities should note that the fact that a tenant has a right to remain in occupation does not necessarily mean that he or she is not homeless.** In assessing whether an applicant is homeless in cases where he or she is a tenant who has a right to remain in occupation pending execution of a warrant for possession, the housing authority will also need to consider whether it would be reasonable for him or her to continue to occupy the accommodation in the circumstances (see paragraphs 8.30–8.32 below).

8.15 Some tenants may face having to leave their accommodation because their landlord has defaulted on the mortgage of the property they rent. Where a mortgage lender starts possession proceedings, the lender is obliged to give written notice of the proceedings to the occupiers of the property before an order for possession is granted. The notice must be given after issue of the possession summons and at least 14 days before the court hearing. As for tenants given notice that the landlord requires possession of the accommodation (see paragraph 8.14 above), authorities will need to consider whether it would be reasonable for a tenant to continue to occupy the accommodation after receiving notice of possession proceedings from the lender.

Inability to secure entry to accommodation

8.16 Under s.175(2), a person is homeless if he or she has a legal entitlement to accommodation, but is unable to secure entry to it, for example:
– those who have been evicted illegally, or
– those whose accommodation is being occupied illegally by squatters.
Although legal remedies may be available to the applicant to regain possession of the accommodation, housing authorities cannot refuse to assist while he or she is actually homeless.

Accommodation consisting of a moveable structure

8.17 Section 175(2)(b) provides that a person is homeless if he or she has accommodation available for his or her occupation which is a moveable structure, vehicle or vessel designed or adapted for human habitation (e.g. a caravan or houseboat), and there is nowhere that he or she is entitled or permitted to place it and reside in it. The site or mooring for the moveable structure need

---

7 There is no equivalent in the Welsh Code.

not be permanent in order to avoid homelessness. In many cases the nature of the structure may reflect the itinerant lifestyle of the applicant, who may not be looking for a permanent site but somewhere to park or moor on a temporary basis.

Reasonable to continue to occupy

8.18   Section 175(3) provides that a person shall not be treated as having accommodation unless it is accommodation which it would be reasonable for him or her to continue to occupy. There are a number of provisions relating to whether or not it is reasonable for someone to continue to occupy accommodation and these are discussed below. There is no simple test of reasonableness. It is for the housing authority to make a judgement on the facts of each case, taking into account the circumstances of the applicant.

Domestic violence or other violence

8.19   Section 177(1) provides that it is not reasonable for a person to continue to occupy accommodation if it is probable that this will lead to domestic violence or other violence against:

i)   the applicant;

ii) a person who normally resides as a member of the applicant's family; or

iii) any other person who might reasonably be expected to reside with the applicant.

Section 177(1A) provides that violence means violence from another person or threats of violence from another person which are likely to be carried out. Domestic violence is violence from a person who is associated with the victim and also includes threats of violence which are likely to be carried out. Domestic violence is not confined to instances within the home but extends to violence outside the home.

8.20   Section 178 provides that, for the purposes of defining domestic violence, a person is associated with another if:

(a) they are, or have been, married to each other;

(b) they are or have been civil partners of each other;

(c) they are, or have been, cohabitants (including same sex partners);

(d) they live, or have lived, in the same household;

(e) they are relatives, i.e. father, mother, stepfather, stepmother, son, daughter, stepson, stepdaughter, grandmother, grandfather, grandson, granddaughter, brother, sister, uncle, aunt, niece or nephew (whether of full blood, half blood or by affinity) of that person or of that person's spouse or former spouse. A person is also included if he or she would fall into any of these categories in relation to cohabitees or former cohabitees if they were married to each other;

(f) they have agreed to marry each other whether or not that agreement has been terminated;

(g) they have entered into a civil partnership agreement between them whether or not that agreement has been terminated;

(h) in relation to a child, each of them is a parent of the child or has, or has had, parental responsibility for the child (within the meaning of the Children Act 1989). A child is a person under 18 years of age;

(i) if a child has been adopted or freed for adoption (s.16(1) *Adoption Act 1976*), two persons are also associated if one is the natural parent or grandparent of the child and the other is the child of a person who has become the parent by virtue of an adoption order (s.72(1) *Adoption Act 1976*) or has applied for an adoption order or someone with whom the child has been placed for adoption.

8.21   The Secretary of State considers that the term 'violence' should not be given a restrictive meaning, and that 'domestic violence' should be understood to include threatening behaviour, violence or abuse (psychological, physical, sexual, financial or emotional) between persons who are, or have been, intimate partners, family members or members of the same household, regardless of gender or sexuality.[8]

8.22   An assessment of the likelihood of a threat of violence being carried out should not be based on whether there has been actual violence in the past. An assessment must be based on the facts of the case and devoid of any value judgements about what an applicant should or should not do, or should or should not have done, to mitigate the risk of any violence (e.g. seek police help or apply for an injunction against the perpetrator). Inquiries into cases where violence is alleged will need careful handling. See Chapter 6 for further guidance.

8.23   In cases involving violence, housing authorities may wish to inform applicants of the option of seeking an injunction, but should make clear that there is no obligation on the applicant to do so. Where applicants wish to pursue this option, it is advisable that they obtain independent advice as an injunction may be ill-advised in some circumstances. Housing authorities should recognise that injunctions ordering a person not to molest, or enter the home of, an applicant may not be effective in deterring perpetrators from carrying out further violence or incursions, and applicants may not have confidence in their effectiveness. Consequently, applicants should not be expected to return home on the strength of an injunction. To ensure applicants who have experienced actual or threatened violence get the support they need, authorities should inform them of appropriate organisations in the area such as agencies offering counselling and support as well as specialist advice.

8.24   When dealing with cases involving violence, or threat of violence, from outside the home, housing authorities should consider the option of improving the security of the applicant's home to enable him or her to continue to live there safely, where that is an option that the applicant wishes to pursue. In some cases, immediate action to improve security within the victim's home may prevent homelessness. A fast response combined with support from the housing authority, police and the voluntary sector may provide a victim with the confidence to remain in their home. When dealing with domestic violence within the home, where the authority is the landlord, housing authorities should consider the scope for evicting the perpetrator and allowing the victim to remain in their home. **However, where there would be a probability of violence if the applicant continued to occupy his or her present accommodation, the housing authority must treat the applicant as homeless and should not expect him or her to remain in, or return to, the accommodation. In all cases involving violence the safety of the applicant and his or her household should be the primary consideration at all stages of decision making as to whether or not the applicant remains in their own home.**

8   There is no equivalent to this paragraph in the Welsh Code.

8.25   The effectiveness of housing authorities' services to assist victims of domestic violence and prevent further domestic violence is measured by Best Value Performance Indicator BVP1 225. Guidance on BVP1 225 is available at www. communities.gov.uk.

General housing circumstances in the district
8.26   Section 177(2) provides that, in determining whether it is reasonable for a person to continue to occupy accommodation, housing authorities may have regard to the general housing circumstances prevailing in the housing authority's district.
8.27   This would apply, for example, where it was suggested that an applicant was homeless because of poor physical conditions in his or her current home. In such cases it would be open to the authority to consider whether the condition of the property was so bad in comparison with other accommodation in the district that it would not be reasonable to expect someone to continue to live there.
8.28   Circumstances where an applicant may be homeless as a result of his or her accommodation being overcrowded should also be considered in relation to the general housing circumstances in the district. Statutory overcrowding, within the meaning of Part 10 of the *Housing Act 1985*, may not by itself be sufficient to determine reasonableness, but it can be a contributory factor if there are other factors which suggest unreasonableness.

Affordability
8.29   One factor that **must** be considered in all cases is affordability. The *Homelessness (Suitability of Accommodation) Order 1996* (SI 1996 No.3204) requires the housing authority to consider the affordability of the accommodation for the applicant. The Order specifies, among other things, that in determining whether it would be (or would have been) reasonable for a person to continue to occupy accommodation, a housing authority must take into account whether the accommodation is affordable for him or her and must, in particular, take account of:
(a)   the financial resources available to him or her;
(b)   the costs in respect of the accommodation;
(c)   maintenance payments (to a spouse, former spouse or in respect of a child); and
(d)   his or her reasonable living expenses.

Tenant given notice of intention to recover possession
8.30   In cases where the applicant has been occupying accommodation as a tenant and has received a valid notice to quit, or a notice that the landlord intends to recover possession, housing authorities should consider the scope for preventing homelessness through consulting the landlord at an early stage to explore the possibility of the tenancy being allowed to continue or the tenant being allowed to remain for a reasonable period to provide an opportunity for alternative accommodation to be found. If the landlord is not persuaded to agree, the authority will need to consider whether it would be reasonable for the applicant to continue to occupy the accommodation once the valid notice has expired.
8.31   In determining whether it would be reasonable for an applicant to continue to occupy accommodation, the housing authority will need to consider all

the factors relevant to the case and decide the weight that individual factors should attract. As well as the factors set out elsewhere in this chapter, other factors which may be relevant include the general cost to the housing authority, the position of the tenant, the position of the landlord, the likelihood that the landlord will actually proceed with possession proceedings, and the burden on the courts of unnecessary proceedings where there is no defence to a possession claim (see paragraphs 8.14 and 8.15 above for guidance on the right to occupy where notice of possession proceedings has been given).

8.32   Each case must be decided on its facts, so **housing authorities should not adopt a general policy of accepting – or refusing to accept – applicants as homeless or threatened with homelessness when they are threatened with eviction but a court has not yet made an order for possession or issued a warrant of execution.** In any case where a housing authority decides that it would be reasonable for an applicant to continue to occupy their accommodation after a valid notice has expired – and therefore decides that he or she is not yet homeless or threatened with homelessness – that decision will need to be based on sound reasons which should be made clear to the applicant in writing (see Chapter 6 for guidance on housing authorities' duties to inform applicants of their decisions). **The Secretary of State considers that where a person applies for accommodation or assistance in obtaining accommodation, and:**

    (a) the person is an assured shorthold tenant who has received proper notice in accordance with s.21 of the *Housing Act 1988*;

    (b) the housing authority is satisfied that the landlord intends to seek possession; and

    (c) there would be no defence to an application for a possession order; then it is unlikely to be reasonable for the applicant to continue to occupy the accommodation beyond the date given in the s.21 notice, unless the housing authority is taking steps to persuade the landlord to withdraw the notice or allow the tenant to continue to occupy the accommodation for a reasonable period to provide an opportunity for alternative accommodation to be found.

8.32a   Authorities are reminded that an applicant cannot be treated as intentionally homeless unless it would have been reasonable for him or her to have continued to occupy the accommodation. Guidance on 'intentional homelessness' is provided in Chapter 11.

Former armed forces personnel required to leave service accommodation

8.33   The Ministry of Defence recognises that housing authorities will need to be satisfied that entitlement to occupy service accommodation will end on a certain date, in order to determine whether applicants who are service personnel and who are approaching their date of discharge may be homeless or threatened with homelessness. For this purpose, the MOD issues a *Certificate of Cessation of Entitlement to Occupy Service Living Accommodation* six months before discharge (see examples at Annexes 14 and 15). These certificates indicate the date on which entitlement to occupy service accommodation ends, and the Secretary of State considers that housing authorities should not insist upon a court order for possession to establish that entitlement to occupy has ended. Authorities should take advantage of the six-month period of notice of discharge to ensure that service personnel receive timely and comprehensive advice on the housing options available to them when they leave the armed forces.

Other relevant factors

8.34 Other factors which may be relevant in determining whether it would be reasonable for an applicant to continue to occupy accommodation include:[9]

physical characteristics: it would not be reasonable for an applicant to continue to occupy accommodation if the physical characteristics of the accommodation were unsuitable for the applicant because, for example, he or she was a wheelchair user and access was limited.

type of accommodation: some types of accommodation, for example women's refuges, direct access hostels, and night shelters are intended to provide very short-term, temporary accommodation in a crisis and it should not be regarded as reasonable to continue to occupy such accommodation in the medium and longer-term.

people fleeing harassment: in some cases severe harassment may fall short of actual violence or threats of violence likely to be carried out. Housing authorities should consider carefully whether it would be, or would have been, reasonable for an applicant to continue to occupy accommodation in circumstances where they have fled, or are seeking to leave, their home because of non-violent forms of harassment, for example verbal abuse or damage to property. Careful consideration should be given to applicants who may be at risk of witness intimidation. In some criminal cases the police may provide alternative accommodation for witnesses, but usually this will apply for the duration of the trial only. Witnesses may have had to give up their home or may feel unable to return to it when the trial has finished.

This is not an exhaustive list and authorities will need to take account of all relevant factors when considering whether it is reasonable for an applicant to continue to occupy accommodation.

CHAPTER 9
Eligibility for assistance

GENERAL

9.1 Part 7 of the 1996 Act includes provisions that make certain persons from abroad ineligible for housing assistance. Housing authorities will therefore need to satisfy themselves that applicants are eligible before providing housing assistance. The provisions on eligibility are complex and housing authorities will need to ensure that they have procedures in place to carry out appropriate checks on housing applicants.

9.2 Housing authorities should ensure that staff who are required to screen housing applicants about eligibility for assistance are given training in the complexities of the housing provisions, the housing authority's duties and responsibilities under the race relations legislation and how to deal with applicants in a sensitive manner.

---

9 The Welsh Code (para 13.13) refers to physical characteristics and type of accommodation, but not people fleeing harassment. Additionally it refers to overcrowding.

9.3   Local authorities are reminded that Schedule 3 to the *Nationality, Immigration and Asylum Act 2002* provides that certain persons shall not be eligible for support or assistance provided through the exercise of local housing authorities' powers to secure accommodation pending a review (s.188(3)) or pending an appeal to the county court (s.204(4)). See paragraph 9.22 below.

PERSONS FROM ABROAD

9.4   A person will not be eligible for assistance under Part 7 if he or she is a person from abroad who is ineligible for housing assistance under s.185 of the 1996 Act. There are two categories of 'person from abroad' for the purposes s.185:

(i)   *a person subject to immigration control* – such a person is not eligible for housing assistance unless he or she comes within a class prescribed in regulations made by the Secretary of State, and

(ii)   *a person from abroad other than a person subject to immigration control* – the Secretary of State can make regulations to provide for other descriptions of person from abroad who, although they are not subject to immigration control, are to be treated as ineligible for housing assistance.

9.5   The regulations that set out which classes of persons from abroad are eligible or ineligible for housing assistance are the *Allocation of Housing and Homelessness (Eligibility) (England) Regulations 2006* (SI 2006 No.1294) ('the Eligibility Regulations'). Persons subject to immigration control are not eligible for housing assistance unless they fall within a class of persons prescribed in **regulation 5** of the Eligibility Regulations. Persons who are not subject to immigration control will be eligible for housing assistance unless they fall within a description of persons who are to be treated as persons from abroad who are ineligible for assistance by virtue of **regulation 6** of the Eligibility Regulations.

PERSONS SUBJECT TO IMMIGRATION CONTROL

9.6   The term 'person subject to immigration control' is defined in s.13(2) of the *Asylum and Immigration Act 1996* as a person who requires leave to enter or remain in the United Kingdom (whether or not such leave has been given).

9.7   Only the following categories of person do **not** require leave to enter or remain in the UK:

(i)   British citizens;

(ii)   certain Commonwealth citizens with a right of abode in the UK;

(iii)   citizens of an EEA country, ('EEA nationals') and their family members, who have a right to reside in the UK that derives from EC law. The question of whether an EEA national (or family member) has a particular right to reside in the UK (or in another Member State e.g. the Republic of Ireland) will depend on the circumstances, particularly the economic status of the EEA national (e.g. whether he or she is a worker, self-employed, a student, or economically inactive etc.). See Annex 12 for further guidance on rights to reside;

(iv)   persons who are exempt from immigration control under the Immigration Acts, including diplomats and their family members based in the United Kingdom, and some military personnel.

For the purposes of this guidance, 'EEA nationals' means nationals of any of the EU member states (excluding the UK), and nationals of Iceland, Norway, Liechtenstein and Switzerland.

9.8   Any person who **does not** fall within one of the 4 categories in paragraph 9.7 above will be a person subject to immigration control and will be ineligible for housing assistance unless they fall within a class of persons prescribed by regulation 5 of the Eligibility Regulations (see paragraph 9.10 below).

9.9   If there is any uncertainty about an applicant's immigration status, it is recommended that authorities contact the Home Office Immigration and Nationality Directorate, using the procedures set out in Annex 8. In some circumstances, local authorities may be under a duty to contact the Immigration and Nationality Directorate (see paragraph 9.24).

Persons subject to immigration control who are eligible for housing assistance

9.10   Generally, persons subject to immigration control are not eligible for housing assistance. However, by virtue of regulation 5 of the Eligibility Regulations, the following classes of person subject to immigration control are eligible for housing assistance:

(i)   *a person granted refugee status*: a person is granted refugee status when his or her request for asylum is accepted. Persons granted refugee status are granted 5 years' limited leave to remain in the UK. (Prior to 30 August 2005, it was the policy to provide immediate settlement (indefinite leave to remain) for persons granted refugee status.)

(ii)   *a person granted exceptional leave to enter or remain in the UK without condition that they and any dependants should make no recourse to public funds*: this status is granted to persons, including some persons whose claim for asylum has been refused, for a limited period where there are compelling humanitarian and/or compassionate circumstances for allowing them to stay. However, if leave was granted on condition that the applicant and any dependants should not be a charge on public funds, the applicant will not be eligible for homelessness assistance. Since April 2003, exceptional leave to remain (which is granted at the Secretary of State's discretion outside the Immigration Rules) has taken the form of either humanitarian protection or discretionary leave.

(iii)   *a person with current leave to enter or remain in the UK with no condition or limitation, and who is habitually resident in the UK, the Channel Islands, the Isle of Man or the Republic of Ireland*: such a person will have indefinite leave to enter (ILE) or remain (ILR) and will be regarded as having settled status. However, where ILE or ILR status was granted as a result of an undertaking that a sponsor would be responsible for the applicant's maintenance and accommodation, the person must have been resident in the UK, the Channel Islands, the Isle of Man or the Republic of Ireland for five years since the date of entry – or the date of the sponsorship undertaking, whichever is later – for the applicant to be eligible. Where a sponsor has (or, if there was more than one sponsor, all of the sponsors have) died within the first five years, the applicant will be eligible for housing assistance;

(iv)   *a person who left the territory of Montserrat after 1 November 1995 because of the effect on that territory of a volcanic eruption.* (See paragraph 9.19 below.)

Asylum seekers

9.11 Asylum seekers will almost always be persons subject to immigration control. **Asylum seekers who are persons subject to immigration control and whose claim for asylum was made after 2 April 2000 are** *not* **eligible for assistance under Part 7 of the 1996 Act.** Some asylum seekers whose claim for asylum was made before 3 April 2000 would be eligible for assistance under Part 7 in certain limited circumstances, but the number of persons who fall in these classes is likely to be very small (if any). Annex 9 provides guidance on the limited categories of asylum seekers eligible for assistance under Part 7 of the 1996 Act.

9.12 Under s.186 of the 1996 Act, an asylum seeker who would otherwise be eligible for assistance under the Eligibility Regulations, will be ineligible, if he or she has any accommodation available in the UK for his or her occupation, however temporary.

OTHER PERSONS FROM ABROAD WHO MAY BE INELIGIBLE FOR ASSISTANCE

9.13 By virtue of regulation 6 of the Eligibility Regulations, a person who is not subject to immigration control and who falls within one of the following descriptions of persons is to be treated as a person from abroad who is ineligible for housing assistance:

(i) a person who is not habitually resident in the UK, the Channel Islands, the Isle of Man or the Republic of Ireland (subject to certain exceptions – see paragraph 9.14 below);

(ii) a person whose only right to reside in the UK is derived from his status as a jobseeker (or his status as the family member of a jobseeker). For this purpose, 'jobseeker' has the same meaning as for the purpose of regulation 6(1)(a) of the *Immigration (European Economic Area) Regulations 2006* (SI 2006 No. 1003) ('the EEA Regulations');

(iii) a person whose only right to reside in the UK is an initial right to reside for a period not exceeding three months under regulation 13 of the EEA Regulations;

(iv) a person whose only right to reside in the Channel Islands, the Isle of Man or the Republic of Ireland is a right equivalent to one of the rights mentioned in (ii) or (iii) above and which is derived from the Treaty establishing the European Community ('the EC Treaty').

See Annex 12 for guidance on rights to reside in the UK derived from EC law.

Persons exempted from the requirement to be habitually resident

9.14 Certain persons from abroad (not being persons subject to immigration control) will be eligible for housing assistance even though they are not habitually resident in the UK, the Channel Islands, the Isle of Man or the Republic of Ireland. Such a person will be eligible for assistance even if not habitually resident, if he or she is:

(a) an EEA national who is in the UK as a worker (which has the same meaning as it does for the purposes of regulation 6(1) of the EEA Regulations);

(b) an EEA national who is in the UK as a self-employed person (which has the same meaning as it does for the purposes of regulation 6(1) of the EEA Regulations);

(c) a person who is an accession state worker requiring registration who is treated as a worker for the purposes of regulation 6(1) of the EEA Regulations, pursuant to the *Accession (Immigration and Worker Registration) Regulations 2004*, as amended;

(d) a person who is a family member of a person referred to in (a) to (c) above;

(e) a person with a right to reside permanently in the UK by virtue of regulation 15(c), (d) or (e) of the EEA Regulations (see Annex 12);

(f) a person who left Montserrat after 1 November 1995 because of the effect of volcanic activity there (see paragraph 9.19 below);

(g) a person who is in the UK as a result of his or her deportation, expulsion or other removal by compulsion of law from another country to the UK (see paragraph 9.21 below).

On (a) and (b), authorities should note that a person who is no longer working or no longer in self-employment will retain his or her status as a worker or self-employed person in certain circumstances. (See Annex 12 for further guidance.) On (c), authorities should note that accession state workers requiring registration will generally only be treated as a worker when they are actually working and will not retain 'worker' status in the circumstances referred to above. (See annexes 12 and 13 for further guidance.) On (d), authorities should note that 'family member' does not include a person who is an extended family member who is treated as a family member by virtue of regulation 7(3) of the EEA Regulations (see Annex 12 for further guidance).

The habitual residence test

9.15 The term 'habitual residence' is intended to convey a degree of permanence in the person's residence in the UK, the Channel Islands, the Isle of Man or the Republic of Ireland; it implies an association between the individual and the place of residence and relies substantially on fact.

9.16 The Secretary of State considers that it is likely that applicants who have been resident in the UK, Channel Islands, the Isle of Man or the Republic of Ireland continuously during the 2-year period prior to their housing application will be habitually resident. In such cases, therefore, housing authorities may consider it unnecessary to make further enquiries to determine whether the person is habitually resident, unless there are other circumstances that need to be taken into account. A period of continuous residence in the UK, Channel Islands, the Isle of Man or the Republic of Ireland might include periods of temporary absence, e.g. visits abroad for holidays or to visit relatives. Where two years' continuous residency has not been established, housing authorities will need to conduct further enquiries to determine whether the applicant is habitually resident.

9.17 A person will not generally be habitually resident anywhere unless he or she has taken up residence and lived there for a period. There will be cases where the person concerned is not coming to the UK for the first time, and is resuming a previous period of habitual residence.

9.18 Annex 10 provides guidance on the factors that a housing authority should consider in determining whether an applicant is habitually resident.

Persons from Montserrat

9.19   The classes of persons (not being persons subject to immigration control) who are not required to be habitually resident in order to be eligible for assistance under Part 7 include a person who left Montserrat after 1 November 1995 because of the effect of volcanic activity there.

9.20   On 21 May 2002 most British overseas territories citizens, including those from Montserrat, became British Citizens. Since their new EU-style passport will not identify that they are from Montserrat, it has been recommended that they should also retain their old British Overseas Citizen passport, to help them demonstrate eligibility for, among other things, housing assistance in the UK.

Persons deported, expelled or removed to the UK from another country

9.21   Persons who are in the UK as a result of their deportation, expulsion or other removal by compulsion of law from another country to the UK will generally be UK nationals. (However, such persons could include EEA nationals, where the UK immigration authorities were satisfied that the person was settled in the UK and exercising EC Treaty rights prior to deportation from the third country.) Where deportation occurs, most countries will signal this in the person's passport and provide them with reasons for their removal. This should enable such persons to identify their circumstances when making an application for housing assistance.

PERSONS INELIGIBLE UNDER CERTAIN PROVISIONS BY VIRTUE OF SCHEDULE 3 TO THE NATIONALITY, IMMIGRATION AND ASYLUM ACT 2002

9.22   Section 54 of, and Schedule 3 to, the *Nationality, Immigration and Asylum Act 2002* have the effect of making certain applicants for housing assistance ineligible for accommodation under s.188(3) *(power to accommodate pending a review)* or s.204(4) *(power to accommodate pending an appeal to the county court)* of the 1996 Act. The following classes of person will be ineligible for assistance under those powers:

(i)   *a person who has refugee status abroad,* i.e. a person:
  – who does not have the nationality of an EEA State, and
  – who the government of an EEA State other than the UK has determined is entitled to protection as a refugee under the Refugee Convention;

(ii)   *a person who has the nationality of an EEA State other than the UK* (but see paragraph 9.23 below);

(iii)   *a person who was (but is no longer) an asylum seeker and who fails to cooperate with removal directions* issued in respect of him or her;

(iv)   *a person who is in the UK in breach of the immigration laws* (within the meaning of s.11 of the *Nationality, Immigration and Asylum Act 2002) and is not an asylum seeker;*

(v)   *certain persons who are failed asylum seekers with dependent children,* where the Secretary of State has certified that, in his opinion, such a person has failed without reasonable excuse to take reasonable steps to leave the UK voluntarily or place himself or herself in a position where he or she is able to leave the UK voluntarily, and that person has received the Secretary of State's certificate more than 14 days previously;

(vi) *a person who is the dependant of a person who falls within class (i), (ii), (iii) or (v) above.*

9.23 However, s.54 and Schedule 3 do not prevent the exercise of an authority's powers under s.188(3) and s.204(4) of the 1996 Act to the extent that such exercise is necessary for the purpose of avoiding a breach of a person's rights under the European Convention of Human Rights or rights under the EC Treaties. Among other things, this means that a local authority can exercise these powers to accommodate an EEA national who has a right to reside in the UK under EC law (see Annex 12).

9.24 Paragraph 14 of Schedule 3 provides, among other things, that authorities must inform the Secretary of State where the powers under s.188(3) or s.204(4) apply, or may apply, to a person who is, or may come, within classes (iii), (iv) or (v) in paragraph 9.22 (by contacting the Home Office Immigration and Nationality Directorate).

9.25 For further guidance, local authorities should refer to Guidance to Local Authorities and Housing Authorities about the *Nationality, Immigration and Asylum Act*, Section 54 and Schedule 3, and the *Withholding and Withdrawal of Support (Travel Assistance and Temporary Accommodation) Regulations 2002*, issued by the Home Office.

ELIGIBILITY – LIST OF RELATED ANNEXES:

8 – How to contact the home Office Immigration and Nationality Directorate

9 – Asylum seekers

10 – The habitual residence test

11 – European groupings (EU, A8, EEA, Switzerland)

12 – Rights to reside in the UK derived from EC law

13 – Worker registration scheme

CHAPTER 10
Priority need

This chapter provides guidance on the categories of applicant who have a priority need for accommodation under the homelessness legislation.

10.1 Under the homelessness legislation, housing authorities must have a strategy for preventing homelessness and ensuring that accommodation and support are available to **anyone** in their district who is homeless or at risk of homelessness. They must also provide advice and assistance on housing and homelessness prevention to anyone in their district, free of charge. Stronger duties to secure accommodation exist for households who have a priority need for accommodation. Since 2002, the priority need categories have embraced a wider range of people whose age or background puts them at greater risk when homeless, including more single people.

10.2 The main homelessness duties in s.193(2) and s.195(2) of the 1996 Act (to secure accommodation or take reasonable steps to prevent the loss of accommodation) apply only to applicants who have a priority need for accommodation. Section 189(1) and the *Homelessness (Priority Need for Accommodation) (England) Order 2002* provide that the following categories of applicant have a priority need for accommodation:

i)　a pregnant woman or a person with whom she resides or might reasonably be expected to reside (see paragraph 10.5);

ii)　a person with whom dependent children reside or might reasonably be expected to reside (see paragraphs 10.6–10.11);

iii)　a person who is vulnerable as a result of old age, mental illness or handicap or physical disability or other special reason, or with whom such a person resides or might reasonably be expected to reside (see paragraphs 10.12–10.18);

iv)　a person aged 16 or 17 who is not a 'relevant child' or a child in need to whom a local authority owes a duty under section 20 of the *Children Act 1989* (see paragraphs 10.36–10.39);

v)　a person under 21 who was (but is no longer) looked after, accommodated or fostered between the ages of 16 and 18 (except a person who is a 'relevant student') (see paragraphs 10.40–10.41);

vi)　a person aged 21 or more who is vulnerable as a result of having been looked after, accommodated or fostered (except a person who is a 'relevant student') (see paragraphs 10.19–10.20);

vii)　a person who is vulnerable as a result of having been a member of Her Majesty's regular naval, military or air forces (see paragraphs 10.21–10.23);

viii)　a person who is vulnerable as a result of:

(a)　having served a custodial sentence,

(b)　having been committed for contempt of court or any other kindred offence, or

(c)　having been remanded in custody; (see paragraphs 10.24–10.27)

ix)　a person who is vulnerable as a result of ceasing to occupy accommodation because of violence from another person or threats of violence from another person which are likely to be carried out (see paragraphs 10.28–10.29);

x)　a person who is vulnerable for any other special reason, or with whom such a person resides or might reasonably be expected to reside (see paragraphs 10.30–10.35);

xi)　a person who is homeless, or threatened with homelessness, as a result of an emergency such as flood, fire or other disaster (see paragraph 10.42).

10.3　Inquiries as to whether an applicant has a priority need must be carried out in all cases where the housing authority has reason to believe that an applicant may be homeless or threatened with homelessness, and is eligible for assistance (s.184). Moreover, where the housing authority has reason to believe that the applicant is homeless, eligible for assistance and in priority need, they will have an immediate duty to secure interim accommodation, pending a decision on the case (see Chapter 7).

10.4　Once a housing authority has notified an applicant that he or she has a priority need and has been accepted as owed the main homelessness duty (s.193(2)) it cannot – unless the decision is subject to a request for a review – change the decision if the applicant subsequently ceases to have a priority need (e.g. because a dependent child leaves home). Any change of circumstance prior to the decision on the homelessness application should be taken into account. However, once all the relevant inquiries are completed, the housing authority should not defer making a decision on the case in anticipation of a possible change of circumstance. (See Chapter 19 for guidance on reviews.)

PREGNANT WOMEN

10.5   A pregnant woman, and anyone with whom she lives or might reasonably be expected to live, has a priority need for accommodation. This is regardless of the length of time that the woman has been pregnant. Housing authorities should seek normal confirmation of pregnancy, e.g. a letter from a medical professional, such as a midwife, should be adequate evidence of pregnancy. If a pregnant woman suffers a miscarriage or terminates her pregnancy during the assessment process the housing authority should consider whether she continues to have a priority need as a result of some other factor (e.g. she may be vulnerable as a result of an other special reason – see paragraph 10.30).

DEPENDENT CHILDREN

10.6   Applicants have a priority need if they have one or more dependent children who normally live with them or who might reasonably be expected to live with them. There must be actual dependence on the applicant, although the child need not be wholly and exclusively dependent on him or her. There must also be actual residence (or a reasonable expectation of residence) with some degree of permanence or regularity, rather than a temporary arrangement whereby the children are merely staying with the applicant for a limited period (see paragraphs 10.9 and 10.10). Similarly, the child need not be wholly and exclusively resident (or expected to reside wholly and exclusively) with the applicant.

10.7   The 1996 Act does not define dependent children, but housing authorities may wish to treat as dependent all children under 16, and all children aged 16–18 who are in, or are about to begin, full-time education or training or who for other reasons are unable to support themselves and who live at home. The meaning of dependency is not, however, limited to financial dependency. Thus, while children aged 16 and over who are in full-time employment and are financially independent of their parents would not normally be considered to be dependants, housing authorities should remember that such children may not be sufficiently mature to live independently of their parents, and there may be sound reasons for considering them to be dependent. Each case will need to be carefully considered according to the circumstances.

10.8   Dependent children need not necessarily be the applicant's own children but could, for example, be related to the applicant or his or her partner or be adopted or fostered by the applicant. There must, however, be some form of parent/child relationship.

10.9   Housing authorities may receive applications from a parent who is separated from his or her former spouse or partner. In some cases where parents separate, the court may make a residence order indicating with which parent the child normally resides. In such cases, the child may be considered to reside with the parent named in the order, and would not normally be expected to reside with the other parent. However, in many cases the parents come to an agreement themselves as to how the child is to be cared for, and a court order will not be made or required.

10.10 Residence does not have to be full-time and a child can be considered to reside with either parent even where he or she divides his or her time between both parents. However, as mentioned above, there must be some regularity to the arrangement. If the child is not currently residing with the applicant, the housing authority will need to decide whether, in the circumstances, it would be reasonable for the child to do so. An agreement between a child's parents, or a joint residence order by a court, may not automatically lead to a conclusion that it would be reasonable for the child to reside with the parent making the application, and housing authorities will need to consider each case individually. However, housing authorities should remember that where parents separate, it will often be in the best interests of the child to maintain a relationship with both parents.

10.11 Where the applicant's children are being looked after by a social services authority – for example, they are subject to a care order or are being accommodated under a voluntary agreement – and they are not currently living with the applicant, liaison with the social services authority will be essential. Joint consideration with social services will ensure that the best interests of the applicant and the children are served. This may, for example, enable a family to be reunited subject to suitable accommodation being available.

VULNERABILITY

10.12 A person has a priority need for accommodation if he or she is vulnerable as a result of:

i)   old age;

ii) mental illness or learning disability (mental handicap) or physical disability;

iii) having been looked after, accommodated or fostered and is aged 21 or more;

iv) having been a member of Her Majesty's regular naval, military or air forces;

v)   having been in custody or detention;

vi) ceasing to occupy accommodation because of violence from another person or threats of violence from another person which are likely to be carried out; or

vii) any other special reason.

In the case of i), ii) and vii) only, a person with whom a vulnerable person lives or might reasonably be expected to live also has a priority need for accommodation and can therefore make an application on behalf of themselves and that vulnerable person.

10.13 It is a matter of judgement whether the applicant's circumstances make him or her vulnerable. When determining whether an applicant in any of the categories set out in paragraph 10.12 is vulnerable, the local authority should consider whether, when homeless, the applicant would be less able to fend for him/herself than an ordinary homeless person so that he or she would suffer injury or detriment, in circumstances where a less vulnerable person would be able to cope without harmful effects.

10.14 Some of the factors which may be relevant to determining whether a particular category of applicant is vulnerable are set out below. The assessment of an applicant's ability to cope is a composite one taking into account all of the circumstances. **The applicant's vulnerability must be assessed on the basis that he or she is or will become homeless, and not on his or her ability to fend for him or herself while still housed.**

Old age

10.15 Old age alone is not sufficient for the applicant to be deemed vulnerable. However, it may be that as a result of old age the applicant would be less able to fend for him or herself as provided in paragraph 10.13 above. All applications from people aged over 60 need to be considered carefully, particularly where the applicant is leaving tied accommodation. However, housing authorities should not use 60 (or any other age) as a fixed age beyond which vulnerability occurs automatically (or below which it can be ruled out); each case will need to be considered in the light of the individual circumstances.

Mental illness or learning disability or physical disability

10.16 Housing authorities should have regard to any advice from medical professionals, social services or current providers of care and support. In cases where there is doubt as to the extent of any vulnerability authorities may also consider seeking a clinical opinion. However, the final decision on the question of vulnerability will rest with the housing authority. In considering whether such applicants are vulnerable, authorities will need to take account of all relevant factors including:

i) the nature and extent of the illness and/or disability which may render the applicant vulnerable;

ii) the relationship between the illness and/or disability and the individual's housing difficulties; and

iii) the relationship between the illness and/or disability and other factors such as drug/alcohol misuse, offending behaviour, challenging behaviours, age and personality disorder.

10.17 Assessment of vulnerability due to mental health will require close co-operation between housing authorities, social services authorities and mental health agencies. Housing authorities should consider carrying out joint assessments or using a trained mental health practitioner as part of an assessment team. Mental Health NHS Trusts and local authorities have an express duty to implement a specifically tailored care programme (the Care Programme Approach – CPA) for all patients considered for discharge from psychiatric hospitals and all new patients accepted by the specialist psychiatric services (see *Effective care co-ordination in mental health services: modernising the care programme approach*, DH, 1999). **People discharged from psychiatric hospitals and local authority hostels for people with mental health problems are likely to be vulnerable.** Effective, timely, liaison between housing, social services and NHS Trusts will be essential in such cases but authorities will also need to be sensitive to direct approaches from former patients who have been discharged and may be homeless.

10.18 Learning or physical disabilities or long-term acute illnesses, such as those defined by the *Disability Discrimination Act 1995*, which impinge on the applicant's housing situation and give rise to vulnerability may be readily discernible, but advice from health or social services staff should be sought, wherever necessary.

Having been looked after, accommodated or fostered and aged 21 or over

10.19 A person aged 21 or over who is vulnerable as a result of having been looked after, accommodated or fostered has a priority need (other than a person who is a 'relevant student'). The terms 'looked after, accommodated or fostered' are set out in the *Children Act 1989* (s.24) and include any person who has been:

i)   looked after by a local authority (i.e. has been subject to a care order or accommodated under a voluntary agreement);

ii) accommodated by or on behalf of a voluntary organisation;

iii) accommodated in a private children's home;

iv) accommodated for a consecutive period of at least three months:
   – by a health authority, special health authority, primary care trust or local education authority, or
   – in any care home or independent hospital or in any accommodation provided by a National Health Service trust; or

v)   privately fostered.

A 'relevant student' means a care leaver under 24 to whom section 24B(3) of the *Children Act 1989* applies, and who is in full-time further or higher education and whose term-time accommodation is not available during a vacation. Under s.24B(5), where a social services authority is satisfied that a person is someone to whom section 24B(3) applies and needs accommodation during a vacation they must provide accommodation or the means to enable it to be secured.

10.20 Housing authorities will need to make enquiries into an applicant's childhood history to establish whether he or she has been looked after, accommodated or fostered in any of these ways. If so, they will need to consider whether he or she is vulnerable as a result. In determining whether there is vulnerability (as set out in paragraph 10.13 above), factors that a housing authority may wish to consider are:

i)   the length of time that the applicant was looked after, accommodated or fostered;

ii) the reasons why the applicant was looked after, accommodated or fostered;

iii) the length of time since the applicant was looked after, accommodated or fostered, and whether the applicant had been able to obtain and/or maintain accommodation during any of that period;

iv) whether the applicant has any existing support networks, particularly including family, friends or mentor.

Having been a member of the armed forces

10.21 A person who is vulnerable as a result of having been a member of Her Majesty's regular armed forces has a priority need for accommodation. Former members of the armed forces will include a person who was previously a member of the regular naval, military or air forces, including a person who has been released following detention in a military corrective training centre.

10.22 The principal responsibility for providing housing information and advice to Service personnel lies with the armed forces up to the point of discharge and these services are delivered through the Joint Service Housing Advice Office (telephone: 01722 436575). Some people, who have served in the armed forces for a long period, and those who are medically discharged, may be offered assistance with resettlement by Ministry of Defence (MOD) resettlement staff. The MOD issues a *Certificate of Cessation of Entitlement to Occupy Service Living Accommodation* (see examples at Annexes 14 and 15) six months before discharge. Applications from former members of the armed forces will need to be considered carefully to assess whether the applicant is vulnerable as a result of having served in the armed forces.

10.23   In considering whether former members of the armed forces are vulnerable (as set out in paragraph 10.13 above) as a result of their time spent in the forces, a housing authority may wish to take into account the following factors:

i)   the length of time the applicant spent in the armed forces (although authorities should not assume that vulnerability could not occur as a result of a short period of service);

ii)   the type of service the applicant was engaged in (those on active service may find it more difficult to cope with civilian life);

iii)   whether the applicant spent any time in a military hospital (this could be an indicator of a serious health problem or of post-traumatic stress);

iv)   whether HM Forces' medical and welfare advisers have judged an individual to be particularly vulnerable in their view and have issued a Medical History Release Form (F Med 133) giving a summary of the circumstances causing that vulnerability;

v)   the length of time since the applicant left the armed forces, and whether he or she had been able to obtain and/or maintain accommodation during that time;

vi)   whether the applicant has any existing support networks, particularly by way of family or friends.

Having been in custody or detention

10.24   A person who is vulnerable as a result of having served a custodial sentence, been committed for contempt of court or remanded in custody has a priority need for accommodation. This category applies to applicants who are vulnerable as a result of having:

i)   served a custodial sentence within the meaning of the *Powers of Criminal Courts (Sentences) Act 2000*, s.76. (This includes sentences of imprisonment for those aged 21 or over and detention for those aged under 21, including children.);

ii)   been committed for contempt of court or any other kindred offence (kindred offence refers to statutory provisions for contempt as opposed to the inherent jurisdiction of the court, e.g. under the *Contempt of Court Act 1981*, s.12 (magistrates' court) and *County Court Act 1984*, s.118 (county court)). (Committal may arise, e.g. where an applicant has breached a civil injunction.);

iii)   been remanded in custody within the meaning of the *Powers of Criminal Courts (Sentencing) Act 2000*, s.88(1)(b), (c) or (d), i.e. remanded in or committed to custody by an order of a court; remanded or committed to housing authority accommodation under the *Children and Young Persons Act 1969* and placed and kept in secure accommodation; or, remanded, admitted or removed to hospital under the *Mental Health Act 1983*, ss.35, 36, 38 or 48.

10.25   Applicants have a priority need for accommodation only if they are vulnerable (see paragraph 10.13 above) as a result of having been in custody or detention. In determining whether applicants who fall within one of the descriptions in paragraph 10.24 are vulnerable as a result of their period in custody or detention, a housing authority may wish to take into account the following factors:

i)   the length of time the applicant served in custody or detention (although authorities should not assume that vulnerability could not occur as a result of a short period in custody or detention);

ii)   whether the applicant is receiving supervision from a criminal justice agency e.g. the Probation Service, Youth Offending Team or Drug Intervention Programme. Housing authorities should have regard to any advice from criminal justice agency staff regarding their view of the applicant's general vulnerability, but the final decision on the question of vulnerability for the purposes of the homelessness legislation will rest with the housing authority;

iii)   the length of time since the applicant was released from custody or detention, and the extent to which the applicant had been able to obtain and/or maintain accommodation during that time;

iv)   whether the applicant has any existing support networks, for example family or friends, and how much of a positive influence these networks are likely to be in the applicant's life.

10.26   In many cases a housing needs assessment may have been completed in respect of offenders by the Probation Service, Prison Services, Youth Offending Team, Criminal Justice Intervention Team or a voluntary organisation acting on behalf of one of these agencies. Where such an assessment identifies an individual as needing help in finding accommodation and judges the individual to be particularly vulnerable and the applicant makes an application for housing assistance, this information will be made available to the relevant housing authority.

10.27   In addition to the question of priority need, when assessing applicants in this client group difficult issues may arise as to whether the applicant has become homeless intentionally. Housing authorities must consider each case in the light of all the facts and circumstances. **Housing authorities are reminded that they cannot adopt a blanket policy of assuming that homelessness will be intentional or unintentional in any given circumstances** (see Chapter 11 for guidance on intentional homelessness).

Having left accommodation because of violence

10.28   A person has a priority need if he or she is vulnerable (as set out in paragraph 10.13 above) as a result of having to leave accommodation because of violence from another person, or threats of violence from another person that are likely to be carried out. It will usually be apparent from the assessment of the reason for homelessness whether the applicant has had to leave accommodation because of violence or threats of violence (see Chapter 8 for further guidance on whether it is reasonable to continue to occupy accommodation). **In cases involving violence, the safety of the applicant and ensuring confidentiality must be of paramount concern.** It is not only domestic violence that is relevant, but all forms of violence, including racially motivated violence or threats of violence likely to be carried out. Inquiries of the perpetrators of violence should not be made. In assessing whether it is likely that threats of violence are likely to be carried out, a housing authority should only take into account the probability of violence, and not actions which the applicant could take (such as injunctions against the perpetrators). See Chapter 6 for further guidance on dealing with cases involving violence.

10.29 In considering whether applicants are vulnerable as a result of leaving accommodation because of violence or threats of violence likely to be carried out, a housing authority may wish to take into account the following factors:

i) the nature of the violence or threats of violence (there may have been a single but significant incident or a number of incidents over an extended period of time which have had a cumulative effect);

ii) the impact and likely effects of the violence or threats of violence on the applicant's current and future well being;

iii) whether the applicant has any existing support networks, particularly by way of family or friends.

Other special reason

10.30 Section 189(1)(c) provides that a person has a priority need for accommodation if he or she is vulnerable for any 'other special reason'. A person with whom such a vulnerable person normally lives or might reasonably be expected to live also has a priority need. The legislation envisages that vulnerability can arise because of factors that are not expressly provided for in statute. Each application must be considered in the light of the facts and circumstances of the case. Moreover, other special reasons giving rise to vulnerability are not restricted to the physical or mental characteristics of a person. Where applicants have a need for support but have no family or friends on whom they can depend they may be vulnerable as a result of another special reason.

10.31 **Housing authorities must keep an open mind and should avoid blanket policies that assume that particular groups of applicants will, or will not, be vulnerable for any 'other special reason'.** Where a housing authority considers that an applicant may be vulnerable, it will be important to make an in-depth assessment of the circumstances of the case. Guidance on certain categories of applicants who may be vulnerable as a result of any 'other special reason' is given below. The list below is not exhaustive and housing authorities must ensure that they give proper consideration to every application on the basis of the individual circumstances. In addition, housing authorities will need to be aware that an applicant may be considered vulnerable for any 'other special reason' because of a combination of factors which taken alone may not necessarily lead to a decision that they are vulnerable (e.g. drug and alcohol problems, common mental health problems, a history of sleeping rough, no previous experience of managing a tenancy).

10.32 *Chronically sick people, including people with AIDS and HIV-related illnesses.* People in this group may be vulnerable not only because their illness has progressed to the point of physical or mental disability (when they are likely to fall within one of the specified categories of priority need) but also because the manifestations or effects of their illness, or common attitudes to it, make it very difficult for them to find and maintain stable or suitable accommodation. Whilst this may be particularly true of people with AIDS, it could also apply in the case of people infected with HIV (who may not have any overt signs or symptoms) if the nature of their infection is known.

10.33 *Young people.* The 2002 Order makes specific provision for certain categories of young homeless people (see paragraph 10.2). However, there are many other young people who fall outside these categories but who could become homeless and be vulnerable in certain circumstances. When assessing applications from young people under 25[10] who do not fall within any of the specific categories of priority need, housing authorities should give careful consideration to the possibility of vulnerability. Most young people can expect a degree of support from families, friends or an institution (e.g. a college or university) with the practicalities and costs of finding, establishing, and managing a home for the first time. But some young people, particularly those who are forced to leave the parental home or who cannot remain there because they are being subjected to violence or sexual abuse, may lack this back-up network and be less able than others to establish and maintain a home for themselves. Moreover, a young person on the streets without adequate financial resources to live independently may be at risk of abuse or prostitution. See Chapter 12 for further guidance on 16 and 17 year olds.

10.34 *People fleeing harassment.* Authorities should consider whether harassment falls under the general definition of domestic violence (see definition in Chapter 8 and paragraphs 10.28–10.29 above which give guidance on vulnerability as a result of violence). In some cases, however, severe harassment may fall short of actual violence or threats of violence likely to be carried out. Housing authorities should consider carefully whether applicants who have fled their home because of non-violent forms of harassment, for example verbal abuse or damage to property, are vulnerable as a result. Careful consideration should be given to applicants who may be at risk of witness intimidation. In some criminal cases the police may provide alternative accommodation for witnesses, but usually this will apply for the duration of the trial only. Witnesses may have had to give up their home or may feel unable to return to it when the trial has finished.

10.35 *Former asylum seekers.* Former asylum seekers who have been granted refugee status or exceptional leave to remain, humanitarian protection, or discretionary leave will be eligible for homelessness assistance and may be at risk of homelessness as a result of having to leave accommodation that had been provided for them (e.g. by the National Asylum Support Service) in the period before a decision was reached on their asylum claim. They may well have experienced persecution or trauma in their country of origin or severe hardship in their efforts to reach the UK and may be vulnerable as a result. In assessing applications from this client group, housing authorities should give careful consideration to the possibility that they may be vulnerable as a result of another special reason. Authorities should be sensitive to the fact that former asylum seekers may be reluctant to discuss, or have difficulty discussing, their potential vulnerability, if, for example, they have experienced humiliating, painful or traumatic circumstances such as torture, rape or the killing of a family member.

10 The Welsh Code (para 14.19) does not specify a particular age.

16 AND 17 YEAR OLDS

10.36 All 16 and 17 year old homeless applicants have a priority need for accommodation except those who are:

i)   a relevant child, or

ii) a child in need who is owed a duty under s.20 of the *Children Act 1989*.

Relevant child or child in need owed a duty under s.20 of the 1989 Act

10.37 A relevant child is a child aged 16 or 17 who has been looked after by a local authority for at least 13 weeks since the age of 14 and has been looked after at some time while 16 or 17 and who is not currently being looked after (i.e. an 'eligible child' for the purposes of paragraph 19B of Schedule 2 to the *Children Act 1989*). In addition, a child is also a relevant child if he or she would have been looked after by the local authority as an eligible child but for the fact that on his or her 16ᵗʰ birthday he or she was detained through the criminal justice system, or in hospital, or if he or she has returned home on family placement and that has broken down (see the *Children Act 1989*, s.23A and the *Children (Leaving Care) Regulations 2001* regulation 4).

10.38 The *Children Act 1989* (s.20(3)) places a duty on children's services authorities to provide accommodation for a child in need aged 16 or over whose welfare is otherwise likely to be seriously prejudiced if they do not provide accommodation; and s.20(1) places a duty on children's services authorities to provide accommodation for children in need in certain other circumstances.

10.39 Responsibility for providing suitable accommodation for a relevant child or a child in need to whom a local authority owes a duty under s.20 of the *Children Act 1989* rests with the children's services authority. In cases where a housing authority considers that a section 20 duty is owed, they should verify this with the relevant children's services authority. In all cases of uncertainty as to whether a 16 or 17 year old applicant may be a relevant child or a child in need, the housing authority should contact the relevant children's services authority and, where necessary, should provide interim accommodation under s.188, pending clarification. A framework for joint assessment of 16 and 17 year olds will need to be established by housing and children's services authorities (and housing and children's services departments within unitary authorities) to facilitate the seamless discharge of duties and appropriate services to this client group.

See Chapter 12 for more detailed guidance on 16 and 17 year olds.

HAVING BEEN LOOKED AFTER, ACCOMMODATED OR FOSTERED AND AGED UNDER 21

10.40 A person under 21 who was (but is no longer) looked after, accommodated or fostered between the ages of 16 and 18 has a priority need for accommodation (other than a person who is a 'relevant student'). The terms 'looked after', 'accommodated' or 'fostered' are set out in the *Children Act 1989* (s.24) and include any person who has been:

i)   looked after by a local authority (i.e. has been subject to a care order or accommodated under a voluntary agreement);

ii) accommodated by or on behalf of a voluntary organisation;

iii) accommodated in a private children's home;

iv) accommodated for a consecutive period of at least three months:
   - by a health authority, special health authority, primary care trust or local education authority, or
   - in any care home or independent hospital or in any accommodation provided by a National Health Service trust; or

v) privately fostered.

A 'relevant student' means a care leaver under 24 to whom section 24B(3) of the *Children Act 1989* applies, and who is in full-time further or higher education and whose term-time accommodation is not available during a vacation. Under s.24B(5), where a social services authority is satisfied that a person is someone to whom s.24B(3) applies and needs accommodation during a vacation they must provide accommodation or the means to enable it to be secured.

10.41 Housing authorities will need to liaise with the social services authority when dealing with homeless applicants who may fall within this category of priority need.

HOMELESS AS A RESULT OF AN EMERGENCY

10.42 Applicants have a priority need for accommodation if they are homeless or threatened with homelessness as a result of an emergency such as fire, flood or other disaster. To qualify as an 'other disaster' the disaster must be in the nature of a flood or fire, and involve some form of physical damage or threat of damage. Applicants have a priority need by reason of such an emergency whether or not they have dependent children or are vulnerable for any reason.

CHAPTER 11
Intentional homelessness

11.1 This chapter provides guidance on determining whether an applicant became homeless, or threatened with homelessness, *intentionally* or *unintentionally*.

11.2 The duty owed towards those who are homeless, or threatened with homelessness, and who have a priority need for accommodation will depend upon whether they became homeless, or threatened with homelessness, intentionally or unintentionally. Section 191 defines the circumstances in which an applicant is to be regarded as having become homeless intentionally. Section 196 frames the same definitions in regard to someone who is threatened with homelessness.

11.3 The duty owed to applicants who have a priority need for accommodation but have become homeless, or threatened with homelessness, intentionally is less than the duty owed to those who have a priority need for accommodation and have become homeless, or threatened with homelessness, unintentionally. This recognises the general expectation that, wherever possible, people should take responsibility for their own accommodation needs and ensure that they do not behave in a way which might lead to the loss of their accommodation.

11.4 Where a housing authority finds an applicant to be homeless, or threatened with homelessness, intentionally they have a duty to provide the applicant (or secure that the applicant is provided) with advice and assistance in any attempts he or she may make to secure that accommodation becomes available (or does not cease to be available) for his or her occupation. Before this advice and assistance is given, the authority must assess the applicant's housing needs. The advice and assistance must include information about the likely availability in the authority's district of types of accommodation appropriate to the applicant's housing needs (including, in particular, the location and sources of such types of accommodation). Authorities should consider what best advice and assistance the authority could provide, for example, providing information about applying for social housing, local lettings in the private rented sector, rent deposit schemes or housing benefit eligibility – to help the applicant avoid homelessness or secure accommodation (see Chapter 2 for further guidance on preventing homelessness). Where such an applicant also has a priority need for accommodation the authority will also have a duty to secure accommodation for such period as will give the applicant a reasonable opportunity of securing accommodation for his or her occupation. See Chapter 14 for guidance on the main duties owed to applicants on completion of inquiries.

11.5 It is for housing authorities to satisfy themselves in each individual case whether an applicant is homeless or threatened with homelessness intentionally. Generally, it is not for applicants to 'prove their case'. The exception is where an applicant seeks to establish that, as a member of a household previously found to be homeless intentionally, he or she did not acquiesce in the behaviour that led to homelessness. In such cases, the applicant will need to demonstrate that he or she was not involved in the acts or omissions that led to homelessness, and did not have control over them.

11.6 **Housing authorities must not adopt general policies which seek to pre-define circumstances that do or do not amount to intentional homelessness or threatened homelessness (for example, intentional homelessness should not be assumed in cases where an application is made following a period in custody – see paragraph 11.14).** In each case, housing authorities must form a view in the light of all their inquiries about that particular case. Where the original incident of homelessness occurred some years earlier and the facts are unclear, it may not be possible for the housing authority to satisfy themselves that the applicant became homeless intentionally. In such cases, the applicant should be considered to be unintentionally homeless.

DEFINITIONS OF INTENTIONAL HOMELESSNESS

11.7 Sections 191(1) and 196(1) provide that a person becomes homeless, or threatened with homelessness, intentionally if:
   i)   he or she deliberately does or fails to do anything in consequence of which he or she ceases to occupy accommodation (or the likely result of which is that he or she will be forced to leave accommodation),
   ii) the accommodation is available for his or her occupation, and
   iii) it would have been reasonable for him or her to continue to occupy the accommodation.

However, for this purpose, an act or omission made in good faith by someone who was unaware of any relevant fact must not be treated as deliberate (see paragraph 11.20).

11.8   Sections 191(3) and 196(3) provide that a person must be treated as homeless, or threatened with homelessness, intentionally if:

i)   the person enters into an arrangement under which he or she is required to cease to occupy accommodation which it would have been reasonable for the person to continue to occupy,

ii)   the purpose of the arrangement is to enable the person to become entitled to assistance under Part 7, and

iii)   there is no other good reason why the person is homeless or threatened with homelessness.

WHOSE CONDUCT RESULTS IN INTENTIONAL HOMELESSNESS?

11.9   Every applicant is entitled to individual consideration of his or her application. This includes applicants where another member of their family or household has made, or is making, a separate application. It is the **applicant** who must deliberately have done or failed to do something which resulted in homelessness or threatened homelessness. Where a housing authority has found an applicant to be homeless intentionally, nothing in the 1996 Act prevents another member of his or her household from making a separate application. Situations may arise where one or more members of a household found to be intentionally homeless were not responsible for the actions or omissions that led to the homelessness. For example, a person may have deliberately failed to pay the rent or defaulted on the mortgage payments, which resulted in homelessness or threatened homelessness, against the wishes or without the knowledge of his or her partner. However, where applicants were not directly responsible for the act or omission which led to their family or household becoming homeless, but they acquiesced in that behaviour, then they may be treated as having become homeless intentionally themselves. In considering whether an applicant has acquiesced in certain behaviour, the Secretary of State recommends that the housing authority take into account whether the applicant could reasonably be expected to have taken that position through a fear of actual or probable violence.

CESSATION OF OCCUPATION

11.10   For intentional homelessness to be established there must have been actual occupation of accommodation which has ceased. However, occupation need not necessarily involve continuous occupation at all times, provided the accommodation was at the disposal of the applicant and available for his or her occupation. The accommodation which has been lost can be outside the UK.

CONSEQUENCE OF A DELIBERATE ACT OR OMISSION

11.11   For homelessness, or threatened homelessness, to be intentional it must be a consequence of a deliberate act or omission. Having established that there was a deliberate act or omission, the housing authority will need to decide whether the loss of the applicant's home, or the likelihood of its loss, is the reasonable result of that act or omission. This is a matter of cause and effect. An example would be where a person voluntarily gave up settled accommodation that it would have been reasonable for them to continue to occupy, moved into alternative accommodation of a temporary or unsettled nature and subsequently became homeless when required to leave the alternative accommodation. Housing authorities will, therefore, need to look back to the last period of settled accommodation and the reasons why the applicant left that accommodation, to determine whether the current incidence of homelessness is the result of a deliberate act or omission.

11.12 Where a person becomes homeless intentionally, that condition may persist until the link between the causal act or omission and the intentional homelessness has been broken. It could be broken, for example, by a period in settled accommodation which follows the intentional homelessness. Whether accommodation is settled will depend on the circumstances of the particular case. Factors such as security of tenure and length of residence will be relevant. It has been established that a period in settled accommodation after an incidence of intentional homelessness would make the deliberate act or omission which led to that homelessness irrelevant in the event of a subsequent application for housing assistance. Conversely, occupation of accommodation that was merely temporary rather than settled, for example, staying with friends on an insecure basis, may not be sufficient to break the link with the earlier intentional homelessness. However, a period in settled accommodation is not necessarily the only way in which a link with the earlier intentional homelessness may be broken: some other event, such as the break-up of a marriage, may be sufficient.

Probability of violence

11.13 In cases where there is a probability of violence against an applicant if they continue, or had continued, to occupy their accommodation, and the applicant was aware of measures that could have been taken to prevent or mitigate the risk of violence but decided not to take them, their decision cannot be taken as having caused the probability of violence, and thus, indirectly, having caused the homelessness. Authorities must not assume that measures which could have been taken to prevent actual or threatened violence would necessarily have been effective.

Ex-offenders[11]

11.14 Some ex-offenders may apply for accommodation or assistance in obtaining accommodation following a period in custody or detention because they have been unable to retain their previous accommodation, due to that period in custody or detention. In considering whether such an applicant is homeless intentionally, the housing authority will have to decide whether, taking into account all the circumstances, there was a likelihood that ceasing to occupy the accommodation could reasonably have been regarded at the time as a likely consequence of committing the offence.

Former members of the armed forces[12]

11.15 Where service personnel are required to vacate service quarters as a result of taking up an option to give notice to leave the service, and in so doing are acting in compliance with their contractual engagement, the Secretary of

11 There is no equivalent in the Welsh Code of Guidance.
12 There is no equivalent in the Welsh Code of Guidance.

State considers that they should not be considered to have become homeless intentionally.

DELIBERATE ACT OR OMISSION

11.16 For homelessness to be intentional, the act or omission that led to homelessness must have been deliberate, and applicants must always be given the opportunity to explain such behaviour. An act or omission should not generally be treated as deliberate, even where deliberately carried out, if it is forced upon the applicant through no fault of their own. Moreover, an act or omission made in good faith where someone is genuinely ignorant of a relevant fact must not be treated as deliberate (see paragraph 11.24).

11.17 Generally, an act or omission should not be considered deliberate where:

i)   the act or omission was non-payment of rent which was the result of housing benefit delays, or financial difficulties which were beyond the applicant's control;

ii) the housing authority has reason to believe the applicant is incapable of managing his or her affairs, for example, by reason of age, mental illness or disability;

iii) the act or omission was the result of limited mental capacity; or a temporary aberration or aberrations caused by mental illness, frailty, or an assessed substance abuse problem;

iv) the act or omission was made when the applicant was under duress;

v)   imprudence or lack of foresight on the part of an applicant led to homelessness but the act or omission was in good faith.

11.18 An applicant's actions would not amount to intentional homelessness where he or she has lost his or her home, or was obliged to sell it, because of rent or mortgage arrears resulting from significant financial difficulties, and the applicant was genuinely unable to keep up the rent or mortgage payments even after claiming benefits, and no further financial help was available.

11.19 Where an applicant has lost a former home due to rent arrears, the reasons why the arrears accrued should be fully explored. Similarly, in cases which involve mortgagors, housing authorities will need to look at the reasons for mortgage arrears together with the applicant's ability to pay the mortgage commitment when it was taken on, given the applicant's financial circumstances at the time.

11.20 Examples of acts or omissions which may be regarded as deliberate (unless any of the circumstances set out in paragraph 11.17 apply) include the following, where someone:

i)   chooses to sell his or her home in circumstances where he or she is under no risk of losing it;

ii) has lost his or her home because of wilful and persistent refusal to pay rent or mortgage payments;

iii) could be said to have significantly neglected his or her affairs having disregarded sound advice from qualified persons;

iv) voluntarily surrenders adequate accommodation in this country or abroad which it would have been reasonable for the applicant to continue to occupy;

v)   is evicted because of his or her anti-social behaviour, for example by nuisance to neighbours, harassment etc.;

vi) is evicted because of violence or threats of violence by them towards another person;

vii) leaves a job with tied accommodation and the circumstances indicate that it would have been reasonable for him or her to continue in the employment and reasonable to continue to occupy the accommodation (but note paragraph 11.15).

AVAILABLE FOR OCCUPATION

11.21   For homelessness to be intentional the accommodation must have been available for the applicant and anyone reasonably expected to live with him or her. Further guidance on 'availability for occupation' is provided in Chapter 8.

REASONABLE TO CONTINUE TO OCCUPY THE ACCOMMODATION

11.22   An applicant cannot be treated as intentionally homeless unless it would have been reasonable for him or her to have continued to occupy the accommodation. Guidance on 'reasonable to continue to occupy' is provided in Chapter 8. It will be necessary for the housing authority to give careful consideration to the circumstances of the applicant and the household, in each case, and with particular care in cases where violence has been alleged.

11.23   Authorities are reminded that, where the applicant has fled his or her home because of violence or threats of violence likely to be carried out, and has failed to pursue legal remedies against the perpetrator(s) which might have prevented the violence or threat of violence, although these decisions (to leave the home and not pursue legal remedies) may be deliberate, the homelessness would not be intentional if it would not have been reasonable for the applicant to continue to occupy the home.

ACTS OR OMISSIONS IN GOOD FAITH

11.24   Acts or omissions made in good faith where someone was genuinely unaware of a relevant fact must not be regarded as deliberate. Provided that the applicant has acted in good faith, there is no requirement that ignorance of the relevant fact be reasonable.

11.25   A general example of an act made in good faith would be a situation where someone gave up possession of accommodation in the belief that they had no legal right to continue to occupy the accommodation and, therefore, it would not be reasonable for them to continue to occupy it. This could apply where someone leaves rented accommodation in the private sector having received a valid notice to quit or notice that the assured shorthold tenancy has come to an end and the landlord requires possession of the property, and the former tenant was genuinely unaware that he or she had a right to remain until the court granted an order and warrant for possession.

11.26   Where there was dishonesty there could be no question of an act or omission having been made in good faith.

11.27   Other examples of acts or omissions that could be made in good faith might include situations where:

i) a person gets into rent arrears, being unaware that he or she may be entitled to housing benefit or other social security benefits;

ii) an owner-occupier faced with foreclosure or possession proceedings to which there is no defence, sells before the mortgagee recovers possession through the courts or surrenders the property to the lender; or

iii) a tenant, faced with possession proceedings to which there would be no defence, and where the granting of a possession order would be mandatory, surrenders the property to the landlord.

In (iii) although the housing authority may consider that it would have been reasonable for the tenant to continue to occupy the accommodation, the act should not be regarded as deliberate if the tenant made the decision to leave the accommodation in ignorance of material facts, e.g. the general pressure on the authority for housing assistance.

APPLICANT ENTERS INTO AN ARRANGEMENT

11.28   Housing authorities will need to be alert to the possibility of collusion by which a person may claim that he or she is obliged to leave accommodation in order to take advantage of the homelessness legislation. Some parents and children, for example, may seek to take advantage of the fact that 16 and 17 year old applicants have a priority need for accommodation. Collusion is not confined to those staying with friends or relatives but can also occur between landlords and tenants. Housing authorities, while relying on experience, nonetheless need to be satisfied that collusion exists, and must not rely on hearsay or unfounded suspicions. For collusion to amount to intentional homelessness, s.191(3) specifies that there should be no other good reason for the applicant's homelessness. Examples of other good reasons include overcrowding or an obvious breakdown in relations between the applicant and his or her host or landlord. In some cases involving collusion the applicant may not actually be homeless, if there is no genuine need for the applicant to leave the accommodation. See paragraphs 8.9–8.12 for further guidance on applicants asked to leave by family or friends.

FAMILIES WITH CHILDREN UNDER 18

11.29   It is important that social services are alerted as quickly as possible to cases where the applicant has children under 18 and the housing authority considers the applicant may be homeless, or threatened with homelessness, intentionally. Section 213A(2) therefore requires housing authorities to have arrangements in place to ensure that all such applicants are invited to agree to the housing authority notifying the social services authority of the essential facts of their case. The arrangements must also provide that, where consent is given, the social services authority are made aware of the essential facts and, in due course, of the subsequent decision on the homelessness case. See Chapter 13 for further guidance on section 213A.

FURTHER APPLICATIONS FOR ASSISTANCE

11.30   There is no period of disqualification if someone wants to make a fresh application after being found intentionally homeless. Where a person whose application has just been decided makes a fresh application, the authority will need to decide whether there are any new facts in the fresh application which render it different from the earlier application. If no new facts are revealed, or any new facts are of a trivial nature, the authority would not be required to consider the new application. However, where the fresh application does reveal substantive new facts, the authority must treat the fresh application in the same way as it would any other application for accommodation or assistance in obtaining accommodation. Therefore, if the authority have reason to believe that the person is homeless or threatened with homelessness, the authority must make inquiries under s.184 and decide whether any interim duty is owed under s.188(1). See Chapter 6 for guidance on inquiries and Chapter 7 for guidance on the interim duty.

CHAPTER 12
16 & 17 Year olds

12.1 This chapter provides guidance on specific duties towards 16 and 17 year old applicants.
Priority need
12.2 All 16 and 17 year old homeless applicants have a priority need for accommodation except those who are:
   i)   a relevant child, or
   ii) a child in need who is owed a duty under s.20 of the *Children Act 1989*.
   See Chapter 10 for more detailed guidance on priority need.

Relevant child or child in need owed a duty under s.20 of the 1989 Act
12.3 A relevant child is a child aged 16 or 17 who has been looked after by a local authority for at least 13 weeks since the age of 14 and has been looked after at some time while 16 or 17 and who is not currently being looked after (i.e. an 'eligible child' for the purposes of paragraph 19B of Schedule 2 to the *Children Act 1989*). In addition, a child is also a relevant child if he or she would have been looked after by the local authority as an eligible child but for the fact that on his or her 16th birthday he or she was detained through the criminal justice system, or in hospital, or if he or she has returned home on family placement and that has broken down (see the *Children Act 1989*, s.23A and the *Children (Leaving Care) Regulations 2001*, Regulation 4).
12.4 The *Children Act 1989* (s.20(3)) places a duty on children's services authorities to provide accommodation for a child in need aged 16 or over whose welfare is otherwise likely to be seriously prejudiced if they do not provide accommodation; and s.20(1) places a duty on children's services authorities to provide accommodation for children in need in certain other circumstances.
12.5 Responsibility for providing suitable accommodation for a relevant child or a child in need to whom a local authority owes a duty under s.20 of the *Children Act 1989* rests with the children's services authority. In cases where a housing authority considers that a s.20 duty is owed, they should verify this with the relevant children's services authority.
12.6 In all cases of uncertainty as to whether a 16 or 17 year old applicant may be a relevant child or a child in need, the housing authority should contact the relevant children's services authority and, where necessary, should provide interim accommodation under s.188, pending clarification. A framework for joint assessment of 16 and 17 year olds will need to be established by housing and children's services authorities (and housing and children's services departments within unitary authorities) to facilitate the seamless discharge of duties and appropriate services to this client group.

Family relationships

12.7   The Secretary of State considers that, generally, it will be in the best interests of 16 and 17 year olds to live in the family home, unless it would be unsafe or unsuitable for them to do so because they would be at risk of violence or abuse. It is not unusual for 16 and 17 year olds to have a turbulent relationship with their family and this can lead to temporary disagreements and even temporary estrangement. Where such disagreements look likely to lead to actual or threatened homelessness the housing authority should consider the possibility of reconciliation with the applicant's immediate family, where appropriate, or the possibility of him or her residing with another member of the wider family.

Reconciliation

12.8   In all cases involving applicants who are 16 or 17 years of age a careful assessment of the young person's circumstances and any risk to them of remaining at home should be made at the first response. Some 16 and 17 year olds may be at risk of leaving home because of a temporary breakdown in their relationship with their family. In such cases, the housing authority may be able to effect a reconciliation with the family. In some cases, however, relationships may have broken down irretrievably, and in others it may not be safe or desirable for the applicant to remain in the family home, for example, in cases involving violence or abuse.

12.9   Therefore, any mediation or reconciliation will need careful brokering and housing authorities may wish to seek the assistance of social services in all such cases.

Collusion

12.10   Where homelessness can not be avoided, local authorities should work with 16 and 17 year olds, and their families where appropriate, to explore alternative housing options. Where the main homelessness duty is owed young people need to be given the chance to consider a range of housing options including but not limited to any accommodation to be offered under s.193. Clear and accurate information is essential to allow young people to identify the right housing solution for them.

12.11   Some parents and children may seek to take advantage of the fact that 16 and 17 year old applicants have a priority need for accommodation. Housing authorities will therefore need to be alive to the possibility of collusion when assessing applications from this client group. Section 191(3) (intentional homelessness) will apply in cases where there is no genuine basis for homelessness and parents have colluded with a child and fabricated an arrangement under which the child has been asked to leave the family home (see Chapter 11 for guidance on intentional homelessness).

Care and support needs

12.12   Where young people actually become homeless and are provided with accommodation, local authorities should consider whether they have any care or support needs. Many young people who have experienced homelessness may lack skills in managing their affairs and require help with managing a tenancy and operating a household budget. Those estranged from their family, particularly care leavers, may lack the advice and support normally available to young people from family, friends and other mentors. 16 and 17 year olds who are homeless and estranged from their family will be particularly vulnerable and in need of support.

12.13   Housing authorities will need to recognise that accommodation solutions for this client group are likely to be unsuccessful if the necessary support is not provided. Close liaison with social services, the Supporting People team and agencies working with young people will be essential. Most 16 and 17 year old applicants are likely to benefit from a period in supported accommodation before moving on to a tenancy of their own, but housing authorities should consider the circumstances of each case.

12.14   **Housing authorities are reminded that Bed and Breakfast (B&B) accommodation is unlikely to be suitable for 16 and 17 year olds who are in need of support. Where B&B accommodation is used for this group it ought to be as a last resort for the shortest time possible and housing authorities will need to ensure that appropriate support is provided where necessary.** See Chapter 17 on the suitability of accommodation for further guidance on the use of B&B accommodation.

12.15   16 and 17 year olds (including lone parents) who apply for housing assistance may also have care and support needs that need to be assessed. **The Secretary of State recommends that housing authorities and social services authorities (and the relevant departments within unitary authorities) have arrangements in place for joint assessments of such young people's needs, whether the application is made initially to the housing department or social services department.** In all cases where an applicant may have care, health or other support needs, it is recommended that the housing authority liaise with the social services authority, the Supporting People team and other agencies (for example, the Primary Care Trust, Criminal Justice Services, and voluntary and community organisations), as appropriate, as part of their inquiries. A joint consideration of an applicant's housing and support needs may be crucial to assist the authority in establishing whether the applicant has a priority need for accommodation and any non-housing support needs (see Chapter 4 for guidance on securing support services and Chapter 5 for guidance on joint working).

Lone teenage parents under 18

12.16   The provision of suitable accommodation with support for lone parents under 18 is a key part of the Government's Teenage Pregnancy Strategy. Providing accommodation with support for 16 and 17 year old lone parents is important for a very vulnerable group at risk of social isolation. It increases the likelihood of them making a successful transition to an independent tenancy and reduces the risk of subsequent homelessness.

12.17   The Government's objective is that all 16 and 17 year old lone parents who cannot live with their parents or partner should be offered accommodation with support. Housing authorities should work with social services, RSLs, the local teenage pregnancy co-ordinator and relevant voluntary organisations in their district to ensure that the Government's objective is met. The allocation of appropriate housing and support should be based on consideration of the young person's housing and support needs, their individual circumstances and their views and preferences. Young parents under the age of 16 must always be referred to social services so that their social care needs may be assessed. Housing authorities may find it helpful to refer to *Guidelines for Good Practice in Supported Accommodation for Young Parents*, separate guidance published jointly by DTLR and the Teenage Pregnancy Unit in September 2001 (available from **www.teenagepregnancyunit.gov.uk**).

CHAPTER 13
Co-operation in certain cases involving children

13.1   This chapter provides guidance on the duty housing authorities and social services authorities have to co-operate in certain cases involving children.

13.2   Section 10 of the *Children Act 2004* establishes a duty on county level and unitary authorities to make arrangements to promote co-operation between the authority, relevant partners (including district authorities) and other persons or bodies engaged in activities in relation to children, to improve the well-being of children and young people in the authority's area. Relevant partners are required to co-operate with the authority. Section 11 of the 2004 Act requires a range of agencies – including county level and unitary authorities and district authorities where there are two tiers of local government – to make arrangements for ensuring that their functions are discharged having regard to the need to safeguard and promote the welfare of children. See Chapter 5 for guidance on joint working.

13.3   Where an applicant is eligible for assistance and unintentionally homeless, and has a priority need because there is one or more dependent child in his or her household, the housing authority will owe a main homelessness duty to secure that accommodation is available to them. However, not all applicants with dependent children will be owed a main homelessness duty. Applicants who are found to be ineligible for assistance are not entitled to homelessness assistance under Part 7 of the 1996 Act. Where an applicant with a priority need is found to be eligible but homeless intentionally, s.190(2) requires the housing authority to secure accommodation for such period as will give the applicant a reasonable opportunity to secure accommodation for him/herself and to ensure that the applicant is provided with advice and assistance in any attempts he or she may make to secure accommodation for his or her occupation. Where an applicant with a priority need is found to be eligible but threatened with homelessness intentionally, s.195(5) requires the housing authority to ensure that the applicant is provided with advice and assistance in any attempts he or she may make to secure that accommodation does not cease to be available for his or her occupation. See Chapter 14 for guidance on the main duties owed to applicants on completion of inquiries, including the duty to provide advice and assistance.

13.4   In each of the above cases, there is a possibility that situations could arise where families may find themselves without accommodation and any prospect of further assistance from the housing authority. This could give rise to a situation in which the children of such families might become children in need, within the meaning of the term as set out in s.17 of the *Children Act 1989*.

13.5   In such cases, it is important that local authority children's services are alerted as quickly as possible because the family may wish to seek assistance under Part 3 of the *Children Act 1989*, in circumstances in which they are owed no, or only limited, assistance under the homelessness legislation. This will give local authority children's services the opportunity to consider the circumstances of the child(ren) and family, and plan any response that may be deemed by them to be appropriate.

13.6   Section 213A of the 1996 Act applies where a housing authority has reason to believe that an applicant for assistance under Part 7 with whom a person under the age of 18 normally resides, or might reasonably be expected to reside:

a)   may be ineligible for assistance;

b)   may be homeless and may have become so intentionally; or

c)   may be threatened with homelessness intentionally.

In these circumstances, a housing authority is required to have arrangements in place to ensure that the applicant is invited to consent to the referral of the essential facts of his or her case to the social services authority for the district (or, in the case of a unitary authority, the social services department of the authority). The arrangements must also provide that, where consent is given, the social services authority or department is made aware of the essential facts and, in due course, of the subsequent decision in relation to the homelessness case.

13.7   The requirement to obtain the applicant's consent to the referral of the essential facts of his or her case under section 213A(2) or (3) does not affect any other power for the housing authority to disclose information about a homelessness case to the social services authority or department. For example, even where consent is withheld, the housing authority should disclose information about a homelessness case to the social services authority, if they have reason to believe that a child is, or may be, at risk of significant harm, as laid out in Chapter 5 of *Working Together to Safeguard Children: A guide to inter-agency working to safeguard and promote the welfare of children* (2006). *Working Together* was recently revised to reflect developments in legislation, policy and practice. It was published in April 2006 and can be found on the *Every Child Matters* website at http://www.everychildmatters.gov.uk/socialcare/safeguarding/workingtogether/

13.8   Where a family with one or more children has been found ineligible for assistance under Part 7 or homeless, or threatened with homelessness, intentionally and approaches the social services authority, that authority will need to decide whether the child is a 'child in need' under the terms of the *Children Act 1989*, by carrying out an assessment of their needs in accordance with the *Framework for the Assessment of Children in Need and their Families* (2000), Department of Health. The findings of the assessment should provide the basis for the decision as to whether the child is a 'child in need' and what, if any, services should be offered to the child in order to safeguard and promote his/her welfare. Section 17 of the *Children Act 1989* requires a local authority to promote the upbringing of children within their family, in so far as this is consistent with their general duty to safeguard and promote their welfare. The social services authority might wish to consider, for example, whether the best way of meeting the child's needs would be by assisting the family to obtain accommodation, for example by providing temporary accommodation or a rent deposit, as part of the exercise of its duty set out in s.17 of the Children Act 1989. *Local Authority Circular 2003(13): Guidance on accommodating children in need and their families* provides further guidance to social services authorities on the effect of s.17.

13.9 Where a social services authority has been made aware of a family found to be ineligible for assistance or homeless, or threatened with homelessness, intentionally by the housing authority, and they consider the needs of a child or children could best be met by helping the family to obtain accommodation, they can request the housing authority to provide them with such advice and assistance as is reasonable in the circumstances. Under s.213A(5), the housing authority must comply with such a request. Advice and assistance as is reasonable in the circumstances might include, for example, help with locating suitable accommodation and making an inspection of the property to ensure that it meets adequate standards of fitness and safety. However, the housing authority is not under a duty to provide accommodation for the family in these circumstances.

13.10 Section 213A(6) requires unitary authorities to have similar arrangements in place so that the housing department provide the social services department with such advice and assistance as they may reasonably request.

13.11 Housing authorities may also wish to consider alerting social services authorities to cases where an applicant whose household includes a child has refused an offer of accommodation which the authority is satisfied is suitable, and the authority has made a decision that it has discharged its homelessness duty under Part 7. In such cases the household could find itself without accommodation and any prospect of further assistance from the housing authority. The applicant would, however, need to consent to the housing authority notifying the social services authority of the essential facts of his or her case (unless the housing authority has any other powers to disclose the information without consent).

CHAPTER 14
Main duties owed to applicants on completion of inquiries

14.1 This chapter provides guidance on the main duties owed to applicants where the housing authority has completed its inquiries and is satisfied that an applicant is eligible for assistance and homeless or threatened with homelessness. The chapter also provides guidance on the circumstances that will bring the s.193(2) duty ('the main homelessness duty') to an end.

14.2 In many cases early, effective intervention can prevent homelessness occurring. The Secretary of State considers that housing authorities should take steps to prevent homelessness wherever possible, and offer a broad range of advice and assistance to those who face the prospect of losing their current home. However, where a housing authority has completed inquiries made under s.184 (see Chapter 6 for guidance on applications) and is satisfied that an applicant is eligible for assistance and homeless or threatened with homelessness, then one or more of the duties outlined in this chapter will apply under Part 7.

14.3 No duty is owed under Part 7 to applicants who are ineligible for assistance or not homeless or threatened with homelessness. However, homelessness strategies should aim to prevent homelessness amongst all households in the district and under s.179 advice and information about homelessness and the prevention of homelessness must be available free of charge to any person in the district, including these applicants. Housing authorities may also choose to offer other assistance to help them obtain accommodation, such as a rent deposit.

DUTIES TO PROVIDE ADVICE AND ASSISTANCE[13]

14.4 Housing authorities have a duty to ensure that the applicant is provided with advice and assistance in a number of different circumstances, and these are dealt with below. These duties require an assessment to be made of the housing needs of the applicant before advice and assistance is provided. This assessment may need to range wider than the housing authority's inquiries into the applicant's homelessness carried out for the purpose of s.184, and should inform the provision of appropriate advice and assistance for that particular applicant. Among other things, the Secretary of State considers the assessment should identify any factors that may make it difficult for the applicant to secure accommodation for him or herself, for example, poverty, outstanding debt, health problems, disabilities and whether English is not a first language. In particular, housing authorities are advised to take account of the circumstances that led to the applicant's homelessness, or threatened homelessness, since these may impact on his or her ability to secure and maintain accommodation and may indicate what types of accommodation would be appropriate.

DUTIES OWED TO APPLICANTS WHO ARE THREATENED WITH HOMELESSNESS

14.5 Under s.175(4), a person is 'threatened with homelessness' if he or she is likely to become homeless within 28 days. However, the Secretary of State considers that housing authorities should not wait until homelessness is a likelihood or is imminent before providing advice and assistance. Early intervention may enable homelessness to be prevented, or delayed sufficiently to allow for a planned move to be arranged. However, where a housing authority has completed its inquiries under s.184 and is satisfied that an applicant is eligible for assistance and threatened with homelessness, then the specific duties outlined in paragraphs 14.6–14.9 below will apply.

Unintentionally threatened with homelessness and has priority need (s.195(2))

14.6 Where the authority are satisfied that an applicant is threatened with homelessness unintentionally, eligible for assistance and has a priority need for accommodation, it has a **duty** under s.195(2) *to take reasonable steps to secure that accommodation does not cease to be available for the applicant's occupation.*

14.7 Such reasonable steps may include for example, negotiation with the applicant's landlord or, in cases where the applicant has been asked to leave by

---

13 The Welsh Guidance (paras 16.32–16.36) is slightly more detailed.

family and friends, by exploring the scope for mediation and the provision of support to the household in order to ease any pressures that may have led to the applicant being asked to leave. Where a housing authority is able to identify the precise reasons why the applicant is being required to leave his or her current accommodation – for example, by interviewing the applicant and visiting his or her landlord or family or friends (as appropriate) – there may be specific actions that the housing authority or other organisations can take, for example, addressing rent arrears due to delays in housing benefit payments or providing mediation services through the voluntary sector, that can prevent the threat of homelessness being realised. See Chapter 2 for further guidance on preventing homelessness.

14.8   Under s.195(3A), as soon as an authority has become subject to a duty under s.195(2), the authority must give the applicant a copy of the statement included in their allocation scheme about their policy on offering choice to people allocated housing accommodation under Part 6. Authorities are required to include such a statement in their allocation scheme by virtue of s.167(1A) of the 1996 Act.

14.9   Where the housing authority is under a duty under s.195(2) and they are unable to prevent the applicant losing his or her current accommodation, the authority will need to secure alternative suitable accommodation for the applicant. Authorities should not delay; arrangements to secure alternative accommodation should begin as soon as it becomes clear that it will not be possible to prevent the applicant from losing their current home. Section 195(4) provides that, where alternative suitable accommodation is secured, the provisions of s.193(3) to (9) will apply in relation to the duty under s.195(2) as they apply in relation to the duty under s.193(2) (see paragraphs 14.17 to 14.24 below).

Unintentionally threatened with homelessness, no priority need (s.195(5) and s.195(9))

14.10   Where the housing authority are satisfied that an applicant is threatened with homelessness, eligible for assistance and does not have a priority need for accommodation, it has a **duty** under s.195(5) *to ensure that the applicant is provided with advice and assistance in any attempts he or she may make to secure that accommodation does not cease to be available for his or her occupation.*

14.11   In addition, where the housing authority are satisfied that an applicant is threatened with homelessness unintentionally, it has a **power** under s.195(9) *to take reasonable steps to secure that accommodation does not cease to be available for the applicant's occupation.* See Chapter 2 for guidance on preventing homelessness and paragraph 14.7 above.

Intentionally threatened with homelessness and has priority need (s.195(5))

14.12   Where the authority are satisfied that an applicant is threatened with homelessness intentionally, eligible for assistance and has a priority need for accommodation, the housing authority has a **duty** under s.195(5) *to ensure that the applicant is provided with advice and assistance in any attempts he or she may make to secure that accommodation does not cease to be available for his or her occupation.* See Chapter 2 for guidance on preventing homelessness.

DUTIES OWED TO APPLICANTS WHO ARE HOMELESS

14.13   Under s.175 a person is 'homeless' if he or she has no accommodation in the UK or elsewhere which is available for his or her occupation and which that person has a legal right to occupy. Where a housing authority has completed its inquiries under s.184 and is satisfied that an applicant is eligible for assistance and homeless then the specific duties outlined below will apply.

Unintentionally homeless and has priority need (s.193(2))

14.14   Where an applicant is unintentionally homeless, eligible for assistance and has a priority need for accommodation, the housing authority has a **duty** under s.193(2) *to secure that accommodation is available for occupation by the applicant* (unless it refers the application to another housing authority under s.198). This is commonly known as 'the main homelessness duty'. In all cases, the accommodation secured must be available for occupation by the applicant together with any other person who normally resides with him or her as a member of his or her family, or any other person who might reasonably be expected to reside, with him or her, and must be suitable for their occupation. See Chapter 16 for guidance on discharging the duty to secure accommodation and Chapter 17 for guidance on suitability of accommodation.

14.15   Acceptance of a duty under s.193(2) does not prevent an immediate allocation of accommodation under Part 6 of the 1996 Act if the applicant has the necessary priority under the housing authority's allocation scheme. Under s.193(3A), as soon as an authority has become subject to a duty under s.193(2), the authority must give the applicant a copy of the statement included in their allocation scheme about their policy on offering choice to people allocated housing accommodation under Part 6. Authorities are required to include such a statement in their allocation scheme by virtue of s.167(1A) of the 1996 Act.

14.16   If the housing authority has notified the applicant that it proposes to refer the case to another housing authority, the authority has a duty under s.200(1) to secure that accommodation is available for the applicant until he or she is notified of the decision whether the conditions for referral of his case are met. The duty under s.200(1) is therefore an interim duty only. Once it has been established whether or not the conditions for referral are met, a duty under s.193(2) will be owed by either the notified housing authority or the notifying housing authority. See Chapter 18 for guidance on referrals to another housing authority.

How the s.193(2) duty ends (this also applies where alternative accommodation has been secured under s.195(2))

14.17   The housing authority will cease to be subject to the duty under s.193(2) (the main homelessness duty) in the following circumstances:

i)   *the applicant accepts an offer of accommodation under Part 6 (an allocation of long term social housing)* (s.193(6)(c)): this would include an offer of an assured tenancy of a registered social landlord property via the housing authority's allocation scheme (see current guidance on the allocation of accommodation issued under s.169 of the 1996 Act);

ii) *the applicant accepts an offer of an assured tenancy (other than an assured shorthold tenancy) from a private landlord* (s.193(6)(cc): this could include an offer of an assured tenancy made by a registered social landlord;

iii) *the applicant accepts a qualifying offer of an assured shorthold tenancy from a private landlord* (s.193(7B)). The local authority must not approve an offer of an assured shorthold tenancy for the purposes of s.193(7B), unless they are satisfied that the accommodation is suitable and that it would be reasonable for the applicant to accept it (s.193(7F)) (see paragraph 14.25 below);

iv) *the applicant refuses a final offer of accommodation under Part 6 (an allocation of long term social housing)*: the duty does not end unless the applicant is informed of the possible consequences of refusal and of his or her right to ask for a review of the suitability of the accommodation (s.193(7)), the offer is made in writing and states that it is a final offer (s.193(7A)), and the housing authority is satisfied that the accommodation is suitable and that it would be reasonable for the applicant to accept it (s.193(7F)) (see paragraph 14.25 below);

v) *the applicant refuses an offer of accommodation to discharge the duty which the housing authority is satisfied is suitable for the applicant* (s.193(5)): the duty does not end unless the applicant is informed of the possible consequences of refusal and of his or her right to ask for a review of the suitability of the accommodation. The housing authority must also notify the applicant that it regards itself as having discharged its duty, before it can end;

vi) *the applicant ceases to be eligible for assistance as defined in s.185 of the 1996 Act*;

vii) *the applicant becomes homeless intentionally from accommodation made available to him or her under s.193 or s.195*; see Chapter 11 for guidance on determining whether an applicant became homeless intentionally;

viii) *the applicant otherwise voluntarily ceases to occupy as his or her principal home accommodation made available under s.193 or s.195.*

14.18 The Secretary of State recommends that applicants are given the chance to view accommodation before being required to decide whether they accept or refuse an offer, and before being required to sign any written agreement relating to the accommodation (e.g. a tenancy agreement). Under s.202(1A), an applicant who is offered accommodation can request a review of its suitability whether or not he or she has accepted the offer. See Chapter 17 for guidance on suitability and Chapter 19 for guidance on reviews.

Qualifying offer of an assured shorthold tenancy

14.19 An offer of an assured shorthold tenancy is a qualifying offer if:

i) it is made, with the approval of the authority, in pursuance of arrangements made by the authority with the landlord with a view to bringing the authority's duty under s.193 to an end;

ii) it is for a fixed term within the meaning of Part 1 of the *Housing Act 1988* (i.e. not a periodic tenancy) and

iii) it is accompanied by a written statement that states the term of the tenancy being offered and explains in ordinary language that there is no obligation on the applicant to accept the offer, but if the offer is accepted the housing authority will cease to be subject to the s.193 duty.

14.20 The s.193 duty will not end with acceptance of an offer of a qualifying tenancy unless the applicant signs a statement acknowledging that he or she has understood the written statement accompanying the offer.

Reasonable to accept an offer

14.21 Housing authorities must not make a final offer under Part 6 or approve a qualifying offer of an assured shorthold tenancy unless they are satisfied that the accommodation is suitable for the applicant and that it is reasonable for him or her to accept the offer (s.193(7F)) (see Chapter 17 for guidance on suitability). Where an applicant has contractual or other obligations in respect of his or her existing accommodation (e.g. a tenancy agreement or lease), the housing authority can reasonably expect the offer to be taken up only if the applicant is able to bring those obligations to an end before he is required to take up the offer (s.193(8)).

14.22 Housing authorities must allow applicants a reasonable period for considering offers of accommodation made under Part 6 that will bring the homelessness duty to an end whether accepted or refused.[14] There is no set reasonable period; some applicants may require longer than others depending on their circumstances, whether they wish to seek advice in making their decision and whether they are already familiar with the property in question. Longer periods may be required where the applicant is in hospital or temporarily absent from the district. In deciding what is a reasonable period, housing authorities must take into account the applicant's circumstances in each case.

Other circumstances that bring the s.193(2) duty to an end

14.23 Under s.193(6) the housing authority will also cease to be subject to the duty under s.193 in the following circumstances:

i) *the applicant ceases to be eligible for assistance as defined in s.185 of the 1996 Act;*

ii) *the applicant becomes homeless intentionally from accommodation made available to him or her under s.193 or s.195:* see Chapter 11 for guidance on determining whether an applicant became homeless intentionally;

iii) *the applicant otherwise voluntarily ceases to occupy as his or her only or principal home accommodation made available under s.193 or s.195.*

Further applications

14.24 Under s.193(9) a person who ceases to be owed a duty under s.193(2) can make a fresh application for accommodation or assistance in obtaining accommodation (see Chapter 6 for guidance on applications).

Unintentionally homeless and has no priority need (s.192(2) and s.192(3))

14.25 Where an applicant is unintentionally homeless, eligible for assistance and does not have a priority need for accommodation, the housing authority has a **duty** under s.192(2) *to ensure that the applicant is provided with advice and assistance in any attempts he or she may make to secure that accommodation becomes available for his or her occupation.* The housing authority might, for

14 The Welsh Code (para 16.19) still refers to a reasonable period to consider all offers.

example, provide assistance with a rent deposit or guarantee to help the applicant to obtain accommodation in the private rented sector, or advice on applying for an allocation of accommodation through the social housing waiting list or through another social landlord (see Chapter 2 for guidance on advisory services).

14.26   In addition, housing authorities have a **power** under s.192(3) *to secure that accommodation is available for occupation by the applicant.* Authorities should consider whether to use this power in all relevant cases.

Intentionally homeless and has priority need (s.190(2))

14.27   Where an applicant is intentionally homeless, eligible for assistance and has a priority need for accommodation, the housing authority has a **duty** under s.190(2) to:

   a)   *secure that accommodation is available for the applicant's occupation for such period as it considers will give him or her a reasonable opportunity of securing accommodation for his or her occupation (s.190(2)(a)); and*

   b)   *provide the applicant, or secure that the applicant is provided with, advice and assistance in any attempts he or she may make to secure that accommodation becomes available for his or her occupation (s.190(2)(b)).*

14.28   The accommodation secured must be suitable. Housing authorities must consider each case on its merits when determining the period for which accommodation will be secured.[15] A few weeks may provide the applicant with a reasonable opportunity to secure accommodation for him or herself. However, some applicants might require longer, and others, particularly where the housing authority provides pro-active and effective advice and assistance, might require less time. In particular, housing authorities will need to take account of the housing circumstances in the local area, including how readily other accommodation is available in the district, and have regard to the particular circumstances of the applicant, including the resources available to him or her to provide rent in advance or a rent deposit where this may be required by private landlords.

14.29   In addition to securing accommodation, the housing authority must ensure the applicant is provided with advice and assistance to help him or her secure accommodation for him/herself. This might include, for example, assistance with a rent deposit or guarantee to help the applicant to obtain accommodation in the private rented sector, or advice on applying for an allocation of long term social housing or accommodation through another social landlord. See Chapter 2 for guidance on advisory services.

Intentionally homeless and has no priority need (s.190(3))

14.30   Where an applicant is intentionally homeless, eligible for assistance and does not have a priority need for accommodation, the housing authority has a **duty** under s.190(3) *to ensure that the applicant is provided with advice and assistance in any attempts he or she may make to secure that accommodation becomes available for his or her occupation.* This might include, for example, assistance with a rent deposit or guarantee to help the applicant to obtain accommodation in

---

15 The Welsh Code (para 16.39) still refers to a 28-day period.

the private rented sector, or advice on applying for an allocation of long term social housing accommodation or through another social landlord. See Chapter 2 for guidance on advisory services.

CHAPTER 15
Discretionary powers to secure accommodation

15.1   This chapter provides guidance on the discretionary *powers* housing authorities have to secure accommodation for a household where they do not have a *duty* to secure accommodation for that household (see Chapter 16 for guidance on discharge of duties to secure accommodation).

15.2   Housing authorities have powers to secure accommodation for:
   i) applicants who are eligible for assistance, unintentionally homeless and do not have a priority need for accommodation;
   ii) applicants who request a review of the housing authority's decision on their case and who satisfy the relevant conditions, pending a decision on the review; and
   iii) applicants who appeal to the county court against the housing authority's decision and who satisfy the relevant conditions, pending the determination of the appeal.

15.3   The fact that a housing authority has decided that an applicant is ineligible for housing assistance under Part 7 does not preclude it from exercising its powers to secure accommodation pending a review or appeal. However, housing authorities should note that s.54 of, and Schedule 3 to, the *Nationality, Immigration and Asylum Act 2002* prevent them from exercising their powers to accommodate an applicant pending a review or appeal to the county court, where the applicant is a person who falls within one of a number of classes of person specified in Schedule 3. See paragraphs 9.20–9.23 in Chapter 9 on eligibility for assistance for further details.

WAYS OF SECURING ACCOMMODATION
15.4   A housing authority may only discharge its housing functions under Part 7 in the following ways:
   a) by securing that suitable accommodation provided by them is available for the applicant (s.206(1)(a));
   b) by securing that the applicant obtains suitable accommodation from some other person (s.206(1)(b)); or
   c) by giving the applicant such advice and assistance as will secure that suitable accommodation is available from some other person (s.206(1)(c)).

See Chapter 17 for guidance on the suitability of accommodation and Chapter 8 for guidance on when accommodation is available for occupation. In so far as is reasonably practicable, accommodation should be secured within the authority's own district (s.208(1)).

POWER TO SECURE ACCOMMODATION FOR APPLICANTS WHO ARE UNINTENTIONALLY HOMELESS AND DO NOT HAVE PRIORITY NEED

15.5   Under s.192(3), housing authorities may secure that accommodation is made available for applicants who are eligible for assistance, unintentionally homeless and do not have a priority need for accommodation. Where a housing authority decides to exercise this power it will still have a duty under s.192(2) to provide advice and assistance to the applicant in any attempts that he or she may make to secure accommodation for him/herself. See Chapter 14 for guidance on this duty.

15.6   By virtue of paragraph 4 of Schedule 1 to the *Housing Act 1985*, a tenancy granted under the power in s.192(3) will not be a secure tenancy. Housing authorities are reminded that all secure and introductory tenancies must be allocated in accordance with their allocation scheme, as framed under Part 6.

15.7   Housing authorities should consider using this power in all relevant cases. Any exercise of, or decision not to exercise, a power may be open to challenge by way of judicial review. In considering the use of this power, housing authorities must have regard to the legitimate expectations of others in housing need who have applied for an allocation of housing under Part 6, and to any need for accommodation to meet their obligations under Part 7.

15.8   Housing authorities should, in particular, consider exercising the s.192(3) power in circumstances where to do so would enable compliance with the obligations imposed on them by virtue of s.6 of the *Human Rights Act 1998* and where not doing so would mean acting in a way that may be incompatible with the applicant's Convention rights. The same is true of the power in s.195(8) (see paragraph 15.17 below).

15.9   Housing authorities may also wish to consider exercising the s.192(3) power to provide accommodation for a limited period to applicants such as key workers who are unintentionally homeless but do not have priority need under Part 7, or priority for an allocation under Part 6. This would be particularly appropriate where it would be in the interests of the local community for such persons to be accommodated in the district.

15.10   Non-secure tenancies will generally be suitable for a limited period only. They should be provided as part of a managed programme of accommodation to give the applicant an opportunity to secure a more settled housing solution in due course. This should be explained to the applicant from the outset and the housing authority should assist him or her to secure alternative accommodation. Reasonable notice should be given of a decision to stop exercising the power.

15.11   Housing authorities should not provide accommodation under s.192(3) as an alternative to allocating accommodation under Part 6 and should not allow non-secure tenancies to continue over the long-term.

POWERS TO ACCOMMODATE PENDING A REVIEW

15.12   Under s.202, applicants have the right to ask for a review of a housing authority's decision on a number of issues relating to their case (see Chapter 19 for guidance on reviews). Housing authorities have three powers to accommodate applicants pending a decision on the review. The relevant powers are found in s.188(3), s.195(8)(b) and s.200(5).

15.13 Under s.188(1), housing authorities must secure that accommodation is available for occupation by an applicant who they have reason to believe is:

(a) homeless,

(b) eligible for assistance, and

(c) in priority need,

pending their decision as to what duty, if any, is owed to that applicant under Part 7. See Chapter 7 for further guidance on this interim duty. Under s.188(3), if the applicant requests a review of the housing authority's decision on the duty owed to them under Part 7, the authority has the power to secure that accommodation is available for the applicant's occupation pending a decision on the review.

15.14 Section 188(3) includes a power to secure that accommodation is available where the applicant was found to be intentionally homeless and in priority need and:

(a) a duty was owed under s.190(2)(a);

(b) the s.190(2)(a) duty has been fully discharged; and

(c) the applicant is awaiting a decision on a review.

15.15 In considering whether to exercise their s.188(3) power, housing authorities will need to balance the objective of maintaining fairness between homeless persons in circumstances where they have decided that no duty is owed to them against proper consideration of the possibility that the applicant might be right. The Secretary of State is of the view that housing authorities should consider the following, although other factors may also be relevant:

(a) the merits of the applicant's case that the original decision was flawed and the extent to which it can properly be said that the decision was one which was either contrary to the apparent merits or was one which involved a very fine balance of judgment;

(b) whether any new material, information or argument has been put to them which could alter the original decision; and

(c) the personal circumstances of the applicant and the consequences to him or her of a decision not to exercise the discretion to accommodate.

The Secretary of State considers that when determining the merits of the applicant's case that the original decision was flawed, housing authorities should take account of whether there may have been procedural irregularities in making the original decision which could have affected the decision taken.

15.16 Housing authorities should give applicants reasonable notice to vacate accommodation provided under s.188(3) following an unsuccessful s.202 review. The Secretary of State considers that reasonableness should be judged against the particular applicant's circumstances. The applicant will require time to enable him or her to make alternative accommodation arrangements and housing authorities should take account of the fact that this may be easier for some applicants than others. Housing authorities may also require time to consider whether they should exercise their discretion under s.204(4) where the applicant appeals to the county court under s.204(1) (see paragraph 15.21).

15.17 Under s.195(5)(b), where a housing authority is satisfied that an applicant is:

(a) threatened with homelessness,

(b) eligible for assistance, and

(c) has a priority need, but

(d) became threatened with homelessness intentionally,

the authority is under a duty to provide the applicant (or secure that he or she is provided with) advice and assistance so that accommodation does not cease to be available for his or her occupation. Under s.195(8)(b), if the applicant requests a review of the housing authority's decision and, pending a decision on the review, becomes homeless, the housing authority may secure that accommodation is available for his or her occupation.

15.18 Under s.200(1), where a housing authority notifies another authority of its opinion that the conditions for the referral of an applicant's case to that authority are met, the authority has a duty to secure that accommodation is available for occupation by the applicant until a decision on the referral is reached. See Chapter 18 for guidance on local connection and referrals. If the applicant subsequently requests a review of the decision reached on the referral of his or her case, the notifying authority has the power under s.200(5) to secure that accommodation is available for the applicant's occupation pending the decision on that review.

15.19 Where, generally, only a small proportion of requests for a review are successful, it may be open to housing authorities to adopt a policy of deciding to exercise their powers to accommodate pending a review only in exceptional circumstances. However, such a policy would need to be applied flexibly and each case would need to be considered on its particular facts. In deciding whether there were exceptional circumstances, the housing authority would need to take account of all material considerations and disregard all those which were immaterial.

15.20 Where an applicant is refused accommodation pending a review, he or she may seek to challenge the decision by way of judicial review.

POWER TO ACCOMMODATE PENDING AN APPEAL TO THE COUNTY COURT

15.21 Applicants have the right to appeal to the county court on a point of law against a housing authority's decision on a review or, if they are not notified of the review decision, against the original homelessness decision (see Chapter 19 for guidance on appeals). Under s.204(4), housing authorities have the power to accommodate certain applicants:

(a) during the period for making an appeal against their decision, and

(b) if an appeal is brought, until it and any subsequent appeals are finally determined.

This power may be exercised where the housing authority was previously under a duty to secure accommodation for the applicant's occupation under s.188 (interim duty pending initial inquiries), s.190 (duty owed to applicants intentionally homeless and in priority need), or s.200 (interim duty owed pending decision on a referral). The power may also be exercised in a case where the applicant was owed a duty under s.195(5)(b) (intentionally threatened with homelessness and in priority need), the applicant requested a review and subsequently become homeless, and, in consequence, the housing authority had a power under s.195(8)(b) to secure accommodation pending the decision on the review.

15.22 The power under s.204(4) may be exercised whether or not the housing authority has exercised its powers to accommodate the applicant pending a review.

15.23 In deciding whether to exercise this power, housing authorities will need to adopt the same approach, and consider the same factors, as for a decision whether to exercise their power to accommodate pending a review (see paragraph 15.12).

15.24 Under s.204A, applicants have a right to appeal to the county court against a decision not to secure accommodation for them pending their main appeal. In deciding a s.204A appeal, the court must apply the principles that would be applied by the High Court on an application for judicial review. The county court cannot substitute its own decision as such. However, where the court quashes the decision of the housing authority, it may order the housing authority to accommodate the applicant, but only where it is satisfied that failure to do so would substantially prejudice the applicant's ability to pursue the main appeal on the homelessness decision.

CHAPTER 16
Securing accommodation

16.1 This chapter provides guidance on the different ways in which housing authorities can ensure that suitable accommodation is available for applicants. In the case of the main homelessness duty the obligation to secure such accommodation will continue until such time as the duty ends in accordance with s.193.

WAYS OF SECURING ACCOMMODATION

16.2 Section 206(1) provides that a housing authority may only discharge its housing functions under Part 7 in the following ways:

(a) by securing that suitable accommodation provided by them is available for the applicant (s.206(1)(a));

(b) by securing that the applicant obtains suitable accommodation from some other person (s.206(1)(b)); or

(c) by giving the applicant such advice and assistance as will secure that suitable accommodation is available from some other person (s.206(1)(c)).

16.3 Accommodation secured must be available for occupation by the applicant and any other person who normally resides with them as a member of their family, or might reasonably be expected to reside with them. The accommodation must also be suitable for their occupation. See Chapter 8 for guidance on when accommodation is available for occupation and Chapter 17 for guidance on the suitability of accommodation.

16.4 In deciding what accommodation needs to be secured housing authorities will need to consider whether the applicant has any support needs. Housing authorities will therefore need to make arrangements for effective links with the Supporting People team, the social services authority or other bodies (for example, Primary Care Trusts, Criminal Justice Services, RSLs and voluntary and community organisations) to ensure that a joint assessment of an applicant's housing and support needs can be made where necessary. See Chapter 4 for guidance on securing support services.

16.5 Where a housing authority has a duty under s.193(2) to secure accommodation for an applicant ('the main homelessness duty'), the Secretary of State recommends that the authority considers, where availability of suitable housing allows, securing settled (rather than temporary) accommodation that will bring the duty to an end in the immediate or short term. For example, an offer of accommodation under the housing authority's allocation scheme or a qualifying offer of an assured shorthold tenancy from a private landlord. See Chapter 14 for guidance on bringing the s.193(2) duty to an end.

16.6   The Secretary of State considers that, generally, it is inappropriate for social housing to be used as temporary accommodation for applicants other than for short periods (see paragraph 16.18 below). Except in limited circumstances where social housing is only going to be available for use for a short period, where an authority has placed a household in social housing as a temporary arrangement to fulfil a duty under s.193(2), the Secretary of State recommends that the authority considers offering the household a settled home under the terms of its allocation scheme as soon as possible.

ACCOMMODATION SECURED OUT OF DISTRICT

16.7   Section 208(1) requires housing authorities to secure accommodation within their district, in so far as is reasonably practicable. Housing authorities should, therefore, aim to secure accommodation within their own district wherever possible, except where there are clear benefits for the applicant of being accommodated outside of the district. This could occur, for example, where the applicant, and/or a member of his or her household, would be at risk of domestic or other violence in the district and need to be accommodated elsewhere to reduce the risk of further contact with the perpetrator(s) or where ex-offenders or drug/alcohol users would benefit from being accommodated outside the district to help break links with previous contacts which could exert a negative influence.

16.8   Where it is not reasonably practicable for the applicant to be placed in accommodation within the housing authority's district, and the housing authority places the applicant in accommodation elsewhere, s.208(2) requires the housing authority to notify the housing authority in whose district the accommodation is situated of the following:

i)   the name of the applicant;

ii)   the number and description of other persons who normally reside with the applicant as a member of his or her family or might reasonably be expected to do so;

iii)   the address of the accommodation;

iv)   the date on which the accommodation was made available;

v)   which function the housing authority is discharging in securing the accommodation.

The notice must be given in writing within 14 days of the accommodation being made available to the applicant.

16.9   The Secretary of State considers that applicants whose household has a need for social services support or a need to maintain links with other essential services within the borough, for example specialist medical services or special schools, should be given priority for accommodation within the housing authority's own district. In particular, careful consideration should be given to applicants with a mental illness or learning disability who may have a particular need to remain in a specific area, for example to maintain links with health service professionals and/or a reliance on existing informal support networks and community links. Such applicants may be less able than others to adapt to any disruption caused by being placed in accommodation in another district.[16]

ACCESS TO SUPPORT SERVICES

16.10 The Secretary of State recommends that housing authorities consider what arrangements need to be in place to ensure that households placed in temporary accommodation, within their district or outside, are able to access relevant support services, including health, education and social services. The Secretary of State considers that all babies and young children placed in temporary accommodation, for example, should have the opportunity to receive health and developmental checks from health visitors and/or other primary health care professionals. See Chapter 4 for further guidance on securing support services.

ACCOMMODATION PROVIDED BY THE HOUSING AUTHORITY

16.11 Housing authorities may secure accommodation by providing suitable accommodation for the applicant themselves (s.206(1)(a)), in which case the housing authority will be the immediate landlord of the applicant, for example, where the housing authority place the applicant in:

i) a house or flat from its own stock (i.e. held under Part 2 of the *Housing Act 1985*);

ii) a hostel owned by the housing authority; or

iii) accommodation leased by the housing authority from another landlord (e.g. under a private sector leasing agreement) and sub-let to the applicant.

Housing authority's own stock

16.12 In considering whether to provide accommodation from their own stock, housing authorities will need to balance the requirements of applicants owed a duty under Part 7 against the need to provide accommodation for others who have priority for an allocation under Part 6 of the 1996 Act. **The Secretary of State considers that, generally, it is inappropriate for social housing to be used as temporary accommodation for applicants other than for short periods.**[17]

16.13 Paragraph 4 of Schedule 1 to the *Housing Act 1985* provides that a tenancy granted by a housing authority in pursuance of any function under Part 7 is not a secure tenancy unless the housing authority notifies the tenant that it is such. Housing authorities are reminded that the allocation of secure and introductory tenancies must be made in accordance with their allocation scheme framed under the provisions of Part 6.

Housing authority hostels

16.14 Some housing authorities operate their own hostels and may wish to use these to accommodate certain applicants, particularly where they consider an

---

16 See in Wales, Welsh Code para 18.12 making further recommendations about accommodation in close proximity to previous addresses.

17 The Welsh Code (para 18.16) is not as strongly worded.

applicant would benefit from a supported environment. See paragraphs 16.25 and 16.26 for further guidance on the use of hostel accommodation.

Accommodation leased from a private landlord

16.15   Accommodation leased from a private landlord can provide housing authorities with a source of good quality, self-contained accommodation which can be let to applicants. Where there is a need for temporary accommodation, housing authorities are encouraged to maximise their use of this type of leasing, in so far as they can secure cost-effective arrangements with landlords.

16.16   Under the prudential capital finance system (introduced by the *Local Government Act 2003* on 1 April 2004) local authorities are free to borrow without Government consent, provided that they can service the debts without extra Government support. The authority must determine how much it can afford to borrow. The new system ended the former financial disincentives to use leasing (and other forms of credit). Consequently, there is no longer any need for special concessions relating to leases of property owned by private landlords where that property is used to accommodate households owed a duty under Part 7. When entering into leases, as when borrowing, the capital finance rules simply require authorities to be satisfied that the associated liabilities are affordable.

ACCOMMODATION SECURED FROM ANOTHER PERSON

16.17   Housing authorities may secure that the applicant obtains suitable accommodation from some other person (s.206(1)(b)). Housing authorities can make use of a wide range of accommodation, including housing in the private rented sector and accommodation held by RSLs. The following paragraphs outline a number of options for securing accommodation from another landlord, which are available to housing authorities.

Registered social landlords

16.18   As the proportion of housing stock in the social sector held by RSLs increases, housing authorities should ensure that they maximise the opportunities for securing housing from RSLs. Under s.213 of the 1996 Act, where requested by a housing authority, an RSL must assist the housing authority in carrying out their duties under the homelessness legislation by co-operating with them as far as is reasonable in the circumstances. Housing Corporation regulatory guidance, issued with the consent of the Secretary of State under s.36 of the 1996 Act, requires RSLs, on request, to provide a proportion of their stock for nominations and as temporary accommodation for people owed a homelessness duty under Part 7 of the 1996 Act – to such extent as is reasonable in the circumstances. **The Secretary of State considers that, generally, it is inappropriate for social housing to be used as temporary accommodation other than for short periods** (see paragraph 16.6 above).[18] Where a longer-term stay occurs or seems likely, the authority and RSL should consider offering an assured tenancy to bring the main homelessness duty to an end. See Annex 5 for further guidance on RSL co-operation with housing authorities.

---

18 The Welsh Code (para 18.23) is not as strongly worded.

16.19 Housing authorities may wish to consider contracting with RSLs for assistance in discharging their housing functions under arrangements whereby the RSL lease and/or manage accommodation owned by private landlords, which can be let to households owed a homelessness duty and nominated by the housing authority. A general consent under s.25 of the *Local Government Act 1988 (The General Consent under Section 25 of the Local Government Act 1988 for Financial Assistance to Registered Social Landlords or to Private Landlords to Relieve or Prevent Homelessness 2005)* allows housing authorities to provide RSLs with financial assistance in connection with such arrangements. Housing authorities must reserve the right to terminate such agreements, without penalty, after 3 years.

Private lettings

16.20 Housing authorities may seek the assistance of private sector landlords in providing suitable accommodation direct to applicants. A general consent under s.25 of the *Local Government Act 1988 (The General Consent under Section 25 of the Local Government Act 1988 for Financial Assistance to Registered Social Landlords or to Private Landlords to Relieve or Prevent Homelessness 2005)* allows housing authorities to provide financial assistance to private landlords in order to secure accommodation for people who are homeless or at risk of homelessness. This could involve, for example, the authority paying the costs of leases; making small one-off grants ('finders' fees') to landlords to encourage them to let dwellings to households owed a homelessness duty; paying rent deposits or indemnities to ensure accommodation is secured for such households; and making one-off grant payments which would prevent an eviction. There is no limit set on the amount of financial assistance that can be provided, however authorities are obliged to act reasonably and in accordance with their fiduciary duty to local tax and rent payers. Housing authorities may also make Discretionary Housing Payments (DHP) to a private landlord to meet a shortfall between the rent and the amount of housing benefit payable to a person who is homeless or at risk of homelessness. DHPs are intended to provide extra financial assistance where there is a shortfall in a person's eligible rent and the housing authority consider that the claimant is in need of further financial assistance. They are governed by the *Discretionary Housing Payment (Grant) Order 2001*. Housing authorities should also consider working with private landlords to arrange qualifying offers of assured shorthold tenancies which would bring the main homelessness duty to an end if accepted by the applicant. See paragraph 14.19 for guidance on qualifying offers.

Tenancies granted by private landlords and registered social landlords to assist with interim duties

16.21 Section 209 governs security of tenure where a private landlord provides accommodation to assist a housing authority discharge an **interim** duty, for example, a duty under s.188(1), s.190(2), s.200(1) or 204(4). Any such accommodation is exempt from statutory security of tenure until 12 months from the date on which the applicant is notified of the authority's decision under s.184(3) or s.198(5) or from the date on which the applicant is notified of the decision of any review under s.202 or an appeal under s.204, unless the landlord notifies the applicant that the tenancy is an assured or assured shorthold tenancy.

16.22   Where a private landlord or RSL lets accommodation directly to an applicant to assist a housing authority discharge any other homelessness duty, the tenancy granted will be an assured shorthold tenancy unless the tenant is notified that it is to be regarded as an assured tenancy.

Other social landlords

16.23   Under s.213 other social landlords, i.e. new town corporations and housing action trusts, have a duty to co-operate, as far as is reasonable in the circumstances, with a housing authority in carrying out their housing functions under Part 7 of the 1996 Act, if asked to do so.

Lodgings

16.24   Lodgings provided by householders may be suitable for some young and/or vulnerable single applicants. Housing authorities may wish to establish a network of such landlords in their district, and to liaise with social services who may operate supported lodgings schemes for people with support needs.

Hostels

16.25   Some applicants may benefit from the supportive environment which managed hostels can provide. Hostels can offer short-term support to people who are experiencing a temporary crisis, and provide an opportunity for them to regain their equilibrium and subsequently move on to live independently. Where an applicant appears to need support, particularly on-going support, and there is no social worker or support worker familiar with their case, the housing authority should request a community care assessment by the social services authority. However, housing authorities should not assume that a hostel will automatically be the most appropriate form of accommodation for vulnerable people, particularly in relation to young people, people with mental health problems and those who have experienced violence and/or abuse. In addition, where hostel accommodation is used to accommodate vulnerable young people or families with children, the Secretary of State considers that it would be inappropriate to accommodate these groups alongside adults with chaotic behavioural problems.

16.26   Housing authorities will need to take into account that some hostels are designed to meet short-term needs only. In addition to the question of whether the hostel accommodation would be suitable for the applicant for other than a short period, housing authorities should have regard to the need to ensure that bed spaces continue to be available in hostels for others who need them.

Women's refuges

16.27   Housing authorities should develop close links with women's refuges within their district, and neighbouring districts, to ensure they have access to emergency accommodation for women applicants who are fleeing domestic or other violence or who are at risk of such violence. However, housing authorities should recognise that placing an applicant in a refuge will generally be a temporary expedient only, and a prolonged stay could block a bed space that was urgently needed by someone else at risk. Refuges should be used to provide accommodation for the minimum period necessary before alternative suitable accommodation is secured elsewhere. Housing authorities should not delay in securing alternative accommodation in the hope that the applicant might return to her partner.

Bed and breakfast accommodation

16.28   Bed and Breakfast (B&B) accommodation caters for very short-term stays only and generally will afford residents only limited privacy and may lack certain important amenities, such as cooking and laundry facilities. Consequently, where possible, housing authorities should avoid using B&B hotels to discharge a duty to secure accommodation for applicants, unless, in the very limited circumstances where it is likely to be the case, it is the most appropriate option for an applicant. The Secretary of State considers B&B hotels as particularly unsuitable for accommodating applicants with family commitments and applicants aged 16 or 17 years who need support. See paragraphs 17.23 *et seq* in Chapter 17 for guidance on suitability and Chapter 12 for more detailed guidance on 16 and 17 year olds.

Accommodation provided by other housing authorities

16.29   Other housing authorities experiencing less demand for housing may be able to assist a housing authority by providing temporary or settled accommodation for homeless applicants. This could be particularly appropriate in the case of applicants who would be at risk of violence or serious harassment in the district of the housing authority to whom they have applied for assistance. Other housing authorities may also be able to provide accommodation in cases where the applicant has special housing needs and the other housing authority has accommodation available which is appropriate to those needs. Under s.213(1), where one housing authority requests another to help them discharge a function under Part 7, the other housing authority must co-operate in providing such assistance as is reasonable in the circumstances. Housing authorities are encouraged to consider entering into reciprocal and co-operative arrangements under these provisions. See Chapter 5 for guidance on the statutory provisions on co-operation between authorities.

Mobile homes

16.30   Although mobile homes may sometimes provide emergency or short-term accommodation, e.g. to discharge an interim duty, housing authorities will need to be satisfied that the accommodation is suitable for the applicant and his or her household, paying particular regard to their needs, requirements and circumstances and the conditions and facilities on the site. Caravans designed primarily for short-term holiday use should not be regarded as suitable as temporary accommodation for applicants.

Tenancies for minors

16.31   There are legal complications associated with the grant of a tenancy to a minor because a minor cannot hold a legal estate in land. However, if a tenancy is granted it is likely to be enforceable as a contract for necessaries (ie. the basic necessities of life) under common law. In some circumstances, social services authorities may consider it appropriate to underwrite a tenancy agreement for a homeless applicant who is under 18.

ADVICE AND ASSISTANCE THAT WILL SECURE ACCOMMODATION FROM ANOTHER PERSON

16.32   Housing authorities may secure accommodation by giving advice and assistance to an applicant that will secure that accommodation becomes available for him or her from another person (s.206(1)(c)). However, where an authority has a duty to secure accommodation, they will need to ensure that the advice and assistance provided results in suitable accommodation actually being secured. Merely assisting the applicant in any efforts that he or she might make to find accommodation would not be sufficient if suitable accommodation did not actually become available.

16.33   One example of securing accommodation in this way is where house purchase is a possibility for the applicant. Advice on all options for financing house purchase should be made available, especially those financial packages which may be suited to people on lower incomes.

16.34   One option to help people into home ownership is shared equity schemes (e.g. part buy/part rent or equity loans to assist with purchase). These schemes are mainly funded by the Housing Corporation and generally offered by RSLs. The Housing Corporation publishes booklets (available from their publication section) giving further details of the existing shared ownership and Homebuy schemes. A new HomeBuy scheme offering further opportunities for home ownership and building on the current schemes commenced on 1st April 2006.

16.35   In other cases, applicants may have identified suitable accommodation but need practical advice and assistance to enable them to secure it, for example the applicant may require help with understanding a tenancy agreement or financial assistance with paying a rent deposit.

16.36   Housing authorities should bear in mind that the advice and assistance must result in suitable accommodation being secured, and that applicants who wish to pursue this option may need alternative accommodation until this result is achieved.

APPLICANTS WHO NORMALLY OCCUPY MOVEABLE ACCOMMODATION (E.G. CARAVANS, HOUSEBOATS)

16.37   Under s.175(2) applicants are homeless if the accommodation available for their occupation is a caravan, houseboat, or other movable structure and they do not have a place where they are entitled, or permitted, to put it and live in it. If a duty to secure accommodation arises in such cases, the housing authority is not required to make equivalent accommodation available (or provide a site or berth for the applicant's own accommodation). However, the authority must consider whether such options are reasonably available, particularly where this would provide the most suitable solution to the applicant's accommodation needs.

Gypsies and Travellers[19]

16.38   The circumstances described in paragraph 16.37 will be particularly relevant in the case of Gypsies and Travellers. Where a duty to secure accommoda-

---

19 There is no equivalent in the Welsh Code.

tion arises but an appropriate site is not immediately available, the housing authority may need to provide an alternative temporary solution until a suitable site, or some other suitable option, becomes available. Some Gypsies and Travellers may have a cultural aversion to the prospect of 'bricks and mortar' accommodation. In such cases, the authority should seek to provide an alternative solution. However, where the authority is satisfied that there is no prospect of a suitable site for the time being, there may be no alternative solution. Authorities must give consideration to the needs and lifestyle of applicants who are Gypsies and Travellers when considering their application and how best to discharge a duty to secure suitable accommodation, in line with their obligations to act consistently with the *Human Rights Act 1998*, and in particular the right to respect for private life, family and the home.

Temporary to settled accommodation

16.39 Housing authorities are encouraged to test new approaches that would enable temporary accommodation to become settled accommodation. This would reduce the uncertainty and lack of security that households in temporary accommodation can face, and provide them with a settled home more quickly. Such approaches could be developed with housing associations through a range of 'temporary to settled' housing initiatives.

16.40 Each year approximately a quarter to a third of all leases of private sector accommodation held by social landlords expire. This presents an opportunity for the leased accommodation to be converted from use as temporary accommodation to the provision of settled housing, through negotiation with the landlord and the tenant during the final months of the lease. Where the household would be content to remain in the accommodation when the lease ends if it could be provided on a more settled basis, and the landlord would be prepared to let directly to the household, the local authority may wish to arrange for the landlord to make a 'qualifying offer' of an assured shorthold tenancy, for the purposes of s.193(7B). See paragraph 14.19 for guidance on 'qualifying offer'.

16.41 Where scope for conversion of temporary accommodation to settled accommodation is explored, the interests of the household must take priority, and the household should not be pressured to accept offers of accommodation that would bring the homelessness duty to an end.

16.42 There may also be limited potential for converting temporary accommodation leased from the private sector to a qualifying offer of an assured shorthold tenancy at the beginning or mid-point of a lease. However, this would probably require the lease to include a break clause to facilitate early termination.

16.43 While the local authority holds the lease of accommodation owned by a private sector landlord, the accommodation would not be capable of being offered to a household as a qualifying offer of an assured shorthold tenancy under s.193(7B). However, where a registered social landlord held such a lease, the accommodation may be capable of being offered to a household as a qualifying offer of an assured shorthold tenancy under s.193(7B) during the period of the lease, if all the parties agreed and the qualifying offer met the terms of s.193(7D).

CHAPTER 17
Suitability of accommodation

17.1 This chapter provides guidance on the factors to be taken into account when determining the suitability of temporary accommodation secured under the homelessness legislation. Key factors include: the needs, requirements and circumstances of each household; space and arrangement; health and safety considerations; affordability, and location. Annex 16 sets out the statutory definition of overcrowding and Annex 17 sets out the minimum recommended standards for Bed and Breakfast accommodation.

17.2 Section 206 provides that where a housing authority discharges its functions to secure that accommodation is available for an applicant the accommodation must be suitable. This applies in respect of all powers and duties to secure accommodation under Part 7, including interim duties such as those under s.188(1) and s.200(1). The accommodation must be suitable in relation to the applicant and to all members of his or her household who normally reside with him or her, or who might reasonably be expected to reside with him or her.

17.3 Suitability of accommodation is governed by s.210. Section 210(2) provides for the Secretary of State to specify by order the circumstances in which accommodation is or is not to be regarded as suitable for someone, and matters to be taken into account or disregarded in determining whether accommodation is suitable for someone.

17.4 Space and arrangement will be key factors in determining the suitability of accommodation. However, consideration of whether accommodation is suitable will require an assessment of all aspects of the accommodation in the light of the relevant needs, requirements and circumstances of the homeless person and his or her family. The location of the accommodation will always be a relevant factor (see paragraph 17.41).

17.5 Housing authorities will need to consider carefully the suitability of accommodation for applicants whose household has particular medical and/or physical needs. The Secretary of State recommends that physical access to and around the home, space, bathroom and kitchen facilities, access to a garden and modifications to assist sensory loss as well as mobility need are all taken into account. These factors will be especially relevant where a member of the household is disabled.

17.6 Account will need to be taken of any social considerations relating to the applicant and his or her household that might affect the suitability of accommodation. Any risk of violence or racial harassment in a particular locality must also be taken into account. Where domestic violence is involved and the applicant is not able to stay in the current home, housing authorities may need to consider the need for alternative accommodation whose location can be kept a secret and which has security measures and staffing to protect the occupants. For applicants who have suffered domestic violence who are accommodated temporarily in hostels or bed and breakfast accommodation, the accommodation may need to be gender-specific as well as have security measures.

17.7 Accommodation that is suitable for a short period, for example bed and breakfast or hostel accommodation used to discharge an interim duty pending inquiries under s.188, may not necessarily be suitable for a longer period, for example to discharge a duty under s.193(2).

17.8 As the duty to provide suitable accommodation is a continuing obligation, housing authorities must keep the issue of suitability of accommodation under review. If there is a change of circumstances of substance the authority is obliged to reconsider suitability in a specific case.

STANDARDS OF ACCOMMODATION

17.9 Section 210(1) requires a housing authority to have regard to the following provisions when assessing the suitability of accommodation for an applicant:

   – Parts 9 and 10 of the *Housing Act 1985* (the '1985 Act') (slum clearance and overcrowding), and

   – Parts 1 to 4 of the *Housing Act 2004* (the '2004 Act') (housing conditions, licensing of houses in multiple occupation, selective licensing of other residential accommodation and additional control provisions in relation to residential accommodation.)

Fitness for habitation[20]

17.10 Part 1 of the *Housing Act 2004* (the '2004 Act') contains provisions that replace the housing fitness regime in s.604 of the 1985 Act. From 6th April 2006, the fitness standard in the 1985 Act is replaced by a new evidence-based assessment of risks to health and safety in all residential premises (including HMOs), carried out using the Housing Health and Safety Rating System (HHSRS). Part 9 of the 1985 Act is retained, with amendments, to deal with hazards for which demolition or area clearance is the most appropriate option.

Housing Health and Safety Rating System (HHSRS)

17.11 Action by local authorities is based on a three-stage consideration: (a) the hazard rating determined under HHSRS; (b) whether the authority has a duty or power to act, determined by the presence of a hazard above or below a threshold prescribed by Regulations (Category 1 and Category 2 hazards); and (c) the authority's judgment as to the most appropriate course of action to deal with the hazard.

17.12 The purpose of the HHSRS assessment is to generate objective information in order to determine and inform enforcement decisions. HHSRS allows for the assessment of twenty nine categories of housing hazard and provides a method for rating each hazard. It does *not* provide a single rating for the dwelling as a whole or, in the case of HMOs, for the building as a whole. A hazard rating is expressed through a numerical score which falls within a band, ranging from Band A to J. Scores in Bands A to C are Category 1 hazards. Scores in Bands D to J are Category 2 hazards. If a housing authority considers that a Category 1 hazard exists on any residential premises, they have a duty under the 2004 Act to take appropriate enforcement action in relation to the hazard. They also have a power to take particular kinds of enforcement action in cases where they consider that a Category 2 hazard exists.

17.13 The HHSRS assessment is based on the risk to the *potential occupant who is most vulnerable to that hazard*. For example, stairs constitute a greater risk to the elderly, so for assessing hazards relating to stairs they are considered the

---

20 The Welsh Code (Chapter 19) does not reflect the implementation of the Housing Act 2004.

most vulnerable group. The very young as well as the elderly are susceptible to low temperatures. A dwelling that is safe for those most vulnerable to a hazard is safe for all.

17.14 Housing authorities should be familiar with the principles of the HHSRS and with the operational guidance issued under s.9 of the 2004 Act.

17.15 **The Secretary of State recommends that when determining the suitability of accommodation secured under the homelessness legislation, local authorities should, as a minimum, ensure that all accommodation is free of Category 1 hazards.** In the case of an out of district placement it is the responsibility of the placing authority to ensure that accommodation is free of Category 1 hazards.

Overcrowding

17.16 Part 10 of the 1985 Act is intended to tackle the problems of overcrowding in dwellings. Section 324 provides a definition of overcrowding which in turn relies on the room standard specified in s.325 and the space standard in s.326 (the standards are set out in Annex 17).

17.17 A room provided within an HMO may be defined as a 'dwelling' under Part 10 of the 1985 Act and the room and space standards will therefore apply. Housing authorities should also note that 'crowding and space' is one of the hazards assessed by the HHSRS. Any breach of the room and space standards under Part 10 is likely to constitute a Category 1 hazard.

Houses in Multiple Occupation (HMOs)[21]

17.18 Parts 2, 3 and 4 of the 2004 Act – which came into force on 6 April 2006 – contain provisions to replace Part 11 of the 1985 Act which relates to HMOs.

17.19 The 2004 Act introduces a new definition of an HMO. A property is an HMO if it satisfies the conditions set out in sections 254(2) to (4), has been declared an HMO under s.255 or is a converted block of flats to which s.257 applies.

17.20 Privately owned Bed and Breakfast or hostel accommodation that is used to accommodate a household pursuant to a homelessness function, and which is the household's main residence, will fall within this definition of an HMO. Buildings managed or owned by a public body (such as the police or the NHS), local housing authority, registered social landlord or buildings which are already regulated under other legislation (such as care homes or bail hostels) will be exempt from the HMO definition. Buildings which are occupied entirely by freeholders or long leaseholders, those occupied by only two people, or by a resident landlord with up to two tenants will also be exempt. Most student accommodation (housing students undertaking a course in higher or further education) will also be exempt if it is managed and controlled by the establishment in accordance with a code of management practice.

17.21 From 6 April 2006, local authorities have been required to undertake the mandatory licensing of all privately rented HMOs (except converted blocks of flats to which s.257 applies) of three or more storeys and occupied by five or more people who form two or more households. Local authorities will also have discretionary powers to introduce additional licensing schemes covering smaller HMOs. In order to be a licence holder, a landlord will have to be a 'fit and

---

21 The Welsh Code (Chapter 19) does not reflect the changes implemented by the Housing Act 2002.

proper' person, as defined in s.89 of the Act and demonstrate that suitable management arrangements are in place in their properties.

17.22   In addition a local authority will have to be satisfied that the HMO is suitable for the number of occupants it is licensed for and meets statutory standards relating to shared amenities and facilities, e.g. that it has an adequate number, type and quality of shared bathrooms, toilets and cooking facilities. These standards are set out in Schedule 3 to the *Licensing and Management of Houses in Multiple Occupation and Other Houses (Miscellaneous Provisions) (England) Regulations 2006* (SI No 2006/373). These 'amenity standards' will run alongside the consideration of health and safety issues under HHSRS. *The Housing (Management of Houses in Multiple Occupation) Regulations 1990* are to be replaced by the *Management of Houses in Multiple Occupation (England) Regulations 2006* (SI 2006/372). Neither the amenity standards nor the new management regulations apply to HMOs that are converted blocks of flats to which s.257 applies. It is intended that separate regulations will be made by July 6th to modify Part 2 of the 2004 Act (which deals with mandatory licensing) in so far as it relates to these types of HMO, and to extend, with modifications, the application of the new amenity standards and management regulations to these types of HMO. Until then they will continue to be subject to the registration schemes made under Part 11 of the 1985 Act. Transitional arrangements have been in place since April 2006 so that most HMOs that are registered in a 1985 scheme will automatically be licensed under the 2004 Act.

17.23   Local authorities also have discretion to extend licensing to privately rented properties in all, or part of, their area to address particular problems, such as low housing demand or significant incidence of anti-social behaviour. However, licensing in these selective circumstances is concerned only with property management and not the condition of the property.

BED AND BREAKFAST ACCOMMODATION

17.24   Bed and Breakfast (B&B) accommodation caters for very short-term stays only and generally will afford residents only limited privacy and may lack certain important amenities, such as cooking and laundry facilities. Consequently, where possible, housing authorities should avoid using B&B hotels to discharge a duty to secure accommodation for homeless applicants, unless, in the very limited circumstances where it is likely to be the case, it is the most appropriate option for the applicant.

17.25   Living in B&B accommodation can be particularly detrimental to the health and development of children. Under s.210(2), the Secretary of State has made the *Homelessness (Suitability of Accommodation) (England) Order 2003* (SI 2003 No. 3326) ('the Order'). The Order specifies that when accommodation is made available for occupation under certain functions in Part 7, B&B accommodation is not to be regarded as suitable for applicants with family commitments.

17.26   Housing authorities should, therefore, use B&B hotels to discharge a duty to secure accommodation for applicants with family commitments only as a last resort. Applicants with family commitments means an applicant –
(a) who is pregnant;
(b) with whom a pregnant woman resides or might reasonably be expected to reside; or

(c) with whom dependent children reside or might reasonably be expected to reside.

17.27 For the purpose of the Order, B&B accommodation means accommodation (whether or not breakfast is included):

(a) which is not separate and self-contained premises; and

(b) in which any of the following amenities is shared by more than one household:

(i)   a toilet;

(ii) personal washing facilities;

(iii) cooking facilities.

B&B accommodation does not include accommodation which is owned or managed by a local housing authority, a registered social landlord or a voluntary organisation as defined in section 180(3) of the *Housing Act 1996*.

17.28 B&B accommodation is not to be regarded as suitable for applicants with family commitments (except as specified in paragraph 17.29 below) for the purpose of discharging a duty under the following duties:

– section 188(1) (interim duty to accommodate in case of apparent priority need);

– section 190(2)(a) (duties to persons becoming homeless intentionally);

– section 193(2) (duty to persons with priority need who are not homeless intentionally);

– section 200(1) (duty to applicant whose case is considered for referral or referred); and

– section 195(2) (duties in case of threatened homelessness) where the accommodation is other than that occupied by the applicant at the time of making his or her application.

17.29 The Order provides that if no alternative accommodation is available for the applicant the housing authority may accommodate the family in B&B for a period, or periods, not exceeding six weeks in result of a single homelessness application. **Where B&B accommodation is secured for an applicant with family commitments, the Secretary of State considers that the authority should notify the applicant of the effect of the Order, and, in particular, that the authority will be unable to continue to secure B&B accommodation for such applicants any longer than 6 weeks, after which they must secure alternative, suitable accommodation.**

17.30 When determining whether accommodation other than B&B accommodation is available for use, housing authorities will need to take into account, among other things, the cost to the authority of securing the accommodation, the affordability of the accommodation for the applicant and the location of the accommodation. An authority is under no obligation to include in its considerations accommodation which is to be allocated in accordance with its allocation scheme, published under s.167 of the 1996 Act.

17.31 If there is a significant change in an applicant's circumstances that would bring the applicant within the scope of the Order (e.g. a new pregnancy), the six week period should start from the date the authority was informed of the change of circumstances not the date the applicant was originally placed in B&B accommodation.

17.32 If the conditions for referring a case are met and another housing authority accepts responsibility for an applicant under s.200(4), any time spent in B&B

accommodation before this acceptance should be disregarded in calculating the six week period.

17.33 B&B accommodation is also unlikely to be suitable for 16 and 17 year olds who are in need of support. Where B&B accommodation is used for this group it ought to be as a last resort for the shortest time possible and housing authorities will need to ensure that appropriate support is provided where necessary. See Chapter 12 for guidance on the use of B&B for 16 and 17 year olds.

17.34 The Secretary of State considers that the limited circumstances in which B&B hotels may provide suitable accommodation could include those where:

(a) emergency accommodation is required at very short notice (for example to discharge the interim duty to accommodate under s.188); or

(b) there is simply no better alternative accommodation available and the use of B&B accommodation is necessary as a last resort.

17.35 The Secretary of State considers that where housing authorities are unable to avoid using B&B hotels to accommodate applicants, they should ensure that such accommodation is of a good standard (see paragraphs 17.36–17.38 below) and is used for the shortest period possible. The Secretary of State considers that where a lengthy stay seems likely, the authority should consider other accommodation more appropriate to the applicant's needs.

Standards of B&B accommodation

17.36 Where housing authorities are unable to avoid using B&B hotels to accommodate applicants they should ensure that such accommodation is of a suitable standard. Where a B&B hotel is used to accommodate an applicant and is their main residence, it falls within the definition of an HMO. Paragraphs 17.18–17.23 above explain the legislation that applies to HMOs with regard to health and safety and overcrowing. Since April 2006, local authorities have a power under the 2004 Act to issue an HMO Declaration confirming HMO status where there is uncertainty about the status of a property.

17.37 The Government recognises that living conditions in HMOs should not only be healthy and safe but should also provide acceptable, decent standards for people who may be unrelated to each other and who are sharing basic facilities. As noted at paragraph 17.22 above, the Government has set out in regulation the minimum 'amenity standards' required for a property to be granted an HMO licence. These standards will only apply to 'high-risk' HMOs covered by mandatory licensing or those HMOs that will be subject to additional licensing, and will not apply to the majority of HMOs. However, housing authorities (or groups of authorities) can adopt their own local classification, amenity specification or minimum standards for B&B and other shared accommodation provided as temporary accommodation under Part 7. In London, for example, boroughs have, since 1988, had a code of practice on the use of B&B and other shared temporary accommodation used to accommodate households under Part 7. This establishes clear benchmarks for standards across the Capital. Under the code of practice, properties are graded from A to E, with the grading dependent upon a wide range of considerations and factors relating to the facilities and services provided by an establishment. Placements are expected to be made only in those properties that meet the required standard. Setting the Standard (STS), a new automated system administered by the Greater London Authority (GLA), assists boroughs to comply with the code of practice. It collects and collates information from environmental health officers' annual inspections of properties and then makes this easily accessible to relevant borough officers across London. For further information on STS contact STS@london.gov.uk. The Secretary of State welcomes these arrangements and encourages other housing authorities to consider adopting similar systems to support the exchange of information and improve standards of temporary accommodation.

17.38 The Government considers that the size and occupancy levels of rooms, the provision and location of cooking, toilet and bathing facilities, and management standards are particularly important factors for determining whether B&B accommodation is suitable for accommodating households under Part 7. The Secretary of State therefore recommends that housing authorities have regard to the recommended minimum standards set out in Annex 17 when assessing whether B&B accommodation is suitable.

AFFORDABILITY

17.39 Under s.210(2), the Secretary of State has made the *Homelessness (Suitability of Accommodation) Order 1996* (SI 1996 No. 3204). The 1996 Order specifies that in determining whether it would be, or would have been, reasonable for a person to occupy accommodation that is considered suitable, a housing authority must take into account whether the accommodation is affordable by him or her, and in particular must take account of:

(a) the financial resources available to him or her (*i.e. all forms of income*), including, but not limited to:

    i)   salary, fees and other remuneration (*from such sources as investments, grants, pensions, tax credits etc.*);

    ii) social security benefits (*such as housing benefit, income support, income-based Jobseekers Allowances or Council Tax benefit etc.*);

    iii) payments due under a court order for the making of periodical payments to a spouse or a former spouse, or to, or for the benefit of, a child;

    iv) payments of child support maintenance due under the *Child Support Act 1991*;

    v) pensions;

    vi) contributions to the costs in respect of the accommodation which are or were made or which might reasonably be expected to be, or have been, made by other members of his or her household (*most members can be assumed to contribute, but the amount depends on various factors including their age and income. Other influencing factors can be drawn from the parallels of their entitlement to housing benefit and income support in relation to housing costs. Current rates should be available from housing authority benefit sections*);

    vii) financial assistance towards the costs in respect of the accommodation, including loans, provided by a local authority, voluntary organisation or other body;

    viii) benefits derived from a policy of insurance (*such as cover against unemployment or sickness*);

    ix) savings and other capital sums (*which may be a source of income or might be available to meet accommodation expenses. However, it should be borne in mind that, again drawing from the parallel social securities assistance, capital savings below a threshold amount are disregarded for the purpose of assessing a claim)*;

(b) the costs in respect of the accommodation, including, but not limited to:

   i)   payments of, or by way of, rent *(including rent default/property damage deposits)*;

   ii) payments in respect of a licence or permission to occupy the accommodation;

   iii) mortgage costs *(including an assessment of entitlement to Income Support Mortgage Interest (ISMI))*;

   iv) payments of, or by way of, service charges *(e.g. maintenance or other costs required as a condition of occupation of the accommodation)*;

   v) mooring charges payable for a houseboat;

   vi) where the accommodation is a caravan or a mobile home, payments in respect of the site on which it stands;

   vii) the amount of council tax payable in respect of the accommodation;

   viii) payments by way of deposit or security in respect of the accommodation;

   ix) payments required by an accommodation agency;

(c) payments which that person is required to make under a court order for the making of periodical payments to a spouse or former spouse, or to, or for the benefit of, a child and payments of child support maintenance required to be made under the *Child Support Act 1991*; and

(d) his or her other reasonable living expenses.

17.40 In considering an applicant's residual income after meeting the costs of the accommodation, the Secretary of State recommends that housing authorities regard accommodation as not being affordable if the applicant would be left with a residual income which would be less than the level of income support or income-based jobseekers allowance that is applicable in respect of the applicant, or would be applicable if he or she was entitled to claim such benefit. This amount will vary from case to case, according to the circumstances and composition of the applicant's household. A current tariff of applicable amounts in respect of such benefits should be available within the authority's housing benefit section. Housing authorities will need to consider whether the applicant can afford the housing costs without being deprived of basic essentials such as food, clothing, heating, transport and other essentials. The Secretary of State recommends that housing authorities avoid placing applicants who are in low paid employment in accommodation where they would need to resort to claiming benefit to meet the costs of that accommodation, and to consider opportunities to secure accommodation at affordable rent levels where this is likely to reduce perceived or actual disincentives to work.

LOCATION OF ACCOMMODATION

17.41 The location of the accommodation will be relevant to suitability and the suitability of the location for all the members of the household will have to be considered. Where, for example, applicants are in paid employment account will need to be taken of their need to reach their normal workplace from the accommodation secured. The Secretary of State recommends that local authorities take into account the need to minimise disruption to the education of young people, particularly at critical points in time such as close to taking GCSE examinations. Housing authorities should avoid placing applicants in isolated accommodation away from public transport, shops and other facilities, and, wherever possible, secure accommodation that is as close as possible to where they were previously living, so they can retain established links with schools, doctors, social workers and other key services and support essential to the well-being of the household.

HOUSEHOLDS WITH PETS[22]

17.42 Housing authorities will need to be sensitive to the importance of pets to some applicants, particularly elderly people and rough sleepers who may rely on pets for companionship. Although it will not always be possible to make provision for pets, the Secretary of State recommends that housing authorities give careful consideration to this aspect when making provision for applicants who wish to retain their pet.

ASYLUM SEEKERS

17.43 Since April 2000 the National Asylum Support Service (NASS) has had responsibility for providing support, including accommodation, to asylum seekers who would otherwise be destitute, whilst their claims and appeals are being considered. Some local authorities may still be providing accommodation to asylum seekers who applied for asylum prior to April 2000 and whose cases have not yet been resolved. However, the number of these cases, if any, will be small and declining.

17.44 Section 210(1A) provides that, in considering whether accommodation is suitable for an applicant who is an asylum seeker, housing authorities:

(a) shall also have regard to the fact that the accommodation is to be temporary pending the determination of the applicant's claim for asylum; and

(b) shall not have regard to any preference that the applicant, or any person who might reasonably be expected to reside with him or her, may have as to the locality of the accommodation secured.

RIGHT TO REQUEST A REVIEW OF SUITABILITY

17.45 Applicants may ask for a review on request of the housing authority's decision that the accommodation offered to them is suitable under s.202(1)(f), although this right does not apply in the case of accommodation secured under s.188, the interim duty to accommodate pending inquiries, or s.200(1), the interim duty pending the decision on a referral. Under s.202(1A) an applicant may request a review as to suitability regardless of whether or not he or she accepts the accommodation. This applies equally to offers of accommodation made under s.193(5) to discharge the s.193(2) duty and to offers of an allocation of accommodation made under s.193(7) that would bring the s.193(2) duty to an end. This means that the applicant is able to ask for a review of suitability without inadvertently bringing the housing duty to an end (see Chapter 19 for guidance on reviews). Housing authorities should note that although there is no right of review of a decision on the suitability of accommodation secured

22 There is no equivalent in the Welsh Code.

under s.188 or s.200(1), such decisions could nevertheless be subject to judicial review in the High Court.

CHAPTER 18
Local connection and referrals to another housing authority

18.1 This chapter provides guidance on the provisions relating to an applicant's 'local connection' with an area and explains the conditions and procedures for referring an applicant to another housing authority.

18.2 Where a housing authority ('the notifying authority') decide that s.193 applies to an applicant (i.e. the applicant is eligible for assistance, unintentionally homeless and has a priority need) but it considers that the conditions for referral of the case to another housing authority are met, they may notify the other housing authority ('the notified authority') of their opinion.

18.3 Notwithstanding that the conditions for a referral are apparently met, it is the responsibility of the notifying authority to determine whether s.193 applies before making a reference. **Applicants can only be referred to another authority if the notifying authority is satisfied that the applicant is unintentionally homeless, eligible for assistance and has a priority need.** Applicants cannot be referred while they are owed only the interim duty under s.188, or any duty other than the s.193 duty (e.g. where they are threatened with homelessness or found to be homeless intentionally).

18.4 **Referrals are discretionary only: housing authorities are not required to refer applicants to other authorities. Nor are they, generally, required to make any inquiries as to whether an applicant has a local connection with an area.** However, by virtue of s.11 of the *Asylum and Immigration (Treatment of Claimants, etc.) Act 2004*, housing authorities will need to consider local connection in cases where the applicant is a former asylum seeker:
i)   who was provided with accommodation in Scotland under s.95 of the *Immigration and Asylum Act 1999*, and
ii) whose accommodation was not provided in an accommodation centre by virtue of s.22 of the *Nationality, Immigration and Asylum Act 2002*.
In such cases, by virtue of s.11(2)(d) and (3) of the *Asylum and Immigration (Treatment of Claimants, etc) Act 2004*, local connection to a district in England, Wales or Scotland will be relevant to what duty is owed under s.193. (See paragraph 18.21 below.)

18.5 Housing authorities may have a policy about how they may exercise their discretion to refer a case. This must not, however, extend to deciding in advance that in all cases where there is a local connection to another district the case should be referred.

18.6 The Local Government Association (LGA) has issued guidelines for housing authorities about procedures for referring a case. These include guidance on issues such as local connection and invoking the disputes procedure when two housing authorities are unable to agree whether the conditions for referral are met. (A copy of the LGA guidelines is at Annex 18 for information).

CONDITIONS FOR REFERRAL

18.7   Sections 198(2) and (2A) describe the conditions which must be satisfied before a referral may be made. A notifying authority may refer an applicant to whom s.193 applies to another housing authority if all of the following are met:

i)   neither the applicant nor any person who might reasonably be expected to live with him or her has a local connection with its district; and

ii)   at least one member of the applicant's household has a local connection with the district of the authority to be notified; and

iii)   none of them will be at risk of domestic or non-domestic violence, or threat of domestic or non-domestic violence which is likely to be carried out, in the district of the authority to be notified.

LOCAL CONNECTION

18.8   When a housing authority makes inquiries to determine whether an applicant is eligible for assistance and owed a duty under Part 7, it may also make inquiries under s.184(2) to decide whether the applicant has a local connection with the district of another housing authority in England, Wales or Scotland.

18.9   Section 199(1) provides that a person has a local connection with the district of a housing authority if he or she has a connection with it:

i)   because he or she is, or was in the past, normally resident there, and that residence was of his or her own choice; or

ii)   because he or she is employed there; or

iii)   because of family associations there; or

iv)   because of any special circumstances.

18.10   For the purposes of (i), above, residence in temporary accommodation provided by a housing authority under s.188 can constitute normal residence of choice and therefore contribute towards a local connection. With regard to (ii) the applicant should actually work in the district: it would not be sufficient that his or her employers' head office was located there. For the purposes of (iii), where the applicant raises family associations, the Secretary of State considers that this may extend beyond parents, adult children or siblings. They may include associations with other family members such as step-parents, grandparents, grandchildren, aunts or uncles provided there are sufficiently close links in the form of frequent contact, commitment or dependency.[23] Family associations may also extend to unmarried couples, provided that the relationship is sufficiently enduring, and to same sex couples. With regard to (iv), special circumstances might include the need to be near special medical or support services which are available only in a particular district.

18.11   The grounds in s.199(1) should be applied in order to establish whether the applicant has the required local connection. However, the fact that an applicant may satisfy one of these grounds will not necessarily mean that he or she has been able to establish a local connection. For example, an applicant may be 'normally resident' in an area even though he or she does not intend to settle there permanently or indefinitely, and the local authority could therefore determine that he or she does not have a local connection. The overriding consideration should always be whether the applicant has a real local connection with an area – the specified grounds are subsidiary to that overriding consideration.

---

23 The Welsh Code provides no guidance on who are family members.

18.12 In assessing whether an applicant's household has a local connection with either its district or a district to which the case might be referred, a housing authority should also consider whether any person who might reasonably be expected to live with the applicant has such a connection.

18.13 A housing authority may not seek to transfer responsibility to another housing authority where the applicant has a local connection with their district but they consider there is a stronger local connection elsewhere. However, in such a case, it would be open to a housing authority to seek assistance from the other housing authority in securing accommodation, under s.213.

18.14 Where a person has a local connection with the districts of more than one other housing authority, the referring housing authority will wish to take account of the applicant's preference in deciding which housing authority to notify.

Ex-service personnel

18.15 Under s.199(2) and (3), serving members of the armed forces, and other persons who normally live with them as part of their household, do not establish a local connection with a district by virtue of serving, or having served, there while in the forces.

Ex-prisoners and detainees under the Mental Health Act 1983

18.16 Similarly, detention in prison (whether convicted or not) does not establish a local connection with the district the prison is in. However, any period of residence in accommodation prior to imprisonment may give rise to a local connection under s.199(1)(a). The same is true of those detained under the *Mental Health Act 1983*.

Former asylum seekers[24]

18.17 Sections 199(6) and (7) were inserted by section 11 of the *Asylum and Immigration (Treatment of Claimants, etc.) Act 2004*. Section 199(6) provides that a person has a local connection with the district of a housing authority if he or she was (at any time) provided with accommodation there under s.95 of the *Immigration and Asylum Act 1999* ('s.95 accommodation').

18.18 Under s.199(7), however, a person does not have a local connection by virtue of s.199(6):

(a) if he or she has been subsequently provided with s.95 accommodation in a different area. Where a former asylum seeker has been provided with s.95 accommodation in more than one area, the local connection is with the area where such accommodation was last provided; or

(b) if they have been provided with s.95 accommodation in an accommodation centre in the district by virtue of s.22 of the *Nationality, Immigration and Asylum Act 2002*.

18.19 A local connection with a district by virtue of s.199(6) does not override a local connection by virtue of s.199(1). Thus, a former asylum seeker who has a local connection with a district because he or she was provided with accommodation there under s.95 may also have a local connection elsewhere for some other reason, for example, because of employment or family associations.

---

24 The Welsh Code provides no guidance on former asylum-seekers.

Former asylum seekers provided with s.95 accommodation in Scotland

18.20 Under Scottish legislation, a person does not establish a local connection with a district in Scotland if he or she is resident there in s.95 accommodation. Consequently, if such a person made a homelessness application to a housing authority in England, and he or she did not have a local connection with the district of that authority, the fact that he or she had been provided with s.95 accommodation in Scotland would not establish conditions for referral to the relevant local authority in Scotland.

18.21 Sections 11(2) and (3) of the *Asylum and Immigration (Treatment of Claimants, etc) Act 2004* provides that where a housing authority in England or Wales is satisfied that an applicant is eligible for assistance, unintentionally homeless and in priority need and:

i)   the applicant has been provided with s.95 accommodation in Scotland at any time;

ii) the s.95 accommodation was not provided in an accommodation centre by virtue of s.22 of the *Nationality, Immigration and Asylum Act 2002*;

iii) the applicant does not have a local connection anywhere in England and Wales (within the meaning of s.199 of the 1996 Act); and

iv) the applicant does not have a local connection anywhere in Scotland (within the meaning of s.27 of the *Housing (Scotland) Act 1987*);

then the duty to the applicant under s.193 (the main homelessness duty) shall not apply. However, the authority:

(a) may secure that accommodation is available for occupation by the applicant for a period giving him or her a reasonable opportunity of securing accommodation for his or her occupation; and

(b) may provide the applicant (or secure that he or she is provided with) advice and assistance in any attempts he or she may make to secure accommodation for his or her occupation.

When dealing with an applicant in these circumstances, authorities will need to take into account the wishes of the applicant but should consider providing such advice and assistance as would enable the applicant to make an application for housing to the Scottish authority in the district where the s.95 accommodation was last provided, or to another Scottish authority of the applicant's choice. If such a person was unintentionally homeless and in priority need, it would be open to them to apply to any Scottish housing authority and a main homelessness duty would be owed to them.

No local connection anywhere

18.22 If an applicant, or any person who might reasonably be expected to live with the applicant, has no local connection with any district in Great Britain, the duty to secure accommodation will rest with the housing authority that has received the application.

RISK OF VIOLENCE

18.23 A housing authority cannot refer an applicant to another housing authority if that person or any person who might reasonably be expected to reside with him or her would be at risk of violence. The housing authority is under a positive duty to enquire whether the applicant would be at such a risk and, if he or she would, it should not be assumed that the applicant will take steps to deal with the threat.

18.24 Section 198(3) defines violence as violence from another person or threats of violence from another person which are likely to be carried out. This is the same definition as appears in s.177 in relation to whether it is reasonable to continue to occupy accommodation and the circumstances to be considered as to whether a person runs a risk of violence are the same.

18.25 Housing authorities should be alert to the deliberate distinction which is made in s.198(3) between actual violence and threatened violence. A high standard of proof of actual violence in the past should not be imposed. The threshold is that there must be:

(a) no risk of domestic violence (actual or threatened) in the other district; and

(b) no risk of non-domestic violence (actual or threatened) in the other district. Nor should 'domestic violence' be interpreted restrictively (see definitions in the introduction to this Code).

DUTIES WHERE CASE REFERRED TO ANOTHER HOUSING AUTHORITY

18.26 If a housing authority decide to refer a case to another housing authority, they will need to notify the other housing authority that they believe the conditions for referral are met (s.198(1)). They must also notify the applicant that they have notified, or intend to notify, another housing authority that they consider that the conditions for referral are met (s.184(4)). At that point, the notifying authority would cease to be subject to the interim duty to accommodate under s.188(1) but will owe a duty under s.200(1) to secure that accommodation is available for the applicant until the question of whether the conditions for referral are met is decided.

18.27 Under s.200(4), if the referral is accepted by the notified authority they will be under a duty to secure accommodation for the applicant under s.193(2). Regardless of whether the notified authority had reached a different decision on a previous application, it is not open to it to re-assess the notifying authority's decision that the applicant is eligible, unintentionally homeless and in priority need. Nor may the notified authority rely on an offer of accommodation which was refused having been made in pursuance of a previous application to it.

18.28 Under s.200(3), if it is decided that the conditions for referral are not met, the notifying authority will be under a duty to secure accommodation for the applicant under s.193(2).

18.29 When the question of whether the conditions for referral to the notified authority are met has been decided, the notifying housing authority must notify the applicant of the decision and the reasons for it (s.200(2)). The notification must also advise the applicant of his or her right to request a review of the decision, and the timescale within which such a request must be made. The interim duty to accommodate under s.200(1) ends regardless of whether the applicant requests a review of the decision. However, where the applicant does request a review the notifying authority has a power under s.200(5) to secure that accommodation is available pending the review decision. (See Chapter 15 for guidance on powers to secure accommodation).

18.30 Notifications to the applicant must be provided in writing and copies made available at the housing authority's office for collection by the applicant, or his or her representative, for a reasonable period.

DISPUTES

18.31 Applicants have the right to request a review of various decisions relating to local connection and referrals (see Chapter 19 for further guidance). There is not a right to request a review of a housing authority's decision not to refer a case, although a failure by a housing authority to consider whether it has the discretion to refer an applicant may be amenable to challenge by way of judicial review. The same is true of an unreasonable use of the discretion.

18.32 The question of whether the conditions for referral are met in a particular case should be decided by agreement between the housing authorities concerned. If they cannot agree, the decision should be made in accordance with such arrangements as may be directed by order of the Secretary of State (s.198(5)).

18.33 The *Homelessness (Decisions on Referrals) Order 1998* (SI 1998 No. 1578) directs that the arrangements to be followed in such a dispute are the arrangements agreed between the local authority associations (i.e. the Local Government Association, the Convention of Scottish Local Authorities, the Welsh Local Government Association and the Association of London Government).

18.34 The arrangements are set out in the Schedule to the Order. Broadly speaking, they provide that in the event of two housing authorities being unable to agree whether the conditions for referral are met, they must agree on a person to be appointed to make the decision for them. If unable to agree on that, they should agree to request the LGA to appoint someone. In default of this, the notifying housing authority must make such a request of the LGA. In all cases the appointed person must be drawn from a panel established by the LGA for the purpose. The Local Government Association has issued guidelines for housing authorities on invoking the disputes procedure (a copy is at Annex 18 for information).

18.35 The arrangements set out in the Schedule to SI 1998 NO. 1578 apply where a housing authority in England, Wales or Scotland seek to refer a homelessness case to another housing authority in England or Wales, and they are unable to agree whether the conditions for referral are met. A similar Order, the *Homelessness (Decisions on Referrals) (Scotland) Order 1998*, SI 1998 No. 1603 applies under the Scottish homelessness legislation. The arrangements in the latter apply in cases where a housing authority in England, Wales or Scotland refer a homelessness case to a housing authority in Scotland, and they are unable to agree whether the conditions for referral are met.

18.36 Where an English or Welsh housing authority seek to refer a case to a Scottish housing authority, a request to the local authority association to appoint an arbitrator should be made to the Convention of Scottish Local Authorities.

18.37 A notified authority which wishes to refuse a referral because it disagrees on a finding as to the application of s.193 to the applicant must challenge the notifying authority's finding (for example as to intentionality) by way of judicial review.

CHAPTER 19
Review of decisions and appeals to the county court

19.1 This chapter provides guidance on the procedures to be followed when an applicant requests the housing authority to review their decision on the homelessness case.

RIGHT TO REQUEST A REVIEW
19.2 Applicants have the right to request the housing authority to review their decisions on homelessness cases in some circumstances. If the request is made in accordance with s.202 the housing authority must review the relevant decision.

19.3 When a housing authority have completed their inquiries into the applicant's homelessness case they must notify the applicant of:
   (a) their decision and, if any decision is against the applicant's interest, the reasons for it;
   (b) the applicant's right to request a review; and
   (c) the time within which such a request must be made.
   Housing authorities should also advise the applicant of his or her right to request a review of the suitability of any accommodation offered as a discharge of a homelessness duty, whether or not the offer is accepted. Authorities should also advise the applicant of the review procedures.

19.4 Under s.202 an applicant has the right to request a review of:
   (a) any decision of a housing authority about his or her eligibility for assistance (i.e. whether he or she is considered to be a person from abroad who is ineligible for assistance under Part 7);
   (b) any decision of a housing authority as to what duty (if any) is owned to him or her under s.190, s.191, s.192, s.193, s.195 and s.196 (duties owed to applicants who are homeless or threatened with homelessness);
   (c) any decision of a housing authority to notify another housing authority under s.198(1) (i.e. a decision to refer the applicant to another housing authority because they appear to have a local connection with that housing authority's district and not with the district where they have made the application);
   (d) any decision under s.198(5) whether the conditions are met for the referral of the applicant's case (including a decision taken by a person appointed under the *Homelessness (Decisions on Referrals) Order 1998* (SI 1998 No. 1578));
   (e) any decision under s.200(3) or (4) (i.e. a decision as to whether the notified housing authority or the notifying housing authority owe the duty to secure accommodation in a case considered for referral or referred);
   (f) any decision of a housing authority as to the suitability of accommodation offered to the applicant under any of the provisions in (b) or (e) above or the suitability of accommodation offered under s.193(7) (allocation under Part 6). Under s.202(1A), applicants can request a review of the suitability of accommodation whether or not they have accepted the offer.

19.5 An applicant must request a review before the end of the period of 21 days beginning with the day on which he or she is notified of the housing authority's decision. The housing authority may specify, in writing, a longer period during which a review may be requested. Applicants do not have a right to request a review of a decision made on an earlier review.

19.6   In reviewing a decision, housing authorities will need to have regard to any information relevant to the period before the decision (even if only obtained afterwards) as well as any new relevant information obtained since the decision.

THE REVIEW REGULATIONS

19.7   The *Allocation of Housing and Homelessness (Review Procedures) Regulations 1999* (SI 1999 No.71) set out the procedures to be followed by housing authorities in carrying out reviews under Part 7.

Who may carry out the review

19.8   A review may be carried out by the housing authority itself or by someone acting as an agent of the housing authority (see Chapter 21 on contracting out homelessness functions). Where the review is to be carried out by an officer of the housing authority, the officer must not have been involved in the original decision, and he or she must be senior to the officer (or officers) who took that decision. Seniority for these purposes means seniority in rank or grade within the housing authority's organisational structure. The seniority provision does not apply where a committee or sub-committee of elected members took the original decision.

19.9   Where the decision under review is a joint decision by the notifying housing authority and the notified housing authority as to whether the conditions of referral of the case are satisfied, s.202(4) requires that the review should be carried out jointly by the two housing authorities. Where the decision under review was taken by a person appointed pursuant to the arrangements set out in the Schedule to the *Homelessness (Decisions on Referrals) Order 1998* (SI 1998 No. 1578), the review must be carried out by another person appointed under those arrangements (see paragraph 19.15).

Written representations

19.10   The applicant should be invited to make representations in writing in connection with his or her request for a review. The relevant provisions in Part 7 give a person an unfettered right to request a review of a decision, so he or she is not required to provide grounds for challenging the housing authority's decision. The purpose of the requirement is to invite the applicant to state his or her grounds for requesting a review (if he or she has not already done so) and to elicit any new information that the applicant may have in relation to his or her request for a review.

19.11   Regulation 6 requires the housing authority to notify the applicant that he or she, or someone acting on his or her behalf, may make written representations in connection with the request for a review. The notice should also advise the applicant of the procedure to be followed in connection with the review (if this information has not been provided earlier). Regulation 6 also provides that:

   i)   where the original decision was made jointly by the notifying and notified housing authorities under s.198(5), the notification should be made by the notifying housing authority; and

ii) where the original decision was made by a person appointed pursuant to the *Homelessness (Decisions on Referrals) Order 1998* (SI 1998 No. 1578), the notification should be made by the person appointed to carry out the review.

Oral hearings

19.12 Regulation 8 provides that in cases where a review has been requested, if the housing authority, authorities or person carrying out the review consider that there is a deficiency or irregularity in the original decision, or in the manner in which it was made, but they are minded nonetheless to make a decision that is against the applicant's interests on one or more issues, they should notify the applicant:

(a) that they are so minded and the reasons why; and,

(b) that the applicant, or someone acting on his or her behalf, may, within a reasonable period, make oral representations, further written representations, or both oral and written representations.

19.13 Such deficiencies or irregularities would include:

i) failure to take into account relevant considerations and to ignore irrelevant ones;

ii) failure to base the decision on the facts;

iii) bad faith or dishonesty;

iv) mistake of law;

v) decisions that run contrary to the policy of the 1996 Act;

vi) irrationality or unreasonableness;

vii) procedural unfairness, e.g. where an applicant has not been given a chance to comment on matters relevant to a decision.

19.14 The reviewer must consider whether there is 'something lacking' in the decision, i.e. were any significant issues not addressed or addressed inadequately, which could have led to unfairness.

Period during which review must be completed

19.15 Regulation 9 provides that the period within which the applicant must be notified of the decision on review is:

i) eight weeks from the day of the request for a review, where the original decision was made by the housing authority;

ii) ten weeks, where the decision was made jointly by two housing authorities under s.198(5) (a decision whether the conditions for referral are met);

iii) twelve weeks, where the decision is taken by a person appointed pursuant to the Schedule to the *Homelessness (Decisions on Referrals) Order* (SI 1998 No.1578).

The regulations provide that in all of these cases it is open to the reviewer to seek the applicant's agreement to an extension of the prescribed period; any such agreement must be given in writing.

Late representations

19.16 The regulations require the reviewer(s) to consider any written representations received subject to compliance with the requirement to notify the applicant of the decision on review within the period of the review, i.e. the period prescribed in the regulations or any extended period agreed in writing by the applicant. It may in some circumstances be necessary to make further enquiries of the applicant about information he or she has provided. The reviewer(s) should be flexible about allowing such further exchanges, having regard to the time limits for reviews prescribed in the regulations. If this leads to significant delays, the applicant may be approached to agree an extension in the period for the review. Similarly, if an applicant has been invited to make oral representations and this requires additional time to arrange, the applicant should be asked to agree an appropriate extension.

PROCEDURES FOR REVIEW OF DECISIONS MADE UNDER THE DECISIONS ON REFERRALS ORDER

19.17 Where the original decision under s.198(5) was made by a person appointed pursuant to the Schedule to the *Homelessness (Decisions on Referrals) Order 1998* (SI 1998 No.1578), regulation 7 provides that a review should be carried out by another person appointed by the notifying housing authority and the notified housing authority. This requirement applies even where the original decision was carried out by a person appointed from the panel by the chairman of the Local Government Association, or his or her nominee. If, however, the two housing authorities fail to appoint a person to carry out the review within five working days of the date of the request for a review, the notifying housing authority must request the chairman of the Local Government Association to appoint a person from the panel. The chairman, in turn, must within seven working days of that request appoint a person from the panel to undertake the review. The housing authorities are required to provide the reviewer with the reasons for the original decision, and the information on which that decision is based, within five working days of his or her appointment.

19.18 Any person thus appointed must comply with the procedures set out in regulations 6, 7, 8 and 9. Specifically, he or she must invite written representations from the applicant and send copies of these to the two housing authorities, inviting them to respond. The reviewer is also required to notify in writing the two housing authorities of his or her decision on review and the reasons for it at least a week before the end of the prescribed period of twelve weeks (or of any extended period agreed by the applicant). This allows the housing authorities adequate time to notify the applicant of the decision before expiry of the period.

NOTIFICATION OF DECISION ON REVIEW

19.19 Section 203 requires a housing authority to notify the applicant in writing of their decision on the review. The authority must also notify the applicant of the reasons for their decision where it:

i)   confirms the original decision on any issue against the interests of the applicant;

ii) confirms a previous decision to notify another housing authority under s.198; or,

iii) confirms a previous decision that the conditions for referral in s.198 are met in the applicant's case.

Where the review is carried out jointly by two housing authorities under s.198(5), or by a person appointed pursuant to the *Homelessness (Decisions on Referrals) Order 1998* (SI 1998 No.1578), the notification may be made by either of the two housing authorities concerned.

At this stage, the authority making the notification should advise the applicant of his or her right to appeal to the County Court against a review decision under s.204 and of the period in which to appeal.

POWERS TO ACCOMMODATE PENDING A REVIEW

19.20   Sections 188(3) and 200(5) give housing authorities powers to secure accommodation for certain applicants pending the decision on a review. See Chapter 15 for guidance on powers to secure accommodation.

APPEALS TO THE COUNTY COURT

19.21   Section 204 provides an applicant with the right of appeal on a point of law to the County Court if:

(a) he or she is dissatisfied with the decision on a review; or

(b) he or she is not notified of the decision on the review within the time prescribed in regulations made under s.203.

In the latter case, an applicant will be entitled to appeal against the original decision.

19.22   An appeal must be brought by an applicant within 21 days of:

(a) the date on which he or she is notified of the decision on review; or

(b) the date on which he or she should have been notified (i.e. the date marking the end of the period for the review prescribed in the regulations, or any extended period agreed in writing by the applicant).

19.23   The court may give permission for an appeal to be brought after 21 days, but only where it is satisfied that:

(a) (where permission is sought within the 21-day period), there is good reason for the applicant to be unable to bring the appeal in time; or

(b) (where permission is sought after the 21-day period has expired), there was a good reason for the applicant's failure to bring the appeal in time and for any delay in applying for permission.

19.24   On an appeal, the County Court is empowered to make an order confirming, quashing or varying the housing authority's decision as it thinks fit. It is important, therefore, that housing authorities have in place review procedures that are robust, fair, and transparent.

POWER TO ACCOMMODATE PENDING AN APPEAL TO THE COUNTY COURT

19.25   Section 204(4) gives housing authorities the power to accommodate certain applicants during the period for making an appeal, and pending the appeal and any subsequent appeal. Applicants have a right to appeal against a housing authority's decision not to secure accommodation for them pending an appeal to the County Court (s.204A). Applicants can also appeal against a housing authority's decision to secure accommodation for them for only a limited period which ends before final determination of the appeal. See Chapter 15 for guidance on powers to secure accommodation.

LOCAL GOVERNMENT OMBUDSMAN

19.26 Applicants may complain to a Local Government Ombudsman if they consider that they have been caused injustice as a result of maladministration by a housing authority. The Ombudsman may investigate the way a decision has been made, but may not question the merits of a decision properly reached. For example, maladministration would occur where a housing authority:

i)   took too long to do something;

ii) did not follow their own rules or the law;

iii) broke their promises;

iv) treated the applicant unfairly;

v)   gave the applicant the wrong information.

19.27 There are some matters an Ombudsman cannot investigate. These include:

i)   matters the applicant knew about more than twelve months before he or she wrote to the Ombudsman or to a councillor, unless the Ombudsman considers it reasonable to investigate despite the delay;

ii) matters about which the applicant has already taken court action against the housing authority, for example, an appeal to the County Court under s.204;

iii) matters about which the applicant could go to court, unless the Ombudsman considers there are good reasons why the applicant could not reasonably be expected to do so.

19.28 Where there is a right of review the Ombudsman would expect an applicant to pursue the right before making a complaint. If there is any doubt about whether the Ombudsman can look into a complaint, the applicant should seek advice from the Ombudsman's office.

CHAPTER 20
Protection of personal property

20.1 **This chapter provides guidance on the duty and powers housing authorities have to protect the personal property of an applicant.**

20.2 Under s.211(1) and (2), where a housing authority has become subject to a duty to an applicant under specified provisions of Part 7 and it has reason to believe that:

i)   there is a danger of loss of, or damage to, the applicant's personal property because the applicant is unable to protect it or deal with it, and

ii) no other suitable arrangements have been, or are being, made,

then, whether or not the housing authority is still subject to such a duty, it must take reasonable steps to prevent the loss of, or to prevent or mitigate damage to, any personal property of the applicant.

20.3 The specified provisions are:

– s.188 (interim duty to accommodate);

– s.190, s.193 or s.195 (duties to persons found to be homeless or threatened with homelessness); or

– s.200 (duties to applicant whose case is considered for referral or referred).

20.4 In all other circumstances, housing authorities have a power to take any steps they consider reasonable to protect in the same ways an applicant's personal property (s.211(3)).

20.5   Section 212 makes provisions supplementing s.211. For the purposes of both s.211 and s.212, the personal property of an applicant includes the personal property of any person who might reasonably be expected to reside with him or her (s.211(5) and s.212(6)).

20.6   A danger of loss or damage to personal property means that there is a likelihood of harm, not just that harm is a possibility. Applicants may be unable to protect their property if, for example, they are ill or are unable to afford to have it stored themselves.

20.7   Under s.212(1), in order to protect an applicant's personal property, a housing authority can enter, at all reasonable times, the applicant's current or former home, and deal with the property in any way which seems reasonably necessary. In particular, it may store the property or arrange for it to be stored; this may be particularly appropriate where the applicant is accommodated by the housing authority in furnished accommodation for a period. In some cases, where the applicant's previous home is not to be occupied immediately, it may be possible for the property to remain there, if it can be adequately protected.

20.8   Where a housing authority does take steps to protect personal property, whether by storing it or otherwise, it must take reasonable care of it and deliver it to the owner when reasonably requested to do so.

20.9   The applicant can request the housing authority to move his or her property to a particular location. If the housing authority considers that the request is reasonable, they may discharge their responsibilities under s.211 by doing as the applicant asks. Where such a request is met, the housing authority will have no further duty or power to protect the applicant's property, and it must inform the applicant of this consequence before complying with the request (s.212(2)).

20.10   Housing authorities may impose conditions on the assistance they provide where they consider these appropriate to the particular case. Conditions may include making a reasonable charge for storage of property and reserving the right to dispose of property in certain circumstances specified by the housing authority – e.g. if the applicant loses touch with them and cannot be traced after a certain period (s.211(4)).

20.11   Where a request to move personal property to another location is either not made or not carried out, the duty or power to take any action under s.211 ends when the housing authority believes there is no longer any danger of loss or damage to the property because of the applicant's inability to deal with or protect it (s.212(3)). This may be the case, for example, where an applicant recovers from illness or finds accommodation where he or she is able to place his or her possessions, or becomes able to afford the storage costs him/herself. However, where the housing authority has discharged the duty under s.211 by placing property in storage, it has a discretionary power to continue to keep the property in storage. Where it does so, any conditions imposed by the housing authority continue to apply and may be modified as necessary.

20.12   Where the housing authority ceases to be under a duty, or ceases to have a power, to protect an applicant's personal property under s.211, it must notify the applicant of this and give the reasons for it. The notification must be delivered to the applicant or sent to his or her last known address (s.212(5)).

CHAPTER 21
Contracting out homelessness functions

21.1   This chapter provides guidance on contracting out homelessness functions and housing authorities' statutory obligations with regard to the discharge of those functions.

21.2   The *Local Authorities (Contracting Out of Allocation of Housing and Homelessness Functions) Order 1996* (SI 1996 No. 3215) ('the Order') enables housing authorities to contract out certain functions under Parts 6 and 7 of the 1996 Act. The Order is made under s.70 of the *Deregulation and Contracting Out Act 1994* ('the 1994 Act'). In essence, the Order allows the contracting out of executive functions while leaving the responsibility for making strategic decisions with the housing authority.

21.3   The Order provides that the majority of functions under Part 7 can be contracted out. These include:
   – making arrangements to secure that advice and information about homelessness, and the prevention of homelessness, is available free of charge within the housing authority's district;
   – making inquiries about and deciding a person's eligibility for assistance;
   – making inquiries about and deciding whether any duty, and, if so, what duty is owed to a person under Part 7;
   – making referrals to another housing authority;
   – carrying out reviews of decisions;
   – securing accommodation to discharge homelessness duties.

21.4   Where decision-making in homelessness cases is contracted out, authorities may wish to consider retaining the review function under s.202 of the 1996 Act. This may provide an additional degree of independence between the initial decision and the decision on review.

21.5   The 1994 Act provides that a contract made:
   i)   may authorise a contractor to carry out only part of the function concerned;
   ii) may specify that the contractor is authorised to carry out functions only in certain cases or areas specified in the contract;
   iii) may include conditions relating to the carrying out of the functions, e.g. prescribing standards of performance;
   iv) shall be for a period not exceeding 10 years and may be revoked at any time by the Minister or the housing authority. Any subsisting contract is to be treated as having been repudiated in these circumstances;
   v)   shall not prevent the housing authority from exercising themselves the functions to which the contract relates.

21.6   Schedule 2 to the Order lists the homelessness functions in Part 7 that may **not** be contracted out. These are:
   – s.179(2) and (3): the provision of various forms of assistance to anyone providing advice and information about homelessness and the prevention of homelessness to people in the district, on behalf of the housing authority;
   – s.180: the provision of assistance to voluntary organisations concerned with homelessness; and
   – s.213: co-operation with relevant housing authorities and bodies by rendering assistance in the discharge of their homelessness functions.

21.7   Local authorities also **cannot** contract out their functions under the *Homelessness Act 2002* which relate to homelessness reviews and strategies. Chapter 1 provides guidance on homelessness reviews and strategies and outlines the main functions. These include:

- – s.1(1): carry out a homelessness review for the district, and formulate and publish a homelessness strategy based on the results of that review;
- – s.1(4): publish a new homelessness strategy within 5 years from the day on which their last homelessness strategy was published; and
- – 3(6): keep their homelessness strategy under review and modify it from time to time.

Reviews and the formulation of strategies can, however, be informed by research commissioned from external organisations.

21.8   The 1994 Act also provides that the housing authority is responsible for any act or omission of the contractor in exercising functions under the contract, except:

- i)   where the contractor fails to fulfil conditions specified in the contract relating to the exercise of the function; or,
- ii)   where criminal proceedings are brought in respect of the contractor's act or omission.

21.9   Where there is an arrangement in force under s.101 of the *Local Government Act 1972* by virtue of which one local authority exercises the functions of another, the 1994 Act provides that the authority exercising the function is not allowed to contract it out without the principal authority's consent.

21.10   **Where a housing authority has contracted out the operation of any homelessness functions the authority remains statutorily responsible and accountable for the discharge of those functions**. This is the case whether a housing authority contracts with a Large Scale Voluntary Transfer registered social landlord, an Arms Length Management Organisation or any other organisation. The authority will therefore need to ensure that the contract provides for delivery of the homelessness functions in accordance with both the statutory obligations and the authority's own policies on tackling and preventing homelessness. The performance of a housing authority's homeless functions will continue to be part of its Comprehensive Performance Assessment and will need to be covered by Best Value reviews, whether or not it discharges the homelessness functions directly.

21.11   When contracting out homelessness functions, housing authorities will need to ensure that:

- – proposed arrangements are consistent with their obligations under the 2002 Act to have a strategy for preventing homelessness and ensuring that accommodation and any necessary support will be available to everyone in their district who is homeless or at risk of homelessness;
- – a high quality homelessness service will be provided, in particular the assessment of applicants and the provision of advice and assistance; and
- – both short-term and settled accommodation services will be available for offer to all applicants owed the main homelessness duty.

21.12   Housing authorities should also ensure they have adequate contractual, monitoring and quality assurance mechanisms in place to ensure their statutory duties are being fully discharged.

21.13 In deciding whether to contract out homelessness functions, housing authorities are encouraged to undertake an options appraisal of each function to decide whether it would best be provided in-house or by another organisation. *Housing Allocation, Homelessness and Stock Transfer – A guide to key issues (ODPM 2004)* provides guidance on the key issues that housing authorities need to consider when deciding whether to retain or contract out the delivery of their homelessness functions.

ANNEX 1
Good Practice/Guidance Publications

DEPARTMENT FOR COMMUNITIES AND LOCAL GOVERNMENT
Homelessness prevention: a guide to good practice (2006)

OFFICE OF THE DEPUTY PRIME MINISTER
Homelessness publications
www.communities.gov.uk/index.asp?id=1162505
Sustainable Communities: settled homes, changing lives. A strategy for tackling homelessness (2005)
Tackling homelessness amongst ethnic minority households – a development guide (2005)
Resources for homeless ex-service personnel in London (2004)
Effective Co-operation in Tackling Homelessness: Nomination Agreements and Exclusions (2004)
Achieving Positive Shared Outcomes in Health and Homelessness (2004)
Local Authorities' Homelessness Strategies: Evaluation and Good Practice (2004)
Reducing B&B use and tackling homelessness – What's working: A Good Practice Handbook (2003)
Housing Associations and Homelessness Briefing (2003)
Achieving Positive Outcomes on Homelessness – A Homelessness Directorate Advice Note to Local Authorities (2003)
Addressing the health needs of rough sleepers (2002)
Care leaving strategies – a good practice handbook (2002)
Drugs services for homeless people – a good practice handbook (2002)
Homelessness Strategies: A Good Practice Handbook (2002)
More than a roof: a report into tackling homelessness (2002)
Helping rough sleepers off the streets: A report to the Homelessness Directorate – Randall, G and Brown, S. (2002)
Preventing tomorrow's rough sleepers – Rough Sleepers Unit (2001)
Blocking the fast track from prison to rough sleeping – Rough Sleepers Unit (2000)

Homelessness and housing support directorate policy briefings
Briefing 15: Summary of Homelessness Good Practice Guidance (June 2006)
Briefing 14: Sustainable Communities: settled homes; changing lives – one year on (March 2006)
Briefing 13: Survey of English local authorities about homelessness (December 2005)

Briefing 12: Hostels Capital Improvement Programme (HCIP) (September 2005)

Briefing 11: Providing More Settled Homes (June 2005)

Briefing 10: Delivering on the Positive Outcomes (December 2004)

Briefing 9: Homelessness Strategies: Moving Forward (November 2004)

Briefing 8: Improving the Quality of Hostels and Other Forms of Temporary Accommodation (June 2004)

Briefing 7: Addressing the Health Needs of Homeless People Policy (April 2004)

Briefing 6: Repeat Homelessness Policy (January 2004)

Briefing 5: Improving Employment Options for Homeless People (September 2003)

Briefing 4: Prevention of Homelessness Policy (June 2003)

Briefing 3: Bed and Breakfast Policy (March 2003)

Briefing 2: Domestic Violence Policy (December 2002)

Briefing 1: Ethnicity and Homelessness Policy (September 2002)

Supporting people publications
www.spkweb.org.uk

Supporting People: Guide to Accommodation and Support Options for People with Mental Health Problems (2005)

Guide to Housing and Housing Related Support Options for Offenders and People at Risk of Offending (2005)

Supporting People: Guide to Accommodation and Support Options for Homeless Households (2003)

Supporting People: The Support Needs of Homeless Households (2003)

Supporting People: Guide to Accommodation and Support Options for Households Experiencing Domestic Violence (2002)

Reflecting the Needs and Concerns of Black and Minority Ethnic Communities in Supporting People (2002)

Other ODPM publications
www.communities.gov.uk

Sustainable Communities: Homes for All. A Five Year Plan (2005)

Improving the Effectiveness of Rent Arrears Management (2005)

Housing Allocation, Homelessness and Stock Transfer – A guide to key issues (2004)

Guidance on Arms Length Management of Local Authority Housing (2004)

Allocation of Accommodation – Code of Guidance for local housing authorities (2002)

Working together, Connexions and youth homelessness agencies, London, Department for Transport, Local Government and the Regions (DTLR) and Connexions (2001)

Other government publications
Audit commission
www.audit-commission.gov.uk

Homelessness: Responding to the New Agenda (2003)

ALMO Inspections. The Delivery of Excellent Housing Management Services (2003)

Housing Services After Stock Transfer (2002)

Department for education and skills
www.dfes.gov.uk
Safeguarding Children, The second joint Chief Inspectors' Report on arrangements to Safeguard Children, Commission for Social Care Inspection (2005)
Every Child Matters: Change for Children (2004)
Working with Voluntary and Community Organisations to Deliver Change for Children and Young People (2004)

Department of Health
www.dh.gov.uk/Home/fs/en
Our health, our care, our say: a new direction for community (2006)
Working together to safeguard children (2005)
Government response to Hidden Harm: the Report of an inquiry by the Advisory Council on the Misuse of Drugs (2005)
Making a Difference: Reducing Bureaucracy in Children, Young People and Family Services (2005)
Independence, well-being and choice: Our vision for the future of social care for adults in England (2005)
Commissioning a patient-led NHS (2005)
Health reform in England: update and next steps (2005)
National service framework for mental health: modern standards and service models (1999)
National service framework for children, young people and maternity services (2004)
From Vision to Reality: Transforming Outcomes for Children and Families (2004)
What to do if you're worried a child is being abused (2003)
Tackling Health Inequalities: a programme for action (2003)
Guidance on accommodating children in need and their families – Local Authority Circular 13 (2003)
Children Missing from Care and Home – a guide for good practice published in tandem with the Social Exclusion Unit's report *Young Runaways* (2002)
Getting it Right: good practice in leaving care resource pack (2000)
The framework for assessment of children in need and their families (2000)
Valuing People: A New Strategy for Learning Disability for the 21st Century (2000)
Working Together to Safeguard Children: a guide to interagency working to safeguard and promote the welfare of children (1999) Department of Health, Home Office and Department for Education and Employment

Home Office
www.homeoffice.gov.uk
Advice note on accommodation for vulnerable young people (2001)

Housing Corporation
www.housingcorp.gov.uk
Tenancy management: eligibility and evictions (2004)
Local Authority Nominations. Circular 02/03/Regulation (2003)

Non-Government publications

Centrepoint
www.centrepoint.org.uk
Joint protocols between housing and social services departments: a good practice guide for the assessment and assistance of homeless young people aged 16 and 17 years, Bellerby, N. London (2000)

Chartered institute of housing
www.cih.org
The Housing Manual (2005)
Housing and Support Services for asylum seekers and refugees: a good practice guide. John Perry (2005)
Strategic Approaches to Homelessness; Good Practice Briefing 24 (2002)

Commission For Racial Equality
www.cre.gov.uk
CRE Code of Practice on Racial Equality in Housing (2006)

Disability Rights Commission
www.dre-gb.org/
The Duty to Promote Disability Equality: Statutory Code of Practice (2005)

National housing federation
www.housing.org.uk
Level threshold: towards equality in housing for disabled people: good practice guide (2005)
Flexible allocation and local letting schemes (2000)

Homeless link
www.homeless.org.uk
Hospital admission and discharge: Guidelines for writing a protocol for the hospital admission and discharge of people who are homeless (2006)

Shelter
http://england.shelter.org.uk/home/index.cfm
Sexual exclusion: issues and best practice in lesbian, gay and bisexual housing and homelessness (2005)
Youth housing: a good practice guide (2004)
Local authorities and registered social landlords – best practice on joint working (2002)

ANNEX 2
Other Strategies and Programmes that may Address Homelessness

- Local and Regional Housing Strategy
- Regional Homelessness Strategy
- Regional Economic Development Plan
- Local Strategic Partnership and Community Strategy
- Local Area Agreements

- Supporting People Strategy
- Children and Young People's Plan
- Sure Start
- Connexions
- Education and Employment programmes (e.g. The Princes Trust, New Deal, The Careers Service)
- Progress2work, for drug misusers, and where available, Progress2work-Link Up for alcohol misusers, offenders and homeless people
- Local health schools programme
- Quality Protects
- NHS Local Delivery Plan
- Teenage Pregnancy Strategy
- Drug Action Team Plan
- Crime and Disorder Strategy
- Regional Reducing Reoffending Strategy
- Domestic Violence Strategy
- Anti-Social Behaviour Strategy
- Anti-Poverty Strategy
- Social Inclusion Strategy
- Valuing People Plan
- Town Centre Management Strategy
- Voluntary and community sector plans
- Gypsy and Traveller Accommodation Strategy (where required by s. 225 *Housing Act 2004*)

ANNEX 3
Other Authorities, Organisations and Persons whose Activities may contribute to Preventing/Tackling Homelessness

- Registered social landlords
- Private landlords
- Lettings agencies
- Self build groups
- Housing Co-operatives
- Housing Corporation
- Supported housing providers
- Home improvement agencies
- Primary Care Trusts, health centres and GP practices
- NHS Trusts – Acute and Mental Health
- Local mental health organisations (e.g. Mind)
- Local disability groups
- Care Services Improvement Partnership Regional Development Centres
- Learning Disability Partnership Boards
- Children's Trusts
- Youth Services and youth advice groups

- Education Welfare Services
- LEA Pupil Referral Units
- Schools
- Sure Start
- Connexions
- Youth Offending Team
- Police
- Crime and Disorder Reduction Partnerships
- Drug Action Teams
- National Offender Management Service (incorporating The Prison and Probation Services)
- Victim support groups
- Anti-Social Behaviour Team
- Street Wardens
- Jobcentre Plus
- Learning and Skills Councils
- Environmental Health Team
- Housing Management Team
- Housing Benefits Team
- Armed Forces resettlement services
- National Asylum Support Service
- Refugee Community Organisations
- Law Centres
- Advice/advocacy services (e.g. Citizens Advice Bureaux and Shelter)
- Local voluntary sector infrastructure bodies (e.g. CVS)
- Faith groups
- Women's groups
- Local domestic violence fora
- Ethnic minority groups
- Age groups (e.g. Age Concern, Help the Aged)
- Lesbian, gay and bisexual groups
- Emergency accommodation providers (such as the Salvation Army)
- Day centres for homeless people
- Refuges
- The Samaritans
- Mediation Services
- Local Strategic Partnerships
- Local businesses/Chambers of Commerce
- Regional Housing Board
- Regional planning bodies
- People living in insecure accommodation (and their representative bodies)
- Rough sleepers (and their representative bodies)
- Residents/tenants organisations
- Self help/user groups
- Services supporting sex workers

ANNEX 4
Specific Objectives and Actions for Local Authorities that might be included in a Homelessness Strategy

This Annex provides suggestions for objectives and actions that local authorities may wish to consider including in their homelessness strategies.

HOUSING AUTHORITY
- **Facilitate the effective co-ordination of all service providers, across all sectors in the district, whose activities contribute to preventing homelessness and/or meeting the accommodation and support needs of people who are homeless or at risk of homelessness (objective).**
- establish a homelessness forum to co-ordinate the activities of all the key players, across all sectors, who are contributing to meeting the aims of the homelessness strategy.
- ensure the homelessness strategy is consistent with other relevant local plans and strategies and that all relevant stakeholders are aware of how they work together.
- **Ensure that people who are at risk of homelessness are aware of, and have access to, the services they may need to help them prevent homelessness (objective).**
- provide comprehensive advice and information about homelessness and the prevention of homelessness, free to everyone in the district.
- provide mediation and reconciliation services (e.g. to tackle neighbour disputes and family relationship breakdown).
- implement an effective tenancy relations service (and good liaison with private landlords).
- **Ensure that the supply of accommodation, including affordable accommodation, in the district reflects estimated housing need (objective).**
- in conjunction with RSLs operating in the district, maximise the number of social lettings available for people who have experienced homelessness or at risk of homelessness, consistent with the need to meet the reasonable aspirations of other groups in housing need.
- ensure that provision of specialised and supported accommodation for people who have experienced homelessness or at risk of homelessness (e.g. refuges and wet hostels) reflects estimated need.
- maximise the provision of affordable housing through planning requirements for new private developments.
- **Work with the social services authority to ensure that the needs of clients who have both housing and social services support needs are fully assessed and taken into account (objective)**
- develop a framework for effective joint working with the social services authority, including screening procedures to identify at an early stage where there is a need for case specific joint working.
- put in place arrangements for carrying out joint assessments of people with support needs who are homeless or have experienced homelessness.
- establish a protocol for the referral of clients and the sharing information between services.

SOCIAL SERVICES AUTHORITY

– **Work with the housing authority to ensure that the needs of clients who have both housing and social services support needs are fully assessed and taken into account (objective)**
– develop a framework for effective joint working with the housing authority, including screening procedures, to identify at an early stage where there is a need for case specific joint working.
– put in place arrangements for carrying out joint assessments of people with support needs who are homeless or have experienced homelessness.
– establish a protocol for the referral of clients and the sharing information between services.
– **Ensure that, subject to relevant eligibility criteria, vulnerable people who are homeless, or at risk of homelessness, receive the support they need to help them sustain a home and prevent homelessness recurring (objective).**
– provide a reconciliation service for young people estranged from their families.
– exercise powers under the *Children Act 1989* to make payments to assist young people who are homeless or at risk of homelessness to sustain/find accommodation.
– operate a supported lodgings scheme for homeless 16 and 17 year olds who need a supportive environment.
– provide assistance to enable families with children who have become homeless intentionally (or are ineligible for housing assistance) to secure accommodation for themselves (e.g. financial assistance with rent deposit/guarantees).

ANNEX 5
Co-operation between Registered Social Landlords and Housing Authorities

HOUSING: THE STRATEGIC CONTEXT

1   Housing authorities have a statutory obligation to consider the housing needs of their district (s.8 *Housing Act 1985*). Under the *Homelessness Act 2002* ('the 2002 Act'), they also have a statutory duty to formulate a strategy for preventing homelessness and ensuring that accommodation and support are available for people who are homeless or at risk of homelessness in their district. A homelessness strategy may include actions which the authority expects to be taken by various other organisations, with their agreement.

2   Most social housing is provided by housing authorities and by Registered Social Landlords (RSLs). Virtually all provision of new social housing is delivered through RSLs and, under the transfer programme, ownership of a significant proportion of housing authority stock is being transferred from housing authorities to RSLs, subject to tenants' agreement. This means that, increasingly, RSLs will become the main providers of social housing. Consequently, it is essential that housing authorities work closely with RSLs, as well as all other housing providers, in order to meet the housing needs in their district

and ensure that the aims and objectives of their homelessness strategy are achieved.

STATUTORY FRAMEWORK FOR CO-OPERATION

3   Section 170 of the *Housing Act 1996* ('the 1996 Act') provides that where an RSL has been requested by a housing authority to offer accommodation to people with priority under its allocation scheme, the RSL must co-operate to such extent as is reasonable in the circumstances. Similarly, s.213 provides that where an RSL has been requested by a housing authority to assist them in the discharge of their homelessness functions under Part 7, it must also co-operate to the same extent. Section 3 of the 2002 Act requires housing authorities to consult appropriate bodies and organisations before publishing a homelessness strategy, and this will inevitably need to include RSLs.

HOUSING CORPORATION REGULATORY GUIDANCE

4   RSLs are regulated by the Housing Corporation which, under s.36 of the 1996 Act, and with the approval of the Secretary of State, has issued guidance to RSLs with respect to their management of housing accommodation. The Housing Corporation's Regulatory Code and guidance requires housing associations to work with local authorities to enable them to fulfil their statutory duties to, among others, homeless people and people who have priority for an allocation of housing. In particular, RSLs must ensure that:

- their lettings policies are flexible, non-discriminatory and responsive to demand while contributing to inclusivity and sustainable communities;
- they can demonstrate their co-operation with local authorities on homelessness reviews, homelessness strategies and the delivery of authorities' homelessness functions;
- when requested, and to such extent as is reasonable in the circumstances, they provide a proportion of their stock (at least 50% – see paragraph 9 below) to housing authority nominations and as temporary accommodation for people owed a homelessness duty;
- following consultation with local authorities, criteria are adopted for accepting or rejecting nominees and other applicants for housing;
- applicants are excluded from consideration for housing only if their unacceptable behaviour is serious enough to make them unsuitable to be a tenant; and
- their lettings policies are responsive to authorities' housing duties, take account of the need to give reasonable priority to transfer applicants, are responsive to national, regional and local mobility and exchange schemes, and are demonstrably fair and effectively controlled.

5   Therefore, the overriding requirement for RSLs in relation to homelessness is to demonstrate that they are co-operating with local authorities to enable them to fulfil their statutory duties.

CO-OPERATION AND PARTNERSHIPS

6   Housing authorities need to draw on these regulatory requirements to form constructive partnerships with RSLs. It is also recommended that authorities refer to the strategic document 'A Framework for Partnership' published jointly by the Local Government Association, the National Housing Federation

and the Housing Corporation and available at www.lga.gov.uk/Documents/
Briefing/framework.pdf

7   Where RSLs participate in choice-based lettings schemes, the Corporation
     will expect any protocols for joint working with housing authorities to make
     proper provision to meet the needs of vulnerable groups, and ensure that sup-
     port is available to enable tenants and applicants to exercise choice. Housing
     authorities should involve RSLs in the implementation of choice-based let-
     tings schemes at an early stage.

NOMINATION AGREEMENTS

8   Whilst legislation provides the framework for co-operation between housing
     authorities and RSLs, nomination agreements set out the way in which this
     co-operation is given effect. It is crucial that a housing authority has a compre-
     hensive nomination agreement with each of its partner RSLs to ensure that
     both sides know what is expected of them. The need for a robust nomination
     agreement applies in all circumstances, but will be particularly important
     where the housing authority has transferred ownership of its housing stock
     and is reliant on the transfer RSL (and any other partner RSLs) to provide
     housing for their applicants. ODPM guidance on *Housing Allocation, Home-
     lessness and Stock Transfer – A Guide to Key Issues (2004)* sets out the policy
     and operational matters which the nomination agreement between the hous-
     ing authority and their transfer RSL should cover.

9   RSLs are required to offer at least 50% of vacancies in their stock (net of inter-
     nal transfers) to housing authority nominations, unless some lower figure
     is agreed between the two bodies.[25] In some circumstances, they may agree
     a substantially higher figure. However, housing authorities should bear in
     mind that RSLs are required to retain their independence. They must honour
     their constitutional obligations under their diverse governing instruments,
     and will make the final decision on the allocation of their housing, within
     their regulatory framework.

10   Where requested by a housing authority, RSLs should consider the possible
     use of a proportion of their own stock to provide temporary accommodation
     for people owed a homelessness duty under Part 7 of the 1996 Act. This may
     be necessary in some areas, particularly those where demand for housing is
     very high and there is a significant number of homeless families with chil-
     dren who need to be placed in temporary accommodation. RSLs and housing
     authorities will have joint responsibility for determining the appropriate use
     of settled housing stock for temporary lettings, taking into account that such
     use will reduce the volume of RSL housing stock available for nominations
     into long-term tenancies. Housing authorities should ensure that their part-
     nerships take maximum advantage of the flexibility that such arrangements
     can provide. The Secretary of State expects that, wherever possible, social
     housing should be allocated on a settled basis rather than used to provide
     temporary accommodation in the medium to long term. Where medium to
     long term accommodation is required, the authority and RSL should consider
     whether it is possible to offer a secure or an assured tenancy under the terms
     of the authority's allocations scheme.

25 Housing Corporation Regulatory Circular, 02/03, February 2003.

11   Housing authorities should ensure that the details of nominated households given to RSLs are accurate and comprehensive. Details should include information about the applicant's priority status under the housing authority's policy, as well as indications of vulnerability, support needs and arrangements for support.

12   The Corporation expects that RSLs' approach to exclusions and evictions will generally reflect the principles to which housing authorities work. Housing Corporation Circular 07/04 *Tenancy management: eligibility and evictions* sets out the Corporation's expectations of RSLs when assessing the eligibility of applicants and when working to prevent or respond to breaches of tenancy.

EFFECTIVE COLLABORATION

13   It is important that housing authorities foster good partnership working with RSLs, to help them prevent and tackle homelessness in the district. The housing management and care and support approaches undertaken by RSLs are key to sustaining tenancies, reducing evictions and abandonment, and preventing homelessness. To ensure effective collaboration between themselves and partner RSLs operating in their district, housing authorities should consider the following:

nominations agreements: housing authorities should ensure that they have a formal nominations agreement with all partner RSLs and that there are robust arrangements in place to monitor effective delivery of the terms of the agreement. These should be clearly set out, and should include the proportion of lettings that will be made available, any conditions that will apply, and how any disputes about suitability or eligibility will be resolved. Housing authorities should negotiate for the maximum number of lettings that will be required to enable them to discharge their housing functions and which would be reasonable for the RSL to deliver.

exclusion criteria: when negotiating nominations agreements housing authorities should aim for any exclusion criteria (that may be applied to nominees by the RSL) to be kept to a minimum. To prevent new tenancies from failing and to minimise the likelihood of exclusion, housing authorities should also ensure that adequate support packages are in place for vulnerable applicants before a nominee is expected to take up their tenancy.

eviction policies: to help prevent homelessness, housing authorities should encourage RSLs to seek to minimise any need for eviction of their tenants by employing preventative strategies and taking early positive action where breaches of tenancy agreement have occurred. Associations should act to support and sustain, rather than terminate, a tenancy.

In cases involving anti-social behaviour eviction should, where possible, be used as a last resort, although in particularly serious cases or where perpetrators refuse to co-operate it may be necessary. A number of measures have been introduced which may be used to tackle anti-social behaviour without removing the perpetrator from their home and moving the problem to somewhere else. These include Acceptable Behaviour Contracts, Anti-Social Behaviour Orders, housing injunctions and demotion. Further information on the tools and powers available to tackle anti-social behaviour can be found on the TOGETHER website, a resource for practitioners working to tackle anti-social behaviour (www.together.gov.uk).

Similarly, in cases involving rent arrears eviction should, where possible, be used as a last resort. RSLs should employ strategies to maximise their income and to prevent and manage rent arrears. Where arrears have accrued they should seek early intervention through personal contact with the tenant(s) offering support and advice. They should offer practical ways for recovering the arrears through debt management plans, referrals to debt advice agencies and ensuring that tenants are claiming all the benefits to which they are entitled. ODPM published guidance for local authorities and RSLs on *Improving the Effectiveness of Rent Arrears Management* (June 2005).

Supporting People programme: housing authorities should ensure they work closely with RSLs in implementing the Supporting People programme to ensure that housing-related support can be delivered, where appropriate, for people who would be at risk of homelessness without such support.

mobility: housing authorities should work with RSLs in considering the scope for mobility – including moves to other areas, moves to other tenures, and joint action to reduce under-occupation and over-crowding – in meeting housing need and reducing homelessness. Larger RSLs, which operate in a number of different areas, may be uniquely placed to facilitate cross-boundary moves, including voluntary moves from high demand areas to areas of lower demand. ODPM, in conjunction with the Housing Corporation, National Housing Federation and Local Government Association, published a good practice guide for local authorities and housing associations on *Effective Co-operation in Tackling Homelessness: Nomination Agreements and Exclusions (2004)*.

ANNEX 6
Homelessness Strategy: Specific Action that might be expected to be taken by Others

PUBLIC SECTOR
Registered social landlords
- ensure allocation policies meet the needs of people accepted as homeless including specialist provision for vulnerable groups, e.g. drug misusers;
- ensure allocation policies are inclusive, defensible and do not operate 'blanket bans' for particular groups;
- ensure arrears policies take into account the aims of the homelessness strategy (and facilitate early access to money and housing advice).

Primary care trusts
- develop health services for homeless people, (e.g. Personal Medical Service pilots, walk-in centres, GP service that visits hostels and day centres);
- ensure access to primary health care for all homeless people including rough sleepers and those using emergency access accommodation;
- liaise with social services and special needs housing providers to ensure access to dependency and multiple needs services where needed;
- ensure that hospital discharge policies and protocols are developed and put in place for those leaving hospital who are in housing need;
- ensure access to mental health services, including counselling and therapy where needed.

Children's trusts
–   ensure children's services and housing strategies are integrated to achieve better outcomes for children.

Youth and community services
–   develop peer support schemes;
–   raise awareness of homelessness issues with young people at risk.

National offender management service
–   complete a basic housing needs assessment on entry to custody in all local establishments;
–   share information with other agencies on risk of harm, potential homelessness and vulnerability;
–   develop local protocols regarding dealing with potentially homeless offenders and information sharing;
–   as part of the local Supporting People Commissioning bodies, provide specialist knowledge to help commission new services for vulnerable offender and victim groups.

Regional offender managers
–   ensure regional strategic representation of the needs of offenders in custody and the community.

Community safety team/anti-social behaviour team
–   develop steps/interventions to reduce anti-social behaviour and therefore reduce the risk of evictions.

Youth offending team
–   work with children and young people to prevent their offending, effectively integrate them and their families within the community and ultimately prevent evictions.

Drug action team
–   consider the need to commission treatment for homeless people, or whether mainstream services can be extended to meet their needs;
–   develop accommodation options for substance misusers including such provision as Rent Deposit Schemes;
–   develop, in collaboration with Supporting People teams, specialist housing provision for substance misusers;
–   ensure that the children of adults with substance misuse problems are taken into account when planning services.

Jobcentre plus
–   ensure that clients are helped to find and keep a job;
–   ensure that clients claim and receive the benefits they are entitled to.

Connexions service
–   provide advice and information on housing and related benefits (or referral to other agencies where appropriate) to all 13 to 19 year olds who need it;
–   ensure vulnerable young people have access to a personal adviser with the aim of preventing those young people becoming homeless.

National asylum support service (NASS)
- ensure NASS accommodation providers notify local authorities of the planned withdrawal of NASS accommodation within two days of a positive asylum decision;
- encourage NASS accommodation providers to help prevent homelessness amongst new refugees (e.g. via tenancy conversion or delaying evictions);
- ensure that homelessness and housing pressures are taken into account by Regional Strategic Co-ordination Meetings when decisions are taken on future asylum seeker dispersal areas.

VOLUNTARY SECTOR
- Provision of a range of services including:
  - Rent in advance/deposit bond schemes;
  - Night stop schemes;
  - Supported lodgings schemes;
  - Homelessness awareness/preventative input to schools;
  - Advice services (housing/debt/benefits etc.);
  - Counselling, mediation, reconciliation services;
  - Provision of floating support;
  - Lay advocacy services;
  - Dependency services;
  - Hospital discharge services;
  - Women's refuges;
  - Day Centres;
  - Outreach to those sleeping rough;
  - Provision of emergency accommodation (e.g. night shelters);
  - Hostels;
  - Foyers;
  - Resettlement services (including pre-tenancy, move-on accommodation and tenancy sustainment);
  - Mental health services;
  - Peer support, self-help and user groups;
  - Meaningful occupation/personal development work/job training/skills for employment/ work placements;
  - Support for parents of young people at risk of homelessness;
  - Support for victims of crime.

PRIVATE SECTOR
- provision of hostels;
- making lettings available to people who are homeless or at risk of homelessness (e.g. through landlord accreditation schemes);
- working with tenants to address rent arrears.

ANNEX 7
Tackling Common Causes of Homelessness

1   This annex provides guidance on how authorities might tackle some of the more common causes of homelessness at an early stage.

Parents, relatives or friends not being able to provide accommodation

2   Housing authorities are advised to consider a range of approaches aimed at avoiding the crisis of homelessness, resolving problems in the long-term or providing respite and time for a planned, and often more sustainable move. Home visits and mediation services can play an important role in delaying or preventing homelessness by helping people find solutions and resolve difficulties.

3   Family tensions can make living conditions intolerable for young people and their parents. Housing authorities are advised to work closely with children's trusts at strategic level to ensure that housing need and homelessness prevention are included in the strategic planning process through the Children and Young People's Plan. They are also advised to work closely with children's trusts at delivery level as part of local multi-agency teams that provide joined up services focusing on improving outcomes for children and young people. As part of this work, they may consider developing partnerships with key agencies in the voluntary sector who work with young people at risk of homelessness. Trained staff and peer mentors can often help young people in difficult relationships restore some links to their families or supporters, resolve family conflict or facilitate planned moves into alternative accommodation.

Relationship breakdown

4   Relationships may often be strained or break down due to periods of separation, e.g. long-term hospital or drug treatment or because of the behaviour of family members, e.g. offending or violence. Local authorities should develop systems for assessing appropriate forms of intervention and the assessment of risks to vulnerable family members to inform decisions about intervention, e.g. where domestic violence or child safety is involved.

5   Local authorities should consider the use of home visits, mediation and counselling services to help couples and families reconcile their differences or facilitate planned moves to alternative accommodation.

6   Housing authorities are advised to consider the provision of specialist advice targeted at young people at risk of homelessness. Local Connexions services, for example, can play a key role in reaching vulnerable young people; helping them access information and advice, providing one-to-one support or brokering appropriate specialist support from key services such as welfare, health, substance and/or alcohol misuse services, education and employment. Housing authorities might also consider working with local schools in order to provide young people with information about the implications of leaving home and the housing choices available to them.

Domestic violence

7   As well as being a direct and underlying cause of homelessness, it is becoming increasingly apparent that domestic violence is a major factor among people who experience 'repeat' homelessness. In many cases, the provision of advice and outreach services to support people who experience domestic violence before they reach crisis point, for example on ex-partner rent arrears, tenancy agreements and property rights, can help to prevent homelessness.

8   Housing authorities are encouraged to offer people who have experienced domestic violence a range of accommodation and support options. For some, escaping domestic violence will involve leaving their home, often as a last resort,

and those who have experienced domestic violence may be placed in a refuge or another form of appropriate temporary accommodation where necessary. Many people who have experienced domestic violence would, however, prefer to remain in their own homes with their social and support networks around them. From 1 April 2005 local authorities have been strongly encouraged to develop, launch and promote a sanctuary type scheme in order to meet part of the revised domestic violence Best Value Performance Indicator 225. The scheme provides security measures to allow those experiencing domestic violence to remain in their own homes where they choose to do so, where safety can be assured and where the perpetrator no longer lives within the accommodation.

9   It is important that when developing policies, strategies and practice-based interventions, housing authorities work with all relevant bodies. For example, when considering the safety, security and confidentiality of people who have experienced domestic violence and their children, especially those children who may be vulnerable and/or at risk, housing authorities will need to work with Crime and Disorder Reduction Partnerships, the Local Domestic Violence Fora and with the Local Safeguarding Children Board. BVPI 225 encourages further work in this area.

End of an assured shorthold tenancy

10   The use of home visits, landlord-tenant mediation services and tenancy sustainment services may enable tenants who have been asked to leave their home to remain with their existing private landlords, through negotiation, mediation and the offer of practical solutions, such as clearing a debt, providing the tenant with advice on managing budgets or fast-tracking a Housing Benefit claim.

11   Housing authorities should also establish services to provide tenants in housing difficulties with advice and information about available housing options and, where necessary, assistance to help them access alternative accommodation. Advice might include, for example, advice about private landlords and letting agents, including any accreditation schemes, within the district; the availability of rent guarantee or rent deposit schemes; or how to apply for social housing through the local authority housing waiting list or from other social landlords).

Rent and mortgage arrears

12   Early intervention by the housing authority could help prevent difficulties with rent or mortgage arrears from triggering a homelessness crisis for tenants or home owners.
Options might include:
    – personal contact with tenants or homeowners to offer support and advice:;
    – mediation with private landlords;
    – welfare benefits advice and assistance with making claims;
    – debt counselling and money advice (either in-house or through referrals to specialist advice agencies);
    – advice on practical ways of recovering rent arrears through debt management plans, attachment to earnings or benefits orders or by referrals to a debt advice agencies.

13   Many approaches to the prevention and management of rent arrears among tenants can apply equally whether the landlord is a social sector or a private sector landlord. ODPM published guidance for local authorities and RSLs on *Improving the Effectiveness of Rent Arrears Management (June 2005)*.

14   In some cases rent arrears may be the result of an underlying problem such as alcohol or drug misuse, death of a partner, relationship breakdown, change in employment status, or physical or mental health problems. In such cases the housing authority may wish to contact the appropriate health and social services departments and other relevant agencies for advice, assistance and specialist support. The Secretary of State considers that housing authorities should always consult the Children's Trust before considering the eviction of a family with children. Vital work helping vulnerable children can be affected if families with children are forced to move out of the local area. Effective, ongoing liaison arrangements and collaborative working will be important in such instances.

Housing Benefit administration

15   Rent arrears can arise from delays in the calculation and payment of housing benefit. It is therefore in housing authorities' interests to develop prompt and efficient systems for the payment of benefit in order to avoid a risk of homelessness arising as a result of such delays. Where the administration of housing benefit and the provision of housing assistance are dealt with by different departments of the local authority, it will be necessary for the authority to ensure that effective liaison arrangements are in place. Efficient housing benefit payments systems can also help to increase the confidence of private sector landlords in letting accommodation to tenants who may rely on benefits to meet their rent costs.

Anti-social behaviour and offending

16   Tenants may be at risk of becoming homeless as a result of their own or others' anti-social or offending behaviour. Housing authorities are urged to contact tenants in these circumstances at the earliest possible stage where they have received a complaint or where it has been brought to their attention that a tenant is causing a nuisance or annoyance. This will enable them to inform such tenants of the possible consequences of continuing with the reported behaviour and may prevent homelessness resulting in some instances. Authorities will need to be aware of the need for discretion about the source of any complaint, particularly where there is concern about threatening or aggressive behaviour.

17   In cases where a housing authority is satisfied that there is a substantive complaint of anti-social behaviour they will need to consider a range of options to address the problem with the tenant before embarking on action to terminate the tenancy. Housing authorities are advised, where possible, to use eviction as a last resort, although in particularly serious cases or where perpetrators refuse to co-operate it may be necessary.

18   Mediation services may help to resolve neighbour disputes which have led to complaints of anti-social behaviour. A number of measures have been introduced which may be used to tackle anti-social behaviour without removing the perpetrator from their home and simply moving the problem somewhere else. These include: Acceptable Behaviour Contracts, Anti-Social Behaviour

Orders, housing injunctions and demotion. Further information can be found on the TOGETHER website, a resource for practitioners working to tackle anti-social behaviour (www.together.gov.uk).

19 Where local authority tenants are at risk of homelessness as a result of other tenants' anti-social behaviour, authorities should be aware of the powers they have to take action against the perpetrators and make urgent housing transfers to protect victims of violence or harassment, where requested.

20 Housing authorities will need to work closely with the National Offender Management Service (NOMS) and their partners in the voluntary and community sector to manage the housing arrangements of offenders in the community, and ensure they receive any support necessary to avoid a risk of homelessness. Where an authority may be considering the eviction of an offender, it will need to consult closely with NOMS to ensure this can be avoided wherever possible. This will also help reduce re-offending and promote community safety.

Leaving an institutional environment

21 People leaving an institutional environment can be particularly at risk of homelessness and may seek assistance from the housing authority to obtain accommodation when they move on. Authorities should have systems in place to ensure that they have advance notice of such people's needs for accommodation in such circumstances to allow them to take steps well in advance to ensure that arrangements are in place to enable a planned and timely move.

Young people leaving care
22 It is important that, wherever possible, the housing needs of care leavers are addressed before they leave care. All care leavers must have a pathway plan prepared by appropriate staff of the authority responsible for their care, setting out the support they will be provided with to enable them make a successful transition to a more independent lifestyle. Making arrangements for accommodation and ensuring that, where necessary, care leavers are provided with suitable housing support will be an essential aspect of the pathway plan. Where care leavers may require social housing, their housing and related support needs should be discussed with the appropriate agencies. Where necessary, arrangements will need to be made for joint assessment between social services and housing authorities, as part of a multi-agency assessment necessary to inform the pathway plan of individual young people.

23 Consideration of an individual care leaver's housing needs should take account of their need for support and reasonable access to places of education, employment, training and health care. As far as possible, pathway plans should include contingency plans in the event of any breakdown in the young person's accommodation arrangements. It is recommended that housing and social services authorities (and relevant departments within unitary authorities) develop joint protocols for meeting the needs of care leavers to ensure that each agency (or department) plays a full role in providing support to – and building trust with – this client group.

Custody or detention
24 Around a third of prisoners lose their housing on imprisonment, so it is important that prisoners receive effective advice and assistance about housing

options, either prior to or when being remanded or sentenced to custody. Assessing an offender's housing needs at this point will help to identify those prisoners who may require assistance to bring to an end, sustain or transfer an existing tenancy, make a claim for Housing Benefit to meet rent costs while in prison, or to help a prisoner transfer or close down an existing tenancy appropriately. Local authorities are advised to assist the Prison Service in providing advice to prisoners and taking action to ensure they can sustain their accommodation while in custody.

25 It is recommended that housing advice be made available to offender through-out the period of custody or detention to ensure that any housing needs are addressed. It is important that early planning takes place between prison staff and housing providers to identify housing options on release, to prevent homelessness and enable them to make a smooth transition from prison, or remand, to independent living.

26 All prisoners in local prisons and Category C prisons have access to housing advice. And, from April 2005 all local prisons have been required to carry out a housing needs assessment for every new prisoner, including those serving short sentences. Local authorities are advised to assist the Prison Service in delivering these services.

27 All Youth Offending Teams (YOTs) now have named accommodation officers. YOTs can offer both practical support to children, young people and their families and can increasingly play a key strategic role in ensuring that young offenders are effectively resettled through accessing mainstream provision and services.

28 Joint working between the National Offender Management Service/Youth Offending Teams and their local housing authorities is essential to help prevent homelessness amongst offenders, ex-offenders and others who have experience of the criminal justice system. Options might include:
   – having a single contact point within the housing authority to provide housing advice and assistance for those who have experience of the criminal justice system;
   – Probation staff offering information on securing or terminating tenancies prior to custody;
   – running housing advice sessions in local prisons to further enable prisoners to access advice on housing options prior to their release;
   – prisons granting prisoners Release On Temporary Licence to attend housing interviews with landlords;
   – developing tenancy support services for those who have experienced the criminal justice system.

Armed forces
29 Members of Her Majesty's regular naval, military and air forces are generally provided with accommodation by the Ministry of Defence (MOD), but are required to leave this when they are discharged from the service. The principal responsibility for providing housing information and advice to Service personnel lies with the armed forces up to the point of discharge and these services are delivered through the Joint Service Housing Advice Office (telephone: 01722 436575). Some people, who have served in the armed forces for a long period, and those who are medically discharged, may be offered assistance

with resettlement by Ministry of Defence (MOD) resettlement staff. The MOD issues a *Certificate of Cessation of Entitlement to Occupy Service Living Accommodation* (see examples at Annexes 14 and 15) six months before discharge.

30　Housing authorities that have a significant number of service personnel stationed in their area will need to work closely with relevant partners, such as the Joint Service Housing Advice Office and MOD's resettlement services, to ascertain likely levels of need for housing assistance amongst people leaving the forces and plan their services accordingly. In particular, housing authorities are advised to take advantage of the six-month period of notice of discharge to ensure that service personnel receive timely and comprehensive advice on the housing options available to them when they leave the armed forces. Authorities may also wish to consider creating links with the employment and business communities to assist people leaving the armed forces to find work or meaningful occupation, enabling them further to make a successful transition to independent living in the community.

31　The Veterans Agency should be the first point of contact for all former armed forces personnel who require information about housing issues. The agency provide a free help line (telephone: 0800 169 2277) which offers former armed forces personnel advice and signposting to ex-Service benevolent organisations who may be able to offer assistance with housing matters.

Hospital

32　Some people who are admitted to hospital – even for a short time – may be in housing need or at risk of homelessness. And some people who may not be in housing need when they are admitted may become at risk of losing their home during a protracted stay in hospital, for example, if they are unable to maintain their rent or mortgage payments. This can apply, in particular, to people admitted to hospital for mental health reasons and for whom family, tenancy or mortgage breakdown is an accompanying factor to the admission to hospital.

33　Housing authorities are advised to work closely with social services and NHS Trusts in order to establish good procedures for the discharge of patients, and to ensure that former patients are not homeless or at risk of homelessness on leaving hospital. This could involve agreeing joint protocols for hospital admissions and discharge of patients to ensure that the housing and support needs of inpatients are identified as early as possible after admission, and that arrangements are put in place to meet the needs of patients in good time prior to discharge. Measures might include, for example, setting up a multi-agency discharge team as part of the homelessness strategy action plan or funding a dedicated post to support patients who may be at risk of homelessness when discharged from hospital.

34　Further guidance is provided in Department of Health publications on *Achieving timely simple discharge from hospital: A toolkit for the multi-disciplinary team (2004)* and *Discharge from hospital: pathway, process and practice (2003)*.

Accommodation provided by National Asylum Support Service (NASS)

35　Asylum seekers who receive leave to remain in the UK must move on from their NASS accommodation within 28 days of the decision on their case. Former asylum seekers will therefore have little time to find alternative accommodation and are unlikely to have had any experience of renting or buying accommodation in the UK, or experience of related matters such as claiming benefits or arranging essential services such as gas, water and electricity. These difficulties are likely to be compounded by the fact that many former asylum seekers may face cultural barriers such as language.

36   In order to prevent these factors leading to homelessness amongst former asylum seekers, housing authorities are advised to develop protocols with NASS accommodation providers, refugee support services and NASS regional managers to ensure that, where possible, a planned and timely move to alternative accommodation or the sustainment of existing accommodation can take place. Housing benefit, rent deposits, homeless prevention loans and discretionary housing benefit payments can all help to fund temporary extensions of the NASS notice period or longer-term tenancy conversion through the establishment of assured shorthold tenancies.

37   Former asylum seekers will need effective and timely advice on the range of housing options available. It is vital that housing authorities ensure that this advice and information can be readily translated into community languages and delivered in locations accessible to asylum seekers and refugees. Authorities are also advised to consider whether there may be a need for ongoing resettlement support in order to maximise the chances of tenancy sustainment. As standard, authorities are advised to ensure that new refugees are made fully aware of the steps that they need to take to maintain a UK tenancy.

38   Authorities may wish to refer to *Housing and Support Services for asylum seekers and refugees: a good practice guide (2005)* published by the Chartered Institute of Housing.

Ethnic minority populations

39   Statistics provided by local authorities show that people from ethnic minority backgrounds are around three times more likely to be accepted as owed a main homelessness duty than their White counterparts. This pattern is found across all regions in England and the reasons are varied and complex. It is therefore critical that housing authorities and their partner agencies develop comprehensive strategies to better prevent and respond to homelessness among people from ethnic minority communities.

40   ODPM published *Tackling homelessness amongst ethnic minority households – a development guide (2005)* to assist local authorities and their partner agencies in the development of inclusive, evidence-based and cost-effective homelessness services for their local ethnic minority populations.

Drug users

41   Drug use can both precede and occur as a result of homelessness. Between half and three quarters of single homeless people have in the past been problematic drug misusers. Many have a wide range of support needs, which reinforce each other and heighten the risk of drug use and homelessness. For those who are engaging in drug treatment, or have stabilised their use, homelessness increases their chances of relapse and continued problematic drug use. Housing authorities are advised to work closely with Drug Action Teams (multi-agency partnerships who co-ordinate the drug strategy at the local level) to ensure that housing and homelessness strategies are aligned with DAT treatment plans and Supporting People strategies help address the needs of homeless drug users as a shared client group.

ANNEX 8
How to Contact the Home Office Immigration and Nationality Directorate

1   The Home Office's Immigration and Nationality Directorate (IND) will exchange information with housing authorities subject to relevant data protection and disclosure policy requirements being met and properly managed, provided that the information is required to assist with the carrying out of statutory functions or prevention and detection of fraud.

2   The Evidence and Enquiries Unit (EEU) will provide a service to housing authorities to confirm the immigration status of an applicant from abroad (Non-Asylum Seekers). In order to take advantage of the service, housing authorities first need to register with the Evidence and Enquiries Unit, Immigration and Nationality Directorate, 12th Floor Lunar House, Croydon, CR9 2BY either by letter or **Fax: 020 8196 3049**

3   Registration details required by the EEU's Local Authorities' Team are:
     (a) Name of enquiring housing authority on headed paper;
     (b) Job title/status of officer registering on behalf of the local housing authority; and
     (c) Names of housing authority staff and their respective job titles/status who will be making enquiries on behalf of the housing authority.

4   Once the housing authority is registered with the EEU, and this has been confirmed, then the authorised personnel can make individual enquiries by letter or fax, but replies will be returned by post.

5   The EEU will not usually indicate that someone is an asylum seeker unless the applicant has signed a disclaimer and it is attached to the enquiry or if the enquirer has specifically asked about asylum.

6   If a response indicates that the applicant has an outstanding asylum claim, or there are any queries regarding an ongoing asylum case, enquiries should be made to NASS LA Comms on 020 8760 4527. Local authorities will also need to be registered with this team before any information can be provided.

7   The Home Office (IND) can only advise whether an EEA/foreign national has a right of residence in the United Kingdom. IND does not decide whether an EEA/Foreign national qualifies for benefits or for local authority housing.

ANNEX 9
Asylum Seekers

OVERVIEW

1   Generally, asylum seekers can be expected to be *persons subject to immigration control* who have been given *temporary admission* but have not been granted leave to enter or remain in the UK.

2   **Asylum seekers who are** *persons subject to immigration control* **and whose claim for asylum was made** *after 2 April 2000* **are not eligible for assistance under Part 7.** However, some asylum seekers who are *persons subject to immigration control* and whose claim for asylum was made before 3 April 2000 may be eligible (see below).

3   Broadly speaking, an asylum seeker is a person claiming to have a well-founded

fear of being persecuted for reasons of race, religion, nationality, membership of a particular social group, or political opinion, and who is unable or unwilling to avail him or her self of the protection of the authorities in his or her own country.

4   A person only becomes an asylum seeker when his or her claim for asylum has been recorded by the Home Secretary, and he or she remains an asylum seeker until such time as that application has been finally resolved (including the resolution of any appeal). The recording, consideration and resolution of such claims is a matter for the Home Office Immigration and Nationality Directorate (IND).

5   If there is any uncertainty about an applicant's immigration or asylum status, housing authorities should contact the Home Office Immigration and Nationality Directorate, using the procedures set out in Annex 8. Before doing so, the applicant should be advised that an inquiry will be made: if at this stage the applicant prefers to withdraw his or her application, no further action will be required

ASYLUM SEEKERS WHO ARE ELIGIBLE FOR PART 7 ASSISTANCE

6   The *Allocation of Housing and Homelessness (Eligibility) (England) Regulations 2006* (SI 2006 No.1294) ('the Eligibility Regulations') provide that asylum seekers who are *persons subject to immigration control* and who claimed asylum before 3 April 2000 are eligible for assistance under Part 7 in certain circumstances (set out below). However, by virtue of s.186(1), an asylum seeker is not eligible for Part 7 assistance if he or she has any accommodation in the UK – however temporary – available for his or her occupation. This would include a place in a hostel or bed and breakfast hotel.

7   Subject to s.186(1), such asylum seekers are eligible for assistance under Part 7, if they claimed asylum *before 3 April 2000*, and:

i)   the claim for asylum was made at the port on initial arrival in the UK (but not on re-entry) from a country outside the United Kingdom, the Channel Islands, the Isle of Man or the Republic of Ireland; **or**

ii) the claim for asylum was made within 3 months of a declaration by the Secretary of State that he would not normally order the return of a person to the country of which he or she is a national because of a fundamental change of circumstances in that country, and the asylum seeker was present in Great Britain on the date the declaration was made; **or**

iii) the claim for asylum was made on or before 4 February 1996 and the applicant was entitled to housing benefit on 4 February 1996 under regulation 7A of the *Housing Benefit (General) Regulations 1987*.

8   Generally, a person ceases to be an asylum seeker for the purposes of the Eligibility Regulations when his claim for asylum is recorded by the Secretary of State as having been decided (other than on appeal) or abandoned. However, a person does not cease to be an asylum seeker in these circumstances for the purposes of paragraph 7(iii) if he continues to be eligible for housing benefit by virtue of:

–   regulation 10(6) of the *Housing Benefit Regulations 2006* (SI 2006 No. 213), or

–   regulation 10(6) of the *Housing Benefit (persons who have attained the qualifying age for state pension credit) Regulations 2006* (SI 2006 No. 214).

as amended by the *Housing Benefit and Council Tax Benefit (Consequential Provisions) Regulations 2006* (SI 2006 No.217).

FORMER ASYLUM SEEKERS

9   Where an asylum claim is successful – either initially or following an appeal – the claimant will normally be granted refugee status. If a claim is unsuccessful, leave to remain in the UK may still be granted, in accordance with published policies on Humanitarian Protection and Discretionary Leave. Former asylum seekers granted refugee status, or those granted Humanitarian Protection or Discretionary Leave which is not subject to a condition requiring him to maintain and accommodate himself without recourse to public funds will be eligible for homelessness assistance.

10 Prior to April 2003, Exceptional Leave to Remain was granted rather than Humanitarian Protection or Discretionary Leave. Those with Exceptional Leave to Remain which is not subject to a condition requiring him to maintain and accommodate himself without recourse to public funds will also be eligible for homelessness assistance.

INFORMATION

11 Under s.187 of the *Housing Act 1996*, the Home Office Immigration and Nationality Directorate (IND) will, on request, provide local housing authorities with the information necessary to determine whether a particular housing applicant is an asylum seeker, or a dependant of an asylum seeker, and whether he or she is eligible for assistance under Part 7. In cases where it is confirmed that a housing applicant is an asylum seeker, or the dependant of an asylum seeker, any subsequent change in circumstances which affect the applicant's housing status (eg. a decision on the asylum claim) will be notified to the authority by the IND. The procedures for contacting the IND are set out in Annex 8.

ANNEX 10
The Habitual Residence Test

1   In practice, when considering housing applications from persons who are subject to the habitual residence test, it is only necessary to investigate habitual residence if the applicant has arrived or returned to live in the UK during the two year period prior to making the application.

DEFINITION OF HABITUALLY RESIDENT

2   The term 'habitually resident' is not defined in legislation. Local authorities should always consider the overall circumstances of a case to determine whether someone is habitually resident in the UK, the Channel Islands, the Isle of Man or the Republic of Ireland.

GENERAL PRINCIPLES

3   When deciding whether a person is habitually resident in a place, consideration must be given to all the facts of each case in a common sense way. It should be remembered that:–

- the test focuses on the fact and nature of residence;
- a person who is not resident somewhere cannot be habitually resident there. Residence is a more settled state than mere physical presence in a country. To be resident a person must be seen to be making a home. It need not be the only home or a permanent home but it must be a genuine home for the time being. For example, a short stay visitor or a person receiving short term medical treatment is not resident;
- the most important factors for habitual residence are the length, continuity and general nature of actual residence rather than intention;
- the practicality of a person's arrangements for residence is a necessary part of determining whether it can be described as settled and habitual;
- established habitual residents who have periods of temporary or occasional absence of long or short duration may still be habitually resident during such absences.

ACTION ON RECEIPT OF AN APPLICATION

Applicant came to live in the UK during the previous two years

4   If it appears that the applicant came to live in the UK during the previous two years, authorities should make further enquiries to decide if the applicant is habitually resident, or can be treated as such.

Factors to consider

5   The applicant's stated reasons and intentions for coming to the UK will be relevant to the question of whether he or she is habitually resident. If the applicant's stated intention is to live in the UK, and not return to the country from which they came, that intention must be consistent with their actions.

6   To decide whether an applicant is habitually resident in the UK, authorities should consider the factors set out below. However, these do not provide an exhaustive check list of the questions or factors that need to be considered. Further enquiries may be needed. The circumstances of each case will dictate what information is needed, and all relevant factors should be taken into account.

Why has the applicant come to the UK?

7   If the applicant is returning to the UK after a period spent abroad, and it can be established that the applicant was previously habitually resident in the UK and is returning to resume his or her former period of habitual residence, **he or she will be immediately habitually resident.**

8   In determining whether an applicant is returning to resume a former period of habitual residence authorities should consider:
- when did the applicant leave the UK?
- how long did the applicant live in the UK before leaving?
- why did the applicant leave the UK?
- how long did the applicant intend to remain abroad?
- why did the applicant return?
- did the applicant's partner and children, if any, also leave the UK?
- did the applicant keep accommodation in the UK?
- if the applicant owned property, was it let, and was the lease timed to coincide with the applicant's return to the UK?
- what links did the applicant keep with the UK?

     – have there been other brief absences? If yes, obtain details

     – why has the applicant come to the UK?

9   If the applicant has arrived in the UK within the previous two years and is not resuming a period of habitual residence, consideration should be given to his or her reasons for coming to the UK, and in particular to the factors set out below.

Applicant is joining family or friends

10   If the applicant has come to the UK to join or rejoin family or friends, authorities should consider:

     – has the applicant sold or given up any property abroad?

     – has the applicant bought or rented accommodation or is he or she staying with friends?

     – is the move to the UK intended to be permanent?

Applicant's plans

11   Authorities should consider the applicant's plans, e.g.:

     – if the applicant plans to remain in the UK, is the applicant's stated plan consistent with his or her actions?

     – were any arrangements made for employment and accommodation (even if unsuccessful) before the applicant arrived in the UK?

     – did the applicant buy a one-way ticket?

     – did the applicant bring all his or her belongings?

     – is there any evidence of links with the UK, eg membership of clubs?

12   The fact that a person may intend to live in the UK for the foreseeable future does not, of itself, mean that habitual residence has been established. However, the applicant's intentions along with other factors, for example the disposal of property abroad, may indicate that the applicant is habitually resident in the UK.

13   An applicant who intends to reside in the UK for only a short period, for example for a holiday or to visit friends is unlikely to be habitually resident in the UK.

Length of residence in another country

14   Authorities should consider the length and continuity of an applicant's residence in another country:

     – how long did the applicant live in the previous country?

     – does the applicant have any remaining ties with his or her former country of residence?

     – has the applicant stayed in different countries outside the UK?

15   It is possible that a person may own a property abroad but still be habitually resident in the UK. A person who has a home or close family in another country would normally retain habitual residence in that country. A person who has previously lived in several different countries but has now moved permanently to the UK may be habitually resident here.

Centre of interest

16   An applicant is likely to be habitually resident in the UK, the Channel Islands, the Isle of Man or the Republic of Ireland, despite spending time abroad, if his or her centre of interest is located in one of these places.

17   People who maintain their centre of interest in the UK, the Channel Islands, the Isle of Man or the Republic of Ireland, for example a home, a job, friends, membership of clubs, are likely to be habitually resident there. People who have retained their centre of interest in another country and have no particular ties with the UK, the Channel Islands, the Isle of Man or the Republic of Ireland, are unlikely to be habitually resident in the UK, the Channel Islands, the Isle of Man or the Republic of Ireland.

18   Authorities should take the following into account when deciding the centre of interest:
- home;
- family ties;
- club memberships;
- finance accounts

19   If the centre of interest appears to be in the UK, the Channel Islands, the Isle of Man or the Republic of Ireland but the applicant has a home somewhere else, authorities should consider the applicant's intentions regarding the property.

20   In certain cultures, e.g. the Asian culture, it is quite common for a person to live in one country but have property abroad that they do not intend to sell. Where such a person has lived in the UK, the Channel Islands, the Isle of Man or the Republic of Ireland for many years, the fact that they have property elsewhere does not necessarily mean that they intend to leave, or that the applicant's centre of interest is elsewhere.

ANNEX 11
European Groupings (EU, A8, EEA, Switzerland)

THE EUROPEAN UNION (EU)
Austria, Belgium, Cyprus, the Czech Republic, Denmark, Estonia, Finland, France, Germany, Greece, Hungary, Ireland, Italy, Latvia, Lithuania, Luxembourg, Malta, the Netherlands, Poland, Portugal, Slovakia, Slovenia, Spain, Sweden, the United Kingdom and the A8 or Accession States.

THE 'A8' OR 'ACCESSION STATES'
The 8 eastern European States that acceded to the EU in 2004 (and whose nationals may be subject to the UK Worker Registration Scheme for a transitional period):
the Czech Republic, Estonia, Hungary, Latvia, Lithuania, Poland, Slovakia and Slovenia.

THE EUROPEAN ECONOMIC AREA (EEA)
All EU countries, plus: Iceland, Norway and Liechtenstein

SWITZERLAND
Note: Although not an EEA State, Switzerland should be treated as an EEA State for the purpose of this guidance. (See the *Immigration (European Economic Area) Regulations 2006* (S.I. 2006 No. 1003), regulation 2(1))

ANNEX 12
Rights to Reside in the UK Derived from EC Law

1   EEA nationals and their family members who have a right to reside in the UK that derives from EC law are not persons subject to immigration control. This means that they will be eligible for assistance under Part 7 of the *Housing Act 1996* ('housing assistance') unless they fall within one of the categories of persons to be treated as a person from abroad who is ineligible for assistance by virtue of regulation 6 of the *Allocation of Housing and Homelessness (Eligibility) (England) Regulations 2006* ('the Eligibility Regulations').

GENERAL
Nationals of EU countries

2   Nationals of EU countries enjoy a number of different rights to reside in other Member States, including the UK. These rights derive from the EC Treaty, EC secondary legislation (in particular *Directive 2004/38/EC*), and the case law of the European Court of Justice.

3   Whether an individual EU national has a right to reside in the UK will depend on his or her circumstances, particularly his or her economic status (e.g. whether employed, self-employed, seeking work, a student, or economically inactive etc.).

The accession states

4   A slightly different regime applies to EU nationals who are nationals of the accession states. For the purposes of this guidance, 'the accession states' are the 8 eastern European countries that acceded to the EU on 1 May 2004: Poland, Lithuania, Estonia, Latvia, Slovenia, Slovakia, Hungary and the Czech Republic.

The Immigration (European Economic Area) Regulations 2006

5   The Immigration (European Economic Area) Regulations 2006 ('the EEA Regulations') implement into UK domestic law EC legislation conferring rights of residence on EU nationals. Broadly, the EEA Regulations provide that EU nationals have the right to reside in the UK without the requirement for leave to remain under the *Immigration Act 1971* for the first 3 months of their residence, and for longer, if they are a 'qualified person' or they have acquired a permanent right of residence.

Nationals of Iceland, Liechtenstein and Norway.

6   The EEA Regulations extend the same rights to reside in the UK to nationals of Iceland, Liechtenstein and Norway as those afforded to EU nationals (The EU countries plus Iceland, Liechtenstein and Norway together comprise the EEA.)

Nationals of Switzerland

7   The EEA Regulations also extend the same rights to reside in the UK to nationals of Switzerland.

8   For the purposes of this guidance, 'EEA nationals' means nationals of any of the EU member states (excluding the UK), and nationals of Iceland, Norway, Liechtenstein and Switzerland.

INITIAL 3 MONTHS OF RESIDENCE

9   Regulation 13 of the EEA Regulations provides that EEA nationals have the right to reside in the UK for a period of up to 3 months without any conditions or formalities other than holding a valid identity card or passport. Therefore, during their first 3 months of residence in the UK, EEA nationals will not be subject to immigration control (unless the right to reside is lost following a decision by an immigration officer in accordance with regulation 13(3) of the EEA Regulations).

10   However, regulations 6(1)(b)(i) and (c) of the Eligibility Regulations provide that a person who is not subject to immigration control is not eligible for housing assistance if:

i)   his or her **only** right to reside in the UK is an initial right to reside for a period not exceeding 3 months under regulation 13 of the EEA Regulations, or

ii)   his or her **only** right to reside in the Channel Islands, the Isle of Man or the Republic of Ireland is a right equivalent to the right mentioned in (i) above which is derived from the Treaty establishing the European Community.

On (ii), article 6 of *Directive 2004/38/EC* provides that EU citizens have the right of residence in the territory of another Member State (e.g. the Republic of Ireland) for a period of up to 3 months without any conditions or formalities other than holding a valid identity card or passport.

RIGHTS OF RESIDENCE FOR 'QUALIFIED PERSONS'

11   Regulation 14 of the EEA Regulations provides that 'qualified persons' have the right to reside in the UK so long as they remain a qualified person. Under regulation 6 of the EEA Regulations, 'qualified person' means:

a)   a jobseeker,
b)   a worker,
c)   a self-employed person,
d)   a self-sufficient person,
e)   a student.

Jobseekers

12   For the purposes of regulation 6(1)(a) of the EEA Regulations, 'jobseeker' means a person who enters the UK in order to seek employment and can provide evidence that he or she is seeking employment and has a genuine chance of being employed.

13   Accession state nationals who need to register to work (see paragraph 20 below) do not have a right to reside in the UK as a jobseeker (see regulation 5(2) of the Accession Regulations, as amended). However, accession state nationals seeking work may have a right to reside by virtue of another status, e.g. as a self-sufficient person.

14   Although a person who is a jobseeker for the purposes of the definition of 'qualified person' in regulation 6(1)(a) of the EEA Regulations is not subject to immigration control, regulation 6 of the Eligibility Regulations provides that a person is not eligible for housing assistance if:

(i)   his or her only right to reside in the UK is derived from his status as a jobseeker or the family member of a jobseeker, or

(ii) his or her only right to reside in the Channel Islands, the Isle of Man or the Republic of Ireland is a right equivalent to the right mentioned in (i) above which is derived from the Treaty establishing the European Community.

Workers

15 In order to be a worker for the purposes of the EEA Regulations, a person must be employed, that is, the person is obliged to provide services for another person in return for monetary reward and who is subject to the control of that other person as regards the way in which the work is to be done.

16 Activity as an employed person may include part-time work, seasonal work and cross-border work (i.e. where a worker is established in another Member State and travels to work in the UK). However, the case law provides that the employment must be effective and genuine economic activity, and not on such a small scale as to be regarded as purely marginal and ancillary.

17 Provided the employment is effective and genuine economic activity, the fact that a person's level of remuneration may be below the level of subsistence or below the national minimum wage, or the fact that a person may be receiving financial assistance from public benefits, would not exclude that person from being a 'worker'. Housing authorities should note that surprisingly small amounts of work can be regarded as effective and genuine economic activity.

18 Applicants in the labour market should be able to confirm that they are, or have been, working in the UK by providing, for example:
- payslips,
- a contract of employment, or
- a letter of employment.

Retention of worker status

19 A person who is no longer working does not cease to be treated as a 'worker' for the purpose of regulation 6(1)(b) of the EEA Regulations, if he or she:
(a) is temporarily unable to work as the result of an illness or accident; or
(b) is recorded as involuntarily unemployed after having being employed in the UK, provided that he or she has registered as a jobseeker with the relevant employment office, and:
   (i)   was employed for one year or more before becoming unemployed, or
   (ii) has been unemployed for no more than 6 months, or
   (iii) can provide evidence that he or she is seeking employment in the UK and has a genuine chance of being engaged; or
(c) is involuntarily unemployed and has embarked on vocational training; or
(d) has voluntarily ceased working and embarked on vocational training that is related to his or her previous employment.

Accession state workers requiring registration who are treated as workers

20 By virtue of the *Accession (Immigration and Worker Registration) Regulations 2004* (SI 2004/1219) ('the Accession Regulations'), accession state nationals (with certain exceptions) are required to register their employment in the UK until they have accrued a period of 12 months' continuous employment. The exceptions are set out in Annex 13.

21 An accession state national requiring registration is only treated as a worker if he or she is actually working and:

(a) has registered his or her employment and is working in the UK for an authorised employer (see regulation 5(2) of the Accession Regulations, as amended), or

(b) is not registered for employment, but has been working for an employer for less than one month (regulation 7(3) of the Accession Regulations), or

(c) has applied to register under the Worker Registration Scheme and is working for the employer with whom he or she has applied to register (regulation 7(2)(b) of the Accession Regulations).

22   To demonstrate eligibility for housing assistance, accession state workers requiring registration should be able to:

(a) provide a valid worker registration card, and a valid worker registration certificate showing their current employer (see Annex 13 for specimens of these documents), or

(b) (where the accession state worker has applied to register but not yet received the registration certificate) provide a copy of their application to register, or

(c) show they have been working for their current employer for less than one month.

23   Authorities may need to contact the employer named in the registration certificate, to confirm that the applicant continues to be employed.

24   See Annex 13 for guidance on the Worker Registration Scheme.

25   A person who is a 'worker' for the purposes of the definition of a qualified person in regulation 6(1) of the EEA Regulations is not subject to immigration control, and is eligible for housing assistance whether or not he or she is habitually resident in the UK, the Channel Islands, the Isle of Man or the Republic of Ireland.

Self-employed persons

26   'Self-employed person' means a person who establishes himself in the UK in order to pursue activity as a self-employed person in accordance with Article 43 of the Treaty establishing the European Union.

27   A self-employed person should be able to confirm that he or she is pursuing activity as a self-employed person by providing documents relating to their business such as:

a) invoices,

b) tax accounts, or

c) utility bills.

28   A person who is no longer in self-employment does not cease to be treated as a self-employed person for the purposes of regulation 6(1)(c) of the EEA regulations, if he or she is temporarily unable to pursue his or her activity as a self-employed person as the result of an illness or accident.

29   Accession state nationals are not required to register in order to establish themselves in the UK as a self-employed person.

30   A person who is a self-employed person for the purposes of the definition of a qualified person in regulation 6(1) of the EEA Regulations is not subject to immigration control, and is eligible for housing assistance whether or not he or she is habitually resident in the UK, the Channel Islands, the Isle of Man or the Republic of Ireland.

Self-sufficient persons

31 Regulation 4(1)(c) of the EEA regulations defines 'self-sufficient person' as a person who has:

(i) sufficient resources not to become a burden on the social assistance system of the UK during his or her period of residence, and

(ii) comprehensive sickness insurance cover in the UK.

32 By regulation 4(4) of the EEA Regulations, the resources of a person who is a self-sufficient person or a student (see below), and where applicable, any family members, are to be regarded as sufficient if they exceed the maximum level of resources which a UK national and his or her family members may possess if he or she is to become eligible for social assistance under the UK benefit system.

33 Where an EEA national applies for housing assistance as a self-sufficient person and does not appear to meet the conditions of regulation 4(1)(c), the housing authority will need to consider whether he or she may have some other right to reside in the UK.

34 Where the applicant does not meet the conditions of regulation 4(1)(c) but has previously done so during his or her residence in the UK, the case should be referred to the Home Office for clarification of their status.

35 A person who is a self-sufficient person for the purposes of the definition of a qualified person in regulation 6(1) of the EEA Regulations is not subject to immigration control, but must be habitually resident in the UK, the Channel Islands, the Isle of Man or the Republic of Ireland to be eligible for housing assistance.

Students

36 Regulation 4(1)(d) of the EEA regulations defines 'student' as a person who:

(a) is enrolled at a private or public establishment included on the Department of Education and Skills' Register of Education and Training Providers, or is financed from public funds, for the principal purpose of following a course of study, including vocational training, and

(b) has comprehensive sickness insurance cover in the UK, and

(c) assures the Secretary of State, by means of a declaration or such equivalent means as the person may choose, that he or she (and if applicable his or her family members) has sufficient resources not to become a burden on the social assistance system of the UK during his or her period of residence.

37 A person who is a student for the purposes of the definition of a qualified person in regulation 6(1) of the EEA Regulations is not subject to immigration control. The eligibility of such a person for housing assistance should therefore be considered in accordance with regulation 6 of the Eligibility Regulations.

PERMANENT RIGHT OF RESIDENCE

38 Regulation 15 of the EEA Regulations provides that the following persons shall acquire the right to reside in the UK permanently:

(a) an EEA national who has resided in the UK in accordance with the EEA regulations for a continuous period of 5 years;

(b) a non-EEA national who is a family member of an EEA national and who has resided in the UK with the EEA national in accordance with the EEA regulations for a continuous period of 5 years;

(c) a worker or self-employed person who has ceased activity (see regulation 5 of the EEA Regulations for the definition of worker or self-employed person who has ceased activity);

(d) the family member of a worker or self-employed person who has ceased activity;

(e) a person who was the family member of a worker or self-employed person who has died, where the family member resided with the worker or self-employed person immediately before the death and the worker or self-employed person had resided continuously in the UK for at least 2 years before the death (or the death was the result of an accident at work or an occupational disease);

(f) a person who has resided in the UK in accordance with the EEA regulations for a continuous period of 5 years, and at the end of that period was a family member who has retained the right of residence (see regulation 10 of the EEA Regulations for the definition of a family member who has retained the right of residence).

Once acquired, the right of permanent residence can be lost through absence from the UK for a period exceeding two consecutive years.

39 A person with a right to reside permanently in the UK arising from (c), (d) or (e) above is eligible for housing assistance whether or not he or she is habitually resident in the UK, the Channel Islands, the Isle of Man or the Republic of Ireland. Persons with a permanent right to reside by virtue of (a),(b), or (f) must be habitually resident to be eligible.

RIGHTS OF RESIDENCE FOR CERTAIN FAMILY MEMBERS
The right to reside

40 Regulation 14 of the EEA Regulations provides that the following family members are entitled to reside in the UK:

(i) a family member of a qualified person residing in the UK;

(ii) a family member of an EEA national with a permanent right of residence under regulation 15; and

(iii) a family member who has retained the right of residence (see regulation 10 of the EEA Regulations for the definition).

41 A person who has a right to reside in the UK as the family member of an EEA national under the EEA Regulations will not be subject to immigration control. The eligibility of such a person for housing assistance should therefore be considered in accordance with regulation 6 of the Eligibility Regulations.

42 When considering the eligibility of a family member, local authorities should consider whether the person has acquired a right to reside in their own right, for example a permanent right to reside under regulation 15 of the EEA Regulations (see paragraph 38 above).

Who is a 'family member'?

43 Regulation 7 of the EEA regulations provides that the following persons are treated as the family members of another person (with certain exceptions for students – see below):

(a) the spouse of the person;

(b) the civil partner of the person (part of a registered partnership equivalent to marriage);

(c) a direct descendant of the person, or of the person's spouse or civil partner, who is under the age of 21;

(d) a direct descendant of the person, or of the person's spouse or civil partner,
who is over 21 and dependent on the person, or the spouse or civil partner;

(e) an ascendant relative of the person, or of the person's spouse or civil partner, who is dependent on the person or the spouse or civil partner.

(f) a person who is an extended family member and is treated as a family
member by virtue of regulation 7(3) of the EEA regulations (see below).

Family members of students

44 Regulation 7(2) of the EEA regulations provides that a person who falls within
(c), (d) or (e) above shall not be treated as a family member of a student residing in the UK after the period of 3 months beginning on the date the student
is admitted to the UK unless:

(i) in the case of paragraph 43 (c) and (d) above, the person is the dependent
child of the student, or of the spouse or civil partner, or

(ii) the student is also a qualified person (for the purposes of regulation 6(1)
of the EEA regulations) other than as a student.

Extended family members

45 Broadly, extended family members will be persons who:

(a) do not fall within any of the categories (a) to (e) in paragraph 43 above,
and

(b) are either a relative of an EEA national (or of the EEA national's spouse or
civil partner) or the partner of an EEA national, and

(c) have been issued with an EEA family permit, a registration certificate or a
residence card which is valid and has not been revoked.

Family members' eligibility for housing assistance

Relationship with other rights to reside

46 This section concerns the eligibility of an applicant for housing assistance
whose right to reside is derived from his or her status as the family member
of an EEA national with a right to reside. In some cases, a family member will
have acquired a right to reside in his or her own right. In particular, a person
who arrived in the UK as the family member of an EEA national may have
subsequently acquired a permanent right of residence under regulation 15 of
the EEA Regulations, as outlined in paragraph 38(a)–(f) above. The eligibility
for housing assistance of those with a permanent right of residence is discussed at paragraph 39.

Family members who must be habitually resident

47 For family members with a right to reside under regulation 14 of the EEA
Regulations, the following categories of persons must be habitually resident
in the UK, the Channel Islands, the Isle of Man or the Republic of Ireland in
order to be eligible for housing assistance:

a) a person whose right to reside derives from their status as a family member of an EEA national who is a self-sufficient person for the purposes of
regulation 6(1)(d) of the EEA regulations;

b) a person whose right to reside derives from their status as a family member of an EEA national who is a student for the purposes of regulation
6(1)(e) of the EEA regulations;

c) a person whose right to reside is dependent on their status as a family member of an EEA national with a permanent right to reside;

d) a person whose right to reside is dependent on their status as a family member who has retained the right of residence.

Family members who are exempt from the habitual residence requirement

48   A person with a right to reside under regulation 14 as a family member of an EEA national who is a worker or a self-employed person for the purposes of regulation 6(1) of the EEA regulations is exempted from the requirement to be habitually resident by regulation 6(2)(d) of the Eligibility Regulations. However, authorities should note that an extended family member (see above) is not counted as a family member for the purposes of regulation 6(2)(d) of the Eligibility Regulations (see regulation 2(3) of the Eligibility Regulations).

Family members of UK nationals exercising rights under the EC Treaty

49   There are some limited cases in which the non-EEA family member of a UK national may have a right to reside under EU law. Under regulation 9 of the EEA Regulations, the family member of a UK national should be treated as an EEA family member where the following conditions are met:

(i) the UK national is residing in an EEA State as a worker or self-employed person, or was so residing before returning to the UK; and

(ii) if the family member of the UK national is his spouse or civil partner, the parties are living together in the EEA State, or had entered into a marriage or civil partnership and were living together in that State before the UK national returned to the UK.

50   Where the family member of a UK national is to be treated as an EEA family member by virtue of regulation 9 of the EEA Regulations, that person is not subject to immigration control, and his or her eligibility for housing assistance should therefore be determined in accordance with regulation 6 of the Eligibility Regulations.

ANNEX 13
Worker Registration Scheme

Introduction

1   On 1 May 2004, 10 new countries acceded to the European Union: Cyprus, Malta, Poland, Lithuania, Estonia, Latvia, Slovenia, Slovakia, Hungary and the Czech Republic.

2   Nationals of all of these countries have the right to move freely among all member states. Nationals of 2 of the Accession countries – Malta and Cyprus – enjoyed full EU Treaty rights from 1 May 2004. These include the right to seek work and take up employment in another Member State.

3   However, under the EU Accession Treaties that apply to the other 8 Accession states ('the A8 Member States'), existing Member States can impose limitations on the rights of nationals of the A8 Member States to access their labour markets (and the associated rights of residence), for a transitional period. (The EU Accession Treaties do not allow existing Member States to restrict access to their labour markets by nationals of Malta or Cyprus.)

4 Under the *Accession (Immigration and Worker Registration) Regulations 2004* (SI 2004/1219) as amended ('the Accession Regulations'), nationals of the A8 Member States (with certain exceptions) are required to register with the Home Office if they work in the UK during the transitional period. While looking for work (or between jobs) their right to reside will be conditional on them being self-sufficient and not imposing an unreasonable burden on the UK social assistance system. These conditions cease to apply once they have worked in the UK continuously for 12 months.

The Accession (Immigration and Worker Registration) Regulations 2004

5 The *Accession (Immigration and Worker Registration) Regulations 2004* provide that, from 1 May 2004, nationals of the A8 Member States can take up employment in the UK provided they are authorised to work for their employer under the Worker Registration scheme.

6 The Accession Regulations also give workers from the A8 Member States the right to reside in the UK. Workers from the A8 Member States who are working lawfully have the same right to equal treatment as other EEA workers while they are working.

The Worker Registration scheme

7 The Worker Registration scheme applies only to nationals of: Poland, Lithuania, Estonia, Latvia, Slovenia, Slovakia, Hungary and the Czech Republic (the A8 Member States). It is a transitional scheme under which the UK Government allows nationals of the A8 Member States access to the UK labour market provided they comply with the registration scheme.

8 The derogation from EC law allowed by the Treaties of Accession does not apply to nationals of existing EEA states. Workers from those states, therefore, have an EC right to work and reside in the UK.

9 The Worker Registration scheme is a transitional measure. The *Accession (Immigration and Worker Registration) Regulations 2004* provide for the registration scheme to operate for up to five years from 1 May 2004 (i.e. until 30 April 2009). The Government reviewed the scheme within its first two years of operation and decided that the scheme will continue beyond 1 May 2006, and may continue throughout the second phase of the transitional arrangements. However, the need to retain the scheme during the whole of the second phase will be kept under review.

10 Nationals of A8 Member States who are self-employed are not required to register. (Under the Accession Treaties, there is no derogation from the right of EU citizens to establish themselves in another Member State (including the UK) as self-employed persons.) However, nationals of A8 Member States who are self-employed cannot take paid employment unless they register (unless they are exempt from registration, see below).

Registration under the scheme

11 Nationals of A8 Member States (except those who are exempt from the scheme, see below) must apply to register with the Home Office as soon as they start work in the UK, and within one month of taking up employment at the very latest. They will be issued with a **worker registration card** and a **worker registration certificate**, authorising them to work for the employer concerned.

12   If they change employers they will have to apply to for a new **registration certificate** authorising them to work for their new employer. They will then be provided with a new certificate for that employer. If they change employer or have a break in employment and resume working for the same employer, they must apply for a new registration certificate.

13   Workers from the A8 Member States have the same right to equal treatment as other EEA workers while they are working.

14   After 12 months' uninterrupted work in the UK, a worker from an A8 Member State will acquire full EU Treaty rights, and will be free from the requirement to register to work. At that stage, they will be able to apply to the Home Office for an EEA residence permit to confirm their right to equal treatment on the same basis as other EEA nationals.

15   The Worker Registration Team issues applicants with a secure **worker registration card** containing:
   – Name;
   – Date of Birth;
   – Nationality;
   – Date of issue;
   – Unique identification number;
   – A facial identifier (photograph);
   and
   a **certificate** (on secure paper) which states:
   – Worker's name;
   – Worker's Date of Birth;
   – Nationality;
   – Worker's unique identification number;
   – Name and address (head or main office) of employer;
   – Job title;
   – Start date;
   – Date of issue.

16   The **registration card** is a secure document that provides applicants with a unique identification reference number. This is valid for as long as the applicant requires registration under the scheme.

17   The **registration certificate** is specific to a particular employer. The certificate expires as soon as the person stops working for that employer. If the person changes employers or has a break in employment and resumes working for the same employer, he or she must apply for a new registration certificate.

18   Specimen copies of the registration card and registration certificate are provided at the end of this annex.

12 months' uninterrupted work

19   A worker from an A8 Member State (who is subject to the registration scheme) must not be out of wormore than a total of 30 days in a 12-month period, in order to establish '12 months' uninterrupted work'.

20   If a national of an A8 Member State has worked for a period of less than 12 months when the employment comes to an end, he or she will need to find another job within 30 days to be able to count the first period of work towards accruing a period of 12 months' uninterrupted employment.

21   If the worker's second (or subsequent) employment comes to an end before he

or she has accrued a period of 12 months' uninterrupted employment, he or she must ensure that there has been no more than a total of 30 days between all of the periods of employment. If more than 30 days between periods of employment occur before a 12-month period of uninterrupted employment is established, a fresh period of 12 months' uninterrupted employment would need to commence from that point.

22 The Worker Registration scheme is based on continuity of employment – there is no restriction on the number of different jobs (or employers) that a worker can have during a 12-month period of continuous employment.

23 When an A8 Member State worker has worked for 12 months without interruption he or she can apply to the Home Office for an EEA residence permit. Evidence of 12 months' uninterrupted employment would include the worker registration card, registration certificates for each of the jobs they have undertaken, letters from employers and pay slips.

A8 nationals who must register

24 The Worker Registration Scheme applies to nationals of the following accession states: Poland; Lithuania; Estonia; Latvia; Slovenia; Slovakia; Hungary; and the Czech Republic.

25 Nationals of A8 Member States need to apply for a registration certificate under the Worker Registration Scheme, if they are a citizen of one of the countries listed above and they:
- start a new job on or after 1 May 2004;
- have been working in the UK before 1 May 2004 without authorisation or in breach of their immigration conditions;
- are working on a short-term or temporary basis; or
- are a student who is also working.

A8 nationals exempt from registration

26 The following are the categories of nationals of an A8 Member State who are not required to register under the Worker Registration Scheme:
- those working in a self-employed capacity;
- those who have been working with permission in the UK for 12 months or more without interruption;
- those who have been working with permission in the UK for their current employer since before 1 May 2004;
- those who have leave to enter the UK under the *Immigration Act 1971* on 30 April 2004 and their leave was not subject to any condition restricting their employment;
- those who are providing services in the UK on behalf of an employer who is not established in the UK;
- those who are a citizen of the UK, another EEA state (other than an A8 state) or Switzerland;
- those who are a family member (spouse, civil partner, or child under the age of 21 or dependant) of a Swiss or EEA national (other than an A8 national) who is working in the UK;
- those who are a family member (spouse, civil partner or dependant child) of a Swiss or EEA national who is in the UK and is a student, self-employed, retired, or self-sufficient.

Home Office
BUILDING A SAFE, JUST
AND TOLERANT SOCIETY

[First Name] [Surname]	DATE OF ISSUE	: [Issue Date]
[House Number] [Street Name]	REFERENCE No	: [URN]
[Town]	WORK CARD SERIAL No	: ▓▓▓▓▓
[County]		
[Post Code]	TELEPHONE	: 0114 207 6022

Accession State Worker Registration Scheme

Thank you for your application to register on the Accession State Worker Registration scheme. I am pleased to inform you that we have approved your application and that you are now registered.

Your worker registration card is attached below. If you have any queries about this document, then please contact Work Permits (UK) on the telephone number above.

- -

Accession State Worker Registration Scheme
Registration Card

SURNAME	:	[Surname]
FORENAME(S)	:	[First Name]
DATE OF BIRTH	:	[Date of Birth]
NATIONALITY	:	[Nationality]
REFERENCE No	:	[URN]
DATE OF ISSUE	:	[Issue Date]

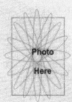

This worker registration card should be retained as evidence of your registration with the Accession State Worker Registration Scheme.

PLEASE DO NOT LOSE - REPLACEMENTS MAY NOT BE ISSUED

WORK CARD SERIAL No

Home Office
BUILDING A SAFE, JUST
AND TOLERANT SOCIETY

Managed Migration
Home Office
PO Box 3468
Sheffield S3 8WA

www.workingintheuk.gov.uk

[First Name] [Surname]
[House Number] [Street]
[Town]
[County]
[Post Code]

Date of Issue: [Issue Date]

ACCESSION STATE WORKER REGISTRATION SCHEME
REGISTRATION CERTIFICATE

Thank you for your application to register on the Accession State Worker Registration Scheme. I am pleased to inform you that we have approved your application.

This is your worker registration certificate. It authorises you to work for the employer specified in this certificate.

This certificate ceases to be valid if you are no longer working for the employer specified in this certificate on the date on which it is issued.

This certificate expires on the date you cease working for the specified employer.

This certificate should be retained with your worker registration card.

Name	: [First Name] [Surname]
Date of Birth	: [Date of Birth]
Nationality	: [Nationality]
Unique Reference Number	: [URN]
Job start date	: [Date Started Employment]
Employer's Name	: [Employer Name]
Employer's Address	: [Unit Number] [Street Name] [Town] [County] [Post Code]

ANNEX 14
MOD Certificate: Certificate of Cessation of Entitlement for Single Personnel to Occupy Service Living Accommodation

MINISTRY OF DEFENCE

MOD Form 1166
Introduced 5/97
Revised 4/03

CERTIFICATE OF CESSATION OF ENTITLEMENT FOR SINGLE PERSONNEL TO OCCUPY SERVICE LIVING ACCOMMODATION

I certify that (Name)

(Rank & Number)

Of (Unit)

Will cease to be entitled to occupy Service Living Accommodation (Address)

From (Date)

By reason of

An application for housing was made to .... Housing

Authority/Housing Association on .... (copy of letter attached)

The person has the following special circumstances ....

....

Signed	UNIT STAMP
Name	
Position	
Date	

1. This certificate provides evidence of cessation of entitlement to occupy Service Living Accommodation.

2. The certificate should be completed by the unit admin authority and sent at the earliest possible date to the Housing Authority/Association to which application for accommodation has been made, preferably as soon as it is known that entitlement to occupy Service Living Accommodation will cease.

3. Copies of this form are published in the Homelessness Code of Guidance For Local Authorities issued by DCLG, and in guidance issued by the Welsh Assembly and Scottish Executive.

ANNEX 15
Certificate of Cessation of Entitlement to Occupy Service Families Accommodation or Substitute Service Families Accommodate (SFA/SSFA)

	MINISTRY OF DEFENCE	MOD Form *Introduced 4/03*

CERTIFICATE OF CESSATION OF ENTITLEMENT TO OCCUPY SERVICE FAMILIES ACCOMMODATION OR SUBSTITUTE SERVICE FAMILIES ACCOMMODATION(SFA/SSFA)

I certify that　　　　(Name)

(Rank & Number) #

Of　　　　(Unit) #
(# Omit if only family involved)

Will cease to be entitled　(Address of SFA or
to occupy　　　　SSFA)

From　　　　(Date)
By reason of loss of entitlement to occupy Service Families Accommodation.

An application for housing was made to ....Housing Authority/
Housing Association on .... (copy of letter attached)

The following special circumstances apply ....
....

The household is as follows ....
....
....

	DHE STAMP
Signed	
Name	
Designation	
Date	

1. **This certificate provides evidence of cessation of entitlement to occupy Service Families Accommodation or Substitute Service Families Accommodation. Authorities should not insist on a Court Order for possession to establish a threat of homelessness.**

2. The certificate should be completed by the Licences Officer of the Defence Housing Executive and sent at the earliest possible date to the Housing Authority/Association to which application for accommodation has been made, preferably as soon as it is known that entitlement to occupy Service Families Accommodation will cease.

3. A period of at least six months notice should normally be allowed so that the appropriate arrangements can be made.

4. Copies of this form are published in the Homelessness Code of Guidance For Local Authorities issued by DCLG, and in guidance issued by the Welsh Assembly and Scottish Executive.

ANNEX 16
Definition of Overcrowding

Under s.324 of the *Housing Act 1985* a dwelling is overcrowded when the number of persons sleeping in the dwelling is such as to contravene –
(a) the standard specified in s.325 (the room standard), or
(b) the standard specified in s.326 (the space standard).

a) The room standard

(1) The room standard is contravened when the number of persons sleeping in a dwelling and the number of rooms available as sleeping accommodation is such that two persons of opposite sexes who are not living together as husband and wife must sleep in the same room.
(2) For this purpose –
    (a) children under the age of ten shall be left out of account, and
    (b) a room is available as sleeping accommodation if it is of a type normally used in the locality either as a bedroom or as a living room.

b) The space standard

(1) The space standard is contravened when the number of persons sleeping in a dwelling is in excess of the permitted number, having regard to the number and floor area of the rooms of the dwelling available as sleeping accommodation.
(2) For this purpose –
    (a) no account shall be taken of a child under the age of one and a child aged one or over but under ten shall be reckoned as one-half of a unit, and
    (b) a room is available as sleeping accommodation if it is of a type normally used in the locality either as a living room or as a bedroom.
(3) The permitted number of persons in relation to a dwelling is whichever is the less of –
    (a) the number specified in Table I in relation to the number of rooms in the dwelling available as sleeping accommodation, and

Table I

Number of rooms	Number of persons
1	2
2	3
3	5
4	7½
5 or more	2 for each room

    (b) the aggregate for all such rooms in the dwelling of the numbers specified in column 2 of Table II in relation to each room of the floor area specified in column 1.

Table II

Floor area of room	Number of persons
110 sq ft or more	2
90 sq ft or more but less than 110 sq ft	1½
70 sq ft or more but less than 90 sq ft	1
50 sq ft or more but less than 70 sq ft	½

No account shall be taken for the purposes of either Table of a room having a floor area of less than 50 square feet.

(4) The Secretary of State may by regulations prescribe the manner in which the floor area of a room is to be ascertained for the purposes of this section; and the regulations may provide for the exclusion from computation, or the bringing into computation at a reduced figure, of floor space in a part of the room which is of less than a specified height not exceeding eight feet.

(5) Regulations under subsection (4) shall be made by statutory instrument which shall be subject to annulment in pursuance of a resolution of either House of Parliament.

(6) A certificate of the local housing authority stating the number and floor areas of the rooms in dwelling, and that the floor areas have been ascertained in the prescribed manner, is prima facie evidence for the purposes of legal proceedings of the facts stated in it.

ANNEX 17
Recommended Minimum Standards for Bed and Breakfast Accommodation

The Secretary of State recommends that housing authorities apply the standards set out below as minimum standards in deciding whether Bed and Breakfast accommodation is suitable for an applicant for the purposes of Part 7 of the Housing Act 1996 ('the homelessness leglislation') in the very limited circumstances where an authority may use such accommodation for this purpose.

Space standards for sleeping accommodation
1   *Room sizes where cooking facilities provided in a separate room/kitchen*

Floor Area of Room	*Maximum No of Persons*
Less than 70 sq ft (6.5 m²)	Nil persons
Not less than 70 sq ft (6.5 m²)	1 person
Not less than 110 sq ft (10.2 m²)	2 persons
Not less than 160 sq ft (14.9 m²)	3 persons
Not less than 210 sq ft (19.6 m²)	4 persons
Not less than 260 sq ft (24.2 m²)	5 persons

Room sizes where cooking facilities provided within the room

Floor Area of Room	Maximum No of Persons
Less than 110 sq ft (10.2 m²)	Nil persons
Not less than 110 sq ft (10.2 m²)	1 persons
Not less than 150 sq ft (13.9 m²)	2 persons
Not less than 200 sq ft (18.6 m²)	3 persons
Not less than 250 sq ft (23.2 m²)	4 persons
Not less than 300 sq ft (27.9 m²)	5 persons

2   In no case should a room be occupied by more than 5 persons. The standard is to be applied irrespective of the age of the occupants. The sharing of rooms in bed and breakfast accommodation is not desirable, but it is accepted that where accommodation is not self-contained families may find it preferable to share.

3   No persons of the opposite sex who are aged 12 and over should have to share a room unless they are living together as partners and both are above the age of consent or are lawfully married.

4   All rooms must have a minimum floor to ceiling height of at least 7 feet (2.14 metres) over not less than 75% of the room area. Any floor area where the ceiling height is less than 5 feet (1.53 metres) should be disregarded.

5   Separate kitchens, bathrooms, toilets, shower rooms, communal rooms and en-suite rooms are deemed unsuitable for sleeping accommodation.

Installation for heating

6   The premises should have adequate provision for heating. All habitable rooms and baths or shower rooms should be provided with a fixed space-heating appliance. The appliance must be capable of efficiently maintaining the room at a minimum temperature of 18°C when the outside temperature is −1°C. 'Fixed space heating appliance' means fixed gas appliance, fixed electrical appliance or an adequate system of central heating, operable at all times.

Facilities for the storage, preparation and cooking of food and disposal of waste water

7   Wherever practicable, each household should have exclusive use of a full set of kitchen facilities including:
   –   cooking facilities – a gas or electric cooker with a four-burner hob, oven and grill. In single person lettings, a cooker with a minimum of two burners, oven and grill is permissible. Where the establishment caters for fewer than 6 persons, a small guest house for example, a microwave may be substituted for a gas or electric cooker for periods of stay not exceeding 6 weeks for any homeless household;
   –   sink and integral drainer – with a constant supply of hot and cold water and properly connected to the drainage system;
   –   storage cupboard, minimum capacity 0.4 m³ (400 litres/15 ft³). This provision is in addition to any base unit cupboards provided below the sink/drainer;
   –   refrigerator – minimum capacity 0.14 m³ (140 litres/5 ft³);
   –   electrical power sockets – minimum of two double 13 amp sockets situated at worktop height. These are in addition to electrical power sockets provided elsewhere in the letting;
   –   worktop – minimum surface area 1000 mm x 600 mm.

8   There may be circumstances where the housing authority is satisfied that the provision of kitchen facilities for exclusive use is not practicable or appropriate. These circumstances could, for example, include where a property is very small, no more than two or three letting rooms, or where the overall standard of the property is considered reasonable in all other respects and the costs of provision of exclusive use kitchens would be prohibitive or detrimentally affect the remaining amenity space. In circumstances such as these, the following standards for communal kitchens may be applied.

9   Kitchen facilities may be provided in the ratio of no less than one set for every 10 persons, irrespective of age. Such kitchen facilities should comprise a minimum of shared:
   – gas or electric cooker with four burners, oven and grill. Where the establishment caters for fewer than 6 persons, a small guest house for example, a microwave may be substituted for a gas or electric cooker for periods of stay not exceeding 6 weeks for any homeless household;
   – sink and integral drainer – with a constant supply of hot and cold water and properly connected to the drainage system;
   – storage cupboard, minimum capacity 0.4 m^3 (400 litres/15 ft^3). This provision is in addition to any base unit cupboards provided below the sink/drainer;
   – electrical power sockets – minimum of two double 13 amp sockets situated at worktop height. These are in addition to electrical power sockets provided elsewhere in the letting;
   – worktop – minimum surface area 1000 mm   600 mm;
   – lockable storage cupboards, minimum capacity 0.14 m^3 (140 litres/5 ft^3) for each bedroom whose occupants use the kitchen. In calculating the required provision of storage cupboards, base unit cupboards below sinks/drainers should be discounted.

10   In addition, the following facilities should be provided within each bedroom, or within the total accommodation occupied exclusively by each household:
   – worktop – minimum surface area 1000 mm   600 mm;
   – refrigerator – minimum capacity 0.14 m^3 (140 litres/5 ft^3);
   – storage cupboard – minimum capacity 0.4 m^3 (400 litres/15 ft^3).

11   The kitchen used by management to provide breakfast may be included when calculating the one in ten ratio, unless it is not available, does not meet the conditions above or is deemed unsuitable for use by residents because:
   – of the size of the kitchen and the equipment provided in it. In a commercial kitchen some equipment may be dangerous or unsatisfactory for use by residents; or
   – the unsatisfactory location of the kitchen in relation to the accommodation it is supposed to serve.

12   In schemes providing a mix of kitchens for shared and exclusive use, one set of kitchen facilities should be provided for every 10 persons sharing. The number of persons who have kitchen facilities provided for their exclusive use should not be included in the calculations. Again, the kitchen used by management to provide breakfast may be included in the one in ten calculation subject to the above conditions.

13   Cooking facilities which are provided should be reasonably located in relation to the room(s) occupied by the person(s) for whom they are provided and in

any event not more than one floor distant from these rooms. Please note the exception for smaller establishments described below.

14   In smaller establishments of not more than three storeys and not more than 30 bed spaces, communal cooking facilities may be provided in one area of the premises more than one floor distant from some bedrooms. In such cases, these kitchens must be provided in association with a suitable dining room or dining rooms of adequate size calculated on the basis of 1 m² per bed space. This should include one area of at least 15 m². Only effective usable space will be considered when calculating the areas for the purpose of this requirement. Dining room facilities should be provided with adequate seating provision.

15   Kitchen facilities should be made available for use 24 hours per day, subject to any representation from the owner/manager, which must be agreed by the receiving and placing authorities.

Toilet and personal washing facilities

16   One internal water closet should be provided for every five persons irrespective of age. The water closet must be within a reasonable distance from its users and not more than one floor distant and, where practicable, a water closet should not be situated within a bathroom. At least 50% of the water closets that are required to be provided should be situated in separate accommodation. The number of persons occupying a bedroom where this facility is provided for their exclusive use should not be included in the calculations.

17   A suitable wash hand basin (minimum dimensions 500 mm   400 mm) with constant hot and cold water supplies, should be provided in every bedroom, except where an en suite bathroom is available, when the wash hand basin may be provided in that bathroom.

18   Each separate water closet compartment and bathroom should be provided with a suitable wash hand basin (minimum dimensions 500 mm x 400 mm), together with constant supplies of hot and cold running water. A tiled splashback (minimum 300 mm high) is to be provided to each wash hand basin.

19   One bath (minimum dimensions 1700 mm   700 mm) or one shower (minimum dimensions 800 mm   800 mm) should be provided for every eight persons, irrespective of age. These facilities must be within a reasonable distance of each user and not more than one floor distant. The number of persons having the exclusive use of a bath or shower should not be included in the calculations.

20   Where the operator chooses to provide showers for the exclusive use of each separate household or the majority of households, a minimum provision of baths, rather than showers will always be required. In such circumstances a minimum of one communal bath should be provided for every 20 persons, irrespective of age, with a minimum of one bath per property. These facilities must be within a reasonable distance of each user and ideally no more than one floor distant.

Other facilities

21   In the case of families with young children, the facilities should include a safe play area(s) that is located away from sleeping accommodation and cooking areas.

Management standards

22   In any B&B accommodation, suitability for the purposes of Part 7 will depend upon the management standards operated within an establishment as well as the adequate provision of basic amenities. The minimum management standards set out below should apply and it is the responsibility of the housing authority to monitor the management of the property.

– Operators are required to ensure the property complies with all relevant statutory and regulatory requirements especially in relation to fire, gas and electrical safety. The supply of gas or electricity to any resident should never be interfered with.

– A clear emergency evacuation plan should be in place setting out action upon hearing the fire alarm, escape routes and safe assembly points. The manager must ensure that each person newly arriving at the premises is told what to do in the event of a fire and about the fire precautions provided.

– Residents should have access to their rooms at all times except when rooms are being cleaned. Provision should be made to accommodate residents at these times.

– Refuse and litter should be cleared from the property and not allowed to accumulate in, or in the curtilage, of the property, except in adequately sized and suitable bulk refuse container(s).

– All communal areas (including, hallways, kitchens, bathrooms/showers, WCs, dining areas, lounges if provided) should be regularly cleaned.

– Appropriate officers of the authority in whose area the premises are situated should have access to inspect the premises as and when they consider necessary, to ensure that the requirements are being complied with. The manager should allow such inspections to take place, if necessary without notice.

– Officers of the health authority, local authority and authorised community workers for the area in which the premises are situated should have access to visit the occupiers of the premises and interview them in private in the room(s) they occupy.

– A manager with adequate day to day responsibility to ensure the good management of the property should be contactable at all times. A notice giving the name, address and telephone number of the manager should be displayed in a readily visible position in the property.

– Procedures should be in place to deal with any complaints relating to harassment on racial, sexual or other discriminatory grounds by either residents or staff.

– There should be a clear complaints procedure for the resolution of disputes between residents and/or staff.

– There should be available within the premises a working telephone available for use by the occupiers and a notice should be displayed by the telephone with information on the address and telephone numbers of: the local Environmental Health Department, Fire Brigade, Gas Company, Electricity Company, Police Station and local doctors.

ANNEX 18
This is not guidance issued by the Secretaries of State.
Procedures for Referrals of Homeless Applicants on the Grounds of Local Connection with Another Local Authority
Guidelines for Local Authorities and Referees

AGREED BY

ASSOCIATION OF LONDON GOVERNMENT (ALG)
CONVENTION OF SCOTTISH LOCAL AUTHORITIES (CoSLA)
LOCAL GOVERNMENT ASSOCIATION (LGA)
WELSH LOCAL GOVERNMENT ASSOCIATION (WLGA)
(*'the local authority associations'*)

INDEX

Standard Notification Form

Procedures for Referrals of Homeless Applicants on the Grounds of Local Connection with Another Local Authority Guidelines for Local Authorities on Procedures for Referral

AGREED BY

ASSOCIATION OF LONDON GOVERNMENT (ALG)
CONVENTION OF SCOTTISH LOCAL AUTHORITIES (CoSLA)
LOCAL GOVERNMENT ASSOCIATION (LGA)
WELSH LOCAL GOVERNMENT ASSOCIATION (WLGA)
(*'the local authority associations'*)

This procedure concerns the situation where, under Part 7 of the *Housing Act 1996*, a housing authority is satisfied that a housing applicant is eligible for assistance, homeless and has a priority need for accommodation, is not satisfied that the applicant is homeless intentionally and the authority consider that the conditions for referral of the case to another housing authority are met, and notifies the other housing authority of its opinion. Referrals are discretionary only. Housing authorities are not required to make inquiries as to whether an applicant has a local connection with another district, and where they decide to do so, there is no requirement to refer applicants to another authority, if the conditions for referral are met. Authorities may have a policy about how they may exercise their discretion. However, they cannot decide in advance that a referral will be made in all cases where an applicant who is eligible for assistance, unintentionally homeless and in priority need may have a local connection with another district.

1 PURPOSE OF THE GUIDELINES

1.1   For English and Welsh authorities s.198 of the *Housing Act 1996* provides that:

'(5) The question whether the conditions for referral of a case are satisfied shall be determined by agreement between the notifying authority and the notified authority or, in default of agreement, in accordance with such arrangements as the Secretary of State may direct by order.

(6) An order may direct that the arrangements shall be:

(a) those agreed by any relevant authorities or associations of relevant authorities, or

(b) in default of such agreement, such arrangements as appear to the Secretary of State to be suitable, after consultation with such associations representing relevant authorities, and such other persons, as he thinks appropriate.'

1.2   Subsections 33(4) and (5) of the *Housing (Scotland) Act 1987* make the same provision for Scotland. However, s.8 of the *Homelessness (Scotland) Act 2003* gives Scottish ministers the power to suspend or vary the circumstnaces under which a homeless applicant may be referred by a Scottish local authority to another authority in Scotland. Please note any future orders made will need to be taken into account.

1.3   The ALG, CoSLA, LGA and the WLGA, the local authority associations in England, Scotland and Wales, have agreed guidelines for referrals which they recommend to local housing authorities. Section 198 *Housing Act 1996* and s.33 *Housing (Scotland) Act 1987* lay down the general procedures to be followed where it appears that s.192(2) (England and Wales) or s.31 (Scotland) applies to the applicant and the applicant does not have a local connection with the area of the authority receiving the housing application but does have one with another area in England, Scotland or Wales. There are, however, considerable areas of possible disagreement and dispute in determining whether the conditions of referral are met in any particular case. Although, in the last resort, disagreements can only be resolved by the courts, the associations are anxious to avoid, as far as possible, legal disputes between local authorities. The associations therefore issue these agreed guidelines on the procedures and criteria to be followed, and recommend them for general adoption by all their members. **These Guidelines are without prejudice to the duty of local authorities to treat each case on its merits and to take into account existing and future case law.** Furthermore, these Guidelines only apply to the issues of local connection and whether the conditions for referral are met for the purposes of Part 7 of the *Housing Act 1996* (England and Wales) and s.33 of the *Housing (Scotland) Act 1987*.

1.4   *In Re Betts (1983) the House of Lords considered the application of the referral arrangements agreed between the local authority associations. Their Lordships decided that a rigid application of the arrangements would constitute a fetter on an authority's discretion. The agreement could be taken into account, and applied as a guideline, provided its application to each case is given individual consideration.*

2 DEFINITIONS

2.1   All references in this agreement to an 'applicant' are to be taken as references to a housing applicant to whom s.193 of the *Housing Act 1996* (England and Wales) or s.28 *Housing (Scotland) Act 1987* or s.31 *Housing (Scotland) Act 1987* would apply but for the decision to refer the case to another authority. For the purposes of this agreement the 1996 Act and 1987 (Scotland) Act definitions apply.

2.2   The authority to whom the applicant applies for accommodation or assistance (for the purposes of s.183 *Housing Act 1996* or s.28 *Housing (Scotland) Act 1987*) and which decides to refer the case to another authority is the '*notifying authority*'.

2.3   Where the notifying authority consider that neither the applicant nor any person who might reasonably reside with the applicant, has a local connection with its district but does have one with another local authority district and notifies the other local authority of its opinion, the authority which they notify is known as the '*notified authority*'.

2.4   Section 199 *Housing Act 1996* and s.27 *Housing (Scotland) Act 1987* set out the circumstances when a person may have a 'local connection' with a district. These guidelines provide a framework within which the local connection referral procedures may be applied.

3 CRITERIA FOR NOTIFICATION

3.1   Before a local authority can consider referring an applicant to another local authority it must first be satisfied that the applicant is:

(i)   eligible for assistance
(ii)   homeless, and
(iii) in priority need,
(iv)   not homeless intentionally.

3.2 Before making a referral the notifying authority must be satisfied that the conditions of referral are met. Broadly, the conditions for referral will be met if:

(a) neither the applicant nor any person who might reasonably be expected to reside with the applicant has a local connection with the district of the authority receiving the application,

(b) either the applicant or any person who might reasonably be expected to reside with the applicant has a local connection with the district of another authority in England, Scotland or Wales

(c) neither the applicant nor any person who might reasonably be expected to reside with the applicant would run the risk of domestic violence/domestic abuse (Scotland) or face a probability of other violence in the district of the other authority (Refer to s.198 of the 1996 Act as amended by s.10 subsection (2&3) *Homelessness Act 2002* (England and Wales)). However, there are exceptions to these conditions, for example, where an applicant applies to an English or Welsh authority for assistance and has been provided with NASS support in Scotland

(d) **For Welsh authorities only**, the conditions for referral to another authority will also be met if the applicant was placed in accommodation in the district of the notifying authority by the other authority as a discharge of a duty to secure accommodation under Part 7 of the 1996 Act following an application to the other authority made within the last five years. The period of 5 years is prescribed by the *Homelessness (Wales) Regulations 2000 SI 2000 No.1079.*)

3.3 3.2(a)(b) and (c) above apply to Scottish authorities. 3.2(d) above does not apply in Scotland.

3.4 In deciding whether or not to make a referral authorities should also consider the court judgment in the case of *R v LB Newham ex parte LB Tower Hamlets* (1990). The notifying authority should have regard to any decisions made by the notified authority that may have a bearing on the case in question (e.g. a previous decision that the applicant was intentionally homeless) as well as any other material considerations, which should include the general housing circumstances prevailing in the district of the notifying authority and in the district of the notified authority. The notifying authority should also consider whether it is in the public interest to accept a duty to secure accommodation under s.193(2) (England and Wales)

3.5 Should a local authority wish to accept a duty to secure accommodation for an applicant who does not have a local connection with its district, nothing in this agreement shall prevent the authority from providing such assistance. The decision to make a referral is discretionary and could be challenged if the discretion was considered to have been exercised unreasonably.

3.6 Under s.202 of the 1996 Act, housing applicants in England and Wales have the right to request a review of certain decisions made by the local authority about their application, including a decision to notify another authority under s.198 and a decision that the conditions are met for referral of the case. The equivalent right to review in Scotland is set out in s.4 of the *Housing (Scotland) Act 2001.*

4 LOCAL CONNECTION

4.1   The relevant date for deciding whether or not a local connection has been established is not the date when the application for housing assistance was made but the date of the decision or, if there is a review, the date of the review decision (cf. House of Lords' judgment in *Mohamed v Hammersmith and Fulham London Borough Council 2001*). Moreover, if inquiries prior to a decision have been prolonged, the notifying authority should also consider whether there may have been any material change in circumstances that might affect the question of whether a local connection has been established. A local connection may be established where the following grounds apply, subject to the exceptions outlined in paragraph 4.2:

(i)   the applicant or a person who might reasonably be expected to reside with the applicant is, or in the past was, normally resident in the district. It is suggested that a working definition of 'normal residence' should be residence for at least 6 months in the area during the previous 12 months, or for not less than 3 years during the previous 5 year period. The period taken into account should be up to the date of the authority's decision. This should include any periods living in temporary accommodation secured by the authority under s.188 (interim duty pending inquiries);

(ii)   the applicant or a person who might reasonably be expected to reside with the applicant is at present employed in the district. The local authority should obtain confirmation from the employer that the person is in employment and that the employment is not of a casual nature;

(iii) the applicant or a person who might reasonably be expected to reside with the applicant has family associations in the district. Family associations normally arise where an applicant or a person who might reasonably be expected to reside with the applicant has parents, adult children or brothers or sisters who have been resident in the district for a period of at least 5 years at the date of the decision, and the applicant indicates a wish to be near them. Only in exceptional circumstances would the residence of relatives other than those listed above be taken to establish a local connection. The residence of dependent children in a different district from their parents would not be residence of their own choice and therefore would not establish a local connection with that district. However, a referral should not be made to another local authority on the grounds of a local connection because of family associations if the applicant objects to those grounds. **NB:** A Scottish authority, when considering the application of this clause, is advised to bear in mind the definition of 'family' in s.83 of the *Housing (Scotland) Act 1987* as amended.

(iv)   there are special circumstances which the authority considers establish a local connection with the district. This may be particularly relevant where the applicant has been in prison or hospital and his or her circumstances do not conform to the criteria in (i) – (iii) above. Where, for example, an applicant seeks to return to a district where he or she was brought up or lived for a considerable length of time in the past, there may be grounds for considering that the applicant has a local connection with that district because of special circumstances. An authority must exercise its discretion when considering whether special circumstances apply.

4.2 A notifying authority should not refer an applicant to another authority on grounds of a local connection because of special circumstances without the prior consent of the notified authority. Alternatively, authorities may come to an informal arrangement in such cases on a reciprocal basis, subject to the agreement of the applicants.

4.3 There are certain circumstances where a local connection is not established because of residence or employment in a district. For these purposes:

(i) a person is not employed in a district if he or she is serving in the Regular Armed Forces of the Crown; and

(ii) residence in a district is not of a person's own choice if he or she (or anyone who might reasonably be expected to reside with them) becomes resident there because he or she is serving in the Regular Armed Forces of the Crown or is detained under the authority of any Act of Parliament (e.g. held in prison, or a secure hospital).

4.4 **For Welsh authorities only** the conditions for referral to another authority are met if the applicant was placed in accommodation in the district of the notifying authority by the other authority as a discharge of a duty to secure accommodation under Part 7 of the 1996 Act following an application to the other authority made within the last five years. This is without prejudice to whether or not the applicant may have established a local connection with a particular district.

4.5 **Former asylum seekers (England and Wales).** Broadly, s.199(6) of the 1996 Act (inserted by s.11 of the *Asylum and Immigration (Treatment of Claimants, etc.) Act 2004* ('the 2004 Act')) (England and Wales) provides that a person has a local connection with the district of a local housing authority if that person was provided with accommodation there under s.95 of the *Immigration and Asylum Act 1999* (NASS accommodation). Where a person has been provided with NASS accommodation in more than one area, the local connection is with the area where accommodation was last provided. A local connection with a district by virtue of s.199(6) does not override a local connection by virtue of s.199(1). So, a former asylum seeker who has a local connection with a district because he or she was provided with NASS accommodation there could also have a local connection elsewhere for some other reason, for example, because of employment or family associations.

4.6 **Former asylum seekers (Scotland).** Under s.27(2)(a)(iii) of the *Housing (Scotland) Act 2001*, as inserted by s.7 of the *Homelessness etc (Scotland) Act 2003*, residence in accommodation provided in pursuance of s.95 of the *Immigration and Asylum Act 1999* does not constitute a local connection as it is deemed to be residence which is not of the applicant's own choice. A local connection could be formed for other reasons, such as family association.

4.7 **Former asylum seekers (cross-border arrangements).** If a former asylum seeker who was provided with asylum support in England or Wales seeks homelessness assistance in Scotland the Scottish local authority could refer the application to another area where a local connection is established, if there was no local connection with the authority applied to. However under Scottish legislation, a local connection would not be formed by virtue of residence in accommodation provided in pursuance of s.95 of the *Immigration and Asylum Act 1999*.

4.8 This paragraph explains the position where a former asylum seeker who was provided with asylum support in Scotland seeks homelessness assistance in England or Wales. The provisions of s.11(2) and (3) of the 2004 Act provide that where a local housing authority in England or Wales are satisfied that an applicant is eligible for assistance, unintentionally homeless and in priority need, the s.193 duty to secure accommodation does not apply if the authority are satisfied that the applicant: has been provided with s.95 accommodation in Scotland at any time and does not have a local connection anywhere in England and Wales (within the meaning of s.199(1) of the 1996 Act) or anywhere in Scotland (within the meaning of s.27 of the *Housing (Scotland) Act 1987*). However, the authority may secure that accommodation is available for the applicant for a period giving him a reasonable opportunity of securing accommodation for himself, and provide the applicant (or secure that he is provided with) advice and assistance in any attempts he may make to secure accommodation for himself.

4.9   Subject to paragraphs 4.6 to 4.9 above (former asylum seekers), once the local authority is satisfied that the applicant is eligible, unintentionally homeless, falls within a priority need category, and does not have a local connection with the district, the authority may notify another authority under s.198 *Housing Act 1996* or s.33 *Housing (Scotland) Act 1987*, provided it is satisfied that all the conditions for referral set out in paragraph 3.3 above are met.

4.10   Once the local authority has established that the applicant is eligible, homeless, in a priority need category, not intentionally homeless and does not have any local connection in its own area it may notify another authority under s.198 *Housing Act 1996* or s.33 *Housing (Scotland) Act 1987*, provided it has satisfied itself that a local connection with the notified authority exists and that no member of the household would be at risk of domestic violence or threat of domestic violence in returning to that area. In determining whether or not there is such a risk authorities should have regard, where relevant, to the advice in the Homelessness Code of Guidance.

4.11   The notifying authority must consider that neither the applicant nor any person who might reasonably be expected to reside with the applicant has **any** local connection with its own district but **does** have a local connection with another local authority district in England, Scotland or Wales, in accordance with the criteria and exceptions listed above. The strength of local connection is irrelevant except where an applicant has no local connection with the notifying authority's district but has a local connection with more than one other local authority district. In such a scenario, the notifying authority must weigh up all the relevant factors in deciding to which authority it would be appropriate to refer the applicant.

4.12   Any relevant changes in an applicant's circumstances, e.g. obtaining employment, will need to be taken into account in determining whether the applicant has a local connection. Authorities should always consider whether special circumstances may apply.

5   PROCEDURES PRIOR TO MAKING A REFERRAL

5.1   If an authority considers that the conditions for referral s.198 *Housing Act 1996* or s.33 *Housing (Scotland) Act 1987* are likely to be met in a particular case it should make any necessary enquiries in the area/s where there may be a local connection. This should be undertaken as soon as possible. An authority that is considering making a referral must investigate all the circumstances of the case with the same thoroughness as if it were not considering a referral.

5.2 The notifying authority has a duty under s.200(1)(England and Wales) or s.34 *Housing (Scotland) Act 1987* to ensure that suitable accommodation is available for occupation by the applicant until the question of whether the conditions for referral are met have been decided.

5.3 Under section 184(4) *Housing Act 1996* or s.34 *Housing (Scotland) Act 1987*, if a housing authority notify, or intend to notify another authority that they consider that the conditions for referral of a case are met, the authority must notify the applicant of this decision, and the reasons for it, at the same time. For English and Welsh authorities, under s.184(5) of the 1996 Act, the notice must also inform the applicant of his right, under s.202, to request a review of the decision and that any request must be made within 21 days (or such longer period as the authority allows in writing). Regulations made under s.203 of the 1996 Act set out the procedure to be followed when making a review and the period within which a request for review must be carried out and the decision made. The *Allocation of Housing and Homelessness (Review Procedures) Regulations 1999 (SI 1999 No. 71)* establishes for England and Wales the period within which the review must be carried out and the decision made. For England and Wales s.204 of the 1996 Act gives applicants the right to appeal to the county court on a point of law if dissatisfied with the decision on the review (or the initial decision, if a review decision is not made within the prescribed time limit).

5.4 Scottish local authorities have a duty to review homelessness decisions under s. 35A of the *Housing (Scotland) Act 1987* as amended by s. 4 of the *Housing (Scotland) Act 2001*. This process does not affect the rights of a homeless applicant to seek judicial review or to seek the redress of the Scottish Public Services Ombudsman.

5.5 Once the notifying authority is has decided that the applicant is eligible, unintentionally homeless, and in priority need, there is no provision for the notified authority to challenge the decision other than judicial review in the High Court. The local authority associations' disputes procedure should be used only where there is a disagreement over the question of whether the conditions for referral are met and not for resolving disagreement on any other matter.

6 MAKING THE NOTIFICATION

6.1 All notifications and arrangements concerning an applicant should be made by telephone and then confirmed in writing. A specimen standard notification form is attached, which authorities are advised to use. If telephone contact cannot be made a fax or e-mail should be sent. Where the notified authority accepts the conditions for referral are met, it should not wait for the receipt of written confirmation of notification before making appropriate arrangements to secure accommodation for the applicant and his or her household.

6.2 Each authority should nominate an officer responsible for making decisions about applications notified by another authority. Appropriate arrangements should also be put in place to ensure cover during any absences of the designated officer.

6.3 The notified authority should normally accept the facts of the case relating to residence, employment, family associations etc., as stated by the notifying authority, unless they have clear evidence to the contrary. It is the notifying authority's duty to make inquiries into the circumstances of homelessness with the same degree of care and thoroughness before referring a case to another authority as it would for any other case.

6.4   Local authorities should try to avoid causing undue disruption to the applicant which could arise from the operation of the criteria and procedures set out above. For instance, where it is agreed that the conditions for referral are met two authorities involved could agree, subject to the applicants' consent, to enter into a reciprocal arrangement so as to avoid having to move a household which may already have made arrangements within the notifying authority's area for schooling, medical treatment etc. Such arrangements could involve provision via nominations to other social housing providers such as registered social landlords. Authorities are reminded that there is no requirement to refer applicants to another authority even where it is agreed that the conditions for referral are met.

6.5   Once written confirmation of notification has been received the notified authority should, within 10 days, reply to the notifying authority. If, despite reminders, there is an unreasonable delay by the notified authority in formally responding to the notification, the notifying authority may ask its local authority association to intercede on its behalf.

7 ARRANGEMENTS FOR SECURING ACCOMMODATION

7.1   As soon as the notifying authority has advised the applicant that it intends to notify, or has already notified, another authority that it considers that the conditions for referral are met, the notifying authority has a duty (under s.200 (1) of the 1996 Act) (England and Wales) and s.34 *Housing (Scotland) Act 1987* to secure accommodation until the applicant is informed of the decision whether the conditions for referral are met. During this period, the notifying authority also has a duty (under s.211) (England and Wales) and s.36 of the *Housing (Scotland) Act 1987* to take reasonable steps for the protection of property belonging to the applicant or anyone who might reasonably be expected to reside with the applicant.

7.2.1   When it has been decided whether the conditions for referral are met the notifying authority must inform the applicant of the decision and the reason for it (s.200(2), England and Wales or s.34 of the *Housing (Scotland) Act 1987*). The applicant must also be informed of his right to ask for a review of the decision and that any request must be made within 21 days or such longer period as the authority may allow in writing

7.2.2   If it is decided that the conditions for referral are not met, under s.200(3) England and Wales or s.34(2) of the *Housing (Scotland) Act 1987* the notifying authority will be subject to the s.193 duty (England and Wales) or s.31 of the *Housing (Scotland) Act 1987* and must ensure that suitable accommodation is available for the applicant.

7.2.3   If it is decided that the conditions for referral are met, under s.200(4) or s.34(2) of the *Housing (Scotland) Act 1987*), the notified authority will be subject to the s.193 duty (England and Wales) s.31 of the *Housing (Scotland) Act 1987* and must ensure that suitable accommodation is available for the applicant.

7.3   The local authority associations recommend that once a notified authority has accepted that the conditions of referral are met it shall reimburse the notifying authority for any expenses which may reasonably have been incurred in providing temporary accommodation, including protection of property. If the notifying authority unduly delays advising an authority of its intention to refer an applicant then the notified authority shall only be responsible for expenses incurred after the receipt of notification. In normal circumstances a period of more than 30 working days, commencing from the date when the notifying authority had reason to believe that the applicant may be homeless or threatened with homelessness and commenced inquiries under s.184, (England & Wales), s.28 of the *Housing (Scotland) Act 1987*, should be considered as constituting undue delay.

8 RIGHT OF REVIEW OF REFERRAL DECISIONS (England and Wales)

8.1 Under s.202(1)(c) *Housing Act 1996*, applicants in England and Wales have the right to request a review of any decision by the authority to notify another authority of its opinion that the conditions for referral are met. And, under s.202(1)(d), applicants in England and Wales have the right to request a review of any decision whether the conditions for referral are met. In Scotland (under s.34(3A) and s.35A(2)(b) of the *Housing (Scotland) Act 1987*) as inserted by s.4 of the *Housing Scotland Act 2001* the applicant must be notified that they can request a review of any decision to refer their case to another authority, any determination reached following referral and the time within which this request should be made – the authority should also notify the applicant of advice and assistance available to him in connection with this review. In both cases the request for review will be made to the notifying authority.

9 STATUTORY PROCEDURE ON REVIEW

9.1 **Review procedure for England** – The procedural requirements for a review are set out in the *Allocation of Housing and Homelessness (Review Procedures) Regulations 1999* (SI 1999 No. 71).

9.2 The notifying authority shall notify the applicant:
(i) that the applicant, or someone acting on the applicant's behalf, may make written representations,
(ii) of the review procedures

9.3 If the reviewer acting for the notifying authority considers that there is an irregularity in the original decision, or in the manner in which it was made, but is nevertheless minded to make a decision which is against the interests of the applicant, the reviewer shall notify the applicant:
(i) that the reviewer is so minded, and the reasons why
(ii) that the applicant, or someone acting on the applicant's behalf, may make further written or oral representations.

9.4 In carrying out a review the reviewer shall:
(i)   consider any representations made by, or on behalf of, the applicant,
(ii) consider any further written or oral representations made by, or on behalf of, the applicant in response to a notification referred to in paragraph 9.2 (b) above
(iii) make a decision on the basis of the facts known at the date of the review.

9.5 The applicant should be notified of the decision on a review within: eight weeks from the date on which a request for review was made under s.202(1)(c), ten weeks from the date on which a request for review was made under s.202(1)(d), or such longer period as the applicant may agree in writing.

9.6   **Review procedure for Scotland** – Procedures are set out in s.35A and s.35B of the *Housing (Scotland) Act 1987*. Good practice guidance on the procedures is set out in Chapter 11 of the Code of Guidance on Homelessness.

9.7   **Review Procedure for Wales.** The procedures are set out in *The Allocation of Housing and Homelessness (Review Procedures) Regulations 1999* (SI 1999 No 71).

9.8   Where the decision under review is a joint decision by the notifying housing authority and the notified housing authority s202 (4) requires that the review should be carried out jointly by the two housing authorities.

9.9   The notifying authority shall notify the applicant:
(i)   that the applicant, or someone acting on the applicant's behalf, may make written representations,
(ii) of the review procedures

9.10 If the reviewer acting for the notifying authority considers that there is an irregularity in the original decision, or in the manner in which it was made, but is nevertheless minded to make a decision which is against the interests of the applicant, the reviewer shall notify the applicant:
(i)   that the reviewer is so minded, and the reasons why
(ii) that the applicant, or someone acting on the applicant's behalf, may make further written and/or oral representations.

9.11 In carrying out a review the reviewer shall:
(i)   consider any representations made by, or on behalf of, the applicant,
(ii)   consider any further written or oral representations made by, or on behalf of, the applicant in response to a notification referred to in paragraph 9.9 (ii) above
(iii) make a decision on the basis of the facts known at the date of the review.

9.12 The applicant should be notified of the decision on a review within:
(i)   eight weeks from the date on which a request for review, where the original decision was made by the housing authority,
(ii)   ten weeks from the date on which a request for review was made where the decision was made jointly by two housing authorities
(iii) twelve weeks, where the decision is taken by a person appointed pursuant to the Schedule to the *Homelessness (Decisions on Referrals) Order 1998* (SI 1998 No. 1578).
In all these cases it is open to the reviewer to seek the applicant's agreement to an extension of the proscribed period; any such agreement must be given in writing.

10 DISPUTES BETWEEN AUTHORITIES

10.1 *The Homelessness (Decisions on Referrals (Scotland) Order 1998* and the *Homelessness (Decisions on Referrals) Order 1998* (SI 1998 No.1578) (England and Wales) set out the arrangements for determining whether the conditions for referral are met, should the notifying and the notified authority fail to agree. These arrangements allow the question to be decided either by a person agreed between the two authorities concerned or, in default of such agreement, by a person appointed from a panel established by the LGA.

10.2 Where a notified authority considers the conditions for referral are not met it should write to the notifying authority giving its reasons in full, within 10 days. The letter should contain all the reasons for its opinion, to avoid delaying the appointment of a referee and to minimise any inconvenience for the applicant.

10.3 Where two authorities cannot reach agreement on whether the conditions for referral are met they must seek to agree on a referee who will make the decision. CoSLA and the LGA have jointly established an independent panel of referees for this purpose. A referee should be appointed within 21 days of the notified authority receiving the notification.

10.4 Authorities invoking the disputes procedure should, having first agreed on the proposed referee, establish that he or she is available and willing to accept the case. Each authority is then responsible for providing the referee with such information as he or she requires to reach a decision, making copies of the submission available to the applicant and ensuring prompt payment of fees and expenses. Sections 10–19 (Guidelines for Invoking the Disputes Procedure) set out in greater detail the requirements and timescale for the disputes procedure.

10.5 Authorities invoking the disputes procedure should be bound by the decision of the referee, including the apportionment of fees and expenses, subject to a further decision by a referee where the applicant asks for a review of the initial decision.

10.6 If the authorities are unable to agree on the choice of a referee, they must jointly request that CoSLA (for Scottish authorities) or the LGA (for English or Welsh authorities) appoint a referee on their behalf as outlined in paragraph 10.8 below.

10.7 If a referee has not been appointed within six weeks of the notified authority receiving the referral the notifying authority may request CoSLA or the LGA, as appropriate, to appoint a referee as outlined in paragraph 10.8 below.

10.8 Where two authorities fail to agree on the appointment of a referee CoSLA (if the dispute is between Scottish authorities) or the LGA (if the dispute is between English or Welsh authorities) may appoint a referee from the panel. Where the **notified** authority is Scottish then the local authority association responsible for appointing a referee will be CoSLA, even if the notifying authority is in England or Wales. The LGA will be the responsible association if the notified authority is English or Welsh.

10.9 The local authority associations should only be involved in the direct appointment of referees as a last resort. Under normal circumstances authorities should jointly agree the arrangements between themselves in accordance with the Guidelines for Invoking the Disputes Procedure.

Procedures for Referrals of Homeless Applicants on the Grounds of Local Connection with Another Local Authority Guidelines for Invoking the Disputes Procedure

AGREED BY

ASSOCIATION OF LONDON GOVERNMENT (ALG)
CONVENTION OF SCOTTISH LOCAL AUTHORITIES (CoSLA)
LOCAL GOVERNMENT ASSOCIATION (LGA)
WELSH LOCAL GOVERNMENT ASSOCIATION (WLGA)
(*'the local authority associations'*)

11 DETERMINING DISPUTES

11.1   The local authority associations have been concerned to establish an inexpensive, simple, speedy, fair and consistent way of resolving disputes between authorities arising from the referral of homeless applicants under s.198 *Housing Act 1996* (England and Wales). In Scotland the provisions of s.33 *Housing (Scotland) Act 1987* apply.

11.2   For the purpose of this Disputes procedure, arbitrators are referred to as 'referees'. Referees will not normally be entitled to apply the criteria set out in this agreed procedure without the consent of the local authorities involved in the dispute. Where the issues in the case are evenly balanced, referees may have regard to the wishes of the applicant.

11.3   In determining disputes referees will need to have regard to:

a)   for English and Welsh authorities
  - Part 7 *Housing Act 1996*
  - regulation 6 of the *Homelessness Regulations 1996* (SI 1996 No. 2754) for Wales
  - the *Homelessness (Decisions on Referrals) Order 1998* (SI 1998 No. 1578)
  - the *Allocation of Housing and Homelessness (Review Procedures) Regulations 1999* (SI 1999 No. 71)
  - *Code of Guidance for Local Authorities on Allocation of Accommodation and Homelessness 2003 (Wales)* – currently under review
  - *Homelessness Code of Guidance for Local Authorities 2006 (England)*

b)   for Scottish authorities
  - *Housing (Scotland) Act 1987*
  - the *Homelessness (Decisions on Referrals) (Scotland) Order 1998*
  - the *Persons subject to Immigration Control (Housing Authority Accommodation and Homelessness) Order 2000* (SI 2000 706)
  - *Homelessness etc (Scotland) Act 2003*
  - *Code of Guidance on Homelessness: Guidance on legislation, policies and practices to prevent and resolve homelessness 2005 (Scotland)*

c)   for all authorities
  - the *Procedures for s.198 (Local Connection) Homeless Referrals: Guidelines for Local Authorities and Referees* produced by the local authority associations
  - *Asylum and Immigration (Treatment of Claimants, etc.) Act 2004*

11.4 Where there is a cross border dispute between a Scottish authority and an English or Welsh authority then the legislation relevant to the location of the *notified* authority should be applied in determining whether the conditions for referral are met.

11.5 Scottish authorities need to be aware of any orders exercised by s.8 of the *Homelessness (Scotland) Act 2003* that may effect referrals between Scottish authorities in the future.

12 ARRANGEMENTS FOR APPOINTING REFEREES

12.1 Referees will be approached by the authorities in dispute, both of which must agree that the referee should be invited to accept the appointment, to establish whether they are willing and able to act in a particular dispute. The referee should be appointed within 21 days of the notified authority receiving the referral. If the local authorities are unable to agree on the choice of referee they should contact CoSLA or the LGA, as appropriate, in accordance with section 10 of the Guidelines for Local Authorities on Procedures for Referral.

12.2 A referee will be given an initial indication of the reason for the dispute by the relevant authorities or the local authority association. The referee's jurisdiction is limited to the issue of whether the conditions for referral are met.

12.3 A referee must not have any personal interest in the outcome of the dispute and should not accept the appointment if he or she is, or was, employed by, or is a council tax payer in, one of the disputing local authorities, or if he or she has any connection with the applicant.

13 PROCEDURES FOR DETERMINING THE DISPUTE

13.1 The general procedures to be followed by a referee in determining a dispute are outlined in the Schedule to the *Homelessness (Decisions on Referrals) Order 1998* (SI 1998 No. 1578). (England and Wales) and SI 1998 No. 1603 *(Scotland)*. It is recommended that the following, more detailed, procedures are applied to *all* cases.

13.2 Following appointment, the referee shall invite the notifying and notified authorities to submit written representations within a period of *fourteen* working days, specifying the closing date, and requiring them to send copies of their submission to the applicant and to the other authority involved in the dispute. Authorities must have the opportunity to see each other's written statements, and should be allowed a further period of *ten* working days to comment thereon before the referee proceeds to determine the issue. The referee may also invite further written representations from the authorities, if considered necessary.

13.3 The homeless applicant to whom the dispute relates is not a direct party to the dispute but the referee may invite written or oral representations from the applicant, or any other person, which is proper and relevant to the issue. Where the referee invites representations from a person they may be made by another person acting on the person's behalf, whether or not the other person is legally qualified.

13.4 The disputing authorities should make copies of their submissions available to the applicant. The authorities should have the opportunity to comment on any information from the applicant (or any other source) upon which the referee intends to rely in reaching his/her decision.

13.5 Since the applicant's place of abode is in question, and temporary accommodation and property storage charges may be involved, it is important that a decision should be reached as quickly as possible – normally within *a month* of the receipt of the written representations and comments from the notifying and notified authority. This period will commence at the end of the process described in point 13.2. In the last resort, a referee may determine a dispute on the facts before him/her if one authority has, after reminders, failed to present its case without reasonable cause.

14 ORAL HEARINGS

14.1 Where an oral hearing is necessary or more convenient (e.g. where the applicant is illiterate, English is not his/her first language or further information is necessary to resolve issues in dispute), it is suggested that the notifying authority should be invited to present its case first, followed by the notified authority and any other persons whom the referee wishes to hear. The applicant may be invited to provide information on relevant matters. The authorities should then be given a right to reply to earlier submissions.

14.2 The referee's determination must be in writing even when there is an oral hearing. The referee will have to arrange the venue for the hearing and it is suggested that the offices of the notifying authority would often be the most convenient location.

14.3 Where a person has made oral representations the referee may direct either or both authorities to pay reasonable travelling expenses. The notifying and notified authorities will pay their own costs.

15 NOTIFICATION OF DETERMINATION

15.1 The written decision of the referee should set out:
(a) the issue(s) which he has been asked to determine
(b) the findings of fact which are relevant to the question(s) in issue
(c) the decision
(d) the reasons for the decision.
The referee's determination is binding upon the participating local authorities, subject to the applicant's right to ask for a review of the decision under s.202 of the 1996 Act (and possible right of appeal to the county court on a point of law under s.204). The statutory right to review does not apply to Scottish legislation.

16 COSTS OF DETERMINATION

16.1 Referees will be expected to provide their own secretarial services and to obtain their own advice on points of law. The cost of so doing, however, will be costs of the determination and recoverable as such.

17 CIRCULATION OF DETERMINATION

17.1 Referees should send copies of the determination to both disputing authorities and to the LGA. The LGA will circulate copies to other members of the Panel of Referees as an aid to settling future disputes and promoting consistency in decisions.

17.2 The notifying authority should inform the applicant of the outcome promptly.

18 PAYMENT OF FEES AND COSTS

18.1 The local authority associations recommend a flat rate fee of £500 per determination (including determinations made on a review) which should be paid in full and as speedily as possible after the determination has been received. However, in exceptional cases where a dispute takes a disproportionate time to resolve, a referee may negotiate a higher fee. In addition, the referee may claim the actual cost of any travelling, secretarial or other incidental expenses which s/he has incurred, including any additional costs arising from the right of review or the right of appeal to a county court on a point of law.

18.2 The LGA will determine such additional fees as may be appropriate for any additional work which may subsequently arise should there be a further dispute or appeal after the initial determination has been made or should a referee be party to an appeal, under s.204 *Housing Act 1996*, to the county court on a point of law.

18.3 The referee's fees and expenses, and any third party costs, would normally be recovered from the unsuccessful party to the dispute, although a referee may choose to apportion expenses between the disputing authorities if he considers it warranted. Referees are advised, when issuing invoices to local authorities, to stipulate that payment be made within **28 days**.

19 REOPENING A DISPUTE

19.1 Once a determination on a dispute is made, a referee is not permitted to reopen the case, even though new facts may be presented to him or her, unless a fresh determination is required to rectify an error arising from a mistake or omission.

20 RIGHT OF REVIEW OF REFEREE'S DECISION

20.1 Section 202(1)(d) *Housing Act 1996* gives an applicant the right to request a review of any decision made under these procedures. The right to review does not apply to Scottish legislation.

20.2 If an applicant asks for a review of a referee's decision the notifying and notified authority must, within five working days, appoint another referee ('the reviewer') from the panel. This applies even if the original referee was appointed by the LGA. The reviewer must be a different referee from the referee who made the initial decision. If the two authorities fail to appoint a reviewer within this period then the notifying authority must, within five working days, request the LGA to appoint a reviewer and the LGA must do so within seven days of the request.

20.3 The authorities are required to provide the reviewer with the reasons for the initial decision, and the information on which the decision is based, within five working days of his or her appointment. The two authorities should decide between them who will be responsible for notifying the applicant of the reviewer's decision, once received.

21 STATUTORY PROCEDURE ON REVIEW

21.1 The procedural requirements for a review are set out in the *Allocation of Housing and Homelessness (Review Procedures) Regulations 1999* (SI 1999 No.71).

21.2   The reviewer is required to:
- (i)   notify the applicant that he or she, or someone acting on his or her behalf, may make written representations,
- (ii)   notify the applicant of the review procedures, and
- (iii) send copies of the applicant's representations to the two authorities and invite them to respond.

21.3   If the reviewer considers that there is an irregularity in the original decision, or in the manner in which it was made, but is nevertheless minded to make a decision which is against the interests of the applicant, the reviewer shall notify the applicant:
- (a) that the reviewer is so minded and the reasons why, and
- (b) that the applicant, or someone acting on his behalf, may make further written or oral representations.

21.4   In carrying out a review, the reviewer is required to:
- (i)   consider any representations made by, or on behalf of, the applicant,
- (ii)   consider any responses to (i) above,
- (iii) consider any further written or oral representations made by, or on behalf of, the applicant in response to a notification referred to in paragraph 21.3 (b), and
- (iv)   make a decision on the basis of the facts known at the date of the review.

21.5   The applicant should be notified of the decision on a review within twelve weeks from the date on which the request for the review was made, or such longer period as the applicant may agree in writing. The two authorities should be advised in writing of the decision on the review, and the reasons for it, **at least a week before the end of the period** in order to allow them adequate time to notify the applicant. Copies of the decision should also be sent to the LGA.

Procedures for Referrals of Homeless Applicants on the Grounds of Local Connection with Another Local Authority Standard Notification Form

AGREED BY

ASSOCIATION OF LONDON GOVERNMENT (ALG)
CONVENTION OF SCOTTISH LOCAL AUTHORITIES (CoSLA)
LOCAL GOVERNMENT ASSOCIATION (LGA)
WELSH LOCAL GOVERNMENT ASSOCIATION (WLGA)
(*'the local authority associations'*)

A   NOTIFYING AUTHORITY DETAILS

Contact Name _____

Authority _____

Telephone Number _____ Fax Number _____

E-mail _____

Address for Correspondence _____

_____

B   APPLICANT DETAILS

Name of Main Applicant _____ Date of Birth _____

Current Address _____

_____

_____

_____

_____

C   FAMILY MEMBERS

Name	Relationship	Date of Birth

D   ADDRESS IN LAST 5 YEARS (include dates and type of tenure)

_____

_____

_____

_____

_____

_____

_____

_____

E   PRESENT/PREVIOUS EMPLOYMENT DETAILS

Employer _____ Tel No _____

Address _____

Contact name _____ Job Title _____

Previous Employer _____

Date from _____ Date to _____

Address _____

F   REASONS FOR HOMELESSNESS

_____

_____

_____

_____

_____

_____

H   PRIORITY NEED CATEGORY

_____

_____

_____

_____

_____

I   LOCAL CONNECTION DETAILS

J   WISHES OF THE APPLICANT(S) (in the context of the referral)

K   THE NOTIFYING AUTHORITY CONSIDER THE CONDITIONS FOR REFERRAL ARE MET BECAUSE:

L   ANY SUPPLEMENTARY INFORMATION
(attach supporting documentation if relevant)

I confirm that, in accordance with s.198 Housing Act 1996, this authority considers that neither the applicant nor any person who might reasonably be expected to reside with the applicant would run the risk of domestic violence or face a probability of other violence in the district of your authority, if this referral is made.

Signed _____   Date _____

Homelessness Code of Guidance for Local Authorities: Supplementary Guidance on Intentional Homelessness: August 2009*

Applicants who face homelessness following difficulties in meeting mortgage commitments

In response to the current economic climate, and the robust framework of financial support the Government has put in place to help homeowners in financial difficulty,[1] this note provides guidance on how local housing authorities should exercise their homelessness functions, and apply the various statutory criteria, when considering whether applicants who are homeless having lost their home because of difficulties in meeting mortgage commitments are intentionally or unintentionally homeless.

Introduction

1. This guidance is issued by the Secretary of State under section 182 of the *Housing Act* 1996 ('the 1996 Act'). Under section 182(1) of the 1996 Act, housing authorities are required to have regard to this guidance in exercising their functions under Part 7 of the 1996 Act.

2. This statutory guidance supplements chapter 11 of the *Homelessness Code of Guidance for Local Authorities* issued in July 2006 ('the 2006 Code'), and should be read in conjunction with that chapter.

Homelessness following mortgage difficulties

3. Homeowners may be at risk of homelessness if they experience difficulties in meeting their mortgage commitments, for example, because a member of the household loses their employment or suffers an income shock. Individual homeowners may respond in different ways when faced with such difficult circumstances.

4. Some homeowners may voluntarily give up possession of the property (hand back the keys to the lender). Some homeowners may decide to sell the property. Others may seek help to remain in their home, including help under the Mortgage Rescue Scheme (MRS) or Homeowner Mortgage Support (HMS), but decide – if found eligible for the scheme – not to accept an offer because they consider that continuing with home ownership would be unsustainable or would entail unacceptable financial risk. Where homeowners who have experienced such circumstances become homeless or threatened with homelessness and apply to a local housing authority for assistance, the authority will need to give careful consideration to the substantive cause(s) of homelessness before coming to a decision on intentionality.

Definition of intentional homelessness

5. Authorities are reminded that by sections 191(1) and 196(1) of the 1996 Act, a person becomes homeless intentionally or threatened with homelessness intentionally, if:

---

i) the person deliberately does or fails to do anything in consequence of which the person ceases to occupy accommodation (or the likely result of which is that the person will be forced to leave accommodation);

ii) the accommodation is available for the person's occupation; and

iii) it would have been reasonable for the person to continue to occupy the accommodation.

However, an act or omission made in good faith by someone who was unaware of any relevant fact must not be treated as deliberate.

6. Authorities are also reminded that they must not adopt general policies that seek to pre-define circumstances that do or do not amount to intentional homelessness or threatened homelessness (see paragraph 11.5 of the *Homelessness Code of Guidance for Local Authorities*).

Principles established by case law

7. The broad thrust of section 191 is to ascribe intentional homelessness to a person who on the facts is responsible for his homelessness by virtue of his own act or omission. Whilst it is not part of the purpose of the legislation to require local authorities to house people whose homelessness is brought upon them by their own fault, equally, it is not part of the legislation that authorities should refuse to accommodate people whose homelessness has been brought upon them without fault on their part, for example, by an inability to make ends meet.

8. Nobody may be presumed to be intentionally homeless; the local housing authority must be satisfied of intentionality and must ask and answer the questions set out in the legislation. The decision maker in the local authority must look for the substantive cause of the homelessness and the effective cause will not always be the most immediate proximate cause.

9. Intentionality does not depend on whether applicants have behaved wisely or prudently or reasonably. Where an applicant's failure to seek help may have been foolish, imprudent or even unreasonable, this would not necessarily mean his or her conduct was not in good faith.

Some possible scenarios

10. As mentioned above, some former homeowners may seek housing assistance from a local housing authority having lost their home in one of the following circumstances:

i) having voluntarily surrendered the property (handed the keys back);

ii) having sold the property;

iii) where the property was repossessed after the applicant refused an offer under the MRS;

iv) where the property was repossessed after the applicant refused an offer of HMS;

v) where the property was repossessed and the applicant had not sought help.

There should be no general presumption that a homeowner will have brought homelessness on him or herself in any of the above scenarios. A person cannot be found to have become intentionally homeless from a property where he or she was already statutorily homeless: eg because it was not reasonable for him to continue to occupy the property (see paragraph 8.18 et seq of the

Homelessness Code of Guidance for Local Authorities). Consequently, where someone was already homeless before surrendering or selling their home or refusing an offer under MRS or HMS, the 'acts' of surrender or sale, and the 'omission' of refusing an offer of MRS or HMS cannot be treated as the cause of homelessness.

11. In particular, authorities will need to satisfy themselves on two questions as applied at the point in time immediately before the applicant ceased to occupy accommodation (i.e. prior to the surrender, sale or refusal of help). First, was the applicant's home available as accommodation for the applicant, any other person who normally resides with him as a member of his family and any person who might reasonably be expected to reside with him? Second, did the applicant's home constitute accommodation that it would have been reasonable for him or her to continue to occupy? It would not have been reasonable for the applicant to continue to occupy his or her home, for example, if the home was not affordable, for example, because the applicant could not meet the cost of his or her mortgage commitments.

12. If the answer to either of the two questions above is in the negative, the applicant will have been homeless prior to the surrender or sale of the property or refusal of an offer of assistance under the MRS or HMS. In such a case, the authority may still consider whether the applicant's homelessness was intentional but will need to look at the substantive causes of that homelessness prior to surrender or sale of the property or refusal of an offer of assistance under the MRS or HMS.

Allocation of Accommodation: Code of Guidance for Local Housing Authorities*

CONTENTS

Chapters

Annexes

* ODPM, November 2002. © Crown Copyright.

CHAPTER 1

[Omitted. Replaced by *Fair and Flexible: statutory guidance on social housing allocations for local authorities in England* (December 2009).]

CHAPTER 2

[Omitted. Replaced by *Fair and Flexible: statutory guidance on social housing allocations for local authorities in England* (December 2009).]

CHAPTER 3
Allocations: general

Partnership working

3.1 Most social housing is provided by housing authorities using their own stock and by RSLs. Even where a housing authority has transferred its stock to an RSL, it retains responsibility for its statutory housing duties. A housing authority has a strategic responsibility for meeting its districts housing needs and the Secretary of State regards it as essential that housing authorities work closely with RSLs, other housing providers and voluntary agencies to meet those needs.

3.2 Housing authorities will need to develop working relationships with other organisations at a strategic and operational level to ensure that the housing, care and support needs of vulnerable people are appropriately met. These organisations will include Supporting People teams, Connexions partnerships, housing related support providers, health authorities, social services authorities, the police and probation service.

3.3 There need to be effective mechanisms in place for developing an interface with other services and providers. The Supporting People process provides a useful model (see www.spkweb.org.uk). Housing authorities will also wish to take advantage of the partnership working arrangements which they develop in drawing up their homelessness strategies.

Definition of allocation

3.4 For the purposes of Part 6 the allocation of housing accommodation by housing authorities is defined in s159 as:
   (a) selecting a person to be a secure or introductory tenant of housing accommodation held by a housing authority;
   (b) nominating a person to be a secure or introductory tenant of housing accommodation held by another person (ie, one of the authorities or bodies fulfilling the landlord condition mentioned in the Housing Act 1985, s80); or
   (c) nominating a person to be an assured tenant of housing accommodation held by an RSL.

Transfers

3.5 Provisions in relation to transfers are now contained in s159(5). As a result, Part 6 now applies to most allocations to existing tenants of housing authorities and RSLs seeking to move to other social housing. This entitles existing social housing tenants to apply to transfer to other social housing stock, which may be in the same district or in another housing authority's district. However, s167(2A) of the 1996 Act means that housing authorities may take into account any local connection which exists between the applicant and the housing authority's district in determining priorities in relation to applicants who fall within the reasonable and additional preference categories (see Chapter 5, para 5.23).

3.6   Those applying for a transfer must be treated on the same basis as other applicants in accordance with the provisions set out in the housing authority's allocation scheme, which should reflect a sensible balance between meeting the housing needs of existing tenants and new applicants, whilst ensuring the efficient use of stock. Transfers that the housing authority initiates for management purposes do not fall within Part 6. These would include a temporary decant to allow repairs to a property to be carried out. Mutual exchanges between existing tenants also do not fall within Part 6 (see annex 1 for a full list of exemptions).

Joint tenants

3.7   The Secretary of State considers joint tenancies can play an important role in the effective use and equitable allocation of housing. Where household members have long term commitments to the home, for example, when adults share accommodation as partners (including same sex partners), friends or unpaid live-in carers, housing authorities should normally grant a joint tenancy. In this way the ability of other adult household members to remain in the accommodation on the death of the tenant would not be prejudiced. Housing authorities should ensure that there are no adverse implications from the joint tenancy for the good use of their housing stock and for their ability to continue to provide for housing need.

3.8   Housing authorities should ensure that applicants, including where they are existing tenants, are made aware of the option of joint tenancies. When doing so, the legal and financial implications and obligations of joint tenancies must be made clear, including the implications for succession rights of partners and children. Where housing authorities refuse an application for a joint tenancy, clear, written reasons for the refusal should be given.

3.9   Where a joint tenant serves notice to quit, housing authorities have a discretion to grant a sole tenancy to the remaining tenant. In exercising this discretion, they should ensure that there are no adverse implications for the good use of their housing stock and their ability to continue to provide for housing need. Where housing authorities decide that they may wish to exercise their discretion in this respect, they must reflect this in their allocation scheme.

3.10   Where a tenant dies and another household member (who does not have succession rights to the tenancy) has:
(a) been living with the tenant for the year prior to the tenants death; or
(b) been providing care for the tenant; or
(c) accepted responsibility for the tenants dependants and needs to live with them in order to do so,
housing authorities should consider granting a tenancy to the remaining person or persons, either in the same home or in suitable alternative accommodation, provided the allocation has no adverse implications for the good use of

the housing stock and has sufficient priority under the allocation scheme. In the case of (a) and (b), the accommodation in question must be the principal or only residence of the survivor at the time the tenant dies.

Period for considering an offer of accommodation

3.11 Applicants must be allowed a reasonable period to make a decision about accommodation offered to them under Part 6. There is no statutory time limit but it is important that applicants are given sufficient time for careful consideration. Applicants who have had the opportunity to make an informed, positive decision to accept an offer are more likely to be committed to making a success of the tenancy.

3.12 Some applicants may require longer than others depending on their circumstances: they may wish to take advice in making their decision particularly in the case of vulnerable applicants; or they may be unfamiliar with the property. Longer periods may be required, for example, where the applicant is currently in hospital, on in some form of temporary accommodation, such as a hostel or refuge.

CHAPTER 4
Eligibility for an allocation of accommodation

General overview

4.1 Section 166(3) places an obligation on housing authorities to consider all applications for social housing that are made in accordance with the procedural requirements of the housing authority's allocation scheme. In considering applications, however, housing authorities must ascertain if an applicant is eligible for accommodation or whether he is excluded from allocation under s160A(1)(a), (3) or (5). Housing authorities may decide to treat the applicant as ineligible for an allocation under s160A(7) (unacceptable behaviour). Otherwise, housing authorities must treat all applicants as eligible.

Nationality and immigration status/persons from abroad

4.2 Under s160A(3) persons from abroad who are subject to immigration control within the meaning of the Asylum and Immigration Act 1996 are ineligible for allocations, but the Secretary of State has prescribed classes of persons who are subject to immigration control but are nonetheless to be eligible for an allocation. Under s160A(5) the Secretary of State has also prescribed that certain persons from abroad, who are not subject to immigration control, have to be habitually resident in the Common Travel Area (CTA) (ie, the UK, the Channel Islands, the Isle of Man and the Republic of Ireland) in order to be eligible (see annex 6).

4.3 The following are the main categories of applicants to whom a housing authority may allocate accommodation taking account of nationality and immigration status (see also annex 4):

(a) **Existing tenants** All existing secure and introductory tenants of a housing authority and assured tenants of accommodation allocated by a housing authority;

(b) **British Nationals** British Nationals, who are habitually resident in the CTA;

(c) **EEA Nationals** Any person, who is a national of any of the countries in the European Economic Area (EEA), and is habitually resident in the CTA; or is a worker, or has a right to reside in the UK;

(d) **Persons subject to immigration control** who have been granted:
   (i) **Refugee status**;
   (ii) **Exceptional leave to remain** provided that there is no condition that they shall not be a charge on public funds; or
   (iii) **Indefinite leave to remain** provided that they are habitually resident in the CTA and their leave to remain was not granted in the previous 5 years on the basis of a sponsorship given in relation to maintenance and accommodation (or, if so, that their sponsor has (or in the case of more than one sponsor, all of them have) died);

(e) **Persons subject to immigration control who are nationals of a country that has ratified the European Convention on Social and Medical Assistance (ECSMA) or the European Social Charter (ESC)** provided that they are habitually resident in the CTA and are lawfully present in the UK (see also annex 6).

The habitual residence test

4.4   While the majority of the categories eligible for housing require the applicant to be habitually resident in the CTA, most applicants for social housing will not be persons from abroad and there will be no reason to apply the test. It is also likely that persons who have been resident in the CTA continuously during the 2 years prior to their housing application will be habitually resident in the CTA. In such cases, therefore, housing authorities may consider it unnecessary to make further enquiries to establish habitual residence, unless there are other circumstances that need to be taken into account. A period of continuous residence in the CTA might include visits abroad e.g. for holidays or to visit relatives. Where 2 years continuous residency in the UK is not established, housing authorities may need to conduct further enquiries to determine whether the applicant is habitually resident in the CTA.

4.5   The term habitual residence is intended to convey a degree of permanence in the persons residence in the CTA; it implies an association between the individual and the country and relies substantially on fact. When deciding whether an applicant is habitually resident, housing authorities should take account of the applicants period of residence and its continuity, his employment prospects, his reason for coming to the UK, his future intentions and his centre of interest.

4.6   A person cannot claim to be habitually resident in any country unless he has taken up residence and lived there for a period. There will be cases where the person concerned is not coming to the UK for the first time, but is resuming a habitual residence previously had. Annex 11 provides detailed guidance on the factors which a housing authority should consider in determining whether an applicant is habitually resident in these circumstances. However, the fact that a person has ceased to be habitually resident in another country does not imply habitual residence in the country to which he has travelled.

4.7   A person who is in stable employment is more likely to be able to establish habitual residence than someone whose employment is, for whatever reason, transitory (ie, an au pair or someone who is on a fixed short-term contract).

Equally, a person, one of whose apparent aims in coming to the UK is to claim benefits, is less likely to be able to establish habitual residence.

4.8 A person who intends to take up permanent work is more likely to be able to establish habitual residence, as is a person who can show that he has immediate family or other ties in the UK.

4.9 The habitual residence test does not apply to:

(a) a worker for the purposes of EC law (see Council Regulation (EEC) No 1612/68 or (EEC) No 1251/70);

(b) a person with a right to reside in the United Kingdom under treaty rights (see Council Directive No 68/360/EEC or No 73/148/EEC); or

(c) a person who left the territory of Monserrat after 1 November 1995 because of the effect of the volcanic activity there.

4.10 On 21 May 2002 most British Overseas Territories Citizens, including all citizens of Monserrat, became British Citizens. Since their new EU-style passport will not identify that they are from Monserrat, it has been recommended that they should also retain their old British Overseas Territories Citizen passport, to help them demonstrate eligibility for social security benefits and social housing in the UK.

Eligible categories

4.11 **Existing tenants** Section 160A(6) provides that none of the provisions relating to the eligibility of tenants with respect to their immigration status is to affect the eligibility of an applicant who is already a secure or introductory tenant or an assured tenant of housing accommodation allocated to him by a housing authority. It is therefore the case that where such a tenant applies for an allocation the housing authority does not need to question eligibility and an allocation can be made regardless of immigration status or habitual residence.

4.12 **British Nationals** Where a British National arrives from abroad, as with all nationals of an EEA country, he must establish habitual residence in order to be eligible for an allocation, even in cases where he was born in the CTA.

4.13 **EEA Nationals** These are the Nationals of the EU countries plus Iceland, Norway and Liechtenstein. They are not subject to immigration control, but are not eligible for accommodation unless they can establish habitual residence.

4.14 **Persons subject to immigration controls prescribed as eligible** Generally, persons subject to immigration control are not eligible for housing accommodation. However, under s160A(3) the Secretary of State has prescribed classes of person who are to be eligible and they are:

(i) Persons granted refugee status A person is granted refugee status when his request for asylum is accepted.

(ii) Persons granted exceptional leave to enter or remain (ELR) This will be either someone who has failed in his request for asylum, but nonetheless been given leave to remain, or someone who has been granted leave to remain where there are compelling, compassionate circumstances. However, it may be the case that when ELR was granted it was on condition that the applicant should not be a charge on public funds. If that is the case, the applicant is not eligible for an allocation.

(iii) Persons granted indefinite leave to enter or remain (ILR) This will be someone who has permission to remain in the UK for an indefinite period and is regarded as having settled status. In order to be eligible, however, the applicant will still have to be able to establish habitual residence. It is also the case that if ILR status was obtained as a result of sponsorship five years must have elapsed since the persons arrival in the UK or the date of the sponsorship undertaking, whichever is later. However, where a sponsor dies (or where there is more than one sponsor, where all of them die) within the first five years, the applicant will be eligible provided he can establish habitual residence.

(iv) Persons subject to immigration control who are nationals of a country that has ratified ECSMA or ESC Such persons have to be lawfully present in the UK as well as habitually resident. This means that the applicant must have leave to enter or remain in the UK.

4.15 Annex 8 provides guidance on identifying persons subject to immigration control who are eligible for an allocation. Annex 7 lists classes of persons subject to immigration control who are not eligible for an allocation. Annex 9 identifies the countries which have ratified ECSMA and ESC, and lists other European groupings.

4.16 The provisions on eligibility are complex and housing authorities will need to ensure that they have procedures in place to carry out appropriate checks on housing applicants.

4.17 If there is any uncertainty about an applicants immigration status, housing authorities are recommended to contact the Home Office Immigration and Nationality Directorate, using the procedures set out in annex 10. Before doing so, the applicant should be advised that an inquiry will be made; if at this stage the applicant prefers to withdraw his or her application, no further action will be required. Where there is reason to believe that the applicant may be an asylum seeker, they should be referred to the National Asylum Support Service (see annex 10).

4.18 Housing authorities should ensure that staff who are required to screen housing applicants about eligibility for an allocation are given training in the complexities of the housing provisions, the housing authority's duties and responsibilities under the race relations legislation and how to deal with applicants in a sensitive manner. Housing authorities may wish to refer to annex 5, which provides model questions that can provide a pathway to determining eligibility. Annex 12 provides a pathway for determining eligibility in the form of a flow chart.

Unacceptable behaviour

4.19 Most applicants for social housing will not be persons from abroad, and will have been resident in the UK (or elsewhere in the CTA) for 2 years prior to their application. Such applicants, together with those eligible applicants from abroad may nonetheless be treated as ineligible by the housing authority on the basis of unacceptable behaviour.

4.20 Where a housing authority is satisfied that an applicant (or a member of the applicants household) is guilty of unacceptable behaviour serious enough to make him unsuitable to be a tenant, section 160A(7) permits the authority to decide to treat the applicant as ineligible for an allocation.

4.21 Section 160A(8) provides that the only behaviour which can be regarded as unacceptable for these purposes is behaviour by the applicant or by a member of his household that would if the applicant had been a secure tenant of the housing authority at the time have entitled the housing authority to a possession order under s84 of the Housing Act 1985 in relation to any of the grounds in Part I of Schedule 2, other than Ground 8. These are fault grounds and include behaviour such as conduct likely to cause nuisance or annoyance, and use of the property for immoral or illegal purposes. Housing authorities should note that it is not necessary for the applicant to have actually been a tenant of the housing authority when the unacceptable behaviour occurred. The test is whether the behaviour would have entitled the housing authority to a possession order if, whether actually or notionally, the applicant had been a secure tenant.

4.22 Where a housing authority has reason to believe that s160A (7) may apply; there are a number of steps that will need to be followed.

(i) They will need to satisfy themselves that there has been unacceptable behaviour which falls within the definition in s160A(8). In considering whether a possession order would be granted in the circumstances of a particular case, the housing authority would have to consider whether, having established the grounds, the court would decide that it was reasonable to grant a possession order. It has been established in case law that, when the court is deliberating, reasonable means having regard to the interests of the parties and also having regard to the interests of the public. So, in deciding whether it would be entitled to an order the housing authority would need to consider these interests, and this will include all the circumstances of the applicant and his or her household. In practice, courts are unlikely to grant possession orders in cases which have not been properly considered and are not supported by thorough and convincing evidence. It is acknowledged that in cases involving noise problems, domestic violence, racial harassment, intimidation and drug dealing, courts are likely to grant a possession order. Rent arrears would probably lead to a possession order, although in many cases it will be suspended giving the tenant the opportunity to pay the arrears. In taking a view on whether it would be entitled to a possession order, the housing authority will need to consider fully all the factors that a court would take into account in determining whether it was reasonable for an order to be granted. In the Secretary of States view, a decision reached on the basis of established case law would be reasonable.

(ii) Having concluded that there would be entitlement to an order, the housing authority will need to satisfy itself that the behaviour is serious enough to make the person unsuitable to be a tenant of the housing authority. For example, the housing authority would need to be satisfied that, if a possession order were granted, it would not be suspended by the court. Behaviour such as the accrual of rent arrears which have resulted from factors outside the applicants control for example, delays in housing benefit payments; or liability for a partners debts, where the applicant was not in control of the households finances or was unaware that arrears were accruing should not be considered serious enough to make the person unsuitable to be a tenant.

(iii) The housing authority will need to satisfy itself that the applicant is unsuitable to be a tenant by reason of the behaviour in question in the circumstances at the time the application is considered. Previous unacceptable behaviour may not justify a decision to consider the applicant as unsuitable to be a tenant where that behaviour can be shown to have improved.

4.23   The housing authority must be satisfied on all three aspects set out in para 4.22. Only then can the housing authority consider exercising its discretion to decide that the applicant is to be treated as ineligible for an allocation. In reaching a decision on whether or not to treat an applicant as ineligible, the housing authority will have to act reasonably, and will need to consider all the relevant matters before it. This will include all the circumstances relevant to the particular applicant, whether health, dependants or other factors. In practice, the matters before the housing authority will normally mean the information provided with the application.

4.24   If an applicant, who has, in the past, been deemed by the housing authority to be ineligible, considers his unacceptable behaviour should no longer be held against him as a result of changed circumstances, he can make a fresh application. Unless there has been a considerable lapse of time it will be for the applicant to show that his circumstances or behaviour have changed.

4.25   Where a housing authority has reason to believe that an applicants unacceptable behaviour is due to a physical, mental or learning disability, they must not treat that person as ineligible for an allocation without first considering whether he would be able to maintain a tenancy with appropriate care and support. In considering the applicants case, the housing authority will need to consult with relevant agencies, including social services, health professionals, and providers of suitable housing, care and housing related support services.

4.26   Housing authorities should note, however, that they are not required to treat an applicant as ineligible where they are satisfied that he is guilty of unacceptable behaviour serious enough to make him unsuitable to be a tenant; instead they may decide to proceed with the allocation but give the applicant no preference for an allocation. This option is considered further at Chapter 5, paras 5.19 to 5.22.

4.27   A housing authority may also take into account the behaviour of an applicant (or a member of his household) which affects his suitability to be a tenant when determining priorities in relation to applicants who fall within the reasonable preference categories. This option is considered further at Chapter 5, para 5.23(b).

Joint tenancies

4.28   Under s160A(1)(c), a housing authority shall not grant a joint tenancy to two or more people if any one of them is a person from abroad who is ineligible or is a person who is being treated as ineligible because of unacceptable behaviour.

Reviews of decisions on eligibility

4.29   Under s160A(9) and (10), and s167(4A) housing authorities, who decide that applicants are ineligible by virtue of s160A(3) or (5) or are to be treated as ineligible because of unacceptable behaviour, must give them written notification of the decision. The notification must give clear grounds for the decision which must be based firmly on the relevant facts of the case.

4.30 Under s167(4A)(d) applicants have the right to request a review under the allocation scheme of any decision as to eligibility and a right to be informed of the decision on review and the grounds for that decision.

CHAPTER 5
Allocation scheme

General overview
5.1–5.12 [Omitted. Replaced by *Fair and Flexible: statutory guidance on social housing allocations for local authorities in England* (December 2009).]

Medical and welfare grounds
5.13 Where it is necessary to take account of medical advice, housing authorities should contact the most appropriate health or social care professional who has direct knowledge of the applicants condition, as well as the impact his condition has on his housing needs.

5.14 Welfare grounds is intended to encompass not only care or support needs, but also other social needs which do not require ongoing care and support, such as the need to provide a secure base from which a care leaver or other vulnerable person can build a stable life. It would include vulnerable people (with or without care and support needs) who could not be expected to find their own accommodation.

5.15 Where accommodation is allocated to a person who needs to move on medical or welfare grounds, it is essential to assess any support and care needs, and housing authorities will need to liaise with social services, the Supporting People team and other relevant agencies, as necessary, to ensure the allocation of appropriate accommodation. Housing authorities should also consider, together with the applicant, whether his needs would be better served by staying put in his current accommodation if appropriate aids and adaptations were put in place.

Hardship grounds
5.16 This would include, for example, a person who needs to move to a different locality in order to give or receive care, to access specialised medical treatment, or to take up a particular employment, education or training opportunity.

5.17 Possible indicators of the criteria which apply to categories (c) and (d) are given in annex 3.

Additional preference
5.18 [Omitted. Replaced by *Fair and Flexible: statutory guidance on social housing allocations for local authorities in England* (December 2009).]

Unacceptable behaviour
5.19 By virtue of s167(2B) and (2C) an allocation scheme may provide that no preference is given to an applicant where the housing authority is satisfied that he, or a member of his household, has been guilty of unacceptable behaviour serious enough to make him unsuitable to be a tenant of the housing authority; and the housing authority is satisfied that, in the circumstances at the time the case is considered, he deserves not to be treated as a person who should be given reasonable preference.

5.20   By virtue of s167(2D), the same provisions apply for determining what is unacceptable behaviour for the purposes of deciding whether to give preference to an applicant, as apply to a decision on eligibility, that is to say s160A(8).

5.21   Section 160A(8) provides that the only behaviour which can be regarded as unacceptable for these purposes is behaviour by the applicant or by a member of his household that would if the applicant had been a secure tenant of the housing authority at the time have entitled the housing authority to a possession order under s84 of the Housing Act 1985 in relation to any of the grounds in Part I of Schedule 2, other than Ground 8.

5.22   Chapter 4, paras 4.21 and 4.22 provide guidance, for the purposes of determining eligibility under s160A(7), on what constitutes unacceptable behaviour serious enough to make an applicant unsuitable to be a tenant, and sets out the steps which housing authorities should take to satisfy themselves in this regard. This guidance applies equally to decisions under s167(2B) and (2C).

5.23–5.32   [Omitted. Replaced by *Fair and Flexible: statutory guidance on social housing allocations for local authorities in England* (December 2009).]

5.33   Households may include a child with a need for settled accommodation on medical or welfare grounds.

5.34   Under s27 of the Children Act 1989, housing authorities are required to respond to social services authorities, who have duties towards children under that Act (see s18). Section 17 of that Act imposes a general duty on social services authorities to safeguard and promote the welfare of children within their area who are in need. Consistent with that duty, they must promote the upbringing of such children by their families, by providing a range and level of services appropriate to those children's needs. Subject to an amendment in the Adoption and Children Bill, families in this context are to include adoptive families, and prospective adoptive families.

5.35   A child in need is defined in the Children Act 1989 as someone who is unlikely to achieve or maintain, or to have the opportunity of achieving or maintaining, a reasonable standard of health or development without the provision of certain services by a local authority; or someone whose health or development is likely to be significantly impaired, or further impaired, without the provision of such services; or someone who is disabled. A child in need may require settled accommodation on medical or welfare grounds.

5.36   Housing authorities will need to consult with social services about the appropriate level of priority for an allocation in such cases, and how any support needs will be met.

Carers

5.37   In making accommodation offers to applicants who receive support from carers who do not reside with them, housing authorities should, wherever possible, take account of the applicants need for a spare bedroom.

Lone teenage parents under 18

5.38   The provision of suitable accommodation with support for lone parents under 18 is a key part of the Governments Teenage Pregnancy Strategy. While lone teenage parents will normally be young women which is why this guidance uses the terms she and her in this section housing authorities need to recognise that there may be some occasions when the applicant is a young man.

5.39   The Governments objective is that all 16 and 17 year-old lone parents who cannot live with their parents or partner and who require social housing should be offered semi-independent accommodation with support. Housing authorities should work with social services, Supporting People teams, RSLs and relevant voluntary organisations in their district to ensure that the Governments objective is met.

5.40   The allocation of appropriate housing and support should be based on consideration of the young persons housing and support needs, her individual circumstances and her views and preferences. Housing authorities must ensure that the accommodation is suitable for babies and young children. Wherever possible, housing authorities should take account of the education and employment needs and opportunities of the applicant when identifying suitable accommodation.

5.41   Where an application for housing is received from a lone parent aged 16 or 17, the Secretary of State recommends that housing authorities have arrangements in place to ensure that they can undertake a joint assessment of the applicants housing, care and support needs with social services. Housing authorities should obtain the consent of the young parent before involving social services, unless child protection concerns are present and to seek such consent might endanger the welfare of the child of the young parent.

5.42   Where RSLs in the district have vacancies in a suitable supported housing scheme, housing authorities should use their nomination rights to secure accommodation for young parents in such accommodation. Support may be provided on site or on a floating basis.

5.43   Where there is no suitable RSL accommodation available, housing authorities should consider allocating the young parent a place in other similar accommodation where appropriate support is available.

5.44   The Secretary of State believes that the young person should not normally be allocated an independent tenancy without floating support. In exceptional cases, however, it may be decided that supported housing would not be appropriate. Such a decision should only be made after careful consideration of the housing and support needs of that individual and her views and preferences. In such circumstances, housing authorities should ensure that the young person is aware of relevant sources of support and advice and how to access them. This might include social services, health visitors, the Connexions service, and relevant voluntary agencies and local providers.

5.45   Housing authorities should also, in consultation with the relevant RSLs in their district, make provision for appropriate move-on accommodation for young parents who have been assessed as ready to leave supported accommodation and live independently. In some cases, where the young parent has made good progress, it may be appropriate for her to live independently before she reaches the age of 18. When allocating move-on accommodation to a young parent, the housing authority should consider whether the parent or child have any continuing support needs, in consultation with the young person, social services and relevant providers.

5.46   If, with the young persons consent, a joint assessment is carried out with social services of the housing, care and support needs of a lone parent aged 16 or 17, it may be considered more appropriate for her to be accommodated by social services, for example, in foster care.

5.47 Young parents under the age of 16 must always be referred to social services so that their social care needs may be assessed.

5.48 Further guidance is set out in *Guidelines for Good Practice in Supported Accommodation for Young Parents*, published jointly by DTLR and the Teenage Pregnancy Unit in September 2001 (available from www.teenagepregancyunit. gov.uk or www.housingcorp.gov.uk).

Tenancies for minors

5.49 In some circumstances, social services authorities may consider it appropriate to underwrite a tenancy agreement for an applicant who is under 18. There are legal complications associated with the grant of a tenancy to a minor because a minor cannot hold a legal estate in land. However, if a tenancy is granted, it probably takes effect as a contract for a lease and would be fully enforceable as a contract for necessaries (ie, the basic necessities of life) under common law. Any guarantee given in those circumstances would remain valid in respect of any liability incurred by the minor notwithstanding that he or she may repudiate the agreement on or shortly after reaching 18.

Rough sleeping

5.50 Housing authorities homelessness strategies have a key role to play in preventing homelessness and rough sleeping. Access to good quality, affordable housing will be vital for rough sleepers and people at risk of sleeping rough.

5.51 Housing authorities should ensure that allocation schemes make provision to enable access to housing authority and RSL accommodation for this client group. Where appropriate, schemes should also ensure that vulnerable people have access to the assistance they need to apply for housing. Often, people at risk of homelessness will require support, for example to address mental health, alcohol or drug problems, or simply to cope with bill paying and basic life skills. Allocation schemes should be developed with strong links to such support services provided under local homelessness strategies and Supporting People.

Sex offenders

5.52 Where sex offenders are allocated accommodation, this should be in the light of considered decisions about managing any risks associated with their release from prison into the community, involving multi-agency arrangements with the police, probation services, social services, health professionals and other relevant bodies. Housing authorities should have regard to DETR guidance issued to Chief Housing Officers in November 1999 about the management of risk in such cases.

Rent (Agriculture) Act 1976

5.53 The Rent (Agriculture) Act 1976 (referred to as the 1976 Act) requires housing authorities to use their best endeavours to provide accommodation for displaced agricultural workers. Section 27 of the 1976 Act requires the housing authority to be satisfied that:

(a) the dwelling-house from which the worker is displaced is needed to accommodate another agricultural worker;

(b) the farmer cannot provide suitable alternative accommodation for the dis-placed worker; and

(c) the displaced worker needs to be re-housed in the interests of efficient agriculture.

5.54   In reaching a decision, the housing authority must have regard to advice of an Agricultural Dwelling-House Advisory Committee (ADHAC). The ADHACs role is to provide advice on whether the interests of efficient agriculture are served by re-housing the worker, and on the applications urgency. If the hous-ing authority is satisfied that the applicants case is substantiated, it is its duty under s28 of the 1976 Act to use its best endeavours to provide suitable alter-native accommodation for the displaced worker. In assessing the applications priority the housing authority is required to consider (a) the cases urgency; (b) the competing claims on the accommodation: and (c) its resources.

5.55   A housing authority would not be properly discharging its duty under s.28 of the 1976 Act if it refused, on the grounds of the displaced worker having insufficient priority under the allocation scheme, to offer that person suit-able alternative accommodation. There must be proper consideration of all relevant s28 factors in the light of the ADHACs advice. It is important, where relevant, for housing authorities to include in their allocation scheme a policy statement in respect of cases arising under the 1976 Act.

General information about particular applications

5.56   Under s167(4A)(a), allocation schemes must be framed so as to give appli-cants the right to request from housing authorities general information that will enable them to assess:

(a) how their application is likely to be treated under the scheme and, in par-ticular, whether they are likely to fall within the reasonable preference categories;

(b) whether accommodation appropriate to their needs is likely to be made available and, if so, how long it is likely to be before such accommodation becomes available.

5.57   Housing authorities which operate an open advertising scheme, whereby applicants can apply for particular properties, would usually be expected to provide information about the properties which have been let; for example, what level of priority the successful applicants had, or the date on which they had applied to go on the housing authority's waiting list. Such feedback is cru-cial as it enables applicants to assess their chances of success in subsequent applications. It can also assist applicants in refining their preferences, and all housing authorities are therefore recommended to consider the extent to which they are able to provide information about properties which have been let. However, s166(4) prohibits housing authorities from divulging to other members of the public that a particular individual is an applicant for social housing, unless they have the applicants consent, and therefore personal information about applicants should always be kept confidential.

Notification about decisions and the right to a review of a decision

5.58   Under s167(4A), allocation schemes must also be framed so as to give appli-cants the following rights about decisions which are taken in respect of their application:

(a) the right to be notified in writing of any decision not to give an applicant any preference under the scheme because of unacceptable behaviour serious enough to make him unsuitable to be a tenant of the housing authority;

(b) the right, on request, to be informed of any decision about the facts of the applicants case which has been, or is likely to be, taken into account in considering whether to make an allocation to him; and

(c) the right, on request, to review a decision mentioned in (a) or (b) above, or a decision to treat the applicant as ineligible because of unacceptable behaviour serious enough to make him unsuitable to be a tenant of the housing authority. The applicant also has the right to be informed of the decision on the review and the grounds for it.

CHAPTER 6

[Omitted. Replaced by *Fair and Flexible: statutory guidance on social housing allocations for local authorities in England* (December 2009).]

CHAPTER 7
Contracting out and stock transfer

Contracting out

7.1   The Local Authorities (Contracting Out of Allocation of Housing and Homelessness Functions) Order 1996 (SI No 3205) enables housing authorities to contract out certain functions under Part 6 of the 1996 Act. The Order is made under s70 of the Deregulation and Contracting Out Act 1994 (the 1994 Act). In essence, the Order allows the contracting out of executive functions, while leaving the responsibility for making strategic decisions with the housing authority.

7.2   Schedule 1 to the Order lists the allocation functions which may not be contracted out:

(i)   adopting or altering the allocation scheme, including the principles on which the scheme is framed, and consulting RSLs; and,

(ii)   making the allocation scheme available at the authority's principal office.

7.3   The Order therefore provides that the majority of functions under Part 6 may be contracted out. These include:

(iii) making enquiries about and deciding a persons eligibility for an allocation;

(iv)   carrying out reviews of decisions;

(v)   making arrangements to secure that advice and information is available free of charge to persons within the housing authority's district on how to apply for housing;

(vi)   making arrangements to secure that any necessary assistance is made available free of charge to anyone who is likely to have difficulty in making a housing application without such assistance; and

(vii) making individual allocations in accordance with the allocation scheme.

7.4   The 1994 Act provides that a contract made:
(i)   may authorise a contractor to carry out only part of the function concerned;
(ii)   may specify that the contractor is authorised to carry out functions only in certain cases or areas specified in the contract;
(iii)   may include conditions relating to the carrying out of the functions, eg, prescribing standards of performance;
(iv)   shall be for a period not exceeding 10 years and may be revoked at any time by the Minister or the housing authority. Any subsisting contract is to be treated as having been repudiated in these circumstances;
(v)   shall not prevent the authority from itself exercising the functions to which the contract relates.

7.5   The 1994 Act also provides that the authority is responsible for any act or omission of the contractor in exercising functions under the contract, except:
(i)   where the contractor fails to fulfil conditions specified in the contract relating to the exercise of the function; or
(ii)   where criminal proceedings are brought in respect of the contractors act or omission.

7.6   Where there is an arrangement in force under s101 of the Local Government Act 1972 by virtue of which one authority exercises the functions of another, the 1994 Act provides that the authority exercising the function is not allowed to contract it out without the principal authority's consent.

Stock transfer

7.7   Housing authorities that have transferred all or part of their housing stock, or are in the process of transferring their stock, are still required under Part 6 to have an allocation scheme where they continue to allocate housing within the meaning of s159 of the 1996 Act. The requirement in s167(7) of the 1996 Act to consult RSLs before adopting or altering their allocation scheme will be particularly important in the case of a transferring housing authority. Whilst transfer RSLs must operate as independent bodies, housing authorities seeking to transfer may wish to consider including in the contract an obligation on the transfer RSL to consult the housing authority if the RSL wishes to amend its allocation policy.

7.8   Nomination arrangements between the transferring housing authority and the transfer RSL must reflect the requirement that nominations of assured tenancies must be to eligible persons in accordance with the housing authority's allocation scheme. It is important to remember that the housing authority may have nomination arrangements with other RSLs in the district, and these should be included in any agreement to contract out the allocation function.

7.9   The transfer agreement will need to include monitoring arrangements. Monitoring arrangements will be important, to ensure that housing authorities can demonstrate that they are meeting their statutory obligations under Part 6, and in particular the requirement to give reasonable preference to persons in the categories set out in s167(2). The monitoring arrangements will also need to cover nominations to all RSL stock.

7.10   Where a housing authority has delegated or contracted out the operation of its allocation functions to an external contractor, the contractor must be made aware of the provisions of Part 6 and advised how the legislation and this guidance may apply to them.

7.11 Good practice guidance on arrangements for contracting out homelessness and allocation functions will be published in Autumn 2003.

ANNEX 1
Scope of Part 6 exemptions

1   Part 6 of the 1996 Act (as amended) does not apply to mutual exchanges within an RSLs stock or between housing authorities and RSLs.

Primary Legislation Exemptions

2   The 1996 Act (as amended), s159(5) states that Part 6 provisions do not apply to a person who is already a secure or introductory tenant unless the allocation involves a transfer of housing accommodation for that person and is made on his application.

3   Similarly, s160 (as amended) exempts from Part 6 provisions cases:
   (a) where a secure tenant dies, the tenancy is a periodic one, and there is a person qualified to succeed the tenant under the Housing Act 1985, s89;
   (b) where a secure tenant with a fixed term tenancy dies and the tenancy remains secure by virtue the Housing Act 1985, s90;
   (c) where a secure tenancy is assigned by way of exchange under the Housing Act 1985, s92;
   (d) where a secure tenancy is assigned to someone who would be qualified to succeed to the tenancy if the secure tenant died immediately before the assignment; or
   (e) where a secure tenancy vests or is otherwise disposed of in pursuance of an order made under:
   the Matrimonial Causes Act 1973, s24 (property adjustment orders in connection with matrimonial proceedings);
   the Matrimonial and Family Proceedings Act 1984, s17(1) (property adjustment orders after overseas divorce); or
   the Children Act 1989, Schedule 1, paragraph 1 (orders for financial relief against parents), or
   (f) where an introductory tenancy:
   (i) becomes a secure tenancy on ceasing to be an introductory tenancy;
   (ii) vests under the 1996 Act, s133(2) (succession to an introductory tenancy on death of tenant); or
   (iii) is assigned to someone who would be qualified to succeed the introductory tenancy if the introductory tenant died immediately before the assignment; or
   (iv) meets the criteria in paragraph 3(e) above.

Secondary legislation exemptions

4   The Allocation of Housing Regulations 1996 SI No 2753, Regulation 3 exempts the following allocations from Part 6 provisions:
   (a) cross-border transfers of secure or assured tenants belonging to the Northern Ireland Housing Executive; Scottish local authorities; housing associations registered with Scottish Homes; or housing companies who

acquired the said accommodation from a Scottish local authority, or from Scottish Homes;

(b) where a housing authority secure the provision of suitable alternative accommodation under the Land Compensation Act 1973, s39 (duty to re-house residential occupiers);

(c) the grant of a secure tenancy under the Housing Act 1985, s554 or s555 (grant of a tenancy to a former owner-occupier or statutory tenant of defective dwelling-house).

ANNEX 2

[Omitted. Replaced by *Fair and Flexible: statutory guidance on social housing allocations for local authorities in England* (December 2009).]

ANNEX 3
Indicators of the criteria in the reasonable preference categories (s167(2)(c) and (d))

Local housing authorities may devise their own indicators of the criteria in the reasonable preference categories in the 1996 Act (as amended), s167(2). The following list is included for illustrative purposes and to assist housing authorities in this task: it is by no means comprehensive or exhaustive, and local housing authorities may have other, local factors to consider and include as indicators of the categories.

Insanitary, overcrowded and unsatisfactory housing conditions
Lacking bathroom or kitchen
Lacking inside WC
Lacking cold or hot water supplies, electricity, gas, or adequate heating
Lack of access to a garden for children
Overcrowding
Sharing living room, kitchen, bathroom/WC
Property in disrepair
Property unfit
Poor internal or external arrangements
Under-occupation
Children in flats or maisonettes above ground floor.

People who need to move on medical or welfare grounds (criteria may apply to any member of the household)
A mental illness or disorder
A physical or learning disability
Chronic or progressive medical conditions (eg, MS, HIV/AIDS)
Infirmity due to old age
The need to give or receive care
The need to recover from the effects of violence (including racial attacks) or threats of violence, or physical, emotional or sexual abuse
Ability to fend for self restricted for other reasons
Young people at risk

People with behavioural difficulties
Need for adapted housing and/or extra facilities, bedroom or bathroom
Need improved heating (on medical grounds)
Need sheltered housing (on medical grounds)
Need ground floor accommodation (on medical grounds)
Need to be near friends/relatives or medical facility on medical grounds.

ANNEXES 4–9

[Omitted. Replaced by *Fair and Flexible: statutory guidance on social housing allocations for local authorities in England* (December 2009).]

ANNEX 10
How to contact the Home Offices Immigration and Nationality Directorate

1   The Home Offices Immigration and Nationality Directorate (IND) will exchange information with housing authorities subject to relevant data protection and disclosure policy requirements being met and properly managed, provided that the information is required to assist with the carrying out of statutory functions or prevention and detection of fraud.
2   The Evidence and Enquiries Unit (EEU) will provide a service to housing authorities to confirm the immigration status of an applicant from abroad (Non Asylum-seekers). In order to take advantage of the service, housing authorities first need to register with the Evidence and Enquiries Unit, Immigration and Nationality Directorate, C Block 3rd Floor, Whitgift Centre, Wellesley Road, Croydon, CR9 2AT either by letter or Fax: 020 8604 5783.
3   Registration details required by the EEUs Local Authorities Team are;
    (a) Name of enquiring housing authority on headed paper,
    (b) Job title/status of officer registering on behalf of the housing authority,
    (c) Names of housing authority staff and their respective job titles/status who will be making enquiries on behalf of the housing authority.
4   Once the housing authority is registered with the EEU, then the authorised personnel can make individual enquiries by letter or fax, but replies will be returned by post.
5   In cases where the EEU indicate that the applicant may be an asylum seeker, enquiries of their status can be made to the National Asylum Support Service (NASS) by **Fax: 020 8633 0014**. Copies of the EEUs correspondence must accompany the request.

ANNEX 11
Habitual Residence Test

Allocation of Housing (England) Regulations 2002 provide that some classes of applicant will be eligible for an allocation subject to their being habitually resident in the Common Travel Area (CTA). However, in practice, when considering applications from these classes of applicant it is only necessary to investigate habitual residence if the applicant has entered the UK in the last two years.

A person can satisfy the Habitual Residence Test (HRT) if they are habitually resident in the CTA. The CTA includes:
- the UK
- Channel Islands
- Isle of Man
- Republic of Ireland

ACTION ON RECEIPT OF AN APPLICATION
Applicant came to live in the UK in the last two years
If it appears that the applicant came to live in the UK in the last two years, make further enquiries to decide if the applicant is habitually resident, or can be treated as such.
- If it appears that the applicant came to live in the UK in the last two years, make further enquiries to decide if the applicant is habitually resident, or can be treated as such.

Factors to consider
It is important to consider the applicant's stated reasons and intentions for coming to the UK.

If the applicant's stated intention is to live in the UK, and not return to the country from which they came, that intention must be consistent with their actions. To decide whether an applicant is habitually resident in the UK, consider the following factors.

Why has the applicant come to the UK?
A   If the applicant is returning to the UK after a period spent abroad, where it can be established that the applicant was previously habitually resident in the UK and is returning to resume his former period of habitual residence, he is immediately habitually resident. In determining whether an applicant is returning to resume a former period of habitual residence consider
- when did the applicant leave the UK?
- how long did the applicant live in the UK before leaving?
- why did the applicant leave the UK?
- how long did the applicant intend to remain abroad?
- why did the applicant return?
- did the applicant's partner and children, if any, also leave the UK?
- did the applicant keep accommodation in the UK?
- if the applicant owned property, was it let, and was the lease timed to coincide with the applicant's return to the UK?
- what links did the applicant keep with the UK?
- have there been other brief absences? If yes, obtain details
- why has the applicant come to the UK?

B   If the applicant has arrived in the UK within the previous two years and is not resuming a period of habitual residence, consideration should be given to his reasons for coming to the UK, and in particular to the factors set out below.

Work arrangements

If the applicant states that they have a job, consider:
- is the work full time or part time?
- how many hours do/will they work?
- is the work short term employment, eg au pair, seasonal work?
- is the applicant on a short term contract with a current employer?

The applicant's employment record and in particular the nature of any previous occupation and plans for the future are relevant. A person with the offer of genuine and effective work in the UK, whether full time or part time, is likely to be habitually resident here.

Pattern of work

Consider the pattern of work, ie:
- has the applicant had a succession of casual or short term jobs either in the UK or the previous country? Be aware that a history of working in short term jobs does not always mean an applicant is not habitually resident
- what is the name and address of the employer are they well known for employing casual labour?
- has the applicant worked in the UK previously? If so:
  - how long ago
  - for what period, either casual or short term
- has the applicant work prospects? If the applicant has come to the UK to seek work:
  - has a job been arranged?
  - who has the job been arranged with?
  - if a job has not been secured, have enquiries been made about a job?
  - who were the enquiries made with?
  - does the applicant have qualifications to match their job requirements?
  - does the applicant, in your opinion, have realistic prospects of finding work?
  - are prospects of finding work in the UK any better than in the country they have left?

Joining family or friends

If the applicant has come to the UK to join or rejoin family or friends, consider:
- has the applicant sold or given up any property abroad?
- has the applicant bought or rented accommodation or are they staying with friends?
- is their move to the UK permanent?

Applicant's plans

Consider the applicant's plans, ie:
- if the applicant plans to remain in the UK, is their stated plan consistent with their actions?
- were any arrangements made for employment and accommodation before the applicant arrived in the UK?
- did they buy a one-way ticket?

– did they bring all their belongings with them?
– is there any evidence of links with the UK, eg, membership of clubs?
The fact that a person may intend to live in the UK for the foreseeable future does not, of itself, mean that habitual residence has been established. However, the applicant's intentions along with other factors, for example the purchase of a home in the UK and the disposal of property abroad may indicate that the applicant is habitually resident in the UK.

An applicant who intends to reside in the UK for only a short period, for example on holiday, to visit friends or for medical treatment, is unlikely to be habitually resident in the UK.

Length of residence in another country
Consider the length and continuity of an applicant's residence in another country:
– how long did the applicant live in the previous country?
– have they lived in the UK before, if so for how long?
– are there any remaining ties with their former country of residence?
– has the applicant stayed in different countries outside the UK?
It is possible that a person may own a property abroad but still be habitually resident in the UK. A person who has a home or close family in another country would normally retain habitual residence in that country. A person who has previously lived in several different countries but has now moved permanently to the UK may be habitually resident here.

Centre of interest
An applicant is likely to be habitually resident in the CTA, despite spending time abroad, if their centre of interest is located in the CTA.

People who maintain their centre of interest in the UK, for example a home, a job, friends, membership of clubs, are likely to be habitually resident in the UK. People who have retained their centre of interest in another country and have no particular ties here are unlikely to be habitually resident in the UK.

Take the following into account when deciding the centre of interest:
– home
– family ties
– club memberships
– finance accounts
If the centre of interest appears to be in the CTA but the applicant has a home abroad, consider the applicant's intentions regarding that property.

In certain cultures, eg, the Asian culture, it is quite common for a person to have property abroad which they do not intend to sell, even if they have lived in the CTA for many years and do not intend to leave. This does not mean that an applicant's centre of interest is anywhere but in the CTA.

Definition of habitually resident
The term habitually resident is not defined in legislation. Always consider the overall circumstances of a case to determine whether someone is habitually resident in the CTA.

The above is not an exhaustive check list of questions or factors which will need to be considered. Further enquiries may be needed. The circumstances of each case will dictate what information is needed, and it is vital all relevant factors are taken into account.

General principles

When deciding whether a person is habitually resident in a place consideration must be given to all the facts of each case in a common sense way. It should be remembered that:

– the test focuses on the fact and nature of residence and not the legal right of abode
– a person who is not resident in this country at all cannot be habitually resident. Residence is a more settled state than mere physical presence in a country. To be resident a person must be seen to be making a home. It need not be the only home or a permanent home but it must be a genuine home for the time being. For example a short stay visitor or a person receiving short term medical treatment is not resident
– it is a question of fact whether a person who has established residence in a country has also become habitually resident; this must be decided by reference to all the circumstances of the particular case
– the most important factors for habitual residence are the length, continuity and general nature of actual residence
– the practicality of a persons arrangements for residence is a necessary part of determining whether it can be described as settled and habitual
– established habitual residents of this country who have periods of temporary or occasional absence of long or short duration may still be habitually resident during such absences.

ANNEX 12

[Omitted. Replaced by *Fair and Flexible: statutory guidance on social housing allocations for local authorities in England* (December 2009).]

ANNEX 13
Information about decisions and the right to a review of a decision

INFORMATION ABOUT DECISIONS

1   Under s160(A)(9) and s167(4A)(b), a housing authority must notify an applicant in writing of any decision:

(i)   to treat him as ineligible by virtue of s160A (3) or (5) (ie, persons from abroad);

(ii)   to treat him as ineligible because of unacceptable behaviour serious enough to make him unsuitable to be a tenant of the housing authority;

(iii)   not to give an applicant any preference under the scheme because of unacceptable behaviour serious enough to make him unsuitable to be a tenant of the housing authority.

2   The notification must give clear grounds for the decision, which must be based firmly on the relevant facts of the case.

3   An applicant also has the right, on request, to be informed of any decision about the facts of the applicant's case which has been, or is likely to be, taken into account in considering whether to make an allocation to him.

THE RIGHT TO A REVIEW OF A DECISION

4   Under s167 (4A)(d) an applicant has the right to request a review of a decision

(i)   to treat him as ineligible because of unacceptable behaviour serious enough to make him unsuitable to be a tenant of the housing authority;

(ii)   not to give him any preference under the scheme because of unacceptable behaviour serious enough to make him unsuitable to be a tenant of the housing authority;

(iii) about the facts of his case which has been, or is likely to be taken into account in considering whether to make an allocation to him;

and to be informed of the decision on the review and the grounds for it.

5   By virtue of s166(2), a housing authority must inform an applicant that he has the rights set out in s1674A, that is to say the right to a review of a decision, and the right to be informed of any decision about the facts of his case.

Allocation of Accommodation: Choice Based Lettings Code of Guidance for Local Housing Authorities*

CONTENTS

---

* Department for Communities and Local Government: August 2008. © Crown Copyright.

Restricting choice
Choice and mobility

Chapter 5: Managing a Choice Based Lettings scheme
Consultation
Information, advice and assistance/support
Information and advice about stock availability and other housing options
Advice
Information about accommodation which has been allocated under a choice based lettings scheme – 'Feedback' information
Application form
Support and assistance
Undue influence
Monitoring
Information sharing and data protection

Chapter 6: Delivering choice in partnership with Registered Social Landlords (RSLs) and Private Sector Landlords
Joint/partnership CBL schemes with RSLs
Statutory framework for co-operation
Applicant prioritisation and eligibility criteria
Nomination agreements
Common housing registers
Stock transfer, contracting out
Private sector landlords

Chapter 7: Regional and sub-regional choice based lettings schemes
Policy objective
Different models of sub-regional and regional CBL
Delegating functions to a central body
Regional and sub-regional allocation schemes
Cross-boundary mobility
RSL involvement in regional CBL schemes

Chapter 1: Purpose of the code

1.1 The Secretary of State is issuing this guidance to local housing authorities in England (referred to in this guidance as 'housing authorities') under s.169 of the Housing Act 1996 (the 1996 Act). Housing authorities must have regard to this guidance for the purposes of exercising their functions under sections 167(1A) and 167(2E) of the 1996 Act. This guidance is also relevant to the duties in sections 193(3A) and 195(3A) of the 1996 Act.

1.2 This code of guidance ('the Code') provides information about those factors which housing authorities should take into account in framing their allocation scheme to offer a choice of accommodation to applicants, and factors which they may wish to consider. Accordingly the guidance is primarily for those authorities which have in place or propose to have in place a policy of offering choice to applicants. It is not a substitute for legislation and in so far as it comments on the law can only reflect the Department's understanding at the time of issue. Housing authorities will still need to keep up to date with any developments in the law in this area.

1.3 Housing authorities which offer a choice of accommodation to applicants continue to allocate accommodation within the meaning of Part 6 of the 1996 Act and must comply with the provisions of Part 6. This guidance is therefore supplementary to the Allocation of Accommodation Code of Guidance for Local Housing Authorities[1] issued in November 2002 (referred to in this guidance as the 'Allocations Code').

Who the guidance is for

1.4 This guidance is specifically for housing authority members and staff. It is also of direct relevance to registered social landlords (referred to as RSLs). Where a housing authority requests it, RSLs have a duty under section 170 of the 1996 Act to co-operate to such extent as is reasonable in the circumstances in offering accommodation to people with priority under the authority's allocation scheme. Other private landlords may also work in partnership with housing authorities to enable applicants to be offered a choice of accommodation and this guidance may be of interest to these landlords.

1.5 Many of the activities covered by this guidance require joint planning and operational co-operation between housing authorities and other bodies. These are likely to include social services departments, health authorities, other referral agencies and voluntary sector organisations, and RSL 'HomeBuy Agents'[2], although this list is not exhaustive. This guidance will be relevant to these organisations as well.

Legislation in context

1.6 In framing their allocation scheme to offer a choice of accommodation to applicants, housing authorities should ensure that their policies and procedures

---

1 *Allocation of Accommodation Code of Guidance for Local Housing Authorities*, ODPM 2002.
2 HomeBuy Agents are appointed RSLs which provide a point of contact for affordable housing options in a given area in England and handle the application process for the Open Market and New Build Homebuy products.

are compatible with obligations imposed on them by other existing legislation, in addition to Part 6 of the 1996 Act, including but not limited to:

- The Race Relations Act 1976 (in particular section 71)
- The Disability Discrimination Act 1995 (in particular section 49A)
- The Sex Discrimination Act 1975 (in particular section 76A)
- The Equality Act (Sexual Orientation) Regulations 2007 (in particular reg-
  ulations 5 and 8)
- The Human Rights Act 1998
- The Freedom of Information Act 2000 (in particular section 19)
- The Data Protection Act 1998 (see paragraph 5.36 below)

1.7   Section 71 of the Race Relations Act 1976 (as amended by the Race Relations
(Amendment) Act 2000) requires specified bodies, including local authorities,
to have due regard to the need to eliminate unlawful racial discrimination
and to promote equality of opportunity and good relations between people of
different racial groups. The aim of this provision is to make the promotion of
racial equality central to the way relevant services are designed and delivered.
Local authorities are also required to publish a race equality scheme which
must be reviewed every three years. Policies and procedures on offering
choice to housing applicants should have regard both to wider duties imposed
on public bodies in terms of race relations, and to the local authority's own
race equality scheme.

1.8   Section 49A of the Disability Discrimination Act 1995 (inserted by the Disability Discrimination Act 2005) introduces a new duty to promote disability
equality which is applicable to all public bodies, including housing authorities. This duty came into force in December 2006. It includes, amongst other
things, the requirement to have due regard to:

- the need to promote equality of opportunity between disabled persons and
  other persons
- the need to eliminate unlawful discrimination and
- the need to take steps to take account of disabled persons disabilities, even
  where that involves treating disabled persons more favourably than other
  persons

1.9   The Equality Act (Sexual Orientation) Regulations 2007 (which are made under
section 81 of the Equality Act 2006) make it unlawful to discriminate on the
grounds of sexual orientation in the provision of goods, facilities and services,
the disposal and management of premises and the exercise of public functions
(amongst other things). Sexual orientation is defined in section 35 of the Equality Act 2006 as meaning an individual's sexual orientation towards persons of
the same sex as him or her, persons of the opposite sex, or both. Lesbian, gay
and bisexual applicants may often be reluctant to access services, including social
housing, for fear of discrimination and/or fear of a lack of awareness or sensitivity to their issues among housing and support providers. Housing authorities
should be aware of this when framing their allocation policies and when considering the support and assistance available to applicants (see further Chapter 5).

1.10   Section 19 of the Freedom of Information Act 2000 requires public authorities
to adopt and maintain a scheme which relates to the publication of information
by the authority, and to publish information in accordance with that scheme.
The publication scheme must specify the classes of information which the
authority publishes or intends to publish; the manner in which information

of each class is, or is intended to be, published; and whether the material is, or is intended to be, available to the public free of charge or on payment. The type of information covered by a publication scheme would include the authority's allocation scheme. This is in addition to the duties under section 168 of the Housing Act1996 to make information available about the authority's allocation scheme.

1.11   The following guidance on the equalities duties is available on the Equality and Human Rights Commission website at www.equalityhumanrights.com:
- The Duty to Promote Disability Equality: Statutory Code of Practice
- Housing and the Disability Equality Duty: A guide to the Disability Equality Duty and Disability Discrimination Act 2005 for the social housing sector
- Gender Equality Duty: Code of Practice for England and Wales
- The gender equality duty and local government: Guidance for public authorities in England
- The Statutory Code of Practice on Racial Equality in Housing (England).

1.12   The policies and procedures on offering a choice of accommodation should be seen in the context of the authority's other housing functions. They should be compatible with the local authority's housing strategy and the relevant regional (and sub-regional) housing strategy. Since the allocation of accommodation under Part 6 is one of the ways in which the main homelessness duty can be discharged, the policies and procedures on choice should also be considered as part of the housing authority's homelessness strategy.

1.13   For a wide range of vulnerable people, housing, care and support are inextricably linked, and housing authorities will want to consider how their policies on offering choice to applicants interacts with other programmes of care and support.

Chapter 2: Overview of the legislative provisions in Part 6 of the 1996 Act relating to offering choice to applicants and the Government's 'choice based lettings' policy

Introduction

2.1   This chapter provides an overview of the Government's policy on offering social housing tenants a choice of accommodation and sets out the obligations imposed on, and powers granted to, housing authorities under Part 6 of the 1996 Act which are particularly relevant to offering choice.

Housing authority's obligations under section 167(1A) of the 1996 Act and powers under section 167(2E)

2.2   Sections 167(1A) and 167(2E) of the 1996 Act were inserted by section 16 of the Homelessness Act 2002 ('the 2002 Act').

2.3   Section 167(1A) provides that an allocation scheme must include a statement as to the housing authority's policy on offering people who are to be allocated housing accommodation a choice of accommodation, or the opportunity to express preferences about the accommodation to be allocated to them. This means that the housing authority must take a policy decision on this issue and address it within their allocation scheme.

2.4   A policy of allowing applicants an opportunity to express their preferences on areas or types of property is not the same as offering applicants a choice of accommodation. In the Secretary of State's view all housing authorities should adopt an allocation scheme which offers a choice of accommodation and she has set a target for all housing authorities to have done so by 2010. In the meantime, however, housing authorities which do not offer a choice of accommodation should consider giving the applicant an opportunity to express preferences in relation to accommodation. This means allowing the applicant to express a preference about, for example, the location and type of accommodation to be allocated. Wherever possible, such preferences should be taken into account in allocating accommodation to that person.

2.5   Section 167(2E) provides that an allocation scheme may contain provision about the allocation of particular accommodation to a person who makes a specific application for that accommodation. This is intended to facilitate choice by providing for the adoption of 'advertising schemes' whereby applicants can apply for particular properties which have been advertised as vacant by the housing authority.

2.6   Section 167(2E) does not specify how authorities should offer a choice of accommodation. However, in the Secretary of State's view the most effective way of doing so is by adopting an advertising scheme and accordingly she expects that all housing authorities will adopt allocation policies and procedures which incorporate an advertising scheme.

Definition of 'choice based lettings scheme'

2.7   The term 'choice based lettings scheme' will be used in this guidance to mean that an authority has adopted allocation policies and procedures which incorporate an advertising scheme.

The Government's policy on offering a choice of accommodation to applicants

2.8   The Secretary of State believes that allocation policies for social housing should provide for applicants to be given more of a say and a greater choice over the accommodation which they are allocated, while continuing to ensure that the primary purpose of social housing is to meet housing need. This is the best way to ensure sustainable tenancies and to build settled, viable and inclusive communities. Research carried out for Communities and Local Government[3] into the longer impact of choice based lettings found that tenants who were offered a choice of accommodation were more likely to be satisfied with their home and remain in that home for a longer period. Satisfied tenants, it is suggested, are more likely to meet their tenancy obligations and maintain the property in good condition.

2.9   In January 2005, ODPM published *Sustainable Communities: Homes for All.*[4] Paragraphs 5.18 to 5.21 of that document set out the Government's choice based lettings policy objectives. These objectives are:

---

3   *Monitoring the Longer Term Impact of Choice Based Lettings*, Heriot-Watt University and BMRB, October 2006.

4   *Sustainable Communities: Homes for All*, Office of the Deputy Prime Minister, January 2005.

- to make it as easy as possible for applicants and tenants to move between local authority, housing association and privately owned accommodation by encouraging the extension of choice based lettings to cover low cost home ownership options and properties for rent from private landlords, as well as social housing
- to develop choice based lettings schemes on a regional and/or sub-regional basis, recognising that housing markets do not follow local authority boundaries
- to support prospective applicants to choose the housing option which is best for them, including: promoting a wide range of options within the district (including low cost home ownership, mutual exchange, the private sector); providing information about 'staying put' options such as aids and adaptations; mobility schemes, including moves from high to low demand areas; property shops and housing advice centres.

Chapter 3: Choice based lettings: general

The extent of a policy to offer choice to applicants

3.1 Where housing authorities adopt a policy of offering a choice of accommodation, the policy should, as far as possible, extend to all applicants and to all available accommodation. Policies which restrict choice to certain categories of applicant or certain types of dwelling are likely to be more difficult for applicants to understand, and may be regarded as less open and transparent. Local authorities should ensure that any policy of restricting choice does not have a discriminatory impact on a particular group or community.

3.2 The fact that certain applicants – for example, people with physical or mental impairments – may have difficulty in making an application for accommodation without assistance, should not preclude them from being offered a choice of accommodation. Instead applicants should have access to any necessary assistance to enable them to make an application (see paragraphs 5.22 to 5.28). Likewise, the fact that certain applicants may have difficulty in living independently in the community without care and/or support should not preclude them from being offered a choice of accommodation. Rather housing authorities should work together with other relevant agencies and providers to ensure that people can apply for appropriate accommodation and receive the support and care necessary to allow them to live as independently as possible. To this end, wherever practicable, specialist and supported accommodation should be advertised to extend choice to as many people as possible. However, where specialist or supported accommodation is advertised alongside other accommodation, it is important to make clear that only those applicants with relevant housing and/or support needs may apply for it. This may be done, for example, by making clear in the details of the advert that only certain categories of applicants will be considered for the accommodation (see paragraphs 4.62, 4.72 and 4.73).

3.3 There may be occasions, however, when it is not advisable or practicable to offer a choice of accommodation to a particular applicant or category of applicants. This category could include sexual or violent offenders where the need to manage the risk which they pose to other individuals or the community in general could limit the amount of choice they can reasonably be allowed. Applicants who pose a risk should not necessarily be precluded from taking part in a choice based lettings scheme but it may be necessary to restrict the properties they can apply for or reserve the right to reject their bid[5] in certain circumstances. Housing authorities must ensure that they have given due consideration to any application made in accordance with the procedural requirements of their allocation scheme (see section 166(3) of the 1996 Act). It therefore follows that, where an authority decides to reject a bid on risk grounds which would otherwise have been successful, the applicant should be informed of the reasons for the decision and preferably informed of the properties they can bid for.

3.4   Local authorities may wish to reserve the right to make direct lets to manage the risk posed by some applicants or for other management reasons.[6] Examples might include: people whose property has been compulsorily purchased (where the local authority is required to offer a specific property to meet the legal requirements) or reluctant decants (ie people who have been required to leave their original property to facilitate an area regeneration scheme, for example, and who are reluctant to participate in the bidding process to move out of temporary into permanent accommodation); people seeking a move under a witness mobility scheme; and MAPPA[7] clients who pose a very serious risk to the community.

3.5   Housing authorities should try to keep to a minimum the circumstances in which choice may have to be restricted and should ensure that these are clearly set out in the published allocation scheme.

Applications for housing accommodation

3.6   Section 166(3) of the 1996 Act requires a housing authority to consider every application for an allocation of accommodation, provided it is made in accordance with the procedural requirements of the allocation scheme.

3.7   Applying for an allocation of accommodation where an authority operates a choice based lettings scheme will normally involve applicants in a two-stage process: in the first instance they will be required to apply to join the scheme; and in the second stage they will be required to express an interest in particular accommodation (a process which may be referred to as 'bidding') if they wish to be considered for an allocation of that accommodation. It is important that the procedural requirements of the allocation scheme cover both parts of this process and distinguish clearly between them.

---

5   For a definition of 'bid' see paragraph 3.7 below.
6   For the purposes of this guidance, the term 'direct let' refers to accommodation which is not let through the authority's choice based lettings scheme, that is to say where the applicant is not offered a choice of accommodation. Where a letting does not constitute an allocation under Part 6 of the 1996 Act (eg, where an existing tenant is moved for management reasons, rather than at his/her own request, or where the letting is excluded from Part 6 by virtue of regulations made under section 160(4) of the 1996 Act) it will be referred to as a 'management let'.
7   Multi Agency Public Protection arrangements for assessing and managing the risks posed by sexual and violent offenders.

Open v closed advertising

3.8 Housing authorities are encouraged to adopt an 'open advertising' approach whereby all applicants and interested members of the wider local population can find out about vacancies which are advertised (eg in a local newspaper or on a public website). Open advertising is more likely to engender trust and confidence in the choice based lettings scheme. It also helps ensure that applicants, and those who may be considering applying for social housing, are aware of what accommodation is, or is likely to become, available, thus making it easier for authorities to manage expectations.

Eligibility

3.9 Housing authorities must ascertain if an applicant is eligible for an allocation of accommodation, or whether he or she is excluded from an allocation under section 160(A)(1), (3) or (5) of the 1996 Act. Housing authorities may also decide to treat an applicant as ineligible for an allocation because of serious unacceptable behaviour under section 160A(7) of the 1996 Act.

3.10 Section 160A of the 1996 Act prevents an authority from allocating housing to a person who is not eligible. In the Secretary of State's view, an authority should consider an applicant's eligibility, both:

a) at the time he or she applies to join the choice based lettings scheme; and

b) at the point at which he or she is considered for an allocation of particular accommodation.

It is important to consider whether an applicant is eligible at registration because an applicant who is accepted onto a choice based lettings scheme has a reasonable expectation that he or she will be eligible to be allocated accommodation under that scheme. However, it is also important to check again on the applicant's eligibility when considering making an allocation to him or her, particularly where a substantial amount of time has elapsed since the applicant registered with the scheme.

3.11 Where a housing authority concludes, at the time that the applicant joins the scheme, that he or she is a person from abroad but is nonetheless eligible for housing, it is recommended that the authority inform the applicant that changes to his or her immigration status or the statutory eligibility criteria prior to an allocation could affect his or her eligibility.

Offers of accommodation and refusals

3.12 As a general rule, accommodation which has been advertised should be offered to the bidder who:

• has the highest priority under the allocation scheme, and

• matches the lettings criteria for that property

So, for example, a couple without children will not usually be permitted to bid successfully for property which has more than one bedroom. In some circumstances, it may be appropriate to attach more restrictive lettings criteria to individual properties, for example, where a section 106 agreement is in place, or where the property belongs to an RSL which operates different and more restrictive eligibility criteria. Where this is the case, the advert should, wherever possible, set out clearly the particular criteria which apply to that property (see paragraph 4.71). However, there may be other reasons why it would be necessary or advisable to reject a bid which would otherwise have been successful: where, for example, the property would not be suitable for that particular applicant (see paragraphs 3.3 and 4.77 about applicants who pose a risk to others and themselves). However, an authority should not reject such a bid, unless there are sound reasons for doing so, in accordance with the allocation scheme. Where an authority does pass over a bid which would otherwise have been successful, they should provide the applicant with the reasons for this decision.

3.13   Housing authorities should not, as a matter of course, impose penalties on applicants who refuse an offer of accommodation which they have applied for under a choice based lettings scheme[8]. This is particularly the case where applicants are expected to apply for properties before they have had a chance to view them. Rather, authorities should ensure that applicants receive sufficient information about the property which is advertised to enable them to make an informed decision as to whether or not to bid for it. This is the best way to ensure that applicants do not bid for properties which do not meet their needs or aspirations.

3.14   The Secretary of State is aware that some authorities restrict the number of bids which applicants can make at any particular time. There may be sound reasons for doing this: for example, to limit the number of refusals; and to minimise the administrative burden, and/or potential for delay, associated with managing a large number of bids. However, authorities are reminded that such an approach may restrict the amount of choice available to applicants, and may distort the feedback on properties which have been let. Authorities should also bear in mind that some applicants will be better equipped than others to use their limited bids to the best effect. Where authorities decide to restrict the number of bids which applicants can make, they should ensure that applicants who might be disadvantaged by such an approach have access to the appropriate advice and assistance to enable them to participate effectively.

3.15   As stated at paragraph 3.11 of the Allocations Code, applicants must be allowed a reasonable period to make a decision about accommodation offered to them under Part 6 of the 1996 Act. This applies equally to accommodation offered under a choice based lettings scheme. The Secretary of State considers that the fact that an applicant has expressed an interest in particular accommodation by bidding for it should not be treated as meaning that he or she has made a final decision to accept it. This is particularly the case where applicants have not had the opportunity to view the property before submitting an application.

3.16   Some applicants may require a longer period than others. For example, applicants requiring additional assistance and/or support may wish to take advice in making their decision. Housing authorities should allow sufficient time for such applicants to arrange for an adviser or advocate (who may be a friend or family member) to accompany them when viewing accommodation. This would be in line with a housing authority's duty to make reasonable adjustments for disabled people, including changes to their practices policies and procedures. Applicants may also need more time to view properties, where they need to travel long distances to do so (see further at paragraph 7.17).

8   For further advice on offers of accommodation to applicants owed the main homelessness duty, see paragraphs 4.50 to 4.59.

Chapter 4: Choice based lettings: policy content and scheme design

Introduction

[Paragraphs 4.1–4.49 have been replaced by *Fair and Flexible: statutory guidance on social housing allocations for local authorities in England* (December 2009). See below.]

Choice for applicants owed the main homelessness duty

4.50   By virtue of sections 193(3A) and 195(3A) of the 1996 Act, housing authorities are required to give people, to whom they owe a homelessness duty under sections 193 or 195, a copy of the statement included in their allocation scheme under section 167(1A) about their policy on offering choice or the opportunity to express preferences about Part 6 housing accommodation. Housing authorities must therefore ensure that their allocation scheme addresses the extent to which they are able to offer choice (or the ability to express preferences) to people to whom they owe one of these homelessness duties (see paragraph 5.7 of the Allocations Code of Guidance).

4.51   The Secretary of State considers that people owed the main homelessness duty (under section 193(2)) should, wherever possible, be offered a choice of Part 6 accommodation where they are awaiting an allocation that will bring the homelessness duty to an end.

4.52   Authorities are reminded that the main homelessness duty may also be brought to an end where the applicant accepts a 'qualifying offer' of an assured shorthold tenancy made by a private landlord (in accordance with section 193(7B)-(7F)).

4.53   Some people owed the main homelessness duty may need advice and assistance in order to participate actively in a choice based lettings scheme. Authorities are, therefore, advised to pay particular attention to the guidance in paragraphs 5.22 to 5.28 to ensure that people owed the main homelessness duty are not disadvantaged under a choice based lettings system.

4.54   The Secretary of State recognises that in certain circumstances (for example, where there is a shortage of social housing and/or where applicants owed the main homelessness duty do not have high priority under an authority's allocation scheme) providing choice for applicants owed the main homelessness duty for an unrestricted period could mean that such applicants wait an unreasonably long time before they are offered suitable Part 6 accommodation. This is unlikely to be in the best interests of applicants or authorities, particularly where it leads to extended periods in temporary accommodation. Accordingly, authorities will need to consider whether, in these circumstances, it would be appropriate to limit the period during which applicants can exercise choice and refuse offers without bringing the homelessness duty to an end.

4.55   Applicants should not be put under pressure so that they feel constrained to bid for accommodation that may not be suitable for them and their household. This would be unacceptable for the applicant and would not discharge the homelessness duty (which requires that the authority is satisfied that the accommodation offered is suitable). Accordingly, the period during which they are allowed to take part in the choice based lettings scheme (referred to hereafter as 'the bidding period') should be realistic. In determining how long the bidding period should be, authorities should take into account the pressure on social housing in the district and the time it would normally take before an opportunity to bid on a suitable property became available for someone with similar priority under the scheme. Larger households and those with special needs which are difficult to meet (eg those who need accessible accommodation) may need a longer time to bid for properties since the availability of suitable vacancies is likely to be limited.

4.56   It is important that there is a process for examining why an applicant has failed to be successful in being offered a suitable CBL property during the bidding period. Where it becomes clear that nothing suitable has been advertised during the bidding period; that the applicant has not fully understood what he or she was expected to do under the scheme; or that the applicant was incapable of accessing the scheme without advice and assistance, the authority should consider extending the period. The authority should also address any need for further advice and assistance to enable the applicant to participate effectively in the choice based lettings scheme.

4.57   Where the authority does not extend the bidding period, they should ensure that the applicant is aware that the period has ended and that he or she will no longer be able to bid for properties. The authority should also ensure that the applicant is aware of what is to happen next. Since the authority is still under a duty to secure that accommodation is available for occupation by the applicant, the options available to the authority are to offer the applicant:

- an allocation of suitable accommodation under Part 6 in accordance with the applicant's priority under the allocation scheme or
- a 'qualifying offer' of an assured shorthold tenancy in the private rented sector

The tenant should be made aware that the offer of Part 6 accommodation is a 'final' offer which will bring the authority's duty to an end (see following paragraph). In respect of a qualifying offer the duty only ends where the tenant accepts the offer.

4.58   Where the authority makes a 'final' offer of accommodation under Part 6, the main homelessness duty will come to an end if:

- the applicant accepts the offer, or
- having been informed of the possible consequences of refusal and of the right to request a review of the suitability of the accommodation, the applicant refuses the offer

Under section 193(7A), an offer of accommodation is a 'final' offer of accommodation only if it is in writing and states that it is a 'final' offer for the purposes of section 193(7). However, by section 193(7F) of the 1996 Act, an authority cannot make a 'final' offer unless they are satisfied that the accommodation is suitable for the applicant and that it is reasonable for the applicant to accept the offer.

4.59   Where the homelessness duty has come to an end following refusal of a final offer, applicants should not be precluded from participating in the choice based lettings scheme – although it should be made clear to them that they will no longer have the reasonable preference which had been accorded to them as a person who was owed the main homelessness duty.

Providing choice for disabled people with access needs

4. 60   Section 167(2)(d) of the 1996 Act provides that people who need to move on 'medical and welfare' grounds must be given reasonable preference for an allocation. Section 167(2) has been revised (by section 223 of the Housing Act 2004) to make clear that 'medical and welfare grounds' include grounds relating to a disability. The amendment, which came into effect on 27 April 2005, is intended to ensure that disabled people with access needs are given appropriate priority for social housing.

4.61   The Secretary of State encourages housing authorities to include accessible properties (ie housing which has been designed or adapted to meet the needs of disabled people) within their choice based lettings scheme. She believes that this is the best way to ensure that disabled people have the widest possible choice of accommodation.

4.62   The Secretary of State believes that accessible housing should be allocated to people with relevant access needs. Accordingly, the Secretary of State encourages housing authorities to design their choice based lettings scheme in such a way that priority for accessible accommodation is given to people who have access needs. This is consistent with the duty to promote disability equality. One way to do this would be by means of the advertising criteria.

4.63   While it would be lawful to provide that only disabled people can apply for accessible vacancies, it would not be lawful to provide that disabled people can only apply for accessible property. However, where a disabled applicant applies for accommodation which does not meet his or her access needs, the housing authority will need to take into account whether it is reasonable and practicable to adapt that property when assessing his or her bid (and must do so in accordance with their duties under the Disability Discrimination Act 1995 and the Housing Grants, Construction and Regeneration Act 1996). If it is reasonable and practicable for the property to be adapted, the disabled applicant should be considered for the vacancy on the same basis as other applicants who have submitted a bid. Where there is a shortage of accessible property, and failure to adapt a property would lead to unreasonable delays in housing for a disabled person then the local authority should take steps to identify properties which are suitable to be adapted, and consider giving priority to disabled persons who bid for such properties.

4.64   Where an accessible property is advertised, it is important that the property is identified as such in the advertisement and that the advertisement gives sufficient information about the level of adaptations and/or accessibility features in the accommodation for disabled applicants to make an informed decision on whether or not to apply for the particular property. In the Secretary of State's view, this is the best way to ensure that:

- the most effective and efficient use is made of accessible housing stock; and
- disabled people are allocated accommodation which meets their needs, while giving them the widest possible choice and a greater say over where they live

4.65   In the case of accessible accommodation, it is also particularly important to include information about external access to the property (eg whether there is a ramp up to the property and whether there is accessible parking nearby) and relevant information about the surrounding area (eg are local shops and public transport easily accessible).

4.66   Housing authorities are also encouraged to maintain lists or databases of accessible housing within their district. This is likely to be of assistance to disabled applicants even where property is allocated under a choice based lettings scheme. Disabled applicants should be able to see the full range of accessible properties (the number and type of properties; accessibility features and level of adaptations of each property; and location) and be informed about the time they are likely to wait for any type of property to become available. Such information can assist people in determining whether to apply for a particular vacancy which is advertised.

4.67   Disabled people may need additional assistance and support to participate in a choice based lettings scheme on an equal footing with other applicants. The nature and degree of assistance they require will depend on the nature and degree of their disability. The following is a non-exhaustive list of the type of assistance and support which housing authorities should consider making available, some of which they will, in any case, be required to do under disability equality legislation:

- advising individual disabled applicants when suitable accessible property is about to or has been advertised
- making arrangements to enable applicants with disabilities to visit properties
- ensuring that websites are accessible for people who have visual impairments or learning disabilities
- using symbols rather than words in adverts
- providing large print maps on websites
- enabling text messaging for people who have hearing impairments
- providing documents in large or clear print, Moon or Braille
- making information available on computer disk or audiotape
- training appropriate staff in the use of British Sign Language and/or Makaton
- ensuring that advice and information is available over the telephone – for those who cannot use a website or cannot get to a property or advice shop easily
- mailing out literature to the housebound and physically disabled
- ensuring that people with learning disabilities who do not have support from any other source (eg friend, relative or social worker) are assigned a suitably trained member of staff to support them.

Local lettings policies and advertising criteria, labelling

[Paragraphs 4.68–4.71 have been replaced by *Fair and Flexible: statutory guidance on social housing allocations for local authorities in England* (December 2009). See below.]

Advertising criteria – 'restrictive labelling'

4.72   Where accommodation is allocated by means of a choice based lettings scheme, housing authorities may wish to attach criteria (known as 'advertising criteria' or 'restrictive labelling') to particular accommodation which is advertised specifying, for example, that:

- only people of a particular description may apply for that particular accommodation or
- people of a particular description will be given preference for that particular accommodation

4.73   Restrictive labelling may be used, for example, to give effect to a local lettings policy (see paragraphs 4.67 to 4.71) or to a target-based system (see paragraph 4.38 to 4.43), or to match people with access needs to accessible accommodation. It is important that the practical application of such labelling should be operated in accordance with criteria or policies which are set out clearly in the authority's allocation scheme, and that the effect should not be directly or indirectly discriminatory. Where an authority uses restrictive labelling, it should monitor the impact to ensure that it continues to comply with its duty to give reasonable preference to applicants in the reasonable preference categories.

Restricting choice

4.74   The fact that a housing authority adopts a policy of offering choice does not mean that applicants should be able to express an interest in and be considered for any and every available vacancy.

4.75   In framing and operating a policy of choice, a housing authority should be mindful of the need to ensure that there are no adverse implications for the good use of their stock and that it does not conflict with their ability to continue to provide for housing need.

4.76   So, for example, applicants should not be permitted to apply for vacancies which would result in statutory overcrowding. Conversely authorities will normally wish to ensure that applicants are not permitted to apply for vacancies which would result in under-occupation, although there may be occasions where this makes good housing management sense (eg in the case of hard-to-let properties or where the authority wishes to bring down the child density ratio on an estate). The information which is provided when a property is advertised ('the advertising criteria') should assist applicants in establishing whether or not they are entitled to express an interest in a particular vacancy.

4.77   The duty to confer reasonable preference on certain categories of people means that an authority should ensure that they are allocated accommodation which meets their identified needs. It is for the authority to make a final judgement on whether it is appropriate to allocate particular accommodation to a particular individual even under a choice based lettings scheme. So, for example, an authority may decide that it is inappropriate to house a drug user on an estate which is known to have a large proportion of other users or where there is a known drug dealer. However, it is important that an authority does not second-guess an individual's needs and should normally take into account his or her views before making a final decision. The authority may find that the drug user's main source of support lives on that estate as well.

4.78   There may be policy justification for designing a choice based lettings scheme to ensure that not all the popular properties go to those in greater housing need (eg by providing that priority cards will cease to have effect where more than a specified number of bids are received for an advertised vacancy). However, such an approach may limit the scope for those who must be given reasonable preference for an allocation to access housing which meets their needs, and may, for example, inadvertently lead to concentrations of homeless applicants in unpopular areas or in areas where there is already a high concentration of deprivation. Where authorities do adopt such an approach, it should be monitored carefully to ensure, for example, that it does not produce outcomes which are discriminatory on racial or other grounds, or conflict with the authority's ability to continue to provide for housing need. Such an approach is not recommended in areas where there is high demand for social housing or where a large proportion of housing applicants are in housing need.

Choice and mobility
[Paragraphs 4.79–4.80 have been replaced by *Fair and Flexible: statutory guidance on social housing allocations for local authorities in England* (December 2009). See below.]

Chapter 5: Managing a Choice Based Lettings scheme

Consultation
5.1 Paragraphs 6.4-6.6 of the Allocations Code provide guidance on considerations which authorities should take into account when consulting on changes to their allocation scheme, or before they adopt a new scheme, and this will include the adoption of a policy of offering choice to applicants.

5.2 Authorities are required to consult RSLs with which they have nomination arrangements. When considering whether to adopt a policy of offering choice to applicants, authorities are urged to go further than the statutory requirement to consult and explore the possibility of entering into partnership with all or most of the RSLs in their district so as to offer all those who are seeking social housing the widest possible choice of accommodation. It is important to do this at an early stage, so that RSLs are given the opportunity to contribute to the design of the choice based lettings scheme.

5.3 Organisations and individuals who provide advice and support to applicants will be crucial to the success of a choice based lettings scheme. In addition to their relevant statutory partners (such as social services, prisons, probation and primary care trusts) and voluntary bodies which provide care and support, authorities should consider whether there are other organisations which represent the interests of existing or potential applicants who may be socially excluded or disadvantaged by a choice based lettings system. Examples may include groups which represent ethnic minority communities, the gypsy and traveller community, veterans, ex-offenders, and drug or alcohol misusers. Bodies which represent the views of older people and people with physical and learning disabilities and mental health problems, and their carers, should also be included. Involving these groups will help authorities meet their race equality, disability and gender equality duties.

5.4 Authorities are also urged to consult existing tenants, applicants and residents. It may also be helpful to involve users in designing and testing various aspects of the scheme, in particular any supporting technology (eg a website). It will be particularly helpful to involve users who may have particular communication requirements, for example, people with visual impairments, those with learning disabilities, or those who cannot understand or speak English well, as well as people with poor literacy and computer skills.

Information, advice and assistance/support

5.5 Section 166(1) of the 1996 Act provides that housing authorities must ensure that advice and information about the right to apply for accommodation is available free of charge to everyone in their district.

5.6 Housing authorities should also ensure that sufficient information is available to all applicants to enable them to apply for accommodation. This includes general information about the procedures for applying to go on the scheme and for applying for advertised vacancies; information about how applicants are prioritised under the scheme and how successful applicants are selected; and the rationale for advertising criteria, for example that priority for bungalows is given to older people or those with disabilities (see paragraphs 4.72 to 4.73 above). Information about review procedures should also be included. If RSL vacancies are included in the scheme, it will be helpful for applicants to know whether each RSL operates specific exclusion policies and, if so, what these are. Information should be easy to understand and should be available in translation where relevant and in alternative formats (Braille;large print, and audiotapes etc).

5.7 It is also important that information can be accessed by all applicants. Choice based lettings schemes which rely entirely, or to a large extent, on web-based information, for example, may restrict participation by applicants who have difficulty accessing or operating a computer. Likewise, authorities which rely on local papers or freesheets to advertise accommodation should ensure that they are widely available at locations across the district, or directly mailed to applicants who would otherwise have difficulty accessing them (eg the housebound). Prisoners are a particular group who are likely to have difficulty accessing information. This is because many prisoners cannot obtain newspapers or access the internet, neither can they contact the choice based lettings scheme directly. One way around this might be to arrange for housing advice surgeries in prison. Such outreach work might also be appropriate in the case of other applicants who are traditionally considered to be hard to reach, such as the gypsy and traveller community.

5.8 Ideally information should be available using a variety of media, including printed hard copy form, on a website or via the telephone. While authorities should provide user-friendly information about their choice based lettings scheme, this is in addition to, rather than an alternative to, the duties in sections 167 and 168 to have and publish an allocation scheme. However, in the spirit of openness and to ensure that applicants have access to as much information as possible, authorities are also encouraged to publish their allocation scheme on their website as well as in hard copy form.

5.9 Applicants also need information about particular vacancies which are advertised in order to determine:
- whether they are entitled to bid for the property
- whether the property meets their needs and any other requirements and
- what their likelihood of success would be if they expressed an interest for the property
- information in the advert will be important and should include basic details about the property such as:
- location
- type (flat, bungalow etc)

- size (eg number of bedrooms)
- floor, and whether or not it has a lift
- type of heating
- whether it has a garden
- the amount of rent payable

The information required will depend on the nature of the applicant. So, for example, disabled applicants will need to know about the type and level of adaptations. The more information provided (eg about the condition of the property or about access to services) the easier it is for applicants to make an informed decision. Information about local services and opportunities, such as transport, education and employment, may be provided through signposting to other websites, for example. Advertising criteria could be used to indicate what type of applicant is entitled or excluded from bidding for a property, or who will be given preference for a property. Authorities must be careful to ensure that advertising criteria are not unlawfully discriminatory. Adverts should be unambiguous and easy to understand. Authorities should consider how to address the needs of applicants, for example, who are deaf, who are blind or partially sighted, who have learning disabilities, or who cannot read English. Symbols rather than words, the use of Braille and translations may all assist; or information on available vacancies could be provided to applicants by telephone.

Information and advice about stock availability and other housing options

5.10   Many housing authorities have found that the introduction of choice based lettings has led to an immediate and significant increase in the number of applications for social housing. In some areas, this has included a marked rise in the numbers of applications from people who are traditionally under-represented in social housing, such as people in employment, indicating that choice based lettings schemes can have a positive impact on the way social housing is viewed. However, it is also clear that housing authorities which introduce choice based lettings schemes need to put in place strategies to manage expectations, recognising that those who bid unsuccessfully over a long period of time may become frustrated or disillusioned.

5.11   An applicant has the right to information to help him or her assess whether accommodation appropriate to his or her needs is likely to be made available and, if so, how long this is likely to take. 'Feedback' about advertised properties which have been let (see paragraphs 5.14 to 5.18 below) may assist applicants to assess how long they are likely to have to wait for a particular type of property or property in a particular location. Authorities should also consider making available general information about the profile of their stock. This might include the type, size and location of the stock, whether it is accessible or could be adapted, whether there is access to a shared or private garden, and how old it is. In the case of stock which is in short supply, an indication of how frequently it is likely to become available would also be helpful.

5.12   Some applicants may have to wait a considerable time before appropriate accommodation is made available to them, particularly in areas of high demand for social housing and/or where the applicant has low priority. In some cases, applicants may have little prospect of ever being allocated accommodation. It could assist such applicants to know about other appropriate housing options which might be available to them. This might include:

- private rented accommodation
- low cost home ownership options
- mobility schemes which enable applicants to move out of the district
- home improvement schemes or aids and adaptations services which enable applicants to remain in their existing accommodation for longer

Authorities are encouraged to make general information about housing options available to all applicants, for example, when they apply to join a choice based lettings scheme, or more generally via the website or weekly freesheets. Authorities are also encouraged to offer more specialised housing options advice to individual applicants whenever this may be appropriate (for example, in the case of applicants who bid frequently but without success).

Advice

5.13   A choice based lettings approach requires applicants to be more proactive than a traditional allocations approach in which allocation decisions are made by housing officers on the basis of need. For this reason all applicants may need advice as well as information to assist them to participate successfully. This is likely to be particularly important for applicants when they first join a choice based lettings scheme. Advice could be provided by staff of the authority or another partner landlord, or by the voluntary sector. It is likely to be most effective if the person providing the advice has appropriate housing related experience and is properly trained to sensitively meet the needs of a diverse client group.

Information about accommodation which has been allocated under a choice based lettings scheme – 'Feedback' information

5.14   It is recommended that housing authorities publish information about accommodation which has been allocated through a choice based lettings scheme (more commonly known as 'feedback'). This might specify the number of applications/bids received for the property and give an indication of the reason why the property was allocated to the successful applicant which will normally relate to their level of priority under the scheme. An example might be the band and waiting time of the applicant, or their points level. This information can be extremely useful both to those applicants who have expressed an interest in the vacancy, because it notifies them that the particular vacancy has been let, and to applicants generally, because it assists them to make judgements about what sort of property to bid for in future. Since this information is likely to be of interest to most if not all applicants, it should be easily accessible and authorities may want to consider using a variety of media, such as the local newspaper and website.

5.15   However, housing authorities need to bear in mind that section 166(4) prohibits them from divulging to other members of the public that a person is an applicant for social housing, unless they have the applicant's consent. Furthermore, authorities should process any personal data which they hold about applicants consistently with the Data Protection Act 1998. This means that, where housing authorities publish information about particular accommodation which has been allocated under a choice based lettings scheme, they must be careful not to provide information which would enable a member of the public to ascertain the identity of the individual applicant who has been allocated the accommodation. In particular, housing authorities should guard against providing information which might put the successful applicant at risk of violence or intimidation by other individuals or members of the public. In extreme cases, it may be advisable not to publish the fact that a property has been let. However, authorities should avoid doing this unnecessarily as it is likely to detract from the transparency of the scheme.

5.16   Where direct lettings are made for whatever reason, information about these lettings should normally be published alongside information about lettings made through the choice based lettings scheme. If providing information about individual lettings could lead to intimidation or harassment, or otherwise put vulnerable tenants at risk, then it might be preferable to generalise the feedback information, for example by publishing the number of direct lets made in any period.

5.17   Individual applicants who have expressed an interest in a particular vacancy but are unsuccessful may want more personalised feedback, for example, about their relative position on the shortlist, or on why they were unsuccessful. It would be helpful if authorities were able to provide this wherever possible. Authorities should also consider providing more detailed feedback to all unsuccessful bidders at regular intervals – perhaps after they have submitted a certain number of unsuccessful bids. This might involve advising applicants about the need to change their bidding strategy, or providing them with advice about alternative housing options available to them, eg low cost home ownership options or the private rented sector (see paragraph 5.12 above).

5.18   Authorities may wish to go further and extract generalised information from feedback data to help inform applicants' bidding strategies generally. For example, authorities could produce and publish tables giving estimated waiting times by estate or parish and/or property type.

Application form

5.19   While application forms should not be so complex/complicated that applicants have difficulty in completing them, it is important that they are drafted to obtain sufficient information from applicants to enable authorities to identify those applicants who are likely to have:
- priority under the authority's scheme and/or
- difficulty in making an application or choosing their accommodation without additional assistance

and to assess an applicant's access or support needs, or at least to alert authorities to the need to make further inquiries.

5.20   Application forms should also obtain sufficient information to enable authorities to determine applicants' eligibility and to monitor the fairness of allocations and compliance with equal opportunities requirements. So, for example, information about ethnicity, disability and gender should be collected through the application form. Best practice might also encourage the collection of data by age, religion and sexual orientation.

5.21   Where application forms obtain sufficiently detailed information, they can be a useful tool in assessing the housing needs of the district.

Support and assistance

5.22   Section 166(1)(b) of the 1996 Act requires a housing authority to secure that any necessary assistance is made available free of charge to persons in its district who are likely to have difficulty in making an application without assistance. Paragraph 6.9 of the Allocations Code provides that, where authorities adopt an allocation policy which requires the active participation of housing applicants in choosing their accommodation, the level of assistance needed by those who are likely to have difficulty in making an application will normally be greater, and housing authorities will need to provide for this. In providing for this, authorities are advised to consider:

- which individuals or group of applicants are likely to have difficulty in making an application without assistance
- how to identify individuals who need assistance
- what type and level of assistance are they likely to require and
- whether that assistance is currently available and from what organisation

5.23   Some people in the reasonable preference categories may need a high level of additional assistance. In such cases failure to provide such assistance could result in an individual failing to participate in the choice based letting scheme. Authorities must ensure that applicants are given the assistance they need to make certain they receive the reasonable preference to which they are entitled.

5.24   However, housing authorities are advised not to equate those who may have difficulty in participating in a choice based lettings scheme with those who are in the reasonable preference categories. It is not necessarily the case that only those in the reasonable preference categories will have difficulty participating in a choice based lettings scheme; neither is it necessarily the case that everyone in the reasonable preference categories will need assistance to participate. The following is a list of people who may have difficulty in making an application without assistance of some sort – the list is illustrative and not exhaustive:

- those for whom English is not their first language (eg refugees)
- people who have literacy problems
- people with learning disabilities
- people who lead chaotic lifestyles, such as those who misuse drugs or alcohol
- people with mental health problems
- those who are currently undergoing a crisis in their lives and for whom their housing situation may be only one of many problems, such as victims of domestic violence
- those who are socially excluded such as rough sleepers
- the gypsy and traveller community
- older people and those suffering from a long-term disability
- vulnerable young people

5.25   The appropriate type and level of assistance will depend on the type of difficulty the applicant is likely to experience. In some cases it may simply be a matter of ensuring that information and advice is available in translation or that people are given information about translation services; or that any relevant written material is delivered to those who are housebound. However, someone with a severe learning disability or acute mental health problem is likely to require intensive support throughout the process.

5.26   It is important that housing authorities work together with social services, prisons, probation and relevant health bodies and professionals, other housing providers, the community and voluntary sector, and carers and users groups to:

- identify which applicants are likely to need assistance in order to choose accommodation that is appropriate to their needs and
- ensure that suitable assistance is available

5.27   An authority may provide assistance itself. This could include a range of activities, from training applicants on use of the website, for example, to operating housing advice surgeries in prisons, making home visits to those with chaotic lifestyles, or making bids on applicants' behalf (with their agreement). However, while, under section 166(1)(a), an authority must secure that assistance is available, there is no requirement for the authority to provide that assistance itself. Where an authority relies on other organisations and individuals to provide such assistance, the authority will need to be very careful to ensure that the support needs of all applicants can be addressed. Authorities should consider and provide for the training needs of organisations and individuals (eg social services, prisons, probation, mental health teams, voluntary agencies, advocates and carers) about how the choice based lettings scheme operates in order to help them advise and assist their clients, friends and family.

5.28   Authorities should consider maintaining a list of applicants who require assistance and support. In many cases it may be relatively simple to identify those individuals who need assistance at the initial application stage. However, this may not always be the case. Similar considerations are likely to apply as those set out in paragraph 4.6 about assessing need. Otherwise, an applicant's behaviour may give an indication that they have a need for assistance which is not being met. So, for example, the fact that an applicant in priority housing need has failed to bid at all or bids for inappropriate accommodation is a good indication that the person may be experiencing difficulties.

Undue influence

5.29   Housing authorities should ensure that, when providing information, advice and assistance, they do not seek to unduly influence an applicant's choice of accommodation. So, for example, authorities which act as 'proxy bidders' on behalf of vulnerable applicants, will need to safeguard against bidding for properties which do not meet the applicants' needs and aspirations.

Monitoring

5.30   Authorities are encouraged to monitor their choice based lettings schemes. Monitoring will assist authorities in assessing:

- whether the scheme is meeting its aims and objectives and working well or
- whether changes need to be made

Data collected may help to inform the authority's homelessness strategy as well as its wider housing strategy. In particular, data on which types of properties are hard to let or in short supply, and which areas are unpopular, will feed decisions on new stock, redevelopment and redesignation, or demolition. Data – appropriately generalised – could also form part of customer feedback at regular intervals.

5.31   Monitoring is crucial to ensure that authorities comply with:
- the duty to give reasonable preference to certain applicants
- the various equality duties

5.32   The following is a range of matters which authorities could usefully include in their monitoring arrangements – it is illustrative and not exhaustive:
- **Housing management performance** – relet times, refusals
- **Support mechanisms** – are the mechanisms which are put in place to support applicants to participate in choice based lettings effective?
- **Nomination arrangements** – the number of successful nominations, proportion going to people in the reasonable preference categories, number of failed nominations and reasons for the failure
- **Lettings outcomes, policies and quotas** – the proportion of lettings (and separately, direct lettings outside CBL[9]) overall going to, for example: homeless applicants and other applicants in the reasonable preference categories; applicants on the 'assisted list'; transferring tenants and new applicants; and the size and quality of properties going to each group. More specifically the proportion of disabled applicants let accessible properties, and conversely the proportion of accessible properties let to disabled applicants
- **Comparative data** about applicants on the waiting list should also be collected. Taken together the waiting list and lettings data may be used to determine whether existing lettings policies and quotas are effective or whether they need to be revised. For example, are existing policies having a disproportionate impact on certain groups or communities, are disabled people having to wait disproportionately long for suitable property, is the authority still able to give effect to its duty to give reasonable preference?
- **Ethnicity data** – particularly numbers on the waiting list, lettings outcomes, and bidding behaviour. The website of the Equalities and Human Rights Commission provides good practice on monitoring ethnicity and the categories to use
- **New communities** – authorities should identify the existence of any new communities within the district and monitor their involvement in choice based lettings. Authorities which use the census categories to define ethnicity may need to reconsider their ethnicity categories as the census categories do not capture this level of detail
- **Community cohesion issues** – whether ethnic minority applicants are moving into predominantly white areas and vice versa
- **Other equality and diversity data** – in particular disability, age and gender. Again this should include numbers on the waiting list, lettings outcomes, and bidding behaviour
- **Potentially disadvantaged/assisted list applicants** – given the pro-active nature of CBL, it is particularly important to monitor the activity levels (ie bidding) and lettings outcomes for potentially disadvantaged groups. Authorities may be able to use demographic and socio-economic data on new applicants to assist in identifying potentially disadvantaged applicants
- **Tenancy sustainment** – are tenancies lasting longer or are there more applications to transfer

---

9   See footnote 6 on page [846] for the meaning of 'direct let'.

- **Bidding behaviour** – ie the number or proportion of households which are actively bidding in any given period. This can be compared to the numbers on the housing waiting list; and can also be used to look at patterns of bidding over time. Also the proportion of applicants in various categories (eg homeless households, other reasonable preference categories, on the 'assisted list', and minority ethnic applicants) who are not bidding or bidding infrequently and what reasons they are giving for not bidding
- **Inter-authority, or inter-regional mobility** – ie numbers/proportions of out-of-borough applicants on the waiting list, making bids, and achieving lettings
- **Customer satisfaction** – do applicants find the system easy to understand and to use, are ethnic minority applicants and/or disabled applicants as satisfied with the system and/or outcomes as other groups

5.33   Authorities which are introducing a choice based lettings scheme are strongly encouraged to establish a baseline to monitor from; and to retain historical data from the period before the choice based lettings scheme is introduced for comparative purposes.

5.34   Rigorous management of the waiting list is important to ensure that the usefulness of waiting list numbers, as a measure of local housing need and/or an indicator of demand, is not compromised. Authorities are also reminded that data protection legislation (see following paragraphs) requires that personal information is kept up-to-date and is not held for longer than necessary. It is, therefore, strongly recommended that authorities review their waiting list on an annual basis.

Information sharing and data protection

5.35   Housing authorities may need to share information about applicants with other agencies and organisations, for example, to ensure that applicants are properly assisted to participate in a choice based lettings scheme and that they are housed appropriately. Such organisations could include social services, other statutory agencies, and voluntary agencies. Information sharing between housing authorities and partner RSLs will be particularly important and failure to get this right could undermine the success of a choice based lettings scheme. Adopting effective information sharing protocols can help ensure that housing authorities and other agencies are clear about the type of information which can be shared with whom and for what purposes.

5.36   In devising information sharing protocols, and when passing on information about individual applicants, housing authorities will need to be mindful of their responsibilities under the Data Protection Act 1998. However, this should not be seen as a complete barrier to sharing any information. If landlords are unclear about their obligations and responsibilities under the Act they should contact the Information Commissioner. Advice on data sharing can also be found on the website for the Department for Constitutional Affairs: www.dca.gov.uk/foi/sharing/toolkit/infosharing.htm

Chapter 6: Delivering choice in partnership with Registered Social Landlords (RSLs) and Private Sector Landlords

Joint/partnership CBL schemes with RSLs

6.1 The Secretary of State recommends that housing authorities work together with RSLs in their district to provide joint choice based lettings schemes which extend to all or the majority of the social housing vacancies to ensure that:

- best use is made of the available social housing in the district and
- applicants are offered the widest choice of accommodation and, as far as possible, a single point of access to that accommodation

6.2 However, where RSLs are involved in choice based lettings schemes with one or more housing authorities, the housing authorities will need to ensure that this does not affect their ability to meet their statutory obligations under Part 6 of the 1996 Act.

Statutory framework for co-operation

6.3 Section 170 of the 1996 Act provides that where a housing authority so request, an RSL must co-operate to such extent as is reasonable in the circumstances in offering accommodation to people with priority under the authority's allocation scheme. Similarly, section 213 of the 1996 Act provides that where an RSL has been requested by a housing authority to assist them in the discharge of their homelessness functions under Part 7, it must also co-operate to the same extent.

6.4 The Housing Corporation has issued regulatory guidance which sets out the requirements on RSLs in respect of local authority nominations (Housing Corporation Regulatory Circular 02/03, February 2003). This provides that in areas where evidence of local housing need is reflected in local planning criteria for affordable housing provision, nomination agreements should provide for 50 per cent or more of true voids for nominations. The circular recognises that agreed percentages may be considerably higher in areas of housing stress.

6.5 Housing authorities which have, or plan to adopt, a choice based lettings scheme will want to ensure that RSLs agree that those vacancies to which the authority has nomination rights are made available through the scheme. The Secretary of State would also encourage housing authorities to negotiate with RSLs to make their other vacancies available through a joint choice based lettings scheme as well. However, it is important that where RSLs let all or the majority of their stock through a joint choice based lettings scheme, there is a means for distinguishing those RSL vacancies to which the authority has nomination rights. It is in the interest of housing authorities, RSLs, applicants and tenants to be clear about the basis on which a tenancy is being allocated, not least in those instances where an applicant may seek to challenge the basis on which a property has been let. One way of distinguishing between the different types of letting would be to have one section of the newsletter or website for local authority lettings which would include 'nomination' lettings, and a separate section for other RSL lettings. In the local authority section, the relevant RSL landlord would be identified in the advertisement for each individual 'nomination' letting.

Applicant prioritisation and eligibility criteria

6.6　Housing authorities must comply with the requirements of Part 6 of the 1996 Act when they nominate an applicant to be the tenant of an RSL. This means that when advertising vacancies through a choice based lettings scheme to which the authority has nomination rights, it is important that applicants for those vacancies are prioritised in accordance with section 167 of the 1996 Act.

6.7　Under section 160A(7) of the 1996 Act, housing authorities are entitled to treat applicants as ineligible (ie to exclude them from an allocation) where they have been guilty of serious unacceptable behaviour. RSLs may operate exclusion policies which are wider than the provisions in section 160A(7). Where this is the case, the exclusion policy of each participating RSL should be clearly set out in the published CBL scheme details. In addition, where this is feasible, the exclusion criteria applied by an RSL should be stated in the advertisement of any relevant vacancy, so that applicants are clear about the basis on which the property is offered.

Nomination agreements

6.8　A local authority nominates a person to RSL accommodation when it does so 'in pursuance of any arrangements (whether legally enforceable or not) to require that housing accommodation, or a specified amount of housing accommodation, is made available to a person or one of a number of persons nominated by the authority', (section 159(4)).

6. 9　It is important that nomination agreements are in place between the housing authority and all RSLs participating in a joint choice based lettings scheme. This is the case even where RSL partners have agreed to put all or the majority of their stock through the choice based lettings scheme.

6.10　Such agreements should set out the proportion of lettings that will be made available; any criteria which the RSLs have adopted, following consultation with the housing authority, for accepting or rejecting nominees; and how any disputes about suitability and eligibility will be resolved.

6.11　When negotiating nominations agreements, housing authorities should try to ensure that criteria for rejecting nominees are kept to a minimum. This will be particularly important where the housing authority have transferred their housing stock.

6.12　Housing authorities should ensure that the details of nominated households given to RSLs are accurate, comprehensive and up-to-date, and in particular provide information about any vulnerability, support needs and arrangements for support, where this information is available. To prevent new tenancies from failing and to minimise the likelihood of the RSL rejecting a nomination, housing authorities should ensure, wherever possible, that adequate support packages are in place for applicants who need them before a nominee is expected to take up their tenancy.

6.13　Housing authorities should ensure that robust monitoring arrangements are in place to monitor effective delivery of the terms of the nomination agreement or protocol. This will be crucial, to ensure that housing authorities can demonstrate that they are meeting their statutory obligations under Part 6, and in particular the requirement to give reasonable preference to persons in the categories set out in section 167(2). Monitoring arrangements should cover successful and 'failed' nominations.

6.14 A 'failed' nomination occurs when an RSL applies its own criteria to reject an applicant who has applied for particular accommodation and who would otherwise be allocated that accommodation, because he or she has appropriate priority under the choice based lettings scheme and is eligible for an allocation under Part 6. It is particularly important to monitor failed nominations to identify whether any particular applicants in the reasonable preference categories are being consistently denied access to accommodation for which they should be given priority.

6.15 The monitoring arrangements will also need to cover nominations to any RSL stock which is not included in the joint choice based lettings scheme.

Common housing registers

6.16 Where housing authorities and RSLs pool together their available accommodation in a single choice based lettings scheme, they are advised to consider developing a single list or database of all applicants who have applied and been accepted onto the joint choice based lettings scheme (referred to here as 'a common housing register').

6.17 A common housing register is a useful administrative tool which facilitates the operation of a joint choice based lettings scheme and improves co-ordination between participating landlords. For applicants, a common housing register, together with a single application form, provides a single point of access to all participating landlords and obviates the need to register separately with each of them. For housing authorities, a common housing register provides a more reliable assessment of housing need in their district, providing important information for the development of their housing strategy, and enabling the best use to be made of existing stock. However, it is important to remember that applicants on the common housing register who wish to bid for local authority allocations (including RSL vacancies to which the local authority has nomination rights) will need to meet the section 160A eligibility criteria.

Stock transfer, contracting out

6.18 Choice based lettings schemes which involve a housing authority and partner RSLs may operate in different contexts, including where the housing authority has contracted out some of its allocation functions and/or where the housing authority has transferred part or all of its stock.

6.19 Housing authorities which have transferred all or part of their stock, as well as those which have contracted out allocation functions, retain their statutory obligations regarding the allocation of accommodation, homelessness and the provision of housing advice. They also retain the responsibility for broader strategic duties such as the duty to undertake a periodic review of housing conditions and to consider aggregate housing needs.

6.20 All housing authorities are required to have an allocation scheme regardless of whether or not they retain ownership of the housing stock and whether or not they contract out the delivery of any of their allocation functions. Authorities are prohibited from contracting out certain allocation functions, including adopting and altering the allocation scheme, which includes the principles on which the scheme is framed.

6.21 In so far as a joint choice based lettings scheme applies to accommodation which is allocated within the meaning of section 159, housing authorities must ensure that:

- the principles of the choice based lettings scheme, and in particular the principles for determining priorities between applicants, comply with the requirements of Part 6 of the 1996 Act
- the principles of the choice based lettings scheme are set out in the authority's allocation scheme and
- accommodation which is allocated within the meaning of section 159 under a choice based lettings scheme is allocated in accordance with the authority's allocation scheme and in accordance with the requirements of Part 6

6.22   In circumstances where a stock transfer landlord – or an RSL to which a housing authority has contracted out some of its allocation functions – has, or proposes to, set up or participate in a choice based lettings scheme, housing authorities are strongly advised to actively participate in the scheme as well. This is the best way to ensure that they can properly carry out their statutory allocation and homelessness functions and duties as well as their strategic housing responsibilities.

Private sector landlords

6.23   Private rented sector housing already performs an important role in providing accommodation for those in housing need. In particular, the private rented sector can provide types and sizes of dwellings which may not be readily available within the social rented sector. For those who have lower priority under an authority's allocation scheme, and who may have to wait a considerable time before they are allocated a social tenancy, a vacancy in the private rented sector may offer a quicker and equally suitable housing solution. The private rented sector can also provide a way into independent living for vulnerable households, particularly where it is coupled with appropriate housing related support. Accordingly, the Secretary of State is of the view that it is appropriate and beneficial for vacancies in the private rented sector to be advertised through an authority's choice based lettings scheme, wherever possible, in order to ensure that all applicants have the widest possible range of housing options.

6.24   Where private rented sector vacancies are advertised in a choice based lettings scheme, authorities should consider putting in place appropriate safeguards to ensure that the housing on offer meets satisfactory standards of condition and management. Where authorities make extensive use of the private rented sector in their housing options approach, appropriate safeguards are likely to be in place already. In these circumstances, the Secretary of State believes private rented vacancies should be included, wherever possible, within the choice based lettings scheme.

6.25   Otherwise, housing authorities should consider putting in place such safeguards with a view to incorporating private rented vacancies within their choice based lettings scheme as soon as this is appropriate.

6.26   A nomination to a private sector landlord is outside the scope of Part 6 of the 1996 Act, and the letting is likely to take the form of an assured shorthold tenancy. Accordingly, where vacancies in the private rented sector are advertised as part of a choice based lettings scheme, the differences between the types of tenure should be made clear to applicants. In particular, authorities should ensure that applicants are aware of:

- the fact that the tenant will acquire more limited tenancy rights than in respect of local authority or RSL accommodation and
- the basis on which the landlord will select the successful bid, if this differs from the basis on which successful bids for social housing vacancies are selected

6.27   When advertising private sector vacancies, authorities will want to ensure that the advertisement includes broadly the same information about the particular vacancy – in terms of the size and nature of the property and level of rent – as for social rented vacancies (see paragraph 5.9). Additional information which it would be helpful to provide in the advertisement include:

- the name of the landlord or letting agent responsible for managing the property
- the form of the tenancy
- any restrictions on who may apply for the property, in particular whether applicants in receipt of Local Housing Allowance will be considered

6.28   In order to minimise confusion for applicants, authorities should consider creating within their advertising a separate and distinct section for private rented vacancies, rather than advertising them together with social rented vacancies. This might include general information about matters which would be of interest to applicants, such as:

- the particular features of assured shorthold tenancies
- a summary of the accreditation scheme, or other standards or safeguards in place
- the availability of rent deposits/bonds and guarantees
- information about tenancy deposit protection
- any housing related support available for private tenants
- any dispute resolution/mediation service (between landlord and tenant)
- an explanation of Local Housing Allowance and current rates

Chapter 7: regional and sub-regional choice based lettings schemes

Policy objective

7.1   The Government's policy objective is for choice based lettings schemes to develop on a sub-regional and/or regional basis. The Secretary of State believes that such schemes, involving a partnership of housing authorities and registered social landlords – and working together with private landlords wherever possible – are the best way to achieve the greatest choice and flexibility in meeting tenants' housing needs.

7.2   There are likely to be a number of benefits from larger, sub-regional or regional schemes which span housing authorities' boundaries:

- they bring together a larger pool of available housing, giving tenants more choice and helping to ease localised problems of high demand
- they break down artificial boundaries and recognise existing housing and labour markets
- they enable greater mobility
- for RSLs, they reduce the costs and complexities associated with being involved in several different schemes and

- they enable partners to share the costs associated with developing and implementing choice based lettings schemes

Different models of sub-regional and regional CBL

7.3   The Secretary of State recognises that housing authorities which plan to set up a sub-regional or regional choice based lettings scheme should have the flexibility to determine how far they wish to coordinate their allocation functions with partner authorities, in line with local policy objectives. In some instances, authorities may decide to retain their own individual allocation schemes. In other circumstances, authorities may decide to adopt a single regional or sub-regional allocation scheme.

Delegating functions to a central body

7.4   A common feature of most sub-regional or regional choice based lettings schemes is likely to be the designation of a single body or organisation to carry out some of the administrative tasks in relation to the scheme. There are two principal options available to housing authorities seeking to delegate their allocation functions to a central body. The constitution of the central body will depend to a large extent on who the partners to the scheme are and which functions the partners choose to delegate to the body.

7.5   Firstly, housing authorities have powers to delegate some of their allocations functions to another body under the Local Authorities (Contracting Out of Allocation of Housing and Homelessness Functions) Order 1996 ('the Contracting Out Order'). Schedule 1 of the Order lists the allocation functions which cannot be contracted out, namely: adopting or altering an allocation scheme; consulting with relevant RSLs before adopting or altering an allocation scheme; and making the allocation scheme available at the authority's principal office, or providing a copy of the scheme on request.

7.6   Housing authorities may wish to use the powers under the Contracting Out Order to delegate allocation functions to an RSL or to a special purpose vehicle set up specifically for this purpose. The functions which could be delegated would include, for example, the central advertising of available properties on behalf of all partners, processing of applications and the compiling of a short-list of bids for each advertised vacancy. Alternatively, housing authorities have the power to delegate to another housing authority under section 101 of the Local Government Act 1972.

7.7   Secondly, local authorities have general powers to work together in the discharge of their functions.[10] Subject to the constitutional arrangements of the authorities concerned, an authority may be able to arrange for the discharge of its functions by another authority, or two or more authorities may be able to arrange for the joint discharge of their functions by a joint committee. These powers could be used to establish a regional or sub-regional choice based lettings scheme involving two or more housing authorities which could

10 In most cases, the relevant statutory powers will be sections 19 and 20 of the Local Government Act 2000. These sections apply to local authorities which have adopted new constitutions which prove for 'executive arrangements'. Local authorities which have not adopted executive arrangements have similar powers under section 101 of the Local Government Act 1972. In practice, most local authorities in England do now have executive arrangements in place.

be operated either by a lead authority discharging the functions of the other authorities, or by a joint committee set up by all the partner authorities. If the authorities wished to do so, they could delegate all of their Part 6 functions to this type of central CBL body.

7.8 Housing authorities may not use these general powers to operate a regional or sub-regional choice based lettings scheme together with RSLs or private sector landlords as partners to the scheme. However, it would be possible to include within such a scheme RSL vacancies to which a local authority had nomination rights (see paragraphs 6.8 to 6.15).

Regional and sub-regional allocation schemes

7.9 Where two or more housing authorities operate a choice based lettings scheme on a regional or sub-regional basis, they are encouraged to consider the benefits of adopting a single, common allocation scheme across all the participating authorities. Such an approach should have a number of advantages for local authorities and RSL partners, and for applicants. For instance, it is likely to:

- be more efficient and cost-effective for landlords
- be more transparent and simpler to understand for applicants, particularly those seeking to move between local authority districts
- promote greater mobility and thus provide greater choice for applicants

7.10 In the Secretary of State's view, the requirements:

- in section 167(1) for every local housing authority to have an allocation scheme, and
- in section 167(8) to allocate in accordance with that scheme

can be effectively discharged by two or more local authorities acting jointly to produce a common allocation scheme. Where a joint regional or sub-regional allocation scheme is adopted by partner authorities, it is important that this is clearly stated on the face of the document. The allocation scheme should explain, for example, that it is a joint scheme for the region or sub-region made up of the named authorities. The role of any central body allocating on behalf of the partner authorities should also be outlined in the joint allocation scheme.

7.11 When framing a joint allocation scheme, housing authorities must ensure that reasonable preference is secured for all applicants to the partner authorities who are entitled to it under section 167 of the 1996 Act. In particular, the joint allocation scheme will still need to meet the requirement for reasonable preference to be secured for 'people who need to move to a particular locality in the district of the housing authority, where failure to meet that need would cause hardship (to themselves or to others)' (section 167(2)(e)). One way this could be achieved in the context of a sub-regional or regional allocation scheme would be to give reasonable preference to an applicant who needs to live in a specific area within the region or sub-region when the applicant bids for a property advertised in that area.

7.12 Where authorities enter into a joint scheme, the same allocations criteria will apply to all allocations in the region, since authorities can only allocate in accordance with their scheme (section 167(8)). The only exception to this will be where the common allocations scheme itself makes provision for local differences under section 167(2E) (ie where the scheme provides for local lettings policies). This would allow authorities to continue to give priority to people with a local connection when allocating accommodation in certain rural parishes, for example.

7.13   Where authorities have adopted a joint allocation scheme, a person who applies for housing under the scheme should be treated as applying to all of the partner housing authorities. This would argue strongly for the partner authorities adopting a common housing register and a single application form. Once the application was accepted, the applicant would then be entitled to bid for vacancies advertised by all of the partner authorities, including partner authorities with which the applicant had no previous connection.

7.14   Another option would be for partner authorities to maintain separate allocation schemes but for each authority to adopt the same banding scheme or points system, preferably together with a common housing register, across the partner authorities. This would have a number of benefits, particularly where partner authorities also delegate their allocation functions to a central body. For partner authorities and the central body, it would be more cost-effective and easier to administer. For applicants, it would be easier to understand and to operate, particularly for those seeking to move across local authority boundaries. It could also be the first step towards a common allocation policy across the region or sub-region.

Cross-boundary mobility

7.15   Housing authorities which are partners in a regional or sub-regional scheme may wish to maintain separate allocation schemes but provide for cross-boundary mobility, that is to say they may wish to make it easier for applicants living within one partner authority's district to apply for and be allocated accommodation in the district of another partner authority. Authorities who have chosen not to adopt a joint allocation scheme are strongly urged to consider the advantages to applicants of facilitating mobility in this way.

7.16   The arrangements for cross-boundary mobility must be capable of being operated in line with the statutory requirements of Part 6. Authorities should note the following points in particular:

   • if allocations under a particular allocation scheme are usually subject to a local connection rule, the scheme should make specific provision for dealing with cross-boundary moves

   • an authority cannot rely on its partner authority's assessment of the applicant's priority, since it can only allocate in accordance with its own scheme. In practice, both authorities may have delegated some of their allocation functions to a central body (see paragraphs 7.4 to 7.8 above). Where this is the case, since the central body only has the powers which are delegated to it, it will still have to consider each application in accordance with the allocation scheme of the allocating authority

   • any provision for cross-boundary moves must not affect the authority's ability to ensure reasonable preference for the classes of person specified in section 167(2). This is unlikely to be a problem if the cross-boundary applicants are all persons who are entitled to reasonable preference

   • the basis for determining priority between cross-boundary applicants should be set out in the allocation scheme

7.17   Applicants who are looking to make longer distance moves may need infor-
        mation and support to help them do so. This may simply mean access to
        information about the new area which they are less likely to be familiar with.
        This might include information on schools, health facilities, transport, train-
        ing and employment. Applicants may also need more time to view proper-
        ties, where they need to travel long distances; and authorities should consider
        whether there is other support which it would be appropriate to offer. Partner
        authorities should build these factors into the sub-regional or regional choice
        based lettings scheme. Partner authorities should ensure that there is close
        co-operation between the choice based lettings scheme and other statutory
        and voluntary agencies, to ensure that applicants with care and support needs
        can be enabled to move across local authority boundaries. Housing authori-
        ties should also consider developing links with the providers of other services
        operating in partner authority areas. Examples might be training and educa-
        tion providers, as well as employers.

RSL involvement in regional CBL schemes

7.18   Where RSL property is advertised through a joint choice based lettings scheme
        by housing authorities which each have their own allocation scheme, the part-
        ners in the scheme should be clear as to which housing authority is the nomin-
        ating authority. There should be clear information available for applicants as
        to which authority's allocation scheme applies to that property (and therefore
        how priority will be determined).

7.19   Housing authorities are encouraged to work with their local HomeBuy Agents
        on sub-regional or regional choice based lettings schemes. HomeBuy Agents
        are appointed RSLs funded by the Housing Corporation (in future the Homes
        and Community Agency) who provide a 'one stop shop' and point of con-
        tact in a given area in England for all applicants for the Government funded
        HomeBuy programme.

Fair and flexible: statutory guidance on social housing allocations for local authorities in England*

Contents

Summary

Scope of the guidance

Introduction

Objectives and outcomes which allocation policies must achieve

Objectives and outcomes which the Government believes allocation policies should achieve

Involving, consulting and raising awareness with local communities

Framing an allocation scheme

Partnership working with RSLs

Summary

1. This statutory guidance covers a number of issues:
    (i) It sets out the Government's strategic view of the objectives and outcomes which local authorities must and those they should seek to achieve in their allocation policies. These are:
        - providing support for those in greatest housing need, including people who have experienced homelessness
        - ensuring allocation policies comply with equality legislation
        - promoting greater choice for prospective and existing tenants
        - creating more mixed and sustainable communities
        - promoting greater mobility for existing tenants
        - making better use of the housing stock
        - supporting people in work or seeking work
        - delivering policies which are fair and considered to be fair
    (ii) It sets out the importance of local authorities' responsibilities under the Local Government Act 1999 (as amended by the Local Government and Public Involvement in Health Act 2007) to involve, inform and consult with local people; and it draws attention to the main legislative provisions governing the allocation of social housing, including the requirement to provide for 'reasonable preference'.
    (iii) It emphasises the importance of communicating facts about allocations (including regular updates on how properties have been allocated), to tackle false perceptions which may arise about the way social housing is allocated.
    (iv) It highlights the implications of the House of Lords judgment in the case of *R (Ahmad) v Newham LBC*,[1] which, among other things, removes the requirement to provide for cumulative preference to be taken into account in prioritising applicants.

---

* Department for Communities and Local Government: December 2009. © Crown Copyright.

1 [2009] UKHL 14.

(v)   It reinforces the flexibilities local authorities have within the allocation legislation to meet local pressures by:
- adopting local priorities alongside the statutory reasonable preference categories
- taking into account other factors in prioritising applicants, including waiting time and local connection
- operating local lettings policies

(vi)   It emphasises the importance of close working between authorities and registered social landlords.

Scope of the guidance

2.   This is statutory guidance provided under section 169 of the Housing Act 1996 (the 1996 Act). It applies to local authorities in England. Local authorities are required to have regard to this guidance in exercising their functions under Part 6 of the 1996 Act. In so far as this guidance comments on the law it can only reflect the Department's understanding of the law at the time of issue. Local authorities will still need to keep up to date on any developments in the law in these areas.

3.   This guidance replaces the following parts of the *Code of Guidance on the Allocation of Accommodation* which was issued in November 2002 (the 2002 code):[2]
- chapters 1, 2 and 6
- paragraphs 5.1 to 5.12 , paragraph 5.18 and paragraphs 5.23 to 5.32 of chapter 5
- annexes 2, 4, 5, 6, 7, 8 9 and 12

4.   This guidance also replaces the following paragraphs of the *Code of Guidance on Choice Based Lettings* which was issued in August 2008 (the 2008 code):[3]
- 4.1 to 4.49
- 4.68 to 4.71
- 4.79 and 4.80

5.   *Circular 04/2009: Housing Allocations – Members of the Armed Forces* remains in effect.

6.   This guidance is specifically for local authority Members and staff. It is also of direct relevance to registered social landlords[4] (referred to as RSLs). On a local authority's request, RSLs have a duty under section 170 of the 1996 Act to co-operate with local authorities to such extent as is reasonable in the circumstances in offering accommodation to people with priority under the authority's allocation scheme.

7.   For local authorities, developing their allocation scheme and carrying out their allocation functions often requires joint planning and operational co-operation between local authorities and other bodies. These are likely to include social services departments, health authorities, the probation service,

---

2 *Allocation of Accommodation: Code of Guidance for Local Housing Authorities,* ODPM, November 2002.

3 *Allocation of Accommodation: Choice Based Lettings: Code of Guidance for Local Housing Authorities,* CLG, August 2008.

4 Subject to Parliamentary approval, from April 2010 RSLs will cease to exist in England. Any references to RSLs will after that date be understood as references to private registered providers.

children's services, other referral agencies and voluntary sector organisations, although this list is not exhaustive. This guidance will be of interest to these organisations as well.

8.   We believe that local authorities will welcome the additional flexibilities which this guidance promotes and would encourage them to review their existing policies as soon as possible and to revise them, where appropriate, in the light of this guidance.

9.   The Audit Commission will consider, through its agreed programmes of monitoring and inspection, which will be reflected in comprehensive area assessments, how well local authorities allocate social housing and therefore their response to this guidance.

Introduction

10.   Social rented housing is an asset of great significance to the country, to local communities, to families and to individual people. It provides an essential part of the welfare safety net that supports many of the most vulnerable in our society. It provides a firm foundation, with the security and stability that can help people to overcome disadvantage and to build successful lives for themselves and their families. And it can help to create prosperous, healthy local communities, as part of a balanced housing market.

11.   In any circumstances, the way that social housing is allocated would be a matter of real importance. That importance is greatly increased by the pressure of demand that we currently face in all parts of England. Almost every local authority has experienced significant growth in applications for social housing over the past five or six years. In *Building Britain's Future*, we set out ambitious plans to invest a further £1.5bn in building thousands of new affordable homes over this year and the next. In total we are committing more than £7.5bn over these years (2009/2011) to deliver 112,000 affordable homes, including 63,000 homes for social rent to be delivered by the Homes and Communities Agency (HCA) over the next two years. However, despite this ambitious programme of affordable housing delivery we can expect continued excess of demand over supply to continue for the medium term.

12.   High levels of demand, often from families with pressing needs, mean decisions on the allocation of social housing need to be taken carefully. Because of the impact such decisions may have, people care deeply about how they are made. Whilst many local authorities are responding positively to this increased demand, we must ensure not only that decisions taken achieve the best overall outcomes for our communities: but also that they are made fairly, and in ways that can be explained and justified to all concerned.

13.   The Government takes the view that decisions on the allocation of social housing – having, as they do, profound impacts at national and at local level – should rightly be taken in a framework which balances national and local interests.

14.   It is important that local authorities continue to play a strong role in housing. They are best placed to assess housing need across the district, in light of demographic and economic change. Councils now have access to specific grant funding to build new council homes. We have also proposed a devolved system of accountability and funding for the existing stock. This would give more power to councils to plan long term, manage their assets and meet the

housing needs of local people. They should also be working with partners to address such needs, including ensuring that the best use is made of existing housing stock. Local authorities also have responsibility for framing local allocation policies within the context set by legislation and taking into account the reality of their local circumstances. It is only at local level that many of the key decisions can be taken, and balances can be struck between competing priorities. Many people find allocation policies complex and confusing. While the Government has a role to play in dispelling the myths which can arise around the allocation of social housing, the task of explaining local allocation policies to local people ultimately depends on effective communication and engagement by local authorities with their communities.

15. In recent years, many local authorities have felt constrained in their decisions on allocations and the way in which their allocation scheme is devised because of the way in which the legislation has been interpreted by the courts. A recent judgment by the House of Lords (see paragraph 58), which we strongly welcome, provides clarity on the allocation legislation and the extent of local authorities' discretion under the legislation. The Government's view is that this is an opportune time, as well as an important one, for local authorities to re-examine their allocation policies and to make changes which take full advantage of the scope for local decision-making.

Objectives and outcomes which allocation policies must achieve

16. There are a number of objectives and outcomes which local authorities must achieve when framing their allocation schemes.

Support for those in greatest housing need

17. We believe it is right that social housing – which brings with it the dual benefits of security of tenure and sub-market rents – should continue to provide a stable base for those who are likely to have more difficulty fending for themselves in the private market. For this reason, we remain of the view that, overall, priority for social housing should go to those in greatest housing need. The current statutory reasonable preference categories are set out in section 167(2) of the 1996 Act. These were rationalised in the Homelessness Act 2002 (and further refined by the Housing Act 2004) to ensure that they are squarely based on housing need. The reasonable preference categories are:

(a) people who are homeless (within the meaning of Part 7 of the 1996 Act); this includes people who are intentionally homeless, and those who do not have a priority need for accommodation

(b) people who are owed a duty by any local authority under section 190(2), 193(2) or 195(2) of the 1996 Act (or under section 65(2) or 68(2) of the Housing Act 1985) or who are occupying accommodation secured by any local authority under section 192(3)

(c) people occupying insanitary or overcrowded housing or otherwise living in unsatisfactory housing conditions

(d) people who need to move on medical or welfare grounds, including grounds relating to a disability

(e) people who need to move to a particular locality in the district of the local authority, where failure to meet that need would cause hardship (to themselves or to others).

18.   This means that a scheme must be framed to give reasonable preference to applicants who fall within the categories set out in section 167(2), over those who do not. While local authorities must demonstrate that, overall, reasonable preference is given to applicants in all the reasonable preference categories, this does not mean that they must give equal weight to each of the reasonable preference categories. Local authorities may wish to take into account local pressures. So, for example, where overcrowding is a particularly serious problem, they may wish to give more priority to overcrowded households in their allocation scheme. Authorities might give effect to this policy objective, for example, by assigning overcrowded households to a higher band, or by including a specific target in respect of overcrowded households in their annual lettings plan.

19.   In addition, section 167(2) gives local authorities the power to frame their allocation scheme so as to give additional preference to particular descriptions of people who fall within the reasonable preference categories and who have urgent housing needs. While there is no requirement for an allocation scheme to be framed to provide for additional preference, all local authorities should consider, in the light of local circumstances, whether there is a need to give effect to this provision.

Providing settled homes for people who have experienced homelessness

20.   The Government places great emphasis on the prevention of homelessness and local authorities are generally responding very positively to this agenda. Through their housing options services, local authorities are increasingly helping people at risk of homelessness by intervening earlier to resolve their difficulties before they reach crisis point. This is reflected by the significant reduction in the number of households accepted as owed the main duty to secure accommodation under the homelessness legislation since acceptances peaked in 2003-04. Local authorities are increasingly harnessing the private rented sector to help meet housing needs and we are looking at how this work could be extended and made more effective. Nevertheless, there are people at risk of homelessness or living in temporary accommodation for whom an allocation of social housing continues to be the most appropriate option to meet their need for a settled home. It is right, therefore, that people who are homeless or placed in temporary accommodation under the homelessness legislation should continue to be entitled to reasonable preference for social housing.

Promoting greater equality and clearly meeting equalities duties

21.   In framing their allocation scheme, local authorities need to ensure that it is compatible with the requirements in the equality legislation. In particular, as well as the other duties to eliminate unlawful discrimination, local authorities are reminded that they are subject to a duty to promote equality of opportunity and good relations between people of different racial groups, as well as a duty to promote equality of opportunity between disabled persons and other persons, and between men and women. Local authorities are strongly recommended to carry out an equality impact assessment of any change to their allocation policies to ensure compliance with the local authority's legal equality duties; and to monitor lettings outcomes under the allocation scheme and ensure that this information is made regularly and publicly available.

22.   Local authorities should bear in mind that, subject to Parliamentary approval, the general public sector equality duty in the Equality Bill will mean that they will need, when carrying out their allocation function and reviewing and revising their allocation policies, to consider the impact of their decisions on people with the protected characteristics of age, race, disability, sex, pregnancy and maternity, sexual orientation, religion or belief or gender reassignment. Local authorities should also be aware of the provision in the Equality Bill which will require all local authorities to give due regard to the desirability of tackling socio-economic inequalities, when making strategic decisions about how to exercise their functions. The Government believes that the way in which local authorities frame their allocation scheme will be significant in ensuring they discharge this duty.

Objectives and outcomes which the Government believes allocation policies should achieve

23.   There are also a number of objectives and outcomes which local authorities should seek to achieve when framing their allocation schemes.

Greater choice and wider options for prospective and existing tenants

24.   The Government believes that allocation policies for social housing should provide for applicants to be given more of a say and a greater choice over the accommodation which they are allocated. This is the best way to ensure sustainable tenancies and to build settled, viable and inclusive communities. Research carried out for Communities and Local Government into the longer term impact of choice based lettings[5] found that tenants who were offered a choice of accommodation were more likely to be satisfied with their home and remain in that home for a longer period. Satisfied tenants are more likely to meet their tenancy obligations and maintain the property in good condition.

25.   It is also important that the allocation of social housing is set within a wider enhanced housing options approach, so that people receive joined-up advice and information about all the options open to them across sectors, including:
- renting in the private sector
- low cost home ownership options
- mobility schemes which enable applicants to move out of the district
- mutual exchange options for existing social tenants
- home improvement schemes or adaptations services which enable applicants to remain in their existing accommodation and
- supported/sheltered housing for older and disabled people

Creating more mixed and sustainable communities

26.   The way in which social housing is allocated can be instrumental in helping to create safe, prosperous and cohesive communities in which people want to live and work, now and in the future. The research into the longer term impacts of CBL suggests that the policy is encouraging applicants to think more flexibly about their housing options. It found that, where applicants have the opportunity to see details about all available vacancies, they will consider moving to areas beyond their immediate locality and beyond areas

---

5   *Monitoring the Longer Term Impact of Choice Based Lettings*, Heriot-Watt University and BMRB, October 2006.

which, under a traditional allocations system, they would have specified as their 'preferred area'.

27.   Alongside CBL, making greater use of the existing flexibilities within the allocation legislation can help to tackle concentrations of deprivation, creating more mixed and sustainable communities. This might include:

- setting local priorities alongside the reasonable preference categories, such as promoting job-related moves
- setting aside a small proportion of lettings to enable existing tenants to move even where they do not have reasonable preference
- using local lettings policies to achieve a wide variety of policy objectives, including dealing with concentrations of deprivation or creating mixed communities by setting aside a proportion of vacancies for applicants who are in employment, or to enable existing tenants to take up an offer of employment.

Greater mobility

28.   Providing social housing tenants with greater opportunities to move within the social sector can help to promote social and economic mobility, as well as meeting individual tenants' specific needs and aspirations. It can also help make the best use of social housing stock.

29.   One way of increasing the opportunities for mobility between local authority areas is to develop choice based lettings schemes on a regional or sub-regional basis and our aim is to expand choice based lettings so that people can move nationwide. However, even where local authorities do not participate in regional or sub-regional choice based lettings schemes, there are ways in which they can frame their allocation scheme to increase the opportunities for mobility across local authority boundaries. So, for example, authorities could use local lettings policies to allow for a small proportion of properties to be prioritised for essential workers (or people with skills in short supply) to attract them into the district; or they could develop arrangements with other authorities or RSLs to make a proportion of their lettings available for cross-boundary nominations.

Making better use of the housing stock

30.   Making better use of the social housing stock could mean giving existing tenants who are under-occupying social housing appropriate priority to secure a transfer within an authority's allocation scheme and ensuring that scarce accessible and adapted accommodation is prioritised for people with access needs. This might be coupled with personal support, incentives and financial payments to encourage people who under-occupy family-sized homes to downsize or vacate adapted homes they no longer need. Authorities may want to consider other approaches such as 'chain lets' – an approach under which a large property released by an under-occupying household can be reserved for existing overcrowded social rented tenants, where the resulting vacancy is then used to house another household with priority under the allocation scheme. For overcrowded households waiting for an allocation of larger accommodation, authorities can assist in mitigating the impacts through a range of measures. Improvements can be made to existing properties in order to improve liveability: additional toilets or wash basins, partitions or space saving furniture can all contribute to alleviating the pressures of overcrowding.

Policies which are fair and considered to be fair

31. There are widespread perceptions that the current allocation system is unfair and favours certain groups (such as the unemployed or migrants). An Ipsos MORI survey carried out for Communities and Local Government in 2008 showed that less than a quarter (23%) of the public agreed that the way social housing is allocated is fair. One in three (32%) did not agree that it is fair. Just under a half (45%) said they did not know if it is fair or were unwilling to give an opinion and opted for 'neither agree nor disagree'.[6] While these perceptions may not always be founded on fact, we recognise that they are strongly felt.

32. It is important that local authorities engage fully with their local community in developing their allocation priorities and drawing up their allocation scheme; and in providing regular, accurate, and generalised information on how housing is being allocated, working actively to dispel any myths and misperceptions which may arise. Policies which are easily understood and sensitive to local needs and local priorities are more likely to achieve acceptance across the wider community and to be, not just fair, but seen to be fair.[7]

Support for people in work or seeking work

33. Local authorities should consider how they can use their allocation policies to support those who are in work or who are seeking work. This could involve using local lettings policies to ensure that particular properties are allocated to essential workers or to those who have skills which are in short supply, regardless of whether they are currently resident in the authority's district. Alternatively, authorities may choose to give some preference within their scheme to existing tenants who are willing to move to take up employment or training opportunities – where, for example, the authority has identified need to address skills shortages and worklessness, perhaps as part of their skills strategy.

Involving, consulting and raising awareness with local communities

34. For many people, the frustration engendered by long waiting times for social housing, the complexity and lack of transparency of many allocation policies, and poorly trained or supported front line housing officers, can contribute to false perceptions of unfairness or generate myths about 'queue jumping' by other groups. These myths and false perceptions need to be countered through effective, transparent communication.

35. Local authorities need to do more to help people locally understand how social housing is allocated.[8] The public are more likely to accept that allocation

6 Communities and Local Government (2009) *Attitudes to housing: Findings from Ipsos MORI Public Affairs Monitor Omnibus Survey* (England).

7 An Ipsos MORI survey for *Inside Housing* shows that people consider the most important factors for prioritising social housing (where demand is greater than supply) as: how long someone has been on the waiting list (23%); whether they are currently living in inadequate accommodation (22%); how long someone has lived in the local area (15%); and being a key worker (eg, nurse or teacher) (14%). *Inside Housing*, 6 June 2008, pp22–25.

8 The Ipsos Mori survey reports that 8% of the general public said they know a lot about the way social housing is allocated, 48% know a little and 41% said they know nothing, with 3% giving a 'don't know' response.

policies are fair if they have a clear understanding of what those policies are and what the justification for those policies is. Clarity about why social housing is prioritised for certain groups is key. To give a specific example, if an authority provided information about the amount of housing they have which is, not only accessible, but capable of being made accessible, and explained why priority for this accommodation is given to those with access needs, it is likely that people would view it as a fair and sensible use of that stock.

36.   That is why it is important to engage fully with the whole community in developing allocation policies. It is also why it is important to provide feedback on properties let through choice based lettings,[9] and wider statistics about who is actually accessing social housing. Simple banding schemes play a role here too, since they can be more easily explained to applicants. Front line staff need to be properly trained and supported so that they provide accurate and consistent messages about how social housing is allocated, and elected members need to take a leading role in explaining to local people how social housing is being allocated and managed in their district – and what their local authority is doing to help increase availability of social housing.

The requirement to have an allocation scheme

37.   Local authorities must have an allocation scheme for determining priorities and the procedures to be followed in allocating housing accommodation; and they must allocate in accordance with that scheme (section 167 of the 1996 Act).

38.   The requirement to have an allocation scheme applies to all local authorities, regardless of whether or not they retain ownership of the housing stock and whether or not they contract out the delivery of any of their allocation functions. Authorities are prohibited from contracting out certain allocation functions, including adopting and altering the allocation scheme, which includes the principles on which the scheme is framed. 'Procedure' includes all aspects of the allocation process, including the people, or descriptions of people, by whom decisions are taken. It is essential that the scheme reflects all the local authority's policies and procedures, including information on whether the decisions are taken by elected members or officers acting under delegated powers.

Involving and consulting about the allocation scheme

39.   Part 6 of the 1996 Act imposes certain requirements on local authorities when consulting on changes to their allocation scheme, or before they adopt a new scheme. Authorities are required to consult with RSLs with which they have nomination arrangements (s167(7)); while anyone likely to be affected by an alteration to the allocation scheme which reflects a major change of policy must be notified of it (s168(3)).

40.   Under section 3 of the Local Government Act 1999 (as amended by the Local Government and Public Involvement in Health Act 2007) an authority is under a general duty to make arrangements to secure continuous improvement in the way in which its functions are exercised, having regard to a combination of economy, efficiency and effectiveness. Under section 3A of the Local Government Act 1999, where an authority considers it appropriate for representatives of local persons to be involved in the exercise of any of its functions

9   Further guidance on feedback in the context of choice based lettings is provided at paragraphs 5.14–5.18 of the 2008 code.

by being provided with information, consulted or involved in another way, it must take such steps as it considers appropriate to secure that such representatives are involved in the exercise of the function in that way. Statutory guidance published by the Government in July 2008[10] sets out the issues which local authorities should consider under the 'duty to involve'.

41. Engaging with and involving local communities in the development of allocation policies will contribute to:

- better awareness among local people of the facts around social housing, including a clearer understanding of the amount of housing available
- reduced opportunities for the circulation of misunderstandings and myths about the ways in which social housing is allocated
- local allocation policies which better reflect local pressures and priorities
- a greater sense among local people that housing is allocated fairly
- stronger community cohesion.

42. Some local authorities currently make significant efforts to engage with local communities in the development of allocation policies, using techniques such as questionnaires and surveys aimed at residents or those on the waiting list, citizens' panels and focus groups. There is scope for all authorities to develop their approaches further, drawing on good practice from within the housing sector and more broadly.[11]

43. Anyone who is affected by or interested in the way social housing is allocated should be included when consulting on changes to an authority's allocation scheme. It will be important to engage with a wide range of stakeholders in the statutory and voluntary and community sector, as well as applicants and the general public. Consultation gives people the opportunity to have their views heard but it also gives local authorities the opportunity to engage the community, to raise awareness about the pressures on social housing, and to ensure that people have a better understanding of why certain groups are prioritised for social housing.

44. However, authorities should also engage with and involve the wider community before they produce their allocation scheme so that people are given the opportunity to contribute to the development of the allocation priorities. Only in this way can authorities ensure that the allocation scheme properly reflects local priorities and issues. An important aspect of engagement will be managing expectations. Providing clear information about allocations, including which households must be given priority under the allocation legislation and what social housing is available in the district, may be helpful here; as also ensuring that any consultation on allocation priorities is set firmly within the context of the local authority's overarching strategic priorities.

45. It will be important to take action to ensure that all groups within the area are engaged. Voluntary and community organisations can be useful here as they often have strong links with their particular communities or client groups. Authorities will need to give particular thought to how to engage those who can often be marginalised but for whom social housing may be particularly relevant (such as substance misusers, gypsies and travellers and ex-offenders).

10 *Creating Strong and Prosperous Communities*, July 2008.
11 *The Duty to Involve: Making it Work* published by the Community Development Foundation (2009) provides advice and examples of effective engagement.

Again, the voluntary and community sector may be in touch with hard to reach groups and can help ensure that they are involved in the consultation process. For this reason, it is particularly important that third sector organisations are involved at an early stage in the consultation process.

46.   Where local authorities involve individuals or groups in developing their allocation priorities or consult them on their allocation scheme, they should consider how they can feed back the outcomes of such involvement or consultation. In doing so they should make clear how the input to consultation and involvement has contributed to the published allocation scheme.

Information about allocations

47.   It is important that applicants and the wider community understand what social housing is available in their district, how social housing is allocated, and who is getting that social housing. Accordingly local authorities are encouraged to make appropriate information about allocations widely available in a way which is easy to access and to understand.[12] This is in addition to the duty in s.168 to make the full allocation scheme available for inspection and a summary of the scheme available free of charge. However, to ensure that local people have access to as much information as possible, authorities should publish their full allocation scheme on their website as well as in hard copy.

48.   Local authorities must ensure that advice and information is available free of charge to everyone in their district about the right to apply for an allocation of accommodation (s166(1)). This includes general information about the procedures for making an application; as well as information about how applicants are prioritised under the allocation scheme.

49.   If applicants are to view the system as fair, they need to know how their application will be treated under the allocation scheme, what their rights and expectations are under the scheme, and they need reassurance that the scheme is being complied with and applied consistently across all applicants. So, for example, applicants have the right to be informed of certain decisions in relation to their application[13] and the right to a review of such decisions (s167(4A)(d)). It is important that applicants have clear information about these rights as well as the procedure upon review. Applicants should also be provided with information about any other relevant complaints procedures which are available to them.

50.   However, information about allocations should go beyond publication of the allocation scheme itself or information about how to apply for an allocation. Most applicants will want to know how long they are likely to have to wait to be allocated accommodation which meets their needs and aspirations (this is in line with their rights under s167(4A)). Authorities can help applicants assess whether particular accommodation is likely to be available and how

12 Chapter 5 of the 2008 code provides detailed guidance on how to ensure that information is provided in a way which is accessible and that advice, assistance and support are available to those who need them in order to apply for social housing.

13 Applicants have the right to be informed of any decision and the grounds for it, relating to their eligibility (s160A(9)) and to be informed of a decision not to give them preference on grounds of unacceptable behaviour (s167(4A(b))). Applicants also have the right on request to be informed of any decision about the facts of their case which are likely to be, or have been, taken into account in considering whether to allocate accommodation to them (s167(4A)(c)).

long they are likely to wait for it, by making available general information about the profile of their stock (amount, type, size, location and accessibility); together with information about how often property of that type/size/location becomes available and estimated waiting times. Information should be kept up-to-date and published on a regular basis. It should be widely available as it may be of interest to people who may be considering applying for social housing as well as those who are already on the waiting list.

51.   It is important that local authorities go wider than simply informing applicants, and consider how they can share information about allocation policies and outcomes with the wider community. Where tensions are associated with housing allocations, communication may need to be part of a wider community cohesion strategy.

52.   Key individuals and organisations need information and training to ensure that they understand how the allocation system works and that they provide consistent messages both to applicants and to the wider public. Training needs to be ongoing, recognising that allocation policies change over time and that council staff and other personnel move on. When communicating messages about why certain groups have access to social housing, it is important to work together with the statutory bodies or community organisations which support those groups and individuals. So, for example, local authorities should work together with local drug action teams and crime and disorder reduction partnerships to explain why providing a stable base for substance misusers or ex-offenders can reduce crime and anti-social behaviour.

Monitoring and evaluation

53.   Monitoring and evaluation systems should be put in place and lettings outcomes published so that people can see that the allocation scheme is being complied with and is fair, and that the authority is meeting its duties under the equality legislation (see paragraph 21). Local authorities should give people the opportunity to feedback comments about how the allocation scheme is working. This might include periodically carrying out surveys of people on the waiting list to find out about their experience over time, or people who have bid for social housing through a choice based lettings scheme (both successfully and unsuccessfully).

Framing an allocation scheme

54.   An authority's allocation priorities should be developed in the context of the authority's other housing functions. Consideration should be given to the wider objectives of meeting the district's housing needs, as set out in the strategic housing market assessment. The allocation scheme should also be compatible with the local authority's housing strategy and the relevant regional housing strategy. Furthermore, since the allocation of accommodation under Part 6 of the 1996 Act is one of the ways in which the main homelessness duty can be discharged, allocation policies and procedures should also be consistent with the local authority's homelessness strategy.

55.   It is also important that the allocation scheme is compatible with and flows from the authority's sustainable community strategy[14] which sets the overall

14 Local Government Act 2000 s4.

strategic direction and long-term vision for the economic, social and environmental well-being of the local area.

56. It is strongly recommended that local authorities put in place allocation schemes which, not only meet the requirements in the legislation to ensure that reasonable preference for an allocation goes to those in the reasonable preference categories, but also:
    • reflect the Government's objectives, and
    • take into account the particular needs and priorities of the local area

57. We recognise that getting the balance right will be challenging, particularly given the constraints within which local authorities operate in terms of the supply of and demand for social housing. Nevertheless, we believe that there is considerable flexibility within the existing statutory framework, particularly following the recent decision in *Ahmad*.

R (Ahmad) v London Borough of Newham

58. In March 2009 the House of Lords gave judgment in the case of *R (Ahmad) v London Borough of Newham LBC*[15] (*'Ahmad'*. The case has significant implications for the way local authorities frame their allocation scheme. In particular the House of Lords found:
    • there is no requirement for local authorities to frame their allocation scheme to provide for cumulative preference, ie affording greater priority to applicants who fall into more than one reasonable preference category.
    • an allocation scheme which allows for priority to be determined between applicants in the reasonable preference categories on the basis of waiting time (alone) is not unlawful or irrational
    • an allocation scheme is not unlawful if it allows for a small percentage of lets to be allocated to existing social housing tenants who wish to transfer and who do not fall within any of the reasonable preference categories
    • where a local authority's allocation scheme complies with the requirements of section 167 and any other statutory requirements, the courts should be very slow to interfere on the ground that it is irrational

59. Through their judgment in the *Ahmad* case, the House of Lords have recognised the complexity of allocation policy and the need for local decision-making.

60. The following paragraphs consider the factors which local authorities should consider in developing their allocation priorities and the different tools and mechanisms available to them to allow for greater flexibility within their allocation scheme and to adapt their scheme to respond to local needs.

Removal of the requirement to provide for 'cumulative preference'

61. The House of Lords decision in *Ahmad* reverses a line of Court of Appeal authority that has held that allocation schemes were required to provide for cumulative preference. This means that it is no longer necessary to distinguish between degrees of housing need, or to provide that those applicants who fall within more than one reasonable preference category are given greater priority for an allocation than those who have reasonable preference on a single, non-urgent basis (indeed there is no requirement for any system of determining priority between those in the reasonable preference groups). In the light of the decision in *Ahmad*, what is important is that an allocation

15 [2009] UKHL 14.

scheme makes an appropriate distinction between those applicants in the reasonable preference categories and those who are not. It is no longer necessary to make a detailed prioritisation of applicants within the reasonable preference categories (instead it is open to local authorities to determine between applicants in the reasonable preference categories by waiting time alone (see paragraph 65).

62. Removing the requirement to provide for cumulative preference gives scope for local authorities to develop simpler, more transparent, systems of applicant prioritisation which are easier for applicants to understand and for housing staff to operate.

Determining priorities between households with a similar level of need

63. For practical purposes, allocation schemes will need to have some mechanism for determining priorities between applicants with a similar level of need, for example between applicants who are in the same band.

64. Section 167 (2A) provides that authorities may frame their allocation scheme to take into account certain factors for the purposes of determining relative priorities between applicants in the reasonable (or additional) preference categories. Examples of factors which may be taken into account are given in the legislation: local connection,[16] financial resources and behaviour. However, these examples are not exclusive and authorities may take into account other factors instead or as well as these.

Waiting time

65. The simplest way of determining priorities between those with a similar level of need would be to take into account the length of time which applicants have been waiting for an allocation (in the case of new applicants this will normally be the date of their original application or date into band, and in the case of transferring tenants, the date they applied to transfer).

66. Waiting time has the benefits of being simple, transparent, and easy to understand. It also accords with the view held by some sections of the public about how social housing should be prioritised. Of course, we recognise that waiting time will already play a role in most allocation schemes. However, authorities may wish to consider the scope for giving more weight to it in the light of *Ahmad*, where this is seen locally as the fairest means of distinguishing between otherwise similar applicants.

Behaviour

67. This would allow local authorities to take account of good as well as bad behaviour. So, for example, authorities could provide for greater priority to be given to applicants who can demonstrate that they have been model tenants or whose actions have directly benefited other residents on their estate or the community more generally. Bad behaviour would include unacceptable behaviour which was not serious enough to justify a decision to treat the applicant as ineligible, or to give him no preference for an allocation, but which could be taken into account in assessing the level of priority which was deserved relative to other applicants. An example could be minor rent arrears or low level anti-social behaviour.

16 For these purposes, local connection is defined in accordance with section 199 of the 1996 Act.

Local connection

68.   Some local authorities may wish to give more priority to 'local connection', ensuring that, wherever possible, social housing goes to those people who live or work in the district, or to those who have close family associations with it or have other special circumstances. While local authorities cannot exclude people who do not have a local connection from applying for social housing, there is nothing to prevent them from framing their allocation scheme to include local connection as a policy priority, provided that overall the scheme continues to meet the reasonable preference requirements in section167.

69.   An allocation scheme which attaches particular weight to local connection could disadvantage individual applicants. One example might be someone who has been placed out of the district they would normally live in for a period of time, while being looked after by children's services – although each case would need to be considered on its merits (care leavers might be able to establish a local connection through family association or special circumstances). Local authorities may wish to provide for circumstances such as these by setting aside a proportion of lettings (eg by including a specific target in their lettings plan, or by means of an appropriate local lettings policy) to help meet the housing needs of such applicants where they meet the reasonable preference criteria.

Banding schemes

70.   An appropriate method of applicant prioritisation could be a system that groups applicants into a number of 'bands' that reflect different levels of housing need or relative priorities within a housing authority's allocation scheme. Such systems are commonly referred to as 'banding schemes.

71.   The House of Lords in *Ahmad* recognised that simple banding schemes could have a number of advantages over more nuanced systems. They are clear, relatively simple to administer and highly transparent. Whereas banding schemes, which involve a large number of bands based on degrees of housing need, are likely to be more expensive and time consuming to operate, more based on value judgement, more open to argument, and more opaque. The House of Lords also considered that more complex banding systems may need to be monitored more closely to take account of the fact that applicants' circumstances are liable to change over time.

72.   In addition to the benefits identified in *Ahmad*, simpler banding schemes may also make it easier for authorities to work together to put in place subregional and regional choice based lettings schemes.

73.   Authorities should bear in mind that a banding scheme must be consistent with and give effect to the principles in the authority's allocation scheme for determining priorities for an allocation. The greater the number and complexity of these principles, the more complex the banding scheme will normally need to be.

Points based approaches

74.   Many local authorities have adopted a points-based approach to the prioritisation of applicants. Points-based systems can be complex and consequently lacking in transparency and difficult for applicants to understand. Local authorities that wish to continue with a points-based system should consider whether there is any scope to simplify it.

Including local priorities alongside the statutory reasonable preference categories

75. Section 167(6) of the Housing Act 1996 makes it clear that, subject to the reasonable preference requirements, it is for local authorities to decide on what principles their allocation scheme is to be framed.

76. An allocation scheme may provide for other factors than those set out in s.167(2) to be taken into account in determining which applicants are to be given preference under a scheme, provided they do not dominate the scheme and that overall the scheme operates to give reasonable preference to people in the reasonable preference categories. This means that an allocation scheme may include other policy priorities, such as promoting job-related mobility, prioritising under-occupiers, or providing move-on accommodation for people leaving supported housing, provided that:
    • they do not dominate the scheme and
    • overall, the scheme operates to give reasonable preference to those in the statutory reasonable preference categories over those who are not

77. The House of Lords in *Ahmad* accepted that local authorities are entitled to allocate to people who do not fall within the reasonable preference groups. For example, Newham's very favourable treatment of under-occupiers was not unlawful, notwithstanding the fact that they were unlikely to fall within any of the reasonable preference groups. It was accepted that account could be taken of wider housing management considerations (as well as the needs of those in the reasonable preference categories), and the judgment made the point that encouraging people in larger homes to transfer to smaller ones could be to the advantage of those in housing need because it produces an overall increase in the accommodation available.

78. Lettings outcomes should be evaluated over time to ensure that the authority is able to meet the priorities and principles set out in its allocation scheme and the reasonable preference requirements in section 167(2). Robust monitoring systems are essential here.

Existing tenants seeking a move

79. Part 6 of the 1996 Act extends to existing tenants of local authorities and RSLs who apply to transfer within the social rented sector. This means existing tenants applying for a transfer must be treated on the same basis as other applicants in accordance with the reasonable preference requirements in s.167. However, the House of Lords in *Ahmad* recognised that there could be good housing management reasons for enabling existing tenants to move, even where they do not have reasonable preference – provided that overall those in the reasonable preference categories continued to receive some preference. This is because such moves are broadly stock neutral (every transfer creates another void which can be used to meet housing needs). The House of Lords also recognised that people who are allowed to move to properties or locations which they prefer are likely to be happier and, as a result, better tenants.

80. In the light of *Ahmad* we consider that authorities have the scope to provide within their allocation scheme for existing tenants to transfer to similar sized accommodation where they can demonstrate good reason for seeking a move, for example, where they want to move to take up an offer of employment. The extent to which there is scope to allow existing tenants to move within the stock will depend on the particular circumstances in the district, taking into

account the demand from other applicants in greater housing need and the effect which this could have on lost revenue from increased void periods. In *Ahmad*, the court considered that setting aside a small proportion of lettings for transferring tenants was not unreasonable.

Quotas, targets and lettings plans

81.   An authority may want to set targets for the proportion of properties which it expects to allocate to the various groups within the allocation scheme as part of an annual lettings plan. So, for example, this might set a target for the proportion of large family-sized accommodation to be allocated to over-crowded households, or for the proportion of lettings to be given to transfer-ring tenants.

82.   Authorities should avoid setting rigid quotas which cannot be amended in the light of changing circumstances. However, they may wish to set broad targets which should be published alongside the authority's allocation scheme. Targets should be published as part of an annual lettings plan and monitored, and lettings outcomes against the targets should be published. Published targets, together with information about lettings outcomes, help make the allocation process more transparent.

83.   In setting targets, authorities should take into account:
   • the size and composition of the waiting list
   • the profile of their stock and the vacancies which are likely to become available.

Local lettings policies

84.   Section 167(2E) of the 1996 Act enables local authorities to allocate particular accommodation to people of a particular description, whether or not they fall within the reasonable preference categories, provided that overall the author-ity is able to demonstrate compliance with the requirements of s.167. This is the statutory basis for so-called 'local lettings policies'. This could mean set-ting aside houses on a particular estate, or certain types of property across the stock, for applicants who meet specified criteria.

85.   A study carried out by Heriot Watt University[17] for Communities and Local Government in 2008, based in two regions, found that about half of respond-ing authorities (23 out of 52) operated local lettings policies. This would sug-gest that local authorities may not be making as much use as they could of the flexibilities which the allocation legislation allows them.

86.   Local lettings policies may be used to achieve a wide variety of policy objec-tives. So for example, they may be used to:
   • deal with concentrations of deprivation or create more mixed communities by setting aside a proportion of vacancies for applicants who are in employ-ment or to enable existing tenants to take up an offer of employment
   • attract essential workers into the district by giving them priority for a small number of properties even though they may not fall within any of the reasonable preference categories
   • deal sensitively with lettings in rural villages and on s106 exception sites by giving priority to those with a local connection to the parish

---

17 *Exploring local authority policy and practice on allocations* (Hal Pawson and Anwen Jones) (CLG 2009).

- ensure that properties which are particularly suited to being made accessible (e.g. ground floor flats) are prioritised for those with access needs
- set aside a proportion of properties to help meet the housing needs of people whose employment requires them to be mobile, such as members of the Armed Forces.[18]

88. Where a number of local authorities have agreed a common allocation policy or common prioritisation criteria, as part of a sub-regional CBL scheme, local lettings policies can be useful as a means of incorporating local priorities.

89. Before adopting a local lettings policy, authorities should consult with those who are likely to be affected by it. So for example, where a local lettings policy is to apply to a particular estate, they should consult with tenants and residents on that estate. RSLs should also be consulted in relation to and, where appropriate (eg where stock they own is included in a relevant estate) involved in developing local lettings policies.

90. The proportion of stock or lettings which may be made available through a local lettings policy to people who are not in the reasonable preference categories will depend on the particular circumstances and factors at play in the district. Authorities will need to take into account factors such as: the size and composition of the waiting list (ie the proportion of applicants in the reasonable preference categories); the stock profile; and the number and type/size of vacancies which are available overall.

91. In the interests of transparency, local lettings policies should be published. Since they will often be time limited, it may not be practicable for the detailed policies to be included in the allocation scheme. One way to get around this would be for the allocation scheme to include a general statement about the intention to implement local lettings policies and to set out the detail in a separate published document or documents which could be revoked or revised as appropriate. Authorities should include an explanation of the local lettings policy which should be evidence-based wherever possible. Where it is intended that the policy is time limited, it should include an appropriate exit strategy.

92. Local lettings policies should also be monitored as to their effectiveness and reviewed regularly so that they can be revised or revoked where they are no longer appropriate or necessary.

Partnership working with RSLs

93. It is important that local authorities take a strong strategic approach to meeting housing needs in their district. To do this, they will need to develop close working partnerships – both at the strategic and operational level – with RSLs, given their key role in the supply and management of social housing, to ensure that:
- best use is made of the available social housing in the district and
- applicants are offered the widest choice of accommodation

94. This will be important for all local authorities but for those who have transferred their stock it will be crucial.

18 For further information on the Government's commitment to ensure that Service personnel are not disadvantaged when accessing public services, authorities are referred to *The Nation's Commitment to the Armed Forces Community: Consistent and Enduring Support*, Cm7674, published 16 July 2009.

95.   RSLs should be involved at an early stage in developing allocation priorities and must be consulted on the allocation scheme. RSLs which manage a large number of properties in the district are likely to be well informed about the general housing needs of the area; while specialist RSLs may have significant knowledge of the needs of minority or marginalised groups. Allocation policies which are framed to take account of local needs and priorities are more likely to gain the support of RSLs.

96.   RSLs have a duty under s.170 of the 1996 Act to co-operate with local authorities – where the authority requests it – to such extent as is reasonable in the circumstances – in offering accommodation to people with priority under the authority's allocation scheme. This is reflected in the Tenant Services Authority's (TSA) draft allocation standard (issued for consultation on 12 November) which requires 'registered providers' to co-operate with local authorities' strategic function and their duties to meet identified housing needs, including meeting obligations in nomination agreements.

97.   Local authorities should ensure that they have nomination agreements in place with RSLs in their district and these should be updated regularly to ensure that they reflect changing housing markets.[19] Nomination agreements should set out the proportion of lettings that will be made available which should reflect the existing housing market circumstances; any criteria which the RSLs have adopted, following consultation with the housing authority, for accepting or rejecting nominees; and how any disputes about suitability and eligibility will be resolved. The TSA's draft allocation standard requires registered providers to clearly set out, and give reasons for, the criteria they use for excluding actual and potential tenants from consideration for allocations, mobility or mutual exchange schemes. When negotiating nominations agreements, local authorities should try to ensure that the criteria for rejecting nominees are kept to a minimum. This will be particularly important where the housing authority has transferred its housing stock. Robust monitoring arrangements should be put in place to measure the effectiveness of the nomination agreement.

98.   Authorities should also agree information sharing protocols with RSLs in their district, covering issues such as rent arrears, anti-social behaviour and support needs. Information sharing between local authorities and RSLs is particularly important and failure to get this right could undermine the nomination process or the success of a joint choice based lettings scheme; while effective information sharing should help ensure that tenancies have the best chance of being sustained. The former Housing Corporation issued a national standard protocol for sharing information about applicants which authorities may wish to follow.[20] Amongst other things, it provides helpful advice on data protection issues.

99.   Local authorities are strongly encouraged to consider – together with RSLs in their district – the scope for developing common approaches to the allocation

19 *Effective Co-operation in Tackling Homelessness: Nomination Agreements and Exclusions*, published by CLG in November 2004 and available on the CLG website, identifies good practice in co-operation between housing authorities and RSLs in relation to nomination agreements and exclusions.

20 *Access to Housing: Information Sharing Protocol*, Campbell Tickell for the Housing Corporation, November 2007.

of social housing. This could include the adoption of a common housing register and a common allocation policy, and local lettings policies which cover RSLs as well as local authority stock. Providing a single point of access to social housing and one set of rules, should help make the process of applying for social housing simpler and more transparent for applicants, and can reduce wasteful duplication of effort by social landlords and applicants. This may help remove some of the confusion and frustration which applicants currently experience. The TSA made clear in *Building a new regulatory framework – a discussion paper* (June 2009), that it views agreement locally between social landlords and local authorities on how accommodation should be allocated as desirable and important for fairness and transparency within local areas.

100. Common housing registers and common allocation policies are particularly relevant in the context of choice based lettings. Developing common approaches requires trust between the partners which can be built by partnerships agreeing clear accountable governance structures and cost sharing arrangements and by delivering a high quality service which is viewed by applicants and by all partner landlords as an improvement on those delivered by local authorities and RSLs on their own.[21]

---

21 Further guidance on partnership working with both RSLs and private landlords is provided in chapter 6 of the 2008 code.

Housing Allocations – Members of the Armed Forces: Circular 4/2009*

Introduction

1. This circular is guidance by the Secretary of State for Communities and Local Government under section 169 of the Housing Act 1996 (the 1996 Act). Local housing authorities are required to have regard to it in exercising their functions under Part 6 of the 1996 Act.

2. In addition to the Code of Guidance for Local Authorities on the Allocation of Accommodation (the Code of Guidance) issued in November 2002, this circular provides updated guidance to housing authorities to which they should have regard when considering applications for an allocation of accommodation made by members of Her Majesty's Armed Forces or by persons who were formerly serving in the Armed Forces. The purpose of this circular is twofold:
   (a) to give effect to a commitment in: 'The Nation's Commitment: Cross-Government Support to our Armed Forces, their Families and Veterans' (the Command Paper) issued by the Ministry of Defence in July 2008; and
   (b) to take account of amendments to section 199 of the 1996 Act made by section 315 of the Housing and Regeneration Act 2008 (the 2008 Act) which change the application of the local connection test in respect of members of the armed forces.

Background

3. The Command Paper sets out a framework for action across Government Departments to:
   a) remove any disadvantage that Service personnel, their families, and veterans may suffer as a result of service in the Armed Forces, and particularly as a consequence of being required to move around the country and the world; and
   b) support those existing and former members of the Armed Forces who have been injured in the service of their country.

4. The Command Paper contains a number of housing related commitments. Paragraph 2.15 sets out the Government's view that seriously injured personnel should be given high priority for social housing and contains a commitment to issue statutory guidance to reinforce this message. Paragraph 2.19 refers to the amendment to the local connection provision in section199 of the 1996 Act in relation to members of the Armed Forces (as amended by section 315 of the 2008 Act).

Seriously injured and disabled servicemen

5. The Secretary of State believes that it is important that Service personnel who have been seriously injured or disabled in action and who have an urgent need for social housing should be given high priority within local authorities' allocation schemes in recognition of their service.

---

* Department for Communities and Local Government (April 2009). © Crown Copyright.

6.   Section 167(2) of the 1996 Act provides that, in framing their allocation scheme so as to determine priorities in the allocation of accommodation, housing authorities must ensure that reasonable preference is given to specified categories of applicants, including people who need to move on medical or welfare grounds, including grounds relating to a disability. Section 167(2) further provides that housing authorities may frame their allocation scheme so as to give additional preference to people who fall within the reasonable preference categories and who have urgent housing needs.

7.   Paragraph 5.18 of the Code of Guidance provides advice on the additional preference provision in section 167(2). It states that housing authorities must consider, in the light of local circumstances, the need to give effect to this provision. It also provides examples of people with urgent housing needs to whom housing authorities should consider giving additional preference within their allocation scheme including those who need to move because of urgent medical reasons.

8.   The Secretary of State is of the view that, where an allocation scheme is framed to provide for additional preference to be given to applicants in urgent housing need, housing authorities should ensure that the categories of applicants to be given additional preference include the following:
     – any applicant who needs to move to suitable adapted accommodation because of a serious injury, medical condition or disability which he or she, or a member of their household, has sustained as a result of service in the Armed Forces.

Section 315 of the Housing Act 2008 – local connection

9.   Section 167(2A) of the 1996 Act allows allocation schemes to make provision for determining priorities in relation to applicants who fall within the reasonable preference and additional preference categories. It gives examples of factors which may be taken into account in determining priorities, including any local connection between the applicant and the authority's district. For these purposes, local connection is defined by reference to section 199 of the 1996 Act.

10. Paragraph 5.23 of the Code of Guidance provides advice on implementing section 167(2A) and sub-paragraph (c) sets out a brief summary of the local connection provisions in s.199. It states that, broadly speaking, a person has a local connection with the district of a housing authority if he has a connection because of normal residence there (either current or previous) of his own choice, employment there, family connections or special circumstances. It goes on to state that residence in an area is not of a person's own choice if it is the consequence of serving in the Armed Forces. This exemption no longer applies.

11. Section 315 of the 2008 Act amends s.199 of the 1996 Act so that a person serving in the Armed Forces can establish a local connection with a district through residence or employment there, in the same way as a civilian person. The amendments apply in respect of all applications for housing under Part 6 made on or after 1 December 2008.

12. Where housing authorities frame their allocation scheme to give greater priority to applicants with a local connection, the effect of the amendments to section 199 of the 1996 Act will be:

(a) applicants who are serving in the Armed Forces and who are either employed or resident in the district will be able to establish a local connection with the district

(b) when considering applications from serving or former members of the Armed

Forces, who are not currently employed or resident in the district, the local housing authority will need to consider whether they have a local connection through previous residence in the district as a result of a former posting in the area while serving in the Armed Forces.

13.   Such authorities should also consider whether there is a need to revise their allocation scheme in light of the amendments to section 199.

14.   [not reproduced.]

15.   [not reproduced.]

Index